MyMarketingLab Improves Student Engagement Before, During, an

Prep and Engagement

Video exercises – engaging videos that bring business concepts to life and explore business topics related to the theory students are learning in class. Quizzes then assess students' comprehension of the concepts covered in each video.

Learning Catalytics – a "bring your own device" student engagement, assessment, and classroom intelligence system helps instructors analyze students' critical-thinking skills during lecture.

Dynamic Study Modules (DSMs) – through adaptive learning, students get personalized guidance where and when they need it most, creating greater engagement, improving knowledge retention, and supporting subject-matter mastery. Also available on mobile devices.

Business Today – bring current events alive in your classroom with videos, discussion questions, and author blogs. Be sure to check back often, this section changes daily.

Decision-making simulations – place your students in the role of a key decision-maker. The simulation will change and branch based on the decisions students make, providing a variation of scenario paths. Upon completion of each simulation, students receive a grade, as well as a detailed report of the choices they made during the simulation and the associated consequences of those decisions.

Decision Making

Critical Thinking

turnitin

- **Writing Space** – better writers make great learners—who perform better in their courses. Providing a single location to develop and assess concept mastery and critical thinking, the Writing Space offers automatic graded, assisted graded, and create your own writing assignments, allowing you to exchange personalized feedback with students quickly and easily.

  Writing Space can also check students' work for improper citation or plagiarism by comparing it against the world's most accurate text comparison database available from **Turnitin**.

- **Additional Features** – included with the MyLab are a powerful homework and test manager, robust gradebook tracking, comprehensive online course content, and easily scalable and shareable content.

http://www.pearsonmylabandmastering.com

PEARSON

► Corporations don't make decisions. **People do.**

Stephanie Nashawaty A decision maker at Oracle

Meet the Real Marketer

Who makes big marketing decisions?
What makes them tick?
How did they get there?
How would you get there?
Get to know the people behind the decisions.

You Make the Call

What would you do?
Hear from a real marketer about a business problem he or she faced, get the options and decide what you would do.

Chapter 3

Strategic Market Planning

Objective Outline

1. Explain business planning and its three levels pp. 72–74
BUSINESS PLANNING: COMPOSE THE BIG PICTURE p. 72

2. Describe the steps in strategic planning pp. 74–80
STRATEGIC PLANNING: FRAME THE PICTURE p. 74

3. Describe the steps in market planning pp. 81–88
MARKET PLANNING: DEVELOP AND EXECUTE MARKETING STRATEGY p. 81

Check out the Chapter 3 Study Map on page 89.

Stephanie Nashawaty
▼ A Decision Maker at Oracle

Stephanie Stewart Nashawaty is group vice president of customer experience (CX) transformation sales at Oracle. She has over 15 years of software sales experience and extensive expertise in enterprise marketing solutions for Global 2000 leading companies.

Stephanie is currently responsible for CX sales at Oracle (this includes Oracle's application solutions for customer-facing functions, such as sales, services, and marketing). She leads an elite sales team of enterprise sales executives who are tasked with creating and delivering $1 million to $30 million Cloud deals with Oracle's most strategic customers. In this capacity, Stephanie also works on joint business development opportunities with selected systems integrators, such as Accenture and Deloitte, as well as digital agencies.

Prior to joining Oracle, Stephanie was a vice president with Unica Corporation, which was acquired by IBM in 2010. She helped to build and launch IBM's Enterprise Marketing Management (EMM) business unit. The unit's focus on "Smarter Marketing" is a key foundational pillar of IBM's current "Smarter Planet" campaign and go-to-market strategy. Stephanie led the EMM global sales team ($400 million in annual revenues), which focused on selling to the office of the chief marketing officer (CMO). She was recognized for her achievements and team contribution by her selection for IBM's Acquisition Talent Acceleration Program. During this time, she was also the executive sales leader for the acquisitions and integrations of three companies in the marketing domain (DemandTec, Tealeaf, and Xtify). Stephanie has significant international experience working with CMOs in retail, travel, telecommunications, and other industries focused on optimizing the customer experience with a brand across all channels.

Stephanie holds a BA in political science from the University of Vermont and was a candidate in the master's degree program at Stanford University. She and her family reside in Needham, Massachusetts.

Stephanie's Info

What I do when I'm not working?
Spend time with my two teenage daughters, ideally doing something outside like hiking, swimming, skiing, and tennis.

First job out of school?
Management trainee, Enterprise Rent-A-Car.

Career high?
Selected for IBM's Acquisition Talent Acceleration Program. Less than 1 percent of IBM employees were selected for this program.

Business book I'm reading now?
Converge: Transforming Business at the Intersection of Marketing and Technology by Bob Lord and Ray Velez.

My motto to live by?
"Don't let the perfect be the enemy of the good," that is, execute and iterate rather than be stuck in overanalyzing decisions.

What drives me?
Fear of failure.

My management style?
Collaborative and decisive.

2

Find Out What Happened

Discover the choice the real marketer made and see how it worked out.

Here's my **choice...**

Real **People**, Real **Choices**

1 Option   **(2)** Option   **3** Option

Why do you think Stephanie chose option 2?

How It Worked Out at Oracle

Stephanie chose option 2. Since 2013, Oracle has acquired several leading SaaS marketing automation companies, and it now labels its new business the Oracle Marketing Cloud™. Its cloud-based services allow clients to customize their communications with different customers, coordinate these messages across multiple channels, and monitor the effectiveness of their campaigns over time (**www.forbes.com/sites/oracle/2014/05/05/6-key-steps-to-customer-centric-modern-marketing/2** [accessed May 8, 2014]).

Marketing

Real People, Real Choices

Global Edition
Eighth Edition

Marketing

Real People, Real Choices

Global Edition
Eighth Edition

Michael R. **SOLOMON**
SAINT JOSEPH'S UNIVERSITY

Greg W. **MARSHALL**
ROLLINS COLLEGE

Elnora W. **STUART**
THE UNIVERSITY OF SOUTH CAROLINA UPSTATE

PEARSON

Boston Columbus Indianapolis New York San Francisco
Amsterdam Cape Town Dubai London Madrid Milan Munich Paris Montréal Toronto
Delhi Mexico City São Paulo Sydney Hong Kong Seoul Singapore Taipei Tokyo

Vice President, Business Publishing: Donna Battista
Editor-in-Chief: Stephanie Wall
Acquisitions Editor: Mark Gaffney
Development Editor: Jennifer Lynn
Program Manager Team Lead: Ashley Santora
Program Manager: Jennifer Collins
Editorial Assistant: Daniel Petrino
Vice President, Product Marketing: Maggie Moylan
Director of Marketing, Digital Services and Products: Jeanette Koskinas
Executive Product Marketing Manager: Anne Fahlgren
Field Marketing Manager: Lenny Ann Raper
Senior Strategic Marketing Manager: Erin Gardner
Project Manager Team Lead: Judy Leale
Project Manager: Becca Groves
Senior Acquisitions Editor, Global Edition: Steven Jackson
Assistant Project Editor, Global Edition: Amrita Kar
Manager, Media Production, Global Edition: Vikram Kumar

Senior Manufacturing Controller, Production, Global Edition: Trudy Kimber
Operations Specialist: Carol Melville
Creative Director: Blair Brown
Senior Art Director: Janet Slowik
Cover Designer: Lumina Datamatics
Vice President, Director of Digital Strategy & Assessment: Paul Gentile
Manager of Learning Applications: Paul Deluca
Digital Editor: Brian Surette
Digital Studio Manager: Diane Lombardo
Digital Studio Project Manager: Robin Lazrus
Digital Studio Project Manager: Alana Coles
Digital Studio Project Manager: Monique Lawrence
Digital Studio Project Manager: Regina DaSilva
Full-Service Project Management and Composition: S4Carlisle Publishing Services
Printer/Binder/Cover Printer: Printpack Malaysia
Text Font: Palatino LT Std

Pearson Education Limited
Edinburgh Gate
Harlow
Essex CM20 2JE
England

and Associated Companies throughout the world

Visit us on the World Wide Web at: www.pearsonglobaleditions.com

ISBN-10: 1-292-09775-2
ISBN-13: 9781-292-09775-6

British Library Cataloguing-in-Publication Data
A catalogue record for this book is available from the British Library

10 9 8 7 6 5 4 3 2 1

Typeset by Lumina Datamatics
Printed and bound in Malaysia (CTP-VVP)

▶Brief Contents

▶ Contents

PART 2 Determine the Value Propositions Different Customers Want 118

▶ Preface

WHAT'S **NEW** IN THE EIGHTH EDITION?

What's new in the eighth edition is what's new in marketing. To put it simply, we feel a newcomer to marketing today needs to grapple with three core issues: Value, ethics, and metrics.

Here's just a sample of what we changed in this edition:

- First and foremost, we've totally reorganized the Table of Contents to be even more concise and user-friendly. The entire book now consists of just 14 chapters—a very convenient size for most undergraduate basic marketing courses. This "lean and mean" structure will allow an instructor who teaches a semester course to cover important marketing concepts from soup to nuts yet still retain enough flexibility to include time for in-class exercises and discussions as well as assessments of students' learning. No more rushing through the last few chapters at the end of the term. A 14-chapter book hits the "sweet spot" for learning!

- We strongly believe that the exchange of value is the essence of marketing. Prior editions have recognized the centrality of the value proposition, but in the eighth edition, we've more clearly structured the book around that core concept. Our new organizational design hinges on the sequential process of creating and delivering value. Hence, the eighth edition is divided into four sections:

  1. Understand the Value Proposition
  2. Determine the Value Propositions Different Customers Want
  3. Develop the Value Proposition for the Customer
  4. Deliver and Communicate the Value Proposition to the Customer

- Within this new organizational paradigm, we make it clear to the student how the traditional "four-Ps" framework relates to the ultimate goal to align the value needs of a specific customer with the organization's offering. To this end, the four-Ps structure is integrated with the updated emphasis on the value proposition. Chapters 8 through 14 cover Product, Price, Place, and Promotion—but with the real-world decision-making emphasis for which our book is famous.

- The eighth edition shines an even larger spotlight on the importance of ethical marketing. The topic is so important to today's students that we moved our coverage of ethical issues right up front to Chapter 2. As soon as the student understands basically what marketing *is*, he or she learns how it *should be*. And each chapter provides a boxed feature called Ripped from the Headlines: Ethical/Sustainable Decisions in the Real World. Here we describe a questionable marketing practice and then ask students to weigh in on MyMarketingLab in a polling feature so they can assess their response versus that of their peers.

- Today's marketer needs to be "a numbers person." Increasingly, the field is data driven, and sophisticated analytics are revolutionizing the options organizations have at their fingertips to create, deliver, and measure value. We're proud to say that we've literally doubled our coverage of market research and analytics in this edition: We now couple our Market Research chapter with an entirely new chapter that focuses on how marketers use the exciting new tools they have available to understand and harness "Big Data" as they strive to identify and meet their customers' needs—often literally on a one-to-one basis.

- Last but certainly not least, as always we pride ourselves on the currency of our content. Today's student deserves to know what is going on in the marketing world *today*—and also tomorrow to the extent we can predict it. Here is a sample of new Key Terms we introduce in the eighth edition:

Chapter 1
barter
Big Data
collaborative consumption
consumer addiction
crowdsourcing
nongovernmental organization (NGO)
rentrepreneurs
shrinkage
social media
societal marketing concept
sustainability

Chapter 2
consumer ethnocentrism
foreign exchange rate (forex rate)
radio frequency identification (RFID)
sachet

Chapter 4
bounce rate
customer insights
data
database
information
neuromarketing
reverse engineering

Chapter 5
click-through
conversion
cost per order
information overload
Internet of Things
marketing analytics
marketing control
marketing metrics
predictive analytics
scanner data
structured data
unstructured data

Chapter 6
encryption
firewall
malware
offshoring
sensory branding

Chapter 7
badge
gamer segment

Generation Z
geographic information system (GIS)
geotargeting
M geographic segmentation
micromarketing
Millennials
usage rate

Chapter 8
adoption pyramid
consumer packaged good (CPG)
creativity
fast-moving consumer good (FMCG)
research and development (R&D)
shopbot
specialized services
value co-creation

Chapter 9
ingredient branding
internal customer mind-set
internal customers
stock-keeping unit (SKU)

Chapter 10
Bitcoin
internet price discrimination
market share
surge pricing

Chapter 11
administered VMS
channel conflict
channel cooperation
channel leader or channel captain
channel power
communication and transaction
    functions
corporate VMS
distribution center
distribution intensity
distribution planning
dual or multiple distribution
    systems
franchise organizations
retailer cooperative
reverse logistics
risk-taking functions
stock-outs
transportation and storage

Chapter 12
experiential shoppers
retailtainment
virtual experiential marketing (VEM)

Chapter 13
authenticated streaming
embedded marketing
native advertising
product placement

Chapter 14
brand polarization
location-based social networks
input measures
output measures
ambient advertising

Features of the Eighth Edition of *Real People, Real Choices*

Meet Real Marketers

Many of the Real People, Real Choices vignettes are new to this edition, featuring a variety of decision makers, from CEOs to brand managers. Here is just a sample of the marketers we feature:

- Joe Kennedy, Pandora
- Keith Sutter, Johnson & Johnson
- Ryan Garton, Discover
- David Clark, General Mills
- Neal Goldman, Under Armour
- Mark Brownstein, Brownstein Group
- Stephanie Nashawaty, Oracle
- Stan Clark, Eskimo Joe's

Ethics and Sustainability in Marketing

Because the role of ethics and sustainability in business and in marketing is so important, we focus on these topics not just in a single chapter but in *every chapter* of the book. These Ripped from the Headlines boxes feature real-life examples of ethical and sustainable decisions marketers are faced with on a day-to-day basis.

Cutting-Edge Technology

With technology evolving at a rapid-fire pace, it's now more important than ever for today's marketers to stay on the cutting edge of the latest technological developments. Viral marketing campaigns are just the tip of the iceberg! The Cutting Edge boxes feature the most current technological advances and explain how companies are using them to deliver value and creatively get their messages out to consumers.

Easy-to-Follow Marketing Plan Template

Marketing: Real People, Real Choices, eighth edition, includes a handy tear-out template of a marketing plan you can use as a road map as you make your way through the book. The template provides a framework that will enable you to organize marketing concepts by chapter and create a solid marketing plan of your own. On the back of the template is a contemporary world map as a reminder that all marketing today is global. We encourage you to keep this tear-out as a handy reference after the class.

Marketing Plan Appendix

Appendix A, The Marketing Plan, provides a basic marketing plan for the fictitious S&S Smoothie Company. This plan gives students the foundation they need to craft a complete marketing plan for a class project. In this edition, the plan is updated to include helpful "how to" guidelines that answer many of the questions that students ask while developing their own plans.

New Career Appendix

Appendix B, You, Marketing, and Your Career, provides guidance for students on how to plan for a successful and rewarding career, whether in marketing or another field. Career success is framed as developing a unique brand that meets the needs of the job market. Career guidance recommendations follow the steps in the marketing plan with suggestions at each step for critical thinking and specific actions.

End-of-Chapter Study Map

Each chapter has an integrative study map for students that includes an Objective Summary, Key Terms, and student assessment opportunities of several types: Concepts: Test Your Knowledge; Activities: Apply What You've Learned; Apply Marketing Metrics (more on this one below); Choices: What Do You Think?, and Miniproject: Learn by Doing. By completing these assessments, students and instructors achieve maximum assurance of learning.

Measuring the Value of Marketing through Marketing Metrics

Just how do marketers add value to a company, and how can that value be quantified? More and more, businesses demand accountability, and marketers respond as they develop a variety of "scorecards" that show how specific marketing activities directly affect their company's ROI—return on investment. And on the job, the decisions that marketers make increasingly come from data and calculations and less from instinct. Each chapter provides a Metrics Moment box that describes some important ways to measure important marketing concepts, followed by an Apply the Metric exercise that asks the student to actually work with some of these measures. And every end-of-chapter includes an Apply Marketing Metrics exercise that provides additional opportunities for students to practice measures that marketers use to help them make good decisions. New to this edition, pricing exercises included at the end of the Marketing Math Supplement following Chapter 10 provide the opportunity for students to work real-life pricing problems.

New and Updated End-of-Chapter Cases in This Edition

Each chapter concludes with an exciting Marketing in Action mini-case about a real firm facing real marketing challenges. Questions at the end let you make the call to get the company on the right track.

Instructor Resources

At the Instructor Resource Center, www.pearsonglobaleditions.com/Solomon, instructors can easily register to gain access to a variety of instructor resources available with this text in downloadable format. If assistance is needed, our dedicated technical support team is ready to help with the media supplements that accompany this text. Visit http://247.pearsoned.com for answers to frequently asked questions and toll-free user support phone numbers.

The following supplements are available with this text:

- Instructor's Resource Manual
- Test Bank
- TestGen® Computerized Test Bank
- PowerPoint Presentation
- Instructor Video Library

Michael R. Solomon, Elnora W. Stuart, Greg W. Marshall

Michael R. Solomon

MICHAEL R. SOLOMON, PhD, joined the Haub School of Business at Saint Joseph's University in Philadelphia as professor of marketing in 2006, where he also serves as director of the Center for Consumer Research. From 2007 to 2013, he also held an appointment as professor of consumer behaviour at the University of Manchester in the United Kingdom. From 1995 to 2006, he was the Human Sciences Professor of Consumer Behavior at Auburn University. Prior to joining Auburn in 1995, he was chairman of the Department of Marketing in the School of Business at Rutgers University, New Brunswick, New Jersey. Professor Solomon's primary research interests include consumer behavior and lifestyle issues; branding strategy; the symbolic aspects of products; the psychology of fashion, decoration, and image; services marketing; and the development of visually oriented online research methodologies. He currently sits on the editorial boards of the *Journal of Consumer Behaviour*, the *European Business Review*, and the *Journal of Retailing*, and he recently completed a six-year term on the Board of Governors of the Academy of Marketing Science. In addition to other books, he is also the author of Prentice Hall's text *Consumer Behavior: Buying, Having, and Being*, which is widely used in universities throughout the world. Professor Solomon frequently appears on television and radio shows, such as *The Today Show*, *Good Morning America*, Channel One, the *Wall Street Journal* Radio Network, and National Public Radio to comment on consumer behavior and marketing issues.

Greg W. Marshall

GREG W. MARSHALL, PhD, is the Charles Harwood Professor of Marketing and Strategy in the Crummer Graduate School of Business at Rollins College in Winter Park, Florida, and is also academic director of the Executive DBA program there. For three years, he also served as vice president for strategic marketing for Rollins. Before joining Rollins, he was on the faculty of Oklahoma State University, the University of South Florida, and Texas Christian University. He also holds a visiting professorship in the Marketing Group at Aston Business School, Birmingham, United Kingdom. Professor Marshall earned a BSBA in marketing and an MBA from the University of Tulsa and a PhD in marketing from Oklahoma State University. His research interests include sales management, marketing management decision making, and intraorganizational relationships. He is editor of the *Journal of Marketing Theory and Practice* and former editor of the *Journal of Personal Selling & Sales Management* and currently serves on the editorial boards of the *Journal of the Academy of Marketing Science*, the *Journal of Business Research*, and *Industrial Marketing Management*. Professor Marshall is past president of the American Marketing Association Academic Division, a distinguished fellow and past president of the Academy of Marketing Science, and a fellow and past president of the Society for Marketing Advances. His industry experience prior to entering academe includes product management, field sales management, and retail management positions with firms such as Warner-Lambert, the Mennen Company, and Target Corporation.

Elnora W. Stuart

ELNORA W. STUART, PhD, is professor of marketing and associate dean of the George Dean Johnson, Jr., College of Business and Economics at the University of South Carolina Upstate. Prior to joining USC Upstate in 2008, she was professor of marketing and the BP Egypt Oil Professor of Management Studies at the American University in Cairo and professor of marketing at Winthrop University in Rock Hill, South Carolina, and on the faculty of the University of South Carolina. She has also been a regular visiting professor at Instituto de Empresa in Madrid, Spain. She earned a BA in theaterspeech from the University of North Carolina at Greensboro and both an MA in journalism and mass communication and a PhD in marketing from the University of South Carolina. Professor Stuart's research has been published in major academic journals, including the *Journal of Consumer Research*, the *Journal of Advertising*, the *Journal of Business Research*, and the *Journal of Public Policy and Marketing*. For over 25 years, she has served as a consultant for numerous businesses and not-for-profit organizations in the United States and in Egypt.

►Acknowledgments

We feature many talented marketers and successful companies in this book. In developing it, we also were fortunate to work with a team of exceptionally talented and creative people at Pearson. Mark Gaffney, Executive Editor, was instrumental in helping us solidify the vision for the eighth edition, and his assistance with decisions about content, organization, features, and supplements was invaluable. Kudos to Jennifer Collins for managing the project with great efficiency and patience. Becca Richter did yeoman work to smoothly integrate all the pieces of this project into one book. Jennifer Lynn worked with the authors to ensure that each chapter was submitted to production in top shape. And Anne Fahlgren, Erin Gardner, and Lenny Ann Raper deserve thanks for marketing the book successfully.

A special note of appreciation goes to Phillip Wiseman of the Crummer Graduate School of Business at Rollins College for his substantial contributions to the new Chapter 5—Apply Market Research for Decision Making—as well as his able assistance in operationally converting the 16-chapter seventh-edition structure to this new 14-chapter framework. And thank you to Leroy Robinson of the University of Houston–Clear Lake, who worked on the Marketing in Action cases for this edition.

No book is complete without a solid supplements package. We extend our thanks to our dedicated supplement authors who devoted their time and shared their teaching ideas.

Finally, our utmost thanks and appreciation go to our families for their continued support and encouragement. Without them, this project would not be possible.

Many people worked to make this eighth edition a reality. Guidance and recommendations by the following professors and focus group participants helped us update and improve the chapters and the supplements:

REVIEWERS

Pia A. Albinsson, Appalachian State University
Gary Benson, Southeast Community College
Greta Blake, York College of Pennsylvania
Norm Borin, California State Polytechnic University
Rich Brown, Harding University
C. Brad Cox, Midlands Technical College
Mayukh Dass, Texas Tech University
Mark Davis, Harding University
Mark DeFanti, Providence College
George D. Deitz, The University of Memphis
Michael Dotson, Appalachian State University
Angel M. Fonseca, MSCTE, Jackson College
Jie G. Fowler, Valdosta State University
Marlene Frisbee, AB-Tech College
Thomas F. Frizzell, Sr., Massasoit Community College
Patricia Galitz, Southeast Community College
Kenneth C. Gehrt, San Jose State University
Kimberly Goudy, Central Ohio Technical College
Arlene Green, Indian River State College
Jeffrey S. Harper, Texas Tech University
Dana L. E. Harrison, East Tennessee State University
Kelli S. Hatin, SUNY Adirondack
Tarique Hossain, California State Polytechnic University, Pomona
Jacqueline J. Kacen, University of Houston
Laura Lynn Kerner, Athens State University
Cheryl Keymer, North Arkansas College
Nancy P. LaGuardia, Capital Community College
Doug Martin, Forsyth Technical Community College
Jane McKay-Nesbitt, Bryant University
Juan (Gloria) Meng, Minnesota State University, Mankato
Rex T. Moody, Angelo State University
Lynn M. Murray, Pittsburg State University
Jun Myers, California State Polytechnic University, Pomona

Hieu P. Nguyen, California State University, Long Beach
David A. Norton, University of Connecticut
Elaine M. Notarantonio, Bryant University
Jason Keith Phillips, West Chester University
Abe Qastin, Lakeland College
Kevin Raiford, College of Southern Nevada
Rosemary P. Ramsey, Wright State University
Matthew Roberts, California Polytechnic State University, San Luis Obispo
L. Renee J. Rogers, Forsyth Technical College
Mary Schramm, Quinnipiac University
Joseph A. Schubert, Delaware Technical Community College, Wilmington Campus
Lisa R. Simon, California Polytechnic State University
Nancy J. Thannert, Robert Morris University Illinois
Mary Jean Thornton, Capital Community College
Beth Ghiloni Wage, University of Hartford
Mary K. Wachter, Pittsburg State University
James R. Walton, Arkansas Tech University
Jefrey R. Woodall, York College of Pennsylvania
Srdan Zdravkovic, Bryant University

EXECUTIVES

In addition to our reviewers and focus group participants, we want to extend our gratitude to the busy executives who gave generously of their time for the Real People, Real Choices features.

Executives Featured in Real People, Real Choices Vignettes

Chapter 1: Joe Kennedy, Pandora
Chapter 2: Keith Sutter, Johnson & Johnson
Chapter 3: Stephanie Nashawaty, Oracle
Chapter 4: Ryan Garton, Discover Financial

Chapter 5: Lisa Arthur, Teradata
Chapter 6 Adam Wexler, Intellipool
Chapter 7: Margaret Molloy, Siegel+Gale
Chapter 8: Neal Goldman, Under Armour
Chapter 9: David Clark, General Mills
Chapter 10: Betsy Fleming, Converse College
Chapter 11: Marc Brownstein, Brownstein Group
Chapter 12: Rohan Deuskar, Stylitics
Chapter 13: Dan Marks, First Tennessee Bank
Chapter 14: Stan Clark, Eskimo Joe's

REVIEWERS OF PREVIOUS EDITIONS

The following individuals were of immense help in reviewing all or part of previous editions of this book and the supplement package:

Camille Abbruscato, Stony Brook University
Roy Adler, Pepperdine University
Lydia Anderson, Fresno City College
Gerald Athaide, Loyola College
Carole S. Arnone, Frostburg State University
Christopher Anicich, California State University–Fullerton
Nathan Austin, Morgan State University
Xenia Balabkins, Middlesex County College
Fred Beasley, Northern Kentucky University
Jas Bhangal, Chabot College
Gregory Spencer Black, Metropolitan State College of Denver
Koren Borges, University of North Florida
Silvia Borges, Miami Dade CC–Wolfson Campus
Deborah Boyce, State University of New York Institute of Technology, Utica, New York
Tom Boyd, California State University–Fullerton
Henry C. Boyd III, University of Maryland–College Park
Val Calvert, San Antonio College
Charles R. Canedy, University of Hartford
Richard Celsi, California State University–Long Beach
Swee-Lim Chia, LaSalle University
Paul Cohen, Florida Atlantic University
Brian Connett, California State University–Northridge
Ruth Clottey, Barry University
Robert M. Cosenza, University of Mississippi
Brent Cunningham, Jacksonville State University
Patricia Doney, Florida Atlantic University
Laura Dwyer, Rochester Institute of Technology
Rita Dynan, LaSalle University
Jill S. Dybus, Oakton Community College
Joyce Fairchild, Northern Virginia Community College
Elizabeth Ferrell, Southwestern Oklahoma State University
Joanne Frazier, Montgomery College
Jon Freiden, Florida State University
Mary Patricia Galitz, Southeast Community College
Debbie Gaspard, Southeast Community College
Mike Gates, South Hills School of Business and Technology
Michael Goldberg, Berkeley College
Karen Welte Gore, Ivy Tech Community College
Kimberly D. Grantham, University of Georgia
David Hansen, Texas Southern University
John Hardjimarcou, University of Texas, El Paso
Manoj Hastak, American University
John Heinemann, Keller Graduate School of Management

Dorothy Hetmer-Hinds, Trinity Valley Community College
Mark B. Houston, Texas Christian University
Gary Hunter, Case Western Reserve University
Annette Jajko, Triton College
Janice M. Karlen, LaGuardia Community College/ City University of New York
Jack E. Kant, San Juan College
Gail Kirby, Santa Clara University
David Knuff, Oregon State University–Cascades
Kathleen Krentler, San Diego State University
Sandra J. Lakin, Hesser College
Linda N. LaMarca, Tarleton State University
Debra A. Laverie, Texas Tech University
Freddy Lee, California State University–Sacramento
David Lehman, Kansas State University
Ron Lennon, Barry University
Marilyn Liebrenz-Himes, George Washington University
Anne Weidemanis Magi, University of South Florida
Cesar Maloles, California State University–East Bay
Norton Marks, California State University–San Bernardino
Kelly Duggan Martin, Washington State University
Carolyn Massiah, University of Central Florida
Mohan K. Menon, University of South Alabama
Laura M. Milner, University of Alaska
Timothy R Mittan, Southeast Community College
Jakki Mohr, University of Montana
Linda Morable, Richland College
Michael Munro, Florida International University
Jeff B. Murray, University of Arkansas
Mark A. Neckes, Johnson & Wales University
Linda Newell, Saddleback College
Eric Newman, California State University–San Bernardino
David Oliver, Edison College
Beng Ong, California State University–-Fresno
A. J. Otjen, Montana State University–Billings
Lucille Pointer, University of Houston–Downtown
Mohammed Rawwas, University of Northern Iowa
John E. Robbins, Winthrop University
Bruce Robertson, San Francisco State University
Leroy Robinson, University of Houston–Clear Lake
Carlos M. Rodreguez, Delaware State University
Ann Renee Root, Florida Atlantic University
Barbara Rosenthal, Miami Dade Community College–Kendall Campus
Behrooz Saghafi, Chicago State University
Ritesh Saini, George Mason University
Charles Jay Schafer, Johnson & Wales University
Marcianne Schusler, Prairie State College
Susan Silverstone, National University
Samuel A. Spralls III, Central Michigan University
Melissa St. James, California State University–Dominguez Hills
Frank Svestka, Loyola University of Chicago
James Swartz, California State Polytechnic University–Pomona
Kim Taylor, Florida International University–Park Campus
Steven Taylor, Illinois State University
Susan L. Taylor, Belmont University
John Thanopoulos, University of Piraeus, Greece
Jane Boyd Thomas, Winthrop University
Scott Thorne, Southeast Missouri State University
Judee A. Timm, Monterey Peninsula College
Sue Umashankar, University of Arizona

Sal Veas, Santa Monica College
D. Roger Waller, San Joaquin Delta College
Leatha Ware, Waubonsee Community College
Steve Wedwick, Heartland Community College
Casey Wilhelm, North Idaho University
Kathleen Williamson, University of Houston–Clear Lake
Mary Wolfinbarger, California State University–Long Beach

Kim Wong, Albuquerque TVI Community College
Steve Wong, Rock Valley College
Richard Wozniak, Northern Illinois University
Brent M. Wren, University of Alabama in Hunstville
Merv Yeagle, University of Maryland at College Park
Mark Young, Winona State University
Marybeth Zipperer, Montgomery College

Pearson would like to thank and acknowledge Steven Ng Kok Toong and Jon and Diane Sutherland for their contribution to the Global Edition, and Ronan Jouan de Kervenoael (Sabancı Üniversitesi), Patrick Poon (Lingan University), Jie Liu (Manchester Metropolitan University), and Ayantunji Gbadamosi (University of East London) for reviewing the Global Edition.

Marketing

Real People, Real Choices

Global Edition

Eighth Edition

Welcome to the World of Marketing
Create and Deliver Value

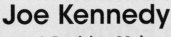

Joe Kennedy
▼ A Decision Maker at Pandora

Joe Kennedy is chief executive officer and president of Pandora, the Internet radio company that more than 65 million people use to create personalized radio stations that they can listen to from their computers, phones, TVs, and cars. Just type the name of one of your favorite songs or artists into Pandora, and it will instantly generate a station with music pulled from its collection of more than 800,000 songs. Enter Rihanna and connect to similar artists like Loer Velocity and The Cab. Is Ludacris more your speed? Discover 112 or Sensational.

How does Pandora customize stations to each individual listener? It all has to do with the Music Genome Project (MGP); Pandora describes it as the most comprehensive analysis of music ever undertaken. Over the past decade, MGP's team of musician-analysts has classified each song based on up to 400 distinct musical characteristics. It takes an analyst 20 to 30 minutes to analyze a song and record the details that define it, such as melody, harmony, instrumentation, rhythm, vocals, and lyrics. Artists receive royalties from Pandora every time one of their songs is played on a station.

Joe Kennedy joined Pandora in 2004 following a five-year stint at E-LOAN, where he was president and chief operating officer. From 1995 to 1999, he was the vice president of sales, service, and marketing for Saturn Corporation, which he grew to more than $4 billion in revenue and established as the top brand for customer satisfaction in the auto industry. Joe joined the initial start-up team at Saturn, four months after it was founded, as a marketing manager and held positions of increasing marketing responsibility over the course of his 11-year tenure there.

Joe has an MBA from Harvard Business School and a BS degree in electrical engineering and computer science from Princeton University, where he dabbled in music theory and learned to compose his own Gregorian chants. According to his bio on the Pandora site, he is Pandora's resident pop music junkie. Joe has also been playing the piano for more than 30 years, spending a majority of that time attempting to master Gershwin's "Rhapsody in Blue."

Joe's Info

What I do when I'm not working?
Work on my tennis game, trying to finally reach that elusive top 10 national ranking in my age-group.

Business book I'm reading now?
Checklist Manifesto by Atul Gawande.

My hero?
Lee Fauve, the president of Saturn from 1986 to 1995.

What drives me?
Bringing about game-changing innovation in categories that consumers are passionate about.

My management style?
Hire senior, experienced, self-motivated leaders who know more about their functional areas than I do and let them do their thing.

My pet peeve?
People who are always running late. It's a clear sign of self-centeredness when someone always keeps other people waiting.

Here's my problem...

Real **People**, Real **Choices**

The company was founded in January 2000 by Tim Westergren, a pianist who played in rock and jazz bands for 10 years before he became a film composer. As he analyzed music to decide what film directors would like, he got the idea of creating a technology that would reflect people's tastes and deliver music that fit those tastes. Tim raised $1.5 million and started Savage Beast Technologies, which sold music recommendations services to companies like Best Buy. But the company struggled as the dot-com boom of the late 1990s burst. Tim and his employees worked on an unpaid basis for several years before they got more financial backing in 2004 (after Tim made 347 unsuccessful pitches to investors!). Tim paid his employees, switched the company's name to Pandora, and changed its focus to consumers instead of businesses. To lead this strategic shift, the newly christened Pandora hired Joe Kennedy, who had solid experience building consumer products. The company knew it was on to something when it first released Pandora in a beta version for family and friends. Within a week, 5,000 people had used the service to discover new music.

That was encouraging, but a 5,000-user base isn't nearly enough to entice advertisers to buy space on the site. Pandora needed to make money by attracting enough people to capture the interest of potential advertising clients; these companies in turn would pay to place ads that would reach Pandora's users. The challenge was to avoid the fate of many other Internet start-ups that offered cool features but never grew to the scale where they could turn a profit. Joe needed to build a solid customer base so he could develop a firm business model for Pandora. He knew that if he could just make music lovers aware of the value Pandora offered, he would be able to turn the fledgling service into a marketing success.

Things to **remember**

Pandora doesn't charge people to use its service. It makes its money by attracting advertisers who want to reach users. In order for the company to entice companies to advertise, it has to offer them access to large numbers of consumers who are likely to tune in to the ads they will encounter on the site.

Part of Pandora's unique product offering is the ability to customize music for each individual user. Everyone who registers can create their own "stations" that play songs with similar characteristics. This enables users to learn about artists they might not otherwise stumble on, so potentially Pandora can create new audiences for independent musicians and for music labels.

Word of mouth is the least expensive way to attract large numbers of Web surfers to Pandora's site. However, it's difficult to build buzz in an environment where many other products and services compete for the consumer's scarce attention.

Joe considered his **Options** 1·2·3

1 Option — **Launch an advertising campaign on radio stations, in music magazines, and at record stores.** Advertising is a great way to create awareness of a new product or service, but it takes a lot of money to cut through the clutter of competing messages. To afford advertising, Pandora would have had to convince financial backers that a substantial up-front investment would pay off as droves of users flocked to the site once they heard or read about it.

2 Option — **Build a buzz about Pandora through word of mouth.** Put Tim Westergren, the company's founder, in front of groups of music lovers to tell the unique story of Pandora and how the MGP makes it work. Cultivate a dedicated fan base by reaching out to social networks on Twitter and Facebook and then rely on these converts to spread the word to their friends. A buzz-building strategy is very inexpensive, and, if done well, it can create a large group of devoted followers almost overnight. On the other hand, a start-up has to compete with the thousands of others that are trying to recruit fans, and it might be difficult to reach a mass audience as opposed to hard-core music lovers without any catchy advertising.

3 Option — **Sell the service to a large chain of record stores, a music magazine, or even a record label.** Pandora could return to its roots as a music recommendation service for businesses. If a large company (like Virgin Records) could offer the service exclusively to its customers, almost instantly Pandora would have access to many thousands of music buyers. In the same way that *USA Today* is able to claim a huge circulation (and thus attract a lot of advertising dollars) because it is distributed free to hotel guests across the country, Pandora would inherit an impressive distribution network. However, this choice would entail giving up control of the unique MGP and its sophisticated database that the company had worked so hard to build. Hard-core music fans might accuse Pandora of "selling out," and they might question how objective its recommendations were.

Now, put yourself in Joe's shoes. Which option would you consider, and why?

You Choose

Which **Option** would you choose, and **why**?

1. ☐YES ☐NO   2. ☐YES ☐NO   3. ☐YES ☐NO

See what **option** Joe chose on **page 50** ➡

MyMarketingLab™

⭐ **Improve Your Grade!**

Over 10 million students improved their results using the Pearson MyLabs. Visit **mymktlab.com** for simulations, tutorials, and end-of-chapter problems.

Chapter 1

1 Marketing: What Is It?

OBJECTIVE

Explain what marketing is, the marketing mix, what can be marketed and the value of marketing.

(pp. 28–34)

consumer
The ultimate user of a good or service.

marketing
Marketing is the activity, set of institutions, and processes for creating, communicating, delivering, and exchanging offerings that have value for customers, clients, partners, and society at large.

Marketing. Lots of people talk about it, but what is it? You already know a lot about marketing—it's been a part of your life from day one. As one of millions of **consumers**, you are the ultimate user of a good or service. Every time you purchase or use your car, your clothes, your lunch at the cafeteria (whether an old-school burger or a vegan version), a movie, or a haircut, you are part of the marketing process. In this book, we'll tell you why—and why you should care.

Indeed, consumers like you (and your humble authors!) are at the center of all marketing activities. Of course, when we refer to consumers, we don't just mean individuals. Organizations, whether a company, government, sorority, or charity, also are consumers.

Here's the key: *Marketing is first and foremost about satisfying consumer needs.* We like to say that the consumer is king (or queen), but it's important not to lose sight of the fact that the seller also has needs—to make a profit, to remain in business, and even to take pride in selling the highest-quality products possible. Products are sold to satisfy both consumers' and marketers' needs—it's a two-way street.

When you ask people to define **marketing**, you get many answers. Some people say, "That's what happens when a pushy salesman tries to sell me something I don't want." Many people say, "Oh, that's simple—TV commercials." Students might answer, "That's a course I have to take before I can get my business degree." Each of these responses has a grain of truth in it, but the official definition of marketing the American Marketing Association adopted in 2013 is as follows:

> Marketing is the activity, set of institutions, and processes for creating, communicating, delivering, and exchanging offerings that have value for customers, clients, partners, and society at large.[1]

The basic idea behind this somewhat complicated definition is that marketing is all about delivering value to everyone whom a transaction affects. We'll dig deeper into that definition to understand exactly what marketing is all about.

Marketing Is the Activity, Institutions, and Processes . . .

As we will discuss throughout this book, marketing includes a great number of activities—from top-level market planning to simple tasks, such as a salesperson calling on a customer or a copywriter creating a magazine ad. What role does marketing play in a firm? The importance organizations assign to marketing activities varies a lot. Top management in some firms is very marketing oriented (especially when the chief executive officer, or CEO, comes from the marketing ranks), whereas in other companies marketing is an afterthought. However, analysts estimate that at least one-third of CEOs come from a marketing background—so stick with us!

Sometimes a company uses the term *marketing* when what it really means is sales or advertising. In some small organizations, no one may specifically be designated as "the marketing person." And some firms realize that marketing applies to all aspects of the firm's activities and integrates it with other business functions (such as management and accounting).

No matter what size the firm, a marketer's decisions affect—and are affected by—the firm's other operations. Marketing managers must work with financial and accounting officers to figure out whether products are profitable, to set marketing budgets, and to determine prices. They must work with people in manufacturing to be sure that products are produced on time and in the right quantities. Marketers also must work with research-and-development specialists to create products that meet consumers' needs.

...for Creating, Communicating, Delivering, and Exchanging: The Marketing Mix...

As we said, marketing is about satisfying needs. To do this, marketers need many tools. The **marketing mix** is the marketer's strategic toolbox. It consists of the tools the organization uses to create a desired response among a set of predefined consumers. These tools include the product itself, the price of the product, the promotional activities that introduce it to consumers, and the places where it is available. We commonly refer to the elements of the marketing mix as the **four Ps**: *product*, *price*, *promotion*, and *place*. As 📷 Figure 1.1 shows, each P is a piece of the puzzle that the marketer must combine with other pieces. Just as a radio DJ puts together a collection of separate songs (a musical mix) to create a certain mood, the idea of a mix in this context reminds us that no single marketing activity is sufficient to accomplish the organization's objectives.

Although we talk about the four Ps as separate parts of a firm's marketing strategy, in reality, product, price, promotion, and place decisions are totally interdependent. Decisions about any single one of the four are affected by and affect every other marketing mix decision. For example, what if Superdry (a rapidly growing apparel company) decides to introduce a leather biker jacket that is higher end than the ones it makes now? If the company uses more expensive materials to make this item, it has to boost the selling price to cover these higher costs—this also signals to consumers that the garment is more upscale. In addition, Superdry would have to create advertising and other promotional strategies to convey a top-quality image. Furthermore, the firm must include high-end retailers like Bloomingdale's in its distribution strategy to ensure that shoppers who seek out high-end items will come across the jacket. Thus, all the pieces in the puzzle we call the marketing mix work together.

We'll examine these components of the marketing mix in detail later in this book. For now, let's briefly look at each of the four Ps to gain some more insight into their role in the marketing mix.

Product

A **product** can be a good, a service, an idea, a place, a person—whatever a person or organization offers for sale in the exchange. Creating new products is vital to the success and even the very life of an organization. This aspect of the marketing mix includes the design and packaging of a good as well as its physical features and any associated services, such as free delivery.

The product is a combination of many different elements, all of which are important to the product's success. For example, when the British airline Virgin Atlantic set out to reposition itself as the world's "most irresistible airline," the company focused on standing out from the competition through its superior customer service both in the air and in its advertising. The airline's "Flying in the Face of Ordinary" campaign features children with special extraordinary talents that they put to use one day as future employees.[2] Whether the focus is on customer service or some other element, the product is an important part of the marketing mix.

marketing mix
A combination of the product itself, the price of the product, the promotional activities that introduce it and the place where it is made available, that together create a desired response among a set of predefined consumers.

four Ps
Product, price, promotion, and place.

product
A tangible good, service, idea, or some combination of these that satisfies consumer or business customer needs through the exchange process; a bundle of attributes including features, functions, benefits, and uses.

Figure 1.1 📷 *Snapshot* | The Marketing Mix

The marketing mix is the marketer's strategic toolbox.

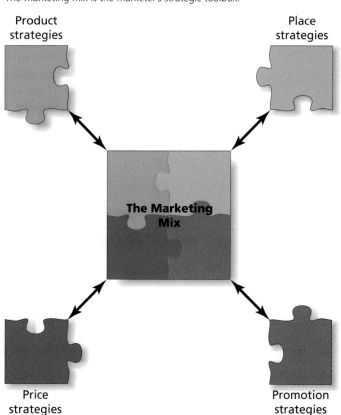

Product strategies

Place strategies

The Marketing Mix

Price strategies

Promotion strategies

▼ Promotional Elements

to decide on a communications ...gy for Pandora. Part of this decision is ...choose which promotional elements he should use to attract more users. His options include paid advertising, publicity releases and "buzz building."

promotion
The coordination of a marketer's communication efforts to influence attitudes or behavior.

place
The availability of the product to the customer at the desired time and location.

price
The assignment of value, or the amount the consumer must exchange to receive the offering.

exchange
The process by which some transfer of value occurs between a buyer and a seller.

Promotion

Promotion, often referred to as marketing communications includes all the activities marketers undertake to inform consumers about their products and to encourage potential customers to buy these products. Marketing communications can take the form of many different promotional elements, including personal selling, TV advertising, store coupons, billboards, magazine ads, publicity releases, and an increasing number of online communications including social media. Today's marketers recognize that many consumers, especially young ones, don't watch TV or read magazines except via the Internet. As a result, advertising budgets today include fewer dollars invested in traditional media and increases in online expenditures.

Place

Place refers to the availability of the product to the customer at the desired time and location. This P relates to a *supply chain*—the set of firms that work together to get a product from a producer to a consumer. For clothing or electronics, this channel includes local retailers as well as other outlets, such as retail sites on the Web that strive to offer the right quantity of products in the right styles at the right time.

Price

Price is the assignment of value, or the amount the consumer must exchange to receive the offering. Marketers often turn to price to increase consumers' interest in a product. This happens when they put an item on sale, but in other cases marketers actually try to sell a product with a *higher* price than people are used to if they want to communicate that it's high quality or cutting edge. For example, Universal Studios Hollywood offers VIP Experience tickets to its park goers—premium perks that come with premium pricing to the tune of $349 per person. VIP ticket holders get a personal tour guide, exclusive back-lot entrée, unlimited front-of-line access to rides, and more.[3]

At the heart of every marketing act—big or small—is something we refer to as an "exchange relationship." An **exchange** occurs when a person gives something and gets something else in return. The buyer receives an object, service, or idea that satisfies a need, and the seller receives something he or she feels is of equivalent value. Today, most but not all exchanges occur as a monetary transaction when one party surrenders currency (in the form of cash, check, or credit card) in return for a good or a service. But there are also other kinds of exchanges. A politician, for example, can agree to work toward certain goals in exchange for your vote, city officials may offer you a cleaner environment if you recycle, and health officials tell you that you can save lives if you wash your hands properly.

For an exchange to occur, at least two people or organizations must be willing to make a trade, and each must have something the other wants. Both parties must agree on the value of the exchange and how it will be carried out. Each party also must be free to accept or reject the other's terms for the exchange. Under these conditions, a gun-wielding robber's offer to "exchange" your money for your life does not constitute a valid exchange. In contrast, although someone may complain that a store's prices are "highway robbery," an exchange occurs if he still forks over the money to buy something there—even if he still grumbles about it weeks later.

To complicate things a bit more, everyone does not always agree on the terms of the exchange. Think, for example, about *music piracy*, which is a huge headache for music labels. On the one hand, they claim that they lose billions of dollars a year when consumers download songs without paying for them. On the other hand, a lot of people who engage in this practice don't feel that they participate in an unfair exchange that deprives manufacturers of the value of their products. They argue that music piracy is the fault of record companies that charge way too much for new songs. What do you think?

. . . Offerings . . . : What Can We Market?

Is there any limit to what marketers can market? Marketing applies to more than just canned peas or Doritos. Some of the best marketers come from the ranks of services companies such as American Express or not-for-profit organizations like Greenpeace. Politicians, athletes, and performers use marketing to their advantage (just think about that $30 T-shirt you may have bought at a baseball game or rock concert). Ideas such as political systems (democracy, totalitarianism), religion (Christianity, Islam), and art (realism, abstract) also compete for acceptance in a "marketplace." In this book, we'll refer to any good, service, or idea that we can market as a product, even though what you buy may not take a physical form.

Consumer Goods and Services

Consumer goods are the tangible products that individual consumers purchase for personal or family use. **Services** are intangible products that we pay for and use but don't own. Service transactions contribute on average more than 60 percent to the gross national product of all industrialized nations. Marketers need to understand the special challenges that arise when they market an intangible service rather than a tangible good.[4] Because both goods and services are products, it's correct to say "goods and services" rather than "products and services."

In both cases, though, keep in mind that the consumer expects to obtain some underlying value, such as convenience, security, or status, from a marketing exchange. That value can come from a variety of competing goods and services, even those that don't resemble one another on the surface. For example, a new CD and a ticket to a local concert may cost about the same, and each may provide the benefit of musical enjoyment, so consumers often have to choose among competing alternatives if they can't afford (or don't want) to buy them all.

See less of your neighbours. Call Ben Towell at Fence Me In for a quote on 07920 423 627

© Brass Agency

Marketing an intangible service like the assistance this British fence company offers poses unique challenges.

consumer goods
The goods individual consumers purchase for personal or family use.

services
Intangible products that are exchanged directly between the producer and the customer.

Business-to-Business Goods and Services

Business-to-business marketing is the marketing of goods and services from one organization to another. Although we usually relate marketing to the thousands of consumer goods begging for our dollars every day, the reality is that businesses and other organizations buy a lot more goods than consumers do. They purchase these **industrial goods** for further processing or to use in their own business operations. For example, automakers buy tons of steel to use in the manufacturing process, and they buy computer systems to track manufacturing costs and other information essential to operations.

Similarly, there is a lot of buzz about **e-commerce** and the buying and selling of products—books, CDs, cars, and so forth—on the Internet. However, just like in the offline world, much of the real online action is in the area of business-to-business marketing.

business-to-business marketing
The marketing of goods and services from one organization to another.

industrial goods
Goods that individuals or organizations buy for further processing or for their own use when they do business.

e-commerce
The buying or selling of goods and services electronically, usually over the Internet.

Not-for-Profit Marketing

As we noted earlier, you don't have to be a businessperson to use marketing principles. Many **not-for-profit organizations** (also known as **nongovernmental organizations** or **NGOs**), including museums, zoos, and even churches, practice the marketing concept. Local governments are adopting marketing techniques to create more effective taxpayer services and to attract new businesses and industries to their counties and cities. Even states are getting into the act: We've known for a long time that I ♥ NY, but recently Kentucky and Oregon hired advertising agencies to develop statewide branding campaigns (the official state motto of Oregon is now "Oregon. We love dreamers.").[5] The intense competition for

not-for-profit organizations
Organizations with charitable, educational, community, and other public service goals that buy goods and services to support their functions and to attract and serve their members.

nongovernmental organizations (NGOs)
Another name for not-for-profit organizations.

support of civic and charitable activities means that only the not-for-profits that meet the needs of their constituents and donors will survive.

Idea, Place, and People Marketing

Marketing principles also encourage people to endorse ideas or to change their behaviors in positive ways. Many organizations work hard to convince consumers not to litter our highways, to avoid texting while driving, or to believe that one political system is preferable to another. In addition to ideas, places and people also are marketable. We are all familiar with tourism marketing that promotes exotic resorts like Club Med ("the antidote for civilization"). For many developing countries like Thailand, tourism provides an important opportunity for economic growth.

You may have heard the expression "Stars are made, not born." There's a lot of truth to that. Beyoncé may have a killer voice and Ryan Braun may have a red-hot baseball bat, but talent alone doesn't make thousands or even millions of people buy CDs or stadium seats. Some of the same principles that go into "creating" a celebrity apply to you. An entertainer—whether Miranda Lambert, Selena Gomez, or Drake—must "package" his or her talents, identify a market that is likely to be interested, and work hard to gain exposure to these potential customers by appearing in the right musical venues.

In the same way, everyday people like you "package" themselves when they sum up their accomplishments on LinkedIn and join professional groups to link with as many "buyers" as they can. And this person marketing perspective is more valid than ever—now that almost everyone can find "15 minutes of fame" on a Web site, a blog, or a YouTube video. We even have a new word—*microcelebrity*—to describe those who are famous, not necessarily to millions of people but certainly to hundreds or even thousands who follow their comings and goings on Facebook, Flickr, or Twitter.

... Value for Customers ...

marketing concept
A management orientation that focuses on identifying and satisfying consumer needs to ensure the organization's long-term profitability.

need
The recognition of any difference between a consumer's actual state and some ideal or desired state.

want
The desire to satisfy needs in specific ways that are culturally and socially influenced.

Most successful firms today practice the **marketing concept**—that is, marketers first identify consumer needs and then provide products that satisfy those needs to ensure the firm's long-term profitability. A **need** is the difference between a consumer's actual state and some ideal or desired state. When the difference is big enough, the consumer is motivated to take action to satisfy the need. When you're hungry, you buy a snack. If you're not happy with your hair, you get a new hairstyle. When you need a job (or perhaps just get mad at your boss), you network on LinkedIn.

Needs relate to physical functions (such as driving) or to psychological ones (such as the need for security). Subaru is one company that tries to meet the psychological needs of consumers to feel safe (as well as their need for reliable transportation). While many Americans feel a connection with their automobiles, Subaru owners maintain a special bond. Browse the Subaru website, and you'll see story after story and photo after photo of people involved in a car crash who wrote in to say that their Subaru saved their lives. Now that's a car worth loving!

The specific way a person satisfies a need depends on his or her unique history, learning experiences, and cultural environment. That explains why Nestlé's Kit Kat is the number one candy brand in Japan—but the flavors you buy there include green tea, soy sauce, yubari melon, and sweet potato.[6] A **want** is a desire for a particular product

Courtesy of UAB "Milk Agency"

This Italian ketchup brand illustrates how the condiment satisfies a simple need.

we use to satisfy a need in specific ways that are culturally and socially influenced. For example, two classmates' stomachs rumble during a lunchtime lecture, and both need food. However, each of the two may satisfy this need in quite a different way. The first student may be a health nut who fantasizes about gulping down a big handful of trail mix, while the second person may lust for a greasy cheeseburger and fries. The first student's want is trail mix, whereas the second student's want is fast food (and some antacid for dessert).

The late management guru Peter Drucker observed, "The aim of marketing is to make selling superfluous."[7] A product delivers a **benefit** when it satisfies a need or want. For marketers to be successful, they must develop products that provide one or more benefits that are important to consumers. The challenge is to identify what benefits people look for and then develop a product that delivers those benefits while also convincing consumers that their product is better than a competitor's product—this makes the choice of which product to buy obvious. For example, in order to satisfy customers' desires for menu offerings that match their healthy lifestyle, McDonald's introduced its line of customizable Premium McWraps. Known as the "Subway buster," these low-priced, fresh McWraps go head to head with Subway's offerings.[8]

Everyone can want your product, but that doesn't ensure sales unless consumers have the means to obtain it. When you couple desire with the buying power or resources to satisfy a want, the result is **demand**. So the potential customers looking for a snappy red BMW convertible are the people who want the car minus those who can't afford to buy or lease one (no, stealing the car doesn't count). A **market** consists of all the consumers who share a common need that can be satisfied by a specific product and who have the resources, willingness, and authority to make the purchase.

A *marketplace* used to be a location where buying and selling occurs face-to-face. In today's "wired" world, however, many buyers and sellers most likely will never meet in person. The modern **marketplace** may take the form of a glitzy shopping mall, a mail-order catalog, a TV shopping network, an eBay auction, or a phone app. In developing countries, the marketplace may be a street corner or an open-air market where people sell fruits and vegetables much as they did thousands of years ago. Indeed, a marketplace may not even exist in the physical world—as players of online games will tell you. Residents of cyberworlds like *Second Life* and *Habbo Hotel* buy and sell virtual real estate, home furnishings, and bling for their digital avatars; in 2012 alone, they bought about $2.9 billion worth of **virtual goods** that exist only on a computer server.

Marketplaces are evolving in another interesting way as well: Increasingly consumers, especially younger ones, would rather rent than purchase the products they use. One of the biggest changes is in the domain of car sales, which are plummeting among newer drivers. Innovative start-ups like Zipcar figured out that many people, especially those who live in urban areas, would rather rent a ride by the hour instead of dealing with the hassles of car loans and hunting for parking spots when they weren't using their cars. Now the big guys are testing the waters. Volkswagen's Quicar project rents cars in Hanover, Germany, while BMW continues its international expansion of the DriveNow electric vehicle car-sharing program from Europe to the U.S.

Similar models for bike sharing (Vélib in Paris, Citi Bike in New York), music sharing (Spotify, Pandora) and even apartment sharing (Airbnb) are upending business models all over the place as consumers figure out that it often makes a lot more sense to lease what you need only when you need it.[9] Millions of enterprising consumers in turn are becoming **rentrepreneurs** as they make money by renting out their stuff when they aren't using it—they're offering everything from barbecue grills and power tools to Halloween costumes and who knows what else on sites like Zilok in France and Craigslist in the U.S. Some analysts refer to this mushrooming trend as **collaborative consumption**.

benefit
The outcome sought by a customer that motivates buying behavior that satisfies a need or want.

demand
Customers' desires for products coupled with the resources needed to obtain them.

market
All the customers and potential customers who share a common need that can be satisfied by a specific product, who have the resources to exchange for it, who are willing to make the exchange, and who have the authority to make the exchange.

marketplace
Any location or medium used to conduct an exchange.

virtual goods
Digital products consumers buy for use in online contexts.

APPLYING ▼ Demand

Joe needs to understand the potential demand for Pandora's services so he can develop a plan that will maximize the number of these consumers who actually visit the site on a regular basis.

rentrepreneurs
enterprising consumers who make money by renting out their possessions when they aren't using them.

collaborative consumption
A term used to refer to the activities practiced by rentrepreneurs.

utility
The usefulness or benefit that consumers receive from a product.

Marketing Creates Utility

Marketing transactions create **utility**, which refers to the sum of the benefits we receive when we use a good or service. When it ensures that people have the type of product they want, where and when they want it, the marketing system makes our lives easier. Utility is what creates value. Marketing processes create several different kinds of utility to provide value to consumers:

- *Form utility* is the benefit marketing provides by transforming raw materials into finished products, as when a dress manufacturer combines silk, thread, and zippers to create a bridesmaid's gown.

- *Place utility* is the benefit marketing provides by making products available where customers want them. The most sophisticated evening gown sewn in New York's garment district is of little use to a bridesmaid in Kansas City if it isn't shipped to her in time.

- *Time utility* is the benefit marketing provides by storing products until they are needed. Some women rent their wedding gowns instead of buying them and wearing them only once (they hope!).

stakeholders
Buyers, sellers, or investors in a company; community residents; and even citizens of the nations where goods and services are made or sold—in other words, any person or organization that has a "stake" in the outcome.

- *Possession utility* is the benefit marketing provides by allowing the consumer to own, use, and enjoy the product. The bridal store provides access to a range of styles and colors that would not be available to a woman outfitting a bridal party on her own.

As we've seen, marketers provide utility in many ways. Now, let's see how customers "take delivery" of this added value.

Value for Clients and Partners

Marketing doesn't just meet the needs of consumers—it meets the needs of diverse stakeholders. The term **stakeholders** here refers to buyers, sellers, or investors in a company, community residents, and even citizens of the nations where goods and services are made or sold—in other words, any person or organization that has a "stake" in the outcome. Thus, marketing is about satisfying everyone involved in the marketing process.

Value for Society at Large

Is it possible to contribute in a positive way to society and the earth and still contribute to your paycheck? Target, one of the nation's largest retailers, seems to think so. The company announced in its 2012 corporate responsibility report that two of its top five priorities are environmental sustainability and responsible sourcing. For example, one goal Target set for 2015 is to ensure that the seafood sold in its stores is 100 percent sustainable (caught without negatively impacting ecosystems) and traceable (the product can be traced through the supply chain from point of harvest to final product). Also, the retailer is giving back to its customers and helping them save money. Through its reusable-bag program, Target has returned more than $7 million to customers (those who bring their reusable bags save five cents per bag off their bill). And more than half of the chain's apparel line is labeled "machine wash cold," meaning customers reduce energy when they wash their clothes (thereby lowering customers' electricity bills).[10]

© Hemis/Alamy

Rent the Runway is a new service started by two recent business school grads. It rents high-end dresses from designers like Diane Von Furstenberg, for about one-tenth of the cost of buying the same garment in a store. A woman can rent a dress for four nights; it's shipped directly to her doorstep much like a Netflix video. The customer returns the dress in a prepaid envelope and the rental price includes the cost of dry cleaning. Place utility at work![6]

2 *When* Did Marketing Begin? The Evolution of a Concept

OBJECTIVE

Explain the evolution of the marketing concept.
(pp. 35–40)

Now that we have an idea of how the marketing process works, let's take a step back and see how this process worked (or didn't work) in "the old days." Although it just sounds like common sense to us, believe it or not, the notion that businesses and other organizations succeed when they satisfy customers' needs actually is a pretty recent idea. Before the 1950s, marketing was basically a means of making production more efficient. Let's take a quick look at how the marketing discipline has developed since then. Table 1.1 tells us about some of the more recent events in this marketing history.

The Production Era

Many people say that Henry Ford's Model T changed America forever. Even from the start in 1908, when the "Tin Lizzie," or "flivver" as the T was known, sold for $825, Ford continued to make improvements in production. By 1912, he got so efficient that the car sold for $575, a price even the Ford employees who made the car could afford.[11] As the price continued to drop, Ford sold even more flivvers. By 1921, the Model T Ford owned 60 percent of the new-car market.

Ford's focus illustrates a **production orientation**, which works best in a seller's market when demand is greater than supply because it focuses on the most efficient ways to produce and distribute products. Essentially, consumers have to take whatever is available—there weren't a whole lot of other Tin Lizzies competing for drivers in the 1920s. Under these conditions, marketing plays a relatively insignificant role—the goods literally sell themselves because people have no other choices. Firms that focus on a production orientation tend to view the market as a homogeneous group that will be satisfied with the basic function of a product. Sometimes this view is too narrow. For example, Colgate-Palmolive Company's market share of its Hill's Science Diet pet food brand has "gone to the dogs" in recent years. This decrease in share is due to the company's reliance on its tried-and-true scientifically formulated dog food product in a world where consumers increasingly seek foods with all-natural ingredients.[12]

production orientation
A management philosophy that emphasizes the most efficient ways to produce and distribute products.

The Sales Era

When product availability exceeds demand in a buyer's market, businesses may engage in the "hard sell," in which salespeople aggressively push their wares. During the Great Depression in the 1930s, when money was scarce for most people, and again in the 1950s, firms shifted their focus from a product orientation toward moving their goods in any way they could.

This **selling orientation** means that management views marketing as a sales function, or a way to move products out of warehouses so that inventories don't pile up. The selling orientation gained in popularity after World War II. During the war, the U.S. dramatically increased its industrial capacity to manufacture tanks, combat boots, parachutes, and countless other wartime goods. After the war, this industrial capacity was converted to producing consumer goods.

Consumers eagerly bought all the things they couldn't get during the war years, but once they satisfied these initial needs and wants, they got more selective. The race for consumers' hearts and pocketbooks was on. The selling orientation prevailed well into the 1950s. But consumers as a rule don't like to be pushed, and the hard sell gave marketing a bad image.

selling orientation
A managerial view of marketing as a sales function, or a way to move products out of warehouses to reduce inventory.

Table 1.1 | Highlights of Marketing History

Year	Marketing Event
1955	Ray Kroc opens his first McDonald's.
1956	Lever Brothers launches Wisk, America's first liquid laundry detergent.
1957	Ford rolls out Edsel, loses more than $250 million in two years.
1959	Mattel introduces Barbie.
1960	The Food and Drug Administration approves Searle's Enovid as the first oral contraceptive.
1961	Procter & Gamble launches Pampers.
1962	Walmart, Kmart, Target, and Woolco open their doors.
1963	The Pepsi Generation kicks off the cola wars.
1964	Blue Ribbon Sports (now known as Nike) ships its first shoes.
1965	Donald Fisher opens The Gap, a jeans-only store in San Francisco.
1971	Cigarette advertising is banned on radio and TV.
1973	Federal Express begins overnight delivery services.
1976	Sol Price opens the first warehouse club store in San Diego.
1980	Ted Turner creates CNN.
1981	MTV begins.
1982	Gannett launches *USA Today.*
1983	Chrysler introduces minivans.
1984	Apple Computer introduces the Macintosh.
1985	New Coke is launched; old Coke rebranded as Coca-Cola Classic is brought back 79 days later.
1990	Saturn, GM's first new car division since 1919, rolls out its first car.
1993	Phillip Morris reduces price of Marlboros by 40 cents a pack and loses $13.4 billion in stock market value in one day.
1994	In the largest switch in ad history, IBM yanks its business from scores of agencies worldwide and hands its entire account to Ogilvy & Mather.
1995	eBay goes online as an experimental auction service.
1997	McDonald's gives away Teenie Beanie Babies with Happy Meals. Consumer response is so overwhelming that McDonald's is forced to take out ads apologizing for its inability to meet demand. Nearly 100 million Happy Meals are sold during the promotion.[a]
1998	Germany's Daimler-Benz acquires America's Chrysler Corporation for more than $38 billion in stock to create a new global automaking giant called Daimler-Chrysler.[b]
2003	Amazon debuts its "Search Inside the Book" feature, which allows you to search the full text of more than 33 million pages from over 120,000 printed books.
2004	Online sales in the U.S. top $100 billion.[c]
2007	About 30 open-source companies were purchased for more than $1 billion.[d]
2008	MySpace boasts over 225 million members worldwide.[d]
2010	Apple launches the iPad; sells 300,000 of the tablets on the first day and 1 million iPads in 28 days—less than half of the 74 days it took to sell 1 million iPhones. Consumers watch more than 30 billion videos online per month.[e]
2012	Retailer J. C. Penney tosses out its old marketing strategy of discounts and promotions in favor of everyday "fair and square" pricing—no coupons needed. (This strategy lasts only about 15 months.)[f]
2013	Sales of carbonated soft drinks continue their nine-year decline, down another 3 percent, despite major advertising and marketing investments.[g]
2014	Facebook spends $2 billion to buy Oculus Rift, a manufacturer of virtual reality headsets, as it signals the next frontier for social networks.[h]

Sources: Patricia Sellers, "To Avoid Trampling, Get Ahead of the Mass," *Fortune,* 1994, 201–2, except as noted. [a]Tod Taylor, "The Beanie Factor," *Brandweek,* June 16, 1997, 22–27. [b]Jennifer Laabs, "Daimler-Benz and Chrysler: A Merger of Global HR Proportions," *Workforce,* July 1998, 13. [c]Keith Regan, "Report: Online Sales Top $100 Billion," June 1, 2004, **www.ecommercetimes.com/ story/34148.html.** [d]Frank Rose, "Wired Business Trends 2008," December 2007, **www.wired.com/techbiz/it/magazine/16-04/bz_opensource.** [e]Eliot Van Buskirk, "Apple iPad Reaches '1 Million Sold' Twice as Fast as iPhone," May 3, 2010, **www.wired.com/epicenter/2010/05/apple-ipad-reaches-one-million-sold-twice-as-fast-as-iphone/#ixzz0qBrfv3tj** (accessed June 7, 2010); **Mashable.com,** April 5, 2010, **http://mashable.com/2010/04/05/ipad-stats-300000-sold** (accessed June 7, 2010); Center for Media Research, "30 Billion Videos Watched Online in April," June 11, 2010, **www.mediapost.com/publications/?fa5Articles.showArticle&art_aid5129561** (accessed June 11, 2010); Brad Tuttle, "J. C. Penney Reintroduces Fake Prices (and Lots of Coupons Too, of Course," May 2, 2013, **http://business.time.com/2013/05/02/jc-penney-reintroduces-fake-prices-and-lots-of-coupons-too-of-course** (accessed April 5, 2014). [f]Natalie Zmuda, "Decline in Soft Drink Sales Accelerates despite Big Marketing Investments," March 31, 2014, **http://adage.com/article/cmo-strategy/ soft-drink-sales-decline-accelerates/292409** (accessed April 5, 2014). [h]Victor Luckerson, "Facebook Buying Oculus Virtual-Reality Company for $2 Billion," March 25, 2014, **http://time .com/37842/facebook-oculus-rift** (accessed April 11, 2014).

Companies that still follow a selling orientation tend to be more successful at making one-time sales rather than at building repeat business. We are most likely to find this focus among companies that sell *unsought goods*—products that people don't tend to buy without some prodding. For example, most of us aren't exactly "dying" to shop for cemetery plots, so some encouragement may be necessary to splurge on a final resting place.

The Relationship Era

At Plaza Fiesta outside Atlanta, Georgia, Hispanic customers are in for a treat: Instead of shopping at a mall, it's more like they're visiting a traditional Mexican village. With a bus station for ease of access, services like hairdressers or a doctor's office, and live music on Sundays, customers come for the experience, not just the shopping.[13] Plaza Fiesta found that it pays to have a **consumer orientation** that satisfies customers' needs and wants.

As the world's most successful firms began to adopt a consumer orientation, marketers had a way to outdo the competition—and firms began to develop more of an appreciation for the ways they could contribute to profits. Marketers did research to understand the needs of different consumers, assisted in tailoring products to the needs of these various groups, and did an even better job of designing marketing messages than in the days of the selling orientation.

The marketing world was humming along nicely, but then inflation in the 1970s and recession in the 1980s took their toll on company profits. The marketing concept needed a boost. Firms had to do more than meet consumers' needs—they had to do this better than the competition—and do it repeatedly. Companies increasingly concentrated on improving the quality of their products. By the early 1990s, many in the marketing community followed an approach termed **total quality management (TQM)**. The TQM perspective takes many forms, but essentially it's a management philosophy that involves all employees from the assembly line onward in continuous product quality improvement. We'll learn more about TQM in Chapter 9.

Indeed, rapid improvements in manufacturing processes give forward-thinking firms—even small ones—a huge edge in the marketplace because they are more nimble and thus able to create products consumers want when they want them and at the price they want. One way they do this is to manufacture *on demand*—this means that they don't actually produce a product until a customer orders it. The Japanese pioneered this idea with their *just-in-time model*, which we'll learn more about in Chapter 11.

Today, however, even small mom-and-pop companies can compete in this space. Technology is creating a new class of businessperson that we call an **instapreneur**. All you need is a design; even amateurs can produce jewelry, T-shirts, furniture, and indeed almost anything we can imagine. They don't have to pay to store their inventory in huge warehouses, they don't need any money down, and they don't have to pay licensing fees.

The Triple-Bottom-Line Orientation

Over time, many forward-thinking organizations began to view their commitment to quality as more than "just" satisfying consumers' needs during a single transaction. A few realized that making monetary profit is important—but there's more to think about than just the financial bottom line. Instead, they began to focus on a **triple-bottom-line orientation**,

consumer orientation
A business approach that prioritizes the satisfaction of customers' needs and wants.

total quality management (TQM)
A management philosophy that focuses on satisfying customers through empowering employees to be an active part of continuous quality improvement.

instapreneur
A businessperson who only produces a product when it is ordered.

triple-bottom-line orientation
A business orientation that looks at financial profits, the community in which the organization operates, and creating sustainable business practices.

Warby Parker is a lifestyle brand with a lofty objective: to offer designer eyewear at a revolutionary price, while leading the way for socially conscious businesses. The company also offers a Home-Try-on Program, which allows customers to try on frames at home before purchasing. With glasses starting as low as $95, the company appeals to the needs of the thrifty as well as the socially conscious—for every pair of eyewear purchased, Warby Parker distributes a pair to someone in need.[14]

Green marketing in action.

societal marketing concept

A management philosophy that marketers must satisfy customers' needs in ways that also benefit society and also deliver profit to the firm.

sustainability

A product design focus that seeks to create products that meet present consumer needs without compromising the ability of future generations to meet their needs.

green marketing

A marketing strategy that supports environmental stewardship, thus creating a differential benefit in the minds of consumers.

which means building long-term bonds with customers rather than merely selling them stuff today.[15] This new way of looking at business emphasizes the need to maximize three components:

1. *The financial bottom line:* Financial profits to stakeholders

2. *The social bottom line:* Contributing to the communities in which the company operates

3. *The environmental bottom line:* Creating sustainable business practices that minimize damage to the environment or that even improve it

One result of this new way of long-term thinking is the **societal marketing concept**, which maintains that marketers must satisfy customers' needs in ways that also benefit society while they still deliver a profit to the firm. A similar important trend now is for companies to think of ways to design and manufacture products with a focus on **sustainability**, which we define as "meeting present needs without compromising the ability of future generations to meet their needs."[16] One way to think about this philosophy is "doing well by doing good." Many big and small firms alike practice sustainability through their efforts that include satisfying society's environmental and social needs for a cleaner, safer environment.

When Canadian hockey players in the 2014 Winter Olympics skated onto the ice, they wore Nike jerseys made from plastic bottles. The jerseys, each made from up to 17 plastic water bottles, were 15 percent lighter in weight than previous jerseys.[17] Walmart is another leader in sustainability practices. The giant retail chain makes and sells photo frames from plastic waste products it creates and recycles materials left over from manufacturing its private label diapers into building materials when it constructs new stores. Sustainability is good business because it reduces costs while conserving resources. Walmart estimates savings of $100 million in one year when it switched to a recyclable variety of cardboard it uses to ship goods to its stores. Consumers love it too: In the U.S. alone, we spend more than $500 billion per year on sustainable products.[18]

Sustainability applies to many aspects of doing business, including social and economic practices (e.g., humane working conditions and diplomacy to prevent wars that deplete food supplies, atmospheric quality, and, of course, lives). One other crucial pillar of sustainability is the environmental impact of the product. **Green marketing** develops marketing strategies that support environmental stewardship by creating an environmentally founded differential benefit in the minds of consumers. Green marketing is one aspect of a firm's overall commitment to sustainability. A recent study on the impact of green marketing uncovered some interesting results:

- About half the companies reported that they consciously take steps to become more green.

- More than 80 percent of respondents indicated they expect to spend more on green marketing in the future.

- Companies with smaller marketing budgets tend to spend more on green marketing and also think green marketing is more effective than do larger companies.

- By far the most popular medium for green marketing was the Internet; about three-fourths of the respondents bought an eco-friendly product online.

- Marketers tend to lead green initiatives; 50 percent of firm managers surveyed agree that control of the green (sustainability) program is in the hands of marketers.[19]

In addition to building long-term relationships and focusing on social responsibility, triple-bottom-line firms place a much greater focus on *accountability*—measuring just how much value an organization's marketing activities create. This means that marketers at these organizations ask hard questions about the true value of their efforts and their impact on the bottom line. These questions all boil down to the simple acronym of **ROI (return on investment)**. Marketers now realize that if they want to assess just how much value they create for the firm, they need to know exactly what they are spending and what the concrete results of their actions are.

return on investment (ROI)
The direct financial impact of a firm's expenditure of a resource, such as time or money.

However, it's not always so easy to assess the value of marketing activities. Many times, managers state their marketing objectives using vague phrases like "increase awareness of our product" or "encourage people to eat healthier snacks." These goals are important, but their lack of specificity makes it pretty much impossible for senior management to determine marketing's true impact. Because management may view these efforts as costs rather than investments, marketing activities often are among the first to be cut out of a firm's budget. To win continued support for what they do (and sometimes to keep their jobs), marketers in triple-bottom-line firms do their best to prove to management that they generate measurable value by aligning marketing activities with the firm's overall business objectives.[20]

What's Next in the Evolution of Marketing?

With the advent of the Internet, more and more firms started to rely heavily on the Web to build long-term bonds with consumers. The Internet provides the ultimate opportunity to implement the marketing concept because it allows a firm to personalize its messages and products to better meet the needs of each individual consumer. More on this in Chapter 14.

Indeed, some marketing analysts suggest that the Internet creates a *paradigm shift* for business. This means that companies must adhere to a new model to profit in a wired world. They argue that we live in an **attention economy**, one in which a company's success will be measured by its *share of mind* rather than share of market, where companies make money when they attract eyeballs rather than just dollars. For example, Google sells advertising to many other companies, so the more consumers it can persuade to "Google" rather than "Bing" or "Yahoo!," the more it can charge to place ads on search pages.

attention economy
A company's success is measured by its share of mind rather than share of market, where companies make money when they attract eyeballs rather than just dollars.

In many marketers' minds, the next era is already here—the era of *Big Data!* You'll have a chance to learn a lot about Big Data in Chapter 5 but for now please know that it is the popular term to describe the exponential growth of data—both structured and unstructured—in massive amounts that are hard or impossible to process using traditional database techniques. Some suggest that Big Data may be as important to business and to society as the Internet. Of course, it's not the data itself that are important—it's the ability to analyze the massive amounts of information for better decision making. Auto manufacturer Ford, for example, has been collecting and analyzing Big Data since 2007. Currently, the company employs about 200 Big Data and analytics experts. Based on the information Ford gets from analyzing Big Data, the company has been able to build better turn signals, make sure the right car is available when a customer with a specific profile visits a particular dealership, and generate more accurate assembly plant schedules and parts forecasts.[21] We'll do a deeper dive into big data in Chapter 5.

Ripped from the Headlines

Ethical/Sustainable Decisions in the Real World

The next time you see someone taking a drag on a cigarette on campus, take another look: That someone might just be "vaping." Vaping, which is the process of inhaling vapors from an e-cigarette (electronic cigarette) or a similar device, is the new "in" thing. And with flavors like Red Energy, Pink Bubblegum, or Java Jolt to choose from and celebrities like Robert Pattinson, Leonardo Di Caprio, and Katherine Heigl doing it, what young adult wouldn't be tempted to give vaping a try?

Originally marketed as a way for traditional cigarette smokers to kick their smoking habit, e-cigarettes are finding their way into the hands of college students and teens. In fact, according to the Centers for Disease Control and Prevention, "e-cigarette experimentation and recent use doubled among U.S. middle and high school students during 2011–2012."[22] But young people aren't always smoking e-cigarettes; they often use "hookah pens," "vape pens," or "vape pipes"; they see these new devices as entirely different from e-cigarettes. "The technology and hardware is the same," said Adam Querbach, head of sales and marketing for hookah maker Romman Inc. "A lot of the difference is branding."[23]

Thanks to some clever and currently unregulated marketing, including those flashy devices and fun flavors, some young people don't believe these devices are dangerous or at least not as dangerous as e-cigarettes. And yet many of these flavors still contain nicotine (the addictive substance found in traditional cigarettes) and other chemicals. Try one, and you could easily get hooked on a product whose long-term effects are as yet unknown and whose use could ultimately lead to more harmful, traditional cigarette smoking.

ETHICS CHECK:

Find out what other students taking this course *would do* and *why* at **mymktlab.com.**

Should e-cigarettes be marketed like any other widely available product such as milk or music?

☐YES ☐NO

3

OBJECTIVE

Understand value from the perspectives of customers, producers, and society. (pp. 40–48)

The Value of Marketing and the Marketing of Value

We said earlier that marketing is all about delivering value to everyone who is affected by a transaction. That includes the customer, the seller, and society at large.

How do customers (such as your potential employers) decide how much value they will get from a purchase? One way to look at value is to think of it simply as a ratio of benefits to costs—that is, customers "invest" their precious time and money to do business with a firm, and they expect a certain bundle of benefits in return.

Let's look at value from the different perspectives of the parties that are involved in an exchange: the customers, the sellers, and society.

Value from the Customer's Perspective

Think about something you would like to buy, say, a new pair of shoes. You have narrowed the choice down to several options. Your purchase decision no doubt will be affected by the ratio of costs versus benefits for each type of shoe. When you buy a pair of shoes, you consider the price (and other costs) along with all the other benefits (utilities) that each competing pair of shoes provides you.

value proposition
A marketplace offering that fairly and accurately sums up the value that will be realized if the good or service is purchased.

Marketers communicate these benefits to the customer in the form of a **value proposition**, a marketplace offering that fairly and accurately sums up the value that the customer will realize if he or she purchases the product. The value proposition includes the whole bundle of benefits the firm promises to deliver, not just the benefits of the product itself. For example, although most people probably won't get to their destination sooner if they drive a BMW versus a Mercedes-Benz or Audi, many die-hard loyalists swear by their favorite brand. These archrival brands are largely marketed in terms of their images—meaning their respective advertising agencies have carefully crafted them with the help of slickly produced commercials and millions of dollars. When you buy a BMW, you do more than choose a car to get you around town—you may also make a statement about the type of person you are or wish you were. In addition to providing a luxury ride or superior maintenance services, that statement also is part of the value the product delivers to you.

The challenge to the marketer is to create a killer value proposition. A big part of this challenge is to convince customers that this value proposition is superior to others they might choose from competitors.

Value from the Seller's Perspective

We've seen that marketing transactions produce value for buyers, but how do sellers experience value, and how do they decide whether a transaction is valuable? One answer is obvious: They determine whether the exchange is profitable to them. Has it made money for the company's management, its workers, and its shareholders?

That's a very important factor but not the only one. Just as we can't measure value from the consumer's perspective only in functional terms, value from the seller's perspective can take many forms. For example, in addition to making a buck or two, many firms measure value along other dimensions, such as prestige among rivals or pride in doing what they do well. Smart companies today understand that making money from a single transaction doesn't provide the kind of value they desire. As we said earlier, the goal of many successful firms is to satisfy the customer over and over again so that they can build a long-term relationship rather than just having a "one-night stand."

Some organizations by definition don't even care about making money, or they may not even be allowed to make money; nonprofits like Greenpeace, the Smithsonian Institution, or National Public Radio regard value in terms of their ability to motivate, educate, or delight the public.

In recent years, many firms have transformed the way they do business. They now regard consumers as *partners* in the transaction rather than as passive "victims." That explains why it's becoming more common for companies to host events (sometimes called **brandfests**) to thank customers for their loyalty. For example, Jeep builds strong bonds with its Jeep 4×4 owners when it holds several off-road adventure weekends every year. These Jeep Jamborees are where other Jeep owners get to challenge the limits of their 4×4s on off-road trails and commune with fellow brand loyalists.[24]

Jeep's cultivation of its 4×4 enthusiasts reflects an important lesson the company understands very well: *It is more expensive to attract new customers than it is to retain current ones.* This notion has transformed the way many companies do business, and we'll repeat it several times in this book. However, there is an important exception to the rule: In recent years, companies have been working harder to calculate the true value of their relationships with customers by asking, "How much is this customer *really* worth to us?" Firms recognize that it can be very costly in terms of both money and human effort to do whatever it takes to keep some customers loyal to the company. Very often these actions pay off, but there are cases in which keeping a customer is a losing proposition.

Companies that calculate the **lifetime value of a customer** look at how much profit they expect to make from a particular customer, including each and every purchase he or she will make from them now and in the future. To calculate lifetime value, companies estimate the amount the person will spend and then subtract what it will cost to maintain this relationship. The Metrics Moment box illustrates one approach to how marketers measure customer value.

Provide Value through Competitive Advantage

How does a firm go about creating a competitive advantage? The first step is to identify what it does really well. A **distinctive competency** is a firm's capability that is superior to that of its competition. For example, Coca-Cola's success in global markets—Coke commands 50 percent of the world's soft-drink business—is related to its distinctive competencies in distribution and marketing communications. Coke's distribution system got a jump on the competition during World War II. To enable U.S. soldiers fighting overseas to enjoy a five-cent Coke, the U.S. government assisted Coca-Cola in building 64 overseas bottling

brandfests
Events that companies host to thank customers for their loyalty.

APPLYING ▼ Customer Value

Joe understands that it's more expensive to attract new customers than it is to retain current ones. He needs to find ways to motivate Pandora's users to visit the site more often and to recommend it to their friends in order to build a loyal customer base.

lifetime value of a customer
The potential profit a single customer's purchase of a firm's products generates over the customer's lifetime.

distinctive competency
A superior capability of a firm in comparison to its direct competitors.

Metrics Moment

This section highlights the concepts of value and the value proposition that firms and their offerings bring to customers. But how do marketers actually measure value? Increasingly, they develop **marketing scorecards** that report (often in the form of numerical values) how the company or brand is actually doing in achieving various goals. We can think of a scorecard as a marketing department's report card. Scorecards tend to be short and to the point, and they often include charts and graphs to summarize information in an easy-to-read format. They might report "grades" on factors such as actual cost per sale, a comparison of Web hits (the number of people who visit an e-commerce site) versus Web transactions (the number who actually buy something at the site), a measure of customers' satisfaction with a company's repair facilities, or perhaps even a percentage of consumers who respond to a mail piece that asks them to make a donation to a charity that the firm sponsors. You can see an example of a simple scorecard in Table 1.2. Throughout this book, we'll give you the opportunity to "get your hands dirty" as you calculate various kinds of scores, or **metrics**.

Apply the Metrics

1. Using Table 1.2 as a template, develop a scorecard for customer satisfaction with your marketing class. You will need to develop your own relevant items for satisfaction measurement.
2. Then have the students in your class complete the scorecard now and again in the middle of the semester.
3. Summarize, interpret, and present the results.

marketing scorecards
Feedback vehicles that report (often in quantified terms) how the company or brand is actually doing in achieving various goals.

metrics
Measurements or "scorecards" that marketers use to identify the effectiveness of different strategies or tactics.

differential benefit
Properties of products that set them apart from competitors' products by providing unique customer benefits.

value chain
A series of activities involved in designing, producing, marketing, delivering, and supporting any product. Each link in the chain has the potential to either add or remove value from the product the customer eventually buys.

plants. Coke's skillful marketing communications program, a second distinctive competency, has contributed to its global success. In addition to its TV commercials, Coke blankets less developed countries such as Tanzania with signs posted on roads and on storefronts so that even people without TVs will think of Coke when they get thirsty.

The second step to develop a competitive advantage is to turn a distinctive competency into a **differential benefit**—value that competitors don't offer. Differential benefits set products apart from competitors' products by providing something unique that customers want. Differential benefits provide reasons for customers to pay a premium for a firm's products and exhibit a strong brand preference. For many years, loyal Apple computer users benefited from superior graphics capability compared to their PC-using counterparts. Later, when PC manufacturers caught up with this competitive advantage, Apple relied on its inventive product designers to create another differential benefit—futuristic-looking computers in a multitude of colors. This competitive advantage even tempted many loyal PC users to take a bite of the Apple (see Table 1.3).

Add Value through the Value Chain

Many different players—both within and outside a firm—need to work together to create and deliver value to customers. The **value chain** is a useful way to appreciate all the players that work together to create value. This term refers to a series of activities involved in

Table 1.2 | An Example of a Customer Service Scorecard

Item Text	Quarterly Scores		
	1st Qtr.	2nd Qtr.	3rd Qtr.
Satisfaction with			
C1 Employee responsiveness	60%	65%	68%
C2 Product selection	60%	62%	63%
C3 Service quality	60%	62%	55%
C4 Cleanliness of facility	75%	80%	85%
C5 Knowledge of employees	62%	62%	58%
C6 Appearance of employees	60%	62%	63%
C7 Convenience of location	60%	65%	68%

Source: Adapted From C. F. Lunbdy and C. Rasinowich, "The Missing Link," *Marketing Research*, Winter 2003, 14–19, p. 18. Copyright © 2003 American Marketing Association.

Table 1.3 | How Some Firms Achieve a Competitive Advantage with a Distinctive Competency

Company	Distinctive Competency	Differential Benefit	Competitive Advantage
Coca-Cola	Distribution and marketing communications	Convenience and brand awareness for customers all over the world	Coke has over 50 percent of world soft-drink market.[a]
Apple	Product quality and ease of use	Easy access to cutting-edge technology	Apple's sales of its Mac computer increased 28.5 percent as the overall market for PCs decreased.[b]
Southwest Airlines	Price point	Appeals to budget-conscious consumers	Southwest is the number one domestic carrier in the U.S...[c]
Amazon.com	Fulfillment and distribution	Availability, convenience, and ease of access of product	Amazon holds about a 50 percent market share for books sold via the Internet.[d]
Starbucks	Product quality	Customer satisfaction	Starbucks has just under 33 percent of the market share in its industry.[e]

Sources: [a]Siddharth Cavale, "Coke Revenue Misses Estimates as Soda Sales Slow," February 18, 2014, **www.reuters.com/article/2014/02/18/us-cocacola-results-idUSBREA1H0WH20140218** (accessed April 7, 2014). [b]Neil Hughes, "Apple's Domestic Mac Sales Surge 28.5% as Overall PC Market Shrinks 7.5%," January 9, 2014, **http://appleinsider.com/articles/14/01/09/apples-domestic-mac-sales-surge-285-as-overall-pc-market-shrinks-75** (accessed April 7, 2014). [c]Southwest Airlines, "2014 Media Kit," **www.southwest.com/assets/pdfs/customer_service/swcom_media_kit.pdf** (accessed April 7, 2014). [d]Andrew Rhomberg, "Is Amazon Invincible?," July 23, 2013, **www.digitalbookworld/2013/is-amazon-invincible** (accessed April 7, 2014). [e]Annalyn Censky, "Dunkin' Donuts to Double U.S. Locations," January 4, 2012, **http://money.cnn.com/2012/01/04/news/companies/dunkin_donuts_locations** (accessed April 7, 2014).

designing, producing, marketing, delivering, and supporting any product. In addition to marketing activities, the value chain includes business functions such as human resource management and technology development.[25]

The value chain concept reminds us that every product starts with raw materials that are of relatively limited value to the end customer. Each link in the chain has the potential to either add or remove value from the product the customer eventually buys. The successful firm is the one that can perform one or more of these activities better than other firms—this is its distinctive competency and thus provides an opportunity to gain a competitive advantage. The main activities of value chain members include the following:

- *Inbound logistics:* Bringing in materials to make the product

- *Operations:* Converting the materials into the final product

- *Outbound logistics:* Shipping out the final product

- *Marketing:* Promoting and selling the final product

- *Service:* Meeting the customer's needs by providing any additional support required

For example, when you buy a new iPad at your local Apple store, do you think about all the people and steps involved in designing, manufacturing, and delivering that product to the store—not to mention other people who create brand advertising, conduct consumer research to figure out what people like or dislike about their mobile music players, or even make the box it comes in or the packaging that keeps the unit from being damaged in shipment?

As Figure 1.2 shows, all these companies (and more) belong to Apple's value chain. This means that Apple must make a lot of decisions. What electronic components will go into its music players? What accessories will it include in the package? What trucking companies, wholesalers, and retailers will deliver the iPods to stores? What service will it provide to customers after the sale? And what marketing strategies will it use? In some cases, members of a value chain will work together to coordinate their activities to be more efficient and thus create a competitive advantage.

APPLYING ▼ Distinctive Competency

Pandora's distinctive competency is the site's ability to build customized "radio stations" that offer the listener the specific types of music he or she likes to hear based on a similar song or artist.

Figure 1.2 📷 *Snapshot* | Apple's Value Chain

Apple's value chain includes inbound logistics, operations, outbound logistics, marketing and sales, and service.

Inbound Logistics	Operations	Outbound Logistics	Marketing and Sales	Service
• Planar lithium battery (Sony) • Hard drive (Toshiba) • MP3 decoder and controller chip (PortalPlayer) • Flash memory chip (Sharp Electronics Corp.) • Stereo digital-to-analog converter (Wolfson Microelectronics Ltd.) • Firewire interface controller (Texas Instruments)	• Consumer research • New product development team • Engineering and production	• Trucking companies • Wholesalers • Retailers	• Advertising • Sales force	• Computer technicians

Source: Based on information from Erik Sherman, "Inside the Apple iPod Design Triumph," May 27, 2006, www.designchain.com/coverstory.asp?issue=summer02.

We've organized this book around the sequence of steps necessary to ensure that the appropriate value exchange occurs and that both parties to the transaction are satisfied—making it more likely they'll continue to do business in the future. 📈 Figure 1.3 shows these steps. Basically, we're going to learn about what marketers do as a product makes its way through the value chain from manufacturers into your hands. We'll start with a focus on how companies plan for success with global and ethical marketing strategies. Next, we'll see how research and Big Data help marketers understand and meet the different needs of different customers. Then we'll take a look at how firms decide to "position" the product in the marketplace, including choices about what it should look like, how its value should be communicated to customers, and how much to charge for it. As we reach the end of our marketing journey, we'll talk about how the product gets delivered and promoted to consumers.

Figure 1.3 📈 *Process* | Create and Deliver Value

This book is organized around the sequence of steps necessary to ensure that the appropriate value exchange occurs and that both parties to the transaction are satisfied. Each step corresponds to one of the book's five parts.

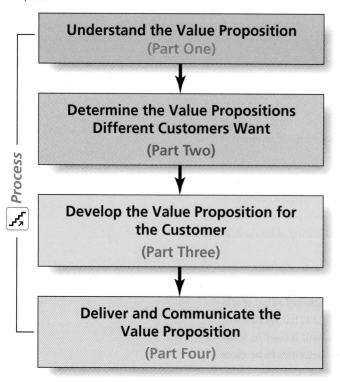

Consumer-Generated Value: From Audience to Community

Undoubtedly, one of the most exciting changes in the world of marketing is that everyday people actually *generate* value instead of just buying it—consumers are turning into advertising directors, retailers, and new-product-development consultants. They create their own ads (some flattering, some not) for products and post them on sites like YouTube. They buy and sell merchandise ranging from Beatles memorabilia to washing machines (to body parts, but that's another story) on eBay. They share ideas for new styles with fashion designers, design new advertising, and customize their own unique versions of products on websites. Some even proudly announce the latest stuff they've bought in "haul videos" they shoot and post on YouTube (if you don't believe us, just search for "haul videos" and see how many people take the time to do this).

These profound changes mean that marketers must adjust their thinking about customers: They need to stop thinking of buyers as a passive audience and start thinking of them as a community that is motivated to participate in both the production and the consumption of what companies sell. Some of these consumers are **amafessionals**: They contribute ideas for the fun and challenge rather than to receive a paycheck, so their motivation is to gain *psychic income* rather than financial income. We'll talk more about this phenomenon later, but for now think about these recent examples of **consumer-generated content**:

- Ghirardelli Chocolate broadcast consumer-generated comments in New York's Times Square about when and where they most enjoyed eating its chocolate squares.[26]

- At iReport, budding citizen journalists can upload photos and videos to CNN in response to breaking news. The most timely and compelling of these stories have the potential to be vetted (cleared) and aired on the CNN TV network.[27]

- Rite-Solutions, a software company that builds advanced command-and-control systems for the U.S. Navy, sets up an internal "prediction market" in which any employee can propose that the company acquire a new technology, enter a new business, or make an efficiency improvement. These proposals become stocks, complete with ticker symbols, discussion lists, and e-mail alerts. Employees buy or sell the stocks, and prices change to reflect the sentiments of the company's engineers, computer scientists, and project managers—as well as its marketers, accountants, and even the receptionist. One "stock" resulted in the development of a new product that now accounts for 30 percent of the company's sales.[28]

- For almost a decade, Doritos has been cashing in on its "Crash the Super Bowl" contest, where fans submit their best 30-second commercials. The winning commercial (as voted on by fans) is aired during the Super Bowl game, and the winner not only gets bragging rights but also takes home a cool $1 million.[29]

Consumer-Generated Value: Social Networking

Consumers also create value through **social media**, Internet-based platforms that allow users to create their own content and share it with others who access their sites. Social media include, among others, social networks such as Facebook and Twitter and product review sites such as TripAdvisor. On **social networking platforms**, a user posts a profile on a website and he or she provides and receives links to other members of the network to share input about common interests. The odds are that you and most of your classmates checked your Facebook page before (or during?) class today.

Social media platforms like this are very hot today; more and more advertisers realize that these sites are a great way to reach an audience that tunes in regularly and enthusiastically to catch up with friends, check out photos of what they did at that outrageous party Saturday night (ouch!), proclaim opinions about political or social issues, or share discoveries of new musical artists.

Social networking is an integral part of what many call **Web 2.0**, which is like the Internet on steroids. The key difference between Web 1.0 and the new version is the interactivity we see among producers and users, but these are some other characteristics of a Web 2.0 site:[30]

- It improves as the number of users increases. For example, Amazon's ability to recommend books to you based on what other people with similar interests have bought gets better as it tracks more and more people who enter search queries.

- Its currency is eyeballs. Google makes its money by charging advertisers according to the number of people who see their ads after they type in a search term.

amafessionals
Consumers who contribute ideas to online forums for the fun and challenge rather than to receive a paycheck, so their motivation is to gain *psychic income* rather than financial income.

consumer-generated content
Everyday people functioning in marketing roles, such as participating in creating advertisements, providing input to new product development, or serving as wholesalers or retailers.

social media
Internet-based platforms that allow users to create their own content and share it with others who access these sites.

social networking platforms
Online platforms that allow a user to represent him- or herself via a profile on a website and provide and receive links to other members of the network to share input about common interests.

Web 2.0
The new generation of the World Wide Web that incorporates social networking and user interactivity.

folksonomy
A classification system that relies on users rather than preestablished systems to sort contents.

wisdom of crowds
Under the right circumstances, groups are smarter than the smartest people in them, meaning that large numbers of consumers can predict successful products.

crowdsourcing
A practice where firms outsource marketing activities (such as selecting an ad) to a community of users.

open-source model
A practice used in the software industry in which companies share their software codes with one another to assist in the development of a better product.

- It's version free and in perpetual beta. Unlike static websites or books, content is always a work in progress. Wikipedia, the online encyclopedia, gets updated constantly by users who "correct" others' errors.

- It categorizes entries according to **folksonomy** rather than "taxonomy." In other words, sites rely on users rather than preestablished systems to sort contents. Listeners at Pandora create their own "radio stations" that play songs by artists they choose as well as other similar artists.[31]

This last point highlights a key change in the way some new media companies approach their businesses: Think of it as marketing strategy by committee. The **wisdom of crowds** perspective (from a book by that name) argues that under the right circumstances, groups are smarter than the smartest people in them. If this is true, it implies that large numbers of (nonexpert) consumers can predict successful products.[32] Marketers rely on **crowdsourcing** when they outsource marketing activities to a large group of people, often through a social networking community. For example, Lego offers up its Lego CUUSOO crowdsourcing platform to solicit product and concept ideas from fans. The company periodically reviews the ideas that garner 10,000 supporters to see which ones might merit the chance to become a real Lego product, such as the Ghostbusters 30th Anniversary set, and "winners" earn 1 percent of the profits on net sales.[33]

Open-Source Business Models

Another related change is the rise of the **open-source model** that turns our conventional assumptions about the value of products and services on their heads. This model started in the software industry, where the Linux system grows by leaps and bounds—even IBM uses it now. Unlike the closely guarded code that companies like Microsoft use, open-source developers post their programs on a public site, and a community of volunteers is free to tinker with it, develop other applications using the code, and then give their changes away for free. For example, did you know that Microsoft Word isn't your only choice when it comes to type up your next research paper? Both OpenOffice and LibreOffice are open-source productivity suites that include word-processing programs to rival Word—and they're free! We'll talk more about this—and answer the question of how in the world you can make money from something when you give it away—in Chapter 10.

Value from Society's Perspective

Every company's activities influence the world around it in ways both good and bad. Therefore, we must also consider how marketing transactions add or subtract value from society. In many ways, we are at the mercy of marketers because we trust them to sell us products that are safe and perform as promised. We also trust them to price and distribute these products fairly. Conflicts often arise in business when the pressure to succeed in the marketplace provokes dishonest business practices—the huge failure of major financial services organizations like AIG and Goldman Sachs is a painful case in point.

The **Cutting Edge**

Users Build Brands That Customers Trust

Your smart phone and a little creativity can earn you some awesome prizes—all while helping companies build their brands. Consider the "Your Door to More" contest, when car manufacturer Nissan put out a call to design videos for its all-new 2014 Nissan Versa Note. Participants were challenged to create a video that featured a paper cutout of a Versa Note and then share it via Instagram or Vine. The prize? One of three $1,000 Amazon gift cards and a spot in a national TV ad. The upside for Nissan? A lot of word-of-mouth advertising for little investment. But does this strategy pay off? In a word, yes. A recent study shows that Millennials trust information they find in user-generated content 50 percent more than they do content from traditional media.[34]

Companies usually find that stressing ethics and social responsibility also is good business, at least in the long run. Some find out the hard way: Home Depot, for example, found itself in a storm of backlash after the company sent out an offensive and racist tweet. Although Home Depot apologized and fired the parties involved, they blamed the agency that created the tweet.[35] GM found itself the target of some seriously bad press when customers learned that the company knew, for more than a decade, about a faulty ignition switch on thousands of its car models and didn't issue a recall. The faulty switch was blamed for at least 12 deaths and 31 crashes and had GM executives apologizing to families and testifying before Congress.[36] In contrast, Procter & Gamble voluntarily withdrew its Rely tampons from the market following reports of women who had suffered toxic shock syndrome (TSS). Although scientists did not claim a causal link between Rely and TSS, the company agreed with the Food and Drug Administration that they would undertake extensive advertising notifying women of the symptoms of TSS and asking them to return their boxes of Rely for a refund. The company took a $75 million loss and sacrificed an unusually successful new product that had already captured about one-quarter of the billion-dollar sanitary product market.[37]

The Dark Side of Marketing

For some—hopefully not many and hopefully not *you* after you read this book—marketing is a four-letter word. Whether intentionally or not, some marketers *do* violate their bond of trust with consumers, and unfortunately the "dark side" of marketing often is the subject of harsh criticism.[38] In some cases, these violations are illegal, such as when a retailer adopts a "bait-and-switch" selling strategy, luring consumers into the store with promises of inexpensive products with the sole intent of getting them to switch to higher-priced goods.

In other cases, marketing practices have detrimental effects on society even though they are not actually illegal. Some alcohol and tobacco companies advertise in low-income neighborhoods where abuse of these products is a big problem. Others sponsor commercials that depict groups of people in an unfavorable light or sell products that encourage antisocial behavior. An online game based on the Columbine High School massacre drew criticism from some who say it trivializes the actions of the two teen killers.

Despite the best efforts of researchers, government regulators, and concerned industry people, sometimes consumers' worst enemies are themselves. We tend to think of ourselves as rational decision makers, calmly doing our best to obtain products and services that will maximize our health and well-being and that of our families and society. In reality, however, our desires, choices, and actions often result in negative consequences to ourselves and the society in which we live. Some of these actions are relatively harmless, but others have more onerous consequences. Some harmful consumer behaviors, such as excessive drinking or cigarette smoking, stem from social pressures, and the cultural value that people place on money encourages activities such as shoplifting or insurance fraud. Exposure to unattainable ideals of beauty and success can create dissatisfaction with the self. Let's briefly review some dimensions of the "dark side" of consumer behavior:

Terrorism: The terrorist attacks of 2001 revealed the vulnerability of nonmilitary targets and reminded us that disruptions of our financial, electronic, and supply networks can potentially be more damaging to our way of life than the fallout from a conventional battlefield. The hours many of us spend as we wait to pass through security lines in airports are but one consequence of these attacks.

Addictive consumption: **Consumer addiction** is a physiological or psychological dependency on goods or services. These problems, of course, include alcoholism, drug addiction, and cigarettes—and many companies profit from addictive products or

consumer addiction
A physiological or psychological dependency on goods or services including alcoholism, drug addiction, cigarettes, shopping, and use of the Internet.

by selling solutions. Although most people equate addiction with drugs, consumers can use virtually anything to relieve (at least temporarily) some problem or satisfy some need to the point that reliance on it becomes extreme. "Shopaholics" turn to shopping much the way addicted people turn to drugs or alcohol.[39] Numerous treatment centers in China, South Korea, and Taiwan (and now a few in the U.S. also) deal with cases of Internet addiction—some hard-core gamers have become so hooked that they literally forget to eat or drink and die of dehydration. There is even a Chap Stick Addicts support group with approximately 250 active members![40]

Exploited people: Sometimes people are used or exploited, willingly or not, for commercial gain in the marketplace; these situations range from traveling road shows that feature dwarfs and little people to the selling of body parts and babies on eBay. *Consumed consumers* are people who themselves become commodities.

Illegal activities: The cost of crimes that consumers commit against businesses has been estimated at more than $40 billion per year. A survey the McCann-Erickson advertising agency conducted revealed the following tidbits:[41]

- Ninety-one percent of people say they lie regularly. One in three fibs about their weight, one in four fudges their income, and 21 percent lie about their age. Nine percent even lie about their natural hair color.

- Four out of 10 Americans have tried to pad an insurance bill to cover the deductible.

- Nineteen percent say they've snuck into a theater to avoid paying admission.

- More than three out of five people say they've taken credit for making something from scratch when they have done no such thing. According to Pillsbury's CEO, this "behavior is so prevalent that we've named a category after it—speed scratch."

shrinkage
Losses experienced by retailers due to shoplifting, employee theft, and damage to merchandise.

Shrinkage: Someone steals from a store every five seconds. **Shrinkage** is the industry term for inventory and cash losses from shoplifting and employee theft. As we'll see in Chapter 12, this is a massive problem for businesses, one that they in turn pass on to consumers in the form of higher prices. Analysts attribute about 40 percent of the losses to employees rather than shoppers.

anticonsumption
The deliberate defacement of products.

Anticonsumption: Some types of destructive consumer behavior are **anticonsumption**, when people deliberately deface products. This practice ranges from relatively mild acts like spray-painting graffiti on buildings and subways, to serious incidences of product tampering or even the release of computer viruses that can bring large corporations to their knees.

4 Marketing As a Process

OBJECTIVE

Explain the basics of market planning.
(pp. 48–49)

Our definition of marketing also refers to *processes*. This means that marketing is not a one-shot operation. When it's done right, marketing is a decision process in which marketing managers determine the strategies that will help the firm meet its long-term objectives and then execute those strategies using the tools they have at their disposal. In this section, we'll look at how marketers make business decisions and plan actions and the tools they use to execute their plans. We'll build on this brief overview in Chapter 3, where we'll also provide you with a "road map" in the form of a pullout planning template you can use to understand the planning process as you work your way through the book.

A big part of the marketing process is *market planning*, where we think carefully and strategically about the "big picture" and where our firm and its products fit within it. The first phase of market planning is to analyze the marketing environment. This means understanding the firm's current strengths and weaknesses by assessing factors that might help or hinder the development and marketing of products. The analysis must also take into account the opportunities and threats the firm will encounter in the marketplace, such as the actions of competitors, cultural and technological changes, and the economy.

Firms (or individuals) that engage in market planning ask questions like these:

- What product benefits will our customers look for in three to five years?

- What capabilities does our firm have that set it apart from the competition?

- What additional customer groups might provide important market segments for us in the future?

- How will changes in technology affect our production process, our communication strategy, and our distribution strategy?

- What changes in social and cultural values are occurring now that will impact our market in the next few years?

- How will customers' awareness of environmental issues affect their attitudes toward our manufacturing facilities?

- What legal and regulatory issues may affect our business in both domestic and global markets?

Answers to these and other questions provide the foundation for developing an organization's **marketing plan**. This is a document that describes the marketing environment, outlines the marketing objectives and strategy, and identifies who will be responsible for carrying out each part of the marketing strategy. As we noted earlier in Chapter 3, we'll give you a template you can use to construct your own marketing plan that will help bring this important process to life. If you want, you can even use it to develop a plan to market yourself as a brand to potential employers. In fact, Appendix B guides you through these same steps to develop your personal marketing plan for a great career.

A major marketing decision for most organizations is which products to market to which consumers without simultaneously turning off other consumers. Some firms choose to reach as many customers as possible, so they offer their goods or services to a **mass market** that consists of all possible customers in a market regardless of the differences in their specific needs and wants. Market planning then becomes a matter of developing a basic product and a single strategy to reach everyone.

Although this approach can be cost effective, the firm risks losing potential customers to competitors whose marketing plans instead try to meet the needs of specific groups within the market. A **market segment** is a distinct group of customers within a larger market who are similar to one another in some way and whose needs differ from other customers in the larger market. For example, automakers such as Ford, General Motors, and BMW offer different automobiles for different market segments. Depending on its goals and resources, a firm may choose to focus on one or on many segments. A **target market** is the segment(s) on which an organization focuses its marketing plan and toward which it directs its marketing efforts. A product's **market position** is how the target market perceives the product in comparison to competitors' brands. We'll learn more about these ideas in Chapter 7.

marketing plan
A document that describes the marketing environment, outlines the marketing objectives and strategy, and identifies who will be responsible for carrying out each part of the marketing strategy.

mass market
All possible customers in a market, regardless of the differences in their specific needs and wants; the way in which the target market perceives the product in comparison to competitors' brands.

market segment
A distinct group of customers within a larger market who are similar to one another in some way and whose needs differ from other customers in the larger market.

target market
The market segments on which an organization focuses its marketing plan and toward which it directs its marketing efforts.

market position
The way in which the target market perceives the product in comparison to competitors' brands.

Here's my choice...

Real **People**, Real **Choices**

1   (2)   3

Option   Option   Option

Why do you think Joe chose option 2?

How It Worked Out at Pandora

Joe chose option 2. To build awareness, *Pandora* relied exclusively on personal communication, via town halls led by the company's founder, email, blog posts, *Twitter*, and eventually a *Facebook* fan page. *Pandora* also counts on its fanatical listeners to serve as "walking billboards," who wear the company's branded T-shirts, caps and other "swag." Rather than "selling out" to a retailer or another media company, Pandora solved its distribution problem by making the service available on as many Internet-enabled devices as possible. When it unveiled its app for the iPhone, the number of registered listeners doubled overnight. Today more than 100 consumer electronic devices stream *Pandora*, including TVs, Blu-Ray players, TV hotboxes, and alarm clocks. One of the firm's current major initiatives is to expand distribution even farther by making the service available to drivers. Since 50 percent of all radio listening happens in the car, it's vital for *Pandora* to be there as well. Through its relationship with Ford and other auto companies, *Pandora* will soon be incorporated into car dashboards where listeners will be able to access their personalized Pandora radio stations as they drive.

Refer back to **page 26** for Joe's story ➡

MyMarketingLab™

Go to **mymktlab.com** to complete the problems marked with this icon ★ as well as additional Marketing Metrics questions only available in MyMarketingLab.

Objective Summary ➡ Key Terms ➡ Apply

CHAPTER 1
Study Map

---

1. Objective Summary (pp.28–34)

Explain what marketing is, the marketing mix, what can be marketed and the value of marketing.

Marketing is the activity, set of institutions, and processes for creating, communicating, delivering, and exchanging offerings that have value for customers, clients, partners, and society at large. Therefore, marketing is all about delivering value to stakeholders, that is, to everyone who is affected by a transaction. Organizations that seek to ensure their long-term profitability by identifying and satisfying customers' needs and wants adopt the marketing concept.

The marketing mix includes product, price, place, and promotion. The product is what satisfies customer needs. The price is the assigned value or amount to be exchanged for the product. The place or channel of distribution gets the product to the customer. Promotion is the organization's efforts to persuade customers to buy the product.

Any good, service, or idea that can be marketed is a product, even though what is being sold may not take a physical form. Consumer goods are the tangible products that consumers purchase for personal or family use. Services are intangible products that we pay for and use but never own. Business-to-business goods and services are sold to businesses and other organizations for further processing or for use in their business operations. Not-for-profit organizations, ideas, places, and people can also be marketed.

Marketing provides value for customers when they practice the marketing concept and focus on identifying and satisfying customer needs. Marketing provides form, place, time, and possession utility. In addition, marketing provides value through satisfying the needs of diverse stakeholders, society, and the earth.

Key Terms

consumer, p. 28

marketing, p. 28

marketing mix, p. 29

four Ps, p. 29

product, p. 29

promotion, p. 30

place, p. 30

price, p. 30

exchange, p. 30

consumer goods, p. 31

services, p. 31

business-to-business marketing, p. 31

industrial goods, p. 31

e-commerce, p. 31

not-for-profit organizations, p. 31

nongovernmental organizations (NGOs), p. 31

marketing concept, p. 32

need, p. 32

want, p. 32

benefit, p. 33

demand, p. 33

market, p. 33

marketplace, p. 33

virtual goods, p. 33

rentrepreneurs, p. 33

collaborative consumption, p. 33

utility, p. 34

stakeholders, p. 34

2. Objective Summary (pp.35–40)

Explain the evolution of the marketing concept.

Early in the twentieth century, firms followed a production orientation in which they focused on the most efficient ways to produce and distribute products. Beginning in the 1930s, some firms adopted a selling orientation that encouraged salespeople to aggressively sell products to customers. In the 1950s, organizations adopted a consumer orientation that focused on customer satisfaction. This led to the development of the marketing concept. Today, many firms are moving toward a triple-bottom-line orientation that includes not only a commitment to quality and value but also a concern for both economic and social profit. The societal marketing concept maintains that marketers

must satisfy customers' needs in ways that also benefit society while still delivering a profit to the firm. Similarly, companies think of ways to design and manufacture products with a focus on *sustainability*, or "doing well by doing good." Many suggest that the Internet has created another major shift for business and that firms are now entering the "Big Data" era.

Key Terms

production orientation, p. 35

selling orientation, p. 35

consumer orientation, p. 37

total quality management (TQM), p. 37

instapreneur, p. 37

triple-bottom-line orientation, p. 37

societal marketing concept, p. 38

sustainability, p. 38

green marketing, p. 38

return on investment (ROI), p. 39

attention economy, p. 39

3. Objective Summary (pp.40–48)

Understand value from the perspectives of customers, producers, and society.

Value is the benefits a customer receives from buying a good or service. Marketing communicates these benefits as the value proposition to the customer. For customers, the value proposition includes the whole bundle of benefits the product promises to deliver, not just the benefits of the product itself. Sellers determine value by assessing whether their transactions are profitable, whether they are providing value to stakeholders by creating a competitive advantage, and whether they are providing value through the value chain. Customers generate value when they turn into advertising directors, retailers, and new-product-development consultants, often through social networking using social media. Society receives value from marketing activities when producers stress ethics and social responsibility. Criticisms of both marketing and consumer activities may be valid in a few instances, but most are unfounded.

Key Terms

value proposition, p. 40

brandfests, p. 41

lifetime value of a customer, p. 41

distinctive competency, p. 41

marketing scorecards, p. 42

metrics, p. 42

differential benefit, p. 42

value chain, p. 42

amafessionals, p. 45

consumer-generated content, p. 45

social media, p. 45

social networking platforms, p. 45

4. Objective Summary (pp. 48–49)

Explain the basics of market planning.

The strategic process of market planning begins with an assessment of factors within the organization and in the external environment that could help or hinder the development and marketing of products. On the basis of this analysis, marketers set objectives and develop strategies. Many firms use a target marketing strategy in which they divide the overall market into segments and then target the most attractive one. Then they design the marketing mix to gain a competitive position in the target market.

Key Terms

Chapter **Questions** and **Activities**

Concepts: Test Your Knowledge

1-1. Briefly explain which elements of a marketing mix generate revenue and which generate cost.

1-2. List and describe the elements of the marketing mix.

1-3. Define the terms *consumer goods*, *services*, and *industrial goods*.

1-4. Explain production orientation and selling orientation. What are their main drawbacks?

1-5. Briefly explain how marketing is different for a non-profit organization.

1-6. Trace the evolution of the marketing concept.

1-7. What are the main phases of a typical marketing plan?

1-8. Describe the Internet and Big Data and how they will change marketing in the future.

1-9. To what does the *lifetime value of the customer* refer, and how is it calculated?

1-10. What are the key phases of market planning?

1-11. What is involved in market planning?

Activities: Apply What You've Learned

1-12. *In Class, 10–25 Minutes for Teams* Assume that you are a marketing consultant employed by a local art museum. The museum hopes to increase the number of individuals who visit the museum. As a marketing expert, you know that there are issues involving product, price, promotion, and place (distribution) that are important in selling both physical products and intangibles. Next week you have an opportunity to speak to the directors of the museum. What product, price, promotion, and place recommendations would you have for "Marketing a Museum?"

1-13. *In Class, 10–25 Minutes for Teams* Successful firms have a competitive advantage because they are able to identify distinctive competencies and use these to create differential benefits for their customers. Consider your business school or your university. What distinctive competencies does it have? What differential benefits does it provide for students? What is its competitive advantage? What are your ideas as to how your university could improve its competitive position? Write an outline of your ideas.

1-14. *In Class, 10–25 Minutes for Teams For* college students living away from home, shopping for groceries becomes a common activity. From your various visits to the local supermarket, consider the store's value proposition based on the perspective of customers, producers, and society. As a role-playing exercise, each group will give a class presentation on the three different perspectives.

1-15. *For Further Research (Individual)* Recent reports indicate that companies are falling short on their green marketing initiatives. Find at least one example of a company or not-for-profit group that is bucking this trend and write up a short case study about the various methods the organization is employing to deliver on its green marketing promises.

1-16. *For Further Research (Groups)* Today's marketers recognize that the Internet and Big Data have changed marketing and will continue to change it in the years to come. Your team assignment is to first find examples of how the Internet and Big Data have improved marketing for some for-profit and not-for-profit organizations. Then develop your ideas on how the Internet and Big Data could make contributions to society as a whole in the future. Develop a short presentation for your class.

Apply Marketing Metrics

The chapter discusses the growing importance of sustainability, and it notes that companies and consumers increasingly consider other costs in addition to financial kinds when they decide what to sell or buy. One of these cost categories is damage to the environment. How can marketers make it easier for shoppers to compute these costs? The answer is more apparent in some product categories than in others. For example, American consumers often are able to compare the power consumption and annual costs of appliances by looking at their EnergyStar™ rating. In other situations, we can assess the *carbon footprint* implications of a product or service; this tells us how much CO_2 our purchase will emit into the atmosphere (e.g., if a person flies from New York to London). The average American is responsible for 9.44 tons of CO_2 per year![42] A carbon footprint comes from the sum of two parts, the direct, or primary, footprint and the indirect, or secondary, footprint:

- The *primary footprint* is a measure of our direct emissions of CO_2 from the burning of fossil fuels, including domestic energy consumption and transportation (e.g., cars and planes).
- The *secondary footprint* is a measure of the indirect CO_2 emissions from the whole life cycle of products we use, from their manufacture to their eventual breakdown.[43]

Although many of us are more aware today that our consumption choices carry unseen costs, there is still a lot of confusion about the best way to communicate the environmental costs of our actions—and in many cases consumers aren't motivated to take these issues into account unless the costs impact them directly and in the short term.

1-17. As a consumer, what other metrics would you suggest that might reflect benefits of sustainability initiatives that would motivate you to purchase from one provider or the other?

1-18. Would you buy from a demonstrably more expensive provider just because they exhibited a higher level of commitment to sustainability?

Choices: What Do You Think?

1-19. *Critical Thinking* Journalists, government officials, and consumers have been highly critical of companies for gathering and storing large amounts of data on consumers (i.e., Big Data). Others argue that such practices are essential for firms to provide high-quality, affordable products that satisfy consumers' varied needs. What do you think? Should the government regulate such practices? How can such practices hurt consumers? How can these practices help consumers?

1-20. *Ethics* Despite best efforts to ensure product safety, products that pose a danger to consumers sometimes reach the marketplace. At what point should marketers release information about a product's safety to the public? How should marketers be held accountable if their product harms a consumer?

1-21. *Critical Thinking* The marketing concept focuses on the ability of marketing to satisfy customer needs. As a typical college student, how does marketing satisfy your needs? What areas of your life are affected by marketing? What areas of your life (if any) are not affected by marketing?

1-22. *Critical Thinking* Ideally, each member of a value chain adds value to a product before someone buys it. Thinking about electronics such as a flat-screen TV, a tablet computer, or a smart phone, what kind of value does the producer add? What about the marketing activities? The bricks-and-mortar retailer? The online retailer?

1-23. *Critical Thinking* User-generated commercials seem to be part of a broader trend toward user-generated content of all sorts. Examples include MySpace, Flickr (where users post photos and comment on others' pictures), blogging, and video-sharing sites like YouTube. Do you think this is a passing fad or an important trend? How (if at all) should marketers be dealing with these activities?

1-24. *Ethics* The American Psychological Association formally recognizes Internet addiction as a psychological disorder. Should it?

1-25. *Ethics* There are cases of marketing practices that have detrimental effects on society, such as cigarette smoking, excessive drinking, the ideals of beauty, the acquisition of wealth, and the possession of material objects. Are the negative perceptions or the notion of the "dark side" of marketing justifiable? Choose any of the examples above and present your view in class.

Miniproject: Learn by Doing

The purpose of this miniproject is to develop an understanding of the practice of marketing and the importance of societal marketing and sustainability to different organizations.

1-26. Working as a team with two or three other students, select an organization in your community. It may be a manufacturer, a service provider, a retailer, a not-for-profit organization—almost any organization will do. Then schedule a visit with someone within the organization who is involved in the marketing activities. Arrange for a short visit during which the person can give your group a tour of the facilities and explain the organization's marketing activities.

1-27. Divide the following list of topics among your team and ask each person to be responsible for developing a set of questions to ask during the interview to learn about the company's program:
- What customer segments the company targets.
- How it determines customer needs and wants.
- What products it offers, including features, benefits, and goals for customer satisfaction.
- What its pricing strategies are.
- How it uses consumer-generated content to engage customers.
- How it distributes products and whether it has encountered any problems.
- How it determines whether the needs and wants of customers are being met.
- Explain what marketers mean by the "societal marketing concept" and "sustainability" and ask if these are areas of concern to the organization. If so, how do they address them in their organization's activities? If not, ask if they have any plans to move in this direction in the future and, if so, how.

1-28. Develop a team report of your findings. In each section of the report, share what you learned that is new or surprising to you compared to what you expected.

1-29. Develop a team presentation for your class that summarizes your findings. Conclude your presentation with comments on what your team believes the company was doing that was particularly good and what was not quite so good.

Marketing in **Action** Case Real Choices at Nestlé

Americans prefer their coffee "grande," the Italian word for "large." The average coffee drinker in the U.S. consumes more coffee per cup than his or her European counterpart. In European markets, Nestlé sells an espresso machine under the family brand name of Nespresso. The machine brews coffee from capsules, a type of preapportioned single-use container of ground coffee and flavorings. To attract the American consumer, Nestlé is "supersizing" the brewer as part of its new VertuoLine system. This strategic move is to take advantage of the rapidly increasing growth of the portioned coffee market (the drink ready in the cup). This coffee market is estimated to be roughly $5 billion in the U.S.

Nespresso is the brand name of Nestlé Nespresso S.A., an operating unit of the Nestlé Group, based in Lausanne, Switzerland. Over 28 years ago, "a simple but revolutionary idea: enable anyone to create the perfect cup of espresso coffee just like skilled baristas" created the Nespresso brand. Nespresso pioneered the premium portioned coffee segment. The fundamental objective of the company is to deliver the highest-quality coffee and ultimate coffee experience to consumers on a consistent basis. The system includes the VertuoLine brewing machine and the companion aluminum capsules. Use of the capsules provides for better consistency in the quality of each individual cup of coffee. Analysts estimate that Nespresso represents about 25 percent of Nestlé's coffee sales.

Although U.S. consumers can purchase the Nespresso machine if they want it, the VertuoLine system of machines and capsules is designed to appeal to the different coffee-drinking habits of North Americans. The system produces 7.8-fluid-ounce cups of coffee and smaller 1.4-fluid-ounce espressos. The coffees are characterized by a rich and generous foam called crema—naturally formed during the brewing process. To support the product debut, eight coffee and four espresso blends in specially designed VertuoLine capsules will be introduced along with the brewing system. The eight large-cup coffee varieties and the four espresso blends will include flavored coffees as well as half-caffeinated varieties.

The VertuoLine system will retail for $299. This is in comparison to Green Mountain's $229 Keurig Rivo R500 espresso maker and Starbucks's Verismo 600 machine that sells for $199. This pricing strategy reflects that Nestlé desires for the Nespresso VertuoLine to be recognized by consumers as a premium product. To reinforce this perception of the product, the system will be sold directly to consumers through a network of Nespresso boutiques and on the Internet at www .nespresso.com. In addition, having the system offered at selected U.S. retailers, including Macy's, Bloomingdales, Sur La Table, and Williams-Sonoma, will strengthen the premium profile.

According to Julien Liew, corporate public relations and public affairs manager for Nestlé Nespresso S.A., "The portioned coffee market is booming and continues to be the fastest growing part of the coffee market, by both value and volume." Euromonitor, a market intelligence firm, reports that single-serve coffee capsules have "exploded" in the U.S. marketplace and that this trend will continue to grow. However, the growth in coffee consumption in the U.S.—one of the world's largest coffee markets—has attracted a great deal of opposition. In addition to Green Mountain's Keurig and Starbucks's Verismo, Nestlé faces competition from companies like Cuisinart, Hamilton Beach, and KitchenAid, to name a few. Due to the amount of growing competition, success is not guaranteed. Nestlé's marketing strategy of product, price, place, and promotion needs to be superior to its rivals to ensure the success of the VertuoLine.

You Make the Call

1-30. What is the decision facing Nestlé?
1-31. What factors are important in understanding this decision situation?
1-32. What are the alternatives?
1-33. What decision(s) do you recommend?
1-34. What are some ways to implement your recommendation?

Sources: Based on Matthew Boyle, "Nestle Supersizes Nespresso for U.S. Coffee Drinkers," February 19, 2014, **www.businessweek.com/ news/2014-02-19/nestle-supersizes-its-nespresso-machine-for-u-dot-s-dot-coffee-drinkers** (accessed April 4, 2014); Nestlé, "New Nespresso System Aims to Reshape North American Coffee Industry," **www.nestle.com/media/newsandfeatures/nespresso-us-launch** (accessed April 4, 2014); Nestlé Nespresso SA, "Our Company," **www.nestle-nespresso.com/about-us/our-company** (accessed April 4, 2014); and Euromonitor International, "Coffee in the US.," **www.euromonitor.com/coffee-in-the-us/report** (accessed April 4, 2014).

MyMarketingLab™

Go to **mymktlab.com** for Auto-graded writing questions as well as the following Assisted-graded writing questions:

1-35.   *Creative Homework/Short Project.* An old friend of yours has been making and selling vitamin-fortified smoothies to acquaintances and friends of friends for some time. He is now thinking about opening a shop in a small college town, but he is worried about whether just having a great smoothie is enough to be successful. Knowing that you are a marketing student, he's asked you for some advice. What can you tell him about product, price, promotion, and place (distribution) strategies that will help him get his business off the ground?

1-36.   *Creative Homework/Short Project.* As a marketing professional, you have been asked to write a short piece for a local business newsletter about the state of marketing today. You think the best way to address this topic is to review how the marketing concept has evolved and to discuss the triple-bottom-line orientation. Write the short article you will submit to the editor of the newsletter.

Global, Ethical, and Sustainable Marketing

Keith Sutter

▼ A Decision Maker at Johnson & Johnson

Keith Sutter is the senior product director for sustainable brand marketing at Johnson & Johnson. In that role, Keith leads Johnson & Johnson's 250 operating companies in developing sustainable products, business, and marketing strategies. He translates the value of Johnson & Johnson's extensive product stewardship and environmental successes to the company's trade customers and consumers, including championing the Earthwards® process.

Keith began his career at Johnson & Johnson in 2001 as a marketing associate. He subsequently held positions of increasing responsibility as a brand marketer on brands such as Band-Aid®, Neutrogena®, Lactaid®, and Ludens®.

Keith has a BS in economics from the Wharton School at the University of Pennsylvania and an MBA from the S.C. Johnson Graduate School of Management at Cornell University. He lives in Center City, Philadelphia, with his wife, Amy, and two sons, Leo and Charlie.

Keith's Info

What I do when I'm not working?
Triathlons and other outdoor sports.

First job out of school?
Marketing associate at Johnson & Johnson on the Decorated Band-Aid® Brand bandages, which was a great job working with licensees and cartoon characters like SpongeBob SquarePants and Elmo.

Business book I'm reading now?
David & Goliath by Malcom Gladwell.

What drives me?
New business opportunities and innovative new products and business models.

My management style?
Pacesetting. I like to set a good example for my team while allowing them the

freedom to develop innovative solutions to our business problems that drive results.

Don't do this when interviewing with me?
Neglect to provide detailed examples of results you drove when asked for specific experiences.

Here's my problem...

Johnson & Johnson is one of the world's leading manufacturers of health care products. It sells many familiar consumer brands such as Band-Aid®, Neutrogena®, Listerine®, Splenda®, and Tylenol®, as well as medical devices and prescription drugs. Within this global company, the Earthwards® approach motivates employees to improve the sustainability of products. It defines how Johnson & Johnson thinks about and addresses its environmental and social impacts and challenges its people to design innovative and more sustainable solutions across a product's life cycle—from formulation and manufacturing to product use and safe disposal.

When Johnson & Johnson launched the Earthwards® process in 2009, Keith and his team used it to encourage J&J's product teams to make significant improvements to 60 products. Today, Johnson & Johnson has integrated and expanded the original process across the company. It uses the Earthwards® approach to drive continuous innovation by doing the following:

Requiring every new product to:

- *Meet product stewardship requirements.* Every new product must achieve regulatory compliance and deliver on Johnson & Johnson's high standards.
- *Understand life cycle impact areas.* The life cycle impacts of products are reviewed at the category level, and opportunities to drive improvements are considered at the design, procurement, manufacturing, and marketing stages of a product's development.

Inviting every product team to:

- *Implement and validate improvements.* Product teams collaborate with sustainability experts to implement recommended improvements, and environmental marketing claims are reviewed and approved in accordance with applicable guidelines.

Encouraging the most sustainable product teams to:

- *Achieve Earthwards® recognition, an honor celebrating our most innovative and improved products.* If a product achieves at least three significant improvements across seven impact areas (materials used, packaging, energy reduction, waste reduction, water reduction,

positive social impact or benefit, and product innovation), a board of internal and external experts determines if the product warrants Earthwards® recognition and provides suggestions for additional improvements. Teams who receive Earthwards® recognition are publicly congratulated on Earthwards.com and rewarded for their innovations by Johnson & Johnson leadership.

As he considered the best strategy to promote Earthwards®, Keith knew that one of his biggest challenges was to convince J&J's 127,000 employees around the globe to buy in to the idea. He needed a way to drive awareness and interest in the Earthwards® approach to sustainable product development across Johnson & Johnson. Generating awareness, understanding, and adoption of the process across J&J's business units was a key performance metric against which his team would be measured.

Keith had only limited resources to accomplish this objective.

Keith considered his **Options** 1·2·3

1 Option
Continue a successful tactic from the early roll-out of Earthwards®: Host regional green marketing conferences to bring together key stakeholders once per year. These meetings would showcase key tools and resources available that would then be distributed as requested by e-mail to other employees. This is high touch and engaging but hard to scale effectively across such a large company.

2 Option
Develop a customer intranet site, including an online scorecard to take Earthwards® submissions from an Excel spreadsheet to an online database accessible by all employees. The site would also house all the tools and materials Keith and his team had developed to date to explain Earthwards® and drive its adoption across J&J's varied businesses. This solution is low-touch and not very engaging, but it is efficient because everyone in the company can access it easily. This database would free up resources that Keith and his team could use to further develop the Earthwards® program both internally and in the marketplace.

3 Option
Develop a high-touch strategy of identifying 20 to 30 influential leaders within Johnson & Johnson. Then set up multiple in-person meetings and training sessions with the goal of making the case for adoption of Earthwards® into each leader's business process and then encouraging each of these leaders to drive adoption of the program within J&J. This option would really engage people, but its impact would be hard to measure.

Now, put yourself in Keith's shoes. Which option would you choose, and why?

You Choose

Which **Option** would you choose, and **why**?
1. ☐YES ☐NO   2. ☐YES ☐NO   3. ☐YES ☐NO

See what **option** Keith chose on **page 88** ➡

Things to remember

Johnson & Johnson's Earthwards® approach defines how Johnson & Johnson thinks about and addresses its environmental and social impacts while motivating employees to improve the sustainability of products.

The Earthwards® approach drives continuous innovation by

- requiring that every new product achieve regulatory compliance and deliver on Johnson & Johnson's high standards,
- driving improvements at all stages of a product's development through an understanding of life cycle impact areas,
- facilitating the collaboration of product teams with sustainability experts to implement recommended improvements,
- reviewing and approving environmental marketing claims, and
- recognizing the most improved products

Keith also knew that one of his biggest challenges was to convince J&J's 127,000 employees around the globe to buy into the Earthwards® approach.

MyMarketingLab™

⭐ **Improve Your Grade!**

Over 10 million students improved their results using the Pearson MyLabs.
Visit **mymktlab.com** for simulations, tutorials, and end-of-chapter problems.

Chapter 2

1

OBJECTIVE

Understand the big picture of international marketing and the decisions firms must make when they consider globalization.
(pp. 58–60)

Take a Bow: Marketing on the Global Stage

Here's an important question: Do you primarily see yourself only as a resident of Smalltown, USA, or as a member of a global community? The reality is that you and all your classmates are citizens of the world and participants in a global marketplace. It is very likely that you eat bananas from Ecuador, drink beer from Mexico, and sip wine from Australia, South Africa, or Chile. When you come home, you may take off your shoes that were made in Thailand, put your feet up on the cocktail table imported from Indonesia, and watch the World Cup football (soccer) match being played in Brazil or Canada on your HDTV made in China. Hopefully, you have some knowledge and concern for important world events such as the Arab Spring and recent developments in Crimea. And you may even be looking for an exciting career with a firm that does business around the globe.

Of course, living in a global community creates both opportunities and challenges. Many consumers and world leaders argue that the development of free trade and a single global marketplace will benefit us all because it allows people who live in developing countries to enjoy the same economic benefits as citizens of more developed countries. Others express concern for the loss of manufacturing in the U.S. and other developed nations as factories relocate where labor and materials are less expensive. The recent downturn in the global economy has reignited demands for greater government protection for domestic industries. Today there is increasing concern around the world about problems such as global warming and the need for international agreements that would force industries and governments to develop and adhere to environmental standards to protect the future of the planet.

The global marketing game is exciting, the stakes are high—and it's easy to lose your shirt. Competition comes from both local and foreign firms, and differences in national laws, customs, and consumer preferences can make your head spin. Like many American companies that feel they can significantly improve their growth by expanding into global markets, U.S. auto manufacturer Ford is aggressively working to expand its international presence, especially in China, which in 2013 surpassed the U.S. as the largest market for autos in the world. But you can be sure that when Ford's planners plot future growth, they're keenly aware of competitors in their external environment who have other ideas. Although Ford—with its Ford Focus—had the top-selling passenger vehicle in China and in the world in 2013, other carmakers, like GM and Volkswagen, had more market share in China overall—and you can bet they'll be working hard to stay on top.

In his best-selling book *The World Is Flat: A Brief History of the Twenty-First Century*, Thomas Friedman argues that technology creates a level playing field for all countries and that marketers must recognize that national borders are not as important as they once were. Today, even very small businesses must seek new and improved ways to attract customers down the street and around the globe in order to stay relevant. In this section, we will first discuss the status of world trade today and then look at the decisions firms must make as they consider their global opportunities.

World Trade

world trade
The flow of goods and services among different countries—the value of all the exports and imports of the world's nations.

World trade refers to the flow of goods and services among different countries—the total value of all the exports and imports of the world's nations. In 2009, the world suffered a global economic crisis that resulted in dramatic decreases in worldwide exports. Today, we

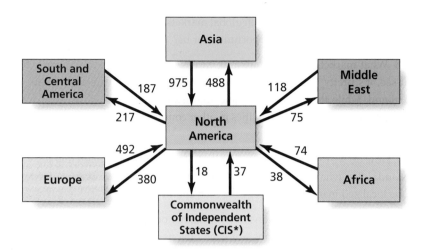

* Armenia, Azerbaijan, Belarus, Kazakhstan, Kyrgyzstan, Republic of Moldova, Russian Federation, and Ukraine

Figure 2.1 📷 *Snapshot* | North American Merchandise Trade Flows (in $ Billions)

Knowing who does business with whom is essential to develop an overseas marketing strategy. As this figure shows, North America trades most heavily with Asia, Europe, and Latin America.

see increasing growth in world trade with world exports of merchandise increasing from $12 trillion in 2009 to nearly $18 trillion in 2012.

Of course, not all countries participate equally in the trade flows among nations. Understanding the "big picture" of who does business with whom is important to marketers when they devise global trade strategies. 📷 Figure 2.1 shows the amount of merchandise North American countries traded with major partners around the world in 2012.

It's often a good thing to have customers in remote markets, but to serve their needs well requires flexibility because you have to run your business differently to adapt to local social and economic conditions. For example, you often have to accommodate the needs of trading partners when those foreign firms can't pay cash for the products they want to purchase. Believe it or not, the currencies of as many as 100 countries—from the Albanian lek to the Uzbekistan sum—are not *convertible*; you can't spend or exchange them outside the country's borders. In other countries, because sufficient cash or credit simply is not available, trading firms work out elaborate deals in which they trade (or *barter*) their products with each other or even supply goods in return for tax breaks from the local government. This **countertrade** accounts for as much as 25 percent of all world trade.[1]

Our ever-increasing access to products from around the world does have a dark side: The growth in world trade in recent years has been accompanied by a glut of unsafe products, like toys tainted with lead, many of which have come from China. In 2014, the European Commission's early warning system for dangerous products (RAPEX) reported a notable increase in alerts of unsafe products; of the more than 2,000 alert issues the commission received, almost two-thirds of the unsafe products came from China.[2] Although most Chinese manufacturers make quality products, some unscrupulous producers have damaged the reputation of Chinese manufacturers and prompted U.S. and European officials to increase their inspections of Chinese imports.

Should We Go Global?

🎯 Figure 2.2 shows that when firms consider going global they must think about this in four steps:

- *Step 1.* "Go" or "no go"—is it in our best interest to focus exclusively on our home market or should we cast our net elsewhere as well?

countertrade
A type of trade in which goods are paid for with other items instead of with cash.

Figure 2.2 🎯 *Process* | Steps in the Decision Process to Enter Global Markets

Entering global markets involves a sequence of decisions.

- *Step 2.* If the decision is "go," which global markets are most attractive? Which country or countries offer the greatest opportunity for us?

- *Step 3.* What market-entry strategy and, thus, what level of commitment is best? As we'll see, it's pretty low risk to simply export products to overseas markets. On the other hand, while the commitment and the risk is substantial if the firm decides to build and run manufacturing facilities in other countries, the potentially greater payoff may be worth the extra risk.

- *Step 4.* How do we develop marketing mix strategies in these foreign markets—should we standardize what we do across all the countries where we operate or develop a unique localized marketing strategy for each country?

We'll look at the first of these decisions now—whether or not to go global.

Although the prospect of millions—or even billions—of consumers salivating for your goods in other countries is very tempting, not all firms can or should go global, and certainly not all global markets are alike. When they make these decisions, marketers need to consider a number of factors that may enhance or detract from their success abroad. Let's review some of the largest ones now: domestic demand and the competitive advantage of the firm.

Look at Domestic and Global Market Conditions

Many times, a firm decides it's time to go global because domestic demand is declining while demand in foreign markets grows. For example, Starbucks has served coffee to just about every American who drinks coffee. To expand its business, Starbucks is now going after the Chinese market, expected to become its second largest in 2014, where the new middle class has extra yuan (the official currency) to spend.[3] But Starbucks isn't just in growing in China. Take a spin around the globe—you can find a Starbucks in more than 50 countries. That's a lot of lattes.

Identify Your Competitive Advantage

In Chapter 1, we saw how firms hope to create a competitive advantage over rivals. When firms enter a global marketplace, this challenge is even greater. There are more players involved, and typically local firms have a "home-court advantage." It's like soccer—increasing numbers of Americans play the game, but they are up against an ingrained tradition of soccer fanaticism in Europe and South America, where kids start dribbling a soccer ball when they start to walk.

If it wants to go global, a firm needs to examine the competitive advantage that makes it successful in its home country. Will this leg up "travel" well to other countries? As we just discussed, Starbucks is experiencing great growth overseas as well as strong sales in the U.S. Long known for its product quality, superior customer service, and fair treatment of employees (whom it calls *partners*), all of these values translate successfully around the world. As Starbucks continues to conquer the globe, product variety and innovation will become increasingly important components of its success.

Chinese automakers like Chery hope to export their cars around the world.

2

OBJECTIVE

Explain how both international organizations such as the World Trade Organization (WTO) and economic communities and individual country regulations facilitate and limit a firm's opportunities for globalization.

(pp. 61–62)

Understand International, Regional, and Country Regulations

Even the most formidable competitive advantage does not guarantee success in foreign markets. Many governments participate in activities that support the idea that the world should be one big open marketplace where companies from every country are free to compete for business. The actions of others frequently say the reverse. In many countries, the local government may "stack the deck" in favor of domestic competitors. Often, they erect roadblocks (or at least those pesky speed bumps) designed to favor local businesses over outsiders that hinder a company's efforts to expand into foreign markets.

Initiatives in International Cooperation and Regulation

In recent years, a number of international initiatives have diminished barriers to unfettered world trade. Most notably, after World War II, the United Nations established the **General Agreement on Tariffs and Trade (GATT)**, which did a lot to establish free trade among nations. During a meeting in 1984 known as the Uruguay Round, GATT created the **World Trade Organization (WTO)**. With 159 members (and over 20 more countries negotiating membership now), the WTO member nations account for 95 percent of world trade. The WTO has made giant strides in creating a single, open world market and is the only international organization that deals with the global rules of trade between nations. Its main function is "to ensure that trade flows as smoothly, predictably and freely as possible."[4]

If you spend any time in Asia, you immediately notice the huge numbers of luxury watches, leather bags, and current music CDs that sell for ridiculously low prices. Who can resist a Rolex watch for $20? Of course, there is a catch: They're fake or pirated illegally. Protection of copyright and patent rights is a huge headache for many companies, and it's a priority the WTO tries to tackle. *Pirating* is a serious problem for U.S. companies because illegal sales significantly erode their profits. All too often, we see news headlines from New York, Rome, or Dubai about police confiscating millions of dollars' worth of goods—from counterfeit luxury handbags to fake Viagra.

General Agreement on Tariffs and Trade (GATT)
International treaty to reduce import tax levels and trade restrictions.

World Trade Organization (WTO)
An organization that replaced GATT; the WTO sets trade rules for its member nations and mediates disputes between nations.

Protected Trade: Quotas, Embargoes, and Tariffs

While the WTO works for free trade, some governments adopt policies of **protectionism** when they enforce rules on foreign firms to give home companies an advantage. Many governments set **import quotas** on foreign goods to reduce competition for their domestic industries. Quotas can make goods more expensive to a country's citizens because the absence of cheaper foreign goods reduces pressure on domestic firms to lower their prices.

We can look at Russia as an example. As the economy of the country has improved, the demand for meat has increased much faster than the production capacity of Russian meat producers. To protect the local industry and to encourage its growth, Russia instituted

protectionism
A policy adopted by a government to give domestic companies an advantage.

import quotas
Limitations set by a government on the amount of a product allowed to enter or leave a country.

import quotas. In 2014, Russia's import quotas on meat products allowed a maximum of 364,000 tons of foreign poultry, 570,000 tons of beef, and 430,000 tons of pork to make their way to Russian dinner tables.

embargo
A quota completely prohibiting specified goods from entering or leaving a country.

An **embargo** is an extreme quota that prohibits commerce and trade with a specified country altogether. Much to the distress of hard-core cigar smokers in the U.S., the U.S. government prohibits the import of Cuban cigars as well as rum and other products because of political differences with its island neighbor.

tariffs
Taxes on imported goods.

Governments also use **tariffs**, or taxes on imported goods, to give domestic competitors an advantage in the marketplace by making foreign competitors' goods more expensive than their own products. For example, in November 2012, the U.S. Commerce Department ruled in favor of imposing tariffs on Chinese imports of solar panels in order to protect American jobs in that industry. This tariff came after Chinese manufacturers were accused of selling the solar panels at below cost in order to drive U.S. manufacturers out of business—and, in fact, about a dozen U.S. manufacturers had gone bankrupt or made significant job cuts in the previous year.[6]

Economic Communities

economic communities
Groups of countries that band together to promote trade among themselves and to make it easier for member nations to compete elsewhere.

Groups of countries may also band together to promote trade among themselves and make it easier for member nations to compete elsewhere. These **economic communities** coordinate trade policies and ease restrictions on the flow of products and capital across their borders. Economic communities are important to marketers because they set policies in areas such as product content, package labeling, and advertising regulations. The U.S., for example, is a member of the *North American Free Trade Agreement (NAFTA)*, which includes the U.S., Canada, and Mexico. *The European Union (EU)* represents 490 million consumers, over 300 million of whom use the euro as their currency. Table 2.1 lists the world's major economic communities.

Table 2.1 | Some Major Economic Communities around the World

Community	Member Countries
Andean Community (www.comunidadandina.org)	Bolivia, Colombia, Ecuador, Peru
Association of Southeast Asian Nations (ASEAN) (www.aseansec.org)	Brunei, Cambodia, Indonesia, Lao PDR, Malaysia, Myanmar, Philippines, Singapore, Thailand, Vietnam
Central American Common Market (CACM)	Costa Rica, El Salvador, Guatemala, Honduras, Nicaragua
Common Market for Eastern and Southern Africa (COMESA) (www.comesa.int)	Burundi, Comoros, Democratic Republic of Congo, Djibouti, Egypt, Eritrea, Ethiopia, Kenya, Libya, Madagascar, Malawi, Mauritius, Rwanda, Seychelles, Sudan, Swaziland, Uganda, Zambia, Zimbabwe
European Union (EU) (www.Europa.eu.int)	Austria, Belgium, Bulgaria, Cyprus, Czech Republic, Denmark, Estonia, Finland, France, Germany, Greece, Hungary, Ireland, Italy, Latvia, Lithuania, Luxembourg, Malta, Netherlands, Poland, Portugal, Romania, Slovak Republic, Slovenia, Spain, Sweden, U.K.
MERCOSUR (www.mercosur.org)	Brazil, Paraguay, Uruguay, Argentina
NAFTA North American Free Trade Agreement (NAFTA) (www.nafta-sec-alena.org)	Canada, Mexico, U.S.
SAPTA South Asian Preferential Trade Arrangement (SAPTA) (www.saarc-sec.org)	Afghanistan, Bangladesh, Bhutan, India, Maldives, Nepal, Pakistan, Sri Lanka

3

OBJECTIVE
Understand how factors in a firm's external business environment influence marketing strategies and outcomes in both domestic and global markets.
(pp. 63–73)

Analyze the Marketing Environment: Internal and External Scans

Whether or not you've decided to venture into a foreign market, it's essential to understand your external environment. For firms that choose to limit themselves to their domestic market, having a sharp picture of the marketing environment allows them to make good decisions about marketing strategies. If you've decided to go global, understanding local conditions in a potential new country or in regional markets helps you to figure out where to go. 📷 Figure 2.3 provides a snapshot of these different external environments. In this section, we'll look at economic, competitive, technological, political/legal, and sociocultural factors in the external environment.

The Economic Environment

After several rocky years of economic stumbling caused by the Great Recession of 2008–2009, the global economy is finally starting to make a comeback. It's slow—the global economy is expected to grow by only 3.0 percent in 2014 and 3.3 percent in 2015—but it's a comeback nonetheless. Not surprisingly, some of the developing countries are expected to the biggest drivers of growth. Even though countries like China, India, and Brazil continue to experience economic slowdowns, these countries continue to grow at a rate that exceeds the global average.[7] Marketers need to understand the state of the economy from two different perspectives: (1) the overall economic health and level of development of a country and (2) the current stage of its business cycle. Let's take a look at each now.

Figure 2.3 📷 *Snapshot* | Elements of the External Environment

It's essential to understand elements of the firm's external environment to succeed in both domestic and global markets.

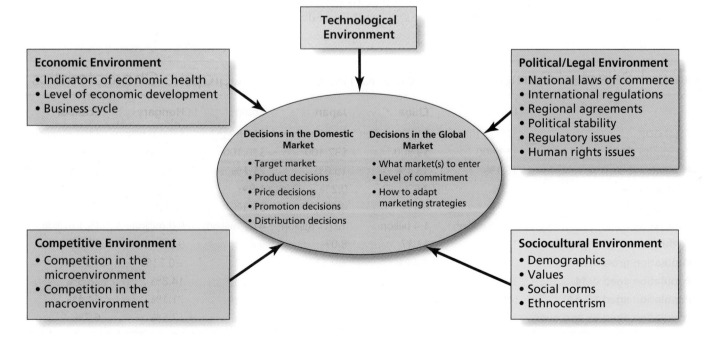

Indicators of Economic Health

Just as a doctor takes your temperature during a medical checkup, companies need to know about the overall "health" of a country's *economic environment* before they conduct a more detailed exam. You can easily find information about most countries in the *World Factbook* of the Central Intelligence Agency (CIA) (no, you don't need high-level security clearance to access this information online).

gross domestic product (GDP)
The total dollar value of goods and services produced by a nation within its borders in a year.

The most commonly used measure of economic health is a country's **gross domestic product (GDP)**: the total dollar value of goods and services it produces within its borders in a year. Table 2.2 shows the GDP and other economic and demographic characteristics of a sampling of countries. In addition to total GDP, marketers may also compare countries on the basis of *per capita GDP*: the total GDP divided by the number of people in a country. The per capita GDP is often the better indicator of economic health since it is adjusted for the population size of each country.

Still, these comparisons may not tell the whole story. Per capita GDP can be deceiving because the wealth of a country may be concentrated in the hands of a few while most of its citizens don't have the means to obtain basic necessities. Furthermore, the costs of the same goods and services are much lower in some global markets. This is why it's important for companies that want to enter a foreign market to consider exchange rates as well.

foreign exchange rate (forex rate)
The price of a nation's currency in terms of another currency.

The **foreign exchange rate**, also referred to as the **forex rate**, is simply the price of a nation's currency in terms of another currency. For example, if we want to know how much a U.S. dollar is worth in countries that are members of the European Union, we might find that it is only worth 72 cents in Europe ($1 = €0.72). If our neighbors in Europe look at the same exchange rate with the euro as the base currency, they would find that a euro is worth over one-third more in the U.S. (i.e., the forex rate would be €1 = $1.38). Why does the exchange rate matter? The rate determines the price of a product in a different country and thus a firm's ability to sell outside its borders. If the dollar becomes stronger so that you can get more euros for your dollars, then a dollar will buy more French wine or escargot, and customers in the U.S. will buy more of it. If the dollar drops in value compared to the euro, then the dollar will buy less when you hike through Italy, while European tourists will flock to the U.S. for a "cheap" vacation.

The Economist magazine developed its Big Mac Index based on the theory that with purchasing power parity, the exchange rate would equalize prices for goods and services. The Big Mac Index shows that a McDonald's Big Mac, which costs an average of $4.62 in the U.S., would cost nearly $8.00 in Norway, over $5.00 in Brazil, and $2.16 in South Africa, while the Maharaja Mac is around a $1.50 in India.[8]

Table 2.2 | Selected Comparisons of Economic and Demographic Characteristics

	U.S.	China	Japan	Spain	Hungary	Ecuador
Total GDP	$16.72 trillion	$13.37 trillion	$4.73 trillion	$1.389 trillion	$196.6 billion	$157.6 billion
Per capita GDP	$52,800	$9,800	$32,100	$30,100	$19,800	$10,600
Population below poverty level	15.1%	13.4%	16.0%	21.1%	14%	27.3%
Inflation rate	1.5%	2.6%	0.2%	1.8%	1.9%	2.6%
Unemployment rate	7.3%	6.4%	4.1%	26.3%	10.5%	4.9%
Population	318.9 million	1.4 billion	127.1 million	47.7 million	9.9 million	15.7 million
Birthrate per 1,000 population	13.42	12.17	8.07	9.88	9.26	18.87
Population growth rate	0.77%	0.44%	−0.13%	0.81%	−0.21%	1.37%
Population aged 0–14	19.4%	17.1%	13.2%	15.4%	14.8%	28.5%
Population aged 15–64	68.1%	71.5%	73.6%	73.1%	71.1%	64.4%
Population aged 65 and over	13.9%	9.4%	24.8%	17.5%	17.5%	6.7%

Source: Data based on, https://www.cia.gov/library/publications/the-world-factbook/index.html (accessed April 15, 2014). *The World Factbook* is updated biweekly.

Of course, GDP and exchange rates alone do not provide the information marketers need to decide if a country's economic environment makes for an attractive market. They also need to consider whether they can conduct "business as usual" in another country. A country's **economic infrastructure** refers to the quality of its distribution, financial, and communications systems. For example, as we saw earlier countries with less developed financial institutions may still operate on a cash economy in which consumers and business customers must pay for goods and services with cash rather than with credit cards or checks. In poorer countries without good road systems, sellers may use donkey carts, hand trucks, or bicycles to deliver goods to the many small retailers who are their customers.

economic infrastructure
The quality of a country's distribution, financial, and communications systems.

Level of Economic Development

When marketers scout the world for opportunities, it helps to consider a country's **level of economic development**. Economists look past simple facts such as growth in GDP to decide this; they also look at what steps the country is taking to reduce poverty, inequality, and unemployment. Analysts also take into account a country's **standard of living**, an indicator of the average quality and quantity of goods and services a country consumes. They describe the following three basic levels of development:

level of economic development
The broader economic picture of a country.

standard of living
An indicator of the average quality and quantity of goods and services consumed in a country.

1. A country at the lowest stage of economic development is a **least developed country (LDC)**. In most cases, its economic base is agricultural. Analysts consider many nations in Africa and South Asia to be LDCs. In LDCs, the standard of living is low, as are literacy levels. Opportunities to sell many products, especially luxury items such as diamonds and caviar, are minimal because most people don't have enough spending money. They grow what they need and barter for the rest. These countries are attractive markets for staples such as rice and inexpensive goods such as shoes and fabrics from which people can make clothing. They may export important raw materials, such as minerals or rubber and even diamonds, to industrialized nations.

least developed country (LDC)
A country at the lowest stage of economic development.

2. When an economy shifts its emphasis from agriculture to industry, standards of living, education, and the use of technology rise. These countries are **developing countries**. In such locales, there may be a viable middle class, often composed largely of entrepreneurs working hard to run successful small businesses. Because more than 8 of 10 consumers now live in developing countries, the number of potential customers and the presence of a skilled labor force attract many firms to these areas. Marketers see these developing countries as the future market for consumer goods like skin care products and laundry detergents.

developing countries
Countries in which the economy is shifting its emphasis from agriculture to industry.

bottom of the pyramid (BOP)
The collective name for the group of consumers throughout the world who live on less than $2 a day.

Within these LDCs and developing countries is a group of consumers known as the **bottom of the pyramid (BOP)**, which is the collective name for the group of over 4 billion consumers throughout the world who live on less than $2 a day.[9] These BOP consumers represent a potentially huge marketing opportunity with purchasing power parity of $5 billion. They also present a big challenge for marketers, as unlike other consumer groups, they generally are unable to afford to purchase "inventory," such as a bottle of shampoo. Procter & Gamble, Unilever, and other companies meet these needs when they offer cleaning products, fabric softeners, and shampoo in affordable one-use **sachet** packaging.

sachet
Affordable one-use packages of cleaning products, fabric softeners, shampoo, etc., for sale to consumers in least developed and developing countries.

BRIC countries
Refers to Brazil, Russia, India, and China, the largest and fastest growing of the developing countries with over 40 percent of the world's population.

The largest of the developing countries—Brazil, Russia, India, and China—are referred to as the **BRIC countries**, or simply as the BRICs. These four countries are the fastest growing of the developing countries, and they represent over 40 percent of the world's population. Marketers are attracted to these countries because of the masses of consumers who are not wealthy but who are beginning their move toward economic prosperity.

Companies like Unilever and Procter & Gamble sell small amounts of personal care products such as shampoos in individual-use sachet packaging.

Vivek Prakash/Bloomberg/Getty Images

developed countries
A country that boasts sophisticated marketing systems, strong private enterprise, and bountiful market potential for many goods and services.

Group of 8 (G8)
An informal forum of the eight most economically developed countries that meets annually to discuss major economic and political issues facing the international community.

business cycle
The overall patterns of change in the economy—including periods of prosperity, recession, depression, and recovery—that affect consumer and business purchasing power.

A **developed country** boasts sophisticated marketing systems, strong private enterprise, and bountiful market potential for many goods and services. Such countries are economically advanced, and they offer a wide range of opportunities for international marketers.

In 1976, the most economically developed countries in the world—France, West Germany, Italy, Japan, the U.K., and the U.S.—formed what became known as the Group of Six, or G6. Later with the addition of Canada in 1976 and Russia in 1998, the G6 became the **Group of Eight (G8)**. The purpose of the G8 is to provide a way for these countries, democracies with highly developed economies, to deal with major economic and political issues that the countries and the international community face. In 2014, Russia's membership was revoked due to its involvement in the Crimean crisis.[10] In addition to topics of the world economy and international trade, G8 summits have more recently included discussions of other issues, such as energy, terrorism, unemployment, the information highway, crime and drugs, arms control, and the environment.[11]

The Business Cycle

The **business cycle** describes the overall pattern of changes or fluctuations of an economy. All economies go through cycles of *prosperity* (high levels of demand, employment, and income), *recession* (falling demand, employment, and income), and *recovery* (gradual improvement in production, lowering unemployment, and increasing income). A severe recession is a *depression*, a period during which prices fall but there is little demand because few people have money to spend and many are out of work.

Inflation occurs when prices and the cost of living rise while money loses its purchasing power because the cost of goods escalates. For example, between 1960 and 2004, prices increased over 5 percent per year so that an item worth $1.00 in 1960 would cost over $6.00 in 2004. During inflationary periods, dollar incomes may increase, but real income—what the dollar will buy—decreases because goods and services cost more.

The business cycle is especially important to marketers because of its effect on customer purchase behavior. During times of prosperity, consumers buy more goods and services. Marketers try to grow the business and maintain inventory levels and even to develop new products to meet customers' willingness to spend. During periods of recession, such as that experienced by countries all over the globe beginning in 2008, consumers simply buy less. They may also "trade down" as they substitute less expensive or lower-quality brands in order to stretch a dollar (or euro etc.).

The challenge to most marketers during a recession is to maintain their firm's level of sales by convincing the customers who *do* buy to select their firm's product over the competition. Of course, even recessions aren't bad for everyone. The Great Recession of 2009 actually was pretty great for some businesses, including dollar stores and frozen foods manufacturers (as more people chose to skip eating out and to cook at home to save money).

The Competitive Environment

A second important element of a firm's external environment is the *competitive environment*. For products ranging from toothpaste to sport-utility vehicles, firms must keep abreast of what the competition is doing so they can develop new product features, new pricing schedules, or new advertising to maintain or gain market share. As we will see, marketers need to understand their competitive position among product alternatives in their microenvironment and in the structure of their industries, that is, their macroenvironment.

Analyze the Market and the Competition

Before we can create a competitive advantage in the marketplace, we need to know who our competitors are and what they're doing. Like players in a global chess

© Glyn Thomas Photography/Alamy

The low wages they can pay to local workers often entice U.S. firms to expand their operations overseas. Although they provide needed jobs, some companies have been criticized for exploiting workers when they pay wages that fall below local poverty levels, for damaging the environment, or for selling poorly made or unsafe items to consumers. Gap responded to criticism by establishing programs that help workers and their families in developing countries.

game, marketing managers size up their competitors according to their strengths and weaknesses, monitor their marketing strategies, and try to predict their next moves.

An increasing number of firms around the globe engage in **competitive intelligence (CI)** activities where they gather and analyze publicly available information about rivals from such sources as the Internet, the news media, and publicly available government documents, such as building permits and patents. Banks continually track home loan, auto loan, and certificate of deposit (CD) interest rates of their competitors. Major airlines change hundreds of fares daily as they respond to competitors' price cuts or increases. Successful CI means that a firm learns about a competitor's new products, its manufacturing processes, or the management styles of its executives. Then the firm uses this information to develop superior marketing strategies (we'll learn more about collecting marketing intelligence in Chapter 4).

competitive intelligence (CI)
The process of gathering and analyzing publicly available information about rivals.

Competition in the Microenvironment

Competition in the *microenvironment* means the product alternatives from which members of a target market may choose. We think of these choices at three different levels:

1. As competition for consumers' **discretionary income**, or the amount of money people have left after they pay for necessities such as housing, utilities, food, and clothing. Do we plow "leftover" money into a new MP3 player, donate it to charity, or turn over a new leaf and lose those extra pounds by investing in a healthy lifestyle?

2. As **product competition**, where competitors offer different products, attempting to satisfy the same consumers' needs and wants. So, for example, if a couch potato decides to use some discretionary income to get buff, joining a health club or buying a Soloflex machine and pump iron at home might be a good idea.

3. As **brand competition**, where competitors offer similar goods or services, vying for consumer dollars. So, our flabby friend who decides to join a gym still must choose among competitors within this industry, such as between Gold's Gym and the YMCA, or may forgo the exercise thing altogether and count on the South Beach diet to work its magic by itself—or just buy bigger pants.

discretionary income
The portion of income people have left over after paying for necessities such as housing, utilities, food, and clothing.

product competition
When firms offering different products compete to satisfy the same consumer needs and wants.

brand competition
When firms offering similar goods or services compete on the basis of their brand's reputation or perceived benefits.

Competition in the Macroenvironment

When we talk about examining competition in the *macroenvironment*, we mean that marketers need to understand the big picture—the overall structure of their industry. This structure can range from one firm having total control to numerous firms that compete on an even playing field.

1. No, it's not just a board game: A **monopoly** exists when one seller controls a market. Because the seller is "the only game in town," it feels little pressure to keep prices low or to produce quality goods or services. In most U.S. industries today, the government attempts to ensure consumers' welfare by limiting monopolies through the prosecution of firms that engage in activities that would limit competition and thus violate antitrust regulations. For example, when the giant cable operator Comcast attempted to buy Time Warner in 2014, the government examined the consequences of this acquisition very closely.

monopoly
A market situation in which one firm, the only supplier of a particular product, is able to control the price, quality, and supply of that product.

2. In an **oligopoly**, there are a relatively small number of sellers, each holding substantial market share, in a market with many buyers. Because there are few sellers, the actions of each directly affect the others. Oligopolies most often exist in industries that require substantial investments in equipment or technology to produce a product. The airline industry is an oligopoly. It is pretty hard for an entrepreneur with little start-up cash to enter—that's left to billionaires like Richard Branson, who can afford to launch a start-up like Virgin Airlines.

oligopoly
A market structure in which a relatively small number of sellers, each holding a substantial share of the market, compete in a market with many buyers.

3. In a state of **monopolistic competition**, many sellers compete for buyers in a market. Each firm, however, offers a slightly different product, and each has only a small share of the market. For example, many athletic shoe manufacturers, including Nike,

monopolistic competition
A market structure in which many firms, each having slightly different products, offer unique consumer benefits.

New Balance, Under Armour, vigorously compete with one another to offer consumers some unique benefit—even though only Adidas (at least for now) offers you a $250 computerized running shoe that senses how hard the ground is where you are running and adapts to it.

perfect competition
A market structure in which many small sellers, all of whom offer similar products, are unable to have an impact on the quality, price, or supply of a product.

4. Finally, **perfect competition** exists when there are many small sellers, each offering basically the same good or service. In such industries, no single firm has a significant impact on quality, price, or supply. Although true conditions of perfect competition are rare, agricultural markets (in which there are many individual farmers, each producing the same corn or jalapeño peppers) come the closest. Even in the case of food commodities, though, there are opportunities for marketers to distinguish their offerings. Egg-Land's Best Inc., for example, says it feeds its hens a high-quality, all-vegetarian diet, so the eggs they lay contain less cholesterol and six times more vitamin E than regular eggs.[12] It brands each egg with a red "EB" seal. The company scrambled the competition when it created an "egg-straordinary" difference where none existed before.

The Technological Environment

The *technological environment* profoundly affects marketing activities. Of course, the Internet is the biggest technological change in marketing within recent times. It allows consumers to buy virtually anything they want (and even some things they don't want) without ever leaving home. Increasingly, marketers use social media such as Facebook and Twitter to have two-way conversations with customers and prospective customers. And distribution has improved because of automated inventory control afforded by advancements such as bar codes, **RFID (radio frequency identification)** chips, and computer light pens. RFID chips are electronic tags or labels that can be placed on objects, people, or even a pet to relay identifying information to an electronic reader by means of radio waves. RFID tags, like bar codes, are used to identify items, but unlike bar codes, they can be embedded within packages or items and can be read even when hidden in the back of a stockroom or high on a shelf.

radio frequency identification (RFID)
RFID chips are electronic tags or labels that can be embedded within packages or items and are used to identify items even when hidden in the back of a stockroom or high on a shelf.

Successful marketers continuously scan the external business environment in search of ideas and trends to spark their own research efforts. When inventors feel they have come across something exciting, they usually want to protect their exclusive right to produce and sell the invention by applying for a **patent**. This is a legal document that grants inventors exclusive rights to produce and sell a particular invention in that country.

patent
A legal mechanism to prevent competitors from producing or selling an invention, aimed at reducing or eliminating competition in a market for a period of time.

The Political and Legal Environment

The *political and legal environment* refers to the local, state, national, and global laws and regulations that affect businesses. Legal and regulatory controls can be prime motivators for many business decisions. Although firms that choose to remain at home have to worry about local regulations only, global marketers must understand more complex political issues that can affect how they are allowed to do business around the world.

American Laws

Laws in the U.S. governing business generally have two purposes. Some, such as the Sherman Antitrust Act and the Wheeler-Lea Act, make sure that businesses compete fairly with each other. Others, such as the Food and Drug Act and the Consumer Products Safety Commission Act, make sure that businesses don't take advantage of consumers. Although some businesspeople argue that excessive legislation only limits competition, others say that laws ultimately help firms because they maintain a level playing field for businesses and support troubled industries.

Table 2.3 lists some of the major federal laws that protect and preserve the rights of U.S. consumers and businesses. Federal and state governments have created a host of regulatory

Table 2.3 | Significant American Legislation Relevant to Marketers

Law	Purpose
Sherman Antitrust Act (1890)	Developed to eliminate monopolies and to guarantee free competition. Prohibits exclusive territories (if they restrict competition), price fixing, and predatory pricing.
Food and Drug Act (1906)	Prohibits harmful practices in the production of food and drugs.
Clayton Act (1914)	Prohibits tying contracts that require a dealer to take other products in the seller's line. Prohibits exclusive dealing if it restricts competition.
Federal Trade Commission Act (FTC) (1914)	Created the Federal Trade Commission to monitor unfair practices.
Robinson-Patman Act (1936)	Prohibits price discrimination (offering different prices to competing wholesalers or retailers) unless cost justified.
Wheeler-Lea Amendment to the FTC Act (1938)	Revised the FTC Act. Makes deceptive and misleading advertising illegal.
Lanham Trademark Act (1946)	Protects and regulates brand names and trademarks.
Fair Packaging and Labeling Act (1966)	Ensures that product packages are labeled honestly.
National Traffic and Motor Vehicle Safety Act (1966)	Sets automobile and tire safety standards.
Cigarette Labeling Act (1966)	Requires health warnings on cigarettes.
Child Protection Act (1966)	Bans dangerous products children use.
Child Protection and Toy Safety Act (1969)	Sets standards for child-resistant packaging.
Consumer Credit Protection Act (1968)	Protects consumers by requiring full disclosure of credit and loan terms and rates.
Fair Credit Reporting Act (1970)	Regulates the use of consumer credit reporting.
Consumer Products Safety Commission Act (1972)	Created the Consumer Product Safety Commission to monitor and recall unsafe products. Sets product safety standards.
Magnuson-Moss Consumer Product Warranty Act (1975)	Regulates warranties.
Prescription Drug Marketing Act (1987)	Prevents introduction and retail sale of substandard, ineffective, or counterfeit drugs.
Children's Television Act (1990)	Limits the amount of TV commercials aired on children's programs.
Nutrition Labeling and Education Act (1990)	Requires that new food labeling requirements be set by the Food and Drug Administration.
National Do Not Call Registry (2003)	Established by the Federal Trade Commission to allow consumers to limit number of telemarketing calls they receive.
Controlling the Assault of Non-Solicited Pornography and Marketing Act of 2003 (CAN-SPAM)	While it makes spam legal, the CAN–SPAM Act regulates commercial e-mail and makes misleading e-mail illegal.
Consumer Product Safety Improvement Act (2008)	Sets safety standards and requirements for children's products and reauthorizes and modernizes the Consumer Products Safety Commission.
Family Smoking and Prevention and Tobacco Control Act of 2009	Bans candy and fruit-flavored cigarettes.
Credit Card Accountability, Responsibility, and Disclosure Act of 2009	Bans unfair rate increases, prevents unfair fee traps, requires disclosures be in plain language, and protects students and young people.
The Affordable Care Act of 2013	Mandates health care coverage for Americans who do not receive benefits through an employer. Revises insurance regulations by eliminating denial of coverage for preexisting conditions, ending lifetime limits on coverage, and so on.[13]
Data Broker and Accountability Act of 2014 (DATA Act)	Gives consumers access to files of personal information a data broker compiles, the ability to correct inaccuracies, and the chance to opt out of the sale of that data to other companies.

Table 2.4 | U.S. Regulatory Agencies and Responsibilities

Regulatory Agency	Responsibilities
Consumer Product Safety Commission (CPSC)	Protects the public from potentially hazardous products. Through regulation and testing programs, the CPSC helps firms make sure their products won't harm customers.
Environmental Protection Agency (EPA)	Develops and enforces regulations aimed at protecting the environment. Such regulations have a major impact on the materials and processes that manufacturers use in their products and thus on the ability of companies to develop products.
Federal Communications Commission (FCC)	Regulates telephone, radio, and TV. FCC regulations directly affect the marketing activities of companies in the communications industries, and they have an indirect effect on all firms that use broadcast media for marketing communications.
Federal Trade Commission (FTC)	Enforces laws against deceptive advertising and product labeling regulations. Marketers must constantly keep abreast of changes in FTC regulations to avoid costly fines.
Food and Drug Administration (FDA)	Enforces laws and regulations on foods, drugs, cosmetics, and veterinary products. Marketers of pharmaceuticals, over-the-counter medicines, and a variety of other products must get FDA approval before they can introduce products to the market.
Interstate Commerce Commission (ICC)	Regulates interstate bus, truck, rail, and water operations. The ability of a firm to efficiently move products to its customers depends on ICC policies and regulations.

agencies—government bodies that monitor business activities and enforce laws. Table 2.4 lists some of the agencies whose actions affect marketing activities.

Sometimes firms learn the hard way that government watchdog activities can put a stop to their marketing plans. The Federal Trade Commission (FTC), for example, cried foul over ads from the makers of four weight-loss products in a sting aptly titled "Operation Failed Resolution." While the makers of Sensa advertised that users could simply sprinkle the product on their food, eat, and lose weight, the FTC charged that there was no competent or reliable scientific evidence to back up the claims. Now it's Sensa that's on the end of a losing battle. In addition to settling with the FTC and paying a $26.5 million fine, the product's manufacturer is banned from making such statements in the future unless it can produce two clinical trials that provide evidence to back up the product's claims.[14]

Political Constraints on Trade

Global firms know that the political actions a government takes can drastically affect their business operations. At the extreme, of course, when two countries go to war, the business environment changes dramatically.

Short of war, a country may impose *economic sanctions* that prohibit trade with another country (as the U.S. has done with several countries, including Cuba, North Korea, and, more recently, Russia) so that access to some markets may be cut off. In some situations, internal pressures may prompt the government to take over the operations of foreign companies that do business within its borders. **Nationalization** occurs when the domestic government reimburses a foreign owned company (often not for the full value) for its assets after taking it over. One of the more famous examples of nationalization occurred when Egyptian president Gamal Abdel Nasser nationalized the Suez Canal Company in 1956. Similarly, following World War II, Germany and other European countries nationalized privately owned businesses.

Expropriation is when a domestic government seizes a foreign company's assets without any reimbursement (and that firm is just out of luck). In 1959, following the Cuban Revolution, the Cuban government expropriated all foreign-owned private companies, most of which were owned by U.S. companies or individuals. To keep track of the level of political stability or instability in foreign countries, firms often engage in formal or informal analyses

nationalization
When a domestic government reimburses a foreign company (often not for the full value) for its assets after taking it over.

expropriation
When a domestic government seizes a foreign company's assets without any reimbursement.

of the potential political risk in various countries or hire specialized consulting firms to do this for them. Today, many firms are monitoring the stability of the governments in the Middle East where governments have changed due to the revolutions of the Arab Spring.

Regulatory Constraints on Trade

Governments and economic communities regulate what products are allowed in the country, what products should be made of, and what claims marketers can make about them. Other regulations ensure that the host country gets a piece of the action. **Local content rules** are a form of protectionism that stipulates that a certain proportion of a product must consist of components supplied by industries in the host country or economic community. For example, Brazil has recently tightened its local content rules regarding the manufacture and assembly of wind turbines. Under these rules, a minimum of 70 percent of the steel plates and 100 percent of the cement used to build the towers must be of Brazilian origin. In addition, the tower's nacelles (the assemblies that house the machinery) must be assembled locally.[15] Such rules ensure that Brazil is able to create more domestic manufacturing jobs for its citizens.

local content rules
A form of protectionism stipulating that a certain proportion of a product must consist of components supplied by industries in the host country or economic community.

Human Rights Issues

Some governments and companies are vigilant about denying business opportunities to countries that mistreat their citizens. They are concerned about conducting trade with local firms that exploit their workers or that keep costs down by employing children or prisoners for slave wages or by subjecting workers to unsafe working conditions, like locked factory doors. Nike, once the poster child for unsafe labor practices, has spent almost two decades admitting to and correcting its formerly abusive practices with increased wages and factory audits, among others, and is now a company others can learn from and look up to.[16]

The **U.S. Generalized System of Preferences (GSP)** is a program Congress established to promote economic growth in the developing world. GSP regulations allow developing countries to export goods duty free to the U.S. The catch is that each country must constantly demonstrate that it is making progress toward improving the rights of its workers. On the other side of the coin, the low wages that U.S. firms can pay to local workers often entices them to expand or entirely move their operations overseas. Although they provide needed jobs, some companies have been criticized for exploiting workers when they pay wages that fall below local poverty levels, for damaging the environment, or for selling poorly made or unsafe items to consumers.

U.S. Generalized System of Preferences (GSP)
A program to promote economic growth in developing countries by allowing duty-free entry of goods into the U.S.

demographics
Statistics that measure observable aspects of a population, including size, age, gender, ethnic group, income, education, occupation, and family structure.

The Sociocultural Environment

The *sociocultural environment* refers to the characteristics of the society, the people who live in that society, and the culture that reflects the values and beliefs of the society. Whether at home or in global markets, marketers need to understand and adapt to the customs, characteristics, and practices of its citizens. Basic beliefs about cultural priorities, such as the role of family or proper relations between the sexes, affect people's responses to products and promotional messages in any market.

Demographics

The first step toward understanding the characteristics of a society is to look at its **demographics**. These are statistics that measure observable aspects of a population, such as population size, age, gender, ethnic group, income, education, occupation, and family structure. The information

Amnesty International campaigns for human rights around the world. This Swiss ad aims to combat domestic abuse.

demographic studies reveal is of great value to marketers when they want to predict the size of markets for many products, from home mortgages to brooms and can openers. We'll talk more about how demographic factors impact marketing strategies in Chapter 7.

Values

Every society has a set of **cultural values**, or deeply held beliefs about right and wrong ways to live, that it imparts to its members.[17] Those beliefs influence virtually every aspect of our lives, even the way we mark the time we live them. For example, for most Americans, *punctuality* is a core value; indeed, business leaders often proclaim that "time is money." For countries in Latin America and other parts of the world, this is not at all true. If you schedule a business meeting at 10:00, you can be assured most people will not arrive until around 10:30—or later.

These differences in values often explain why marketing efforts that are a big hit in one country can flop in another. Italian housewives spend about five times as many hours per week as do their American counterparts on household chores. On average, they wash their kitchen and bathroom floors at least four times a week. This dedication (obsession?) should make them perfect customers for cleaning products—but when Unilever Procter & Gamble (P&G) tested its top-selling Swiffer Wet mop, which eliminates the need for a clunky bucket of water, the product bombed so badly in Italy that P&G took it off the market. P&G failed to realize that the benefit of labor-saving convenience is a huge turnoff to Italian women who want products that are tough cleaners, not time-savers.[18]

One important dimension on which cultures differ is their emphasis on collectivism versus individualism. In **collectivist cultures**, such as those we find in Venezuela, Pakistan, Taiwan, Thailand, Turkey, Greece, and Portugal, people tend to subordinate their personal goals to those of a stable community. In contrast, consumers in **individualist cultures**, such as the U.S., Australia, Great Britain, Canada, and the Netherlands, tend to attach more importance to personal goals, and people are more likely to change memberships when the demands of the group become too costly.[19]

cultural values
A society's deeply held beliefs about right and wrong ways to live.

collectivist cultures
Cultures in which people subordinate their personal goals to those of a stable community.

individualist cultures
Cultures in which people tend to attach more importance to personal goals than to those of the larger community.

social norms
Specific rules dictating what is right or wrong, acceptable or unacceptable.

Social Norms

Values are general ideas about good and bad behaviors. From these values flow **social norms**, or specific rules that dictate what is right or wrong, acceptable or unacceptable, within a society. Social norms indicate what ways to dress, how to speak, what to eat (and how to eat), and how to behave.

A custom dictates the appropriate hour at which the meal should be served—many Europeans, Middle Easterners, and Latin Americans do not begin dinner until around 9:00 p.m. or later, and they are amused by American visitors whose stomachs growl by 7:00 p.m. Customs tell us how to eat the meal, including such details as the utensils, table etiquette, and even the appropriate apparel for dinnertime (no thongs at the dinner table!).

Conflicting customs can be a problem when U.S. marketers try to conduct business in other countries where executives have different ideas about what is proper or expected. These difficulties even include body language; people in Latin countries tend to stand much closer to each other than do Americans, and they will be insulted if their counterpart tries to stand farther away. In many countries, even casual friends greet each other with a kiss (or two) on the cheek. In the U.S., one should kiss only a person of the opposite sex—and one kiss only, please. In Spain and other parts of Europe, kissing includes a kiss on each cheek for both people of the same and the opposite sex, while in the Middle East, unless a very special friend, it is unacceptable for a man to kiss a woman or a woman to kiss a man. Instead, it is the norm to see two men or two women holding hands or walking down the street with their arms entwined.

AMERICANO, MAS COM UM TOQUE DE MÉXICO.

Mustang Sally

Marketers often "borrow" imagery from other cultures to communicate with local customers. This ad is for a Mexican restaurant in Brazil.

Language

The language barrier is one obvious problem that confronts marketers who wish to break into foreign markets. Travelers abroad commonly encounter signs in tortured English, such as a note to guests at a Tokyo hotel that said, "You are invited to take advantage of the chambermaid"; a notice at a hotel in Acapulco that proclaimed, "The manager has personally passed all the water served here"; or a dry cleaner in Majorca that urged passing customers to "drop your pants here for best results."

These translation snafus are not just embarrassing. They can affect product labeling and usage instructions, advertising, and personal selling as well. It's vital for marketers to work with local people who understand the subtleties of language to avoid confusion.

Consumer Ethnocentrism

Ethnocentrism refers to the belief that one's own national or ethnic group is superior to others. Similarly, **consumer ethnocentrism** refers to consumers' beliefs about products produced in their country versus those from another. Consumers may feel that products from their own country are superior, or they may feel it is wrong, immoral, or unpatriotic to buy products produced in another country. Consumer ethnocentrism can cause consumers to be unwilling to try products made elsewhere. For example, the French tend to be a bit finicky about their cuisine, and they evaluate food products from other countries critically. However, the upscale British department store Marks & Spencer is making inroads in France by selling English-style sandwiches, such as egg and watercress on whole-wheat bread, and ethnic dishes, such as chicken tikka masala. Young office workers view these as convenience foods, and they are less expensive than the traditional French loaf split down the middle and lathered with butter and ham or Camembert cheese.

consumer ethnocentrism
Consumers' feeling that products from their own country are superior or that it is wrong to buy products produced in another country.

4 OBJECTIVE

Explain some of the strategies and tactics that a firm can use to enter global markets.
(pp. 73–79)

Is the World Flat or Not? How "Global" Should a Global Marketing Strategy Be?

Going global is not a simple task. Even a company known for its keen marketing prowess can make blunders when it reaches beyond its familiar borders. Disney, for example, learned several lessons from mistakes it made when it opened Hong Kong Disneyland:[20]

- Bigger is better. Unlike giant American parks, which Chinese visitors are accustomed to, Hong Kong Disneyland is Disney's smallest park, easily seen in a single day.

- Cinderella who? Chinese visitors know characters from recent movies like *Toy Story*, but they didn't grow up hearing about Cinderella, so that emotional connection to Disney's traditional characters is lacking, even though they're seen throughout the park.

- Speak the language. Songs, like those from *The Lion King*, are sung in Cantonese and English but not Mandarin. That means a significant number of young visitors not only get left out but also are left feeling lost.

If a firm decides to expand beyond its home country, it must make important decisions about how to structure its business and whether to adapt its product marketing strategy to accommodate local needs. First, the company must decide on the level of its commitment, which dictates the type of entry strategy it will use. Is the firm better off to simply export to another country, to partner with another firm, or to go it alone in the foreign market? It also has to make specific decisions about the marketing mix for a particular product. In this final

Many consumers today hunger for new variations of familiar products from around the world. This German ad for crisps (i.e., potato chips) reads, "Discover Africa's spiciest secret."

section, we'll consider issues related to these two crucial aspects of global strategy: decisions at the company level and the product level.

Company-Level Decisions: The Market Entry Strategy

Just like a romantic relationship, a firm must determine the level of commitment it is willing to make to operate in another country. This commitment ranges from casual involvement to a full-scale "marriage." At one extreme the firm simply exports its products, while at the other extreme it directly invests in another country by buying a foreign subsidiary or opening its own stores or manufacturing facility. This decision about the extent of commitment entails a trade-off between *control* and *risk*. Direct involvement gives the firm more control over what happens in the country, but its risk also increases if the operation is not successful.

Let's review four globalization strategies representing increased levels of involvement: exporting, contractual arrangements, strategic alliances, and direct investment. Table 2.5 summarizes these options.

Table 2.5 | Market-Entry Strategies

Strategy	Exporting Strategy	Contractual Agreements		Strategic Alliances	Direct Investment
Level of risk	Low	Medium		Medium	High
Level of control	Low	Medium		Medium	High
Options	Sell on its own	Licensing	Franchising	Joint venture, where firm and local partner pool their resources	Complete ownership often buying a local company
	Rely on export merchants	License a local firm to produce the product	A local firm adopts your entire business model		
Advantages	Low investment, so presents the lowest risk of financial loss	Avoid barriers to entry	Local franchisee avoids barriers to entry	Easy access to new markets	Maximum freedom and control
	Can control quality of product	Limit financial investment and thus risk	Limit financial investment and risk	Preferential treatment by governments and other entities	Avoid import restrictions
	Avoid difficulties of producing some products in other countries				
Disadvantages	May limit growth opportunities	Lose control over how product is produced and marketed, which could tarnish company and brand image	Franchisee may not use the same-quality ingredients or procedures, thus damaging brand image	High level of financial risk	Highest level of commitment and financial risk
	Perceived as a "foreign" product	Potential unauthorized use of formulas, designs, or other intellectual property			Potential for nationalization or expropriation if government is unstable

Choosing a market-entry strategy is a critical decision for companies that want to go global. Decisions vary in terms of risk and control.

Exporting

If a firm chooses to export, it must decide whether it will attempt to sell its products on its own or rely on intermediaries to represent it in the target country. These specialists, or **export merchants**, understand the local market and can find buyers and negotiate terms. An exporting strategy allows a firm to sell its products in global markets and cushions it against downturns in its domestic market. Because the firm actually makes the products at home, it is able to maintain control over design and production decisions.

export merchants
Intermediaries a firm uses to represent it in other countries.

Contractual Agreements

The next level of commitment a firm can make to a foreign market is a contractual agreement with a company in that country to conduct some or all of its business there. These agreements take several forms. Two of the most common are licensing and franchising:

1. In a **licensing agreement**, a firm (the *licensor*) gives another firm (the *licensee*) the right to produce and market its product in a specific country or region in return for royalties on goods sold. Because the licensee produces the product in its home market, it can avoid many of the barriers to entry that the licensor would have encountered. However, the licensor also loses control over how the product is produced and marketed, so if the licensee does a poor job, this may tarnish the company's reputation. Often licensors must provide the licensee with its formulas, designs, or other intellectual property, thus risking unauthorized use for production of copied products.

licensing agreement
An agreement in which one firm gives another firm the right to produce and market its product in a specific country or region in return for royalties.

2. **Franchising** is a form of licensing that gives the franchisee the right to adopt an entire way of doing business in the host country. Again, there is a risk to the parent company if the *franchisee* does not use the same-quality ingredients or procedures, so firms monitor these operations carefully. McDonald's, perhaps the best known of all franchises, has over 34,000 restaurants that serve nearly 70 million people in more than 100 countries daily.[21] In India, where Hindus do not eat beef, the McDonald's menu features vegetarian specialties such as McAloo Tikki (a spiced-potato burger); in Morocco, you can order a McArabia (a pita bread sandwich); and in Malaysia, you can sample some Bubur Ayam (chicken strips in porridge).[22]

franchising
A form of licensing involving the right to adapt an entire system of doing business.

Strategic Alliances

Firms that choose to develop an even deeper commitment to a foreign market enter a **strategic alliance** with one or more domestic firms in the target country. These relationships often take the form of a **joint venture**: Two or more firms create a new entity to allow the partners to pool their resources for common goals. Strategic alliances also allow companies easy access to new markets, especially because these partnerships often bring with them preferential treatment in the partner's home country. For example, after a business partnership in which lifestyle company Hakkasan Group (founded in London) opened a successful restaurant and nightclub at Las Vegas hotel and casino MGM Grand, the two companies decided to extend their partnership. And so with the union of MGM Resorts International and Hakkasan Group, MGM Hakkasan Hospitality, was born. The new company, which includes the Bellagio, Hakkasan, MGM Grand, and Skylofts brands, aims to build luxury, nongaming hotels across the globe, starting with developments in the Americas and the United Arab Emirates.[23]

strategic alliance
Relationship developed between a firm seeking a deeper commitment to a foreign market and a domestic firm in the target country.

joint venture
A strategic alliance in which a new entity owned by two or more firms allows the partners to pool their resources for common goals.

Direct Investment

An even deeper level of commitment occurs when a firm expands internationally through ownership, often when it buys a business in the host country outright. Instead of starting from scratch in its quest to become multinational, buying part or all of a domestic firm allows a foreign firm to take advantage of a domestic company's political savvy and market position in the host country.

Sometimes firms have no option other than to invest directly in a local business. In most countries, McDonald's purchases its lettuce and pickles from local farms. When the company entered Russia in 1990, there were no private businesses to supply the raw ingredients for its burgers. McDonald's had to build its own facility, the McComplex, outside Moscow. As the country's economy booms, however, domestic businesses develop to take up the slack. Today, McDonald's purchases 80 percent of its ingredients from local farmers, some of whom have become millionaires as a result.[24]

The Marketing Mix Strategies

In addition to "big-picture" decisions about how a company will operate in other countries, managers must decide how to market their product in each country. Do they need to modify or create new four Ps—product, price, promotion, and place—to suit local conditions?

Standardization versus Localization

When they go global, marketers ask such questions as these:

1. To what extent will the company need to adapt its marketing communications to the specific styles and tastes of each local market?

2. Will the same product appeal to people there?

3. Will it have to be priced differently?

4. And, of course, how does the company get the product into people's hands?

Let's consider each of these questions in turn. The executive in charge of giant VF Corporation's overseas operations recently observed that when most American brands decide to branch out to other countries, they "tend to take every strategy used in their home market—products, pricing, marketing—and apply it in the same way." VF, which owns several fashion brands, including Tommy Hilfiger and Nautica, discovered that this doesn't necessarily work very well because local tastes can differ so dramatically. On the other hand, Spanish fashion retailer Zara, which prides itself on being able to design, manufacture, and deliver new clothing designs to its stores within just two weeks, provides trendy consumers the same designs worldwide.[25]

So which strategy is right? Advocates of standardization argue that the world has become so small that basic needs and wants are the same everywhere. A focus on the similarities among cultures certainly is appealing. After all, if a firm doesn't have to make any changes to its marketing strategy to compete in foreign countries, it will realize large economies of scale because it can spread the costs of product development and promotional materials over many markets. Widespread, consistent exposure also helps create a global brand because it forges a strong, unified image all over the world—Coca-Cola signs are visible on billboards in London and on metal roofs deep in the forests of Thailand.

In contrast, those in favor of localization feel that the world is not *that* small; you need to tailor products and promotional messages to local environments. These marketers argue that each culture is unique, with a distinctive set of behavioral and personality characteristics. For example, Egyptians like their beverages very sweet, but alcoholic beverages are prohibited for Muslims. When the Al Ahram Beverage Company introduced its Farouz brand beer alternative—a super-sweet nonalcoholic malt

Courtesy of CNN Turk

This Turkish ad for CNN implies that everyone has at least some things in common.

beverage—the local firm enjoyed surprising success. In less than five years, Farouz captured a 12 percent market share from giants Coke and Pepsi.

To P or Not to P: Tweak the Marketing Mix

Once a firm decides whether it will adopt standardization or a localization strategy, it is time to plan for the four Ps.

Product Decisions

One company in China is betting on the success of its TV series *Fei Cheng Wu Rao* (*If You Are the One*) in international markets such as Italy and Spain. The popular dating show, which is known for its ability to "arouse public interest in many contemporary issues," has already toured Australia, the U.S., South Korea, and France.[26] Whether it will truly take off across the globe is yet to be seen, but the show's producers are hopeful.

A firm has three localization/standardization choices when it decides on a product strategy:

1. Sell the same product in the new market.

2. Modify it for that market.

3. Develop a brand-new product to sell there.

A **straight extension strategy** retains the same product for domestic and foreign markets. The Apple iPod is a good example of a straight extension strategy. No matter where you go in the world, every iPod is basically the same. A **product adaptation strategy** recognizes that in many cases people in different cultures do have strong and different product preferences. Sometimes these differences can be subtle yet important. In South Korea, for example, the familiar pink and orange neon Dunkin' Donuts sign beckons customers inside to sample its gourmet coffee and traditional glazed donuts, but also on the menu is more Korean fare, such as black rice donuts, jalapeño sausage pie donuts, and rice sticks.[27]

A **product invention strategy** means a company develops a new product as it expands to foreign markets. In some cases, a product invention strategy takes the form of **backward invention**. For example, there are still nearly one and a half billion people or over 20 percent of the world's population who have no access to reliable electricity, primarily in Africa, Asia, and the Middle East. This provides a challenge for firms to develop products such as refrigerators and air-conditioning systems that can operate without electric power.[28]

Many of these people use kerosene lamps for light that are hazardous to both themselves and the environment. Here are just a few startling statistics:

- Fumes from kerosene lamps kill approximately 1.5 million African women and children annually.

- More than 1.5 million people in India suffer burns from kerosene lamps each year.

- Kerosene lamps burn fossil fuels and emit carbon dioxide (over two pounds annually when used daily for four hours), contributing to greenhouse gas emissions.[29]

To combat these and other serious problems cocreators Jim Reeves and Martin Riddiford developed the $5 GravityLight, a small, batteryless LED that is powered by gravity. The light, which is attached to a bag filled with up to 28 pounds of sand, dirt, or rock (or whatever you

straight extension strategy
Product strategy in which a firm offers the same product in both domestic and foreign markets.

product adaptation strategy
Product strategy in which a firm offers a similar but modified product in foreign markets.

product invention strategy
Product strategy in which a firm develops a new product for foreign markets.

backward invention
Product strategy in which a firm develops a less advanced product to serve the needs of people living in countries without electricity or other elements of a developed infrastructure.

Local customs provide opportunities for product invention strategies. Most American consumers would not be familiar with this Indian product: Cooling hair oil.

McCann Worldgroup India

have handy), works when the bag is hoisted into the air. As gravity pulls the weight of the bag downward, a notched belt spins a series of gears that drives the motor for the light. After you've used up approximately 25 minutes of light, you simply raise up the weight for another go.[30] As long as you've got a little muscle, you've got sustainable light. Gravity-Lights are currently being tested in 25 countries around the world.

Promotion Decisions

Marketers must also decide whether it's necessary to modify how they speak to consumers in a foreign market. Some firms endorse the idea that the same message will appeal to everyone around the world, while others feel the need to customize it. Unilever, maker of Lipton tea, is doing a bit of both in its first-ever global ad campaign to encourage its current and would-be tea drinkers to "Be More Tea"—that is, to "get off autopilot." The ads, which star Kermit the Frog from *The Muppets*, target both hot-tea and iced-tea drinkers. While all of the global ads will include the same "Be More Tea" slogan (or translations thereof), only those global markets where *The Muppets* is well known will feature ads starring Kermit.[31]

Price Decisions

It's often more expensive to manufacture a product in a foreign market than at home. This is because there are higher costs stemming from transportation, tariffs, differences in currency exchange rates, and the need to source local materials. To ease the financial burden of tariffs on companies that import goods, some countries have established **free trade zones**. These are designated areas where foreign companies can warehouse goods without paying taxes or customs duties until they move the goods into the marketplace.

One danger of pricing too high is that competitors will find ways to offer their product at a lower price, even if they do so illegally. **Gray market goods** are items that are imported without the consent of the trademark holder. While gray market goods are not counterfeit, they may be different from authorized products in warranty coverage and compliance with local regulatory requirements. The Internet offers exceptional opportunities for marketers of gray market goods ranging from toothpaste to textbooks. But, as the saying goes, "If it seems too good to be true, it probably is." Consumers may be disappointed when they find that gray market goods may not be of the same quality, so the deal they got may not look as good after they take delivery.

Another unethical and often illegal practice is **dumping**, through which a company prices its products lower than it offers them at home. This removes excess supply from home markets and keeps prices up there. And dumping isn't relegated to just retail products like the solar panels we discussed earlier—agricultural products can be dumped, too. For example, starting in late 2012, one Chinese company "flooded" the U.S. market with 60 million pounds of "cheap garlic." California, a large U.S. grower of garlic, said it just couldn't compete with Chinese prices because of the state's high property values and U.S. food safety laws.[32] Now that's a stinky situation!

Place/Distribution Decisions

Getting your product to consumers in a remote location can be quite a challenge. It's essential for a firm to establish a reliable distribution system if it's going to succeed in a foreign market. Marketers used to dealing with a handful of large wholesalers or retailers in their domestic market may have to rely instead on thousands of small "mom-and-pop" stores or distributors, some of whom transport goods to remote rural areas on oxcarts, wheelbarrows, or bicycles. In LDCs, marketers may run into problems when they want to package, refrigerate, or store goods for long periods.

Even the retailing giant Walmart occasionally stumbles when it expands to new markets. In 2013, Walmart backed out of its joint venture to open several new retail stores in

---

free trade zones
Designated areas where foreign companies can warehouse goods without paying taxes or customs duties until they move the goods into the marketplace.

gray market goods
Items manufactured outside a country and then imported without the consent of the trademark holder.

dumping
A company tries to get a toehold in a foreign market by pricing its products lower than it offers them at home.

India. In India, investment rules mandate that foreign retailers, like Walmart, purchase 30 percent of their products from local small businesses, for example. Rather than face fines for being noncompliant, Walmart put its India expansion plans on hold.[33]

5 Ethics Is Job One in Marketing Planning

OBJECTIVE

Understand the importance of ethical marketing practices.
(pp. 79–84)

It's hard to overemphasize the importance of ethical marketing decisions. Businesses touch many stakeholders, and they need to do what's best for all of them where possible. On a more selfish level, unethical decisions usually come back to bite you later. The consequences of low ethical standards become very visible when you consider the number of highly publicized corporate scandals that have made news headlines since the turn of the century. In the past few years alone, Walmart was the target of an investigation by the U.S. Department of Justice regarding bribes it allegedly made to get its hands on permits to open new stores in Mexico, JPMorgean Chase shelled out almost $1 billion in fines as a result of its "London Whale" scandal, and pharmaceutical company GlaxoSmithKline plead guilty to the promotion of its drugs for unapproved uses, failure to report safety data, and improper marketing.

The fallout from these and other cases raises the issue of how damaging unethical practices can be to society at large. The business press is filled with articles about accountability, corporate accounting practices, and government regulation as the public and corporate worlds rethink what we define as ethical behavior. When major companies defraud the public, everyone suffers. Thousands of people lose their jobs, and in many cases the pensions they counted on to support them in retirement vanish overnight.

Other stakeholders are punished as well, including stockholders who lose their investments and consumers who end up paying for worthless merchandise or services. Even confidence in our political system suffers, as was the case with the 2007–2008 government bailouts of major financial institutions while some of these same firms continued to pay managers healthy performance bonuses.[34]

While these examples of unethical businesses make headlines, there are many examples of highly ethical companies. Since 2011, *Forbes* magazine has published the Ethisphere Institute's list of the world's most ethical companies. Of the 600 companies nominated in 2013, only 144 made the list. Some shining examples from the U.S. include 3M Company (the maker of Post-It Notes), Kellogg Company, Microsoft Corporation, UPS, and Visa. What did these companies have to do to earn their way onto the list? To start, companies had to have robust corporate compliance programs as well as strong corporate social responsibility programs, and they had to be free of any pending legal charges. Other stringent requirements made sure that only the best of the best made the list.

Ethical Philosophies

Of course, what constitutes ethical behavior is often different for different people. We can point to various ethical philosophies and look at how each guides people to make their decisions. Table 2.6 presents a few of these different philosophies and how they reflect on ethical decision making.

For example, if one uses utilitarianism as a means of making a decision on different safety features to include in a new product, the ethical choice is the one that provides the most good and the least harm. As another example, the fairness or justice approach suggests that the ethical decision about employee compensation is to pay everyone the same or to be able to justify why one salary is higher than another.

Table 2.6 | Some Common Ethical Philosophies

Ethical Philosophy	Description of the Ethical Decision	Questions for Decision Making
Utilitarian approach	The decision that provides the most good or the least harm (i.e., the best balance of good and harm).	Which option will produce the most good and do the least harm?
Rights approach	The decision that does the best job of protecting the moral rights of all affected. These include the following: • The rights to decide what kind of life to lead • The right to be told the truth • The right not to be injured • The right to privacy	Which option best respects the rights of all who have a stake?
Fairness or justice approach	The decision that treat all human beings equally—or, if unequally, then fairly based on some standard that is defensible.	Which option treats people equally?
Common good approach	The decision that contributes to the good of all in the community.	Which option best serves the community as a whole, not just some members?
Virtue approach	The decision is in agreement with certain ideal virtues. Honesty, courage, compassion, generosity, tolerance, love, fidelity, integrity, fairness, self-control, and prudence are all examples of virtues.	Which option leads me to act as the sort of person I want to be?

utilitarian approach
Ethical philosophy that advocates a decision that provides the most good or the least harm.

rights approach
Ethical philosophy that advocates the decision that does the best job of protecting the moral rights of all.

fairness or justice approach
Ethical philosophy that advocates the decision that treats all human beings equally.

common good approach
Ethical philosophy that advocates the decision that contributes to the good of all in the community.

virtue approach
Ethical philosophy that advocates the decision that is in agreement with certain ideal values.

ethical relativism
Suggests that what is ethical in one culture is not necessarily the same as in another culture.

business ethics
Basic values that guide a firm's behavior.

code of ethics
Written standards of behavior to which everyone in the organization must subscribe.

Of course, there are other factors that influence behavior. **Ethical relativism** suggests that what is ethical in one culture is not necessarily the same as in another culture. In other words, what is right or wrong is relative to the moral norms within the culture. Business leaders who have experienced a sheltered life in American companies are often shocked to find that they cannot expect the same ethical standards of others in the global community. Westerners, for example, are often painfully honest. If an American business contact cannot meet a deadline or attend a meeting or provide the needed services, he or she will normally say so. In other cultures the answer, even if untrue, will always be "yes." Westerners see such dishonest answers as unethical, but in some areas of the world, people just believe saying "no" to any request is extremely rude—even if there's no way they intend to honor the request.

Codes of Business Ethics

Ethics are rules of conduct—how most people in a culture judge what is right and what is wrong. **Business ethics** are basic values that guide a firm's behavior. These values govern all sorts of marketing planning decisions that managers make, including what goes into their products, where they source raw materials, how they advertise, and what type of pricing they establish. Developing sound business ethics is a major step toward creating a strong relationship with customers and others in the marketplace.

With many rules about doing business—written and unwritten—floating around, how do marketers know what upper management, investors, and customers expect of them? In order to answer this question definitively, many firms develop their own **code of ethics**— written standards of behavior to which everyone in the organization must subscribe—as part of the planning process. These documents eliminate confusion about what the firm considers to be ethically acceptable behavior by its people and also set standards for how the organization interacts with its stakeholders. For example, AT&T's *Code of Business Conduct*, an 11-page document available via its Web site at **www.att.com**, details its commitments to honesty and to each other (to act with integrity and create a safe workplace), to the business and its shareholders (to work lawfully and to protect physical assets and intellectual property), to its customers (to follow ethical sales practices and guard customer communications), to its communities (to be responsible for the environment), to others (to maintain integrity in recording and reporting and to comply with antitrust laws), and to the code itself.[35]

To help marketers adhere to ethical behavior in their endeavors, the American Marketing Association (AMA) developed the code of ethics that we reproduce in Table 2.7. Note that this code spells out norms and expectations relating to all aspects of the marketing process, from pricing to marketing research.

Table 2.7 | Statement of Ethics

Ethical Norms and Values for Marketers

PREAMBLE

The American Marketing Association commits itself to promoting the highest standard of professional ethical norms and values for its members (practitioners, academics, and students). Norms are established standards of conduct that are expected and maintained by society and/or professional organizations. Values represent the collective conception of what communities find desirable, important and morally proper. Values also serve as the criteria for evaluating our own personal actions and the actions of others. As marketers, we recognize that we not only serve our organizations but also act as stewards of society in creating, facilitating, and executing the transactions that are part of the greater economy. In this role, marketers are expected to embrace the highest professional ethical norms and the ethical values implied by our responsibility toward multiple stakeholders (e.g., customers, employees, investors, peers, channel members, regulators, and the host community).

ETHICAL NORMS

As Marketers, we must:

1. **Do no harm.** This means consciously avoiding harmful actions or omissions by embodying high ethical standards and adhering to all applicable laws and regulations in the choices we make.

2. **Foster trust in the marketing system.** This means striving for good faith and fair dealing so as to contribute toward the efficacy of the exchange process as well as avoiding deception in product design, pricing, communication, and delivery of distribution.

3. **Embrace ethical values.** This means building relationships and enhancing consumer confidence in the integrity of marketing by affirming these core values: honesty, responsibility, fairness, respect, transparency, and citizenship.

ETHICAL VALUES

Honesty—to be forthright in dealings with customers and stakeholders. To this end, we will:

- Strive to be truthful in all situations and at all times.
- Offer products of value that do what we claim in our communications.
- Stand behind our products if they fail to deliver their claimed benefits.
- Honor our explicit and implicit commitments and promises.

Responsibility—to accept the consequences of our marketing decisions and strategies. To this end, we will:

- Strive to serve the needs of customers.
- Avoid using coercion with all stakeholders.
- Acknowledge the social obligations to stakeholders that come with increased marketing and economic power.
- Recognize our special commitments to vulnerable market segments such as children, seniors, the economically impoverished, market illiterates, and others who may be substantially disadvantaged.
- Consider environmental stewardship in our decision making.

Fairness—to balance justly the needs of the buyer with the interests of the seller. To this end, we will:

- Represent products in a clear way in selling, advertising, and other forms of communication; this includes the avoidance of false, misleading, and deceptive promotion.
- Reject manipulations and sales tactics that harm customer trust.
- Refuse to engage in price fixing, predatory pricing, price gouging, or "bait-and-switch" tactics.
- Avoid knowing participation in conflicts of interest.
- Seek to protect the private information of customers, employees, and partners.

(continues)

Table 2.7 | Statement of Ethics (continued)

Ethical Norms and Values for Marketers

Respect—to acknowledge the basic human dignity of all stakeholders. To this end, we will:

- Value individual differences and avoid stereotyping customers or depicting demographic groups (e.g., gender, race, sexual orientation) in a negative or dehumanizing way.
- Listen to the needs of customers and make all reasonable efforts to monitor and improve their satisfaction on an ongoing basis.
- Make every effort to understand and respectfully treat buyers, suppliers, intermediaries, and distributors from all cultures.
- Acknowledge the contributions of others, such as consultants, employees, and coworkers, to marketing endeavors.
- Treat everyone, including our competitors, as we would wish to be treated.

Transparency—to create a spirit of openness in marketing operations. To this end, we will:

- Strive to communicate clearly with all constituencies.
- Accept constructive criticism from customers and other stakeholders.
- Explain and take appropriate action regarding significant product or service risks, component substitutions or other foreseeable eventualities that could affect customers or their perception of the purchase decision.
- Disclose list prices and terms of financing as well as available price deals and adjustments.

Citizenship—to fulfill the economic, legal, philanthropic, and societal responsibilities that serve stakeholders. To this end, we will:

- Strive to protect the ecological environment in the execution of marketing campaigns.
- Give back to the community through volunteerism and charitable donations.
- Contribute to the overall betterment of marketing and its reputation.
- Urge supply chain members to ensure that trade is fair for all participants, including producers in developing countries.

IMPLEMENTATION

We expect AMA members to be courageous and proactive in leading and/or aiding their organizations in the fulfillment of the explicit and implicit promises made to those stakeholders. We recognize that every industry sector and marketing sub-discipline (e.g., marketing research, e-commerce, Internet selling, direct marketing, and advertising) has its own specific ethical issues that require policies and commentary. An array of such codes can be accessed through links on the AMA Web site. Consistent with the principle of subsidiarity (solving issues at the level where the expertise resides), we encourage all such groups to develop and/or refine their industry and discipline-specific codes of ethics to supplement these guiding ethical norms and values.

The American Marketing Association helps its members adhere to ethical standards of business through its Code of Ethics.

Source: Copyright © American Marketing Association.

Is Marketing Unethical?

Most marketers want to be ethical. Some behave ethically because it's the right thing to do, while others are motivated by a desire not to get into trouble with consumers or government regulators. Still there are examples of questionable or unethical marketing. We'll discuss some of these criticisms here:

1. *Marketing serves the rich and exploits the poor:* Many marketers are concerned about their bottom line, but they also want to provide a better quality of life for all consumers, that is, the societal marketing concept that we discussed in Chapter 1. But there are exceptions. For example, because of decreasing sales of cigarettes in developed countries, tobacco companies target smokers in LDCs and developing countries and thus contribute to the health problems of those populations. In Indonesia, there is limited regulation of tobacco products, so cigarette ads run freely on TV and litter billboards, and cartoon characters show up on packaging—all practices that are banned in developed countries like the U.S.[36]

2. *Products are not safe:* Whether marketers are truly dedicated to providing their customers with the safest products possible or because of the fear of government regulation and liability issues, most firms do make safe products and, if they find a problem, quickly notify customers and recall the defective product. GM, however, in 2014 found

itself embroiled in a huge scandal after it chose in 2005 not to recall 2.6 million cars with ignition switches that were known to be faulty. Instead, GM continued to use the switches, which could cut off power to the engine, disabling the airbags and power steering and brakes. The faulty switches were linked to at least 13 deaths.[37]

3. *Poor-quality products:* Many people bemoan the loss of U.S. manufacturing, feeling that imported products such as textiles and furniture are of poor quality. Product quality, however, is determined by what consumers want in a product. Do you want a refrigerator that lasts 50 years? Home appliance manufacturers could design and sell that, but would consumers be willing to pay what it would cost? Until consumers are willing to pay for higher quality, marketers have to provide products at the prices consumers want.

4. *Planned obsolescence:* In order to remain profitable, marketers must offer new products after an existing product has been on the market a period of time. For example, just when we all decided we had to trade in our old HCD TV for an LED smart TV, the OLED (organic light-emitting diode) TVs are hitting the market at prices beginning around $5,000. For many people, this is a good thing, as it increases their pleasure and enjoyment of TV. Others who can't tell the difference in picture quality can choose to spend their hard-earned money on other things.

5. *Marketing creates interest in products that pollute the environment:* Yes, it is true that those gas-guzzling SUVs remain on the market and that commercial fertilizers, pesticides, and insecticides continue to pollute the environment as farmers try to produce more and better food. Many would argue, however, that those chemicals would not be available unless there were a demand for them.

6. *Easy consumer credit makes people buy things they don't need and can't afford:* Many are concerned about businesses such as payday loan and car title loan companies that charge interest rates that can exceed 400 percent annually. Their customers typically are people with limited financial resources and even less knowledge about how to manage their money. We even know of an entrepreneur who leases tires to consumers who can't afford to buy them. Of course, by the time the tires are paid off, the customer has spent enough to buy several sets of tires.

When Is a Bribe Not a Bribe? Ethical Issues for Global Business

Whether the organization operates in one's own home market or in a global environment, marketers face ethical dilemmas on an almost daily basis. Thus, understanding the environment where you do business means you need to stay on top of the ethical values and norms of the business culture in the marketplace—often not an easy task. Indeed, there are vast differences in what people around the world consider ethical business behavior.

In many LDCs and developing countries, salaries for midlevel people are sadly very low; the economy runs on a system we would call *blatant bribery*. Some of these "payments" are only petty corruption, and the "favors" are inconsequential, while others may involve high-level government or business officials and can have devastating consequences. If you need to park your car or your delivery truck illegally where there is no parking space, you give a little money to the policeman. If the shopkeeper wants the policeman to watch out for his store, he gives the policeman a shirt from his stock once in a while. If an importer wants to get her merchandise out of customs before it spoils, she pays off the government worker who can hold up her shipment for weeks. And if someone wants the contract to build a new building or wants an unsafe building to pass inspection—well, you get the idea.

Bribery occurs when someone voluntarily offers payment to get an illegal advantage. **Extortion** occurs when someone in authority extracts payment under duress. Some

bribery
When someone voluntarily offers payment to get an illegal advantage.

extortion
When someone in authority extracts payment under duress.

Table 2.8	The Transparency International 2011 *Bribe Payers Index*: Some Winners and Some Losers

2011 Country Rank	Country	2011 BPI Score*
1	Netherlands	8.8
1	Switzerland	8.8
3	Belgium	8.7
4	Germany	8.6
4	Japan	8.6
10	U.S.	8.1
15	Hong Kong	7.6
15	Italy	7.6
15	Malaysia	7.6
15	South Africa	7.6
27	China	6.5
28	Russia	6.1
Average		7.8

*A lower score such as those for China and Russia indicates a higher propensity to pay bribes.

Source: Data based on Transparency International, *Bribe Payers Index*, http://bpi.transparency.org/bpi2011 (accessed April 7, 2014).

businesspeople give bribes to speed up required work, secure a contract, or avoid having a contract canceled. Such payments are a way of life in many countries because many people consider them as natural as giving a waiter a tip for good service. The Foreign Corrupt Practices Act of 1977 (FCPA), however, puts U.S. businesses at a disadvantage because it bars them from paying bribes to sell overseas. The FCPA does, however, allow payments for "routine governmental action . . . such as obtaining permits, licenses, or other official documents; processing governmental papers, such as visas and work orders; [and] providing police protection." But the FCPA does not permit payment to influence "any decision by a foreign official to award new business or to continue business with a particular party."[38] So under U.S. rules, bribes are out.

Transparency International, an anticorruption organization, publishes an annual survey, the *Bribe Payers Index*, that measures the propensity of firms from 30 various countries to pay bribes. Table 2.8 provides the results of a recent survey and shows that even among developed countries, there is great variation in the frequency of this practice. Top countries include the Netherlands, Switzerland, Belgium, Germany, and Japan. The most likely to engage in bribery abroad are China and Russia.

OBJECTIVE

Explain the role of sustainability in marketing planning.
(pp. 84–87)

Sustainability: Marketers Do Well by Doing Good

In Chapter 1, we saw that many firms today have adopted a *triple-bottom-line orientation*. These firms don't just look at their financial successes but also focus on how they contribute to their communities (their social bottom line) and create sustainable business practices (the environmental bottom line). Today, many believe that sustainability is no longer an option. It's necessary, it's happening, and it will continue to be a part of strategic planning into the future.

Why are sustainable business practices so important? It's really simple. All of the things we need today or in the future to maintain life as we know it depend on the natural resources of our planet—air, water, our mineral resources in the earth, and ore reserves that we mine. Today, our earth's population continues to grow at staggering rates. Economic growth, especially the growth in developing countries, means we consume our natural resources at higher rates. The massive growth of developing countries like China and India doesn't just provide expanding marketing opportunities; the growing middle classes in these countries look at the lives the consumers of developed countries and want that same life, thus creating even greater levels of unsustainable consumption.

Sustainability Is a Sensible Business Decision

To understand sustainable marketing better, we might go back to the marketing concept: identifying and satisfying consumer needs to ensure the organization's long-term profitability. Sustainability adds to this the need of the firm to sustain itself and the long-term future of society. Sustainable companies that satisfy the long-term needs of customers will survive. Those organizations that fail to meet customer needs or that intentionally or unintentionally harm consumers, harm others in society, and/or the needs of future generations will not be around for long.

Today we see an increasing number of firms moving toward greater sustainability by increasing operational efficiencies, decreasing use of raw materials, conserving energy, increasing the use of recycled materials, and preventing the discharge of wastes into the natural and social environment. General Mills, for example, stopped using genetically modified organism (GMO) crops in Cheerios.[39] IKEA launched an ad campaign in the U.K. to get consumers to swap incandescent light bulbs for LEDs to save energy.[40] Levi-Strauss, Walmart, and Nike are working to clean up their industries. Levi-Strauss not only practices sustainability in cotton fields and its supply chain but designs its products this way as well. Levi's Waste<Less jeans are made from recycled plastic bottles. Nike's FlyKnit shoes use yarn instead of leather uppers, which also creates less waste.[41]

A campaign for fair trade bananas from New Zealand.

Advertising Agency - The Special Group; Illustrator: James Stewart

Ethical/Sustainable Decisions in the Real World

You're headed out to the store to purchase a new pair of denim jeans. But where do you go? And what do you do with the old ones you no longer wear? Why not go to H&M and trade in your worn-out jeans for a discount?

H&M, the world's second-largest clothing retailer, rolled out a global garment recycling program that allows consumers with a conscience to bring in a bag of their old clothes—any brand, any condition—in exchange for a 15 percent discount on the next item they purchase.[42]

But H&M's green efforts don't just stop as it saves used clothing from ending up in landfills (more than 7.7 million pounds of unwanted wares have been collected so far). In its latest initiative, the company used recycled fibers to launch a new line of jeans and other denim products. These items contain up to 20 percent recycled cotton.[43]

H&M is the epitome of a company "doing well while doing good." Sales after the launch of its recycling program actually increased because the discount encouraged shoppers to buy even more jeans and other apparel from the store.

ETHICS CHECK: Find out what other students taking this course *would do* and *why* at **mymktlab.com**.

Are you more likely to shop at a store that offers recycling?

☐YES ☐NO

Developing a Sustainable Marketing Mix

We can examine how some companies already implement sustainable marketing practices to gather some clues about the best ways to do that as we tweak our target marketing and Four Ps to do well by doing good:

- *Target marketing strategies:* Marketers need to understand the attitudes of their customers toward sustainability. What is the potential market for sustainability-focused goods and services? What environmentally friendly products will consumers be likely to purchase, and which will they not? Then they can successfully target **green customers**—those consumers who are most likely to actively look for and buy products that are eco-friendly.

- *Product strategies:* Sustainable product strategies include the production of more environmentally friendly products, such as electric automobiles, and the use of environmentally friendly and recycled materials in products and in packaging. Long-term sustainability requires that marketers also understand how consumers use, store, and dispose of products. Some firms also strive to choose **fair trade** suppliers. This term refers to companies that pledge to pay a fair price to producers in developing countries, to ensure that the workers who produce the goods receive a fair wage, and to ensure that these manufacturers rely where possible on environmentally sustainable production practices.

- *Price strategies:* Many consumers would like to buy green products, but they don't because the price is higher than comparable traditional products. Sustainable marketing practices aim to establish prices for green products that are the same or close to the prices of other products. A truly sustainable strategy actually reduces prices in the long term because it encourages more efficiency and less waste.

- *Place/distribution strategies:* Sustainable distribution strategies can include retailers who focus on a reduction in the use of energy in order to benefit from both monetary savings and the loyalty of green consumers. Both producers and retailers can choose to buy from nearby suppliers to reduce dependence on long-haul trucking, which is a major source of air pollution. Within the food industry in particular, the growing trend of **locavorism** means that many shoppers actively look for products that come from farms within 50 to 100 miles of where they live.[44]

- *Promotion strategies:* The most obvious sustainable promotion strategies are those that inform customers of the firm's commitment to the planet and future generations through advertising and other messages. But there are other opportunities. The cost of creating a TV commercial is enormous and may take two or three days of shooting to complete. Some firms have begun to "reuse" old commercials while letting customers know that this is their way of practicing sustainability.

Sustainable Customer Behavior

A sustainability approach doesn't end with an improvement in manufacturing processes. Marketers also need to understand what will motivate customers to seek out, pay for, and use sustainable options. Many but certainly not all consumers, like corporations, do buy products that minimize the use of natural resources; encourage the use of recycled, reused, and repurposed products; purchase fair trade and organic food; use environmentally friendly cleaning products and toiletries not tested on animals; and

---

green customers
Those consumers who are most likely to actively look for and buy products that are eco-friendly.

fair trade
Companies that pledge to pay a fair price to producers in developing countries, to ensure that the workers who produce the goods receive a fair wage, and to ensure that these manufacturers rely where possible on environmentally sustainable production practices.

locavorism
The situation when many shoppers actively look for products that come from farms within 50 to 100 miles of where they live.

APPLYING ▼ Sustainable Marketing Mix

Keith understands that at Johnson & Johnson is more than just a producer of health care products. The company's top priority is health of people *and the planet.* To create sustainable products, teams collaborate with sustainability experts and develop opportunities to drive improvements at the design, procurement, manufacturing, and marketing stages of a product's development.

Metrics Moment

Most organizations today measure business success using the traditional bottom line—profitability—as profits are essential for the survival of both nonprofit and for-profit organizations. However, sustainable businesses take two other bottom lines into consideration: natural capital and social capital. As we said in Chapter 1, this concept is called the triple-bottom-line orientation. Every decision made by a sustainable business must not harm (or may even improve) environmental quality and must have a social/community building component. Companies should treat their employees as valuable resources and give back to their community. Luckily, the same business practices that improve environmental and social capital have been shown to also improve long-term firm profitability. When implemented, sustainable business practices provide an avenue to achieve mutual benefits in the natural world, the community, and the economy.

Sustainability metrics are tools that measure the benefits an organization achieves through the implementation of sustainability. Unfortunately, unlike many widely used financial metrics, today there is no *standardized* method of measuring the other two elements of the triple bottom line. Hence, it is extremely hard to compare one company working toward sustainability with another. The social capital metrics are possibly the hardest set of metrics to develop—there are simply too many variables to measure societal progress, and, as a result, it is extremely difficult to develop standardized metrics. Nonetheless, here are five examples of fairly common sustainability metrics:

- *Material intensity:* Pounds of material wasted per unit of organizational output

- *Energy intensity:* Net fuel energy in BTUs consumed to provide organizational heat and power requirements
- *Water consumption:* Gallons of fresh water consumed per unit of organizational output
- *Toxic emissions:* Pounds of toxic materials emitted in the process of creating organizational output
- *Pollutant (greenhouse gas) emissions:* Pounds of pollutants emitted in the process of creating organizational output

Complementary metrics within each of these categories can be developed by a firm to customize a dashboard of metrics to meet its needs.[45]

Apply the Metrics

1. Today most large firms have a section on their website that points to their sustainability initiative. Select any large company that manufactures products (i.e., not a purely service firm like a bank or retail store). Review their website and find their section on sustainability (if the first firm you select doesn't have one, pick another firm to investigate).
2. What are several of the key specific activities the firm points to as evidence that they are engaged in sustainability-related activities?
3. What specific evidence do they report (i.e., what metrics do you find reported) that quantify their level of success in sustainability?

---

share cars, even at the expense of higher prices, less convenience, and lower product performance. Consumers can be an important part of sustainable marketing practices when they do the following:

- Become knowledgeable about environmental concerns, product offerings that are more environmentally friendly, and firms that have a focus on sustainability

- Purchase and use green products and choose products that come in green packaging, including these:
  - Products that use less energy and less water
  - Products made from recycled materials

- Use products such as detergents in the amounts suggested or less

- Reuse products when possible

- Recycle clothing, appliances, household items, and even larger items, such as automobiles, by giving them to organizations that will distribute them for use by others rather than consigning them to a junkyard

- Dispose of all products—including hazardous ones—in an appropriate manner

sustainability metrics
Tools that measure the benefits an organization achieves through the implementation of sustainability.

Here's my choice...

Real **People**, Real **Choices**

Why do you think Keith chose option 2?

1 Option **2** Option **3** Option

How It Worked Out at Johnson & Johnson

Keith chose option 2, as he decided it was the most scalable solution; that is, it would be able to communicate about the program to the maximum number of Johnson & Johnson employees. By developing a custom online resource, branding it effectively (**www.earthwards.jnj.com**), and making the tools more approachable and easier to use, Keith's team drove 100 percent gains in awareness from 7 percent in 2012 to 14 percent of all J&J employees in 2013.

How Johnson & Johnson Measures Success

The Earthwards® intranet site was one of the first in the company to integrate Google analytics tracking. This means the group is able to track visitors, visits, downloads, and other key metrics it combines into a weighted average it tracks monthly called *Website Engagement*. This engagement index increased by 84 percent from 2012 to 2013.

Table 2.9 summarizes actual visits to the intranet site during this period. These metrics allow Keith and his team to assess on an ongoing basis how effective their efforts are to drive changes in sustainability marketing across a huge company.

Table 2.9 | Metrics for the Earthwards® Intranet Site

Metrics	2012 Average	Jan	Feb	Mar	Apr	May	Jun	Jul	Aug	Sept	Oct	Nov	Dec	2013 Average	Change (%)	Weight (%)	Weighted Average (%)
Visits	440	760	472	670	1,155	764	801	854	690	795	1019	816	650	**787**	78.90	30	23.67
Visitors	197	313	209	279	489	270	269	354	290	328	467	366	320	**330**	67.26	30	20.18
New Visitors (%)	29.1	27.8	25	28.5	30.6	24.1	22.7	26.6	29.97	28	34.45	31.71	30.1	**28**	−2.77	10	−0.28
Pageviews	1,940	2,931	1,873	3,492	7,469	4,945	7,071	5,895	2,777	5,432	5,022	3,983	2,600	**4458**	129.77	30	38.93
Avg. Time on Site (s)	358	297	433	544	473	545	592	495	419	584	396	372	368	**460**	28.45	10	2.84
Bounce Rate (%)	36.08	46.63	44.07	37.22	34.81	30.5	30.1	38.6	39.47	41.37	47.51	41.23	47.5	**40**	10.64	−10	−1.06
Mon. Click through rate							41%	33%	NA	NA	27%	20%	13%				
																	84.28

Refer back to **page 56** for Keith's story

Objective Summary ➡ Key Terms ➡ Apply

1. Objective Summary (pp. 58–60)

Understand the big picture of international marketing and the decisions firms must make when they consider globalization.

The increasing amount of world trade—the flow of goods and services among countries—may take place through cash, credit payments, or countertrade. A decision to go global often comes when domestic market opportunities dwindle and the firm perceives likelihood for success in foreign markets due to a competitive advantage. After a firm has decided to go global, they must consider which markets are most attractive, what market-entry strategy is best, and how to best develop the marketing mix.

Key Terms

world trade, p. 58

countertrade, p. 59

2. Objective Summary (pp. 61–62)

Explain how both international organizations such as the World Trade Organization (WTO) and economic communities and individual country regulations facilitate and limit a firm's opportunities for globalization.

Established by the General Agreement on Tariffs and Trade (GATT) in 1984, the World Trade Organization with its 159 members seeks to create a single open world market where trade flows "smoothly, predictably and freely as possible." Some governments, however, adopt policies of protectionism with rules designed to give home companies an advantage. Such policies may include trade quotas, embargoes, or tariffs that increase the costs of foreign goods. Many countries have banded together to form economic communities to promote free trade.

Key Terms

General Agreement on Tariffs and Trade (GATT), p. 61

World Trade Organization (WTO), p. 61

protectionism, p. 61

import quotas, p. 61

embargo, p. 62

tariffs, p. 62

economic communities, p. 62

3. Objective Summary (pp. 63–73)

Understand how factors in a firm's external business environment influence marketing strategies and outcomes in both domestic and global markets.

The economic environment refers to the economic health of a country that may be gauged by its gross domestic product (GDP) and its economic infrastructure, its level of economic development, and its stage in the business cycle. Marketers use competitive intelligence to examine brand, product, and discretionary income competition in the microenvironment. They also consider the structure of the industry that is competition in the macroenvironment. A country's political and legal environment includes laws and regulations that affect business. Marketers must understand any local political constraints, that is, the prospects for nationalization or expropriation of foreign holdings, regulations such as local content rules, and labor and human rights regulations. Because technology can affect every aspect of marketing, marketers must be knowledgeable about technological changes, often monitoring government and private research findings. Marketers also examine a country's sociocultural environment, including demographics, values, social norms and customs, language, and ethnocentricity. The ethical environment in some countries can cause problems for marketers if they do not understand the differences in the ethical perspective of such things such as honesty. In many least developed and developing countries, corruption is a major stumbling block for Western businesses. Bribery and extortion present ethical dilemmas for U.S. companies who must abide by the Foreign Corrupt Practices Act of 1977 (FCPA).

Key Terms

gross domestic product (GDP), p. 64

foreign exchange rate (forex rate), p. 64

economic infrastructure, p. 65

level of economic development, p. 65

standard of living, p. 65

least developed country (LDC), p. 65

developing countries, p. 65

bottom of the pyramid (BOP), p. 65

sachet, p. 65

BRIC countries, p. 65

developed countries, p. 66

Group of 8 (G8), p. 66

business cycle, p. 66

competitive intelligence (CI), p. 67

discretionary income, p. 67

product competition, p. 67

brand competition, p. 67

monopoly, p. 67

oligopoly, p. 67

monopolistic competition, p. 67

perfect competition, p. 68

radio frequency identification (RFID), p. 68

patent, p. 68

nationalization, p. 70

expropriation, p. 70

local content rules, p. 71

U.S. Generalized System of Preferences (GSP), p. 71

demographics, p. 71

cultural values, p. 72

collectivist cultures, p. 72

individualist cultures, p. 72

social norms, p. 72

consumer ethnocentrism, p. 73

4. Objective Summary (pp. 73–78)

Explain some of the strategies and tactics that a firm can use to enter global markets.

Different foreign-market-entry strategies represent varying levels of commitment for a firm. Exporting of goods entails little commitment but allows little control over how products are sold. Contractual agreements such as licensing or franchising allow greater control. With strategic alliances through joint ventures, commitment increases. Finally, the firm can choose to invest directly by buying an existing company or starting a foreign subsidiary in the host country. Firms that operate in two or more countries can choose to standardize their marketing strategies by using the same approach in all countries or choose to localize by adopting different strategies for each market. The firm needs to decide whether to sell an existing product, change an existing product, or develop a new product. In many cases, the promotional strategy, the pricing strategy, the place/distribution strategy, and the product itself must be tailored to fit the needs of consumers in another country.

Key Terms

export merchants, p. 75

licensing agreement, p. 75

franchising, p. 75

strategic alliance, p. 75

joint venture, p. 75

straight extension strategy, p. 77

product adaptation strategy, p. 77

product invention strategy, p. 77

backward invention, p. 77

free trade zones, p. 78

gray market goods, p. 78

dumping, p. 78

5. Objective Summary (pp. 78–84)

Understand the importance of ethical marketing practices.

Ethical business practices are important in order for the firm to do the best for all stakeholders and to avoid the consequences of low ethical standards the firm and to society. Differing philosophies of ethics provide different results in ethical decision making. Business ethics, values that guide the firm, are often used to develop a business code of ethics. While most marketers do make ethical decisions, there are examples of actions that justify some of the criticisms of marketing. In many countries, bribery and extortion are an accepted way of doing business.

Key Terms

utilitarian approach, p. 80

rights approach, p. 80

fairness or justice approach, p. 80

common good approach, p. 80

virtue approach, p. 80

ethical relativism, p. 80

business ethics, p. 80

code of ethics, p. 80

bribery, p. 83

extortion, p. 83

6. Objective Summary (pp. 84–87)

Explain the role of sustainability in marketing planning.

With growing world populations and increasing demand for products, sustainable business practices are necessary for life in the future. Many firms practice sustainability when then develop target marketing, product, price, place/distribution, and promotion strategies designed to protect the environment and the future of our communities.

Key Terms

green customers, p. 86

fair trade, p. 86

locavorism, p. 86

sustainability metrics, p. 87

Chapter **Questions** and **Activities**

Concepts: Test Your Knowledge

2-1. What is the difference between world trade and countertrade? Discuss whether countertrades are riskier than world trade.

2-2. Explain what world trade means. What is the role of the WTO and economic communities in encouraging free trade? What is protectionism? Explain import quotas, embargoes, and tariffs.

2-3. Explain how GDP, the categories of economic development, and the business cycle influence marketers' decisions in entering global markets. What are the BRIC countries? What is the Group of Eight (G8)?

2-4. What are the common reasons for implementing import quotas over embargoes?

2-5. What are the advantages of strategic alliances as a form of market-entry strategy?

2-6. The political system and the legal environment can cause major constraints and risks in the international market. Describe the four political-legal constraints—nationalization, expropriation, local content laws, and human rights issues—faced by international firms.

2-7. What do marketers mean when they refer to technological and sociocultural environments? What is RFID, and how does it improve marketing? Why do they need to understand these environments in a global marketplace?

2-8. What is ethnocentrism? What is consumer ethnocentrism?

2-9. Unlike in Singapore, the right to chew gum is taken for granted in most countries. Similarly, the right to carry guns does not exist in most Asian countries. Which ethical philosophies explain these contrasting situations?

2-10. What are the arguments for standardization of marketing strategies in the global marketplace? What are the arguments for localization? What are some ways a firm can standardize or localize its marketing mix?

2-11. Describe the utilitarianism, rights, fairness or justice, common good, and virtue approaches to ethical decision making. What is ethical relativism?

2-12. What could consumers do as part of their contribution to sustainability?

Activities: Apply What You've Learned

2-13. *In Class, 10–25 Minutes for Teams* Tide laundry detergent, McDonald's food, and Dell computers are very different U.S. products that are marketed globally. Develop ideas about why the marketers for each of these products
   a. Standardize product strategies.
   b. Localize product strategies.
   c. Standardize promotion strategies.
   d. Localize promotion strategies.

2-14. *Creative Homework/Short Project* You work for a company that manufactures and sells low-cost mobile phones. Think about how the firm's offering in the product category would need to differ for LDCs, developing countries, and developed countries. Develop a proposal that provides recommendations for the product, pricing, promotion, and place/distribution in each of these different markets.

2-15. *In Class, 10–25 Minutes for Teams* Consider the pros and cons of localization and standardization of marketing strategies. Are the advantages and disadvantages different for different products? In different countries? Organize a debate in your class to argue the merits of the standardization perspective versus the localization perspective.

2-16. *In Class, 10–25 Minutes for Teams* Assume you are the director of marketing for a firm that produces tablets. Your firm is considering going after the Indian market and is faced with the decision of the best entry strategy. Should they simply export their products, or would a strategic alliance, licensing, or a joint venture be a better choice? Develop your ideas for a best entry strategy. Be specific in your recommendations for a strategy, how to implement the strategy, and your reasons for your recommendations.

2-17. *Creative Homework/Short Project* Consumer ethnocentrism is the tendency for individuals to prefer products from one's own culture. Sometimes people think products made at home are better than imported goods. Develop a small study to find out what students at your university think about products made at home and abroad. Develop a survey that asks other students to evaluate 10 or more products (not brands) that are imported versus made at home. You might wish to ask if they feel the domestic or imported products are superior in quality and which they would purchase. Prepare a report on your study for your class.

2-18. *In Class, 10–25 Minutes for Teams* Some marketers argue the merits of international marketing, whereas others are in support of national interests and protectionism. Plan a debate in your class with two teams, one arguing for international marketing, the other against.

2-19. *For Further Research (Individual)* As a marketing manager, you are interested in exploring marketing opportunities in the international market. Using the Internet, identify 10 countries from the Americas, Europe, and Asia that are member countries of the World Trade Organization (WTO). Is each classified as a developed, developing, or least developed country? What are their main currencies of exchange, and their main imports and main exports?

2-20. *For Further Research (Groups)* You are part of an up-and-coming coffeehouse chain in the U.S., and you know that you need to participate in competitive intelligence activities to learn more about your competitors. Using the Internet, collect at least five distinct pieces of information about either Starbucks or Dunkin' Donuts that will enable you to improve your marketing strategy.

Apply Marketing Metrics

Many Western firms see their futures in the growing populations of developing countries, where 8 out of 10 consumers now live. Consumers from the BRIC countries—Brazil, Russia, India, and China—offer new opportunities for firms because growing numbers of them are accumulating significant amounts of disposable income. Firms such as worldwide cosmetics giant Beirsdorf, the producer of Nivea products, are adapting their products and their marketing activities to meet the needs of these populations. Often this means selling miniature or even single-use sachet packages of shampoo, dishwashing detergent, or fabric softener for only a few cents. The huge Swiss company Nestlé sells shrimp-flavored instant soup cubes for two cents each in Ghana, while the financial company Allianz, in a joint program with CARE, sells microinsurance for five cents a month to the very poor in India.

How do these firms measure their success in these new markets? Firms in developed countries normally use standard marketing metrics such as customer awareness, customer satisfaction, increases in market share or profits, or return on customer investment or return on marketing investment. But these metrics are based on standard market-entry strategies with full-size products and correspondingly typical pricing and promotional strategies—very different from the approach just described. Hence, these metrics are likely not too useful for the new markets in the developing world, where many millions of people buy streamlined versions of a firm's products at a fraction of their usual price.

⭐ **2-21.** Do you think the approach described above is effective for entering BRIC markets to appeal to consumers with small but growing disposable income?

⭐ **2-22.** How would the success of this approach be better measured—that is, what metrics would be more useful than the typical metrics used in developed countries? Be creative and develop a list of several possible metrics that firms might use to measure their success in these new developing markets. Hint: Keep closely in mind what firms hope to accomplish by increasing their presence and sales in those markets.

Choices: What Do You Think?

⭐ **2-23.** *Critical Thinking* What role has technology played in the globalization of businesses? Has technology leveled the economic playing field, or has it merely increased the distance between the "haves" and the "have-nots"? Give at least one example of each and explain your position.

2-24. *Ethics* Discuss whether real estate firms should be allowed to clear virgin forests for property development or whether oil companies should be able to inject high-pressure liquid into the earth for oil and gas extraction.

2-25. *Critical Thinking* Some countries have been critical of the exporting of American culture by U.S. businesses. What about American culture might be objectionable? Can you think of some products that U.S. marketers export that can be objectionable to some foreign markets?

2-26. *Critical Thinking* The WTO seeks to eventually remove all barriers to world trade. Do you think this will ever be a reality? What do you think are the positive and negative aspects of a totally free marketplace? Which countries will win and which will lose in such a world?

2-27. *Critical Thinking* In 1999, several single European nations banded together to form the European Union and converted their individual monetary systems over to the euro. Do you believe there will ever be other economic communities that would follow this path? Explain your reasoning and, if necessary, provide some possible examples. What about the possibility of a single world currency? Could this happen? Why or why not?

2-28. *Ethics* Ethical relativism suggests that what is ethical in one culture may not be considered ethical in another. What should the attitude of businesses be when differences occur? Should businesses follow the ethical values and practices of their own country or of the host country? What should governments do about this if anything? What is the role of the WTO?

2-29. *Ethics* Review the *AMA Code of Ethical Norms and Values for Marketers*, provided in the chapter. Which of the areas represented within the document do you anticipate are the most challenging for marketers to consistently follow? What makes these issues particularly troublesome? Do you think marketing in general does a good job adhering to the *AMA Code*? Provide specific evidence from your knowledge and experience to support your position.

Miniproject: Learn by Doing

The purpose of this miniproject is to gain experience in understanding what it takes to move a product that is successful in its home market into a global market in which it will continue to be successful. Assume that you oversee a number of up-and-coming hair salons and have decided to take your services global.

2-30. Describe your local competitive advantage and why you believe this competitive advantage will serve you globally.

2-31. Determine which global market(s) is most attractive for your service. Will you target a single country or an economic community? Describe your reasoning.

2-32. Decide which market-entry strategy you will pursue. Again, explain your reasoning.

2-33. Describe your marketing mix strategy:
- How might you need to adapt your services?
- What product decisions do you need to make?
- How will you promote your services?
- How will you price your services?
- What place/distribution decisions must you consider?

Prepare a short presentation to share with your class.

Marketing in **Action** Case   Real Choices at Mattel

In 1945, Mattel's founders, Ruth and Elliot Handler, were manufacturing picture frames out of a garage workshop. The couple also ran a side business making dollhouse furniture from the frame scraps; this became so successful that they turned to making toys. Ten years later, Mattel began advertising its toys

through the *Mickey Mouse Club* TV show and thus revolutionized the way toys were sold. In 1959, Ruth Handler, noting her own daughter Barbara's love for cutout paper dolls, created the idea of a three-dimensional paper doll. Barbie was born and very quickly propelled Mattel to the forefront of the toy industry. The 1960s saw Mattel grow with such new products as Barbie's boyfriend Ken, See-and-Say toys, and Hot Wheels toy cars. Mattel became a global company in the 1980s with the purchase of Hong Kong–based ARCO industries; Correlle, SA, a maker of collector-quality dolls based in France; a British company, Corgi Toys Ltd; and a joint venture with Japan's largest toy company, Bandai.

The company's responsibility mission states, "Mattel's Corporate Responsibility mission is to positively impact our people, our products and our planet by playing responsibly. This commitment resonates in our actions and through our company values each and every day." In 2013, Mattel was ranked number two among *Corporate Responsibility* magazine's "100 Best Corporate Citizens." Mattel and the Mattel Children's Foundation made a total cash donation of $750,000 for multiyear disaster support to Save the Children and the American Red Cross. In addition, over 10,000 Mattel employees have engaged in social impact activities to make a meaningful difference in the lives of children globally.

Nevertheless, despite Mattel's actions to support children and the resulting recognition, there are some problems with Mattel's corporate responsibility record. In 2007, Mattel commissioned Chinese companies to produce its products. By August, Mattel was forced to recall 1.5 million of its Fisher-Price toys, including such favorites as Elmo and Big Bird, because they were suspected of containing hazardous levels of lead paint. Later in August, Mattel recalled over 19 million more Chinese-made toys because they contained magnets that could be swallowed by children or because they were made with dangerous lead paint. In 2010, Mattel recalled over 10 million of its Fisher-Price products, including about 7 million Fisher-Price Trikes and Tough Trikes. The tricycles have a plastic ignition key near the seat that kids can sit or fall on, potentially leading to injuries. This also included recalls of its little People Wheelies Stand 'n Play Rampway due to a possible choking hazard.

In 2011, Mattel's Fisher-Price recalled for repair its Little People Builders' Load 'n Go Wagons due to a possible laceration hazard. Both the play rampway and the wagons were manufactured in Mexico and sold in mass-merchandise retail stores nationwide. In 2013, Mattel voluntarily announced a recall to inspect its Fisher-Price Newborn Rock 'n Play Sleeper. It was discovered that "mold can develop between the removable seat cushion and the hard plastic frame of the sleeper when it remains wet/moist or is infrequently cleaned."

Such product recalls can damage a firm's reputation and its bottom line. Mattel must continue to work hard to recover from these incidents. Are apologies and claims for new safety regulations enough? Because some but not all of the recalls were due to production in other countries, should the company stop producing its toys in China and other developing countries where costs are low? Or should Mattel return to its roots and produce the millions of Polly Pockets, "Sarge" toy cars, and Barbie play sets in the U.S., where costs are substantially higher but standards are tougher? How should Mattel protect its social responsibility reputation into the future?

You Make the Call

2-34. What is the decision facing Mattel?

2-35. What factors are important in understanding this decision situation?

2-36. What are the alternatives?

2-37. What decision(s) do you recommend?

2-38. What are some ways to implement your recommendation?

Sources: Based on Mary Bellis, "History of the Mattel Toy Company," http://inventors.about.com/od/bstartinventions/a/The-History-Of-Barbie-Dolls_3.htm (accessed April 7, 2014); Mattel, Inc., "Corporate Responsibility," https://corporate.mattel.com/about-us/corporate-responsibility.aspx (accessed April 7, 2014); *CR Magazine*, "100 Best Corporate Citizens List," www.thecro.com/content/cr-magazine-corporate-citizenship-lists-methodology (accessed April 7, 2014); Associated Press, "Fisher-Price Recalls 10 Million Items," *New York Times*, October 1, 2010, B6; and Nicholas Casey and Nicholas Zamiska, "Mattel Does Damage Control after Recall," August 15, 2007, http://online.wsj.com/news/articles/SB118709567221897168 (accessed April 4, 2014).

MyMarketingLab™

Go to **mymktlab.com** for Auto-graded writing questions as well as the following Assisted-graded writing questions:

2-39. *Creative Homework/Short Project.* As a marketing manager, you must consider whether to delay the production and introduction of a new automobile because of a small problem with the door locks—they could become nonfunctional when temperatures drop very low. Using (1) the utilitarian approach, (2) the rights approach, and (3) the common good approach, what would the different decisions be?

2-40. *Ethics.* Some companies have been criticized for moving their manufacturing to other countries where laws protecting the environment are more lenient and goods can be produced more cheaply because the firms do not have to invest in ways to protect the environment. What do you think of this practice? What can governments and/or consumers do to prevent such actions?

Strategic Market Planning

Check out the Chapter 3 **Study Map** on page 113.

Stephanie Nashawaty
▼ A Decision Maker at Oracle

Stephanie Stewart Nashawaty is group vice president of customer experience (CX) transformation sales at Oracle. She has over 15 years of software sales experience and extensive expertise in enterprise marketing solutions for Global 2000 leading companies.

Stephanie is currently responsible for CX sales at Oracle (this includes Oracle's application solutions for customer-facing functions, such as sales, services, and marketing). She leads an elite sales team of enterprise sales executives who are tasked with creating and delivering $1 million to $30 million Cloud deals with Oracle's most strategic customers. In this capacity, Stephanie also works on joint business development opportunities with selected systems integrators, such as Accenture and Deloitte, as well as digital agencies.

Prior to joining Oracle, Stephanie was a vice president with Unica Corporation, which was acquired by IBM in 2010. She helped to build and launch IBM's Enterprise Marketing Management (EMM) business unit. The unit's focus on "Smarter Marketing" is a key foundational pillar of IBM's current "Smarter Planet" campaign and go-to-market strategy. Stephanie led the EMM global sales team ($400 million in annual revenues), which focused on selling to the office of the chief marketing officer (CMO). She was recognized for her achievements and team contribution by her selection for IBM's Acquisition Talent Acceleration Program. During this time, she was also the executive sales leader for the acquisitions and integrations of three companies in the marketing domain (DemandTec, Tealeaf, and Xtify). Stephanie has significant international experience working with CMOs in retail, travel, telecommunications, and other industries focused on optimizing the customer experience with a brand across all channels.

Stephanie holds a BA in political science from the University of Vermont and was a candidate in the master's degree program at Stanford University. She and her family reside in Needham, Massachusetts.

Stephanie's Info

What I do when I'm not working?
Spend time with my two teenage daughters, ideally doing something outside like hiking, swimming, skiing, and tennis.

First job out of school?
Management trainee, Enterprise Rent-A-Car.

Career high?
Selected for IBM's Acquisition Talent Acceleration Program. Less than 1 percent of IBM employees were selected for this program.

Business book I'm reading now?
Converge: Transforming Business at the Intersection of Marketing and Technology by Bob Lord and Ray Velez.

My motto to live by?
"Don't let the perfect be the enemy of the good," that is, execute and iterate rather than be stuck in overanalyzing decisions.

What drives me?
Fear of failure.

My management style?
Collaborative and decisive.

Here's my problem...

Oracle is a huge player in a booming industry that helps businesses manage the vast amount of information they need to operate. Its initial business focus was on relational databases. For example, the global communications company British Telecom (BT) uses Oracle's database solution to increase control and improve customer service with a streamlined global information technology (IT) infrastructure and standardized database administration. With Oracle's help, BT can now deploy a database in 20 minutes as compared to the several weeks this task required before the company used Oracle's solution.

Things to remember

Stephanie and her team have the task of creating and delivering $1 million to $30 million Cloud deals with Oracle's most strategic customers. Companies today can access an incredible amount of information about customers and prospects from their interactions with a brand including online Web-surfing behavior, interactions in stores and kiosks, calls into service call centers, and social media such as Twitter. Today, companies are moving toward a new model called software as a service (SaaS). This "soft-ware-on-demand" approach, referred to as "cloud comput-ing" because data live "in the cloud" rather than being physically stored in a machine, makes it easier for clients to coordinate data management across locations.

Companies now have the ability to access an incredible amount of information about customers and prospects. These data points come from all of our interactions with a brand, including online Web-surfing behavior, interactions in stores and kiosks, our calls into service call centers, and even when we tweet about an airline losing our baggage. Marketing departments need automation technology to help them make sense of all of the data and to interact with their loyal customers on an almost constant basis. Today, U.S. companies spend over $1.5 trillion per year on marketing technologies. The research firm Gartner predicts that by 2017, a typical firm's CMO will spend more on technology than will its chief information officer (CIO).

As business operations become more complex, the demand for change in IT increases, along with the associated risks a company has to address. Today's IT professionals are asked to manage a flood of information and to deliver it to their users in a timely manner with ever-increasing quality of service. And in today's economic climate, IT must also reduce budgets and derive greater value out of existing investments.

Over the years, Oracle has moved into offering software applications that help all of the various lines of business, such as human resources and sales, to do their jobs better. Oracle acquired its customer relationship management (CRM) application when it bought Siebel Systems in 2005. Siebel CRM is an on-premise application that allows salespeople to manage their prospects and accounts and forecast their business. It is the key to maintaining contact with the client's customers. For example, a company that maintains a loyalty program where it tracks consumers' transactions and awards points and other goodies in return has to monitor thousands and sometimes even millions of interactions every month.

It's a huge understatement to say that the technological environment is changing rapidly. In particular, the industry is moving toward a new model called software as a service (SaaS). Instead of purchasing and installing software on its own computers, this "software-on-demand" approach allows a company to take advantage of new "distributed computing" technology. This approach stores these programs remotely so that a user can access the software from any location. Users can customize the software, obtain faster answers, and analyze larger volumes of data, making it easier for clients with global operations to coordinate data management across locations. Many people refer to this revolution in information storage as "cloud computing" because data live "in the cloud" rather than being physically stored in a machine in the building.

This sea change in the technological environment creates both a huge opportunity and a big headache for Oracle. The opportunity is that Oracle traditionally sold its products exclusively to the CIO. Now that the CMO and his team is so attuned to data-driven decision making, Oracle suddenly finds itself with an entirely new set of potential customers. Companies will be increasing their "spend" on sophisticated technology to keep up with a wired world, and the relative amount of this money they spend across functions will shift toward fatter marketing budgets for data-related products and services.

The downside: Oracle ironically faces a challenge because it is so successful in the on-premise product space, with hundreds of major corporate clients that equate the company with this traditional solution to data management. The company has faced challenges for the past few years as it struggles with concerns about its ability to compete in a new cloud-based business environment.

If Oracle tries to change with the times and move its vast number of clients "to the cloud," these companies may now think twice about sticking with the company. A CIO who wants to totally revamp the way her company manages information probably will explore what competing SaaS solutions companies have to offer. In that case, it would be open season on Oracle's clients.

Oracle needs to make important adjustments in its strategic planning to move to where the market is going. It needs to figure out how to structure its sales force to go after this new source of revenue, and at the same time Oracle has to rebrand itself as a leader in cloud computing technology. The company needs to increase its focus on developing new cloud computing capabilities or perhaps acquiring other companies that already have SaaS-based solutions and a sales team that understands this new marketing space.

Oracle needs to win in the emerging cloud-based market but at the same time retain the loyalty of its existing client base. The company needs to convince CMOs that it still has the ability to solve their most pressing database marketing challenges and that Oracle's solutions will help them acquire, upsell, and retain customers as the business world continues to move to the cloud.

Stephanie considered their **Options** 1·2·3

1 Option **Stay the course with marketing clients.** Oracle is extremely successful as a premise-based solutions provider. The company still boasts a huge roster of corporate clients that are very satisfied with what it does for them. A shift to cloud-based solutions will confuse these clients and open the door to a host of competitors. Of course, the long-term writing is on the wall: CMOs will continue to move their operations to the cloud and over time Oracle may be stuck with obsolete technologies and lose its reputation as an industry innovator.

You Choose

Which **Option** would you choose, and **why**?

1. ☐YES ☐NO 2. ☐YES ☐NO 3. ☐YES ☐NO

See what **option** Stephanie chose on **page 113** ➡

2 Option

Acquire companies that already offer new SaaS marketing technologies. Go to market with a dedicated sales team that focuses only on selling cloud solutions to current and new clients. If Oracles buys up companies with this expertise, it will quickly acquire a customer base, products, and organization that were designed exclusively for this technology. These new products also will cross-pollinate across Oracle so that its own software engineers will come up to speed quickly on state-of-the-art applications. This choice would also create an immediate revenue stream from SaaS clients, and Oracle will be able to rebrand itself as an organization that truly is on the cutting edge of database management. On the other hand, it will be very expensive to acquire these companies. Oracle's biggest rivals, including IBM, Salesforce.com, Adobe, and SAP, also are on the lookout for them, so the company might find itself in bidding wars that could up the ante quite a bit. An acquisition strategy might also create market confusion about what Oracle sells, and in addition the company's strategic partners are not as familiar with these new offerings as they are with legacy applications like Siebel. In fact, Oracle might lose clients who use the Seibel system now if they decide the company is not committed to the platform for the long haul. Finally, it was unclear if the salespeople at these smaller companies would stick with Oracle after it acquired their employers. Some of them might prefer to work for a young start-up rather than a huge corporation.

3 Option

Stick to your knitting. Continue to promote the Siebel system for basic data management function. "Deinvest" in the marketing solutions category, where it will be expensive to compete against the numerous other companies that were gearing up to swoop into this market.

This would be a much less costly decision, since Oracle would not have to spend the billions of dollars it would probably take to acquire new companies as in option 2. As is the case with option 1, Oracle already is well known as a market leader in database solutions. The messages it would send to the market would be much simpler and more straightforward, and it would benefit from a sales force that already knows the product and is familiar to clients.

However, Oracle would have to counter the perception that the company is trying to "ride an old horse" in a technology industry that richly rewards innovative solutions. In a few years, it may find itself the market leader in an obsolete category as all kinds of businesses eventually migrate to the cloud. Oracle might well find itself "penny wise and pound foolish" if it focuses on what it does well right now but fails to invest in the marketing category. By all indications, marketing functions will account for a steadily increasing share of the money that organizations spend on technology. If Oracle decides to enter this lucrative but competitive category down the road, it may discover that the ship has already sailed.

Now put yourself in the team's shoes. Which option would you choose, and why?

1

OBJECTIVE

Explain business planning and its three levels.

(pp. 96–98)

Business Planning: Compose the Big Picture

There's an old saying in business that "planning is everything"—well, almost. Planning allows a firm like Oracle to define its distinctive identity and purpose. Careful planning enables a firm to speak in a clear voice in the marketplace so that customers understand what the firm is and what it has to offer that competitors don't—especially as it decides how to create value for customers, clients, partners, and society at large. In this chapter, you will experience the power of effective business planning—and especially market planning—and lay the groundwork for your own capability to do successful planning.

We think this process is really important. That's why we're starting with a discussion about what planners do and the questions they need to ask to be sure they keep their companies and products on course. In many ways, developing great business planning is like taking an awesome digital photo with your smart phone (maybe a "selfie"?)—hence the title of this section. The metaphor works because success in photography is built around capturing the right information in the lens of your camera, positioning the image correctly, and snapping the picture you'll need to set things in motion. A business plan is a lot like that.

The knowledge you gain from going through a formal planning process is worth its weight in gold. Without market planning as an ongoing activity in a business, there's no real way to know where you want the firm to go, how it will get there, or even if it is on the right or wrong track right now. There's nothing like a clear road map when you're lost in the wilderness. And speaking of road maps, we even include a handy tear-out guide later in this chapter that shows you step-by-step how to build a marketing plan and where to find the information throughout the book to be able to do it. This tear-out road map will be highly useful as you make your way through the book, keeping the "big-picture" viewpoint of marketing in mind no matter which chapter you're reading.

What exactly is **business planning**? Put simply, it's an ongoing process of decision making that guides the firm in both the short term and the long term. Planning identifies and builds on a firm's strengths, and it helps managers at all levels to make informed decisions in a changing business environment. *Planning* means that an organization develops objectives before it takes action. In large firms like IBM and Ford, which operate in many markets, planning is a complex process involving many people from different areas of the company's operations. At a very small business like Mac's Diner in your hometown, however, planning is quite different. Yet regardless of firm size or industry, great planning can only increase the chances of success.

In the sections that follow, we'll look at the different steps in an organization's planning. First, we'll see how managers develop a **business plan** to specify the decisions that guide the entire organization or its business units. Then we'll examine the entire strategic planning process and the stages in that process that lead to the development and implementation of a **marketing plan**—a process and resulting document that describes the marketing environment, outlines the marketing objectives and strategies, and identifies how the company will implement and control the strategies embedded in the plan.

business planning
An ongoing process of making decisions that guides the firm both in the short term and in the long term.

business plan
A plan that includes the decisions that guide the entire organization.

marketing plan
A document that describes the marketing environment, outlines the marketing objectives and strategy, and identifies who will be responsible for carrying out each part of the marketing strategy.

The Three Levels of Business Planning

We all know in general what planning is—we plan a vacation or a great Saturday night party. Some of us even plan how we're going to study and get our assignments completed without stressing out at the last minute. When businesses plan, the process is more complex. As ⟨📷⟩ Figure 3.1 shows, planning occurs at three levels: strategic, functional, and operational. The top level is big-picture stuff, while the bottom level specifies the "nuts-and-bolts" actions the firm will need to take to achieve these lofty goals:

- *First-level planning:* **Strategic planning** is the managerial decision process that matches the firm's resources (such as its financial assets and workforce) and capabilities (the things it is able to do well because of its expertise and experience) to its market opportunities

strategic planning
A managerial decision process that matches an organization's resources and capabilities to its market opportunities for long-term growth and survival.

Figure 3.1 ⟨📷⟩ *Snapshot* | Levels of Planning

During planning, an organization determines its objectives and then develops courses of action to accomplish them. In larger firms, planning takes place at the strategic, functional, and operational levels.

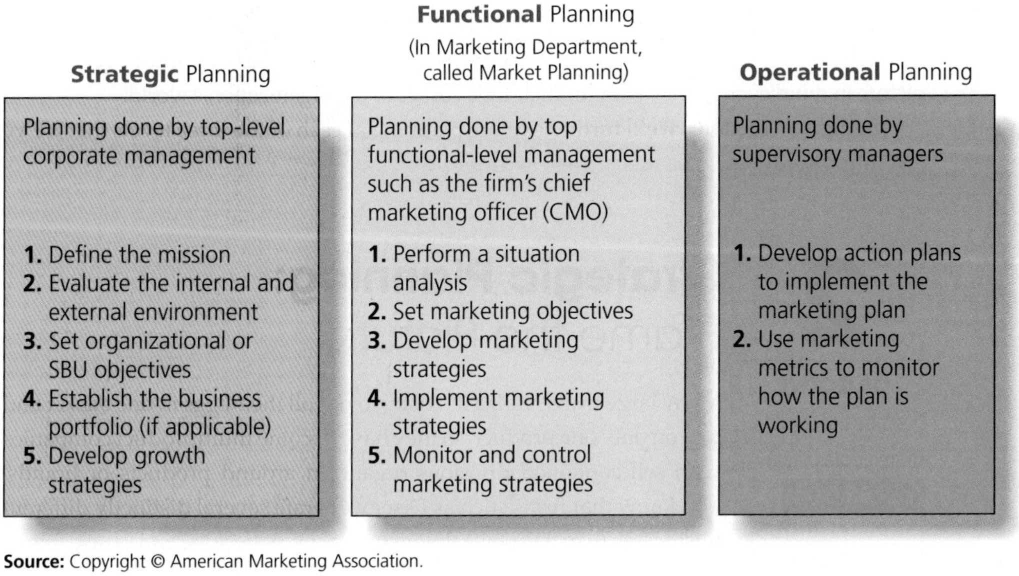

Strategic Planning	**Functional** Planning (In Marketing Department, called Market Planning)	**Operational** Planning
Planning done by top-level corporate management	Planning done by top functional-level management such as the firm's chief marketing officer (CMO)	Planning done by supervisory managers
1. Define the mission	1. Perform a situation analysis	1. Develop action plans to implement the marketing plan
2. Evaluate the internal and external environment	2. Set marketing objectives	2. Use marketing metrics to monitor how the plan is working
3. Set organizational or SBU objectives	3. Develop marketing strategies	
4. Establish the business portfolio (if applicable)	4. Implement marketing strategies	
5. Develop growth strategies	5. Monitor and control marketing strategies	

Source: Copyright © American Marketing Association.

for long-term growth. In a strategic plan, top management—usually the chief executive officer (CEO), president, and other top executives—define the firm's purpose and specify what the firm hopes to achieve over the next five years or so. For example, Oracle's strategic plan may set an objective to increase total revenues by 20 percent in the next five years.

strategic business units (SBUs)
Individual units within the firm that operate like separate businesses, with each having its own mission, business objectives, resources, managers, and competitors.

Large firms, such as the Walt Disney Company, have a number of self-contained divisions we call **strategic business units (SBUs)**—individual units that represent different areas of business within a firm that are unique enough to each have their own mission, business objectives, resources, managers, and competitors. Disney's SBUs include its theme parks, TV networks, and cruise line divisions, and strategic planning occurs both at the overall corporate level (Disney headquarters plans for the whole corporation globally) and at the individual business unit level (at the theme park, TV networks, and cruise line level). We'll discuss these two levels later in the chapter.

functional planning
A decision process that concentrates on developing detailed plans for strategies and tactics for the short term, supporting an organization's long-term strategic plan.

- *Second-level planning:* The next level of planning is **functional planning**. This level gets its name because it involves the various functional areas of the firm, such as marketing, finance and human resources. Vice presidents or functional directors usually do this. We refer to what the functional planning marketers do as *market planning*. The person in charge of such planning may have the title of director of marketing, vice president of marketing, chief marketing officer, or something similar. Such marketers might set an objective to gain 40 percent of a particular market by successfully introducing three new products during the coming year. This objective would be part of a marketing plan. Market planning typically includes both a broad three- to five-year plan to support the firm's strategic plan and a detailed annual plan for the coming year.

operational planning
A decision process that focuses on developing detailed plans for day-to-day activities that carry out an organization's functional plans.

- *Third-level planning:* Still farther down the planning ladder are the managers who are responsible for planning at a third level we call **operational planning**. In marketing, these include people such as sales managers, marketing communications managers, brand managers, and market research managers. This level of planning focuses on the day-to-day execution of the functional plans and includes detailed annual, semiannual, or quarterly plans. Operational plans might show exactly how many units of a product a salesperson needs to sell per month or how many TV commercials the firm will place on certain networks during a season. At the operational planning level, a manager may develop plans for a marketing campaign to promote the product by creating buzz via social networking outlets.

Of course, marketing managers don't just sit in their offices dreaming up plans without any concern for the rest of the organization. Even though we've described each layer separately, *all business planning is an integrated activity*. This means that at an organization like Oracle, strategic, functional, and operational plans must work together for the benefit of the whole, always within the context of the organization's mission and objectives. So planners at all levels must consider good principles of accounting, the value of the company to its stockholders, and the requirements for staffing and human resource management—that is, they must keep the big picture in mind even as they plan for their little corner of the organization's world.

In the next sections, we'll further explore planning at each of the three levels that we've just introduced.

2 Strategic Planning: Frame the Picture

OBJECTIVE
Describe the steps in strategic planning.
(pp. 98–104)

Many large firms realize it's risky to put all their eggs in one basket and rely on only one product, so they have become multiproduct companies with self-contained divisions organized around products or brands. You know that firms such as Disney operate several distinctly different businesses (e.g., Disney's theme parks, TV networks, and cruise line).

In firms with multiple SBUs, the first step in strategic planning is for top management to establish a mission for the entire corporation. Top managers then evaluate the internal and external environments of the business and set corporate-level objectives that guide decision making within each individual SBU. In small firms that are not large enough to have separate SBUs, strategic planning simply takes place at the overall firm level. Whether or not a firm has SBUs, the process of strategic planning is basically the same. Let's look at the planning steps in a bit more detail, guided by Figure 3.2.

Step 1: Define the Mission

Theoretically, top management's first step in the strategic planning stage is to answer questions such as the following:

- What business are we in?
- What customers should we serve?
- How should we develop the firm's capabilities and focus its efforts?

In many firms, the answers to questions such as these become the lead items in the organization's strategic plan. The answers become part of a **mission statement**—a formal document that describes the organization's overall purpose and what it hopes to achieve in terms of its customers, products, and resources. For example, the mission of Mothers Against Drunk Driving (MADD) is "to stop drunk driving, support the victims of this violent crime, and prevent underage drinking."[1] The ideal mission statement is not too broad, too narrow, or too shortsighted. A mission that is too broad will not provide adequate focus for the organization. It doesn't do much good to claim, "We are in the business of making high-quality products" or "Our business is keeping customers happy," as it is hard to find a firm that doesn't make these claims. It's also important to remember that the need for a clear mission statement applies to virtually any type of organization, even those like MADD, whose objective is to serve society rather than to sell goods or services.

Step 2: Evaluate the Internal and External Environment

The second step in strategic planning is to assess the firm's internal and external environments. We refer to this process as a **situation analysis**, *environmental analysis*, or sometimes a *business review*. The analysis includes a discussion of the firm's internal environment, which can identify a firm's strengths and weaknesses, as well as the external environment in which the firm does business so the firm can identify opportunities and threats.

By **internal environment** we mean all the controllable elements inside a firm that influence how well the firm operates. Internal strengths may lie in the firm's technologies. What is the firm able to do well that other firms would find difficult to duplicate? What patents does it hold? A firm's physical facilities can be an important strength or weakness, as can its level of financial stability, its relationships with suppliers, its corporate reputation, its ability to produce consistently high-quality products, and its ownership of strong brands in the marketplace. Internal elements include a firm's structure, organizational culture, and all sorts of assets—financial and otherwise.

Internal strengths and weaknesses often reside in the firm's employees—the firm's *human and intellectual capital*. What skills do the employees have? What kind of training have they had? Are they loyal to the firm? Do they feel a sense of ownership? Has the firm been able to attract top researchers and good decision makers?

The **external environment** consists of elements outside the firm that may affect it either positively or negatively. For Oracle and many other firms, the external environment for today's businesses is global, so managers/marketers must consider elements such as the economy, competition, technology, law, ethics, and sociocultural trends. Unlike elements of the internal

Figure 3.2 *Process* | Steps in Strategic Planning

The strategic planning process includes a series of steps that results in the development of growth strategies.

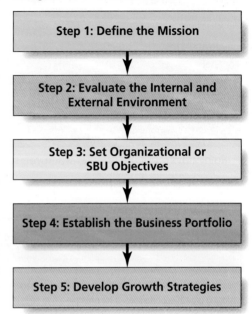

Step 1: Define the Mission

Step 2: Evaluate the Internal and External Environment

Step 3: Set Organizational or SBU Objectives

Step 4: Establish the Business Portfolio

Step 5: Develop Growth Strategies

mission statement
A formal statement in an organization's strategic plan that describes the overall purpose of the organization and what it intends to achieve in terms of its customers, products, and resources.

situation analysis
An assessment of a firm's internal and external environments.

internal environment
The controllable elements inside an organization, including its people, its facilities, and how it does things that influence the operations of the organization.

external environment
The uncontrollable elements outside an organization that may affect its performance either positively or negatively.

APPLYING ▼ Examining the External Environment

Stephanie knows that good decisions about future growth of Oracle are tied to an accurate assessment of the external environment. Understanding industry movement toward a "distributed computing" technology and the changing customer base as CMO's move toward data-driven technology is critical to planning for Oracle's future.

A mission statement that is *too narrow* may prevent managers from envisioning growth opportunities. If for example a firm sees itself only in terms of the products it currently makes rather than the underlying benefits it provides, it can be caught flat-footed when technology moves on. Although consumers know Xerox primarily as a maker of photocopier and printers, the company views itself as a leader in document technology and business services. By staying true to its mission of giving their clients the freedom to focus on their real business, Xerox is now the world's leading enterprise for business process and document management, offering global services from health insurance claims reimbursement and automated toll transaction to customer care centers and HR benefits management.

SWOT analysis

An analysis of an organization's strengths and weaknesses and the opportunities and threats in its external environment.

environment that management can control to a large degree, the firm can't directly control these external factors, so management must respond to them through its planning process.

In Chapter 2, you read in depth about the various elements of the external environment in which marketing takes place, within the context of today's global enterprise. You gained an appreciation of why it is important for you to be aware that opportunities and threats can come from any part of the external environment. On the one hand, trends or currently unserved customer needs may provide opportunities for growth. On the other hand, if changing customer needs or buying patterns mean customers are turning away from a firm's products, it's a signal of possible danger or threats down the road. Even very successful firms have to change to keep up with external environmental pressures. Oracle's business, like that of most marketing-related suppliers, is greatly impacted by the marketing budgets of its clients, which in turn are driven by economic conditions and ultimately consumer demand.

What is the outcome of an analysis of a firm's internal and external environments? Managers often synthesize their findings from a situation analysis into a format we call a **SWOT analysis**. This document summarizes the ideas from the situation analysis. It allows managers to focus clearly on the meaningful strengths (S) and weaknesses (W) in the firm's internal environment and opportunities (O) and threats (T) coming from outside the firm (the external environment). A SWOT analysis enables a firm to develop strategies that make use of what the firm does best in seizing opportunities for growth while at the same time avoiding external threats that might hurt the firm's sales and profits. Table 3.1 shows an example of a partial SWOT analysis for McDonald's.

Step 3: Set Organizational or SBU Objectives

After they construct a mission statement, top management translates it into *organizational* or *SBU objectives*. These goals are a direct outgrowth of the mission statement and broadly identify what the firm hopes to accomplish within the general time frame of the firm's long-range business plan. If the firm is big enough to have separate SBUs, each unit will have its own objectives relevant to its operations.

To be effective, objectives need to be *specific*, *measurable* (so firms can tell whether they've met them), *attainable*, and *sustainable*. Attainability is especially important—firms that establish "pie-in-the-sky" objectives they can't realistically obtain can create frustration for their employees (who work hard but get no satisfaction of accomplishment) and other stakeholders in the firm, such as vendors and shareholders who are affected when the firm doesn't meet its objectives. That a firm's objectives are sustainable is also critical—what's the point of investing in attaining an objective for only a very short term? This often happens when a firm underestimates the likelihood that a competitor will come to market with a better offering. Without some assurance that an objective is sustainable, the financial return on an investment likely will not be positive.

Objectives may relate to revenue and sales, profitability, the firm's standing in the market, return on investment, productivity, product development, customer satisfaction, social responsibility, and many other attributes. To ensure measurability, marketers increasingly try to state objectives in numerical terms. For example, a firm might have as an objective a 10 percent increase in profitability. It could reach this objective by increasing productivity, by reducing costs, or by selling off an unprofitable division. Or it might meet this 10 percent objective by developing new products, investing in new technologies, or entering a new market.

| **Table 3.1** | Example of a Partial SWOT Analysis for McDonald's |

Strengths	World-class research and product development.
	Global franchise system that is second to none.
	Strong cash position.
	Consistency of product and service quality across the globe.
	World's largest global supply chain in food
	Growing presence in the coffee/bistro market.
Weaknesses	Until recently, slow to react to changing consumer trends and preferences (organics, low-fat options).
	Image as purely a burger provider.
Opportunities	Changing consumer tastes and dining preferences signals an opportunity to enhance the customer experience while inside the store.
	Reconnecting with Baby Boomers and Gen X while cultivating Gen Y and Millennials provides opportunity for product innovation and more flexibility by market area.
	High cost of gasoline means more people are seeking dining experiences closer to home.
	The image of McDonald's is inextricably linked to the image of America globally (could also be a threat).
Threats	The image of McDonald's is inextricably linked to the image of America globally (could also be an opportunity).
	Strongly negative media coverage surrounding obesity and unhealthy eating, especially among children and teens, has tarnished the brand (e.g., the documentary film "Super Size Me").
	Wendy's has recovered its footing with the new "Wendy" girl imagery and food innovations.

For many years, one of the objectives of Procter & Gamble (P&G) was to have a number one brand in every product category in which it competed—a goal that was certainly specific and attainable. However, realistic it was not. External factors like the recent global recession and internal factors like top management changes put P&G behind on its goals. But P&G is still on top under the leadership of CEO A. G. Lafley, whose current target objective is to "grow the base"—that is, focus on those brands and markets (including developing countries) that make up the biggest chunk of the company's sales and profits.[3] More specifically P&G will work toward ". . . value creation for consumers and shareowners, productivity and innovation, significant improvements to operating discipline and investments in research and development and go-to-market capabilities."[4] So even though P&G admits it might not be number one everywhere, it strives to be number one overall.

Step 4: Establish the Business Portfolio

For companies with several different SBUs, strategic planning includes making decisions about how to best allocate resources across these businesses to ensure growth for the total organization. Each SBU has its own focus within the firm's overall strategic plan, and each has its own target market and strategies to reach its objectives. Just like an independent business, each SBU is a separate *profit center* within the larger corporation—that is, each SBU within the firm is responsible for its own costs, revenues, and profits. These items can be accounted for separately for each SBU.

Just as we call the collection of different stocks an investor owns a portfolio, the range of different businesses that a large firm operates is its **business portfolio**. These different businesses usually represent very different product lines, each of which operates with its own budget and management. Having a diversified business portfolio reduces the firm's dependence on one product line or one group of customers. For example, if the economy sours and consumers don't travel as much in a bad year for Disney theme park attendance and cruises, its managers hope that the sales will be made up by stay-at-homers who watch Disney's TV

Southwest Airlines has always been very focused on hiring and developing employees who reflect the "Southwest Spirit" to customers. Anyone who has flown on Southwest can attest to the fact that the atmosphere is lively and fun, and flight attendants are likely to do most any crazy stunt—bowling in the aisle, or serenading the captain and first officer (and passengers) with a favorite tune. One of our favorites is a guy who does galloping horse hooves and neighing sounds during takeoff and landing to promote a fun atmosphere. For Southwest, a real strength—one that's hard for the competition to crack—lies in this employee spirit.

business portfolio
The group of different products or brands owned by an organization and characterized by different income-generating and growth capabilities.

Figure 3.3 📷 *Snapshot* | BCG Matrix

The Boston Consulting Group's (BCG) growth–market share matrix is one way a firm can examine its portfolio of different products or SBUs. By categorizing SBUs as stars, cash cows, question marks, or dogs, the matrix helps managers make good decisions about how the firm should grow.

Stars: SBUs whose products have a dominant market share in high-growth markets

Question Marks: SBUs whose products have a low market share in high-growth markets

Cash Cows: SBUs whose products have a dominant market share in a low-growth market

Dogs: SBUs nobody wants

Market Growth Rate — High / Low

Relative Market Share — High / Low

Source: Product Portfolio Matrix, © 1970, The Boston Consulting Group.

networks and who purchase Mickey Mouse collectibles from the Disney website.

Portfolio analysis is a tool management uses to assess the potential of a firm's business portfolio. It helps management decide which of its current SBUs should receive more—or less—of the firm's resources and which of its SBUs are most consistent with the firm's overall mission. There are a host of portfolio models available. To illustrate how one works, let's examine the especially popular model the Boston Consulting Group (BCG) developed: the **BCG growth–market share matrix**.

The BCG model focuses on determining the potential of a firm's existing successful SBUs to generate cash that the firm can then use to invest in other businesses. The BCG matrix in 📷 Figure 3.3 shows that the vertical axis represents the attractiveness of the market: the *market growth rate*. Even though the figure shows "high" and "low" as measurements, marketers might ask whether the total market for the SBU's products is growing at a rate of 10, 50, 100, or 200 percent annually.

The horizontal axis in Figure 3.3 shows the SBU's current strength in the market through its relative market share. Here, marketers might ask whether the SBU's share is 5, 25, or perhaps 75 percent of the current market. Combining the two axes creates four quadrants representing four different types of SBUs. Each quadrant of the BCG grid uses a symbol to designate business units that fall within a certain range for market growth rate and market share. Let's take a closer look at each cell in the grid:

portfolio analysis
A management tool for evaluating a firm's business mix and assessing the potential of an organization's strategic business units.

BCG growth–market share matrix
A portfolio analysis model developed by the Boston Consulting Group that assesses the potential of successful products to generate cash that a firm can then use to invest in new products.

stars
SBUs with products that have a dominant market share in high-growth markets.

cash cows
SBUs with a dominant market share in a low-growth-potential market.

question marks
SBUs with low market shares in fast-growth markets.

dogs
SBUs with a small share of a slow-growth market. They are businesses that offer specialized products in limited markets that are not likely to grow quickly.

- **Stars** are SBUs with products that have a dominant market share in high-growth markets. Because the SBU has a dominant share of the market, stars generate large revenues, but they also require large amounts of funding to keep up with production and promotion demands. Hence, stars need investment capital from other parts of the business as they don't generate it themselves. Of course, any profits generated directly by stars presumably would be reinvested right back in the star. For example, in recent years, Disney has viewed its TV operations as a star, so it invested heavily in such franchise players as *Sophia the First* and *Doc McStuffins*. Likewise, at Marvel Entertainment, blockbuster movies like *The Avengers* and *Iron Man 3* continued the sensational success of that business unit as a contributor to overall Disney profits.[5]

- **Cash cows** have a dominant market share in a low-growth potential market. Because there's not much opportunity for new companies, competitors don't often enter the market. At the same time, the SBU is well established and enjoys a high market share that the firm can sustain with minimal funding. Firms usually milk cash cows of their profits to fund the growth of other SBUs. Of course, if the firm's objective is to increase revenues, having too many cash cows with little or no growth potential can become a liability. For Disney, its theme parks unit fits into the cash cow category in that sales have been basically steady for an extended period of time. Recently, Walt Disney World in Orlando completed a major upgrade of its oldest park there—Magic Kingdom—with an all-new Fantasyland in order to keep the park fresh and appealing for its visitors.[6]

- **Question marks**—sometimes called "problem children"—are SBUs with low market shares in fast-growth markets. When a business unit is a question mark, they key issue is whether through investment and new strategy it can be transformed into a star. For example, the firm could pump more money into marketing the product and hope that relative market share will improve. But the problem with question marks is that despite investment many times they make a beeline straight into the annals of market failures. Hence, the firm must carefully evaluate the likelihood that investment in a question mark will pay off else it may find itself "throwing good money after bad" if it gains nothing but a negative cash flow and disappointment. For Disney, its retailing store operation falls into the question-mark category, as its performance compared to the overall specialty retail market has somewhat lagged. Like most retail operators today, the online version of the Disney Store provides a better growth trajectory than the bricks-and-mortar version.

- **Dogs** command a small share of a slow-growth market. They are businesses that offer specialized products in limited markets that are not likely to grow quickly. When possible, large firms may sell off their dogs to smaller firms that may be able to nurture them—or they may take the SBU's products off the market. Disney, being a savvy strategic planner, apparently identified its Miramax film studio as a long-term dog (to Pluto and Goofy: no pun intended), as they sold it off in 2010 ending a 17-year involvement with that studio.[7] In addition, in 2011, Disney Vacation Club (its time-share unit) scrapped plans to launch a major new facility at National Harbor near Washington, D.C.[8] This move was no doubt reflective of the general malaise in the time-share market (also called "vacation ownership") since the Great Recession.

Like Disney, Oracle could use the BCG matrix to evaluate its product lines in order to make important decisions about where to invest for future growth. It would look across Oracle's various offerings to assess the market growth rate and relative market share, determine the degree to which each is a cash generator or a cash user, and decide whether to invest further in these or other business opportunities.

The recent acquisition of Marvel Comics by Disney most likely will add to the entertainment company's stable of stars.

Step 5: Develop Growth Strategies

Although the BCG matrix can help managers decide which SBUs they should invest in for growth, it doesn't tell them much about *how* to make that growth happen. Should the growth of an SBU come from finding new customers, from developing new variations of the product, or from some other growth strategy? Part of strategic planning at the SBU level entails evaluating growth strategies.

Marketers use the product–market growth matrix, shown in 📷 Figure 3.4, to analyze different growth strategies. The vertical axis in Figure 3.4 represents opportunities for growth either in existing markets or in new markets. The horizontal axis considers whether the firm would be better off putting its resources into existing products or whether it should acquire new products. The matrix provides four fundamental marketing strategies: market penetration, market development, product development, and diversification:

- **Market penetration strategies** seek to increase sales of existing products to existing markets, such as current users, nonusers, and users of competing brands within a market. To accomplish penetration in the super-competitive yogurt market, Dannon has very aggressively promoted its Activia yogurt with probiotics. The product, which contains a probiotic culture called Bifidus Regularis, has been shown to help set the balance of the intestinal microflora within the digestive system when consumed daily over a period of two weeks.[9] The Activia website is filled with information about digestive health and good nutrition.

- **Market development strategies** introduce existing products to new markets. This strategy can mean expanding into a new geographic area, or it may mean reaching new customer segments within an existing

market penetration strategies
Growth strategies designed to increase sales of existing products to current customers, nonusers, and users of competitive brands in served markets.

Figure 3.4 📷 *Snapshot* | Product–Market Growth Matrix

Marketers use the product–market growth matrix to analyze different growth strategies.

Product Emphasis

	Existing **Products**	New **Products**
Existing Markets	**Market penetration strategy** • Seek to increase sales of existing products to existing markets	**Product development strategy** • Create growth by selling new products in existing markets
New Markets	**Market development strategy** • Introduce existing products to new markets	**Diversification strategy** • Emphasize both new products and new markets to achieve growth

Market Emphasis

market development strategies
Growth strategies that introduce existing products to new markets.

product development strategies
Growth strategies that focus on selling new products in existing markets.

diversification strategies
Growth strategies that emphasize both new products and new markets.

APPLYING ▼ Growth Strategies

Stephanie recognizes that choosing the right growth strategy is not an easy decision. If Oracle targets marketing clients with existing technology, a market development strategy, Oracle could lose its reputation as an innovator. Offering new technologies to new clients, a diversification strategy, would be costly and Oracle could lose current clients. Maintaining focus on its data management function would be less costly but might leave Oracle, the market leader, in an obsolete product category.

---

geographic market. For example, Boeing sells its airplanes in many countries throughout the world, but it just recently entered the African market for the first time. With an initial order by South Africa's Comair worth $830 million, Boeing hopes its most recent market development strategy will take flight.[10]

- **Product development strategies** create growth by selling new products in existing markets. *Product development* may mean extending the firm's product line by developing new variations of the item, or it may mean altering or improving the product to provide enhanced performance. McDonald's, for example, has begun testing its McCafé Petite Pastries in its San Diego, California, restaurants in hopes that the product will further support its premium roast coffee and line of McCafé coffee drinks.[11]

- **Diversification strategies** emphasize both new products and new markets to achieve growth. After a long period of sluggish performance in the fast-food market, McDonald's has reenergized itself over the past several years through successful strategic planning. For example, planners at McDonald's in the past decided that the company was starting to max out in the hamburger business. The company tried to attract different customers when it offered new lines of business to diversify its portfolio of food offerings. Among those were Donato's Pizza, Boston Market, and a controlling interest in Chipotle Mexican Grills. However, McDonald's discovered that it wasn't very good at managing a portfolio of SBUs. The company divested these other brands as it shifts from a diversification strategy back to more of a product development strategy around the core McDonald's brand, as we've seen with its new Petite Pastries.[12]

To review what we've learned so far, strategic planning includes developing the mission statement, assessing the internal and external environment (resulting in a SWOT analysis), setting objectives, establishing the business portfolio, and developing growth strategies. In the next section, we'll look at marketers' functional plans as we examine the process of market planning.

Ripped from the Headlines

Ethical/Sustainable Decisions in the Real World

Let's face it. We all love the crunch of a good potato chip. Or two. Or a handful. Or . . .? As the Lay's slogan claims, "Betcha can't eat just one." And there's a reason for that. Food and beverage manufacturers spend big money to make sure that you not only like their products but also—literally—become addicted to them. The science doesn't lie.

Known as the "bliss point," manufacturers strive to create the "greatest amount of crave." That crave might result in a true addiction, such as with added salt, sugar, and fat, where ingesting the food or beverage actually lights up the pleasure centers in the brain. Or it could be a sensory addiction. Frito-Lay, for example, has a $40,000 device that simulates the human mouth. The company's studies show that it takes four pounds of pressure per square inch to make the perfect "snap," that glorious crunch sound that people want to hear when they bite into a chip. Either way, you've got the craving.

And that craving has led, at least in part, to an obesity epidemic. At least one in three American adults and one in five children are now considered to be clinically obese. If that weren't enough, 24 million Americans have type 2 diabetes, and 79 million have prediabetes—most cases of which are caused by poor diets.

But are marketers the only ones to blame? As General Mills's CEO Stephen Sanger pointed out at a meeting attended by the leaders of the top food and beverage companies, it's not as if his company only sells bad-for-you food. For example, General Mills also has a line of diet foods, as well as foods that are low in sugar and others that contain whole grains. Says Sanger, "People bought what they liked, and they liked what tasted good."[13]

So where does the ultimate responsibility lie: with the junk food marketers or the consumers who buy it?

ETHICS CHECK: ➤
Find out what other students taking this course *would do* and *why* at **mymktlab.com**.

Are marketers to blame for America's obesity epidemic?

☐YES ☐NO

3

Market Planning:
Develop and Execute Marketing Strategy

Until now, we have focused on fairly broad strategic plans. This big-picture perspective, however, does not provide details about how to reach the objectives we set. Strategic plans "talk the talk" but put the pressure on lower-level functional-area managers, such as the marketing manager, production manager, and finance manager, to "walk the walk" by developing the functional plans—the nuts and bolts—to achieve organizational and SBU objectives. Since you're taking a marketing course and this is a marketing book, our focus at the functional planning level is naturally on developing marketing plans, which is the next step in planning as we showed back in Figure 3.1.

The four Ps of the marketing mix we discussed in Chapter 1 remind us that successful firms must have viable *products* at *prices* consumers are willing to pay, a way to *promote* the products to the right consumers, and the ability to get the products to the *place* where consumers want to buy them.

Making this happen requires a tremendous amount of planning by the marketer. The steps in this market planning process are quite similar to the steps at the strategic planning level. An important distinction between strategic planning and market planning, however, is that marketing professionals focus much of their planning efforts on issues related to the *marketing mix*— the firm's product, its price, promotional approach, and distribution (place) methods. In the end, as you learned in Chapter 1, marketing focuses on creating, communicating, delivering, and exchanging offerings that have value, and market planning plays a central role in making these critical components of marketing successful. Let's use  Figure 3.5 as a guide to look at the steps involved in the market planning process in a bit more detail.

Lee jeans diversifies its product portfolio.

Step 1: Perform a Situation Analysis

The first step to develop a marketing plan is to conduct an analysis of the *marketing environment*. In Chapter 2, you learned about four key external elements that impact marketers: the economic, technological, political and legal, and sociocultural environments. To do this, managers build on the company's SWOT analysis and search out information about the environment that specifically affects the marketing plan. For example, for Oracle to develop an effective marketing communication program for any one of its products, it's not enough to have just a general understanding of the target market. Oracle needs to know *specifically* what media potential customers like to connect with, what messages about the product are most likely to make them buy, and how they prefer to communicate with the firm about new services and customer care issues. Oracle also must know how competitors market to customers so that the company can plan effectively.

Step 2: Set Marketing Objectives

Once marketing managers have a thorough understanding of the marketing environment, the next step is to develop specific marketing objectives. How do marketing objectives differ from corporate objectives? Generally, marketing objectives are more specific to the firm's brands, sizes, product features, and other marketing mix–related elements. Think of the connection between business objectives and marketing objectives this way: Business objectives guide the entire firm's operations, while marketing objectives state what the marketing function

Figure 3.5 Process | Steps in Market Planning

The steps in market planning are quite similar to those in strategic planning, with the important distinction that marketing professionals focus much of their planning efforts on issues related to the marketing mix—the firm's product, price, promotional approach, and distribution (place) methods. Market planning facilitates creating, communicating, delivering, and exchanging offerings that have value.

Step 1: Perform a Situation Analysis

Step 2: Set Marketing Objectives

Step 3: Develop Marketing Strategies

Step 4: Implement and Control the Marketing Plan

California's almond growers have a marketing strategy to increase consumption by promoting the nut's health benefits.

must accomplish if the firm is ultimately to achieve these overall business objectives. So for Oracle, setting marketing objectives means deciding what the firm wants to accomplish in terms of a product line's marketing mix–related elements: product development, pricing strategies, or specific marketing communication approaches.

Step 3: Develop Marketing Strategies: Target Markets and the Marketing Mix

In the next stage of the market planning process, marketing managers develop their actual marketing strategies—that is, they make decisions about what activities they must accomplish to achieve the marketing objectives. Usually this means they decide which markets to target and actually develop the marketing mix strategies (product, price, promotion, and place [supply chain]) to support how they want to position the product in the market. At this stage, marketers must figure out how they want consumers to think of their product compared to competing products.

As we mentioned in Chapter 1, the target market is the market segment(s) a firm selects because it believes its offerings are most likely to win those customers. The firm assesses the potential demand—the number of consumers it believes are willing and able to pay for its products—and decides if it is able to create a sustainable competitive advantage in the marketplace among target consumers.

Marketing mix decisions identify how marketing will accomplish its objectives in the firm's target markets by using product, price, promotion, and place. To make the point, we'll compare several different airlines' approaches:

- Because the product is the most fundamental part of the marketing mix—firms simply can't make a profit without something to sell—carefully developed *product strategies* are essential to achieve marketing objectives. Product strategies include decisions such as product design, packaging, branding, support services (e.g., maintenance); if there will be variations of the product; and what product features will provide the unique benefits targeted customers want. For example, product planners for JetBlue Airways decided to include in-seat video games and TV as a key product feature during the flight. Their planes get you from point A to point B just as fast (or slow) as the other airlines—that is, the basic product is the same—but the flight seems shorter because there is more to do while you're in the air.

- A *pricing strategy* determines how much a firm charges for a product. Of course, that price has to be one that customers are willing to pay. If not, all the other marketing efforts are futile. In addition to setting prices for the final consumer, pricing strategies usually establish prices the company will charge to wholesalers and retailers. A firm may base its pricing strategies on costs, demand, or the prices of competing products. In recent years, airlines started to charge extra fees (checked baggage anyone?) for services and perks they used to include in the ticket price, a practice known as *debundling*, in an effort to increase their revenues. However, many passengers being "nickeled-and-dimed" for additional charges, so bundling—this time for a fee—is on its way back. Delta Air Lines, for example, offers its fliers the $199 Smart Travel Pack, which allows customers to package value-added options like free checked baggage, priority boarding, or preferred seating with their airfare.[14]

- A *promotional strategy* is how marketers communicate a product's value proposition to the target market. Marketers use promotion strategies to develop the product's message and the mix of advertising, sales promotion, public relations and publicity, direct marketing, and personal selling that will deliver the message. Many firms use all these elements to communicate their message to consumers. American Airlines, which rebranded itself "The New American" as part of its combination with U.S. Airways, strives to portray an image of quality and luxury for the serious business travelers—especially on international trips. To do so, it combines TV ads focused on that target with sales promotion in the form of the AAdvantage™ loyalty program, personal selling to companies and conventions to promote usage of American as the "official carrier" for the group events, direct marketing via mail and e-mail providing information to loyal users, and (its managers hope) positive publicity through word of mouth about the airline's good service and dependability. A panel of wine judges *Global Traveler Magazine* created recently named American as the airline with the "Best Wine Selections." And the airline also offers amenity kits from Dermalogica and Akhassa as well as Fully Lie-Flat seats and Wi-Fi so that you can "Fly Better. Feel better."[15]

- *Distribution strategies* outline how, when, and where the firm will make the product available to targeted customers (the *place* component). When they develop a distribution strategy, marketers must decide whether to sell the product directly to the final customer or to sell through retailers and wholesalers. And the choice of which retailers should be involved depends on the product, pricing, and promotion decisions. Back in the day, airlines used to sell tickets in person or by phone directly to customers or through independent travel agents, but customers now largely purchase tickets online, often through third-party vendors such as Travelocity. And there are benefits to this strategy, especially for consumers. For example, travelers can see at a glance the best airlines fares and flight schedules; they can get discounts for booking multiple travel services, such as flights, hotels, and car rentals; and they can get access to top deals like "April Showers of Cruise Savings."[16]

Step 4: Implement and Control the Marketing Plan

Once the marketing plan is developed, it's time to get to work and make it succeed. In practice, marketers spend much of their time managing the various elements involved in implementing the marketing plan. Once Oracle understands the marketing environment, determines the most appropriate objectives and strategies, and gets its ideas organized and on paper in the formal plan, the rubber really hits the road. Like all firms, how Oracle actually implements its plan is what will make or break it in the marketplace.

During the implementation phase, marketers must have some means to determine to what degree they actually meet their stated marketing objectives. Often called **control**, this formal process of monitoring progress entails three steps:

1. Measure actual performance.

2. Compare this performance to the established marketing objectives or strategies.

3. Make adjustments to the objectives or strategies on the basis of this analysis. This issue of making adjustments brings up one of the most important aspects of successful market planning: Marketing plans aren't written in stone, and marketers must be flexible enough to make such changes when changes are warranted.

control
A process that entails measuring actual performance, comparing this performance to the established marketing objectives, and then making adjustments to the strategies or objectives on the basis of this analysis.

The Cutting Edge

Strengthen Your Message with Twitter Cards

Today more than ever, marketers use social media to get the word out about their products and services. In fact, 80 percent of marketers are turning to Twitter as part of their marketing plans (Facebook, at 91 percent, is the number one platform).[17] But how much can you really say when your message is limited to 140 characters (just a little bit more than the length of this question)?

For one, you can say it with pictures—which everyone knows are worth a thousand words—courtesy of Twitter Cards. By adding a few lines of simple HTML code to your website, anyone who then tweets links to your content will have a Product Card, with a product photo and description of your choice, added to their tweet. And which tweet are followers more apt to give their eyeballs to—the plain-text tweet or the media-enhanced tweet? Our bet is on the latter.

For effective control, Oracle has to establish appropriate *metrics* related to each of its marketing objectives and then track those metrics to know how successful the marketing strategy is and determine whether it needs to change the strategy along the way. For example, what happens if Oracle sets an objective for the first quarter of a year to increase its market share for a particular product line by 20 percent but after the first quarter sales are only even with those of last year? The *control process* means that market planners would have to look carefully at *why* the company isn't meeting its objectives. Is it due to internal factors, external factors, or a combination of both? Depending on the cause, Oracle would then have to adjust the marketing plan's strategies (such as to implement product alterations, modify the price, change distribution channels, or increase or alter promotion). Alternatively, Oracle could decide to adjust the marketing objective so that it is more realistic and attainable. This scenario illustrates the important point we made earlier in our discussion of strategic planning: Objectives must be specific and measurable but also *attainable* (and *sustainable over time*) in the sense that if an objective is not realistic, it can become very demotivating for everyone involved in the marketing plan.

For Oracle and all firms, effective control requires appropriate *marketing metrics*, which, as we discussed in Chapter 1, are concrete measures of various aspects of marketing performance. You will note throughout the book we place a strong emphasis on metrics. But marketing control and the measurement of marketing performance must be tempered with an eye toward sustainability. Recall from earlier chapters that sustainability has to do with firms doing well by doing good—that is, paying attention to important issues such as ethics, the environment, and social responsibility as well as the bottom line. In market planning, we certainly don't want to drive firms toward strategies that compromise sustainability by focusing only on controlling relatively short-term aspects of performance.

Today's CEOs are keen to quantify just how an investment in marketing has an impact on the firm's success, financially and otherwise, over the long haul. You've heard of the financial term *return on investment (ROI)*—in a marketing context we refer to **return on marketing investment (ROMI)**. *In fact, it's critical to consider marketing as an investment rather than an expense*—this distinction drives firms to use marketing more strategically to enhance the business. For many firms today, ROMI is the metric du jour to analyze how the marketing function contributes to the bottom line.

So, what exactly is ROMI? It is the revenue or profit margin (both are widely used) generated by investment in a specific marketing campaign or program divided by the cost of that program (expenditure) at a given risk level (the risk level is determined by management's analysis of the particular program). Again, the key word is *investment*—that is, in the planning process, thinking of marketing as an investment rather than an expense keeps managers focused on using marketing dollars to achieve specific goals.[18]

Here's a quick and simple example of the ROMI concept. Let's say that a relatively routine marketing campaign costs $30,000 and generates $150,000 in new revenue. Thus, the ROMI for the program is 5.0 (the ROI is five times the investment). If the firm has a total marketing budget of $250,000 and an objective for new revenue of $1,000,000, then the ROMI hurdle rate could be considered 4.0 ($1,000,000/$250,000), meaning that each program should strive to meet or exceed that ROMI benchmark of $4.00 in revenue for every $1.00 in marketing expenditure. Because the marketing campaign above exceeds the ROMI hurdle rate, it would be deemed acceptable to proceed with that investment.[19]

For an organization to use ROMI properly it must (1) identify the most appropriate and consistent measure to apply, (2) combine review of ROMI with other critical marketing metrics (one example is marketing payback—how quickly marketing costs are recovered),

return on marketing investment (ROMI)
Quantifying just how an investment in marketing has an impact on the firm's success, financially and otherwise.

Metrics Moment

Is return on marketing investment (ROMI) always appropriate or sufficient to judge marketing's effectiveness and efficiency? Here are six common objections to relying *exclusively* on ROMI to measure marketing success:

1. In a company's accounting statements, marketing expenditures tend to appear as a cost, not an investment. This practice perpetuates the "marketing-is-an-expense" mentality in the firm.
2. ROMI requires the profit to be divided by expenditure, yet all other bottom-line performance measures (like the ones you learned in your finance course) consider profit or cash flow after deducting expenditures.
3. Calculating ROMI requires knowing what would have happened if the marketing expenditure in question had never taken place. Few marketers have those figures.
4. ROMI has become a fashionable term for marketing productivity in general, yet much evidence exists that firms interpret how to calculate ROMI quite differently. When executives discuss ROMI with different calculations of it in mind, only confusion can result.

5. ROMI, by nature, ignores the effect of marketing assets of the firm (e.g., its brands) and tends to lead managers toward a more short-term decision perspective. That is, it typically considers only short-term incremental profits and expenditures without looking at longer-term effects or any change in brand equity.
6. And speaking of short-term versus long-term decisions, ROMI (like a number of other metrics focused on snapshot information—in this case, a particular marketing campaign) often can lead to actions by management to shore up short-term performance to the detriment of a firm's sustainability commitment. Ethics in marketing should not be an oxymoron—but often unethical behavior is driven by the demand for quick, short-term marketing results.[20]

Apply the Metrics

1. Review the six objections to ROMI above and discuss them with your classmates.
2. Select any two of the objections and develop a specific example of how they might lead to a bad decision in market planning.

and (3) fully consider the potential long-term impact of the actions ROMI drives (i.e., is the impact sustainable for the organization over the long term).[21] Fortunately for the marketer, there are many other potential marketing metrics beyond ROMI that measure specific aspects of marketing performance. Just to give you a sense of a few of them, Table 3.2 provides some examples of metrics that managers apply across an array of market planning situations, including all the marketing mix variables.

Action Plans

How does the implementation and control step actually manifest itself within a marketing plan? One very convenient way is through the inclusion of a series of **action plans** that support the various marketing objectives and strategies within the plan. We sometimes refer to action plans as "marketing programs." The best way to use action plans is to include a separate action plan for each important element involved in implementing the marketing plan. Table 3.3 provides a template for an action plan.

action plans
Individual support plans included in a marketing plan that provide the guidance for implementation and control of the various marketing strategies within the plan. Action plans are sometimes referred to as "marketing programs."

For example, let's consider the use of action plans in the context of supporting the objective we came up with for Oracle earlier to increase market share of a particular product line by 20 percent in the first quarter of the year. To accomplish this, the marketing plan would likely include a variety of strategies related to how Oracle will use the marketing mix elements to reach this objective. Important questions will include the following:

- What are the important needs and wants of this target market?
- How will the product be positioned in relation to this market?
- What will be the product and branding strategies?
- What will be the pricing strategy for this group?
- How will the product be promoted to them?
- What is the best distribution strategy to access the market?

Any one of these important strategic issues may require several action plans to implement.

Table 3.2 | Examples of Marketing Metrics

- Cost of a prospect
- Value of a prospect
- ROI of a campaign
- Value of telesales
- Conversion rates of users of competitor products
- Long-term value of a customer
- Customer commitment to relationship/partnership
- Referral rate
- Response rates to direct marketing
- Perceived product quality
- Perceived service quality
- Customer loyalty/retention
- Customer turnover
- Customer/segment profitability
- Customer mind-set/customer orientation
- Customer satisfaction
- Company/product reputation
- Customer word-of-mouth (buzz) activity
- Salesperson's self-ratings of effectiveness
- Timeliness and accuracy of competitive intelligence
- Usage rates of technology in customer initiatives
- Reach and frequency of advertising
- Recognition and recall of message
- Sales calls per day/week/month
- Order fulfillment efficiency/stock-outs
- Timeliness of sales promotion support

Action plans also help managers when they need to assign responsibilities, time lines, budgets, and measurement and control processes for market planning. Notice in Table 3.3 that these four elements are the final items an action plan documents. Sometimes when we view a marketing plan in total, it can seem daunting and nearly impossible to actually implement. Like most big projects, implementation of a marketing plan is best done one step at a time, paying attention to maximizing the quality of executing that step. In practice, what happens is that marketers combine the input from these last four elements of each action plan to form the overall implementation and control portion of the marketing plan. Let's examine each element a bit further.

Assign Responsibility

A marketing plan can't be implemented without people. And not everybody who will be involved in implementing a marketing plan is a marketer. The truth is, marketing plans touch most areas of an organization. Upper management and the human resources department will need to deploy the necessary employees to accomplish the plan's objectives. You learned in Chapter 1 that marketing isn't the responsibility only of a marketing department. Nowhere is that idea more apparent than in marketing plan implementation. Sales, production, quality control, shipping, customer service, finance, information technology—the list goes on—all will likely have a part in making the plan successful.

Table 3.3 | Template for an Action Plan

Title of action plan	Give the action plan a relevant name.
Purpose of action plan	What do you hope to accomplish by the action plan—that is, what specific marketing objective and strategy within the marketing plan does it support?
Description of action plan	Be succinct—but still thorough—when you explain the action plan. What are the steps involved? This is the core of the action plan. It describes what must be done in order to accomplish the intended purpose of the action plan.
Responsibility for the action plan	What person(s) or organizational unit(s) are responsible for carrying out the action plan? What external parties are needed to make it happen? Most importantly, who specifically has final "ownership" of the action plan—that is, who within the organization is accountable for it?
Time line for the action plan	Provide a specific timetable of events leading to the completion of the plan. If different people are responsible for different elements of the time line, provide that information.
Budget for the action plan	How much will implementation of the action plan cost? This may be direct costs only or may also include indirect costs, depending on the situation. The sum of all the individual action plan budget items will ultimately be aggregated by category to create the overall budget for the marketing plan.
Measurement and control of the action plan	Indicate the appropriate metrics, how and when they will be measured, and who will measure them.

Create a Time Line

Notice that each action plan requires a time line to accomplish the various tasks it requires. This is essential to include in the overall marketing plan. Most marketing plans portray the timing of tasks in flowchart form so that it is easy to visualize when the pieces of the plan will come together. Marketers often use *Gantt charts* or *PERT charts*, popular in operations management, to portray a plan's time line. These are the same types of tools that a general contractor might use to map out the different elements of building a house from the ground up. Ultimately, managers develop budgets and the financial management of the marketing plan around the time line so they know when cash outlays are required.

Set a Budget

Each element of the action plan links to a *budget item*, assuming there are costs involved in carrying out the plan. Forecasting the needed expenditures related to a marketing plan is difficult, but one way to improve accuracy in the budgeting process overall is to ensure estimates for expenditures for the individual action plans that are as accurate as possible. At the overall marketing plan level, managers create a master budget and track it throughout the market planning process. They report variances from the budget to the parties responsible for each budget item. For example, a firm's vice president of sales might receive a weekly or monthly report that shows each sales area's performance against its budget allocation. The vice president would note patterns of budget overage and contact affected sales managers to determine what, if any, action they need to take to get the budget back on track. The same approach would be repeated across all the different functional areas of the firm on which the budget has an impact. In such a manner, the budget itself becomes a critical element of control.

Decide on Measurements and Controls

Earlier, we described the concept of control as a formal process of monitoring progress to measure actual performance, compare the performance to the established marketing objectives or strategies, and make adjustments to the objectives or strategies on the basis of this analysis. The metric(s) a marketer uses to monitor and control individual action plans ultimately forms the overall control process for the marketing plan. It is an unfortunate fact that many marketers do not consistently do a good job of measurement and control, which, of course, compromises their market planning. And remember that selection of good metrics needs to take into account short-term objectives balanced against the firm's focus on long-term sustainability.

Operational Planning: Day-to-Day Execution of Marketing Plans

operational plans
Plans that focus on the day-to-day execution of the marketing plan. Operational plans include detailed directions for the specific activities to be carried out, who will be responsible for them, and time lines to accomplish the tasks.

Recall that planning happens at three levels: strategic, functional (such as market planning), and operational. In the previous section, we discussed market planning—the process by which marketers perform a situation analysis, set marketing objectives, and develop, implement, and control marketing strategies. But talk is cheap: The best plan ever written is useless if it's not properly carried out. That's what **operational plans** are for. They put the pedal to the metal by focusing on the day-to-day execution of the marketing plan.

The task of operational planning falls to the first-line managers we discussed earlier, such as sales managers, marketing communications managers, brand managers, and market research managers. Operational plans generally cover a shorter period of time than either strategic plans or marketing plans—perhaps only one or two months—and they include detailed directions for the specific activities to be carried out, who will be responsible for them, and time lines for accomplishing the tasks. In reality, the action plan template we provide in Table 3.3 is most likely applied at the operational level.

Significantly, many of the important marketing metrics managers use to gauge the success of plans actually get used at the operational planning level. For example, sales managers in many firms are charged with the responsibility of tracking a wide range of metrics related to the firm–customer relationship, such as number of new customers, sales calls per month, customer turnover, and customer loyalty. The data are collected at the operational level and then sent to upper management for use in planning at the functional level and above.

Make Your Life Easier! Use the Market Planning Template

Ultimately, the planning process we've described in this section is documented in a formal, written marketing plan. You'll find a tear-out template for a marketing plan in the foldout located in this chapter. The template will come in handy as you make your way through the book, as each chapter will give you information you can use to "fill in the blanks" of a marketing plan. You will note that the template is cross-referenced with the questions you must answer in each section of the plan. It also provides you with a general road map of the topics covered in each chapter that need to flow into building the marketing plan. By the time you're done, we hope that all these pieces will come together and you'll understand how real marketers make real choices.

As we noted earlier, a marketing plan should provide the best possible guide for the firm to successfully market its products. In large firms, top management often requires such a written plan because putting the ideas on paper encourages marketing managers to formulate concrete objectives and strategies. In small entrepreneurial firms, a well-thought-out marketing plan is often the key to attracting investors who will help turn the firm's dreams into reality.

The decision makers at Oracle elected to leap forward into the cloud.

Here's my **choice...**

Real **People**, Real **Choices**

1 Option   **2** Option   **3** Option

Why do you think Stephanie chose option 2?

How It Worked Out at Oracle

Stephanie chose option 2. Since 2013, Oracle has acquired several leading SaaS marketing automation companies, and it now labels its new business the Oracle Marketing Cloud™. Its cloud-based services allow clients to customize their communications with different customers, coordinate these messages across multiple channels, and monitor the effectiveness of their campaigns over time (**www.forbes.com/sites/oracle/2014/05/05/6-key-steps-to-customer-centric-modern-marketing/2** [accessed May 8, 2014]).

The company gambled that its large investment to buy SaaS firms would reap big rewards. It hoped that its dramatic shift toward cloud-based computing would convince the market that Oracle remains on the cutting edge of database management innovation. This bet seems to be paying off for Oracle. Its stock price is rebounding—a good sign that industry analysts are confident in the company's future. As one prominent analyst recently wrote, "We believe that Oracle has significantly improved their cloud offerings and has now or will within the next twelve months (as they continue to expand, integrate and upgrade these offerings) have competitive offerings that will drive revenue growth. We believe that Oracle has already assembled one of the most complete digital marketing offerings."[22] Oracle looks like it is ready to take up residence in the cloud.

Refer back to **page 94** for Stephanie's story ➡

MyMarketingLab™

Go to **mymktlab.com** to complete the problems marked with this icon ⭐ as well as additional Marketing Metrics questions only available in MyMarketingLab.

Objective Summary ➡ Key Terms ➡ Apply

CHAPTER 3
Study Map

1. Objective Summary (pp. 96–98)

Explain business planning and its three levels.

Business planning is the ongoing process of decision making that guides the firm in both the short term and the long term. A business plan, which includes the decisions that guide the entire organization or its business units, is different from a marketing plan, which is a process and resulting document that describes the marketing environment, outlines the marketing objectives and strategies, and identifies how the company will implement and control the strategies embedded in the plan.

Planning takes place at three key levels. Strategic planning is the managerial decision process that matches the firm's resources and capabilities to its market opportunities for long-term growth. Large firms may have a number of self-contained divisions called *strategic business units (SBUs)*. In such cases, strategic planning takes place at both the overall corporate level and within the SBU. Functional planning gets its name because the various functional areas of the firm, such as marketing, finance, and human resources, get involved. And operational planning focuses on the day-to-day execution of the functional plans and includes detailed annual, semiannual, or quarterly plans.

Key Terms

business planning, p. 97

business plan, p. 97

marketing plan, p. 97

strategic planning, p. 97

strategic business units (SBUs), p. 98

functional planning, p. 98

operational planning, p. 98

2. Objective Summary (pp. 98–104)

Describe the steps in strategic planning.

For large firms that have a number of self-contained business units, the first step in strategic planning is for top management to establish a mission for the entire corporation. Top managers then evaluate the internal and external environment of the business and set corporate-level objectives that guide decision making within each individual SBU. In small firms that are not large enough to have separate SBUs, strategic planning simply takes place at the overall firm level.

The first step in strategic planning is defining the mission—a formal document that describes the organization's overall purpose and what it hopes to achieve in terms of its customers, products, and resources. Step 2 is to evaluate the internal and external environment through a process known as situational analysis, which is later formatted as a SWOT analysis that identifies the organization's strengths, weaknesses, opportunities, and threats. Step 3 is to set organizational or SBU objectives that are specific, measurable, attainable, and sustainable. Step 4 is to establish the business portfolio, which is the range of different businesses that a large firm operates. To determine how best to allocate resources to the various businesses, or units, managers use the Boston Consulting Group (BCG) growth–market share matrix to classify SBUs as stars, cash cows, question marks, or dogs. The final step, Step 5, in strategic planning is to develop growth strategies. Marketers use the product–market growth matrix to analyze four fundamental marketing strategies: market penetration, market development, product development, and diversification.

Key Terms

mission statement, p. 99

situation analysis, p. 99

internal environment, p. 99

external environment, p. 99

SWOT analysis, p. 100

business portfolio, p. 101

portfolio analysis, p. 102

BCG growth–market share matrix, p. 102

stars, p. 102

cash cows, p. 102

question marks, p. 102

dogs, p. 103

market penetration strategies, p. 103

market development strategies, p. 103

product development strategies, p. 104

diversification strategies, p. 104

3. Objective Summary (pp. 105–112)

Describe the steps in market planning.

Once big-picture issues are considered, it's up to the lower-level functional-area managers, such as the marketing manager, production manager, and finance manager, to develop the functional marketing plans—the nuts and bolts—to achieve organizational and SBU objectives. The steps in this market planning process are quite similar to the steps at the strategic planning level. An important distinction between strategic planning and market planning, however, is that marketing professionals focus much of their planning efforts on issues related to the four Ps of the marketing mix. Managers start off by performing a situational analysis of the marketing environment. Next, they develop marketing objectives specific to the firm's brand, sizes, and product features. Then marketing managers select the target market(s) for the organization and decide what marketing mix strategies they will use. Product strategies include decisions about products and product characteristics that will appeal to the target market. Pricing strategies state the specific prices to be charged to channel members and final consumers. Promotion strategies include plans for advertising, sales promotion, public relations, publicity, personal selling, and direct marketing used to reach the target market. Distribution (place) strategies outline how the product will be made available to targeted customers when and where they want it. Once the marketing strategies are developed, they must be implemented, which is the last step in developing the marketing plan. Control is the measurement of actual performance and comparison with planned performance. Maintaining control implies the need for concrete measures of marketing performance called "marketing metrics."

Operational planning is done by first-line supervisors such as sales managers, marketing communication managers, and market research managers and focuses on the day-to-day execution of the marketing plan. Operational plans generally cover a shorter period of time and include detailed directions for the specific activities to be carried out, who will be responsible for them, and time lines for accomplishing the tasks. To ensure effective implementation, a marketing plan must include individual action plans, or programs, that support the plan at the operational level. Each action plan necessitates providing a budget estimate, schedule, or time line for its implementation and appropriate metrics so that the marketer can monitor progress and control for discrepancies or variation from the plan. Sometimes, variance from a plan requires shifting or increasing resources to make the plan work; other times, it requires changing the objectives of the plan to recognize changing conditions.

Key Terms

control, p. 107

return on marketing investment (ROMI), p. 108

action plans, p. 109

operational plans, p. 112

Chapter **Questions** and **Activities**

Concepts: Test Your Knowledge

3-1. What is first-level planning, and what is it normally called in business jargon?

3-2. In marketing, what is likely to be involved in terms of third-level or operational planning?

3-3. What is a business review, an environmental analysis or a situation analysis? What does it aim to investigate?

3-4. What is a business portfolio? Why is a diversified portfolio desirable over one that is focused on a very specific product or service?

3-5. What is the aim of a growth strategy?

3-6. Why might it be the case that a business would seek to divest itself of products designated as dogs?

3-7. What are the two key areas under consideration if a business opts for a diversification strategy?

3-8. Explain the four steps in the market planning process.

3-9. What is return on marketing investment (ROMI)? How does considering marketing as an investment instead of an expense affect a firm?

3-10. Give several examples of marketing metrics. How might a marketer use each metric to track progress of some important element of a marketing plan?

3-11. What is an action plan? Why are action plans such an important part of market planning? Why is it so important for marketers to break the implementation of a marketing plan down into individual elements through action plans?

3-12. How does operational planning support the marketing plan?

Activities: Apply What You've Learned

⭐ **3-13.** *Creative Homework/Short Project* As a marketing student, you know that large firms often organize their operations into a number of strategic business units (SBUs). A university might develop a similar structure in which different academic schools or departments are seen as separate businesses. Consider how your university or college might divide its total academic units into separate SBUs. What would be the problems with implementing such a plan? What would be the advantages and disadvantages for students and for faculty? Be prepared to share your analysis of university SBUs to your class.

3-14. *In Class, 10–25 Minutes for Teams* As an employee of a business consulting firm that specializes in helping people who want to start small businesses, you have been assigned a client who is interested in introducing a new concept in health clubs—one that offers its customers both the usual exercise and weight-training opportunities and certain related types of medical assistance, such as physical therapy, a weight-loss physician, and basic diagnostic testing. As you begin thinking about the potential for success for this client, you realize that developing a marketing plan is going to be essential. Take a role-playing approach to present your argument to the client as to why he or she needs to spend the money on your services to create a formal marketing plan.

3-15. *For Further Research (Individual)* All businesses—big and small—need to plan if they want to be profitable and sustainable. Contact one of your favorite local businesses and make an appointment with someone who has a hand in developing the firm's business plan. Find out how much time the planning process takes, how often the business plan is updated, and what types of information the business plan contains. Summarize your findings in a short report.

3-16. *For Further Research (Groups)* Identify a large company, find its website, and read through its press releases and corporate brochures. From the information, try to identify the company's marketing activities. Identify the elements of the marketing plan. Identify the target markets and the marketing mix. Prepare a short presentation to share with your class.

Apply Marketing Metrics

You learned in the chapter that most marketers today feel pressure to measure (quantify) their level of success in market planning. They do this by setting and then measuring marketing objectives. One very popular metric is market share, which in essence represents the percentage of total product category sales your products represent versus category competitors. For example, recent statistics indicate that Lenovo holds the number one market share in global PC sales with about 17 percent, slightly topping HP with about 16 percent. Ranked third through fifth are Dell, Acer, and Asus, respectively.[23] But, despite its common appearance in marketing objectives, market share has been heavily criticized as a metric. Often it can become more of a "bragging right" for a firm than a profit enhancer. This is because—especially in situations like the global PC market that is seeing heavy annual declines in sales as tablets and other devices replace PCs—investing in being number one in market share may deflect focus away from more lucrative new and growing product lines. In particular, in recent years HP has waffled back and forth about its long-term commitment to being a presence in the PC market, probably hanging in too long now that PCs are essentially a declining market. As a result, for HP the PC is a "dog" based on the BCG matrix.

⭐ **3-17.** Under what conditions do you believe market share as a metric is important to a firm? What are the potential pitfalls of relying too much on market share as a key metric? What self-defeating behaviors might this over-reliance lead a firm to undertake?

⭐ **3-18.** Come up with some other product categories besides PCs that are declining and identify the firms within those categories that have the highest market share. What does their profit picture look like?

Choices: What Do You Think?

⭐ **3-19.** The Boston Consulting Group matrix identifies products as stars, cash cows, question marks, and dogs. Do you think this is a useful way for organizations to examine their businesses? What are some examples of product lines that fit in each category?

3-20. In this chapter, we saw that different businesses, as an integral part of their marketing planning, frame their marketing mix in different ways. What makes a certain mix more appropriate for one business compared to another one?

3-21. Most planning involves strategies for growth. But is growth always the right direction to pursue? Can you think of some organizations that should have contraction rather than expansion as their objective? Do you know of any organizations that have planned to get smaller rather than larger in order to be successful?

3-22. When most people think of successful marketing, internal firm culture doesn't immediately come to mind as a contributing factor. You may have learned about corporate culture in a management course. What is a corporate culture? What are some reasons a firm's culture is important to the capability of doing good marketing? Give some examples of aspects that you consider indicate a good corporate culture for marketing.

3-23. Many companies operate on the mentality that "marketing is an expense." Do you agree that marketing is an expense, or should marketing be treated as an investment? Should there be a business standard as to whether marketing is treated as an expense/investment, or should individual organizations be given the freedom to choose which line item to assign it to? Explain your reasoning.

Miniproject: Learn by Doing

The purpose of this miniproject is to gain an understanding of market planning through actual experience.

3-24. a. Select one of the following for your market planning project:
   - Yourself (in your search for a career)
   - Your university
   - A specific department in your university

b. Next, develop the following elements of the market planning process:
   - A mission statement
   - A SWOT analysis
   - Objectives
   - A description of the target market(s)
   - A positioning strategy
   - A brief outline of the marketing mix strategies—the product, pricing, distribution, and promotion strategies—that satisfy the objectives and address the target market

c. Prepare a brief outline of a marketing plan using the basic template provided in this chapter as a guide.

Marketing in **Action** Case Real Choices at Amazon

Right now a lot of big companies are fighting a fierce battle to get into your home. They're not burglars, but they do want you to let them in so they can control how you access TV shows, movies, online shopping, and video games. One group knocking on your door is the manufacturers of streaming media set-top boxes. These companies include some of the titans of the tech world, including Apple and Google. Now Amazon is joining this elite group as it rolls out its Fire TV product. Amazon's streaming media set-top box is an Internet-connected device that lets you watch services such as Netflix, Prime Instant Video, Hulu Plus, and low-cost movie rentals.

The set-top box supports 1,080-pixel high-definition video streaming, Dolby Digital Plus surround sound, 2 gigabytes of RAM, MIMO dual-band Wi-Fi, and a Bluetooth remote control with a microphone for voice search. Due to a quad-core processor with three times the processing power of Apple TV, Fire TV is relatively fast and fluid. The Bluetooth-enabled remote has all the controls customers need to search, watch, navigate, and play games. Additionally, Fire TV also allows users to play video games via a mobile app or with an optional $39 game controller. Amazon Fire TV arrives preregistered to the customer's Amazon account, and setup is easy.

When members pair Fire TV with Amazon's Prime service, they enjoy unlimited, commercial-free streaming of 200,000 popular movies and TV shows, millions of songs, and over a hundred games. Advanced Streaming and Prediction (ASAP) learns what movies and shows customers select most often. The more the customer uses Fire TV, the better ASAP can dynamically adapt to his viewing habits. The interface allows the user to browse popular movies and TV, and it offers personalized recommendations for each viewer. Users can instantly add new discoveries to a watch list, and any content they purchase from Amazon will be listed in the video library.

Fire TV puts Amazon in close competition with industry powerhouses that offer their own streaming media set-top boxes, including Apple (Apple TV), Google (Google Chromecast), and Roku (Roku 3). Along with others, each of these competitors is attempting to "reach into consumers' homes and to tie customers to a package of services." According to Peter Larsen, Amazon vice president, "The retailer sells millions of streaming media devices each year, and its own box is an effort to address three complaints it commonly hears from customers: search is too clunky, there is not an open ecosystem that allows people to use several different streaming systems, and performance isn't good enough."

While the market for streaming media set-top boxes is small right now (8 percent of American consumers own one), the potential is big and the field is crowded. Ooyala, a California-based company that specializes in online video and online video analytics, found that the streaming media market is poised for rapid growth. Growth attracts competitors. Amazon currently pegs Apple TV as its principal competitor, so it offers Fire TV at the same $99 price point as Apple TV. Both devices share the same design structure, and on first glance they are hard to distinguish from one another. However, there are other options out there as well: Don't forget that Google's Chromecast ($35) also lets you stream content from a phone, computer, or laptop. In addition, Internet-connected or "smart" TVs offer similar access to streaming media without the need for extra hardware.

How will Amazon distinguish itself in this market? Will its gaming capabilities set it apart from other streaming media options? Fire TV is its connection to customers' homes and a tie-in to many other sources of revenue. Nevertheless, for success to materialize, Amazon must carefully consider what long-term strategies are necessary to make Fire TV a profitable winner in a crowded marketplace. Who will you let into your living room?

You Make the Call

3-25. What is the decision facing Amazon?

3-26. What factors are important in understanding this decision situation?

3-27. What are the alternatives?

3-28. What decision(s) do you recommend?

3-29. What are some ways to implement your recommendation?

Sources: Based on Molly Wood, "Expressway to Amazon in a Box," **www.nytimes.com/2014/04/07/technology/personaltech/the-amazon-fire-tv-streaming-media-set-top-box.html?hpw&rref=technology&_r=1** (accessed April 10, 2014); "Amazon Fire TV," **www.amazon.com/Amazon-CL1130-Fire-TV/dp/B00CX5P8FC#whatis** (accessed April 10, 2014); and Adam Satariano and Edmund Lee, "Amazon Introduces Fire TV Device to Take on Apple, Google," April 2, 2014, **www.bloomberg.com/news/2014-04-02/amazon-said-set-to-debut-tv-viewing-living-room-device.html** (accessed April 11, 2014).

MyMarketingLab™

Go to **mymktlab.com** for Auto-graded writing questions as well as the following Assisted-graded writing questions:

3-30. *Creative Homework/Short Project.* Assume that you are the marketing director for Mattel Toys. Your boss, the company vice president for marketing, has decided that it's time to develop some new objectives for some of their product lines as the company begins market planning. Your VP has asked you to help out by writing several initial objectives. Select any product line at Mattel and develop several objectives that fulfill the criteria for objectives discussed in the chapter.

3-31. *Creative Homework/Short Project.* An important part of planning is a SWOT analysis, understanding an organization's strengths, weaknesses, opportunities, and threats. Prepare a SWOT analysis for Panera Bread that includes three or four items in each of the four SWOT categories.

Market Research

Ryan Garton

▼ A Decision Maker at Discover Financial Services

Ryan Garton is director of consumer insights at Discover Financial Services. Promoted to his current position in January 2008, Ryan and the consumer insights team are responsible for all market research activities for the firm, including brand and advertising tracking/effectiveness, new product development/innovation screeners, financial attitudes and usage studies, overall voice of the customer, and other ad hoc quantitative and qualitative studies as requested by business lines. Prior to this assignment, Ryan joined Discover Financial Services as the director of corporate brand strategy, where he and his team of brand specialists were responsible for overall corporate brand strategy for all Discover Card products and programs, including Discover More Card, Miles by Discover, Discover Open Road Card, Discover Motiva Card, and Stored Value card products. Additionally, the team was responsible for brand and marketing strategy for Discover Banking products, such as student loans, deposits, and personal loans. The brand team is also responsible for integrating product development, innovation cycles, and marketing strategy and ensuring that communication efforts are fully leveraged across all business activities.

Prior to joining Discover Financial Services, Ryan had an 11-year career at United Airlines, which spanned several marketing leadership roles in international marketing—STAR Alliance, market research, product development, and brand marketing strategy. He and his team were responsible for all United branding, the new United aircraft livery, development of airport lounge products, EasyCheck-in, subbrand development (TED), and overall partnership strategy (Starbucks, Pepsi, and AOL). His assignment prior to joining the Marketing Division was as the marketing and sales manager for the Midwest Region–Chicago, where he was responsible for revenue and profitability within United's largest North American region.

Before his airline career, Ryan worked for Gallup, Inc. in survey research and political tracking. He worked with several key accounts, including Volkswagen, NationsBank, CNN News, and numerous political polls. He has an MBA from the University of Nebraska with an emphasis on international marketing and strategy and an undergraduate degree from St. Olaf College in economics and political science.

Ryan's Info

What I do when I'm not working?
Activities with my three kids—soccer, dance, swimming, and music lessons. Restoring our 1910 home. (I am a bit of a carpenter! Think of *This Old House*.)

First job out of school?
Market research for the Gallup Organization.

Business book I'm reading now?
Buyology by Martin Lindstrom.

My motto to live by?
"Make no small plans, for they have not the power to stir the hearts and minds of men." Daniel Burnham

My management style?
Competitive—strategic—achiever—individualization—relator.

Don't do this when interviewing with me?
Make excuses.

My pet peeve?
Others not taking ownership of their actions.

Here's my problem...

Ryan's problem at Discover Card was simple: too much of a good thing. The company had a lot of very good new product and services ideas: new card products, new technologies to help people manage their finances/ bills, enhancements to its website, new insurance products, and new banking products. However, Ryan lacked an integrated approach to determine which of the ideas would be most likely to fit cardholders' desires, fit with the Discover brand image as the card that is all about cash back and other rewards to cardholders, and fit with company resources (financial and technical).

In fact, Ryan had such a good thing that he didn't have the internal resources to evaluate each product idea. In particular, he was missing a crucial piece of the puzzle: customer input. Typically, Discover would prioritize new product ideas using metrics such as revenue projections, resource consumption estimates, and internal assessments of strategic fit. But these estimates occur largely in a vacuum because they don't include the "reality check" that actual users could provide.

Ryan knew he had to seriously consider whether it was worthwhile to invest crucial resources to develop a system that could screen a large number of new product ideas with input from current or potential users of these products. He convened a cross-functional team of colleagues from consumer insights, brand strategy, and new product strategy to outline what this new screening process might look like. The "old" process was one where Ryan would gather these business partners together to look at the financial information and technology resources available. They would then determine the best course of action, typically without necessarily considering consumers' needs.

Things to remember

Like many companies, Discover Financial collected a lot of data from different sources to stay on top of changes in the financial services industry and to monitor the types of credit card options competitors offered to customers. But (also like many companies), the recognition that consumers' preferences should play a role when decisions are made regarding which products to take to market is a fairly new one for Discover. The market research process also gets more complicated when more input is included, so Ryan has to decide if his internal organization has the resources to make the best use of all the information. He also recognizes that internal decision making often has a "political" side to it, as executives often have a vested interest in which paths the company will choose to follow.

to undergo another evaluation. Decision makers wouldn't have to learn a new process. But decisions about new features would continue to rely on internal projections and the intuition of managers without benefiting from input by actual consumers.

2 Option **Modify the current process to include existing consumer input that Discover can easily access.** The team could look more carefully at feedback the company received in blogs, letters, and telephone calls to help it gauge the likelihood of success. Again, this extra layer of information wouldn't significantly hold up the progress of product ideas in the pipeline. And, if the information contradicted management's priorities, at least this would be a red flag to force decision makers to take a second look. However, some of the new ideas broke new ground, so there was no primary or syndicated research to indicate if they would fly. Consumers can't spontaneously provide feedback about products that don't yet exist.

3 Option **Engage an outside firm to assist Discover in developing a new process.** Ideally, Ryan wanted to test consumers' reactions to several key measures: market potential, consumer likability, brand fit, and comparisons with launches by other financial services companies. This new process would involve hiring an outside firm to apply a standardized set of measures to assess all potential offerings so that Discover could use an "apples-to-apples" comparison. Decision makers could access one score for each concept that encompasses all relevant research results. They could more easily identify how a concept might be improved so that cardholders would think more highly of it. And the score would include an assessment of how well each concept fits with the Discover brand. But this radical new approach would be politically challenging within the organization because it would challenge some internal stakeholders' existing beliefs and priorities regarding which offerings they would like to develop. And a new approach would involve a big financial investment, most likely in the neighborhood of $100,000. There would also be a potential cost in that it would add weeks to the decision-making process, so a competitor might get to market with the idea first.

Now, put yourself in Ryan Garton's shoes. Which option would you choose, and why?

Ryan considered his **Options** 1·2·3

1 Option **Don't muddy the waters.** Continue to use the same project prioritization process that Discover had been using for many years. A passive approach would not put additional roadblocks in front of project time lines; new card features and other offerings could get to market faster because they wouldn't have

You Choose

Which **Option** would you choose, and **why**?
1. ☐YES ☐NO 2. ☐YES ☐NO 3. ☐YES ☐NO

See what **option** Ryan chose on **page 142** ➡

MyMarketingLab™

⭐ **Improve Your Grade!**

Over 10 million students improved their results using the Pearson MyLabs.
Visit **mymktlab.com** for simulations, tutorials, and end-of-chapter problems.

1 Knowledge Is Power

OBJECTIVE

Explain the role of a marketing information system and a marketing decision support system in marketing decision making.
(pp. 120–124)

By now we know that successful market planning means that managers make informed decisions to guide the organization. But how do marketers actually make these choices? Specifically, how do they find out what they need to know to develop marketing objectives, select a target market, position (or reposition) their product, and develop product, price, promotion, and place strategies?

The answer is (drumroll . . .): information. Information is the fuel that runs the marketing engine. There's a famous acronym in the marketing information systems field: GIGO, which stands for Garbage In, Garbage Out. To make good decisions, marketers must have information that is not "garbage"—rather, it must be accurate, up to date, and relevant. To understand these needs, marketers first must engage in various forms of research and data collection to identify them. In this chapter, we will discuss some of the tools that marketers use to get that information. In Chapter 5, we'll drill down further on applying market research for decision making via marketing analytics. Then in the chapters that follow, we will look closely at how and why both consumers and organizations buy and then how marketers sharpen their focus via target marketing.

Before we jump into the topic of market research, here's a question for you. A marketer who conducts research to learn more about his customers shouldn't encounter any ethical challenges, right? Well, maybe in a perfect world. In reality though, several aspects of market research are fraught with the *potential* for ethics breaches. **Market research ethics** refers to taking an ethical and aboveboard approach to conducting market research that does no harm to the participant in the process of conducting the research.

When the organization collects data, important issues of privacy and confidentiality come into play. Marketers must be very clear when they work with research respondents about how they will use the data and give respondents full disclosure on their options for confidentiality and anonymity. For example, it is unethical to collect data under the guise of market research when your real intent is to develop a **database** of potential customers for direct marketing. A database is an organized collection (often electronic) of data that can be searched and queried to provide information about contacts, products, customers, inventory, and more. Firms that abuse the trust of respondents run a serious risk of damaging their reputation when word gets out that they are engaged in unethical research practices. This makes it difficult to attract participants in future research projects—and it "poisons the well" for other companies when consumers believe that they can't trust them.

market research ethics
Taking an ethical and aboveboard approach to conducting market research that does no harm to the participant in the process of conducting the research.

database
An organized collection (often electronic) of data that can be searched and queried to provide information about contacts, products, customers, inventory, and more.

The Marketing Information System

Many firms use a **marketing information system (MIS)** to collect information. The MIS is a process that first determines what information marketing managers need. Then it gathers, sorts, analyzes, stores, and distributes relevant and timely marketing information to users. As you can see in Figure 4.1, the MIS system includes three important components:

1. Four types of data (internal company data, market intelligence, market research, and acquired databases)

2. Computer hardware and software to analyze the data and to create reports

3. Output for marketing decision makers

marketing information system (MIS)
A process that first determines what information marketing managers need and then gathers, sorts, analyzes, stores, and distributes relevant and timely marketing information to system users.

Various sources "feed" the MIS with data, and then the system's software "digests" it. MIS analysts use the output to generate a series of regular reports for various decision makers. For example, Frito-Lay's MIS generates daily sales data by product line and by region. Its managers then use this information to evaluate the market share of different Frito-Lay products compared to one another and to competing snack foods in each region where the company does business.[1]

Let's take a closer look at each of the four different data sources for the MIS.

Internal Company Data

The *internal company data system* uses information from within the organization to produce reports on the results of sales and marketing activities. Internal company data include a firm's sales records—information such as which customers buy which products in what quantities and at what intervals, which items are in stock and which are back-ordered because they are out of stock, when items were shipped to the customer, and which items have been returned because they are defective.

Often, an MIS allows salespeople and sales managers in the field to access internal records through a company **intranet**. This is an internal corporate communications network that uses Internet technology to link company departments, employees, and databases. Intranets are secured so that only authorized employees have access. When salespeople and sales managers in the field can use an intranet to access their company's MIS, they can better serve their customers because they have immediate access to information on pricing, inventory levels, production schedules, shipping dates, and the customer's sales history. Related to the company intranet concept is the concept of *customer relationship management (CRM)*, which we'll develop more fully in Chapter 5.

Marketing managers at company headquarters also can see daily or weekly sales data by brand or product line from the internal company data system. They can view monthly sales reports to measure progress toward sales goals and market share objectives. For example, buyers and managers at Walmart's headquarters in Arkansas use up-to-the-minute sales information they obtain from store cash registers around the country so they can quickly detect problems with products, promotions, price competitiveness, and even the firm's distribution system.

Market Intelligence

As we saw in Chapter 2, to make good decisions, marketers need to have information about the marketing environment. Thus, a second important element of the MIS is the **market intelligence system**, a method by which marketers get information about what's going on in the world that is relevant to their business. Although the name *intelligence* may suggest cloak-and-dagger spy activities, in reality nearly all the information that companies need about their environment—including the competitive environment—is available by monitoring everyday sources: company websites, industry trade publications, or direct field observations of the competitive marketplace.

And because salespeople are the ones "in the trenches" every day, talking with customers, distributors, and prospective customers, they are a key to sourcing this valuable information. Retailers often hire "mystery shoppers" to visit their stores and those of their competitors posing as customers to see how people are treated. (Imagine being paid to shop!) Other information may come from speaking with organizational buyers about competing products, attending trade shows, or simply purchasing, using, and even **reverse engineering** competitors' products, which means physically deconstructing the product to determine how it's put together.

Figure 4.1 *Process* | The Marketing Information System

A firm's marketing information system (MIS) stores and analyzes data from a variety of sources and turns the data into information for useful marketing decision making.

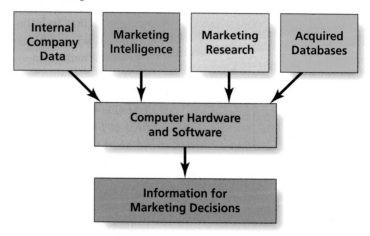

intranet
An internal corporate communication network that uses Internet technology to link company departments, employees, and databases.

market intelligence system
A method by which marketers get information about everyday happenings in the marketing environment.

reverse engineering
The process of physically deconstructing a competitor's product to determine how it's put together.

Marketing managers may use market intelligence data to predict fluctuations in sales due to a variety of external environmental factors you read about in Chapter 2, including economic conditions, political issues, and events that heighten consumer awareness, or to forecast the future so that they will be on top of developing trends. For example, knowledge of trends in consumer preferences, driven by the younger generation that lives on their phones, prompted plucky cellular provider T-Mobile to best AT&T and Verizon Wireless with a first-of-its kind no-annual-contract plan that offers "unlimited everything"—that's unlimited talk, text, and data on their network, plus unlimited international data and text—all for $50 per month and all without the typical two-year contract. T-Mobile will even cover your early termination fee. T-Mobile is betting that its "unleash" marketing campaign will speak to consumers tired of the rules that other providers tie them to: "Other wireless carriers just can't let go of their lame rules. They say that's just the way it is. We say, not cool." Nothing speaks to young consumers like an easier or cheaper way to text their friends—except maybe being able to break all the rules![2]

Market Research

market research

The process of collecting, analyzing, and interpreting data about customers, competitors, and the business environment in order to improve marketing effectiveness.

Market research refers to the process of collecting, analyzing, and interpreting data about customers, competitors, and the business environment to improve marketing effectiveness. (Note that the term "marketing research" is often used interchangeably with "market research," but to be precise marketing research refers to the type of research that academics in marketing conduct.) Although companies collect market intelligence data continuously to keep managers abreast of happenings in the marketplace, market research also is called for when managers need unique information to help them make specific decisions. Whether their business is selling cool fashion accessories to teens or industrial coolant to factories, firms succeed when they know what customers want, when they want it, where they want it—and what competing firms are doing about it. In other words, the better a firm is at obtaining valid market information, the more successful it will be. Therefore, virtually all companies rely on some form of market research, though the amount and type of research they conduct varies dramatically. In general, market research data available in an MIS come in two flavors: syndicated research reports and custom research reports.

syndicated research

Research by firms that collect data on a regular basis and sell the reports to multiple firms.

Syndicated research is general information specialized firms collect on a regular basis and then sell to other firms. INC/The QScores Company, for instance, reports on consumers' perceptions of over 1,800 celebrity performers for companies that want to feature a well-known person in their advertising. The company also rates consumer appeal of cartoon characters, sports stars, and even deceased celebrities.[3] Comedian Bill Cosby holds the record for the highest QScore ever recorded, while other controversial celebrities, like Woody Allen and Martha Stewart, don't fare quite so well.[4] Other examples of syndicated research reports include Nielsen's TV ratings and Nielsen Audio's (formerly Arbitron's) radio ratings. Experian Simmons Market Research Bureau and GfK Mediamark Research & Intelligence are two syndicated research firms that combine information about consumers' buying behavior and their media usage with geographic and demographic characteristics.

Boomberg via Getty Images

Telecommunications companies work hard to ride the trend of booming mobile usage. Customers today rely on their phones for much more than calls so telcos need to understand the future of texting, online gaming, and other smart phone–based activities.

As valuable as it may be, syndicated research doesn't provide all the answers to marketing questions because the information it collects typically is broad but shallow; it gives good insights about general trends, such as who is watching what TV shows or what brand of perfume is hot this year. In contrast, a firm conducts **custom research** to provide answers to specific questions. This kind of research is especially helpful for firms when they need to know more about *why* certain trends have surfaced.

Some firms maintain an in-house research department that conducts studies on its behalf. Many firms, however, hire outside research companies that specialize in designing and conducting projects based on the needs of the client. These custom research reports are another kind of information an MIS includes. Marketers may use market research to identify opportunities for new products, to promote existing ones, or to provide data about the quality of their products, who uses them, and how.

Acquired Databases

A large amount of information that can be useful in marketing decision making is available in the form of external databases. Firms may acquire these databases from any number of sources. For example, some companies are willing to sell their customer database to noncompeting firms. Government databases, including the massive amounts of economic and demographic information the U.S. Census Bureau, Bureau of Labor Statistics, and other agencies collect, are available at little or no cost. State and local governments may make information such as automobile license data available for a fee.

In recent years, the use of databases for marketing purposes has come under increased government scrutiny as some consumer advocates become more and more concerned about potential invasion of privacy these may cause. Using the data to analyze overall consumer trends is one thing—using it for outbound direct mailings and unsolicited phone calls and e-mails has evoked a backlash resulting in a plethora of "do-not-call" lists and antispam laws. Maybe you have noticed that when you sign up for most anything online that requires your contact information, you receive an invitation to "opt out" of receiving promotional mailings from the company or from others who may acquire your contact information from the organization later. By law, if you decide to opt out, companies cannot use your information for marketing purposes.

We'll further develop the overall issue of database usage by marketers in the context of the popular phrase "Big Data" in Chapter 5. It's a good bet that every website or mobile link you search—and maybe even every tweet or Facebook message you post today—will wind up in a marketer's database.

The Marketing Decision Support System

As we have seen, a firm's MIS generates regular reports for decision makers on what is going on in the internal and external environment. But sometimes these reports alone are inadequate. Different managers may want different information, and in some cases the problem they must address is too vague or unusual for the MIS process to easily answer. As a result, many firms beef up their MIS with a **marketing decision support system (MDSS)**. An MDSS includes analysis and interactive software that allows marketing managers, even those who

custom research
Research conducted for a single firm to provide specific information its managers need.

APPLYING ▼ Custom Research

In order to decide which of the new product and service ideas for Discover to introduce, Ryan felt it was necessary to gain customer insight. This meant conducting custom research. Because Discover did not have the resources internally to conduct the research, it would be necessary to hire an outside research firm costing Discover around $100,000 and delaying the introduction of new products.

---

marketing decision support system (MDSS)
The data, analysis software, and interactive software that allow managers to conduct analyses and find the information they need.

Sophisticated companies like Harrah's closely track what people do in venues like Las Vegas. If the data show that some of the company's clientele favor one property over another, one form of gaming over another, or even one type of show over another, those customers will receive promotional materials tailored to their specific preferences. Slot players are notified of slot tournaments, while fans of magic shows get a heads up when Lance Burton is scheduled to appear.

Paul DrinkWater/Wireimage/Getty Image

Figure 4.2  *Process* | The MDSS

Although an MIS provides many reports managers need for decision making, it doesn't answer all their information needs. The marketing decision support system (MDSS) is an enhancement to the MIS that makes it easy for marketing managers to access the MIS system and find answers to their questions.

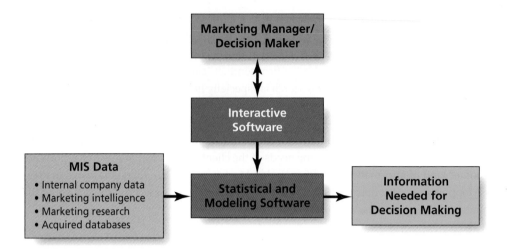

are not computer experts, to access MIS data and conduct their own analyses, often within the context of the company intranet. Figure 4.2 shows the elements of an MDSS.

Typically, an MDSS includes sophisticated statistical and modeling software tools. Statistical software allows managers to examine complex relationships among factors in the marketplace. For example, a marketing manager who wants to know how consumers perceive her company's brand in relation to the competition's brand might use a sophisticated statistical technique called "multidimensional scaling" to create a "perceptual map," or a graphic presentation of the various brands in relationship to each other. You'll see an example of a perceptual map in Chapter 7.

Modeling software allows decision makers to examine possible or preconceived ideas about relationships in the data—to ask "what-if" questions. For example, media modeling software allows marketers to see what would happen if they made certain decisions about where to place their advertising. A manager may be able to use sales data and a model to find out how many consumers stay with his brand and how many switch, thus developing projections of market share over time. A media company like Netflix wants to understand what factors influence viewers' ratings of movies so it can tweak its offerings and attract more subscribers (more on that later in the chapter, so stay with us): The company even sponsored the Netflix Prize with a purse of $1 million to anyone who could develop a model that would improve its ability to predict by 10 percent (the winning team boosted accuracy by "only" 8.43 percent, but they pocketed the cash anyway).[5] Table 4.1 gives some examples of the different marketing questions an MIS and an MDSS might answer.

Table 4.1 | Examples of Questions an MIS and an MDSS Might Answer

Questions an MIS Answers	Questions an MDSS Answers
What were our company sales of each product during the past month and the past year?	Has our decline in sales simply reflected changes in overall industry sales, or is there some portion of the decline that industry changes cannot explain?
What changes are happening in sales in our industry, and what are the demographic characteristics of consumers whose purchase patterns are changing the most?	Do we see the same trends in our different product categories? Are the changes in consumer trends very similar among all our products? What are the demographic characteristics of consumers who seem to be the most and the least loyal?
What are the best media to reach a large proportion of heavy, medium, or light users of our product?	If we change our media schedule by adding or deleting certain media buys, will we reach fewer users of our product?

2

OBJECTIVE

Understand the concept of customer insights and the role it plays in making good marketing decisions.

(p. 125)

The Role of the Customer Insights Function in a Marketing Organization

It's getting easier all the time for organizations to collect huge amounts of data. **Data** are raw, unorganized facts that need to be processed. Data are then processed, organized, structured, and presented in order to become useful for decision making. This transformation creates **information**, which is interpreted data. But there is a downside to knowing too much! All of these data can be overwhelming—and not very useful—if no one has any idea what they all mean. As some describe the ocean, "water, water everywhere and not a drop to drink!" can be repurposed "data, data everywhere and nothing insightful to find!"

Enter the customer insight specialists to save the day. At its essence, the idea of **customer insights** refers to the collection, deployment, and interpretation of information that allows a business to acquire, develop, and retain its customers. Like Ryan Garton at Discover, most companies today maintain a dedicated team of experts whose jobs are to sift through all the information available in order to support market planning decisions. This group does its best to understand how customers interact with the organization (including the nasty encounters they may have) and to guide planners when they think about future initiatives.

The job is more complicated than it sounds. Traditionally, most companies have operated in "silos" so that, for example, the people in new product development would have zero contact with anyone in customer service who actually had to deal with complaints the items designed by the new product folks. The insights manager is like an artist who has to work with a lot of different colors on her palette—her job is to integrate feedback from syndicated studies, marketing research, customer service, loyalty programs, and other sources to paint a more complete picture the organization can use. As such, this function in the organization usually plays a supporting role across the firm's SBUs (strategic business units).

For example, Discover offers prepaid credit cards that businesses can buy to reward employees or even loyal customers. A manager in this division might want to know more about the types of businesses that are the most likely to purchases these cards and perhaps to avoid some of the problems prior clients may have encountered. She would call on Ryan and his group to answer these questions by sifting through an ocean of data in order to formulate and provide *insights* to guide future marketing decisions. By the way, many organizations are "catching the wave" by adding customer insights departments—this growing trend in turn offers a lot of promising job opportunities for graduates who know how to fish for usable knowledge in the huge information ocean.

data
Raw, unorganized facts that need to be processed.

information
Interpreted data.

customer insights
The collection, deployment, and interpretation of information that allows a business to acquire, develop, and retain their customers.

3

OBJECTIVE

List and explain the steps and key elements of the market research process.

(pp. 125–141)

Steps in the Market Research Process

The collection and interpretation of information is hardly a one-shot deal that managers engage in "just out of curiosity." Ideally, market research is an ongoing process; a series of steps marketers take repeatedly to learn about the marketplace. Whether a company conducts the research itself or hires another firm to do it, the goal is the same: to help managers make informed marketing decisions. Figure 4.3 provides a great road map of the steps in the research process. You can use it to track our discussion of each step.

Figure 4.3 *Process* | Steps in the Market Research Process

The market research process includes a series of steps that begins with defining the problem or the information needed and ends with the finished research report for managers.

Define the Research Problem

- Specify the research objectives
- Identify the consumer population of interest
- Place the problem in an environmental context

↓

Determine the Research Design

- Determine whether secondary data are available
- Determine whether primary data are required
  —Exploratory research
  —Descriptive research
  —Causal research

↓

Choose the Method to Collect Primary Data

- Determine which survey methods are most appropriate
  —Mail questionnaires
  —Telephone interviews
  —Face-to-face interviews
  —Online questionnaires
- Determine which observational methods are most appropriate
  —Personal observation
  —Unobtrusive measures
  —Mechanical observation

↓

Design the Sample

- Choose between probability sampling and nonprobability sampling

↓

Collect the Data

- Translate questionnaires and responses if necessary
- Combine data from multiple sources (if available)

↓

Analyze and Interpret the Data

- Tabulate and cross-tabulate the data
- Interpret or draw conclusions from the results

↓

Prepare the Research Report

- In general, the research report includes the following:
  —An executive summary
  —A description of the research methods
  —A discussion of the results of the study
  —Limitations of the study
  —Conclusions and recommendations

Step 1: Define the Research Problem

The first step in the market research process is to clearly understand what information managers need. We refer to this step as defining the research problem. You should note that the word *problem* here does not necessarily refer to "something that is wrong" but instead refers to the overall questions for which the firm needs answers. Defining the problem has three components:

1. *Specify the research objectives:* What questions will the research attempt to answer?

2. *Identify the consumer population of interest:* What are the characteristics of the consumer group(s) of interest?

3. *Place the problem in an environmental context:* What factors in the firm's internal and external business environment might influence the situation?

It's not as simple as it may seem to provide the right kind of information for each of these pieces of the problem. Suppose a luxury car manufacturer wants to find out why its sales fell off dramatically over the past year. The research objective could center on any number of possible questions: Is the firm's advertising failing to reach the right consumers? Is the right message being sent? Do the firm's cars have a particular feature and related benefit (or lack of one) that turns customers away? Does a competitor offer some features and benefits that have better captured customer imaginations? Is there a problem with the firm's reputation for providing quality service? Do consumers believe the price is right for the value they get? The particular objective researchers choose depends on a variety of factors, such as the feedback the firm gets from its customers, the information it receives from the marketplace, and sometimes even the intuition of the people who design the research.

Often the focus of a research question comes from marketplace feedback that identifies a possible problem. Volvo, long known for the safety records of its cars, had a tough time competing with luxury brands like Mercedes-Benz, BMW, Lexus, and Audi. How could Volvo improve its market share among luxury car buyers?

The *research objective* determines the consumer population the company will study. In the case of Volvo, the research could have focused on current owners to find out what they especially like about the car. Or it could have been directed at nonowners to understand their lifestyles, what they look for in a luxury automobile, or their beliefs about the Volvo brand that discourage them from buying the cars. Instead, the company chose to focus on why consumers didn't buy the competing brands. Managers figured it would be a good idea to identify the "pain points" shoppers experienced when they looked at rivals so that they could try to address these objections with their own marketing activities.

So what did Volvo find out? Its research showed that many car shoppers were too intimidated by the "ostentatious" image of Mercedes and BMW to consider actually buying one. Others felt that too many of their neighbors were driving a Lexus, and they wanted to make more of an individual statement. Volvo's vice president of marketing explained that Volvo owners' ". . . interpretation of luxury is different but very real. They're more into life's experiences, and more into a Scandinavian simple design [of vehicles] versus a lot of clutter. They are very much luxury customers and love luxury products, but they don't feel a need to impress others." Based on the research findings, Volvo developed a new ad campaign, showing consumers that it was OK—and even desirable—to be different. The company even pokes fun at rival luxury brands. In one TV commercial, a sophisticated woman sits at a stoplight in her Mercedes-Benz SUV and checks out her makeup in the rear-view mirror. Another woman pulls up next to her in a Volvo XC60—but she's more down to earth. The Volvo driver looks into her own rear-view mirror. The difference is she makes a funny face in order to make her kids in the backseat crack up. The voice-over says, "Volvos aren't for everyone, and we kinda like it that way."[6]

Step 2: Determine the Research Design

Once we isolate specific problems, the second step of the research process is to decide on a "plan of attack." This plan is the **research design**, which specifies exactly what information marketers will collect and what type of study they will do. Research designs fall into two broad categories based on whether the analysts will utilize primary or secondary data (see ⚡ Figure 4.4). All marketing problems do not call for the same research techniques, and marketers solve many problems most effectively with a combination of approaches.

Research with Secondary Data

The first question marketers must ask when they determine their research design is whether the information they require to make a decision already exists. For example, a coffee producer who needs to know the differences in coffee consumption among different demographic and geographic segments of the market may find that the information it needs is available from one or more studies already conducted by the National Coffee Association, the leading trade association of U.S. coffee companies and a major generator of industry research. We call information that has been collected for some purpose other than the problem at hand **secondary data**.

Many marketers thrive on going out and collecting new, "fresh" data from consumers. In fact, getting new data seems to be part of the marketing DNA. However, if secondary data are available, it saves the firm time and money because it has already incurred the expense to design a study and collect the data. Sometimes the information that marketers need may be "hiding" right under the organization's nose in the form of company reports; previous company research studies; feedback received from customers, salespeople, or stores; or even in the memories of longtime employees (it's amazing how many times a manager commissions a study without knowing that someone else who was working on a different problem already submitted a similar report!).

APPLYING ▼ Define the Research Problem

Ryan knows that the first step in marketing research is to define the research problem. Ryan's identified the problem as Discover's need for consumer information to assist in determining which product ideas would be most likely to fit cardholders' desires, fit with the Discover brand image as the card that is all about cash back and other rewards to cardholders, and fit with company's financial and technical resources.

research design
A plan that specifies what information marketers will collect and what type of study they will do.

secondary data
Data that have been collected for some purpose other than the problem at hand.

Figure 4.4 ⚡ *Process* | Market Research Designs

For some research problems, secondary data may provide the information needed. At other times, one of the primary data collection methods may be needed.

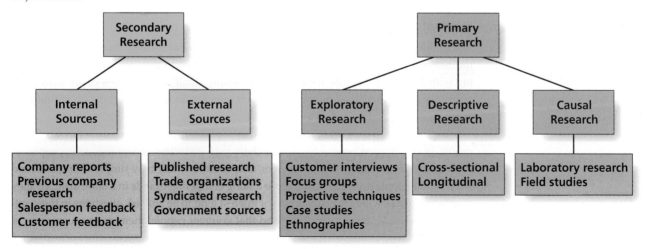

Table 4.2 | Helpful Websites for Secondary Data

URL	Description
www.opinionresearch.com	ORC International offers numerous industry and trend reports that are useful as secondary data sources.
www.census.gov	The U.S. Census Bureau publishes separate reports on specific industries (such as agriculture, construction, and mining) as well as on housing, population growth and distribution, and retail trade. One challenge with census data is that the full data collection process occurs only every 10 years, although interim data are collected on some issues.
www.ama.org	The American Marketing Association provides many resources to its members on a variety of industry topics.
www.lexisnexis.com	LexisNexis is a large database featuring information from sources such as Dun & Bradstreet, the *New York Times*, CNN, and National Public Radio transcripts.

More typically, though, researchers need to look elsewhere for secondary data. They may obtain reports published in the popular and business press, studies that private research organizations or government agencies conduct, and published research on the state of the industry from trade organizations. For example, many companies subscribe to reports such as the *National Consumer Study*, a survey conducted by syndicated research firm Experian Simmons. The company publishes results that it then sells to marketers, advertising agencies, and publishers. Access to its' data is even available in some college libraries. This database contains over 60,000 data variables with usage behavior on all major media, over 500 product categories, and over 8,000 brands. Data from Experian Simmons can give a brand manager a profile of who uses a product, identify heavy users, or even provide data on what information sources a target market is likely to consult prior to purchase.[7] Table 4.2 lists several websites helpful to marketers when they look for secondary data.

Research with Primary Data

primary data
Data from research conducted to help make a specific decision.

Of course, secondary data are not always the answer. When a company needs to make a specific decision, marketers often collect **primary data**: information they gather directly from respondents to specifically address the question at hand. Primary data include demographic and psychological information about customers and prospective customers, customers' attitudes and opinions about products and competing products, as well as their awareness or knowledge about a product and their beliefs about the people who use those products. In the next few sections, we'll talk briefly about the various designs options to collect primary data.

Exploratory Research

exploratory research
A technique that marketers use to generate insights for future, more rigorous studies.

Marketers use **exploratory research** to come up with ideas for new strategies and opportunities or perhaps just to get a better handle on a problem they are currently experiencing with a product. Because the studies are usually small scale and less costly than other techniques, marketers may do this to test their hunches about what's going on without too much risk or expense.

Exploratory studies often involve in-depth probing of a few consumers who fit the profile of the "typical" customer. Researchers may interview consumers, salespeople, or other employees about products, services, ads, or stores. They may simply "hang out" and watch what people do when they choose among competing brands in a store aisle. Or they may locate places where the consumers of interest tend to be and ask questions in these settings. For example, some researchers find that younger people often are too suspicious or skeptical in traditional research settings, so they may interview them while they wait in line to buy concert tickets or in clubs.[8]

We refer to most exploratory research as *qualitative*; that is, the results of the research project tend to be nonnumeric and instead might be detailed verbal or visual information about consumers' attitudes, feelings, and buying behaviors in the form of words rather than in numbers. For example, Procter & Gamble (P&G) conducted personal interviews with consumers after the initial product launch of its Febreze odor neutralizer flopped. When marketers visited dozens of homes—many of them downright smelly—they found out the people who lived in them couldn't even smell the bad odors from cigarettes or a house full of cats because they had become desensitized to the smells. These people didn't know they needed the product (and they must have had very polite friends). But during one interview, the researchers visited the home of a woman who used Febreze as part of her general cleaning routine. She sprayed the product after she cleaned up as a sort of "mini-celebration" for a job well done. On learning this, P&G went back and reformulated the original Febreze by adding more perfume. Febreze the air freshener, along with a new ad campaign, was born, and sales skyrocketed.[9] The rest of us are grateful!

The **focus group** is the technique that market researchers employ most often for exploratory research. Focus groups typically consist of five to nine consumers who have been recruited because they share certain characteristics (they all play golf at least twice a month, are women in their twenties, and so on). These people sit together to discuss a product, ad, or some other marketing topic a discussion leader introduces. Typically, the leader records (by videotape or audiotape) these group discussions, which may be held at special interviewing facilities that allow for observation by the client who watches from behind a one-way mirror.

Today it's common to find focus groups in cyberspace as well. Firms such as IKEA and Volvo use online focus group sites that bear a resemblance to other social networking sites. IKEA used consumer consulting boards (also known as a *market research online community or MROC*) in five different countries to solicit feedback about the newest version of its catalog.[10] Volvo, on the other hand, launched its focus group via Twitter Chat to gather feedback about its new ads. Volvo marketers say the instant feedback from consumers helps to strike the right balance in its ads. The rapid back-and-forth between the company and the online community allows for real-time data collection.[11]

The **case study** is a comprehensive examination of a particular firm or organization. In business-to-business market research in which the customers are other firms, for example, researchers may try to learn how one particular company makes its purchases. The goal is to identify the key decision makers, to learn what criteria they emphasize when they choose among suppliers, and perhaps to learn something about any conflicts and rivalries among these decision makers that may influence their choices.

Another qualitative approach is **ethnography**, which uses a technique that marketers borrow from anthropologists who go to "live with the natives" for months or even years. Some market researchers visit people's homes or participate in real-life consumer activities to get a handle on how they really use products. Imagine having a researcher follow you around while you shop and then, while you use the products you bought, see what kind of consumer you are. This is basically marketing's version of a reality show—though, we hope, the people they study are a bit more "realistic" than the ones on TV!

Descriptive Research

We've seen that marketers have many qualitative tools in their arsenal, including focus groups and observational techniques, to help them better define a problem or opportunity. These are usually modest studies of a small number of people, enough to get some indication of what is going on but not enough for the marketer to feel confident about generalizing what she observes to the rest of the population.

focus group
A product-oriented discussion among a small group of consumers led by a trained moderator.

case study
A comprehensive examination of a particular firm or organization.

ethnography
An approach to research based on observations of people in their own homes or communities.

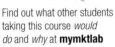

Ripped from the Headlines

Ethical/Sustainable Decisions in the Real World

What are the ingredients for a successful advertising campaign? It has to grab your attention. It has to be cutting edge. It has to be unforgettable. It has to be—offensive?[12]

In the battle to create advertising that generates buzz and captures the almighty consumer dollar, there's often a fine line between being on the cutting edge and stepping over the edge. Consider this ad from Hyundai that aired in the UK: A man starts his car in an enclosed garage, sits back, and closes his eyes—in an apparent suicide attempt. Sometime later, the same man, defeated, emerges from his garage and goes back into his house. The tagline "The new ix35 with 100% water emissions" and the Hyundai logo follow.

ETHICS **CHECK:**
Find out what other students taking this course *would do* and *why* at **mymktlab .com**.

Or take this three-part online ad for Mountain Dew: An irate goat (with voice-over by the rapper Tyler, the Creator) beats up a waitress after she cuts the goat off from his gotta-have soda. In the second part, the cops pull over the goat for a "DewUI." In the last ad, the goat, shown in a lineup with five African American men, tries to intimidate the waitress so that she won't call him out.

After an almost immediate backlash from the public, both the Hyundai and Mountain Dew ads were pulled, the first for being insensitive to mental health issues and the latter after being accused of being possibly the most racist commercial in history. And these are just two examples.

Over the years, advertising agencies have continually pushed the boundaries of decency in an effort to get more eyeballs. These edgy ads, sometimes known as *shock advertising*, are "shocking" because they violate our social norms (unwritten rules about how to behave) or focus on topics that many people consider inappropriate. For better or for worse, they do get people to sit up and pay attention.

As a marketing director, would you sign off an ad that's so edgy it's sure to get attention but that some people are sure to consider offensive?

☐ **YES**   ☐ **NO**

descriptive research
A tool that probes more systematically into the problem and bases its conclusions on large numbers of observations.

cross-sectional design
A type of descriptive technique that involves the systematic collection of quantitative information.

longitudinal design
A technique that tracks the responses of the same sample of respondents over time.

The next step in market research, then, often is to conduct **descriptive research**. This kind of research probes systematically into the marketing problem and bases its conclusions on a large sample of participants. Results typically are expressed in quantitative terms—averages, percentages, or other statistics that result from a large set of measurements. In such *quantitative approaches* to research, the project can be as simple as counting the number of Listerine bottles sold in a month in different regions of the country or as complex as statistical analyses of responses to a survey mailed to thousands of consumers about their flavor preferences in mouthwash. In each case, marketers conduct the descriptive research to answer a specific question, in contrast to the "fishing expedition" they may undertake in exploratory research. However, don't downplay the usefulness of qualitative approaches—initial qualitative market research serves to greatly inform and shape subsequent quantitative approaches.

Market researchers who employ descriptive techniques most often use a **cross-sectional design**. This approach usually involves the systematic collection of responses to a consumer survey instrument, such as a *questionnaire*, from one or more samples of respondents at one point in time. They may collect the data on more than one occasion but usually not from the same pool of respondents.

In contrast to these one-shot studies, a **longitudinal design** tracks the responses of the same sample of respondents over time. Market researchers sometimes create consumer panels to get information; in this case, a sample of respondents that are representative of a larger market agrees to provide information about purchases on a weekly or monthly basis. Major consumer package goods firms like P&G, Unilever, Colgate Palmolive, and Johnson & Johnson, for example, recruit consumer advisory panels on a market-by-market basis to keep their fingers on the pulse of local shoppers. P&G, for example, maintains two key advisory panels: one for teens (Tremor) and one for moms (Vocalpoint). With more than 750,000 members weighing in on everything from package design to promotional material, P&G estimates that the loyalty and advocacy of these members have boosted P&G's sales by 10 to 30 percent.[13]

Causal Research

It's a fact that purchases of both diapers and beer peak between 5:00 P.M. and 7:00 P.M. Can we say that purchasing one of these products caused shoppers to purchase the other as well—and, if so, which caused which? Does taking care of a baby drive a parent to drink?

Or is the answer simply that this happens to be the time when young fathers stop at the store on their way home from work to pick up some brew and Pampers?[14]

And what about hemlines? Since the 1920s, George Taylor's "hemline theory" has posited that the length of women's hemlines reflects overall economic health. The theory originated at a time when women wore silk stockings—when the economy was strong, they shortened their hemlines to show off the stockings; when the economy took a dive, so did the hemlines, to cover up the fact that women couldn't afford the fancy stockings. Don't believe it? The same was true in 2009—when runway designs were "shockingly short"—the stock market rallied 15 percent for the year.[15]

Sales of diapers and beer are correlated, but does one cause the other?

The descriptive techniques we've mentioned do a good job of providing valuable information about what is happening in the marketplace, but by its very nature descriptive research can only *describe* a marketplace phenomenon—it cannot tell us *why* it occurs. Sometimes marketers need to know if something they've done has brought about some change in behavior. For example, does placing one product next to another in a store mean that people will buy more of each? We can't answer this question through simple observation or description.

Causal research attempts to identify cause-and-effect relationships. Marketers use causal research techniques when they want to know if a change in something (e.g., placing cases of beer next to a diaper display) is responsible for a change in something else (e.g., a big increase in diaper sales). They call the factors that might cause such a change *independent variables* and the outcomes *dependent variables*. The independent variable(s) cause some change in the dependent variable(s). In our example, then, the beer display is an independent variable, and sales data for the diapers are a dependent variable—that is, the study would investigate whether an increase in diaper sales "depends" on the proximity of beer. Researchers can gather data and test the causal relationship statistically.

causal research
A technique that attempts to understand cause-and-effect relationships.

This form of causal research often involves using experimental designs. **Experiments** attempt to establish causality by ruling out alternative explanations, and to maintain a high level of control, experiments may entail bringing subjects (participants) into a lab so that researchers can control precisely what they experience. For the diaper example, a group of men might be paid to come into a testing facility and enter a "virtual store" on a computer screen. Researchers would then ask the men to fill a grocery cart as they click through the virtual aisles. The experiment might vary the placement of the diapers—next to shelves of beer in one scenario and near paper goods in another scenario. The objective of the experiment is to find out which placement gets more of the guys to put diapers into their carts.

experiments
A technique that tests predicted relationships among variables in a controlled environment.

Step 3: Choose the Method to Collect Primary Data

When the researcher decides to work with primary data, the next step in the market research process is to figure out just how to collect it. We broadly describe primary data collection methods as either *survey* or *observation*. There are many ways to collect data, and marketers try new ones all the time. In fact, today, more and more marketers are turning to sophisticated brain scans to directly measure consumers' brain's reactions to various advertisements or products. This **neuromarketing**, or brain research, uses technologies such as functional magnetic resonance imaging (fMRI) to measure brain activity to better understand why consumers make the decisions they do, and some firms have even invested in their own labs and in-house scientists to perform an ongoing neuromarketing research

neuromarketing
A type of brain research that uses technologies such as functional magnetic resonance imaging (fMRI) to measure brain activity to better understand why consumers make the decisions they do.

Sophisticated new technologies like virtual stores allow marketers to re-create shopping experiences on a respondent's computer screen or mobile device.

program. Google, CBS, Frito-Lay, and many others have used neuromarketing research approaches to measure consumer reactions to their ads or products.[16] Since most of us don't have access to fMRI machines to conduct market research, in this section we'll focus more on explaining other methods to collect primary data.

Survey Methods

Survey methods involve some kind of interview or other direct contact with respondents who answer questions. Questionnaires can be administered on the phone, in person, through the mail, or over the Internet. Table 4.3 summarizes the advantages and disadvantages of different survey methods to collect data.

Questionnaires

Questionnaires differ in their degree of structure. With a totally *unstructured questionnaire*, the researcher loosely determines the items in advance. Questions may evolve from the respondent's answers to previous questions. At the other extreme, the researcher uses a *completely structured questionnaire*, asking every respondent the exact same questions, and each participant responds to the same set of fixed choices. You have probably experienced this kind of questionnaire, where you might have had to respond to a statement by saying if you "strongly agree," "somewhat agree," and so on. *Moderately structured questionnaires* ask each respondent the same questions, but the respondent is allowed to answer the questions in his own words.

Mail questionnaires are easy to administer and offer a high degree of anonymity to respondents. On the downside, because the questionnaire is printed and mailed, researchers have little flexibility in the types of questions they can ask and little control over the circumstances under which the respondent answers them. Mail questionnaires also take a long time to get back to the company and are likely to have a much lower response rate than other types of data collection methods because people tend to ignore them.

Telephone interviews usually consist of a brief phone conversation in which an interviewer reads a short list of questions to the respondent. There are several problems with using telephone interviews as a data collection method. The respondent also may not feel comfortable speaking directly to an interviewer, especially if the survey is about a sensitive subject.

telemarketing
The use of the telephone to sell directly to consumers and business customers.

Another problem with this method is that the growth of **telemarketing**, in which businesses sell directly to consumers over the phone, has eroded consumers' willingness to participate in phone surveys. In addition to aggravating people by barraging them with telephone sales messages (usually during dinnertime!), some unscrupulous telemarketers disguise their pitches as research. They contact consumers under the pretense of doing a study when, in fact, their real intent is to sell the respondent something or to solicit funds for some cause. This in turn prompts increasing numbers of people to use voice mail and caller ID to screen calls, further reducing the response rate. And, as we noted earlier, state and federal *do-not-call lists* allow many would-be research subjects to opt out of participation in both legitimate market research and unscrupulous telemarketing.[17]

Using *face-to-face interviews*, a live interviewer asks questions of one respondent at a time. Although in "the old days" researchers often went door-to-door to ask questions, that's much less common today because of fears about security and because the large numbers of two-income families make it less likely to find people at home during the day. Typically, today's face-to-face interviews occur in a **mall intercept** study in which researchers recruit shoppers in malls or other public areas. You've probably seen this going on in your

mall intercept
A study in which researchers recruit shoppers in malls or other public areas.

Table 4.3 | Advantages and Disadvantages of Survey Data Collection Methods

Data Collection Method	Advantages	Disadvantages
Mail questionnaires	• Respondents feel anonymous • Low cost • Good for ongoing research	• It may take a long time for questionnaires to be returned • Low rate of response; many consumers may not return questionnaires • Inflexible questionnaire format • Length of questionnaire is limited by respondents' interest in the topic • Unclear whether respondents understand the questions • Unclear who is responding • No assurance that respondents are being honest
Telephone interviews	• Fast • High flexibility in questioning • Low cost • Limited interviewer follow-up • Limited questionnaire length	• Decreasing levels of respondent cooperation • High likelihood of respondent misunderstanding • Respondents cannot view materials • Cannot survey households without phones • Consumers screen calls with answering machines and caller ID • Do-not-call lists allow many research subjects to opt out of participation
Face-to-face interviews	• Flexibility of questioning • Can use long questionnaires • Can determine whether respondents have trouble understanding questions • Take a lot of time • Can use visuals or other materials	• High cost • Interviewer bias a problem
Online questionnaires	• Instantaneous data collection and analysis • Questioning very flexible • Low cost • No interviewer bias • No geographic restrictions • Can use visuals or other materials	• Unclear who is responding • No assurance that respondents are being honest • Limited questionnaire length • Unable to determine whether respondent understands the question • Self-selected samples

local mall, where a smiling person holding a clipboard stops shoppers to see if they are willing to answer a few questions.

Mall intercepts offer good opportunities to get feedback about new package designs, styles, or even reactions to new foods or fragrances. However, because only certain groups of the population frequently shop at malls, a mall intercept study does not provide the researcher with a representative sample of the population (unless the population of interest is mall shoppers). In addition to being more expensive than mail or phone surveys, respondents may be reluctant to answer questions of a personal nature in a face-to-face context.

Online questionnaires are growing in popularity, but the use of such questionnaires is not without concerns. Many researchers question the quality of responses they will receive—particularly because (as with mail and phone interviews) no one can be really sure who is typing in the responses on the computer. In addition, it's uncertain whether savvy online consumers are truly representative of the general population.[18] However, these concerns are rapidly evaporating as research firms devise new ways to verify identities; present surveys in novel formats, including the use of images, sound, and animation; and recruit more diverse respondents.[19]

Observational Methods

As we said earlier, the second major primary data collection method is *observation*. This term refers to situations where the researcher simply records the consumer's behaviors.

When researchers use *personal observation*, they simply watch consumers in action to understand how they react to marketing activities. Although a laboratory allows researchers to exert control over what test subjects see and do, marketers don't always have the luxury of conducting this kind of "pure" research. But it is possible to conduct field studies in the real world, as long as the researchers still can control the independent variables. For example, a diaper company might choose two grocery stores that have similar customer bases in terms of age, income, and so on. With the cooperation of the grocery store's management, the company might place its diaper display next to the beer in one store and next to the paper goods in the other and then record diaper purchases men make over a two-week period. If a lot more guys buy diapers in the first store than in the second (and the company was sure that nothing else was different between the two stores, such as a dollar-off coupon for diapers being distributed in one store and not the other), the diaper manufacturer might conclude that the presence of beer in the background does indeed result in increased diaper sales.

When they suspect that subjects will probably alter their behavior if they know someone is watching them, researchers may use **unobtrusive measures** to record traces of physical evidence that remain after people have consumed something. For example, instead of asking a person to report on the alcohol products currently in her home, the researcher might go to the house and perform a "pantry check" by actually counting the bottles in her liquor cabinet. Another option is to sift through garbage to search for clues about each family's consumption habits. The "garbologists" can tell, for example, which soft drink is accompanied by what kind of food. Since people in these studies don't know that researchers are looking through products they've discarded, the information is totally objective—although a bit smelly!

Mechanical observation is a method of primary data collection that relies on nonhuman devices to record behavior. For example, one of the classic applications of mechanical observation is the Nielsen Company's famous use of "people meters"—boxes the company attaches to the TV sets of selected viewers to record patterns of TV watching. The data that Nielsen obtains from these devices indicate who is watching which shows. These "television ratings" help network clients determine how much to charge advertisers for commercials and which shows to cancel or renew. The service is so popular that Nielsen has more than tripled the size of its reporting panel between since 2007 and 2014—currently over 40,000 homes and over 100,000 people are involved in the data collection.[20] Nielsen also measures user activity on digital media. The research company's U.S. panel alone is comprised of over 200,000 Internet users across 30,000 sites.[21] This allows Nielsen to give clients a more updated understanding of how viewers interact with their favorite TV shows. For example, it tracks the number of TV-related tweets people post—in a three-month period, almost 20 million people tweet about a TV show.[22]

unobtrusive measures
Measuring traces of physical evidence that remain after some action has been taken.

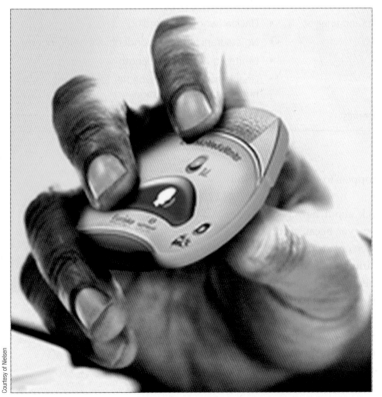

Courtesy of Nielsen

Nielsen's "People Meter" monitors what a large sample of American consumers watch.

Similarly, Nielsen Audio (formerly Arbitron) deploys thousands of "portable people meters" (PPMs). PPMs resemble pagers and automatically record the wearer's exposure to any media that has inserted an inaudible code into its promotion such as TV ads or shelf displays. Thus, when the consumer is exposed to a broadcast commercial, cinema ad, Internet banner ad, or other form of commercial, the PPM registers, records, and time-stamps the signal. At day's end, a home docking station downloads the media history. Portability ensures that all exposures register; this eliminates obtrusive people meters and written diaries that participants often forget to fill out.[23]

Online Research

Many companies find that an online approach is a superior way to collect data—it's fast, it's relatively cheap, and it lends itself well to forms of research from simple questionnaires to online focus groups. In fact, some large companies like P&G now collect a large portion of their consumer intelligence online. Developments in online research are happening quickly, so let's take some time now to see where things are headed.

There are two major types of online research. One type is information that organizations gather when they track consumers while they surf the Web. The second type is information they gather more selectively through questionnaires on websites, including of course social media sites, through e-mail, or from focus groups that virtual moderators conduct in chat rooms. Most social media platforms, such as Twitter or Facebook, offer numerous ways to analyze trends and conduct market research. By simply searching the latest posts and popular terms—or, as marketers refer to it, "scraping the Web"—you can gain insight into emerging trends and see what customers are talking about in real time. One example of this is conducting hashtag searches on Twitter. By setting up a few searches with hashtags related to your brand, industry, or product, you can receive instant notifications when customers, clients, or competitors use key terms.[24]

Across all of its platforms and forms, the Internet offers us unprecedented ability to track consumers as they search for information on Google, Bing, YouTube and other search engines. We've become so accustomed to just looking up stuff online that "google" has become a verb (as has "friend"). As consumers enter search terms like "lowest prices on J Brand jeans" or "home theaters," these queries become small drops in the ocean of data available to marketers that engage in online behavioral tracking. How do they know what we're looking at online? Beware the Cookie Monster! **Cookies** are text files that a website sponsor inserts into a user's hard drive when the user connects with the site. Cookies remember details of a visit to a website and track which pages the user visits. Some sites request or require that visitors "register" on the site by answering questions about themselves and their likes and dislikes. In such cases, cookies also allow the site to access these details about the customer.

cookies
Text files inserted by a website sponsor into a Web surfer's hard drive that allows the site to track the surfer's moves.

The Cutting Edge

Cookies That Track You 24/7

Cookies have been tracking your online habits for years, but now one company has created "persistent cookies" that track your movements 24/7 via an app on your smart phone—when you go to school, to your favorite coffee shop, and even to the movies at midnight. In exchange for giving up information about their personal whereabouts, participants can earn gift cards and be entered into drawings for prizes like Apple iPads. The company responsible for collecting all this data—a firm called "Placed"—then sells this information to businesses and mobile advertisers.

For example, by tracking its participants, Placed knows that Asian American moms like to shop at Trader Joe's and that if you're between the ages of 25 and 34, you're likely to head to Taco Bell. But how does the app know exactly where you are? For phones that have a compass, Placed can access that data; for other phones, Placed makes some educated guesses to pinpoint where you are within a broader area. If it's 1:00 A.M., for example, you're more likely to be at Joe's Local Bar than next door getting a manicure.

While some people think it's downright creepy, others see it as marketing genius. Placed has already had more than 125,000 people sign on.[25]

The technology associated with Cookies allows websites to customize services, such as when Amazon recommends new books to users on the basis of what books they have ordered in the past. Consider this one: It is late evening, and you should be studying, but you just can't make yourself do it. So you grab your tablet and sign in to Netflix. And like every other time you sign in, Netflix offers up a bunch of movies and TV shows to tempt you away from the textbooks. But how does Netflix know what you want to see—sometimes they seem to anticipate your tastes better than your friends can!

No, there isn't someone sitting at their office whose only job is to follow you around online in order to guess what you'll want to see next. These surprising connections are the results of **predictive technology**, which uses shopping patterns of large numbers of people to determine which products are likely to be purchased if others are—except in this case what you're "shopping" for is movies to watch. To figure out what movies or TV shows you are likely to enjoy, Netflix trained teams of people to watch thousands of movies and tag them according to attributes such as "goriness" or "plot conclusiveness." Netflix then combines those attributes with the viewing habits of millions of users.[26] And voilà—Netflix knows just what to serve up to satisfy your viewing fix.

You can block cookies or curb them by changing settings on your computer, although this can make life difficult if you are trying to log on to many sites, such as online newspapers or travel agencies that require this information to admit you. The information generated from tracking consumers' online journeys has become big business, and in massive quantities it has become popularly known as "big data," a topic we will discuss in more detail in Chapter 5. To date, the Federal Trade Commission has relied primarily on firms and industries to develop and maintain its own standards instead of developing its own extensive privacy regulations, but many would like to see that situation changed, and much discussion is afoot at all levels of government regarding online privacy rights. Proponents advocate the following guiding principles:

- Information about a consumer belongs to the consumer.

- Consumers should be made aware of information collection.

- Consumers should know how information about them will be used.

- Consumers should be able to refuse to allow information collection.

- Information about a consumer should never be sold or given to another party without the permission of the consumer.

No data collection method is perfect, and online research is no exception—though many of the criticisms of online techniques also apply to offline techniques. One potential problem is the representativeness of the respondents. Many segments of the consumer population, mainly the economically disadvantaged and elderly, do not have the same level of access to the Internet as other groups. In addition, in many studies (just as with mail surveys or mall intercepts), there is a *self-selection bias* in the sample. That is, because respondents have agreed to receive invitations to take part in online studies, by definition they tend to be the people who like to participate in surveys. As with other kinds of research, such as live focus groups or panel members, it's not unusual to encounter "professional respondents"—people who just enjoy taking part in studies (and getting paid for it). Quality online research specialists such as Harris Interactive, SSI—Survey Sampling International, and Toluna address this problem by monitoring their participants and regulating how often they are allowed to participate in different studies over a period of time. However, unfortunately, with the proliferation of online data collection, many new and unproven data providers continue to come into the industry—therefore, in terms of online research, the venerable phrase *caveat emptor* (let the buyer beware) rules.

There are other disadvantages of online research. Hackers can actually try to influence research results. Competitors can learn about a firm's marketing plans, products,

---

predictive technology
Analysis techniques that use shopping patterns of large numbers of people to determine which products are likely to be purchased if others are.

advertising, and other proprietary elements when they intercept information from these studies (though this can occur in offline studies just as easily). Because cheating has become so rampant, some companies today use fraud-busting software that creates a digital finger-print of each computer involved in a survey to identify respondents who fake responses or professionals who game the industry by doing as many surveys as possible.[27]

Metrics Moment

More and more, marketing is responsible for the e-commerce aspect of firms' Web strategies. **Bounce rate** is a marketing metric for analyzing website traffic. It represents the percentage of visitors who enter the site (typically at the home page) and "bounce" (leave the site) rather than continue viewing other pages within the same overall site. It is a straight-forward metric to understand and is based on the following formula:

$$\text{Bounce rate} = \frac{\text{Total number of visitors viewing one page only}}{\text{Total entries to the Web page}}$$

A site's bounce rate is easy to track with tools like Google Analytics. Such tools can show the bounce rates on different pages of a website, how the user came to the site (organic search, paid search, banner ad, etc.), how the bounce rate has changed over time, and other data so that the mar-keter can really dig into where the leak is occurring.

Marketers can use bounce rates to determine whether an entry page effectively generates visitors' interest. A bounce rate, simply put, is the mea-sure of how many visitors come to a page on a website and leave without viewing any other pages. An entry page with a low bounce rate means that this first page encourages visitors to view still more pages and continue deeper into the website. High bounce rates, on the other hand, typically indicate that whatever visitors encounter on that first "hit" isn't interesting enough to make them want to check out more.[28]

Apply the Metrics

1. A rule of thumb for website effectiveness is that great websites should fulfill three basic criteria: (1) the site should be attractive, (2) the site should be easy to navigate and get where you want to go, and (3) the site should have up-to-date information (no old stuff). When you bounce off of a website, does it tend to be for one or more of these reasons? Are any of them more important than others to you?

2. Consider the bounce rate metric we describe above. Like any mar-keting metric, decisions should not be made based on the bounce rate alone. What other considerations should the marketer use to evaluate the effectiveness of a website?

Data Quality: Garbage In, Garbage Out

We've seen that a firm can collect data in many ways, including focus groups, ethnographic approaches, observational studies, and controlled experiments. But how much faith should marketers place in what they find out from the research?

All too often, marketers who commission a study assume that because the researchers give them a massive report full of impressive-looking numbers and tables, they must be looking at the "truth." Unfortunately, there are times when this "truth" is really just one person's interpretation of the facts. At other times, the data researchers use to generate recommendations are flawed. Earlier in the chapter we brought up GIGO: "garbage in, gar-bage out."[29] That is, your conclusions can be only as good as the *quality* of the information you use to make them. Typically, three factors influence the quality of research results—validity, reliability, and representativeness.

Validity is the extent to which the research actually measures what it was intended to measure. This was part of the problem underlying the famous New Coke fiasco in the 1980s, in which Coca-Cola underestimated people's loyalty to its flagship soft drink after it replaced "Old Coke" with a new, sweeter formula. In a blind taste test, the com-pany assumed that testers' preferences for one anonymous cola over another was a valid measure of consumers' preferences for a cola brand. Coca-Cola found out the hard way that measuring taste only is not the same as measuring people's deep allegiances to their favorite soft drinks. After all, Coke is a brand that elicits strong consumer loyalty and is nothing short of a cultural icon. Tampering with the flavors was like assaulting Mom and apple pie. Sales eventually recovered after the company brought back the old version as "Coca-Cola Classic."[30]

bounce rate
A marketing metric for analyzing website traffic. It represents the percentage of visitors who enter the site (typically at the home page) and "bounce" (leave the site) rather than continue viewing other pages within the same overall site.

validity
The extent to which research actually measures what it was intended to measure.

reliability
The extent to which research measurement techniques are free of errors.

Reliability is the extent to which the research measurement techniques are free of errors. Sometimes, for example, the way in which a researcher asks a question creates error by biasing people's responses. Imagine that an attractive female interviewer who works for Trojans condoms stops male college students on campus and asks them if they use contraceptive products. Do you think their answers might change if they were asked the same questions on an anonymous survey they received in the mail? Most likely, their answers would be different because people are reluctant to disclose what they actually do when their responses are not anonymous. Researchers try to maximize reliability by thinking of several different ways to ask the same questions, by asking these questions on several occasions, or by using several analysts to interpret the responses. Thus, they can compare responses and look for consistency and stability.

Reliability is a problem when the researchers can't be sure that the consumer population they're studying even understands the questions. For example, kids are difficult subjects for market researchers because they tend to be undependable reporters of their own behavior, they have poor recall, and they often do not understand abstract questions. In many cases, the children cannot explain why they prefer one item over another (or they're not willing to share these secrets with grown-ups).[31] For these reasons, researchers have to be especially creative when they design studies involving younger consumers.  Figure 4.5 shows part of a completion test that a set of researchers used to measure children's preferences for TV programming in Japan.

representativeness
The extent to which consumers in a study are similar to a larger group in which the organization has an interest.

Representativeness is the extent to which consumers in the study are similar to a larger group in which the organization has an interest. This criterion underscores the importance of **sampling**: the process of selecting respondents for a study. The issue then becomes how large the sample should be and how to choose these people. We'll talk more about sampling in the next section.

sampling
The process of selecting respondents for a study.

Step 4: Design the Sample

probability sample
A sample in which each member of the population has some known chance of being included.

Once the researcher defines the problem, decides on a research design, and determines how to collect the data, the next step is to decide from whom to obtain the needed information. Of course, he or she *could* collect data from every single customer or prospective customer, but this would be extremely expensive and time consuming if possible at all (this is what the U.S. Census spends millions of dollars to do every 10 years). Not everyone has the resources of the U.S. government to poll *everyone* in their market. So they typically collect most of their data from a small proportion, or *sample*, of the population of interest. Based on the answers from this sample, researchers generalize to the larger population. Whether such inferences are accurate or inaccurate depends on the type and quality of the study sample. There are two main types of samples: probability and nonprobability samples.

Figure 4.5 📷 *Snapshot* | Completion Test

It can be especially difficult to get accurate information from children. Researchers often use visuals, such as this Japanese completion test, to encourage children to express their feelings. The test asked boys to write in the empty balloon what they think the boy in the drawing will answer when the girl asks, "What program do you want to watch next?"

Probability Sampling

In a **probability sample**, each member of the population has some known chance of being included. Using a probability sample ensures that the sample represents the population and that inferences we make about the population from what members of the sample say or do are justified. For example, if a larger percentage of males than females in a probability sample say they prefer action movies to "chick flicks," one can infer with confidence that a larger percentage of males than females in the general population also would rather see a character get sliced and diced than kissed and dissed (okay, we wouldn't really use these descriptions in a study, but you get the idea).

The most basic type of probability sample is a *simple random sample*, in which every member of a population has a known and equal chance of being included in the study. For example, if we simply take the names of all 40 students in a class, put them in a hat, and draw one out, each member of the class has a 1 in 40 chance of being included in the sample. In most studies, the population from which the sample will be drawn is too large for a hat, so marketers use a computer program to generate a random sample from a list of members.

Sometimes researchers use a *systematic sampling procedure* to select members of a population; they select the *n*th member of a population after a random start. For example, if we want a sample of 10 members of your class, we might begin with the second person on the roll and select every fourth name after that—the second, sixth, tenth, fourteenth, and so on. Researchers know that studies that use systematic samples are just as accurate as those that use simple random samples. But unless a list of members of the population of interest is already in a computer data file, it's a lot simpler just to create a simple random sample.

Yet another type of probability sample is a *stratified sample*, in which a researcher divides the population into segments that relate to the study's topic. For example, imagine you want to study what movies most theatergoers like. You have learned from previous studies that men and women in the population differ in their attitudes toward different types of movies—men like action flicks, and women like romantic comedies. To create a stratified sample, you would first divide the population into male and female segments. Then you would randomly select respondents from each of the two segments in proportion to their percentage of the population. In this way, you have created a sample that is proportionate to the population on a characteristic that you know will make a difference in the study results.

Nonprobability Sampling

Sometimes researchers do not believe that the time and effort required to develop a probability sample is justified, perhaps because they need an answer quickly or just want to get a general sense of how people feel about a topic. They may choose a **nonprobability sample**, which entails the use of personal judgment to select respondents—in some cases, they just ask anyone they can find. With a nonprobability sample, some members of the population have no chance at all of being included. Thus, there is no way to ensure that the sample is representative of the population. Results from nonprobability studies can be generally suggestive of what is going on in the real world but are not necessarily definitive.

A **convenience sample** is a nonprobability sample composed of individuals who just happen to be available when and where the data are being collected. For example, if you were to simply stand in front of the student union and ask students who walk by to complete your questionnaire, the "guinea pigs" you get to agree to do it would be a convenience sample.

Finally, researchers may also use a *quota sample*, which includes the same proportion of individuals with certain characteristics as in the population. For example, if you are studying attitudes of students in your university, you might just go on campus and find freshmen, sophomores, juniors, and seniors in proportion to the number of members of each class in the university. The quota sample is much like the stratified sample except that, with a quota sample, the researcher uses his or her individual judgment to select respondents.

Step 5: Collect the Data

At this point, the researcher has determined the nature of the problem to be addressed. She chose a research design that will specify how to investigate the problem and what kinds of information (data) will be needed. The researcher has also selected the data collection and sampling methods. Once these decisions have been made, the next task is to collect the data.

nonprobability sample
A sample in which personal judgment is used to select respondents.

convenience sample
A nonprobability sample composed of individuals who just happen to be available when and where the data are being collected.

Conducting market research in other countries can pose a real challenge.

We noted earlier that the quality of your conclusions is only as good as the data you use. The same logic applies to the people who collect the data: *The quality of research results is only as good as the poorest interviewer in the study.* Careless interviewers may not read questions exactly as written, or they may not record respondent answers correctly. So marketers must train and supervise interviewers to make sure they follow the research procedures exactly as outlined. In the next section, we'll talk about some of the problems in gathering data and some solutions.

Challenges to Gathering Data in Foreign Countries

Conducting market research around the world is big business for U.S. firms—more than half of their revenues come from projects outside the U.S.[32] However, market conditions and consumer preferences vary worldwide, and there are major differences in the sophistication of market research operations and the amount of data available to global marketers. In Mexico, for instance, because there are still large areas where native tribes speak languages other than Spanish, researchers may end up bypassing these groups in surveys. In Egypt, where the government must sign off on any survey, the approval process can take months or years. And in many developing countries, infrastructure is an impediment to executing phone or mail surveys, and lack of online connectivity blocks Web-based research.

For these and other reasons, choosing an appropriate data collection method is difficult. In some countries, many people may not have phones, or low literacy rates may interfere with mail surveys. Understanding *local customs* can be a challenge, and *cultural differences* also affect responses to survey items. Both Danish and British consumers, for example, agree that it is important to eat breakfast. However, the Danish sample may be thinking of fruit and yogurt, while the British sample has toast and tea in mind. Sometimes marketers can overcome these problems by involving local researchers in decisions about the research design.

Another problem with conducting market research in global markets is *language*. Sometimes translations just don't come out right. In some cases, entire subcultures within a country might be excluded from the research sample. In fact, this issue is becoming more and more prevalent inside the U.S. as non-English speakers increase as a percentage of the population.

back-translation
The process of translating material to a foreign language and then back to the original language.

To overcome language difficulties, researchers use a process of **back-translation**, which requires two steps. First, a native speaker translates the questionnaire into the language of the targeted respondents. Then someone fluent in the second language translates this new version back into the original language to ensure that the correct meanings survive the process. Even with precautions such as these, researchers must interpret the data they obtain from other cultures with care.

Step 6: Analyze and Interpret the Data

Once market researchers collect the data, what's next? It's like a spin on the old "if a tree falls in the woods" question: "If results exist, but there's no one to interpret them, do they have a meaning?" Let's leave the philosophers out of it and just say that marketers would answer "no." Data need interpretation if the results are going to be useful.

To understand the important role of data analysis, let's take a look at a hypothetical research example. Say a company that markets frozen foods wishes to better understand consumers' preferences for varying levels of fat content in their diets. They conducted a descriptive research study where they collected primary data via telephone interviews. Because they know that dietary preferences relate to gender (among other aspects), they used a stratified sample that includes 175 males and 175 females.

Table 4.4 | Examples of Data Tabulation and Cross-Tabulation Tables

Fat Content Preference (number and percentages of responses)

Do you prefer a meal with high-fat content, medium-fat content, or low-fat content?

Questionnaire Response	Number of Responses	Percentage of Responses
High fat	21	6
Medium fat	179	51
Low fat	150	43
Total	350	100

Fat Content Preference by Gender (number and percentages of responses)

Do you prefer a meal with high-fat content, medium-fat content, or low-fat content?

Questionnaire Response	Number of Females	Percentage of Females	Number of Males	Percentage of Males	Total Number	Total Percentage
High fat	4	2	17	10	21	6
Medium fat	68	39	111	64	179	51
Low fat	103	59	47	27	150	43
Total	175	100	175	100	350	100

Typically, marketers first tabulate the data as Table 4.4 shows—that is, they arrange the data in a table or other summary form so they can get a broad picture of the overall responses. The data in Table 4.4 show that 43 percent of the sample prefers a low-fat meal. In addition, there may be a desire to cross classify or cross tabulate the answers to questions by other variables. *Cross tabulation* means that we examine the data that we break down into *subgroups*, in this case males and females separately, to see how results vary between categories. The cross tabulation in Table 4.4 shows that 59 percent of females versus only 27 percent of males prefer a meal with low-fat content. Researchers may wish to apply additional statistical tests that you may learn about in subsequent courses (something to look forward to).

Based on the tabulation and cross tabulations, the researcher interprets the results and makes recommendations. For example, the study results in Table 4.4 may lead to the conclusion that females are more likely than males to be concerned about a low-fat diet. Based on these data, the researcher might then recommend that the firm target females when it introduces a new line of low-fat foods.

Step 7: Prepare the Research Report

The final step in the market research process is to prepare a report of the research results. In general, a research report must clearly and concisely tell the readers—top management, clients, creative departments, and many others—what they need to know in a way that they can easily understand and that won't bore you to tears (just like a good textbook should keep you engaged). A typical research report includes the following sections:

- An executive summary of the report that covers the high points of the total report
- An understandable description of the research methods
- A complete discussion of the results of the study, including the tabulations, cross tabulations, and additional statistical analyses
- Limitations of the study (no study is perfect)
- Conclusions drawn from the results and the recommendations for managerial action based on the results

Here's my choice...

Real **People**, Real **Choices**

Why do you think Ryan choose option 3?

1 Option 2 Option **3** Option

How It Worked Out at Discover Card

Ryan chose option 3. The firm's leadership decided it was worth taking on additional costs and delays to maximize the chances that consumers would adopt new card offerings. After all, a new product that bombs can cost a company millions of dollars, so investing up front to prevent this can be well worth the money and time.

Ryan's team undertook the first Innovation Screening in Discover's history. The company interviewed numerous marketing research companies and eventually selected Ipsos, which had impressive prior experience in working with clients from the financial services industry. This company also maintained an online panel that would allow them to create a statistically representative panel of over 1,600 respondents who were current customers of Discover as well as those who used competing card products. The consumer panelists evaluated a total of 16 concepts: three benchmark cards (card products that Chase, Citibank, and American Express already had in the market), seven new product ideas, and six new feature ideas. Each respondent evaluated three concepts, for a total of about 300 evaluations per concept. In order to get at the true potential of the ideas, participants assessed them without being told which card company was thinking about introducing them. At a later point in the study, they rated the attractiveness of these ideas when they were paired with actual card companies.

The consumer research showed that in fact some of management's initial estimates about the likely appeal of new products was significantly off the mark: Some were less appealing than sponsors assumed, while some showed evidence of greater demand than Discover's internal finance teams predicted—one potential product moved from the back of the list to be Discover's highest priority based on this work. In addition, when the team tested some new offerings that competing card companies had recently launched, it found that they weren't all that appealing—and indeed about a year later, the other companies closed these down. Ryan was gratified that Discover lived up to its name and invested in discovering what its customers actually liked and disliked.

Refer back to **page 118** for Ryan's story ➡

MyMarketingLab™

Go to **mymktlab.com** to complete the problems marked with this icon ⭐ as well as additional Marketing Metrics questions only available in MyMarketingLab.

Objective Summary ➥ Key Terms ➥ Apply

CHAPTER 4
Study Map

1. Objective Summary (pp. 120–124)

Explain the role of a marketing information system and a marketing decision support system in marketing decision making.

A marketing information system (MIS) is composed of internal data, market intelligence, market research data, acquired databases, and computer hardware and software. Firms use an MIS to gather, sort, analyze, store, and distribute information needed by managers for marketing decision making. The marketing decision support system (MDSS) allows managers to use analysis software and interactive software to access MIS data and to conduct analyses and find the information they need about their products and services.

Key Terms

market research ethics, p. 120

database, p. 120

marketing information system (MIS), p. 120

intranet, p. 121

market intelligence system, p. 121

reverse engineering, p. 121

market research, p. 122

syndicated research, p. 122

custom research, p. 123

marketing decision support system (MDSS), p. 123

2. Objective Summary (p. 125)

Understand the concept of customer insights and the role it plays in making good marketing decisions.

Organizations today are collecting massive amounts of data, but they need customer insight specialists to sift through that data in order to make it useful. The concept of customer insights refers to the collection, deployment, and interpretation of information that allows a business to acquire, develop, and retain its customers. This information supports market planning decisions and guides planners about future business initiatives.

Key Terms

data, p. 125

information, p. 125

customer insights, p. 125

3. Objective Summary (pp. 125–141)

List and explain the steps and key elements of the market research process.

The research process begins by defining the problem and determining the research design or type of study. Next, researchers choose the data collection method—that is, whether there are secondary data available or whether primary research with a communication study or through observation is necessary. Then researchers determine what type of sample is to be used for the study and then collect the data. The final steps in the research are to analyze and interpret the data and prepare a research report.

Exploratory research typically uses qualitative data collected by individual interviews, focus groups, or observational methods, such as ethnography. Descriptive research includes cross-sectional and longitudinal studies. Causal research goes a step further by designing controlled experiments to understand cause-and-effect relationships between independent marketing variables, such as price changes, and dependent variables, such as sales.

Researchers may choose to collect data via survey methods and observation approaches. Survey approaches include mail questionnaires, telephone interviews, face-to-face interviews, and online questionnaires. A study may use a probability sample, such as a simple random or stratified sample, in which inferences can be made to a population on the basis of sample results. Nonprobability sampling methods include a convenience sample and a quota sample. The researcher tries to ensure that the data are valid, reliable, and representative.

Internet-based research, including via various social media platforms, accounts for a rapidly growing proportion of all market research. Online tracking uses cookies to record where consumers go on a website. Consumers have become increasingly concerned about privacy and how this information is used and made available to others. Online approaches also provide an attractive alternative to traditional communication data collection methods because of its speed and low cost. Many firms use the Internet to conduct online focus groups.

Key Terms

research design, p. 127

secondary data, p. 127

primary data, p. 128

exploratory research, p. 128

focus group, p. 129

case study, p. 129

Chapter **Questions** and **Activities**

Concepts: Test Your Knowledge

4-1. What is the difference between market research, syndicated research, and custom research?

4-2. How does a marketing decision support system (MDSS) allow marketers to easily get the information they need?

4-3. Define the concept of customer insights and the role it plays in market planning decisions.

4-4. Why is defining the problem to be researched so important to ultimate success with the research project?

4-5. Explain the difference between primary data and secondary data.

4-6. What techniques can marketers use to gather data in exploratory research? How is this type of data collection useful?

4-7. Explain what descriptive research is.

4-8. What are the advantages and disadvantages of mail questionnaires and telephone interviews?

4-9. What are the main methods of secondary research?

4-10. GIGO—garbage in, garbage out—is mentioned in the chapter. What is the significance of this concept to market research?

4-11. What is a (computer) cookie? What ethical and privacy issues relate to cookies?

4-12. What important issues must researchers consider when they plan to collect data online?

4-13. When we consider data quality, what are the differences among validity, reliability, and representativeness? How can you know the data have high levels of these characteristics?

4-14. How do probability and nonprobability samples differ? What are some types of probability samples? What are some types of nonprobability samples?

4-15. Under what conditions would exploratory research be used instead of descriptive research?

Activities: Apply What You've Learned

4-16. *In Class, 10–25 Minutes for Teams* The syndicated research company where you are working is interested in conducting a case study research project on an overseas firm. In a role-playing situation, present the potential research challenges encountered in the overseas firm. Would you expect fewer research challenges if the case study was conducted on a local firm?

4-17. *Creative Homework/Short Project* As an account executive with a market research firm, you are responsible for deciding on the type of research to be used in various studies conducted for your clients. For each of the following client questions, list your choices of research approaches.

  a. Will TV or magazine advertising be more effective for a local bank to use in its marketing communication plan?

  b. Could a new package design for dry cereal do a better job of satisfying the needs of customers and, thus, increase sales?

  c. Are consumers more likely to buy brands from firms that support strong sustainability initiatives?

  d. How do female consumers determine if a particular perfume is right for them?

4-18. *Creative Homework/Short Project* For each of the topics you selected in item 4-17, how might you use a more passive (observation) approach to support the communication methods you employ?

4-19. *Creative Homework/Short Project* To what degree could secondary data sources be used to address the topics you selected in item 4-17? What specific secondary sources (if any) might be most useful to help address your selected issues?

4-20. *In Class, 10–25 Minutes for Teams* Your market research firm is planning to conduct surveys to gather information for a number of clients. Your boss has asked you and a few other new employees to do some preliminary work. She has asked each of you to choose three of the topics (from among the six listed next) that will be included in the project and to prepare an analysis of the advantages and disadvantages of each these communication methods of collecting primary data: mail questionnaires, telephone interviews, face-to-face interviews, and online questionnaires.

  a. The amount of sports nutrition drinks consumed in a city
  b. Why a local bank has been losing customers
  c. How heavily the company should invest in manufacturing and marketing home fax machines
  d. The amount of money being spent "over the state line" for lottery tickets
  e. What local doctors would like to see changed in the city's hospitals
  f. Consumers' attitudes toward several sports celebrities

4-21. *For Further Research (Individual)* The financial institution you work for is planning to open a new branch at an identified location at the city center. You were instructed to do further research at the location using a personal observation technique throughout the next 90 days. What sort of information will you look for? Justify your reasoning.

Apply Marketing Metrics

Marketers historically have tended to overrely on click-through rates as a metric for success of Web advertising. *Click-through rate* means the proportion of visitors who initiated action with respect to an advertisement that redirected them to another page where they might purchase an item or learn more about a product or service. Technically, click-through rate is the number of times a click is made on the advertisement divided by the total impressions (the times an advertisement was served up to the consumer during the visit to the website). Thus,

$$\text{Click-through rate (\%)} = \frac{\text{Number of click-throughs}}{\text{Number of impressions}}$$

While providing useful information, click-through rates merely measure quantity, not quality, of consumer response. Consider what you learned in this chapter about various approaches to market research.

4-22. What other two or three data collection approaches to measuring the success of a Web advertising campaign might be fruitful in providing more meaningful data than just clicks? Hint: Just because the metric relates to the Web doesn't mean non-Web-based research approaches are inappropriate.[33]

Choices: What Do You Think?

4-23. *Ethics* Suppose that you had conducted an ethnographic research study on an ethnic community. After months of living with the community members and participating in their real-life consumer activities, the research is now concluded. What ethical challenges did you likely face during the study, and how would you conduct a graceful exit?

⭐ **4-24.** *Critical Thinking* What is your overall attitude toward market research? Do you think it is a beneficial activity from a consumer's perspective? Or do you think it merely gives marketers new insights on how to convince consumers to buy something they really don't want or need?

4-25. *Critical Thinking* More and more companies are starting to employ customer insight specialists to make sense of the data collected about their customers. Do you think this position is really needed within companies, or is it just a fad? Explain your reasoning.

4-26. *Ethics* Other than children, what groups of people would you consider to be prone to ethical challenges? Explain why you chose these groups.

4-27. *Critical Thinking* Are you willing to divulge personal information to market researchers? How much are you willing to tell, or where would you draw the line?

4-28. *Critical Thinking* Would you alter the settings on your computer to disallow cookies? Why or why not?

⭐ **4-29.** *Critical Thinking* During the 2014 legislative session, the Data Broker and Accountability Act of 2014 was introduced in the hopes of giving consumers more control over the types of information data brokers collect about them as well as letting consumers opt out of the sale of such information to other companies. Would you support such legislation? Why or why not?

4-30. *Ethics* Reverse engineering is one form of market intelligence and involves, physically deconstructing a competitor's product to discover how it is put together. Is this ethical? Why or why not?

4-31. *Critical Thinking* Consider the approach to tracking consumers' exposure to promotions via portable people meters (PPMs). Would you be willing to participate in a study that required you to use a PPM? Why or why not?

Miniproject: Learn by Doing

The purpose of this miniproject is to familiarize you with market research techniques and to help you apply these techniques to managerial decision making.

4-32. With a group of three other students in your class, select a small retail business or quick-serve restaurant to use as a "client" for your project. (Be sure to get the manager's permission before you conduct your research.) Then choose one topic from among the following possibilities to develop a study problem:
  • Employee–customer interactions
  • The busiest periods of customer activity
  • Customer perceptions of service

- Customer likes and dislikes about the menu
- Customer likes and dislikes about the environment in the place of business
- The benefits customers perceive to be important
- The age-groups that frequent the place of business
- The buying habits of a particular age group
- How customer complaints are handled

Develop a plan for the research.
   a. Define the research question as you will study it.
   b. Choose the type of research approach you will use.
   c. Select the techniques you will use to gather data.
   d. Develop the mode and format for data collection.
Conduct the research.

Write a report (or develop a class presentation) that includes the five parts shown in step 7 of the market research process covered in the chapter.

Marketing in **Action** Case Real Choices at GetFeedback

The world is going mobile. What's a traditional market researcher to do? According to the BI Intelligence research service, as of 2014, 6 percent of the global population will own a tablet, 20 percent will own PCs, and 22 percent will own smart phones. Consumers are changing how they interact with companies, products, and services. However, Forrester Research estimates that as few as 17 percent of marketing researchers have taken their survey processes mobile. That means that most companies still use outdated technology and techniques. Roxana Strohmenger, a Forrester analyst says, "Consumers have already decided for us: If you want to connect with them, mobile is the way." Any information gap between the companies and consumers increases the likelihood that researchers are not getting the best information possible. Remember GIGO (garbage in, garbage out): Insights drawn from poor information may lead to bad marketing decisions.

In 2013, Kraig Swensrud and Sean Whiteley recognized the information gap in the marketplace and decided that it needed to be closed with mobile-first customer surveys. The two former Salesforce.com employees created a start-up called GetFeedback. Their goal was to be on the front lines of the changeover to mobile computing. GetFeedback is a service that creates surveys for smartphones, tablets, and mobile Web browsers. As of 2014, the company had more than 1,000 users that include high-profile companies like Salesforce.com, LinkedIn, Facebook, and Dropbox. A range of available services includes packages from free ($0 per month) for up to 10 responses per month to enterprise ($120 per month) for up to 10,000 responses per month. Additionally, service plans may include Web, e-mail, and telephone technical support.

Swensrud believes that mobile surveys present many challenges, including how to optimize questions for smaller screen sizes so that respondents can scroll down and answer them quickly. GetFeedback offers templates to integrate video clips, photographs, or images to reinforce a company's marketing. Clients can create surveys and then add style by adding colors, fonts, logos, and images. In order to attain a deeper engagement and higher completion rates of online surveys, imagery and video are essential. The objective is to have the survey reflect the personality of the brand. Other key features of GetFeedback include push notifications that provide alerts and a set of analytical tools that allow clients to fully utilize the collected information. All of this can happen in real time, which gives GetFeedback's customers an advantage over their competitors. And the client owns the information it collects, so it is readily available to share within the company. The information can easily be downloaded and exported into Microsoft Excel or any analytical software that can handle comma-separated values (CSV).

The Council of American Survey Research Organizations estimates that globally $19 billion is spent annually on telephone polls, online surveys, questionnaires, and other market research. According to IBISWorld, a market research firm, approximately $2 billion is spent annually on online surveys in the U.S. alone. The market for consumer research is immense and steadily growing. However, GetFeedback is not alone in its attempts to succeed in this ever-changing marketplace. SurveyMonkey is the existing market leader with more than 15 million customers, including Kraft Foods, Sirius XM, and Facebook. The CEO of SurveyMonkey, Dave Goldberg, believes that companies should keep the survey process under 10 minutes. If not, he says that "people are going to resist long, complex surveys."

GetFeedback has to challenge a market leader, figure out how to shorten surveys, maintain information quality, and deliver great value to its customers. At the same time, the company must generate attractive shareholder gains. In an environment as dynamic as this one, the picture is always unclear. GetFeedback must consider its future strategy and discover how to succeed as more and more consumers make the leap to an "always-on" world.

You Make the Call

4-33. What is the decision facing GetFeedback?

4-34. What factors are important in understanding this decision situation?

4-35. What are the alternatives?

4-36. What decision(s) do you recommend?

4-37. What are some ways to implement your recommendation?

Sources: Based on Heather Clancy, "With Mobile Surveys, Market Research Gets a Makeover," March 25, 2014, **http://tech.fortune.cnn .com/2014/03/25/with-mobile-surveys-market-research-gets-a-makeover** (accessed April 13, 2014); Ingrid Lunden, "Salesforce's Ex-CMO Launches GetFeedback, a New Mobile-First Customer Survey Platform," December 12, 2013, **http://techcrunch.com/2013/12/12/ getfeedback** (accessed April 13, 2014); and *Plans & Pricing, Features,* **https://getfeedback.com** (accessed April 4, 2014).

MyMarketingLab™

Go to **mymktlab.com** for Auto-graded writing questions as well as the following Assisted-graded writing questions:

4-38. *Creative Homework/Short Project.* Your company recently launched a new "dry" shampoo. Although initial sales were strong, they have steadily declined over the last year and a half. You have decided to conduct further market research, but first you have to define the research problem. What are your research objectives? What is the population of interest? How does the problem fit within the environmental context? Prepare a short report that clearly and fully defines the research problem for your product.

4-39. *Creative Homework/Short Project.* You work for a small company that designs and sells women's trendy rubber rain boots throughout the U.S. Sales have been strong, but you think they could be stronger. You have begun the market research process and are now ready to design the sample. Will you design a probability sample or a nonprobability sample? What type of probability or nonprobability sample will you use? What are the advantages of the method that you chose? What are the limitations of the method you chose?

Marketing Analytics: Welcome to the Era of Big Data!

Lisa Arthur

▼ A Decision Maker at Teradata Corporation

As Teradata's chief marketing officer (CMO), Lisa Arthur drives global market and demand strategy, product and solutions marketing, and customer-centric initiatives and serves as global industry thought leader around data-driven marketing and Teradata's Integrated Marketing Cloud solutions. A 30-year marketing veteran, she has also served as CMO for Internet leader Akamai Technologies, B2B2C application provider Mindjet, and, most recently, Aprimo (now Teradata). She is the author of *Big Data Marketing; Engage Your Customers More Effectively to Drive Value* (2013).

Lisa spent nearly seven years at Oracle, where as a vice president of marketing she managed the market entry and growth for Oracle CRM and E-Business Suite On-Demand. Also, as the founder of Cinterim, she applied her market-centric processes and insight to provide strategic counsel for Silicon Valley start-ups and *Fortune 50* technology companies.

A seasoned keynote speaker, Lisa has addressed diverse topics at Web 2.0, Office 2.0, the Direct Marketing Association, the Australian Direct Marketing Association, the American Marketing Association (AMA) Strategy Conference, Stanford University, and the MIT Sloan CMO Summit and various CMO Executive Forums. She is frequently quoted in industry media, has a syndicated blog in *B2C Community*, and has appeared on Asia's *Wall Street Journal* broadcast and published numerous papers with the AMA. Her industry thought-leadership blogs have appeared on the Forbes.com CMO Network, and she is a contributor to *Lean back*, a marketing blog of The Economist Group. Lisa's recent honors include the *Direct Marketing News* 2013 "Marketing Hall of Femme," honoring today's top women marketers, and the American Business Association's 2012 Gold "Stevie Award" for Marketing Executive of the Year. And, in 2014, 2012, and 2011, she was named a "Woman to Watch" by the Sales and Lead Management Association. She is also a trustee with the Marketing Sciences Institute. She earned a BA degree from Ohio State University.

Lisa's Info

What I do when I'm not working?
Writing, cooking, and photography.

First job out of school?
I had school loans, and it was a tough job market, so I began my professional career as a temporary employment recruiter and placement professional. Needless to say, I'm thrilled I switched to marketing.

Career high?
Publishing my first book, *Big Data Marketing*, in October 2013.

A job-related mistake I wish I hadn't made?
Not listening to my intuition. I've made this mistake a couple of times, and while data is essential for decision making, so is gut instinct.

Business book I'm reading now?
The Singularity Is Near by Ray Kurtzweil.

My hero?
My husband. Every day, he is the "superman" in my life, and I couldn't do what I do without his love and support.

My motto to live by?
It's never too late.

What drives me?
I'm on a quest along with my company, Teradata, to make marketing a more valued function through the use of data to innovate and transform customer engagement and experiences.

My management style?
Collaborative coach.

My pet peeve?
The word *can't*.

Here's my problem...

Real People, Real Choices

When Lisa joined Aprimo in 2009 (now part of Teradata Corporation, a public company listed on the New York Stock Exchange) as its CMO, the company had been in business for 11 years and had enjoyed strong success in the marketing resource management (MRM), the multichannel campaign management, and in the enterprise marketing management space. It boasted a blue-chip client list of more than 200 companies that used its marketing software and services to improve their marketing results and effectiveness. Acquired in 2011 by Teradata, the applications have expanded to also include Big Data discovery and marketing attribution through its TeradataAster solutions. Marketers are both the consumers and the generators of Big Data and can gain insight and then take action with consumers and buyers to engage in real time to provide next-best offer or next-best message. Since Teradata is the leader in data and analytic platforms as well as its own leading multichannel campaign management solution, the combination of marketing applications along with Big Data and advanced analytics adds value to the company's already robust marketing solution.

Prior to the Teradata acquisition, Lisa was recruited to be a change agent—to reposition Aprimo, the company, and its brand as *the* platform for marketers. There had been branding and positioning work that had created a great logo, but the company still was missing a clear connection between what it could offer to marketing executives and their teams.

The company was growing quickly and needed to broaden its appeal to a wider market. At the same time, it was launching a next-generation cloud offering comprised of marketing operations, campaign management, and digital messaging solutions, along with associated analytics to help make real-time sense of customer data. The cloud analytics category was an emerging market with all the hallmarks of a sector ready to explode. But the Aprimo brand was not well known, and most people in the marketing analytics industry perceived that the firm was only an MRM technology solutions provider. In reality, the company offered a lot more—a marketing software platform to enable global companies to manage the entire business of marketing, immediately and for the long term. Beyond managing marketing operations, Aprimo offered clients advanced campaign management capabilities to communicate online or offline with their consumers and prospects as well as integrated digital messaging for its online platform to simplify and accelerate the delivery of e-mails and Short Message Service.

The company was gearing up for the launch of Aprimo Marketing Studio On Demand, a cloud-based platform. The launch of its cloud product was strategically important to the company to provide more flexible implementation and usage of its marketing solutions. The launch was scheduled to happen within the quarter during which Lisa joined the company, and the annual global user conference was just six months away. Resources in the marketing department were extremely limited, as the leadership team of the company had awaited the arrival of the incoming CMO to staff up. In Lisa's strategic view, the Aprimo brand needed to be refreshed, evolved, and invigorated. Clearly, this market was ready for a true thought leader. The challenge was limited human and capital resources and not much time to "relaunch the company."

Lisa considered her Options 1·2·3

Option 1
Continue on the current course and pace and focus only on the launch of the product for the short term in order to provide more time and resources to relaunch the brand. Wait 9 to 12 months to do the more extensive brand work that would do a better job of communicating the company's abilities. This choice would allow Lisa and her team to focus on a "big-bang" product launch that would generate a lot of interest among potential clients in the short term. Since the marketing department was understaffed, this choice would allow the team to focus on getting the product launch right. On the other hand, the new cloud product was going to spearhead a major repositioning for Aprimo, and Lisa feared that the impact of the launch would get lost without a more full-scale, integrated approach.

Option 2
Launch the product and the brand in a "two-prong" release. Aprimo could use the revenue it would earn from the new cloud product to fund aggressive growth plans it had for the following year. This choice would allow the company to meet its revenue goals and also provide two (rather than one) anchor points for the relaunch of the company—there would be some buzz generated by the new cloud product, and then the brand relaunch a few months later could build on that. This decision would also give the company time to tweak its cloud product among early adopter clients so it could be confident that it was rolling on all cylinders when the entire Aprimo brand relaunched. Still, it wasn't clear if the team's minimal staff could pull off two separate launches within a fairly short period of time. And, this was a fairly unusual strategy, so it was a high-risk move for a brand-new CMO.

Option 3
Delay the cloud product launch, accelerate efforts to rebrand Aprimo, and then launch both the cloud product and the new brand together. This option was a big-bang approach that would energize the company. The relaunch would be even more impactful because it would be accompanied by the release of an innovative product to signal the company's arrival in the cloud. All of the company's event planning resources could focus on one truly integrated plan. On the other hand, this delay would probably result in a loss of revenue for Aprimo. The time lag might give competitors an opportunity to bring out similar products beforehand and steal Aprimo's thunder. Also, the delay would force Teradata to miss the industry's big autumn trade show, DreamForce, where people in the industry traditionally expected to see big new launches announced.

You Choose

Which **Option** would you choose, and **why**?
1. ☐YES ☐NO   2. ☐YES ☐NO   3. ☐YES ☐NO

See what **option** Lisa chose on **page 168** ➤

Chapter 5

1

Customer Relationship Management (CRM): A Key Decision Tool for Marketers

customer relationship management (CRM)
A systematic tracking of consumers' preferences and behaviors over time in order to tailor the value proposition as closely as possible to each individual's unique wants and needs.

one-to-one marketing
Facilitated by CRM, one-to-one marketing allows for customization of some aspect of the goods or services that are offered to each customer.

In Chapter 1, you learned that a *consumer orientation* is a business approach that prioritizes the satisfaction of customers' needs and wants. Now it's time to drill down a bit more on how firms actually accomplish this prioritization. Toward this end, most highly successful firms embrace **customer relationship management (CRM)** programs that involve systematically tracking consumers' preferences and behaviors over time in order to tailor the value proposition as closely as possible to each individual's unique wants and needs. CRM allows firms to talk to individual customers and to adjust elements of their marketing programs in light of how each customer reacts.[1] The CRM trend facilitates **one-to-one marketing**, which includes several steps:[2]

1. Identify customers and get to know them in as much detail as possible.

2. Differentiate among these customers in terms of both their needs and their value to the company.

3. Interact with customers and find ways to improve cost efficiency and the effectiveness of the interaction.

4. Customize some aspect of the goods or services that you offer to each customer. This means treating each customer differently based on what the organization has learned about him or her through prior interactions.[3]

Table 5.1 suggests some specific activities to implement these four steps of one-to-one marketing. Remember, successful one-to-one marketing depends on CRM, which allows a company to identify its best customers, stay on top of their needs, and increase their satisfaction.[4]

At its core, CRM is about communicating with customers and about customers being able to communicate with a company "up close and personal." CRM systems are applications that use computers, specialized computer software, databases, and often the Internet to capture information at each **touchpoint**, which is any point of direct interface between customers and a company (online, by phone, or in person).

touchpoint
Any point of direct interface between customers and a company (online, by phone, or in person).

These systems include everything from websites that let you check on the status of a bill or package to call centers that solicit your business. When you log on to the FedEx website to track a lost package, that's part of a CRM system. When you get a phone message from the dentist reminding you about your appointment tomorrow to get a root canal, that's CRM (sorry about that). And when you get a call from the car dealer asking how you like your new vehicle, that's also CRM. Remember how we said in Chapter 4 that information is the fuel that runs the marketing engine? It is through CRM that companies act on and manage the information they gather from their customers.

To fully appreciate the value of a CRM strategy, consider the experience of USAA, which began as an insurance company catering to the military market and today is a leading global financial services powerhouse. In 1922, when 25 army officers met in San Antonio and decided to insure each other's vehicles, they could not have imagined that their tiny organization would one day serve 6 million members and become the only fully integrated financial services company in America. Unlike State Farm, Allstate, and other traditional insurance providers, USAA does not provide field agents with an office you can go to, sit down, and shoot the breeze about your latest fishing trip. In fact, USAA's employees conduct business almost entirely over the phone. But just ask any USAA member how they feel about the service, and you'll get a glowing report.

Table 5.1	The Four Steps of One-to-One Marketing	

Step	Suggested Activities
Identify	Collect and enter names and additional information about your customers.
	Verify and update, deleting outdated information.
Differentiate	Identify top customers.
	Determine which customers cost the company money.
	Find higher-value customers who have complained about your product more than once.
	Find customers who buy only one or two products from your company but a lot from other companies.
	Rank customers into A, B, and C categories based on their value to your company.
Interact	Call the top three people in the top 5 percent of dealers, distributors, and retailers that carry your product and make sure they're happy.
	Call your own company and ask questions; see how hard it is to get through and get answers.
	Call your competitors and compare their customer service with yours.
	Use incoming calls as selling opportunities.
	Initiate more dialogue with valuable customers.
	Improve complaint handling.
Customize	Find out what your customers want.
	Personalize your direct mail.
	Ask customers how and how often they want to hear from you.
	Ask your top 10 customers what you can do differently to improve your product.
	Involve top management in customer relations.

Source: Adapted by permission of *Harvard Business Review* from Don Peppers, Martha Rogers, and Bob Dorf, "Is Your Company Ready for One-to-One Marketing?," *Harvard Business Review* (January–February 1999), 151–60. Copyright © 1999 by the Harvard Business School Publishing Corporation. All rights reserved.

The secret sauce in USAA's success is largely its state-of-the-art CRM system. No matter where on the globe you are, no matter what time of day or night, a USAA representative will pull up your profile, and you'll feel that he or she knows you. Of course, it takes a good dose of employee training to enable those folks to use the system to its potential. But USAA does a great job of building and maintaining long-term customer relationships and, more important, getting customers to move many or all of their business over to USAA, including banking, credit cards, money management, investments, and financial planning. To further build loyalty, USAA even runs an online company store that sells all sorts of popular product lines and brands for which members get purchase discounts.[5]

USAA's success helps illustrate and explain why CRM has become a driving philosophy in many successful firms. Gartner, a leading information technology (I.T.) research firm, notes that the CRM market grew from $16 billion to $18 billion between 2011 and 2012.[6] In addition, the firm forecasts that the global market for CRM systems will grow to $36.5 billion by 2017.[7] Clearly, CRM is increasingly becoming an important part of how businesses operate, and there does not seem to be any signs of that trend slowing down. Here are some recent examples of CRM at work:

- Amazon.com is the world champion master of the happy customer approach to CRM. For loyal users, Amazon tracks visits so that it can customize advertisements, product promotions, and discounts for each shopper. This helps keep customers engaged during each of their visits and helps ensure that they continue to come back for more. For instance, if you happen to have a passion for, say, grunge bands of the 1990s, the website is quick to recommend that new retrospective on Pearl Jam the next time you visit.[8]

- Coca-Cola launched its My Coke Rewards online program, the multiyear customer loyalty marketing blitz into which it poured millions of dollars. The organization is now in the process of developing a new version of My Coke Rewards that is in its beta version. This new version is oriented toward providing a more social and interactive experience that connects users to the things that they love (and because it is online, the company can track the activity of users for valuable data).[9]

- In 2014, Disney launched MyMagic+, a new system that allows Disney World visitors to more efficiently plan out their vacation experience and reduce the need to carry around

tickets and other items previously necessary to tour the park. Visitors can book events in advance, reserve times on rides, and review the park activities that they have experienced in the past, to name a few of the main features. MyMagic+ is designed to be partnered with a wearable computer called the Disney Magic Band, which enables users to verify all of the actions they have taken through the MyMagic+ system without carrying around receipts or other forms of proof. In addition, they can use the wearable Magic Band to make transactions while in the park. The benefits and convenience for visitors is obvious, but for Disney another big advantage is the amount of data it can collect on visitors' behavior and actions. These data better enable the firm to understand how to communicate with each customer and manage each relationship more effectively.[10] Yep—one-to-one marketing even within a massive theme park!

Disney's Magic Band is a wearable computer that allows visitors to interact with the theme park.

Characteristics of CRM

In addition to having a different mind-set, companies that successfully practice CRM have different goals, use different measures of success, and look at customers in some different ways from firms that do not. Followers of CRM look at four critical elements (see 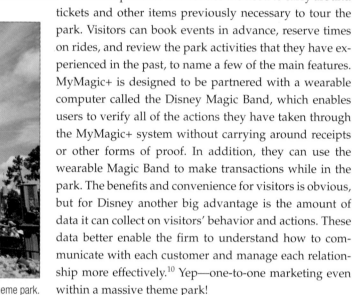 Figure 5.1): share of customer, lifetime value of a customer, customer equity, and customer prioritization. Let's have a look at each of these ideas now.

Figure 5.1 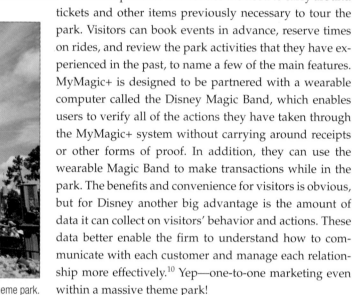 *Snapshot* |
Characteristics of CRM

Followers of CRM look at share of customer, lifetime value of a customer, customer equity, and customer prioritization.

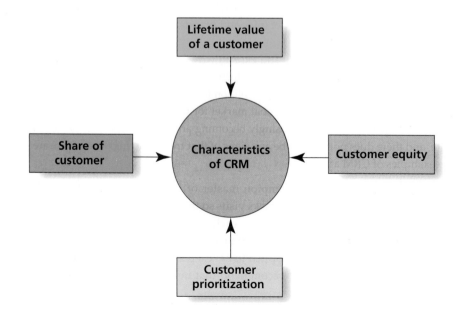

Share of Customer

Because it is always easier and less expensive to keep an existing customer than to get a new one, CRM firms try to increase their **share of customer**, not share of market; this is the percentage of an individual customer's purchase of a product over time that is the same brand. Let's say that a consumer buys six pairs of shoes a year—two pairs from each of three different manufacturers. Assume that one shoemaker has a CRM system that allows it to send letters to its current customers inviting them to receive a special price discount or a gift if they buy more of the firm's shoes during the year. If the firm can get the consumer to buy three or four or perhaps all six pairs from it, it has increased its *share of customer*. And that may not be too difficult because the customer already likes the firm's shoes. Without the CRM system, the shoe company would probably use traditional advertising to increase sales, which would be far more costly than the customer-only direct mail campaign. So the company can increase sales and profits at a much lower cost than it would spend to get one, two, or three new customers.

share of customer
The percentage of an individual customer's purchase of a product that is a single brand.

Lifetime Value of a Customer

As you'll recall from Chapter 1, the *lifetime value of a customer* represents how much profit a firm expects to make from a particular customer, including each and every purchase he or she will make from them now and in the future. Thus, this metric describes the potential profit that a single customer's purchase of a firm's products generates over the customer's lifetime. It just makes sense that a firm's profitability and long-term success will be far greater if it develops long-term relationships with its customers so that those customers buy from it again and again. Costs will be far higher and profits lower if each customer's purchase is a first-time sale. That's why we keep repeating this mantra: *It's much more profitable to retain an existing customer than to acquire a new one.*

How do marketers calculate the lifetime value of a customer? Using data from the CRM system, they first estimate a customer's future purchases across all products from the firm over the next 20 or 30 years. The goal is to try to figure out what profit the company could make from the customer in the future (obviously this will just be an estimate). For example, an auto dealer might calculate the lifetime value of a single customer by first calculating the total revenue the customer will generate for the company during his or her life. This figure includes the number of automobiles he will probably buy times their average price plus the service the dealership would provide over the years and even possibly the income from auto loan financing. The lifetime value of the customer would be the total profit the revenue stream generates.

customer equity
The financial value of a customer throughout the lifetime of the relationship.

Customer Equity

Today, an increasing number of companies consider their relationships with customers as financial assets. These firms measure success by calculating the value of their **customer equity**—the financial value of a customer throughout the lifetime of the relationship.[11] To do this, they compare the investments they make to acquire customers and then to retain them to the financial return they'll get on those investments.

Customer Prioritization

Using a CRM approach, the organization prioritizes its customers and customizes its communications to them accordingly. For example, any banker will tell you that not all customers are equal when it comes to profitability. Some generate a lot of revenue because they pay interest on loans or credit cards, while others simply use the bank as a convenient place to store a small amount of money and take out a little bit each week to buy beer. Banks use CRM systems to generate a profile of each customer based on factors such as value, risk, attrition, and interest in buying new

A bank's customers are not equal when it comes to profitability. Some use it primarily as a place to pick up cash for the weekend.

financial products. This automated system helps the bank decide which current or potential customers it will target with certain communications or how much effort it will expend to retain an account—all the while cutting its costs by as much as a third. It just makes sense to use different types of communication contacts based on the value of each individual customer. For example, personal selling (the most expensive form of marketing communication per contact) may constitute 75 percent of all contacts with high-volume customers, while direct mail or telemarketing is more often the best way to talk to low-volume customers.

Big Data
A popular term to describe the exponential growth of data—both structured and unstructured—in massive amounts that are hard or impossible to process using traditional database techniques.

APPLYING ▼ Big Data

Lisa knows that marketers are both consumers and generators of Big Data that allow them to gain insight and take action with consumers and buyers. She also recognized that offering Teradata's customers a combination of the firm's existing marketing applications along with Big Data and advanced analytics would provide greater value for customers and more success for Teradata.

Internet of Things
Describes a system in which everyday objects are connected to the Internet and in turn are able to communicate information throughout an interconnected system.

2

OBJECTIVE

Understand Big Data, data mining, and how marketers can put these techniques to good use.

(pp. 154–162)

Big Data: Terabytes Rule

CRM systems provide a great internal organizational data repository. But as more consumer experiences shift into the digital space and new means of connecting and interacting with both individuals and corporations becomes possible and widely accepted, it is no surprise that *Big Data* is becoming an increasingly important concept. You were briefly introduced to **Big Data** in Chapter 1, learning that it is the popular term to describe the exponential growth of data—both structured and unstructured—in massive amounts that are hard or impossible to process using traditional database techniques.

According to SAS, a leading provider of data analytics software, "Big Data refers to the ever-increasing volume, velocity, variety, variability and complexity of information."[12] Think about the amount of time that you spend online looking up information through search engines such as Google, connecting with friends through social media sites such as Facebook, listening to music on sites such as Pandora, or myriad other online activities that all of us engage in, and you'll begin to comprehend the sheer volume of data that we are (perhaps unwittingly) creating each and every day. Each action you take online leaves a digital imprint, and all of those imprints have the potential to yield valuable insights for a wide range of stakeholders within society. We see a successful application of Big Data when we look at the Oakland Athletics, a Major League Baseball team that used the analysis of large data sets to help identify undervalued players and make strategic decisions in games. In 2002, the Oakland Athletics won a record 20 games in a row thanks in part to their Big Data–driven strategy. You can even read about the team's Big Data–enabled exploits in the best-selling book *Moneyball* (also adapted into a major motion picture starring Brad Pitt).[13]

For marketers, Big Data has potential to provide competitive advantages in three main areas:

1. Identifying new opportunities through analytics that yield greater return on investment (ROI) on marketing efforts

2. Turning insights they gain into products and services that are better aligned with the desires of consumers

3. Delivering communications on products and services to the marketplace more efficiently and effectively

The amount of data that all of us produce does not appear to be slowing down either, as new technologies continue to enhance the ways we connect to people, machines, and organizations. The **Internet of Things** is a term that is increasingly used in articles and stories on technology trends to describe a system in which everyday objects are connected to the Internet and in turn are able to communicate information throughout an interconnected system.[14] Areas that would become part of this network include medical devices, cars, toys, video games—the list goes on and on. Within the context of

"Smart refrigerators" that can scan product codes are part of the "Internet of Things." It may not be long before your fridge will compile a shopping list for you as you run out of staples and even e-mail the grocery store to arrange for a delivery.

The **Cutting Edge**

Big Data Predicts Outbreaks of Infectious Diseases

You may have heard of Google Flu, which maps possible levels of flu activity around the world in real time—all based on search terms. You search for "flu symptoms," and Google assumes that you or someone you know is probably sick. Google then combines this information with other, similar searches in your area and, bam, your location gets added to the map as a known flu outbreak. Unfortunately, it turns out that Google Flu isn't all that accurate, mainly because people who think they have the flu and search for it actually tend to have something else, which skews the searches.[15] So is it possible to develop such a predictor? In a word, yes.

Enter BioMosaics, a new project that merges Big Data from three separate tools into a single app. BioMosaics combines airline records and disease reports with demographic data to help public health official visualize health risks, such as West Nile virus or SARS. With this information, health officials can then deploy preventive measures where they're most needed, be it cities, counties, or even hospitals.

For example, a cholera epidemic broke out after a major earthquake in Haiti in 2010. You might ask, "What does that have to do with the rest of the world?" Well, BioMosaics was able to show where Haitian-born residents in the U.S. were most likely to live, and, when combined with air and sea routes to and from Haiti, it could pinpoint where cholera outbreaks were possible in the U.S., making preventive measures possible.

"It really helps you get right to the heart of the matter: that concept that a global event in Haiti becomes a local event in five counties in Florida and five counties in New York," says Dr. Marty Cetron, who works for the Centers for Disease Control and Prevention and came up with the idea for the project. "When you see it, you get these aha! moments of appreciation."[16]

Now if only there were an app to help you feel better once you do get sick!

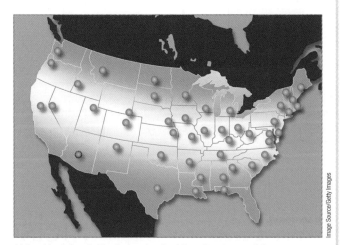

A Visual from Google Flu displays localized flu outbreaks on a U.S. map.

Big Data, this means that an even larger amount of data will be accessible, offering insight into the extent and ways in which everyday objects are being utilized and potentially allow for processes that were previously done manually to be automated.

For marketers, this interconnection of objects and collection of data could mean gaining insights into how we use products via data captured through sensors embedded in products that track a user's interaction with the product. This information would then be transmitted via an Internet connection at or near real time. Not only would this enable greater knowledge to be gained on how a product is used (which could be used to develop products and messaging more closely aligned with how consumers use that product), but also it could be done on a scale that traditional market research could achieve only through astronomical financial investments—essentially tracking the actions of each and every product user! So it's easy to begin to see how much data we would produce in a world where the Internet of Things has fully taken hold.

Big Data Creation, Sources, and Usage

The millions of pieces of information that make up Big Data originate from both direct and indirect paths. Here are two examples to illustrate how this works:

1. *Direct path:* You shop for a car online and see a model that you like. You submit a request for information form in which you supply personal information, including features of the car that appeal to you. That information is stored in the car dealership's database, and a salesperson pulls it up later on before she contacts you about the car.

2. *Indirect path:* On the other hand, data creation can be a by-product of another action. A company that uses Big Data might know, for example, that consumers who purchase green detergent products, register as Democrats, and hold college degrees are more likely than average to purchase a hybrid vehicle. A person who fits this profile might receive a communication about a Honda Prius or other hybrid car even though he or she has not (yet) specifically requested information about these vehicles.

Figure 5.2  *Snapshot* | Sources of Big Data for Marketers

Big Data can come from many sources. These sources can be both within and outside of the organization and created and compiled from different groups.

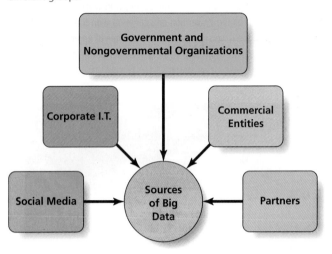

Some of the most important sources of Big Data for marketers are listed below and illustrated in  Figure 5.2:

1. *Social media sources:* With an increasing array of social media sites that boast large number of consumers interacting with each other, with brands, and with other entities, a wealth of information is being produced about how individuals feel about products and just about everything else in their lives. It is not uncommon today for consumers to either praise or condemn a product online. That information can be very valuable to marketers not only in terms of what they're saying but also in terms of the sorts of factors that triggered them to say it. Today, several companies engage in **Web scraping** (using computer software to extract large amounts of data from websites), **sentiment analysis** (a process of identifying a follower's attitude toward a brand by assessing the context or emotion of comments provided), and other cutting-edge techniques that involve analyzing and mapping millions of posts on Facebook, Twitter, and other social media platforms to track what people say about their experiences with products and services. They depict the themes in these posts visually so that managers can easily see the kinds of words customers use in

Web scraping
The process of using computer software to extract large amounts of data from websites.

sentiment analysis
The process of identifying a follower's attitude toward a brand by assessing the context or emotion of her comments.

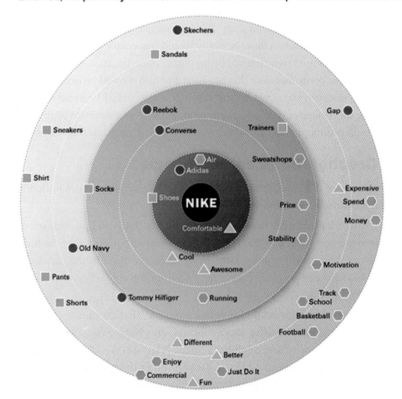

Nielsen's BAM (Brand Association Map) analyzes consumer conversations online and plots the words and phrases that most closely relate to a client's brand. The closer a word appears to the map's center, the stronger the association. And the proximity of words to each other also indicates the strength of their relationship in online posts.

Source: Courtesy of Nielsen

their posts. (Hint: If your brand's name appears a lot of time with terms like "awful" or "sucks," you probably have a problem.)

2. *Corporate I.T. sources:* 📷 Figure 5.3 provides a list of some of the different places and tools that are used to store corporate data. These sources that live within the organization might include CRM databases, back-end websites, Web analytic databases (e.g., Google Analytics), enterprise resource planning databases, and even accounting-related databases. Each of these and more can contain a treasure trove of information on an organization's consumers. Unfortunately, too often these systems live in departmental "silos"; one group in the company may not share this information with others in the firm, so each group gets only an incomplete picture of its customers. Hence, marketing needs to be the function within the organization that cuts across these groups in order to mine these databases and connect the dots.

Figure 5.3 📷 *Snapshot* | Examples of Corporate I.T. Sources

Corporate I.T. Data Sources

- **CRM Databases**
- **Backend Website Databases**
- **Web Analytic Databases**
- **ERP Databases**
- **Accounting Databases**

Corporate I.T. sources of data can span the entire organization or can be held by specific groups in an organization.

3. *Government and nongovernmental organization sources:* Provided by the government, these types of data could be most anything from extracted U.S. Census results to data on the economic conditions in developing countries that allow marketers to better understand the demographics of consumers at home and the opportunities for global expansion. Ever-increasing types and amounts of government-generated data that are accessible and machine readable will continue to provide new opportunities for enterprising marketers.[17]

4. *Commercial entity sources:* Many companies today collect data in large quantities to sell to organizations that can derive value from them. For some provider firms, this activity is their primary source of revenue; for others, it is a nice additional source of revenue over and above their principal business activities. For example (and this may or may not come as a surprise to you), many credit card companies, such as American Express and MasterCard, sell your purchase data to advertisers so that they can better target their ads. And supermarkets like Safeway for years have sold **scanner data**—data derived from all those items that are scanned at the cash register when you check out with your loyalty card (which just happens to have your demographic profile information in its record!). The data are sold in aggregated form so that it's not possible to identify the actions of a specific consumer, but scanner data still provide extremely useful information to both manufacturers and retailers about how much shoppers buy in different categories and which brands they choose.[18]

scanner data
Data derived from items that are scanned at the cash register when you check out with your loyalty card.

5. *Partner database sources:* In Chapter 11, you will read about different members of a channel of distribution. Many firms today have adopted a channel partner model in which there is a two-way exchange of information between purchasing organizations and their vendors through shared I.T. systems (more on channel relationships in Chapter 11). If you're the producer of a product that is sold by a large retailer such as Walmart, think about the information and insights you could gain from access to the consumer information that Walmart gathers from its interactions with shoppers in its stores.

Indeed, Walmart in particular is already well known for employing this approach through its vendor management system known as Retail Link, which provides real-time purchase data to suppliers, making it possible for them to track purchase data for their products in real time. Vendors are able manage the process of replenishment so that they can ensure that their products are available for consumers exactly when and where they need them. In addition, for marketers, this provides a valuable source of purchase data in real time that they can use to analyze purchase patterns within different Walmart locations. It also saves Walmart the costs of having to manage this process themselves.[19]

For organizations, being able to leverage large amounts of data to yield new insights and provide a clearer understanding of both consumers and internal business operations is a very attractive proposition and a potential source of competitive advantage. As we noted in the previous section, increased integration among organizations within supply chains that allows them to more efficiently track the movement of goods at every point in the supply chain all the way to the end user consumer helps to create a more efficient balance between supply and demand. Ultimately, this means cost savings that retailers can pass down to the consumer in the form of lower prices.

Marketers today have the tools at their disposal to develop complex automated correspondences with both current and potential customers via automated e-mail interactions using software that combines complex logic with data captured about the respective consumer. These communications can mirror the correspondences that a consumer might have with a salesperson or customer service representative by harnessing the data collected about the consumer prior to and even during the correspondence sequence. As more sources of data within an organization are integrated that contain different pieces of information, more complex interactions can be achieved that will even more closely mimic the interactions that a person might have with a knowledgeable "live" customer service representative or salesperson.

IBM's Watson computer is well known for having competed against and outsmarted a number of former *Jeopardy!* champions (trivia point for your future *Jeopardy!* appearance—the computer was named "Watson" after IBM's iconic founder Thomas J. Watson). The technology is capable of thinking in a way that is closer to how humans think by understanding the complexity of natural language, generating hypotheses based on evidence that Watson discovers, and continually learning over time.[20] Although it was certainly enjoyable to watch Watson best some of the brightest minds on *Jeopardy!*, it is also worth knowing about some of the real-world applications that IBM is developing based on this *intelligent agent* approach to machine learning. For instance, The North Face partnered with IBM to explore the possibility of using the Watson technology to develop a site in which Watson functions as a sort of shopping concierge capable of helping consumers identify the right products to purchase based on continually asking them questions and observing their actions. The technology in a sense would develop a relationship with each consumer and be able to learn from past interactions and purchases in order to better understand individual needs and then make appropriate proactive suggestions each time.[21] Who needs to hire a professional shopper when Watson is available 24/7?

Data Mining

For organizations today, the challenge with data is not about having enough but rather about determining what to do with all of the data it collects. Big Data can easily exacerbate the problem of **information overload**, in which the marketer is buried in so much data that it becomes nearly paralyzing to decide which of it provides useful information and which does not. Most *marketing information systems* include internal customer transaction databases, and many include acquired databases. Often, these databases are extremely large. To take advantage of the massive amount of data now available, a sophisticated analysis technique called **data mining** is now a priority for many firms. This refers to a process in which analysts sift through Big Data (often measured in terabytes—much larger than kilobytes or even gigabytes) to identify unique patterns of behavior among different customer groups. To give you a sense of the scale, 1 terabyte = 1,024 gigabytes!

In a marketing context, data mining uses computers that run sophisticated programs so that analysts can combine different databases to understand relationships among buying decisions, exposure to marketing messages, and in-store promotions. These operations are so complex that often companies need to build a **data warehouse** (which can cost more than $10 million) simply to store and process the data.[22] As you've no doubt read in the news because it can be controversial, marketers at powerful consumer data generators Google,

information overload
A state in which the marketer is buried in so much data that it becomes nearly paralyzing to decide which of the data provide useful information and which do not.

data mining
Sophisticated analysis techniques to take advantage of the massive amount of transaction information now available.

data warehouse
A system to store and process the data that result from data mining.

Yahoo!, Facebook, and Twitter are into data mining big time. For example, Yahoo! collects between 12 and 15 terabytes of data each day, and Facebook has access to valuable information that its over 50 million users post. Both firms want to use the data to facilitate targeted advertising by clients who are willing to pay big bucks to get their online ads in front of people who are likely to buy.[23]

Even cellular providers are into the data mining act. Signals among phones and base stations can be detected by commercial sensing devices. Recent U.S. Supreme Court action has supported the position that the detailed records of who is calling whom belong entirely to the phone companies. Right now, they make little use of such data, in part because they fear alienating subscribers who worry about privacy infringement. But cellular operators have begun signing deals with business partners who are eager to market products based on specific phone users' location and calling habits. Such **reality mining** is the collection and analysis of machine-sensed environmental data pertaining to human social behavior with the goal of identifying predictable patterns of behavior. It was declared to be one of the "10 technologies most likely to change the way we live" by *Technology Review Magazine*.[24] If reality mining catches on, phone companies' calling records will become precious assets. And these will only grow in value as customers use their phones to browse the Web, purchase products, and update their Facebook pages—and as marketers apply reality mining's tool kit to these activities.[25]

reality mining
The collection and analysis of machine-sensed environmental data pertaining to human social behavior with the goal of identifying predictable patterns of behavior.

data brokers
Companies that collect and sell personal information about consumers.

structured data
Data that (1) are typically numeric or categorical; (2) can be organized and formatted in a way that is easy for computers to read, organize, and understand; and (3) can be inserted into a database in a seamless fashion.

Ripped from the Headlines

Ethical/Sustainable Decisions in the Real World

When you sign up for a loyalty card at your favorite retailer, you are giving away your personal information. When you like a product or company on Facebook, you are again giving up information about yourself. And when you make a purchase online—you guessed it. Meanwhile, data brokers are having a field day.

Data brokers are companies that collect and sell personal information about consumers, including their religion, ethnicity, user names, income, the medications they take, and more. And while companies and marketers have collected such information for years, with the popularity of the Internet, where you volunteer personal information on practically a daily basis, data brokers are able to collect more information about you than ever before. Have you downloaded the Angry Birds app or the Brightest Flashlight Free app? If so, you probably didn't know these apps were tracking your movements and selling them to other companies. According to Federal Trade Commissioner Julie Brill, "Your smartphones are basically little mini tracking devices. And it's collecting information about where you are traveling through the day."[26] Such information is a hot commodity to data brokers.

Data brokers then buy and sell such data from other data brokers to generate ever more detailed profiles of you, most often without your knowledge. Acxiom, the largest of the data brokers, acknowledges that it has, on average, 1,500 piece of information, or data points, on more

than 200 million Americans. Want to get a glimpse into some of the things the company knows about you? Go to **www.aboutthedata.com** and prepare to be surprised.

In many cases, the collection of this information all boils down to a question of consumer privacy. For example, Target used data it had collected about female consumers to determine whether these customers were pregnant. In one case, the data were too accurate—a girl still in high school received coupons for baby clothes and cribs. Her father, who was initially outraged at the mailer and at Target, later found out from his teenage daughter that she was indeed pregnant.[27]

Other companies use such information to recruit for clinical trials. Blue Chip Marketing Worldwide found 9,000 patients whom its client needed to participate in a trial for a diet drug. By applying an algorithm to consumer profiles it had purchased, Blue Chip was able to flag clues about a person's weight by identifying fast-food dining habits and a history of shopping online for clothes.[28] (That's one way to get around the Health Insurance Portability and Accountability Act, which prevents health care providers from sharing or selling personally identifiable information about patients.)

Still, the fact is that consumers leave clues about their health—and more—everywhere they go. But do others have a right to collect and profit from this information? What ethical issues arise in such cases?

ETHICS CHECK:
Find out what other students taking this course *would do* and *why* at **mymktlab.com**.

Should it be legal for companies to collect and sell your personal information without your knowledge?

☐ YES ☐ NO

Primary Data Types for Data Mining

As data mining techniques improve and software becomes more adept at understanding and analyzing information in its various formats, the ability to gain deeper insights about consumers from data is increasing. Data in electronic format can be considered either structured or unstructured. **Structured data** are what you might find in an Excel spreadsheet or in a statistics table on a sports website such as ESPN.com. Such data: are typically either numeric or categorical; usually are organized and formatted in a way that is easy for computers

Figure 5.4 *Process* | Structured and Unstructured Data Examples

Far more unstructured data than structured data are created on a daily basis through different business processes, but both have the potential to offer marketers greater insights into their customers and markets.

Structured Data	Unstructured Data
• Date	• Body of Emails
• Time	• Tweets
• Census Data	• Facebook Status Update Messages
• Facebook "Likes"	• Video Transcripts

unstructured data
Nonnumeric information that is typically formatted in a way that is meant for human eyes and not easily understood by computers.

to read, organize, and understand; can be inserted into a database in a seamless fashion; and typically can be easily placed within rows and columns.

Unstructured data contain nonnumeric information that is typically formatted in a way that is meant for human eyes and not easily understood by computers.[29] A good example of unstructured data is the body of an e-mail message. The e-mail carries a lot of meaning to a human but poses a greater challenge for a machine to understand or organize. Figure 5.4 lists other examples of different types of structured and unstructured data.

In the past, data mining and data analysis were focused on structured data because computers could easily analyze a large number of data points at one time. For instance, a baseball statistician can put into a computer all of the "at bats" that a player has had throughout the course of a season along with their outcomes and easily tell the computer to predict his batting average for the year (as well as a number of other useful measures). This output yields a better understanding of each player's performance on the field.

It becomes more challenging—but also potentially more interesting—to derive meaning from large quantities of *unstructured* data. For instance, imagine that you are the social media manager for a company that sells candy bars and you spend a lot of time engaging with customers through Facebook and Twitter. You are lucky to have a lot of likes and followers and a high level of interaction as well, but you're not satisfied with these data and believe that this is only the tip of the iceberg. In addition, you know that all of these comments from your customers could be a source of a lot of great information—the only problem is that there are thousands of them flooding in, and you're only one person. How could you possibly find the time to effectively analyze their contents and discern valuable patterns from all of this information? Even a huge team would have significant challenges trying to cull through the vast amount of unstructured data customers create every day when they talk about different companies online.

Technology to the rescue! Significant advances in data-analytic technologies make the process of unstructured data analysis easier through the development of computer logic that can search through and extract patterns from large amounts of textual data. It also makes it more cost effective through the use of automated processes as opposed to manual intervention (imagine having to sift through every message by hand to pull out and record the information that you believed was meaningful).[30] The other advantage is that these types of technologies give unstructured data a "structure," enabling it to be shared and leveraged when combining it with data sources held elsewhere in an organization. Being able to leverage both structured and unstructured data in data mining efforts offers marketers the opportunity to gain a deeper understanding of their customers.

Data Scientists: Transforming Big Data into Winning Information

In Chapter 4, we talked about the important role of customer insights to marketing decision making. Being able to transform data into insights and leveraging data to enhance the way that organizations interact with consumers is a really challenging proposition. It is one that is executed by analysts with the help of powerful databases and complex software. These analysts (also known as business intelligence developers or data scientists) are employed by the biggest names in technology. A **data scientist** is someone who searches through multiple, disparate data sources in order to discover hidden insights that will provide a competitive advantage.[31] These individuals frequently have PhDs, often command six-figure starting salaries (according to Glassdoor.com, the median salary as of 2014 was $115,000), and are becoming an increasingly important source of competitive advantage for organizations that want to leverage Big Data. Traditional data analysts often looked at one data source, whereas data scientists typically look at multiple sources of data across the organization.[32]

If you have ever used LinkedIn, you'll be interested to learn that one of the most frequently used features on the site was developed through experimentation by one of the organization's data scientists named Jonathan Goldman. Specifically, Goldman developed the "People You May Know" feature on the site, where LinkedIn users whom you may know in real life are shown three profiles at a time. Goldman accomplished this by developing a way to assess and score users based on common elements, such as shared tenures at educational institutions, and then sorting the profiles displayed through the feature from the highest to the lowest scores (to a limit). The idea was originally implemented as an advertisement on the site to generate interest in the message. Sure enough, the site's managers discovered that this feature had a click rate that was 30 percent higher than average. Soon after that, top management within the organization signed off on adding "People You May Know" as a standard feature.[33]

These and many other insights exemplify what data scientists are able to generate and the value they can yield for organizations. As more data become available from multiple sources, organizations will most likely continue to need people with the skill and curiosity to transform data into information (any interest on your part in being a data scientist?).

Data Mining: Applications for Marketers

A key theme of this chapter and the previous chapter is that better understanding of both current and potential customers should be a central goal for all marketers. Every interaction the firm has with a consumer—every touchpoint, regardless of which department might facilitate the interaction—can provide valuable information for marketers to leverage. Data mining techniques that enhance the value of Big Data provide opportunities for marketers to increase organizational performance. To help identify the data needed for these efforts and bring them together, organizations often assemble teams of individuals from different functions, such as marketing, sales, in-store operations, and I.T. to help identify and gather the needed data sources for analysis.[34]

As illustrated in 📷 Figure 5.5, data mining has four important applications for marketers:[35]

1. *Customer acquisition:* Many firms include demographic and other information about customers in their database. For example, a number of supermarkets offer weekly special price discounts for store "members." These stores' membership application forms require that customers indicate their age, family size, address, and so on. With this information, the supermarket determines which of its current customers respond best to specific offers and then sends the same offers to noncustomers who share the same demographic characteristics.

2. *Customer retention and loyalty:* The firm identifies big-spending customers and then targets them for special offers and inducements other customers won't receive. Keeping the most profitable customers coming back is a great way to build business success because—here we go again!—keeping good customers is less expensive than constantly finding new ones.[36]

data scientist
An individual who searches through multiple, disparate data sources in order to discover hidden insights that will provide a competitive advantage.

Figure 5.5 📷 *Snapshot* | Uses of Data Mining

Data mining has four primary applications for marketers.

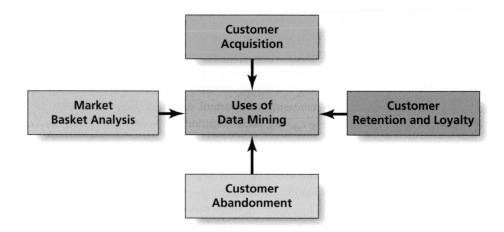

3. *Customer abandonment:* Strange as it may sound, sometimes a firm wants customers to take their business elsewhere because servicing them actually costs the firm too much. Today, this is popularly called "firing a customer." For example, a department store may use data mining to identify unprofitable customers—those who don't spend enough or who return most of what they buy. Data mining has allowed Sprint to famously identify its customers as "the good, the bad, and the ugly."[37]

4. *Market basket analysis:* Develops focused promotional strategies based on the records of which customers have bought certain products. Hewlett-Packard, for example, carefully analyzes which of its customers recently bought new printers and targets them to receive e-mails about specials on ink cartridges and tips to get the most out of their machines.

3 Marketing Analytics

OBJECTIVE

Describe what marketing analytics include and how organizations can leverage both marketing analytics and predictive analytics to improve marketing performance.
(pp. 162–166)

marketing analytics

A group of technologies and processes that enable marketers to collect, measure, analyze, and assess the effectiveness of marketing efforts.

Marketing analytics have become an increasingly important part of a marketer's toolbox as technological advances enable consumers to engage in an increasing number of activities online that were previously possible only within the physical space. At its core, **marketing analytics** comprises a group of technologies and processes that enable marketers to collect, measure, analyze, and assess the effectiveness of marketing efforts. Marketing analytic solutions provide marketers with a holistic means of looking at the performance of different marketing initiatives.[38] They are capable of providing a level of analysis and a degree of accuracy and speed that is crucial in our data-driven world. Put simply, then, marketing analytics takes the Big Data and makes sense out of it for use in marketing decision making! That is, the breadth and depth of information that today's marketers have at their disposal require the ability to leverage technology that can move through massive and often disparate data sets to provide useful information that can power decisions and help marketers better understand the value of their investments.

There's an old saying among marketers credited to John Wanamaker, a famous Philadelphia retailer of the late 1800s, that goes, "Half the money I spend on advertising is wasted; the trouble is, I don't know which half." The issue that this quote highlights—the need to be able to tie specific actions in advertising to measurable results (such as sales)—has been a long-standing challenge for marketers, and especially for those who have spent money on TV advertising, billboards, and other forms of traditional advertising, there is a real challenge in quantifying the value of those efforts. You may have seen a TV advertisement for

McDonald's featuring a Big Mac and chosen the next day to purchase one because of the advertisement, but how would anyone else know that it was that advertisement as opposed to any of the other marketing investments that McDonald's has made? Enabling marketers to get a better sense through marketing analytics of what the ROI of each of their marketing channels is makes digital marketing an increasingly attractive option.

Connect Digital Marketing Channels to Marketing Analytics

One of the perennial primary challenges of marketers in the past (and still today) is being able to determine the effectiveness of different marketing campaigns and channels. This is because it is not always clear where a lead came from or what led to a purchase by a consumer without being able to track it from its origin. For instance, did a consumer learn about and ultimately purchase a product because of the commercial he or she saw on TV or because of the ad he or she viewed in a magazine, or perhaps both? For traditional media such as TV and magazines, it is still not always clear what actions yield the greatest impact for the marketer. However, with the proliferation of digital media and digital marketing channels, it has become more straightforward to understand what actions on the part of marketers drive consumers to ultimately make a decision that aligns with the interests of the organization.

For example, if a marketer places a banner ad on a website for a product and a user clicks on that ad (bringing up the product's page on the website), where he or she ultimately purchases the product, marketers have the ability to trace that process directly back to the banner ad. All of those data can be captured digitally, and the marketer can gain assurance that his or her organization is getting satisfactory ROI for the ad. Better yet, the marketer can now measure that investment relative to its cost and identify how the company might make further improvements.

In order to understand the value that marketing analytics offers to organizations, it is important to recognize how much the way that we ingest information has changed over time. With more individuals having access to and spending time on the Internet, digital marketing has become an increasingly important element of the marketer's toolbox. According to a survey conducted by Pew Research Center, 86 percent of Americans use the Internet (up from 14 percent in 1995), and 73 percent of Americans use at least one social networking site, with 42 using multiple social networking sites.[39]

Across the globe, more people use the Internet for an increasingly wider array of purposes. Who knows how many more functions will be made faster, easier, or more intuitive as developers continually introduce new apps. A survey by Gartner, a leading I.T. research and consulting firm, noted that in 2014, digital marketing budgets would increase by 10 percent, following up on a double-digit increase in digital marketing budgets for 2013. The data were compiled based on a survey conducted of respondents who answered for their organizations. Especially enlightening is the finding that 11 percent of those respondents noted that more than half of their budget was dedicated to digital marketing.[40]

The options for investment in digital marketing channels are diverse with consumers spending large amounts across a variety of options. 📷 Figure 5.6 illustrates the four major groupings of different digital marketing channels: social media, pay-per-click advertisements, search engines, and Email.

Figure 5.6 📷 *Snapshot* | Major Digital Marketing Channels

Digital marketing channels are typically broken up into four main categories. Within these, there are multiple types of marketing efforts and campaigns that marketers can develop and track.

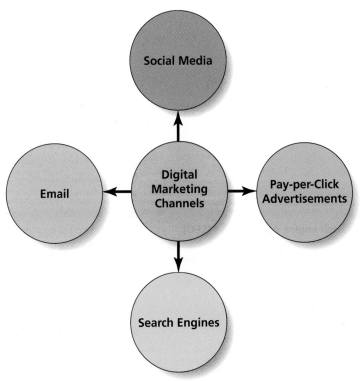

cost-per-click
An online ad purchase in which the cost of the advertisement is charged only each time an individual clicks on the advertisement and is directed to the Web page that the marketer placed within the advertisement.

cost-per-impression
An online ad purchase in which the cost of the advertisement is charged each time the advertisement shows up on a page that the user views.

Note that we will discuss digital advertising options that are available to marketers in detail in Chapter 13. For all of these entities, there is a lot of money to be made through the selling of advertising space to organizations. Facebook, which is used by over a billion people, offers users the ability to create a profile for free, but its business model relies heavily on being able to generate revenue through the selling of advertisements on the site. Increasingly, social networking sites are looking for creative ways to provide advertisements on their sites in a way that does not turn off users. The objective is to create a source of value for organizations that does not compromise the website's user experience and relevance.

For marketers, investments in digital marketing are especially attractive because their cost is often directly tied to specific actions users take. For instance, Google's paid search ads can be purchased or bid on based on a **cost-per-click** in which the cost of the advertisement is charged only each time an individual clicks on the advertisement and is directed to the Web page that the marketer placed within the advertisement. This method of charging for advertisements is common for online vendors of advertisement space. Other methods of purchasing advertisements digitally include **cost-per-impression**, in which the cost of the advertisement is charged each time the advertisement shows up on a page that the user views.

Companies that sell online advertising space commonly use both of these methods of charging for advertisements. Cost-per-click purchases of advertisements are typically more expensive, as they demand a higher level of interaction from the user (i.e., the users have actually visited the page on which the ad appears and hence are one step closer to becoming a customer). Cost-per-impression purchases of advertisements can provide a good value. However, advertisements that are purchased with a cost-per-impression structure typically require a greater leap of faith because it's not so easy to measure the value of an impression (or view of an advertisement). For instance, if a marketer knew (or had a good idea) that a certain number of impressions from an advertisement translated into a specific number of clicks, then he or she would be able more accurately estimate the cost of the ad in terms of clicks even while using a cost-per-impression structure to price advertisements. In this way, the marketer would be able to obtain a better value through cost-per-impression pricing as opposed to cost-per-click pricing.

One advantage of digital marketing is that data come in at the speed at which data travel, which is almost instantaneous. This means that marketers can track the performance of digital marketing initiatives and determine their performance both in the very short term and over the long term. Marketing analytics enable them to capture these data across all of the channels in which they have invested and present the data in a way that provides valuable insights into the performance of each channel.

Determine the Value of Digital Marketing Investments across Channels

Imagine you have an e-commerce website selling specialty headphones and you have begun to invest in attracting new customers to your website. You've purchased some online banner advertisements that are being strategically shown to individuals who visit different music websites, and you've also purchased some ads on Facebook that are showing up as sponsored posts in people's feeds who frequently "like" different indie rock bands' pages. You've even looked into **search engine optimization (SEO)**, which is a systematic process of ensuring that your firm comes up at or near the top of lists of typical search phrases related to your business. As a result, you've hired a SEO specialist to help ensure that your website ranks highly on search engines such as Google and Bing when people type in search phrases such as "high-quality headphones" and "best way to listen to music."

Now that you have invested in your different marketing channels, you start to see that sales are increasing. It seems as though your investment in all of these different digital

search engine optimization (SEO)
A systematic process of ensuring that your firm comes up at or near the top of lists of typical search phrases related to your business.

marketing channels is paying off, but what if some are paying off more than others because their efforts are engaging more effectively with your target audience and in turn helping to create more sales? How would you determine this? Answer: Marketing analytics would enable you to analyze the performance of all of these channels to help you make the best investment of your marketing dollars moving forward. To understand what's really working on your e-commerce site, you might look to see whether more sales come from your customers who arrive at your site because they typed a search term into Google or whether those who come there because they clicked on a Facebook ad spend more. Or you might find that the banner advertisements bring in relatively few customers and that the transactions they make are relatively small. If you compare the average cost per customer transaction from each of these channels against the average value of the customer transaction from each channel, it would become clear which channel provides your e-commerce site with the most value. You might even discover that one of these channels costs more than it wins in sales!

Without marketing analytics and data produced by digital marketing initiatives, this would have been more challenging to determine, and as a result there would have been more waste within your e-commerce site's marketing mix. These are the types of challenging questions that companies such as Zappos.com and Overstock.com deal with every day as they look to ensure that their marketing investments provide a healthy ROI. Marketing analytics help them to better understand how their different marketing channels are performing.

It is worth noting that some caution can be beneficial when we examine marketing analytics data. For example, suppose an individual sees a TV advertisement for a product and decides to go online to learn more about it. At that point, he comes across a banner advertisement online that includes a coupon for the product. Then he clicks on the banner advertisement to redeem the coupon and buy the product. On the surface, to a marketer it might look as though all of the credit for the sale should go to the banner advertisement because the marketer has no awareness of the influence that the TV advertisement has had on the consumer, but, as we can see, that is not entirely accurate. The risk illustrated here is the misappropriation of the value that one particular effort has had in delivering a specific result.

Being able to determine the effectiveness of digital marketing depends on having clear goals that can be tracked and measured. In the case of an e-commerce site, the defined goal would most likely be a transaction with a consumer. However, for a business consulting company's website, it might be getting a prospective client to submit a request for information about what the consulting company can do to help with their particular problem. And being able to tie these data into a CRM system that tracks the individual from the point of filling out a request for information to when he or she ultimately becomes a customer enables the company to look back at the specific digital marketing initiative that motivated that customer to come to the website in the first place, providing greater insight into what particular channels and factors help create new business.

This example serves to illustrate how different pieces of Big Data—in the form of the comprehensive information about a customer that resides in different parts of the organization (in this case, in the CRM system along with what is currently captured in the marketing analytics system for Web-based interactions)—can be brought together. Through the use of marketing analytics, these data can be transformed into a more complete picture of each customer as well as each marketing channel in order to better understand where future investments should be made or how current marketing campaigns should be adjusted. Understanding each customer's full story enables marketers to better understand how to weave their own actions and communications into the fabric of that story in a way that is meaningful and compelling.

Predictive Analytics

Up to this point, we've looked how marketing analytics can be leveraged to better understand how *current* marketing channels and initiatives are performing—in other words, to understand how to validate the value of what decisions have already been made and potentially create fact-based triggers that will enable a marketer to better determine how to make future investments. Another intriguing area for any marketer is the ability to actually *predict* the future and thus better understand the value of their marketing campaigns even *before* they implement them. A harbinger of such clairvoyance came in the form of a highly publicized patent application by Amazon for a process it calls "anticipatory package shipping." The idea is to develop a data driven system that will allow for starting delivery of packages even before customers click "buy." Essentially, Amazon will be able to box and ship products it expects customers in a specific area will want but for which a specific customer order has not actually yet been placed. Getting the right goods moving like this could cut delivery time and thus dissuade customers from visiting brick-and-mortar retailers instead of shopping online.[41]

predictive analytics
Uses large quantities of data within variables that have identified relationships to more accurately predict specific future outcomes.

This crystal-ball scenario is where **predictive analytics** can increasingly provide significant value to marketers. These techniques use large quantities of data and variables that the analysts know relate to one another to more accurately predict specific *future* outcomes (the key with "predictive" analytics is this focus on the future, not just the present).[42] To return to our earlier example, we may be able to make a very highly educated guess that a consumer will strongly consider the purchase of a hybrid vehicle. We can estimate this event even though we know nothing about his or her prior history of car buying—*if* we know enough about other things he or she buys and we can establish a pattern.

Now, organizations have used these techniques for decades in order to help forecast sales and other important measures of business performance and outcomes, but don't fool yourself into thinking there's nothing new or exciting within this area. Thanks to Big Data and the new-age data mining capabilities we've discussed, the types of future outcomes that can be predicted and the level of accuracy possible with those predictions now enables marketers to obtain more accuracy than ever before when they forecast successful future marketing investments.

Vodafone Netherlands is the second-largest mobile carrier in the Netherlands, and predictive analytics solutions seemed to be a strong choice to better understand the behavior of their customers and better predict future behaviors. As the organization's senior information architect for business intelligence noted, "We have a reasonably large number of customers, a limited marketing budget, and the need to understand how to apply the money effectively and get the best results."[43] Vodafone had a wealth of information and wanted to have the capabilities to identify opportunities in order to more effectively predict consumer behavior and better tailor service offerings to consumers based on the information. One way that Vodafone was able to create value from predictive analytics was through the understanding of winter roaming patterns and, in particular, which of their customers were most likely to go skiing. Through the firm's analysis, they were better able to identify and predict which customers would fall within the category of going skiing in the winter and target them exclusively with a campaign that was tailored to offer great value for winter roamers. What if they had they reached out with this offering to customers within their base who did not fall within this group? Most likely, it would have been a disaster, including not only additional costs but also potentially aggravated customers who felt they were being unnecessarily bothered (Marketing Rule #1: Never upset your current profitable customers). For phone carriers such as Vodafone, as well as most all marketers, finding that sweet spot of providing valuable services to customers when they are needed by those particular customers who would most appreciate them is mission critical in today's global competitive marketplace. Predictive analytics and marketing analytics in general enable great execution of marketing strategies.

marketing metrics
Specific measures that help marketers watch the performance of their marketing campaigns, initiatives, and channels and, when appropriate, serve as a control mechanism.

4

OBJECTIVE

Identify how organizations can use marketing metrics to measure performance and achieve marketing control.

(pp. 167–168)

Metrics for Marketing Control

Throughout this chapter and also at different points throughout the text, we touch on different types of metrics and the benefit they provide to marketers (e.g., the "Metrics Moment" features in each chapter and the "Apply the Metrics" exercises at the end of each chapter). In a data-rich and data-driven world, organizations have the ability to gain a more detailed understanding than ever before of what's going on both inside and outside their operations. For marketers, this means having the ability to show more clearly a return on their various investments and to use this knowledge to develop and execute marketing plans and strategies. **Marketing metrics** are specific measures that help marketers keep an eye on the performance of their marketing campaigns, initiatives, and channels and, when appropriate, serve as a control mechanism for when corrective action is necessary. **Marketing control** means the ability to identify deviations in expected performance, both positive and negative, as soon as they occur, thus enabling marketers to adjust their actions before greater losses or inefficiencies are realized. Another

marketing control
The ability to identify deviations in expected performance, both positive and negative, as soon as they occur.

click-through
A metric that indicates the percentage of website users who have decided to click on an advertisement in order to visit the website or Web page associated with it.

conversion
Signifies an event that occurs on a Web page that indicates the meeting of a predefined goal associated with the consumer's interaction with that page.

cost-per-order
The cost of gaining an order in terms of the marketing investment made to turn a website visitor into a customer who has chosen to make a transaction.

Metrics Moment

Three Examples of Metrics

Here are three great examples of metrics that are relevant to a chapter on Big Data and marketing analytics. In them, the following symbols are used: $ = a monetary figure, % = a percentage figure, and # = a figure in units. Table 5.2 provides a summary of the metrics listed below as a point of reference.

Click-Through Rate

Within digital marketing, the **click-through** rate is a metric that indicates the percentage of users (viewers of the advertisement or the page that the link is on) who have decided to click on the advertisement in order to visit the website or Web page associated with the advertisement:[44]

Click-through rate (%) = (Click-throughs (#)/Impressions (#)) × 100

Most digital marketing campaigns or initiatives use click-through rates as a means of determining marketing effectiveness. Specifically, they indicate what percentage of users who viewed the ad found it relevant and interesting enough to click on it in order to be redirected to another Web page. However, from that point of landing on the Web page or website, the visitor could have chosen to immediately leave the Web page due to a lack of interest in the content on the page or for some other reason. Other metrics taken in tandem with click-through rates can provide a more complete picture.

Conversion Rate

A popular metric used to look at the effectiveness of digital marketing is the conversion rate, which is expressed as a percentage. A **conversion** based on a consumer's interaction with a Web page might be the purchase of a product or a service (or multiple purchases in one sitting), the choice to sign up for a mailing list, or the decision to become a follower of the company via social media.[45] The conversion rate is calculated by taking the number of visitors to a website who complete the identified desired activity and dividing that by the total number of visitors to the website and then multiplying the result by 100 to arrive at percentage value:

Conversion rate (%) = (Number of goal achievements/Number of website visitors) × 100

Conversion rate can be tracked on a day-to-day basis or provided as a cumulative value and tied back to different marketing campaigns or channels in order to measure the impact of those activities and to answer questions, such as what is bringing customer to your site. It can also alert marketers to opportunities to take corrective action in order to improve the performance of their marketing efforts.

Cost-per-Order

Cost-per-order indicates the cost of gaining an order in terms of the marketing investment made to turn a visitor to a website into a customer who has chosen to make a transaction.[46] Within digital marketing, this metric can be broken down by specific campaigns or marketing channels to help marketers to get a more precise idea of how effective their marketing investments are:

Cost-per-order ($) = Advertising costs ($)/Orders (#)

For marketers, it provides a clearer idea of what the average cost in advertising dollars is to generate an order. For instance, one might learn that Facebook ads have a lower cost per order than YouTube video ads, and as a result more resources are directed toward Facebook.

Apply the Metrics

Consider the information generated by calculating click-through rate, conversion rate, and cost per order.

1. How does knowledge of the results of calculating these three aid marketers in making better investment decisions in Web strategies?
2. Do you think one of these metrics is more useful than the others? If so, what leads you to this opinion?

reason digital marketing is seeing increased growth in investment from marketers is the speed at which they can modify their investments in different media channels. For example, a charitable organization that detects an unusually high flow of donations from a Facebook campaign can almost instantly shift more resources to that channel to capitalize on the sudden interest.

Before we dive into marketing metrics, one point worth making is that it is typically not practical to use too many metrics at once to measure marketing effectiveness. Identifying the right metrics that are aligned with the desired outcomes of your marketing strategies ensures that the right controls are in place and that the organization focuses on aligning the most important outcomes with its marketing decisions.

For instance, imagine you're the CMO for a laundry detergent producer. In order to bring in more business, you have decided to give your team full latitude to use the department's resources to ramp up sales. You tell them that they are going to be judged by their ability to increase the number of detergent bottles sold. In the following few weeks, you're pleased to see that the detergent seems to be flying off of supermarket shelves. But on further inspection, you also learn that despite the surge in sales, profits have not increased. As it turns out, your marketing team has been saturating the market with coupons for half-off detergent bottles, and this price promotion is what drove the influx of business. You console yourself that, although profits may not have been positively impacted due to the reduced prices people are paying for the brand, surely this effort will bring in more business over the *long run* as new customers try the brand because they received a coupon. Unfortunately, the marketing team did not do an effective job of targeting new customers. It turns out that the shoppers who redeemed the coupons were primarily regulars (existing users) of the product who just bought as they normally would but at a reduced price. As a result, sales actually decline over the next month. The reason: Customers who stocked up on laundry detergent in the past month continue to use their reserves of the product they purchased at a promotional price! Had the goals of the effort been more clearly defined and the right metrics selected related to both gaining market share and increasing sales, then perhaps a more targeted approach with better controls could have been implemented.

Why do you think Lisa choose option 2?

Here's What Happened at Teradata Corporation

Lisa chose option 2. Based on both qualitative and quantitative research, it became clear that there was a real opportunity to satisfy the market and to drive short-term revenue if Aprimo released the new cloud product first and then focused on rebranding the entire company. Aprimo needed to know how its new product would compare against others in the market and how to differentiate its offering. Lisa's team, which included internal brand experts and an agency, analyzed category competitors' brands and offerings to determine where best to position the cloud product. This analysis resulted in a brand promise the team labeled "change navigators." As she interacted with people in the industry, Lisa also realized that the traditional term *enterprise marketing management* wasn't a good label to convey what the new product would offer to the target audience. This term conveyed the idea of "big and heavy," highly complex software, which was the opposite of the simplicity marketers wanted from the cloud. The company's researchers discovered that if Teradata simply substituted the word *integrated* for *enterprise*, customers would feel much better about the offering. This insight led Lisa's team to develop a new category it called *integrated marketing management (IMM)* that Teradata could offer to clients. The revised description encouraged CMOs and their terms who truly wanted to integrate marketing—its processes, its technology data, and its people—to think about Aprimo's services in terms of a forward-looking cloud-based technology option for all of their organization's marketing needs.

Teradata's new website was a key component of Lisa's brand relaunch strategy.

Lisa's team launched the cloud product at a major industry trade show, even as they continued to apply the data from their research to the creative development of the Teradata brand. The team followed the show with a media and analyst tour to communicate the new direction the brand was heading and to solicit feedback from industry thought leaders. This groundwork allowed the team to relaunch the Teradata brand at the Aprimo Marketing Summit, which is the company's major customer conference. The relaunch took the form of a visually impactful, emotion-based branding and repositioning campaign known as "The Marketing Revolution."

The market took notice. Analysts described the visuals as "arresting" and "visceral," and the launch captured the market's attention. A major analyst firm welcomed the new approach so much that it renamed its annual category research report "Integrated Marketing Management." Teradata was well positioned as the thought leader in this emerging IMM space within 10 months of the relaunch.

How Teradata Measures Success

Lisa developed a six-prong scorecard to measure the following:

- *Demand generation:* Based on marketing qualified leads.
- *Customer satisfaction:* Based on a NetPromoterScore (as an aside, *everyone* in the company had their compensation tied to this metric, not just marketing).
- *Sales productivity:* Based on conversions, that is, moving from identified opportunities to closed business/wins.
- *Market leadership:* The team benchmarked brand awareness (aided and unaided) in the industry.
- *Marketing effectiveness:* This metric was measured on the health of the outcomes of the four categories and on measuring the return on marketing investment.
- *Return on marketing investment:* The team tracked the demand generation spend and then the value it brought in from revenue.

Refer back to **page 168** for Lisa's story ▶

MyMarketingLab™

Go to **mymktlab.com** to complete the problems marked with this icon ⬤ as well as additional Marketing Metrics questions only available in MyMarketingLab.

Objective Summary ➡ Key Terms ➡ Apply

1. Objective Summary (pp. 150–154)

Explain how marketers increase long-term success and profits by practicing customer relationship management.

Companies using CRM programs establish relationships and differentiate their behavior toward individual customers on a one-to-one basis through dialogue and feedback. Success is often measured one customer at a time using the concepts of share of customer, lifetime value of the customer, and customer equity. In CRM strategies, customers are prioritized according to their value to the firm, and communication is customized accordingly. CRM also provides marketers with the means to better tailor their communications to customers based on the wealth of data that is being effectively captured and organized within the system.

Key Terms

customer relationship management (CRM), p. 150

one-to-one marketing, p. 150

touchpoint, p. 150

share of customer, p. 153

customer equity, p. 153

2. Objective Summary (pp. 154–162)

Understand Big Data, data mining, and how marketers can put these techniques to good use.

Big Data refers to data that are growing in terms of both volume and velocity. It comes from a wider range of sources within different functions within organizations as well as society at large. Big Data offers marketers the ability to gain a deeper understanding of their customers when properly leveraged through methods such as data mining. When marketers utilize data mining, they methodically sift through large data sets using computers that run sophisticated programs to understand relationships among things like consumer buying decisions, exposure to marketing messages, and in-store promotions. Data mining leads to the ability to make important decisions about which customers to invest in further, which to abandon, and where the greatest opportunities for new investments lie.

Key Terms

Big Data, p. 154

Internet of Things, p. 154

Web scraping, p. 156

sentiment analysis, p. 156

scanner data, p. 157

information overload, p. 158

data mining, p. 158

data warehouse, p. 158

reality mining, p. 159

data brokers, p. 159

structured data, p. 159

unstructured data, p. 160

data scientist, p. 161

3. Objective Summary (pp. 162–166)

Describe what marketing analytics include and how organizations can leverage both marketing analytics and predictive analytics to improve marketing performance.

Marketing analytics offer marketers the means of better understanding and analyzing the wealth of data that are now at their disposal. With the proliferation of digital marketing and the speed at which data can be captured and analyzed, marketers are able to gain insights at or near real time in regard to the performance of their marketing investments. This capability to analyze across channels the performance of their different marketing initiatives provides a means through which to more precisely identify *where value is being created*. Predictive analytics have the potential to help marketers identify outcomes before they occur and in turn make smarter decisions as they plan marketing campaigns and investments.

Key Terms

marketing analytics, p. 162

cost-per-click, p. 164

cost-per-impression, p. 164

search engine optimization (SEO), p. 164

predictive analytics, p. 166

4. Objective Summary (pp. 167–168)

Identify how organizations can use marketing metrics to measure performance and achieve marketing control.

Marketing metrics provide marketers with the means to further understand the performance of their marketing campaigns and channels and a means of identifying potential red flags or opportunities as they arise. Increases in the popularity of digital marketing as well as tools that are able to easily capture data online have enabled marketers to track marketing performance at a level of detail that was either not possible or not cost effective in the past. The marketing metrics provided in this section were just a small sampling, but they do provide some examples of what kinds of metrics can be used to help ensure that marketing control is achieved. Through the selection of the right metrics, marketers are better able to understand the performance of their marketing activities, identify opportunities for improvement, and take corrective actions at a point where greater benefits can be realized.

Key Terms

marketing metrics, p. 167

marketing control, p. 167

click-through, p. 167

conversion, p. 167

cost-per-order, p. 167

Chapter Questions and Activities

Concepts: Test Your Knowledge

5-1. What is meant by one-to-one marketing?

5-2. Why do many businesses view their relationships with customers as financial assets?

5-3. What is the Internet of Things? What are its components? What are the Big Data implications, and how might it be used?

5-4. Within the Big Data context, distinguish between the direct and indirect paths.

5-5. Companies collect data in large quantities to sell to organizations. How does this process work?

5-6. What is a data scientist? Briefly explain the qualifications and provide a job description.

5-7. What is search engine optimization? Why is it vital that a firm spends time and money on it?

5-8. What is the difference between purchasing digital advertisements with a cost-per-impression structure versus a cost-per-click structure? Is one better than the other?

5-9. Define marketing metrics. How can marketing metrics help marketers understand the performance of different marketing initiatives and provide greater control?

5-10. What is a click-through rate, and how is it calculated?

5-11. What is a conversion? What are some examples of conversions on an e-commerce website?

5-12. What is a cost-per-order? What kind of information do marketers gain from this metric?

Activities: Apply What You've Learned

5-13. *Creative Homework/Short Project* Assume that you are in charge of developing and opening a new restaurant concept for a large national restaurant company. The concept will be opened for a test-pilot run in a city that your boss has picked out. Not being familiar with the city or its inhabitants, you are hesitant to proceed without collecting some data first.

   a. Outline the sources of data that you would use to help determine what the concept should be in terms of food, appearance, service, and where the test pilot location should be placed.

   b. For each source of data, list specific information that you would try to look for and explain how it would enable you to make a better decision in regard to all the previously mentioned considerations.

5-14. *Creative Homework/Short Project* Choose a company based in your own country that has a wide range of different products or services. Write down 20 to 30 of the key products or services it sells. Try not to use brand names as part of your list; use generic words or names to describe these products or services. Create a table with four columns and as many rows as you need. Across the first column write "product/service," and label the remaining columns 1, 2, and 3. Using a search engine, systematically search each of your key words. Write down, in order, the companies that appear first, second, and third in the search results. Is there a pattern? Do you think search optimization is a factor?

⭐ **5-15.** *Creative Homework/Short Project* Consider that you are in charge of all paid search advertising through Google for your company. One of your colleagues is in charge of Instagram advertising. Your boss is in the process of putting together the marketing budget and has asked you to weigh in on how much should be allotted for Facebook advertising. He tells you that he feels that the organization's funds would be better put toward increasing spending on Instagram as opposed to Google paid search advertisements. He says, "Pictures on Instagram are just more compelling than little blocks of text in a search engine's results." You couldn't agree less with that sentiment, and you have the data to back it up.

   a. How would you go about making the argument that Google paid search advertisements should receive more of the marketing budget compared to Instagram advertisements? What factors in your boss's statement above are potentially not taking this into consideration?

   b. What metrics would you use to help make your case, and how would you explain their relevance and importance?

5-16. *In Class, 10–25 Minutes for Teams* As a brand manager, you are interested in conversion rates. With another student who is acting as your marketing manager, discuss how conversion rates are calculated, how often they should be calculated, and what to do with the results. Is the conversion rate useful for specific marketing campaigns?

Apply Marketing Metrics

In the chapter discussion about CRM, you read about four key characteristics of CRM: share of customer, lifetime value of a customer, customer equity, and customer prioritization. Each of these elements is discussed in the context of monitoring and assessing the effectiveness of a CRM initiative.

Consider J. C. Penney's loyalty program, JCP Rewards. Go to their website (**www.jcprewards.com**) and review the information about their reward program.

5-17. In what ways could J. C. Penney expect to measure the four elements of CRM above within the context of a reward program such as this?

5-18. How would data be collected for each element, and how might management at J. C. Penney utilize that data to provide loyal customers with a very strong relationship with the firm?

Choices: What Do You Think?

5-19. *Ethics* CRM relies on data collected from customers to create customized or one-to-one experiences for those customers. Data are collected at various touchpoints—places in which the customer interfaces with the firm to provide information, such as at a checkout lane, on the phone, on the website, and so on. Do firms have an obligation to explain to customers that they are collecting information from them to populate and drive their CRM initiative, or is it inherently obvious in today's world that such practices are routine? In general, what is your personal viewpoint of database-driven positioning strategies? What are the potential pros and cons to the company and to the customer?

⭐ **5-20.** *Ethics* The Internet of Things means the increased proliferation of devices that are connected to the Internet and that in turn can be connected to each other. While there are a number of benefits to this level of connectivity for both society and businesses, there are also a number of risks and ethical issues. What are some of the risks and ethical issues that stem from this? Do the benefits outweigh the costs? What physical objects would you consider not allowing to be connected through the Internet, and why?

⭐ **5-21.** *Critical Thinking* Spending on digital marketing has trended upward in recent years, and with so many individuals using the Internet for extended periods of time, it is easy to understand why. In some cases, some organizations spend more than half of their budget on digital marketing. How do you think they justify committing more than half of their budget to marketing to digital efforts? Do you believe that more companies should invest primarily in digital marketing? What groups or factors would indicate to you that digital marketing does not make sense as an investment?

5-22. *Critical Thinking* A study conducted by Adobe found that 77 percent of marketers surveyed believe that data on customer purchase histories can improve marketing performance, yet only 21 percent actually use it. Similarly, 88 percent believe that behavioral data can have a similar impact, but only 20 percent use it.[47] These statistics highlight a contradiction between the perception of marketing analytics' value and the actual frequency of execution of marketing analytics. Why do you think this is? If you were in charge of implementing marketing analytics into an organization, what hurdles would you expect to encounter and from whom, and how would you overcome them?

Miniproject: Learn by Doing

Different types of businesses use different approaches to engaging with both current and potential consumers online. A company's website is usually a key source of information for potential and current customers. The purpose of this project is to gain a deeper understanding of how marketing analytics can be implemented in order to gain greater insights into and enable more effective control of marketing efforts.

a. Select three company websites. These should include one ecommerce site (e.g., Amazon), one consulting company (e.g., IBM), and one consumer packaged goods company (e.g., Tide).

b. For each company's website, list what you believe the objectives of the organization are as communicated through the website and identify specific conversion actions on the website that would most closely align with these goals. For example, customer acquisition might be supported and ultimately achieved by getting users to sign up for an e-mail newsletter, which would be defined as a conversion action.

5-23. Rank the conversion actions in order of importance and include an explanation of why you have ordered them as such. Identify whether they are short-term oriented as they relate to the organization's objectives or long term-oriented (or, in some cases, both) and why.

5-24. If you could choose only two marketing metrics (remember metrics, not conversions) to track for each of these websites, identify which two you would select for each website and explain why.

5-25. Some of the websites visited should have a request-for-information form on them. Often, this is one of the ways that marketers begin to collect information on a customer to place within their CRM system. Locate this form and identify what information it is asking for. Write down the different potential uses of this information for the organization and in what ways it might be used by marketers to further engage with the customer. What are some creative ways that you would recommend leveraging these data for each website analyzed in terms of future communications?

Marketing in **Action** Case Real Choices at State Farm

How safe is your driving? State Farm wants to use customers' Big Data to find out. Some drivers are willing to have a small device installed into their cars to monitor, record, and analyze all of their driving habits. This assortment of information is at the center of State Farm's "Drive Safe & Save" program. The program uses a vehicle's communication system (i.e., OnStar) to collect basic information about the customer's driving.

Drivers believe that the collection of their own Big Data will lead to substantial discounts. The phenomenon of collecting as much customer data as possible is sweeping through the $167 billion industry. The use of Big Data to improve insurance offerings by insurers may not be well received by privacy advocates. Some critics see this as an overreaching effort by Big Brother to infiltrate customers' lives.

State Farm was founded in 1922 by retired farmer and insurance salesman George J. Mecherle. His original vision for the company was to operate fairly and do the right thing for its customers. The company is owned by its policyholders and has over 17,000 agent offices servicing 81 million policies and accounts throughout the U.S. and Canada. Since 1942, the company is the largest auto insurer in the U.S. About one of every five cars on the road in the U.S. is insured with State Farm. In this effort, State Farm handles nearly 35,000 claims per day.

Historically, the pricing of insurance rates relied primarily on customer characteristics such as driving record, age, gender, marital status, and residence. To a lesser extent, the make and model of car, credit-based insurance score, car usage, and prior insurance history are also used. The information is then correlated with potential losses. However, many insurers recognized that those factors do not always lead to the best rates. The "Drive Safe & Save" program is voluntary to customers. According to State Farm, each good driver is able to earn discounts, and bad drivers are charged only the rates they are currently paying. State Farm's potential discounts can run as high

as 50 percent. The company believes that the feedback from the data will alert poor drivers to their actual driving habits and thus make them better drivers. Better drivers lead to fewer claims. Fewer claims lead to more profits for State Farm.

The advent of Big Data has led to many privacy fears. For example, the Privacy Rights Clearinghouse, a nonprofit consumer education and advocacy project, suggests that insurers could easily track a customer's driving routes, potentially leading to a log of a customer's travels. How will these data be shared? For instance, will the data be shared with law enforcement? In response, State Farm says that it receives only data "about the broad geographic areas" of drivers, not exact vehicle locations.

State Farm is not the only insurance company implementing Big Data. Progressive is the pioneer in tracking driving data with its "Snapshot" program. It has over 10 years of experience with the process. Allstate has released its "Drivewise" program across the country and is gaining experience. How will State Farm get the "Drive Safe & Save" program to stand out in a crowded field? How will State Farm use these customer data to lead to the best prices for customers while growing profits?

You Make the Call

5-26. What is the decision facing State Farm?

5-27. What factors are important in understanding this decision situation?

5-28. What are the alternatives?

5-29. What decision(s) do you recommend?

5-30. What are some ways to implement your recommendation?

Sources: Based on Leslie Scism, "State Farm Is There: As You Drive." August 4, 2013, **http://online.wsj.com/news/articles/SB100014241 2788732342060457864795049754195 8** (accessed April 28, 2014); State Farm Mutual Automobile Insurance Company, "About Us," **www.statefarm.com/about-us/company-overview** (accessed May 1, 2014); and Brad Tuttle, "Big Data Is My Copilot: Auto Insurers Push Devices That Track Driving Habits," **http://business.time.com/2013/08/06/big-data-is-my-copilot-auto-insurers-push-devices-that-track-driving-habits** (accessed May 3, 2014).

MyMarketingLab™

Go to **mymktlab.com** for Auto-graded writing questions as well as the following Assisted-graded writing questions:

5-31. *Creative Homework/Short Project.* Assume that a firm hires you as marketing manager for a chain of retail bookstores. You believe that the firm should develop a CRM strategy. Outline the steps you would take in developing that strategy.

5-32. *Creative Homework/Short Project.* Your boss has been hearing about the importance of Big Data and data mining to marketers. Write a memo to your boss that describes the various applications that data mining has for marketers in order to convince him that the company should explore this topic.

Understand Consumer and Business Markets

Adam Wexler
▼ A Decision Maker at Insightpool

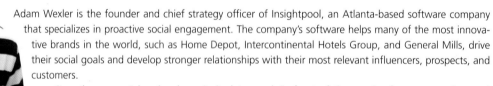

Adam Wexler is the founder and chief strategy officer of Insightpool, an Atlanta-based software company that specializes in proactive social engagement. The company's software helps many of the most innovative brands in the world, such as Home Depot, Intercontinental Hotels Group, and General Mills, drive their social goals and develop stronger relationships with their most relevant influencers, prospects, and customers.

Over the years, Adam has been invited to speak in front of thousands of event attendees and students about subjects such as social media and entrepreneurship. Additionally, Adam has written for a wide variety of publications, such as the *Huffington Post*, *Digiday*, and *Direct Marketing News*. At different times, Adam has also been the voice behind numerous brands on social media, including Sprite, NCAA March Madness, and Cracker (the band). He graduated in 2007 with a Bachelor of Business Administration (BBA) degree in real estate from the University of Georgia, where he also completed the Music Business and Institute for Leadership Advancement Certificate programs.

Adam's Info

What I do when I'm not working?
Go to the gym (basketball, biking, weightlifting) and reading.

First job out of school?
GoRankem (my original Web-based company).

Career high?
Scoring 33 of my team's 39 points in my third-grade basketball game.

Business book I'm reading now?
The Founder's Dilemmas by Noam Wasserman.

My hero?
Steve Nash.

My motto to live by?
Fail fast.

What drives me?
To do what I want to do when I want to do it.

My management style?
Lead by example.

Here's my problem...

One of our clients, DocuSign, Inc., The Global Standard for Digital Transaction Management™ (DTM), enables organizations of every size, industry, and geography to securely sign, send, and manage transactions and documents in the cloud. This client asked Insightpool to identify and engage existing or potential customers about subjects of interest. Whether they're trying to build a meaningful social audience, promote their latest white paper, or host an event, DocuSign has plenty of initiatives going at any time. These all are targeted to the company's target market of professionals who work in industries including financial services, insurance, health care, high tech, real estate, and the public sector as well as in business departments including human resources, procurement, legal, IT and more. All of these B2B consumers share the same need: to complete mission-critical transactions with others and ensure that they will be conducted safely, securely, and reliably in the cloud. This isn't an easy proposition and is one of the many reasons why DocuSign has invested more than $100 million in its platform and technology and why there are few real competitors in the space.

One of DocuSign's ongoing marketing objectives is to generate demand for its service. Because the idea of transacting business and storing documents in the cloud rather than on secure servers that sit in a person's office is still fairly new to a lot of people, it's usually necessary to persuade a prospective user to see a demo of the service. If DocuSign can get someone to take the time to try a one-minute demo, it's much more likely they will understand the benefits of the company's industry-leading DTM platform and also feel more comfortable about the company's security. In terms of consumer decision making, it moves people through several steps in the process: They recognize that they have a need to send documents quickly and securely to transact business (problem recognition), they can obtain information to identify DocuSign as a potential vendor (information search), and they can see how the company's service can do a superior job of meeting their need (evaluation of alternatives). From there, it's much easier to move them to the next step, which is to actually purchase the service.

The trick is to entice people to sign up for a demo, especially if they have been sending important documents in more traditional ways and don't see a need to learn about an alternative. Digital and social advertising helps to build awareness of the DocuSign brand, but these messages don't necessarily create motivation to learn more about it. The client clearly understood this problem, as the click-through rates (CTRs) on ads it posted were achieving less-than-desirable results. Mass posting to DocuSign's Facebook and Twitter pages also didn't work very well.

Insightpool worked with DocuSign to target executives with the greatest likelihood of interest in the service to engage in a one-to-one dialogue using social media. Here was an example of an initial message:

Things to remember

Insightpool specializes in proactive social engagement, that is, it helps companies drive their social goals and develop stronger relationships with their most relevant influencers, prospects, and customers. One of Insightpool's clients, DocuSign, Inc., The Global Standard for Digital Transaction Management™ (DTM), enables organizations to securely sign, send, and manage transactions and documents in the cloud. DocuSign's target market includes industry and public sector professionals. DocuSign asked Insightpool to identify and engage existing or potential customers about subjects of interest and to entice them to sign up for a DocuSign demo.

Hey [name], Coffee is for closers. Demo @docusign now for a chance to win a $10 gift card to Starbucks: esign.docusign.com/coffeenow

While the results of Insightpool's initial direct marketing efforts were good, we knew there was still room for improvement. The original message templates were too "salesy," and the content was not resonating with the target audience. The Insightpool team wasn't sure if the gift card angle was doing enough to attract executives to sit through a demo. Clearly, more needed to be done to move these busy professionals down the path to purchase.

We considered our **Options** 1·2·3

1 **Option** **Make the message sound like less of a sales pitch.** Attract the target's attention by personalizing the content. Include the prospect's first name and other information from their bio or what they were tweeting about. People tend to be turned off by blatant sales appeals, even though they love the chance to win free stuff. Rather than pointing out up front that they need to sign up for a demo to enter the sweepstakes, DocuSign could let them figure out this requirement after they clicked through. This would be a fairly easy fix, although it wouldn't do much if the basic offer needed to be adjusted rather than just the invitation copy.

2 **Option** **Boost the incentive to a $50 Starbucks gift card.** Many individuals value their time too much to be interested in the chance of winning $10, so a larger prize might be enough to entice a click and submission. A bigger prize might persuade some people who weren't very interested in the demo to sit through it just to get a chance to win the money. If the demo itself was interesting enough, some proportion of those people might want to think about using DocuSign even though they didn't originally intend to. On the other hand, since many of the target audience members are senior executives, it wasn't clear if even a $50 card would be hefty enough to attract their interest. And a larger budget would be required to deliver the more expensive gift cards.

3 **Option** **Drop the sweepstakes approach in favor of a more brand-focused campaign.** Offer a series of content-oriented programs in the form of webinars or white papers that would be valuable to busy executives. DocuSign could compliment the targets by asking for their perspective on topics of interest, such as how to engage sales prospects (ironically, just what DocuSign was trying to do). People tend to be narcissistic, and a recognizable brand name reaching out for their opinion would be flattering. Of course, there wouldn't be a monetary incentive to contribute to these programs, so the only currency would be "ego." It would also require a lot of additional effort to draw up the strategy and implement the new outreach campaign.

You Choose

Which **Option** would you choose, and **why**?
1. ☐YES ☐NO   2. ☐YES ☐NO   3. ☐YES ☐NO

See what **option** Adam chose on **page 210** ➡

MyMarketingLab™

⭐ **Improve Your Grade!**

Over 10 million students improved their results using the Pearson MyLabs.
Visit **mymktlab.com** for simulations, tutorials, and end-of-chapter problems.

Chapter 6

1

The Consumer Decision-Making Process

OBJECTIVE

Define *consumer behavior* and explain the purchase decision-making process.
(pp. 176–182)

Compelling new products, clever packaging, and creative advertising surround us, clamoring for our attention—and our money. But consumers don't all respond in the same way. Each of us is unique, with our own reasons to choose one product over another. Remember: The focus of the marketing concept is to satisfy consumers' wants and needs. To accomplish that crucial goal, first we need to appreciate what those wants and needs are. What causes one consumer to step into Denny's for a huge cholesterol-laden breakfast while another opts for a quick Starbucks latte and Danish and a third will only eat a healthy serving of "natural" Kashi cereal and fruit? And what, other than income, will cause one consumer to buy that box of Kashi cereal only when it's "on deal" while her neighbor never even looks at the price?

consumer behavior

The process involved when individuals or groups select, purchase, use, and dispose of goods, services, ideas, or experiences to satisfy their needs and desires.

Consumer behavior is the process individuals or groups go through to select, purchase, use, and dispose of goods, services, ideas, or experiences to satisfy their needs and desires. Marketers recognize that consumer decision making is an ongoing process—it's much more than what happens at the moment a consumer forks over the cash and in turn receives a good or service.

Let's go back to the shoppers who want to buy a box of dry cereal. Although this may seem like a simple purchase, in reality there are quite a few steps in the process that cereal marketers need to understand. The first decision in the process is where to buy your cereal. If you eat a lot of it, you may choose to make a special trip to a warehouse-type retailer that sells super-duper-sized boxes rather than just picking up a box while you're at the local supermarket. Of course, if you get a craving for cereal in the middle of the night, you may dash to the local convenience store. Then, what type of cereal do you buy? Do you eat only low-fat, high-fiber bran cereals, or do you go for the sugar-coated varieties with marshmallows? Of course, you may also like to have a variety of cereals available so you can "mix and match."

Marketers also need to know how and when you consume their products. Do you eat cereal only for breakfast, or do you snack on it while you sit in front of the TV at night? Do you eat certain kinds of cereal only at certain times (like sugary kids' cereals that serve as comfort food when you pull an all-nighter)? What about storing the product (if it lasts that long)? Do you have a kitchen pantry where you can store the supersized box, or is space an issue?

And there's more. Marketers also need to understand the many factors that influence each of these steps in the consumer behavior process—internal factors unique to each of us, situational factors at the time of purchase, and the social influences of people around us. In this chapter, we'll talk about how all these factors influence how and why consumers do what they do. But first we'll look at the types of decisions consumers make and the steps in the decision-making process.

Not All Decisions Are the Same

Traditionally, researchers assumed that consumers carefully collect information about competing products, determine which products possess the characteristics or product attributes important to their needs, weigh the pluses and minuses of each alternative, and arrive at a satisfactory decision. But how accurate is this picture of the decision-making process? Is this the way *you* buy cereal?

Although it does seem that people take these steps when they make an important purchase such as a new car, is it realistic to assume that they do this for everything they buy, like that box of cereal? Today, we realize that decision makers actually employ a set of approaches that range from painstaking analysis to pure whim, depending on the importance of what they are buying and how much effort they choose to put into the decision.[1] Researchers find it convenient to think in terms of an "effort" continuum that is anchored on one end by *habitual decision making*, such as deciding to purchase a box of cereal, and at the other end by *extended problem solving*, such as deciding to purchase a new car.

When consumers engage in extended problem solving, indeed they do carefully go through the steps Figure 6.1 outlines: problem recognition, information search, evaluation of alternatives, product choice, and postpurchase evaluation.

When we make habitual decisions, however, we make little or no conscious effort. Rather, the search for information and the comparison of alternatives may occur almost instantaneously as we recall what we have done in the past and the satisfaction we received. You may, for example, simply throw the same brand of cereal in your shopping cart week after week without thinking about it too much. Figure 6.2 provides a summary of the differences between extended problem solving and habitual decision making.

Many decisions fall somewhere in the middle and are characterized by *limited problem solving*, which means that we do *some* work to make a decision but not a great deal. This is probably how you decide on a new pair of running shoes or a new calculator for math class. Just how much effort do we put into our buying decisions? The answer depends on our level of **involvement**—how important we perceive the consequences of the purchase to be. As a rule, we are more involved in the decision-making process for products that we think are risky in some way. **Perceived risk** may be present if the product is expensive or complex and hard to understand, such as a new computer or a sports car. Perceived risk also can play a role when we think that making a bad choice will result in embarrassment or social rejection. For example, a young woman might decide against purchasing a nice-looking and functional Nine West purse from Kohl's for fear that she might be teased or ridiculed by her sorority sisters who all sport trendy Coach handbags.

When perceived risk is low—such as when we buy a box of cereal—we experience a low amount of involvement in the decision-making process. In these cases, we're not overly concerned about which option we choose because it is not especially important or risky. The worst-case scenario is that you don't like the taste and pawn off the box on your unsuspecting roommate! In *low-involvement* situations, the consumer's decision is often a response to environmental cues, such as when you decide to try a new type of cereal because the grocery store prominently displays it at the end of the aisle, known as an *end cap*. Under these circumstances, managers must concentrate on how a store displays products

Figure 6.1 *Process* | The Consumer Decision-Making Process

The consumer decision-making process involves a series of steps.

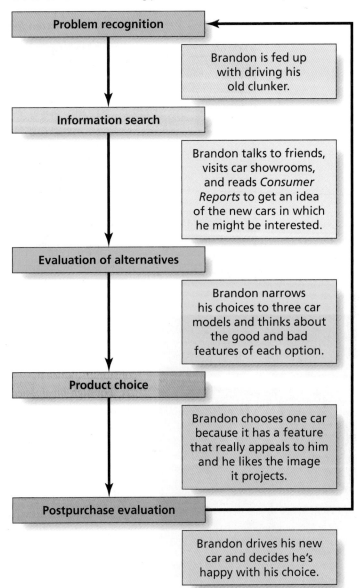

involvement
The relative importance of perceived consequences of the purchase to a consumer.

perceived risk
The belief that choice of a product has potentially negative consequences, whether financial, physical, and/or social.

Figure 6.2 ⚡ *Process* | Extended Problem Solving versus Habitual Decision Making

Decisions characterized as extended problem solving versus habitual decision making differ in a number of ways.

	Extended Problem Solving	**Habitual Decision Making**
Product	New car	Box of cereal
Level of involvement	High (important decision)	Low (unimportant decision)
Perceived risk	High (expensive, complex product)	Low (simple, low-cost product)
Information processing	Careful processing of information (search advertising, magazines, car dealers, Web sites)	Respond to environmental cues (store signage or displays)
Learning model	Cognitive learning (use insight and creativity to use information found in environment)	Behavioral learning (ad shows product in beautiful setting, creating positive attitude)
Needed marketing actions	Provide information via advertising, salespeople, brochures, Web sites. Educate consumers to product benefits, risks of wrong decisions, etc.	Provide environmental cues at point-of-purchase, such as product display

www.wildwash.co.uk

Many dog owners are highly involved with their companion animals.

problem recognition

The process that occurs whenever the consumer sees a significant difference between his current state of affairs and some desired or ideal state; this recognition initiates the decision-making process.

APPLYING ▼ Problem Recognition

Adam recognizes that the first step toward a purchase decision for consumers and organizations is problem recognition. For their client, DocuSign, Inc., Insightpool seeks to stimulate problem recognition when potential customers view a demo of DocuSign's Digital Transaction Management™ service.

---

at the time of purchase to influence the decision maker. For example, a cereal marketer may decide to spend extra money to be sure its brand stands out in a store display or feature a cool athlete like Olympic skier and gold medalist Mikaela Shiffrin on the box so consumers notice it.

For *high-involvement* purchases, such as when we buy a house or a car, we are more likely to carefully process all the available information and to have thought about the decision well before we buy the item. The consequences of the purchase are important and risky, especially because a bad decision may result in significant financial losses, aggravation, or embarrassment. Most of us would not just saunter into an auto dealer's office at lunchtime and casually plunk down a deposit on a new Tesla Roadster. For high-involvement products, managers must start to reduce perceived risk by educating the consumer about why their product is the best choice well in advance of the time that the person is ready to make a decision.

To understand each of the steps in the decision-making process, we'll follow the fortunes of a consumer named Brandon, who, as Figure 6.1 shows, is in the market for a new ride—a highly involving purchase decision, to say the least.

Step 1: Problem Recognition

Problem recognition occurs whenever a consumer sees a significant difference between his or her current state of affairs and some desired or ideal state. A woman whose 10-year-old Hyundai lives at the mechanic's shop has a problem, as does the man who thinks he'd have better luck getting dates if he traded his Hyundai for a new sports car. Brandon falls into the latter category—his old clunker runs okay, but he wants to sport some wheels that will get him admiring stares instead of laughs.

Do marketing decisions have a role in consumers' problem recognition? Although most problem recognition occurs spontaneously or when a true need arises, marketers often develop creative advertising messages that stimulate consumers to recognize that their current state (that old car) just doesn't equal their desired state (a shiny, new convertible). ⚡ Figure 6.3 provides examples of marketers' responses to consumers' problem recognition and the other steps in the consumer decision-making process.

Stage in the Decision Process	Marketing Strategy	Example
Problem recognition	Encourage consumers to see that existing state does not equal desired state	• Create TV commercials showing the excitement of owning a new car
Information search	Provide information when and where consumers are likely to search	• Target advertising on TV programs with high target-market viewership • Provide sales training that ensures knowledgeable salespeople • Make new-car brochures available in dealer showrooms • Design exciting, easy-to-navigate, and informative Web sites • Provide information on blogs and social networks to encourage word-of-mouth strategies • Use search marketing to ensure that your Web site has preferential search engine positioning • Participate in consumer review/advisory Web sites such as tripadvisor.com
Evaluation of alternatives	Understand the criteria consumers use in comparing brands and communicate own brand superiority	• Conduct research to identify most important evaluative criteria • Create advertising that includes reliable data on superiority of a brand (e.g., miles per gallon, safety, comfort)
Product choice	Understand choice heuristics used by consumers and provide communication that encourages brand decision	• Advertise "Made in America" (country of origin) • Stress long history of the brand (brand loyalty)
Postpurchase evaluation	Encourage accurate consumer expectations	• Provide honest advertising and sales presentations

Figure 6.3 Process

Responses to Decision Process Stages

Understanding the consumer decision process means marketers can develop strategies to help move the consumer from recognizing a need to being a satisfied customer.

Step 2: Information Search

Once Brandon recognizes his problem—he wants a newer car—he needs adequate information to resolve it. **Information search** is the step of the decision-making process in which the consumer checks his or her memory and surveys the environment to identify what options might solve his or her problem. Advertisements in newspapers, on TV or the radio, information we "Google" on the Internet, or a video on YouTube often provide valuable guidance during this step. Brandon might rely on recommendations from his friends, Facebook drivers' clubs, information he finds at **www.caranddriver.com**, brochures from car dealerships, or the manufacturers' websites.

information search
The process whereby a consumer searches for appropriate information to make a reasonable decision.

search marketing
Marketing strategies that involve the use of Internet search engines.

search engine optimization (SEO)
A systematic process of ensuring that your firm comes up at or near the top of lists of typical search phrases related to your business.

search engine marketing (SEM)
Search marketing strategy in which marketers pay for ads or better positioning.

sponsored search ads
Paid ads that appear at the top or beside the Internet search engine results.

comparison shopping agents or shopbots
Web applications that help online shoppers find what they are looking for at the lowest price and provide customer reviews and ratings of products and sellers.

Increasingly, consumers use the Internet to search for information about products. Search engines, sites such as Google (**www.google.com**) and Bing (**www.bing.com**), help us locate useful information as they search millions of Web pages for key words and return a list of sites that contain those key words.

Of course, the problem for marketers is that consumers seldom follow up on more than a page or two of results they get from these searches—we're all bombarded by way too much information these days to ever look at all of it. This has led marketers to develop sophisticated **search marketing** techniques. With **search engine optimization**, marketers first find what key words consumers use most in their searches. Then they edit their site's content or HTML to increase its relevance to those key words so that they can try to place their site high up in the millions of sites the search might generate. With **search engine marketing**, the search engine company charges marketers to display **sponsored search ads** that appear at the top or beside the search results.

Comparison shopping agents (shopbots) such as **Shopzilla.com**, **NexTag.com**, and Australia's **ShopBot.com.au**, are Web applications that can help online shoppers find what they are looking for at the lowest price. In addition to listing where a product is available and the price, these sites often provide customer reviews and ratings of the product and the sellers. They enable consumers to view both positive and negative feedback about the product and the online retailer from other consumers. Increasingly, consumers also search out other consumers' opinions and experiences through networking websites such as YouTube and Facebook. We'll talk more about these sites and others similar to them later in the chapter.

Step 3: Evaluation of Alternatives

Once Brandon identifies his options, it's time to decide on a few true contenders. There are two components to this stage of the decision-making process. First, a consumer armed with information identifies a small number of products in which he or she is interested. Then he or she narrows down one's choices while deciding which of the possibilities are feasible and then compares the pros and cons of each remaining option.

Brandon has always wanted a red Ferrari. But after he allows himself to daydream for a few minutes, he returns to reality and reluctantly admits that an Italian sports car is probably not in the cards for him right now. He decides that the cars he likes—and can actually afford—are the Fiat 500, the Volkswagen Jetta, and the Honda Fit. He narrows down his options as he considers only affordable cars that come to mind or that his buddies suggest.

Now it's decision time. Brandon has to look more systematically at each of the three possibilities and identify the important product characteristics, what marketers refer to as **evaluative criteria**, he will use to decide among them. The characteristics may be power, comfort, price, the style of the car, and yes, even safety. Keep in mind that marketers often play a role in educating consumers about which product characteristics they should use as evaluative criteria—usually they will "conveniently" emphasize the dimensions on which their product excels. To make sure customers like Brandon come to the "right" conclusions in their evaluation of the alternatives, marketers must understand which criteria consumers use and which they believe are more and less important. With this information, sales and advertising professionals can point out a brand's superiority on the most important criteria as *they* have defined them.

evaluative criteria
The dimensions consumers use to compare competing product alternatives.

Step 4: Product Choice

When Brandon examines his alternatives and takes a few test drives, it's time to "put the pedal to the metal." Deciding on one product and acting on this choice is the next step in the decision-making process. After agonizing over his choice for a few weeks, Brandon decides that even though the Jetta and the Fit have attractive qualities, the Fiat 500 offers the affordability he needs, and its carefree image is the way he wants others to think about him. All this thinking about cars is "driving" him crazy, and he's relieved to make a decision to buy the Fiat and get on with his life.

So just how do consumers like Brandon choose among the alternatives they consider? These decisions often are complicated because it's hard to juggle all the product characteristics in your head. One car may offer better gas mileage, another is $2,000 cheaper, while another boasts a better safety record. How do we make sense of all these qualities and arrive at a decision?

We often rely on simple "rules of thumb," or heuristics, instead of painstakingly learning all the ins and outs of every product alternative. These **heuristics** provide consumers with shortcuts that simplify the decision-making process. One such heuristic is "price = quality"; many people willingly buy the more expensive brand because they assume that if it costs more, it must be better (even though this isn't always true). Perhaps the most common heuristic is **brand loyalty**; this occurs when we buy the same brand over and over, and, as you might guess, it's the Holy Grail for marketers. People form preferences for a favorite brand and then may never change their minds in the course of a lifetime, making it extremely difficult for rivals to persuade them to switch.

Still another heuristic is based on *country of origin*. We assume that a product has certain characteristics if it comes from a certain country. In the car category, many people associate German cars with fine engineering and Swedish cars with safety. Brandon assumed that the Italian-made Fiat would be more stylish than the Jetta or Fit, so he factored that into his decision.

Sometimes a marketer wants to encourage a country association even when none exists. For example, U.S. firm General Mills offers consumers Swiss-sounding Yoplait yogurt, while Dannon introduced its Greek-sounding Oikos Organic Greek Yogurt. Häagen-Dazs ice cream comes from that exotic Scandinavian region we call New Jersey!

Step 5: Postpurchase Evaluation

In the last step of the decision-making process, the consumer evaluates just how good a choice he or she made. Everyone has experienced regret after making a purchase ("What was I *thinking*?"), and (it is hoped) we have all been pleased with something we've bought. The evaluation of the product results in a level of **consumer satisfaction/dissatisfaction**. This refers to the overall feelings, or attitude, a person has about a product after he or she purchases it.

Just how do we decide if we're satisfied with what we bought? When we buy a product, we have some *expectations* of product quality. How well a product or service meets or exceeds these expectations determines customer satisfaction. In other words, we tend to assess product quality by comparing what we have bought to a preexisting performance standard. We form this standard via a mixture of information from marketing communications, informal information sources such as friends and family, and our own prior experience with the product category. That's why it's very important that marketers create accurate expectations of their product in advertising and other communications.

Even when a product performs to expectations, consumers may experience regret, or **cognitive dissonance**, after they make a purchase. When we reject product alternatives with attractive features, we may second-guess our decision. Brandon, for example, might begin to think, "Maybe I should have chosen the Honda Fit—everyone says Hondas are great cars." To generate satisfied customers and remove dissonance, marketers often seek to reinforce purchases through direct mail or other personalized contacts after the sale.

So, even though Brandon's new Audi is not exactly as powerful as a Ferrari, he's still happy with the car because he never really expected a fun little car to eat up the highway like a high-performance sports car that costs 10 times as much. Brandon has "survived" the consumer decision-making process: He recognized a problem, conducted an informational

heuristics
A mental rule of thumb that leads to a speedy decision by simplifying the process.

brand loyalty
A pattern of repeat product purchases, accompanied by an underlying positive attitude toward the brand, based on the belief that the brand makes products superior to those of its competition.

consumer satisfaction/dissatisfaction
The overall feelings or attitude a person has about a product after purchasing it.

cognitive dissonance
The anxiety or regret a consumer may feel after choosing from among several similar attractive choices.

Figure 6.4 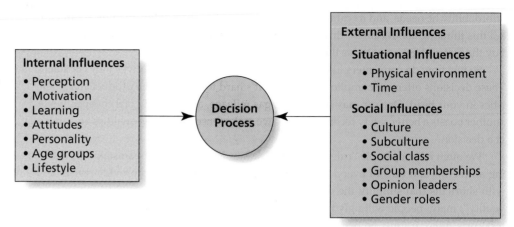 *Process* | Influences on Consumer Decision Making

A number of different factors in consumers' lives influence the consumer decision-making process. Marketers need to understand these influences and which ones are important in the purchase process.

search to resolve it, identified the (feasible) alternatives available, made a product choice, and then evaluated the quality of his decision.

In addition to understanding the mechanics of the consumer decision-making process, marketers need to understand what influences in consumers' lives affect this process. As we see in Figure 6.4, there are three main influences in the decision-making process: internal, situational, and social influences. All of these factors work together to affect the ultimate choice each person makes.

2
OBJECTIVE
Explain how internal factors influence consumers' decision-making processes.
(pp. 182–189)

Internal Influences on Consumers' Decisions

Like Brandon, your dream ride may be a sporty Ferrari. However, your roommate dreams of a tricked-out Mustang, and your dad is set on owning a big Mercedes. As the saying goes, "That's why they make chocolate and vanilla." We can attribute much of these differences to internal influences on consumer behavior—those things that cause each of us to interpret information about the outside world, including which car is the best, differently from one another.

Perception

perception
The process by which people select, organize, and interpret information from the outside world.

Perception is the process by which people select, organize, and interpret information from the outside world. We receive information in the form of sensations, the immediate response of our sensory receptors—eyes, ears, nose, mouth, and skin—to basic stimuli such as light, color, odors, touch, and sound. We try to make sense of the sensations we receive by interpreting them in light of our past experiences.

Take the computer keyboard, for example. When typewriters were introduced in the 1870s, the keys got stuck if you typed too fast. Then, in 1874, an inventor named Christopher Latham Sholes developed the QWERTY keyboard (named for the first six letters on the top row); this layout arranged the letters of the alphabet so that it decreased how fast a person could type. We don't have physical keys in computers and smart phones, so why do we still use QWERTY keyboards? Because we're used to them and it would be really weird to try to learn a different configuration.

We are bombarded with information about products—thousands of ads, in-store displays, special offers, our friends' opinions we read on their Facebook page, and on and on. The perception process has important implications for marketers: As we absorb and make sense of the vast quantities of information that compete for our attention, the odds are that any single message will get lost in the clutter. And, if we do notice the message, there's no guarantee that the meaning we give it will be the same one the marketer intended. Marketers need to understand the three steps that occur during this process: *exposure*, *attention*, and *interpretation*.

Exposure

The stimulus must be within range of people's sensory receptors to be noticed; in other words, people must be physically able to see, hear, taste, smell, or feel the stimulus. For example, the lettering on a highway billboard must be big enough for a passing motorist to read easily, or the message will be lost. **Exposure** is the extent to which a person's sensory receptors are capable of registering a stimulus.

Marketers work hard to achieve exposure for their products, but sometimes it's just a matter of making sure that cool people use your product—and that others observe them doing so. One way marketers get their products into the hands of A-listers is to insert them into both official and unofficial gift bags that celebrities receive when they attend the Academy Awards—and then hope those celebrities like the swag so much they show it off for the cameras. One year, for example, actor Kevin James received as a gift a George Foreman grill that was such a hit that he wrote it into episodes of his hit show *The King of Queens*—where millions of viewers around the world saw it.[2]

Many people believe that even messages they can't see will persuade them to buy advertised products. Claims about **subliminal advertising** of messages hidden in ice cubes (among other places) have been surfacing since the 1950s. A survey of American consumers found that almost two-thirds believe in the existence of subliminal advertising, and over one-half are convinced that this technique can get them to buy things they don't really want.[3]

There is very little evidence to support the argument that this technique actually has any effect at all on our perceptions of products and even less that marketers are or ever have used subliminal advertising methods. But still, concerns persist. ABC once rejected a commercial for KFC that invites viewers to slowly replay the ad to find a secret message, citing the network's long-standing policy against subliminal advertising. The ad (which other networks aired) is a seemingly ordinary pitch for KFC's $.99 Buffalo Snacker chicken sandwich. But if you replay it slowly on a digital video recorder, it tells you that viewers can visit KFC's website to receive a coupon for a free sandwich. Ironically, this technique is really the *opposite* of subliminal advertising because instead of secretly placing words or images in the ad, KFC blatantly publicized its campaign by informing viewers that it contains a message and how to find it.[4] The short story: Hidden messages are intriguing and fun to think about (if a little scary), but they don't really work. Sorry for the letdown—and don't bother trying to read this paragraph backwards.

Attention

As you drive down the highway, you pass hundreds of other cars. But to how many do you pay attention? Probably only one or two—the bright pink and purple VW Bug and the Honda with the broken taillight that cut you off at the exit ramp. **Attention** is the extent to which we devote mental-processing activity to a particular stimulus. Consumers are more likely to pay attention to messages that speak to their current needs. For example, you're far more likely to notice an ad for a fast-food restaurant when you're hungry, while smokers are more likely than nonsmokers to block out messages about the health hazards of smoking.

Grabbing consumers' attention is harder than ever because people's attention spans are shorter than ever. Now that we are accustomed to *multitasking*, flitting back and forth between our e-mails, TV, instant messages, and so on, advertisers have to be more creative by mixing up the types of messages they send. That's why we see both long (60-second) commercials that almost feel like miniature movies and short (some as brief as five seconds)

exposure
The extent to which a stimulus is capable of being registered by a person's sensory receptors.

subliminal advertising
Supposedly hidden messages in marketers' communications.

attention
The extent to which a person devotes mental processing to a particular stimulus.

messages that are meant to have surprise value: They are usually over before commercial haters can zap or zip past them. Indeed, brief blurbs that are long enough to tantalize viewers but short enough not to bore them are becoming commonplace. In contrast to the old days when most commercials on TV networks were 30-second (or even 60-second) spots, today more than one-third of national ads run for only 15 seconds.[5]

Interpretation

interpretation
The process of assigning meaning to a stimulus based on prior associations a person has with it and assumptions he or she makes about it.

Interpretation is the process of assigning meaning to a stimulus based on prior associations we have with it and assumptions we make about it. The Galaxy Gear smart watch was a flop almost as soon as it was released. Besides having limited support—it was compatible only with the Galaxy Note 3 smart phone—it was big and clunky, and the battery lasted only for a single day.[6] While consumers might expect to have to wind a watch from time to time, they certainly don't plan on having to plug it in every day. Products that don't behave in the way consumers expect them to because of their prior experiences just become a waste of marketers' time.

Motivation

motivation
An internal state that drives us to satisfy needs by activating goal-oriented behavior.

Motivation is an internal state that drives us to satisfy needs. Once we activate a need, a state of tension exists that drives the consumer toward some goal that will reduce this tension by eliminating the need.

Think again about Brandon and his old car. He began to experience a gap between his present state (he owns an old car) and a desired state (he craves a car that gets him noticed and is fun to drive). This activated the need for a new car, which in turn motivated Brandon to test different models, to talk with friends about different makes, and finally to buy a new car, thus eliminating the need.

hierarchy of needs
An approach that categorizes motives according to five levels of importance, the more basic needs being on the bottom of the hierarchy and the higher needs at the top.

Psychologist Abraham Maslow developed an influential approach to motivation.[7] He formulated a **hierarchy of needs** that categorizes motives according to five levels of importance, the more basic needs being on the bottom of the hierarchy and the higher needs at the top. The hierarchy suggests that before a person can meet needs at a given level, he or she must first meet the lower level's needs—somehow those hot new 7 For All Mankind jeans don't seem as enticing when you don't have enough money to buy food.

gamification
A strategy in which marketers apply game design techniques, often by awarding of points, badges, or levels, to non-game experiences in order to drive consumer behavior.

As you can see from 📷 Figure 6.5, people start at the lowest level with basic physiological needs for food and sleep. Then they progress to higher levels to satisfy more complex needs, such as the need to be accepted by others or to feel a sense of accomplishment. Ultimately, they can reach the highest-level needs, where they will be motivated to attain such goals as self-fulfillment. As the figure shows, if marketers understand the level of needs relevant to consumers in their target market, they can tailor their products and messages to them.

Marketers use their understanding of consumer needs for prestige, status, and accomplishment when they use gamification. **Gamification** is a strategy in which marketers apply game design techniques, often by awarding points or badges to nongame experiences in order to drive consumer behavior. Nike+, for example, allows consumers to earn points and set goals to motivate themselves to exercise more. Foursquare and Zynga apps use gamification to encourage app usage. Stride gum introduced "Gumulon," the world's first chewing-based mobile game. Players position the camera on their mobile devices to use their mouths to control the intergalactic game. A simple chewing motion

passion for water.

Van Marcke

Consumers purchase many products such as bathtubs for both functional and aesthetic reasons.

Figure 6.5 📷 *Snapshot* | Maslow's Hierarchy of Needs and Related Products

Abraham Maslow proposed a hierarchy of needs that categorizes motives. Savvy marketers know they need to understand the level of needs that motivates a consumer to buy a particular product or brand.
Source: Maslow, Abraham H.; Frager, Robert D.; Fadiman, James, *Motivation and Personality*, 3rd Ed., ©1987. Reprinted and Electronically reproduced by permission of Pearson Education, Inc., Upper Saddle River, New Jersey.

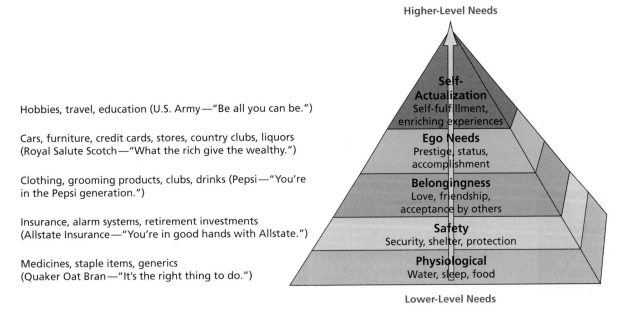

Higher-Level Needs

- **Self-Actualization**
  Self-fulfillment, enriching experiences
- **Ego Needs**
  Prestige, status, accomplishment
- **Belongingness**
  Love, friendship, acceptance by others
- **Safety**
  Security, shelter, protection
- **Physiological**
  Water, sleep, food

Lower-Level Needs

Hobbies, travel, education (U.S. Army—"Be all you can be.")

Cars, furniture, credit cards, stores, country clubs, liquors (Royal Salute Scotch—"What the rich give the wealthy.")

Clothing, grooming products, clubs, drinks (Pepsi—"You're in the Pepsi generation.")

Insurance, alarm systems, retirement investments (Allstate Insurance—"You're in good hands with Allstate.")

Medicines, staple items, generics (Quaker Oat Bran—"It's the right thing to do.")

causes the main character, Ace, to jump and advance through levels of the game, which takes place in a cavernous outer space mine (on the planet "Gumulon"). Many believe that gamification will become an even more significant trend in the future. Would you study more if you could collect badges for your efforts?

Learning

Learning is a change in behavior caused by information or experience. Psychologists who study learning have advanced several theories to explain the learning process, and these perspectives are important because a major goal for marketers is to "teach" consumers to prefer their products. The two major perspectives on how people learn are referred to as behavioral and cognitive learning.

learning
A relatively permanent change in behavior caused by acquired information or experience.

Behavioral Learning

Behavioral learning theories assume that learning takes place as the result of experience and the connections we form between events. In one type of behavioral learning, **classical conditioning**, a person perceives two stimuli at about the same time. After a while, the person transfers his or her response from one stimulus to the other. For example, an ad shows a product and a breathtakingly beautiful scene so that (the marketer hopes) you will transfer the positive feelings you get when you look at the scene to the advertised product. Hint: Did you ever notice that car ads often show a new auto on a beautiful beach at sunset or speeding down a mountain road with brightly colored leaves blowing across the pavement?

Another common form of behavioral learning is **operant conditioning**, which occurs when people learn that their actions result in rewards or punishments. This feedback influences how they will respond in similar situations in the future. Just as a rat in a maze learns the route to a piece of cheese, consumers who receive a "reward," such as

behavioral learning theories
Theories of learning that focus on how consumer behavior is changed by external events or stimuli.

classical conditioning
The learning that occurs when a stimulus eliciting a response is paired with another stimulus that initially does not elicit a response on its own but will cause a similar response over time because of its association with the first stimulus.

operant conditioning
Learning that occurs as the result of rewards or punishments.

Ripped from the Headlines

Ethical/Sustainable Decisions in the Real World

You've no doubt seen them before: loyalty cards from your favorite retailer. Hallmark has them. Panera Bread has them. Even your favorite gas station has them. And now your favorite retailers (and perhaps even your employer) are starting to offer similar reward programs online—but instead of earning discounts on greeting cards or free cinnamon crunch scones, you earn virtual badges or awards. If you think these "*social* loyalty programs" sound like gamification, you're right.

Gamification is an up-and-coming trend among businesses and is a brilliant way to increase brand loyalty, word of mouth, and more. For example, Samsung launched its Samsung Nation, where users who sign up can earn badges (like the Twitterati or Connoisseur badges) for tweeting about or reviewing Samsung products or responding to user Q&As. Those users who beat out others to engage the brand the most then get to appear atop the leaderboard.[8]

But is it all really just fun and games? Some companies that use gamification as part of their marketing strategy go one step further: They develop programs that collect data about user actions, such as Facebook posts, that in effect spy on their users. Still, game players typically are required to sign up in order to participate, and they do so willingly. If you agree to let a company monitor what you do, does this make it ethical?

ETHICS CHECK:
Find out what other students taking this course *would do* and *why* at **mymktlab.com**.

Should companies be allowed to collect and use information about users obtained from gamification activities for marketing purposes?

☐YES ☐NO

cognitive learning theory
Theory of learning that stresses the importance of internal mental processes and that views people as problem solvers who actively use information from the world around them to master their environment.

observational learning
Learning that occurs when people watch the actions of others and note what happens to them as a result.

a reusable plastic container like those you get when you buy some types of lunch meat, will be more likely to buy that brand again. We don't like to think that marketers can train us like lab mice, but that kind of feedback does reward us for the behavior. Will that be American or Swiss for you?

Cognitive Learning

In contrast to behavioral theories of learning, **cognitive learning theory** views people as problem solvers who learn by gaining new information. Supporters of this viewpoint stress the role of creativity and insight during the learning process. *Cognitive learning* occurs when consumers make a connection between ideas or by observing things in their environment.

Observational learning occurs when people watch the actions of others and note what happens to them as a result. They store these observations in memory and at some later point use the information to guide their own behavior. Marketers often use this process to create advertising and other messages that allow consumers to observe the benefits of using their products. Health clubs and manufacturers of exercise equipment feature ripped men and women pounding away on treadmills, while mouthwash makers imply that fresh breath is the key to romance.

Now we've discussed how the three internal processes of perception, motivation, and learning influence consumer behavior. But the results of these processes—the interpretation the consumer gives to a marketing message or action—differ depending on unique consumer characteristics. Let's talk next about some of these characteristics: existing consumer attitudes, the personality of the consumer, and consumer age-groups.

Attitudes

An **attitude** is a lasting evaluation of a person, object, or issue.[9] Consumers have attitudes toward brands, such as whether McDonald's or Wendy's has the best hamburgers. They also evaluate more general consumption-related behaviors, such as whether high-fat foods,

Consumers learn to like or dislike products in part based on how others in their environment react. Marmite is an "acquired taste;" it's a yeast extract that is extremely salty and a local delicacy in the U.K. Australians favor a similar product called vegemite. Americans aren't wild about either.

including hamburgers, are a no-no in a healthy diet. Marketers often measure consumer attitudes because they believe attitudes predict behavior—people like Brandon who think a Fiat 500 is a "cool" car are more likely to buy one than consumers who cherish the plush comfort of a big Buick. In order to make attitude measurement meaningful, marketers understand that a person's attitude has three components: affect, cognition, and behavior.

Affect is the *feeling* component of attitudes. This term refers to the overall emotional response a person has to a product. Affect is usually dominant for expressive products, such as perfume, where we choose a fragrance if it makes us feel happy. These emotional reactions actually cause physiological changes, such as an increase in pulse and sweating when a well-done commercial really gets to us. Joining the ranks of other advertisers, Disney recently built a lab where it will measure heart rate and skin conductivity and track the eye gaze of consumers while they view ads over the Internet, mobile devices, and their TVs.[10] Jasmine, Mulan and Florian—be still my heart!

Cognition, the *knowing* component, refers to the beliefs or knowledge a person has about a product and its important characteristics. You may believe that a Mercedes is built better than most cars or (like Brandon) that a Fiat 500 is slightly stylish yet boasts characteristics such as a five-star safety rating and good fuel economy.[11] Cognition is important for complex products such as computers, for which we may develop beliefs on the basis of technical information.

Behavior, the *doing* component, involves a consumer's intention to do something, as the intention to purchase or use a certain product. For products such as cereal, consumers act (purchase and try the product) on the basis of limited information and then form an evaluation of the product simply on the basis of how the product tastes or performs.

Personality and the Self: Are You What You Buy?

Personality is the set of unique psychological characteristics that consistently influences the way a person responds to situations in the environment. One adventure-seeking consumer may always be on the lookout for new experiences and cutting-edge products, while another is happiest in familiar surroundings using the same brands over and over. Today, popular online matchmaking services like Match.com, Matchmaker.com, and eHarmony.com offer to create your "personality profile" and then hook you up with other members whose profiles are a good match.

A person's **self-concept** is his or her attitude toward him- or herself. The self-concept is composed of a mixture of beliefs about one's abilities and observations of one's own behavior and feelings (both positive and negative) about one's personal attributes, such as body type or facial features. The extent to which a person's self-concept is positive or negative can influence the products he buys and even the extent to which he or she fantasizes about changing his or her life.

Self-esteem refers to how positive a person's self-concept is. Unilever uses a self-esteem pitch to promote its Soft & Beautiful, Just for Me hair relaxer for children. The company's "Just for Moms" blog encourages mothers to provide affirmation of their daughters' beauty to encourage their self-esteem. The site also provides "conversation starters" to help parents talk to their daughters about self-image.[12]

Age

A person's age is another internal influence on purchasing behavior. Many of us feel we have more in common with those of our own age because we share a common set of experiences and memories about cultural events, whether these

---

attitude
A learned predisposition to respond favorably or unfavorably to stimuli on the basis of relatively enduring evaluations of people, objects, and issues.

affect
The feeling component of attitudes; refers to the overall emotional response a person has to a product.

cognition
The knowing component of attitudes; refers to the beliefs or knowledge a person has about a product and its important characteristics.

behavior
The doing component of attitudes; involves a consumer's intention to do something, such as the intention to purchase or use a certain product.

personality
The set of unique psychological characteristics that consistently influences the way a person responds to situations in the environment.

self-concept
An individual's self-image that is composed of a mixture of beliefs, observations, and feelings about personal attributes.

Goods and services often appeal to a specific age-group.

J. Walter Thompson Italia SpA. CANNES ADVERTISING FESTIVAL 2006/SHORTLIST BAYER FITOSONNO "Daughter's Boyfriend" category outdoor

Each stage in the family life cycle presents new challenges.

involve Woodstock, Woodstock II, or even Woodstock III. Goods and services often appeal to a specific age-group. Although there are exceptions, it is safe to assume that most buyers of Rihanna's CDs are younger than those who buy Barbra Streisand discs.

Age is important, but regardless of how old we are, what we buy often depends more on our current position in the **family life cycle**—the stages through which family members pass as they grow older. Singles (of any age) are more likely to spend money on expensive cars, entertainment, and recreation. Couples with small children purchase baby furniture, insurance, and a larger house, while older couples whose children have "left the nest" are more likely to buy a retirement home in Florida.

Lifestyle

Demographic characteristics, such as age, income, and family life cycle, tell marketers *what* products people buy, but they don't reveal *why*. Two consumers can share the same demographic characteristics yet be totally different people—all 20-year-old male college students are hardly identical to one another. That's why marketers often further profile consumers in terms of their lifestyles. A **lifestyle** is a pattern of living that determines how people choose to spend their time, money, and energy and that reflects their values, tastes, and preferences.

To determine the lifestyles of consumers, marketers turn to **psychographics**, which groups consumers according to psychological and behavioral similarities. One way to do this is to describe people in terms of their **activities, interests, and opinions (AIOs)**. These dimensions are based on preferences for vacation destinations, club memberships, hobbies, political and social attitudes, tastes in food and fashion, and so on. Using data from large samples, marketers create profiles of customers who resemble one another in terms of their activities and patterns of product use.[13]

family life cycle
A means of characterizing consumers within a family structure on the basis of different stages through which people pass as they grow older.

lifestyle
The pattern of living that determines how people choose to spend their time, money, and energy and that reflects their values, tastes, and preferences.

psychographics
The use of psychological, sociological, and anthropological factors to construct market segments.

AIOs
Measures of consumer activities, interests, and opinions used to place consumers into dimensions.

uma Press/Newscom

Marketers at the beginning of the walking shoe craze assumed that all recreational walkers were just burned-out joggers. Subsequent psychographic research that examined the AIOs of these walkers showed that there were actually several psychographic segments within the larger group who engaged in the activity for very different reasons.

Metrics Moment

There are many potential metrics available to assess aspects of consumer behavior. Here are some popular ones and an example of each.

- *Overall awareness:* The percentage of all consumers who recognize or know the name of a brand. This can be "aided" or "unaided." A marketer can measure unaided awareness for Sensodyne toothpaste simply by asking consumers to name all the brands of toothpaste that come to mind. Aided recognition is measured by asking consumers questions such as "Have you heard of Tom's of Maine toothpaste?" Then follow-up questions can be asked to ascertain additional pertinent information.
- *Top-of-mind awareness (TOMA):* The first brand that comes to a consumer's mind when he or she thinks of a product category. Marketers measure TOMA with questions such as "What school comes to mind when you think of Ivy League universities?"
- *Consumer knowledge:* Measured by asking consumers if they have some specific knowledge about a brand. To measure brand knowledge, marketers may ask consumers if they believe the brand possesses certain attributes or characteristics, such as "Does the Kia Soul come with Bluetooth wireless technology as a base feature?"
- *Attitude toward a brand:* Often measured with survey questions about (1) beliefs that the brand possesses certain characteristics, (2) the relative importance of those characteristics to the product category, and (3) the overall measure of how much the consumer likes the brand. A resulting question might be "What is your overall feeling toward Chick-fil-A?" (measured on a scale from very unfavorable to highly favorable).
- *Purchase intentions:* A consumer's stated willingness to buy or expressed likelihood of certain behavior. A consumer survey may ask, "If you are in the market for a new pair of running shoes, what is the likelihood that you would purchase a pair of Brooks running shoes?" (measured on a scale from highly unlikely to highly likely). Caution: Stated intent to purchase does not perfectly translate into actual purchase behavior!
- *Purchase habits:* Another measure of a consumer's self-reported behavior. Marketers ask questions such as "On average, how many times a month does your family eat out?," "Which restaurant did you go to the last time you ate out?," and "How much do you normally spend on a dinner out with your family?"
- *Customer loyalty:* A measure of a consumer's commitment to a specific brand. Once the marketer has determined which brand the consumer typically uses, they follow up with questions such as "If on your next trip to the store you plan to purchase hand soap and your favorite brand of hand soap is not available, would you buy another brand or wait until you find your favorite brand to make the purchase?"
- *Customer satisfaction:* A consumer survey may ask questions such as "How satisfied are you with the level of cabin service by JetBlue Airlines?" (measured on a scale from very dissatisfied to very satisfied).

Apply the Metrics

Consider the consumer behavior metrics mentioned above. Pick out several metrics that you think would be most useful to gain a better understand of each item below. How might you use each metric you choose to do the following?

1. Better understand a firm's existing customers
2. Identify potential new customers for a firm
3. Gauge the market potential for a new product

---

3 OBJECTIVE
Show how situational factors and consumers' relationships with other people influence consumer behavior.
(pp. 189–194)

Situational and Social Influences on Consumers' Decisions

We've seen that internal factors, such as how people perceive marketing messages, their motivation to acquire products, and their unique personalities, age-groups, family life cycle, and lifestyle, influence the decisions they make. In addition, situational and social influences—factors external to the consumer—have a big impact on the choices consumers make and how they make them.

Situational Influences

When, where, and how consumers shop—what we call *situational influences*—shape their purchase choices. Some important situational cues are our physical surroundings and time pressures.

Marketers know that dimensions of the physical environment, including factors such as decor, smells, lighting, music, and even temperature, can significantly influence consumption. When casino operators replaced old-school "one-armed bandits" with electronic

sensory marketing
Marketing techniques that link distinct sensory experiences such as a unique fragrance with a product or service.

sensory branding
The use of distinct sensory experiences not only to appeal to customers but also to enhance their brand.

slot machines that no longer made the familiar whirring noises when players pulled the handle, earnings fell by 24 percent.[14] And the Hard Rock Hotel in Orlando, Florida, boosted ice cream sales by 50 percent simply by spraying a waffle cone scent into the air outside its shop.[15]

Sensory marketing is becoming big business. Specialized companies sell scents to hotels, car manufacturers, and even banks (like customers don't know what money smells like). Some offer individual scents, like vanilla, while others sell combinations of popular scents. But for some retailers, like Victoria's Secret and Bloomingdale's, it's not enough to have just any scent; these retailers have actually purchased custom scents that not only appeal to their customers but also enhance their brand. Marketers term this strategy **sensory branding**.[16] Let's see how some other situational factors influence the consumer decision-making process.

The Physical Environment

It's no secret that physical surroundings strongly influence people's moods and behaviors. Despite all their efforts to presell consumers through advertising, marketers know that the store environment influences many purchases. For example, one study of purchasing habits showed that consumers decide on about three out of every four of their supermarket product purchases in the aisles (so always eat before you go to the supermarket). The study also showed that in-store marketing and branding had a strong influence on shoppers' purchasing decisions.[17]

Two dimensions, *arousal* and *pleasure*, determine whether a shopper will react positively or negatively to a store environment. In other words, the person's surroundings can be either dull or exciting (arousing) and either pleasant or unpleasant. Just because the environment is arousing doesn't necessarily mean it will be pleasant—we've all been in crowded, loud, hot stores that are anything but. The importance of these surroundings explains why many retailers focus on packing as much entertainment as possible into their stores. For example, Bass Pro Shops, a growing chain of outdoor sports equipment stores built in the style of an enormous hunting lodge, features giant aquariums, waterfalls, trout ponds, archery and rifle ranges, putting greens, fish and wildlife mounts at every turn, and free classes (for adults and kids) in everything from ice fishing to conservation to meat processing. And if all that sensory overload leaves you famished, many of the Bass Pro Shops stores even offer on-site restaurants at their more than 60 current locations.

Time

Time is one of consumers' most limited resources. We talk about "making time" or "spending time," and we remind one another that "time is money." Marketers know that the time of day, the season of the year, and how much time a person has to make a purchase affects decision making.

Indeed, many consumers believe that they are more pressed for time than ever before. This sense of **time poverty** makes consumers responsive to marketing innovations that allow them to save time, including services such as drive-through lanes at pharmacies, to-your-door grocery delivery, and mobile pet grooming. In fact, a funeral home in Farmville, Virginia, even offers drive-through viewing for mourners who don't want to get out of their cars to see the deceased.[18]

Then of course there is the "always open" convenience of "stores" on the Web, ready to serve you whenever, wherever, and however you want. In fact, online shopping is growing at about seven times the rate of overall retail spending in the U.S. But even though 70 percent of people said that they preferred to shop their favorite retailer online, that doesn't mean your favorite bricks-and-mortar store is going away anytime soon.[19] Instead, these stores are adapting their services to meet your needs. For

time poverty
Consumers' belief that they are more pressed for time than ever before.

The **Cutting Edge**

No More Waiting on Shipping

To save customers time waiting on product shipments—and prevent lost sales to convenient brick-and-mortar stores—Amazon is considering shipping your next book or kitchen gadget *before* you buy it. That way, when you decide you want the product, you'll spend less time waiting on UPS or other shippers to deliver it to your door.

By looking at your previous purchases, items on your wish list, products you've searched, and products you've purchased, Amazon is betting it can predict what you'll buy next (much like the process they use now to recommend items to you). In this case, Amazon will go one step further and ship that item, where it will wait at a shipping hub until your order comes through. This concept, known as "anticipatory shipping," is just in the idea stages, but Amazon did file a patent so it will be ready to meet customers' future needs.[20] Still impatient for your package? Amazon also is testing "Prime Air," a drone delivery service that will literally fly a package from its warehouse to your doorstep—just Google "Amazon Prime Air" to check out a video that shows the new idea in action.[21]

example, many retailers now let you ship your online purchase to the store nearest you free of charge, and you can return items you purchased online at this location as well. And while you're in the store picking up that new summer tank top you ordered online, chances are you'll pick up a few extra items you didn't know you needed, like those matching earrings and to-die-for flip-flops.

Social Influences on Consumers' Decisions

Although we are all individuals, we are also members of many groups that influence our buying decisions. Families, friends, and classmates often sway us, as do larger groups with which we identify, such as ethnic groups and political parties. Now let's consider how social influences, such as culture, social class, influential friends and acquaintances, and trends within the larger society, affect the consumer decision-making process.

Culture

We can think of **culture** as a society's personality. It is the values, beliefs, customs, and tastes a group of people produce or practice. Although we often assume that what people in one culture (especially our own) think is desirable or appropriate will be appreciated in other cultures as well, that's far from the truth. For example, simply translating American marketing messages into Spanish doesn't mean those messages will be accepted—especially among those Hispanic consumers living in the U.S. who have a strong desire to maintain their Hispanic identity. Instead, marketers must "recognize that Hispanics buy brands that empower their cultural relevancy."[22] That means developing relationships with customers and considering their family and religious values.

culture
The values, beliefs, customs, and tastes a group of people values.

Values (Again)

As we also saw in Chapter 2, cultural values are deeply held beliefs about right and wrong ways to live.[23] Marketers who understand a culture's values can tailor their product offerings accordingly. But over time, cultural values do change. Consider, for example, that the values for collectivist countries differ greatly from those of individualistic cultures, where immediate gratification of one's own needs come before all other loyalties. In collectivist cultures, loyalty to a family or a tribe overrides personal goals. Today, we see the economic growth of some collectivist countries such as India, Japan, and China, making many consumers more affluent—and individualistic. For marketers, this means growth opportunities for products such as travel, luxury goods, sports activities like tennis and golf, and entertainment.

subculture
A group within a society whose members share a distinctive set of beliefs, characteristics, or common experiences.

microcultures
Groups of consumers who identify with a specific activity or art form.

Subcultures

A **subculture** is a group that coexists with other groups in a larger culture but whose members share a distinctive set of beliefs or characteristics, such as members of a religious organization or an ethnic group. **Microcultures** are groups of consumers who identify with a specific activity or art form. These form around TV shows like *American Idol* or *Grey's Anatomy*, Facebook games like FarmVille or Candy Crush Saga, or leisure activities such as extreme sports. Social media have been a real boon to subcultures and microcultures; they provide an opportunity for like-minded consumers to share their thoughts, photographs, videos, and so on. More on these important new sharing platforms later in the book.

For marketers, some of the most important subcultures are racial and ethnic groups because many consumers identify strongly with their heritage, and products that appeal to this aspect of their identities appeal to them. To grow its business, Clorox got down and dirty with its Hispanic consumers. After studying how Hispanics traditionally clean their homes, Clorox introduced its Clorox Fraganzia line of cleaning products to meet all of their cleaning needs—a thorough process of cleaning, disinfecting, and aromatizing. Even their toilet-bowl cleaners, in the shape of little baskets, or *canastillas*, look like those used in Latin America.[24]

consumerism
A social movement that attempts to protect consumers from harmful business practices.

Consumerism: An Emerging Lifestyle Trend

Powerful new social movements within a society also contribute to how we decide what we want and what we don't. One such influence is **consumerism**, the social movement directed toward protecting consumers from harmful business practices. Many consumers are becoming very aware of the social and environmental consequences of their purchases—and making their decisions accordingly.

Organized activities that bring about social and political change are not new to the American scene. Women's right to vote, child labor laws, the minimum wage, equal employment opportunity, and the ban on nuclear weapons testing all have resulted from social movements in which citizens, public and private organizations, and businesses worked to change society. In today's connected world, criticisms from consumerists can be especially damaging. A company's best way to combat such attacks and maintain a good image is to be proactive by practicing good business.

social class
The overall rank or social standing of groups of people within a society according to the value assigned to factors such as family background, education, occupation, and income.

Social Class

Social class is the overall rank of people in a society. People who are within the same class tend to exhibit similarities in occupation, education, and income level, and they often have similar tastes in clothing, decorating styles, and leisure activities. Class members also share many political and religious beliefs as well as preferences for AIOs.

Many marketers design their products and stores to appeal to people in a specific social class. Working-class consumers tend to evaluate products in more utilitarian terms, such as sturdiness or comfort, instead of trendiness or aesthetics. They are less likely to experiment with new products or styles, such as modern furniture or colored appliances, because they tend to prefer predictability to novelty.[25] Marketers need to understand these differences and develop product and communication strategies that appeal to different social classes.

status symbols
Visible markers that provide a way for people to flaunt their membership in higher social classes (or at least to make others believe they are members).

Luxury goods often serve as **status symbols**, visible markers that provide a way for people to flaunt their membership in higher social classes (or at least to make others believe they are members). The bumper sticker "He who dies with the most toys wins" illustrates the desire to accumulate these badges of achievement. However, it's important to note that over time, the importance of different status symbols rises and falls. For example, when James Dean starred in the 1956 movie *Giant*, the Cadillac convertible was the ultimate status symbol car in America. Today, wealthy consumers who want to let the world know of their success are far more likely to choose a Mercedes, a BMW, or an Escalade. The "in" car five years from now is anyone's guess—perhaps with today's emphasis on the environment, the Prius hybrid or the all-electric Tesla will emerge as the new status symbols.

Sometimes, group activities create new business opportunities. Due to the increasing popularity of tailgating during football games, many companies have figured out that there's as much, if not more, money to be made in the stadium parking lot as on the field.

In addition, traditional status symbols today are available to a much wider range of consumers around the world with rising incomes. This change fuels demand for mass-consumed products that still offer some degree of panache or style. Think about the success of companies like Nokia, H&M, Zara, ING, Dell Computers, Gap, Nike, EasyJet, or L'Oréal. They cater to a consumer segment that analysts label **mass class**. This term refers to the hundreds of millions of global consumers who now enjoy a level of purchasing power that's sufficient to let them afford high-quality products offered by well-known multinational companies.

mass class
The hundreds of millions of global consumers who now enjoy a level of purchasing power that's sufficient to let them afford high-quality products—except for big-ticket items like college educations, housing, or luxury cars.

Group Membership

Anyone who's ever "gone along with the crowd" knows that people act differently in groups than they do on their own. When there are more people in a group, it becomes less likely that any one member will be singled out for attention, and normal restraints on behavior may evaporate (think about the last wild party you attended). In many cases, group members show a greater willingness to consider riskier alternatives than they would if each member made the decision alone.[26]

A **reference group** is a set of people that a consumer wants to please or imitate. Consumers "refer to" these groups when they decide what to wear, where they hang out, and what brands they buy. This influence can take the form of family and friends, a sorority or fraternity, a respected statesman like Martin Luther King Jr., celebrities like Angelina Jolie, or even (dare we say it) your professors.

reference group
An actual or imaginary individual or group that has a significant effect on an individual's evaluations, aspirations, or behavior.

Opinion Leaders

If, like Brandon, you are in the market for a new car, is there a certain person to whom you'd turn for advice? An **opinion leader** is a person who influences others' attitudes or behaviors because they believe that he or she possesses expertise about the product.[27] Opinion leaders usually exhibit high levels of interest in the product category. They continuously update their knowledge as they read blogs, talk to salespeople, or subscribe to podcasts about the topic. Because of this involvement, opinion leaders are valuable information sources.

Unlike commercial endorsers, who are paid to represent the interests of just one company, opinion leaders have no ax to grind and can impart both positive and negative information about the product (unless they're being compensated to blog on behalf of a brand, which is not unheard of these days!). In addition, these knowledgeable consumers often are among the first to buy new products, so they absorb much of the risk and reduce uncertainty for others who are not as courageous.

opinion leader
A person who is frequently able to influence others' attitudes or behaviors by virtue of his or her active interest and expertise in one or more product categories.

Every culture communicates expectations about the proper roles for men and women, as this ad from Chile for a line of power tools illustrates.

gender roles

Society's expectations regarding the appropriate attitudes, behaviors, and appearance for men and women.

Gender Roles

Some of the strongest pressures to conform come from our **gender roles**, society's expectations regarding the appropriate attitudes, behaviors, and appearance for men and women.[28] Of course, marketers play a part in teaching us how society expects us to act as men and women. Marketing communications and products often portray women and men differently. These influences teach us what the "proper" gender roles of women or men should be and which products are appropriate for each gender. Some of these "sex-typed" products have come under fire from social groups. For example, feminists claim that the Barbie doll reinforces unrealistic ideas about what women's bodies should look like. But even with an "average" Barbie, you still can't win. One budding entrepreneur created the new "it" doll, known as Lammily, who has the average proportions of a 19-year-old woman. However, the tagline "Average Is Beautiful" has stirred up its own controversy; some critics argue that there is no normal and that "everyone is beautiful."[29]

Sex roles constantly evolve—in a complex society like ours, we often encounter contradictory messages about "appropriate" behavior. We can clearly see this in the messages girls have been getting from the media for the last several years: It's cool to be overly provocative. Role models like Paris Hilton, Lindsay Lohan, Britney Spears, and, more recently, Miley Cyrus convey standards about how far preteens and teens should go to broadcast their sexuality. Now we see signs of a backlash. At the Pure Fashion website, girls get style tips, including skirts and dresses that fall no more than four fingers above the knee and no tank tops without a sweater or jacket over them. Several other sites, such as ModestApparelU.S.A.com, offer girls and women a variety of modest clothing items from longer dresses to modest underwear.

RING ON YOUR FINGER, NECKLACE ON YOUR NECK AND MEN ON THEIR KNEES.

APARECIDA jewellery

www.aparecidajoias.com.br

Advertising often reinforces gender roles.

Men's sex roles are changing too. For one, men are concerned as never before with their appearance. In fact, appearance ranks as their second-biggest worry (topped only by money worries and weighing on them more than worries about their family and their health).[30] To prove this point, guys spend $17.5 billion on toiletries globally each year—and that doesn't include the cost of razors, razor blades, or shaving cream.[31] How does this obsession with hair gels and moisturizers coexist with the traditional "macho" guy who can hardly be bothered to comb his hair? Clearly, our cultural definition of masculinity is evolving as men try to redefine sex roles while they stay in a "safety zone" of acceptable behaviors bounded by danger zones of sloppiness at one extreme and effeminate behavior at the other. And, much like the "girls gone milder" trend we just discussed, some cultural observers report the emergence of "retrosexuals"—men who want to emphasize their old-school masculinity as they get plastic surgery to create a more rugged look that includes hairier chests and beards, squarer chins, and more angular jawlines.[32]

4 Business Markets: Buying and Selling When the Customer Is Another Organization

OBJECTIVE

Understand the characteristics of business-to-business markets and business-to-business market demand and how marketers classify business-to-business customers.

(pp. 195–200)

You might think most marketers spend their days dreaming up the best way to promote cutting-edge products for consumers like new apps for your iPhone, a new power drink to keep you fit, or some funky shoes to add to your closet collection. But this is not the whole picture. Many marketers know that the "real action" also lies in products that companies sell to businesses and organizations rather than to end-user consumers like you—software applications to make a business more efficient, safety goggles for industrial plants, the carts shoppers push in supermarkets, or the sensors that keep track of your luggage at the airport. In fact, some of the most interesting and lucrative jobs for young marketers are in businesses you've never heard of because these companies don't deal directly with consumers.

Like an end consumer, a business buyer makes decisions—but with an important difference: The purchase may be worth millions of dollars, and both the buyer and the seller have a lot at stake (maybe even their jobs). A consumer may decide to buy two or three T-shirts at one time, each emblazoned with a different design. *Fortune* 500 companies such as ExxonMobil, PepsiCo Inc., and FedEx buy thousands of employee uniforms embroidered with their corporate logos in a single order.

Consider these transactions: Procter & Gamble contracts with several advertising agencies to promote its brands at home and around the globe. The Metropolitan Opera buys costumes, sets, and programs. Mac's Diner buys a case of canned peas from BJ's Wholesale Club. The U.S. government places an order for 3,000 new HP laser printers. The country of Qatar purchases five new Boeing 787 Dreamliners to add to their fleet—at a price that can exceed $200 million each.[33]

All the above exchanges have one thing in common: they're part of *business-to-business (B2B) marketing*. As we saw in Chapter 1, this is the marketing of goods and services that businesses and other organizations buy for purposes other than personal consumption. Some firms resell these goods and services, so they are part of a *channel of distribution*, a concept we'll revisit in Chapters 11 and 12. Other firms use the goods and services they buy to produce still other goods and services that meet the needs of their customers or to support their own operations. These **business-to-business (B2B) markets**, also called **organizational markets**, include manufacturers and other product producers, wholesalers, retailers, and a variety of other organizations, such as hospitals, universities, and governmental agencies.

To put the size and complexity of business markets into perspective, let's consider a single product—a pair of jeans. A consumer may browse through several racks of jeans and ultimately purchase a single pair, but the buyer who works for the store at which the consumer shops had to purchase many pairs of jeans in different sizes, styles, and brands from different manufacturers. Each of these manufacturers purchases fabrics, zippers, buttons, and thread from other manufacturers, which in turn purchase the raw materials to make these components. In addition, all the firms in this chain need to purchase equipment, electricity, labor, computer systems, legal and accounting services, insurance, office supplies, packing materials, and countless other goods and services. So, even a single purchase of a pair of 7 For All Mankind jeans is the culmination of a series of buying and selling activities among many organizations—many people have been keeping busy while you're out shopping!

business-to-business (B2B) markets
The group of customers that include manufacturers, wholesalers, retailers, and other organizations.

organizational markets
Another name for business-to-business markets.

Factors That Make a Difference in Business Markets

In theory, the same basic marketing principles should hold true in both consumer and business markets—firms identify customer needs and develop a marketing mix to satisfy those needs. For example, take the company that made the desks and chairs in your classroom. Just like a firm that markets consumer goods, the classroom furniture company first must create an important competitive advantage for its target market of universities. Next, the firm develops a marketing mix strategy beginning with a product—classroom furniture that will withstand years of use by thousands of students while it provides a level of comfort that a good learning environment requires (and you thought those hardback chairs were intended just to keep you awake during class). The firm must offer the furniture at prices that universities will pay and that will allow the firm to make a reasonable profit. Then the firm must develop a sales force or other marketing communication strategy to make sure your university (and hundreds of others) considers—and hopefully chooses—its products when it furnishes classrooms.

Although marketing to business customers does have a lot in common with consumer marketing, there are differences that make this basic process more complex.[34] Figure 6.6 summarizes the key areas of difference, and Table 6.1 provides a more extensive set of comparisons between the two types of markets.

Multiple Buyers

In business markets, products often have to do more than satisfy an individual's needs. They must meet the requirements of everyone involved in the company's purchase decision. If you decide to buy a new chair for your room or apartment, you're the only one who has to be satisfied. For your classroom, the furniture must satisfy not only students but also faculty, administrators, campus planners, and the people at your school who actually do the purchasing. If your school is a state or other governmental institution, the furniture may also have to meet certain government-mandated engineering standards. If you have a formal green initiative, the purchase must satisfy environment-friendly criteria.

Number of Customers

Organizational customers are few and far between compared to end-user consumers. In the U.S., there are about 100 million consumer households but less than half a million businesses and other organizations.

Size of Purchases

B2B products dwarf consumer purchases both in the quantity of items ordered and in how much a single item may cost. A company that rents uniforms to other businesses, for example, buys hundreds of large drums of laundry detergent each year to launder its uniforms.

Figure 6.6 *Snapshot* |
Key Differences in Business versus
Consumer Markets

There are a number of differences between business and consumer markets. To be successful, marketers must understand these differences and develop strategies specific to organizational customers.

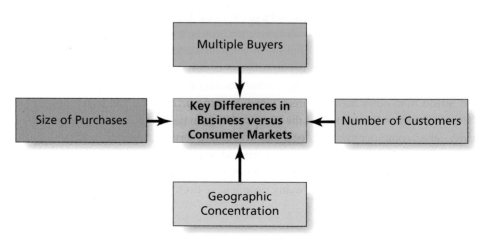

Table 6.1	Differences between Organizational and Consumer Markets
Organizational Markets	**Consumer Markets**
• Purchases made for some purpose other than personal consumption	• Purchases for individual or household consumption
• Purchases made by someone other than the user of the product	• Purchases usually made by ultimate user of the product
• Decisions frequently made by several people	• Decisions usually made by individuals
• Purchases made according to precise technical specifications based on product expertise	• Purchases often based on brand reputation or personal recommendations with little or no product expertise
• Purchases made after careful weighing of alternatives	• Purchases frequently made on impulse
• Purchases based on rational criteria	• Purchases based on emotional responses to products or promotions
• Purchasers often engage in lengthy decision processes	• Individual purchasers often make quick decisions
• Interdependencies between buyers and sellers; long-term relationships	• Buyers engage in limited-term or one-time-only relationships with many different sellers
• Purchases may involve competitive bidding, price negotiations, and complex financial arrangements	• Most purchases made at "list price" with cash or credit cards
• Products frequently purchased directly from producer	• Products usually purchased from someone other than producer of the product
• Purchases frequently involve high risk and high cost	• Most purchases are relatively low risk and low cost
• Limited number of large buyers	• Many individuals or household customers
• Buyers often geographically concentrated in certain areas	• Buyers generally dispersed throughout total population
• Products often complex; classified based on how organizational customers use them	• Products: consumer goods and services for individual use
• Demand derived from demand for other goods and services, generally inelastic in the short run, subject to fluctuations, and may be joined to their demand for other goods and services	• Demand based on consumer needs and preferences, is generally price elastic, steady over time and independent of demand for other products
• Promotion emphasizes personal selling	• Promotion emphasizes advertising

In contrast, even a hard-core soccer mom who deals with piles of dirty socks and shorts goes through a box of detergent only every few weeks.

Organizations purchase many products, such as a highly sophisticated piece of manufacturing equipment or computer-based marketing information systems that can cost a million dollars or more. Recognizing such differences in the size of purchases allows marketers to develop effective marketing strategies.

Geographic Concentration

Another difference between business markets and consumer markets is *geographic concentration*, meaning that many business customers may be located in a single region of the country. Whether they live in the heart of New York City or in a small fishing village in Oregon, consumers buy and use toothpaste and TVs. For years, Silicon Valley, a 50-mile-long corridor close to the California coast, has been home to thousands of electronics and software companies because of its high concentration of skilled engineers and scientists. For B2B marketers who wish to sell to these markets, this means that they can concentrate their sales efforts and perhaps even locate distribution centers in a single geographic area.

Figure 6.7 *Process* | Derived Demand

B2B demand is derived demand. That is, the demand is derived directly or indirectly from consumer demand for another good or service. Some of the demand for forestry products is derived indirectly from the demand for education. At least until the day when all textbooks are available only online, publishers will need to buy paper.

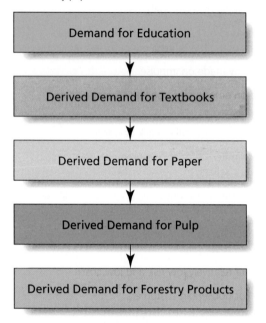

derived demand
Demand for business or organizational products caused by demand for consumer goods or services.

inelastic demand
Demand in which changes in price have little or no effect on the amount demanded.

B2B Demand

Demand in business markets differs from consumer demand. Most demand for B2B products is derived, inelastic, fluctuating, and joint. Understanding how these factors influence B2B demand is important for marketers when they forecast sales and plan effective marketing strategies. Let's look at each of these concepts in a bit more detail.

Derived Demand

Consumer demand is based on a direct connection between a need and the satisfaction of that need. But business customers don't purchase goods and services to satisfy their own needs. Businesses instead operate on **derived demand** because a business's demand for goods and services comes either directly or indirectly from consumers' demand for what it produces.

To better understand derived demand, take a look at *Figure 6.7* (beginning at the bottom). Demand for forestry products comes from the demand for pulp, which in turn is derived from the demand for paper that publishers buy to make the textbooks you use in your classes. The demand for textbooks comes from the demand for education (yes, education is the "product" you're buying—with the occasional party or football game thrown in as a bonus). As a result of derived demand, the success of one company may depend on another company in a different industry. The derived nature of business demand means that marketers must constantly be alert to changes in consumer trends that ultimately will have an effect on B2B sales. So, if fewer students attend college and those who do increasingly choose to purchase digital textbooks, the forestry industry has to find other sources of demand for its products.

Inelastic Demand

Inelastic demand means that it usually doesn't matter if the price of a B2B product goes up or down—business customers still buy the same quantity. Demand in B2B markets is mostly inelastic because what a firm sells often is just one of the many parts or materials that go into producing the consumer product. It is not unusual for a large increase in a business product's price to have little effect on the final consumer product's price.

For example, you can buy a Limited Edition Porsche Boxster S "loaded" with options for about $60,000.[35] To produce the car, Porsche purchases thousands of different parts. If the price of tires, batteries, or stereos goes up or down, Porsche will still buy enough to meet consumer demand for its cars. As you might imagine, increasing the price by $30 or $40 or even $100 won't change consumer demand for Boxsters—so demand for parts remains the same. (If you have to ask how much it costs, you can't afford it!)

Fluctuating Demand

Business demand also is subject to greater fluctuations than is consumer demand. There are two reasons for this. First, even modest changes in consumer demand can create large increases or decreases in business demand. Take, for example, air travel. A rise in jet fuel prices, causing higher ticket prices and a shift by some consumers from flying to driving vacations, can cause airlines to postpone or cancel orders for new equipment. This change in turn creates a dramatic decrease in demand for planes from manufacturers such as Boeing and Airbus.

A product's life expectancy is another reason for fluctuating demand. Business customers tend to purchase certain products infrequently. They may need to replace some types of large machinery only every 10 or 20 years. Thus, demand for such products fluctuates—it may be very high one year when a lot of customers' machinery wears out but low the following year because everyone's old machinery works fine.

Joint Demand

Joint demand occurs when two or more goods are necessary to create a product. For example, Porsche needs tires, batteries, and spark plugs to make that Limited Edition Boxster S that piqued your interest earlier. If the supply of one of these parts decreases, Porsche will be unable to manufacture as many automobiles, so it will not buy as many of the other items either.

joint demand
Demand for two or more goods that are used together to create a product.

Types of Business-to-Business Customers

As we noted before, many firms buy products in business markets so they can produce other goods. Other B2B customers resell, rent, or lease goods and services. Still other customers, including governments and not-for-profit institutions such as the Red Cross or a local church, serve the public in some way. In this section, we'll look at the three major classes of B2B customers shown 📷 Figure 6.8 (producers, resellers, and organizations). Then we'll look at how marketers classify specific industries.

Producers

Producers purchase products for the production of other goods and services that they, in turn, sell to make a profit. For this reason, they are customers for a vast number of products from raw materials to goods that still other producers manufacture. For example, Dell buys microprocessor chips from Intel and AMD that go into its line of computers, and Marriott hotels buys linens, furniture, and food to produce the accommodations and meals their guests expect.

producers
The individuals or organizations that purchase products for use in the production of other goods and services.

Resellers

Resellers buy finished goods for the purpose of reselling, renting, or leasing to consumers and other businesses. Although resellers do not actually produce goods, they do provide their customers with the time, place, and possession utility we talked about in Chapter 1 because they make the goods available to consumers when and where they want them. For example, Walmart buys toothpaste, peanuts, kids' shoes, and about a gazillion other products to sell in its over 10,000 stores worldwide.[36]

resellers
The individuals or organizations that buy finished goods for the purpose of reselling, renting, or leasing to others to make a profit and to maintain their business operations.

Figure 6.8 📷 *Snapshot* | The Business Marketplace

The business marketplace consists of three major categories of customers: producers, resellers, and organizations. B2B marketers must understand the different needs of these customers if they want to build successful relationships with them.

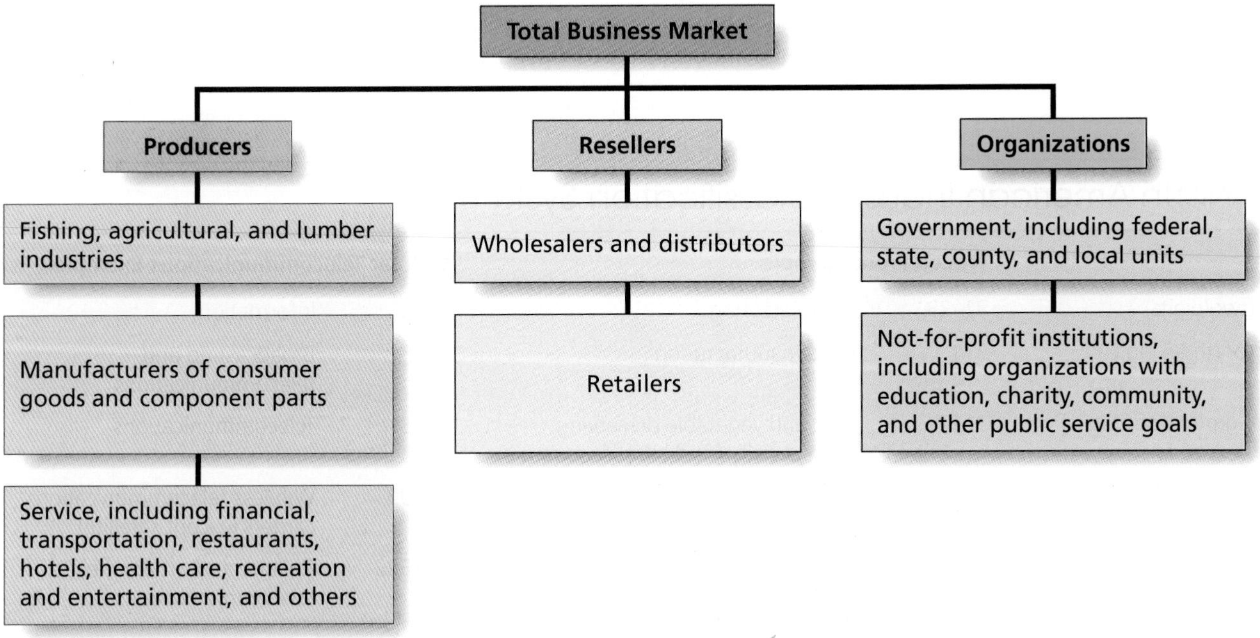

Total Business Market

Producers
- Fishing, agricultural, and lumber industries
- Manufacturers of consumer goods and component parts
- Service, including financial, transportation, restaurants, hotels, health care, recreation and entertainment, and others

Resellers
- Wholesalers and distributors
- Retailers

Organizations
- Government, including federal, state, county, and local units
- Not-for-profit institutions, including organizations with education, charity, community, and other public service goals

Government and Not-for-Profit Organizations

government markets
The federal, state, county, and local governments that buy goods and services to carry out public objectives and to support their operations.

Governments and not-for-profit institutions are two other types of organizations in the business marketplace. **Government markets** make up the largest single business and organizational market in the U.S. The U.S. government market includes more than 3,000 county governments, 35,000 municipalities and townships, 37,000 special district governments, 50 states and the District of Columbia, plus the federal government. State and local government markets alone account for 15 percent of the U.S. gross national product.[37]

And, of course, there are thousands more government customers around the globe, and many of those governments are just about the only customers for certain products, such as jet bombers and nuclear power plants. But many government expenditures are for more familiar items. Pens, pencils, and paper for offices; cots, bedding, and toiletries for jails and prisons; and cleaning supplies for routine facilities maintenance are just a few examples of items that consumers buy one at a time but that governments purchase in bulk.

As we said in Chapter 1, not-for-profit organizations are organizations with educational, community, and other public service goals, such as hospitals, churches, universities, museums, and charitable and cause-related organizations like the Salvation Army and the Red Cross. These institutions tend to operate on low budgets. Because nonprofessional part-time buyers who have other duties often make purchases, these customers may rely on marketers to provide more advice and assistance before and after the sale.

The North American Industry Classification System

North American Industry Classification System (NAICS)
The numerical coding system that the United States, Canada, and Mexico use to classify firms into detailed categories according to their business activities.

In addition to looking at B2B markets within these three general categories, marketers rely on the **North American Industry Classification System (NAICS)** to identify their customers. This is a numerical coding of industries the U.S., Canada, and Mexico developed. Table 6.2 shows the NAICS coding system. NAICS replaced the U.S. Standard Industrial Classification system in 1997 so that the North American Free Trade Agreement (NAFTA) countries could compare economic and financial statistics.[38] The NAICS reports the number of firms, the total dollar amount of sales, the number of employees, and the growth rate for industries, all broken down by geographic region. Many firms use the NAICS to assess potential markets and to determine how well they are doing compared to others in their industry group.

Firms may also use the NAICS to find new customers. A marketer might first determine the NAICS industry classifications of his or her current customers and then evaluate the sales potential of other firms occupying these categories.

Table 6.2 | North American Industry Classification System

	Frozen Fruit Example		Cellular Telecommunications Example	
• Sector (two digits)	31–33	Manufacturing	51	Information
• Subsector (three digits)	311	Food manufacturing	513	Broadcasting and telecommunications
• Industry group (four digits)	3114	Fruit and vegetable preserving and specialty food manufacturing	5133	Telecommunications
• Industry (five digits)	31141	Frozen food manufacturing	51332	Wireless telecommunications carriers (except satellite)
• U.S. industry (six digits)	311311	Frozen fruit, juice, and vegetable manufacturing	513322	Cellular and other wireless telecommunications

5

OBJECTIVE

Identify and describe the different business buying situations and the business buying decision process including the use of e-commerce and social media.

(pp. 201–209)

Business Buying Situations and the Business Buying Decision Process

So far we've talked about how B2B markets are different from consumer markets and about the different types of customers that make up business markets. In this section, we'll discuss some of the important characteristics of business buying situations. This is important because just like companies that sell to end-user consumers, a successful B2B marketer needs to understand how his or her customers make decisions. Armed with this knowledge, the company is able to participate in the buyer's decision process from the start.

The Buyclass Framework

Like end-user consumers, business buyers spend more time and effort on some purchases than on others. This usually depends on the complexity of the product and how often they need to make the decision. A **buyclass** framework, illustrated in Figure 6.9, identifies the degree of effort required of the firm's personnel to collect information and make a purchase decision. These classes, which apply to three different buying situations, are straight rebuys, modified rebuys, and new-task buys.

Straight Rebuy

A **straight rebuy** refers to the routine purchase of items that a B2B customer regularly needs. The buyer has purchased the same items many times before and routinely reorders them when supplies are low, often from the same suppliers. Reordering the items takes little time. Buyers typically maintain a list of approved vendors that have demonstrated their ability to meet the firm's criteria for pricing, quality, service, and delivery. GE Healthcare's customers routinely purchase its line of basic surgical scrubs (the clothing and caps doctors and nurses wear in the operating room) without much evaluation on each occasion.

Because straight rebuys often contribute the "bread-and-butter" revenue a firm needs to maintain a steady stream of income, many business marketers go to great lengths to cultivate and maintain relationships with customers who submit reorders on a regular basis. Salespeople may regularly call on these customers to personally handle orders and to see if there are additional products the customer needs—and to take the purchasing agent to lunch. The goal is to be sure that the customer doesn't even think twice about just buying the same product every time he or she runs low. Rebuys keep a supplier's sales volume up and help cover selling costs.

Modified Rebuy

Life is sweet for companies whose customers automatically do straight rebuys. Unfortunately, these situations don't last forever. A **modified rebuy** occurs when a firm decides to shop around for suppliers with better prices, quality, or delivery times. This situation also can occur when the organization confronts new needs for products it already buys. A buyer who purchased many BlackBerry smart phones, for example, may have to reevaluate several other options if the firm upgrades its cellular telecommunications system.

Modified rebuys require more time and effort than straight rebuys. The buyer generally knows the purchase requirements and

buyclass
One of three classifications of business buying situations that characterizes the degree of time and effort required to make a decision.

straight rebuy
A buying situation in which business buyers make routine purchases that require minimal decision making.

modified rebuy
A buying situation classification used by business buyers to categorize a previously made purchase that involves some change and that requires limited decision making.

Figure 6.9 *Snapshot* | Elements of the Buyclass Framework

The classes of the buyclass framework relate to three different organizational buying situations: straight rebuy, modified rebuy, and new-task buy.

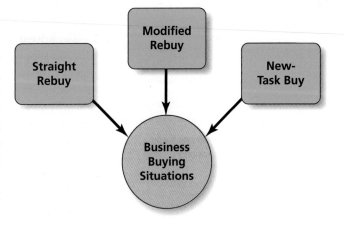

has a few potential suppliers in mind. Marketers know that modified rebuys can mean that some vendors get added to a buyer's approved supplier list while others may be dropped. So even if in the past a company purchased its smart phones from Blackberry, this doesn't necessarily mean it will do so in the future as this company's operating system steadily loses ground to newer rivals. Now, other platforms, like Apple, Palm, and Google's Android, may gain approved supplier status going forward, and the race is on. Astute marketers routinely call on buyers to detect and define problems that can lead to winning or losing in such situations.

New-Task Buy

new-task buy
A new business-to-business purchase that is complex or risky and that requires extensive decision making.

A first-time purchase is a **new-task buy**. Uncertainty and risk characterize buying decisions in this classification, and they require the most effort because the buyer has no previous experience on which to base a decision.

Your university, for example, may decide (if it hasn't done so already) to go into the "distance-learning" business—delivering courses to off-site students. Buying the equipment to set up classrooms with two-way video transmission is an expensive and complex new-task buy for a school. The buyer has to start from scratch to gather information on purchase specifications that may be highly technical and complex and require detailed input from others. In new-task buying situations, not only do buyers lack experience with the product, but they also are often unfamiliar with firms that supply the product. Supplier choice is critical, and buyers gather much information about quality, pricing, delivery, and service from several potential suppliers.

Marketers know that to get the order in a new-buy situation, they must develop a close working relationship with the business buyer. There are many situations in which marketers focus on selling their product by wooing people who recommend their products—over and above the end consumers who actually buy them. To use an example close to home, think about all of the goods and services that make up the higher-education industry. For instance, even though you are the one who shelled out the money for this extremely awesome textbook, your professor was the one who made the exceptionally wise decision to assign it. He or she made this choice (did we mention it was a really wise choice?) only after carefully considering numerous textbooks and talking to several publishers' sales representatives.

Professional Buyers and Buying Centers

Just as it is important for marketers of consumer goods and services to understand their customers, it's essential that B2B marketers understand who handles the buying for their business customers. Trained professional buyers typically carry out buying in B2B markets. These people have titles such as *purchasing agents, procurement officers,* or *directors of materials management.*

While some consumers like to shop 'til they drop almost every day, most of us spend far less time roaming the aisles. However, professional purchasers do it all day, every day—it's their job and their business to buy. These individuals focus on economic factors beyond the initial price of the product, including transportation and delivery charges, accessory products or supplies, maintenance, and other ongoing costs. They are responsible for selecting quality products and ensuring their timely delivery. They shop as if their jobs depend on it—because they do.

buying center
The group of people in an organization who participate in a purchasing decision.

Many times in business buying situations, several people—ranging from a production worker to the CFO—work together to reach a decision. The **buying center** is the group of people in the organization who participate in the decision-making process. Although this term may conjure up an image of "command central" buzzing with purchasing activity, a buying center is not a place at all. Instead, it is a cross-functional team of decision makers. Generally, the members of a buying center have some expertise or interest in the particular decision, and as a group they are able to make the best decision.

Table 6.3 | Roles in the Buying Center

Role	Potential Player	Responsibility
• Initiator	• Production employees, sales manager, almost anyone	• Recognizes that a purchase needs to be made
• User		• Individual(s) who will ultimately use the product
• Gatekeeper	• Production employees, secretaries, almost anyone	• Controls flow of information to others in the organization
• Influencer	• Buyer/purchasing agent	
• Decider	• Engineers, quality control experts, technical specialists, outside consultants	• Affects decision by giving advice and sharing expertise
• Buyer	• Purchasing agent, managers, CEO	• Makes the final purchase decision
	• Purchasing agent	• Executes the purchase decision

Depending on the complexity of the purchase and the size of the buying center, a participant may assume one, several, or all of the six roles that Table 6.3 shows. Let's review them now:

- The *initiator* begins the buying process by first recognizing that the firm needs to make a purchase. A production employee, for example, may notice that a piece of equipment is not working properly and notify a supervisor that it is slowing up the production line. Depending on the initiator's position in the organization and the type of purchase, the initiator may or may not influence the actual purchase decision. For marketers, it's important to make sure that individuals who might initiate a purchase are aware of improved products they offer.

- The *user* is the member of the buying center who actually needs the product. The user's role in the buying center varies. For example, an administrative assistant may give her input on the features a new copier should have because she will be chained to it for several hours a day. Marketers need to inform users of their products' benefits, especially if the benefits outweigh those that competitors offer.

- The *gatekeeper* is the person who controls the flow of information to other members. Typically, the gatekeeper is the purchasing agent, who gathers information and materials from salespeople, schedules sales presentations, and controls suppliers' access to other participants in the buying process. For salespeople, developing and maintaining strong personal relationships with gatekeepers is critical to being able to offer their products to the buying center.

- An *influencer* affects the buying decision when he or she dispenses advice or shares expertise. Highly trained employees, like engineers, quality control specialists, and other technical experts in the firm, generally have a great deal of influence in purchasing equipment, materials, and component parts the company uses in production. The influencers may or may not wind up using the product. Marketers need to identify key influencers in the buying center and persuade them of their product's superiority.

- The *decider* is the member of the buying center who makes the final decision. This person usually has the greatest power within the buying center; he or she often has power within the organization to authorize spending the company's money. For a routine purchase, the decider may be the purchasing agent. If the purchase is complex, a manager or even the CEO may be the decider. The decider is critical to a marketer's success and deserves a lot of attention in the selling process.

- The *buyer* is the person who has responsibility to execute the purchase. The buyer obtains competing bids, negotiates contracts, and arranges delivery dates and payment plans. Once a firm makes the purchase decision, marketers turn their attention to negotiating the details of the purchase with the buyer. Successful marketers are well aware that providing exemplary service in this stage of the purchase can be a critical factor in achieving future sales from this client.

The Business Buying Decision Process

APPLYING ▼ Search for Information

Adam knows that it's the job of marketers to make sure information is available when and where business customers look for it. Insightpool's services are based on the knowledge that business professionals use social media in order to get credible up-to-date information.

We've seen that there are a number of players in the business buying process, beginning with an initiator and ending with a buyer. To make matters even more challenging to marketers, members of the buying team go through several stages in the decision-making process before the marketer gets an order. The *business buying decision process*, as Figure 6.10 shows, is a series of steps similar to those in the consumer decision process we discussed earlier in this chapter. To help understand these steps, let's say you've just started working at the Way Radical Skateboard Company and your boss just assigned you to the buying center for the purchase of new software for Web page design—a new-task buy for your firm.

Step 1: Recognize the Problem

As in consumer buying, the first step in the business buying decision process occurs when someone sees that a purchase can solve a problem. For straight rebuy purchases, this may occur because the firm has run out of paper, pens, or garbage bags. In these cases, the buyer places the order, and the decision-making process ends. Recognition of the need for modified rebuy purchases often comes when the organization wants to replace outdated existing equipment, from changes in technology, or from an ad, brochure, or some other marketing communication that offers the customer a better product or one at a lower price. Two events may occur in the problem-recognition step. First, a firm makes a request or requisition, usually in writing. Then, depending on the complexity of the purchase, the firm may form a buying center. The need for new-task purchases often occurs because the firm wants to enhance its operations in some way or when a smart salesperson tells the business customer about a new product that will increase the efficiency of the firm's operations or improve the firm's end products.

Figure 6.10 *Process* | Steps in the Business Buying Decision Process

The steps in the business buying decision process are the same as those in the consumer decision process. But for business purchases, each step may be far more complex and require more attention from marketers.

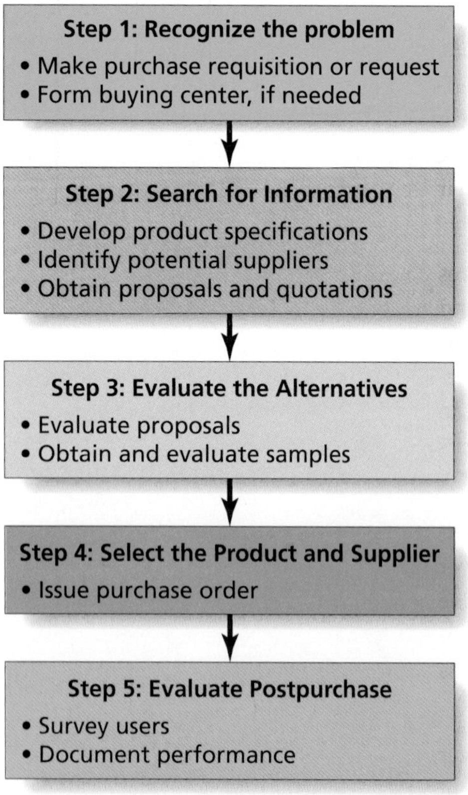
Step 1: Recognize the problem
• Make purchase requisition or request
• Form buying center, if needed
Step 2: Search for Information
• Develop product specifications
• Identify potential suppliers
• Obtain proposals and quotations
Step 3: Evaluate the Alternatives
• Evaluate proposals
• Obtain and evaluate samples
Step 4: Select the Product and Supplier
• Issue purchase order
Step 5: Evaluate Postpurchase
• Survey users
• Document performance

Step 2: Search for Information

In the second step of the decision process (for purchases other than straight rebuys), the buying center searches for information about products and suppliers. Members of the buying center may individually or collectively refer to reports in trade magazines and journals, seek advice from outside consultants, and pay close attention to marketing communications from different manufacturers and suppliers. As in consumer marketing, it's the job of marketers to make sure that information is available when and where business customers want it—by placing ads in trade magazines, by mailing brochures and other printed material to prospects, and by having a well-trained sales force regularly calling on customers to build long-term relationships.

There are thousands of specialized publications out there that cater to just about any industry you can think of. Usually sponsored by leading industry trade associations, each is bursting with information from competing companies that cater to a specific niche. Who needs that fluffy romance novel at the beach? Try leafing through the latest issue of *Chemical Processing* or *Meat and Poultry Magazine* instead.

Of course, sometimes B2B marketers try to get the information about their product into the hands of buyers via less specialized media. For example, in recent years AFLAC—the American Family Life Assurance Company of Columbus (the firm behind the famous duck)—has heavily advertised on TV even though most of its customers are in the B2B space. In fact, many end-user consumers don't have the foggiest notion what AFLAC sells—but they sure love to "quack up" over the duck's antics. The truth is, AFLAC's primary business is working with businesses (over 400,000 of them, in fact) to enhance their employee benefits packages with various types of insurance and other benefits in order to improve recruiting and retention of the firms' people. But their strategy of advertising directly on mass media was brilliant; now when an organizational buyer or human resources manager searches for these services, AFLAC's name will surely be at the top of the list (aided by great search engine optimization). Now there's a duck that's not out of water![39]

Business buyers often develop **product specifications**, that is, a written description of the quality, size, weight, color, features, quantity, training, warranty, service terms, and delivery requirements for the purchase. When the product needs are complex or technical, engineers and other experts are the key players who identify specific product characteristics they require and determine whether the organizations can get by with standardized, off-the-shelf items or if they need to acquire customized, made-to-order goods and services. Once the product specifications are in hand, the next step is to identify potential suppliers and obtain written or verbal proposals, or *bids*, from one or more of them. For standardized or branded products in which there are few if any differences in the products of different suppliers, this may be as simple as an informal request for pricing information, including discounts, shipping charges, and confirmation of delivery dates. At other times, the potential suppliers receive a formal written *request for proposal* or *request for quotation* that requires detailed information from vendors.

product specifications
A written description of the quality, size, weight, and other details required of a product purchase.

Step 3: Evaluate the Alternatives

In this stage of the business buying decision process, the buying center assesses the proposals it receives. Total spending for goods and services can have a major impact on the firm's profitability, so, all other things being equal, price can be a primary consideration. Pricing evaluations must take into account discount policies for certain quantities, returned-goods policies, the cost of repair and maintenance services, terms of payment, and the cost of financing large purchases. For capital equipment, cost criteria also include the life expectancy of the purchase, the expected resale value, and disposal costs for the old equipment. In some cases, the buying center may negotiate with the preferred supplier to match the lowest bidder.

Although a firm often selects a bidder because it offers the lowest price, there are times when it bases the buying decision on other factors. For example, in its lucrative B2B market, American Express wins bids for its travel agency business because it offers extra services other agencies don't or can't, such as a corporate credit card, monthly reports that detail the company's total travel expenses, and perks tied to the company's customer loyalty program.

The more complex and costly the purchase, the more time buyers spend searching for the best supplier—and the more marketers must do to win the order. In some cases, a company may even ask one or more of its current customers to participate in a **customer reference program**. In these situations, customers formally share success stories and actively recommend products to other potential clients, often as part of an online community composed of people with similar needs.

customer reference program
A formalized process by which customers formally share success stories and actively recommend products to other potential clients, usually facilitated through an on-line community.

Marketers often make formal presentations and product demonstrations to the buying center group. In the case of installations and large equipment, they may arrange for buyers to speak with or even visit other customers to examine how the product performs. For less complex products, the buying firm may ask potential suppliers for samples of the products so that its people can evaluate them personally. The buying center may ask salespeople from various companies to demonstrate their software for your Way Radical group so that you can all compare the capabilities of different products.

Step 4: Select the Product and Supplier

Once buyers have assessed all proposals, it's time for the rubber to hit the road. The next step in the buying process is the purchase decision when the group selects the best product and supplier to meet the organization's needs. Reliability and durability rank especially high for equipment and systems that keep the firm's operations running smoothly without interruption. For some purchases, warranties, repair service, and regular maintenance after the sale are important.

One of the most important decisions a buyer makes is how many suppliers can best serve the firm's needs. Sometimes having one supplier is more beneficial to the organization than having multiple suppliers. **Single sourcing**, in which a buyer and seller work quite closely, is particularly important when a firm needs frequent deliveries or specialized products. Single sourcing also helps assure consistency of quality of materials input into the production process. But reliance on a single source means that the firm is at the mercy of the chosen supplier to deliver the needed goods or services without interruption. If the single source doesn't come through, the firm's relationship with its own end users will very likely be affected.

However, using one or a few suppliers rather than many has its advantages. A firm that buys from a single supplier becomes a large customer with a lot of clout when it comes to negotiating prices and contract terms. Having one or a few suppliers also lowers the firm's administrative costs because it has fewer invoices to pay, fewer contracts to negotiate, and fewer salespeople to see than if it uses many sources.

In contrast, **multiple sourcing** means buying a product from several different suppliers. Under this system, suppliers are more likely to remain price competitive. And if one supplier has problems with delivery, the firm has others to fall back on. The automotive industry practices this philosophy: A vehicle manufacturer often won't buy a new product from a supplier unless the vendor's rivals also are capable of making the same item. This policy tends to stifle innovation, but it does ensure a steady supply of parts to feed to the assembly line.

Sometimes supplier selection is based on **reciprocity**, which means that a buyer and seller agree to be each other's customers by saying, essentially, "I'll buy from you, and you buy from me." For example, a firm that supplies parts to a company that manufactures trucks would agree to buy trucks from only that firm.

The U.S. government frowns on reciprocal agreements and often determines that such agreements between large firms are illegal because they limit free competition—new suppliers simply don't have a chance against the preferred suppliers. Reciprocity between smaller firms, that is, firms that are not so large as to control a significant proportion of the business in their industry, is legal in the U.S. if both parties voluntarily agree to it. In other countries, reciprocity is a practice that is common and even expected in B2B marketing.

Outsourcing occurs when firms obtain outside vendors to provide goods or services that might otherwise be supplied in-house. For example, Sodexo is the world's largest outsourcer for food and facilities management services with over 6,000 U.S. client sites. Colleges and universities are a major category of clientele for Sodexo (are they your school's vendor?), as these educational institutions want to focus on educating students rather than preparing and serving food. (Fortunately, your professors don't have to cook as well as teach!)

Outsourcing is an increasingly popular strategy, but in some cases it can be controversial. Many critics object when American companies contract with companies or individuals in remote places like China or India to perform work they used to do at home, a process known as **offshoring**. These tasks range from complicated jobs like writing computer code to fairly simple ones like manning reservations desks, staffing call centers for telephone sales, and even taking drive-through orders at American fast-food restaurants. (Yes, in some cases, it's actually more efficient for an operator in India to relay an order from a customer for a #3 Burger Combo to the restaurant's cooks than for an on-site person to take the order.)

single sourcing
The business practice of buying a particular product from only one supplier.

multiple sourcing
The business practice of buying a particular product from several different suppliers.

reciprocity
A trading partnership in which two firms agree to buy from one another.

outsourcing
The business buying process of obtaining outside vendors to provide goods or services that otherwise might be supplied in-house.

offshoring
A process by which companies contract with companies or individuals in remote places like China or India to perform work they used to do at home.

Controversy aside, many companies find that it's both cost efficient and productive to call on outsiders from around the world to solve problems their own scientists can't handle. We call this process **crowdsourcing**: put simply, a way to harness "crowds" to "source" solutions to business problems. Among the more interesting areas for crowdsourcing by marketers include brainstorming and feedback (**www.kluster.com**), brand names (**www.namethis.com**), product redesign (**www.redesignme.com**), and logo design (**www.99designs.com**), which hawks itself as follows: "Need a logo? No problem. Simply turn your logo/design project needs into a contest on 99designs. Submit a brief and determine a fee for the contest winner (minimum is around $150), then sit back and watch the crowd go to work. More than 40,000 designers use 99designs. After all the submissions are in, you can choose a design. What could be simpler?"[40]

Yet another type of buyer–seller partnership is **reverse marketing**. Instead of sellers trying to identify potential customers and then "pitching" their products, buyers try to find suppliers that can produce specifically needed products and then attempt to "sell" the idea to the suppliers. Often large poultry producers practice reverse marketing. Perdue supplies baby chickens, chicken food, financing for chicken houses, medications, and everything else necessary for farmers to lay "golden eggs" for the company. This assures the farmer that he or she will have a buyer while at the same time Purdue knows it can rely on a steady supply of chickens.

Step 5: Evaluate Postpurchase

Just as consumers evaluate purchases, an organizational buyer assesses whether the performance of the product and the supplier lives up to expectations. The buyer surveys the users to determine their satisfaction with the product as well as with the installation, delivery, and service that the supplier provides. For producers of goods, this may relate to the level of satisfaction of the final consumer of the buying firm's product. Has demand for the producer's product increased, decreased, or stayed the same? By documenting and reviewing supplier performance, a firm decides whether to keep or drop the supplier.

An important element in postpurchase evaluation is measurement. When you think about measuring elements of a customer's experience with a company and its products and brands, we'll bet you automatically think about end-user consumers—like travelers' views of their Marriott hotel stay or the taste of that new Starbucks coffee flavor. Similarly, in the B2B world, managers pay a lot of attention to the feedback they get from their customers about the purchases they've made.

B2B E-Commerce and Social Media

We know that the Internet transformed marketing—from the creation of new products to providing more effective and efficient marketing communications to the actual distribution of some products. This is certainly true in business markets as well. **B2B e-commerce** refers to Internet exchanges of information, goods, services, and payments between two or more businesses or organizations. It's not as glitzy as consumer e-commerce, but it sure has changed the way businesses operate. Using the Internet for e-commerce allows business marketers to link directly to suppliers, factories, distributors, and their customers, radically reducing the time necessary for order and delivery of goods, tracking sales, and getting feedback from customers.

In the simplest form of B2B e-commerce, the Internet provides an online catalog of goods and services that businesses need. Companies find that their Internet site is important to deliver online technical support, product information, order status information, and customer service to corporate customers. Many companies, for example, save millions of dollars a year when they replace hard-copy manuals with electronic downloads. And, of course, B2B e-commerce creates some exciting opportunities for a variety of B2B service industries.

crowdsourcing
A practice in which firms outsource marketing activities (such as selecting an ad) to a community of users.

reverse marketing
A business practice in which a buyer firm attempts to identify suppliers who will produce products according to the buyer firm's specifications.

business-to-business (B2B) e-commerce
On-line exchanges between companies and individual consumers.

Intranets and Extranets

Although the Internet is the primary means of B2B e-commerce, many companies maintain an *intranet*, which provides a more secure means of conducting business. As we said in Chapter 4, this term refers to an internal corporate computer network that uses Internet technology to link a company's departments, employees, and databases. **Intranets** give access only to authorized employees. They allow companies to process internal transactions with greater control and consistency because of stricter security measures than those they can use on the entire Web. Businesses also use intranets to videoconference, distribute internal documents, communicate with geographically dispersed branches, and train employees.

In contrast to an intranet, an **extranet** allows certain suppliers, customers, and others outside the organization to access a company's internal system. A business customer that a company authorizes to use its extranet can place orders online. Extranets can be especially useful for companies that need to have secure communications between the company and its dealers, distributors, and/or franchisees. As you can imagine, intranets and extranets are very cost efficient and save money for organizations.

In addition to saving companies money, extranets allow business partners to collaborate on projects (such as product design) and build relationships. GE's extranet, the Trading Process Network, began as a set of online purchasing procedures and has morphed into an extensive online extranet community that connects GE with large buyers, such as Con Edison.

The Dark Side of B2B E-Commerce

Doing business the Web-enabled way sounds great—perhaps too great. There are also security risks because so much information gets passed around in cyberspace. You've no doubt heard stories about hackers obtaining vast lists of consumers' credit card numbers from a number of retailers including Target and Neiman-Marcus. But companies have even greater worries. When hackers break into company sites, they can destroy company records and steal trade secrets. Both B2C and B2B e-commerce companies worry about *authentication* and ensuring that transactions are secure. This means making sure that only authorized individuals are allowed to access a site and place an order. Maintaining security also requires firms to keep the information transferred as part of a transaction, such as a credit card number, from criminals' hard drives.

Well-meaning employees also can create security problems. They can give out unauthorized access to company computer systems by being careless about keeping their passwords into the system a secret. For example, hackers can guess at obvious passwords—nicknames, birth dates, hobbies, or a spouse's name.

Some employees (and even nonemployees) are not so well-meaning—they deliberately create security breaches by leaking confidential documents or hacking into an organization's computer system for sensitive information. Edward Snowden became famous (or, rather, infamous) for his role in leaking thousands of classified documents to the media while working as a consultant for the National Security Agency. And Target's computer system was breached when hackers installed **malware** (software designed specifically to damage or disrupt computer systems) that captured more than 40 million credit card numbers and other customer data despite safeguards the retailer had in place.[41]

To increase security of their Internet sites and transactions, most companies now have safeguards in place—firewalls and encryption devices, to name the two most common methods, though, as we saw with Target, even these safeguards aren't always 100 percent hacker-proof.

A **firewall** is a combination of hardware and software that ensures that only authorized individuals gain entry into a computer system. The firewall monitors and controls all traffic between the Internet and the intranet to restrict access. Companies may even place additional firewalls within their intranet when they wish only designated employees to

intranet
An internal corporate communication network that uses Internet technology to link company departments, employees, and databases.

extranet
A private, corporate computer network that links company departments, employees, and databases to suppliers, customers, and others outside the organization.

malware
Software designed specifically to damage or disrupt computer systems.

firewall
A combination of hardware and software that ensures that only authorized individuals gain entry into a computer system.

have access to certain parts of the system. Although firewalls can be fairly effective (even though none is totally foolproof), they require costly, constant monitoring.

Encryption means scrambling a message so that only another individual (or computer) with the right "key" can unscramble it. Otherwise, it looks like gobbledygook. The message is inaccessible without the appropriate encryption software—kind of like a decoder ring your favorite superhero might wear. Without encryption, it would be easy for unethical people to get a credit card number by creating a "sniffer" program that intercepts and reads messages. A sniffer finds messages with four blocks of four numbers, copies the data, and voilà!—someone else has your credit card number.

Despite firewalls, encryption, and other security measures, Web security for B2B marketers remains a serious problem. The threat to intranet and extranet usage goes beyond competitive espionage. The increasing sophistication of hackers and Internet criminals who create viruses and worms and other approaches to disrupting individual computers and entire company systems mean that all organizations—and consumers—are vulnerable to attacks and must remain vigilant.

encryption
The process of scrambling a message so that only another individual (or computer) with the right "key" can unscramble it.

B2B and Social Media

While most of us associate business use of social media such as Facebook, LinkedIn, and Twitter with consumer marketing, B2B organizations are increasing their use of and their budgets for social media:[42]

- A recent study found three social media sites that B2B marketers are most likely to use: LinkedIn (91 percent), Twitter (85 percent), and Facebook (81 percent). Effectiveness ratings for the three sites were lower: LinkedIn (62 percent), Twitter (50 percent), and Facebook (30 percent).

- Forty-five percent of B2B marketers have gained a customer through LinkedIn.

- Job postings on LinkedIn for social media marketers have increased by 1,300 percent since 2010.

- Seventy-six percent of B2B marketers say they maintain company blogs, and 52 percent say it is an important to their company for communicating content.

- How do B2B marketers use social media? Eighty-three percent say they use sites to increase brand exposure, 69 percent to increase Web traffic, and 65 percent to gain marketing insights.

- Why are B2B and marketers turning to social media? Many say they are tired of the normal impersonal communication of advertising and that social media allow them to relate to one another.

- In 2013, global Internet ad spending including that by B2B firms grew to second place (20.6 percent) behind TV (40.2 percent), while newspaper advertising dropped to only 17.0 percent of total ad spending.

As with consumer marketing, a number of strategies can be successful in using social media marketing for B2B firms.[43] First, social media sites are good sources of information to identify target audiences. It's very helpful to know which potential customers your competitors interact with on social media. And, one of the most important uses of social media for both consumer marketers and business marketers is to monitor what your customers and others say about your product, your firm, and your competitors. A number of tools, such as Google Analytics, Radian6, and Social Mention, have been developed for this purpose. Social media provide platforms for marketers or consumers to join in conversations, get answers to their questions, and share experiences. Marketers who understand social media contribute to conversations on Twitter, Facebook, and blogs. They give good answers to questions and establish their credibility and a leadership position in the industry.

Here's my choice...

Real People, Real Choices

Why do you think Adam choose option 3?

1 Option   2 Option   3 Option

How It Worked Out at Insightpool

We approached DocuSign with all three options, but we encouraged the client to consider a different approach rather than just tweaking the current campaign. DocuSign agreed and chose option 3. The client was already hosting a sales webinar by a well-known figure in the selling world. Insightpool used its proprietary software to identify the most influential executives who would be the best prospects for DocuSign's services. These individuals were invited to contribute their expertise to the sales program. If enough of these executives participated, Insightpool knew that they would help to spread positive word of mouth about the client and serve as "brand ambassadors" for DocuSign to help the company build interest in its services and engage other potential customers in the decision-making process.

How Insightpool Measures Success

Two constants that relate to any advertising or marketing campaign are CTRs (click-through rate) and total redemptions. While these two were easy to measure, new key performance indicators are emerging every year in the social media space. As a result, we are aggregating totals from the social networks (in this case, the number of retweets, favorites, and @mentions were calculated) while also including new innovative metrics, such as expanded impressions (the total audience reach of those who are retweeting). Overall, Insightpool was able to raise the participation rate to 40 percent of the prospects the company contacted on behalf of the client.

Refer back to **page 174** for Adam's story

MyMarketingLab™

Go to **mymktlab.com** to complete the problems marked with this icon as well as additional Marketing Metrics questions only available in MyMarketingLab.

Objective Summary ➡ Key Terms ➡ Apply

CHAPTER 6
Study Map

1. Objective Summary (pp. 176–182)

Define *consumer behavior* and explain the purchase decision-making process.

Consumer behavior is the process individuals or groups go through to select, purchase, use, and dispose of goods, services, ideas, or experiences to satisfy their needs and desires.

Consumer decisions differ greatly, ranging from habitual, repeat (low-involvement) purchases to complex, extended problem-solving activities for important, risky (high-involvement) purchases. When consumers make important purchases, they go through a series of five steps. First, they recognize there is a problem to be solved. Then they search for information to make the best decision. Next, they evaluate a set of alternatives and judge them on the basis of various evaluative criteria. At this point, they are ready to make their purchasing decision. Following the purchase, consumers decide whether the product matched their expectations and may develop anxiety or regret or cognitive dissonance.

Key Terms

consumer behavior, p. 176

involvement, p. 177

perceived risk, p. 177

problem recognition, p. 178

information search, p. 179

search marketing, p. 180

search engine optimization (SEO), p. 180

search engine marketing (SEM), p. 180

sponsored search ads, p. 180

comparison shopping agents or shopbots, p. 180

evaluative criteria, p. 180

heuristics, p. 181

brand loyalty, p. 181

consumer satisfaction/dissatisfaction, p. 181

cognitive dissonance, p. 181

2. Objective Summary   (pp. 182–189)

Explain how internal factors influence consumers' decision-making processes.

Several internal factors influence consumer decisions. Perception is how consumers select, organize, and interpret stimuli. Motivation is an internal state that drives consumers to satisfy needs. Learning is a change in behavior that results from information or experience. Behavioral learning results from external events, while cognitive learning refers to internal mental activity. An attitude is a lasting evaluation of a person, object, or issue and includes three components: affect, cognition, and behavior. Personality influences how consumers respond to situations in the environment. Marketers seek to understand a consumer's self-concept in order to develop product attributes that match some aspect of the consumer's self-concept.

The age of consumers, family life cycle, and their lifestyle also are strongly related to consumption preferences. Marketers may use psychographics to group people according to activities, interests, and opinions that may explain reasons for purchasing products.

Key Terms

perception, p. 182

exposure, p. 183

subliminal advertising, p. 183

attention, p. 183

interpretation, p. 184

motivation, p. 184

hierarchy of needs, p. 184

gamification, p. 184

learning, p. 185

behavioral learning theories, p. 185

classical conditioning, p. 185

operant conditioning, p. 185

cognitive learning theory, p. 186

observational learning, p. 186

attitude, p. 186

affect, p. 187

cognition, p. 187

behavior, p. 187

personality, p. 187

self-concept, p. 187

family life cycle, p. 188

lifestyle, p. 188

psychographics, p. 188

AIOs, p. 188

3. Objective Summary   (pp. 189–194)

Show how situational factors and consumers' relationships with other people influence consumer behavior.

Situational influences include our physical surroundings and time pressures. Dimensions of the physical environment create arousal and pleasure and can determine how consumers react to the environment. The time of day, the season of the year, and how much time one has to make a purchase also affect decision making.

Consumers' overall preferences for products are determined by their membership in cultures and subcultures and by cultural values such as collectivism and individualism. Consumerism is a social movement directed toward protecting consumers from harmful business practices. Social class, group memberships, and opinion leaders are other types of social influences that affect consumer choices. A reference group is a set of people a consumer wants to please or imitate, and this affects the consumer's purchasing decisions. Purchases also result from conformity to real or imagined group pressures. Another way social influence is felt is in the expectations of society regarding the proper roles for men and women. Such expectations have led to many gender-typed products.

Key Terms

sensory marketing, p. 190

sensory branding, p. 190

time poverty, p. 190

culture, p. 191

subculture, p. 192

microcultures, p. 192

consumerism, p. 192

social class, p. 192

status symbols, p. 192

mass class, p. 193

reference group, p. 193

opinion leader, p. 193

gender roles, p. 194

4. Objective Summary (pp. 195–200)

Understand the characteristics of business-to-business markets and business-to-business market demand and how marketers classify business-to-business customers.

B2B markets include business or organizational customers that buy goods and services for purposes other than personal consumption. There are a number of major and minor differences between organizational and consumer markets. To be successful, marketers must understand these differences and develop strategies that can be effective with organizational customers. For example, business customers are usually few in number, they may be geographically concentrated, and they often purchase higher-priced products in larger quantities. Business demand derives from the demand for another good or service, is generally not affected by price increases or decreases, is subject to great fluctuations, and may be tied to the demand and availability of some other good.

Business customers include producers, resellers, governments, and not-for-profit organizations. Producers purchase materials, parts, and various goods and services needed to produce other goods and services to be sold at a profit. Resellers purchase finished goods to resell at a profit as well as other goods and services to maintain their operations. Governments and other not-for-profit organizations purchase the goods and services necessary to fulfill their objectives. The NAICS, a numerical coding system developed by NAFTA countries, is a widely used classification system for business and organizational markets.

Key Terms

business-to-business (B2B) markets, p. 195

organizational markets, p. 195

derived demand, p. 198

inelastic demand, p. 198

joint demand, p. 199

producers, p. 199

resellers, p. 199

government markets, p. 200

North American Industry Classification System (NAICS), p. 200

5. Objective Summary (pp. 201–209)

Identify and describe the different business buying situations and the business buying decision process including the use of e-commerce and social media.

The buyclass framework identifies the degree and effort required to make a business buying decision. Purchase situations can be straight rebuy, modified rebuy, and new-task buying. A buying center is a group of people who work together to make a buying decision. The roles in the buying center are (1) the initiator, who recognizes the need for a purchase; (2) the user, who will ultimately use the product; (3) the gatekeeper, who controls the flow of information to others; (4) the influencer, who shares advice and expertise; (5) the decider, who makes the final decision; and (6) the buyer, who executes the purchase. The steps in the business buying process are similar to those in the consumer decision process but are often somewhat more complex. For example, in the search for information, B2B firms often develop written product specifications, identify potential suppliers, and obtain proposals and quotations.

B2B e-commerce refers to Internet exchanges of information, goods and services, and payments between two or more businesses or organizations. B2B firms often maintain intranets that give access only to employees or extranets that allow access to certain suppliers and other outsiders. Firms often install firewalls and use encryption to prevent problems from hackers and other threats to the security of the firm's intranets and extranets. B2B firms are increasingly using social media to gather information on target audiences, increase brand exposure and Web traffic, monitor what customers and others are saying, and provide a platform for conversations with customers.

Key Terms

buyclass, p. 201

straight rebuy, p. 201

modified rebuy, p. 201

new-task buy, p. 202

buying center, p. 202

product specifications, p. 205

customer reference program, p. 205

single sourcing, p. 206

multiple sourcing, p. 206

reciprocity, p. 206

outsourcing, p. 206

offshoring, p. 206

crowdsourcing, p. 207

reverse marketing, p. 207

business-to-business (B2B) e-commerce, p. 207

intranet, p. 208

extranet, p. 208

malware, p. 208

firewall, p. 208

encryption, p. 209

Chapter **Questions** and **Activities**

Concepts: Test Your Knowledge

6-1. What is consumer behavior? Why is it important for marketers to understand consumer behavior?

6-2. Explain habitual decision making, limited problem solving, and extended problem solving. What is the role of perceived risk in the decision process?

6-3. Explain the steps in the consumer decision-making process?

6-4. What is perception? Explain the three parts of the perception process: exposure, attention, and interpretation.

6-5. Describe Maslow's hierarchy of needs as it relates to motivation. How does gamification satisfy some of these needs?

6-6. What is behavioral learning? What is cognitive learning?

6-7. What are the three components of attitudes? What is personality?

6-8. What is family life cycle? Explain what lifestyle means.

6-9. How do situational influences, such as the physical environment and time, shape consumer purchase decisions?

6-10. What are cultures, subcultures, and microcultures? What is the significance of social class to marketers?

6-11. What are reference groups, and how do they influence consumers? What are opinion leaders? What are gender roles?

6-12. How do B2B markets differ from consumer markets?

6-13. Explain what we mean by derived demand, inelastic demand, fluctuating demand, and joint demand.

6-14. How do we generally classify B2B markets?

6-15. Describe the buyclass framework. What are new-task buys, modified rebuys, and straight rebuys?

6-16. What is a buying center? What are the roles of the various people in a buying center?

6-17. Explain the steps in the business buying decision process.

6-18. What is consumerism? Why is it important to marketers?

6-19. Explain the role of intranets and extranets in B2B e-commerce. Describe the security issues firms face in B2B e-commerce and some safeguards firms use to reduce their security risks.

Activities: Apply What You've Learned

⭐ **6-20.** *Creative Homework/Short Project* This chapter indicated that consumers go through a series of steps (from problem recognition to postpurchase evaluation) as they make purchases. Write a detailed report describing what you as a consumer would do in each of these steps when deciding to purchase one of the following products:
  a. A suit for an upcoming job interview
  b. A piece of jewelry to be given to a special friend for his or her birthday
  c. A fast-food lunch
  d. A Christmas tree
  Then make suggestions for what marketers might do to make sure that consumers like you who are going through each step in the consumer decision process

move toward the purchase of their brand. (*Hint:* Think about product, place, price, and promotion strategies.)

6-21. *In Class, 10–25 Minutes for Teams* During the last week of class, your professor explains how she wants to employ a gamification strategy next semester to further motivate and engage students, and she is asking for your help. Develop a simple gamification strategy that she can use in the classroom. Describe what the goals should be, how progress will be measured, and what the reward system will be.

6-22. *Creative Homework/Short Project* You probably had more than one school in mind before you ultimately decided on the college or university you are now attending. To better understand how consumers make decisions, prepare an outline that shows how internal influences like perception, motivation, and so on had an impact on the decision you made about which school to attend. Include specific examples for each type of internal influence in your outline.

6-23. *Creative Homework/Short Project* Think about some of the products and services you purchase each month (pizza on Saturday night or your smart phone bill) as well as a few impulse purchases you might make (new music from iTunes). Categorize each of these items according to Maslow's hierarchy of needs. Explain why your budget does or doesn't match this hierarchy of needs (i.e., most of your budget goes toward physiological needs, followed by safety needs, etc.). What does this say about your motivations?

6-24. *In Class, 10–25 Minutes for Teams* Assume you are a sales manager for a firm that is a distributor of hospital equipment and supplies. Your company offers its customers a wide range of products—everything from disposable gloves to high-tech patient monitors. Thus, purchases made by your customers include straight rebuys, modified rebuys, and new-task purchases. Your job is to explain to your new salesperson the differences among these types of purchases and how to effectively "get the business" for all three types of purchases. In a role-playing exercise with another classmate, provide the needed information and advice.

6-25. *For Further Research (Individual)* In this chapter, we learned that some products are status symbols and serve as visible markers that provide a way for people to flaunt their membership in higher social classes. Using the Internet and magazines (your library probably has a collection of magazines), find ads and websites for status symbol products. Examine how the websites and the ads communicate that the product is a status symbol. How do they relate to a higher social class? Make a list of the products and the visuals and words that are used to promote the status symbol products.

6-26. *For Further Research (Groups)* Assume that you work for an established firm that sells running shoes. Your company wants to get a better idea of what its customers and others are saying about your product, your firm, and your competitors. You've heard that tools such as Google Analytics, Radian6, and Social Media can help you gather this information. Using the Internet, research these tools and come to a consensus on which would be the best tool for your organization. Explain your reasoning.

Apply Marketing Metrics

B2B customers (clients) are very busy professionals and thus are notoriously reluctant to take time to provide data to marketers. In order to measure important issues described in the chapter, such as overall client satisfaction, service quality by the vendor firm, level of customer engagement, repurchase intentions, and speed and effectiveness of problem resolution, marketers must employ the most user-friendly and efficient data collection methods available when dealing with these professional business clients. Otherwise, it is highly unlikely that they will take time to provide any useful data for market planning and decision making.

⭐ **6-27.** Take a few minutes to go back and briefly review what you learned in Chapter 4 about the different approaches to collecting data. Propose an approach to collecting the above types of information from a busy B2B customer in a way that is most likely to result in his or her cooperation. Be as specific as you can in describing your chosen approach and explain why you selected it.

Choices: What Do You Think?

⭐ **6-28.** *Critical Thinking* Changing demographics and cultural values are important to marketers. What are some current trends that may affect the marketing of the following products?
  a. Housing
  b. Food
  c. Education
  d. Clothing
  e. Travel and tourism
  f. Automobiles

6-29. *Critical Thinking* Consumers often rely on opinion leaders for information and influence when considering a purchase. Do you consider yourself an opinion leader? If so, which product category? Justify your claim in terms of your knowledge, interest, and expertise.

⭐ **6-30.** *Ethics* Marketers have been shelling out the bucks on sensory marketing techniques for years to appeal to your subconscious mind. And studies show that it works. But is sensory marketing fair? Some say it's a way to enhance the purchasing process, while others say marketers are unethically manipulating consumers. What are some of the pros and cons associated with sensory marketing? What is your position?

6-31. *Critical Thinking* E-commerce is dramatically changing the way B2B transactions take place. What are the advantages of B2B e-commerce to companies? To society? Are there any disadvantages of B2B e-commerce?

6-32. *Critical Thinking* M-commerce (short for mobile commerce) is a rapidly growing category of e-commerce that takes place via a smart phone or tablet instead of a desktop or laptop computer. How has M-commerce changed the way consumers shop? What do marketers need to do now and in the future to better support their M-commerce customers?

6-33. *Critical Thinking* The consumer decision-making process may be quick for some, but long and time consuming for others. Either way, consumers may still experience cognitive dissonance after, post-purchase evaluation. What are the causes of cognitive dissonance? What could consumers and marketers do to address buyers, anxiety and regrets?

6-34. *Ethics* When firms implement a single sourcing policy in their buying, other possible suppliers do not have an opportunity to compete for the business. Is this ethical? What are the advantages to the company? What are the disadvantages?

6-35. *Critical Thinking* In the buying center, the gatekeeper controls information flow to others in the center. Thus, the gatekeeper determines which possible sellers are heard and which are not. Does the gatekeeper have too much power? What policies might be implemented to make sure that all possible sellers are treated fairly?

6-36. *Critical Thinking* Outsourcing and offshoring are practices often surrounded by controversy. What are the benefits of outsourcing for businesses? For consumers? What are the disadvantages of outsourcing for businesses? For consumers? Should outsourcing be regulated to protect American interests both at home and abroad? Why or why not?

Miniproject: Learn by Doing

The purpose of this miniproject is to increase your understanding of the internal factors influencing consumers, purchasing decisions. Internal factors include perception, motivation, learning, attitudes, personality, age, and lifestyle. Consider the internal factors influencing purchasing decisions for the following items (or other items of your choice), and prepare a report to present in class.

- A new car
- A fine-dining restaurant
- Smart phones
- Organic food
- Fitness center
- Retirement home

6-37. How do our sensory receptors influence our perception of a brand new car?

6-38. Motivation is an internal state that drives consumers to take action to satisfy their needs. Explain the five motives of Maslow's hierarchy of needs in relation to a fine dining restaurant.

6-39. How does the classical conditioning theory influence a consumer's decision to purchase a smart phone? To what extent do marketers of smart phones utilize cognitive learning and observational learning theories in advertising their products?

6-40. Explain consumers' attitude toward organic food through the processes of cognition, affection, and behavior. Can the attitude be negative?

6-41. How would marketers utilize the concept of consumer personality in promoting a fitness center? Do you think the pitching of a negative self-concept in advertising is more convincing than pitching a positive self-concept?

6-42. Other than age, how does lifestyle relate to the marketing of a retirement home?

Marketing in **Action** Case | Real Choices at Electrolux

How many customers like to "clean up" after they "clean up?" Not many. For the typical consumer, things can get pretty messy when it's time to empty the family vacuum cleaner. At least that's what Electrolux is counting on.

Electrolux, a Swedish appliance manufacturer headquartered in Stockholm, Sweden, is the world's second-largest household appliance maker. The company sells major appliances and vacuum cleaners under a variety of brand names, including its own, that are intended for consumer and professional use. Formerly, Electrolux vacuums used the brand name of Eureka; however, since 2000, the company sells both Eureka- and Electrolux-branded vacuums.

In its almost 100-year-old history, Electrolux used engineers and accountants to manage the product development process. According to Bill Fischer, a professor at Swiss business school IMD who specializes in innovation management, the idea of seeking insights from its customers ". . . would have been revolutionary." But that's exactly what Electrolux did. Market researchers from the company watched and talked to people vacuuming in Australia, France, and Russia. These observations led to the development of the UltraCaptic bagless vacuum cleaner. The vacuum has a unique "Compact and Go" solution that reduces the dust created when emptying the vacuum. The UltraCaptic compresses the dust into a spongy pellet the company calls a dirt cake, thus eliminating the flyaway particles when the user empties the vacuum.

In addition to "cleaner" emptying, the UltraCaptic is packed full of other innovative features. It is able to be efficient while being quieter that most other high-end vacuums. It offers a bagless cyclonic system that gives customers consistent suction power to thoroughly clean their homes. Customers have the option of moving between wood floors, carpets, tiles, furniture, crevices, and any other surfaces.

All of these advantages are great; however, the success of the UltraCaptic is not a sure thing. A major concern is price; consumers may not be willing to pay the premium price of $700 for the UltraCaptic. While an important feature of the UltraCaptic is its quieter operation, some consumers assume that in order for a vacuum cleaner to perform well, it must make a loud noise. They believe that the noise is required because of the powerful suction coming from the motor. These buyers may not believe that a quiet machine is doing the job they paid for.

Furthermore, the premium vacuum market is highly competitive. Dyson is one of the market leaders and has a perception of high quality among consumers. The brand is bolstered by its cutting-edge design, powerful suction, and premium pricing. Miele, a manufacturer of high-end domestic appliances based in Germany, offers various vacuum cleaners that have a reputation for exceptional quality, performance, and durability.

For Electrolux, the challenge is obvious. Will customers perceive that the UltraCaptic has a difference worth paying for?

You Make the Call

6-43. What is the decision facing Electrolux?

6-44. What factors are important in understanding this decision situation?

6-45. What are the alternatives?

6-46. What decision(s) do you recommend?

6-47. What are some ways to implement your recommendation?

MyMarketingLab™

Go to **mymktlab.com** for Auto-graded writing questions as well as the following Assisted-graded writing questions:

6-48. *Creative Homework/Short Project.* Sometimes advertising or other marketing activities cause problem recognition by showing consumers how much better off they would be with a new product or by pointing out problems with products they already own. Discuss problem recognition for the following product categories. Make a list of some ways marketers might try to stimulate problem recognition for each product. Present your ideas to your class.
   a. Toothpaste
   b. A home security system
   c. A new automobile
   d. An online dating service
   e. A health club membership

6-49. *Creative Homework/Short Project.* As a director of purchasing for a firm that manufactures motorcycles, you have been notified that the price of an important part used in the manufacture of the bikes has nearly doubled from $100 to nearly $200. You see your company having three choices: (1) buying the part and passing the cost on to the customer by increasing your price; (2) buying the part and absorbing the increase in cost, keeping the price of your bikes the same; and (3) buying a lower-priced part that will be of lower quality. Prepare a list of pros and cons for each alternative. Then explain your recommendation and justification for it.

Segmentation, Target Marketing, and Positioning

Margaret Molloy

▼ A Decision Maker at Siegel+Gale

Margaret Molloy is the global chief marketing officer (CMO) at Siegel+Gale, a leading strategic branding firm, where she is responsible for marketing and business development initiatives. Known as "the simplicity company," Siegel+Gale helps clients define, design, and deliver brand experiences that are unexpectedly clear and remarkably fresh. Founded in 1969, the firm has been building leading brands across industries—and the world—for 45 years. Since its founding by branding pioneer Alan Siegel, Siegel+Gale has helped drive business results for brands such as Aetna, Bank of America, Haier, Dell, Dow Chemical Company, Four Seasons Hotels and Resorts, the Internal Revenue Service, King Abdullah University of Science and Technology, Microsoft, Motorola, Pfizer, SAP, Sony PlayStation, Yahoo!, the YMCA, SAG-AFTRA, the Television Academy, and many more. Previously, Margaret was CMO and partner at Velocidi, a digital agency. She also served as senior vice president of marketing at Gerson Lehrman Group, the world's leading expert network. Margaret has led marketing organizations at Siebel Systems—where she was a member of the Siebel Systems CEO's Circle—and served as vice president of Marketing at Telecom Ireland US (eircom). Based in New York, Margaret is also on the advisory board of Sightsavers International and is an active member of the American Ireland Fund.

Margaret has been published in *Forbes*, *Forbes CMO Network*, *Fast Company*, *The Economist Lean back*, *Wired*, and many more leading business publications. A captivating speaker, she is renowned for her skill at convening and moderating provocative panel discussions with industry thought leaders. She has been consistently recognized as one the most influential CMOs on Twitter. Follow her @MargaretMolloy.

A native of Ireland, Margaret earned her MBA from Harvard Business School and received her undergraduate degrees from the University of Ulster, Northern Ireland, and La Universidad de Valladolid, Spain.

Margaret's Info

What I do when I'm not working?
Spend time with young sons and support philanthropic causes in the Irish community.

First job out of school?
Marketing executive with Enterprise Ireland, the Irish state economic development agency.

Career high?
Recognized as one of the top 100 Irish Americans in business by *Irish America* magazine—my heritage is important to me.

A job-related mistake I wish I hadn't made?
Moving to a new company and not taking enough time to appreciate a company's cultural dynamic. A playbook that works in one environment doesn't necessarily translate. You must seek to understand the company culture and modify your management style accordingly before you can affect meaningful change through employees.

Business book I'm reading now?
Simple by Alan Siegel.

My hero?
My parents.

My motto to live by?
Great execution is the ultimate differentiator.

What drives me?
Staying relevant in my profession and being on the edge of what affects modern marketing.

My management style?
Hire the best people and empower and motivate them to be the best they can be.

Don't do this when interviewing with me?
Neglect to research the firm.

My pet peeve?
People who don't keep their promises.

Here's my problem...

Real People, Real Choices

Founded in 1969, Siegel+Gale is a global strategic branding firm specializing in brand development, identity design, naming, simplification, research and insights, and digital strategy. In a highly competitive market, clients want to hire branding professionals who have an established point of view. This means that Siegel+Gale must engage in the new discipline of content marketing, which refers to the strategy of establishing thought leadership in the form of bylines, blogs, commenting opportunities, videos, sharable social images, and infographics. Publishing content that the firm's employees create is a powerful way to differentiate and position the firm and to bring the points of view of the professionals who work there to life. As the executive responsible for marketing the firm to its stakeholders, Margaret saw the need for Siegel+Gale to implement a powerful content marketing strategy in order to harness the intellectual rigor of the firm on a wide range of topics. It needed to demonstrate the value of the firm's services and the relevance of the point of view on creating "simple" brand experiences.

But mobilizing a large number of professionals to publish great content while they juggle other responsibilities is not easy. In an extremely busy firm, where the majority of professionals' time is consumed with billable client deliverables, motivating employees to produce marketing content presented a number of challenges. To propel these activities, the Siegel+Gale marketing team needed to devise a way to encourage employees across the firm to participate.

The first challenge for the marketing team was to inspire a behavioral shift among employees—Margaret needed to enlist team members across practices to become content creators, but balancing this new demand with their client deliverables was essential. The marketing team recognized there were many different segments of employees across the firm based on discipline, comfort level with content creation, and familiarity with various media platforms. Margaret knew it was unlikely that all team members at Siegel+Gale would respond to this change in the same way or participate in the firm's content marketing initiative on the same media platforms. This became a matter of addressing employees as segments in the same way that marketers who sell products and services to outside companies or individuals divide their total customer base into smaller slices.

The second challenge was to raise the company's social media profile. It is not enough to produce insightful content—you have to make that content visible, accessible, and "native" across platforms through which prospective clients access that content. A fundamental goal of the strategy was to increase both the firm's and its employees' social media activity to focus on the opportunity and value of connecting with influencers, that is, CMOs, reporters, and bloggers.

The marketing team therefore decided to train employees to shift their focus and approach daily activities as potential content sources. For example, elements of a pitch could be developed into a point of view for a byline, and photos from cultural events and conferences could become a photo blog. The team devised a plan to sell the idea of content marketing internally with a training program it could customize employees based on their individual roles, preferences, and abilities. This segmentation strategy would provide Margaret's team with valuable raw material in various formats that flowed from employee segments. Her team could use this material to create engaging social media content that would showcase Siegel+Gale's thought leadership to influencers on social media channels, including Twitter, LinkedIn, SlideShare, Facebook, and Pinterest. Employees could contribute by developing blog posts, white papers, research reports, byline articles, and third-party media coverage.

This was an exciting idea, but Margaret knew you can't make great wine from lousy grapes. As the new Global CMO, Margaret's role was to train, empower, and inspire employees across all disciplines to create insightful content her team could use to keep the company front and center in the constantly evolving social media environment. She recognized the fact that not all Siegel+Gale's employees are the same, so the organization must define its own employee "market segments" in terms of the types of content the members of each segment excelled at producing. For example, Siegel+Gale's research practice was experienced at producing detailed studies that could lend themselves to compelling white papers or that could be distilled into visually arresting infographics. The content team was adept at writing compelling blogs. Other team members were more visual, so their sharable content was more likely to take the form of videos or photography. Finally, many strategists could create amazing presentation decks they could post on SlideShare.

Another aspect of the segmentation process was the attitude of team members held toward publishing content and their willingness to dedicate time to doing so. Some professionals would respond positively to firmwide initiatives that "automated" the process of converting their work to content the firm could share externally. Others would respond well to the individual recognition they would receive for contributing to Siegel+Gale's heightened profile in the marketplace. Still another segment would welcome the opportunity to initiate their own content marketing as a creative extension of their work and value the enhanced profile they would receive when they shared their views externally.

You Choose

Which **Option** would you choose, and **why**?

1. ☐YES ☐NO   2. ☐YES ☐NO   3. ☐YES ☐NO

See what **option** Margaret chose on **page 238** ➡

MyMarketingLab™

Margaret considered her **Options** 1·2·3

1 Option

Promote content creation from a top-down approach. Issue a directive from senior management for everyone across the firm to contribute content. This option would make firmwide participation mandatory. For example, all team members across practice areas would be expected to develop a blog or a SlideShare presentation every month. By simply defining this activity as a part of each employee's job description, a steady flow of content would begin almost immediately. Still, Margaret wasn't sure if such a directive would drive long-term results. The ultimate goal was to win the hearts and minds of colleagues across the firm by showing them the power of content marketing. The marketing team didn't want to merely dictate and use the power of authority to affect change. They might be assured of quantity but not quality.

2 Option

Nominate senior directors to lead content-creation initiatives. The marketing team would designate specific senior executives across the firm's global offices to act as drivers of the content strategy. This process would empower the leaders to be role models, and their actions would filter down through all levels of the firm. For example, the company would mandate that each senior leader develop a blog post or byline every week. Hopefully, others who reported to these top-level people would see the value of doing this as well. However, this option runs the risk of missing a lot of talent in the firm. Not everyone would be motivated to emulate what their managers were required to do if it weren't required of them as well. And subject matter expertise is not always directly correlated to seniority. For example, a designer may not be senior in rank but could be deep in expertise.

3 Option

Recruit champions across all levels to contribute. An all-inclusive strategy would recruit advocates across all levels and practice areas. It would provide them with training to produce content that strengthens not only their individual profile but also the firm's. Siegel+Gale would reward employees at all levels by publicly recognizing their efforts every week. If it was successful, this approach eventually would develop a broad base of contributors and thus build the "organizational muscle" in content creation across practice areas. Employees up and down the firm hierarchy would be able to see the value of participating, and the pathway to get themselves involved would be clear since some of their peers already were on board with the process. However, this option was very ambitious because it would take a lot of time and effort to develop this "grassroots" network. Margaret knew that some employees wouldn't respond well to a voluntary addition to their job responsibilities. In addition, this more informal approach would require a lot more hand-holding from her team in terms of individualized training and marketing resources to identify champions and encourage their colleagues to get on the train.

Now, put yourself in Margaret's shoes. Which option would you choose, and why?

1 Target Marketing:
Select and Enter a Market

OBJECTIVE

Identify the steps in the target marketing process.
(pp. 218–219)

In the opening vignette on Margaret Malloy at Siegel+Gale you saw that **content marketing** refers to the strategy of establishing thought leadership in the form of bylines, blogs, commenting opportunities, videos, sharable social images, and infographics. Content marketing is but one way to differentiate and position a brand against its defined target markets. Way back in Chapter 1, we defined a market as all the customers and potential customers who share a common need that can be satisfied by a specific product, who have the resources to exchange for it, who are willing to make the exchange, and who have the authority to make the exchange. And at this point in your study of marketing, you know that key goals of the marketer are to create value, build customer relationships, and satisfy needs. But in our modern, complex society, it's naive to assume that everyone's needs are the same. Today, it's a complex task to understand people's differing needs because technological and cultural advances create a condition of **market fragmentation**. This means that people's diverse interests and backgrounds naturally divide them into numerous groups with distinct needs and wants. Because of this diversity, the same good or service will not appeal to everyone.

Consider, for example, the effects of fragmentation in higher education. Before you faced the big decision of which classes to register for, including this one, you had the even bigger task of deciding on which one of the numerous types of colleges or universities you would attend. Not only did you have the more traditional schools to choose from—

content marketing
The strategy of establishing thought leadership in the form of bylines, blogs, commenting opportunities, videos, sharable social images, and infographics.

market fragmentation
The creation of many consumer groups due to a diversity of distinct needs and wants in modern society.

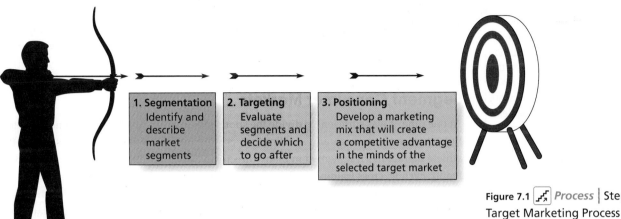

Figure 7.1 Process | Steps in the Target Marketing Process

Target marketing strategy consists of three separate steps. Marketers first divide the market into segments based on customer characteristics, then select one or more segments, and finally develop products to meet the needs of those specific segments.

community or technical colleges and public or private four-year schools—but you also had newer schools, such as the for-profit University of Phoenix or Kaplan University, and several online-only schools, such as Western Governors University. Each of these institutions of higher learning serves a different market need, and what may meet your needs currently might not meet your needs in the future. Fortunately, there are plenty of options to choose from, depending on your abilities, background, and of course the old checkbook!

Marketers must balance the efficiency of mass marketing where they serve the same items to everyone, with the effectiveness that comes when they offer each individual exactly what he or she wants. Mass marketing certainly costs much less—when we offer one product to everyone, we eliminate the need for separate advertising campaigns and distinctive packages for each item. However, consumers see things differently. From their perspective the best strategy would be to offer the perfect product just for them. Unfortunately, that's often not realistic.

For 40 years, Burger King's motto was "Have It Your Way," but in 2014 it scrapped that iconic theme for an updated version of the slogan: "Be Your Way." BK says that the new motto is intended to remind people that "they can and should live how they want anytime. It's ok to not be perfect. . . . Self-expression is most important and it's our differences that make us individuals instead of robots."[1] This change is convenient for BK because the huge chain could deliver on the old promise only to a point: "Having" it your way is fine as long as you stay within the confines of familiar condiments, such as mustard or ketchup. Don't dream of topping your burger with blue cheese, mango sauce, or some other "exotic" ingredient.

So, instead of trying to sell the same thing to everyone, marketers select a **target marketing strategy** in which they divide the total market into different segments based on customer characteristics, select one or more segments, and develop products to meet the needs of those specific segments. Figure 7.1 illustrates the three-step process of segmentation, targeting, and positioning, and it's what we're going to check out in this chapter. Let's start with the first step—segmentation.

target marketing strategy
Dividing the total market into different segments on the basis of customer characteristics, selecting one or more segments, and developing products to meet the needs of those specific segments.

2

OBJECTIVE

Understand the need for market segmentation and the approaches available to do it.

(pp. 219–231)

Step 1: Segmentation

Segmentation is the process of dividing a larger market into smaller pieces based on one or more meaningful, shared characteristics. This process is a way of life for almost all marketers in both consumer and business-to-business markets. The truth is that you can't please all the people all the time, so you need to take your best shot.

Just how do marketers segment a population? How do they divide the whole pie into smaller slices they can "digest"? The marketer must decide on one or more useful **segmentation variables**—that is,

segmentation
The process of dividing a larger market into smaller pieces based on one or more meaningfully shared characteristics.

segmentation variables
Dimensions that divide the total market into fairly homogeneous groups, each with different needs and preferences.

APPLYING ▼ Segmentation

As CMO at Siegel+Gale, Margaret understood the value of segmenting a market into different customer groups. She also knew that there were many different segments of employees across the firm. Using that philosophy, she considered segmenting Siegel+Gale employees in her content marketing program.

Generation Y
The group of consumers born between 1979 and 1994.

dimensions that divide the total market into fairly homogeneous groups, each with different needs and preferences. In this section, we'll take a look at this process, beginning with the types of segmentation variables that marketers use to divide up end-user consumers. Then we'll move on to business-to-business segmentation.

Segment Consumer Markets

At one time, it was sufficient to divide the sports shoe market into athletes and nonathletes. But take a walk through any sporting goods store today and you'll quickly see that the athlete market has fragmented in many directions. Shoes designed for jogging, basketball, tennis, cycling, cross training, and even skateboarding beckon us from the aisles.

Nike, a brand already popular among many different types of athletes and enthusiasts, was in good shape to address this new fragmentation, especially when it came to targeting the extreme or "action" sports (think skateboarding or BMX) that are popular with **Generation Y**—people born between 1979 and 1994.[2] But Nike had to be careful in targeting this market, which doesn't like to be "sold" to. Instead, as part of its new "Chosen" campaign, Nike got directly involved with the athletes to help them showcase their sports and even allowed to athletes to "wear" other sponsors. The lyrics of their new ads, which include "I've got a thing, you've got a thing . . . everybody's got a thing," (translation: "We're not coming into your world to change you.") resonated well with this independent market.[3]

We need several segmentation variables if we want to slice up the market for all the shoe variations available today. First, not everyone is willing or able to drop a few Benjamins on the latest sneakers, so marketers consider income (Note: A pair of Air Jordan Friends and Family edition kicks will run you a cool $6,000).[4] Second, men may be more interested in basketball shoes for shooting hoops with the guys, while women snap up the latest Pilates styles, so marketers also consider gender. Because not all age-groups are equally interested in buying specialized athletic shoes, we slice the larger consumer "pie" into smaller pieces in a number of ways, including demographic, psychographic, and behavioral differences. In the case of demographic segmentation, there are several key subcategories of demographics: age (including generational differences), gender, family life cycle, income and social class, ethnicity, and place of residence, sometimes referred to separately as geographic segmentation. 📷 Figure 7.2 summarizes the dominant approaches to segmenting consumer markets.

In the sections that follow, we'll consider each of these segmentation approaches in turn, but first a note of caution. When it comes to marketing to some groups—in particular, lower-income individuals, the poorly educated, nonnative-language speakers, and children—it is incumbent on marketers to exercise the utmost care not to take undue advantage of their circumstances. In Chapter 2, we introduced a global segment called the *bottom of the pyramid, (BOP)*, which is the collective name for the group of over 4 billion consumers throughout the world who live on less than $2 a day. Ethical marketers must be sensitive to the different conditions in which people find themselves and proactively work to uphold a high level of honesty and trust with all segments of the public. Doing so is nothing short of marketing's social responsibility.

One other caveat is needed before we jump into our discussion of different market segments. Identifying segments is not, repeat *not*, intended by marketers as a form of stereotyping. The idea of segmenting markets is to identify groups of consumers with similar needs so that marketing to them can be done more

Figure 7.2 📷 *Snapshot* | Segmenting Consumer Markets

Consumer markets can be segmented by demographic, psychographic, or behavioral criteria.

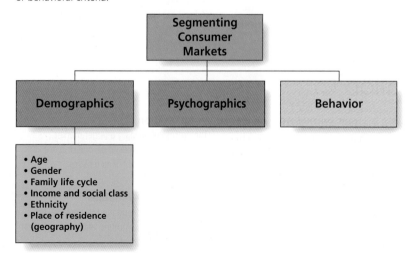

efficiently and effectively versus a mass-market approach. That doesn't necessarily mean that we want to pigeonhole a group of people because they happen to share an important characteristic such as gender or place of residence.

Segment by Demographics: Age

As we stated in Chapter 2, **demographics** are statistics that measure observable aspects of a population, including size, age, gender, ethnic group, income, education, occupation, and family structure. These descriptors are vital to identify the best potential customers for a good or service. Because they represent objective characteristics, they usually are easy to identify, and then it's just a matter of tailoring messages and products to relevant age-groups.

Consumers of different age-groups have different needs and wants. Members of a generation tend to share the same outlook, values, and priorities. We call such a focus **generational marketing**.

For example, *children* are an attractive age segment for many marketers. Although kids obviously have a lot to say about purchases of toys and games, they influence other family purchases as well (just watch them at work in the grocery store!). By one estimate, American children aged 4 to 12 have a say in family-related purchases of more than $1.2 trillion a year.[5] The popularity of shows such as Nickelodeon's *Sam & Cat*, which brings together stars from its *iCarly* and *Victorious* series, is helping to propel star Ariana Grande into a successful singing career. The younger-girl market segment loves the idea of being a pop star, and the girls live their dream vicariously through Grande as well as shows like *American Idol* and *The Voice*.

Teens are also an attractive market segment. The 12- to 17-year-old age-group is growing nearly twice as fast as the general population—and teens and *tweens* (kids between the ages of 8 and 14) spend an average of $5,000 per year.[6] Much of this money goes toward "feel-good" products: music, video games, cosmetics, and fast food—with the occasional tattoo or hookah pen thrown in as well. Because they are so interested in many different products and have the resources to obtain them, many marketers avidly court the teen market.[7] Macy's, for example, caters to tween girls with its Material Girl collection for juniors (represented by Madonna's daughter, Lourdes) as well as the older members of this generation with its mystylelab and Impulse departments.[8] Marketers refer to individuals born after 1994 as **Millennials or Generation Z** although the term "Millennials" is also sometimes (mistakenly) attached to the Generation Y period (confusing, eh?).

As mentioned earlier, Generation Y consists of people born between the years 1979 and 1994. Sometimes also called *Echo Boomers*, this age segment is the first generation to grow up online, and it is more ethnically diverse than earlier generations. Generation Y is an attractive market for a host of consumer products because of its size (approximately 27 percent of the population) and free-spending nature—as a group, it spends about $1.3 trillion annually.[9]

But Generation Y consumers are also hard to reach because they resist reading and increasingly turn off the TV to opt instead for streaming video and digital video recordings. As a result, many marketers have had to develop other ways to reach this generation "where they live," which is in large measure through their smart phones and tablets, using social media and related technology. We'll talk more about the shift to new-age marketing communications techniques later in this book.

We already know that Gen Yers are technology savvy, but what else defines them as a generation? A Pew Research study shows that Millennials are less inclined to associate themselves with a political party (50 percent are politically independent) or a religion (29 percent have no religious affiliation). They are unmarried (only 26 percent are married). And they are a racially diverse generation—43 percent of Gen Yers are nonwhite.[10]

The group of consumers born between 1965 and 1978 consists of 46 million Americans known as **Generation X**, who unfortunately and undeservedly came to be called slackers, or busters (for the "baby bust" that followed the "baby boom"). Many of these

demographics
Statistics that measure observable aspects of a population, including size, age, gender, ethnic group, income, education, occupation, and family structure.

generational marketing
Marketing to members of a generation, who tend to share the same outlook and priorities.

Millennials or Generation Z
The group of consumers born after 1994.

Generation X
The group of consumers born between 1965 and 1978.

The Apple iPhone enables teens to be content creators and empowers them to be masters of their own music world.

The **Cutting Edge**

Chipotle Targets Socially Conscious Gen Y

How do you reach a generation of consumers who shun TV, distrust big-brand advertising, and are highly socially conscious—Gen Y? Chipotle Mexican Grill is finding out. The company is forgoing traditional advertising, like TV, and going out on a limb with "The Scarecrow," its newest online video and accompanying free game app, both of which have gone viral.

Described as both "brilliant" and "creepy," the three-minute video stars a scarecrow who searches for a way to do the right thing: bring homegrown foods to city dwellers who are otherwise forced to get their conventionally processed food from the industrialized "Crow Foods" factory. The popular video also features a sound track by singer/songwriter Fiona Apple, who sings "Pure Imagination" from the movie *Willy Wonka and the Chocolate Factory*. Every download of the song from the iTunes Store means that 60 cents will be donated to the Chipotle Cultivate Foundation.[11] The game app, which focuses on the same message—food integrity—gives players the opportunity to earn free food rewards at Chipotle restaurants.

But what else is so special about this video and the accompanying game app? It's what you don't see. Instead of plastering its brand all over the ad, Chipotle opted to focus on the social message and included only a flash of its logo at the very end. "Chipotle's marketing strategy makes sense because the ecosystem of advertising has fundamentally changed," says brand consultant David Vinjamuri. "Chipotle is relying on social messengers to connect the message to the brand."[12] And with more than 12 million video hits, they just might be onto something.

people have a cynical attitude toward marketing—a chapter in a famous book called *Generation X* is titled "I Am Not a Target Market!"[13]

Despite this tough reputation, members of Generation X, the oldest of whom are now in their early fifties, have mellowed with age. In retrospect, they also have developed an identity for being an entrepreneurial group. One study revealed that Gen Xers led much of the modern technology revolution, and now firms seek them out for their entrepreneurial talents. An industry expert observed, "Today's Gen Xer is both values-oriented and value-oriented. This generation is really about settling down."[14] Many people in this segment were determined to have stable families after being brought up as latchkey children themselves as both their parents put in long days at work. Gen Xers tend to view the home as an expression of individuality rather than material success. More than half are involved in home improvement and repair projects.[15] So much for Gen Xers as slackers!

Baby Boomers

The segment of people born between 1946 and 1964.

Baby Boomers, consumers born between 1946 and 1964 and who are now in their fifties and sixties, are an important segment to many marketers—if for no other reason than that there are so many of them who have a lot of money. The baby boom occurred when soldiers came flooding home after World War II and there was a rush to get married and start families. Back in the 1950s and 1960s, couples started having children younger and had more of them than the previous generation. The resulting glut of kids really changed the infrastructure of the country: more single-family houses, more schools, migration to the suburbs, and freeways to commute from home to work.

One aspect of Boomers marketers should always remember is that they never age. At least, that's the way they look at it. Boomers are willing to invest a ton of money, time, and energy to maintain their youthful image. In fact, the antiaging products market is expected to exceed more than $114 billion by 2015 as Boomers invest in over-the-counter products, cosmetic surgeries such as facelifts and noninvasive procedures such as Botox, and even human growth hormone treatments for men and women alike. One skin care product called Peau Magnifique costs $1,500 for a 28-day supply. This market is increasing at such a fast rate that even *Consumer Reports* magazine is now testing the effectiveness of cosmetics like face serums, which are designed to reduce wrinkles.[16]

Currently, there are just over 40 million Americans aged 65 or older—a 15 percent increase in this age segment since 2000.[17] To better accommodate the senior market, companies are changing their stores and their products. CVS, for example, introduced carpeting in its stores to reduce slipping, and Walgreens added magnifying glasses in aisles that featured products with fine print. Kimberly-Clark not only redesigned its Depends line to look more like regular underwear but also will now shelve the product among other general hygiene products and not in an "old person's" section of the store.[18]

Many *mature consumers* enjoy leisure time and continued good health. Indeed, a key question today is, "Just what is a senior citizen, when people live longer and "80 is the new 60?" As we will see later in the chapter, perhaps it isn't age but rather lifestyle factors, including mobility, that best define this group. More and more marketers offer products that appeal to active-lifestyle seniors. And they often combine the product appeal with a nostalgia theme that includes music popular during the seniors' era of youth. People tend to prefer music that was released when they were teenagers or young adults, with interest peaking between ages 24 and 25. For years, Sandals Resorts has used the song "(I've Had) The Time of My Life" in commercials for its romantic vacation destinations in the Caribbean. The song, recorded by Bill Medley and Jennifer Warnes, was made famous in the classic 1987 movie *Dirty Dancing*. As nostalgia, it does double duty because the movie itself was set in 1963, so it conjures up memories of both the 1980s and the 1960s for Boomers, who are a key demographic for Sandals.[19]

Segment by Demographics: Gender

Many products, from fragrances to fashion apparel and accessories, specifically appeal to men or women. Segmenting by gender starts at a very early age—even diapers come in pink for girls and blue for boys. As proof that consumers take these differences seriously, market researchers report that most parents refuse to put male infants in pink diapers.[20]

In some cases, manufacturers develop parallel products to appeal to each sex. For example, male grooming products have traditionally been Gillette's priority since the company's founder King Gillette (yes, his first name was actually King) introduced the safety razor in 1903. But today, the Venus line by Gillette is a top-selling razor for women of all ages.

Metrosexual as a marketing buzzword gained steam beginning in the late 2000s. The term describes a straight, urban man who is keenly interested in fashion, home design, gourmet cooking, and personal care. Metrosexuals are usually well-educated urban dwellers who are in touch with their feminine side.[21] While many men are reluctant to overtly identify with the metrosexual, there's no denying that a renewed interest in personal care products, fashion accessories, and other "formerly feminine" product categories creates many marketing opportunities. Mainstream newspapers such as the *New York Times* offer regular segments dedicated to male fashion and grooming. And spas at luxury hotels increasingly promote the full pampered treatment for men from facials to nail care. The JW Marriott Grand Rapids, for example, has a microbrew-inspired line of spa treatments just for men, including a brew pedicure, a beer foot bath, and a brew polish and massage.[22] Cheers!

An interesting trend related to gender segmentation has been fueled by the recent recession. Men now are increasingly likely to marry wives with more education and income than they have, and the reverse is true for women. In recent decades, with the rise of well-paid working wives, the economic gains of marriage have been a greater benefit for men. The education and income gap has grown even more in the latest recession, when men held about three in four of the jobs that were lost. In 1960, 13.5 percent of wives had husbands who were better educated, and 6.9 percent were married to men with less education. By 2012, the comparable figures were 19.9 percent and 20.7 percent—for the first time in history, more women "married down," educationally speaking, than men.[23] In 1960, 6.2 percent of husbands had wives who made more money; in 2007, 24 percent did.[24]

metrosexual
A straight, urban male who is keenly interested in fashion, home design, gourmet cooking, and personal care.

Shapes for Women is a South African chain of women-only gyms.

Courtesy of Grey Jhb. Client: Shapes For Women Gyms, Amazing Wellness Brands

Segment by Demographics: Family Life Cycle

Because family needs and expenditures change over time, one way to segment consumers is to consider the stage of the family life cycle they occupy. (You learned about the family life cycle in Chapter 6.) Not surprisingly, consumers in different life cycle segments are unlikely to need the same products, or at least they may not need these things in the same quantities. IKEA, the trendy Swedish home furnishings company, reports that sales of products for its "small-space" living line are on the rise. Norwegian Cruise Lines offers studio staterooms for those who travel alone. And for singles who love Spam (that ham in a can), Hormel introduced individually portioned Spam Single Classic and Spam Single Lite.[25]

But not all attempts at marketing to the family life cycle succeed. Gerber once tried to market single-serving food jars to single seniors—a quick meal for one person who lives alone. The manufacturer called these containers "Singles." However, Gerber's strong identification with baby food worked against it: The product flopped because their target market was embarrassed to be seen buying baby food.[26]

As families age and move into new life stages, different product categories ascend and descend in importance. Young bachelors and newlyweds are the most likely to exercise, go to bars and movies, and consume alcohol (in other words, party while you can). Older couples and bachelors are more likely to use maintenance services. Seniors are a prime market for resort condominiums and golf products. Marketers need to identify the family life cycle segment of their target consumers by examining purchase data by family life cycle group.

Cultural changes continually create new opportunities as people's roles change. For example, boomer women in their sixties are a hot new market for what the auto industry calls "reward cars": sexy and extravagant vehicles. Says president of Women-Drivers.com Anne Fleming, "As they graduate from baseball and ballerina mom, they are seizing their newfound freedom and buying sexy, indulgent 'me-mobiles.'"[27] Vehicle registration records show that the number of women over age 45 who purchased cars in the niche known as "midsized sporty," which includes two-door models like the Mazda RX-8 and the Chrysler Crossfire, is up 277 percent since 2000. Among women 45 and over earning at least $100,000, smaller luxury cars like the BMW 3 Series and the Audi A4 are up 93 percent.[28]

Segment by Demographics: Income and Social Class

The distribution of wealth is of great interest to marketers because it determines which groups have the greatest *buying power*. After a more than 50-year run during which the truly wealthy just kept getting richer, the Great Recession took some of the wind out of their sails due to heavy investment losses. While these losses have been mitigated by a rebound in the stock market, that history of risk and volatility in investments has likely impacted the consumer behavior of the rich just as it has other income segments. Of course, households making $100,000 or more certainly do not in most cases come close to being part of that "truly wealthy" crowd, but marketers mightily depend on their discretionary spending. While they represent only 20 percent of U.S. households, they control more than half of all income and are far less likely than everyone else to be restrained by tight credit markets. On average, historically the affluent are 2.6 times more likely to make purchases in general, and when they do, they spend 3.7 times more.[29]

In the past, it was popular for marketers to consider *social class segments*, such as upper class, middle class, and lower class. However, many consumers buy not according to where they actually fall in that framework but rather according to the image they wish to portray. For example, over the years, readily available credit has facilitated many a sale of a BMW to a consumer whose income doesn't easily support the steep price tag. Low interest rates and relatively free-flowing credit contributed to the "bubble" in the housing market that triggered the Great Recession of 2008, so buyer beware.

Segment by Demographics: Ethnicity

A consumer's national origin is often a strong indicator of his or her preferences for specific magazines or TV shows, foods, apparel, and leisure activities. Marketers need to be aware of these differences and sensitivities—especially when they invoke outmoded stereotypes to appeal to consumers of diverse races and ethnic groups.

African Americans, Asian Americans, and Hispanic Americans are the largest ethnic groups in the U.S. The Census Bureau projects that by the year 2050, non-Hispanic whites will make up just less than 50 percent of the population (compared to 74 percent in 1995) as these other groups grow. Let's take a closer look at each of these important ethnic segments.

African Americans account for about 12 percent of the U.S. population. This percentage has held steady for 20 years. Reflecting the growing consumer power fueled by the hip-hop and urban scene, magazines such as *The Source* in the U.S. and *Hip Hop Connection* in the UK target this market.[30] TV shows that feature African American heroes and heroines, unheard of until the late 1960s, are commonplace today, and BET is an advertising force to be reckoned with as it reaches more than 90 million households.[31] In many cities, urban-sound radio stations are among the elite few in audience ratings.

These media examples demonstrate the opportunities that await those who develop specialized products to connect with segments of consumers who share an ethnic or racial identity. And what had been the original rap culture has migrated from the inner-city streets to mainstream hip-hop clubs, creating substantial opportunities for marketers to parlay what started out as an urban street trend among the African American community to a broader cultural phenomenon that appeals to young people of many ethnicities.

Although their numbers are still relatively small, *Asian Americans* are the fastest-growing minority group in the U.S. The Asian American population is projected to grow from 11.3 million in 2000 to 19.6 million in 2020.[32] The American advertising industry spends between $200 million and $300 million to court these consumers.[33] The Horseshoe Casino in Cleveland, Ohio, is just one business that goes the extra mile to make customers feel welcome. The casino employs Chinese-speaking natives to serve as translators for guests, and it hosts special Asian-inspired events like the Moon Festival.[34]

The *Hispanic American* population is the real emerging superstar segment for this decade, a segment that mainstream marketers today actively cultivate. Hispanics have overtaken African Americans as the nation's largest minority group. In the U.S., Hispanics command well over $1 trillion in purchasing power. In addition to its rapid growth, five other factors make the Hispanic segment attractive to marketers:[35]

- Hispanics tend to be brand loyal, especially to products made in their country of origin.

- They tend to be highly concentrated by national origin, which makes it easy to fine-tune the marketing mix to appeal to those who come from the same country.

- This segment is young (the median age of Hispanic Americans is 23.6, compared with the U.S. average of 32), which is attractive to marketers because it is a great potential market for youth-oriented products, such as cosmetics and music.

- The average Hispanic household contains 3.5 people, compared to only 2.7 people for the rest of the U.S. For this reason, Hispanic households spend 15 to 20 percent more of their disposable income than the national average on groceries and other household products.

- In general, Hispanic consumers are very receptive to relationship-building approaches to marketing and selling. For this reason, there are many opportunities to build loyalty to brands and companies by emphasizing relationship aspects of the customer encounter.[36]

As with any ethnic group, appeals to Hispanic consumers need to take into account cultural differences. For example, Hispanics didn't appreciate the successful mainstream

"Got Milk?" campaign because biting, sarcastic humor is not part of their culture. In addition, the notion of milk deprivation is not funny to a Hispanic mother—if she runs out of milk, this means she has failed her family. To make matters worse, "Got Milk?" translates as "Are You Lactating?" in Spanish. Thus, new Spanish-language versions were changed to "And you, have you given them enough milk today?" with tender scenes centered on cooking *flan* (a popular pudding) in the family kitchen. And Taco Bell's "Yo quiero Taco Bell" uttering Chihuahua dog was put out to pasture years ago.

It is not an overstatement to say that Latino youth are changing mainstream culture. Many of these consumers are "young biculturals" who bounce back and forth between hip-hop and rock en Español, blend Mexican rice with spaghetti sauce, and spread peanut butter and jelly on tortillas. By 2020, the Census Bureau estimates, the number of Hispanic teens will grow by 62 percent, compared with 10 percent growth in teens overall. They seek spirituality, stronger family ties, and more color in their lives—three hallmarks of Latino culture. Music crossovers from the Latin charts to mainstream lead the trend, including pop idols Shakira, Enrique Iglesias, Marc Anthony, Jennifer Lopez, and Reggaeton sensation Daddy Yankee.

A powerhouse media force within the U.S. Latino culture is the TV network Univision. In many markets with large Hispanic populations, it fields some of the highest-rated programs on cable. At the pinnacle is the Saturday night staple *Sabado Gigante*, which airs an eclectic and frenetic mix of various contests, human interest stories, and live entertainment. *Sabado Gigante* is the longest continually running variety show in the world, and current host Don Francisco (stage name of Chilean TV star Mario Kreutzberger) is one of the most recognizable TV personalities on the planet. If you've never watched the show, tune in some Saturday and see how many mainstream U.S. advertisers buy spots in order to convince the lucrative Spanish-speaking market that their products are right for them.

One caution about the Hispanic market is that the term *Hispanic* itself actually is a misnomer. For example, Cuban Americans, Mexican Americans, and Puerto Ricans may share a common language, but their history, politics, and culture have many differences. Marketing to them as though they are a homogeneous segment can be a big mistake. However, the term is still widely used as a demographic descriptive.

An important outcome of the increase in multiethnicity in the U.S. is the opportunity for increased cultural diversity in the workplace and elsewhere. **Cultural diversity**, a management practice that actively seeks to include people of different sexes, races, ethnic groups, and religions in an organization's employees, customers, suppliers, and distribution channel partners, is today business as usual rather than an exception. Marketing organizations benefit from employing people of all kinds because they bring different backgrounds, experiences, and points of view that help the firm develop strategies for its brands that will appeal to diverse customer groups.

Segment by Demographics: Place of Residence

Recognizing that people's preferences often vary depending on where they live, many marketers tailor their offerings to specific geographic areas, an approach called **geographic segmentation**. Google Earth and other similar applications of a **geographic information system (GIS)** have ramped up geographic approaches to segmentation. A GIS system can very elegantly combine a geographic map with digitally stored data about the consumers in a geographic area. Thus, market information by geographic location is much more convenient for use in market planning and decision making than ever before.

When marketers want to segment regional markets even more precisely, they sometimes combine geography with demographics using the technique of **geodemography**. A basic assumption of geodemography is that "birds of a feather flock together"—people who live near one another share similar characteristics. Sophisticated statistical techniques identify geographic areas that share the same preferences for household items, magazines,

cultural diversity
A management practice that actively seeks to include people of different sexes, races, ethnic groups, and religions in an organization's employees, customers, suppliers, and distribution channel partners.

geographic segmentation
An approach in which marketers tailor their offerings to specific geographic areas because people's preferences often vary depending on where they live.

geographic information system (GIS)
A system that combines a geographic map with digitally stored data about the consumers in a particular geographic area.

geodemography
A segmentation technique that combines geography with demographics.

and other products. This lets marketers construct segments of households with a common pattern of preferences. This way, they can hone in on those customers most likely to be interested in its specific offerings, in some cases so precisely that families living on one block will belong to a segment while those on the next block will not.

One widely used geodemographic system is PRIZM, which is a large database developed by Nielsen Claritas. This system classifies the U.S. population into 66 segments based on various socioeconomic data, such as income, age, race, occupation, education, and household composition as well as lifestyle attributes that are critical to marketing strategies, shopping patterns such as where they vacation, what they drive and their favorite brands, and media preferences. The 66 segments range from the highly affluent "Upper Crust" and "Blue Blood Estates" to the lower-income "Big City Blues or "Low-Rise Living" neighborhoods.

Here are a few thumbnail sketches of different segments of relatively younger consumers a marketer might want to reach depending on the specific product or service he or she sells:

- *Young Digerati* are tech-savvy and live in fashionable neighborhoods on the urban fringe. Affluent, highly educated, and ethnically mixed, Young Digerati communities are typically filled with trendy apartments and condos, fitness clubs and clothing boutiques, casual restaurants, and all types of bars—from juice to coffee to microbrew. The Young Digerati are much more likely than the average American consumer to shop at Bloomingdale's, travel to Asia, read *Dwell*, watch the Independent Film Channel, and buy an Audi A3.

- *Kids & Cul-de-Sacs* are upper-middle-class, suburban, married couples with children— that's the skinny on Kids & Cul-de-Sacs, an enviable lifestyle of large families in recently built subdivisions. This segment has a high rate of Hispanics and Asian Americans. It is also is a refuge for college-educated, white-collar professionals with administrative jobs and upper-middle-class incomes. Their nexus of education, affluence, and children translates into large outlays for child-centered products and services. They are much more likely than the average American consumer to order from target.com, play fantasy sports, read *Parents* magazine, watch X Games, and buy a Honda Odyssey.

- *Shotguns & Pickups* came by its moniker honestly: it scores near the top of all lifestyles for owning hunting rifles and pickup trucks. These Americans tend to be young, working-class couples with large families, living in small homes and manufactured housing. Nearly a third of residents live in mobile homes, more than anywhere else in the nation. They are much more likely than the average American consumer to order from Mary Kay, own a horse, read *Four Wheeler*, watch *Maury*, and drive a Ram diesel pickup.

One interesting specific approach to location-based targeting is **geotargeting**, which in Internet marketing refers to determining the geographic location of a website visitor and delivering different content to that visitor based on his or her location, such as country, region/state, city, metro code/ZIP code, organization, IP address, Internet service provider (ISP), or other criteria.[37] McDonald's teamed up with CampusLIVE to geotarget nearby college students with a customized challenge called "McSmile," where students were challenged to visit their closest McDonald's, buy a cup of coffee, take a photo with it, and then post it. In exchange for their efforts, the person with the most votes won a trip for two to Miami, and the top 10 "sharers" won $50 worth of free coffee.[38]

Ultimately, highly precise geodemographic segmentation enables marketers to practice **micromarketing**, which is the ability to identify and target very small geographic segments that sometimes amount to just one or a few individuals—a capability you read about in Chapter 5 that we referred to as one-to-one marketing.

geotargeting
Determining the geographic location of a website visitor and delivering different content to that visitor based on his or her location.

micromarketing
The ability to identify and target very small geographic segments that sometimes amount to individuals

Metrics Moment

It should be clear from your reading that geodemographic and related approaches to segmentation can be very powerful and allow for a high level of precision in identifying potentially fruitful segments to target. When it comes to metrics, good data about the characteristics of the various consumer segments that you may wish to ultimately target is critical because target marketing is ultimately a strategic investment of resources in the segments that appear to have the best ROI.

To make the power of the geodemographic technique and resulting information for decision making come alive, let's try a demonstration of the PRIZM database that gets close to home.

Apply the Metrics

1. Go to the Nielsen My Best Segments website (search for the phrase "Nielsen My Best Segments" website on any search engine).

2. Click on Zip Code Lookup, and then type in your own ZIP code along with the provided security code, then click SUBMIT.

3. Several segments should then come up that comprise your ZIP code. Click on each for more detail.

4. You will also see some quick facts in a box that further describe some basic demographics of your ZIP code (population, median age, median income, and consumer spend total and per household).

5. What is your reaction to the segment profiles and other information about your ZIP code? Are you surprised with the results, or was it what you expected?

6. Given the profile provided, what sort of products and services do you think are most likely to be particularly attractive to the segments represented?

Segment by Psychographics

Demographic information is useful, but it does not always provide enough information to divide consumers into meaningful segments. Although we can use demographic variables to discover, for example, that the female college student segment uses perfume, we won't be able to tell whether certain college women prefer perfumes that express an image of, say, sexiness rather than athleticism.

psychographics
The use of psychological, sociological, and anthropological factors to construct market segments.

As we said in Chapter 6, **psychographics** segments consumers in terms of psychological and behavioral similarities, such as shared activities, interests, and opinions, or AIOs.[39] Marketers often develop profiles of the typical customers they desire to paint a more vivid picture of them. Although some marketers and their creative agencies develop their own psychographic techniques to classify consumers, others subscribe to services that divide the entire U.S. population into segments and then provides this information to clients for use in proprietary marketing project applications such as strategy planning. The best known of these systems is **VALS**™, which is a product of Strategic Business Insights (SBI). VALS™ divides U.S. adults into eight groups according to what drives them psychologically as well as by their economic resources.

VALS™ (Values and Lifestyles)
A psychographic system that divides the entire U.S. population into eight segments.

As  Figure 7.3 shows, three primary consumer motivations are key aspects of the system: ideals, achievement, and self-expression. Consumers who are motivated primarily by ideals are guided by knowledge and principles. Consumers who are motivated primarily by achievement look for goods and services that demonstrate success to their peers. And consumers who are motivated primarily by self-expression desire social or physical activity, variety, and risk.

VALS™ identifies which types of consumers are the best target for various products and services. Clients use VALS™ because it has been validated and because the groups can be replicated reliably. For example, approximately 12 percent of American adults who are Experiencers. These are independent and experimental people, often at the

Digital enhancement portrait of mature bike couple

A Harley rider's profile includes both thrill-seeking and affinity for a countercultural image (at least on weekends).

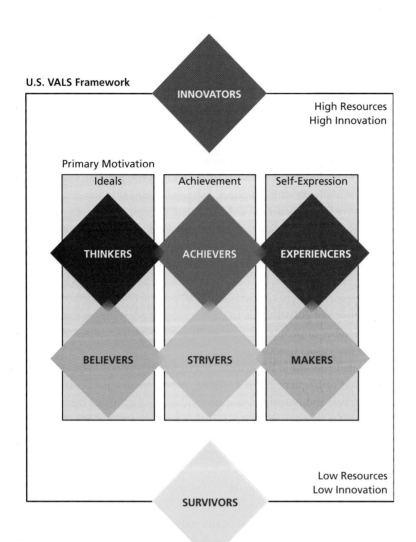

U.S. VALS Framework

Figure 7.3 📷 *Snapshot* | VALS™ Framework

VALS™ uses psychological characteristics to segment the U.S. market into eight unique consumer groups.
Source: Strategic Business Insights (SBI); www.strategicbusinessinsights.com/VALS.

forefront of social change. Another 11 percent are Thinkers (with a median age of 59), who are "informed," "reflective," and "content." Among Thinkers, 46 percent own a dog, and 15 percent buy food labeled as natural or organic.[40] VALS™ used this kind of information to identify target consumers for a Minnesota medical center that was offering a new cosmetic surgery service. By understanding the motivations of the target consumer, the medical center and its ad agency worked together to create an ad campaign that was so successful that the medical center actually had to turn away patients.[41]

One segment that combines a psychographic/lifestyle component with a heavy dose of generational marketing is the **gamer segment**, sometimes referred to as the gamer generation—"gamer" as in "video games," of course. This group grew up playing video games as second nature for primary recreation, and as they have entered college and the workforce, they continue to carry many gaming sensibilities with them. Video gaming is clearly a lifestyle, and much as the company Google turned into the generic verb "to google" in the 2000s, in this decade the buzz term du jour is *gamification*, which, as we saw in Chapter 6, is a strategy in which marketers apply game design techniques, often by awarding points or badges to nongame experiences, to drive consumer behavior (e.g., the gamification of practice exams where you might earn badges for getting right answers and moving to the next level of difficulty in your homework). And, by the way, just in case you didn't know, a **badge** is some type of milestone or reward a player earns when he or she progresses through a gamified application. If you've ever checked into Foursquare

gamer segment
A consumer segment that combines a psychographic/lifestyle component with a heavy dose of generational marketing.

badge
A milestone or reward earned for progressing through a video game.

and earned a badge for a (dubious) achievement like "Gym Rat," "Overshare," or even "Crunked," you know how this works. Marketers would be wise to think about what sorts of badges might appeal to the gamer segment as they become more and more engaged as consumers who are highly likely to do much of their shopping online.

Segment by Behavior

behavioral segmentation
A technique that divides consumers into segments on the basis of how they act toward, feel about, or use a good or service.

People may use the same product for different reasons, on different occasions, and in different amounts. So, in addition to demographics and psychographics, it is useful to study what consumers actually do with a product. **Behavioral segmentation** slices consumer segments on the basis of how they act toward, feel about, or use a product. One way to segment on the basis of behavior is to divide the market into users and nonusers of a product. Then marketers may attempt to reward current users or try to win over new ones. In addition to distinguishing between users and nonusers, marketers can describe current customers as heavy, moderate, and light users. They often do this according to a rule of thumb we call the **80/20 rule**: 20 percent of purchasers account for 80 percent of the product's sales (the ratio is an approximation, not gospel). This rule means that it often makes more sense to focus on the smaller number of people who are really into a product rather than on the larger number who are just casual users.

80/20 rule
A marketing rule of thumb that 20 percent of purchasers account for 80 percent of a product's sales.

usage rate
A measurement that reflects the quantity purchased or frequency of use among consumers of a particular product or service.

Another related concept in behavioral segmentation is **usage rate**, which reflects the quantity purchased or frequency of use among consumers of a particular product or service. The entire travel and hospitality industry cultivates high users through their loyalty programs, such as American Airlines AAdvantage or Marriott Rewards. The high-use segment is often incredibly profitable over the long run.

long tail
A new approach to segmentation based on the idea that companies can make money by selling small amounts of items that only a few people want, provided they sell enough different items.

While the 80/20 rule still holds true in the majority of situations, the Internet's ability to offer an unlimited choice of goods to billions of people has changed how marketers think about segmentation. An approach called the **long tail** turns traditional thinking about the virtues of selling in high volume on its head. The basic idea is that we need no longer rely solely on big hits (like blockbuster movies or best-selling books) to find profits. Companies can also make money when they sell small amounts of items that only a few people want—if they sell enough different items. Apple's iTunes Store is a prime example of a long tail. The online store boasts a catalog of 26 million songs, compared to the fairly limited number of songs that you might find on CDs at your local Best Buy or that you can hear on the radio. And while new releases are certainly popular purchases in the iTunes Store, older, obscure, and independent music is a big part of the store's bread-and-butter sales. For example, consider the 25 billionth song, which was purchased by a German consumer: "Monkey Drums (Goksel Vancin Remix)" by Chase Buch[42]—probably not a huge moneymaker for Apple. Still, even little sales add up to big profits.

usage occasions
An indicator used in behavioral market segmentation based on when consumers use a product most.

B. Anthony Stewart/National Geographics/Getty Images

The Biltmore Estate in Asheville, North Carolina, increased attendance during its annual Christmas celebration as part of a strategy to segment by usage occasion. The estate's marketers developed four separate strategies to target different types of visitors, including heavy users who have made a Christmas pilgrimage an annual family tradition.

Another way to segment a market on the basis of behavior is to look at **usage occasions**, or when consumers use the product most. We associate many products with specific occasions, whether time of day, holidays, business functions, or casual get-togethers. Businesses often divide up their markets according to when and how their offerings are in demand. Ruth's Chris Steakhouse is by far the market leader in the high-end steak restaurant category featuring USDA Prime Beef as its signature dish. Ruth's is well aware that it is a special-occasion location—graduations, birthdays, promotions, you name it—and folks want to celebrate at Ruth's. And they are all too happy to accommodate, often surprising guests with special table decorations for the occasion and a nice dessert treat, compliments of the chef.

And in the online space, Google enables its advertising clients to target certain ads to certain segments of search engine users based on data such as Google domain, query entered, IP address, and language preference. This way, companies can have Google automatically sort and send the intended ad to certain market segments. Thus, it is possible for advertisers on Google to tailor their automatically targeted ads based on seasonality—you will see more TurboTax ads on Google pages during tax season, even if people aren't querying tax software.[43]

Segment B2B Markets

We've reviewed the segmentation variables marketers use to divide up the consumer pie, but how about all those B2B marketers out there? Adding to what we learned about business markets in Chapter 6, it's important to know that segmentation also helps them better understand their customers. Although the specific variables may differ, the underlying logic of classifying the larger market into manageable pieces that share relevant characteristics is the same whether the product you sell is pesto or pesticides.

Organizational demographics also help a B2B marketer understand the needs and characteristics of its potential customers. These classification dimensions include the size of the firms (either in total sales or in number of employees), the number of facilities, whether they are a domestic or a multinational company, their purchasing policies, and the type of business they are in. B2B markets may also be segmented on the basis of the production technology they use and whether the customer is a user or a nonuser of the product.

Many industries use the North American Industry Classification System we discussed in Chapter 6 to obtain information about the size and number of companies operating in a particular industry. B2B marketers often consult general informational business and industry databases on the Web, such as Hoover's or Yahoo! Finance for insight and up-to-date information on private and public companies worldwide.

3 Step 2: Targeting

OBJECTIVE

Explain how marketers evaluate segments and choose a targeting strategy.
(pp. 231–234)

We've seen that the first step in a target marketing strategy is segmentation, in which the firm divides the market into smaller groups that share certain characteristics. The next step is **targeting**, in which marketers evaluate the attractiveness of each potential segment and decide in which of these groups they will invest resources to try to turn them into customers. The customer group or groups they select are the firm's **target market**, which as you learned in Chapter 1, is the segment(s) on which an organization focuses its marketing plan and toward which it directs its marketing efforts.

Figure 7.4 *Process* | Phases of Targeting

Targeting involves three distinct phases of activities.

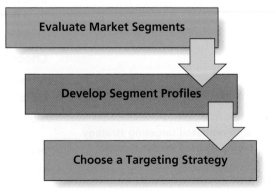

Targeting in Three Steps

In this section, we'll review the three phases of targeting: evaluate market segments, develop segment profiles, and choose a targeting strategy. Figure 7.4 illustrates these three phases.

232 PART TWO | DETERMINE THE VALUE PROPOSITIONS DIFFERENT CUSTOMERS WANT

targeting
A strategy in which marketers evaluate the attractiveness of each potential segment and decide in which of these groups they will invest resources to try to turn them into customers.

target market
The market segments on which an organization focuses its marketing plan and toward which it directs its marketing efforts.

Evaluate Market Segments

Just because a marketer identifies a segment does not necessarily mean that it's a useful target. A viable target segment should satisfy the following requirements:

- *Are members of the segment similar to each other in their product needs and wants and, at the same time, different from consumers in other segments?* Without real differences in consumer needs, firms might as well use a mass-marketing strategy. For example, it's a waste of time to develop two separate lines of skin care products for working women and nonworking women if both segments have the same complaints about dry skin.

- *Can marketers measure the segment?* Marketers must know something about the size and purchasing power of a potential *segment* before they decide if it's worth their efforts.

- *Is the segment large enough to be profitable now and in the future?* For example, a graphic designer who hopes to design Web pages for Barbie-doll collectors must decide whether there are enough hard-core aficionados to make this business worthwhile and whether the trend will continue.

- *Can marketing communications reach the segment?* It is easy to select TV programs or magazines that will efficiently reach older consumers, consumers with certain levels of education, or residents of major cities because the media *they* prefer are easy to identify. However, it is unlikely that marketing communications can reach only left-handed blondes with multiple piercings who listen to Taylor Swift overdubbed in Mandarin Chinese.

- *Can the marketer adequately serve the needs of the segment?* Does the firm have the expertise and resources to satisfy the segment better than the competition? Some years ago, consumer-products manufacturer Warner-Lambert (now a part of Pfizer) made the mistake of trying to enter the pastry business by purchasing Entenmann's Bakery. Entenmann's sells high-end boxed cakes, cookies, pastries, and pies in supermarkets. Unfortunately, Warner-Lambert's expertise at selling Listerine mouthwash and Trident gum did not transfer to baked goods, and it soon lost a lot of "dough" on the deal.

Develop Segment Profiles

segment profile
A description of the "typical" customer in a segment.

Once a marketer identifies a set of usable segments, it is helpful to generate a profile of each to really understand segment members' needs and to look for business opportunities. This segment profile is a description of the "typical" customer in that segment. A **segment profile** might, for example, include customer demographics, location, lifestyle information, and a description of how frequently the customer buys the product. Years ago, Harley-Davidson customers were described as young white men who "didn't fit into society and didn't much care"—they were "large, tough, and dangerous outlaws clad in black leather and covered in tattoos." Today, however, the typical Harley-Davidson customer is a middle-aged man from the affluent middle class.[44]

Choose a Targeting Strategy

undifferentiated targeting strategy
Appealing to a broad spectrum of people.

A basic targeting decision centers on how finely tuned the target should be: Should the company go after one large segment or focus on meeting the needs of one or more smaller segments? Let's look at four targeting strategies, which 📷 Figure 7.5 summarizes.

A company like Walmart that selects an **undifferentiated targeting strategy** appeals to a broad spectrum of people. If successful, this type of operation can be very efficient because production, research, and promotion costs benefit from *economies of scale*—it's cheaper to develop one product or one advertising campaign than to choose

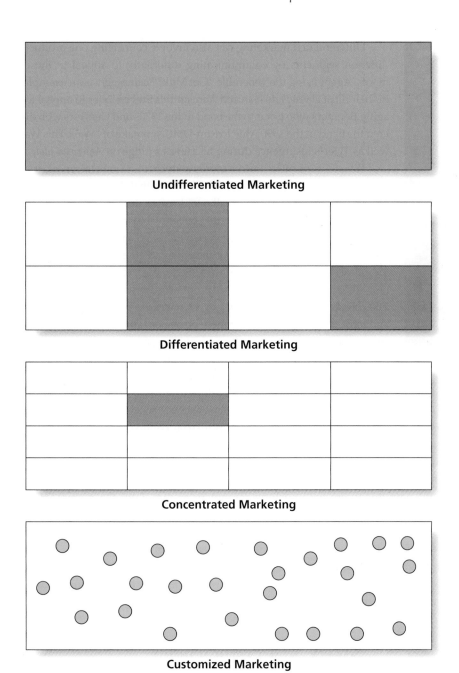

Undifferentiated Marketing

Differentiated Marketing

Concentrated Marketing

Customized Marketing

Figure 7.5 📷 *Snapshot* | Choose a Targeting Strategy

Marketers must decide on a targeting strategy. Should the company go after one total market, one or several market segments, or even target customers individually?

several targets and create separate products or messages for each. But the company must be willing to bet that people have similar needs so that the same product and message will appeal to many customers.

A company that chooses a **differentiated targeting strategy** develops one or more products for each of several customer groups with different product needs. A differentiated strategy is called for when consumers choose among well-known brands that have distinctive images and the company can identify one or more segments that have distinct needs for different types of products.

Despite its highly publicized product safety issues in 2014, GM historically has been a leader in differentiated strategy with distinct product lines that satisfy the needs of multiple customer groups. Its Cadillac and Buick product lines cater to consumers who want luxury. The Chevrolet Volt hybrid provides value to drivers who want to save gas money and the environment. And finally, the GMC product line appeals to drivers who need an everyday truck, crossover, or SUV that is both dependable and stylish.

differentiated targeting strategy
Developing one or more products for each of several distinct customer groups and making sure these offerings are kept separate in the marketplace.

Blacksocks practices a highly concentrated targeting strategy.

concentrated targeting strategy
Focusing a firm's efforts on offering one or more products to a single segment.

customized marketing strategy
An approach that tailors specific products and the messages about them to individual customers.

mass customization
An approach that modifies a basic good or service to meet the needs of an individual.

positioning
Developing a marketing strategy to influence how a particular market segment perceives a good or service in comparison to the competition.

Differentiated marketing can also involve connecting one product with different segments by communicating differently to appeal to those segments. Again using the venerable "Got Milk?" campaign as an example, one of their most classic ads featured Aerosmith's Steven Tyler to appeal to both aging Boomers who got into the band in the 1970s and Gen Yers who discovered the band in the 1990s due to Run-DMC's remake of "Walk This Way" as well as Tyler's resurgence during his run as a judge on *American Idol*.

When a firm offers one or more products to a single segment, it uses a **concentrated targeting strategy**. Smaller firms that do not have the resources or the desire to be all things to all people often do this. Blacksocks.com is a mail-order sock company that started out only making black dress socks, then moved into some other similarly conservative "business" colors, and now has a separate "funky socks" shop for the wild and crazy among us. At the core, they clearly target businessmen who are too busy to go to the store and buy new socks when their old ones wear out—loyalists are called "sockscribers." The company argues that every guy who wears a business suit wears socks, and most wear black socks. For these busy men, going to the store just to buy socks is boring, time consuming, and simply unnecessary.[45]

Ideally, marketers should be able to define segments so precisely that they can offer products that exactly meet the unique needs of each individual or firm. This level of concentration does occur (we hope) in the case of personal or professional services we get from doctors, lawyers, and hairstylists. A **customized marketing strategy** also is common in industrial contexts where a manufacturer often works with one or a few large clients and develops products that only these clients will use.

Of course, in most cases this level of segmentation is neither practical nor possible when mass-produced products such as computers or cars enter the picture. However, advances in computer technology, coupled with the new emphasis on building solid relationships with customers, have focused managers' attention on devising new ways to tailor specific products and the messages about them to individual customers. Thus, some forward-looking, consumer-oriented companies are moving toward **mass customization** in which they modify a basic good or service to meet the needs of an individual.[46] This issue came up earlier in the chapter in the discussion of micromarketing.

4 Step 3: Positioning

OBJECTIVE

Recognize how marketers develop and implement a positioning strategy.
(pp. 234–238)

The final stage of developing a target marketing strategy is to provide consumers who belong to a targeted market segment with a good or service that meets their unique needs and expectations. **Positioning** means developing a marketing strategy to influence how a particular market segment perceives a good or service in comparison to the competition. A key word in this definition is *perceives*—that is, positioning is in the eyes of the beholder. A firm may truly believe that its customers think about its offering in a certain way, but unless market research bears this out, what the marketer "thinks" doesn't matter as it is trumped by what the consumer perceives. To position a brand, marketers must clearly understand the criteria target consumers use to evaluate competing products and then convince them that their product, service, or organization will meet those needs. In addition, the organization has to come up with a plan to communicate this position to its target market.

Positioning happens in many ways. Sometimes it's just a matter of making sure that cool people use your product—and that others observe them doing this. After finding out that a close friend was flying to Los Angeles to audition for the film *Any Given Sunday*, the

Ripped from the Headlines

Ethical/Sustainable Decisions in the Real World

Fast-food restaurants have long been criticized for targeting children and teens with their TV advertisements, with critics arguing—and research supporting—that such marketing contributes to the problem of childhood obesity. But it's not just a problem with TV. And it's not just a problem in Western countries like the U.S.

Today, fast-food chains have more avenues than ever before to promote their products. Consider social media like Facebook, Twitter, Instagram, and YouTube. In 2012, 6 billion fast-food ads appeared on Facebook alone, and Taco Bell's YouTube videos were viewed almost 14 million times.[47] And the fast-food restaurants are getting creative. Ads often come in the form of "advergames," which are video games designed to promote a product or service and engage the user with the brand for as long as possible. Those ads foster feelings of confidence and trendiness among young users; those good feelings then translate into restaurant sales, which then translate into expanded waistlines.

In countries like China and India, youth are experiencing expanding waistlines at an alarming rate as well. As chains like McDonald's, KFC, and Taco Bell move into these countries, they bring their "predatory marketing" with them. Says Samir Kuckreja, president of the National Restaurant Association of India, "Children are a target market for all the quick-service restaurant chains, and more marketing is skewed towards them."[48] Unlike in the U.S., where marketing to children is somewhat regulated by the government, marketing in these emerging economies is often still self-regulated. That means that companies like Domino's Pizza are free to advertise directly to children, with commercials that entice them to attend school for a pizza treat, for example.

As food profits rise, so does the cost of health care. Childhood obesity is linked to diabetes, high blood pressure, heart disease, and more. What began as a simple hamburger ad has turned into potentially the biggest health crisis that these countries will face in the future.

ETHICS CHECK: ↖
Find out what other students taking this course *would do* and *why* at **mymktlab.com**.

Should fast-food marketing to children be regulated by the government?

☐YES ☐NO

---

president of the high-performance sportswear company Under Armour sent along with him a bunch of free samples of its athletic wear to give to the film's casting director as a gift. The director liked the quality of the clothes so much that he gave them to the wardrobe company the filmmakers hired, and they also really liked the clothes. The next thing you know, the movie (starring Al Pacino and Jamie Foxx) featured both the actors wearing Under Armour clothes on screen—and there was even a scene in the film when Jamie Foxx undressed in the locker room with a clear shot of the Under Armour logo on his jock strap. After the movie's release, hits on Under Armour's website spiked, and, as they say, the rest is history.[49]

Steps in Positioning

Figure 7.6 shows the stages marketers use to decide just how to position their product or service: analyze competitors' positions, offer a good or service with a competitive advantage, finalize the marketing mix, and evaluate responses and modify as needed. Let's take a closer look at each of the positioning stages.

Analyze Competitors' Positions

The first stage is to analyze competitors' positions in the marketplace. To develop an effective positioning strategy, marketers must understand the current lay of the land. What competitors are out there, and how does the target market perceive them? Aside from direct competitors in the product category, are there other goods or services that provide similar benefits?

Sometimes the indirect competition can be more important than the direct, especially if it represents an emerging consumer trend. For years, McDonald's developed positioning strategies based only on its direct competition, which it defined as other large fast-food hamburger chains (translation: Burger King and Wendy's). McDonald's failed to realize that in fact many indirect competitors fulfilled consumers' needs for a quick, tasty, convenient meal—from supermarket delis to frozen microwavable single-serving meals to call-ahead takeout from full-service restaurants like Applebee's, T.G.I. Friday's, Outback, and Chili's—all of whom have convenient curbside service instead of backed-up drive-through lines. Only recently,

Figure 7.6 Process | Stages in a Positioning Decision

Four key elements comprise the decision-making process in positioning.

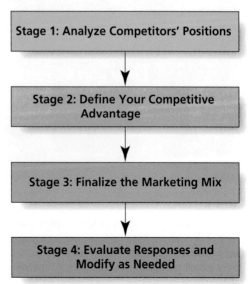

Stage 1: Analyze Competitors' Positions

Stage 2: Define Your Competitive Advantage

Stage 3: Finalize the Marketing Mix

Stage 4: Evaluate Responses and Modify as Needed

McDonald's has begun to understand that it must react to this indirect competition by serving up a wider variety of adult-friendly food and shoring up lagging service. Now the company also offers its McCafé concept, with coffee products aimed squarely at taking business away from morning mainstays Starbucks and Dunkin' Donuts, along with a tasty breakfast menu to compete in a brand-new space.

Define Your Competitive Advantage

The second stage is to offer a good or service with a competitive advantage to provide a reason why consumers will perceive the product as better than the competition. If the company offers only a "me-too product," it can induce people to buy for a lower price. Other forms of competitive advantage include offering a superior image (Giorgio Armani), a unique product feature (Levi's 501 button-fly jeans), better service (Cadillac's roadside assistance program), or even better-qualified people (the legendary salespeople at Nordstrom's department stores).

Finalize the Marketing Mix

repositioning
Redoing a product's position to respond to marketplace changes.

Once they settle on a positioning strategy, the third stage for marketers is to finalize the marketing mix as they put all the pieces into place. The elements of the marketing mix must match the selected segment. This means that the good or service must deliver benefits that the segment values, such as convenience or status. Put another way, it must add value and satisfy consumer needs (sound familiar?). Furthermore, marketers must price this offering at a level these consumers will pay, make the offering available at places they are likely to go, and correctly communicate the offering's benefits in locations where these targets are likely to take notice. In other words, the positioning strategy translates into the organization's marketing mix that we discussed in Chapter 1.

Beginning with Chapter 8, all the remaining chapters in the book provide you with the details of developing strategies for each element of the marketing mix: product, price, physical distribution, and promotion. The sum of these individual marketing mix strategies results in the overall positioning strategy for your offering.

Evaluate Responses and Modify as Needed

In the fourth and final stage, marketers evaluate the target market's responses so they can modify strategies if necessary. Over time, the firm may find that it needs to change which segments it targets or even alter a product's position to respond to marketplace changes. Consider this classic example: Both TGI Fridays and Jim Beam are venerable brands in separate market spaces. But like peanut butter and chocolate in the case of a Reese's peanut butter cup, Fridays and JB partnered to create a set of new menu items like the Jim Beam Bourbon Burger®, which repositioned TGIF from your father's restaurant to a more hip place for the younger urban crowd.

A change in positioning strategy is **repositioning**, and it's fairly common to see a company try to modify its brand image to keep up with changing times. Take as an example Charles Schwab, which used to be pegged primarily as a self-service stock brokerage. Competition in the budget broker business, especially from online brokers, prompted Schwab's repositioning to a full-line, full-service financial services firm that still pays attention to frugal prices for its services. Think of it this way: There's not much value Schwab can add as one of a dozen or more online providers of stock trades. In that environment, customers simply will view the firm as a commodity

The SoBe Beverage Company started in Miami's South Beach (So-Be) in 1996 when the founders saw a lizard on the art deco façade of the Abbey Hotel, and the rest is history. SoBe has masterfully executed the process of segmentation, target marketing, and positioning you've read about in this chapter and today boasts an amazing brand and product line that appeals to a definitive set of demographic/psychographic targets.

Ruaridh Stewart/ZUMA Press/Newscom

(i.e., just a way to buy stocks) with no real differentiation. Schwab still has its no-frills products, but the real growth in sales and profits comes from its expanded product lines and provision of more information—both online and through personal selling—that warrant higher fees and build deeper customer relationships. Repositioning also occurs when a marketer revises a brand thought to be inextricably past its prime. Sometimes these products rise like a phoenix from the ashes to ride a wave of nostalgia and return to the marketplace as **retro brands**—venerable brands like Oxydol laundry detergent, Breck Shampoo, Ovaltine cereal, Frontier airlines, and Tab cola all are examples of brands that were nearly forgotten but got a new lease on life.[50]

retro brands
A once-popular brand that has been revived to experience a popularity comeback, often by riding a wave of nostalgia.

Bring a Product to Life: Brand Personality

In a way, brands are like people: We often describe them in terms of personality traits. We may use adjectives such as *cheap*, *elegant*, *sexy*, or *cool* when we talk about a store, a perfume, or a car. That's why a positioning strategy often tries to create a **brand personality** for a good or service—a distinctive image that captures its character and benefits. An advertisement for *Elle*, an amazingly chic fashion magazine for women, proclaimed, "She is not a reply card. She is not a category. She is not shrink-wrapped. *Elle* is not a magazine. She is a woman." We'll talk a lot more about brands in Chapter 9.

brand personality
A distinctive image that captures a good's or service's character and benefits.

Products as people? It seems funny to say, yet marketing researchers find that most consumers have no trouble describing what a product would be like "if it came to life." People often give clear, detailed descriptions, including what color hair the product would have, the type of house it would live in, and even whether it would be thin, overweight, or somewhere in between.[51] If you don't believe us, try doing this yourself.

Part of creating a brand personality is to develop an identity for the product that the target market will prefer over competing brands. How do marketers determine where their product actually stands in the minds of consumers? One solution is to ask consumers what characteristics are important and how competing alternatives would rate on these attributes, too. Marketers use this information to construct a **perceptual map**—a vivid way to construct a picture of where products or brands are "located" in consumers' minds.

perceptual map
A technique to visually describe where brands are "located" in consumers' minds relative to competing brands.

For example, suppose you want to develop an idea for a new publication that will appeal to American women in their twenties. You might construct a perceptual map of how these target customers perceive the magazines out there now to help you develop an idea for a new publication they would like. After you interview a sample of female readers, you might identify two key questions women ask when they select a magazine: (1) Is it "traditional," that is, oriented toward family, home, or personal issues, or is it "fashion-forward," oriented toward personal appearance and fashion? (2) Is it for "upscale" women who are older and established in their careers or for relatively "downscale" women who are younger and just starting out in their careers?

The perceptual map in 📷 Figure 7.7 illustrates how these ratings might look for a set of major women's magazines. The map provides some guidance as to where you might position your new magazine. You might decide to compete directly with either the cluster of "service magazines" in the lower left or the traditional fashion magazines in the upper right. In this case, you would have to determine what benefits your new magazine might offer that these existing magazines do not. Media firm Condé Nast, for example, positions *Allure* to compete against other fashion magazines by going into more depth than they do on beauty issues, such as the mental, physical, and emotional dangers of cosmetic surgery.

You might try to locate an unserved or underserved area in this perceptual map. There may be room for a magazine that targets "cutting-edge" fashion for college-age women. A neglected segment is the "Holy Grail" for marketers: With luck, they can move quickly to capture a segment and define the standards of comparison for the category. This tactic paid off for Chrysler, which first identified the minivan market for soccer moms; JetBlue,

Figure 7.7 📷 *Snapshot* |
Perceptual Map

Perceptual mapping allows marketers to identify consumers' perceptions of their brand in relation to the competition.

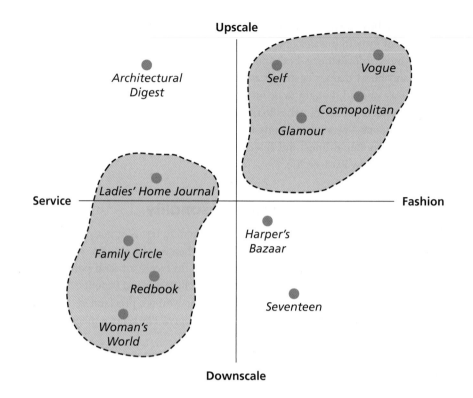

which found a spot for low fares and high tech without the poor-boy service attitude and cattle-call boarding procedure of other budget airlines; and Liz Claiborne, which pioneered the concept of comfortable, "user-friendly" clothing for working women. In the magazine category, perhaps *Marie Claire* comes closest to this position.

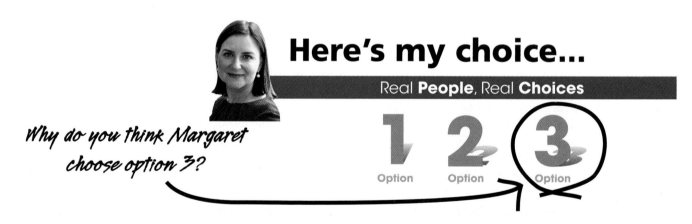

Why do you think Margaret choose option 3?

How It Worked Out at Siegel+Gale

Margaret and her team chose option 3. They met with individual practices, such as the research team and design teams, and presented their 2014 content strategy, its potential benefits, and the specific role that each practice area had in driving its success. This enabled the marketing team to motivate employees and identify champions across all levels and disciplines of the firm. The team customized their overall approach for each practice area, or "segment." For design-related content, for example, they stressed the importance of videos and visuals in blogs. For strategists, they emphasized the importance of generating actionable takeaways and lessons that the reader can apply to his or her brand strategy. This option also ensured that Siegel+Gale was creating content across various types of formats where its audience consumed information. For example, some people like to consume information as a byline or infographic, while others prefer a video.

The team hosted "lunch and learns" to educate employees about distributing the company's content through LinkedIn and other social platforms. Content creators were acknowledged for their participation via company-wide announcements and content updates. For example, the co-CEOs acknowledged active contributors during quarterly town hall meetings. In addition, new content was showcased on TVs in Siegel+Gale's kitchen and lobby areas to enhance the recognition of company employees who raised their external profiles as thought leaders.

How Siegel+Gale Measures Success

Margaret and her team track the volume and quality of employees' content-creation activities using measures such as these (based on the first six months of 2014):

- *Blog posts.* From January to May 2014, 37 percent of Siegel+Gale employees contributed original blog content. This activity resulted in 86 blog posts, which is a 41 percent increase in volume versus the same period in 2013.

- *Website traffic.* Siegel+Gale's corporate website saw a 19 percent increase in unique visitors during the first quarter of 2014 versus the first quarter of 2013 and a 9 percent increase in total visitors.

- *Media mentions.* Since October 2013, Siegel+Gale employees have been published or quoted in top-tier outlets, including *Forbes*, *Time*, the *Wall Street Journal*, Reuters, the *Chicago Tribune*, *Bloomberg Businessweek*, *The Economist*, *USA Today*, *Mashable*, FoxBusiness.com, *Fast Company*, and *Variety*. From January to May 2014, Siegel+Gale was mentioned in the press on 76 occasions, including 26 bylines authored by Siegel+Gale team members.

- *Social media activity.* The period from January to May 2014 saw a 25 percent increase in Twitter followers as well as a marked increase in engagement as reflected by 1,782 Twitter retweets and 2,297 Twitter mentions. During the same time period, the company also posted a 14 percent increase in Facebook fans and a 32 percent increase in LinkedIn followers.

A Typical Post by Siegel+Gale.

Refer back to **page 216** for Margaret's story ➡

MyMarketingLab™

Go to **mymktlab.com** to complete the problems marked with this icon ⭐ as well as additional Marketing Metrics questions only available in MyMarketingLab.

Objective Summary ➡ Key Terms ➡ Apply

CHAPTER 7
Study Map

1. Objective Summary (pp. 218–219)

Identify the steps in the target marketing process.

Marketers must balance the efficiency of mass marketing, serving the same items to everyone, with the effectiveness of offering each individual exactly what she wants. To accomplish this, instead of trying to sell something to everyone, marketers follow these steps: (1) select a target marketing strategy, in which they divide the total market into different segments based on customer characteristics; (2) select one or more segments; and (3) develop products to meet the needs of those specific segments.

Key Terms

content marketing, p. 218

market fragmentation, p. 218

target marketing strategy, p. 219

2. Objective Summary (pp. 219-231)

Understand the need for market segmentation and the approaches available to do it.

Market segmentation is often necessary in today's marketplace because of market fragmentation—that is, the splintering of a mass society into diverse groups due to technological and cultural differences. Most marketers can't realistically do a good job of meeting the needs of everyone, so it is more efficient to divide the larger pie into slices in which members of a segment share some important characteristics and tend to exhibit the same needs and preferences. Marketers frequently find it useful to segment consumer markets on the basis of demographic characteristics, including age, gender, family life cycle, social class, race or ethnic identity, and place of residence. A second dimension, psychographics, uses measures of psychological and social characteristics to identify people with shared preferences or traits. Consumer markets may also be segmented on the basis of how consumers behave toward the product, for example, their brand loyalty, usage rates (heavy, moderate, or light), and usage occasions. B2B markets are often segmented on the basis of industrial demographics, type of business based on the North American Industry Classification codes, and geographic location.

Key Terms

segmentation, p. 219

segmentation variables, p. 219

Generation Y, p. 220

demographics, p. 221

generational marketing, p. 221

Millennials or Generation Z, p. 221

Generation X, p. 221

Baby Boomers, p. 222

metrosexual, p. 223

cultural diversity, p. 226

geographic segmentation, p. 226

geographic information system (GIS), p. 226

geodemography, p. 226

geotargeting, p. 227

micromarketing, p. 227

psychographics, p. 228

VALS™, p. 228

gamer segment, p. 229

badge, p. 229

behavioral segmentation, p. 230

80/20 Rule, p. 230

usage rate, p. 230

long tail, p. 230

usage occasions, p. 230

3. Objective Summary (pp. 231-234)

Explain how marketers evaluate segments and choose a targeting strategy.

To choose one or more segments to target, marketers examine each segment and evaluate its potential for success as a target market. Meaningful segments have wants that are different from those in other segments, can be identified, can be reached with a unique marketing mix, will respond to unique marketing communications, are large enough to be profitable, have future growth potential, and possess needs that the organization can satisfy better than the competition.

After marketers identify the different segments, they estimate the market potential of each. The relative attractiveness of segments also influences the firm's selection of an overall marketing strategy. The firm may choose an undifferentiated, differentiated, concentrated, or custom strategy based on the company's characteristics and the nature of the market.

Key Terms

targeting, p. 231

target market, p. 231

segment profile, p. 232

undifferentiated targeting strategy, p. 232

differentiated targeting strategy, p. 233

concentrated targeting strategy, p. 234

customized marketing strategy, p. 234

mass customization, p. 234

4. Objective Summary (pp. 234-238)

Recognize how marketers develop and implement a positioning strategy.

After marketers select the target market(s) and the overall strategy, they must determine how they wish customers to perceive the brand relative to the competition—that is, should the brand be positioned like, against, or away from the competition? Through positioning, a brand personality is developed. Marketers can compare brand positions by using such research techniques as perceptual mapping. In developing and implementing the positioning strategy, firms analyze the competitors' positions, determine the competitive advantage offered by their product, tailor the marketing mix in accordance with the positioning strategy, and evaluate responses to the marketing mix selected. Marketers must continually monitor changes in the market that might indicate a need to reposition the product.

Key Terms

positioning, p. 234

repositioning, p. 236

retro brands, p. 237

brand personality, p. 237

perceptual map, p. 237

Chapter **Questions** and **Activities**

Concepts: Test Your Knowledge

7-1. What is positioning? How is it related to target marketing?

7-2. Briefly describe which is better: mass marketing or personalized service.

7-3. What is generational marketing, and why is it an important strategy in today's marketplace?

7-4. Distinguish between Generation Z, Y, and X. What is specific about Generation Y that makes its members so attractive?

7-5. What does the term *metrosexual* mean? What are its marketing opportunities?

7-6. What is geographic segmentation?

7-7. What is micromarketing, and how does it help marketers?

7-8. List the criteria marketers use to determine whether a segment may be a good candidate for targeting.

7-9. Explain the differences between undifferentiated, differentiated, concentrated, and customized marketing strategies. What is mass customization?

7-10. What is product positioning?

7-11. What do marketers mean by creating a brand personality? How do marketers use perceptual maps to help them develop effective positioning strategies?

Activities: Apply What You've Learned

⭐ **7-12.** *Creative Homework/Short Project* You are an entrepreneur who is designing a new line of boutique hotels located along Florida's coastlines. Each of the 75 guest rooms in each hotel will offer upscale decor, Wi-Fi, and iPod docks for a nightly rate of $219. The hotels will have an on-site restaurant and a separate full-service bar that features local musicians. Describe in detail the demographics—age, gender, family life cycle, income and social class, ethnicity, and place of residence—of your target customer.

⭐ **7-13.** *Creative Homework/Short Project* As the marketing director for a company that is planning to enter the B2B market for photocopy machines, you are attempting to develop an overall marketing strategy. You have considered the possibility of using mass-marketing, concentrated marketing, differentiated marketing, and custom marketing strategies.

  a. Prepare a summary explaining what each type of strategy would mean for your marketing plan in terms of product, price, promotion, and distribution channel.

  b. Evaluate the desirability of each type of strategy.

  c. Describe your final recommendations for the best type of strategy.

7-14. *In Class, 10–25 Minutes for Teams* To better market a new shopping mall located close to the university to potential businesses to rent, create a geo-demographic profile of your class. According to the profile, what kinds of businesses should the mall owners target? Share your description with the class.

7-15. *In Class, 10–25 Minutes for Teams* As an account executive for a marketing consulting firm, your newest client is a university—your university. You have been asked to develop a positioning strategy for the university. With your team, develop an outline of your ideas, including the following:

  a. Who are your competitors?

  b. What are the competitors' positions?

  c. What target markets are most attractive to the university?

  d. How will you position the university for those segments relative to the competition?

7-16. *For Further Research (Individual)* A global company specializing in men's grooming products sold in a spa or salon environment wants to identify the location for a flagship store in your area. The products are in the mid-high range price and should appeal to men with an existing interest in grooming products. Identify the best geographical location for the store and present a summary to your class.

Apply Marketing Metrics

When it comes to metrics, good data about the characteristics of the various consumer segments that you may wish to ultimately target is critical because target marketing is ultimately a strategic investment of resources in the segments that appear to have the best return on investment. In this chapter, you learned that VALS™ is a well-known approach to psychographic segmentation.

⭐ **7-17.** To make the power of the psychographic technique and resulting information for decision making come alive, let's find out your own VALS™ category.

  a. Go to the VALS™ website (either Google it or go directly to **www.strategicbusinessinsights.com**).

  b. Click on "Take the VALS™ Survey." Complete all the questions and click SUBMIT to view your results.

  c. What is your VALS™ type? Review the information on the website that describes it (found under the tabs About VALS™/VALS™ Types) along with the other VALS™ types.

  d. What is your reaction to learning your own VALS™ type? Are you surprised with the result or was it what consistent with what you would have expected? Why or why not?

  e. What insights does the knowledge of your VALS™ type provide relative to your own consumer behavior?

Choices: What Do You Think?

7-18. *Ethics* Some critics of marketing have suggested that market segmentation and target marketing lead to an unnecessary proliferation of product choices that wastes valuable resources. These critics suggest that if marketers didn't create so many different product choices, there would be more resources to feed the hungry and house the homeless and provide for the needs of people around the globe. Are the results of segmentation and target marketing harmful or beneficial to society as a whole? Should firms be concerned about these criticisms? Why or why not?

⭐ **7-19.** *Critical Thinking* One of the criteria for a usable market segment is its size. This chapter suggested that to be usable, a segment must be large enough to be profitable now and in the future and that some very small segments get ignored because they can never be profitable. So how large should a segment be? How do you think a firm should go about determining if a segment is profitable? Have technological advances made it possible for smaller segments to be profitable? Do firms ever have a moral or ethical obligation to develop products for small, unprofitable segments? When?

7-20. *Ethics* Marketers are in business to make a profit, but they also have an ethical obligation not to take advantage of consumers, especially disadvantaged consumers like those at the bottom of the pyramid. Would you consider it ethical to sell mosquito nets in Africa to prevent the spread of malaria? Would you consider it ethical to sell Coca-Cola or Pepsi to consumers in rural India? Why or why not? Is there a line between what is ethical to sell and what is not? How would you describe that line?

7-21. *Critical Thinking* In this chapter, you learned about the use of geotargeting by McDonald's in its "McSmile" challenge. Part of the success of such campaigns is the word-of-mouth advertising that participants generate with others on social media sites via "shares" and "likes." In what ways are such geotargeting campaigns successful? Why might they fail? Have you ever participated in such a campaign? Was it worth "sharing" the product with your friends in return for a small reward? Would your friends agree with you?

7-22. *Critical Thinking* A few years ago, Anheuser-Busch Inc. created a new division dedicated to marketing to Hispanics and announced it would boost its ad spending in Hispanic media by two-thirds to more than $60 million, while Miller Brewing Co. signed a $100 million, three-year ad package with Spanish-language broadcaster Univision. But Hispanic activists immediately raised public health concerns about the beer ad blitz on the grounds that it targets a population that skews young and is disproportionately likely to abuse alcohol.

Surveys of Hispanic youth show that they are much more likely to drink alcohol, get drunk, and engage in binge drinking than their white or black peers. A senior executive at Anheuser-Busch responded, "We would disagree with anyone who suggests beer billboards increase abuse among Latino or other minority communities. It would be poor business for us in today's world to ignore what is the fastest-growing segment of our population."

a. Manufacturers of alcohol and tobacco products have been criticized for targeting unwholesome products to certain segments of the market—the aged, ethnic minorities, the disabled, and others. Do you view this as a problem? Should a firm use different criteria in targeting such groups? Should the government oversee and control such marketing activities?

Miniproject: Learn by Doing

This miniproject will help you to develop a better understanding of how firms make target marketing decisions. The project focuses on the market for men's athletic shoes.

a. Gather ideas about different dimensions useful for segmenting the men's athletic shoes market. You may use your own ideas, but you probably will also want to examine advertising and other marketing communications developed by different athletic shoe brands.

b. Based on the dimensions for market segmentation that you have identified, develop a questionnaire and conduct a survey of consumers. You will have to decide which questions should be asked and which consumers should be surveyed.

c. Analyze the data from your research and identify the different potential segments.

d. Develop segment profiles that describe each potential segment.

e. Generate several ideas for how the marketing strategy might be different for each segment based on the profiles.

f. Define your competitive advantage.

7-23. Develop a presentation (or write a report) outlining your ideas, your research, your findings, and your marketing strategy recommendations.

Marketing in **Action** Case Real Choices at Subaru

"Love. It's what makes a Subaru, a Subaru." How do companies "share the love" with their buyers? Subaru of America attempts to "share the love" through its marketing efforts. The company wants to "build a connection between Subaru vehicles and the ability they give folks to follow their whims." Subaru has developed more aggressive and effective campaigns by making use of its understanding of current buyers. No-nonsense vehicles designed for loyal, upscale, active buyers is the foundation of the brand's target audience. The main objective of its marketing efforts is to add more members to the Subaru family.

In 1968, Subaru of America began in Philadelphia and subsequently moved its headquarters to Cherry Hill, New Jersey.

In 1986, the company was acquired by Fuji Heavy Industries. Internationally, the Subaru brand is identified by its use of boxer engines and the all-wheel drive train layout. Recently, Subaru sold almost 425,000 vehicles in the U.S. This topped off five consecutive years of sales growth, a feat accomplished by only one U.S. car company. All Subaru products are manufactured in zero-landfill production plants, and the company's main production facility in Indiana is the only U.S. automobile production plant to be designated a backyard wildlife habitat by the National Wildlife Federation.

Michael McHale, a spokesperson for Subaru, says that the company wants to grow as the brand of choice for "adventure-seekers, people who enjoy exploring the outdoors, fishing and hiking and so on . . . we want to take them on the trail . . . we're targeting those guys." Subaru believes that those buyers are "young, idealistic, environmentally minded, and appreciative of companies such as Subaru that publicly stand with them in caring about the causes important to them." The company has a history of a loyal support base with a high core identity. The current cars have a new styling that has enabled Subaru to expand its buyer base and increase its brand awareness in the marketplace. This has led to 60 percent of its car buyers being new to the Subaru brand.

To increase its attractiveness to potential buyers, the car company has added to its range of promotional activities. Subaru has made the interiors of its cars roomier and reduced its pricing to be more competitive with its rivals. Its program to make contributions to a buyer's charity of choice is in contrast to the company's history of not offering cash incentives. Subaru is using digital media to broaden its appeal to younger car buyers. These new promotions work with the company's "unwavering dedication to a quirky, outdoorsy clientele that prizes function over high-tech glitz and plush interiors" to increase its appeal.

Subaru is continually moving from a minor niche player into a key competitor in the tough U.S. marketplace. In 2013, the brand was number 12 in sales, which is up from its number 22 position in 2006. Currently, Subaru is ahead of Ram, Chrysler, Mazda, and Buick, with Volkswagen within its reach. The company is expanding its retail presence in the Sun Belt and southern California. Sales in that part of the country are increasing faster than in Subaru's traditional cold-climate markets. According to Subaru, there are 6 million cause-minded U.S. consumers who fit Subaru's target market. In order to grow market share, the firm will have to attract more buyers. Its past tactics may or may not work in other regions of the country. If Subaru were to adjust its marketing tactics, would it harm its relationships with current buyers?

You Make the Call

7-24. What is the decision facing Subaru?

7-25. What factors are important in understanding this decision situation?

7-26. What are the alternatives?

7-27. What decision(s) do you recommend?

7-28. What are some ways to implement your recommendation?

Sources: Based on: Erik Derr, "For Subaru, Shared Values Outweigh Market Share," November 26, 2013, **http://wardsauto.com/ management-amp-strategy/subaru-shared-values-outweigh-market-share** (accessed April 25, 2014); Subaru of America, Inc., "Company," **www.subaru.com/company/index.html** (accessed April 25, 2014); Diana T. Kurylko, "Subaru's Growth Formula: Keep Tight Focus on U.S.; Price 'em Smart; Cater to the Quirky," September 2, 2013, **www.autonews.com/article/20130902/RETAIL/309029962/ subarus-growth-formula:-keep-tight-focus-on-u.s.;-price-em-smart;#** (accessed April 25, 2014).

MyMarketingLab™

Go to **mymktlab.com** for Auto-graded writing questions as well as the following Assisted-graded writing questions:

7-29. *Creative Homework/Short Project.* Assume that a small regional microbrewery has hired you to help them with their target marketing. They are pretty unsophisticated about marketing—you will need to explain some things to them and provide ideas for their future. In the past, the microbrewery has simply produced and sold a single beer brand to the entire market—a mass-marketing strategy. As you begin work, you come to believe that the firm could be more successful if it developed a target marketing strategy. Write a memo to the owner outlining the following:
  a. The basic reasons for doing target marketing in the first place
  b. The specific advantages of a target marketing strategy for the microbrewery
  c. An initial "short list" of possible target segment profiles

7-30. *Creative Homework/Short Project.* You have been a contributing author to several marketing newsletters, and you have been asked to submit a one-page article on market segmentation. First, describe the need for market segmentation and then, in turn, discuss the various approaches marketers can take, including the advantages of each approach.

Product I: Innovation and New Product Development

Neal Goldman
▼ A Decision Maker at Under Armour

Neal Goldman is director of men's training and team sports apparel at Under Armour. Based in Baltimore, Maryland, Neal has been on the Under Armour men's apparel business for four years. He has held various product category business responsibilities, including those for Baselayer, NFL Combine, and Football. Prior to Under Armour, he worked at Warrior Sports, where he was the product and brand manager for the Brine Lacrosse brand. At Warrior, Neal oversaw everything from product direction to execution to marketing asset activation, doubling Brine's business in three years. Neal graduated with a degree in English literature in 2004 from Georgetown University, where he also was a four-year starter and co-captain of the men's lacrosse team. He graduated in the top 10 all time in scoring and was named the 2004 Georgetown Male Athlete of the Year.

Neal's Info

What I do when I'm not working?
Playing with my wild two-year-old son and still pretending I'm as good of a lacrosse player as I was 10 years ago.

First job out of school?
Wrigley Gum sales rep.

Career high?
I feel like it's an evolving ranking, but currently it's the acknowledgment of being made director.

My motto to live by?
I have two: (1) If it was easy, anybody could do it. (2) Be the thermostat, not the thermometer.

What drives me?
Personally, making my family proud. Professionally, curiosity of the unknown.

My management style?
Lead by actions, not words. I want my team to see what empowerment to make decisions looks like.

My pet peeve?
Meetings where lots of words are said but no decisions are made.

Here's my problem...

In 1996, Kevin Plank, a football player at the University of Maryland, had the thought that there must be a better solution to the 100 percent cotton T-shirt he and his fellow teammates were wearing under their pads. Their shirts were quickly soaked with sweat within minutes of practice, and once they were saturated, it seemed like it took an eternity for them to dry. Not only did the wet, uncomfortable feeling of a heavy shirt bother him, but they also fit poorly; the shirts were constantly poking out of the jersey and becoming a distraction. He knew there had to be a better solution, so he scoured the garment district, found a synthetic blend that met his liking, and took that material along with a small underwear shirt to a tailor. With that, the first run of Under Armour compression shirts was created.

What started as Kevin's idea in 1996 has exploded into a $2 billion-plus empire 18 years later that now encompasses world-class footwear, outerwear, and women's and youth products. But no matter how much Under Armour grows and expands into new markets and categories around the world, the heritage product category, compression Heat-Gear, remains a vital part of the company. This Baselayer apparel line links directly to Under Armour's core message: "Protect This House."

In the spring of 2011, Under Armour started to see a gradual decline in HeatGear Baselayer sales during a time when historically business would begin ramping up. The brand's biggest sporting goods wholesale partners were telling us that for the first time since the company created this category, they were seeing severe competition from other brands. One major threat was Nike, which had just launched a new product campaign called Pro Combat. If Under Armour had created the story of compression apparel, Nike's Pro Combat was aiming to write the next chapter. The company clearly planned to target the next wave of athletes, who might not have ever been exposed to the Under Armour brand, for their new performance gear line.

The challenge we faced was twofold: product and marketing. At least from the consumer's perspective, the HeatGear Baselayer product line had not evolved in over a decade. The core franchise business had been treated like "milk and eggs" in the sense that as long as these basic items were in stock, customers wouldn't forget to pick up key essentials. That mind-set contributed to a lack of new product initiatives within this range, as we had been focusing on creating new category opportunities, such as women's apparel and athletic shoes. Marketing also played a critical role in this challenge, as Nike launched a full-on assault in all touch points with a heavy focus on retail in-store creative and social media. Our bigger rival was forging a new emotional connection

Things to remember

The compression HeatGear Baselayer line of garments was the heritage product category for Under Armour's $2 billion-plus global empire. Over the years the line remained a vital part of the company and had not evolved. Beginning in the spring of 2011, HeatGear Baselayer sales experienced declining sales due to competition. While Under Armour had ignored new product initiatives, Nike's Pro Combat line, marketed using all touch points with a heavy focus on in-store promotions and social media, had become a major competitor. It would take 18 months for Under Armour to take a new product to market.

with customers and leveraging its roster of professional athletes and creative resources to explode into the Baselayer category—and threaten our house.

To make matters worse, the product development calendar is an 18-month process from line architecture briefing to market delivery. When business began to dip, the reality of the situation was that any product line overhaul might be too little too soon. The HeatGear compression line sells millions of units each year. Any product adjustment can send ripple effects through the supply chain, which in turn can affect delivery times, sales, and profit. On the other hand, the longer Under Armour waited to enact a new plan, the more we would see a dip in sales. A delay in responding to the threat had the potential to threaten long-term revenue and decrease Under Armour's overall market share in the athletic apparel category.

As the leader of the business unit, my role was to assess our options and deliver a strategy that took into account all cross-functional groups with the end goal of recouping short-term revenue as well as setting the brand up for long-term success.

Neal considered his **Options** 1·2·3

Option 1

Approach the decision as a product problem. Build new product offerings to get into retail ASAP. Try to reverse the sales trend with new, exciting styles. This emphasis on immediate new product development to produce a new collection of Baselayer apparel could capture *open-to-buy* dollars from retailers (i.e., the budget they have to purchase retail merchandise), who clearly were going to begin allocating more of their funds to Nike. It could also help Under Armour to look more enticing and competitive compared to other products in the market, which would draw shoppers back to our core brand. But because Under Armour's product development team would have to make this happen on an accelerated time line with no opportunity for delays, production expenses would go up. We would need to position materials, trims, and manufacturing with our current supplier so that once designs and fits were completed, production could start immediately. Combine speed to market with the substantial aesthetic and material direction this product line would demand, and the costs of producing these styles could climb anywhere from 25 to 50 percent. Under Armour wouldn't be able to pass these costs on to consumers in such a competitive market, so short-term gains at retail could come at the expense of bottom-line revenue. In addition, we had to assume that we wouldn't acquire more floor space in stores, so some of our current product offerings would have to come off the displays to make room for the new. The company might need to take back the current product and absorb those costs against sales as well as add more inventory to the books.

You Choose

Which **Option** would you choose, and **why**?
1. ☐YES ☐NO 2. ☐YES ☐NO 3. ☐YES ☐NO

See what **option** Neal chose on **page 267** ➡

MyMarketingLab™

⭐ **Improve Your Grade!**

Over 10 million students improved their results using the Pearson MyLabs.
Visit **mymktlab.com** for simulations, tutorials, and end-of-chapter problems.

2

Option

Approach the decision as a marketing problem. Stay the course with the current product line and invest time, money, and resources immediately into ramping up the messaging that Under Armour sent to its target market of active athletes. This would allow us to continue investing in other new business categories and allow one of the brand's strengths—storytelling—to be on display. An overhaul of this presentation of our Baselayer products in stores would create new energy for the brand and encourage shoppers to take a closer look. Styles that had been treated like "milk and eggs" would now take center stage, and launching a social and digital campaign for Baselayer could reach millions of consumers instantly. However, while a marketing blitz could put Baselayer into the product spotlight, this might provide only a temporary shot in the arm to sales. The short-term gain from a marketing blitz could even provide us with a false sense of security about our Baselayer business. The same issues with product inertia and attractive options from competitors could pop up again six to nine months later, and, if so, we would find ourselves in an even deeper hole in terms of our ability to bring new products to market. In addition, other initiatives the marketing teams are working on would need to be put on hold. Finally, cost could be a real issue: Nike's marketing budget dwarfs Under Armour's, so going toe-to-toe with the larger company in a marketing showdown would be tough for us.

3

Option

Start over with a new business plan. Rebuild the Baselayer product from the ground up. Analyze every detail in terms of new fabric selections, design aesthetics, features and benefits, pricing, and consumer positioning. Instead of rushing through the process like option 1 proposes, play the long game: Develop a go-to-market product strategy to ensure that all business needs are addressed without compromising the supply chain and bottom-line revenue. Marketing would have more time, money, and resources to build out the consumer-facing message of what this relaunch means to athletes all over the world. Because this more drawn-out approach would not interrupt their project flow from the previous season, Under Armour's marketing team would have the bandwidth to fully focus on the new deliverables. However, it's nice to have the luxury to step back and reset the game. We didn't necessarily have that; this approach would cause us to lose out in sales and market share in the short term. We don't know how low the floor is yet: Will Under Armour still have the confidence of its retail partners when we come back to the table with new ideas after a tough year of stagnant or declining sales? Another major concern was that in order to overhaul the product line, we would have to move the category into a different direction from when the company was founded. Think about that for a second: Aside from questioning why we need a new course of action after 17 years of doing something the same way, imagine telling the CEO and COO that in order to be successful, we would need to go forward with a different product plan than what these two had built from the ground up! And from the marketing end, conventional branding wasn't going to make enough waves to let consumers know about the new line, so there is much more cost and risk associated with taking a bigger swing. If the product and marketing reset isn't successful, how deep is the hole Under Armour would have to dig itself out of?

Now, put yourself in Neal's shoes. Which option would you choose, and why?

1

Build a Better Mousetrap— and Add Value

OBJECTIVE

Explain how value is derived through different product layers.
(pp. 246–249)

"Build a better mousetrap and the world will beat a path to your door." Although we've all heard that adage, the truth is that just because a product is better there is no guarantee it will succeed. For decades, the Woodstream Company built Victor brand wooden mousetraps. Then the company decided to build a better one. Woodstream's product-development people researched the eating, crawling, and nesting habits of mice (hey, it's a living). They built prototypes of different mousetraps to come up with the best possible design and tested them in homes. Then the company unveiled the sleek-looking "Little Champ," a black plastic miniature inverted bathtub with a hole. When the mouse went in and ate the bait, a spring snapped upward—and the mouse was history.

Sounds like a great new product (unless you're a mouse), but the Little Champ failed. Woodstream studied mouse habits, *not* consumer preferences. The company later discovered that husbands set the trap at night, but in the morning it was the wives who disposed of the "present" they found waiting for them. Unfortunately, many of them thought the

Little Champ looked too expensive to throw away, so they felt they should empty the trap for reuse. This was a task most women weren't willing to do—they wanted a trap they could happily toss into the garbage.[1]

Woodstream's failure in the "rat race" underscores the importance of creating products that provide the benefits people want rather than just new gizmos that sound like a good idea. It also tells us that any number of products, from low-tech cheese to high-tech traps, potentially deliver these benefits. Despite Victor's claim to be the "World's Leader in Rodent Control Solutions," in this case cheese and a shoe box could snuff out a mouse as well as a high-tech trap.

We need to take a close look at how products successfully trap consumers' dollars when they provide value. In Chapter 1, we saw that the *value proposition* is the consumer's perception of the benefits he or she will receive if he or she buys a good or service. So the marketer's task is twofold: first, to create a better value than what's out there already and, second, to convince customers that this is true.

As we defined it in Chapter 1, a *product* is a tangible good, service, idea, or some combination of these that satisfies consumer or business customer needs through the exchange process; it is a bundle of **attributes**, including features, functions, benefits, and uses as well as its brand and packaging.

Products can be physical goods, services, ideas, people, or places. A **good** is a *tangible* product, something that we can see, touch, smell, hear, taste, or possess. It may take the form of a pack of yummy cookies, a shiny new iPad, a house, a part used in production of that Tesla electric sports car you'd like to buy, or a chic but pricey Coach handbag. In contrast, *intangible* products—services, ideas, people, and places—are products that we can't always see, touch, taste, smell, or possess. We'll talk more about intangible products in Chapter 12.

Welcome to Part 3 of this book, "Develop the Value Proposition for the Customer." The key word here is *develop*, and a large part of the marketer's role in developing the value proposition is to create and market products innovatively. In this chapter, we'll first examine what a product is and see how marketers classify consumer and B2B products. Then we'll go on to look at new products, how marketers develop new products, and how markets accept them (or not).

More broadly speaking, Parts 3 and 4 of the book take you systematically through all of the elements of the marketing mix's four Ps: product and price in Part 3 and distribution ("place") and promotion in Part 4. As you learned in Chapter 7, developing and executing a great marketing mix is the heart and soul of positioning strategy. And the place to start is with your product—as an old saying in marketing goes, "If the product ain't right, the rest don't matter."

Layers of the Product Concept

No doubt you've heard someone say, "It's the thought, not the gift that counts." Sometimes that's just an excuse for a lame present, but more broadly it means that the gift is a sign or symbol that the gift giver has remembered you. When we evaluate a gift, we may consider the following: Was it presented with a flourish? Was it wrapped in special paper? Was it obviously a "regift"—something the gift giver had received as a gift for him- or herself but wanted to pass on to you (like last year's fruitcake)? These dimensions are a part of the total gift you receive in addition to the actual goodie in the box.

Like a gift, a product is everything that a customer receives in an exchange. As Figure 8.1 shows, we distinguish among three distinct layers of the product—the core product, the actual product, and the augmented product. When they develop product strategies, marketers need to consider how to satisfy customers' wants and needs at each of these three layers—that is, how they can create value. Let's consider each layer in turn.

attributes
Include features, functions, benefits, and uses of a product. Marketers view products as a bundle of attributes that includes the packaging, brand name, benefits, and supporting features in addition to a physical good.

good
A tangible product that we can see, touch, smell, hear, or taste.

Figure 8.1 📷 *Snapshot* | Layers of the Product

A product is everything a customer receives—the basic benefits, the physical product and its packaging, and the "extras" that come with the product.

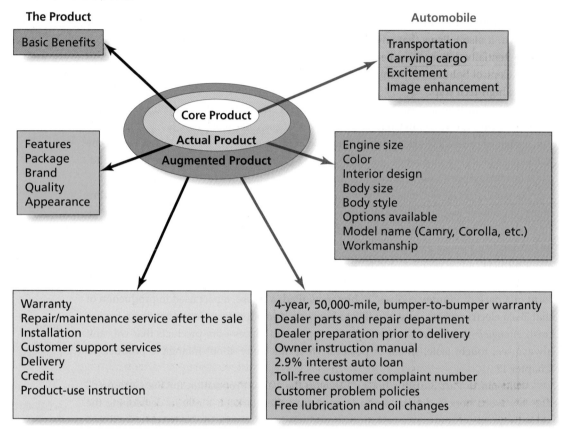

The Core Product

The **core product** consists of all the benefits the product will provide for consumers or business customers. As we noted in Chapter 1, a *benefit* is an outcome that the customer receives from owning or using a product. Wise old marketers (and some young ones, too) will tell you, "A marketer may make and sell a half-inch drill bit, but a customer buys a half-inch hole." This tried-and-true saying reminds us that people buy the core product, in this case, the ability to make a hole. If a new product, such as a laser, comes along that provides that outcome in a better way or more cheaply, the drill-bit maker has a problem. The moral of this story? *Marketing is about supplying benefits*, not *attributes*. And benefits are the foundation of any value proposition.

Many products actually provide multiple benefits. For example, the primary benefit of a car is transportation—all cars (in good repair) offer the ability to travel from point A to point B. But products also provide customized benefits—benefits customers receive because manufacturers add "bells and whistles" to win them over. Some drivers simply want economical transportation, others appreciate an environmentally friendly hybrid car, and still others want a top-of-the-line, all-terrain vehicle or perhaps a hot sports car that will be the envy of their friends. And some just like the expandable cup holder's ability to accommodate everything from your Red Bull to a Big Gulp!

The Actual Product

The second layer—the **actual product**—is the physical good or the delivered service that supplies the desired benefit. For example, when you buy a washing machine, the core product is the ability to get clothes clean, but the actual product is a large, square metal

core product
All the benefits the product will provide for consumers or business customers.

actual product
The physical good or the delivered service that supplies the desired benefit.

apparatus. When you get a medical exam, the core service is maintaining your health, but the actual one is a lot of annoying poking and prodding. The actual product also includes the unique features of the product, such as its appearance or styling, the package, and the brand name. Samsung makes a wide range of flat-screen TVs in dozens of sizes from low-end low-price to other models that might cause you to mortgage your house. But in the end, all offer the same core benefit of enabling you to catch Sheldon Cooper's antics on the latest episode of *The Big Bang Theory*.

The Augmented Product

Finally, marketers offer customers an **augmented product**—the actual product plus other supporting features, such as a warranty, credit, delivery, installation, and repair service after the sale. Marketers know that adding these supporting features to a product is an effective way for a company to stand out from the crowd.

For example, Apple truly revolutionized the music industry when it created its iTunes Store, which enabled consumers to download titles directly to their digital music and video libraries. It also conveniently saves you the trouble of correctly inserting, labeling, and sorting the new music. This innovation no doubt dealt a blow to firms that manufactured stands designed to hold hundreds of CDs. Apple's augmented product (convenience, extensive selection, and ease of use) pays off handsomely for the company in sales and profits, and customers adore the fact that you can do it all on your device of choice. Apple continues to add layers to its core music product, most recently with its purchase of the headphone maker and music-streaming service Beats for a "mere" $3.2 billion.[2]

This diet dessert offers the value proposition of good taste without the extra calories.

augmented product
The actual product plus other supporting features such as a warranty, credit, delivery, installation, and repair service after the sale.

2 | How Marketers Classify Products

OBJECTIVE
Describe how marketers classify products.
(pp. 249–252)

So far, we've learned that a product may be a tangible good or an intangible service or idea and that there are different layers to the product through which a consumer can derive value. Now we'll build on these ideas as we look at how products differ from one another. Marketers classify products into categories because they represent differences in how consumers and business customers feel about products and how they purchase different products. Such an understanding helps marketers develop new products and a marketing mix that satisfies customer needs.

Let's first consider differences in consumer products based on how long the product will last and on how the consumer shops for the product. Then we will discuss the general types of B2B products.

How Long Do Products Last?

Marketers classify consumer goods as durable or nondurable depending on how long the product lasts. You expect a refrigerator to last many years, but a gallon of milk will last only a week or so until it turns into a science project. **Durable goods** are consumer products that provide benefits over a period of months, years, or even decades, such as cars, furniture, and appliances. In contrast, we consume **nondurable goods**, such as *People* magazine and fresh sushi, in the short term.

durable goods
Consumer products that provide benefits over a long period of time, such as cars, furniture, and appliances.

nondurable goods
Consumer products that provide benefits for a short time because they are consumed (such as food) or are no longer useful (such as newspapers).

We are more likely to purchase durable goods under conditions of *high involvement* (as we saw in Chapter 5), while nondurable goods are more likely to be *low-involvement* decisions. When consumers buy a new car or a house, most will spend a lot of time and energy on the decision process. When they offer high-involvement products, marketers need to understand consumers' desires for different product benefits and the importance of warranties, service, and customer support. So they must be sure that consumers can find the information they need. One way is to provide a "Frequently Asked Questions" (FAQ) section on a company website. Another is to host a Facebook page, Twitter feed, message board, or blog to build a community around the product. When a company itself sponsors such forums, odds are that the content will be much more favorable and the firm can keep track of what people say about its products. For example, as part of the "Funville" section of its website, Carnival Cruise Lines has a special forums section that allows users to interact with staff, cruise experts, and other current and would-be cruisers in order to get information about Carnival's ships, ports of call, and all things related to cruising.[3]

In contrast, consumers usually don't "sweat the details" so much when they choose among nondurable goods. There is little if any search for information or deliberation. Sometimes this means that consumers buy whatever brand is available and is reasonably priced. In other instances, they base their decisions largely on past experience. Because a certain brand has performed satisfactorily before, customers often see no reason to consider other brands, and they choose the same one out of habit.

How Do Consumers Buy Products?

Marketers also classify products based on where and how consumers buy the product. Figure 8.2 portrays product classifications in the consumer and business marketplaces. We'll consider the consumer market first in which we think of both goods and services as convenience products, shopping products, specialty products, or unsought products. Recall that in Chapter 6 we talked about how consumer decisions differ in terms of effort they put into habitual decision making versus limited problem solving versus extended problem solving—a useful idea on which to base our understanding of why it's important to classify products.

A **convenience product** typically is a nondurable good or service that consumers purchase frequently with a minimum of comparison and effort. As the name implies, consumers expect these products to be handy, and they will buy whatever brands are easy to obtain. In general, convenience products are low priced and widely available. You can buy a gallon of milk or a loaf of bread at most any grocery store, drugstore, or convenience store. Consumers generally already know all they need or want to know about a convenience product, devote little effort to purchases, and willingly accept alternative brands if their preferred brand is not available in a convenient location. What's the most important thing for marketers of convenience products? You guessed it—make sure the product is easily obtainable in all the places where consumers are likely to look for it. It's a good guess that shoppers don't put a lot of thought into buying convenience products, so a company that sells products like white bread might focus its strategy on promoting awareness of a brand name as opposed to providing a detailed "spec sheet" we might expect to find for a smart phone or other durable product.

convenience product
A consumer good or service that is usually low priced, widely available, and purchased frequently with a minimum of comparison and effort.

Figure 8.2 📷 *Snapshot* | Classification of Products

Products are classified differently depending on whether they are in the consumer or business market.

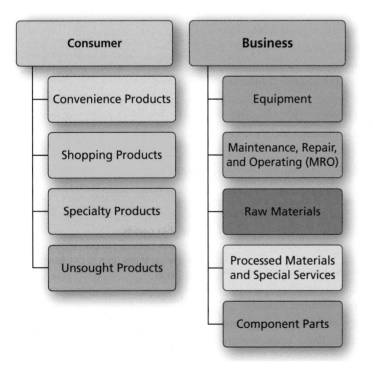

There are several types of convenience products:

- **Staple products**, such as milk, bread, and gasoline, are basic or necessary items that are available almost everywhere. Most consumers don't perceive big differences among brands. A particular category of staple products is called consumer packaged goods. A **consumer packaged good (CPG) or fast-moving consumer good (FMCG)** is a low-cost good that we consume quickly and replace frequently.

  Like staple products in general, CPGs (or FMCGs) are also frequently purchased but are less basic, with more variations than general staples. Importantly, they are also more brand-centric, and consumers tend to perceive more differences in product quality, features, and benefits, so the brands are heavily advertised. And in terms of distribution, giant retailers use CPGs/FMCGs to bring shoppers into the store, thus building foot traffic and increasing the chances that other types of products (see impulse and shopping products below) will also end up in shopping baskets. Walmart, for example, promoted the arrival of Twinkies at its stores the weekend before Twinkies were set to make their nationwide re-debut.[4] If your Twinkie crave was on, Walmart was the place to be. And who can go into Walmart and purchase just one item?

- While a staple is something we usually decide to buy in advance (or at least before the fuel needle sits on "E" for too long), we buy **impulse products** on the spur of the moment. When you throw a copy of *People* magazine into your shopping cart because it has a cool photo of Brad Pitt and Angelina Jolie on the cover, you're acting on impulse. When they want to promote impulse products, marketers have two challenges: (1) to create a product or package design that "reaches out and grabs the customer" and (2) to make sure their product is highly visible, for example, by securing prime end-aisle or checkout-lane space. That's why you'll often find brightly colored packages of yellow creme Oreos on end caps in the spring or cheery packages of gum and candy in the checkout lines. Package design and placement is becoming ever more important as customers come through the lines with "mobile blinders" on—that is, customers with mobile phones in hand are more likely to send texts or check Facebook while they stand in line, so they don't even notice the impulse products beckoning for their attention.[5] It's getting harder and harder for a package of Juicy Fruit gum to compete with a juicy Facebook post.

- As the name suggests, we purchase **emergency products** when we're in dire need; examples include bandages, umbrellas, and something to unclog the nasty bathroom sink. Because we need the product badly and immediately, price and sometimes product quality may be irrelevant to our decision to purchase.

In contrast to convenience products, **shopping products** are goods or services for which consumers will spend time and effort to gather information on price, product attributes, and product quality. For these products, consumers are likely to compare alternatives before they buy.

Tablet computers are a good example of a shopping product. They offer an ever-expanding array of features and functions, and new versions constantly enter the market. The shopper has many trade-offs and decisions to make about a variety of features that can be bundled, including speed, screen size, functionality, weight, and battery life. And tablet manufacturers understand your decision dilemma: They take great pains to communicate comparisons to you in their advertising—and, as you might expect, they usually find a way to make their version seem superior.

Specialty products have unique characteristics that are important to buyers at almost any price. You can buy a Swiffer Wet Jet mop starter kit at Target for about $20, right? Yet the iRobot Scooba Model 450 floor-scrubbing robot sells for $600 on the iRobot website.[6] Other examples of specialty products include Rolex watches and Big Bertha golf clubs.

staple products
Basic or necessary items that are available almost everywhere.

consumer packaged good (CPG) or fast-moving consumer good (FMCG)
A low-cost good that is consumed quickly and replaced frequently.

impulse products
A product people often buy on the spur of the moment.

emergency products
Products we purchase when we're in dire need.

shopping products
Goods or services for which consumers spend considerable time and effort gathering information and comparing alternatives before making a purchase.

specialty products
Goods or services that has unique characteristics and is important to the buyer and for which he or she will devote significant effort to acquire.

252 **PART THREE** | DEVELOP THE VALUE PROPOSITION FOR THE CUSTOMER

Consumers usually know a good deal about specialty products, and they tend to be loyal to specific brands. Generally, a specialty product is an extended problem-solving purchase that requires a lot of effort to choose, meaning that firms that sell these kinds of products need to create marketing strategies that make their products stand apart from the rest.

Unsought products are goods or services (other than convenience products) for which a consumer has little awareness or interest until a need arises. When a college graduate lands his or her first "real" job, typically retirement plans and disability insurance are unsought products. It requires a good deal of advertising or personal selling to interest young people in these kinds of products—just ask any life insurance salesperson. One solution may be to make pricing more attractive; for example, reluctant consumers may be more willing to buy an unsought product for "only pennies a day" than if they have to think about their yearly or lifetime cash outlay.

How Do Businesses Buy Products?

Although consumers purchase products for their own use, as we saw in Chapter 6 organizational customers purchase items to enable them to produce still other goods or services. Marketers classify B2B products based on how organizational customers *use* them. As with consumer products, when marketers know how their business customers use a product, they are better able to design products and craft an appropriate marketing mix. Let's briefly review the five different types of B2B products that Figure 8.2 depicts.

- **Equipment** refers to the products an organization uses in its daily operations. *Heavy equipment*, sometimes called *installations* or *capital equipment*, includes items such as the sophisticated robotics Ford uses to assemble automobiles. Installations are big-ticket items and last for a number of years. Computers, photocopy machines, and water fountains are examples of *light* or *accessory equipment*; they are portable, cost less, and have a shorter life span than capital equipment.

- **Maintenance, repair, and operating (MRO) products** are goods that a business customer consumes in a relatively short time. *Maintenance products* include lightbulbs, mops, cleaning supplies, and the like. Repair products are items such as nuts, bolts, washers, and small tools. *Operating supplies* include computer paper and oil to keep machinery running smoothly. Although some firms use a sales force to promote MRO products, others rely on catalog sales, the Internet, and telemarketing in order to keep prices as low as possible.

- **Raw materials** are products of the fishing, lumber, agricultural, and mining industries that organizational customers purchase to use in their finished products. For example, a food company transforms soybeans into tofu, and a steel manufacturer changes iron ore into large sheets of steel that other firms use to build automobiles, washing machines, and lawn mowers.

- Firms produce **processed materials** when they transform raw materials from their original state. A builder uses treated lumber to add a deck onto a house. A company that creates aluminum cans for Red Bull buys aluminum ingots to make them.

- In addition to tangible processed materials, some business customers purchase **specialized services** from outside suppliers. These may be equipment based, such as repairing a copy machine or fixing an assembly line malfunction, or non–equipment based, such as market research and legal services. These services are essential to the operation of an organization but are not part of the production of a product.

- **Component parts** are manufactured goods or subassemblies of finished items that organizations need to complete their own products. For example, a computer manufacturer needs silicon chips to make a computer, and an automobile manufacturer needs batteries, tires, and fuel injectors.

---

unsought products
Goods or services for which a consumer has little awareness or interest until the product or a need for the product is brought to his or her attention.

equipment
Expensive goods that an organization uses in its daily operations that last for a long time.

maintenance, repair, and operating (MRO) products
Goods that a business customer consumes in a relatively short time.

raw materials
Products of the fishing, lumber, agricultural, and mining industries that organizational customers purchase to use in their finished products.

processed materials
Products created when firms transform raw materials from their original state.

specialized services
Services that are essential to the operation of an organization but are not part of the production of a product.

component parts
Manufactured goods or subassemblies of finished items that organizations need to complete their own products.

3

OBJECTIVE

Understand the importance and types of product innovations.
(pp. 253–255)

"New and Improved!" The Process of Innovation

"New and improved!" What exactly do we mean when we use the term *new product*? The Federal Trade Commission says that (1) a product must be entirely new or changed significantly to be called new and that (2) a product may be called new for only six months.

That definition is fine from a legal perspective. From a marketing standpoint, though, a new product or an **innovation** is *anything* that customers perceive as new and different. Innovation has its roots in an even more elemental concept that is a hot topic in boardrooms of most organizations today: creativity. **Creativity** describes a process that results in something new. Creative outcomes can take on many forms, but most often we experience them as something we can see, hear, smell, touch, or taste.[7] The outcome can be most anything—an idea, a joke, an artistic or literary work, a painting or musical composition, a novel solution to a problem, an invention, and, of course, a new product. Scientific research into creativity provides strong evidence of the importance of creative processes in the production of novel, useful products.[8]

An innovation may relatively minor, such as the thousands of new versions of current products, such as Chocolate Cheerios, we see on the market each year. Or it can be something game changing like the Apple Watch. It may come in the form of a new way to transmit information, such as when Skype VoIP telephony became available as a free service over the Internet, or as a new way to power a vehicle, such as the hydrogen fuel cells in the Honda FCX Clarity. In some cases, an innovation may be a completely new product that provides benefits never available before, like the original HP scientific calculator that nearly overnight made the slide rule obsolete (if the term *slide rule* is foreign to you, we suggest Googling it—a slide rule is how engineers used to make complex calculations prior to HP's innovation). In this section and the next, we focus heavily on the concept and process of product innovation, which, if done well, contributes mightily to organizational success.

Types of Innovations

Innovations differ in their degree of newness, and this helps determine how quickly the target market will adopt them. Because innovations that are more novel require us to exert

innovation
A product that consumers perceive to be new and different from existing products.

creativity
A phenomenon whereby something new and valuable is created.

Even minor innovations can add value to a product.

Courtesy of Publicis Conseil

The **Cutting Edge**

Innovating for a Better Shave

In 1901, King C. Gillette invented the world's first safety razor with a single disposable blade. And in the decades since, innovation in the razor industry has typically meant adding another blade—two blades, three blades, four blades, and even five blades! (After all, the more blades there are, the better the performance you get from the razor.) So it was a true innovation when Procter & Gamble's (P&G's) Gillette turned the razor industry on its head in 2014 and instead innovated a new razor handle. "Innovation is our life blood," says Patrice Louvet, group president of global grooming and shave care.[9]

After five years of development—with tests on 24,000 real men—Gillette introduced the Fusion ProGlide FlexBall, a razor that has an orange swiveling head that allows the blades to pivot left and right as well as up and down. What does this mean? It means that the razor misses 20 percent fewer hairs and cuts hairs 23 microns shorter. At $11.49, it is one of the most expensive razors on the market, but that doesn't worry Gillette marketers, who spent $200 million in its biggest-ever launch of a new razor to make sure the product was a hit with their target markets: boomers and Millennials.[10] As part of the product launch, Gillette also shared its favorite famous "shave faces" on Twitter and Facebook, starting with tennis great Roger Federer, and sponsored a six-city "Shaving Rebuilt" tour.[11]

Figure 8.3 📷 *Snapshot* | Types of Innovations

Three types of innovations are continuous, dynamically continuous, and discontinuous, based on their degree of newness.

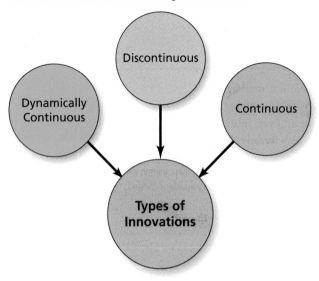

greater effort to figure out how to use them, they are slower to spread throughout a population than new products that are similar to what is already available.

As 📷 Figure 8.3 shows, marketers classify innovations into three categories based on their degree of newness: continuous innovations, dynamically continuous innovations, and discontinuous innovations. However, it is better to think of these three types as ranges along a continuum that goes from a very small change in an existing product to a totally new product. We can then describe the three types of innovations in terms of the amount of change they bring to people's lives. For example, the first automobiles caused tremendous changes in the lives of people who were used to getting places by "horse power." Then airplanes came along and opened the entire world to us. And now, with recent innovations like the TripLingo app, you can communicate easily while traveling abroad. TripLingo comes with a real-time translator—just speak into your phone, and it speaks back to you, at whatever speed you choose. It even has a Slangslider so that you can set the level of formality.[12] On the idea side, Airbnb is changing how travelers book a place to stay at their destinations (by allowing virtually anyone to rent out space in their own homes), and Uber's app provides a new way to get to this destination (by allowing virtually anyone to become a taxi driver and pick up fares when people summon a ride on their phones).

Continuous Innovations

continuous innovation
A modification of an existing product that sets one brand apart from its competitors.

A **continuous innovation** is a modification to an existing product, such as when Samsung and others reinvigorated the TV market by offering thinner sets that featured high-definition viewing. This type of modification can set one brand apart from its competitors. For example, people associate Volvo cars with safety—in fact, their taglines include "Safety first, always" and "You're not just driving a car, you're driving a promise." Those are strong words, and Volvo backs them up with a steady stream of safety-related innovations.

The consumer doesn't have to learn anything new to use a continuous innovation. From a marketing perspective, this means that it's usually relatively easy to convince consumers to adopt this kind of new product. For example, the current generation of high-definition plasma flat-screen monitors didn't require computer users to change their behaviors. We all know what a computer monitor is and how it works. The system's continuous innovation simply gives users the added benefits of taking up less space and being easier on the eyes than old-style monitors.

knockoff
A new product that copies, with slight modification, the design of an original product.

A **knockoff** is a new product that copies, with slight modification, the design of an original product. Firms deliberately create knockoffs of clothing and jewelry, often with the intent to sell to a larger or different market. For example, companies may copy the haute couture clothing styles of top designers and sell them at lower prices to the mass market. It's likely that a cheaper version of the gown Jennifer Lawrence wears to the Academy Awards ceremony will be available at numerous websites within a few days after the event. It is difficult to legally protect a design (as opposed to a technological invention) because an imitator can argue that even a very slight change—different buttons or a slightly wider collar on a dress or shirt—means the knockoff is not an exact copy.

Dynamically Continuous Innovations

A **dynamically continuous innovation** is a pronounced modification to an existing product that requires a modest amount of learning or change in behavior to use it. The history of audio equipment is a series of dynamically continuous innovations. For many years, consumers enjoyed listening to their favorite Frank Sinatra songs on record players (actually, when first introduced, they were called Gramophones). In the 1960s, teeny boppers screamed and swooned as they listened to the Beatles on a continuous-play eight-track tape (requiring the purchase of an eight-track tape player, of course). Then came cassette tapes to listen to the Eagles (oops, now a cassette player is needed). In the 1980s, consumers could hear Metallica songs digitally mastered on compact discs (that, of course, required the purchase of a new CD player).

But of course, in the 1990s, recording technology moved one big step forward with MP3 technology; it allowed Madonna fans to download music from the Internet or to exchange electronic copies of the music with others, and when mobile MP3 players hit the scene in 1998, fans could download the tunes directly into a portable player. Then, in November 2001, Apple Computer introduced its first iPod (can you believe it's been that long!). With the original iPod, music fans could take 1,000 songs with them wherever they went. By 2010, iPods could hold 40,000 songs, 25,000 photos, and 200 hours of video.[13] Music fans go to the Apple iTunes Store or elsewhere to download songs and to get suggestions for new music they might enjoy. Of course, today you can do all this on your smart phone—and although iPods still sell well and are popular in microsizes for sports, you certainly don't need an iPod to have a portable music player. From Gramophone to smart phone—an amazing journey in dynamically continuous innovation.

Are record albums doomed to the fate of the dinosaur? Maybe, but old-style phonograph records from the '80s and earlier are something of a cult product on sites like eBay, and connoisseurs of real "albums" swear that the analog sound is "richer" (static and all) than the crisp digital recordings of today.

Discontinuous Innovations

To qualify as a **discontinuous innovation**, the product must create *major changes* in the way we live. Consumers have to learn a great deal to be able to effectively use a discontinuous innovation because no similar product has ever been on the market. Major inventions, such as the airplane, the car, and the TV, are the sort of innovations that radically changed modern lifestyles. Another discontinuous innovation, the personal computer—developed in fairly close parallel to the rise of the Internet—changed the way we shop and allowed more people to work from home or anywhere else. Since the advent of PCs, the move toward processing the same information on tablets and on handheld devices became a follow-up journey in dynamically continuous innovation. One particular type of discontinuous innovation is **convergence**, which means the coming together of two or more technologies to create new systems that provide greater benefit than the original technologies alone.

What's the next discontinuous innovation? Is there a product out there already that will gain that distinction? Usually, marketers know for sure only through 20/20 hindsight; in other words, it's tough to plan for the next really big one (what the computer industry calls the "killer app").

dynamically continuous innovation
A change in an existing product that requires a moderate amount of learning or behavior change.

discontinuous innovation
A totally new product that creates major changes in the way we live.

convergence
The coming together of two or more technologies to create a new system with greater benefits than its separate parts.

Convergence is one of the most talked-about forms of dynamically continuous innovations in the digital world. Originally, the phone, organizer, and camera all came together in the Palm Treo and then the Motorola Q. Cable companies now provide cellular service, land phone lines, and highspeed Internet. Today devices like Apple's iPad integrate numerous functions on one platform.

4 New Product Development

OBJECTIVE
Show how firms develop new products.
(pp. 255–261)

Building on our knowledge of the concept of creativity and the different types of innovations, we'll now turn our attention to how firms actually develop new products. The process described is

Metrics Moment

How do marketers measure innovation? Short answer: It's pretty complex. This is because it involves not only marketing but also the firm's overall culture, leadership, and processes in place that foster innovation. Here's a short list of measures that when taken as a whole can provide a firm's "Innovation Score Card":

Firm Strategy

- How aware are organization members of a firm's goals for innovation?
- How committed is the firm and its leadership to those goals?
- How actively does the firm support innovation among its organization members? Are there rewards and other incentives in place to innovate? Is innovation part of the performance evaluation process?
- To what degree do organization members perceive that resources are available for innovation (money and otherwise)?

Firm Culture

- Does the organization have an appetite for learning and trying new things?

- Do organization members have the freedom and security to try things, fail, and then go forward to try different things?

Outcomes of Innovation

- How many innovations have been launched in the past three years?
- What is the percentage of revenue attributable to launches of innovations during the past three years?[14]

Apply the Metrics

1. Select a firm that you are particularly interested in and that you believe is pretty innovative.
2. Do a little research on its website and elsewhere to get a sense for the evidence about how it performs on the above criteria for innovativeness.
3. Summarize your findings—how does the firm score on the Innovation Score Card?
4. In general, do you find that the firm is more or less innovative than you expected?

---

research and development (R&D)
A well-defined and systematic approach to how innovation is done within the firm.

APPLYING ▼ New Product Development

David understands that developing successful new products is a multistep process that would take Under Armour 18 months to deliver. While new products would help Under Armour compete with Nike's new products, the product development process would be expensive and increase the cost of the new product.

new product development (NPD)
The phases by which firms develop new products, including idea generation, product concept development and screening, marketing strategy development, business analysis, technical development, test marketing, and commercialization.

idea generation (ideation)
A phase of product development in which marketers use a variety of sources to come up with great new product ideas that provide customer benefits and that are compatible with the company mission.

value co-creation
The process by which benefits-based value is created through collaborative participation by customers and other stakeholders in the new product development process.

based on expenditures in **research and development (R&D)**, which in most organizations is a well-defined and systematic approach to how it innovates. Investors and financial markets closely scrutinize R&D investments because these expenditures tend to predict how robust the firm's oncoming new product stream will be. In fact, R&D investment in and of itself is often a central metric for organizational commitment to innovation. Higher levels of R&D activity are inherently more competitively important in some industries versus others (high tech and pharmaceuticals are examples on the high side), but, as we saw in the case of Under Armour at the beginning of the chapter, in any firm new product development is fueled by investment in R&D.

There are seven phases in the process of **new product development (NPD)**, as Figure 8.4 shows: idea generation, product concept development and screening, marketing strategy development, business analysis, technical development, test marketing, and commercialization. Let's take a quick look at what goes on during each of these phases.

Phase 1: Idea Generation (Ideation)

In the initial **idea generation** (or **ideation**) phase of product development, marketers use a variety of sources to come up with great new product ideas that provide customer benefits and that are compatible with the company mission. Sometimes ideas come from customers. Ideas also come from salespeople, service providers, and others who have direct customer contact. **Value co-creation** refers to the process by which an organization creates worth through collaborative participation by customers and other stakeholders in the new product development process.

Marketers at Ford, for example, reached out to customers to test design concepts for the luxury Lincoln brand. The program, which is called "Virtual Voice of the Customer" and runs on an iPad, shows drivers design concepts and asks them to choose among sportier or more modern looks. Ford then records the design concepts they prefer, along with demographic data, to get a better feel for consumer preferences in real time.[15] This value co-creation approach runs counter to "traditional" approaches in which firms develop products behind a curtain and send them to market, hoping that customers connect with the intended value proposition of the new offering.

Often firms use marketing research activities, such as the *focus groups* we discussed in Chapter 4, in their search for new product ideas. For example, a company like ESPN that wants to develop new channels or change the focus of its existing channels might hold focus group discussions across different groups of sports-minded viewers to get ideas for new types of programs.

Phase 2: Product Concept Development and Screening

The second phase in developing new products is **product concept development and screening**. Although ideas for products initially come from a variety of sources and, it is hoped, through co-creation with customers and others, ultimately the responsibility usually falls to marketers to manage the process and expand these ideas into more complete product concepts. Product concepts describe what features the product should have and the benefits those features will provide for consumers.

In new product development, failures often come as frequently (or more so) than successes, and it is critical to screen ideas for *both* their technical and commercial value. When screening, marketers examine the chances that a new product concept might be successful while they weed out concepts that have little chance to make it in the market. They estimate *technical success* when they decide whether the new product is technologically feasible—is it possible to actually build this product? Then they estimate *commercial success* when they decide whether anyone is likely to buy the product. And speaking of technology-driven product innovation, take a look at Table 8.1 for some examples of "pushing out the envelope"—new products that have their roots in some pretty old-fashioned ones. But caution: Any new product today can easily be obsolete tomorrow!

Phase 3: Marketing Strategy Development

The third phase in new product development is to develop a marketing strategy to introduce the product to the marketplace, a process we began to talk about back in Chapter 2. This means that marketers must identify the target market, estimate its size, and determine how they can effectively position the product to address the target market's needs. And, of course, marketing strategy development includes planning for pricing, distribution, and promotion expenditures both for the introduction of the new product and for the long run.

Phase 4: Business Analysis

Once a product concept passes the screening stage, the next phase is a **business analysis**. Even though marketers have evidence that there is a market for the product, they still must find out if the product can make a profitable contribution to the organization's product mix. How much potential demand is there for the product? Does the firm have the resources it will need to successfully develop and introduce the product?

The business analysis for a new product begins with assessing how the new product will fit into the firm's total product mix. Will the new product increase sales, or will it simply take away sales of existing products (a concept called *cannibalization* that we'll discuss further in Chapter 9)? Are there possible synergies between the new product and the company's existing offerings that may improve visibility and the image of both? And what are the marketing costs likely to be?

Figure 8.4  *Process* | Phases in New Product Development

New product development generally occurs in seven phases.

- **Phase 1:** Idea Generation
- **Phase 2:** Product Concept Development and Screening
- **Phase 3:** Marketing Strategy Development
- **Phase 4:** Business Analysis
- **Phase 5:** Technical Development
- **Phase 6:** Test Marketing
- **Phase 7:** Commercialization

The director of culinary innovation at McDonald's recently came up with a simple idea: He took the breaded chicken the chain uses in its Chicken Selects strips, topped it with shredded cheddar jack cheese and lettuce, added a few squirts of ranch sauce, and wrapped it in a flour tortilla. McDonald's dubbed it the "Snack Wrap" and put it on the menu at a starter price of $1.29. A hit was born—the Snack Wrap is one of the most successful new product launches in company history with sales exceeding projections by 20 percent.

Table 8.1 | Products Yesterday and Beyond

Old Hat	More Recent	Fresh
Typewriter	Personal computer	**Dragon Naturally Speaking 12** This software for computers, MP3 players, and smart phones allows you to send e-mails and instant messages and to surf the Web with voice commands. $60, **www.shop.nuance.com**
Drinking fountain	Bottled water	**AquaSafeStraw** This portable, reusable straw removes 99.9 percent of waterborne bacteria from any water. $40, **www.aquasafestraw.com**
Wine cork	Synthetic cork and screw cap	**Skybar Wine Preservation and Optimization System** A wine bar that stores, refrigerates, pours, and preserves a bottle of wine for up to 10 days after opening. $300, **www.skybarhome.com**
Blackboard	Dry-erase board	**Interactive Smart Board 6065** This whiteboard lets you write in multiple colors, erase, zoom, and move objects around with your fingers or with one of its ink-free pens. $4,500, **www.smarttech.com**
Pay phone	Cell phone	**Google's Nexus 5** This smart phone with a 4.95-inch touch screen, an eight-megapixel camera, and Wi-Fi connectivity will help you forget the scary parts of the movie *Phone Booth.* $350, **www.play.google.com/store/devices**
Mechanical bell	Electronic bell (alarm clock)	**Soleil Sun Alarm Ultima SA-2008** Instead of a bell, the high-intensity LED bulb grows brighter (just like the sunrise) as time to rise and shine approaches. $80, **www.sunalarmstore.com**
Boombox	Sony Walkman	**Sony Ericsson Portable Bluetooth Speaker MBS-100** Set the speakers around the room, keep your MP3 player or smart phone in your pocket, and DJ from the dance floor. $55, **www.amazon.com**
Hotel key	Electronic key card	**Openways** This system sends a secure Mobile Key to guests' cell phones, alleviating the need to stop at the front desk to check in. **www.openways.com**
Road map	GPS navigation device	**Garmin nüvi 3597LMTHD** This GPS provides real-time traffic updates and detailed images of junctions, along with hands-free control. $330, **www.bestbuy.com**
Checkbook	Debit card	**RedLaser App** This iPhone application lets you scan a barcode for an item, comparison-shop online, and purchase with your phone. Free, **www.iTunes.com**
Lick-and-stick stamp	Peel-and-press stamp	**Stamps.com** Pay a monthly service charge on this site, and you can print official U.S. postage directly onto your envelopes. No licking, no peeling, no nothing. $16 per month, **www.stamps.com**
Photo film	Digital camera	**Sony Cyber-shot DSC-HX50V/B** This still camera was the first of its kind to include a GPS, a compass, and full advanced video codec high-definition video capability. $370, **www.sonystyle.com**

Source: Lauren Parajon, "Last Tech," *Southwest Airlines Spirit Magazine*, March 2010, pp. 82–92, updated to 2014.

product concept development and screening
The second step of product development in which marketers test product ideas for technical and commercial success.

business analysis
The step in the product development process in which marketers assess a product's commercial viability.

technical development
The step in the product development process in which company engineers refine and perfect a new product.

Phase 5: Technical Development

If a new product concept survives the scrutiny of a business analysis, it then undergoes **technical development**, in which a firm's engineers work with marketers to refine the design and production process. LG, for example, is one of many electronics companies that has moved from traditional light-emitting diode (LED) technology in its TVs to OLED technology. What's the difference? OLED introduces an organic substance (hence the O in OLED) that, when met by an electric current, glows to produce high-definition imagery. This technology also makes it possible to switch off individual pixels of color, which makes blacks truly black and creates a higher contrast ratio. The translation of technical developments like this into terms that consumers can easily understand and respond to is a critical marketing challenge. Rather than get into the nitty-gritty of how the OLED works, LG marketers instead poetically describe the technology by citing life's significant moments such as one's first kiss or a child's first steps, or the majestic beauty of a western sunset."[19]

Ripped from the Headlines

Ethical/Sustainable Decisions in the Real World

New product development has never been easy, but today it's an even greater challenge because marketers also must keep sustainability in mind. Adidas Group, a leading maker of sports apparel and equipment, is one company that is doing it right.

As part of its new product development process, Adidas uses the Design for Environment (DfE) approach. This approach systematically applies environmental and human health considerations at the product design stage. It encourages designers to minimize environmental impact at all stages of a product's life cycle—raw material extraction and processing, innovation, design, development, manufacturing, packaging and distribution, product use, and end of life.[16]

Here are some examples of how Adidas uses DfE in new product development and manufacturing:

- The DryDye fabric for T-shirts eliminates the need for water in the dyeing process. In contrast, the conventional dyeing process uses up to 25 liters of water per shirt.
- New clothing lines employ a new approach called pattern efficiency, which reduces fabric waste when machines cut out clothing patterns.
- Instead of physical prototypes, Adidas employs virtual images showcase new products that save water and energy and reduce greenhouse gas emissions normally required to produce real-life prototypes.[17]

One new Adidas product designed with DfE in mind is the Element Voyager shoe, which is made from sustainable fabrics and includes recycled polyester and recycled rubber. The upper part of the shoe alone achieves 95 percent pattern efficiency. The result is a shoe that contains 60 fewer components than a traditional running shoe.[18] Better for Adidas. Better for the consumer. Better for the planet.

ETHICS CHECK: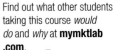
Find out what other students taking this course *would do* and *why* at **mymktlab.com**.

Do you believe marketers are doing enough to develop sustainable products?

☐YES ☐NO

The better a firm understands how customers will react to a new product, the better its chances of commercial success. For this reason, typically a company allocates resources to develop one or more physical versions or **prototypes** of the product. Prospective customers may evaluate these mock-ups in focus groups or in field trials at home.

Prototypes also are useful for people within the firm. Those involved in the technical development process must determine which parts of a finished good the company will make and which ones it will buy from other suppliers. In the case of manufacturing goods, the company may have to buy new production equipment or modify existing machinery. Someone has to develop work instructions for employees and train them to make the product. When it's a matter of a new service process, technical development includes decisions such as which activities will occur within sight of customers versus in the "backroom" and whether the company can automate parts of the service to make delivery more efficient.

Technical development sometimes requires the company to apply for a **patent**. Because patents legally prevent competitors from producing or selling the invention, this legal mechanism may reduce or eliminate competition in a market for many years so that a firm gains some time to recoup its investments in technical development.

prototypes
Test versions of a proposed product.

patent
A legal mechanism to prevent competitors from producing or selling an invention, aimed at reducing or eliminating competition in a market for a period of time.

Phase 6: Test Marketing

The next phase of new product development is **test marketing**. This usually means the firm tries out the complete marketing plan—the distribution, advertising, and sales promotion—in a small slice of the market that is similar to the larger market it ultimately hopes to enter with full force.

There are both pluses and minuses to test marketing. On the negative side, test marketing is extremely expensive. It can cost over a million dollars to conduct a test market even in a single city. A test market also gives the competition a free look at the new product, its introductory price, and the intended promotional strategy—and an opportunity to get to the market first with a competing product. On the positive side, when they offer a new product in a limited area, marketers can evaluate and improve the marketing program. Sometimes, test marketing uncovers a need to improve the product itself. At other times, test marketing indicates product failure; this advanced warning allows the firm to save millions of dollars by "pulling the plug."

test marketing
Testing the complete marketing plan in a small geographic area that is similar to the larger market the firm hopes to enter.

New flavors need to undergo rigorous technical development so companies can be sure they will satisfy consumers' expectations.

simulated test marketing
Application of special computer software to imitate the introduction of a product into the marketplace allowing the company to see the likely impact of price cuts and new packaging—or even to determine where in the store it should try to place the product.

commercialization
The final step in the product development process in which a new product is launched into the market.

crowdfunding
Online platforms that allow thousands of individuals to each contribute small amounts of money in order to fund a new product from a startup company.

For years, the manufacturer of Listerine wanted to introduce a mint-flavored version of its classic gold formulation to compete more directly with P&G's pleasant-tasting Scope (it originally introduced this alternative under the brand Listermint). Unfortunately, every time they tried to run a test market, P&G found out, and the rival poured substantial extra advertising and coupons for its Scope brand into the test market cities. This counterattack reduced the usefulness of the test market results for Listerine when its market planners tried to decide whether to introduce Listermint nationwide. Because P&G's aggressive response to Listermint's test marketing actually *increased* Scope's market share in the test cities, there was no way to determine how well Listermint would actually do under normal competitive conditions. The company went ahead and introduced Listermint nationally anyway, but the new brand achieved only marginal success, and the company ultimately pulled it from the market. Today, thanks to better product development, the Listerine brand itself is available in mint flavor as well as several other choices and is the top-selling mouthwash.[20]

Because of the potential problems and expense of test marketing, marketers instead may use special computer software to conduct **simulated test marketing** that imitates the introduction of a product into the marketplace. These simulations allow the company to see the likely impact of price cuts and new packaging—or even to determine where in the store it should try to place the product. The process entails gathering basic research data on consumers' perceptions of the product concept, the physical product, the advertising, and other promotional activity. The test market simulation model uses that information to predict the product's success much less expensively (and more discreetly) than a traditional test market. As this technology improves, traditional test markets may become a thing of the past.

Phase 7: Commercialization

The last phase in new product development is **commercialization**. This means the launching of a new product, and it requires full-scale production, distribution, advertising, sales promotion—the works. For this reason, commercialization of a new product cannot happen overnight. A launch requires planning and careful preparation.

Commercialization is very expensive, but the Internet makes it much easier for start-ups to obtain the funding they need to get their new products into the market. Today, we witness the explosive growth of **crowdfunding**, where innovative websites such as Kickstarter.com, Indiegogo.com, and Crowdfunder.com have raised more than $5 billion for entrepreneurs and small companies (not to mention the popular TV show *Shark Tank*, which also provides funding for select contestants). On these sites, individuals can choose to either donate money (often in exchange for a product sample) or invest in the company.[21] Under this model, even small contributions add up when hundreds or thousands of people like an idea and pitch in.

As launch time nears, preparations gain a sense of urgency. First, the social media campaigns are likely to crank up and hopefully insiders will then start to buzz about the new product on Twitter and in the blogosphere. Then sales managers will have to explain special incentive programs to salespeople, who in turn will educate all of their customers in the channel of distribution. Soon the media announce to prospective customers why they should buy and where they can find the new product. And all of this has to be orchestrated with the precision of a symphony, with every player spot on his or her part, or else the introduction into the market can easily disappoint customers when they first try to buy.

The late Apple innovation genius Steve Jobs was never one to squelch precommercialization hype about his new product introductions. It has been estimated that Apple achieved prelaunch publicity worth over $500 million on the original iPhone before it spent a single penny on any actual paid advertising. And the introduction of the original iPad back in 2010 was no exception to the Apple hype-creation machine. Jobs claimed that the iPad would offer an experience superior to that of netbooks. He argued that the 751 million people who at that time already owned iPhones and iPod Touches already knew how to use the iPad since it uses the same operating system and touch-screen interface. Well, as they say, the rest is history. Since 2010, the iPad and its bevy of competitors have had a major impact on how we work and entertain ourselves.[22] The reflection on the iPad introduction provides a perfect segue to the next section on adoption and diffusion of innovation.

5 Adoption and Diffusion of New Products

OBJECTIVE

Explain the process of product adoption and the diffusion of innovations.
(pp. 261–267)

In the previous section, we talked about the steps marketers take to develop new products from generating ideas to launch. Now we'll look at what happens *after* that new product hits the market—how an innovation spreads throughout a population.

A painting is not a work of art until someone views it. A song is not music until someone sings it. In the same way, new products do not satisfy customer wants and needs until the customer actually uses (consumes) them—hence the word *consumer*. **Product adoption** is the process by which a consumer or business customer begins to buy and use a new good, service, or idea.

The term **diffusion** describes how the use of a product spreads throughout a population. One way to understand how this process works is to think about a new product as if it were a computer virus that spreads from a few computers to infect many machines. A brand might just slog around—sometimes for years and years. At first, only a small number of people buy it, but change happens in a hurry when the process reaches the moment of critical mass. This moment of truth is called the **tipping point**.[23] After they spend months or even years to develop a new product, the real challenge for firms is to get consumers to buy and use the product and to do so quickly and in sufficient quantities so they can recover the costs of product development and launch. To accomplish this, marketers must understand the product adoption process.

Next we'll discuss the stages in this process. We'll also see how consumers and businesses differ in their eagerness to adopt new products and how the characteristics of a product affect its adoption (or "infection") rate.

Stages in Consumers' Adoption of a New Product

Whether the innovation is the next breakthrough in smart phones or a better mousetrap, individuals and organizations pass through six stages in the adoption process. 🔀 Figure 8.5 shows the **adoption pyramid**, which reflects how a person goes from being unaware of an innovation through stages from the bottom up of awareness, interest, evaluation, trial, adoption, and confirmation. At every stage in building the pyramid, people drop out of the process, so the proportion of consumers who wind up actually using the innovation on a consistent basis is a mere fraction of those who are exposed to it.

product adoption
The process by which a consumer or business customer begins to buy and use a new good, service, or idea.

diffusion
The process by which the use of a product spreads throughout a population.

tipping point
In the context of product diffusion, the point when a product's sales spike from a slow climb to an unprecedented new level.

adoption pyramid
Reflects how a person goes from being unaware of an innovation through stages from the bottom up of awareness, interest, evaluation, trial, adoption, and confirmation.

Figure 8.5 🔀 *Process* | Adoption Pyramid

Consumers pass through six stages in the adoption of a new product—from being unaware of an innovation to becoming loyal adopters. The right marketing strategies at each stage help ensure a successful adoption.

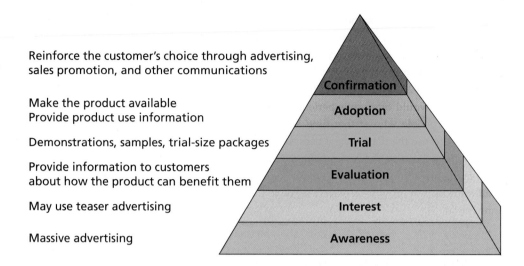

Reinforce the customer's choice through advertising, sales promotion, and other communications — **Confirmation**

Make the product available
Provide product use information — **Adoption**

Demonstrations, samples, trial-size packages — **Trial**

Provide information to customers about how the product can benefit them — **Evaluation**

May use teaser advertising — **Interest**

Massive advertising — **Awareness**

media blitz

A massive advertising campaign that occurs over a relatively short time frame.

Awareness

Awareness that the innovation exists at all is the first step in the adoption process. To educate consumers about a new product, marketers may conduct a massive advertising campaign: a **media blitz**. In spring 2014, Chick-fil-A rolled out a much-anticipated launch of its New Grilled Recipe Chicken (sandwiches and nuggets), hawking the "unmatched backyard grilled taste . . . cooked on a state-of-the-art, proprietary grill developed by Chick-fil-A." Under product development and testing for over seven years, the new recipe hit the quick-serve market like a storm backed by massive initial advertising and social media activity. So far so good—initial reviews are good, and critics give the product strong marks for quality and taste.[24]

At this stage, though, some consumers will say, "So there's a chicken sandwich out there. So what?" Many of these consumers—a good portion of whom are probably not current Chick-fil-A users—of course will fall by the wayside and thus drop out of the adoption process. But this strategy works for new products when at least some consumers see a new product as something they want and need and just can't live without. As their spokes-cows say, "Eat mor chikn!"

Interest

For some of the people who become aware of a new product, a second stage in the adoption process is *interest*. In this stage, a prospective adopter begins to see how a new product might satisfy an existing or newly realized need. Interest also means that consumers look for and are open to information about the innovation. To pique consumer interest in the all-electric Tesla, for example, marketers take the vehicle to the people, right where they shop—the mall. Instead of selling cars though dealerships, Tesla Motors opens boutique-size showrooms at upscale malls (so far 35 across the U.S., Europe, and Asia), where thousands of people walk past on a daily basis.[25] People who initially had "zero interest" in the car can see it, sit in it, talk with a salesperson and, incredibly, actually buy the car right then and there if they want.[26] Talkabout going from 0 to 60 in record time!

However, this approach doesn't work with all products, so marketers often design teaser advertisements that give prospective customers just enough information about the new product to make them curious and to stimulate their interest. Despite marketers' best efforts, however, some more consumers drop out of the process at this point.

Evaluation

In the *evaluation* stage, we weigh the costs and benefits of the new product. On the one hand, for complex, risky, or expensive products, people think about the innovation a great deal before they will try it. For example, a firm will carefully evaluate spending hundreds of thousands of dollars on manufacturing robotics prior to purchase. Marketers for such products help prospective customers see how such products can benefit them.

But as we've seen in the case of impulse products, sometimes little evaluation may occur before someone decides to buy a good or service. A person may do very little thinking before he or she makes an **impulse purchase**, like the virtual *Tamagotchi* (Japanese for "cute little egg") pets. For these goods, marketers design the product to be eye-catching and appealing to get consumers to notice the product quickly. Tamagotchis certainly did grab the attention of consumers, who bought over 79 million of them since the first generation came out.[27] And now Toymaker Bandai Co. is coming out with a whole new generation of Tamagotchis—Tamagotchi Friends, which feature a new lineup of characters—and, they look like Hello Kitty but with bigger eyes and mouths! These new Tamagotchis can even send text messages and earn in-game rewards, such as virtual meals and jewelry, so that you can feed your Tamagotchis and dress them up.[28]

Some potential adopters will evaluate an innovation positively enough to move on to the next stage. Those who do not think the new product will provide adequate benefits drop out at this point.

impulse purchase
A purchase made without any planning or search effort.

Trial

Trial is the stage in the adoption process when potential buyers will actually experience or use the product for the first time. Often marketers stimulate trial when they provide opportunities for consumers to sample the product. Such is the case with test-driving groundbreaking electric vehicles (EVs) like the Teslas we just mentioned. We all know they're good for the environment, but you're probably not likely to buy one until you know how well they really perform. And to find out, you have to test-drive them. In northern Colorado, Drive Electric Northern Colorado (DENC) makes this possible. DENC has teamed up with marketers of EVs like General Motors, Nissan, BMW, Ford, Mitsubishi, and Tesla to host ride-and-drive events. One survey shows that after a test-drive, more than 50 percent of consumers are willing to consider purchasing an EV.[29] Even if the trial is satisfactory, however, some prospective buyers still won't actually adopt the new product because it costs too much (like the Tesla, which starts at around $70,000).

Adoption

In the *adoption* stage, a prospect actually buys the product (hooray, a sale!). Does this mean that all individuals or organizations that first choose an innovation are permanent customers? No, and that's a mistake many firms make. Marketers need to provide follow-up contacts and communications with adopters to ensure they are satisfied and remain loyal to the new product over time.

Confirmation

After adopting an innovation, a customer weighs expected versus actual benefits and costs. Favorable experiences make it more likely that the customer will become a loyal adopter as his or her initially positive opinions result in *confirmation*. Of course, nothing lasts forever—even a loyal customer may decide that a new product no longer meets his or her expectations and reject it. Hence, marketers understand that reselling the customer in the confirmation stage is often quite important. They provide advertisements, sales presentations, and other communications to reinforce a customer's choice.

Adopter Categories

As we saw earlier, *diffusion* describes how the use of a product spreads throughout a population. Of course, marketers prefer their entire target market to immediately adopt a new

Figure 8.6 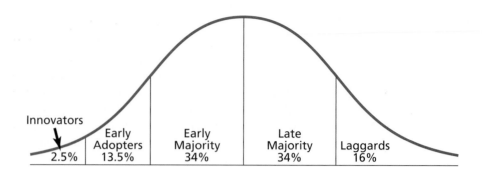 *Snapshot* | Categories of Adopters

Because consumers differ in how willing they are to buy and try a new product, it often takes months or years for most of the population to adopt an innovation.

product, but this is not the case. Both consumers and business customers differ in how eager or willing individuals are to try something new, lengthening the diffusion process by months or even years. Based on adopters' roles in the diffusion process, experts classify them into five categories, as shown in 📷 Figure 8.6: innovators, early adopters, early majority, late majority, and laggards.[30]

Some people like to try new products. Others are so reluctant that you'd think they're afraid of anything new (know anyone like that?). To understand how the adopter categories differ, we'll focus below on a threaded example of the adoption of one specific technology from the past that has had a big impact on all of us today—Wi-Fi (wireless fidelity). What would we do without it?

Innovators

innovators
The first segment (roughly 2.5 percent) of a population to adopt a new product.

Innovators make up roughly the first 2.5 percent of adopters. This segment is extremely adventurous and willing to take risks with new products. Innovators are typically well educated, younger, better off financially than others in the population, and worldly. Innovators who were into new technology knew all about Wi-Fi well before other people had even heard of it. Because innovators pride themselves on trying new products, they purchased laptops with Wi-Fi cards way back in ancient history (1999) when Apple first introduced them in its Mac laptops.

Early Adopters

early adopters
Those who adopt an innovation early in the diffusion process but after the innovators.

Early adopters, approximately 13.5 percent of adopters, buy product innovations early in the diffusion process but not as early as innovators. Unlike innovators, early adopters are very concerned about social acceptance, so they tend to gravitate toward products they believe will make others think they are cutting-edge or fashionable. Typically, they are heavy media users and often are heavy users of the product category. Others in the population often look to early adopters for their opinions on various topics, making early adopters critical to a new product's success. For this reason, marketers often heavily target them in their advertising and other communications efforts. Remember that the innovators pretty much already have the new product in hand before most early adopters purchase.

Columnists who write about personal technology for most popular magazines and tech websites were testing Wi-Fi in mid-2000. They experienced some problems (like PCs crashing when they set up a wireless network at home), but still they touted the benefits of wireless connectivity. Road warriors adopted the technology as Wi-Fi access spread into airports, hotels, city parks, and other public spaces. Intel, maker of the Centrino mobile platform, launched a major campaign with field-leading Condé Nast's *Traveler* magazine and offered a location guide to T-Mobile hot spots nationwide.

Early Majority

The **early majority**, roughly 34 percent of adopters, avoid being either first or last to try an innovation. They are typically middle-class consumers and are deliberate and cautious. Early majority consumers have slightly above-average education and income levels. When the early majority adopts a product, we no longer consider it new or different—that is, when it gets into their hands, it is, in essence, "established." By 2002, Wi-Fi access was available in over 500 Starbucks cafés, and monthly subscription prices were dropping rapidly (from $30 to $9.95 per month).

early majority
Those whose adoption of a new product signals a general acceptance of the innovation.

Late Majority

Late majority adopters, about 34 percent of the population, are older, are even more conservative, and typically have lower-than-average levels of education and income. The late majority adopters avoid trying a new product until it is no longer risky. By that time, the product has become an economic necessity for them, or there is pressure from peer groups to adopt. By 2004, Wi-Fi capability was being bundled into almost all laptops, and you could connect in mainstream venues like McDonald's restaurants and sports stadiums. Cities across the country began considering blanket Wi-Fi coverage throughout the entire town through WiMax (Worldwide Interoperability for Microwave Access) technology, a wireless communication standard.

late majority
The adopters who are willing to try new products when there is little or no risk associated with the purchase, when the purchase becomes an economic necessity, or when there is social pressure to purchase.

Laggards

Laggards, about 16 percent of adopters, are the last in a population to adopt a new product. Laggards are typically lower in income level and education than other adopter categories and are bound by tradition. By the time laggards adopt a product, it may already be superseded by other innovations. By 2006, it would have seemed strange if Wi-Fi or a similar capability was not part of the standard package in even the lowest-priced laptop computer, and people began to become annoyed if Wi-Fi access wasn't available just about everywhere they might go.[31]

laggards
The last consumers to adopt an innovation.

Understanding these adopter categories allows marketers to develop strategies that will speed the diffusion or widespread use of their products. For example, early in the diffusion process, marketers may put greater emphasis on gaining buzz through targeted social media and in advertising in special-interest magazines and websites to attract innovators and early adopters. Later, they may lower the product's price or come out with lower-priced models with fewer "bells and whistles" to attract the late majority. We will talk more about more strategies for new and existing products in the next chapter.

Product Factors That Affect the Rate of Adoption

Not all products are successful, to say the least. Let's see if you've ever heard of these classic boo-boos in new product introduction:

- *Clairol Look of Buttermilk shampoo:* Consumers pondered what exactly *was* the "Look of Buttermilk" and why they would want it.

- *Betamax video player:* Sony refused to allow anyone else to make the players, and the rest of the industry went to VHS format.

- *Snif-T-Panties:* Yes, women's underwear that smelled like bananas, popcorn, whiskey, or pizza. What were they thinking![32]

- *Heinz multicolored ketchup:* What's better than red ketchup? Blue, green, or purple, of course! Consumers, however, didn't equate the look with the flavor.

- *Wow! Chips:* Frito-Lay thought fat-free chips would be a smash hit among the health conscious. Too bad the main ingredient, Olestra, caused stomach cramping and other abdominal issues.[33]

The reason for most product failures is really pretty simple—consumers did not perceive that the products satisfied a need better than competitive products already on the market. If you *could* predict which new products will succeed and which will fail, you'd quickly be in high demand as a marketing guru by companies worldwide. That's because companies make large investments in new products, but failures are all too frequent. Experts suggest that between one-third and one-half of all new products fail. As you might expect, a lot of people try to develop research techniques that enable them to predict whether a new product will be hot or not.

Researchers identify five characteristics of innovations that affect the rate of adoption: relative advantage, compatibility, complexity, trialability, and observability.[34] The degree to which a new product has each of these characteristics affects the speed of diffusion. It may take years for a market to widely adopt a new product. Let's take a closer look at the humble microwave oven—a product that was highly innovative in its early days but now is generally a low-priced staple of every kitchen (and every college apartment and dorm)—as an example to better understand why each of these five factors is important:

- **Relative advantage** describes the degree to which a consumer perceives that a new product provides superior benefits. In the case of the microwave oven, consumers in the 1960s did not believe that the product provided important benefits that would improve their lives. But by the late 1970s, that perception had changed because more women had entered the workforce. In the 1960s, a woman had all day to prepare the evening meal, so she didn't need the microwave (yes, at that time there were very few males in the "househusband" role—that's really changed today!). In the 1970s, however, when many women left home for work at 8:00 A.M. and returned home at 6:00 P.M., an appliance that would "magically" defrost a frozen chicken and cook it in 30 minutes provided a genuine advantage.

- **Compatibility** is the extent to which a new product is consistent with existing cultural values, customs, and practices. Did consumers see the microwave oven as being compatible with existing ways of doing things? Hardly. Cooking on paper plates? If you put a paper plate in a conventional oven, you'll likely get a visit from the fire department. By anticipating compatibility issues early in the new-product-development stage, marketing strategies can address such problems in planning communications and consumer education programs, or there may be opportunities to alter product designs to overcome some consumer objections.

- **Complexity** is the degree to which consumers find a new product or its use difficult to understand. Many microwave users today haven't a clue about how a microwave oven cooks food. When appliance manufacturers introduced the first microwaves, they explained that this new technology causes molecules to move and rub together, which creates friction that produces heat. Voilà! Cooked pot roast. But that explanation was too complex and confusing for the homemaker of the Beaver Cleaver days back in the 1960s.

- **Trialability** is the ease of sampling a new product and its benefits. Marketers took a very important step in the 1970s to speed up adoption of the microwave oven—product trial. Just about every store that sold microwaves invited shoppers to visit the store and sample an entire meal a microwave cooked. Finally, consumers began to understand what the product even was and what it could do!

relative advantage
The degree to which a consumer perceives that a new product provides superior benefits.

compatibility
The extent to which a new product is consistent with existing cultural values, customs, and practices.

complexity
The degree to which consumers find a new product or its use difficult to understand.

trialability
The ease of sampling a new product and its benefits.

APPLYING ▼ Relative Advantage

David understands the necessity that new products provide an important relative advantage for customers. In 1996, founder Kevin Plank developed the Under Armour compression shirt that provided a significant relative advantage over the 100 percent cotton T-shirt. Since then, Under Armour has grown to a $2 billion-plus empire.

- **Observability** refers to how visible a new product and its benefits are to others who might adopt it. The ideal innovation is easy to see. For example, for a generation of kids, scooters like the Razor became the hippest way to get around as soon as one preteen saw her friends flying by. That same generation observed its friends trading Pokémon cards and wanted to join in (were you part of this craze when you were younger?). In the case of the microwave, it wasn't quite so readily observable for its potential adopters—only close friends and acquaintances who visited someone's home would likely see an early adopter using it. But the fruits of the microwave's labors—tasty food dishes—created lots of buzz at office watercoolers and social events, and its use spread quickly. Too bad they didn't have social media back then— if they had, it's a sure bet that the rate of adoption of microwaves would have been a whole lot faster.

observability
How visible a new product and its benefits are to others who might adopt it.

Here's my choice...

Real **People**, Real **Choices**

1 Option 2 Option ③ Option

Why do you think Neal chose option 3?

How It Worked Out at Under Armour

We took a step back, evaluated, and then chose option 3. When the negative sales reads became more consistent week over week, we rewrote the Baselayer business plan with a new go-to-market date. Setting the go-live date gave us a deadline to work from so that we could ensure that we met the key milestones along the way. We titled our new business plan "The House of Baselayer." It entailed a full-year global product and marketing approach that outlined new textile/fabric decisions, wear-test schedules, design philosophy, pricing hierarchy, event and athlete integration, and, finally, a new section we called "The X Factor." The X factor represented some innovations we felt would give us a competitive edge above and beyond just making new styles. An example of this approach was bringing novelty, such as printed/pattern fabrics and bright neon colors, into the Baselayer category, which had historically been a team/core color–dominated business. Another critical X factor idea that we decided to pursue involved creating a subcategory within Baselayer called "Alter Ego," which was our initiative to create a graphic Baselayer product line. This was a chance for us to be first to market with something no one had seen before, so we worked closely with the marketing team on a launch strategy. The end result was a product and marketing partnership with DC Comics and Marvel Entertainment that enabled us to offer versions of our new Baselayer products emblazoned with licensed superhero characters. This was a

The House of Baselayer goes live in stores.

perfect match for Under Armour because it enables athletes to feel "super" when they don their Baselayer apparel.

How Under Armour Measures Success

There were two phases we focused on to gauge whether our House of Baselayer plan was successful. The first phase was to assess how our retail accounts purchased our new product line. Because we had lost some market share over the previous year, we wanted to see if our orders after we launched the House of Baselayer initiative would show growth over a prior year when our business was booming and retail accounts were investing in us as business drivers or if they would they be slightly larger than if we did nothing at all because buyers were spending their dollars on competing brands, including Nike.

The second metric we used was our market share data captured by new product development, which is made up of point-of-sale information and consumer surveys. This measure allowed us to see monthly and quarterly views of how we were selling compared to our performance in the prior year and also how we were performing versus Nike.

The results were overwhelmingly positive on both metrics. Sales grew in line with our projections, and we took back significant market share. The program also impacted how we looked at the multiyear product plan going forward. It has helped us to establish more overarching principles on product life cycle, pricing barriers, and go-to-market activation strategies. We've protected our house, and now we can continue to build it.

Refer back to **page 244** for Neal's story ➡

MyMarketingLab™

Go to **mymktlab.com** to complete the problems marked with this icon ⭐ as well as additional Marketing Metrics questions only available in MyMarketingLab.

Objective Summary ➡ Key Terms ➡ Apply

CHAPTER 8
Study Map

1. Objective Summary (pp. 246–249)

Explain how value is derived through different product layers.

Products can be physical goods, services, ideas, people, or places. A good is a *tangible* product, something that we can see, touch, smell, hear, taste, or possess. In contrast, *intangible* products—services, ideas, people, and places— are products that we can't always see, touch, taste, smell, or possess. Marketers think of the product as more than just a thing that comes in a package. They view it as a bundle of attributes that includes the packaging, brand name, benefits, and supporting features in addition to a physical good. The key issue is the marketer's role in creating the value proposition in order to develop and market products appropriately.

The core product is the basic product category benefits and customized benefit(s) the product provides. The actual product is the physical good or delivered service, including the packaging and brand name. The augmented product includes both the actual product and any supplementary services, such as warranty, credit, delivery, installation, and so on.

Key Terms

attributes, p. 247

good, p. 247

core product, p. 248

actual product, p. 248

augmented product, p. 249

2. Objective Summary (pp. 249–252)

Describe how marketers classify products.

Marketers generally classify goods and services as either consumer or B2B products. They further classify consumer products according to how long they last and by how they are purchased. Durable goods provide benefits for months or years, whereas nondurable goods are used up quickly or are useful for only a short time. Consumers purchase convenience products frequently with little effort. Customers carefully gather information and compare different brands on their attributes and prices before buying shopping products. Specialty products have unique characteristics that are important to the buyer. Customers have little interest in unsought products until a need arises. Business products are for commercial uses by organizations. Marketers classify business products according to how they are used, for example, equipment: maintenance, repair, and operating (MRO) products; raw materials; processed materials; specialized services; and component parts.

Key Terms

durable goods, p. 249

nondurable goods, p. 249

convenience product, p. 250

staple products, p. 251

consumer packaged good (CPG) or fast-moving consumer good (FMCG), p. 251

impulse products, p. 251

emergency products, p. 251

shopping products, p. 251

specialty products, p. 251

unsought products, p. 252

equipment, p. 252

maintenance, repair, and operating (MRO) products, p. 252

raw materials, p. 252

processed materials, p. 252

specialized services, p. 252

component parts, p. 252

3. Objective Summary (pp. 253–255)

Understand the importance and types of product innovations.

Innovations are anything consumers perceive to be new. Understanding new products is important to companies because of the fast pace of technological advancement, the high cost to companies of developing new products, and the contributions to society that new products can make. Marketers classify innovations by their degree of newness. A continuous innovation is a modification of an existing product, a dynamically continuous innovation provides a greater change in a product, and a discontinuous innovation is a new product that creates major changes in people's lives.

Key Terms

innovation, p. 253

creativity, p. 253

continuous innovation, p. 254

knockoff, p. 254

dynamically continuous innovation, p. 254

discontinuous innovation, p. 255

convergence, p. 255

4. Objective Summary (pp. 255–261)

Show how firms develop new products.

In new product development, marketers generate product ideas from which product concepts are first developed and then screened. Next, they develop a marketing strategy and conduct a business analysis to estimate the profitability of the new product. Technical development includes planning how the product will be manufactured and may mean obtaining a patent. Next, an actual or a simulated test market may be conducted to assess the effectiveness of the new product in the market. Finally, in the commercialization phase the product is launched, and the entire marketing plan is implemented.

Key Terms

research and development (R&D), p. 256

new product development (NPD), p. 256

idea generation (ideation), p. 256

value co-creation, p. 256

product concept development and screening, p. 257

business analysis, p. 257

technical development, p. 258

prototypes, p. 259

patent, p. 259

test marketing, p. 259

simulated test marketing, p. 260

commercialization, p. 260

crowdfunding, p. 260

5. Objective Summary (pp. 261–267)

Explain the process of product adoption and the diffusion of innovations.

Product adoption is the process by which an individual begins to buy and use a new product, whereas the diffusion of innovations is how a new product spreads throughout a population. The stages in the adoption process are awareness, interest, trial, adoption, and confirmation. To better understand the diffusion process, marketers classify consumers—according to their readiness to adopt new products—as innovators, early adopters, early majority, late majority, and laggards.

Five product characteristics that have an important effect on how quickly (or if) a new product will be adopted by consumers are relative advantage, compatibility, product complexity, trialability, and observability. Similar to individual consumers, organizations differ in their readiness to adopt new products based on characteristics of the organization, its management, and characteristics of the innovation.

Key Terms

product adoption, p. 261

diffusion, p. 261

tipping point, p. 261

adoption pyramid, p. 261

media blitz, p. 262

impulse purchase, p. 263

innovators, p. 264

early adopters, p. 264

early majority, p. 265

late majority, p. 265

laggards, p. 265

relative advantage, p. 266

compatibility, p. 266

complexity, p. 266

trialability, p. 266

observability, p. 267

Chapter **Questions** and **Activities**

Concepts: Test Your Knowledge

8-1. "Marketing is about supplying benefits, not attributes." Discuss whether these benefits are of paramount importance.

8-2. Why are most products and services augmented in some way? Give examples of augmentation.

8-3. What are the categories of products or services that are bought by businesses? What are MROs?

8-4. What are emergency products, and why are they purchased? Give some consumer examples.

8-5. What are the challenges to marketers in creating impulse products?

8-6. What are the three different ways in which marketers classify innovations? What are the categories based upon?

8-7. What is a knockoff in product terms? What makes a knockoff legal or illegal?

8-8. List and explain the steps marketers undergo to develop new products.

8-9. What is a test market? What are some pros and cons of test markets?

8-10. Explain the stages a consumer goes through in the adoption of a new product.

8-11. List and explain the categories of adopters.

8-12. What product factors affect the rate of adoption of innovations?

Activities: Apply What You've Learned

⭐ **8-13.** *Creative Homework/Short Project* Assume that you are employed in the marketing department of a firm that is producing a lawnmower. In developing this product,

you realize that it is important to provide a core product, an actual product, and an augmented product that meets the needs of customers. Develop an outline of how your firm might provide these three product layers in the lawnmower.

8-14. *In Class, 10–25 Minutes for Teams* Firms go to great lengths to develop new product ideas. Sometimes new ideas come from brainstorming, in which groups of individuals get together and try to think of as many different, novel, creative, and, it is hoped, profitable ideas for a new product as possible. With a group of other students, participate in brainstorming for new product ideas for one of the following (or some other product of your choice):

a. An exercise machine with some desirable new features

b. A combination shampoo and body wash

c. A new type of university

Then, with your class, screen one or more of the ideas for possible further product development.

8-15. *In Class, 10–25 Minutes for Teams* As the board of directors of a new company, come up with a new product or service idea. Think through all of the product development stages for the product or service. At what point would your chosen product or service begin to struggle and perhaps not make it through the phase? Identify how you might adapt or amend the product or service and how it might differ at the end of the process compared to your initial thoughts.

⭐ **8-16.** *Creative Homework/Short Project* As a member of a new product team with your company, you are working to develop an electric car jack that would make changing car tires easier. You are considering conducting a test market for this new product. Outline the pros and cons for test marketing this product. What are your recommendations?

8-17. *For Further Research (Individual)* Every year, niche or small-market products and services break into the mainstream and, temporarily, may become a significant and profitable trend if they are marketed in the right way. Using the Internet, find a good example and present your findings to the rest of the class.

Apply Marketing Metrics

In the chapter, we define creativity and discuss how it relates to innovation. Innovation can be measured in terms of number of successful new products as well as a variety of secondary measures related to those products (e.g., new product launches per year, per employee, and success rate versus failure rate—cast on the basis of how the firm defines product success and failure). Innovation is fueled by R&D expenditures, as the chapter notes.

But what about measuring creativity itself? Some experts have argued that an overfocus on metrics can kill creativity.[35] They might argue that the phrase "creativity metric" is an oxymoron. There's always been a right-brain/left-brain argument that marketing, to be optimally successful, has to nurture both the creative and the analytical. Has the obsession with marketing metrics over the past decade squelched essential creativity emanating from the right brain?

8-18. What is your viewpoint about measuring creativity? Do you believe it is more constructive or damaging to organizational innovation? Support your opinions.

8-19. Point out a few well-known organizations that you believe are quite creative. How do you know that they are creative—that is, what specific evidence can you cite that indicates that a high level of creativity is practiced?

Choices: What Do You Think?

8-20. *Critical Thinking* Technology is moving at an ever-increasing speed, and this means that new products enter and leave the market faster than ever. What are some products you think technology might be able to develop in the future that you would like? Do you think these products could add to a company's profits?

8-21. *Critical Thinking* In this chapter, we talked about the core product, the actual product, and the augmented product. Does this mean that marketers are simply trying to make products that are really the same seem different? When marketers understand these three layers of the product and develop products with this concept in mind, what are the benefits to consumers? What are the hazards of this type of thinking?

⭐ **8-22.** *Critical Thinking* Discontinuous innovations are totally new products—something seldom seen in the marketplace. What are some examples of discontinuous innovations introduced in the past 50 years? Why are there so few discontinuous innovations? What products have companies recently introduced that you believe will end up being regarded as discontinuous innovations?

⭐ **8-23.** *Critical Thinking* "Mobile blinders" is the phrase used to describe individuals who, when standing in checkout lanes, spend their time waiting by sending text messages or checking Facebook on their smart phones. And in doing so, they tune out the checkout displays designed to get them to buy impulse items like magazines or candy bars. As a marketer, what would you do to combat this problem and increase your sales of impulse products?

8-24. *Ethics* For several decades, consumer products—everything from vaccines to cosmetics—have been tested on animals. Do you think product testing on animals should be legal or illegal? Does your position change depending on what kind of animal the product is tested on (e.g., a mouse versus dog)? What are some instances of when it would be acceptable or unacceptable to test products on animals (e.g., medical necessity versus enhancing one's looks)?

8-25. *Critical Thinking* Consider the differences in marketing to consumer markets versus business markets. Which aspects of the processes of product adoption and diffusion apply to both markets? Which aspects are unique to one or the other? Provide evidence of your findings.

8-26. *Ethics* In this chapter, we explained that knockoffs are slightly modified copies of original product designs. Should knockoffs be illegal? Who is hurt by knockoffs? Is the marketing of knockoffs good or bad for consumers in the short run? In the long run?

8-27. *Critical Thinking* It is not necessarily true that all new products benefit consumers or society. What are some new products that have made our lives better? What are some new products that have actually been harmful to consumers or to society? Should there be a way to monitor or "police" new products that are introduced to the marketplace?

8-28. *Critical Thinking* Patent trolling is the practice of acquiring patents with the sole purpose of making money off of them either by suing those who infringe on the patent or by licensing the patent. What do you think of the practice of patent trolling? What effect does patent trolling have on product innovation?

Miniproject: Learn by Doing

What product characteristics do consumers think are important in a new product? What types of service components do they demand? Most important, how do marketers know how to develop successful new products? This miniproject is designed to let you make some of these decisions as you walk through several steps of the new product development process.

8-29. Develop a presentation that summarizes your efforts for each of the following phases of new product development:

   a. Phase 1: Idea generation: Create (in your mind) a new product item that might be of interest to college students such as yourself. Develop a written description and possibly a drawing of this new product. Describe the benefits of the product.

b. Phase 2: Product concept development and screening: Describe what features the product should have and the benefits those features will provide for consumers. Estimate both the technical success and the commercial success of the product.

c. Phase 3: Marketing strategy development: Develop a simple marketing plan that identifies the target market and how you can position the product to meet that market's needs.

Assume now that you have undergone a thorough business analysis (phase 4) and have built a prototype of the product (phase 5).

d. Phase 6: Test marketing: Describe your product to five other college students, as if you had an actual prototype of the product. What is their overall opinion of the new product? Would they try the product? How could you influence them to buy the product?

e. Phase 7: Commercialization: Based on the information you have collected, determine whether you are ready to launch the product. If not, describe the reasons why.

Marketing in **Action** Case   Real Choices at Chobani

What's for dessert? If Chobani gets its way, the after-dinner choice will include yogurt. This company is currently the top seller of Greek yogurt in the U.S., but until recently it had not deviated much from its focus on a fruit-infused, single-serving creation.

Now Chobani is working feverishly to expand its product line; the company wants its products to be on consumers' minds other than at breakfast or snack time. According to Peter McGuinness, Chobani's chief marketing and brand officer, "We want to inspire consumers to eat yogurt throughout the day, and increase per capita consumption."

The company is creating products for such varied food categories as desserts, dips, and cooking ingredients:

- To compete with ice cream, the new Chobani Indulgent line is a pudding-like yogurt that comes in flavors like Dulce de Leche, Raspberry Dark Chocolate Chunk, Mint Dark Chocolate Chunk, and Banana Dark Chocolate Chunk. This dessert offering combines yogurt with ingredients like real cream, dark chocolate, and ripe fruits.
- Chobani Kitchen is a whole-milk yogurt for use in recipes, like baked goods. It can also be used on a baked potato, in chili, or in fajitas.
- For customers who like oatmeal and protein bars, Chobani Greek Yogurt Oats is its product blended with mixed fruit and whole-grain steel-cut oats. Flavors include Banana Maple, Apple Cinnamon, Blueberry, and Cranberry.
- Chobani Kids is a mix of low-fat, hormone-free Greek yogurt and fruit, in "fun, finger-friendly" packaging. Nutritionally, it is high in protein and low in sugar. Flavors include Grape, Watermelon, and Vanilla Chocolate Dust.

- In the near future, Chobani plans to introduce a line of Chobani-branded savory dips targeted toward customers who desire hummus, guacamole, and Greek tzatziki.

But Chobani has company. In the U.S. today, less yogurt is consumed annually per capita than in Canada, Germany, and France. Rivals also see opportunities to expand the yogurt market. Dannon has a partnership with the Starbucks Coffee Company to offer a selection of "Evolution Fresh, Inspired by Dannon"–branded, ready-to-eat Parfait Greek yogurt products. Yoplait recently reformulated its Greek yogurt and introduced Yoplait Greek 100, a new lower-calorie product. It has also launched an advertising campaign targeted against Chobani, and the rival added comparative "taste tests" to its promotional efforts.

Now that Chobani has taken the steps to develop its new products, it has to find ways to convince customers that its new range of yogurt products belongs in their refrigerators.

You Make the Call

8-30. What is the decision facing Chobani?

8-31. What factors are important in understanding this decision situation?

8-32. What are the alternatives?

8-33. What decision(s) do you recommend?

8-34. What are some ways to implement your recommendation?

Sources: Based on Annie Gasparro, "Chobani Expands into New Yogurt Products," April 18, 2014, **http://online.wsj.com/news/article_email/ SB10001424052702304626304579509243369295888-IMyQjAxMTA0MDAwMzEwNDMyWj** (accessed May 4, 2014); Venessa Wong, "Chobani Greek Yogurt for Lunch, Dinner, and Dessert?," **www.businessweek.com/articles/2014-04-22/chobani-greek-yogurt-for-lunch-dinner-and-dessert** (accessed May 4, 2014); and Chobani, LLC, "Chobani History," **www.chobani.com/history** (accessed May 4, 2014).

MyMarketingLab™

Go to **mymktlab.com** for Auto-graded writing questions as well as the following Assisted-graded writing questions:

8-35. *Creative Homework/Short Project.* Assume that you are the director of marketing for the company that has developed a smart phone to outdo the iPhone. How would you go about convincing the late majority to go ahead and adopt it—especially since they still haven't quite caught onto the iPhone yet?

8-36. *Creative Homework/Short Project.* You work for a large retailer and have been asked by a professor at the local university to give a presentation on how your business classifies products. Prepare a slide show that defines the various product categories, including any subcategories, and give at least three examples of each. Include photos of the products where possible.

Product II: Product Strategy, Branding, and Product Management

David Clark
▼ A Decision Maker at General Mills

David Clark is vice president of Big G Adult Cereals at General Mills. Since July 2007, he has been responsible for leading the development and execution of growth strategies for several iconic brands, including Wheaties, Total, Chex, and Fiber One. In November 2008, he was recognized as being among the Marketing Top 50 by *Advertising Age*.

Prior to his responsibilities in the Big G division, David was the marketing director for General Mills Foodservice from November 2003 to July 2007. In this assignment, he led the Brand Marketing, Channel Marketing, and Promotions Marketing teams in driving growth across 13 product platforms within the Foodservice Distributor channel.

From June 1997 to November 2003, David held various marketing roles, including marketing manager for Progresso Soup, marketing manager for Green Giant Frozen Vegetables, and associate marketing manager for Old El Paso Mexican Food.

Although David has spent the majority of his career in marketing and general management leadership positions, his early career experience in marketing research, category management, and sales were instrumental in building a foundational understanding of consumer behavior and the consumer packaged-goods industry.

David holds a bachelor's degree from the University of Tennessee, Knoxville, and an MBA from the University of Minnesota Carlson School. He currently resides in Minneapolis, Minnesota, with his wife, Molly, and three children.

David's Info

What I do when I'm not working?
Tennis, running, and all things digital.

Career high?
Leading the Wheaties brand and working with five top athletes (Peyton Manning, Albert Pujols, Kevin Garnett, Bryan Clay, and Hunter Kemper) to co-create a new Breakfast of Champions, Wheaties Fuel.

A job-related mistake I wish I hadn't made?
Thinking that it's easier to gain new consumers than keep current ones—a lesson no one wants to learn twice.

My hero?
My mom, who taught me that honest, hard work and treating others with respect are the real secrets to success.

My motto to live by?
See what everyone sees; think what no one has thought.

What drives me?
The possibilities that can come from a great idea.

Here's my problem...

Fiber One cereal was launched in 1985. One of the first high-fiber cereals on the market, the product delivered 57 percent of one's daily value of fiber per bowl. It gained a small but intensely loyal following of older consumers who often learned about the brand from a doctor or pharmacist.

Fiber One sat quietly on the shelf as an average performer until 2002. Then the Atkins Diet generated a lot of interest in fiber as a tool to offset carbohydrate levels in foods. Fiber One sales started to grow. In the years following, increased coverage in the media and medical community about the benefits of fiber increased consumer awareness and interest in the nutrient.

Due to the boom in consumer interest in fiber, Fiber One was uniquely positioned for growth from increased marketing investment that would build awareness about the brand. General Mills launched new brand extensions, including Fiber One Honey Clusters Cereal and Fiber One Oats and Chocolate Snack Bars. The brand took on a fresh, more contemporary look with a packaging redesign. Now, the big question was how the core Fiber One brand should be positioned and grow as it matured through its life cycle.

users tend to be older consumers (age 55 and over) who have the greatest desire to add fiber to their diets. A superiority message would appeal to their greatest need. However, products in the fiber supplement category (Benefiber and Metamucil) already advertised their superiority over other high-fiber foods. And younger consumers who were just beginning to seek more fiber in their diets were less willing to trade off taste; they often described the taste of fiber products as "cardboard." They thought high-fiber products were "old-people food," and this was a turnoff.

2 **Option** **Own the position of "Great Tasting High Fiber."** Consumers pointed to the poor taste of fiber as the number one barrier to getting more fiber in their diets. They rated the taste of recent new product launches, such as Fiber One Honey Clusters Cereal and Oats and Chocolate Snack Bars, as surprisingly good given their high fiber content. On the other hand, fiber delivers many important health benefits to consumers (weight management, heart health, and digestive health). Failure to position against the health benefits of fiber could be an opportunity lost to competition. In addition, consumers might have such a negative association with fiber products that they might not believe a message that stressed its good taste.

3 **Option** **Own the position of "Digestive Health."** Consumers think about fiber mainly in terms of its digestive benefits. This is particularly appealing to the growing baby boomer demographic. They were already snapping up products in other categories (especially yogurt) because of their digestive health benefits. However, other cereal brands already were talking about digestive health benefits, and this topic tended to polarize shoppers. While older consumers valued digestive efficiency, younger consumers found this a turnoff or even comical.

Now put yourself in David's shoes: Which option would you choose, and why?

Things to remember

General Mills' Fiber One cereal, one of the first high-fiber cereals on the market, enjoyed a small but loyal following of older consumers for over 15 years. Beginning in 2002, Fiber One sales began to grow as the Atkins Diet popularized the benefits of fiber as a tool to offset carbohydrate levels in foods. Later the brand enjoyed continued growth due to increased discussion in the media and the medical community about the benefits of fiber. Consumer interest in fiber led General Mills to launch new Fiber One brand extensions, including Fiber One Honey Clusters Cereal and Fiber One Oats and Chocolate Snack Bars. Still General Mills faced the challenge of positioning and growing the core Fiber One brand in a mature market.

You Choose

Which **Option** would you choose, and **why**?

1. ☐YES ☐NO   2. ☐YES ☐NO   3. ☐YES ☐NO

See what **option** David chose on **page 297** ➡

David considered his **Options** 1·2·3

1 **Option** **Own the position of "Fiber Superiority."** Fiber One is very high in fiber. For example, it takes 3.5 cups of broccoli to get the same fiber as one bowl of Fiber One Original Cereal. Bringing this comparison to life could make a powerful marketing visual on which to build a campaign. The cereal's heaviest

MyMarketingLab™

⭐ **Improve Your Grade!**

Over 10 million students improved their results using the Pearson MyLabs.
Visit **mymktlab.com** for simulations, tutorials, and end-of-chapter problems.

1

OBJECTIVE

Discuss the different product objectives and strategies a firm may choose.
(pp. 276–282)

Product Planning: Use Product Objectives to Decide on a Product Strategy

What makes one product fail and another succeed? It's worth reemphasizing what you learned in Chapter 3: *Firms that plan well succeed.* Product planning plays a big role in the firm's *marketing planning.* And among the famous four Ps of the marketing mix, each P is not created equal—that is, the best pricing, promotion, and physical distribution strategies cannot overcome fundamental problems with the product over the long run! Hence, product planning takes on special significance in marketing.

Strategies outlined within the product specify how the firm expects to develop a value proposition that will meet marketing objectives. Product planning is guided by the continual process of **product management**, which is the systematic and usually team-based approach to coordinating all aspects of a product's strategy development and execution. In some companies, product management is sometimes also called *brand management*, and the terms refer to essentially the same thing. The organization members that coordinate these processes are called *product managers* or *brand managers.* We discuss the role of these individuals in more detail later in the chapter.

As more and more competitors enter the global marketplace and as technology moves forward at an ever-increasing pace, firms create products that grow, mature, and then decline at faster and faster speeds. This acceleration underscores that smart product management strategies are more critical than ever. Marketers just don't have the luxury of trying one thing, finding out it doesn't work, and then trying the next thing—they have to multitask when it comes to product management!

In Chapter 8, we talked about how marketers think about products—both core and augmented—and about how companies develop and introduce new products. In this chapter, we finish the product part of the story as we see how companies manage products, and then we examine the steps in product planning, shown in  Figure 9.1. These steps include developing product objectives and the related strategies required to successfully market products as they evolve from "newbies" to tried-and-true favorites—and in some cases finding new markets for these favorites. Next, we discuss branding and packaging, two of the more important tactical decisions product planners make. Finally, we examine how firms organize for effective product management. Let's start with an overview of how firms develop product-related objectives.

product management
The systematic and usually team-based approach to coordinating all aspects of a product's strategy development and execution.

Getting Product Objectives Right

When marketers develop product strategies, they make decisions about product benefits, features, styling, branding, labeling, and packaging. But what do they want to accomplish? Clearly stated product objectives provide focus and direction. They should support the broader marketing objectives of the business unit in addition to being consistent with the firm's overall mission. For example, the objectives of the firm may focus on return on investment (ROI). Marketing objectives then may concentrate on building market share and/or the unit or dollar sales volume necessary to attain that ROI. Product objectives need to specify how product decisions will contribute to reaching a desired market share or level of sales.

To be effective, product-related objectives must be measurable, clear, and unambiguous—and feasible. Also, they must indicate a specific time frame.

Figure 9.1 🎯 *Process* | Steps to Manage Products

Effective product strategies come from a series of orderly steps.

Develop Product Objectives
- For individual products
- For product lines and mixes

↓

Design Product Strategies

↓

Make Tactical Product Decisions
- Product branding
- Packaging and labeling design

↓

Organize for Product Management

Consider, for example, how Amy's, a popular organic and health-conscious frozen ethnic entrée manufacturer, might state its product objectives:

- "In the upcoming fiscal year, reduce the fat and calorie content of our products by 15 percent to satisfy consumers' health concerns."

- "Introduce three new products this quarter to the product line to take advantage of increased consumer interest in Mexican foods."

- "During the coming fiscal year, improve the chicken entrées to the extent that consumers will rate them better tasting than the competition."

Planners must keep in touch with their customers so that their objectives accurately respond to their needs. In Chapter 2, we introduced you to the idea of *competitive intelligence*, and an up-to-date knowledge of competitive product innovations is important to develop product objectives. Above all, these objectives should consider the *long-term implications* of product decisions. Planners who sacrifice the long-term health of the firm to reach short-term sales or financial goals choose a risky course. Product planners may focus on one or more individual products at a time, or they may look at a group of product offerings as a whole. Next, we briefly examine both of these approaches. We also look at one important product objective: product quality.

Objectives and Strategies for Individual Products

Everybody loves the MINI Cooper. But it wasn't just luck or happenstance that turned this product into a global sensation. Just how do you launch a new car that's only 142 inches long and makes people laugh when they see it? Maker BMW succeeded by deliberately but gently poking fun at the MINI Cooper's small size. The original launch of the MINI Cooper included bolting the MINI onto the top of a Ford Excursion with a sign reading, "What are you doing for fun this weekend?" BMW also mocked up full-size MINIs to look like coin-operated kiddie rides you find outside grocery stores with a sign proclaiming, "Rides $16,850. Quarters only." The advertising generated buzz in the 20- to 34-year-old target market, and today the MINI is no joke.

As a smaller brand, the MINI never had a huge advertising budget—in fact it was the first launch of a new car in modern times that didn't include TV advertising. Instead, the MINI launched with print, outdoor billboards, and online ads. It has an active and ongoing social media presence. The objective wasn't a traditional heavy car launch; rather, BMW envisioned a "discovery process" by which target consumers would find out about the brand on their own and fall in love with it. Ads promoted "motoring" instead of driving, and magazine inserts included MINI-shaped air fresheners and pullout games. *Wired* magazine even ran a cardboard foldout of the MINI suggesting that readers assemble and drive it around their desks making "putt-putt" noises. *Playboy* came up with the idea of a six-page MINI "centerfold" complete with the car's vital statistics and hobbies. By the end of its first year on the market, the MINI was rated the second most memorable new product of the year!

Like the MINI, product strategies often focus on a single new product. (As an interesting sidebar, enough customers have complained about the cramped quarters in the MINI's backseat—it is, after all, a "mini"—that BMW acquiesced and introduced a "larger MINI." Now that's an oxymoron—something like a "jumbo shrimp"!)[1] Strategies for individual products may be quite different, depending on the situation: new products, regional products, mature products, or other differences. For new products, not surprisingly, the objectives relate heavily to producing a very successful introduction.

After a firm experiences success with a product in a local or regional market, it may decide to introduce it nationally. Trader Joe's, for example, opened its doors in Pasadena,

California, in 1967 (and it's still there today). But it wasn't until 1993 that the brand moved outside of California, heading east to Phoenix, Arizona. Today, you can find Trader Joe's throughout most of the country, though you won't yet find it in all 50 states.[2]

For mature products like cheddar Goldfish snack crackers that Campbell's Soup Company manufactures under its Pepperidge Farm label, product objectives may focus on bringing new life to a product while holding on to their traditional brand personality. For Goldfish, "The snack that smiles back," this means introducing a host of spin-offs—peanut butter flavored, giant sized, multicolored, and color changing, to name a few. The Goldfish brand has been around since 1962, but it continues to stay fresh with 25 varieties it sells in more than 40 countries. In fact, people eat over 142 billion Goldfish per year—if strung together, enough to wrap around the earth almost 60 times![3]

Objectives and Strategies for Multiple Products

Although a small firm might get away with a focus on one product, larger firms often sell a set of related products. This means that strategic decisions affect two or more products simultaneously. The firm must think in terms of its entire portfolio of products. As Figure 9.2 shows, product planning means developing *product line* and *product mix* strategies to encompass multiple offerings.

A **product line** is a firm's total product offering to satisfy a group of target customers. For example, for decades, Procter & Gamble (P&G) had a line of cleaning products that included three different dishwashing liquid brands: Dawn stresses grease-cutting power, Ivory emphasizes mildness, and Joy is positioned for people who want shiny dishes. To do an even better job of meeting varying consumer needs, each of the three brands comes in more than one formulation. Think that's overkill in dish soap? Guess again—new Gain dishwashing liquid is P&G's first new hand dish brand in nearly 40 years, and its sales are trending ahead of expectations. With this introduction, the scent of Gain was successfully

product line
A firm's total product offering designed to satisfy a single need or desire of target customers.

Figure 9.2 *Process* | Objectives for Single and Multiple Products

Product objectives provide focus and direction for product strategies. Objectives can focus on a single product or a group of products.

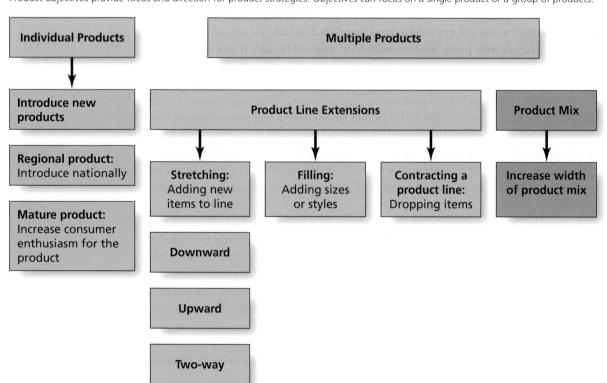

translated from a laundry product to a hand dish product. But more than merely wooing its most loyal fans into the dishwashing category, it has spawned new "Gainiacs," which has in turn strengthened trial across the entire line of Gain products. On track to double its first-year sales, Gain Dish Liquid is already approaching a 5 percent share of the U.S. hand dish market. Now for the first time ever, Gainiacs new and old are enjoying the value and scent experience of Gain at one more familiar place—the kitchen sink.[4] The **product line length** is determined by the number of separate items within the same category, in this case four brands each with multiple **stock-keeping units (SKUs)**. An SKU is a unique identifier for each distinct product. Hence, for Gain Dish Liquid, each SKU represents a unique item within the brand, such as different sizes and scents.

We describe a large number of variations in a product line as a *full line* that targets many customer segments to boost sales potential. A *limited-line strategy*, with fewer product variations, can improve the firm's image if consumers perceive it as a specialist with a clear, specific position in the market. A great example is Rolls-Royce Motor Cars, which BMW also owns (how about that—from MINI Coopers to Rolls—quite a stable of brands!). Rolls-Royce makes expensive, handcrafted cars built to each customer's exact specifications and for decades maintained a unique position in the automobile industry. Every Rolls Phantom that rolls out the factory door is truly a unique work of art.[5]

Organizations may decide to extend their product line by adding more brands or models. For example, Marriott extended its reach and appeal to a new market segment when the company added the Gaylord brand of convention hotels to its product line. Gaylord properties—such as the famous Gaylord Opryland Resort and Convention Center in Nashville—literally define ostentatiousness in hospitality with enormous indoor dining and recreational spaces that can best be described as palatial.

When a firm stretches its product line, it must decide on the best direction to go. If a firm's current product line includes middle- and lower-end items, an *upward line stretch* adds new items—higher-priced entrants that claim better quality or offer more bells and whistles. Kia has been working to stretch its low-priced product line upward with new brand-building activities and a new luxury car. Now branded as "A Different Beat," Kia aims to set itself apart from its competitors by being "vibrant, distinctive and reliable."[6] To achieve that objective, Kia launched its $66,000 luxury K900, positioning it between the BMW 5-Series (at about $50,000) and the BMW 7-Series (at about $75,000).[7] Conversely, a *downward line stretch* augments a line when it adds items at the lower end. Here, the firm must take care not to blur the images of its higher-priced, upper-end offerings. Rolex, for example, may not want to run the risk of cheapening its image with a new watch line to compete with Timex or Swatch. In some cases, a firm may come to the realization that its current target market is too small. In this case, the product strategy may call for a *two-way stretch* that adds products at both the upper and lower ends.

A *filling-out strategy* adds sizes or styles not previously available in a product category. Mars Candy did this when it introduced Reese's Minis as a knockoff of its already crazy-popular full-sized product. In other cases, the best strategy may be to *contract*—meaning reduce the size of a product line, particularly when some of the items are not profitable. For example, P&G spun off its Pringles line of salty snacks when it determined that it could make more money focusing on its growing health and beauty product lines.[8]

We've seen that there are many ways a firm can modify its product line to meet the competition or take advantage of new opportunities. To further explore these product strategy decisions, let's stick with the P&G theme and return to the "glamorous" world of dish detergents. By the way, P&G basically invented the product management system that is widely used in firms around the world, so it's certainly fitting to focus on this giant consumer products company. What does P&G do if the objective is to increase market share? One possibility would be to expand its line of liquid dish detergents—as the company did

product line length
Determined by the number of separate items within the same category.

stock-keeping unit (SKU)
A unique identifier for each distinct product.

with its move to expand Gain's popularity from laundry soap to dishwashing liquid. If the line extension meets a perceived consumer need the company doesn't currently address, this would be a good strategic objective. Gain brought a bevy of laundry loyalists into its new category in dishes, making for a great base of business on which to build.

But whenever a manufacturer extends a product line or a product family, there is risk of **cannibalization**. This occurs when the new item eats up sales of an existing brand as the firm's current customers simply switch to the new product. That may explain why P&G's Gain dishwashing positioning is all about the unique Gain scent. For Gain Flings (basically the Gain equivalent of Tide Pods), the message to consumers is "get 50 percent more of that original Gain scent you love—it's music to your nose!"

cannibalization
The loss of sales of an existing brand when a new item in a product line or product family is introduced.

Product Mix Strategies

product mix
The total set of all products a firm offers for sale.

A firm's **product mix** describes its entire range of products. For example, in addition to a deep line of shaving products, P&G's acquisition of Gillette a few years back gave P&G Oral B toothbrushes, Braun oral care products, and Duracell batteries.

product mix width
The number of different product lines the firm produces.

When they develop a product mix strategy, marketers usually consider the **product mix width**: the number of different product lines the firm produces. If it develops several different product lines, a firm reduces the risk of putting all its eggs in one basket. Normally, firms develop a mix of product lines that have some things in common.

product quality
The overall ability of the product to satisfy customer expectations.

The entry of wine and spirits distributor Constellation Brands into the mainstream supermarket wine space through its acquisition of Robert Mondavi a few years ago is an example of a successful product mix expansion strategy. Americans' consumption of wine has steadily increased over the past decade, and the Mondavi brand gives Constellation a strong presence in the huge and growing supermarket wine channel.[9]

Ripped from the Headlines

Ethical/Sustainable Decisions in the Real World

Would you wear green jeans? No, not jeans that are the color green but jeans that are environmentally friendly "green." Levi-Strauss is betting that you will, and as a way to add relevance to their brand, they are going green with their products.

The company, which created the first blue jeans all the way back in 1873, has developed green jeans as part of its new Waste<Less line.

ETHICS CHECK: ➘
Find out what other students taking this course *would do* and *why* at **mymktlab .com**.

For starters, Levi's uses polyethylene terephthalate (PET) materials to produce its fabrics. That means that 20 percent of each pair of these jeans is made from PET-friendly waste such as brown beer bottles, green soda bottles, clear water bottles, and black food trays. But Levi's doesn't stop there. As part of its denim-finishing process, Levi's has found a way to reduce water consumption by 96 percent for some styles, resulting in a savings of 154 million gallons of water so far.[10]

Levi's is obviously making some great strides toward going green, but how green is green enough? How much of a product do you think must be green in order to label it as such?

Realizing that no product can be 100 percent green, is it ethical for a marketer to promote a product to customers as "green" anyway?

☐YES ☐NO

Quality as a Product Objective: TQM and Beyond

Product objectives often focus on **product quality**, which is the overall ability of the product to satisfy customer expectations. Quality is tied to how customers *think* a product will perform, not necessarily to some technological level of perfection. That is, for all intents and purposes, perception is reality. Product quality objectives coincide with marketing objectives for higher sales and market share and to the firm's objectives for increased profits.

In 1980, just when the economies of Germany and Japan were finally rebuilt from World War II and were threatening American markets with a flood of terrific new products, an NBC documentary on quality titled *If Japan Can Do It, Why Can't We?* fired a first salvo to the American public—and to American CEOs—that American product quality become inferior to other that of other global players.[11] So began the **total quality management (TQM)** revolution in American industry.

TQM is a business philosophy that calls for company-wide dedication to the development, maintenance, and continuous improvement of all aspects of the company's operations. Indeed, some of the world's most admired, successful companies—top-of-industry firms such as Nordstrom, 3M, Boeing, and Coca-Cola, to name a few—endorse a total quality focus.

Product quality is one way that marketing adds value to customers. However, TQM as an approach to doing business is far more sophisticated and impactful than simply paying attention to products that roll off the assembly line. TQM firms promote a culture among employees that *everybody* working there serves its customers—even employees who never interact with people outside the firm. In such cases, employees' customers are **internal customers**—other employees with whom they interact with the attitude that all activities ultimately impact external customers. This **internal customer mind-set** comprises the following four beliefs: (1) employees who receive my work are my customers, (2) meeting the needs of employees who receive my work is critical to doing a good job, (3) it is important to receive feedback from employees who receive my work, and (4) I focus on the requirements of the person who receives my work.

The bottom line is that TQM maximizes external customer satisfaction by involving all employees, regardless of their function, in efforts to continually improve quality, hence resulting in products that perform better and more fully meet customer needs. For example, TQM firms encourage all employees, even the lowest-paid factory workers, to suggest ways to improve products—and then reward them when they come up with good ideas.

TQM fired the first shot on product quality, and since then, around the world, many companies look to the uniform standards of the International Organization for Standardization (ISO) for quality guidelines. This Geneva-based organization developed a set of criteria to improve and standardize product quality in Europe. The **ISO 9000** is a broad set of guidelines that establish voluntary standards for quality management. These guidelines ensure that an organization's products conform to the customer's requirements.

ISO subsequently has developed a variety of other standards, including ISO 14000, which concentrates on environmental management, and ISO 22000 on food safety management and ISO 27001 on information security. This means the organization works to minimize any harmful effects it may have on the environment. Because members of the European Union and other European countries prefer suppliers with ISO 9000 and ISO 14000 certification, U.S. companies must comply with these standards to be competitive there.[12]

One way that companies can improve quality is to use the **Six Sigma** method. The term *Six Sigma* comes from the statistical term *sigma*, which is a standard deviation from the mean. Six Sigma refers to six standard deviations from a normal distribution curve. In practical terms, that translates to no more than 3.4 defects per million—getting it right 99.9997 percent of the time. As you can imagine, achieving that level of quality requires a very rigorous approach (try it on your term papers—even when you use spell-check!), and that's what Six Sigma offers. The method involves a five-step process called "DMAIC" (*define*, *measure*, *analyze*, *improve*, and *control*). The company trains its employees in the method, and as in karate they progress toward "black belt" status when they successfully complete all the levels of training. Employees can use Six Sigma processes to remove defects from services, not just products. In these cases a "defect" means failing to meet customer expectations. For example, hospitals use Six Sigma processes to reduce medical errors, and airlines use the system to improve flight scheduling.

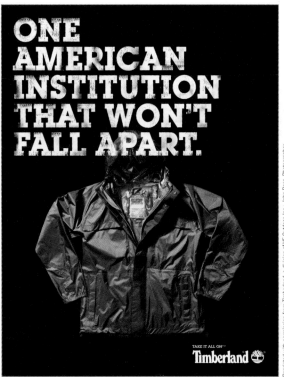

Timberland uses a patriotic message to underscore an emphasis on quality.

total quality management (TQM)
A management philosophy that focuses on satisfying customers through empowering employees to be an active part of continuous quality improvement.

internal customers
Other employees with whom employees interact with the attitude that all activities ultimately impact external customers.

internal customer mind-set
An organizational culture in which all organization members treat each other as valued customers.

ISO 9000
Criteria developed by the International Organization for Standardization to regulate product quality in Europe.

Six Sigma
A process whereby firms work to limit product defects to 3.4 per million or fewer.

Figure 9.3 📷 *Snapshot* | Product Quality

Some product objectives focus on quality, which is the ability of a product to satisfy customer expectations—no matter what those expectations are.

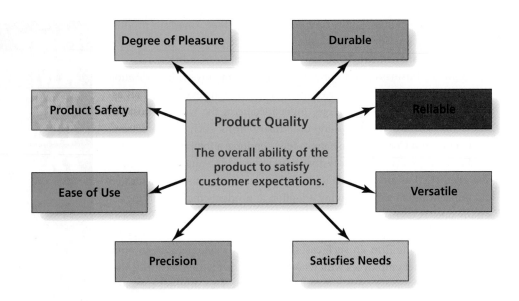

It's fine to talk about product quality, but exactly what is it? 📷 Figure 9.3 summarizes the many aspects of product quality. In some cases, product quality means durability. For example, athletic shoes shouldn't develop holes after their owner shoots hoops for a few weeks. Reliability also is an important aspect of product quality—customers want to know that a McDonald's hamburger is going to taste the same at any location. For many customers, a product's versatility and its ability to satisfy their needs are central to product quality.

For other products, quality means a high degree of precision. For example, purists compare HDTVs in terms of the number of pixels and their refresh rate. Quality, especially in B2B products, also relates to ease of use, maintenance, and repair. Yet another crucial dimension of quality is product safety. Finally, the quality of products, such as a painting, a movie, or even a wedding gown, relates to the degree of aesthetic pleasure they provide. Of course, evaluations of aesthetic quality differ dramatically among people: To one person, the quality of a mobile device may mean simplicity, ease of use, and a focus on reliability in voice signal, while to another it's the cornucopia of apps and multiple communication modes available on the device.

2 Marketing throughout the Product Life Cycle

OBJECTIVE

Understand how firms manage products throughout the product life cycle.
(pp. 282–286)

product life cycle (PLC)
A concept that explains how products go through four distinct stages from birth to death: introduction, growth, maturity, and decline.

Many products have very long lives, while others are "here today, gone tomorrow." The **product life cycle (PLC)** is a useful way to explain how the market's response to a product and marketing activities change over the life of a product. In Chapter 8, we talked about how marketers introduce new products, but the launch is only the beginning. Product marketing strategies must evolve and change as they continue through the product life cycle.

Alas, some brands don't have long to live. Who remembers the Rambler car or Evening in Paris perfume? In contrast, other brands seem almost immortal. For example, Coca-Cola has been the number one cola brand for more than 120 years, General Electric has been the number one lightbulb brand for over a century, and Kleenex has been the number one tissue brand for over 80 years.[13] Let's take a look at the stages of the PLC.

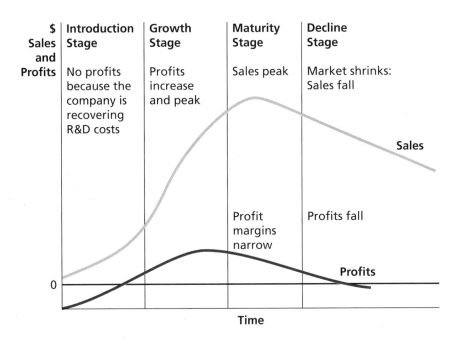

$ Sales and Profits	Introduction Stage	Growth Stage	Maturity Stage	Decline Stage
	No profits because the company is recovering R&D costs	Profits increase and peak	Sales peak	Market shrinks: Sales fall
			Profit margins narrow	Profits fall

Sales

Profits

0

Time

Figure 9.4 📷 *Snapshot* |
The Product Life Cycle

The PLC helps marketers understand how a product changes over its lifetime and suggests how to modify their strategies accordingly.

Introduction Stage

Like people, products are born, they "grow up," and eventually they die. We divide the life of a product into four stages. The first stage we see in 📷 Figure 9.4 is the **introduction stage**. Here, customers get the first chance to purchase the good or service. During this early stage, a single company usually produces the product. If it clicks and is profitable, competitors usually follow with their own versions.

During the introduction stage, the goal is to get first-time buyers to try the product. Sales (hopefully) increase at a steady but slow pace. As is also evident in Figure 9.4, the company usually does not make a profit during this stage. Why? Research-and-development (R&D) costs and heavy spending for advertising and promotional efforts cut into revenue.

As 📷 Figure 9.5 illustrates, during the introduction stage, pricing may be high to recover the R&D costs (demand permitting) or low to attract a large numbers of consumers. For example, the introductory base price of the Lexus GS450h was $54,900, nearly the same as the BMW 550i's base price of $57,400 at the time. Lexus intended the price to appeal to consumers who are willing to pay for the GS450h's unique combination of comfort, great gas mileage, and superb performance. The high price is also necessary so that Lexus can recover its R&D costs for this revolutionary new engineering design and ultimately develop more hybrid products like the LS 600h L, which hit the market at $104,000. And by the way, all three of these cars have gone up in price handily since they first hit the market!

How long does the introduction stage last? As we saw in the microwave oven example in Chapter 8, it can be quite long. A number of factors come into play, including marketplace acceptance and the producer's willingness to support its product during start-up. Sales for hybrid cars started out pretty slowly except for the Prius, but now with gas prices at stratospheric levels and sales reaching new heights, hybrids are well past the introduction stage. Now, electric cars like the Chevy Volt and the Tesla have replaced them in the introduction quadrant.

It is important to note that many products *never* make it past the introduction stage. For a new product to succeed, consumers must first know about it. Then they must believe that it is something

introduction stage
The first stage of the product life cycle, in which slow growth follows the introduction of a new product in the marketplace.

The "Snuggie" blanket was a new product success story, largely due to exceptionally well-executed product planning and management.

Figure 9.5 📷 *Snapshot* | Marketing Mix Strategies through the Product Life Cycle

Marketing mix strategies—the four Ps—change as a product moves through the life cycle.

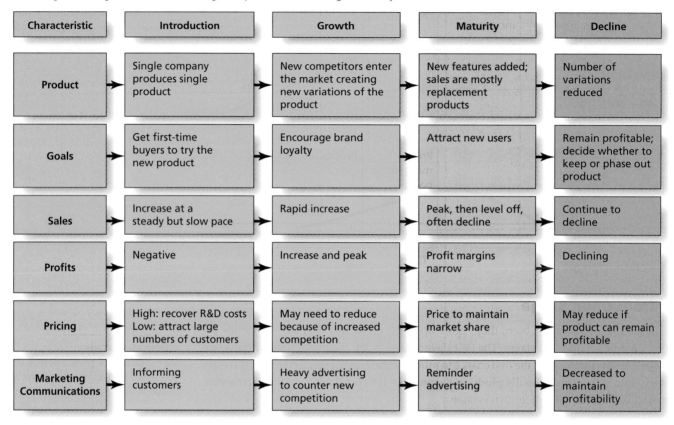

Characteristic	Introduction	Growth	Maturity	Decline
Product	Single company produces single product	New competitors enter the market creating new variations of the product	New features added; sales are mostly replacement products	Number of variations reduced
Goals	Get first-time buyers to try the new product	Encourage brand loyalty	Attract new users	Remain profitable; decide whether to keep or phase out product
Sales	Increase at a steady but slow pace	Rapid increase	Peak, then level off, often decline	Continue to decline
Profits	Negative	Increase and peak	Profit margins narrow	Declining
Pricing	High: recover R&D costs Low: attract large numbers of customers	May need to reduce because of increased competition	Price to maintain market share	May reduce if product can remain profitable
Marketing Communications	Informing customers	Heavy advertising to counter new competition	Reminder advertising	Decreased to maintain profitability

they want or need. Marketing during this stage often focuses on informing consumers about the product, how to use it, and its promised benefits. However, this isn't nearly as easy as it sounds: Would you believe that the most recent data indicate that as many as 95 percent of new products introduced each year fail? Shocking as that number is, it's true. Ever heard of Parfum Bic, Pierre Cardin frying pans, or Jack Daniels mustard? These product blunders—which must have seemed good to some product manager at the time but sound crazy now—certainly didn't last on shelves very long. Ever heard of the Microsoft "Kin" mobile phone, positioned as a product for teens and tweens? It was both introduced and subsequently quickly withdrawn from the market because sales were abysmal (if you have one, keep it—it could be worth a fortune as a collector's item on eBay). It's noteworthy that these (as are many) product failures were backed by big companies and attached to already well-known brands. Just think of the product introduction risks for start-ups and unknown brands![14]

Growth Stage

growth stage
The second stage in the product life cycle, during which consumers accept the product and sales rapidly increase.

In the **growth stage**, sales increase rapidly while profits increase and peak. Marketing's goal here is to encourage brand loyalty by convincing the market that this brand is superior to others. In this stage, marketing strategies may include the introduction of product variations to attract market segments and increase market share. Tablets and smart phones are examples of products that are still in the growth stage, as worldwide sales continue to increase. Continual new product innovations fuel what seems for now to be an endless growth opportunity, and recently Samsung has given Apple a new run for its' money with the sensational launch of the Galaxy s5, which in no time at all will be topped by another and then another model, each with more and more communication features and awesome apps.

When competitors appear on the scene, marketers must heavily rely on advertising and other forms of promotion. Price competition may develop, driving profits down. Some firms may seek to capture a particular segment of the market by positioning their product to appeal to a certain group. And, if it initially set the price high, the firm may now reduce it to meet increasing competition.

Maturity Stage

The **maturity stage** of the product life cycle is usually the longest. Sales peak and then begin to level off and even decline while profit margins narrow. Competition gets intense when remaining competitors fight for their share of a shrinking pie. Firms may resort to price reductions and reminder advertising ("Did you brush your teeth today?") to maintain market share. Because most customers have already accepted the product, they tend to buy to replace a worn-out item or to take advantage of product improvements. For example, almost everyone in the U.S. owns a TV (there are still more homes without indoor toilets than without a TV set), meaning that most people who buy a new set replace an older one—especially when TV stations nationwide stopped using analog signals and began to broadcast exclusively in a digital format. TV manufacturers hope that a lot of the replacements will be sets with the latest-and-greatest new technology—plucky Samsung would love to sell you a 3D TV to replace that worn-out basic model. During the maturity stage, firms try to sell their product through as many outlets as possible because availability is crucial in a competitive market. Consumers will not go far to find one particular brand if satisfactory alternatives are close at hand.

To remain competitive and maintain market share during the maturity stage, firms may tinker with the marketing mix in order to extend this profitable phase for their product. Food manufacturers constantly monitor consumer trends, which of late have been heavily skewed toward healthier eating. This has resulted in all sorts of products that trumpet their low-carb, organic, or no-trans-fat credentials.

Decline Stage

The **decline stage** of the product life cycle is characterized by a decrease in overall product category sales. The reason may be obsolescence forced by new technology—where (other than in a museum) do you see a typewriter today? See many people using flip phones recently? Although a single firm may still be profitable, the market as a whole begins to shrink, profits decline, there are fewer variations of the product, and suppliers pull out. In this stage, there are usually many competitors, but none has a distinct advantage.

A firm's major product decision in the decline stage is whether to keep the product at all. An unprofitable product drains resources that the firm could use to develop newer products. If the firm decides to keep the product, it may decrease advertising and other marketing communications to cut costs and reduce prices if the product can still remain profitable. If the firm decides to drop the product, it can eliminate it in two ways: (1) phase it out by cutting production in stages and letting existing stocks run out or (2) simply dump the product immediately. If the established market leader anticipates that there will be some residual demand for the product for a long time, it may make sense to keep the product on the market. The idea is to sell a limited quantity of the product with little or no support from sales, merchandising, advertising, and distribution and just let it "wither on the vine."

Now that e-commerce is a significant factor for marketing, some products that would have died a natural death in brick-and-mortar stores continue to sell online to a cadre of fans, backed by zero marketing support (translation: high profits for the manufacturer). Have a hankering for Beeman's, Blackjack, or Clove gum? At least for now, several online purveyors sell both direct to consumers. In the "old days" (i.e., B.I.—Before the Internet), a brand like Beeman's would have been doomed by aggressive marketing budgets for all the crazy and continuous new product introductions in the gum category by behemoth gum competitors like Wrigley. eBay has certainly helped to extend the life cycle of many products—yes, you can buy Beeman's there too but probably for "vintage display" purposes rather than for human consumption!

maturity stage
The third and longest stage in the product life cycle, during which sales peak and profit margins narrow.

decline stage
The final stage in the product life cycle, during which sales decrease as customer needs change.

The **Cutting Edge**

Social Media Brings Products Back to Life

It used to be that when your favorite product was discontinued, it was gone for good. But today, thanks to social media, you might just be in luck. "It's literally shaping how the market is driven," said Karen Grant, a senior global industry analyst with a market research firm in New York.[15]

For example, Bobbi Brown Cosmetics and MAC Cosmetics (brands of the Estée Lauder Companies) set up campaigns on Facebook—"Bobbi Brings Back: Lip Color" and "MAC by Request"—so that customers could vote on which of their favorite products to bring back from the dead-and-gone products graveyard. The MAC by Request campaign garnered more

than 600,000 votes, and winning shades of lipstick, lip gloss, and eye shadow were made available for sale on the company's website.

It's really a win for both consumers and marketers. Consumers get to have input on the products they love, and marketers not only generate goodwill but also keep themselves from making costly mistakes. Skin care brand Erno Laszlo, for example, planned to drop more than half of its products, but when customers found out, they sent hundreds of e-mails to CEO Charles Denton in an effort to save their faves. As a result, two powders that were on the cut list were spared. "The consequence of a poor decision could take 18 months to two years to filter back to the head office," said Denton. "With social media you can take an instant read. That's fantastically valuable."[16]

3 Branding and Packaging: Create Product Identity

OBJECTIVE

Explain how branding and packaging strategies contribute to product identity.
(pp. 286–295)

Successful marketers keep close tabs on their products' life cycle status, and they plan accordingly. Equally important, though, is to give that product an *identity* and a *personality*. For example, the mere word "Disney" evokes positive emotions around fun, playfulness, family, and casting day-to-day cares out the window. Folks pay a whole lot of money at Disney's theme parks in Florida and California (as well as in France, China, and Japan) to act on those emotions. Disney achieved its strong identity through decades of great branding. Branding along with packaging are extremely important (and expensive) elements of product strategies.

What's in a Name (or a Symbol)?

brand

A name, a term, a symbol, or any other unique element of a product that identifies one firm's product(s) and sets it apart from the competition.

How do you identify your favorite brand? By its name? By the logo (how the name appears)? By the package? By some graphic image or symbol, such as Nike's swoosh? A **brand** is a name, a term, a symbol, or any other unique element of a product that identifies one firm's product(s) and sets it apart from the competition. Consumers easily recognize the Coca-Cola logo, the Jolly Green Giant (a *trade character*), and the triangular red Nabisco logo (a *brand mark*) in the corner of the box. Branding provides the recognition factor products need to succeed in regional, national, and international markets.

A brand name is probably the most used and most recognized form of branding. Smart marketers use brand names to maintain relationships with consumers "from the cradle to the grave." McDonald's would like nothing better than to bring in kids for their Happy Meal and then convert them over time to its more adult Premium Grilled Chicken Ranch BLT (accompanied, it is hoped, by a Side Salad and a McCafé Frappé Chocolate Chip). A good brand name may position a product because it conveys a certain image (Ford Mustang, which just celebrated its fiftieth anniversary) or describes how it works (Drano). Brand names such as Caress and Shield help position these different brands of bath soap by saying different things about the benefits they promise. Irish Spring soap provides an unerring image of freshness (can't you just smell it now?). The Nissan Xterra combines the word *terrain* with the letter *X*, which many young people associate with extreme sports, to give the brand name a cutting-edge, off-road feel. Apple's use of "i-everything" is a brilliant branding strategy, as it conveys individuality and personalization—characteristics that Gen Y buyers prize.

How does a firm select a good brand name? Good brand designers say there are four "easy" tests: *easy to say*, *easy to spell*, *easy to read*, and *easy to remember*—like P&G's Tide,

Cheer, Bold, Gain, Downy, and Ivory Snow, all of which compete in the laundry products category (P&G is probably the undisputed branding king of all time). And the name should also pass the "fit test" on four dimensions:

1. Fit the target market

2. Fit the product's benefits

3. Fit the customer's culture

4. Fit legal requirements

When it comes to graphics for a brand symbol, name, or logo, the rule is that it must be recognizable and memorable. No matter how small or large, the triangular Nabisco logo in the corner of the box is a familiar sight. And it should have visual impact. That means that from across a store or when you quickly flip the pages in a magazine, the brand will catch your attention. Apple's apple with the one bite missing never fails to attract.

A **trademark** is the legal term for a brand name, brand mark, or trade character. The symbol for legal registration in the U.S. is a capital "R" in a circle: ®. Marketers register trademarks to make their use by competitors illegal. Because trademark protection applies only in individual countries where the owner registers the brand, unauthorized use of marks on counterfeit products is a huge headache for many companies.

A firm can claim protection for a brand even if it has not legally registered it. In the U.S., *common-law protection* exists if the firm has used the name and established it over a period of time (sort of like a common-law marriage). Although a registered trademark prevents others from using it on a similar product, it may not bar its use for a product in a completely different type of business. Consider the range of unrelated "Quaker" brands: Quaker Oats (cereals), Quaker Funds (mutual funds), Quaker State (motor oil), Quaker Bonnet (gift food baskets), and Quaker Safety Products Corporation (firemen's clothing). A court applied this principle when Apple Corp., the Beatles' music company, sued Apple Computers in 2006 over its use of the Apple logo. The plaintiff wanted to win an injunction to prevent Apple Computer from using the Apple logo in connection with its iPod and iTunes products; it argued that the application to music-related products came too close to the Beatles' musical products. The judge didn't agree; he ruled that Apple Computer clearly used the logo to refer to the download service, not to the music itself.[17]

Why Brands Matter

A brand is *a lot* more than just the product it represents—the best brands build an emotional connection with their customers. Think about the most popular diapers—they're branded Pampers and Luvs, not some functionally descriptive name like Absorbency Master or Dry Bottom. The point is that Pampers and Luvs evoke the joys of parenting, not the utility of the diaper.

Marketers spend huge amounts of money on new product development, advertising, and promotion to develop strong brands. When they succeed, this investment creates **brand equity**. This term describes a brand's value over and above the value of the generic version of the product. For example, how much extra will you pay for a shirt with the American Eagle Outfitters logo on it than for the same shirt with no logo or, worse, the logo of an "inferior" brand? The difference reflects the eagle's brand equity in your mind.

Brand equity means that a brand enjoys customer loyalty because people believe it is superior to the competition. For a firm, brand equity provides a competitive advantage because it gives the brand the power to capture and hold on to a larger share of the market and to sell at prices with higher profit margins. For example, among pianos, the Steinway name has such powerful brand equity that its market share among concert pianists is 95 percent.[18]

Marketers identify different levels of loyalty (or lack thereof) by observing how customers feel about the product. At the lowest level, customers really have no loyalty to a brand, and they will change brands for any reason—often they will jump ship if they find something else at a lower price. At the other extreme, some brands command fierce devotion, and loyal users will go without rather than buy a competing brand.

trademark
The legal term for a brand name, brand mark, or trade character; trademarks legally registered by a government obtain protection for exclusive use in that country.

brand equity
The value of a brand to an organization.

brand meaning
The beliefs and associations that a consumer has about the brand.

Escalating levels of attachment to a brand begin when consumers become aware of a brand's existence. Then they might look at the brand in terms of what it literally does for them or how it performs relative to competitors. Next, they may think more deeply about the product and form beliefs and emotional reactions to it. The truly successful brands, however, are those that truly "bond" with their customers so that people feel they have a real relationship with the product. Here are some of the types of relationships a person might have with a product:

- *Self-concept attachment:* The product helps establish the user's identity. (For example, do you feel better in Ralph Lauren or Forever 21 clothing?)

- *Nostalgic attachment:* The product serves as a link with a past self. (Does eating the inside of an Oreo cookie remind you of childhood?)[19]

- *Interdependence:* The product is a part of the user's daily routine. (Could you get through the day without a Starbucks coffee?)

- *Love:* The product elicits emotional bonds of warmth, passion, or other strong emotion. (Hershey's Kiss, anyone?)[20]

APPLYING ▼ Brand Meaning

David knows that a key to the Fiber One brand's growth is developing the right brand meaning. The benefits of the brand combined with trends in the marketplace suggested three options: Fiber Superiority, Great Tasting High Fiber, and Digestive Health.

Ultimately, the way to build strong brands is to forge strong bonds with customers—bonds based on **brand meaning**. This concept encompasses the beliefs and associations that a consumer has about the brand. In many ways, the practice of brand management revolves around the management of meanings. Brand managers, advertising agencies, package designers, name consultants, logo developers, and public relations firms are just some of the collaborators in a global industry devoted to the task of *meaning management*. Table 9.1 summarizes some important dimensions of brand meaning.

Today, for many consumers brand meaning builds virally as people spread its story online. "Tell to sell," once a mantra of top Madison Avenue ad agencies, is making a comeback as marketers seek to engage consumers with compelling stories rather than peddle products in hit-and-run fashion with interruptive advertising like 30-second TV commercials—which Gen Y and younger largely block out anyway. The method of **brand storytelling** captures the notion that powerful ideas do self-propagate when the audience is connected by digital technology. It conveys the constant reinvention inherent in interactivity in that

brand storytelling
Compelling stories told by marketers about brands to engage consumers.

Table 9.1 | Dimensions of Brand Meaning

Dimension	Example
Brand identification markers	Coca-Cola's red and white colors, the Nike swoosh logo, Harley-Davidson's characteristic engine roar, Ruth's Chris steak sizzle
Product attribute and benefit	Starbucks as good coffee; BMW as "The Ultimate Driving Machine"
Gender	NASCAR, Harley-Davidson, and Ram pickups and masculinity; Laura Ashley and femininity
Social class	Mercedes and the old-guard elite; Jell-O and the lower middle class
Age	Facebook, Skechers, Sony Walkman, iPod, Adult Swim
Reference group	Dockers and the casual workforce; Williams-Sonoma and the serious cook
Life stage	Dewar's and the coming of age; J&J baby shampoo and new mothers
Lifestyles and taste subcultures	BMW and the yuppie; Red Bull and the club culture
Place	Coke and America; Ben & Jerry's and rural Vermont
Time and decade	Betty Crocker and the 1950s; VW and the 1960s countercultural revolution
Trends	Pottery Barn and cocooning; Starbucks and small indulgences
Traditions and rituals	Häagen-Dazs ice cream and the pampering of self

Source: Parts of the table are adapted from Susan G. Fournier, Michael R. Solomon, and Basil G. Englis, "Brand Resonance," in *Handbook on Brand and Experience Management*, ed. Bernd Schmitt (Cheltenham: Elgar Publishing, 2009).

whether it's blogging, content creation through YouTube, or sharing a board on Pinterest, there will always be new and evolving perceptions and dialogues about a brand in real time. A cadre of start-up firms have emerged over the past few years to aid companies in storytelling about their brand.[21]

If we could name the key elements that make a brand successful, what would they be? Here is a list of 10 characteristics of the world's top brands:[22]

1. The brand excels at delivering the benefits customers truly desire.

2. The brand stays relevant.

3. The pricing strategy is based on consumers' perceptions of value.

4. The brand is properly positioned.

5. The brand is consistent.

6. The brand portfolio and hierarchy make sense.

7. The brand makes use of and coordinates a full repertoire of marketing activities to build equity.

8. The brand's managers understand what the brand means to consumers.

9. The brand is given proper support, and that support is sustained over the long run.

10. The company monitors sources of brand equity.

Products with strong brand equity provide exciting opportunities for marketers. A firm may leverage a brand's equity via **brand extensions**—new products it sells with the same brand name. Because of the existing brand equity, a firm is able to sell its brand extension at a higher price than if it had given it a new brand, and the brand extension will attract new customers immediately. Of course, if the brand extension does not live up to the quality or attractiveness of its namesake, brand equity will suffer, as will brand loyalty and sales.

One other related approach is **sub-branding**, or creating a secondary brand within a main brand that can help differentiate a product line to a desired target group. Virgin is the king of sub-brands, having launched dozens over the history of the company. From Virgin Atlantic to Virgin America, Virgin Mobile, Virgin Megastore, Virgin Wines, Virgin Radio, and on and on—founder Sir Richard Branson has shown the power of thematic threading when the principal brand is robust.[23]

Sometimes a brand's meaning simply becomes so entrenched with a particular consumer group that it can be tough to find ways to branch out and achieve new users through extensions. Take, for example, Quiksilver, whose original line of wetsuits and swimwear started out aimed squarely at teenage boys who identified with the surf and skate cultures. The brand now has migrated to appeal to women who may have never hit the waves with items from sweaters to jeans. The lines are in Quiksilver's owned stores as well as in Nordstrom and other high-end retail outlets. The competition is fierce, though—Urban Outfitters' Anthropologie and Liz Claiborne's Lucky Brand Jeans are formidable in the twenty-something female market and are aimed at the same genre of retailer as Quiksilver's line.[24]

brand extensions
A new product sold with the same brand name as a strong existing brand.

sub-branding
Creating a secondary brand within a main brand that can help differentiate a product line to a desired target group.

APPLYING ▼ Brand Extensions

Growing consumer interest in fiber provided an opportunity for General Mills to grow the Fiber One brand. Part of this growth was to leverage the Fiber One brand equity and launch new brand extensions, Fiber One Honey Clusters Cereal and Fiber One Oats and Chocolate Snack Bars.

Branding Strategies

Because brands contribute to a marketing program's success, a major part of product planning is to develop and execute branding strategies. Marketers have to determine which branding strategy approach(es) to use. 📷 Figure 9.6 illustrates the options: individual or family brands, national or store brands, generic brands, licensing, and cobranding. This decision is critical, but it is not always an easy or obvious choice.

Figure 9.6 📷 *Snapshot* | Branding Strategies

Marketing managers have several options for which branding strategy or strategies to employ.

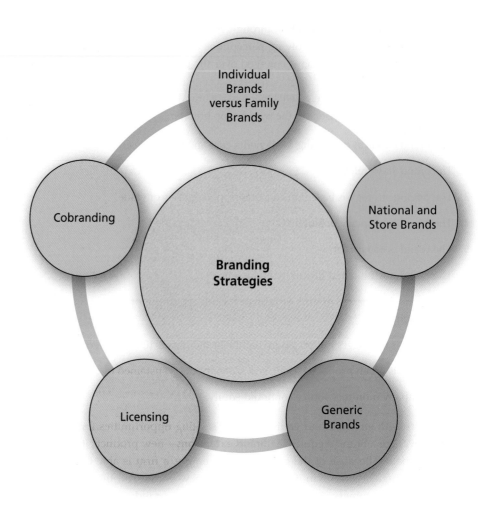

Campbell's uses a family branding strategy to identify its Chunky line of soups.

Individual Brands versus Family Brands

Part of developing a branding strategy is to decide whether to use a separate, unique brand for each product item—an *individual brand strategy*—or to market multiple items under the same brand name—a **family brand** or *umbrella brand* strategy. Individual brands may do a better job of communicating clearly and concisely what the consumer can expect from the product, while a well-known company like Hyatt Hotels may find that its high brand equity and reputation in one category (e.g., Hyatt Regency at the high end) can sometimes "rub off" on a brands in newer categories like Hyatt Place and Hyatt House.

The decision whether to family brand often depends on characteristics of the product and whether the company's overall product strategy calls for introduction of a single, unique product or for the development of a group of similar products. For example, Microsoft serves as a strong umbrella brand for a host of diverse, individually branded products like Windows 8, Office 2013, Xbox 360, and Bing, while Unilever and P&G prefer to brand each of their beauty care and household products separately (for most of the products, you'd never know who the manufacturer is unless you look at the small print on the back label).

But there's a potential dark side to having too many brands, particularly when they become undifferentiated in the eyes of the consumer due to poor positioning. Over the past decade, venerable General Motors continually suffered from muddy differentiation among the brands in its portfolio—namely, Chevrolet, GMC, Pontiac, Saturn, Cadillac, Buick, Hummer, and Saab. The brands often competed with each other—both for customers and for a slice of GM's marketing budget. For example, at one time GM had four mainstream midsize sedans. It backed its top-selling Chevy Malibu with an aggressive ad campaign, while the Buick LaCrosse, Pontiac G6, and Saturn Aura struggled to build the awareness and recognition these lines need to compete. Fast forward to today: When GM got into financial difficulty and was "bailed out" by the U.S. government (i.e., the taxpayers), one of the first moves for the leaner, meaner GM was to cut out all the fat in its product lines. Of the models listed above, only the Malibu is still around! And among the main GM brand lines, only Chevrolet, GMC, Cadillac, and Buick are in production.[25]

National and Store Brands

Retailers today often are in the driver's seat when it comes to deciding what brands to stock and push. In addition to choosing from producers' brands, called **national or manufacturer brands**, retailers decide whether to offer their own versions. **Private-label brands**, also called *store brands*, are the retail store or chain's exclusive trade name. Costco, for example, features a fine line of more than 300 products under its own private label Kirkman Signature. Representative categories include housewares, luggage, pet food and bedding, baby wipes, diapers, baby formula, apparel, wine, snacks, and more.[26] During the Great Recession that began in the late 2000s, store brands gained substantially in popularity for many value-conscious shoppers, and many consumers did not switch back to the parallel national brands as the economy rebounded because they are satisfied with the private labels.

In addition, if you stock a unique brand that consumers can't find in other stores, it's much harder for shoppers to compare "apples to apples" across stores and simply buy the brand where they find it sold for the lowest price. Loblaws, Canada's largest supermarket chain, sells over 4,000 food items under the "premium quality" President's Choice label, from cookies to beef, olive oil, curtains, and kitchen utensils. Sales of President's Choice items run from 30 to 40 percent of total store volumes. Under the private label, Loblaws can introduce new products at high quality but for lower prices than brand names. It can also keep entire categories profitable with its mix of pricing options. Competitors that sell only national brands can cut prices on those brands, but that hurts their overall profitability. Loblaws can reduce prices on national brands but still make money on its private-label products.[27]

Generic Brands

An alternative to either national or store branding is **generic branding**, which is basically no branding at all. Generic branded products are typically packaged in white with black lettering that names only the product itself (e.g., "Green Beans"). Generic branding is one strategy to meet customers' demand for the lowest prices on standard products such as dog food or paper towels. Generic brands first became popular during the inflationary period of the 1980s when consumers became especially price conscious. More recently, Walmart has aggressively disrupted the pharmacy business by offering some types of generic prescriptions, such as basic antibiotics, for $4.[28]

Licensing

Some firms choose to use a **licensing** strategy to brand their products. This means that one firm sells another firm the right to use a legally protected brand name for a specific purpose and for a specific period of time. Why should an organization sell its name? Licensing can provide instant recognition and consumer interest in a new product, and this strategy can quickly position a product for a certain target market as it trades on the high recognition of the licensed brand among consumers in that segment. For example, distiller Brown-Forman licensed its famous Jack Daniel's bourbon name to T.G.I. Friday's to use on all sorts of menu

family brand
A brand that a group of individual products or individual brands share.

national or manufacturer brands
Brands that the product manufacturer owns.

private-label brands
Brands that a certain retailer or distributor owns and sells.

generic branding
A strategy in which products are not branded and are sold at the lowest price possible.

licensing
An agreement in which one firm sells another firm the right to use a brand name for a specific purpose and for a specific period of time.

Jelly Belly cobrands with several soft drink brands to offer new flavor options.

cobranding
An agreement between two brands to work together to market a new product.

ingredient branding
A type of branding in which branded materials become "component parts" of other branded products.

package
The covering or container for a product that provides product protection, facilitates product use and storage, and supplies important marketing communication.

items from shrimp to steak to chicken and is one of the most popular of all food lines sold in Friday's restaurants.[29]

A familiar form of licensing occurs when movie producers license their properties to manufacturers of a seemingly infinite number of products. Remember how each time a blockbuster Harry Potter movie hit the screens, a plethora of Potter products packed the stores? In addition to toys and games, there was Harry Potter candy, clothing, all manner of back-to-school items, home items, and even wands and cauldrons. In 2010, with considerable fanfare, Harry and the gang showed up in the form of a major attraction at Universal Orlando called "The Wizarding World of Harry Potter." The latest addition, called "Dragon Alley," opened for business in the summer of 2014.[30]

Cobranding

Frito-Lay sells K.C. Masterpiece–flavored potato chips. Taco Bell sells Spicy Chicken Cool Ranch Doritos Locos Tacos, and Post sells Oreo O's cereal. Strange marriages? Not at all! Actually, these are examples of an innovative strategy called **cobranding**. Cobranding benefits both partners when combining the two brands provides more recognition power than either enjoys alone. For example, Sony markets its line of digital Cyber-shot cameras that use Zeiss lenses, which are world famous for their sharpness.[31] Sony is known for its consumer electronics. Combining the best in traditional camera optics with a household name in consumer electronics helps both brands.

A new and fast-growing variation on cobranding is **ingredient branding**, in which branded materials become "component parts" of other branded products.[32] This was the strategy behind the classic "Intel inside" campaign, which convinced millions of consumers to ask by name for a highly technical computer part (a processor) that they wouldn't otherwise recognize if they fell over it.[33] Today, consumers can buy Breyer's Ice Cream with Reese's Peanut Butter Cups, M&M's candies, Girl Scout Cookies Thin Mints, and several other decadent ingredients.

The practice of ingredient branding has two main benefits. First, it attracts customers to the host brand because the ingredient brand is familiar and has a strong brand reputation for quality. Second, the ingredient brand's firm can sell more of its product, not to mention the additional revenues it gets from the licensing arrangement.[34]

Packages and Labels: Branding's Little Helpers

How do you know if the soda you are drinking is "regular" or "caffeine free"? How do you keep your low-fat grated cheese fresh after you have used some of it? Why do you like that little blue box from Tiffany's so much? The answer to all these questions is effective packaging and labeling. So far, we've talked about how marketers create product identity with branding. In this section, we'll learn that packaging and labeling decisions also help to create product identity. We also talk about the strategic functions of packaging and some of the legal issues that relate to package labeling.

A **package** is the covering or container for a product, but it's also a way to create a competitive advantage. So the important functional value of a package is that it protects the product. For example, packaging for computers, TV sets, and stereos protects the units from damage during shipping and warehousing. Cereal, potato chips, or packs of grated cheese wouldn't be edible for long if packaging didn't provide protection from moisture, dust, odors, and insects. The multilayered, soft box for the chicken broth you see in 📷 Figure 9.7 prevents the ingredients inside from spoiling. In addition to protecting the product, effective packaging makes it easy for

A range of package sizes allows a company to expand its product line.

Metrics Moment

Recall from our earlier discussion that brand equity represents the value of a product with a particular brand name compared to what the value of the product would be without that brand name (think Coca-Cola versus generic supermarket soda). Companies, market research firms, and creative agencies create metrics of brand equity because this is an important way to assess whether a branding strategy has been successful. For example, Harris Interactive conducts its EquiTrend study annually to measure the brand equity of over 1,500 brands in more than 150 industries. The company interviews over 40,000 consumers to determine how they feel about competing brands.[35] You can review the latest results at **www.harrisinteractive.com**, then click on "Insights" and find the latest year's brand rankings.

If consumers have strong, positive feelings about a brand and are willing to pay extra to choose it over others, marketers are on cloud nine. Each of the following approaches to measuring brand equity has some good points and some bad points:

- *Customer mind-set metrics* focus on consumer awareness, attitudes, and loyalty toward a brand. However, these metrics are based on consumer surveys and don't usually provide a single objective measure that a marketer can use to assign a financial value to the brand.
- *Product-market outcome metrics* focus on the ability of a brand to charge a higher price than that of an unbranded equivalent. This usually involves asking consumers how much more they would be willing to pay for a certain brand compared to others. These measures often rely on hypothetical judgments and can be complicated to use.
- *Financial market metrics* consider the purchase price of a brand if it is sold or acquired. They may also include subjective judgments about the future stock price of the brand.
- A team of marketing professors proposed a simpler measure that they claim reliably tracks the value of a brand over time. Their *revenue premium metric* compares the revenue a brand generates with the revenue generated by a similar private-label product (that doesn't have any brand identification). In this case, brand equity is just the difference in revenue (net price times volume) between a branded good and a corresponding private label.[36]

Apply the Metrics

1. Work with one or more other students to come up with a short list of five to seven of your collective favorite brands.
2. Consider the various aspects of branding you've read about in this chapter. What characteristics of each brand caused you to include it on your short list?

Figure 9.7 📷 *Snapshot* | Functions of Packaging

Great packaging provides a covering for a product, and it also creates a competitive advantage for the brand.

A next-generation bar code called an *Aztec code* is starting to pop up on everything from cereal boxes to airline boarding passes. It holds much more data and can be read by cellphones that have the necessary software.

Universal Product Code (UPC)
A set of black bars or lines printed on the side or bottom of most items sold in grocery stores and other mass-merchandising outlets that correspond to a unique 10-digit number.

consumers to handle and store the product. Review the different elements pointed out in Figure 9.7—collectively, they illustrate how packaging serves a number of different functions.

Over and above these utilitarian functions, however, a package communicates brand personality. Effective product packaging uses colors, words, shapes, designs, and pictures to provide brand and name identification for the product. In addition, packaging provides product facts, including flavor, fragrance, directions for use, suggestions for alternative uses (e.g., recipes), safety warnings, and ingredients. Packaging may also include warranty information and a toll-free telephone number for customer service.

A final communication element is the **Universal Product Code (UPC)**, which is the set of black bars or lines printed on the side or bottom of most items sold in grocery stores and other mass-merchandising outlets. The UPC is a national system of product identification. It assigns each product a unique 10-digit number. These numbers supply specific information about the type of item (grocery item, meat, produce, drugs, or a discount coupon), the manufacturer (a five-digit code), and the specific product (another five-digit code). At checkout counters, electronic scanners read the UPC bars and automatically transmit data to a computer in the cash register so that retailers can easily track sales and control inventory.

Design Effective Packaging

Should the package have a resealable zipper, feature an easy-to-pour spout, be compact for easy storage, be short and fat so it won't fall over, or be tall and skinny so it won't take up much shelf space? Effective package design involves a multitude of decisions.

Planners must consider the packaging of other brands in the same product category. For example, when Pringles potato chips were introduced, they were deliberately packaged in a cylindrical can instead of in bags like Lay's and others. This was largely out of necessity since Pringles doesn't have all the local trucks to deliver to stores that Frito-Lay does, and the cans keep the chips fresher much longer. However, quickly after product introduction, Pringles discovered that not all customers will accept a radical change in packaging, and retailers may be reluctant to adjust their shelf space to accommodate such packages. To partly answer the concern, Pringles now comes in very diverse array of products and package types and sizes, including Stix, Snack Stacks, Grab & Go, and, for the healthier eaters, Lightly Salted, Reduced Fat, Fat Free, and 100 Calorie.[37]

Who says people don't judge a book by its cover? AXE, a line of men's grooming products from Unilever, makes a distinct impression on the shelf. Amidst more traditional packaging, the futuristic-looking (think X-Men) black bottles of shave gel and shampoo that sport cool colors such as blue, purple, green, and red really stand out. While the cylindrical shave gel can looks somewhat like a barbell, the deodorant and shower gel almost look like spaceships set for takeoff. And it just might do that—to promote its new Apollo line, Unilever plans to send 22 consumers into space.[38]

Firms that wish to act in a socially responsible manner must also consider the environmental impact of packaging. Shiny gold or silver packaging transmits an image of quality and opulence, but certain metallic inks are not biodegradable. Some firms are developing innovative *green packaging* that is less harmful to the environment than other materials. Of course, there is no guarantee that consumers will accept such packaging. They didn't take to plastic pouch refills for certain spray bottle products even though the pouches may take up less space in landfills than the bottles do. They didn't like pouring the refill into their old spray bottles. Still, customers have accepted smaller packages of concentrated products, such as laundry detergent, dishwashing liquid, and fabric softener.

What about the shape: Square? Round? Triangular? Hourglass? Toiletry manufacturer Mennen once had an aftershave and cologne line called Millionaire that it packaged in a gold pyramid-shaped box. How about an old-fashioned apothecary jar that consumers can reuse as an attractive storage container? What color should it be? White to communicate purity? Yellow because it reminds people of lemon freshness? Brown because the flavor is chocolate? Sometimes, we can trace these decisions back to personal preferences. The familiar Campbell's Soup label—immortalized as art by Andy Warhol—is red and white because a company executive many years ago liked the football uniforms at Cornell University!

Finally, there are many specific decisions brand managers must make to ensure that a product's packaging reflects well on its brand and appeals to the intended target market. What graphic information should the package show? Someone once quipped, "Never show the dog eating the dog food." Translation: Should there be a picture of the product on the package? Must green bean cans always show a picture of green beans? Should there be a picture that demonstrates the results of using the product, such as beautiful hair? Should there be a picture of the product in use, perhaps a box of crackers that shows them with delicious-looking toppings arranged on a silver tray? Should there be a recipe or coupon on the back? Of course, all these decisions rely on a marketer's understanding of consumers, ingenuity, and perhaps a little creative luck.

Store brands have unique packaging opportunities. Some store brands opt for copycat packaging, mimicking the look of the national branded product they want to knock off. Walgreens is a master of such copycat packaging—look on any shelf in its medicinal categories, and you will see a Walgreens brand proudly merchandised on the shelf right next to the leading national brand in that category, with the package design and colors so similar that you have to look carefully to discern what you are actually buying.[39]

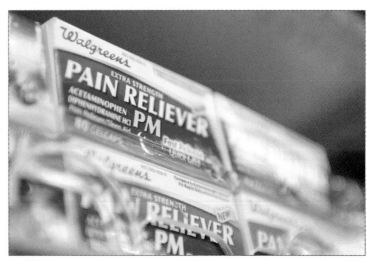

Some store brands opt for copycat packaging, mimicking the look of the national branded product they want to knock off. Walgreens is a master of such copycat packaging—look on any shelf in its medicinal categories and you will see a Walgreens brand proudly merchandised on the shelf right next to the leading national brand in that category, with the package design and colors so similar that you have to look carefully to discern what you are actually buying.

Labeling Regulations

The Federal Fair Packaging and Labeling Act of 1966 controls package communications and labeling in the U.S. This law aims to make labels more helpful to consumers by providing useful information. More recently, the requirements of the *Nutrition Labeling and Education Act of 1990* forced food marketers to make sweeping changes in how they label products. Since August 18, 1994, the U.S. Food and Drug Administration (FDA) requires most foods sold in the U.S. to have labels telling, among other things, how much fat, saturated fat, cholesterol, calories, carbohydrates, protein, and vitamins are in each serving of the product. These regulations force marketers to be more accurate when they describe the contents of their products. Juice makers, for example, must state how much of their product is real juice rather than sugar and water.

As of January 1, 2006, the FDA also requires that all food labels list the amount of trans fat in the food directly under the line for saturated fat content. The new labeling reflects scientific evidence showing that consumption of trans fat, saturated fat, and dietary cholesterol raises "bad" cholesterol levels, which increase the risk of coronary heart disease. The new information is the first significant change on the Nutrition Facts panel since it was established.[40]

4 Organize for Effective Product Management

OBJECTIVE

Describe how marketers structure organizations for new and existing product management.

(pp. 296–297)

Of course, firms don't create great products, brands, and packaging—people do. Like all elements of the marketing mix, product strategies are only as effective as their managers make them and carry them out. In this section, we talk about how firms organize both to manage existing products and to develop new products.

Manage Existing Products

In small firms, a single marketing manager usually handles the marketing function. This individual is responsible for new product planning, advertising, working with the company's few sales representatives, marketing research, and just about everything else. But in larger firms, there are a number of managers who are responsible for different brands, product categories, or markets. As illustrated in Figure 9.8, depending on the organization's needs and the market situation, product management may include brand managers, product category managers, and market managers. Let's take a look at how each operates.

Brand Managers

Sometimes, a firm sells several or even many different brands within a single product category. Take the hair care section in the supermarket, for example. In the shampoo and conditioner category, P&G manufactures and markets these brands (among others): Head & Shoulders, Herbal Essences, and Pantene. In such cases, each brand may have its own **brand manager** who coordinates all marketing activities for a brand; these duties include positioning, identifying target markets, research, distribution, sales promotion, packaging, and evaluating the success of these decisions.

brand manager
An individual who is responsible for developing and implementing the marketing plan for a single brand.

Although this job title and assignment (or something similar) is still common throughout industry, some big firms are changing the way they allocate responsibilities. For example, today P&G's brand managers function more like internal consultants to cross-functional teams located in the field that have responsibility for managing the complete business of key retail clients across all product lines. Brand managers still are responsible for positioning of brands and developing and nurturing brand equity, but they also work heavily with folks from sales, finance, logistics, and others to serve the needs of the major retailers that make up the majority of P&G's business.

By its very nature, the brand management system is not without potential problems. If they act independently and sometimes competitively against each other, brand managers may fight for increases in short-term sales for their own brand, potentially to the detriment of the overall product category for the firm. They may push too hard with coupons, cents-off packages, or other price incentives to a point at which customers will refuse to buy the product when it's not "on deal." Such behavior can hurt long-term profitability and damage brand equity.

Product Category Managers

Some larger firms have such diverse product offerings that they need more extensive coordination. Take IBM, for example. Originally known as a computer manufacturer, IBM now generates much of its revenue from a wide range of consulting and related client services across the spectrum of IT applications (and the company doesn't even sell personal computers anymore,

Figure 9.8 *Snapshot* | Types of Product Management

Product management can take several forms: brand managers, product category managers, and market managers, depending on the firm's needs and the market situation.

Three Types of Product Management

having long ago spun off its ThinkPad business to the Chinese firm Lenovo). In cases such as IBM, organizing for product management may include **product category managers**, who coordinate the mix of product lines within the more general product category and who consider the addition of new product lines based on client needs.

product category managers
Individuals who are responsible for developing and implementing the marketing plan for all the brands and products within a product category.

Market Managers

Some firms have developed a **market manager** structure in which different people focus on specific customer groups rather than on the products the company makes. This type of organization can be useful when firms offer a variety of products that serve the needs of a wide range of customers. For example, Raytheon, a company that specializes in consumer electronics products, special-mission aircraft, and business aviation, sells some products directly to consumer markets, others to manufacturers, and still others to the government. It serves its customers best when it focuses separately on each of these very different markets.

market manager
An individual who is responsible for developing and implementing the marketing plans for products sold to a particular customer group.

Organize for New Product Development

You read in Chapter 8 about the steps in new product development and learned earlier in this chapter about the importance of the introduction phase of the product life cycle (PLC). Because launching new products is so important, the management of this process is a serious matter. In some instances, one person handles new product development, but within larger organizations, new product development almost always requires many people. Often especially creative people with entrepreneurial skills get this assignment.

The challenge in large companies is to enlist specialists in different areas to work together in **venture teams**, which focus exclusively on the new product development effort. Sometimes the venture team is located away from traditional company offices in a remote location called a "skunk works." This colorful term originated with the Skunk Works, an illicit distillery in the comic strip *Li'l Abner*. Because illicit distilleries were bootleg operations, typically located in an isolated area with minimal formal oversight, organizations adopted the colorful description "skunk works" to refer to a small and often isolated department or facility that functions with minimal supervision (not because of its odor).[41]

venture teams
Groups of people within an organization who work together to focus exclusively on the development of a new product.

Why do you think David chose option 2?

How It Worked Out at General Mills

David chose option 2. David chose to position Fiber One as a great-tasting, high-fiber product. By emphasizing Fiber One's great taste, General Mills would offer a solution to the biggest obstacle people associated with eating fiber.

Under the "Surprisingly Great-Tasting High-Fiber" campaign, Fiber One has expanded to over eight product categories, and sales have increased tenfold over four years. The brand now exceeds $500 million in retail sales annually.

Refer back to **page 274** for David's story

MyMarketingLab™
Go to **mymktlab.com** to complete the problems marked with this icon ⭐ as well as additional Marketing Metrics questions only available in MyMarketingLab.

Objective Summary ➡ Key Terms ➡ Apply

CHAPTER 9
Study Map

1. Objective Summary (pp. 276–282)

Discuss the different product objectives and strategies a firm may choose.

Product planning is guided by the continual process of product management. Objectives for individual products may be related to introducing a new product, expanding the market of a regional product, or rejuvenating a mature product. For multiple products, firms may decide on a full- or a limited-line strategy. Often, companies decide to extend their product line with an upward, downward, or two-way stretch or with a filling-out strategy, or they may decide to contract a product line. Firms that have multiple product lines may choose a wide product mix with many different lines or a narrow one with few. Product quality objectives refer to the durability, reliability, degree of precision, ease of use and repair, or degree of aesthetic pleasure. One way that companies can improve quality is to use the Six Sigma method.

Key Terms

product management, p. 276

product line, p. 278

product line length, p. 279

stock-keeping unit (SKU), p. 279

cannibalization, p. 280

product mix, p. 280

product mix width, p. 280

product quality, p. 280

total quality management (TQM), p. 281

internal customers, p. 281

internal customer mind-set, p. 281

ISO 9000, p. 281

Six Sigma, p. 281

2. Objective Summary (pp. 282–286)

Understand how firms manage products throughout the product life cycle.

The product life cycle explains how products go through four stages from birth to death. During the introduction stage, marketers seek to get buyers to try the product and may use high prices to recover R&D costs. During the growth stage, characterized by rapidly increasing sales, marketers may introduce new product variations. In the maturity stage, sales peak and level off. Marketers respond by adding desirable new product features or market-development strategies. During the

decline stage, firms must decide whether to phase a product out slowly, drop it immediately, or, if there is residual demand, keep the product.

Key Terms

product life cycle (PLC), p. 282

introduction stage, p. 283

growth stage, p. 284

maturity stage, p. 285

decline stage, p. 285

3. Objective Summary (pp. 286–295)

Explain how branding and packaging strategies contribute to product identity.

A brand is a name, term, symbol, or other unique element of a product used to identify a firm's product. A brand should be selected that has a positive connotation and that is recognizable and memorable. Brand names need to be easy to say, spell, read, and remember and should fit the target market, the product's benefits, the customer's culture, and legal requirements. To protect a brand legally, marketers obtain trademark protection. Brands are important because they help maintain customer loyalty and because brand equity or value means a firm is able to attract new customers. Firms may develop individual brand strategies or market multiple items with a family or umbrella brand strategy. National or manufacturer brands are owned and sold by producers, whereas private-label or store brands carry the retail or chain store's trade name. Licensing means a firm sells another firm the right to use its brand name. In a cobranding strategy, two brands form a partnership to market a new product.

Packaging is the covering or container for a product and serves to protect a product and to allow for easy use and storage of the product. The colors, words, shapes, designs, pictures, and materials used in package design communicate a product's identity, benefits, and other important product information. Package designers must consider cost, product protection, and communication in creating a package that is functional, aesthetically pleasing, and not harmful to the environment. Product labeling in the U.S. is controlled by a number of federal laws aimed at making package labels more helpful to consumers.

Key Terms

brand, p. 286

trademark, p. 287

4. Objective Summary (pp. 296–297)

Describe how marketers structure organizations for new and existing product management.

To successfully manage existing products, the marketing organization may include brand managers, product category managers, and market managers. Large firms, however, often give new product responsibilities to new product managers or to venture teams, groups of specialists from different areas who work together for a single new product.

Key Terms

Chapter **Questions** and **Activities**

Concepts: Test Your Knowledge

9-1. What are the key stages in creating an effective product strategy? Why are these stages important? What is it about the stages that ensures that product planning works?

9-2. What is Six Sigma, and how is it used? what is DMAIC, and how can it work by involving all employees in the business?

9-3. Which is the third and longest stage of the product life cycle? What steps do marketers take during this stage?

9-4. What are the product decisions in the decline stage of a product?

9-5. What are the easy test and the fit test that can be applied when giving a name to a brand?

9-6. What is brand equity? Why is it important?

9-7. What is brand storytelling? How is it created and how does it work?

9-8. What does it mean to license a brand? What is cobranding?

9-9. What are the functions of packaging? What are some important elements of effective package design?

9-10. What should marketers know about package labeling?

9-11. Describe some of the ways firms organize the marketing function to manage existing products. What are the ways firms organize for the development of new products?

Activities: Apply What You've Learned

9-12. *In Class, 10–25 Minutes for Teams* You have been asked to give a presentation on the product life cycle to a small group of students who are interning at your firm this summer. Describe each of the stages of the product life cycle—introduction, growth, maturity, and decline—and give examples of products in the various stages. Include examples of products that are in transition stages as well as examples of some product failures and some products that have been discontinued.

9-13. *Creative Homework/Short Project* You have been recently promoted at P&G and have been tasked with identifying five cobranding opportunities. These cobranded products could be P&G products or a P&G product cobranded with another firm's brand. Describe each of the cobranding opportunities and define the advantages that would result from each.

9-14. *In Class, 10–25 Minutes for Teams* Assume that you are working in the marketing department of a major beverage chain. Your firm is not introducing a new product line as such, but wants to phase out disposable cups. The idea is called "wash and fill." Consumers will bring their own cups or mugs to the store and you will wash and fill the vessels for them. This is seen as a major step in reducing waste and damage to the local environment. Make a list of the advantages and disadvantages of the strategy. Develop your recommendations.

9-15. *In Class, 10–25 Minutes for Teams* As the board of a major global company with a multitude of different brands being sold in various countries around the world, how would you organize your brand and marketing efforts? Which type of organization would suit the company best, and how would you coordinate the work?

9-16. *Creative Homework/Short Project* Assume that you have been recently hired by Kellogg, the cereal manufacturer. You have been asked to work on a plan for redesigning the packaging for Kellogg's cereals. In a role-playing situation, present the following report to your marketing superior:

   a. Discussion of the problems or complaints customers have with current packaging

   b. Several different package alternatives

c. Your recommendations for changing packaging or for keeping the packaging the same

9-17. *For Further Research (Individual)* You are interested in the role that Six Sigma plays with regard to product quality. Using the Internet, research the concept of Six Sigma and find at least two case studies on companies that employ Six Sigma in their day-to-day activities. Summarize your findings in a short report.

Apply Marketing Metrics

The chapter introduced you to the concept of brand equity, an important measurement of the value vested in a product's brand in and of itself. Different formulas for calculating brand equity exist. One well-publicized approach is that of Interbrand, which annually publishes its Best 100 Global Brands list. Go to the location on the Interbrand website where they provide these rankings for the present and past years (**www.interbrand.com**), then click on "Best Global Brands." Peruse the list of brands and select any five in which you have interest. For each, observe whether brand equity has been trending up or down over the past few years.

9-18. How does Interbrand explain the changes (or stability) in each?

9-19. Do you agree with Interbrand's assessment or do you have another opinion about why your brand's equity is what it is?

Choices: What Do You Think?

⭐ **9-20.** *Critical Thinking* Brand equity means that a brand enjoys customer loyalty, perceived quality, and brand-name awareness. To what brands are you personally loyal? What is it about the product that creates brand loyalty and, thus, brand equity?

9-21. *Critical Thinking* Quality is an important product objective, but quality can mean different things for different products, such as durability, precision, aesthetic appeal, and so on. What does quality mean for the following products?
a. Smart phone
b. Pop-up tent
c. Athletic wear
d. Vacuum cleaner
e. Pet food
f. College education

9-22. *Critical Thinking* Many times firms take advantage of their popular, well-known brands by developing brand extensions because they know that the brand equity of the original or parent brand will be transferred to the new product. If a new product is of poor quality, it can damage the reputation of the parent brand, while a new product that is of superior quality can enhance the parent brand's reputation. What are some examples of brand extensions that have damaged and that have enhanced the parent brand equity?

⭐ **9-23.** *Ethics* According to a U.K. study of 1,000 people, 91 percent felt that "the way company behaves towards its customers and communities is influential when making a purchase."[42] Do you share the same belief? Have you ever looked up, for example, a company's environmental initiatives before making a purchase? How important is a brand's ethical behavior to

you? Have you ever *not* purchased a brand because of the ethics of the company behind the brand?

9-24. *Critical Thinking* Sometimes marketers seem to stick with the same packaging ideas year after year regardless of whether they are the best possible design. Following is a list of products. For each one, discuss what (if any) problems you have with the package of the brand you use. Then think of ways the package could be improved. Why do you think marketers don't change the old packaging? What would be the results if they adopted your package ideas?
a. Dry cereal
b. Laundry detergent
c. Frozen orange juice
d. Gallon of milk
e. Potato chips
f. Loaf of bread

9-25. *Critical Thinking* The FDA is currently working to update the Nutrition Facts label on most food packages. In addition to a redesign of the label to make some information more prominent, the label would contain information about added sugars, potassium, and vitamin D, and serving sizes would be based on what consumers actually eat, not what they should eat (serving sizes on current labels were originally set 20 years ago). Do you think such labeling updates are necessary for today's consumers? How might the proposed changes affect the way people eat or drink?

9-26. *Ethics* You learned in this chapter that it's hard to *legally* protect brand names across product categories—Quaker and Apple, for example, and also Delta—which is an airline and a faucet. But what about the *ethics* of borrowing a name and applying it to some unrelated products? Think of some new business you might like to start up. Now consider some possible names for the business that are already in use as brands in other, unrelated categories. Do you think it would be ethical to borrow one of those names? Why or why not?

Miniproject: Learn by Doing

In any supermarket in any town, you will surely find thousands of examples of product packaging. This miniproject is designed to give you a better understanding of how branding, cobranding, and packaging all work together to compete for your purchasing dollars.

a. Go to a typical supermarket in your community.
b. Select two product categories of interest to you: ice cream, cereal, laundry detergent, soup, frozen meals, and so on.
c. For each product category, visit that area of the store. Write down a list of the three items that attract your attention first. Identify what it was about the product that attracted your attention (the brand, cobrand, or package design).
d. For each of the three products, identify which you are most likely to buy based on the first look alone. Explain why you chose this product.

9-27. Pick up each of three products and study their package design and any information you can find about the product. Now which product are you most likely to buy? Explain why you chose this product.

9-28. Present a summary to your class on what you learned about the brands and packaging in your two product categories.

Marketing in **Action** Case   Real Choices at Starbucks

How much Starbucks can Americans consume? Whatever the answer may be, the company doesn't think the country has reached that point. Troy Alstead, chief operating officer, says, "We are a long ways from saturation." As the company expands its retail locations, it is also expanding its menu choices.

The Starbuck's story began as a local coffee bean roaster and retailer of whole bean and ground coffee, tea, and spices. From 1971, a lone store in Seattle's Pike Place Market has grown into the largest coffeehouse company in the world. The Seattle-based Starbucks Corporation is an international coffee and coffeehouse chain with over 21,000 stores in 64 countries, including approximately 13,000 in the U.S., nearly 1,300 in Canada, and more than 1,000 in Japan. The Starbucks product selection includes drip-brewed coffee, espresso-based hot drinks, other hot and cold drinks, coffee beans, salads, hot and cold sandwiches and paninis, pastry, snacks, and items such as mugs and tumblers.

The VIA platform of Ready Brew instant beverages, first launched in 2009, has been an area of successful expansion. The platform is focused on coffee and espresso and has grown to over $100 million in global sales. Until recently, it was not utilizing a potential growth opportunity, the caffè latte. A latte is a coffee-based drink made with espresso and steamed milk. The latte is the newest addition to the VIA instant-coffee product line in the U.S. and Canada. Customers only have to add water to the new VIA Caffè Mocha Latte and Vanilla Latte packs. This new option contains milk, sugar, and all natural flavors to reproduce the taste of a Starbucks caffè latte. Starbucks hopes that the new offering increases the success it has attained within the VIA format.

Food represents another significant area for growth. As much as 75 percent of all transactions for the retailer contain some type of food item. In 2012, Starbucks purchased the San Francisco–based La Boulange bakery brand for $100 million. This purchase led the company to rebrand its bakery products with the La Boulange name. The initial reaction to the new branding has been positive. According to Scott Maw, chief financial officer, "What we see in the results of La Boulange—the customer reaction, the pride that our partners have in an elevated food experience—has well met all the expectations—rather lofty expectations—we had at launch."

With any product strategy change, there are inevitable obstacles that need to be managed. Choosing the correct ingredients and flavors for the VIA Lattes is not easy. Dealing with different customer groups can also pose dilemmas. For instance, there is a current campaign by vegans for Starbucks to offer the VIA Pumpkin Spice Latte in a gluten-free version.

In addition, the La Boulange branding strategy has been fraught with challenges. The problems range from choosing the correct menu items to educating customers about the correct way to warm the items to various supply chain issues. Whether these changes are successful in the long term will be a function of how well Starbucks manages the situation.

You Make the Call

9-29. What is the decision facing Starbucks?

9-30. What factors are important in understanding this decision situation?

9-31. What are the alternatives?

9-32. What decision(s) do you recommend?

9-33. What are some ways to implement your recommendation?

Sources: Based on Tamara Walsh, "Starbucks Makes a Big Bet on New Product Mix in 2014," January 8, 2014, **www.fool.com/investing/general/2014/01/08/starbucks-makes-a-big-bet-on-new-product-mix-in-20.aspx** (accessed May 11, 2014); Starbucks, "Company Profile," **www.starbucks.com/about-us/company-information** (accessed May 11, 2014); and Eric Schroeder, "Starbucks Still in 'Early Days' of La Boulange Roll-Out," March 13, 2014, **www.foodbusinessnews.net/articles/news_home/Business_News/2014/03/Starbucks_still_in_early_days.aspx?ID={242368C5-383C-4827-AEDF-E01EC234B2A9}&cck=1** (accessed May 12, 2014).

MyMarketingLab™

Go to **mymktlab.com** for Auto-graded writing questions as well as the following Assisted-graded writing questions:

9-34. *Creative Homework/Short Project.* You may think of your college or university as an organization that offers a line of different educational products. Assume that you have been hired as a marketing consultant by your university to examine and make recommendations for extending its product line. Develop alternatives that the university might consider:

    a. Upward line stretch

    b. Downward line stretch

    c. Two-way stretch

    d. Filling-out strategy

    Describe how each extension might be accomplished. Evaluate each alternative.

9-35. *Creative Homework/Short Project.* Assume that you are the vice president of marketing for a firm that markets a large number of specialty food items (gourmet sauces, marinades, relishes, and so on). Your firm is interested in improving its marketing management structure. You are considering several alternatives: using a brand manager structure, having product category managers, or focusing on market managers. Outline the advantages and disadvantages of each type of organization. What is your recommendation?

Price: What Is the Value Proposition Worth?

Betsy Fleming
▼ A Decision Maker at Converse College

Betsy Fleming has served as president of Converse College in Spartanburg, South Carolina, since October 2005. She graduated magna cum laude from Harvard University with an AB in fine arts, received an MA in the history of design from the Royal College of Art in London, and earned a PhD in the history of art from Yale University. Her career began with administrative and curatorial positions at the Frick Collection and the Metropolitan Museum of Art in New York, the J. Paul Getty Trust in Los Angeles, the Yale University Art Gallery, and the Victoria and Albert Museum in London. She has taught at Yale and Parsons School of Design. Immediately prior to her arrival at Converse, Betsy was executive director of the Gibbes Museum of Art in Charleston, South Carolina. An Aspen Institute Liberty Fellow, she has served on the boards of the Women's College Coalition and the National Association of Independent Colleges and currently serves on the Board of Directors for the Federal Reserve Bank of Richmond, Charlotte Branch, and BlueCross BlueShield of South Carolina.

Betsy's Info

What I do when I'm not working?
For the body, biking, power walking, and yoga; for the spirit, indulging my love of the arts; and, for the mind, reading nonfiction, especially biographies.

First job out of school?
Selling expensive socks and gloves at Gorsuch, Ltd. in Vail, Colorado.

A job-related mistake I wish I hadn't made?
Publicly criticizing an important member of my senior leadership team during a team meeting.

Business book I'm reading now?
Mindset: The New Psychology of Success by Carol Dweck and *Lean In* by Sheryl Sandberg.

My heroes?
Teddy Roosevelt and Gloria Steinem.

My motto to live by?
Think and live out of the box.

What drives me?
Empowering and celebrating human creativity, expression and accomplishment.

My management style?
Collaborative with a priority on accountability.

My pet peeve?
Telling me, "But, we've always done it this way."

Here's my problem...

Real **People,** Real **Choices**

In 2013, the administration of Converse College, a private master's university located in South Carolina, realized that escalating tuition costs were creating serious problems for current and potential students. Higher-education costs are exploding, even while median U.S. household income has remained mostly flat for the past 10 years. Betsy and her staff decided to take a serious look at the college's pricing model. Their objective was threefold: (1) address the affordability concerns of private higher education within the marketplace, (2) recapture a greater portion of the middle class market that was feeling priced out of the private college experience, and (3) develop a more sustainable and transparent operating model for the college. Betsy launched a strategic enrollment planning process that involved extensive research to guide data-driven decisions. The outcomes of this work would allow her to partner with the Board of Trustees and key stakeholders to cultivate buy-in and approval for a new pricing model. The working group identified possible solutions to the high-tuition dilemma.

Betsy considered her **Options** 1·2·3

1 Option

Reset tuition to a significantly lower price for traditional undergraduate students. The upward spiral of tuition prices within higher education is of national concern, and being a leader in offering a different business model was an attractive opportunity to help the school stand out from the crowd. Since Converse projected that tuition would increase on average 3.5 percent each year, students would save quite a bit over several years because of the compounded savings that would result from a price drop. This option would enable Converse to promote a discounted tuition to encourage a larger number of qualified applicants to consider the school—many were unwilling to take a first look because they assumed that a small private school like Converse would be too expensive. However, this would be a risky move because some people who equate high tuition with prestige might assume that Converse's quality is lower than private schools with much higher tuition prices. A price reduction would also require Converse to reduce scholarships proportionately to the tuition decrease. This would create a healthier operating model for the school since scholarships would come from endowed funds alone rather than being supplemented by revenue from inflated tuition. But it could hamper the school's ability to recruit well-qualified students from families who still could not afford even reduced private school tuition (which was only marginally higher than in-state public universities).

2 Option

Freeze tuition for each incoming student from the time she matriculated until she graduated. Families would be secure in the knowledge that they would not face annual increases in tuition that leave them challenged to afford college over a four-year period. This action would provide an immediate incentive and financial relief for classes entering Converse in the next year or two. On the other hand, a temporary freeze would provide only a short-term "Band-Aid" for a long-term problem. Converse incurs annual increases in operating costs, and it must generate additional revenue to offset that cost. Rather than having the entire student body share those increased costs through the form of an annual tuition increase, the next incoming class would shoulder the cost in the form of a much higher tuition increase. This would ultimately make tuition spiral upward at an even faster rate.

3 Option

Provide students with a Loan Repayment Program (LRP), which guarantees that any student without employment after college would have her loans covered by an insurance policy. This guarantee would relieve the financial burden for graduates who could not find employment and provide some peace of mind for their families. It would demonstrate quite forcefully that the school had "skin in the game" in terms of preparing its students to be competitive in the workplace. However, Converse would pay an insurance premium for each student who enrolled, which would increase costs and ultimately result in tuition increases (thus perpetuating the upward spiral). And, paradoxically, this benefit contradicted the school's mission to help students find gainful employment—it would only reward graduates who were not successful at finding a job.

Now put yourself in Betsy's shoes. Which option would you choose, and why?

You Choose

Which **Option** would you choose, and **why**?
1. ☐YES ☐NO   2. ☐YES ☐NO   3. ☐YES ☐NO

See what **option** Betsy chose on **page 334** ➡

Bitcoin
The most popular and fastest-growing digital currency.

price
The assignment of value, or the amount the consumer must exchange to receive the offering.

Chapter 10

1

OBJECTIVE

Explain the importance of pricing and how marketers set objectives for their pricing strategies.

(pp. 304–308)

"Yes, But What Does It Cost?"

"If you have to ask how much it is, you can't afford it!" We've all heard that, but how often do you buy something without asking the price? If price weren't an issue, we'd all drive dream cars, take trips to exotic places, and live like royalty. In the real world, though, most of us need to at least consider a product's price before we buy it.

In the past two chapters, we've talked about creating and managing products. But to create value for customers, marketers must do more than just create a fantastic new (or existing) widget with all the bells and whistles consumers want. Equally (if not more) important is pricing the new offering so that consumers are willing to fork over their hard-earned cash to own the product. The question of what to charge for a product is a central part of the marketing plan.

In this chapter, we'll tackle the basic question—what is price? We'll look at pricing objectives and the roles that demand, costs, revenues, and the environment play in the pricing decision process. Then we'll explore specific pricing strategies and tactics. Finally, we'll look at the dynamic world of pricing on the Internet and at some psychological, legal, and ethical aspects of pricing.

The **Cutting Edge**

Digital Currencies: Bitcoin

History shows a series of innovations in how consumers buy shoes, food, and services. Coins replaced bartering and were the first currency. Paper money followed coins, and in the 1950s Diner's Club introduced the first credit card that people could use to pay for meals in restaurants. Today, Americans use plastic more than money, and some airlines and restaurants won't even take cash. So what's next? Most likely the transition to digital cash.

Right now, **Bitcoin** is the currency alternative everyone is talking about. It's a bit hard to understand and quite controversial but is quickly establishing itself as an alternative to traditional Benjamins. The Bitcoin system was created by a shadowy software developer named Satoshi Nakamoto (nobody knows for certain just who he or she really is). The Bitcoin units are generated by open-source software; each additional Bitcoin can enter the system only after a sophisticated computer solves an encryption problem in a process called *mining*. This means there are only a very limited number of them around—as of today, about 12,747,000 XBT (XBT is the abbreviation for Bitcoin)—so some people are trying very hard to snatch them up, as they gamble they will be worth a lot more in the future.[1] You can buy this new digital currency on several *Bitcoin exchanges*, or individuals can purchase them from each other using mobile apps that store their Bitcoins in a "virtual wallet." Note: Don't plan on walking around with a shiny new Bitcoin in your pocket; they don't really exist in the sense that you can touch or see one!

Why are Bitcoins so controversial? The main reason is that unlike other "real" currencies, they are not controlled by a single entity like the U.S. Treasury, which puts Bitcoins beyond the grasp of governmental control. This means there are no "middlemen" (like banks) involved in the process that collect transaction fees (which is why many businesses like this option).

However, it also means that transactions occur only from person to person, so there is no record of them, and this opens the potential for Bitcoins to show up in illegal transactions (such as laundering drug money).

What is the future of Bitcoin? Right now it's a bit like the Wild West. Many large companies (and governments) don't accept them as valid currency, and tax agencies are starting to make noises about regulating them (good luck). On the other hand, some big companies, including Amazon, Target, and even Victoria's Secret, now honor Bitcoins, so the movement is starting to snowball.[2] Like other forms of computer code, Bitcoins can be hacked (i.e., stolen) by clever programmers, and conceivably someone's virtual wallet could be eaten alive by a nasty computer virus. Despite these drawbacks, many think the Bitcoin network will continue to grow in value and in usage because of a number of distinct advantages of digital currency. Perhaps most important to consumers like you is that it eliminates the risk of credit card fraud that attracts criminals to steal personal customer information and credit card numbers. Instead of pulling out your credit card in the checkout lane to pay for your purchase, you use your smart phone to take a picture of the QR code displayed by the cash register. You click "Confirm," and your app pays for your purchase with Bitcoins. There is also a societal benefit from the use of Bitcoin. Many lower-income consumers do not have bank accounts. Instead, they must often pay fees of 10 percent or higher each time they need to send a money order to a payee. With Bitcoin, such payments would cost only a fraction of that amount. Many believe that the advantages of Bitcoin will contribute to increased quality of life for those living in the world's poorest countries. In the future, paper money as we know it may cease to exist.[3] What are the odds of this happening? Just flip a coin to find out.

What Is Price?

As we said in Chapter 1, **price** is the assignment of value, or the amount the consumer must exchange to receive the offering or product. Payment may be in the form of money, goods, services, favors, votes, or anything else that has *value* to the other party. As we also explained in Chapter 1, marketing is the process that creates exchanges of things of value. We usually think of this exchange as people trading money for a good or a service. But in some marketplace practices, price can mean exchanges of nonmonetary value as well. Long before societies minted coins, people exchanged one good or service for another. This practice still occurs today. For example, someone who owns a home at a mountain ski resort may exchange a weekend stay for car repair or dental work. No money changes hands, but there still is an exchange of value (just ask the Internal Revenue Service).

Other nonmonetary costs often are important to marketers. What is the cost of wearing seat belts? What is it worth to people to camp out in a clean national park? It is also important to consider an *opportunity cost*, or the value of something we give up to obtain something else. For example, the cost of going to college includes more than tuition—it also includes the income that the student could have earned by working instead of going to classes (no, we're not trying to make you feel guilty). And what about a public service campaign designed to reduce alcohol-related accidents? The cost to the individual is either agreeing to abstain and be a designated driver or shelling out for taxi fare. The value is reducing the risk of having a serious or possibly fatal accident. Unfortunately, too many people feel the chance of having an accident is so slim that the cost of abstaining from drinking is too high.

As Figure 10.1 shows, the elements of price planning include six steps: developing pricing objectives, estimating demand, determining costs, evaluating the pricing environment, choosing a pricing strategy, and developing pricing tactics. In this chapter, we talk about how marketers go through these steps for successful price planning.

Step 1: Develop Pricing Objectives

The first crucial step in price planning is to develop pricing objectives. These must support the broader objectives of the firm, such as maximizing shareholder value, as well as its overall marketing objectives, such as increasing market share. Figure 10.2 provides examples of different types of pricing objectives. Let's take a closer look at these.

Profit Objectives

As we discussed in Chapter 2, often a firm's overall objectives relate to a certain level of profit it hopes to realize. When pricing strategies are determined by profit objectives, the focus is on a target level of profit growth or a desired net profit margin. A profit objective is important to firms that believe profit is what motivates shareholders and bankers to invest in a company.

Because firms usually produce an entire product line and/or a product mix, profit objectives may focus on pricing for the firm's entire portfolio of products. In such cases, marketers develop pricing strategies that maximize the profits of the entire portfolio rather than focusing on the costs or profitability of each individual product. For example, it may be better to price one product especially high and lose sales on it if that decision causes customers to instead purchase a product that has a higher profit margin.

Although profits are an important consideration in the pricing of all goods and services, they are critical when the product is a *fad*. Fad products, from Tamagotchis

Figure 10.1 *Process* | Elements of Price Planning

Successful price planning includes a series of orderly steps beginning with setting pricing objectives.

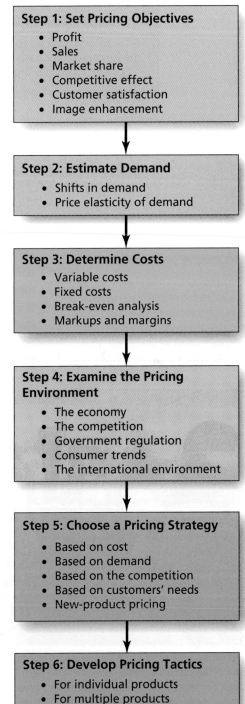

Step 1: Set Pricing Objectives
- Profit
- Sales
- Market share
- Competitive effect
- Customer satisfaction
- Image enhancement

Step 2: Estimate Demand
- Shifts in demand
- Price elasticity of demand

Step 3: Determine Costs
- Variable costs
- Fixed costs
- Break-even analysis
- Markups and margins

Step 4: Examine the Pricing Environment
- The economy
- The competition
- Government regulation
- Consumer trends
- The international environment

Step 5: Choose a Pricing Strategy
- Based on cost
- Based on demand
- Based on the competition
- Based on customers' needs
- New-product pricing

Step 6: Develop Pricing Tactics
- For individual products
- For multiple products
- Distribution-based tactics
- Discounting for channel members

Figure 10.2 *Process* | Pricing Objectives

The first step in price planning is to develop pricing objectives that support the broader objectives of the firm.

Sales or Market Share
Develop bundle pricing offers in order to increase market share

Profit
Set prices to allow for an 8 percent profit margin on all goods sold.

Image Enhancement
Alter pricing policies to reflect the increased emphasis on the product's quality image.

Pricing Objectives

Competitive Effect
Alter pricing strategy during first quarter of the year to increase sales during competitor's introduction of a new product.

Customer Satisfaction
Alter price levels to match customer expectations.

APPLYING ▼ Pricing Objectives

Betsy's objectives in pricing were to 1) address affordability concerns, (2) recapture a greater portion of the middle class market and (3) develop a more sustainable and transparent model for the College.

to Silly Bandz or Slap Wraps, have a short market life; this makes a profit objective essential to allow the firm to recover its investment in a short time. In such cases, the firm must harvest profits before customers lose interest and move on to the next fad. Think about the Snuggie, for example. Although many people like to make fun of this quirky blanket with sleeves, its inventors laughed all the way to the bank. Introduced in just 2008, 25 million Snuggies had been sold by the end of 2010.[4] A company that hawks a snuggly blankey like this has to move quickly to unload its "inventory" before the next cool idea replaces it.

Sales or Market Share Objectives

Often the objective of a pricing strategy is to maximize sales (either in dollars or in units) or to increase market share. Does setting a price intended to increase unit sales or market share simply mean pricing the product lower than the competition? Sometimes, yes. Providers of cable and satellite TV services such as Time Warner, Comcast, DIRECTV, and AT&T U-verse relentlessly offer consumers better deals that include more TV, wireless Internet, and telephone service. But lowering prices is not always necessary to increase market share. If a company's product has a competitive advantage, keeping the price at the same level as other firms may satisfy sales objectives. And such "price wars" can have a negative effect when consumers switch from one producer to another simply because the price changes.

Competitive Effect Objectives

Sometimes strategists design the pricing plan to dilute the competition's marketing efforts. In these cases, a firm may deliberately try to preempt or reduce the impact of a

The plight of U.S. airlines is a good example of how bad pricing decisions can hurt an entire industry. In 1978, the U.S. Congress passed the Airline Deregulation Act, which allowed airlines to set their own fares and fly whatever domestic routes they wished while allowing new airlines to enter the industry. From about 1982 to 1992, the airline industry engaged in a fierce price war, lowering the per-mile fare nearly 25 percent (accounting for inflation of the dollar) while costs such as labor and fuel more than doubled. As a result, during that time period, the airlines lost over $10 billion—more than they had earned since the start of commercial air travel.

dundanim/Shutterstock

Metrics Moment

One criticism of marketing is that these operations lag behind other business areas in terms of measuring performance and how much they contribute to the success of the overall business. In fact, for most of marketing's history as a field, sales volume response to marketing expenditures was the most frequently cited metric, either in sales units or in dollar revenue. But, of course, many factors influence sales volume, so it is hard for marketing to claim a direct one-to-one relationship between marketing effectiveness and increases in sales.

Market share is the percentage of a market (defined in terms of either sales units or revenue) accounted for by a specific firm, product lines, or brands. Market share is quoted within the context of a particular set of competitors.[5] For example, the set of global auto manufacturers (which is only a few firms) might claim market share figures that add up to 100 percent of total U.S. sales. Market share is often a "bragging right"

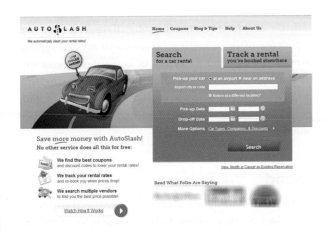

E-commerce sites like Autoslash compete on price in order to increase the size of their customer base.

for a firm—sort of a "We're number one!" cheer. But some strategy gurus question whether a market share number is actually very useful as a marketing performance metric because there are numerous cases in which firms, product lines, or brands that do not have number one bragging rights in market share are consistently more profitable than their higher-share competitors. Why would this be? In this chapter, you will learn about cost concepts like *contribution margin* that tell the full story.

Here's an example. Everybody has heard of the brands Gillette and Schick in the U.S. razor and blade market. For years when Gillette was an independent firm (it has since been acquired by Procter & Gamble), the company boasted about a 60 percent share of the U.S. market versus Schick's share of less than 20 percent. Yet the Schick line consistently outperformed Gillette in bottom-line financial contribution—not just percentage profit but actual dollar profit! This was due largely to huge differences in costs, mainly the research-and-development and marketing expenses Gillette incurred in always trying to be the market innovator and grand advertiser (think Super Bowl ads). As a result, Gillette became a takeover target and the rest is history. Lesson: The old adage that "we'll make it up on volume" doesn't work when your variable costs per unit are ridiculously high versus the competition.

Apply the Metrics

1. Pick any industry and identify the main competitors—this can be any type of product or service line of your choice as long as there are several easily identified competing brands (Hint: Publicly traded firms are easier to research then privately held firms.) Do a little research to find out how their market shares stack up.
2. Then, for the same firms, take a look at their most recent reported profits. Based on your findings, does a higher market share translate into a better profit picture?

rival's pricing changes. That's what happened in Australia when Virgin Australia airlines began undercutting competitor Qantas's prices on domestic routes in 2013 in order to attract Qantas passengers. Qantas fought back to defend its 65 percent market share with plans to add capacity and reduce prices. Early in 2014, Qantas announced a $235 million loss and 5,000 jobs cut. By April 2014, Qantas reported its number of passengers down 1.5 percent.[6]

market share
The percentage of a market (defined in terms of either sales units or revenue) accounted for by a specific firm, product lines, or brands.

Customer Satisfaction Objectives

Many quality-focused firms believe that profits result from making customer satisfaction the primary objective. These firms believe that if they focus solely on short-term profits, they will lose sight of their objective to retain customers for the long term. Retail giant Walmart, long known as the "Every Day Low Price" leader, is hoping to make its customers even more satisfied with its pricing. Following the lead of stores like Target and Best Buy that offer to meet the lower prices of their rivals, Walmart is introducing its Savings Catcher, an online tool that customers can use in the store to compare the prices of 80,000 food and household products to those of the competitors. Customers need only sign on to the Internet site and type in the number on their receipt. Savings Catcher automatically compares the prices on the receipt with the prices at other local stores and issues the customer an online gift card with the savings.[7]

Image Enhancement Objectives

Consumers often use price to make inferences about the quality of a product. In fact, marketers know that price is often an important means of communicating not only quality but also image to prospective customers. The image-enhancement function of pricing is particularly important with **prestige products** (or luxury products) that have a high price and appeal to status-conscious consumers. Most of us would agree that the high price tag on a Rolex watch, a Louis Vuitton handbag, or a Rolls-Royce car, although representing the higher costs of producing the product, is vital to shaping an image of an extraordinary product that only the wealthy can afford (not counting the "real" Rolex you buy for $10 from that guy on the street).

prestige products
Products that have a high price and that appeal to status-conscious consumers.

2

OBJECTIVE

Describe how marketers use costs, demands, revenue, and the pricing environment to make pricing decisions.

(pp. 308–320)

Costs, Demand, Revenue, and the Pricing Environment

Once a marketer decides on its pricing objectives, it is time to begin the actual process of price setting. In order to set the right price, marketers must understand a variety of quantitative and qualitative factors that can mean success or failure for the pricing strategy. As shown in Figure 10.3, these include an estimate of demand, knowledge of costs and revenue, and an understanding of the pricing environment.

Step 2: Estimate Demand

The second step in price planning is to estimate demand. *Demand* refers to customers' desire for a product: How much of a product are they willing to buy as the price of the product goes up or down? Obviously, marketers should know the answer to this question before they set prices. Therefore, one of the earliest steps marketers take in price planning is to estimate demand for their products.

Demand Curves

Economists use a graph of a *demand curve* to illustrate the effect of price on the quantity demanded of a product. The demand curve, which can be a curved or straight line, shows the quantity of a product that customers will buy in a market during a period of time at various prices if all other factors remain the same.

Figure 10.4 shows demand curves for normal and prestige products. The vertical axis for the demand curve represents the different prices that a firm might charge for a product (P). The horizontal axis shows the number of units or quantity (Q) of the product demanded. The demand curve for most goods (that we show on the left side of Figure 10.4) slopes downward and to the right. As the price of the product goes up (P_1 to P_2), the number of units that customers are willing to buy goes down (Q_1 to Q_2). If prices decrease, customers will buy more. This is the *law of demand*. For example, if the price of bananas goes up, customers will probably buy fewer of them. And if the price gets really high, customers will eat their cereal without bananas.

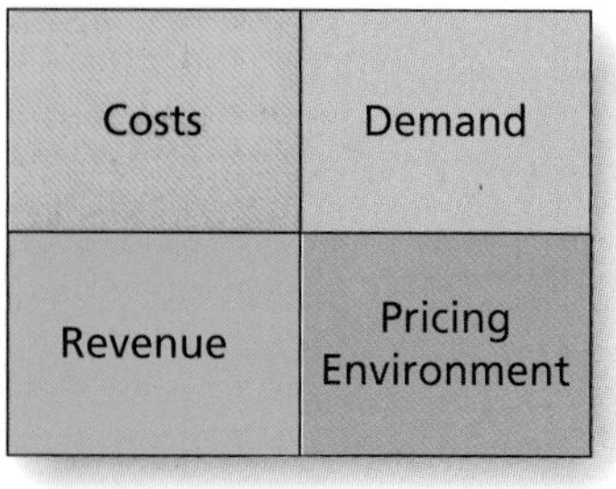

There are, however, exceptions to this typical price–quantity relationship. In fact, there are situations in which (otherwise sane) people desire a product more as it *increases* in price. For prestige products such as luxury cars or jewelry, a price hike may actually result in an *increase* in the quantity consumers demand because they see the product as more valuable. In such cases, the demand curve slopes upward. The right-hand side of Figure 10.4 shows the "backward-bending" demand curve we associate with prestige products. If the price

Figure 10.3 *Process* | Factors in Price Setting

To set the right price, marketers must understand a variety of quantitative and qualitative factors.

Costs	Demand
Revenue	Pricing Environment

Figure 10.4 📷 *Snapshot* | Demand Curves for Normal and Prestige Products

There is an inverse relationship between price and demand for normal products. For prestige products, demand will increase—to a point—as price increases or will decrease as price decreases.

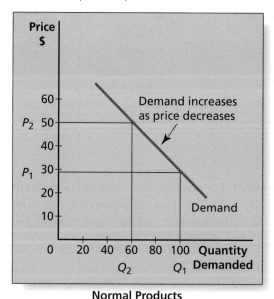

Normal Products

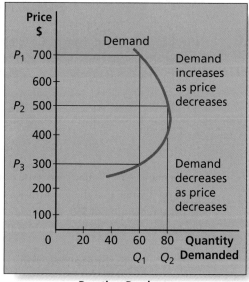

Prestige Products

decreases, consumers perceive the product to be less desirable, and demand may decrease. You can see that if the price decreases from P_2 to P_3, the quantity demanded decreases from Q_2 to Q_1. On the other hand, if the price increases, consumers think the product is more desirable. This is what happens if the price begins at P_3 and then goes up to P_2; quantity increases from Q_1 to Q_2. Still, the higher-price/higher-demand relationship has its limits. If the firm increases the price too much (say, from P_2 to P_1), making the product unaffordable for all but a few buyers, demand will begin to decrease. The direction the backward-bending curve takes shows this.

Shifts in Demand

The demand curves we've shown assume that all factors other than price stay the same. But what if they don't? What if the company improves the product? What happens when there is a glitzy new advertising campaign that turns a product into a "must-have" for a lot of people? What if stealthy paparazzi catch Brad Pitt using the product at home? Any of these things could cause an *upward shift* of the demand curve. An upward shift in the demand curve means that at any given price, demand is greater than before the shift occurs. And the demand shift would no doubt be even more precipitous if Pitt's daughter Shiloh Nouvel Jolie-Pitt were also to make an appearance in the pic!

📷 Figure 10.5 shows the upward shift of the demand curve as it moves from D_1 to D_2. At D_1, before the shift occurs, customers will be willing to purchase the quantity Q_1 (or 80 units in Figure 10.5) at the given price, P (or $60 in Figure 10.5). For example, customers at a particular store may buy 80 barbecue grills at $60 a grill. But then the store runs a huge advertising campaign featuring Queen Latifah on her patio using the barbecue grill. The demand curve shifts from D_1 to D_2. (The store keeps the price at $60.) Take a look at how the quantity demanded has changed to Q_2. In our example, the store is now selling 200 barbecue grills at $60 per grill. From a marketing standpoint, this shift is the best of all worlds. Without lowering prices, the company can sell more of its product. As a result, total revenues go up, and so do profits, unless, of course, the new promotion costs as much as those potential additional profits.

Figure 10.5 📷 *Snapshot* | Shift in the Demand Curve

Changes in the environment or in company efforts can cause a shift in the demand curve. A great advertising campaign, for example, can shift the demand curve upward.

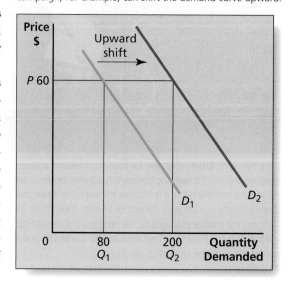

Table 10.1 | Estimating Demand for Pizza

Number of families in market	180,000
Average number of pizzas per family per year	6
Total annual market demand	1,080,000
Company's predicted share of the total market	3 percent
Estimated annual company demand	32,400 pizzas
Estimated monthly company demand	2,700 pizzas
Estimated weekly company demand	675 pizzas

Demand curves may also shift downward. For example, if a rumor spread at warp speed on Twitter that the gas grill was faulty and could cause dangerous fires, even with the price remaining at $60, the curve would shift downward, and the quantity demanded would drop so that the store could sell only 30 or 40 grills.

Estimate Demand

It's extremely important for marketers to understand and accurately estimate demand. Plans for production of the product as well as marketing activities and budgets must all be based on reasonably accurate estimates of potential sales.

So how do marketers reasonably estimate potential sales? Marketers predict total demand first by identifying the number of buyers or potential buyers for their product and then multiplying that estimate times the average amount each member of the target market is likely to purchase. Table 10.1 shows how a small business, such as a start-up pizza restaurant, estimates demand in markets it expects to reach. For example, the pizza entrepreneur may estimate that there are 180,000 consumer households in his market who would be willing to buy his pizza and that each household would purchase an average of six pizzas a year. The total annual demand is 1,080,000 pizzas (hold the anchovies on at least one of those, please).

Once the marketer estimates total demand, the next step is to predict what the company's market share is likely to be. The company's estimated demand is then its share of the whole (estimated) pie. In our pizza example, the entrepreneur may feel that he can gain 3 percent of this market, or about 2,700 pizzas per month—not bad for a new start-up business. Of course, such projections need to take into consideration other factors that might affect demand, such as new competitors entering the market, the state of the economy, and changing consumer tastes, such as a sudden demand for low-carb takeout food.

Price Elasticity of Demand

Marketers also need to know how their customers are likely to react to a price change. In particular, it is critical to understand whether a change in price will have a large or a small impact on demand. How much can a firm increase or decrease its price until it sees a marked change in sales? If the price of a pizza goes up $1, will people switch to subs and burgers? What would happen if the pizza went up $2? Or even $5?

In the real world, factors other than the price and marketing activities influence demand. If it rains, the demand for umbrellas increases and the demand for tee times on a golf course is a wash. The development of new products may influence demand for old ones. Even though a few firms may still produce phonographs, the introduction of cassette tapes and then CDs and iPods has all but eliminated the demand for new vinyl records and turntables on which to play them.

Edyta Pawlowska/Shutterstock

Price elasticity of demand is a measure of the sensitivity of customers to changes in price: If the price changes by 10 percent, what will be the percentage change in demand for the product? The word *elasticity* indicates that changes in price usually cause demand to stretch or retract like a rubber band. We calculate price elasticity of demand as follows:

$$\text{Price elasticity of demand} = \frac{\text{Percentage change in quantity demand}}{\text{Percentage change in price}}$$

Sometimes customers are very sensitive to changes in prices and a change in price results in a substantial change in the quantity they demand. In such instances, we have a case of **elastic demand**. In other situations, a change in price has little or no effect on the quantity consumers are willing to buy. We describe this as **inelastic demand**. Let's use the formula in this example: Suppose the pizza maker finds (from experience or from marketing research) that lowering the price of his pizza 10 percent (from $10 per pizza to $9) will cause a 15 percent increase in demand. He would calculate the price elasticity of demand as 15 divided by 10. The price elasticity of demand would be 1.5. If the price elasticity of demand is greater than one, demand is elastic; that is, consumers respond to the price decrease by demanding more. Or, if the price increases, consumers will demand less. 📷 Figure 10.6 shows these calculations.

As 📷 Figure 10.7 illustrates, when demand is elastic, changes in price and in total revenues (total sales) work in opposite directions. If the price is increased, revenues decrease. If the price is decreased, total revenues increase. With elastic demand, the demand curve

price elasticity of demand
The percentage change in unit sales that results from a percentage change in price.

elastic demand
Demand in which changes in price have large effects on the amount demanded.

inelastic demand
Demand in which changes in price have little or no effect on the amount demanded.

Elastic demand

Price changes from $10 to $9.
$10 − 9 = $1
1/10 = 10% change in price
Demand changes from 2,700 per month to 3,100 per month

	3,100
	− 2,700
Increase	400 pizzas
Percentage increase	400/2,700 = .148 ~ 15% change in demand

$$\text{Price elasticity of demand} = \frac{\text{percentage change in quantity demanded}}{\text{percentage change in price}}$$

$$\text{Price elasticity of demand} = \frac{15\%}{10\%} = 1.5$$

Inelastic demand

Price changes from $10 to $9.
$10 − 9 = $1
1/10 = 10% change in price
Demand changes from 2,700 per month to 2,835 per month

	2,835
	− 2,700
Increase	135 pizzas
Percentage increase	135/2,700 = 0.05 ~ 5% change in demand

$$\text{Price elasticity of demand} = \frac{\text{percentage change in quantity demanded}}{\text{percentage change in price}}$$

$$\text{Price elasticity of demand} = \frac{5\%}{10\%} = 0.5$$

Figure 10.6 📷 *Snapshot* | Price Elasticity of Demand

Marketers know that elasticity of demand is an important pricing metric.

Figure 10.7 📷 *Snapshot* |

Price-Elastic and Price-Inelastic

Price elasticity of demand represents how demand responds to changes in prices. If there is little change in demand, then demand is said to be price inelastic. If there is a large change in demand, demand is price elastic.

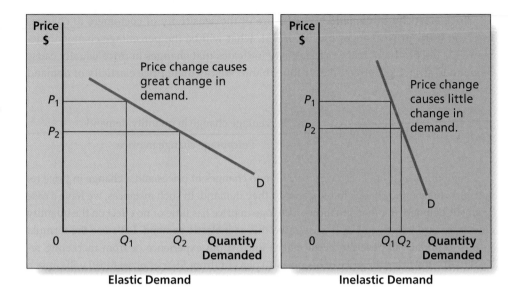

Elastic Demand   Inelastic Demand

shown in Figure 10.7 is more horizontal. With an elasticity of demand of 1.5, a decrease in price will increase the pizza maker's total revenue.

Demand Curves

Price elasticity of demand represents how demand responds to changes in prices. If there is little change in demand, then demand is said to be price inelastic. If there is a large change in demand, demand is price elastic.

We saw earlier that in some instances demand is *inelastic* so that a change in price results in little or no change in demand. For example, if the 10 percent decrease in the price of pizza resulted in only a 5 percent increase in pizza sales, then the price elasticity of demand calculated would be 5 divided by 10, which is 0.5 (less than one), and our pizza maker faces inelastic demand. When demand is inelastic, price and revenue changes are in the same direction; that is, increases in price result in increases in total revenue, while decreases in price result in decreases in total revenue. In the case of inelastic demand, the demand curve in Figure 10.7 becomes more vertical. Generally, the demand for necessities, such as food and electricity, is inelastic. Even large price increases do not cause us to buy less food or to give up our lights and hot water (though we may take fewer bubble baths).

If demand is price inelastic, can marketers keep raising prices so that revenues and profits will grow larger and larger? And what if demand is elastic? Does it mean that marketers can never raise prices? The answer to these questions is no (surprise!). Elasticity of demand for a product often differs for different price levels and with different percentages of change.

As a general rule, pizza makers and other companies can determine the *actual* price elasticity only after they have tested a pricing decision and calculated the resulting demand. Only then will they know whether a specific price change will increase or decrease revenues.

Marketers often do research to estimate what demand is likely to be at different prices for new or existing products. One approach is to conduct a study in which consumers tell marketers how much of a product they would be willing to buy at different prices. For example, researchers might ask participants if they would download fewer iTunes songs if the price per track went from $.89 to $1.50 or how many bags of their favorite chocolate chip cookies they would buy at $3, $4, or $5. At other times, researchers conduct *field studies* in which they vary the price of a product in different stores and measure how much is actually purchased at the different price levels.

Other factors can affect price elasticity and sales. Consider the availability of *substitute* goods or services. If a product has a close substitute, its demand will be elastic; that is, a change in price will result in a change in demand as consumers move to buy the substitute product. For example, all but the most die-hard cola fans might consider Coke and Pepsi close substitutes. If the price of Pepsi goes up, many people will buy Coke instead. Marketers of products with close substitutes are less likely to compete on price because they recognize that doing so could result in less profit as consumers switch from one brand to another.

Changes in prices of other products also affect the demand for an item, a phenomenon we label **cross elasticity of demand**. When products are substitutes for each other, an increase in the price of one will increase the demand for the other. For example, if the price of bananas goes up, consumers may instead buy more strawberries, blueberries, or apples. However, when products are *complements*—that is, when one product is essential to the use of a second—an increase in the price of one decreases the demand for the second. So if the price of gasoline goes up, consumers may drive less, carpool, or take public transportation, and thus demand for tires (as well as gasoline) will decrease.[8]

cross-elasticity of demand
When changes in the price of one product affect the demand for another item.

Step 3: Determine Costs

Estimating demand helps marketers to determine possible prices to charge for a product. It tells them how much of the product they think they'll be able to sell at different prices. Knowing this brings them to the third step in determining a product's price: making sure the price will cover costs. Before marketers can determine price, they must understand the relationship of cost, demand, and revenue for their product. In this next section, we'll talk about different types of costs that marketers must consider in pricing. Then we'll show how marketers use that information to make pricing decisions.

Variable and Fixed Costs

It's obvious that the cost of producing a product plays a big role when firms decide what to charge for it. If an item's selling price is lower than the cost to produce it, it doesn't take a rocket scientist to figure out that the firm will lose money. Before we look at how costs influence pricing decisions, we need to understand the different types of costs that firms incur.

First, a firm incurs **variable costs**—the per-unit costs of production that will fluctuate depending on how many units or individual products a firm produces. For example, if it takes 25 cents worth of nails—a variable cost—to build one bookcase, it will take 50 cents worth for two, 75 cents worth for three, and so on. Make cents? For the production of bookcases, variable costs would also include the cost of lumber and paint as well as the wages the firm would pay factory workers.

variable costs
The costs of production (raw and processed materials, parts, and labor) that are tied to and vary, depending on the number of units produced.

Figure 10.8 shows some examples of the variable cost per unit or average variable cost and the total variable costs at different levels of production (for producing 100, 200, and 500 bookcases). If the firm produces 100 bookcases, the average variable cost per unit is $50, and the total variable cost is $5,000 ($50 × 100). If it doubles production to 200 units, the total variable cost now is $10,000 ($50 × 200).

In reality, it's usually more complex to calculate variable costs than what we've shown here. As the number of bookcases the factory produces increases or decreases, average variable costs may change. For example, if the company buys just enough lumber for one bookcase, the lumberyard will charge top dollar. If it buys enough for 100 bookcases, the guys at the lumberyard will probably offer a better deal. And if it buys enough for thousands of bookcases, the company may cut variable costs even more. Even the cost of labor goes down with increased production, as manufacturers are likely to invest in labor-saving equipment that allows workers to produce bookcases faster. Figure 10.8 shows this is the

Figure 10.8 📷 *Snapshot* | Variable Costs at Different Levels of Production

Variable Costs to Produce 100 Bookcases		Variable Costs to Produce 200 Bookcases		Variable Costs to Produce 500 Bookcases	
Wood	$13.25	Wood	$13.25	Wood	$9.40
Nails	0.25	Nails	0.25	Nails	0.20
Paint	0.50	Paint	0.50	Paint	0.40
Labor (3 hours × $12.00 per hr)	$36.00	Labor (3 hours × $12.00 per hr)	$36.00	Labor (2½ hours × $12.00 per hr)	$30.00
Cost per unit	$50.00	Cost per unit	$50.00	Cost per unit	$40.00
Multiply by number of units	100	Multiply by number of units	200	Multiply by number of units	500
Cost for 100 units	$5,000	Cost for 200 units	$10,000	Cost for 500 units	$20,000

One bookcase = one unit.

case. By purchasing wood, nails, and paint at a lower price (because of a volume discount) and by providing a means for workers to build bookcases more quickly, the company reduces the cost per unit to produce 500 bookcases to $40 each.

Variable costs don't always go down with higher levels of production. Using the bookcase example, at some point the demand for the labor, lumber, or nails required to produce the bookcases may exceed the supply: The bookcase manufacturer may have to pay employees higher overtime wages to keep up with production. The manufacturer may have to buy additional lumber from a distant supplier that will charge more to cover the costs of shipping. The cost per bookcase rises. You get the picture.

fixed costs

Costs of production that do not change with the number of units produced.

Fixed costs are costs that *do not* vary with the number of units produced—the costs that remain the same whether the firm produces 1,000 bookcases this month or only 10. Fixed costs include rent or the cost of owning and maintaining the factory, utilities to heat or cool the factory, and the costs of equipment, such as hammers, saws, and paint sprayers, used in the production of the product. While the wages of factory workers to build the bookcases are part of a firm's variable costs, the salaries of a firm's executives, accountants, human resources specialists, marketing managers, and other personnel not involved in the production of the product are fixed costs. So too are other costs, such as advertising and other marketing activities, at least in the short term. All these costs are constant no matter how many items the factory manufactures.

average fixed cost

The fixed cost per unit produced.

Average fixed cost is the fixed cost per unit—the total fixed costs divided by the number of units (bookcases) produced and sold. Although total fixed costs remain the same no matter how many units are produced, the average fixed cost will decrease as the number of units produced increases. Say, for example, that a firm's total fixed costs of production are $300,000. If the firm produces one unit, it applies the total of $300,000 to the one unit. If it produces two units, it applies $150,000, or half of the fixed costs, to each unit. If it produces 10,000 units, the average fixed cost per unit is $30 and so on. As we produce more and more units, average fixed costs go down, and so does the price we must charge to cover fixed costs.

Of course, like variable costs, in the long term, total fixed costs may change. The firm may find that it can sell more of a product than it has manufacturing capacity to produce, so it builds a new factory, its executives' salaries go up, and more money goes to purchase manufacturing equipment.

total costs

The total of the fixed costs and the variable costs for a set number of units produced.

Combining variable costs and fixed costs yields **total costs** for a given level of production. As a company produces more and more of a product, both average fixed costs and average variable costs may decrease. As output continues to increase, average variable costs may start to increase. These variable costs ultimately rise faster than average fixed costs decline, resulting in an increase to average total costs. As total costs fluctuate with differing levels of production, the price that producers have to charge to cover those costs changes accordingly. Therefore, marketers need to calculate the minimum price necessary to cover all costs—the *break-even price*.

Break-Even Analysis

Break-even analysis is a technique marketers use to examine the relationship between costs and price. This method lets them determine what sales volume the company must reach at a given price before it will completely cover its total costs and past which it will begin to turn a profit. Simply put, the **break-even point** is the point at which the company doesn't lose any money and doesn't make any profit. All costs are covered, but there isn't a penny extra. A break-even analysis allows marketers to identify how many units of a product they will have to sell at a given price to exceed the break-even point and be profitable.

Figure 10.9 uses our bookcase example to demonstrate break-even analysis assuming the manufacturer charges $100 per unit. The vertical axis represents the amount of costs and revenue in dollars, and the horizontal axis shows the quantity of goods the manufacturer produces and sells. In this break-even model, we assume that there is a given total fixed cost and that variable costs do not change with the quantity produced.

In this example, let's say that the total fixed costs (the costs for the factory, the equipment, and electricity) are $200,000 and that the average variable costs (for materials and labor) are constant. The figure shows the total costs (variable costs plus fixed costs) and total revenues if varying quantities are produced and sold. The point at which the total revenue and total costs lines intersect is the break-even point. If sales are above the break-even point, the company makes a profit. Below that point, the firm will suffer losses.

To determine the break-even point, the firm first needs to calculate the **contribution per unit**, or the difference between the price the firm charges for a product (the revenue per unit) and the variable costs. This figure is the amount the firm has after it pays for the wood, nails, paint, and labor to contribute to meeting the fixed costs of production and any profit. For our example, we will assume that the firm sells its bookcases for $100 each. Using the variable costs of $50 per unit that we had before, contribution per unit is $100 − $50 = $50. Using the fixed cost for the bookcase manufacturing of $200,000, we can now calculate the firm's break-even point in units of the product:

$$\text{Break-even point (in units)} = \frac{\text{Total fixed costs}}{\text{Contribution per unit to fixed costs}}$$

$$\text{Break-even point (in units)} = \frac{\$200,00}{\$50} = 4,000 \text{ units}$$

We see that the firm must sell 4,000 bookcases at $100 each to meet its fixed costs and to break even. We can also calculate the break-even point in dollars. This shows us that to break even, the company must sell $400,000 worth of bookcases:

$$\text{Break-even point (in dollars)} = \frac{\text{Total fixed costs}}{1 - \dfrac{\text{Variable cost per unit}}{\text{Price}}}$$

$$\text{Break-even point (in dollars)} = \frac{\$200,000}{1 - \dfrac{\$50}{\$100}} = \frac{\$200,000}{1 - 0.5} = \frac{\$200,000}{0.5} = \$400,000$$

Figure 10.9 📷 *Snapshot* | Break-Even Analysis Assuming a Price of $100

Using break-even analysis, marketers can determine what sales volume must be reached before the company makes a profit. This company needs to sell 4,000 bookcases at $100 each to break even.

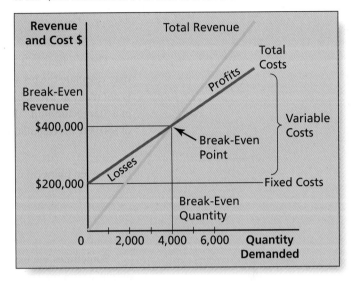

break-even analysis
A method for determining the number of units that a firm must produce and sell at a given price to cover all its costs.

break-even point
The point at which the total revenue and total costs are equal and beyond which the company makes a profit; below that point, the firm will suffer a loss.

contribution per unit
The difference between the price the firm charges for a product and the variable costs.

After the firm's sales have met and passed the break-even point, it begins to make a profit. How much profit? If the firm sells 4,001 bookcases, it will make a profit of $50. If it sells 5,000 bookcases, we calculate the profit as follows:

$$\text{Profit} = \text{Quantity above break-even point} \times \text{Contribution margin}$$

$$= \$1,000 \times 50$$

$$= \$50,000$$

Often a firm will set a *profit goal*, the dollar profit figure it wants to earn. Its managers may calculate the break-even point with a certain dollar profit goal in mind. In this case, it is not really a "break-even" point we are calculating because we're seeking profits. It's more of a "target amount." If our bookcase manufacturer thinks it is necessary to realize a profit of $50,000, his calculations look like this:

$$\text{Break-even point (in units) with target profit included)} = \frac{\text{total fixed costs} + \text{target profit}}{\text{contribution per unit to fixed costs}}$$

$$\text{Break-even point (in units)} = \frac{\$200,000 + 50,000}{\$50} = 5,000 \text{ units}$$

Sometimes we express the target return or profit goal as a *percentage of sales*. For example, a firm may say that it wants to make a profit of at least 10 percent on sales. In such cases, it first calculates what the 10 percent profit is in dollars: 10 percent of $100 is $10. Then the firm adds this profit amount to the variable cost when it calculates the break-even point. In our example, the company wants to earn 10 percent of the selling price of the bookcase, or per unit. We would simply add this $10 to the variable costs of $50 and calculate the new target amount as we calculated the break-even point before. The contribution per unit becomes the following:

$$\text{Contribution per unit with target profit included} = \text{Selling price} - (\text{Variable costs} + \text{Target profit}) = \$100 - (\$50 + \$10) = \$40$$

$$\text{Break-even point (in units)} = \frac{\text{Total fixed costs}}{\text{Contribution per unit to fixed costs}}$$

$$\text{Break-even point (in units)} = \frac{\$200,000}{\$40} = 5,000 \text{ units}$$

Break-even analysis does not provide an easy answer for pricing decisions. Yes, it provides answers about how many units the firm must sell to break even and to make a profit—but without knowing whether demand will equal that quantity at that price, companies can make big mistakes.

Markups and Margins: Pricing through the Channel

So far, we've talked about costs simply from the perspective of a manufacturer selling directly to a consumer. But in reality, most products are not sold directly to consumers or business buyers. Instead, a manufacturer may sell a consumer good to a wholesaler, distributor, or jobber who in turn sells to a retailer who finally sells the product to the ultimate consumer. In organizational markets, the manufacturer may sell his or her product to a distributor who will then sell to the business customer. Each of these members of the channel of distribution buys a product for a certain amount and adds a **markup** amount to create the price at which they will sell a product. This markup amount is the **gross margin**, also referred to as the **retailer margin** or the **wholesaler margin**. The margin must be great enough to cover the fixed costs of the retailer or wholesaler and leave an amount for a profit. When a manufacturer sets a price, he or she must consider these

markup
An amount added to the cost of a product to create the price at which a channel member will sell the product.

gross margin
The markup amount added to the cost of a product to cover the fixed costs of the retailer or wholesaler and leave an amount for a profit.

retailer margin
The margin added to the cost of a product by a retailer.

wholesaler margin
The amount added to the cost of a product by a wholesaler.

margins. To understand pricing through the channel better, we'll look at a simple example of channel pricing.

Many times, a manufacturer builds its pricing structure around list prices. A **list price**, which we also refer to as a **manufacturer's suggested retail price (MSRP)**, is the price that the manufacturer sets as the appropriate price for the end consumer to pay. Let's say we have a consumer good with an MSRP of $10. This means the retailer will sell the product to the consumer for $10. But, as we said, retailers need money to cover their fixed costs and their profits. Thus, the retailer may determine that he must have a certain percentage gross or retailer margin, say 30 percent.

This means that the retailer must be able to buy the product for no more than the following:

$$\text{Price to the retailer} = \$10.00 \times (1.00 - .30)$$
$$= \$10.00 \times .70$$
$$= \$7.00$$

list price or manufacturer's suggested retail price (MSRP)
The price that the manufacturer sets as the appropriate price for the end consumer to pay.

If the channel of distribution also includes a wholesaler, the wholesaler must be able to mark up the product in order to pay for his fixed costs and profits. This means that the wholesaler must also have a certain percentage gross or wholesaler margin, say 20 percent.

This means that the wholesaler must be able to buy the product for no more than the following:

$$\text{Price to the wholesaler} = \$7.00 \times (1.00 - .20)$$
$$= \$7.00 \times .80$$
$$= \$5.40$$

Thus, the manufacturer will sell the product not for $10 but for $5.40. Of course, the manufacturer may sell the product to the wholesaler for less than that, but he cannot sell it for more and meet the margin requirements of the retailer and the wholesaler. If the manufacturer's variable costs for producing the product are $3, then his contribution to fixed costs is $2.40. It is this amount we use to calculate the break-even point.

Step 4: Examine the Pricing Environment

In addition to demand and costs, marketers look at factors in the firm's external environment when they set prices. This is especially important in today's recessionary economic environment. Thus, the fourth step in developing pricing strategies is to examine and evaluate the pricing environment. Only then can marketers set a price that not only covers costs but also provides a *competitive advantage*—a price that meets the needs of customers better than the competition. This section will discuss some important external influences on pricing strategies—the economic environment, competition, and consumer trends. Before we begin this discussion, it is especially important to note that price decisions are interdependent. They must take into account demand and costs and the pricing environment together as a whole.

The Economy

Broad economic trends, like those we discussed in Chapter 2, tend to direct pricing strategies. The business cycle, inflation, economic growth, and consumer confidence all help to determine whether one pricing strategy or another will succeed. Should a firm keep prices stable, reduce them, or

It's common for services like insurance to rely on price as a competitive advantage.

Consumers are very price-sensitive when economic conditions are bleak.

even raise them in today's recessionary economy? Of course, the upswings and downturns in a national economy do not affect all product categories or all regions equally. Marketers need to understand how economic trends will affect their particular business.

In general, during *recessions* like the Great Recession that began in 2008, consumers grow more price sensitive. They switch brands to get a better price and patronize discount stores and warehouse outlets. They are less likely to take luxury vacations; instead, they're happy with a "staycation" where they entertain the family at home. Many consumers lose their jobs, and others are fearful of losing theirs. Even wealthy households, relatively unaffected by the recession, tend to cut back on their consumption. As a result, to keep factories in operation during periods of recession, some firms find it necessary to cut prices to levels at which they cover their costs but don't make a profit.

During Great Recession of 2008, Macy's launched its My Macy's initiative as a way to offer shoppers greater personalization and selection in hopes of improving declining sales. With this strategy, merchandisers would go into stores weekly to learn from sales associates exactly what was and wasn't working. For example, marketers found out that strapless dresses were selling everywhere except in the Salt Lake City and Pittsburgh stores. So it was out with the strapless dresses in those stores and in with a more conservative look that increased sales.[9] This personalization and localization strategy worked out so well for Macy's that the retailer continues to do this today.

There are also some economic trends that allow firms to change prices, altering what consumers see as an acceptable or unacceptable price range for a product. *Inflation* may give marketers causes to either increase or decrease prices. First, inflation gets customers accustomed to price increases. Customers may become insensitive to price increases, even when inflation goes away, allowing marketers to make real price increases, not just those that adjust for the inflation. Of course, during periods of inflation, consumers may grow fearful of the future and worry about whether they will have enough money to meet basic needs. In such a case, they may cut back on purchases. Then, as in periods of recession, inflation may cause marketers to lower prices and temporarily sacrifice profits to maintain sales levels.

The Competition

Marketers try to anticipate how the competition will respond to their pricing actions. They know that consumers' expectations of what constitutes a fair price largely depend on what the competition charges. However, it's not always a good idea to fight the competition with lower and lower prices. Pricing wars, such as those in the fast-food industry, can change consumers' perceptions of what is a "fair" price, leaving them unwilling to buy at previous price levels.

Most industries, such as the airline, restaurant, and wheat farm industries, consist of a number of firms. As we discussed in Chapter 2, these industries can belong to one of three industry structures—an oligopoly, monopolistic competition, or pure competition. The industry

Procter & Gamble is the world's biggest consumer-product maker, producing many premium-priced brands, some at prices twice the category average. But during the 2008 recession, P&G found sales, market share, and profits declining as consumers switched to store brands and other cheaper options. P&G responded with a number of price-cutting and product enhancement strategies. For example, P&G began offering larger packs of Duracell batteries and more absorbent Pamper's diapers without increasing prices. The company has also repositioned both Era and Cheer detergent as bargain brands. But will customers return to premium brands after the recession? Many believe that the recession of 2008, the worst since the Great Depression, will probably have a permanent effect on the American consumer. Consumers, even those whose income has not declined, are spending less and saving more.

structure a firm belongs to will influence price decisions. In general, firms like Delta Airlines that do business in an oligopoly, in which the market has few sellers and many buyers, are more likely to adopt status quo pricing objectives in which the pricing of all competitors is similar. Such objectives are attractive to oligopolistic firms because avoiding price competition allows all players in the industry to remain profitable. In a business like the restaurant industry, which is characterized by monopolistic competition in which there are a lot of sellers each offering a slightly different product, it is possible for firms to differentiate products and to focus on nonprice competition. Then each firm prices its product on the basis of its cost without much concern for matching the exact price of competitors' products. People don't tend to "comparison shop" between the prices of a burger at Applebee's versus one at Chili's before they decide which chain to patronize. Of course, this doesn't mean that firms in an oligopoly can just ignore pricing by the competition. When one fast-food chain offers a "value meal," others often respond with their own versions.

Not everyone cuts prices in a recession. Starbucks' strategy to cope with the downturn was to keep a premium image while the chain retained price-sensitive customers who threatened to defect to lower-priced competitors, such as McDonald's. To do this, Starbucks raised the prices of its sugary coffees with several ingredients, such as frappuccinos and caramel macchiatos, by 10, 15, or even 30 cents. At the same time, the company reduced prices of more popular beverages, such as lattes and brewed coffee, from 5 to 15 cents.

Organizations like wheat farmers that function in a market characterized as pure competition have little opportunity to raise or lower prices. Rather, supply and demand directly influence the price of wheat, soybeans, corn, or fresh peaches. When bad weather decreases the supply of crops, prices go up. And prices for almost any kind of fish have increased dramatically since health-conscious consumers began to turn away from red meat.

Of course, as we said, the elements of the pricing environment are interdependent. When the economy turns down and firms are faced with declining sales from a recession, many will simply lower their prices and sacrifice profits to drive sales. Other firms in the industry have to decide whether to maintain their current prices or follow suit and lower prices. The trick is to balance the two—to maintain customer loyalty and the corresponding sales while ensuring an adequate level of profits.

Government Regulation

Another important factor in the environment that influences how marketers develop pricing strategies is government regulation. Governments in the U.S. and other countries develop two different types of regulations that affect pricing. First, regulations for health care, environmental protection, occupational safety, and highway safety, just to mention a few, cause the costs of producing many products to increase. Other regulations on specific industries, such as those imposed by the Food and Drug Administration on the production of food and pharmaceuticals, increase the costs of developing and producing those products.

In addition, some regulations directly address prices. In 1971, in order to fight what was thought to be an unacceptable level of inflation, President Nixon announced an unprecedented 90-day price freeze on most products that in reality lasted nearly three years. More recently, Congress enacted the Credit Card Responsibility and Disclosure Act, which limits credit card rates and other fees.[10] In March 2010, a massive health care overhaul bill known as the Affordable Care Act was enacted. The legislation, which took effect in 2013–2014, offers all Americans access to health care, including those with preexisting conditions who in the past have often been denied coverage. We have yet to see the full effects (e.g., the predicted layoffs or drastic increases in insurance premiums), but so far the plan seems to be working.[11]

Consumer Trends

Consumer trends also can strongly influence prices. Culture and demographics determine how consumers think and behave, so these factors have a large impact on all marketing decisions. Take, for example, the buying habits of the women who opted for a career in their twenties but who are hearing the ticking of their biological clocks as they enter their late thirties and early forties. Couples who have babies later in their lives are often better off financially than younger parents, and on average they will have fewer children to spoil, so they are more willing to spend whatever it costs to give their babies the best.

Another important trend is that even well-off people no longer consider it shameful to hunt for bargains—in fact, it's becoming trendy to boast that you found one or to recycle a slightly used designer gown from a thrift store. According to one marketing expert, "The old idea that 'if you have to ask the price, then you can't afford it' has been replaced by the wealthy being focused on price and getting the most bang for their buck and sometimes that means asking for a discount, looking to find the lowest price or making strategic brand substitutes to save money."[12] So, affluent customers are just as likely as many others to want to save money, but they don't go "bargain hunting"—they practice the art of "strategic shopping."[13]

The International Environment

As we discussed in Chapter 2, the marketing environment often varies widely from country to country. This can have important consequences in developing pricing strategies. Can a company standardize prices for all global markets, or must it adjust to local conditions?

For some products, such as jet airplanes, companies like Boeing and Airbus standardize their prices. This is possible, first, because about the only customers for the wide-bodies and other popular jets are major airlines and governments of countries that buy for their military or for use by government officials. Second, companies that build planes have little or no leeway to cut their costs without sacrificing safety.

For other products, including most consumer goods, unique environmental factors in different countries mean that marketers must adapt their pricing strategies. As we noted in Chapter 2, the economic conditions in developing countries often mean that consumers simply cannot afford $3 or $4 or more for a bottle of shampoo or laundry detergent. As a result, marketers offer their brands at lower prices, often by providing them in one-use packages called sachets that sell for just a few cents. In other cases, companies must save on costs by using less expensive ingredients in their brands in order to provide toothpaste or soap that is affordable.

The competitive environment in different countries also contributes to different pricing strategies. In countries such as China, long-established manufacturers of packaged foods and toiletries have been successful for decades by providing products at affordable prices. New entrants into these markets must price their products more or less in line with the local firms. There are some exceptions, however. Many consumers from China's new middle class are willing to spend more on Western products (like Starbucks lattes) because of the status they associate with these pricey treats. In one study, Chinese consumers said they either "absolutely" or "somewhat" favored products with the "Made in the USA" label, and 61 percent of them were willing to pay more for those U.S.-made goods.[14]

Another factor that can affect a firm's pricing in the international environment is government regulation. In some countries, the government dictates prices for products such as pharmaceuticals. With this kind of government control, a firm's only options are to use cheaper ingredients to produce the product or not make their products available in that market.

Finally, channels of distribution often vary both in the types and sizes of available intermediaries and in the availability of an infrastructure to facilitate product distribution. Often these differences can mean that trade margins will be higher, as will the cost of getting the products to consumers.

3 Identify Strategies and Tactics to Price the Product

OBJECTIVE
Understand key pricing strategies and tactics.
(pp. 321–327)

An old Russian proverb says, "There are two kinds of fools in any market. One doesn't charge enough. The other charges too much."[15] In modern business, there seldom is any one-and-only, now-and-forever, best pricing strategy. Like playing a chess game, making pricing moves and countermoves requires thinking two and three moves ahead. Figure 10.10 provides a summary of different pricing strategies and tactics. Price planning is influenced by psychological issues and strategies and by legal and ethical issues.

Step 5: Choose a Pricing Strategy

The next step in price planning is to choose a pricing strategy. Some strategies work for certain products, with certain customer groups, in certain competitive markets. When is it best for the firm to undercut the competition and when to just meet the competition's prices? When is the best pricing strategy one that covers costs only, and when is it best to use one based on demand?

Pricing Strategies Based on Cost

Marketing planners often choose cost-based strategies because they are simple to calculate and are relatively risk free. They promise that the price will at least cover the costs the company incurs to produce and market the product.

Cost-based pricing methods have drawbacks, however. They do not consider factors such as the nature of the target market, demand, competition, the product life cycle, and the product's image. Moreover, although the calculations for setting the price may be simple and straightforward, accurate cost estimating may prove difficult.

Think about firms such as 3M, General Electric, and Nabisco, all of which produce many products. How does a cost analysis allocate the costs for the plant, research and development, equipment, design engineers, maintenance, and marketing personnel among the different products so that the pricing plan accurately reflects the cost to produce any one product? For example, how do you allocate the salary of a marketing executive who oversees many different products? Should the cost be divided equally among all products? Should costs be based on the actual number of hours spent working on each product? Or should costs be assigned based on the revenues generated by each product? There is no one

APPLYING ▼ The Pricing Environment

Betsy recognized that higher-education costs were exploding, even while median U.S. household income had remained mostly flat for the past 10 years.

Pricing strategies	Pricing tactics
• Based on cost	• Pricing for individual products
Cost plus	Two-part pricing
• Based on demand	Payment pricing
Target costing	• Pricing for multiple products
Yield management	Price bundling
• Based on the competition	Captive pricing
Price leadership	• Distribution-based pricing
• Based on customers' needs	• Discounting for channel members
Value (EDLP) pricing	
• New product pricing	
Skimming pricing	
Penetration pricing	
Trial pricing	

Figure 10.10 *Snapshot* | Pricing Strategies and Tactics

Marketers develop successful pricing programs by choosing from a variety of pricing strategies and tactics.

cost-plus pricing

A method of setting prices in which the seller totals all the costs for the product and then adds an amount to arrive at the selling price.

right answer. Even with these limitations, though, cost-based pricing strategies often are a marketer's best choice.

The most common cost-based approach to pricing a product is **cost-plus pricing**, in which the marketer totals all the costs for the product and then adds an amount (or marks up the cost of the item) to arrive at the selling price. Many marketers, especially retailers and wholesalers who often must set the price for tens of thousands of products, use cost-plus pricing because of its simplicity—users need only know or estimate the unit cost and add the markup. To calculate cost-plus pricing, marketers usually calculate either a markup on cost or a markup on selling price. With both methods, you calculate the price by adding a predetermined percentage to the cost, but as the names of the methods imply, for one the calculation uses a percentage of the costs and for the other a percentage of the selling price. Which of the two methods is used seems often to be little more than a matter of the "the way our company has always done it." You'll find more information about cost-plus pricing and how to calculate markup on cost and markup on selling price in the *Chapter 10 Supplement* at the end of this chapter.

Pricing Strategies Based on Demand

demand-based pricing

A price-setting method based on estimates of demand at different prices.

Demand-based pricing means that the firm bases the selling price on an estimate of volume or quantity that it can sell in different markets at different prices. To use any of the pricing strategies based on demand, firms must determine how much product they can sell in each market and at what price. As we noted earlier, marketers often use customer surveys, in which consumers indicate whether they would buy a certain product and how much of it they would buy at various prices. They may obtain more accurate estimates by conducting an experiment like the ones we described in Chapter 4. Two specific demand-based pricing strategies are target costing and yield management pricing. Let's take a quick look at each approach.

target costing

A process in which firms identify the quality and functionality needed to satisfy customers and what price they are willing to pay before the product is designed; the product is manufactured only if the firm can control costs to meet the required price.

Today, firms find that they can be more successful if they match price with demand using a **target costing** process.[16] With target costing, firms first use marketing research to identify the quality and functionality needed to satisfy attractive market segments and what price they are willing to pay *before they design the product*. As 📷 Figure 10.11 shows, the next step is to determine what margins retailers and dealers require as well as the profit margin the company requires. On the basis of this information, managers can calculate

Figure 10.11 📷 *Snapshot* | Target Costing Using a Jeans Example

With target costing, a firm first determines the price at which customers would be willing to buy the product and then works backward to design the product in such a way that it can produce and sell the product at a profit.

Step 1: Determine the price customers are willing to pay for the jeans
  $79.99

Step 2: Determine the markup required by the retailer
  40% (.40)

Step 3: Calculate the maximum price the retailer will pay, the price customers are
  willing to pay minus the markup amount

  Formula: Price to the retailer = Selling price × (1.00 − markup percentage)
  Price to the retailer = $79.99   × (1.00 − .40)
           = $79.99   × 0.60 =   **$47.99**

Step 4: Determine the profit required by the firm
  15% (.15)

Step 5: Calculate the target cost, the maximum cost of producing the jeans
  Formula: Target cost = Price to the retailer × (1.00 − profit percentage)
  Target cost = $47.99 × 0.85 =   **$40.79**

the target cost—the maximum it can cost the firm to manufacture the product. If the firm can meet customer quality and functionality requirements and control costs to meet the required price, it will manufacture the product. If not, it abandons the product.

Yield management pricing is another type of demand-based pricing strategy that hospitality companies like airlines, hotels, and cruise lines use. These businesses charge different prices to different customers in order to manage capacity while they maximize revenues. Many service firms practice yield management pricing because they recognize that different customers have different sensitivities to price—some customers will pay top dollar for an airline ticket, while others will travel only if there is a discount fare. The goal of yield management pricing is to accurately predict the proportion of customers who fall into each category and allocate the percentages of the airline's or hotel's capacity accordingly so that no product goes unsold.

> **yield management pricing**
> A practice of charging different prices to different customers in order to manage capacity while maximizing revenues.

For example, an airline may charge two prices for the same seat, say, a full fare of $899 and a discount fare of $299. (In reality, of course, the airlines charge a much greater number of different prices.) The airline must predict how many seats it can fill at full fare and how many it can sell only at the discounted fare. The airline begins months ahead of the date of the flight with a basic allocation of seats—perhaps it will place 25 percent in the full-fare "bucket" and 75 percent in the discount-fare "bucket." As flight time gets closer, the airline might make a series of adjustments to the allocation of seats in the hope of selling every seat on the plane at the highest price possible. If the New York Mets need to book the flight, chances are the airline will be able to sell some of the discount seats at full fare, which in turn decreases the number available at the discounted price. If, as the flight date nears, the number of full-fare ticket sales falls below the forecast, the airline will move some of those seats over to the discount bucket. Then the suspense builds! The pricing game continues until the day of the flight as the airline attempts to fill every seat by the time the plane takes off. This is why you may find one price for a ticket on Travelocity.com or Expedia.com a month before the flight, a much higher price two weeks later, and a very low price the last few days before the flight. This also tells you why you often see the ticket agents frantically looking for "volunteers" who are willing to give up their seats because the airline sold more seats than actually fit in the plane.

> **price leadership**
> A pricing strategy in which one firm first sets its price and other firms in the industry follow with the same or very similar prices.

Pricing Strategies Based on the Competition

Sometimes a firm's pricing strategy involves pricing its wares near, at, above, or below the competition's prices. In the "good old days," when U.S. automakers had the American market to themselves, pricing decisions were straightforward: Industry giant General Motors would announce its new car prices, and Ford, Chrysler, Packard, Studebaker, Hudson, and the others got in line or dropped out. A **price leadership** strategy, which usually is the rule in an oligopolistic industry that a few firms dominate, may be in the best interest of all players because it minimizes price competition. Price leadership strategies are popular because they provide an acceptable and legal way for firms to agree on prices without ever coordinating these rates with each other.

Priceline uses hotels' excess capacity to its advantage as it provides rooms to guests at a discount.

Pricing Strategies Based on Customers' Needs

When firms develop pricing strategies that cater to customers, they are less concerned with short-term results than with keeping customers for the long term. Firms that

value pricing or everyday low pricing (EDLP)

A pricing strategy in which a firm sets prices that provide ultimate value to customers.

APPLYING ▼ Pricing Based on Customers' Needs

Betsy knew that offering a different business model that made the college affordable would help the school stand out from the crowd.

---

skimming price

A very high, premium price that a firm charges for its new, highly desirable product.

penetration pricing

A pricing strategy in which a firm introduces a new product at a very low price to encourage more customers to purchase it.

trial pricing

Pricing a new product low for a limited period of time in order to lower the risk for a customer.

practice **value pricing or everyday low pricing (EDLP)** develop a pricing strategy that promises ultimate value to consumers. What this really means is that in the customers' eyes, the price is justified by what they receive. At Walmart, EDLP is a fundamental part of the company's success. The world's largest retailer demands tens of billions of dollars in cost efficiencies from its supply chain and passes these savings on to its customers. To compete, other retailers must reduce their prices. Grocery stores, for example, often end up reducing their prices by 1 to 1.2 percent when Walmart moves into their community.[17] When you consider the thousands of products grocery stores sell, that's a big chunk of change.

New Product Pricing

New products are vital to the growth and profits of a firm—but they also present unique pricing challenges. When a product is new to the market or when there is no established industry price norm, marketers may use a skimming price strategy, a penetration pricing strategy, or trial pricing.

A **skimming price** means that the firm charges a high, premium price for its new product with the intention of reducing it in the future in response to market pressures. If a product is highly desirable and offers unique benefits, demand is price inelastic during the introductory stage of the product life cycle, allowing a company to recover research and development and promotion costs. When rival products enter the market, the firm lowers the price to remain competitive. Firms that focus on profit objectives when they develop their pricing strategies often set skimming prices for new products The Sony PlayStation 3 was originally sold at $599 in the U.S. market, but it has been gradually reduced to below $200.[18]

Second, for skimming pricing to be successful, there should be little chance that competitors can get into the market quickly. With highly complex, technical products, it will take time for competitors to put a rival product into production. **Penetration pricing** is the opposite of skimming pricing. In this situation, the company prices a new product very low to sell more in a short time and gain market share early. One reason marketers use penetration pricing is to discourage competitors from entering the market. The firm that first introduces a new product has an important advantage. Experience shows that a pioneering brand often is able to maintain dominant market share for long periods. Penetration pricing may act as a *barrier to entry* for competitors if the prices the market will bear are so low that the company will not be able to recover development and manufacturing costs. Campbell's soup with the iconic red label designed in 1898 is a brand that was first to market in 1895 and still dominates the industry today.[19]

Trial pricing means that a new product carries a low price for a limited time to generate a high level of customer interest. Unlike penetration pricing, in which the company maintains the low price, in this case it increases the trial price after the introductory period. The idea is to win customer acceptance first and make profits later, as when a new health club offers an introductory membership to start pulling people in or a cable TV company offers a great low price for six months if you sign up for their TV, Internet, and phone bundle after which you will pay much more.

Step 6: Develop Pricing Tactics

Once marketers have developed pricing strategies, the last step in price planning is to implement them. The methods companies use to set their strategies in motion are their *pricing tactics*.

Secondhand products often meet the price needs of frugal consumers. This ad for a used furniture store ran in Turkey.

Pricing for Individual Products

Once marketers have settled on a product's price, the way they present it to the market can make a big difference:

- *Two-part pricing* requires two separate types of payments to purchase the product. For example, golf and tennis clubs charge yearly or monthly fees plus fees for each round of golf or tennis.

- *Payment pricing* makes the consumer think the price is "do-able" by breaking up the total price into smaller amounts payable over time. For example, at the online shopping channel QVC you can avoid the *sticker shock* (a negative reaction to the total retail price) of an iPad by paying for the product with low installment payments. For five easy payments of $159.99 (plus shipping and handling, of course), you can get a 16-gigabyte Apple iPad 2 with Bluetooth keyboard, case, and more. Just beware: The total cost of the iPad plus accessories totals $799.98—twice the price of the one you could have gotten at Best Buy for only $399![20]

Pricing for Multiple Products

A firm may sell several products that consumers typically buy at one time. As fast-food restaurants like Burger King know, a customer who buys a burger for lunch usually goes for a soft drink and fries as well. The sale of a paper-cup dispenser usually means a package of cups is not far behind. The two most common tactics for pricing multiple products are price bundling and captive pricing.

Price bundling means selling two or more goods or services as a single package for one price—a price that is often less than the total price of the items if bought individually. Traditional cable TV providers like AT&T U-verse, Comcast, and Time Warner have gotten into the price bundling act as they entice their customers to sign on for a package of cable TV, high-speed Internet, and local or, in some cases, wireless phone service.

From a marketing standpoint, price bundling makes sense. If we price products separately, it's more likely that customers will buy some but not all the items. They might choose to put off some purchases until later, or they might buy from a competitor. Whatever revenue a seller loses from the reduced prices for the total package it often makes up for in increased total purchases.

Captive pricing is a pricing tactic a firm uses when it has two products that work only when used together. The firm sells one item at a very low price and then makes its profit on the second high-margin item. This tactic is commonly used to sell shaving products where the razor is relatively cheap but the blades are not. Similarly, companies such as HP and Canon offer consumers a desktop printer that also serves as a fax, copier, and scanner for under $100 in order to keep selling ink cartridges.

Distribution-Based Pricing

Distribution-based pricing is a pricing tactic that establishes how firms handle the cost of shipping products to customers near, far, and wide. Characteristics of the product, the customers, and the competition figure in the decision to charge all customers the same price or to vary according to shipping cost.

F.O.B. pricing is a tactic used in B2B marketing. F.O.B. stands for "free on board," which refers to who pays for the shipping. Also—and this is important—*title passes to the buyer* at the F.O.B. location. F.O.B. factory or **F.O.B. origin pricing** means that the cost of transporting the product from the factory to the customer's location is the responsibility of the customer. **F.O.B. delivered pricing** means that the seller pays both the cost of loading and the cost of transporting to the customer, amounts it includes in the selling price.

price bundling
Selling two or more goods or services as a single package for one price.

captive pricing
A pricing tactic for two items that must be used together; one item is priced very low, and the firm makes its profit on another, high-margin item essential to the operation of the first item.

F.O.B. origin pricing
A pricing tactic in which the cost of transporting the product from the factory to the customer's location is the responsibility of the customer.

F.O.B. delivered pricing
A pricing tactic in which the cost of loading and transporting the product to the customer is included in the selling price and is paid by the manufacturer.

Delivery terms for pricing of products sold in international markets are similar:[21]

- *CIF* (cost, insurance, freight) is the term used for ocean shipments and means the seller quotes a price for the goods (including insurance), all transportation, and miscellaneous charges to the point of debarkation from the vessel.

- *CFR* (cost and freight) means the quoted price covers the goods and the cost of transportation to the named point of debarkation, but the buyer must pay the cost of insurance. The CFR term is also used for ocean shipments.

- *CIP* (carriage and insurance paid to) and *CPT* (carriage paid to) include the same provisions as CIF and CFR but are used for shipment by modes other than water.

When a firm uses **uniform delivered pricing**, it adds an average shipping cost to the price, no matter what the distance from the manufacturer's plant—within reason. For example, when you order a CD from a music supplier, you may pay the cost of the CD plus $2.99 shipping and handling, no matter what the actual cost of the shipping to your particular location. Internet sales, catalog sales, home TV shopping, and other types of nonstore retail sales usually use uniform delivered pricing.

Freight absorption pricing means the seller takes on part or all of the cost of shipping. This policy works well for high-ticket items, for which the cost of shipping is a negligible part of the sales price and the profit margin. Marketers are most likely to use freight absorption pricing in highly competitive markets or when such pricing allows them to enter new markets. More recently, online marketers such as Amazon.com have found that offering free shipping makes a big difference to consumers and to their sales volume.

Discounting for Channel Members

So far, we've talked about pricing tactics used to sell to end customers. Now we'll talk about tactics firms use to price to members of their *distribution channels*:

- *Trade or functional discounts:* We discussed earlier how manufacturers often set a list or suggested retail price for their product and then sell the product to members of the channel for less, allowing the channel members to cover their costs and make a profit. Thus, the manufacturer's pricing structure will normally include **trade discounts** to channel intermediaries. These discounts are usually set percentage discounts off the suggested retail or list price for each channel level. In today's marketing environment dominated by large retail chains such as Walmart, Costco, and Target, the amount of the trade discount is dictated by the retailers who, because of their size, have the most power in the channel. We'll talk more about channel power in Chapter 11.

- *Quantity discounts:* To encourage larger purchases from distribution channel partners or from large organizational customers, marketers may offer **quantity discounts**, or reduced prices for purchases of larger quantities. *Cumulative quantity discounts* are based on a total quantity bought within a specified time period, often a year, and encourage a buyer to stick with a single seller instead of moving from one supplier to another. Cumulative quantity discounts often take the form of *rebates*, in which case the firm sends the buyer a rebate check at the end of the discount period or, alternatively, gives the buyer credit against future orders. *Noncumulative quantity discounts* are based only on the quantity purchased with each individual order and encourage larger single orders but do little to tie the buyer and the seller together.

- *Cash discounts:* Many firms try to entice their customers to pay their bills quickly by offering **cash discounts**. For example, a firm selling to a retailer may state that the terms of the sale are "2 percent 10 days, net 30 days," meaning that if the retailer pays the producer for the goods within 10 days, the amount due is cut by 2 percent. The total amount is due within 30 days, and after 30 days the payment is late.

uniform delivered pricing
A pricing tactic in which a firm adds a standard shipping charge to the price for all customers regardless of location.

freight absorption pricing
A pricing tactic in which the seller absorbs the total cost of transportation.

trade discounts
Discounts off list price of products to members of the channel of distribution who perform various marketing functions.

quantity discounts
A pricing tactic of charging reduced prices for purchases of larger quantities of a product.

cash discounts
A discount offered to a customer to entice them to pay their bill quickly.

- *Seasonal discounts:* **Seasonal discounts** are price reductions offered only during certain times of the year. For seasonal products such as snowblowers, lawn mowers, and water-skiing equipment, marketers use seasonal discounts to entice retailers and wholesalers to buy off-season and either store the product at their locations until the right time of the year or pass the discount along to consumers with off-season sales programs. Alternatively, they may offer discounts when products are in-season to create a competitive advantage during periods of high demand.

seasonal discounts
Price reductions offered only during certain times of the year.

4 Pricing and Electronic Commerce

OBJECTIVE
Understand the opportunities for Internet pricing strategies.
(pp. 327–329)

As we have seen, price planning is a complex process in any firm. But if you are operating in the "wired world," get ready for even more pricing options!

Because sellers are connected to buyers around the globe as never before through the Internet, corporate networks, and wireless setups, marketers can offer deals they tailor to a single person at a single moment. On the other hand, they're also a lot more vulnerable to smart consumers, who can easily check out competing prices with the click of a mouse.

Many experts suggest that technology is creating a consumer revolution that might change pricing forever—and perhaps create the most efficient market ever. The music industry provides the most obvious example: Music lovers from around the globe purchase and download tens of billions of songs from numerous Internet sites, including the iTunes Store, Google Play, and Amazon MP3.[22] More than 70 million people who live in the U.S. alone access music through their phones.[23]

The Internet also enables firms that sell to other businesses (B2B firms) to change their prices rapidly as they adapt to changing costs. For consumers who have lots of stuff in their attics that they need to put in someone else's attic, the Internet means an opportunity for sellers to find ready buyers through C2C sites such as eBay and Etsy. And for B2C firms that sell to consumers, the Internet offers other opportunities. In this section, we will discuss some of the more popular Internet pricing strategies.

Dynamic Pricing Strategies

One of the most important opportunities the Internet offers is **dynamic pricing**, in which the seller can easily adjust the price to meet changes in the marketplace. If a bricks-and-mortar retail store wants to change prices, employees/workers must place new price tags on items, create and display new store signage and media advertising, and input new prices into the store's computer system. For B2B marketers, employees/workers must print catalogs and price lists and distribute to salespeople and customers. These activities can be very costly to a firm, so they simply don't change their prices very often.[24]

dynamic pricing
A pricing strategy in which the price can easily be adjusted to meet changes in the marketplace.

Internet Price Discrimination

Of course, the Internet allows firms to do more than just adjust prices due to external factors such as changing costs or competitive activity. The promise of the Internet is that it allows consumers to quickly comparison shop for the very lowest price, all the while sitting in their pajamas at home. Many firms, it seems, use the same technology to practice **Internet price discrimination**. Internet price discrimination is an Internet pricing strategy that charges different prices to different customers for the same product.[25] A *Wall Street Journal* investigation found that a Swingline stapler on Staples.com was priced at $15.79

Internet price discrimination
An Internet pricing strategy that charges different prices to different customers for the same product.

for one customer and $14.29 for another who lived just a few miles away based on their location and their distance from either an OfficeMax or an Office Depot store.[26] Marketers know that they will maximize profits if they charge each customer the most that person is willing to pay. While this is not practical, placing customers into groups based on where they live, how close they are to the retailer or a competitor, the cost of doing business in the area, or their Internet browsing history can greatly increase profits. Some sites even offer customers a discount if they use a mobile device. A shopper who uses a smart phone to find a hotel room on sites like Orbitz.com or CheapTickets.com may find rooms for as much as 50 percent less than they would otherwise pay.

Is price discrimination illegal? As long as the company doesn't charge different prices based on a demographic characteristic such as gender or race, it is not. Whether it is ethical, however, is debatable. And there's a more practical reason to be concerned: Marketers run the risk of creating a lot of "unhappy campers" if some of their customers discover that others received the same product for a lower price.

Online Auctions

online auctions
E-commerce that allows shoppers to purchase products through online bidding.

Most consumers are familiar with eBay. But what about eCrater, Bonanzle, eBid, and CQout? These too are some of the many **online auctions** that allow shoppers to bid on everything from bobbleheads to health-and-fitness equipment to a Sammy Sosa home-run ball. Auctions are a powerful Internet pricing strategy. Perhaps the most popular auctions are the C2C auctions such as those on eBay. The eBay auction is an *open auction*, meaning that all the buyers know the highest price bid at any point in time. On many Internet auction sites, the seller can set a *reserve price*, a price below which the item will not be sold.

A *reverse auction* is a tool firms use to manage their costs in B2B buying. While in a typical auction buyers compete to purchase a product, in reverse auctions sellers compete for the right to provide a product at, it is hoped, a low price.

Freemium Pricing Strategies

freemium
A business strategy in which a product in its most basic version is provided free of charge but the company charges money (the premium) for upgraded versions of the product with more features, greater functionality, or greater capacity.

Perhaps the most exciting new pricing strategy is **freemium** pricing (a mix of "free" and "premium."). Freemium is a business strategy in which a product in its most basic version is provided free of charge but the company charges money (the premium) for upgraded versions of the product with more features, greater functionality, or greater capacity.[27] The freemium pricing strategy has been most popular in digital offerings such as software media, games, or Web services where the cost of one additional copy of the product is negligible. Companies that have followed the new pricing strategy include Dropbox, Inc., SurveyMonkey, Spotify, and Skype. The idea is that if you give your product away, you will build a customer base of consumers willing to pay for the added benefits. While some products such as Skype have been highly successful, others have found that customers never upgrade to the premium version of the product. Pandora, the firm we met in Chapter 1, found that many consumers were unwilling to pay for their service and changed their business model to include a free service supported by paid advertising plus their Pandora One paid service without the ads.

Pricing Advantages for Online Shoppers

The Internet also creates unique pricing challenges for marketers because consumers and business customers are gaining more control over the buying process. Access to sophisticated "shopbots" and search engines means that consumers are no longer at the mercy of firms that dictate a price they must accept. The result is that customers have become more price sensitive. Many computer-savvy Internet shoppers find that shopbots provide them with the best price on all kinds of products. As one illustration, a comparison study found that the price of an Otter Box Defender Series case for your iPhone 5s ranges from a high of $59.90 at OtterBox.com to a low of $44.20 at Amazon.com. Similarly, the price of a Michael Kors Signature Tote is $165.50 at Amazon.com but $198.00 online from Nordstrom (no, we're not working on commission).

Detailed information about what products actually cost manufacturers, available from sites such as Consumerreports.org, can give consumers more negotiating power when shopping for new cars and other big-ticket items. Finally, e-commerce potentially can lower consumers' costs because of the gasoline, time, and aggravation they save when they avoid a trip to the mall.

5

OBJECTIVE

Describe the psychological, legal, and ethical aspects of pricing.

(pp. 329–334)

Psychological, Legal, and Ethical Aspects of Pricing

So far, we've discussed how marketers use demand, costs, and an understanding of the pricing environment to plan effective pricing strategies and tactics. There are, however, other aspects of pricing that marketers must understand and deal with in order to maximize the effectiveness of their pricing plans. In this section, we discuss a number of psychological, legal, and ethical factors related to pricing that are important for marketers. 📷 Figure 10.12 provides a quick look at these aspects of pricing.

Psychological Issues in Setting Prices

Much of what we've said about pricing depends on economists' notion of a customer who evaluates price in a logical, rational manner. For example, we express the concept of demand by a smooth curve, which assumes that if a firm lowers a product's price from $10 to $9.50 and then from $9.50 to $9 and so on, then customers will simply buy more and more. In the real world, though, it doesn't always work that way—consumers aren't nearly as rational as that! Let's look at some psychological factors that keep economists up at night.

Buyers' Pricing Expectations

Often consumers base their perceptions of price on what they perceive to be the customary or *fair price*. For example, for many years a candy bar or a pack of gum was priced at five cents (yes, five). Consumers would have perceived any other price as too high or low. It was a nickel candy bar—period. So when inflation kicked in and costs went up, some candy makers tried to shrink the size of the bar instead of changing the price.

Psychological Issues in Pricing	Psychological Pricing Strategies
• Buyer' Expectations • Internal Reference Prices • Price-Quality inferences	• Odd-Even Pricing • Price Lining • Prestige Pricing
Legal and Ethical Issues in B2C Pricing	Legal and Ethical Issues in B2B Pricing
• Bait-and-Switch • Loss-Leader pricing	• Price Discrimination • Price-Fixing • Predatory Pricing

Figure 10.12 📷 *Snapshot* |
Psychological, Legal, and Ethical Aspects of Pricing

Price planning is influenced by psychological issues and strategies and by legal and ethical issues.

Eventually, inflation prevailed, consumers' salaries rose, and that candy bar goes for as much as 20 times one nickel today—a price that consumers would have found unacceptable a few decades ago.

When the price of a product is above or even sometimes when it's below what consumers expect, they are less willing to purchase the product. If the price is above their expectations, they may think it is a rip-off. If it is below expectations, consumers may think quality is below par. By understanding the pricing expectations of their customers, marketers are better able to develop viable pricing strategies. These expectations can differ across cultures and countries. For example, in one study researchers did in southern California, they found that Chinese supermarkets charge significantly lower prices (only half as much for meat and seafood) than mainstream American supermarkets in the same areas.[28]

Internal Reference Prices

internal reference price
A set price or a price range in consumers' minds that they refer to in evaluating a product's price.

Sometimes consumers' perceptions of the customary price of a product depend on their **internal reference price**. That is, based on past experience, consumers have a set price or a price range in mind that they refer to when they evaluate a product's cost. The reference price may be the last price paid, or it may be the average of all the prices they know of for similar products. No matter what the brand, the normal price for a loaf of sandwich bread is about $2.00. In some stores it may be $1.89, and in others it is $2.89, but the average is $2.00. If consumers find a comparable loaf of bread priced much higher than this—say, $3.99—they will feel it is overpriced and grab a competing brand. If they find bread priced significantly lower—say, at $.89 or $.99 a loaf—they may shy away from the purchase as they wonder "what's wrong" with the bread (no, we don't think that's why they call it Wonder Bread).

In some cases, marketers try to influence consumers' expectations of what a product should cost when they use reference pricing strategies. For example, manufacturers may compare their price to competitors' prices when they advertise. Similarly, a retailer may display a product next to a higher-priced version of the same or a different brand. The consumer must choose between the two products with different prices.

Two results are likely: On the one hand, if the prices (and other characteristics) of the two products are fairly close, the consumer will probably feel the product quality is similar. This is an *assimilation effect*. The customer might think, "The price is about the same, they must be alike. I'll be smart and save a few dollars." And so the customer chooses the lower-price item because the low price makes it look attractive next to the higher-priced alternative. This is why store brands of deodorant, vitamins, pain relievers, and shampoo sit beside national brands, often accompanied by a shelf talker pointing out how much shoppers can save if they purchase the store brands. On the other hand, if the prices of the two products are too far apart, a *contrast effect* may result, in which the customer equates the gap with a big difference in quality: "Gee, this lower-priced one is probably not as good as the higher-priced one. I'll splurge on the more expensive one." Using this strategy, an appliance store may place an advertised $300 refrigerator next to a $699 model to convince a customer that the bottom-of-the-line model just won't do.

Price–Quality Inferences

Imagine that you go to a shoe store to check out running shoes. You notice one pair that costs $89.99. On another table you see a second pair that looks almost identical to the first pair—but its price is only $24.95. Which pair do you want? Which pair do you think is the better quality? Many of us will pay the higher price because we believe the bargain-basement shoes aren't worth the risk at any price.

Consumers make *price–quality inferences* about a product when they use price as a cue or an indicator of quality. (An inference means we believe something to be true without any direct evidence.) If consumers are unable to judge the quality of a product through examination or prior experience, they usually assume that the higher-priced product is the higher-quality product.

In fact, new research on how the brain works even suggests that the price we pay can subtly influence how much pleasure we get from the product. Brain scans show that—contrary to conventional wisdom—consumers who buy something at a discount experience *less* satisfaction than people who pay full price for the very same thing. For example, in one recent study, volunteers who drank wine that they were told cost $90 a bottle actually registered more brain activity in pleasure centers than did those who drank the very same wine but who were told it only cost $10 a bottle. Researchers call this the *price-placebo effect*. This is similar to the placebo effect in medicine where people who think they are getting the real thing but who are actually taking sugar pills still experience the effects of the real drug.[29]

Psychological Pricing Strategies

Setting a price is part science, part art. Marketers must understand psychological responses to prices when they decide what to charge for their products or services.

Odd–Even Pricing

In the U.S. market, we usually see prices in dollars and cents—$1.99, $5.98, $23.67, or even $599.95. We see prices in even dollar amounts—$2, $10, or $600—far less often. The reason? Marketers assume that there is a psychological response to odd prices that differs from the response to even prices. Habit might also play a role here. Whatever the reason, research on the difference in perceptions of odd versus even prices indeed supports the argument that prices ending in 99 rather than 00 lead to increased sales.[30]

But there are some instances in which even prices are the norm or perhaps a necessity. Theater and concert tickets, admission to sporting events, and lottery tickets tend to be priced in even amounts. Professionals normally quote their fees in even dollars. Would you want to visit a doctor or dentist who charged $39.99 for a visit, or would you be concerned that the quality of medical care was less than satisfactory? Many luxury items, such as jewelry, golf course fees, and resort accommodations, use even dollar prices to set them apart.

Restaurants (and the menu engineers who work with them) have discovered that how prices for menu items are presented has a major influence on what customers order—and how much they pay. When prices are given with dollar signs or even the word dollar, customers spend less. Thus, a simple 9 is better on a menu than $9. For high-end restaurants, the formats that end in 9, such as $9.99, indicate value but not quality.[31]

Price Lining

Marketers often apply their understanding of the psychological aspects of pricing in a practice they call **price lining**, whereby items in a product line sell at different prices, or *price points*. If you want to buy a new digital camera, you will find that most of the leading manufacturers have one "stripped-down" model for $100 or less. A better-quality but still moderately priced model likely will be around $200, while a professional-quality camera with multiple lenses might set you back $1,000 or more. Price lining provides the different ranges necessary to satisfy each segment of the market.

price lining
The practice of setting a limited number of different specific prices, called price points, for items in a product line.

Why is price lining a smart idea? From the marketer's standpoint, it's a way to maximize profits. In theory, a firm would charge each individual customer the highest price that customer is willing to pay. If the maximum one particular person is willing to pay for a digital camera is $150, then that will be the price. If another person is willing to pay $300, that will be his price. But charging each consumer a different price is really not possible. Having a limited number of prices that generally fall at the top of the different price ranges that customers find acceptable is a more workable alternative.

Prestige Pricing

Finally, although a "rational" consumer should be more likely to buy a product or service as the price goes down, in the real world sometimes this assumption gets turned on its head. Remember that earlier in the chapter we talked about situations where we want to meet an image-enhancement objective to appeal to status-conscious consumers. For this reason, sometimes luxury goods marketers use a *prestige pricing strategy*. Contrary to the "rational" assumption that we are more likely to purchase a product or service as the price goes down, in these cases, believe it or not, people tend to buy more as the price goes up!

Legal and Ethical Considerations in B2C Pricing

The free enterprise system is founded on the idea that the marketplace will regulate itself. Prices will rise or fall according to demand. Firms and individuals will supply goods and services at fair prices if there is an adequate profit incentive. Unfortunately, the business world includes the greedy and the unscrupulous.

Deceptive Pricing Practices: Bait and Switch

Unscrupulous businesses may advertise or promote prices in a deceptive way. The Federal Trade Commission (FTC), state lawmakers, and private bodies such as the Better Business Bureau have developed pricing rules and guidelines to meet the challenge. They say retailers (or other suppliers) must not claim that their prices are lower than a competitor's unless that claim is true. A going-out-of-business sale should be the last sale before going out of business. A fire sale should be held only when there really was a fire.

Another deceptive pricing practice is the **bait-and-switch** tactic, whereby a retailer will advertise an item at a very low price—the *bait*—to lure customers into the store. An example might be a budget model TV that has been stripped of all but the most basic features. But it is almost impossible to buy the advertised item—salespeople like to say (privately) that the item is "nailed to the floor." The salespeople do everything possible to get the unsuspecting customers to buy a different, more expensive, item—the *switch*. They might tell the customer "confidentially" that "the advertised item is really poor quality, lacking important features, and full of problems." It's complicated to enforce laws against bait-and-switch tactics because these practices are similar to the legal sales technique of "trading up." Simply encouraging consumers to purchase a higher-priced item is acceptable, but it is illegal to advertise a lower-priced item when it's not a legitimate, bona fide offer that is available if the customer demands it. The FTC may determine if an ad is a bait-and-switch scheme or a legitimate offer by checking to see if a firm refuses to show, demonstrate, or sell the advertised product; disparages it; or penalizes salespeople who do sell it.

Loss-Leader Pricing and Unfair Sales Acts

Not every advertised bargain is a bait and switch. Some retailers advertise items at very low prices or even below cost and are glad to sell them at that price because they know that once in the store, customers may buy other items at regular prices. Marketers call this **loss-leader pricing**; they do it to build store traffic and sales volume. For example, some office-supply stores and mass merchandisers recognize that "back-to-school" shopping means more than pencils and erasers and protractors.[32] These retailers use loss-leader pricing—eight pencils

bait-and-switch
An illegal marketing practice in which an advertised price special is used as bait to get customers into the store with the intention of switching them to a higher-priced item.

loss-leader pricing
The pricing policy of setting prices very low or even below cost to attract customers into a store.

for a penny, 24 Crayola crayons for a quarter, or a watercolor set for 50 cents—in order to entice mothers to fork out $60 for a new Spiderman backpack.

Some states frown on loss-leader practices, so they have passed legislation called **unfair sales acts** (also called *unfair trade practices acts*). These laws or regulations prohibit wholesalers and retailers from selling products below cost. These laws aim to protect small wholesalers and retailers from larger competitors because the "big fish" have the financial resources that allow them to offer loss leaders or products at very low prices—they know that the smaller firms can't match these bargain prices.

unfair sales acts
State laws that prohibit suppliers from selling products below cost to protect small businesses from larger competitors.

Legal Issues in B2B Pricing

Of course, illegal pricing practices are not limited to B2C pricing situations. Some of the more significant illegal B2B pricing activities include price discrimination, price fixing, and predatory pricing.

Illegal B2B Price Discrimination

The *Robinson–Patman Act* includes regulations against price discrimination in interstate commerce. Price discrimination regulations prevent firms from selling the same product to different retailers and wholesalers at different prices if such practices lessen competition. In addition to regulating the price companies charge, the Robinson–Patman Act specifically prohibits offering such "extras" as discounts, rebates, premiums, coupons, guarantees, and free delivery to some but not all customers.

There are exceptions, however:

- The Robinson–Patman Act does not apply to consumers—only resellers.

- A discount to a large channel customer is legal if it is based on the quantity of the order and the resulting efficiencies, such as transportation savings.

- The act allows price differences if there are physical differences in the product, such as different features. A name-brand appliance may be available through a large national retail chain at a lower price than an almost identical item a higher-priced retailer sells because only the chain sells that specific model.

Price-Fixing

Price-fixing occurs when two or more companies conspire to keep prices at a certain level. *Horizontal price-fixing* occurs when competitors making the same product jointly determine what price they each will charge. Of course, parallel pricing among firms in industries in which there are few sellers is not in and of itself considered price-fixing. There must be an exchange of pricing information between sellers to indicate illegal price-fixing actions. The Sherman Antitrust Act of 1890 specifically makes this practice, referred to as collusion, illegal. In 2013, a U.S. district court found Apple guilty of price-fixing due to secret agreements it made with the publishers Macmillan, Penguin, Hachette, HarperCollins, and Simon & Schuster to raise the price of e-books in order to combat Amazon's strategy of discounting titles to sales of its Kindle reader. When the publishers joined forces to raise e-book prices, Amazon had no choice but to follow suit. As a result consumers paid millions of dollars more for e-books regardless of where they purchased them.[33]

Price-fixing can occur in two ways: horizontal and vertical. Horizontal price fixing, illegal under the Sherman Act, occurs when firms in the same industry join to charge the same price. Vertical price fixing occurs when manufacturers or wholesalers attempt to force retailers to charge a certain price for their product. When *vertical price-fixing* occurs, the

price fixing
The collaboration of two or more firms in setting prices, usually to keep prices high.

Ripped from the Headlines

Ethical/Sustainable Decisions in the Real World

You live in a big city, and you need a ride. Quick! What do you do? You pull out your Uber app, and a car appears at your location within minutes. But wait. Now it's next week, and you need a ride in a blinding snowstorm. What do you do? You pull out your Uber app, of course. But this time the ride costs you 8.25 times as much as last week![34] What's the deal?

The deal (or is it?) is **surge pricing**, which occurs when a company, like Uber,

raises the price of its product as demand for that product goes up and then lowers it as demand goes back down. So in times of greatest need—for example, bad weather or New Year's Eve—it's going to cost you more to get a ride. While some riders cry foul play, Uber argues that surge pricing is fair because this ensures that cars will be available during times of greatest demand. Since each Uber driver is an independent contractor who can work whenever he or she chooses, the higher price encourages drivers to make themselves available at more times and locations. Still, many customers are angry about the price increases—one even posted her receipt on Instagram with the hashtag #neveragain.[35]

If you were advising Uber's executives, would you encourage them to end the service's surge pricing strategy to prevent the company from losing customers who are angry about such price hikes?

☐ **YES** ☐ **NO**

surge pricing
A pricing strategy in which the price of a product is raised as demand for that product goes up and lowered as demand goes down.

predatory pricing
An illegal pricing strategy in which a company sets a very low price for the purpose of driving competitors out of business.

retailer that wants to carry the product has to charge the "suggested" retail price. The *Consumer Goods Pricing Act* of 1976 limited this practice, leaving retail stores free to set whatever price they choose without interference by the manufacturer or wholesaler. Today, retailers don't need to adhere to "suggested" prices.

Predatory Pricing

Predatory pricing means that a company sets a very low price for the purpose of driving competitors out of business. Later, when they have a monopoly, they turn around and increase prices. The Sherman Act and the Robinson–Patman Act prohibit predatory pricing. For example, in 1999 the Justice Department accused American Airlines of predatory pricing at its Dallas–Fort Worth hub.[36] In the mid-1990s, three small rivals started flying into the airport. American responded by lowering the prices of its flights on four routes. The Justice Department claimed that the airline planned to scare the three carriers away and monopolize the routes. While American was exonerated in court, the case did send a message to airlines that they must be careful when they set prices.

Here's my choice...

Real **People**, Real **Choices**

Why do you think Betsy chose option 1?

1 Option **2** Option **3** Option

How It Worked Out at Converse College

Betsy chose option 1, and the college reduced undergraduate tuition by 43 percent to a total of $16,500. It arrived at this number on the basis of a price-sensitivity study it commissioned from Noel-Levitz, a consulting firm. In this study, the company presented college-age students and their parents with different combinations of college choices, tuition, and financial aid. Their responses to these scenarios helped the analysts determine how important a tuition decrease would be relative to other possibilities and how much of a cut Converse would have to make to really have an impact. Exhibit 10-11 shows one of the slides from the company's report to Converse that recommended this option.

This decision moved the school away from the high-tuition/high-discount model in which students who pay more than the actual cost of their education ultimately subsidize the aid for students who receive the highest discounts. The decision also priced a private customized college experience comparably to flagship public universities while offering the added value of an 11-to-1 student-to-faculty ratio.

Why such a drastic price cut? The logic was that if Converse was going to make such an unusual move, the school wanted it to be truly meaningful and to make a bold statement. Converse created a multifaceted marketing plan to announce the move to reset tuition that centered on new messaging about a top-quality product for a great value with the tagline "Voice, Value, Vision."

With the tuition reset, Converse took a national lead in helping to solve America's college-affordability issues, as the tuition decrease rewinds the price back to what it was over a decade ago. The $16,500 tuition reset is coupled with a room-and-board price of $9,500 for a total cost of $26,000. This gives Converse one of the lowest prices of any four-year private college or university in the region and is comparable with total costs at premiere public universities both in and out of state.

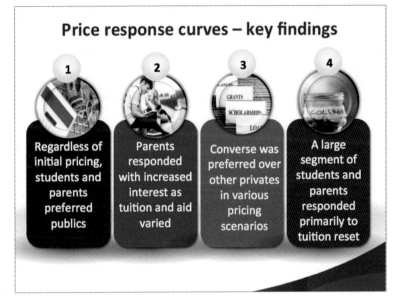

Marketing Metrics: How Converse Measures Success

Converse received immediate increased interest from prospective students, and recruitment numbers are significantly ahead of previous years. The school showed a 6 percent increase in applications and an 11 percent increase in the number of prospective students who visited the campus and is projecting an increase of 5 percent in undergraduate enrollment for the first year. More broadly, here are some important measures the school uses to determine how its new pricing model is working:

Enrollment funnel. Prospective student inquiries, applications, visits, admittances, and tuition deposits.

Retention numbers. First to second year, second to third year, third to fourth year, and overall graduation rates.

Revenue generation. The impact of the tuition reset on college revenue, which Converse anticipates will remain flat if enrollment remains constant and will increase as enrollment numbers increase.

Student billing. Converse will assess whether students find it easier to pay tuition and pay on time by measuring the number and size of past-due balances.

Demographic shifts in student body makeup that may be attributed to the tuition reset. Converse already is seeing an increase in transfer students. The school is receiving more applications from students who are also applying to public colleges, indicating that it has broadened its target market by reducing its cost.

Tuition discount rate. A lower discount rate (the percentage that tuition price is discounted with the awarding of financial aid) is healthier for colleges, and the reduced tuition will result in a healthier discount rate. It likewise creates a more sustainable operating model with transparent and controllable financial levers with which to advance the college and its mission.

Refer back to **page 302** for Betsy's story

MyMarketingLab™

Go to **mymktlab.com** to complete the problems marked with this icon ⭐ as well as additional Marketing Metrics questions only available in MyMarketingLab.

Objective Summary ➡ Key Terms ➡ Apply

1. Objective Summary (pp. 304–308)

Explain the importance of pricing and how marketers set objectives for their pricing strategies.

Pricing is important to firms because it creates profits and influences customers to purchase or not. Prices may be monetary or nonmonetary, as when consumers or businesses exchange one product for another. Effective pricing objectives are designed to support corporate and marketing objectives and are flexible. Pricing objectives often focus on a desired level of profit growth or profit margin, on sales (to maximize sales or to increase market share), on competing effectively, on increasing customer satisfaction, or on communicating a certain image.

Key Terms

Bitcoin, p. 304

price, p. 305

market share, p. 307

prestige products, p. 308

2. Objective Summary (pp. 308–320)

Describe how marketers use costs, demands, revenue, and the pricing environment to make pricing decisions.

In developing prices, marketers must estimate demand and determine costs. Marketers often use break-even analysis to help in deciding on the price for a product. Break-even analysis uses fixed and variable costs to identify how many units must be sold at a certain price in order to begin making a profit. Marketers must also consider the requirements for adequate trade margins for retailers, wholesalers, and other members of the channel of distribution. Like other elements of the marketing mix, pricing is influenced by a variety of external environmental factors. This includes economic trends such as inflation and recession and the firm's competitive environment—that is, whether the firm does business in an oligopoly, a monopoly, or a more competitive environment. Government regulations can also affect prices by increasing the cost of production or through actual regulations of a firm's pricing strategies. Consumer trends that influence how consumers think and behave may also influence pricing. While marketers of some products may develop standardized pricing strategies for global markets, unique environmental factors in different countries mean marketers must localize pricing strategies.

Key Terms

price elasticity of demand, p. 311

elastic demand, p. 311

inelastic demand, p. 311

cross-elasticity of demand, p. 313

variable costs, p. 313

fixed costs, p. 314

average fixed cost, p. 314

total costs, p. 314

break-even analysis, p. 315

break-even point, p. 315

contribution per unit, p. 315

markup, p. 316

gross margin, p. 316

retailer margin, p. 316

wholesaler margin, p. 316

list price or manufacturer's suggested retail price (MSRP), p. 317

3. Objective Summary (pp. 321–327)

Understand key pricing strategies and tactics.

Although easy to calculate and "safe," frequently used cost-based strategies do not consider demand, the competition, the stage in the product life cycle, plant capacity, or product image. The most common cost-based strategy is cost-plus pricing.

Pricing strategies based on demand, such as target costing and yield management pricing, can require that marketers estimate demand at different prices in order to be certain they can sell what they produce. Strategies based on the competition may represent industry wisdom but can be tricky to apply. A price leadership strategy is often used in an oligopoly.

Firms that focus on customer needs may consider everyday low price or value pricing strategies. New products may be priced using a high skimming price to recover research, development, and promotional costs or a penetration price to encourage more customers and discourage competitors from entering the market. Trial pricing means setting a low price for a limited time.

To implement pricing strategies with individual products, marketers may use two-part pricing or payment pricing tactics. For multiple products, marketers may use price bundling, wherein two or more products are sold and priced as a single package. Captive pricing is often chosen when two items must be used together; one item is sold at a very low price and the other at a high, profitable price.

Distribution-based pricing tactics, including F.O.B., basing-point, and uniform delivered pricing, address differences in how far products must be shipped. Similar pricing tactics are used for products sold internationally.

Pricing for members of the channel may include trade or functional discounts, cumulative or noncumulative quantity discounts to encourage larger purchases, cash discounts to encourage fast payment, and seasonal discounts to spread purchases throughout the year or to increase off-season or in-season sales.

Key Terms

cost-plus pricing, p. 322

demand-based pricing, p. 322

target costing, p. 322

yield management pricing, p. 323

price leadership, p. 323

value pricing or everyday low pricing (EDLP), p. 324

skimming price, p. 324

penetration pricing, p. 324

trial pricing, p. 324

price bundling, p. 325

captive pricing, p. 325

F.O.B. origin pricing, p. 325

F.O.B. delivered pricing, p. 325

uniform delivered pricing, p. 326

freight absorption pricing, p. 326

trade discounts, p. 326

quantity discounts, p. 326

cash discounts, p. 326

seasonal discounts, p. 327

4. Objective Summary   (pp. 327–329)

Understand the opportunities for Internet pricing strategies.

E-commerce may offer firms an opportunity to initiate dynamic pricing—meaning prices can be changed frequently with little or no cost. Auctions offer opportunities for customers to bid on items in C2C, B2C, and B2B e-commerce. The Internet also allows firms to practice freemium pricing, in which basic versions of digital products are given to customers for no charge. The Internet allows buyers to compare products and prices, gives consumers more control over the price they pay for items, and has made customers more price sensitive.

Key Terms

dynamic pricing, p. 327

Internet price discrimination, p. 327

online auctions, p. 328

freemium, p. 328

5. Objective Summary   (pp. 329–334)

Describe the psychological, legal, and ethical aspects of pricing.

Consumers may express emotional or psychological responses to prices. Customers may use an idea of a customary or fair price as an internal reference price in evaluating products. Sometimes marketers use reference pricing strategies by displaying products with different prices next to each other. A price–quality inference means that consumers use price as a cue for quality. Customers respond to odd prices differently than to even-dollar prices. Marketers may practice price lining strategies in which they set a limited number of different price ranges for a product line. With luxury products, marketers may use a prestige pricing strategy, assuming that people will buy more if the price is higher.

Most marketers try to avoid unethical or illegal pricing practices. One deceptive pricing practice is the illegal bait-and-switch tactic. Many states have unfair sales acts, which are laws against loss leader pricing that make it illegal to sell products below cost. Federal regulations prohibit predatory pricing, price discrimination, and horizontal or vertical price-fixing.

Key Terms

internal reference price, p. 330

price lining, p. 331

bait-and-switch, p. 332

loss-leader pricing, p. 332

unfair sales acts, p. 333

price fixing, p. 333

surge pricing, p. 334

predatory pricing, p. 334

Chapter **Questions** and **Activities**

Concepts: Test Your Knowledge

10-1. What is opportunity cost? Why is it unavoidable for businesses?

10-2. What are the six steps involved in price planning? Identify them and list them in the correct order.

10-3. What is meant by price elasticity of demand? Explain, with examples of each, price elasticity and price inelasticity. Why is it the case that some products or services are price elastic and others are price inelastic?

10-4. What is meant by cross elasticity of demand? Why is it important?

10-5. What are variable costs?

10-6. What are pricing tactics? Give four examples of pricing tactics used by businesses.

10-7. Delivery terms for pricing of products sold in international markets are similar. Explain what is meant by CIF, CFR, and CIP. Define each term and briefly explain how it works.

10-8. Explain and give an example of cost-plus pricing, target costing, and yield management pricing.

10-9. For new products, when is skimming pricing more appropriate, and when is penetration pricing the best strategy? When would trial pricing be an effective pricing strategy?

10-10. Explain two-part pricing, payment pricing, price bundling, captive pricing, and distribution-based pricing tactics.

10-11. Why do marketers use trade or functional discounts, quantity discounts, cash discounts, and seasonal discounts in pricing to members of the channel?

10-12. What is dynamic pricing? What is discriminatory pricing? What is the difference between the two?

10-13. Explain these psychological aspects of pricing: price–quality inferences, odd–even pricing, internal reference price, price lining, and prestige pricing.

10-14. Explain how unethical marketers might use bait-and-switch tactics, price-fixing, and predatory pricing. What is surge pricing?

Activities: Apply What You've Learned

⭐ **10-15.** *Creative Homework/Short Project* Assume that you are an entrepreneur who runs a bakery that sells gluten-free breads and cakes. You believe that the current economic conditions merit an increase in the price of your baked goods. You are concerned, however, that increasing the price might not be profitable because you are unsure of the price elasticity of demand for your products. Develop a plan for the measurement of price elasticity of demand for your products. What findings would lead you to increase the price? What findings would cause you to rethink the decision to increase prices? Develop a presentation for your class outlining (1) the concept of elasticity of demand, (2) why raising prices without understanding the elasticity would be a bad move, (3) your recommendations for measurement, and (4) the potential impact on profits for elastic and inelastic demand.

10-16. *In Class, 10–25 Minutes for Teams* For each of the following products, determine at least three different prices that might be charged. Then survey each of the individuals within your group to find out how much of each product they would buy at each price point for each of the products. For each product, calculate the price elasticity of demand to determine whether the demand is elastic or inelastic.
   a. Cheese pizzas per month
   b. Movie tickets per month
   c. Concert tickets per year

10-17. *Creative Homework/Short Project* Assume that you have been hired as the assistant manager of a local store that sells fresh fruits and vegetables. As you look over the store, you notice that there are two different displays of tomatoes. In one display, the tomatoes are priced at $2.39 per pound, and in the other, the tomatoes are priced at $1.69 per pound. The tomatoes look very much alike. You notice that many people are buying the $2.39 tomatoes. Write a report explaining what is happening and give your recommendations for the store's pricing strategy.

10-18. *For Further Research (Individual)* Price skimming and price penetration are opposites. Choose a major global brand for each strategy and identify an example. Explain how the pricing tactics work and when they are used. What is it about the nature of the product or service that allows the brand to have this type of pricing? What is it that makes the pricing a success or a failure?

10-19. *For Further research (Individual)* In this chapter, we talked about how the ways in which a manufacturer or a major distributor uses pricing tactics in the distribution chain. Outline the main pricing tactics used an, where possible, find examples of how they work and their effect on sales. In each case, make sure you are clear about the specifics of the pricing tactic as well as when and how the tactic is used. Write a report on your findings and what they tell you about distribution chain pricing.

10-20. *For Further Research (Groups)* Select one of the product categories below. Identify two different firms that offer consumers a line of product offerings in the category. For example, Dell, HP, and Apple each market a line of laptop computers, while Hoover, Dyson, and Bissell offer lines of vacuum cleaners. Using the Internet or by visiting a retailer who sells your selected product, research the product lines and pricing of the two firms. Based on your research, develop a presentation on the price lining strategies of the two firms. Your presentation should discuss (1) the specific price points of the product offerings of each firm and how the price lining strategy maximizes revenue, (2) your ideas for why the specific price points were selected, (3) how the price lining strategies of the two firms are alike and how they are different, and (4) possible reasons for differences in the strategies.
   a. Laptop computers
   b. Vacuum cleaners
   c. LED TVs
   d. Smart phones

Apply Marketing Metrics

Contribution analysis and break-even analysis are very popular and often used marketing metrics. These analyses are essential to determine if a firm's marketing opportunity will mean a financial loss or profit. As explained in the chapter, *contribution* is the difference between the selling price per unit and the variable cost per unit. Break-even analysis that includes contribution tells marketers how much must be sold to break even or to earn a desired amount of profit.

Touch of Beirut Brands is a Los Angeles–based specialty manufacturer of Lebanese specialty foods and ingredients. In the past, the firm has marketed primarily through restaurant distributors to small mom-and-pop Lebanese cuisine restaurants around the U.S. But they've developed a marketing plan to sell a combination hummus and pita slices packaged product that is ready to eat—sort of like the famous boxed Oscar Meyer Lunchables. They've branded the new product "Happy Hummus." Outlets will be Whole Foods and other new-age supermarkets.

The company plans to use social media to gain buzz around the new product but will also be spending money on advertising and sales promotion through coupons to consumers and price incentives to distributors and retailers. Whole Foods would like to be able to sell the boxes at retail for $5. Because the retailer typically requires a 30 percent markup, Touch of Beirut's price to the supermarkets will be $3.50 per box. The unit variable costs for the product including packaging will be $1.25.

The company estimates its advertising and promotion expenses for the first year will be $2,500,000.

⭐ **10-21.** What is the contribution per unit for Happy Hummus?

⭐ **10-22.** What is the break-even volume for the first year that will cover the planned advertising and promotion (1) in units and (2) in dollars?

⭐ **10-23.** How many units of Happy Hummus must Touch of Beirut sell to earn a profit of $1,000,000?

⭐ **10-24.** Does this seem like a good business venture to you? Why or why not?

Choices: What Do You Think?

⭐ **10-25.** *Critical Thinking* Governments sometimes provide price subsidies to specific industries; that is, they reduce a domestic firm's costs so that it can sell products on the international market at a lower price. What reasons do governments (and politicians) use for these government subsidies? What are the benefits and disadvantages to domestic industries in the long run? To international customers? Who would benefit and who would lose if all price subsidies were eliminated? Do you feel that the U.S. government should or should not use price subsidies for some U.S. industries? Why do you feel that way?

10-26. *Ethics* Several online stores now sell products to consumers at different prices based on the user's information, such as geographical location—which determines your proximity to competitors and your area's average income. Although this practice, known as Internet price discrimination, is not illegal, some would say it is unethical. Do you believe this practice is unethical? Should this practice be illegal? If you think the practice should be legal, should retailers be required to put a disclaimer on their site? Explain your reasoning.

⭐ **10-27.** *Critical Thinking* In many oligopolistic industries, firms follow a price leadership strategy, in which an accepted industry leader sets, raises, or lowers prices and the other firms follow. In what ways is this policy good and bad for the industry? In what ways is this good or bad for consumers? What is the difference between price leadership and price fixing? Should governments allow industries to use price leadership strategies? If not, how can they prevent it?

10-28. *Ethics* Many very successful retailers use a loss leader pricing strategy, in which they advertise an item at a price below their cost and sell the item at that price to get customers into their store. They feel that these customers will continue to shop with their company and that they will make a profit in the long run. Do you consider this an unethical practice? Who benefits and who is hurt by such practices? Do you think the practice should be made illegal, as some states have done? How is this different from bait-and-switch pricing?

10-29. *Critical Thinking* Consumers often make price–quality inferences about products. What does this mean? What are some products for which you are likely to make price–quality inferences? Do such inferences make sense, and, if so, how?

10-30. *Critical Thinking* You work as a marketer for a large chain of upscale boutique-like stores that sells all-natural and other fresh beauty products. Your research tells you that the market won't tolerate a price increase, so to save money during tough times you have decided to use cheaper ingredients from new suppliers. What, if anything, do you tell your customers? What are some of the possible ramifications of this decision for your business, your customers, and your suppliers? What will you do when the market rebounds?

10-31. *Critical Thinking* In pricing new products, marketers may choose a skimming or a penetration pricing strategy. While it's easy to see the benefits of these practices for the firm, what are the advantages and/or disadvantages of the practice for consumers? For an industry as a whole?

Miniproject: Learn by Doing

The purpose of this miniproject is to help you become familiar with how consumers respond to different prices by conducting a series of pricing experiments. For this project, you should first select a product category that students such as yourself normally purchase. It should be a moderately expensive purchase, such as athletic shoes, a smart phone, or a piece of luggage. You should next obtain two photographs of items in this product category or, if possible, two actual items. The two items should not appear to be substantially different in quality or in price.

Note: You will need to recruit separate research participants for each of the activities listed in the next section.

10-32. *Experiment 1: Reference Pricing*
   a. Place the two products together. Place a sign on one with a low price. Place a sign on the other with a high price (about 50 percent higher will do). Ask your research participants to evaluate the quality of each of the items and to tell which one they would probably purchase.
   b. Reverse the signs and ask other research participants to evaluate the quality of each of the items and to tell which one they would probably purchase.
   c. Place the two products together again. This time place a sign on one with a moderate price. Place a

sign on the other that is only a little higher (less than 10 percent higher). Again, ask research participants to evaluate the quality of each of the items and to tell which one they would probably purchase.

  d. Reverse the signs and ask other research participants to evaluate the quality of each of the items and to tell which one they would probably purchase.

10-33. *Experiment 2: Odd–Even Pricing:* For this experiment, you will only need one of the items from experiment 1.

  a. Place a sign on the item that ends in $.99 (e.g., $62.99). Ask research participants to tell you if they think the price for the item is very low, slightly low, moderate, slightly high, or very high. Also ask them to evaluate the quality of the item and to tell you,

on a scale of 1 to 10, with 10 being very likely, how likely they would be to purchase the item.

  b. This time place a sign on the item that is slightly lower but that ends in $.00 (e.g., $60). Ask different research participants to tell you if they think the price for the item is very low, slightly low, moderate, slightly high, or very high. Also ask them to evaluate the quality of the item and to tell you how likely they would be to purchase the item.

Develop a presentation for your class in which you discuss the results of your experiments and what they tell you about odd-even pricing and about assimilation and contrast effects in price perceptions.

Marketing in **Action** Case — Real Choices at Procter & Gamble

How many different paper towel choices do you need? The number in the marketplace to choose from is growing. For many product categories, companies use a three-tier pricing system: entry-level, mid-tier, and luxury. This model appears in automobiles (Toyota: Scion, Toyota, Lexus), clothes (Gap: Old Navy, Gap, Banana Republic), and hotels (Marriott: Fairfield Inn, Courtyard, The Ritz-Carlton). Procter & Gamble Co. (P&G) wants to know if the three-tier pricing system would also work for paper towels, detergent, and other household products.

P&G is a global consumer goods company headquartered in Cincinnati, Ohio. Its products include pet foods, cleaning agents, and personal care products. The company has been recognized by the Forbes/Reputation Institute for its ability to foster innovation, nurture talent, and earn consumers' trust and admiration. P&G has a reputation for dominance in many of the consumer goods categories in which it competes. The company's brands, including Bounty, Crest, and Tide, are offered in North America, Latin America, Europe, the Middle East, Africa, Asia, Australia, and New Zealand. Over 25 of P&G's brands individually generate more than a billion dollars in net annual sales.

In response to growing consumer spending and household wealth in the U.S., the company is introducing top-of-the-line versions of many of its household products, such as Tide Pods and Crest 3D White toothpaste, touting "superior product benefits." P&G's Bounty brand has added Bounty DuraTowel, a luxury version of one its standard brands. The paper towel has embossing that resembles a dishcloth and has thicker plastic packaging. Customers pay $10.25 for a six-pack, a 46 percent increase over the intermediate offering and double the price of the basic version. The company is segmenting customers by willingness to pay. P&G hopes that the new sales from customers who desire better features or special indulgences will grow its profits.

In addition to the Bounty brand, P&G has added a "platinum" variety of its Cascade dishwasher detergent. The new version promises not only to scrub away food stuck on dishes for 24 hours but also to clean the stainless-steel tub of the dishwasher. Cascade Platinum costs 30.2 cents per dose, which is 3.1 cents more per use than the next Cascade offering below it. The new pricing is coupled with new packaging consisting of a shiny silver bag. This is in comparison to the basic green packaging of its other Cascade offerings.

P&G may face challenges in justifying its premium pricing strategy in ordinary product categories. Will consumers be willing to pay premium prices for basic household items like paper towels? Burt Flickinger, a retail consultant and managing director of Strategic Resource Group, says, "There's going to be a high degree of difficulty for P&G." He believes that consumers may be willing to pay a premium for beauty products and high-performance goods. However, how will they feel about other products where there are effective and efficient choices at more competitive prices? Of course, P&G's competitors are not sitting still. Kimberly-Clark, Colgate-Palmolive, and others are also introducing premium versions of their offerings to the marketplace. P&G has a lot to think about now that the products have been introduced.

You Make the Call

10-34. What is the decision facing P&G?

10-35. What factors are important in understanding this decision situation?

10-36. What are the alternatives?

10-37. What decision(s) do you recommend?

10-38. What are some ways to implement your recommendation?

Sources: Based on Serena Ng, "Basics Get Luxury Treatment," September 4, 2013, **http://online.wsj.com/news/articles/SB100014 24127887323838204579000421935278090** (accessed April 26, 2014); Procter & Gamble, Inc., "Brands and Innovation," **www .pg.com/en_US/brands/index.shtml** (accessed April 25, 2014); and Kyle Stock, "Procter & Gamble Cleans Up with Luxury Paper Towels," October 28, 2013, **www.businessweek.com/articles/2013-10-28/procter-and-gamble-profits-from-high-end-products** (accessed April 26, 2014).

MyMarketingLab™

Go to **mymktlab.com** for Auto-graded writing questions as well as the following Assisted-graded writing questions:

10-39. This chapter states, "Often consumers base their perception of price on what they believe to be the customary or fair price." Explain the meaning of this statement and provide an example.

10-40. Some firms have profit as a pricing objective, while others set prices for customer satisfaction. What are the major differences between these two? Which is better?

Marketing Math

To develop marketing strategies to meet the goals of an organization effectively and efficiently, it is essential that marketers understand and use a variety of financial analyses. This supplement provides some of these basic financial analyses, including a review of the income statement and balance sheet, as well as some basic performance ratios. In addition, this supplement includes an explanation of some of the specific calculations that marketers use routinely to set prices for their goods and services.

Income Statement and Balance Sheet

The two most important documents used to analyze the financial situation of a company are the income statement and the balance sheet. The *income statement* (which is sometimes referred to as the *profit and loss statement* or the *P&L*) provides a summary of the revenues and expenses of a firm—that is, the amount of income a company received from sales or other sources, the amount of money it spent, and the resulting income or loss that the company experienced.

The major elements of the income statement are as follows:

- **Gross sales** are the total of all income the firm receives from the sales of goods and services.

- **Net sales revenue** is the gross sales minus the amount for returns and promotional or other allowances given to customers.

- **Cost of goods sold** (sometimes called the *cost of sales*) is the cost of inventory or goods that the firm has sold.

- **Gross margin** (also called *gross profit*) is the amount of sales revenue that is in excess of the cost of goods sold.

- **Operating expenses** are expenses other than the cost of goods sold that are necessary for conducting business. These may include salaries, rent, depreciation on buildings and equipment, insurance, utilities, supplies, and property taxes.

- **Operating income** (sometimes called *income from operations*) is the gross margin minus the operating expenses. Sometimes accountants prepare an *operating statement*, which is similar to the income statement except that the final calculation is the operating income—that is, other revenues or expenses and taxes are not included.

- **Other revenue and expenses** are income and/or expenses other than those required for conducting the business. These may include items such as interest income/expenses and any gain or loss experienced from the sale of property or plant assets.

- **Taxes** are the amount of income tax the firm owes calculated as a percentage of income.

- **Net income** (sometimes called *net earnings* or *net profit*) is the excess of total revenue over total expenses.

Table 10S.1 shows the income statement for an imaginary company, DLL Incorporated. DLL is a typical merchandising firm. Note that the income statement is for a specific year and includes income and expenses inclusively from January 1 through December 31. The following comments explain the meaning of some of the important entries included in this statement.

- DLL Inc. has total or gross sales during the year of $253,950. This figure was adjusted, however, by deducting the $3,000 worth of goods returned and special allowances given to customers and by $2,100 in special discounts. Thus, the actual or net sales generated by sales is $248,850.

- The cost of goods sold is calculated by adding the inventory of goods on January 1 to the amount purchased during the year and then subtracting the inventory of goods on December 31. In this case, DLL had $60,750 worth of inventory on hand on January 1. During the year, the firm made purchases in the amount of $135,550. This amount,

Table 10S.1 | DLL Income Statement for the Year Ended December 31, 2008

Gross sales		$253,950	
Less: sales returns and allowances	$ 3,000		
Sales discounts	2,100	5,100	
Net sales revenue			$248,850
Cost of goods sold			
Inventory, January 1, 2008		60,750	
Purchases	135,550		
Less: purchase returns and allowances	1,500		
Purchase discounts	750		
Net purchases	133,300		
Plus: freight-in	2,450	135,750	
Goods available for sale		196,500	
Less: inventory, December 31, 2008		60,300	
Cost of goods sold			136,200
Gross margin			112,650
Operating expenses			
Salaries and commissions		15,300	
Rent		12,600	
Insurance		1,500	
Depreciation		900	
Supplies		825	
Total operating expenses			31,125
Operating income			81,525
Other revenue and (expenses)			
Interest revenue		1,500	
Interest expense		(2,250)	(750)
Income before tax			80,775
Taxes (40%)			32,310
Net income			$ 48,465

however, was reduced by purchase returns and allowances of $1,500 and by purchase discounts of $750, so the net purchases are only $133,300.

There is also an amount on the statement labeled "Freight-In." This is the amount spent by the firm in shipping charges to get goods to its facility from suppliers. Any expenses for freight from DLL to its customers (Freight-Out) would be an operating expense. In this case, the Freight-In expense of $2,450 is added to net purchase costs. Then these costs of current purchases are added to the beginning inventory to show that during the year the firm had a total of $196,500 in goods available for sale. Finally, the inventory of goods held on December 31 is subtracted from the goods available for sale, to reveal the total cost of goods sold of $136,200.

We mentioned that DLL Inc. is a merchandising firm—a retailer of some type. If DLL were instead a manufacturer, calculation of the cost of goods sold would be a bit more complicated and would probably include separate figures for items such as inventory of finished goods, the "work-in-process" inventory, the raw materials inventory, and the cost of goods delivered to customers during the year. Continuing down the previous income statement we have the following:

- The cost of goods sold is subtracted from the net sales revenue to get a gross margin of $112,650.

- Operating expenses for DLL include the salaries and commissions paid to its employees, rent on facilities and/or equipment, insurance, depreciation of capital items, and the cost of operating supplies. DLL has a total of $31,125 in operating expenses, which is deducted from the gross margin. Thus, DLL has an operating income of $81,525.

- DLL had both other income and expenses in the form of interest revenues of $1,500 and interest expenses of $2,250, making a total other expense of $750, which was subtracted from the operating income, leaving an income before taxes of $80,775.

- Finally, the income before taxes is reduced by 40 percent ($32,310) for taxes, leaving a net income of $48,465. The 40 percent is an average amount for federal and state corporate income taxes incurred by most firms.

The *balance sheet* lists the assets, liabilities, and stockholders' equity of the firm. Whereas the income statement represents what happened during an entire year, the balance sheet is like a snapshot; it shows the firm's financial situation at one point in time. For this reason, the balance sheet is sometimes called the *statement of financial position*.

Table 10S.2 shows DLL Inc.'s balance sheet for December 31. Assets include any economic resource that is expected to benefit the firm in the short or long term. *Current assets* are items that are normally expected to be turned into cash or used up during the next 12 months or during the firm's normal operating cycle. Current assets for DLL include cash, securities, accounts receivable (money owed to the firm and not yet paid), inventory on hand, prepaid insurance, and supplies: a total of $84,525. *Long-term assets* include all assets that are not current assets. For DLL, these are furniture and fixtures (less an amount for depreciation) and land, or $45,300. The *total assets* for DLL are $129,825.

A firm's *liabilities* are its economic obligations, or debts that are payable to individuals or organizations outside the firm. *Current liabilities* are debts due to be paid in the coming year or during the firm's normal operating cycle. For DLL, the current liabilities—the accounts payable, unearned sales revenue, wages payable, and interest payable—total $72,450. *Long-term liabilities* (in the case of DLL, a note in the amount of $18,900) are all liabilities that are not due to be paid during the coming cycle. *Stockholders' equity* is the value of the stock and the corporation's capital or retained earnings. DLL has $15,000 in common stock and $23,475 in retained earnings for a total stockholders' equity of $38,475. Total liabilities always equal total assets—in this case $129,825.

Table 10S.2	DLL Inc. Balance Sheet: December 31, 2008		

Assets

Current assets			
Cash		$ 4,275	
Marketable securities		12,000	
Accounts receivable		6,900	
Inventory		60,300	
Prepaid insurance		300	
Supplies		150	
Total current assets			84,525
Long-term assets—property, plant and equipment			
Furniture and fixtures	$42,300		
Less: accumulated depreciation	4,500	37,800	
Land		7,500	
Total long-term assets			45,300
Total assets			$129,825
Liabilities			
Current liabilities			
Accounts payable	$70,500		
Unearned sales revenue	1,050		
Wages payable	600		
Interest payable	300		
Total current liabilities		72,450	
Long-term liabilities			
Note payable		18,900	
Total liabilities			91,350
Stockholders' equity			
Common stock		15,000	
Retained earnings		23,475	
Total stockholders' equity			38,475
Total liabilities and stockholders' equity			$129,825

Important Financial Performance Ratios

How do managers and financial analysts compare the performance of a firm from one year to the next? How do investors compare the performance of one firm with that of another? As the book notes, managers often rely on various metrics to measure performance.

Often, a number of different financial ratios provide important information for such comparisons. Such *ratios* are percentage figures comparing various income statement items to net sales. Ratios provide a better way to compare performance than simple dollar sales or cost figures for two reasons. They enable analysts to compare the performance of large and small firms, and they provide a fair way to compare performance over time without having to take inflation and other changes into account. In this section, we will explain the basic operating ratios. Other measures of performance that marketers frequently use and that are also explained here are the inventory turnover rate and return on investment (ROI).

Operating Ratios

Measures of performance calculated directly from the information in a firm's income statement (sometimes called an operating statement) are called the *operating ratios*. Each ratio compares some income statement item to net sales. The most useful of these are the *gross margin ratio*, the *net income ratio*, the *operating expense ratio*, and the *returns and allowances ratio*. These ratios vary widely by industry but tend to be important indicators of how a firm is doing within its industry. The ratios for DLL Inc. are shown in Table 10S.3.

- **Gross margin ratio** shows what percentage of sales revenues is available for operating and other expenses and for profit. With DLL, this means that 45 percent, or nearly half, of every sales dollar is available for operating costs and for profits.

- **Net income ratio** (sometimes called the *net profit ratio*) shows what percentage of sales revenues is income or profit. For DLL, the net income ratio is 19.5 percent. This means that the firm's profit before taxes is about 20 cents of every dollar.

- **Operating expense ratio** is the percentage of sales needed for operating expenses. DLL has an operating expense ratio of 12.5 percent. Tracking operating expense ratios from one year to the next or comparing them with an industry average gives a firm important information about the efficiency of its operations.

- **Returns and allowances ratio** shows what percentage of all sales is being returned, probably by unhappy customers. DLL's returns and allowances ratio shows that only a little over 1 percent of sales is being returned.

Table 10S.3 | Hypothetical Operating Ratios for DLL Inc.

Gross margin ratio	$= \dfrac{\text{Gross margin}}{\text{Net sales}}$	
Net Income ratio	$= \dfrac{\text{Net income}}{\text{Net sales}}$	$= \dfrac{\$48,465}{248,850} = 19.5\%$
Operating expense ratio	$= \dfrac{\text{Total operating expenses}}{\text{Net sales}}$	$= \dfrac{\$31,125}{248,850} = 12.5\%$
Returns and allowances ratio	$= \dfrac{\text{Return and allowances}}{\text{Net sales}}$	$= \dfrac{\$3,000}{248,850} = 1.2\%$

Inventory Turnover Rate

The *inventory turnover rate*, also referred to as the *stockturn rate*, is the number of times inventory or stock is turned over (sold and replaced) during a specified time period, usually a year. Inventory turnover rates are usually calculated on the basis of inventory costs, sometimes on the basis of inventory selling prices, and sometimes by number of units.

In our example, for DLL Inc. we know that for the year the cost of goods sold was $136,200. Information on the balance sheet enables us to find the average inventory. By adding the value of the beginning inventory to the ending inventory and dividing by 2, we can compute an average inventory. In the case of DLL, this would be as follows:

$$\frac{\$60,750 + \$60,300}{2} = \$60,525$$

Thus,

$$\text{Inventory turnover rate (in cost of goods sold)} = \frac{\text{Costs of goods sold}}{\text{Average inventory at cost}} = \frac{\$136,200}{\$60,525} = 2.25 \text{ times}$$

Return on Investment

Firms often develop business objectives in terms of *return on investment (ROI)*, and ROI is often used to determine how effective (and efficient) the firm's management has been. First, however, we need to define exactly what a firm means by investment. In most cases, firms define investment as the total assets of the firm. To calculate the ROI, we need the net income found in the income statement and the total assets (or investment) found in the firm's balance sheet.

Return on investment is calculated as follows:

$$\text{ROI} = \frac{\text{Net income}}{\text{Total investment}}$$

For DLL Inc., if the total assets are $129,825 then the ROI is as follows:

$$\frac{\$48,465}{\$129,825} = 37.3\%$$

Sometimes, return on investment is calculated by using an expanded formula:

$$\text{ROI} = \frac{\text{Net profit}}{\text{Sales}} \times \frac{\text{Sales}}{\text{Investment}}$$

$$= \frac{\$48,465}{\$248,850} \times \frac{\$248,850}{\$129,825} = 37.3\%$$

This formula makes it easy to show how ROI can be increased and what might reduce ROI. For example, there are different ways to increase ROI. First, if the management focuses on cutting costs and increasing efficiency, profits may be increased while sales remain the same:

$$\text{ROI} = \frac{\text{Net profit}}{\text{Sales}} \times \frac{\text{Sales}}{\text{Investment}}$$

$$= \frac{\$53,277}{\$248,850} \times \frac{\$248,850}{\$129,825} = 41.0\%$$

But ROI can be increased just as much without improving performance simply by reducing the investment—by maintaining less inventory:

$$\text{ROI} = \frac{\text{Net profit}}{\text{Sales}} \times \frac{\text{Sales}}{\text{Investment}}$$

$$= \frac{\$48,465}{\$248,850} \times \frac{\$248,850}{\$114,825} = 42.2\%$$

Sometimes, however, differences among the total assets of firms may be related to the age of the firm or the type of industry, which makes ROI a poor indicator of performance. For this reason, some firms have replaced the traditional ROI measures with *return on assets managed* (ROAM), *return on net assets* (RONA), or *return on stockholders' equity* (ROE).

Price Elasticity

Price elasticity, discussed in Chapter 10, is a measure of the sensitivity of customers to changes in price. Price elasticity is calculated by comparing the percentage change in quantity to the percentage change in price:

$$\text{Price elasticity of demand} = \frac{\text{Percentage change in quantity}}{\text{Percentage change in price}}$$

$$E = \frac{(Q_2 - Q_1)\,Q_1}{(P_2 - P_1)\,P_1}$$

where Q = quantity and P = price.

For example, suppose a manufacturer of jeans increased its price for a pair of jeans from $30.00 to $35.00. But instead of 40,000 pairs being sold, sales declined to only 38,000 pairs. The price elasticity would be calculated as follows:

$$E = \frac{(38{,}000 - 40{,}000)/40{,}000}{(\$35.00 - 30.00)/\$30.00} = \frac{-0.05}{0.167} = 0.30$$

Note that elasticity is usually expressed as a positive number even though the calculations create a negative value.

In this case, a relatively small change in demand (5 percent) resulted from a fairly large change in price (16.7 percent), indicating that demand is inelastic. At 0.30, the elasticity is less than 1.

On the other hand, what if the same change in price resulted in a reduction in demand to 30,000 pairs of jeans? Then the elasticity would be as follows:

$$E = \frac{(30{,}000 - 40{,}000)/40{,}000}{(\$35.00 - 30.00)/\$30.00} = \frac{-0.25}{0.167} = 1.50$$

In this case, because the 16.7 percent change in price resulted in an even larger change in demand (25 percent), demand is elastic. The elasticity of 1.50 is greater than 1.

Note: Elasticity may also be calculated by dividing the change in quantity by the average of Q_1 and Q_2 and dividing the change in price by the average of the two prices. However, we have chosen to include the formula that uses the initial quantity and price rather than the average.

Cost-Plus Pricing

As noted in Chapter 10, the most common cost-based approach to pricing a product is *cost-plus pricing*, in which a marketer figures all costs for the product and then adds an amount to cover profit and, in some cases, any costs of doing business that are not assigned to specific products. The most frequently used type of cost-plus pricing is *straight markup pricing*. The price is calculated by adding a predetermined percentage to the cost. Most retailers and wholesalers use markup pricing exclusively because of its simplicity—users need only estimate the unit cost and add the markup.

The first step requires that the unit cost be easy to estimate accurately and that production rates are fairly consistent. As Table 10S.4 shows, we will assume that a jeans manufacturer has fixed costs (the cost of the factory, advertising, managers' salaries, etc.) of $2,000,000. The variable cost, per pair of jeans (the cost of fabric, zipper, thread, and labor) is $20.00. With the current plant, the firm can produce a total of 400,000 pairs of jeans, so the fixed cost per pair is $5.00. Combining the fixed and variable costs per pair means that the jeans are produced at a total cost of $25.00 per pair and the total cost of producing 400,000 pairs of jeans is $10,000,000.

Table 10S.4	Markup Pricing Using Jeans as an Example	
Step 1: Determine Costs		
1.a: Determine total fixed costs		
Management and other nonproduction-related salaries	$ 750,000	
Rental of factory	600,000	
Insurance	50,000	
Depreciation on equipment	100,000	
Advertising	500,000	
Total fixed costs	**$2,000,000**	
1.b: Determine fixed costs per unit		
Number of units produced = 400,000		
Fixed cost per unit ($2,000,000/400,000)		**$5.00**
1.c: Determine variable costs per unit		
Cost of materials (fabric, zipper, thread, etc.)	$ 7.00	
Cost of production labor	10.00	
Cost of utilities and supplies used in production process	3.00	
Variable cost per unit		**$20.00**
1.d: Determine total cost per unit		
$20.00 + $5.00 = $25.00		
Total cost per unit		**$25.00**
Total cost for producing 400,000 units = $10,000,000		
Step 2: Determine markup and price		
***Manufacturer's markup on cost* (assuming 20% markup)**		
Formula: Price = total cost + (total cost × markup percentage)		
Manufacturer's Price to the Retailer		**$30.00**
= $25.00 + ($25.00 × 0.20) = $25.00 + 5.00 =		
***Retailer's markup on selling price* (assuming 40% markup)**		
Formula: Price = $\dfrac{\text{Total cost}}{(1.00 - \text{Markup percentage})}$		
Retailer's Price to the Consumer = $\dfrac{\$30.00}{(1.00 - 40)} = \dfrac{\$30.00}{0.60} =$		**$50.00**
***Retailer's alternative markup on cost* (assuming 40% markup)**		
Formula: Price = total cost + (total cost × markup percentage)		
Retailer's Price to the Consumer		
$30.00 + ($30.00 × 0.40) = $30.00 + $12.00 =		**$42.00**

The second step is to calculate the markup. There are two methods for calculating the markup percentage: markup on cost and markup on selling price. For *markup on cost pricing*, just as the name implies, a percentage of the cost is added to the cost to determine the firm's selling price. As you can see, we have included both methods in our example shown in Table 10S.4.

Markup on Cost

For markup on cost, the calculation is as follows:

$$\text{Price} = \text{Total cost} + (\text{Total cost} \times \text{Markup percentage})$$

But how does the manufacturer or reseller know which markup percentage to use? One way is to base the markup on the total income needed for profits, for shareholder dividends, and for investment in the business. In our jeans example, the total cost of producing the 400,000 pairs of jeans is $10,000,000. If the manufacturer wants a profit of $2,000,000, what markup percentage would it use? The $2,000,000 is 20 percent of the $10 million total cost, so 20 percent. To find the price, the calculations would be as follows:

$$\text{Price} = \$25.00 + (\$25.00 \times 0.20) = \$25.0 + \$5.00 = \$30.00$$

Note that in the calculations, the markup percentage is expressed as a decimal; that is, 20% = 0.20, 25% = 0.25, 30% = 0.30, and so on.

Markup on Selling Price

Some resellers, that is, retailers and wholesalers, set their prices using a markup on selling price. The markup percentage here is the seller's gross margin, the difference between the cost to the wholesaler or retailer and the price needed to cover overhead items, such as salaries, rent, utility bills, advertising, and profit. For example, if the wholesaler or retailer knows that it needs a margin of 40 percent to cover its overhead and reach its target profits, that margin becomes the markup on the manufacturer's selling price. Markup on selling price is particularly useful when firms negotiate prices with different buyers because it allows them to set prices with their required margins in mind.

Now let's say a retailer buys the jeans from the supplier (wholesaler or manufacturer) for $30.00 per pair. If the retailer requires a margin of 40 percent, it would calculate the price as a 40 percent markup on selling price. The calculation would be as follows:

$$\text{Price} = \frac{\text{Total cost}}{1.00 - \text{Markup percentage}}$$

$$\text{Price} = \frac{\$30.00}{(1.00 - 0.40)} = \frac{\$30.00}{0.60} = \$50.00$$

Therefore, the price of the jeans with the markup on selling price is $50.00.

Just to compare the difference in the final prices of the two markup methods, Table 10S.4 also shows what would happen if the retailer uses a markup on cost method. Using the same product cost and price with a 40 percent markup on cost would yield $42.00, a much lower price. The markup on selling price gives you the percentage of the selling price that the markup is. The markup on cost gives you the percentage of the cost that the markup is. In the markup on selling price the markup amount is $20.00, which is 40 percent of the selling price of $50.00. In the markup on cost, the markup is $12.00, which is 40 percent of the cost of $30.00.

Supplement Problems Test Your Marketing Math

1. Assume that you are in charge of pricing for a firm that produces pickles. You have fixed costs of 2,000,000. Variable costs are $0.75 per jar of pickles. You are selling your product to retailers for $0.89. You sell the pickles in cases of 24 jars per case.
   A. How many jars of pickles must you sell to break even?
   B. How much must you sell in dollars to break even?
   C. How many jars of pickles must you sell to break even plus make a profit of $300,000?

   D. Assume a retailer buys your product for $0.89. His business requires that he prices products with a 35 percent markup on cost. Calculate his selling price.
   E. Assume you have an MSRP of $1.39 for the pickles. If a retailer has a required 35 percent retailer margin on all products he sells, what is the most he is willing to pay the producer for the pickles?
   F. A clothing retailer knows that to break even and make a profit he needs to have a minimum retailer margin (also referred to as a contribution margin or

gross margin) of at least 60 percent. If he is to sell a pair of shorts for the manufacturer's suggested retail price of $49.99, what is the most he can pay the manufacturer for the shorts and maintain his margin?

G. A salesperson is developing a quote for a quantity of disposable hospital gowns. His cost for each case of gowns is $85.00. His firm requires that he have a 20 percent margin so he is using a markup on selling price calculation to price the gowns. What will his quote be per case of gowns if he uses a 20 percent markup on selling price?

2. Executives of Studio Recordings Inc. produced the latest compact disc by the Starshine Sisters Band, titled *Sunshine/Moonshine*. The following cost information pertains to the CD.

a. CD package	$1.25/CD
b. Songwriters' royalties	$0.35/CD
c. Recording artists' royalties	$1.00/CD
d. Advertising and promotion	$275,000
e. Studio Recording Inc.'s overhead	$250,000
f. Selling price to the CD distributor	$9.00

Calculate the following:
1. Contribution per CD unit
2. Break-even volume in CD units and dollars
3. Net profit if 1 million CDs are sold
4. Necessary CD unit volume to achieve a $200,000 profit

Deliver the Goods: Determine Distribution Strategy

Dan Marks
▼ A Decision Maker at First Tennessee Bank

Dan Marks is the chief marketing officer for First Tennessee Bank. First Tennessee is headquartered in Memphis, Tennessee; it is the leading bank in Tennessee with 170 offices primarily in Tennessee and states in the southeastern U.S. It has been nationally recognized by independent research organizations such as J. D. Power and Greenwich Associates for leading customer satisfaction. First Tennessee is a nearly billion-dollar-revenue business unit of First Horizon National Corporation. Dan is responsible for all marketing functions and the consumer digital/e-commerce channels.

Dan has a BS in accounting from Belhaven University and an MBA from Vanderbilt University. He serves as co-chair of the Dallas CMO Executive Summit and is a frequently sought after speaker and thought leader on marketing and digital topics. He has previous work experience with regional boutique consulting companies and a start-up. Dan is happily married with one son, and he also keeps active in the community with board service and mentoring and as an officer at his church.

Dan's Info

First job out of school?
Consultant/business analyst.

Career high?
My current job is a lot of fun.

Business book I'm reading now?
Moneyball by Michael Lewis.

My motto to live by?
Always improve and treat others like you wanted to be treated.

My management style?
Collaborative with a sense of urgency.

Don't do this when interviewing with me?
Tell me you've never had a failure or made a mistake.

Here's my problem...

Decision Time at First Tennessee Bank

Just like other goods and services, the delivery of financial products to customers plays a crucial role in a bank's value proposition. First Tennessee's marketing research clearly showed that online features were an increasingly important decision criterion when customers choose a new bank. First Tennessee had already invested millions of dollars to improve its online banking services. In recent years, the platform had been upgraded, account information functions streamlined, and paperless statements for all account types rolled out, and the website now had the ability to open and fund the full range of deposit products online. This was a solid start, but Dan knew that First Tennessee couldn't rest on its laurels while the digital world continued to evolve and offer new ways for consumers to interact with service providers. Dan knew that the online experience would continue to play a big role in how a bank's customers choose among competitors and also that online banking could be key to expanding the relationship people have with their bank. Still, online enhancements can be tricky, and there are only so many improvements an organization can take on at once. This is especially true in the financial services industry, where security is a huge concern and a provider can't afford to launch a product that doesn't work. The question Dan and his team faced was how to prioritize future development.

bank's website. On the other hand, these relatively cosmetic improvements wouldn't keep First Tennessee at the cutting edge of online banking; competitors were quickly upgrading their systems and offering new services to their customers.

Option 2

Offer customers the option to pay their bills online—both to companies and to other individuals. The ability to make payments online was known to improve customer retention rates and increase the probability that a customer would purchase other products when they logged in to pay their bills. For example, seeing the bank as the central hub to manage account information and make payments would lead to a great chance that customers would consolidate savings accounts that might be held at other banks or to open a First Tennessee credit card. However, about 30 percent of customers who tried to pay their bills online at First Tennessee would eventually stop using the bill-pay feature and go straight to vendors to make online payments at their websites or in some cases revert to just writing a paper check. The research said what customers did but was less clear on the reasons why customers made these choices. Clearly, the existing process was unattractive to some customers but still very valuable to the majority. In addition, person-to-person payments were a new idea that had some potential. Fueled by the success of eBay ad other websites that enabled regular people to buy and sell goods and services, an increasing number of consumers valued the capability to pay other individuals electronically by using just an e-mail address rather than actually mailing them a check. PayPal had grown very rapidly by facilitating electronic person-to-person payments, but it wasn't tightly integrated with the actual bank website. Again, though, this is an unfamiliar process for many, so it posed challenges in terms of devising a system that is easy to use and also secure.

Option 3

Enable banking by smart phone. Pundits had been predicting for years that mobile banking was "just around the corner." Although customer research showed very low levels of awareness and interest from consumers, several banks had started to introduce mobile banking apps that took advantage of smart phones like the popular Blackberry or Apple iPhone. Dan saw the biggest risk as being too early to market; if a newer technology emerged before a lot of the bank's customers started to use the service, First Tennessee would have to invest more in the long term to be compatible. But, smart phones offered unique capabilities that a computer doesn't. In addition to convenience, the iPhone and other new generations of phones have a camera. This feature meant that potentially a customer could use a mobile app to deposit a check just by taking a picture of it and then securely transmitting it to the bank. This new "remote check deposit"

Things to remember

As with physical goods, the delivery of services is an important part of the value proposition. Customers' online opportunities and experience in the delivery of banking services are increasingly important in choosing among competing banks. While First Tennessee had made a number of improvements to its online banking, new ways to interact with customers were needed. The bill pay option would attract new customers but many would likely leave First Tennessee for another service. Banking by smartphone offered customers convenience and because smartphones have cameras, customers could make deposits wherever they were without going to the bank. Such new technology, however, might lack the needed security.

Dan considered his Options 1·2·3

Option 1

Pursue minor refinements in many areas. First Tennessee had identified several small improvements that would address small problems customers experienced when they banked online. For example, feedback from the call center and the bank's customer experience monitoring program indicated that people sometimes had problems linking their online accounts. Also, making address changes on accounts was still a manual process even though the request was submitted online. If Dan's team could make a number of these small tweaks and process improvements, customers would have a more pleasant experience when they logged in to the

You Choose

Which **Option** would you choose, and **why**?
1. ☐YES ☐NO 2. ☐YES ☐NO 3. ☐YES ☐NO

See what **option** Dan chose on **page 378** ⮕

MyMarketingLab™

⭐ **Improve Your Grade!**

Over 10 million students improved their results using the Pearson MyLabs.
Visit **mymktlab.com** for simulations, tutorials, and end-of-chapter problems.

capability had the potential to be a game changer. It could become a highly "buzzworthy" feature to set First Tennessee apart in the crowded banking marketplace. It had the potential to fundamentally transform the banking experience. Rather than having to go to the bank or ATM to make a deposit, suddenly a customer could make a deposit from wherever he or she had cell phone coverage. However, the technology was still very new and not proven. Still, the costs appeared to be reasonable—with development estimated to be no more than about the equivalent to 10 of the new type of ATMs that would allow "envelope-less" deposits. The variable costs had the potential to be significantly less than using a teller or even an ATM to make deposits, but this was not proven either. Mobile banking was getting some traction in the marketplace, but Dan knew that the bank's risk management process would look at any new technology intensely, and this analysis might find a problem with the technology that would make it uneconomical or even expose a security vulnerability.

Now put yourself in Dan's shoes. Which option would you choose, and why?

1

OBJECTIVE

Explain what a distribution channel is, identify types of wholesaling intermediaries, and describe the different types of distribution channels.
(pp. 354–365)

Types of Distribution Channels and Wholesale Intermediaries

So you've done all the work to understand your target market. You've created your product, and you've priced it, too. Your Facebook page is attracting legions of brand fans. But sorry, you're still not done with the marketing mix—now you need to get what you make out into the marketplace (i.e., distribute it). The delivery of goods to customers involves **physical distribution**, which refers to the activities that move finished goods from manufacturers to final customers. A **channel of distribution** is a series of firms or individuals that facilitates the movement of a product from the producer to the final customer. In many cases, these channels include an organized network of producers (or manufacturers), wholesalers, and retailers that develop relationships and work together to make products conveniently available to eager buyers. And, as First Tennessee Bank's decision illustrates, the delivery of value is a vital strategic issue that applies to intangibles as well.

Distribution channels come in different shapes and sizes. The bakery around the corner where you buy your cinnamon rolls is a member of a channel, as is the baked-goods section at the local supermarket, the Starbucks that sells biscotti to go with your double-mocha cappuccino, and the bakery outlet store that sells day-old rolls at a discount.

A channel of distribution consists of, at a minimum, a producer—the individual or firm that manufactures or produces a good or service—and a customer. This is a *direct channel*. For example, when you buy a loaf of bread at a mom-and-pop bakery, you're buying through a direct channel. Firms that sell their own products through websites, catalogs, toll-free numbers, or factory outlet stores use direct channels.

But life (and marketing) usually isn't that simple: Channels often are *indirect* because they include one or more **channel intermediaries**—firms or individuals such as wholesalers, agents, brokers, and retailers who in some way help move the product to the consumer or business user. For example, a bakery may choose to sell its cinnamon buns to a wholesaler that will in turn sell boxes of buns to supermarkets and restaurants that in turn sell them to consumers. Another older term for intermediaries is *middlemen*.

Functions of Distribution Channels

Channels that include one or more organizations or intermediaries often can accomplish certain distribution functions more effectively and efficiently than can a single organization. As we saw in Chapter 2, this is especially true in international distribution channels, where differences among countries' customs, beliefs, and infrastructures can make global

---

physical distribution
The activities that move finished goods from manufacturers to final customers, including order processing, warehousing, materials handling, transportation, and inventory control.

channel of distribution
The series of firms or individuals that facilitates the movement of a product from the producer to the final customer.

channel intermediaries
Firms or individuals such as wholesalers, agents, brokers, or retailers who help move a product from the producer to the consumer or business user. An older term for intermediaries is *middlemen*.

marketing a nightmare. Even small companies can succeed in complex global markets when they rely on distributors that know local customs and laws.

Overall, channels provide the place, time, and possession utility we described in Chapter 1. They make desired products available when, where, and in the sizes and quantities that customers desire. Suppose, for example, you want to buy that perfect bouquet of flowers for a special someone. You *could* grow them yourself or even "liberate" them from a cemetery if you were *really* desperate (very classy!). Fortunately, you can probably accomplish this task with just a simple phone call or a few mouse clicks, and "like magic" a local florist delivers a bouquet to your honey's door.

Distribution channels provide a number of logistics or physical distribution functions that increase the efficiency of the flow of goods from producer to customer (more on this later in the chapter). How would we buy groceries without our modern system of supermarkets? We'd have to get our milk from a dairy, our bread from a bakery, our tomatoes and corn from a local farmer, and our flour from a flour mill. And forget about specialty items such as Coca-Cola or Twinkies (which died and then recently came back to life like a phoenix due to popular demand). The companies that make these items would have to handle literally millions of transactions to sell to every individual who craves a junk-food fix.

Distribution channels create *efficiencies* because they reduce the number of transactions necessary for goods to flow from many different manufacturers to large numbers of customers. This occurs in two ways. The first is **breaking bulk**. Wholesalers and retailers purchase large quantities (usually cases) of goods from manufacturers but sell only one or a few at a time to many different customers. Second, channel intermediaries reduce the number of transactions when they **create assortments**—they provide a variety of products in one location—so that customers can conveniently buy many different items from one seller at one time.

 Figure 11.1 provides a simple example of how distribution channels work. This simplified illustration includes five producers and five customers. If each producer sold

Sometimes firms "delegate" part of the distribution function to the customer. And many customers are happy to cooperate when they can save on shipping charges and get that 60" LCD TV set up immediately.

breaking bulk
Dividing larger quantities of goods into smaller lots in order to meet the needs of buyers.

create assortments
To provide a variety of products in one location to meet the needs of buyers.

Figure 11.1 *Process* | Reduce Transactions via Intermediaries

One of the functions of distribution channels is to provide an assortment of products. Because the customers can buy a number of different products at the same location, this reduces the total costs of obtaining a product.

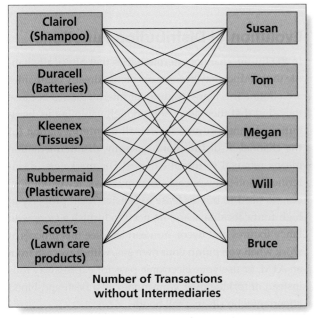

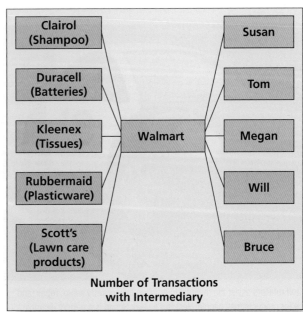

Number of Transactions without Intermediaries

Number of Transactions with Intermediary

APPLYING ▼ Place, time and, possession utility

Dan knew it was important for First Tennessee Bank to provide the place, time and possession utility customers wanted and that online features were increasingly important to the FTB customers and how they chose a bank. Thus, FTB needed to offer new ways for consumers to interact with the bank through online banking.

transportation and storage
Occurs when retailers and other channel members move the goods from the production point to other locations where they can hold them until consumers want them.

facilitating functions
Functions of channel intermediaries that make the purchase process easier for customers and manufacturers.

risk-taking functions
The chance retailers take on the loss of a product when they buy a product from a manufacturer because the product sits on the shelf because no customers want it.

communication and transaction functions
Happens when channel members develop and execute both promotional and other types of communication among members of the channel.

disintermediation (of the channel of distribution)
The elimination of some layers of the channel of distribution in order to cut costs and improve the efficiency of the channel.

its product to each individual customer, 25 different transactions would have to occur—not exactly an efficient way to distribute products. But with a single intermediary who buys from all five manufacturers and sells to all five customers, we quickly cut the number of transactions to 10. If there were 10 manufacturers and 10 customers, an intermediary would reduce the number of transactions from 100 to just 20. Do the math: Channels are efficient.

The **transportation and storage** of goods is another type of physical distribution function. That is, retailers and other channel members move the goods from the production point to other locations where they can hold them until consumers want them. Channel intermediaries also perform a number of **facilitating functions** that make the purchase process easier for customers and manufacturers. For example, intermediaries often provide customer services, such as offering credit to buyers.

Many of us like to shop at bricks-and-mortar department stores because if we are not happy with the product, we can take it back to the store, where cheerful customer service personnel are happy to give us a refund (at least in theory). But the same facilitating function happens online with Zappos, Lands' End, and a host of other customer-friendly retailers. These same customer services are even more important in B2B markets where customers purchase larger quantities of higher-priced products. And channel members perform **risk-taking functions**. For example, if a retailer buys a product from a manufacturer and it just sits on the shelf because no customers want it, he or she is stuck with the item and must take a loss. But hey, that's what outlet malls are for, right? Perishable items present an even greater risk of spoilage and loss, hence potentially a high risk. Blueberries in the U.S. are in season for only a very short period of time. Retailers want to stock up to meet the annual high demand; on the other hand, a carton of semisoft blueberries on the shelf a few weeks past prime is beyond unappealing.

Finally, intermediaries perform **communication and transaction functions** by which channel members develop and execute both promotional and other types of communication among members of the channel. Wholesalers buy products to make them available for retailers, and they sell products to other channel members. Retailers handle transactions with final consumers. Channel members can provide two-way communication for manufacturers. They may supply the sales force, advertising, and other types of marketing communication necessary to inform consumers and persuade them that a product will meet their needs. And the channel members can be invaluable sources of information on consumer complaints, changing tastes, and new competitors in the market.

Some wholesalers and retailers assist the manufacturer when they provide setup, repair, and maintenance service for products they handle. Best Buy's Geek Squad is a perfect example.

Evolution of Distribution Functions

In the future, channel intermediaries that physically handle the product may become obsolete. Already companies are eliminating many traditional intermediaries because they find that they don't add enough value in the distribution channel—a process we call **disintermediation (of the channel of distribution)**. Literally, disintermediation means removal of intermediaries! For marketers, disintermediation reduces costs in many ways: fewer employees, no need to buy or lease expensive retail property in high-traffic locations, and no need to furnish a store with fancy fixtures and decor. You can also see this process at work when you pump your own gas, withdraw cash from an ATM, or use your electronic pass for expressway tolls instead of forking over your money to a flesh-and-blood attendant who sits in a toll booth.

As with many other aspects of marketing, the Internet is radically changing how companies coordinate among members of a supply chain to make it more effective in ways that end consumers never see. These firms develop better ways to implement **knowledge management**, which refers to a comprehensive approach that collects, organizes, stores, and retrieves a firm's information assets. Those assets include databases and company documents as well as the practical knowledge of employees whose past experience may be relevant to solve a new problem. In the world of B2B, this process probably occurs via an **intranet**, which, as you read in Chapter 6, is an internal corporate communication network that uses Internet technology to link company departments, employees, and databases. But it can also be used to facilitate sharing of knowledge among channel partners since it is a secure and password-protected platform. This more strategic management of information results in a win-win situation for all the partners.

But as with most things cyber, the Internet as a distribution channel brings pain with pleasure. One of the more vexing problems with Internet distribution is the potential for **online distribution piracy**, which is the theft and unauthorized repurposing of intellectual property via the Internet. Obviously that's a major concern for financial institutions like First Tennessee Bank that need to transfer real money between accounts thousands of times a day.

Bringing things close to home, the college textbook industry has high potential for online piracy. It's not uncommon for U.S.-produced textbooks to make their way to unscrupulous individuals outside the home country who translate the core content into the native language and post it online for distribution. This practice completely devalues the knowledge contained therein and results in zero return to the knowledge creators (namely, your humble textbook authors!). Many students don't realize that the only people who profits from used or pirated books are the middlemen who have obtained them (sometimes illegally). Used books do sell for less, but since the publisher does not see any revenue from these sales, it is forced to raise prices in order to return a profit. This results in a vicious circle as new books become more and more expensive, which motivates more students to buy them illegitimately, and so the madness continues.

Let's look at a similar distribution issue in a product category that's probably more familiar to you. Unauthorized downloads of music continue to pose a major challenge to the "recording" industry—to the point where the whole nature of the industry has turned topsy-turvy in search of a new business model that works. Many in the music business are rethinking exactly what—and where—is the value added for what they do. To the majority of modern consumers of music, the value of a physical CD has diminished—to the point where many listeners are unwilling to pay anything at all for the artist's work. And more and more musical artists opt to defect from traditional record labels and introduce their tunes online, where they can control at least some of the channel of distribution. As you may know, a few years ago the band Radiohead even tried a "name your own price" strategy when it released its studio album *In Rainbows* on its website.

So far, we've learned what a distribution channel is and talked about some of the functions it performs. Now let's find out about specific types of channel intermediaries and channel structures.

Wholesaling Intermediaries

How can you get your hands on a new Iggy Azalea T-shirt or hoodie? You could pick one up at your local music store, at a trendy clothing store like Hot Topic, or maybe at its online store. You might join hordes of others and buy

knowledge management
A comprehensive approach to collecting, organizing, storing, and retrieving a firm's information assets.

intranet
An internal corporate communication network that uses Internet technology to link company departments, employees, and databases.

online distribution piracy
The theft and unauthorized repurposing of intellectual property via the Internet.

APPLYING ▼ Online Distribution

The Internet has radically changed the way banks and other service providers do business. Dan knew that online banking was important in how customers choose a bank and a key to expanding the relationship between people and their bank. Dan also recognized that in the financial industry, changes must be made slowly to make sure the improvements work and to maintain security of confidential information.

Free shipping provides a competitive advantage for a large retailer.

Figure 11.2 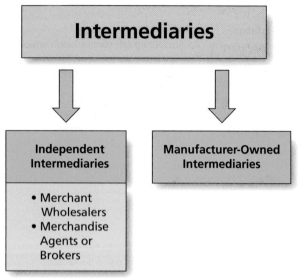 *Snapshot* | Key Types of Intermediaries

Intermediaries can be independent or manufacturer owned.

an "official Iggy Azalea concert T-shirt" from vendors during a show. Alternatively, you might get a "deal" on a bootlegged, unauthorized version of the same shirt that a shady guy who stands *outside* the concert venue sells from a battered suitcase. Perhaps you shop online at www.iggyazalea.com. Each of these distribution alternatives traces a different path from producer to consumer. Let's look at the different types of wholesaling intermediaries and at different channel structures. Note that we will hold off focusing on retailers, which are usually the last link in the chain, until Chapter 12. Retailers are a big deal and deserve a chapter of their own.

Wholesaling intermediaries are firms that handle the flow of products from the manufacturer to the retailer or business user. There are many different types of consumer and B2B wholesaling intermediaries. Some of these are independent, but manufacturers and retailers can own them, too. Figure 11.2 portrays key intermediary types, and Table 11.1 summarizes the important characteristics of each.

Independent Intermediaries

Independent intermediaries do business with many different manufacturers and many different customers. Because no manufacturer owns or controls them, they make it possible for many manufacturers to serve customers throughout the world while they keep prices low.

Merchant wholesalers are independent intermediaries that buy goods from manufacturers and sell to retailers and other B2B customers. Because merchant wholesalers **take title** to the goods (i.e., they legally own them), they assume certain risks and can suffer losses if products are damaged, become outdated or obsolete, are stolen, or just don't sell. On the other hand, because they own the products, they are free to develop their own marketing strategies, including setting the prices they charge their customers. Wait, it gets better: There are several different kinds of merchant wholesalers:

- **Full-service merchant wholesalers** provide a wide range of services for their customers, including delivery, credit, product-use assistance, repairs, advertising, and other promotional support—even market research. Full-service merchant wholesalers often have their own sales force to call on businesses and organizational customers. Some general merchandise wholesalers carry a large variety of different items, whereas specialty wholesalers carry an extensive assortment of a single product line. For example, a candy wholesaler carries only candy and gum products but stocks enough different varieties to give your dentist nightmares for a year.

- In contrast, **limited-service merchant wholesalers** provide fewer services for their customers. Like full-service wholesalers, limited-service wholesalers *take title* to merchandise but are less likely to provide services such as delivery, credit, or marketing assistance to retailers. Specific types of limited-service wholesalers include the following:

  - *Cash-and-carry wholesalers* provide low-cost merchandise for retailers and industrial customers that are too small for other wholesalers' sales representatives to call on. Customers pay cash for products and provide their own delivery. Some popular cash-and-carry product categories include groceries, office supplies, and building materials.

  - *Truck jobbers* carry their products to small business customer locations for their inspection and selection. Truck jobbers often supply perishable items such as fruit and vegetables to small grocery stores. For example, a bakery truck jobber calls on

wholesaling intermediaries
Firms that handle the flow of products from the manufacturer to the retailer or business user.

independent intermediaries
Channel intermediaries that are not controlled by any manufacturer but instead do business with many different manufacturers and many different customers.

merchant wholesalers
Intermediaries that buy goods from manufacturers (take title to them) and sell to retailers and other B2B customers.

take title
To accept legal ownership of a product and assume the accompanying rights and responsibilities of ownership.

full-service merchant wholesalers
Wholesalers that provide a wide range of services for their customers, including delivery, credit, product-use assistance, repairs, advertising, and other promotional support.

limited-service merchant wholesalers
Wholesalers that provide fewer services for their customers.

Table 11.1 | Types of Intermediaries

Intermediary Type	Description	Advantages
Independent intermediaries	Do business with many different manufacturers and many different customers	Used by most small to medium-size firms
• **Merchant wholesalers**	Buy (take title to) goods from producers and sell to organizational customers; either full or limited function	Allow small manufacturers to serve customers throughout the world with competitive costs
• Cash-and-carry wholesalers	Provide products for small-business customers who purchase at wholesaler's location	Distribute low-cost merchandise for small retailers and other business customers
• Truck jobbers	Deliver perishable food and tobacco items to retailers	Ensure that perishable items are delivered and sold efficiently
• Drop shippers	Take orders from and bill retailers for products drop shipped from manufacturer	Facilitate transactions for bulky products
• Mail-order wholesalers	Sell through catalogs, telephone, or mail order	Provide reasonably priced sales options to small organizational customers
• Rack jobbers	Provide retailers with display units, check inventories, and replace merchandise for the retailers	Provide merchandising services to retailers
• **Merchandise agents and brokers**	Provide services in exchange for commissions	Maintain legal ownership of product by the seller
• Manufacturers' agents	Use independent salespeople; carry several lines of noncompeting products	Supply sales function for small and new firms
• Selling agents, including export/import agents	Handle entire output of one or more products	Handle all marketing functions for small manufacturers
• Commission merchants	Receive commission on sales price of product	Provide efficiency primarily in agricultural products market
• Merchandise brokers, including export/import brokers	Identify likely buyers and bring buyers and sellers together	Enhance efficiency in markets where there are many small buyers and sellers
Manufacturer-owned intermediaries	Limit operations to one manufacturer	Create efficiencies for large firms
• **Sales branches**	Maintain some inventory in different geographic areas (similar to wholesalers)	Provide service to customers in different geographic areas
• **Sales offices**	Carry no inventory; availability in different geographic areas	Reduce selling costs and provide better customer service
• **Manufacturers' showrooms**	Display products attractively for customers to visit	Facilitate examination of merchandise by customers at a central location

supermarkets, checks the stock of bread on the shelves, removes outdated items, and suggests how much bread the store needs to reorder.

- *Drop shippers* are limited-function wholesalers that take title to the merchandise but never actually take possession of it. Drop shippers take orders from and bill retailers and industrial buyers, but the merchandise is shipped directly from the manufacturer. Because they take title to the merchandise, they assume the same risks as other merchant wholesalers. Drop shippers are important to both the producers and the customers of bulky products, such as coal, oil, or lumber.

- *Mail-order wholesalers* sell products to small retailers and other industrial customers, often located in remote areas, through catalogs rather than a sales force. They usually carry products in inventory and require payment in cash or by credit card before shipment. Mail-order wholesalers supply products such as cosmetics, hardware, and sporting goods.

- *Rack jobbers* supply retailers with specialty items, such as health and beauty products and magazines. Rack jobbers get their name because they own and maintain the product display racks in grocery stores, drugstores, and variety stores. These wholesalers visit retail customers on a regular basis to maintain levels of stock and refill their racks with merchandise. Think about how quickly magazines turn over on the rack—without an expert who pulls old titles and inserts new ones, retailers would have great difficulty ensuring that you can buy the current issue of *People* magazine on the first day it hits the streets.

Merchandise Agents or Brokers

merchandise agents or brokers
Channel intermediaries that provide services in exchange for commissions but never take title to the product.

Merchandise agents or brokers are a second major type of independent intermediary. Agents and brokers provide services in exchange for commissions. They may or may not take possession of the product, but they *never* take title; that is, they do not accept legal ownership of the product. Agents normally represent buyers or sellers on an ongoing basis, whereas clients employ brokers for a short period of time:

- *Manufacturers' agents*, or *manufacturers' reps*, are independent salespeople who carry several lines of noncompeting products. They have contractual arrangements with manufacturers that outline territories, selling prices, and other specific aspects of the relationship but provide little if any supervision. Manufacturers normally compensate agents with commissions based on a percentage of what they sell. Manufacturers' agents often develop strong customer relationships and provide an important sales function for small and new companies.

- *Selling agents*, including *export/import agents*, market a whole product line or one manufacturer's total output. They often work like an independent marketing department because they perform the same functions as full-service merchant wholesalers but do not take title to products. Unlike manufacturers' agents, selling agents have unlimited territories and control the pricing, promotion, and distribution of their products. We find selling agents in industries such as furniture, clothing, and textiles.

- *Commission merchants* are sales agents who receive goods, primarily agricultural products such as grain or livestock, on *consignment*—that is, they take possession of products without taking title. Although sellers may state a minimum price they are willing to take for their products, commission merchants are free to sell the product for the highest price they can get. Commission merchants receive a commission on the sales price of the product.

- *Merchandise brokers*, including export/import brokers, are intermediaries that facilitate transactions in markets such as real estate, food, and used equipment, in which there are lots of small buyers and sellers. Brokers identify likely buyers and sellers and bring the two together in return for a fee they receive when the transaction is completed.

Manufacturer-Owned Intermediaries

Sometimes manufacturers set up their own channel intermediaries. In this way, they can operate separate business units that perform all the functions of independent intermediaries while still maintaining complete control over the channel:

- *Sales branches* are manufacturer-owned facilities that, like independent wholesalers, carry inventory and provide sales and service to customers in a specific geographic area. We find sales branches in industries such as petroleum products, industrial machinery and equipment, and motor vehicles.

- *Sales offices* are manufacturer-owned facilities that, like agents, do not carry inventory but provide selling functions for the manufacturer in a specific geographic area. Because they allow members of the sales force to locate close to customers, they reduce selling costs and provide better customer service.

- *Manufacturers' showrooms* are manufacturer-owned or leased facilities in which products are permanently displayed for customers to visit. Merchandise marts are often multiple buildings in which one or more industries hold trade shows and many manufacturers have permanent showrooms. Retailers can visit either during a show or all year long to see the manufacturer's merchandise and make B2B purchases.

Types of Distribution Channels

Firms face many choices when they structure distribution channels. Should they sell directly to consumers and business users? Would they benefit if they included wholesalers, retailers, or both in the channel? Would it make sense to sell directly to some customers but use retailers to sell to others? Of course, there is no single best channel for all products. The marketing manager must select a channel structure that creates a competitive advantage for the firm and its products based on the size and needs of the target market. Let's consider some of the factors these managers need to think about.

When they develop distribution (place) strategies, marketers first consider different **channel levels**. This refers to the number of distinct categories of intermediaries that make up a channel of distribution. Many factors have an impact on this decision. What channel members are available? How large is the market? How frequently do consumers purchase the product? What services do consumers require? 📷 Figure 11.3 summarizes the different structures a distribution channel can take. The producer and the customer are always members, so the shortest channel possible has two levels. Using a retailer adds a third level, a wholesaler adds a fourth level, and so on. Different channel structures exist for both consumer and B2B markets.

channel levels
The number of distinct categories of intermediaries that make up a channel of distribution.

And what about services? You will learn in Chapter 12 that services are intangible, so there is no need to worry about storage, transportation, and the other functions of physical distribution. In most cases, the service travels directly from the producer to the customer. However, an intermediary we call an *agent* can enhance the distribution of some services when he helps the parties complete the transaction. Examples of these agents include insurance agents, stockbrokers, and travel agents (no, not everyone books their travel online).

Consumer Channels

As we noted earlier, the simplest channel is a direct channel. Why do some producers sell directly to customers? One reason is that a direct channel may allow the producer to serve its customers better and at a lower price than is possible if it included a retailer. A baker who uses a direct channel makes sure that customers enjoy fresher bread than if the tasty loaves are sold through a local supermarket. Furthermore, if the baker sells the bread through a supermarket, the price will be higher because of the supermarket's costs of doing business and its need to make its own profit on the bread. In fact, sometimes this is the *only* way to sell the product because using channel intermediaries may boost the price above what consumers are willing to pay.

Another reason to use a direct channel is *control*. When the producer handles distribution, it maintains control of pricing, service, and delivery—all elements of the transaction. Because distributors and dealers carry many products, it can be difficult to get their sales forces to focus on selling one product. In a direct channel, a producer works directly with customers, so it gains insights into trends, customer needs and complaints, and the effectiveness of its marketing strategies.

Why do producers choose to use indirect channels to reach consumers? A reason in many cases is that customers are familiar with certain retailers or other intermediaries—it's where they always go to look for what they need. Getting customers to change their normal buying behavior— for example, convincing consumers to buy their laundry detergent or frozen pizza from a catalog or over the Internet instead of from the corner supermarket— can be difficult.

Recording artist Aimee Mann licenses her music rather than work with a major record label in order to retain creative control over her product.

Figure 11.3 📷 *Snapshot* | Different Types of Channels of Distribution

Channels differ in the number of channel members that participate.

Major Types of Channels of Distribution

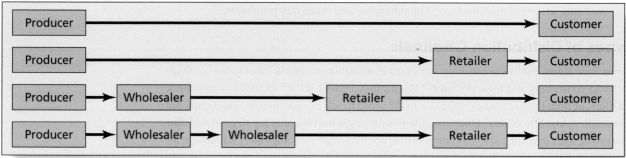

Typical Consumer Channels

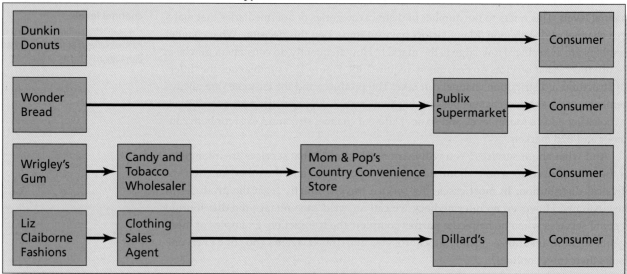

Typical B2B Channels

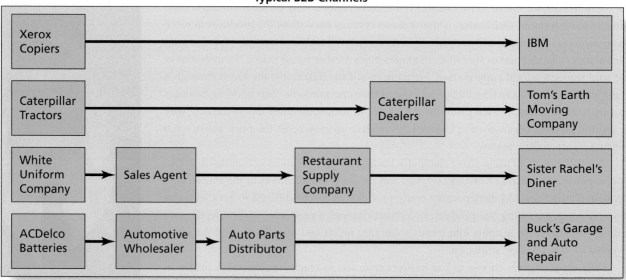

In addition, intermediaries help producers in all the ways we described earlier. By creating utility and transaction efficiencies, channel members make producers' lives easier and enhance their ability to reach customers. The *producer–retailer–consumer channel* in Figure 11.3 is the shortest indirect channel. Samsung uses this channel when it sells TVs through large retailers such as Best Buy (either their bricks-and-mortar stores or their online store). Because the retailers buy in large volume, they can obtain inventory at a low price and then pass these savings on to shoppers (this is what gives them a competitive advantage over smaller, more specialized stores that don't order so many items). The size of these retail giants also means they can provide the physical distribution functions, such as transportation and storage, that wholesalers handle for smaller retail outlets.

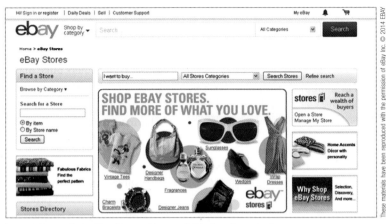

Internet intermediaries like eBay provide new distribution channel options as consumers can buy new or used items from other consumers in addition to producers.

The *producer–wholesaler–retailer–consumer channel* is a common distribution channel in consumer marketing. An example would be a single ice cream factory that supplies, say, four or five regional wholesalers. These wholesalers then sell to 400 or more retailers, such as grocery stores. The retailers, in turn, each sell the ice cream to thousands of customers. In this channel, the regional wholesalers combine many manufacturers' products to supply grocery stores. Because the grocery stores do business with many wholesalers, this arrangement results in a broad selection of products.

B2B Channels

B2B distribution channels, as the name suggests, facilitate the flow of goods from a producer to an organizational or business customer. Generally, B2B channels parallel consumer channels in that they may be direct or indirect. For example, the simplest indirect channel in industrial markets occurs when the single intermediary—a merchant wholesaler we refer to as an *industrial distributor* rather than a retailer—buys products from a manufacturer and sells them to business customers.

Direct channels are more common in B2B markets versus consumer markets. As we saw in Chapter 6, this is because B2B marketing often means that a firm sells high-dollar, high-profit items (a single piece of industrial equipment may cost hundreds of thousands of dollars) to a market made up of only a few customers. In such markets, it makes sense financially for a company to develop its own sales force and sell directly to customers—in this case, the investment in an in-house sales force pays off.

The **Cutting Edge**

Amazon Delivers in 30 Minutes or Less?

You just found the perfect item on Amazon, but you want it now. Not in three to five days. Not overnight. Like *right* now. Is that even possible? It certainly could be thanks to Amazon's Prime Air project, which is currently under development. Prime Air, Amazon's newest delivery system, is designed to get your goods to you in 30 minutes or less thanks to the use of unmanned aerial vehicles—drones.[1]

It works like this: Once you click the "Buy" button, these amazing little "octocopters," as they are known, will pick up your items in a small yellow bucket at Amazon's fulfillment center and deliver them by air to your doorstep—all in less than 30 minutes. Of course, there are some limits. First, the items need to weigh less than five pounds, and although that doesn't sound like much, it's actually the weight of about 86 percent of the items Amazon ships. Oh, and your doorstep needs to be within a 10-mile radius of a fulfillment center, though initially Amazon is considering using "drop spots" instead of actual doorsteps—and it's weather permitting. Still, the technology works, and it works now.[2] Although the Federal Aviation Administration has grounded Amazon's plans for now (commercial drones presently are illegal), who knows what the future might bring?

Dual and Hybrid Distribution Systems

Figure 11.3 illustrates how simple distribution channels work. But, once again, we are reminded that life (or marketing) is rarely that simple: Producers, dealers, wholesalers, retailers, and customers alike may actually participate in more than one type of channel. We call these **dual or multiple distribution systems**.

dual or multiple distribution systems
A system where producers, dealers, wholesalers, retailers, and customers participate in more than one type of channel.

The pharmaceutical industry provides a good example of multiple-channel usage. Pharmaceutical companies distribute their products in at least three types of channels:

1. They sell to hospitals, clinics, and other organizational customers directly. These customers buy in quantity, and they purchase a wide variety of products. Because hospitals and clinics dispense pills one at a time rather than in bottles of 50, these outlets require different product packaging than when the manufacturer sells medications to other types of customers.

2. They rely on an indirect consumer channel when they sell to large drugstore chains, like Walgreens, that distribute the medicines to their stores across the country. Alternatively, some of us would rather purchase our prescriptions in a more personal manner from the local independent drugstore where we can still get an ice cream soda while we wait. In this version of the indirect consumer channel, the manufacturer sells to drug wholesalers that, in turn, supply these independents.

3. Finally, the companies sell directly to third-party payers such as HMOs, PPOs, and insurance companies. After health care reform in the U.S. fully kicks in, who knows what the channel configuration might be!

hybrid marketing system
A marketing system that uses a number of different channels and communication methods to serve a target market.

Instead of serving a target market with a single channel, some companies combine channels—direct sales, distributors, retail sales, and direct mail—to create a **hybrid marketing system**.[3] Believe it or not, the whole world of business actually has not gone paperless (we know it's hard to accept)! Hence, companies actually do still buy copying machines (sounds so 1999)—and in large quantities. At one time, you could buy a Xerox copier only directly through a Xerox salesperson. Today, unless you are a very large business customer, you likely will purchase a Xerox machine from a local Xerox authorized dealer or possibly through the Xerox "Online Store." Xerox turned to an enhanced dealer network for distribution because such hybrid marketing systems offer companies certain competitive advantages, including increased coverage of the market, lower marketing costs, and a greater potential for customization of service for local markets.

SALAMI.COM
The Old Fashioned Flavor You Remember delivered from Cyberspace

Free Send A Virtual Card

Please Sign Our Guestbook

ABOUT US | SHOPPING | GIFT BASKETS | FRESH SAUSAGE | AWARDS | HOLIDAY SPECIALS

Secure Shopping at Salami.com

14-Jun-04 16:09 GMT >>
SECURED BY
GeoTrust QuickSSL

SHOPPING
Only 9 days until Father's Day
▶ GIFT BASKETS
▶ IMPORTED JAMS
NEW ▶ HOLIDAY SPECIALTIES
▶ CHEESE
▶ PASTA
▶ SAUSAGE & SALAMI
▶ FRESH SAUSAGE
▶ IMPORTED COFFEES

Happy Father's

A Special for Father's Day
More Stuff Than Fluff

Hi and Welcome to Salami.com. We have been offering top quality Italian Food on the Internet since 1995!! We are Vinny Barbieri (that's me on the left) and my partner Richie Lodico the owners of Salami.com. We have just spruced up our website and added a whole lot of great food. Please take a look!!

When you need the finest quality ingredients come shop securely with us. Supplying top quality cheeses, meats, breads, and imported Italian specialty items is not our job, but our life! People keep telling us,

© 2003 New York Italian Food Specialties

Entrepreneurs Richie Lodico and Vinny Barbieri, owners of Eastern Meat Farms, Inc., discovered in the very early days of the Internet (they started their online business in 1995) that an online direct channel is a great way to continually expand their business globally. For years prior to going online, Lodico and Barbieri shipped sausages and cheeses across the country, but they didn't feel there was enough volume to justify the expense of direct marketing. However, with the advent of the Internet, **www.salami.com** was born (the URL alone must be worth a fortune today!). The company ships each order using Styrofoam and ice packs to ensure that customers from around the globe receive high-quality, fresh products, often for less than half the price they would have to pay for similar delicacies locally. Hot dog!

Distribution Channels and the Marketing Mix

How do decisions regarding place relate to the other *three Ps*? For one, place decisions affect pricing. Marketers that distribute products through low-priced retailers such as Walmart, T.J. Maxx, and Marshalls will have different pricing objectives and strategies than will those that sell to specialty stores like Tiffany or high-end department stores like Nordstrom. And, of course, the nature of the product itself influences the retailers and intermediaries that are used for distribution. Manufacturers select mass merchandisers to sell mid–price-range products while they distribute top-of-the-line products such as expensive jewelry through high-end department and specialty stores.

Distribution decisions can sometimes give a product a distinct position in its market. For example, Enterprise

Rent-a-Car avoids being overly dependent on the cutthroat airport rental car market, as historically it operated in residential areas and local business centers. This strategy takes advantage of the preferences of customers who are not flying and who want short-term use of a rental vehicle, such as when their primary vehicle is in the repair shop. Enterprise built such a successful following around this business model that loyal customers began to clamor for more Enterprise counters at airports, which the company is all too happy to provide. Now Enterprise is a rising competitive threat to traditional airport car rental agencies such as Hertz and Avis. Enterprise isn't the only threat, however. Consider car-sharing services, such as BMW's DriveNow, that let you "rent" cars by the hour or the day. With such services, you can bypass the rental counter altogether. All you have to do is sign up online and pay a one-time fee, and then you can use the free DriveNow app to locate, reserve, and return any one of BMW's many electric cars—you pay only for the time you need the car.[4]

Ethics in the Distribution Channel

Companies' decisions about how to make their products available to consumers through distribution channels can create ethical dilemmas. For example, because their size gives them great bargaining power when they negotiate with manufacturers, many large retail chains force manufacturers to pay a **slotting allowance**—a fee in exchange for agreeing to place a manufacturer's products on a retailer's valuable shelf space. Although the retailers claim that such fees pay the cost of adding products to their inventory, many manufacturers feel that slotting fees are more akin to highway robbery. Certainly, the practice prevents many smaller manufacturers that cannot afford the slotting allowances from getting their products into the hands of consumers.

Another ethical issue involves the sheer size of a particular channel intermediary—be it manufacturer, wholesaler, retailer, or other intermediary. Walmart, the poster child for giant retailers, has been vilified for years as contributing to the demise of scores of independent competitors (i.e., mom-and-pop stores). But recently, the company has begun a very visible program to help its smaller rivals. The program offers financial grants to hardware stores, dress shops, and bakeries near its new urban stores; training on how to survive with a Walmart in town; and even free advertising in Walmart stores. While certainly beneficial to the small fry, Walmart also hopes to benefit from the program in urban settings like Los Angeles and New York, where its plan to build new stores in inner-city neighborhoods has met with mixed reactions from local communities.[5]

Overall, it is important for all channel intermediaries to behave and treat each other in a professional, ethical manner—and to do no harm to consumers (financially or otherwise) through their channel activities. Every intermediary in the channel wants to make money, but behavior by one to maximize its financial success at the expense of others' success is a doomed approach, as ultimately cooperation in the channel will break down. Instead, it behooves intermediaries to work cooperatively in the channel to distribute products to consumers in an efficient manner—making the channel a success for everybody participating in it (including consumers)! Win-win!

slotting allowance
A fee paid in exchange for agreeing to place a manufacturer's products on a retailer's valuable shelf space.

2
OBJECTIVE

List and explain the steps to plan a distribution channel strategy.

(pp. 365–371)

Develop a Channel Strategy

Do customers want products in large or small quantities? Do they insist on buying them locally, or will they purchase from a distant supplier? How long are they willing to wait to get the product? Inquiring marketers want to know!

Channel of distribution planning works best when marketers follow the steps in 🔀 Figure 11.4. In this section, we first look at how manufacturers decide on distribution objectives and then examine what influences distribution decisions. Finally, we talk about how firms select different distribution strategies and tactics.

Figure 11.4 🎿 *Process* | Steps in Distribution Planning

Distribution planning begins with setting channel objectives and evaluating the environment and results in developing channel strategies and tactics.

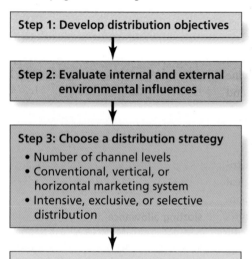

Step 1: Develop distribution objectives

Step 2: Evaluate internal and external environmental influences

Step 3: Choose a distribution strategy
- Number of channel levels
- Conventional, vertical, or horizontal marketing system
- Intensive, exclusive, or selective distribution

Step 4: Develop Distribution Tactics
- Select channel partners
- Manage the channel
- Develop logistics strategies
  - Order processing
  - Warehousing
  - Materials handling
  - Transportation
  - Inventory control

distribution planning
The process of developing distribution objectives, evaluating internal and external environmental influences on distribution, and choosing a distribution strategy.

Firms that operate within a channel of distribution—manufacturers, wholesalers, and retailers—do **distribution planning**, which is a process of developing distribution objectives, evaluating internal and external environmental influences on distribution, and choosing a distribution strategy. In this section, our perspective focuses primarily on distribution planning by producers/manufacturers rather than intermediaries because manufacturers, more often than intermediaries, take a leadership role to create a successful distribution channel. (There are notable exceptions, such as with a retailer like Walmart, which clearly is the biggest fish in any channel in which it operates.)

Step 1: Develop Distribution Objectives

The first step to decide on a distribution plan is to develop objectives that support the organization's overall marketing goals. How can distribution work with the other elements of the marketing mix to increase profits? To increase market share? To increase sales volume? In general, the overall objective of any distribution plan is to make a firm's product available when, where, and in the quantities customers want at the minimum cost. More specific distribution objectives, however, depend on the characteristics of the product and the market.

For example, if the product is bulky, a primary distribution objective may be to minimize shipping costs. If the product is fragile, a goal may be to develop a channel that minimizes handling. In introducing a new product to a mass market, a channel objective may be to provide maximum product exposure or to make the product available close to where customers live and work. Sometimes marketers make their product available where similar products are sold so that consumers can compare prices.

Step 2: Evaluate Internal and External Environmental Influences

After they set their distribution objectives, marketers must consider their internal and external environments to develop the best channel structure. Should the channel be long or short? Is intensive, selective, or exclusive distribution best? Short, often direct channels may be better suited for B2B marketers for whom customers are geographically concentrated and require high levels of technical know-how and service. Companies frequently sell expensive or complex products directly to final customers. Short channels with selective distribution also make more sense with perishable products since getting the product to the final user quickly is a priority. However, longer channels with more intensive distribution are generally best for inexpensive, standardized consumer goods that need to be distributed broadly and that require little technical expertise.

The organization must also examine issues such as its own ability to handle distribution functions, what channel intermediaries are available, the ability of customers to access these intermediaries, and how the competition distributes its products. Should a firm use the same retailers as its competitors? It depends. Sometimes, to ensure customers' undivided attention, a firm sells its products in outlets that don't carry the competitors' products. In other cases, a firm uses the same intermediaries as its competitors because customers expect to find the product there. For example, you will find Harley-Davidson bikes only in selected Harley "boutiques" and Piaggio's Vespa scooters only at Vespa dealers (no sales through Walmart for those two!), but you can expect to find Coca-Cola, Colgate toothpaste, and a Snickers bar in every possible outlet that sells these types of items (remember our discussion in Chapter 8 about the nature of convenience products).

Finally, when they study competitors' distribution strategies, marketers learn from their successes and failures. If the biggest complaint of competitors' customers is delivery speed, developing a system that allows same-day delivery can make the competition pale in comparison.

Step 3: Choose a Distribution Strategy

Planning a distribution strategy means making several decisions. First, of course, distribution planning includes decisions about the number of levels in the distribution channel. We already discussed these options in the earlier section on consumer and B2B channels, illustrated by Figure 11.3. Beyond the number of levels, distribution strategies also involve two additional decisions about channel relationships: (1) whether a conventional system or a highly integrated system will work best and (2) the proper **distribution intensity**, meaning the number of intermediaries at each level of the channel. The next sections provide insight into making these two distribution strategy decisions.

distribution intensity
The number of intermediaries at each level of the channel.

Decision 1: Conventional, Vertical, or Horizontal Marketing System?

Participants in any distribution channel form an interrelated system. In general, these marketing systems take one of three forms: conventional, vertical, or horizontal.

1. A **conventional marketing system** is a multilevel distribution channel in which members work independently of one another. Their relationships are limited to simply buying and selling from one another. Each firm seeks to benefit, with little concern for other channel members. Even though channel members work independently, most conventional channels are highly successful. For one thing, all members of the channel work toward the same goals—to build demand, reduce costs, and improve customer satisfaction. And each channel member knows that it's in everyone's best interest to treat other channel members fairly.

conventional marketing system
A multiple-level distribution channel in which channel members work independently of one another.

2. A **vertical marketing system (VMS)** is a channel in which there is formal cooperation among channel members at two or more different levels: manufacturing, wholesaling, and retailing. Firms develop vertical marketing systems as a way to meet customer needs better by reducing costs incurred in channel activities. Often, a vertical marketing system can provide a level of cooperation and efficiency not possible with a conventional channel, maximizing the effectiveness of the channel while also maximizing efficiency and keeping costs low. Members share information and provide services to other members; they recognize that such coordination makes everyone more successful when they want to reach a desired target market.

vertical marketing system (VMS)
A channel of distribution in which there is formal cooperation among members at the manufacturing, wholesaling, and retailing levels.

In turn there are three types of vertical marketing systems: administered, corporate, and contractual:

a. In an **administered VMS**, channel members remain independent but voluntarily work together because of the power of a single channel member. Strong brands are able to manage an administered VMS because resellers are eager to work with the manufacturer so they will be allowed to carry the product.

administered VMS
A vertical marketing system in which channel members remain independent but voluntarily work together because of the power of a single channel member.

b. In a **corporate VMS**, a single firm owns manufacturing, wholesaling, and retailing operations. Thus, the firm has complete control over all channel operations. Retail giant Macy's, for example, owns a nationwide network of distribution centers and retail stores.

corporate VMS
A vertical marketing system in which a single firm owns manufacturing, wholesaling, and retailing operations.

c. In a **contractual VMS**, cooperation is enforced by contracts (legal agreements) that spell out each member's rights and responsibilities and how they will cooperate. This arrangement means that the channel members can have more impact as a group than they could alone. In a wholesaler-sponsored VMS, wholesalers get retailers to work together under their leadership in a voluntary chain. Retail members of the chain use a common name, cooperate in advertising and other

contractual VMS
A vertical marketing system in which cooperation is enforced by contracts (legal agreements) that spell out each member's rights and responsibilities and how they will cooperate.

retailer cooperative
A group of retailers that establishes a wholesaling operation to help them compete more effectively with the large chains.

franchise organizations
A contractual vertical marketing system that includes a *franchiser* (a manufacturer or a service provider) who allows an entrepreneur (the *franchisee*) to use the franchise name and marketing plan for a fee.

horizontal marketing system
An arrangement within a channel of distribution in which two or more firms at the same channel level work together for a common purpose.

promotion, and even develop their own private-label products. Examples of wholesaler-sponsored chains are IGA (Independent Grocers' Alliance) food stores and Ace Hardware stores.

In other cases, retailers themselves organize a cooperative marketing channel system. A **retailer cooperative** is a group of retailers that establishes a wholesaling operation to help them compete more effectively with the large chains. Each retailer owns shares in the wholesaler operation and is obligated to purchase a certain percentage of its inventory from the cooperative operation. Associated Grocers and True Value Hardware stores are examples of retailer cooperatives.

Franchise organizations are a third type of contractual VMS. Franchise organizations include a *franchiser* (a manufacturer or a service provider) who allows an entrepreneur (the *franchisee*) to use the franchise name and marketing plan for a fee. In these organizations, contractual arrangements explicitly define and strictly enforce channel cooperation. In most franchise agreements, the franchiser provides a variety of services for the franchisee, such as helping to train employees, giving access to lower prices for needed materials, and selecting a good location. In return, the franchiser receives a percentage of revenue from the franchisee. Usually, the franchisees are obligated to follow the franchiser's business format very closely in order to maintain the franchise.

From the manufacturer's perspective, franchising a business is a way to develop widespread product distribution with minimal financial risk while at the same time maintaining control over product quality. From the entrepreneur's perspective, franchises are a helpful way to get a start in business.

3. In a **horizontal marketing system**, two or more firms at the same channel level agree to work together to get their product to the customer. Sometimes, unrelated businesses forge these agreements. Most airlines today are members of a horizontal alliance that allows them to cooperate when they provide passenger air service. For example, American Airlines is a member of the oneworld alliance, which also includes Air Berlin, British Airways, Cathay Pacific, Finnair, Iberia, Japan Airlines, LAN, Malaysia Airlines, Qantas, Qatar Airways, Royal Jordanian, S7 Airlines, SriLankan Airlines, TAM Airlines and, recently added, US Airways. These alliances increase passenger volume for all airlines because travel agents who book passengers on one of the airline's flights will be more likely to book a connecting flight on the other airline. To increase customer benefits, they also share frequent-flyer programs and airport clubs.[6]

Decision 2: Intensive, Exclusive, or Selective Distribution?

How many wholesalers and retailers should carry the product within a given market? This may seem like an easy decision: distribute the product through as many intermediaries as possible. But guess again. If the product goes to too many outlets, there may be inefficiency and duplication of efforts. For example, if there are too many Honda dealerships in town, there will be a lot of unsold Hondas sitting on dealer lots, and no single dealer will be successful. But if there are not enough wholesalers or retailers to carry a product, this will fail to maximize total sales of the manufacturer's products (and its profits). If customers have to drive hundreds of miles to find a Honda dealer, they may instead opt for a Toyota just because of convenience, Thus, a distribution objective may be to either increase or decrease the level of distribution in the market.

The three basic choices are intensive, exclusive, and selective distribution. Table 11.2 summarizes five decision factors—company, customers, channels, constraints, and competition—and how they help marketers determine the best fit between distribution system and marketing goals. Read on, and you will find that these categories connect with the concept of convenience products, shopping products, and specialty products you learned about in Chapter 8.

Table 11.2	Characteristics That Favor Intensive versus Exclusive Distribution	
Decision Factor	**Intensive Distribution**	**Exclusive Distribution**
Company	Oriented toward mass markets	Oriented toward specialized markets
Customers	High customer density	Low customer density
	Price and convenience are priorities	Service and cooperation are priorities
Channels	Overlapping market coverage	Nonoverlapping market coverage
Constraints	Cost of serving individual customers is low	Cost of serving individual customers is high
Competition	Based on a strong market presence, often through advertising and promotion	Based on individualized attention to customers, often through relationship marketing

Intensive distribution aims to maximize market coverage by selling a product through all wholesalers or retailers that will stock and sell the product. Marketers use intensive distribution for *convenience products*, such as chewing gum, soft drinks, milk, and bread, that consumers quickly consume and must replace frequently. Intensive distribution is necessary for these products because availability is more important than any other consideration in customers' purchase decisions.

In contrast to intensive distribution, **exclusive distribution** means to limit distribution to a single outlet in a particular region. Marketers often sell pianos, cars, executive training programs, TV programs, and many other *specialty products* with high price tags through exclusive distribution arrangements. They typically use these strategies with products that are high priced and have considerable service requirements and when a limited number of buyers exist in any single geographic area. Exclusive distribution enables wholesalers and retailers to better recoup the costs associated with long-selling processes for each customer and, in some cases, extensive after-sale service.

Of course, not every situation neatly fits a category in Table 11.2. (You didn't *really* think it would be that simple, did you?) For example, consider professional sports. Customers might not shop for games in the same way they shop for pianos. They might go to a game on impulse, and they don't require much individualized service. Nevertheless, professional sports use exclusive distribution. A team's cost of serving customers is high because of those million-dollar player salaries and multi-million-dollar stadiums.

The alert reader (and/or sports fan) may note that there are some exceptions to the exclusive distribution of sports teams. New York has two football teams and two baseball teams, Chicago fields two baseball teams, and so on. We call market coverage that is less than intensive distribution but more than exclusive distribution **selective distribution** (yes, this type falls between the two). This model fits when demand is so large that exclusive distribution is inadequate but selling costs, service requirements, or other factors make intensive distribution a poor fit. Although a White Sox baseball fan may not believe that the Cubs franchise is necessary (and vice versa), Major League Baseball and even some baseball fans think the Chicago market is large enough to support both teams.

Selective distribution strategies are suitable for most *shopping products*, such as household appliances and electronic equipment, for which consumers are willing to spend time visiting different retail outlets to compare alternatives. For producers, selective distribution means freedom to choose only those wholesalers and retailers that have a good credit rating, provide good market coverage, serve customers well, and cooperate effectively. Wholesalers and retailers like selective distribution because it results in higher profits than are possible with intensive distribution, in which sellers often have to compete on price.

intensive distribution
Selling a product through all suitable wholesalers or retailers that are willing to stock and sell the product.

exclusive distribution
Selling a product only through a single outlet in a particular region.

selective distribution
Distribution using fewer outlets than intensive distribution but more than exclusive distribution.

Step 4: Develop Distribution Tactics

As with planning for the other marketing Ps, the final step in distribution planning is to develop the tactics for distribution necessary to implement the distribution strategy. These decisions are usually about the type of distribution system to use, such as a direct or an indirect channel or a conventional or an integrated channel. Distribution tactics relate to two aspects of the implementation of these strategies: (1) how to select individual channel members and (2) how to manage the channel. We provide insights into making each of these two decisions below.

First, it is essential to understand that these two decisions are important because they often have a *direct impact on customer satisfaction*—nobody wants to have to wait for something they've bought! When Toyota first introduced the now wildly successful Scion, the company wisely came up with a new approach to distribute this youth-oriented vehicle that differs from its traditional Toyota distribution system. The company's overall goal was to cut delivery time to its impatient young customers to no more than a week by offering fewer model variations and doing more customization *at the dealer* rather than at the factory.[7] Today, Scion uses its "Pure Process" method to quickly and efficiently get cars to their new owners. Consumers can go to the Scion website, choose their base model and color, find a dealer, and then customize their Scion with accessories like fog lights or rear spoilers. And all this happens for a "Pure Price"—no negotiating necessary.[8] The continuing success of the Scion brand shows the power of tailoring distribution tactics differently for different markets.

Decision 1: Select Channel Partners

When firms agree to work together in a channel relationship, they become partners in what is normally a long-term commitment. Like a marriage, it is important to both manufacturers and intermediaries to select channel partners wisely, or they'll regret the match-up later (and a divorce can be really expensive!). In evaluating intermediaries, manufacturers try to answer questions such as the following: Will the channel member contribute substantially to our profitability? Does the channel member have the ability to provide the services customers want? What impact will a potential intermediary have on channel control?

For example, what small to midsize firm wouldn't jump at the chance to have retail giant Walmart distribute its products? With Walmart as a channel partner, a small firm could double, triple, or quadruple its business. But believe it or not, some firms that recognize that size means power in the channel actually decide against selling to Walmart because they are not willing to relinquish control of their marketing decision making. There is also a downside to choosing one retailer and selling only through that one retailer. If that retailer stops carrying the product, for example, the company will lose its one and only customer (perhaps after relinquishing other smaller customers), and it will be back to square one.

Another consideration in selecting channel members is competitors' channel partners. Because people spend time comparing different brands when purchasing a shopping product, firms need to make sure they display their products near similar competitors' products. If most competitors distribute their electric drills through mass merchandisers, a manufacturer has to make sure its brand is there also.

A firm's dedication to social responsibility may also be an important determining factor in the selection of channel partners. Many firms run extensive programs to recruit minority-owned channel members. Starbucks's famous organizational commitment to good corporate citizenship translates in one way into its "supplier diversity program" that works to help minority-owned business thrive.[9]

Decision 2: Manage the Channel

Once a manufacturer develops a channel strategy and aligns channel members, the day-to-day job of managing the channel begins. The **channel leader or channel captain** is the dominant firm that controls the channel. A firm becomes the channel captain because it

channel leader or channel captain
The dominant firm that controls the channel.

has more **channel power** relative to other channel members. Channel power is the ability of one channel member to influence, control, and lead the entire channel based on one or more sources of power. This power comes from different potential sources, among which are the following:

- A firm has *economic power* if it has the ability to control resources.

- A firm such as a franchiser has *legitimate power* if it has legal authority to call the shots.

- A producer firm has *reward* or *coercive power* if it engages in exclusive distribution and has the ability to give profitable products and to take them away from the channel intermediaries.

As we mentioned, historically producers have held the role of channel captain. Procter & Gamble, for example, developed customer-oriented marketing programs, tracked market trends, and advised retailers on the mix of products most likely to build sales. As large retail chains have evolved, giant retailers such as Best Buy, Home Depot, Target, Walmart, and Walgreens began to assume a leadership role because of the sheer size of their operations. Today, it is much more common for the big retailers to dictate their needs to producers instead of producers controlling what products they offer to retailers. As an example, Amazon is trying to use its channel power to "persuade" publisher Hachette to meet to Amazon's terms regarding e-book pricing by subjecting their books to artificial purchase delays, and some Hachette titles no longer appear in search results. Other popular titles are no longer available for preorder. Whatever the outcome of this dispute, the fact remains that Amazon has been particularly smart in positioning itself as a nexus for distributing a wide spectrum of products. They've done this through shrewd partnerships and agreements with a huge number of manufacturers and other retailers, and today the world's largest retailer—Walmart—views Amazon as its number one competitor!

Because producers, wholesalers, and retailers depend on one another for success, **channel cooperation** helps everyone. Channel cooperation is stimulated when the channel leader takes actions that make its partners more successful. Examples of this, such as high intermediary profit margins, training programs, cooperative advertising, and expert marketing advice, are invisible to end customers but are motivating factors in the eyes of wholesalers and retailers.

Of course, relations among members in a channel are not always full of sweetness and light. Because each firm has its own objectives, **channel conflict** may threaten a manufacturer's distribution strategy. Such conflict most often occurs between firms at different levels of the same distribution channel. Incompatible goals, poor communication, and disagreement over roles, responsibilities, and functions cause conflict. For example, a producer is likely to feel the firm would enjoy greater success and profitability if intermediaries carry only its brands, but many intermediaries believe they will do better if they carry a variety of brands.

In this section, we've been concerned with the distribution channels firms use to get their products to customers. In the next section, we'll look at the area of logistics—physically moving products through the supply chain—and end by introducing the concept of the supply chain.

channel power
The ability of one channel member to influence, control, and lead the entire channel based on one or more sources of power.

channel cooperation
Occurs when producers, wholesalers, and retailers depend on one another for success.

channel conflict
Incompatible goals, poor communication, and disagreement over roles, responsibilities, and functions among firms at different levels of the same distribution channel that may threaten a manufacturer's distribution strategy.

3

OBJECTIVE

Discuss the concepts of logistics and supply chain.

(pp. 371–378)

Logistics and the Supply Chain

Some marketing textbooks tend to depict the practice of marketing as 90 percent planning and 10 percent implementation. Not so! In the "real world" (and in our book), many managers argue that this ratio should be reversed. Marketing success is very much the art of getting the timing right and delivering on promises—*implementation*.

logistics
The process of designing, managing, and improving the movement of products through the supply chain. Logistics includes purchasing, manufacturing, storage, and transport.

reverse logistics
Includes product returns, recycling and material reuse, and waste disposal.

That's why marketers place so much emphasis on efficient **logistics**: the process of designing, managing, and improving the movement of products through the supply chain. Logistics includes purchasing, manufacturing, storage, and transport. From a company's viewpoint, logistics takes place both *inbound* to the firm (raw materials, parts, components, and supplies) and *outbound* from the firm (work in process and finished goods).

Logistics is also a relevant consideration regarding product returns, recycling and material reuse, and waste disposal—**reverse logistics**.[10] As we saw in earlier chapters, that's becoming even more important as firms start to more seriously consider *sustainability* as a competitive advantage and put more effort into maximizing the efficiency of recycling to save money and the environment at the same time. So you can see that logistics is an important issue across all elements of the supply chain. Let's examine this process more closely.

The Lowdown on Logistics

Have you ever heard the saying, "An army travels on its stomach"? *Logistics* was originally a term the military used to describe everything needed to deliver troops and equipment to the right place, at the right time, and in the right condition. In business, logistics is similar in that its objective is to deliver exactly what the customer wants—at the right time, in the right place, and at the right price. As 🏃 Figure 11.5 shows, logistics activities include order processing, warehousing, materials handling, transportation, and inventory control. This process impacts how marketers physically get products where they need to be, when they need to be there, and at the lowest possible cost.

When a firm does logistics planning, however, the focus also should be on the customer. In the old days when managers thought of logistics as physical distribution only, the objective was to deliver the product at the lowest cost. Today, forward-thinking firms consider the needs of the customer first. The customer's goals become the logistics provider's priorities. And this means that when they make most logistics decisions, firms must decide on the best trade-off between low costs and high customer service. The appropriate goal is not just to deliver what the market needs at the lowest cost but rather to provide the product at the lowest cost possible *as long as the firm meets delivery requirements*. Although it would be nice to transport all goods quickly by air (even by drone, as Amazon wants to do), that is certainly not practical. But sometimes air transport is necessary to meet the needs of the customer, no matter the cost.

order processing
The series of activities that occurs between the time an order comes into the organization and the time a product goes out the door.

Figure 11.5 🏃 *Process* | The Five Functions of Logistics

When developing logistics strategies, marketers must make decisions related to order processing, warehousing, materials handling, transportation, and inventory control.

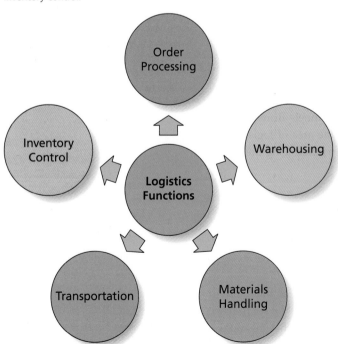

When they develop logistics strategies, marketers must make decisions related to each of the five functions of logistics depicted in Figure 11.5. For each decision, managers need to consider how to minimize costs while maintaining the service customers want. Let's look closely at each of the five logistics functions.

Order Processing

Order processing includes the series of activities that occurs between the time an order comes into the organization and the time a product goes out the door. After a firm receives an order, it typically sends it electronically to an office for record keeping and then on to the warehouse to fill it. When the order reaches the warehouse, personnel there check to see if the item is in stock. If it is not, they put the order on back-order status. That information goes to the office and then to the customer. If the item is available, the company locates it in the warehouse, packages it for shipment, and schedules it for pickup by either in-house or external shippers.

Fortunately, many firms automate this process with **enterprise resource planning (ERP) systems**. An ERP system is a software solution that integrates information from across the entire company, including finance, order fulfillment, manufacturing, and transportation. Data need to be entered into the system only once, and then the organization automatically shares this information and links it to other related data. For example, an ERP system ties information on product inventories to sales information so that a sales representative can immediately tell a customer whether the product is in stock.

enterprise resource planning (ERP) systems
A software system that integrates information from across the entire company, including finance, order fulfillment, manufacturing, and transportation, and then facilitates sharing of the data throughout the firm.

Warehousing

Whether we deal with fresh-cut flowers, canned goods, or computer chips, at some point goods (unlike services) must be stored. Storing goods allows marketers to match supply with demand. For example, gardening supplies are especially big sellers during spring and summer, but the factories that manufacture them operate 12 months of the year. **Warehousing**—storing goods in anticipation of sale or transfer to another member of the channel of distribution—enables marketers to provide *time utility* to consumers by holding on to products until consumers need them.

warehousing
Storing goods in anticipation of sale or transfer to another member of the channel of distribution.

Part of developing effective logistics means making decisions about how many warehouses are needed and where and what type of warehouse each should be. A firm determines the location of its warehouse(s) by the location of customers and access to major highways, airports, or rail transportation. The number of warehouses often depends on the level of service that customers require. If customers generally demand fast delivery (today or tomorrow at the latest), then it may be necessary to store products in a number of different locations from which the company can quickly ship the goods to the customer.

Firms use private and public warehouses to store goods. Those that use private warehouses have a high initial investment, but they also lose less of their inventory due to damage. Public warehouses are an alternative that allows firms to pay for a portion of warehouse space rather than having to own an entire storage facility. Most countries offer public warehouses in all large cities and many smaller cities to support domestic and international trade. A **distribution center** is a warehouse that stores goods for short periods of time and that provides other functions, such as breaking bulk. Most large retailers have their own distribution centers so that their stores do not need to keep a lot of inventory in the back room.

distribution center
A warehouse that stores goods for short periods of time and that provides other functions, such as breaking bulk.

Materials Handling

Materials handling is the moving of products into, within, and out of warehouses. When goods come into the warehouse, they must be physically identified, checked for damage, sorted, and labeled. Next, they are taken to a location for storage. Finally, they are recovered from the storage area for packaging and shipment. All in all, the goods may be handled over a dozen separate times. Procedures that limit the number of times a product must be handled decrease the likelihood of damage and reduce the cost of materials handling.

materials handling
The moving of products into, within, and out of warehouses.

Transportation

Logistics decisions take into consideration options for **transportation**, the mode by which products move among channel members. Again, making transportation decisions entails a compromise between minimizing cost and providing the service customers want. As

transportation
The mode by which products move among channel members.

Table 11.3 | A Comparison of Transportation Modes

Transportation Mode	Dependability	Cost	Speed of Delivery	Accessibility	Capability	Traceability	Most Suitable Products
Railroads	Average	Average	Moderate	High	High	Low	Heavy or bulky goods, such as automobiles, grain, and steel
Water	Low	Low	Slow	Low	Moderate	Low	Bulky, nonperishable goods, such as automobiles
Trucks	High	High for long distances; low for short distances	Fast	High	High	High	A wide variety of products, including those that need refrigeration
Air	High	High	Very fast	Low	Moderate	High	High-value items, such as electronic goods and fresh flowers
Pipeline	High	Low	Slow	Low	Low	Moderate	Petroleum products and other chemicals
Internet	High	Low	Very fast	Potentially very high	Low	High	Services such as banking, information, and entertainment

Table 11.3 shows, modes of transportation, including railroads, water transportation, trucks, airways, pipelines, and the Internet, differ in the following ways:

- *Dependability:* The ability of the carrier to deliver goods safely and on time
- *Cost:* The total transportation costs to move a product from one location to another, including any charges for loading, unloading, and in-transit storage
- *Speed of delivery:* The total time to move a product from one location to another, including loading and unloading
- *Accessibility:* The number of different locations the carrier serves
- *Capability:* The ability of the carrier to handle a variety of different products, such as large or small, fragile, or bulky
- *Traceability:* The ability of the carrier to locate goods in shipment

Each mode of transportation has strengths and weaknesses that make it a good choice for different transportation needs. Table 11.3 summarizes the pros and cons of each mode:

- *Railroads:* Railroads are best to carry heavy or bulky items, such as coal and other mining products, over long distances. Railroads are about average in their cost and provide moderate speed of delivery. Although rail transportation provides dependable, low-cost service to many locations, trains cannot carry goods to every community.
- *Water:* Ships and barges carry large, bulky goods and are very important in international trade. Water transportation is relatively low in cost but can be slow.
- *Trucks:* Trucks or motor carriers are the most important transportation mode for consumer goods, especially for shorter hauls. Motor carrier transport allows flexibility

because trucks can travel to locations missed by boats, trains, and planes. Trucks also carry a wide variety of products, including perishable items. Although costs are fairly high for longer-distance shipping, trucks are economical for shorter deliveries. Because trucks provide door-to-door service, product handling is minimal, and this reduces the chance of product damage.

- *Air:* Air transportation is the fastest and also the most expensive transportation mode. It is ideal to move high-value items such as important mail, fresh-cut flowers, and live lobsters. Passenger airlines, air-freight carriers, and express delivery firms, such as FedEx, provide air transportation. Ships remain the major mover of international cargo, but air transportation networks are becoming more important as international markets continue to develop.

- *Pipeline:* Pipelines carry petroleum products such as oil and natural gas and a few other chemicals. Pipelines flow primarily from oil or gas fields to refineries. They are very low in cost, require little energy, and are not subject to disruption by weather.

- *The Internet:* As we discussed earlier in this chapter, marketers of services such as banking, news, and entertainment take advantage of distribution opportunities the Internet provides.

Inventory Control

Another component of logistics is **inventory control**, which means developing and implementing a process to ensure that the firm always has sufficient quantities of goods available to meet customers' demands—no more and no less. This explains why firms work so hard to track merchandise so that they know where their products are and where they are needed in case a low-inventory situation appears imminent.

Some companies are even phasing in a sophisticated technology (similar to the EZ Pass system many drivers use to speed through tollbooths) known as **radio frequency identification (RFID)**. As we saw in Chapter 2, RFID lets firms tag clothes, pharmaceuticals, or virtually any kind of product with tiny chips that contain information about the item's content, origin, and destination. This technology has the potential to revolutionize inventory control and help marketers ensure that their products are on the shelves when people want to buy them. Great for manufacturers and retailers, right? But some consumer groups are creating a backlash against RFID, which they refer to as "spy chips." Through blogs, boycotts, and other anticompany initiatives, these groups proclaim that RFID is a personification of the privacy violations George Orwell predicted in his classic book *1984*.[11] One blogger, for example, convinced that Gillette is using "spy chips" in the packaging of its razors to spy on and take pictures of customers, decided to start his own "Boycott Gillette" website. The site warns consumers which Gillette products not to buy and lets them know how to contact Gillette as well as their lawmakers to fight against the use of RFID tags.[12]

Firms store goods (i.e., they create an *inventory*) for many reasons. For manufacturers, the pace of production may not match seasonal demand. It may be more economical to produce snow skis year-round than to produce them only during the winter season. For channel members that purchase goods from manufacturers or other channel intermediaries, it may be economical to order a product in quantities that don't exactly parallel demand. For example, delivery costs make it prohibitive for a retail gas station to place daily orders for just the amount of gas that people will use that day. Instead, stations usually order truckloads of gasoline, holding their inventory in underground tanks. **Stock-outs**, which are zero-inventory situations resulting in lost sales and customer dissatisfaction, may be very negative. Ever go to the store based on an ad in the newspaper, only to find the store doesn't have the product on hand?

inventory control
Activities to ensure that goods are always available to meet customers' demands.

radio frequency identification (RFID)
Product tags with tiny chips containing information about the item's content, origin, and destination.

stock-outs
Zero-inventory situations resulting in lost sales and customer dissatisfaction.

just in time (JIT)

Inventory management and purchasing processes that manufacturers and resellers use to reduce inventory to very low levels and ensure that deliveries from suppliers arrive only when needed.

Inventory control has a major impact on the overall costs of a firm's logistics initiatives. If supplies of products are too low to meet fluctuations in customer demand, a firm may have to make expensive emergency deliveries or else lose customers to competitors. If inventories are above demand, unnecessary storage expenses and the possibility of damage or deterioration occur. To balance these two opposing needs, manufacturers turn to **just in time (JIT)** inventory techniques with their suppliers. JIT sets up delivery of goods just as they are needed on the production floor. This minimizes the cost of holding inventory while ensuring the inventory will be there when customers need it.

A supplier's ability to make on-time deliveries is the critical factor in the selection process for firms that adopt this kind of system. JIT systems reduce stock to very low levels (or even zero) and time deliveries very carefully to maintain just the right amount of inventory. The advantage of JIT systems is the reduced cost of warehousing. For both manufacturers and resellers that use JIT systems, the choice of supplier may come down to one whose location is nearest. To win a large customer, a supplier may even have to be willing to set up production facilities close to the customer to guarantee JIT delivery.[13]

Place: Pulling It All Together through the Supply Chain

supply chain

All the activities necessary to turn raw materials into a good or service and put it in the hands of the consumer or business customer.

A **supply chain** includes all the activities necessary to turn raw materials into a good or service and put it into the hands of the consumer or business customer. Sam's Club and its sister company, Walmart, are iconic when it comes to global supply chain effectiveness. In recent years, Walmart has been working to increase the proportion of goods that it buys directly from manufacturers rather than through third-party procurement companies or suppliers. As part of its effort to combine purchasing for the 15 countries in which it operates, Walmart has established four global merchandising centers for general goods and clothing. These include a center in Mexico City focused on emerging markets and a center in the U.K. to serve its George brand. It has also shifted to direct purchasing of a number of lines, such as the following: fresh fruit and vegetables on a global basis; sheets and towels for its stores in the U.S., Canada, and Mexico; its Faded Glory clothing line; licensed Disney

inventory turnover or inventory turns

The number of times a firm's inventory completely cycles through during a defined time frame.

Metrics Moment

One of the most used measures of inventory control is **inventory turnover or inventory turns**, which is the number of times a firm's inventory completely cycles through during a defined time frame (usually in one year). Marketers can measure inventory turnover by using the value of the inventory at cost or at retail, or this metric can even be expressed in units. Just make sure that you're using the same unit of measure in both the numerator and the denominator.[14] One of the most common formulas is the following:

$$\text{Inventory turnover} = \text{Annual cost of sales} \div \text{Average inventory level for the period}$$

However, the above formula requires waiting until the end of the year (or end of the business's fiscal year). An alternative is using the following "snapshot" number, which takes a rolling approach so that turns can be calculated at any time by looking at cost of sales for the immediately prior 12 months and the current inventory at the end of that period:

$$\text{Inventory turnover} = \text{Rolling 12-month cost of sales} \div \text{Current inventory}$$

Benchmarks for inventory turnover vary greatly by industry and product line. High-volume/low-margin settings like supermarkets may have 12 or more inventory turns per year overall, but some staple goods that are bought at every trip (e.g., milk and bread) may have significantly higher turnover rates. All else equal, a firm can up its profitability substantially by targeting increases in inventory turnover—selling through Product X 15 times a year instead of 12 naturally improves the bottom line. However, if price reductions or promotional expense increases are needed to up the turns, management will have to carefully calculate whether increased volume really adds to profits (this is where marketers can get into trouble with the old saying, "We're losing money but we'll make it up in volume!").

Apply the Metrics

1. Spider's Auto Parts Store ended its fiscal year last month with a cost of sales of $3,600,000 and an average inventory of $450,000. What is Spider's inventory turnover for that fiscal year?
2. Spider's would like to boost its turns to 10 during the next fiscal year. What suggestions do you have that will help them accomplish this objective?

character clothing; and eventually other categories, including seafood, frozen food, and dry packaged groceries.[15]

Walmart clearly understands the potential for supply chain practices to enhance organizational performance and profits, and scores of other firms across most every industry with physical products benchmark against them for best practices. The truth is that distribution may be the "final frontier" for marketing success. To understand why, consider these facts about the other three Ps of marketing. After years of hype, many consumers no longer believe that "new and improved" products really *are* new and improved. Nearly everyone, even upscale manufacturers and retailers, tries to gain market share through aggressive pricing strategies. Advertising and many other forms of promotion are so commonplace today that they have lost some of their impact. Even hot new social media strategies can't sell overpriced or poorly made products, at least for long. Marketers have come to understand that *place* (the "distribution P") may be the only one of the *four Ps* to offer an opportunity for really long-term competitive advantage—especially since many consumers now expect "instant gratification" by getting just what they want instantaneously when the urge strikes.

That's why savvy marketers are always on the lookout for novel ways to distribute their products. A large part of the marketer's ability to deliver a value proposition rests on the ability to understand and develop effective supply chain strategies. Often, of course, firms may decide to bring in outside companies to accomplish these activities—this is *outsourcing*, which as we learned about in Chapter 6 occurs when firms obtain outside vendors to provide goods or services that might otherwise be supplied in-house. In the case of supply chain functions, outsource firms are most likely organizations with whom the company has developed some form of partnership or cooperative business arrangement.

Supply chain management is the coordination of flows among the firms in a supply chain to maximize total profitability. These "flows" include not only the physical movement of goods but also the sharing of information about the goods—that is, supply chain partners must synchronize their activities with one another. For example, they need to communicate information about which goods they want to purchase (the procurement function), about which marketing campaigns they plan to execute (so that the supply chain partners can ensure there will be enough product to supply the increased demand that results from the promotion), and about logistics (such as sending advance shipping notices to alert their partners that products are on their way). Through these information flows, a company can effectively manage all the links in its supply chain, from sourcing to retailing.

In his book *The World Is Flat: A Brief History of the Twenty-First Century*, which we discussed in Chapter 2, Thomas Friedman addresses a number of high-impact trends in global supply chain management.[16] One such development is the trend whereby companies we traditionally know for other things remake themselves as specialists who take over the coordination of clients' supply chains for them. UPS is a great example of this trend. UPS, which used to be "just" a package delivery service, today is much more because it also specializes in **insourcing**. This process occurs when companies contract with a specialist who services their supply chains. Unlike the *outsourcing process* where a company delegates nonessential tasks to subcontractors, insourcing means that the client company brings in an external company to run its essential operations. Although we tend to associate UPS with those little brown trucks that zip around town delivering boxes, the company actually positions itself in the B2B space as a broad-based supply chain consultancy!

Finally, in case you're wondering about the difference between a supply chain and a channel of distribution, the major distinguishing feature is the number of members and their functions. A supply chain is broader, consisting of those firms that supply the raw materials, component parts, and supplies necessary for a firm to produce a good or service *plus* the firms that facilitate the movement of that product to the ultimate users of the product. This last part—the firms that get the product to the ultimate users—is the channel of distribution.

supply chain management
The management of flows among firms in the supply chain to maximize total profitability.

insourcing
A practice in which a company contracts with a specialist firm to handle all or part of its supply chain operations.

Ripped from the Headlines

Ethical/Sustainable Decisions in the Real World

Imagine if a company can operate not only a single restaurant that serves locally grown, sustainable gourmet meals but also a whole chain of such restaurants that can serve millions of these healthy, responsibly sourced meals. If—of all people—a former president and CEO of McDonald's thinks it can, then it can. And his vision is coming to life in the form of Lyfe Kitchen.

Lyfe Kitchen (which stands for Love Your Food Everyday) started with one restaurant in California but is now a small chain, growing every year. The founders hope to open hundreds of restaurants within the span of five years. Their aims are twofold: "to build a radically sustainable, health brand of fast food" and to do "for responsibly grown meat and veggies what McDonald's did for factory-farmed beef."[17] All thanks to new methods of supply chain management.

ETHICS CHECK: ✎
Find out what other students taking this course *would do* and *why* at **mymktlab.com**.

Take, as an example, the poultry supply chain. The traditional supply chain would say that you have to get your chicken as quickly and cheaply as possible. But instead of going the traditional route, with suppliers like Tyson or Perdue, Lyfe Kitchens buys its chicken from Mary's Chickens. The difference? At Mary's Chickens, slaughtered chickens are cooled with chilled air rather than dipped in chlorine baths. The result is a better-tasting chicken, with a savings of 30,000 gallons of water daily. And Lyfe Kitchens's cheese comes from a dairy farm called Fiscalini, which uses its waste to produce all of its own electricity.

As you might expect, even the kitchens at Lyfe Kitchens are high-tech. In addition to appliances that sense when to save energy, the dishwashing system captures steam, condenses it, and then recycles the heat for the next batch of dishes. The dishwashers also use about three-quarters of a gallon of water per wash (compared with 1.5 gallons for a typical dishwasher) and sanitize without chlorine.

For now, Lyfe Kitchens seems to be doing well. And the start-up certainly is on track with its sustainability efforts. So, knowing that it's possible to "do well by doing good," do you think other restaurants should be required to step up their sustainability efforts?

Do you think restaurants should be required to purchase their ingredients from sustainable suppliers like Fiscalini, which produces food while it gives back to the environment?

☐ YES ☐ NO

Why do you think Dan choose option 3?

Here's my choice...
Real **People**, Real **Choices**

1 Option   2 Option   ③ Option

How It Worked Out at First Tennessee Bank

Dan and his team chose option 3 and decided to concentrate on mobile banking. They reasoned that the ability to conduct transactions via smart phone could be relatively quickly developed and deployed, and it provided a way to establish leadership with a relatively modest investment. In partnership with the First Tennessee Enterprise Technology division, Dan's team identified a leading developer of mobile technology. The tech firm Mfoundry was doing some very leading edge work in the space, including development of a mobile payment app for Starbucks, and the company retained them to develop the app.

After less than half a year in development, Dan's team went through a disciplined launch process starting with a beta test followed by an "employee customer" soft launch. During the soft launch phase, employee customers used the actual mobile banking product to become familiar with it and to allow the development team to make additional refinements. The feedback from this phase also allowed the launch promotional materials to be fine-tuned and tested on a smaller scale.

When Mobile Banking launched, it used a full multichannel approach, including listing in the Apple AppStore, e-mails to the full First Tennessee Bank e-mail list, inserts in other customer communications, prominent placement on the bank's website **ftb.com**, extensive banner and search advertising, and messages in traditional mass media, such as radio and print ads.

After the initial launch, the bank introduced additional features to add capability to pay bills and make remote check deposits. Each additional feature release offered another opportunity to communicate to customers and prospects about the exciting new reasons to bank with First Tennessee. As a result, Mobile Banking was well received with customers and potential customers. In fact, First Tennessee's mobile banking adoption was twice as high as the initial business case predicted.

How First Tennessee Bank Measures Success

Dan and his team developed a business case for mobile banking that built in certain assumptions. These included an estimate of the number of existing customers who would adopt a mobile banking app plus the number of additional customers the mobile banking feature would attract. Since the market was so new, there were few benchmarks to rely on when they developed these assumptions, so the team used direct customer research on overall level of awareness, current usage of smart phones, other electronic banking behaviors, and attitudes toward adopting new technology to come up with these estimates.

In addition to enticing new people to bank with the company, First Tennessee expected to see an increase in the "stickiness" of existing customers in terms of the number who stayed with the bank. For example, if the average customer tenure was five years and mobile banking could extend the average life to six years, that would represent a 20 percent increase in the lifetime value of the customer. Research and previous experience also showed that customers who used more of the bank's services had a higher probability of purchasing other financial products the bank offered.

To keep tabs on the app's progress, the team created a *launch dashboard* that tracked the number of users who adopted mobile banking and its penetration into the existing customer base. At the three-, six-, and 12-month marks postlaunch, the First Tennessee Customer Insight team conducted an analysis to understand the impact on retention rates, probability of purchasing other products, and the cost-saving potential of moving inquiries from the call center or deposits from the teller line onto the mobile platform.

First Tennessee Bank was one of the first to market with a mobile application.

Refer back to **page 352** for Dan's story ➡

MyMarketingLab™

Go to **mymktlab.com** to complete the problems marked with this icon ⭐ as well as additional Marketing Metrics questions only available in MyMarketingLab.

Objective Summary ➡ Key Terms ➡ Apply

CHAPTER 11
Study Map

1. Objective Summary (pp. 354–365)

Explain what a distribution channel is, identify types of wholesaling intermediaries, and describe the different types of distribution channels.

A channel of distribution is a series of firms or individuals that facilitates the movement of a product from the producer to the final customer. Channels provide place, time, and possession utility for customers and reduce the number of transactions necessary for goods to flow from many manufacturers to large numbers of customers by breaking bulk and creating assortments. Channel members make the purchasing process easier by providing important customer services.

Wholesaling intermediaries are firms that handle the flow of products from the manufacturer to the retailer or business user.

Merchant wholesalers are independent intermediaries that take title to a product and include both full-service merchant wholesalers and limited-service merchant wholesalers. Merchandise agents and brokers are independent intermediaries that do not take title to products. Manufacturer-owned channel members include sales branches, sales offices, and manufacturers' showrooms.

Distribution channels vary in length from the simplest two-level channel to longer channels with three or more channel levels. Distribution channels include direct distribution, in which the producer sells directly to consumers, and indirect channels, which may include a retailer, wholesaler, or other intermediary. B2B distribution channels facilitate the flow of goods from a producer to an organizational or business customer. Producers, dealers, wholesalers, retailers, and customers may participate in more than one type of channel, called a dual or multiple distribution system. Finally, some companies combine channels—direct sales, distributors, retail sales, and direct mail—to create a hybrid marketing system.

Key Terms

physical distribution, p. 354

channel of distribution, p. 354

channel intermediaries, p. 354

breaking bulk, p. 355

create assortments, p. 355

transportation and storage, p. 356

facilitating functions, p. 356

risk-taking functions, p. 356

communication and transaction functions, p. 356

disintermediation (of the channel of distribution), p. 356

knowledge management, p. 357

intranet, p. 357

online distribution piracy, p. 357

wholesaling intermediaries, p. 358

independent intermediaries, p. 358

merchant wholesalers, p. 358

take title, p. 358

full-service merchant wholesalers, p. 358

limited-service merchant wholesalers, p. 358

merchandise agents or brokers, p. 360

channel levels, p. 361

dual or multiple distribution systems, p. 364

hybrid marketing system, p. 364

slotting allowance, p. 365

2. Objective Summary (pp. 365–371)

List and explain the steps to plan a distribution channel strategy.

Firms that operate within a channel of distribution—manufacturers, wholesalers, and retailers—do distribution planning, which is a process of developing distribution objectives, evaluating internal and external environmental influences on distribution, and choosing a distribution strategy. Marketers begin channel planning by developing distribution channel objectives and considering important internal and external environmental factors. The next step is to decide on a distribution strategy, which involves determining the type of distribution channel that is best. Finally, distribution tactics include the selection of individual channel members and management of the channel.

Key Terms

distribution planning, p. 366

distribution intensity, p. 367

conventional marketing system, p. 367

vertical marketing system (VMS), p. 367

administered VMS, p. 367

corporate VMS, p. 367

contractual VMS, p. 367

retailer cooperative, p. 368

franchise organizations, p. 368

horizontal marketing system, p. 368

intensive distribution, p. 369

exclusive distribution, p. 369

selective distribution, p. 369

channel leader or channel captain, p. 370

channel power, p. 371

channel cooperation, p. 371

channel conflict, p. 371

3. Objective Summary (pp. 371–378)

Discuss the concepts of logistics and supply chain.

Logistics is the process of designing, managing, and improving supply chains, including all the activities that are required to move products through the supply chain. Logistics contributes to the overall supply chain through activities including order processing, warehousing, materials handling, transportation, and inventory control.

A supply chain includes all the activities necessary to turn raw materials into a good or service and put it into the hands of the consumer or business customer. Supply chain management is the coordination of flows among the firms in a supply chain to maximize total profitability.

Key Terms

logistics, p. 372

reverse logistics, p. 372

order processing, p. 372

enterprise resource planning (ERP) systems, p. 373

warehousing, p. 373

distribution center, p. 373

materials handling, p. 373

transportation, p. 373

Chapter **Questions** and **Activities**

Concepts: Test Your Knowledge

11-1. What is the purpose of breaking bulk? What is meant by creating assortments?

11-2. What is meant by risk-taking functions in distribution?

11-3. The Internet has affected supply chains. What is knowledge management, and what is an intranet?

11-4. What are full-service and limited-service merchant wholesalers? Distinguish between the two types of wholesalers and explain what they do.

11-5. What is a channel leader or a channel captain?

11-6. What is channel power, and what are the sources of this power?

11-7. What is meant by channel conflict?

11-8. What is logistics? Explain the functions of logistics. What is reverse logistics?

11-9. What are the advantages and disadvantages of shipping by rail? By air? By ship? By truck?

11-10. What is inventory control, and why is it important?

11-11. What is a supply chain, and how is it different from a channel of distribution?

Activities: Apply What You've Learned

11-12. *Creative Homework/Short Project* Assume that you are the director of marketing for a firm that manufactures cleaning chemicals used in industries. You have traditionally sold these products through manufacturer's reps. You are considering adding a direct Internet channel to your distribution strategy, but you aren't sure whether this will create channel conflict. Make a list of the pros and cons of this move. What do you think is the best decision?

11-13. *Creative Homework/Short Project* In many markets in your home country, changes are under way in distribution networks. Gradually, businesses that handled products in the past are being eased out of the network as they fail to add sufficient value. In the role of advisor to one of these intermediaries, come up with a summarized list of added-value services you could offer.

11-14. *In Class, 10–25 Minutes for Teams* Independent intermediaries do business with many different manufacturers and many different customers. Because no manufacturer owns or controls them, they make it possible for many manufacturers to serve customers throughout the world while they keep prices low. In a role-playing situation, each team member should take the role of an independent intermediary. Choose a popular product or service and break up the

distribution by adopting the roles of limited-service wholesalers. How would you split the responsibilities and tasks? You will need to adopt the roles of cash-and-carry wholesalers, truck jobbers, drop shippers, mail-order wholesalers, and rack jobbers. Now consider your own country and the role of these limited-service companies; are they common or rare in most industries?

11-15. *For Further Research (Individual)* Visit the website for UPS (www.ups.com). UPS has positioned itself as a full-service provider of logistics solutions. After reviewing its website, answer the following questions:
   a. What logistics services does UPS offer its customers?
   b. What does UPS say to convince prospective customers that its services are better than those of the competition?

11-16. *In Class, 10–25 Minutes for Teams* Assume that you have recently been hired by a firm that manufactures furniture. You feel that marketing should have an input into supplier selection for the firm's products, but the purchasing department says that should not be a concern for marketing. You need to explain to the department head the importance of the value chain perspective. In a role-playing exercise, explain to the purchasing agent the value chain concept, why it is of concern to marketing, and why the two of you should work together.

11-17. *Creative Homework/Short Project* Your friend is studying for an upcoming marketing test but doesn't quite understand logistics. Write up a summary of the various logistics functions and devise a short multiple-choice quiz that will help him test his comprehension of the subject.

Apply Marketing Metrics

Companies track a wide range of metrics within the supply chain area. Some of the most common ones are the following:

- On-time delivery
- Accuracy of forecasted inventory needs
- Returns processing cost as a percentage of product revenue
- Customer order actual cycle time
- Perfect order measurement

Let's take a look at the last measure in more detail. The perfect order measurement calculates the error-free rate of each stage of a fulfilling a purchase order.[18] This measure helps managers track the multiple steps involved in getting a product from a manufacturer to a customer so that opportunities for process improvement can be pinpointed. For example, a company can calculate its error rate at each stage and then combine these rates to create an overall metric of order quality. Suppose the company identifies the following error rates:

- Order entry accuracy: 99.95 percent correct (translate as 5 errors per 1,000 order lines)
- Warehouse pick accuracy: 99.2 percent (.8 errors per 1,000 items picked by warehouse staff)
- Delivered on time: 96 percent (4 errors per 1,000 deliveries)
- Shipped without damage: 99 percent (1 damaged item per 1,000 deliveries)
- Invoiced correctly: 99.8 percent (.2 errors per 1,000 invoices)

To calculate the perfect order measurement, all the company has to do is combine these individual rates into an overall metric by multiplying them together.

11-18. Calculate the perfect order measurement for the above purchase order process. Interpret your result.

11-19. Do you think the firm should be satisfied with this level of performance? Why or why not? What particular areas need attention, if any?

11-20. Is a zero error rate realistic? How close should a firm be expected to come to zero errors? How do you suggest motivating employees toward reducing these errors?

11-21. Given this particular example, what are some things the manufacturer might work on to bring the overall perfect order measurement higher? What would be the advantages to the firm of investing in making this already good number even better for customers?

Choices: What Do You Think?

11-22. *Critical Thinking* Many entrepreneurs choose to start a franchise business rather than "go it alone." Do you think franchises offer the typical businessperson good opportunities? What are some positive and negative aspects of purchasing a franchise?

11-23. *Critical Thinking* As colleges and universities are looking for better ways to satisfy their customers, an area of increasing interest is the distribution of their product (which of course is a student's education). Describe the characteristics of your school's channel(s) of distribution. What types of innovative distribution might make sense for your school to try?

11-24. *Ethics* RFID tags are extremely useful for retailers, but many consumers have responded negatively to them, even calling them "spy chips." What are the ethical issues that retailers must be aware of when they use

these chips? What responsibility do retailers have to educate consumers about how they will use the information contained in these chips?

11-25. *Critical Thinking* Music, video, or textbook downloading (even when done clandestinely) is just a way to create a more efficient supply chain because it "cuts out the middleman" (e.g., stores that sell music, video, and books). Do you agree? Why or why not?

11-26. *Critical Thinking* The supply chain concept looks at both the inputs of a firm and the firms that facilitate the movement of the product from the manufacturer to the consumer. Do you think *marketers* should be concerned with the total supply chain concept? Why or why not?

11-27. *Ethics* To bring cost-effective products to your door, retailers like Walmart use suppliers, some of which may contract work out to other suppliers and so on. And while the initial suppliers that Walmart contracts with may be socially responsible, not all suppliers are. What should retailers do to protect themselves from working with unethical companies or selling products made by such companies? How far down the supply chain should retailers be responsible for the business practices of their vendors?

Miniproject: Learn by Doing

In the U.S., the distribution of most products is fairly easy. There are many independent intermediaries (wholesalers, dealers, distributors, and retailers) that are willing to cooperate to get the product to the final customer. Our elaborate interstate highway system combines with rail, air, and water transportation to provide excellent means for moving goods from one part of the country to another. In many other countries, the means for distribution of products are far less efficient and effective.

For this miniproject, you should first select a consumer product, probably one you normally purchase. Then use library sources, other people, or both (retailers, manufacturers, dealers, classmates, and so on) to gather information to do the following:

a. Describe the path the product takes to get from the producer to you. Draw a model to show each of the steps the product takes. Include as much as you can about transportation, warehousing, materials handling, order processing, inventory control, and so on.

b. Select another country in which the same or a similar product is sold. Describe the path the product takes to get from the producer to the customer in that country.

c. Determine if the differences between the two countries cause differences in price, availability, or quality of the product.

11-28. Prepare and present a summary of your findings.

Marketing in **Action** Case Real Choices at Elizabeth Arden

Where do you buy your beauty products? Very few people would expect to find a leader in the beauty industry's brands for sale when they visit the doctor. But indeed, Elizabeth Arden is adding to its distribution strategy by offering its new

Rx skin care line exclusively at physicians' offices. The plan is to offer the products in a credible, science-based environment to bolster the customer's confidence in their effectiveness. Elizabeth Arden asserts that this new channel supports "the company's omni-channel growth strategy of selling and marketing Elizabeth Arden branded products in the prestige retail, spa, and now the professional skincare market."

Elizabeth Arden, Inc. is an American-based global prestige beauty products company. The company has a broad collection of prestige beauty brands available in over 120 countries. This portfolio includes Elizabeth Arden skin care, color, and fragrance products; a professional skin care line; and celebrity fragrance brands. Over 100 hundred years ago, Elizabeth Arden, a pioneer and entrepreneur, opened the first Red Door salon in New York City. Thus began the American beauty industry. The fundamental belief of the company is that "beauty should not be a veneer of makeup, but an intelligent cooperation between science and nature in order to develop a woman's finest natural assets." Entrepreneurial spirit, commitment to innovation, quality, and excellence represent the core values of the company.

Elizabeth Arden is a trailblazer in the beauty market. It was the first to introduce eye makeup to American women, the first to incorporate its founder's name into a product name, the first to offer travel-size beauty products, and the first to send out a team of traveling demonstrators and saleswomen. This new physician-based distribution choice is in line with the company's past decision making.

Elizabeth Arden has an investment in US CosmeceuTechs, a skin care company that sells skin care products through professional dermatology and spa channels and the first to expand into the professional medical channel. Elizabeth Arden Rx is the company's initial entry into the global professional skin care market.

The Rx skin care line addresses four skin conditions by offering physician-strength, clinically proven chemical peel treatments and customer applied take-home products and in-office therapies. It provides simple solutions for patients with signs of premature skin aging, uneven skin tone and pigmentation, acne and problem-prone skin, and dry skin. The professional in-office treatments require multiple visits to apply different combinations/concentrations of ingredients to "peel" the outer layer of skin without harming the underlying healthy skin. The first take-home product to launch is the Triple Protection Factor Broad Spectrum SPF 50, accessible only through physicians' offices in the US. The rest of the take-home RX line is made up of various cleansers, creams, and serums.

Elizabeth Arden's new distribution strategy is an attempt to increase efficiency and effectiveness. According to E. Scott Beattie, chairman, president, and CEO, "Our core target is actively shopping in all skincare distribution channels." By broadening its distribution channel profile to include medical professionals, Elizabeth Arden is able to increase its overall market presence. How does the company use this new multiple-channel approach to deliver its value proposition to its customers?

You Make the Call

11-29. What is the decision facing Elizabeth Arden?

11-30. What factors are important in understanding this decision situation?

11-31. What are the alternatives?

11-32. What decision(s) do you recommend?

11-33. What are some ways to implement your recommendation?

Sources: Based on Elizabeth Arden, Inc., "Elizabeth Arden Unveils Next Step in Multi-Channel Distribution Strategy," http://online.wsj.com/article/PR-CO-20140306-913093.html?mod=wsj_share_email (accessed May 17, 2014), and Elizabeth Arden, Inc., "About Elizabeth Arden," www.elizabetharden.com/About-Elizabeth-Arden/about-us,default,pg.html&hasbr=cs-landing (accessed May 17, 2014).

MyMarketingLab™

Go to **mymktlab.com** for Auto-graded writing questions as well as the following Assisted-graded writing questions:

11-34. *Creative Homework/Short Project.* Your new boss thinks that intermediaries cost the company too much money, but you know he is looking only at the bottom line. He has asked you to investigate the issue. In a short memo to your boss, describe the efficiencies that intermediaries create and identify the tangible and intangible benefits that these intermediaries provide.

11-35. *Creative Homework/Short Project.* Assume that your firm recently gave you a new marketing assignment. You are to head up development of a distribution plan for a new product line—a series of do-it-yourself instruction videos for home gardeners. These videos would show consumers how to plant trees, shrubbery, and bulbs; how to care for their plants; how to prune; and so on. You know that as you develop a distribution plan, it is essential that you understand and consider a number of internal and external environmental factors. Make a list of the information you will need before you can begin to write the distribution plan. How will you adapt your plan based on each of these factors?

Deliver the Customer Experience: Bricks and Clicks

Stan Clark

▼ **A Decision Maker at Eskimo Joe's**

Stan Clark is a native of Tulsa, Oklahoma. He graduated from Oklahoma State University (OSU) in May 1975 with a bachelor of science degree in business administration. For more than a decade, Stan's entrepreneurial success story has captivated audiences all over Oklahoma and across the country. Among other honors he was a Regional Finalist for *Inc.* magazine's Entrepreneur of the Year.

Stan's Info

First job out of school?
Eskimo Joe's. I graduated from OSU in May 1975 and opened Joe's about two weeks later. To do that, I turned down an assistantship to go into the OSU MBA program.

A job-related mistake I wish I hadn't made?
Killing the annual Joe's Anniversary Party in 1993. It attracted tens of thousands of people but was getting unwieldy.

My hero?
My dad, who inspired me to be an entrepreneur, and my mom, who gave me a positive outlook on life.

Business book I'm reading now?
Hug Your Customers by Jack Mitchell and *Discovering the Soul of Service* by Len Berry.

Career high?
During his 1990 commencement address at Lewis Field at OSU, President George H. W. Bush mentioned Eskimo Joe's in his speech. In 2006, George W. Bush did the same thing.

My motto to live by?
Live passionately and make a difference.

Here's my problem...

Real People, Real Choices

Stan Clark, the colorful entrepreneur behind the toothy grin of the Eskimo Joe caricature, and his dog Buffy faced a big problem. In 1975, Stan opened Eskimo Joe's bar in Stillwater, Oklahoma—the home of Oklahoma State University (OSU). By the mid-1980s, the watering hole had become a huge favorite among OSU students. Situated right across from the OSU campus, Joe's carved out a niche as *the* place to go for beer, music, pool, and foosball in this college town. Trading on the popularity of the bar as well as its quirky logo, Stan had also begun to sell some logo apparel over the counter. Before long, students, friends, parents, alums, and other visitors simply couldn't get enough of the T-shirts sporting the wide smiles by the boy and his faithful dog. For Stan, life was good and also lots of fun.

So what could possibly go wrong? Try the fact that Oklahoma had just passed a statewide "liquor by the drink" law. Prior to this, Oklahoma had a patchwork quilt of post–Prohibition era liquor laws, including "club card" requirements at bars and bring-your-own-bottle rules. Liquor by the drink opened up normal serving of beer, wine, and spirits at any establishment with a proper state liquor license—however, part of the new law was an increase in the legal drinking age from 18 to 21. Oops—a beer bar in a college town when you have to be 21 to drink? Not exactly an attractive business proposition. But, in the eight years since Eskimo Joe's opening, Stan had come to understand that the place represented a whole lot more to people than just pitchers of cold Bud on hot summer nights. There was a certain mystique and a strong sense of community around the brand that made it more than just a place to drink. Brisk sales of T-shirts and other clothing over the counter were evidence that people saw something else in the retailer—something that made them want to wear these items again and again. The affection and interest reached almost cult-like proportions and were not limited to Stillwater or even to Oklahoma. Stan had hit on something big, but what could he do? Big Brother in the State of Oklahoma was about to regulate him right out of his core business.

Stan had to take a couple of steps back, take a new look at his business, and think about what he might do to ensure that his retail enterprise would survive the new law. The situation could be life or death for Eskimo Joe's.

Things to remember

Stan Clark successfully positioned Eskimo Joe's as the place go for beer, music and good times near the campus of Oklahoma State University. Then, in the mid-1980s the State of Oklahoma raised the legal drinking age from 18 to 21—and Stan had a big problem.

In the ten or so years it took to build the brand, Eskimo Joe's also developed a certain mystique—its toothy spokescharacters appeared on T-shirts all over the world. Clearly people had developed a loyalty and affection for the brand that went well beyond just a place that sold pizza and beer.

As Stan decided how address the new change in his environment he had to think hard about just what he was selling in addition to brews and slices—and repackage those qualities for a new generation.

transformation, Stan would have to extensively remodel the facility. He would have to figure out who the new target market is and what type of menu fare would be most appealing to that customer. This was a risky proposition since restaurants open and close all the time. On the other hand, if Stan could morph the location into a restaurant that also happens to serve alcohol (which, under the new liquor law, would be legal—and potentially quite profitable), he would hopefully be able to continue to build the fledgling logo apparel business around the new restaurant theme, à la the Hard Rock Café.

2 Option
Continue operating as a beer bar at the core and work to offset declining beer sales with an increase in apparel sales. From 1975 to 1984, Joe's was "Stillwater's Jumpin' Little Juke Joint." It was by far one of the highest-volume beer bars in the region, and it had built its entire reputation on this image. As the number-one competitor in this market space, Stan had every reason to believe that the weaker competitors would be forced out of business by the law change, leaving their share of the market to him. Stan could continue to operate the bar in much the way it had always been operated, and if he liked, he could use it as a cash cow to generate revenues and then invest the money elsewhere for growth. The upside of this plan would be that any attempt to rebrand Eskimo Joe's as something other than what it had always been would be risky. However, the downside was the unknown of what it would mean to a retailer over the long run to lose its primary customer base of 18- to 20-year-olds in a town brimming with college students.

3 Option
Close Eskimo Joe's bar and refocus resources on building the growing apparel business. The cult-like status of the Eskimo Joe's brand and image may have begun at the physical location of the bar in Stillwater, but the way to replicate and perpetuate it on a national or international scale is by marketing the now-hip logo. Stan could build a small retail clothing boutique in Stillwater but turn primarily to direct marketing through catalogs focused on his target primary age and demographic groups. A key benefit of this approach is avoiding any unexpected problems with the bar that might occur in the liquor law transition, especially the very negative publicity that would result if Joe's got caught selling beer to underage drinkers. The Eskimo Joe spirit would be maintained through the direct marketing and also through accompanying word of mouth. On the downside, to Joe's loyal fans, closing Stillwater's "Jumpin' Little Juke Joint" would be like Harley-Davidson ceasing to make motorcycles: Who wants the logo apparel when there's no product or place that still sports it? However, this option was tempting in that it would redirect Stan's resources to the high-growth (and high-profit-margin) apparel retailing sector.

Now put yourself in Stan's shoes. Which option would you choose, and why?

Stan considered his Options 1·2·3

1 Option
Convert the beer bar into a full-service restaurant that focuses on selling great food. This option assumes that the equity of the Eskimo Joe's brand would transfer into a brand-new market and product space. To accomplish this

You Choose

Which **Option** would you choose, and **why**?
1. ☐YES ☐NO 2. ☐YES ☐NO 3. ☐YES ☐NO

See what **option** Stan chose on **page 413** ➡

retailing
The final stop in the distribution channel in which organizations sell goods and services to consumers for their personal use.

1

OBJECTIVE
Define retailing; understand how retailing evolves and consider some ethical issues in retailing.
(pp. 386–392)

Retailing, Twenty-First-Century Style

Shop 'til you drop! For many people, obtaining the product is only half the fun. Others, of course, would rather walk over hot coals than spend time in a store. Marketers like Stan Clark need to find ways to deliver goods and services that please both types of consumers. **Retailing** is the final stop on the distribution path—the process by which organizations sell goods and services to consumers for their personal use.

As we said in Chapter 11, planning for distribution of product offerings includes decisions about where to make the product available. Thus, when marketers of consumer goods and services plan their distribution strategy, they talk about the retailers they will include in their channel of distribution. This, of course, means they need to understand retailing and the retailer landscape.

Of course, retailers also develop their own marketing plans. While the sample marketing plan we provided for your use relates to a producer, we find essentially the same elements in retailers' marketing plans. Like producers, they must decide which consumer groups they can best serve, what product assortment and services they will provide for their customers, what pricing policies they will adopt, how they will promote their retail operations, and where they will locate their stores. This chapter will explore the many different types of retailers as we keep one question in mind: How does a retailer—whether store or nonstore (i.e., selling via TV, phone, vending machine, or the Internet)—successfully make its goods or services available to the consumer?

So, this chapter has plenty "in store" for us. Let's start with an overview of where retailing has been and where it's going.

Retailing: A Mixed (Shopping) Bag

Retailing is big business. In 2013, U.S. retail sales totaled $4.53 trillion. E-commerce accounted for 16.9 percent, or over $263 billion, and m-commerce accounted for $42.13 billion.[1] Over 1 million retail businesses employ over 15.3 million workers—more than 1 of every 10 U.S. workers.[2] Although we tend to associate huge stores such as Walmart and Sears with retailing activity, in reality most retailers are small businesses like Eskimo Joe's. Certain retailers, such as Home Depot, also are wholesalers because they provide goods and services to businesses as well as to end consumers.

As we said in Chapter 11, retailers belong to a channel of distribution, and as such they provide time, place, and ownership utility to customers. Some retailers save people time or money when they provide an assortment of merchandise under one roof. Others search the world for the most exotic delicacies; they allow shoppers access to goods they would otherwise never see. Still others, such as Starbucks, Apple or REI, provide us with interesting environments in which to spend our leisure time and, they hope, our money.

Globally, retailing may have a very different face. In some European countries, don't even think about squeezing a tomato to see if it's too soft or picking up a cantaloupe to see if it smells ripe. Such mistakes will quickly gain you a reprimand from the store clerk, who will choose your oranges and bananas for you. In developing countries like those in Asia, Africa, and South America, retailing often includes many small butcher shops where sides of beef and lamb proudly hang in store windows so everyone will be assured that the meat comes from healthy animals; vendors sell lettuce, tomatoes, and cucumbers on the sidewalk or neatly stack watermelons on a donkey cart; and women sell small breakfast items they cook out of the front of their homes for workers and schoolchildren who pass by in the mornings. Neat store shelves stacked with bottles of shampoo may be replaced by hanging displays that hold one-use size sachets of shampoo—as we noted in Chapter 10, the only size that a woman can afford to buy and then only for special occasions. Street vendors may sell cigarettes one at a time. The local pharmacist also gives customers injections and recommends antibiotics and other medicines for patients who come in with a complaint and who can't afford to see a doctor. Don't feel like cooking tonight? There's no drive-through window for pickup but even better—delivery from McDonald's, Hardees, KFC, Pizza Hut, Fuddruckers, Chili's, and a host of local restaurants via motor scooters that dangerously dash in and out of traffic is just a few minutes away. You can even order your Big Mac or a spicy vegetable dragon roll for delivery online through sites such as Egypt's Otlob.com or Mumbai's Foodkamood.com.

The Evolution of Retailing

Retailing has taken many forms over time, including the peddler who hawked his wares from a horse-drawn cart, a majestic urban department store, an intimate boutique, and a huge "hyperstore" that sells everything from potato chips to snow tires. But now the cart you see at your local mall that sells new-age jewelry or monogrammed golf balls to pass-ersby has replaced the horse-drawn cart. As the economic, social, and cultural pictures change, different types of retailers emerge—and they often squeeze out older, outmoded types. How can marketers know what the dominant types of retailing will be tomorrow or 10 years from now?

One of the oldest and simplest explanations for these changes is the **wheel-of-retailing hypothesis**. Figure 12.1 shows that new types of retailers begin at the entry phase, where they find it easiest to enter the market with low-end strategies as they offer goods at lower prices than their competitors.[3] After they gain a foothold, they gradually trade up. They improve their facilities and increase the quality and assortment of merchandise. Finally, retailers move on to a high-end strategy with even higher prices, better facilities, and amenities such as parking and gift wrapping. *Upscaling* results in greater investment and operating costs, so the store must raise its prices to remain profitable. This makes it vulnerable to still newer entrants that can afford to charge lower prices. And so the wheel turns.

That's the story behind Pier 1 Imports. Pier 1 started as a single store in San Mateo, California, that sold low-priced beanbags, love beads, and incense to post–World War II baby boomers. Today, it sells quality home furnishings and decorative accessories to the same customers, who are now among the more affluent of the American population.[4]

wheel-of-retailing hypothesis
A theory that explains how retail firms change, becoming more upscale as they go through their life cycle.

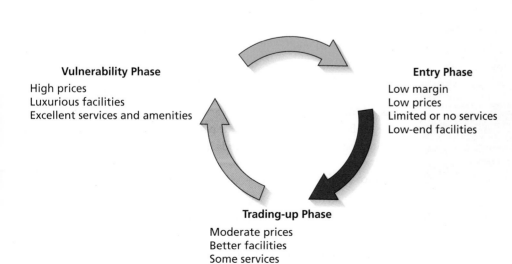

Figure 12.1 *Snapshot* |
The Wheel of Retailing

The Wheel of Retailing explains how retailers change over time.

Vulnerability Phase
High prices
Luxurious facilities
Excellent services and amenities

Entry Phase
Low margin
Low prices
Limited or no services
Low-end facilities

Trading-up Phase
Moderate prices
Better facilities
Some services
Increased quality merchandise

Retailers, however, must be careful not to move too quickly and too far from their roots. Longtime favorite J.C. Penney, under the direction of a new CEO, added new designer brands, chucked its coupons and sales in favor of everyday "fair and square" pricing, and redesigned its stores and its logo.[5] After making the changes, designed to bring more customers into its stores, J.C. Penney instead lost about 1.3 million of its female customers and 10 percent of its share price.[6] Today, that new CEO is out and coupons are back as J.C. Penney struggles to find its way in the marketplace.

The wheel of retailing helps us explain the development of some but not all forms of retailing. For example, some retailers never trade up; they simply continue to occupy a niche as discounters. Others, such as upscale specialty stores, start out at the high end. Of course, some retailers move down after they experience success at the high end. Sometimes they open sister divisions that sell lower-priced products (as when Gap Stores opened Old Navy), or they develop outlets that sell lower-priced versions of their own products (as when Nordstrom creates the Nordstrom Rack or Anne Taylor opens Anne Taylor Loft).

The Evolution Continues: What's "In Store" for the Future?

As our world continues to change rapidly, retailers scramble to keep up. Four factors motivate innovative merchants to reinvent the way they do business: the economic environment, changing demographics, technology, and globalization.

The Changing Economy

As we noted in Chapter 2, all marketers including retailers must understand and respond to changes in the marketing environment. Recently, changes in the economic environment have been especially important. The economic downturn that began in 2008 meant that consumers worldwide were less willing to spend discretionary income. Instead, they chose to lower their level of debt and to save. Retail sales, including the all-important Christmas sales, fell in nearly all retail segments.[7] Sales for most upscale retailers were especially vulnerable, while stores such as TJ Maxx, Marshalls, Dollar General, and online retailer Amazon.com that offer consumers low prices or discounted merchandise thrived. A number of retailers filed for bankruptcy, including Sharper Image, Circuit City, CompUSA, and Waldenbooks.[8]

Other stores changed their merchandise assortment to meet consumers' preferences. Sales of private-label brands continue to grow and in 2013 reached an all-time high in sales of $108 billion, which included 19 percent of supermarket sales.[9] Walmart and other mass merchandisers responded to this trend by allocating more shelf space to their own private-label brands and less to national brands. (Walmart later found that this strategy aggravated many consumers and hurt overall sales, and the chain quickly returned many items to its shelves.[10]) Even private-label wines are becoming more popular. Trader Joe's exclusively carries Charles Shaw, Whole Foods uniquely offers Three Wishes, and Total Wine & More sells its very own Pacific Peak—and all sell for the low price of about $3 a bottle. Can your palate detect the difference between private labels and the pricier brands if you remove the labels first?[11]

Demographics

As we noted in Chapter 7, keeping up with changes in population characteristics is at the heart of many marketing efforts. Retailers can no longer afford to stand by and assume that their customer base is the same as it has always been. They must come up with new ways to sell their products to diverse groups.

Like other marketers, retailers need to stay on top of cultural trends that affect demand for the merchandise they sell, such as fur-free, vegan, or sustainable products.

Here are some of the ways changing demographics are altering the face of retailing:

- *Convenience for working consumers:* Some retailers expand their operating hours and services to meet the needs of working consumers who have less time to shop. Other retailers, including dry cleaners and pharmacies, add drive-up windows. In some areas, mobile furniture stores replace design studios; designers pick out 8 or 10 sofas from their large inventories and bring them to your home so you can see how each will actually look in your living room. Others may use new phone apps like "ShowInRoom" that reproduces your room on your phone and lets you "virtually" rearrange furniture without breaking a sweat. And walk-in medical clinics located at retailer, pharmacy, or grocery stores not only provide convenience but also save both patients and insurers money on routine care.[12]

- *Recognition of ethnic diversity:* Although members of every ethnic group can usually find local retailers that cater to their specific needs, larger companies must tailor their strategies to the cultural makeup of specific areas. For example, in Texas, California, and Florida, where there are large numbers of customers who speak only Spanish, many retailers make sure that there are sales associates who "habla Español."

Technology

In addition to demographics, technology is revolutionizing retailing. As we all know, the Internet has brought us the age of e-tailing. Whether it's a store that sells only on the Web, such as Amazon.com, or a traditional retailer, such as Banana Republic or J. Crew that also sells on the Web, retailing is steadily evolving from bricks to clicks. When you go into J.C. Penney, for example, you may have to look harder to find a traditional checkout counter. All store associates now carry an iPod Touch, and they can quickly ring up a sale from anywhere in the store.[13] No more standing in long checkout lines!

Some of the most profound changes are not even visible to shoppers, such as advanced electronic **point-of-sale (POS) systems**. These devices contain computer brains that collect sales data and connect directly into the store's inventory-control system. Stores may use POS systems to create **perpetual inventory unit control systems** that keep a running total on sales, returns, transfers to other stores, and so on. This technology allows stores to develop computerized **automatic reordering systems** that are activated when inventories reach a certain level.[14] The store of the future will use RFID tags (and other technology) to assist the shopper in ways we haven't even thought of. For example, an RFID tag on a bottle of wine can tip off a nearby plasma screen that will project an ad for Barilla pasta and provide a neat recipe for fettuccine with bell peppers and shrimp. Some restaurants already use technology to let diners order their food tableside directly from a screen complete with photos of the dishes it offers. The *e-menus* help customers because they can see what every item on the menu will look like and, it is hoped, avoid a surprise when the waiter arrives.[15] This innovation also increases sales for the restaurant—who can avoid that mouth-watering picture of the eight-layer chocolate cake with peppermint-stick ice cream on top?

Of course, technology is important to service industries also. Banking, for example, has become much simpler for both consumers and business customers because of electronic banking. For many years, electronic banking offered ATMs and websites where consumers can check their bank balance or transfer funds. Today, most banks offer automatic bill-pay services that allow consumers to schedule to pay their bills online, and the bank will write the check and mail it. Also, many banks now let you make deposits using your smart phone.

Globalization

As we saw in Chapter 2, the world is becoming a much smaller (and flatter) place. Retailers are busy expanding to other countries, and they bring with them innovations and new management philosophies. McDonald's, T.G.I. Friday's, Starbucks, and the Hard Rock Café are global success stories for U.S. retailers. Similarly, Spanish fashion retailers Zara and Mango

point-of-sale (POS) systems
Retail computer systems that collect sales data and are hooked directly into the store's inventory-control system.

perpetual inventory unit control system
Retail computer system that keeps a running total on sales, returns, transfers to other stores, and so on.

automatic reordering system
Retail reordering system that is automatically activated when inventories reach a certain level.

Andre Jenny/Newscom

Planet Hollywood is a retail chain with outposts in London and Paris.

experiential shoppers
Shoppers who shop because it satisfies their experiential needs, that is, their desire for fun.

are now global brands, while Swedish home goods company IKEA furnishes rooms around the world. Even French hyperstore chain Carrefour has stores in Europe, South America, Asia, North Africa, and the U.S.

Still, retailers need to adjust to different conditions around the world. In countries in the Middle East with large Muslim populations, you won't find the riblet basket on the Applebee's menu, and McDonald's offers customers McArabia Kofta sandwiches. And some countries require that certain percentages, often over half, of goods sold in retail stores are locally produced.

Retailtainment to Satisfy Experiential Shoppers

For many customers, shopping is not just about making a purchase. Instead, they shop because it satisfies their experiential needs, that is, their desire for fun. These **experiential shoppers** regard shopping as entertainment. When the retail experience includes surprise, excitement, and a unique experience, experiential shoppers are more likely to make impulsive purchase decisions.[16]

With the tremendous growth on online retailing, bricks-and-mortar retailers have to do more than just sell stuff.[17] **Retailtainment** is all about marketing strategies that enhance the shopping experience. Retailers from Disney to Bass Pro Shops create excitement, impulse purchase, and an emotional connection with the brand through retailtainment. For example, Thirsty Bear, a London pub, installed iPads at tables so customers could set up electronic bar tabs (and check their Facebook pages). Lark Lagerfeld, a London clothing retailer, installed iPads in dressing rooms that allow customers to send "selfies" to friends to get their opinions of the purchase. The new H&M in New York City uses smart dressing rooms with iPads so customers can buy items while still in the dressing room and then leave, wearing their purchase. They also offer customers a DJ booth and a catwalk performance that is projected on external LED screens for passersby to see.[18] Cabela's devotes up to 45 percent of their store space to retailtainment features including taxidermy displays and a shooting gallery.[19] And Toys "R" Us Times Square is a top tourist attraction with a 60-foot Ferris wheel, a 20-foot animatronic T-Rex dinosaur, and a life-size Barbie dollhouse.[20]

Ethical Problems in Retailing

Retailers must deal with ethical problems that involve both their customers and their employees. Losses due to **shrinkage** are a growing problem. *Shrinkage* is the term retailers use to describe stock losses due to shoplifting, employee theft, and damage to merchandise. The *Euromonitor 2012–2013 Global Retail Theft Barometer* found that shrinkage costs retailers $112 billion, or 1.4 percent, of all retail sales.[21] That works out to a loss of $300 per family that shops at these stores: Guess who winds up paying for these mysterious disappearances?

Shoplifting

Shoplifting has grown in recent years to giant proportions. In the U.S., shoplifting accounts for 34 percent of all shrinkage. The National Association of Shoplifting Prevention reports that $13 billion in goods are stolen from retailers annually—that's $35 million a day.[22] These thefts in turn drive consumer prices up and hurt the economy and sometimes even cause smaller retailers to go out of business. At its worst, shoplifting can be an organized criminal activity. About 3 percent of shoplifting in the U.S. is done by professional criminals.[23] These range from drug addicts who steal to buy drugs to organized gangs of thieves that use store floor plans and foil-lined bags to evade security sensors to get away with thousands of dollars in goods in a single day.

In South Florida, several individuals were paid up to $1,000 a day to steal expensive diabetes strips, painkillers, and heartburn medication from area Walgreens, CVS, and

retailtainment
The use of retail strategies that enhance the shopping experience and create excitement, impulse purchases, and an emotional connection with the brand.

shrinkage
Losses experienced by retailers due to shoplifting, employee theft, and damage to merchandise.

Publix stores. The more than $15 million worth of stolen products were then sold online or to wholesale distributors at cut-rate prices. In all, more than 20 people were busted as part of this massive theft ring.[24]

Of course, some shoplifting is more amateurish, and some shoplifters are just not that clever. One woman in California was caught stashing expensive items in her purse each time employees turned their backs. But after three trips into the store to steal, her luck ran out when she wrote down her real name and address while signing up for a raffle contest the store was hosting.[25] It's a safe bet to say she wasn't the sharpest tool in the shed.

Employee Theft

A second major source of shrinkage in retail stores is employee theft of both merchandise and cash. In the U.S., it accounts for 32 percent of all shrinkage, nearly as much as shoplifting.[26] On a case-by-case basis, dishonest employees steal 6.6 times the amount shoplifters do.[27] A current trend in employee theft involves the use of store gift cards. Saks, for example, caught a sales clerk ringing up $130,000 in false merchandise returns and putting the money on a gift card.[28] Employees not only have access to products but also are familiar with the store's security measures. "Sweethearting" is an employee practice in which a cashier consciously undercharges, gives a cash refund, or allows a friend to walk away without paying for items.[29] Sometimes a dishonest employee simply carries merchandise out the backdoor to a friend's waiting car.

Retail Borrowing

A third source of shrinkage is an unethical consumer practice the industry calls **retail borrowing**. Merchants over recent decades have developed liberal policies of accepting returns from customers because the product performs unsatisfactorily or even if the customer simply changes her mind. Retail borrowing refers to the return of nondefective merchandise for a refund after it has fulfilled the purpose for which it was purchased.[30] Popular objects for retail borrowing include a dress for a high school prom, a new suit for a job interview, and or a large-screen TV for a big football game. One study suggests that 12 percent of merchandise returns involve intent to deceive the retailer. For the consumer, the practice provides short-term use of a product for a specific occasion at no cost. For the retailer, the practice results in lower total sales and often in damaged merchandise, unsuitable for resale.

Ethical Treatment of Customers

On the other side of the retail ethics issue is how retailers and their employees treat customers. While it may be illegal if a store doesn't provide equal access to consumers of different ethnic groups, behavior that discourages customers who appear economically disadvantaged or socially unacceptable is not. One study, for example, showed that restaurant servers based their level of service on the customer's perceived ability to pay and leave a good tip.[31] In other **customer profiling** situations, where the level of customer service is tailored based on a customer's perceived ability to pay, some customers were followed around the store by associates and made so uncomfortable that they left before making a purchase, or the customer was ignored altogether to the point he or she left the store disgusted and angry.[32] As a classic scene in the movie *Pretty Woman* starring Julia Roberts depicted, stores that seek to maintain an image of elite

Bricks-and-mortar bookstores, like this chain in Lithuania, struggle to provide unique experiences to buyers who are otherwise tempted to shop online.

retail borrowing
The consumer practice of purchasing a product with the intent to return the nondefective merchandise for a refund after it has fulfilled the purpose for which it was purchased.

customer profiling
The act of tailoring the level of customer service based on a customer's perceived ability to pay.

The online shopping site Motilo tries to make clothes shopping more fun as it offers user-generated suggestions, prizes, and other engaging activities.

Ripped from the Headlines

Ethical/Sustainable Decisions in the Real World

From the moment you walk into an Abercrombie & Fitch store, you're likely to notice a certain "look." The store's layout, the designer clothes, and even the attractive sales associates all have that look. That look is intentional—it's meant to reinforce the retailer's all-American brand. But in 2003, a group of would-be and former employees filed a lawsuit against the company, alleging that the popular retailer discriminated against African American, Asian American, and Latino applicants and employees because they didn't fit the Abercrombie & Fitch "look." The lawsuit also claimed that when minorities were hired, it was for positions back in the stockroom and out of the public eye.[33]

"All-American doesn't mean all-white," says Jennifer Lu, a salesperson who contends she was fired because she didn't have the right look. "A corporate official had pointed to an Abercrombie poster and told our management at our store, 'You need to have more staff that looks like this.' And it was a white Caucasian male on that poster." Not long after that directive, she says, several Asian-American salespeople were fired and several white males were hired.[34]

While it's not illegal to make hiring decisions based on a person's attractiveness, it is illegal not to hire based on race. In a 2004 settlement, Abercrombie & Fitch paid out $40 million to those they had discriminated against, and the retailer was required to institute a number of polices designed to promote diversity and ethical hiring practices.[35] More recently, in 2013, the retailer settled a lawsuit with two women who claimed they were discriminated against for wearing religious head scarves.[36]

Do you think Abercrombie & Fitch's hiring practices are ethical? How does this situation differ from the hiring practices of Hooters and Twin Peaks, which also hire employees based on a certain "look"? Is "employee profiling" any different from "customer profiling"?

ETHICS CHECK: ➤

Find out what other students taking this course *would do* and *why* at **mymktlab.com**.

> Should retailers be free to hire a sales force that is representative of their brand even if this policy means that some applicants won't be hired due to their appearance?
>
> ☐YES ☐NO

sophistication may not offer assistance to customers who enter the premises not meeting the requirements for that image—or they may actually ask the customer to leave.

Similarly, many would suggest that retailers have an obligation not to sell products to customers if the products can be harmful. For example, for many years some teens and young adults abused potentially harmful over-the-counter medicines. While government regulations removed many of these drug products from store shelves in recent years, retailers still have to carefully police their distribution. The same is true for products such as alcohol and cigarettes, which by law are limited to sale to adult customers.

2 Types of Bricks-and-Mortar Retailers

OBJECTIVE

Understand how we classify traditional retailers.
(pp. 392–398)

The field of retailing covers a lot of ground—from mammoth department stores to sidewalk vendors to websites to bars like Eskimo Joe's. Retail marketers need to understand the possible ways they might offer their products in the market, and they also need a way to benchmark their performance relative to other, similar retailers.

Classify Retailers by What They Sell

One of the most important strategic decisions a retailer such as Eskimo Joe's makes is *what* to sell—its **merchandise mix**. This choice is similar to settling on a market segment (as we discussed in Chapter 7, if a store's merchandise mix is too limited, it may not have enough potential customers, whereas if it is too broad, the retailer runs the risk of being a "jack of all trades, master of none"). Because what the retailer sells is central to its identity, one way we describe retailers is in terms of their merchandise mix.

merchandise mix
The total set of all products offered for sale by a retailer, including all product lines sold to all consumer groups.

While we learned in Chapter 9 that a manufacturer's product line consists of product offerings that satisfy a single need, in retailing a *product line* is a set of related products a retailer offers, such as kitchen appliances or leather goods. The *Census of Retail Trade* that the U.S. Bureau of the Census conducts classifies all retailers by North American Industry Classification System (NAICS) codes (the same system we described in Chapter 6 that classifies industrial firms). A retailer that wants to identify direct competition simply looks for other firms with the same NAICS classification codes.

However, a word of caution: As retailers experiment with different merchandise mixes, it's getting harder to make these direct comparisons. For example, even though marketers like to distinguish between food and nonfood retailers, in reality these lines are blurring. **Combination stores** offer consumers food and general merchandise in the same store. **Supercenters**, such as Walmart Supercenters and SuperTargets, are larger stores that combine an economy supermarket with other lower-priced merchandise. Other retailers like CVS, RiteAid, and Walgreens drugstores, carry limited amounts of food.

We can also classify retailers by their **merchandise assortment**, or selection of products they sell. Merchandise assortment has two dimensions: breadth and depth. **Merchandise breadth**, or variety, is the number of different product lines available. A *narrow assortment*, such as we encounter in convenience stores, means that shoppers will find only a limited selection of product lines, such as candy, cigarettes, and soft drinks. A *broad assortment*, such as a warehouse store like Costco or Sam's Club offers, means there is a wide range of items from eyeglasses to barbecue grills.

Merchandise depth is the variety of choices available within each specific product line. A *shallow assortment* means that the selection within a product category is limited, so a factory outlet store may sell only white and blue men's dress shirts (all made by the same manufacturer, of course) and only in standard sizes. In contrast, a men's specialty store may feature a *deep assortment* of dress shirts (but not much else) in varying shades and in hard-to-find sizes. 📷 Figure 12.2 illustrates these assortment differences for one product: science fiction books.

Classify Retailers by Level of Service

Retailers differ in the amount of service they provide for consumers. Firms recognize that there is a trade-off between service and low prices, so they tailor their strategies to the level of service they offer. Customers who demand higher levels of service must be willing to pay for that service, and those who want lower prices must be willing to give up services.

Retailers like Sam's Club that promise cut-rate prices often are self-service operations. When customers shop at *self-service retailers*, they make their product selection without any assistance, they often must bring their own bags or containers to carry their purchases, and they may even handle the checkout process with self-service scanners. Contrast that experience to visiting a *full-service retailer*. Department stores like Bloomingdale's and specialty stores like Victoria's Secret provide supporting services such as gift wrapping, and

combination stores
Retailers that offer consumers food and general merchandise in the same store.

supercenters
Large combination stores that combine economy supermarkets with other lower-priced merchandise.

merchandise assortment
The range of products a store sells.

merchandise breadth
The number of different product lines available.

merchandise depth
The variety of choices available for each specific product line.

Figure 12.2 📷 *Snapshot* | Classification of Book Retailers by Merchandise Selection

Marketers often classify retail stores on the breadth and depth of their merchandise assortment. In this figure, we use the two dimensions to classify types of bookstores that carry science fiction books.

	Breadth	
	Narrow	Broad
Shallow	Airport Bookstore: A few *Lord of the Rings* books	Sam's Club: A few *Lord of the Rings* books and a limited assortment of *Lord of the Rings* T-shirts and toys
Deep	www.legendaryheroes.com: Internet retailer selling only merchandise for *Lord of the Rings*, *The Highlander*, *Zena: Warrior Princess*, *Legendary Swords*, *Conan*, and *Hercules*	www.Amazon.com: Literally millions of current and out-of-print books plus a long list of other product lines including electronics, toys, apparel, musical instruments, jewelry, motorcycles and ATVs

Depth (row label spanning Shallow and Deep)

they offer trained sales associates who can help us select that perfect gift. Other specialized services are available based on the merchandise the store offers. For example, many full-service clothing retailers will provide alteration services. Retailers like Macy's, Bed Bath & Beyond, and Best Buy that carry china, silver, housewares, appliances, electronics, or other items that brides (and grooms) might want also offer special bridal consultants and bridal gift registries.

Limited-service retailers fall in between self-service and full-service retailers. Stores like Walmart, Target, Old Navy, and Kohl's offer credit and merchandise return but little else. Customers select merchandise without much assistance, preferring to pay a bit less rather than have more assistance from sales associates.

Major Types of Retailers

Now that we've seen how retailers differ in the breadth and depth of their assortments, let's review some of the major forms these retailers take. Table 12.1 provides a list of these types and their characteristics.

Convenience Stores

convenience stores
Neighborhood retailers that carry a limited number of frequently purchased items and cater to consumers willing to pay a premium for the ease of buying close to home.

Convenience stores carry a limited number of frequently purchased items, including basic food products, newspapers, and sundries. They cater to consumers willing to pay a premium for the ease of buying staple items close to home. In other words, convenience stores meet the needs of those who are pressed for time, who buy items in smaller quantities, or who shop at irregular hours. But these stores are starting to change, especially in urban areas, where many time-pressed shoppers prefer to visit these outlets even for specialty items. Store chains such as 7-Eleven and Wawa now offer customers a coffee bar, fresh sandwiches, and pastries. A great example of *The Wheel of Retailing* at work!

Think convenience stores are just for convenience and a late-night gallon of milk? Maverik Country Stores, Inc. doesn't think so. The 250-store chain transformed itself from an Old West country store to match its slogan, "Adventure's First Stop." Customers from soccer moms to mountain bikers think it's a fun place. The Adventure First Stop stores feature cascading waterfalls of fountain drinks, a winding river of coffee, and snowy mountains made of frozen yogurt. Unique names are also a part of the fun. Destination areas of the stores include Bodacious Bean coffee stations, Fountain Falls beverage dispensers, Big Moon restrooms (no comment), Big Bear Bakery, and Room with a Brew walk-in beer coolers. The stores even wrap their fuel pumps and tanker delivery trucks in murals of sports images, such as jet skis and snowmobiles.[37]

Supermarkets

supermarkets
Food stores that carry a wide selection of edibles and related products.

Supermarkets are food stores that carry a wide selection of edible and nonedible products. Although the large supermarket is a fixture in the U.S., it has not caught on to the same extent in other parts of the world. In many European countries, for example, consumers walk or bike to small stores near their homes. They tend to have smaller food orders per trip and to shop more frequently, partly because many lack the freezer space to store a huge inventory of products at home. Wide variety is less important than quality and local ambiance to Europeans, but their shopping habits are starting to change as huge hypermarkets become popular around the globe.

Box Stores

box stores
Food stores that have a limited selection of items, few brands per item, and few refrigerated items.

Box stores are food stores that have a limited selection of items, few brands per item, and few refrigerated items. Generally, they are open fewer hours than supermarkets, are smaller, and carry fewer items than warehouse clubs. Items are displayed in open boxes (hence the

Table 12.1 | Different Retailers Offer Varying Product Assortments, Levels of Service, Store Sizes, and Prices

Type	Merchandise	Level of Service	Size	Prices	Examples
Convenience stores	Limited number of choices in narrow number of product lines; frequently purchased and emergency items	Self-service	Small	Low-priced items sold at higher than average prices	7-Eleven
Supermarkets	Large selection of food items and limited selection of general merchandise	Limited service	Medium	Moderate	Publix, Kroger
Box stores	Limited selection of food items; many store brands	Self-service Bag your own purchases	Medium	Low	ALDI
Specialty stores	Large selection of items in one or a few product lines	Full service	Small and medium	Moderate to high	Claire's (accessories), Yankee Candle Co., Things Remembered
Category killers	Large selection of items in one or a few product lines	Full service	Large	Moderate	Toys "R" Us, Home Depot, Best Buy
Leased departments	Limited selection of items in a single product line	Usually full service	Small	Moderate to high	Picture Me portrait studios in Walmart stores
Variety stores	Small selection of items in limited product lines; low-priced items; may have a single price point	Self-service	Small	Low	Dollar General, Dollar Tree
General merchandise discount stores	Large selection of items in a broad assortment of product lines	Limited service	Large	Moderate to low	Walmart, Kmart
Off-price retailers	Moderate selection of limited product lines; buy surplus merchandise	Limited service	Moderate	Moderate to low	T.J. Maxx, Marshall's
Warehouse clubs	Moderate selection of limited product lines; many items in larger than normal sizes	Self-service	Large	Moderate to low	Costco, Sam's Club, BJ's
Factory outlet stores	Limited selection from a single manufacturer	Limited service	Small	Moderate to low	Gap Outlet, Liz Claiborne Outlet, Coach Outlet
Department stores	Large selection or many product lines	Full service	Large	Moderate to high	Macy's, Bloomingdale's, Nordstrom
Hypermarkets	Large selection of items in food and a broad assortment of general merchandise product lines	Self-service	Very large	Moderate to low	Carrefour
Pop-up stores	Often a single line or brand; frequently used for seasonal products	Self-service	Very small	Low to moderate	Halloween costume pop-ups

Retailing is alive and well at Taiwan's airport.

specialty stores
Retailers that carry only a few product lines but offer good selection within the lines that they sell.

category killer
A very large specialty store that carries a vast selection of products in its category.

leased departments
Departments within a larger retail store that an outside firm rents.

variety stores
Stores that carry a variety of inexpensive items.

general merchandise discount stores
Retailers that offer a broad assortment of items at low prices with minimal service.

name), and customers bag their own purchases. ALDI stores, for example, carry only about 1,400 regularly stocked items, while a typical supermarket may carry up to 50,000 items.[38] (About 95 percent of ALDI items are store brands with a few national brands that are special-buy purchases and are available for limited periods.)

Specialty Stores

Specialty stores have narrow and deep inventories. They do not sell a lot of product lines, but they offer a good selection of brands within the lines they do sell. For many women with less-than-perfect figures, shopping at a store that sells only swimsuits means there will be an adequate selection so they can find a suit that really fits. The same is true for larger, taller men who can't find suits that fit in regular department stores but have lots of choices in stores that cater to big-and-tall guys. Specialty stores can tailor their assortment to the specific needs of a targeted consumer, and they often offer a high level of knowledgeable service.

Category Killers

The **category killer** is one type of specialty store that has become especially important in retailing today. A category killer is a very large specialty store that carries a vast selection of products in its category. Some examples of category killers are Home Depot, Toys "R" Us, Best Buy, and Staples.

Leased Departments

Leased departments are departments within a larger retail store that an outside firm rents. This arrangement allows larger stores to offer a broader variety of products than they would otherwise carry. Some examples of leased departments are in-store banks, photographic studios, pet departments, jewelry departments, and watch and shoe repair departments.

Variety Stores

Variety stores originated as the five-and-dime or dime stores that began in the late 1800s. In these early variety stores, such the iconic Woolworth's, all items are sold for a nickel or a dime. Today's variety stores carry a variety of inexpensive items from kitchen gadgets to toys to candy and candles. It's tough to buy something for a dime today, but many variety stores still stick to a single price point, and some offer products that don't cost more than a dollar. Some examples of today's variety stores include Dollar General Stores, Family Dollar stores, and Dollar Tree.

Discount Stores

General merchandise discount stores, such as Target, Kmart, and Walmart, offer a broad assortment of items at low prices and with minimal service and are the dominant outlet for many products. Discounters are tearing up the retail landscape because they appeal to price-conscious shoppers who want easy access to a lot of merchandise. These stores increasingly carry

DZ/Dean Pictures/Newscom

The *category killer* is one type of specialty store that has become especially important in retailing today. A category killer is a very large specialty store that carries a vast selection of products in its category. Some examples of category killers are Home Depot, Toys "R" Us, Best Buy, and Staples.

designer-name clothing at bargain prices as companies like Liz Claiborne create new lines just for discount stores.[39]

Some discount stores, such as T.J. Maxx, Marshalls, HomeGoods, and A.J. Wright, are **off-price retailers**. These stores obtain surplus merchandise from manufacturers and offer brand-name, fashion-oriented goods at low prices.

Warehouse clubs, such as Costco and BJ's, are a newer version of the discount store. These establishments do not offer any of the amenities of a full-service store. Customers buy many of the products in larger-than-normal packages and quantities—nothing like laying in a three-year supply of paper towels or five-pound boxes of pretzels, even if you have to build an extra room in your house to store all this stuff! These clubs often charge a membership fee to consumers and small businesses. A recent survey showed that the typical warehouse shopper shops about once a month, is intrigued by bulk buying, hates long lines, and is drawn to the club retailer because of specific product areas such as fresh groceries.[40] And, consistent with the wheel of retailing, even these stores "trade up" in terms of what they sell today; shoppers can purchase fine jewelry and other luxury items at many warehouse clubs.

The **factory outlet store** is still another type of discount retailer. A manufacturer owns these stores. Some factory outlets enable the manufacturer to sell off defective merchandise or excess inventory, while others carry items not available at full-price retail outlets and are designed to provide an additional distribution channel for the manufacturer. Although the assortment is not wide because a store carries products only one manufacturer makes, we find most factory outlet stores in *outlet malls*, where a large number of factory outlet stores cluster together in the same location.

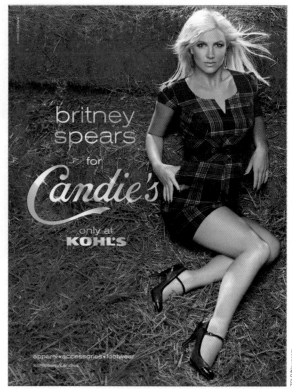

Discount department stores like Kohl's are a go-to source for fashion today.

Department Stores

Department stores sell a broad range of items and offer a deep selection organized into different sections of the store. Grand department stores dominated urban centers in the early part of the twentieth century. In their heyday, these stores sold airplanes and auctioned fine art. Lord & Taylor even offered its customers a mechanical horse to ensure the perfect fit of riding habits.

In many countries, department stores continue to thrive, and they remain consumers' primary place to shop. In Japan, department stores are always crowded with shoppers who buy everything from a takeaway sushi dinner to a string of fine pearls. In Spain, a single department store chain, El Corte Inglés, dominates retailing. Its branch stores include store-size departments for electronics, books, music, and gourmet foods, and each has a vast supermarket covering one or two floors of the store.

In the U.S., however, department stores have struggled in recent years. On the one hand, specialty stores lure department store shoppers away with deeper, more cutting-edge fashion selections and better service. On the other hand, department stores have also been squeezed by discount stores, catalogs, and online stores that offer the same items at lower prices because they don't have the expense of rent, elaborate store displays and fixtures, or high salaries for salespeople. To remain major players in the minds and pocketbooks of consumers, department stores such as Macy's and Neiman Marcus are developing successful online marketing strategies.

Hypermarkets

Hypermarkets combine the characteristics of warehouse stores and supermarkets. A European invention, these are huge establishments several times larger than other stores. A supermarket might be 40,000 to 50,000 square feet, whereas a hypermarket takes up 200,000 to 300,000 square feet, or four football fields. They offer one-stop shopping, often

off-price retailers
Retailers that buy excess merchandise from well-known manufacturers and pass the savings on to customers.

warehouse clubs
Discount retailers that charge a modest membership fee to consumers who buy a broad assortment of food and nonfood items in bulk and in a warehouse environment.

factory outlet store
A discount retailer, owned by a manufacturer, that sells off defective merchandise and excess inventory.

department stores
Retailers that sell a broad range of items and offer a good selection within each product line.

hypermarkets
Retailers with the characteristics of both warehouse stores and supermarkets; hypermarkets are several times larger than other stores and offer virtually everything from grocery items to electronics.

A *popup store* is a temporary retail space a company erects to build buzz for its products. As the sour economy creates a glut of commercial real estate, this concept is an increasingly popular way to test new product ideas or perhaps even to test if a neighborhood will be a good fit for a new store. A range of marketers, from eBay and 7 for All Mankind to upscale Hermés, have bought into the concept.

pop-up stores
Retail stores, such as Halloween costume stores, that "pop up" one day and then disappear after a period of one day to a few months.

nonstore retailing
Any method used to complete an exchange with a product end user that does not require a customer visit to a store.

Figure 12.3 📷 *Snapshot* | Types of Nonstore Retailing

Traditional retailers must compete with a variety of nonstore retailers from automatic vending to dynamic Web sites.

Direct Selling
- Door to door
- Parties and networks
- Multilevel networks and activities

Automatic Vending

B2C E-Commerce

for over 50,000 items, and feature restaurants, beauty salons, and children's play areas. Hypermarkets such as those the French firm Carrefour runs are popular in Europe and Latin America, where big stores are somewhat of a novelty. More recently, Carrefour is expanding to developing countries such as China, where a burgeoning population and a lack of large retailers provide hyper-opportunities. Hypermarkets have been less successful in the U.S., where many other shopping options exist and consumers find them too large and shopping in them too time consuming.

Pop-Up Stores

Pop-up stores are retail experiences that "pop up" one day and then disappear after a period of one day to a few months. In addition to being a low-cost way to start a business, pop-up stores provide a number of advantages, including building consumer interest, creating buzz, and test marketing products and locations. Seasonal pop-up stores are frequently opened to sell Halloween costumes, Christmas gifts and decorations, and fireworks, and traditional retailers, such as Target, Kate Spade, Gucci, and Louis Vuitton, have experimented with pop-ups.

3
OBJECTIVE
Describe the more common forms of nonstore retailing, including B2C e-commerce.
(pp. 398–403)

E-Commerce and Other Types of Nonstore Retailers

Stores like The Limited succeed because they put cool merchandise in the hands of young shoppers who can't get it elsewhere. But competition for shoppers' dollars comes from sources other than traditional stores that range from bulky catalogs to dynamic websites. Debbie in Dubuque can easily log on to Alloy.com at 3:00 A.M. and order the latest belly-baring fashions without leaving home.

As the founder of the Neiman Marcus department store once noted, "If customers don't want to get off their butts and go to your stores, you've got to go to them."[41] Indeed, many products are readily available in places other than stores. Think of the Avon lady who sells beauty products to millions of women around the world. Today, Avon allows customers to place orders by phone, fax, or catalog or through one of Avon's 6 million sales representatives in over 100 countries.

Avon's success at giving customers alternatives to traditional store outlets illustrates the increasing importance of **nonstore retailing**, which is any method a firm uses to complete an exchange that does not require a customer to visit a store. Indeed, many conventional retailers—from upscale specialty stores such as Tiffany's to discounter Walmart—offer nonstore alternatives such as catalogs and websites for customers who want to buy their merchandise. For other companies, such as Internet retailer Amazon.com, nonstore retailing is their entire business. In Chapter 14, we will discuss what direct marketing retailers do through the mail, telephone, and TV. In this section, we'll look at other types of nonstore retailing, shown in 📷 Figure 12.3: direct selling, automatic vending, and B2C e-commerce.

Direct Selling

Direct selling occurs when a salesperson presents a product to one individual or a small group, takes orders, and delivers the merchandise. The Direct Selling Association reported that in 2012, 15.9 million people engaged in direct selling in the U.S., and these activities generated $31.63 billion in sales.[42] Of this, 68 percent of revenues came from face-to-face sales and 27 percent from party plan or group sales. The major product categories for direct sales include home/family care products (such as cleaning products), wellness products (such as weight loss products), personal care products (such as cosmetics, jewelry, and skin care products), and services.

Door-to-Door Sales

Door-to-door selling is still popular in some countries, such as China. But it's declining in the U.S., where two-income households are the norm, because fewer people are home during the day and those who *are* home are reluctant to open their doors to strangers. Door-to-door selling is illegal in communities that have **Green River Ordinances**; they prohibit door-to-door selling unless prior permission is given by the household.

Parties and Networks

At *home shopping parties*, also called *in-home selling*, a company representative known as a consultant, distributor, or adviser makes a sales presentation to a group of people who have gathered in the home of a friend.[43] One reason that these parties are so effective is that people who attend may get caught up in the "group spirit" and buy things they would not normally purchase if they were alone—even Botox injections to get rid of those nasty wrinkles. We call this sales technique a **party plan system**. Perhaps the most famous home shopping parties were the Tupperware parties popular in the 1950s. Today, though, you're more like to go to a Thirty-One or Scentsy party.

Multilevel Marketing

Another form of direct selling, which the Amway Company epitomizes, is **multilevel marketing or network marketing**. In this system, a *master distributor* recruits other people to become distributors. The master distributor sells the company's products to the people he or she entices to join and then receives commissions on all the merchandise sold by the people he or she recruits. Today, Amway has over 3 million independent business owners who distribute personal care, home care, and nutrition and commercial products in more than 100 countries and territories.[44] Amway and other similar network marketers use revival-like techniques to motivate distributors to sell products and find new recruits.[45]

Despite the popularity of this technique, some network systems are illegal. They are really **pyramid schemes**: illegal scams that promise consumers or investors large profits from recruiting others to join the program rather than from any real investment or sale of goods to the public. Often, large numbers of people at the bottom of the pyramid pay money to advance to the top and to profit from others who might join. At recruiting meetings, pyramid promoters create a frenzied, enthusiastic atmosphere complete with promises of easy money. Promoters also use high-pressure tactics to get people to sign up, suggesting that if they don't sign on now, the opportunity won't come around again. Some pyramid schemes are disguised as multilevel marketing—that is, people entering the pyramid do not pay fees to advance, but they are forced to buy large, costly quantities of nonreturnable merchandise.[46] That's one of the crucial differences between pyramid schemes and legitimate network marketers.

direct selling
An interactive sales process in which a salesperson presents a product to one individual or a small group, takes orders, and delivers the merchandise.

Green River Ordinances
Community regulations that prohibit door-to-door selling unless prior permission is given by the household.

party plan system
A sales technique that relies heavily on people getting caught up in the "group spirit," buying things they would not normally buy if they were alone.

multilevel or network marketing
A system in which a master distributor recruits other people to become distributors, sells the company's product to the recruits, and receives a commission on all the merchandise sold by the people recruited.

pyramid schemes
An illegal sales technique that promises consumers or investors large profits from recruiting others to join the program rather than from any real investment or sale of goods to the public.

This ATM dispenses cupcakes rather than cash.

Automatic Vending

Coin-operated vending machines are a tried-and-true way to sell convenience goods, especially cigarettes and drinks. These machines are appealing because they require minimal space and personnel to maintain and operate. Some of the most interesting innovations are state-of-the-art vending machines that dispense everything from baguettes (which are good any time of day) to ballet flats (which you'll want after a late night out dancing).[47] Chinese customers can purchase live crabs from vending machines, and in Japan customers can buy draft beers. In the U.S., vending machines that utilize touch screens and accept credit card or mobile payments dispense pricey items like Beats by Dr. Dre headphones and Ray-Ban sunglasses.[48]

In general, however, vending machines are best suited to the sales of inexpensive merchandise, food, and beverages. Most consumers are reluctant to buy pricey items from a machine. New vending machines may spur more interest, however, as technological developments loom on the horizon, including video kiosk machines that let people see the product in use, have the ability to accept credit card or mobile payments, and have inventory systems that signal the operator when malfunctions or stock-outs occur.

The **Cutting Edge**

Tokyo Vending Machines "Recognize" Customers

In Tokyo, watch out for the vending machines—they just might know who you are. Although these vending machines may look like any other vending machine, they're much more high-tech. As you approach the vending machine, which looks like a digital billboard, motion sensors detect your presence, and a tiny camera in the vending machine estimates your sex and age. The machine then responds with a display of recommendations about

what you might like to drink based on what it knows about you or people like you. You then touch the image of the drink you want, swipe your commuter card or smart phone loaded with cash, and the drink is yours. In the meantime, the real-time data collected about your transaction is sent to JR East Water Business, the maker of the machines, so that the company can refine its "knowledge" of people's purchasing habits. In the future, these vending machines could target their ads based on location and time of day, and the touch-screen menu could offer more customization, such as letting you choose the exact amount of sugar you want in your coffee.[49]

B2C E-Commerce

B2C e-commerce
Online exchanges between companies and individual consumers.

B2C e-commerce is online exchange between companies and individual consumers. Forrester Research reports that in 2012, shoppers bought $231 billion worth of consumer goods online.[50] Furthermore, Forrester estimates that by 2017, 60 percent of all U.S. retail sales will involve the Web in some way—that means either a direct purchase of a product online or doing online research before making a product purchase in a traditional store (a Web-influenced purchase).[51] Forrester also estimates that offline Web-influenced sales will increase to $1.8 trillion by 2017 while online sales will top $370 billion.[52]

A number of factors prevent online sales from growing even more. Most consumers prefer stores where they can touch and feel items and avoid issues with returns and shipping costs. Also, many consumers don't like to buy online because they want the product immediately. To address some of these issues, many retailers, such as Best Buy, have merged their online and in-store sales functions. Consumers can select an item and pay for it online, then pick it up at their local store within hours—no wandering over the store to find the item or waiting in line to pay and no concerns about stock-outs.

Benefits of B2C E-Commerce

For both consumers and marketers, B2C e-commerce provides a host of benefits and some limitations. Table 12.2 lists some of these.

From the consumer's perspective, electronic marketing increases convenience as it breaks down many of the barriers time and location create. You can shop 24/7 without leaving home. Consumers in even the smallest of communities can purchase funky shoes or a hot swimsuit from Bloomingdales.com just like big-city dwellers. The website Ideeli .com offers its customers the chance to buy heavily discounted luxury items in a kind of online "blue-light special" on your cell phone. At the red-hot WarbyParker.com, you can upload your photo and virtually try on different sunglasses before you buy. The company will even send you several pairs if you're undecided; you just return the ones you don't want. In less developed countries, the Internet lets consumers purchase products that may not be available at all in local markets. Thus, the Internet can improve the quality of life without the necessity of developing costly infrastructure, such as opening retail stores in remote locations.

While most online consumers engage in goal-directed behavior and want to satisfy their shopping goal as quickly as possible, between 20 and 30 percent shop online because they enjoy the "thrill of the hunt" as much as or more than the actual acquisition of the item. The desire to be entertained motivates these online experiential shoppers, and they linger at sites longer. Consequently, marketers who wish to attract these customers must design websites that offer surprise, uniqueness, and excitement. Today, marketers provide **virtual experiential marketing** when they use online enhancements including colors, graphics, layout and design, interactive videos, contests, games, and giveaways.[53] Because over half of all retail customers say that friends influence their purchases, some online retailers have developed groups of "brand friends" who will share the news from the retailer.[54]

virtual experiential marketing
An online marketing strategy that uses enhancements, including colors, graphics, layout and design, interactive videos, contests, games, and giveaways, to engage experiential shoppers online.

Marketers realize equally important benefits from e-commerce. Because an organization can reach such a large number of consumers via e-commerce, it is possible to develop very specialized businesses that could not be profitable if limited by geographic constraints.

Table 12.2 | Benefits and Limitations of E-Commerce

Benefits	Limitations
For the Consumer	**For the Consumer**
Shop 24 hours a day	Lack of security
Less traveling	Fraud
Can receive relevant information in seconds from any location	Can't touch items
More product choices	Exact colors may not reproduce on computer monitors
More products available to less developed countries	Expensive to order and then return
Greater price information	Potential breakdown of human relationships
Lower prices, so less affluent can purchase	
Participate in virtual auctions	
Fast delivery	
Electronic communities	
For the Marketer	**For the Marketer**
The world is your marketplace	Lack of security
Decreases costs of doing business	Must maintain site to reap benefits
Very specialized businesses can succeed	Fierce price competition
Real-time pricing	Conflicts with conventional retailers
	Legal issues not resolved

The Internet provides an excellent opportunity to bring merchants with excess merchandise and bargain-hunting consumers together.[55] When retailers become concerned that, due to economic downturns or other factors, consumers may not buy enough, they may utilize online liquidators, such as Overstock.com and Bluefly.com, that offer consumers great bargains on apparel and accessories, items that retailers refer to as "distressed inventory."

Even high-fashion designers whose retail outlets we associate with Rodeo Drive in Los Angeles, Fifth Avenue in New York, and the Magnificent Mile in Chicago are setting up shop on the Internet to sell $3,000 skirts and $5,000 suits. According to Forrester Research, it makes sense to sell luxury online because 8 of 10 affluent customers use the Internet to research and purchase luxury goods.[56] The luxury fashion site Net-a-Porter.com sells designer clothing and accessories from Givency, Jimmy Choo, Victoria Beckman, and other top designers.[57] Bottega Veneta bolero jackets sell for $5,600, while Oscar de la Renta lace and tulle gowns sell for $9,290.

As we discussed in Chapter 11, one of the biggest advantages of e-commerce is that it's easy to get price information. Want to buy a new Hellboy action figure, a mountain bike, an MP3 player, or just about anything else you can think of? Instead of plodding from store to store to compare prices, many Web surfers use search engines or "shopbots," such as Ask.com, that compile and compare prices from multiple vendors. With readily available pricing information, shoppers can browse brands, features, reviews, and information on where to buy that particular product.

E-commerce also allows businesses to reduce costs. Compared to traditional bricks-and-mortar retailers, e-tailers' costs are minimal—no expensive mall sites to maintain and no sales associates to pay. And, for some products, such as computer software and digitized music, e-commerce provides fast, almost instantaneous delivery. Newer entertainment downloads have gone a step further with sites such as Amazon.com, Netflix.com, and iTunes that offer online shoppers the opportunity to purchase or rent movies. Just download a flick to your new high-definition LED smart TV and pop some corn. You're set for the evening.

Limitations of B2C E-Commerce

But all is not perfect in the virtual world. E-commerce does have its limitations. One drawback compared to shopping in a store is that customers must wait a few days to receive most products, which are often sent via private delivery services, so shoppers can't achieve instant gratification by walking out of a store clutching their latest "finds." The electronics chain Best Buy thinks it can address this issue with a new form of hybrid retailing; a customer can order a big-screen TV on the company's website and then drive to a bricks-and-mortar store to pick it up the same day.

Of course, some e-commerce sites still suffer from poor design that people find irritating. Customers are less likely to return to sites that are difficult to navigate or that don't provide easy access to customer service personnel, such as the online chats that better sites provide. Customers are often frustrated with sites where their shopping baskets "disappear" as soon as they leave the site. Retailers need to take these navigational problems seriously. When consumers have problems shopping on a site, they are less likely to return to shop another day.

Security is a concern to both consumers and marketers. We regularly hear news of yet another retail chain's data system being hacked and information from millions of consumers' credit cards stolen. Although in the U.S. an individual's financial liability in most theft cases is limited because credit card companies usually absorb most or all of the loss, the damage to one's credit rating can last for years.

Consumers also are concerned about Internet fraud. Although most of us feel competent to judge a local bricks-and-mortar business by its physical presence, by how long it's been around, and from the reports of friends and neighbors who shop there, we have little or no information on the millions of Internet sites offering their products for sale—even though sites like eBay.com and the Better Business Bureau try to address these concerns by posting extensive information about the reliability of individual vendors.

As with catalogs, even though most online companies have liberal return policies, consumers can still get stuck with large delivery and return shipping charges for items that don't fit or simply aren't the right color. To respond to this, a number of retailers, including Zappos and Neiman Marcus, are offering online customers free shipping to the customer and for returns.

Developing countries with primarily cash economies pose yet another obstacle to the global success of B2C e-commerce. In these countries, few people use credit cards, so they can't easily pay for items they purchase over the Internet. Furthermore, banks are far less likely to offer consumers protection against fraudulent use of their cards, so a hacked card number can literally wipe you out. For consumers in these countries, there are a growing number of alternatives for safely paying for online purchases. PayPal is a global leader in online payments. Founded in 1998 and acquired by eBay in 2002, PayPal has 148 million active accounts and services customers in 193 markets and 26 currencies around the world and processes more than 9 million transactions daily.[58] Twitpay is a service that permits consumers to send payments using the social network site Twitter. Twitpay's RT2Giv service offers consumers the opportunity to easily make payments to nonprofits. For example, the nonprofit group Malaria No More joined with Twitter to raise money for its Help Us End Malaria campaign—donations were used to buy mosquito nets for African children and their families.[59]

As major marketers beef up their presence on the Web, they worry that inventory they sell online will *cannibalize* their store sales (we discussed the strategic problem of cannibalization in Chapter 9). This is a big problem for companies like bookseller Barnes & Noble, which has to be careful as it steers customers toward its website and away from its chain of stores bursting with inventory. Barnes & Noble has to deal with competitors such as Amazon (with 182 million worldwide customers[60] and annual sales of not only books but myriad products from apparel to cell phones of over $74 billion in 2013),[61] which sells its books and music exclusively over its 13 global websites and so doesn't have to worry about this problem. Of course, today, books, including textbooks like the awesome one you're reading now, have gone digital and can be purchased and downloaded online. Tablet e-book readers, such as Amazon's Kindle and Apple's iPad, have made e-books even more attractive.

B2C's Effect on the Future of Retailing

Does the growth of B2C e-commerce mean the death of bricks-and-mortar stores as we know them? Don't plan any funerals for your local stores prematurely. Although some argue that virtual distribution channels will completely replace traditional ones because of their cost advantages, this is unlikely. For example, although a bank saves 80 percent of its costs when customers do business online from their home computers, Wells Fargo found that it could not force its customers to use PC-based banking services. And for many products, people need "touch-and-feel" information before they buy. For now, clicks will have to coexist with bricks.

However, this doesn't mean that physical retailers can rest easy. Stores as we know them will continue to evolve to lure shoppers away from their computer screens. In the future, the trend will be *destination retail*; that is, consumers will visit retailers not so much to buy a product as for the entertainment they receive from the total experience. As we saw in our discussion of retailtainment, many retailers already offer ways to make the shopping in bricks-and-mortar stores an experience rather than just a place to pick up stuff. Bass Pro Shops Mega Outdoor Stores are a store, museum, and art gallery all built into one. Hand-painted murals, 15,000-gallon saltwater aquariums, wildlife exhibits, a full-service restaurant, and a gift and nature center beckon customers to linger. In fact, the average Bass Pro Shop customer spends two and a half hours in the store after driving an average distance of 50-plus miles to get there.[62] This is definitely not your grandfather's bait-and-tackle store!

4 Service as a Core Source of Value

OBJECTIVE
Understand the marketing of services and other intangibles.
(pp. 404–413)

As we said at the beginning of this chapter, retailing is about selling goods and services to consumers for their personal use. Thus, to understand retailing, we must also understand *services* and how marketers provide consumers with quality services (and other intangibles) that meet their needs.

Marketing What Isn't There

What do a Rihanna concert, a college education, a Cubs baseball game, and a visit to Walt Disney World have in common? Easy answer—each is a product that combines experiences with physical goods to create an event that the buyer consumes. You can't have a concert without musical instruments (or maybe a pink wig, in Rihanna's case), a college education without textbooks (Thursday night parties don't count), a Cubbies game without a hot dog, or a Disney experience without the mouse ears. But these tangibles are secondary to the primary product, which is some act that, in these cases, produces enjoyment, knowledge, or excitement.

In this section, we'll consider some of the challenges and opportunities that face marketers whose primary offerings are **intangibles**: services and other experience-based products that we can't touch. The marketer whose job is to build and sell a better football, automobile, or smart phone—all tangibles—deals with issues that are somewhat different from the job of the marketer who wants to sell tickets to a basketball game, limousine service to the airport, or allegiance to a hot new rock band. Services are one type of intangible that also happens to be the fastest-growing sector in our economy. As we'll see, all services are intangible, but not all intangibles are services.

Services are acts, efforts, or performances exchanged from producer to user without ownership rights. In 2013, service industry jobs accounted for four out of every five jobs in the U.S.[63] and almost 80 percent of the gross domestic product.[64] If you pursue a marketing career, it's highly likely that you will work somewhere in the services sector of the economy. Got your interest?

Of course, the service industry includes many consumer-oriented services, ranging from dry cleaning to body piercing. Marketers classify services in terms of whether the service is performed directly on the customer or on something the customer owns. In addition, services are classified based on whether the service leaves tangible or physically perceivable results or is totally intangible. Customers themselves receive tangible services to their bodies—a haircut or a heart transplant. The education (we hope!) you are receiving in this course is an intangible service directed at the consumer. A customer's possessions may also be the recipient of tangible services, such as the repair of a favorite carpet. Intangible services directed at a consumer's possessions include insurance and home security.

But the service industry also encompasses a vast number of services directed toward organizations. Some of the more common *business services* include vehicle leasing, information technology services, insurance, security, Internet transaction services (Amazon.com, Google, online banking, etc.), legal advice, food services, consulting, cleaning, and maintenance. In addition, businesses also purchase some of the same services as consumers, such as electricity, telephone service, and gas (although, as we saw in Chapter 6, these purchases tend to be in much higher quantities). The market for business services has grown rapidly because it is often more cost effective for organizations to hire outside firms that specialize in these services than to hire a workforce and handle the tasks themselves.

APPLYING ▼ Marketing Intangibles

Much like a concert or a ball game, Eskimo Joe's combines a great experience (an intangible) with beer (a tangible). But Stan knows that Eskimo Joe's doesn't fit neatly into traditional service or retail categories. As a bar and restaurant, it provides service but skyrocketing sales of T-shirts and other clothing over the counter means that customers also come looking for just the right breadth and depth of a product assortment.

intangibles
Experience-based products.

services
Intangible products that are exchanged directly between the producer and the customer.

Characteristics of Services

Services come in many forms, from those done *to* you, such as a massage or a teeth cleaning, to those done to *something you own*, such as having your computer tuned or getting a new paint job on your classic 1965 Mustang. Regardless of whether they affect our bodies or our possessions, all services share four characteristics, which are summarized in 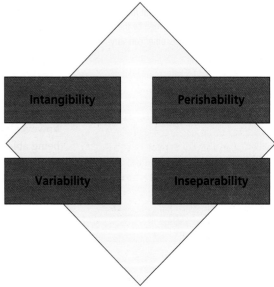 Figure 12.4: intangibility, perishability, inseparability, and variability. The discussion that follows shows how marketers can address the unique issues related to these characteristics of services that don't pop up when they deal with tangible goods.

Intangibility

Marketing of services might be called "marketing the product that isn't there." The essence is that unlike a bottle of Izzo soda or a smart 3D TV—both of which have physical, tangible properties—services do not assume a tangible form. **Intangibility** means customers can't see, touch, or smell good service. We can't inspect or handle services before we buy them. This makes it much more difficult for consumers to evaluate many services. Although it may be easy to evaluate your new haircut, it is far less easy to determine whether the dental hygienist did a great job when she cleaned your teeth.

Because they're buying something that isn't there, customers look for reassuring signs before they purchase—so marketers must ensure that these signs are readily available. That's why they try to overcome the problem of intangibility by providing *physical cues* to reassure the buyer. These cues for a service provider (such as a bank) might be the "look" of the facility; its furnishings, logo, stationery, business cards, or appearance of its employees; or well-designed advertising and websites.

Perishability

Perishability refers to the characteristic of a service that makes it impossible to store for later sale or consumption—it's a case of use it or lose it. When rooms go unoccupied at a ski resort, there is no way to make up for the lost opportunity to rent them for the weekend. Marketers try to avoid these problems when they use the marketing mix to encourage demand for the service during slack times. One popular option is to reduce prices to increase demand for otherwise unsold services. In Chapter 10, we talked about how airlines use yield management pricing and offer more lower-priced seats in the final days before a flight by offering customers last-minute deals through outlets like Priceline.com. Carnival Cruise Lines, after a series of service fiascos including what was dubbed the "Poop Cruise" (where stranded customers had no working toilets for five days), began offering heavily discounted tickets in an effort to lure customers back to its empty ships. Cabins could be purchased for as little as $50 a day—assuming you were willing to chance it, of course.[65]

Capacity management is the process by which organizations adjust their services in an attempt to match supply with demand. This strategy may mean adjusting the product, or it may mean adjusting the price. In the summer, for example, the Winter Park ski resort in Colorado combats its perishability problem when it opens its lifts to mountain bikers who tear down the sunny slopes. Rental car companies offer discounts on days of the week when business travel is light, and many hotels offer special weekend packages to increase weekend occupancy rates.

Figure 12.4 📷 *Snapshot* | Characteristics of Services

Services have four unique characteristics versus products.

Intangibility · Perishability · Variability · Inseparability

intangibility
The characteristic of a service that means customers can't see, touch, or smell good service.

perishability
The characteristic of a service that makes it impossible to store for later sale or consumption.

capacity management
The process by which organizations adjust their offerings in an attempt to match demand.

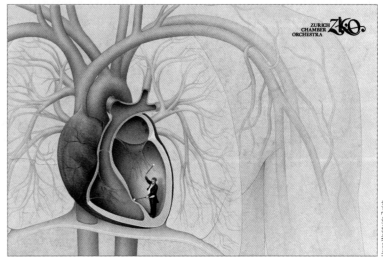

A symphony orchestra provides an intangible service that is also variable from one performance to another.

Havas Worldwide Zurich

variability
The characteristic of a service that means that even the same service performed by the same individual for the same customer can vary.

inseparability
The characteristic of a service that means that it is impossible to separate the production of a service from the consumption of that service.

service encounter
The actual interaction between the customer and the service provider.

disintermediation
The elimination of some layers of the channel of distribution in order to cut costs and improve the efficiency of the channel.

Variability

A National Football League quarterback may be red hot one Sunday and ice cold the next, and the same is true for most services. **Variability** means that over time, even the same service that the same individual performs for the same customer changes—even only in minor ways. It's rare when you get exactly the same cut from a hairstylist each time you visit him or her. Even your physician might let a rough day get in the way of his or her usual charming bedside manner with patients.

It's difficult to standardize services because service providers and customers vary. Think about your experiences in your college classes. A school can standardize its offerings to some degree—course catalogs, course content, and classrooms are fairly controllable. Professors, however, vary in their training, life experiences, and personalities, so there is little hope of being able to make teaching uniform (not that we'd want to do this anyway). And because students with different backgrounds and interests vary in their needs, the lecture that you find fascinating might put your friend to sleep (trust us on this). The same is true for customers of organizational services. Differences in the quality of individual security guards or cleaning personnel mean variability in how organizations deliver these services.

The truth is, if you really stop and think about it, we don't necessarily *want* standardization when we purchase a service. Most of us desire a hairstyle that fits our face and personality and a personal trainer who will address our unique physical training needs. Businesses like McDonald's, Wendy's, and Burger King want their ad agencies to create unique advertising campaigns to set them apart from each other.

Inseparability

In services, **inseparability** means that it is impossible to divide the production of a service from the consumption of that service. Think of the concept of inseparability this way: A firm can manufacture goods at one point in time, distribute them, and then sell them later (likely at a different location than the original manufacturing facility). In contrast, by its nature, a service can take place only at the time the actual service provider performs an act on either the customer or the customer's possession.

Still, it's difficult if not impossible to detach the expertise, skill, and personality of a provider or the quality of a firm's employees, facilities, and equipment from the service offering itself. The central role that employees play in making or breaking a service underscores the importance of the **service encounter**, or the interaction between the customer and the service provider.[66] The most expertly cooked meal is just plain mush if a surly or incompetent waiter brings it to the table.

To minimize the potentially negative effects of bad service encounters and to save on labor costs, some service businesses turn to **disintermediation**, which means removing the "middleman" and thus eliminating the need for customers to interact with people at all. Examples include self-checkouts at the supermarket or home improvement store, self-service gas pumps, and bank ATMs. Even salad and dessert bars reduce reliance on a restaurant server. Although some consumers resist dealing with ATM machines, pumping their own gas, or fixing their own salad, most prefer or at least don't mind the speed and efficiency that disintermediation provides.

The Internet provides many opportunities for disintermediation, especially in the financial services area. Banking customers can access their accounts, transfer funds from one account to another, and pay their bills with the click of a mouse. Many busy consumers can apply for a loan at their convenience online. Online brokerage services are popular, as many consumers seek to handle their investments themselves so they can avoid the commission a full-service brokerage firm charges.

The Service Encounter

Earlier, we said that a service encounter occurs when the customer comes into contact with the organization—which usually means he or she interacts with one or more employees who represent that organization. The *service encounter* has several dimensions that are important to marketers.[67] First, there is the social contact dimension—one person interacting with another person. The physical dimension is also important—customers often pay close attention to the environment where they receive the service.

Despite all the attention (and money) firms pay to create an attractive facility and deliver a quality product, this contact is "the moment of truth"—the employee often determines whether the customer will come away with a positive or a negative impression of the service. Our interactions with service providers can range from the most superficial, such as when we buy a movie ticket, to telling a psychiatrist (or bartender) our most intimate secrets. In each case, though, the quality of the service encounter exerts a big impact on how we feel about the service we receive. In other words, *the quality of a service is only as good as its worst employee*.

However, the customer also plays a part in the type of experience that results from a service encounter. When you visit a doctor, the quality of the health care you receive depends not only on the physician's competence. It's also influenced by your ability to accurately and clearly communicate the symptoms you experience and how well you follow the regimen he or she prescribes to treat you. In the same way, the business customer must provide accurate information to his or her accounting firm.

Physical Elements of the Service Encounter: Servicescapes and Other Tangibles

As we noted earlier, because services are intangible, marketers have to be mindful of the *physical evidence* that goes along with them. An important part of this physical evidence is the **servicescape**: the environment in which the service is delivered and where the firm and the customer interact. Servicescapes include facility exteriors—elements such as a building's architecture, the signage, parking, and even the landscaping. They also include interior elements, such as the design of the office or store, equipment, colors, air quality, temperature, and smells. For hotels, restaurants, banks, airlines, and even schools, the servicescape is quite elaborate. For other services, such as an express mail drop-off, a dry cleaner, or an ATM, the servicescape can be very simple.

servicescape
The actual physical facility where the service is performed, delivered, and consumed.

Marketers know that carefully designed servicescapes can have a positive influence on customers' purchase decisions, their evaluations of service quality, and their ultimate satisfaction with the service. Thus, for a service such as a pro basketball game, much planning goes into designing not only the actual court but also the exterior design and entrances of the stadium, landscaping, seating, restrooms, concession stands, and ticketing area. Similarly, marketers pay close attention to the design of other tangibles that facilitate the performance of the service or provide communications. For the basketball fan, these include the signs that direct people to the stadium, the game tickets, the programs, the team's uniforms, and the hundreds of employees who help to deliver the service.

How We Provide Quality Service

If a service experience isn't positive, it can quickly turn into a *disservice* with nasty consequences. Quality service ensures that customers are satisfied with what they have paid for. However, satisfaction is relative because the service recipient compares the current experience to some prior set of expectations. That's what makes delivering quality service tricky. What may seem like excellent service to one customer may be mediocre to another person who has been "spoiled" by earlier encounters with an exceptional service provider. So, marketers must identify customer expectations and then work hard to exceed them.

In air travel, lots of "little things" that used to be considered a normal part of the service are now treated by most airlines as extras. Many fliers believe the airlines are "nickel and diming" them for extra bag weight, blankets and pillows, small snacks and drinks, and prime seat locations. Soon they'll be charging us to use the restroom in flight! Southwest, though, has continued to offer all these perks as part of the basic service. Thus, by essentially doing nothing different from what they've always done, Southwest now stands out from the crowd and exceeds customer expectations. No surprise that for over five straight years, Southwest has been ranked among the top three in customer satisfaction among low-priced carriers by J.D. Power and Associates.[68]

Strategic Issues When We Deliver Service Quality

We've seen that delivering quality is the goal of every successful service organization. What can the firm do to maximize the likelihood that a customer will choose its service and become a loyal customer? Because services differ from goods in so many ways, decision makers struggle to market something that isn't there. But, just as in goods marketing, the first step is to develop effective marketing strategies. Table 12.3 illustrates how three different types of service organizations might devise effective marketing strategies.

Of course, no one (not even your marketing professor) is perfect, and mistakes happen. Some failures, such as when your dry cleaner places glaring red spots on your new

SERVQUAL
A multiple-item scale used to measure service quality across dimensions of tangibles, reliability, responsiveness, assurance, and empathy.

gap analysis
A marketing research method that measures the difference between a customer's expectation of a service quality and what actually occurred.

Metrics Moment

We can easily measure service quality. The **SERVQUAL** scale is one popular instrument to measure customers' perceptions of service quality. SERVQUAL identifies five dimensions, or components, of service quality:

- *Tangibles:* The physical evidence of service quality, such as the physical facilities and equipment, professional appearance of personnel, and the look and functionality of the website
- *Reliability:* The ability to provide dependably and accurately what was promised to the customer
- *Responsiveness:* The willingness to help customers and provide prompt service
- *Assurance:* The knowledge and courtesy of employees and the ability to convey trust and confidence
- *Empathy:* The degree to which the service provider genuinely cares about customers and takes the customer perspective into account when delivering service.[69]

The SERVQUAL scale is reliable and valid (concepts discussed in Chapter 4), and service businesses usually administer the scale in a survey format through a written, online, or phone questionnaire to customers. Firms often track their own SERVQUAL scores over time to understand how their service quality is, it is hoped, improving. They also can use it to collect data on customers' service quality perceptions of key competitors and then compare those scores to their own to see where to improve.

Gap analysis (no, nothing to do with a Gap clothing store) is a related measurement approach that gauges the difference between a customer's expectation of service quality and what actually occurs. By identifying specific places in the service system where there is a wide gap between what customers expect and what they receive, services marketers can get a handle on what needs improvement.

Disney Parks and Resorts is a real champion of consistency between standards and delivery. Disney makes all employees, or "Cast Members" (whether they sell ice cream on Main Street USA or they come in from another company to fill an executive role), go through "Traditions" training, as well as many other training programs, to help ensure that all Disney cast members know how they should interact with guests. They follow up frequently with refresher seminars and meetings to remind everyone of the company's history and traditions.

Apply the Metrics

1. Think back on a service encounter you've had in the past few days. This could be either in person or by phone.
2. Rate the quality of the service on each of the five SERVQUAL dimensions above (consider if each aspect was low, medium, or high) and then give an overall rating for the service encounter. Explain why you gave the ratings that you did.

Table 12.3	Marketing Strategies for Service Organizations		
	Dry Cleaner	**City Opera Company**	**A State University**
Marketing objective	Increase total revenues by 20 percent within one year by increasing business of existing customers and obtaining new customers	Increase to 1,000 the number of season memberships to opera productions within two years	Increase applications to undergraduate and graduate programs by 10 percent for the coming academic year
Target markets	Young and middle-aged professionals living within a five-mile radius of the business	Clients who attend single performances but do not purchase season memberships	Primary market: prospective undergraduate and graduate students who are residents of the state
		Other local residents who enjoy opera but do not normally attend local opera performances	Secondary market: prospective undergraduate and graduate students living in other states and in foreign countries
Benefits offered	Excellent and safe cleaning of clothes in 24 hours or less	Experiencing professional-quality opera performances while helping ensure the future of the local opera company	High-quality education in a student-centered campus environment
Strategy	Provide an incentive offer to existing customers, such as one suit cleaned for free after 10 suits cleaned at regular price	Correspond with former membership holders and patrons of single performances encouraging them to purchase new season memberships	Increase number of recruiting visits to local high schools; arrange a special day of events for high school counselors to visit campus
	Use newspaper and direct mail advertising to communicate a limited-time discount offer to all customers	Arrange for opera company personnel and performers to be guests for local TV and radio talk shows	Communicate with alumni encouraging them to recommend the university to prospective students they know

white sweater, are easy to see at the time the firm performs the service. Others, such as when the dry cleaner shrinks your sweater, are less obvious, and you recognize them only at a later time when you're running late and get a "surprise." But no matter when or how you discover the failure, the important thing is that the firm takes fast action to resolve the problem. A timely and appropriate response means that the problem won't occur again (it is hoped) and that the customer's complaint will be satisfactorily resolved. The key is speed; research shows that customers whose complaints are resolved quickly are far more likely to buy from the same company again than from those that take longer to resolve complaints.[70]

To make sure that they keep service failures to a minimum and that, when they do blow it, they can recover quickly, managers should first understand the service and the potential points at which failures are most likely to occur so they can plan how to recover ahead of time. That's why it's so important to identify critical incidents. In addition, employees should be trained to listen for complaints and be empowered to take appropriate actions immediately. Many hoteliers allow front-desk employees the discretion to spend up to a certain amount per service failure to compensate guests for certain inconveniences.

Marketing People, Places, and Ideas

By now, you understand that services are intangibles that marketers work hard to sell. But as we said earlier, services are not the only intangibles that organizations need to market.

It's hard to imagine anyone topping Stefani Joanne Angelina Germanotta for pure marketing chutzpah. Oh, by the way, that's Lady Gaga's real name. Her stage name was inspired by the Queen song "Radio Ga Ga" and in 2010 she laid claim to the most Facebook friends of any living person with over 11 million. A lot of corporate marketing gurus could take a lesson or two from Lady Gaga's marketing playbook!

Intangibles such as people, places, and ideas often need to be "sold" by someone and "bought" by someone else. Let's consider how marketing is relevant to each of these.

Marketing People

As we saw in Chapter 1, people are products, too. If you don't believe that, you've never been on a job interview or spent a Saturday night in a singles bar! Many of us find it distasteful to equate people with products. In reality, though, a sizable number of people hire personal image consultants to devise a marketing strategy for them, and others undergo plastic surgery, physical conditioning, or cosmetic makeovers to improve their "market position" or "sell" themselves to potential employers, friends, or lovers.[71] Let's briefly touch on a few prominent categories of people marketing.

Sophisticated consultants create and market politicians when they "package" candidates (clients) who then compete for "market share" as measured by votes. We trace this perspective all the way back to the 1952 and 1956 presidential campaigns of Dwight Eisenhower. Advertising executive Rosser Reeves (one of the original "Mad Men" who shaped the industry) repackaged the bland but amiable U. S. Army general as he invented jingles and slogans such as "I like Ike" and contrived man-on-the-street interviews to improve the candidate's market position.[72] For better or worse, Reeves's strategies revolutionized the political landscape as people realized they could harness the tactics they use to sell soap to sell candidates for public office. Today, the basic idea remains the same, even though the techniques are more sophisticated. From actors and musicians to athletes and supermodels, the famous and near-famous jockey for market position in popular culture. Agents carefully package celebrities as they connive to get their clients exposure on TV, starring roles in movies, recording contracts, or product endorsements.[73] Like other products, celebrities even rename themselves to craft a "brand identity." They use the same strategies marketers use to ensure that their products make an impression on consumers, including memorability (Flo Rida), suitability (fashion designer Oscar Renta reverted to his old family name of de la Renta because it sounded more elegant), and distinctiveness (Alicia Beth Moore became Pink).

In addition to these branding efforts, there are other strategies marketers use to "sell" a celebrity, as Table 12.4 shows. These include the following:

1. The *pure selling approach:* An agent presents a client's qualifications to potential "buyers" until he or she finds one who is willing to act as an intermediary.

2. The *product improvement approach:* An agent works with the client to modify certain characteristics that will increase his or her market value.

3. The *market fulfillment approach:* An agent scans the market to identify unmet needs. After identifying a need, the agent then finds a person or a group that meets a set of minimum qualifications and develops a new "product."

Marketing Places

place marketing
Marketing activities that seek to attract new businesses, residents, or visitors to a town, state, country, or some other site.

Place marketing strategies regard a city, state, country, or other locale as a brand. Marketers use the marketing mix to create a suitable identity so that consumers choose this brand over competing destinations when they plan their travel. Because of the huge

Table 12.4	Strategies to Sell a Celebrity	
Marketing Approach	**Implementation**	
Pure selling approach	Agent presents a client to the following:	
	Record companies	
	Movie studios	
	TV production companies	
	Talk show hosts	
	Advertising agencies	
	Talent scouts	
Product improvement approach	Client is modified:	
	New name	
	New image	
	Voice lessons	
	Dancing lessons	
	Plastic surgery	
	New backup band	
	New music genre	
Market fulfillment approach	Agent looks for market opening:	
	Identify unmet need	
	Develop a new product (band or singer) to the specifications of consumer wants	

amount of money tourism generates, the competition to attract visitors is fierce. There are about 1,600 visitors' bureaus in the U.S. alone that try to brand their locations. In addition, almost every town or city has an economic development office charged with luring new businesses or residents. Marketers invite would-be tourists to come and visit "Pure Michigan." In the commercials, which feature the calm, soothing voice of actor Tim Allen, the state of Michigan shows off its off-the-beaten path outdoor beauty as well as its big-city adventures. And these popular ads pay off—they brought in $1.2 billion in revenue in 2013. In addition to the current U.S. campaign, "Pure Michigan" commercials are set to air soon in Canada, Germany, and China, reaching ever more consumers and bringing in ever more revenue.[74]

Marketing Ideas

You can see people. You can stand in a city. So how do you market something you can't see, smell, or feel? **Idea marketing** refers to strategies that seek to gain market share for a concept, philosophy, belief, or issue. Even religious organizations market ideas about faith and desirable behavior when they adopt secular marketing techniques to attract young people. Some evangelists offer slickly produced services complete with live bands and professional dancers that draw huge audiences.[75]

Pascal Le Segretain/Getty Images

The marketers whose job is to promote Las Vegas as a tourist destination have changed course several times. First they tried to clean up the city's original image as a den of corruption and vice to encourage family visits. Then they switched direction and plugged the city's bawdy roots with the slogan "What happens in Vegas stays in Vegas." Oops, then the recession hit and companies clamped down on business and convention travel to "Sin City." Now, Vegas no longer promotes its famous tagline as it opens its arms to families once again with all sorts of kid-friendly activities and incentives.

idea marketing
Marketing activities that seek to gain market share for a concept, philosophy, belief, or issue by using elements of the marketing mix to create or change a target market's attitude or behavior.

Figure 12.5 📷 *Snapshot* | Factors That Shape the Future of Services

Changing demographics, globalization, technological advances, and proliferation of information all impact services.

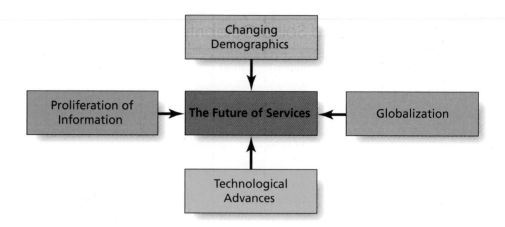

But make no mistake about it; the marketing of ideas can be even more difficult than marketing goods and services. Consumers often do not perceive that the *value* they receive when they recycle garbage or designate a driver or even when they conserve to reduce global warming is worth the *cost*—the extra effort necessary to realize these goals. Governments and other organizations use marketing strategies, often with only limited success, to sell ideas that will save the lives of millions of unwilling consumers or that will save our planet.

The Future of Services

As we look into the future, we recognize that service industries will continue to play a key role in the growth of both the U.S. and the global economy. 📷 Figure 12.5 provides several trends for us to consider that will provide both opportunities and challenges for the marketers of services down the road (that means you). In the future, we can expect services we can't even imagine yet. Of course, they will also provide many new and exciting job opportunities for future marketers. These trends include the following:

- *Changing demographics:* As the population ages, service industries that meet the needs of older consumers will see dramatic growth. Companies that offer recreational opportunities, health care, and living assistance for seniors will be in demand.

- *Globalization:* The globalization of business will increase the need for logistics and distribution services to move goods around the world (discussed in Chapter 11) and for accounting and legal services that facilitate these global exchanges. In addition, global deregulation will affect the delivery of services by banks, brokerages, insurance, and other financial service industries because globalization means greater competition. For example, many "medical tourists" now journey to countries like Thailand and India to obtain common surgical procedures that may cost less than half what they would in the U.S. Meanwhile, hospitals back home often look more like luxury spas as they offer amenities such as adjoining quarters for family members, choice of different ethnic cuisines, and in-room Internet access. In the hotel industry, demand for luxury properties is growing around the world. Hyatt Worldwide is expanding aggressively its Waldorf-Astoria and Conrad brands in China, with at least 16 luxury properties either open or scheduled to open by 2020.[76]

- *Technological advances:* Changing technology provides opportunities for growth and innovation in global service industries, such as telecommunications, health care, banking, and Internet services. And we can also expect technological advances to provide opportunities for services that we haven't even thought of yet but that will dramatically change and improve the lives of consumers.

- *Proliferation of information:* In many ways, we have become an information society. The availability of, flow of, and access to information are critical to the success of organizations. These changes will provide greater opportunities for database services, artificial intelligence systems, communications systems, and other services that facilitate the storage and transfer of knowledge.

Here's my choice...
Real **People**, Real **Choices**

Option 1   Option 2   Option 3

Why do you think Stan choose option 1?

How It Worked Out at Eskimo Joe's

Stan chose option 1 and reopened Eskimo Joe's as a trendy restaurant. Today the company consists of three restaurants that locals call "The Three Amigos." The original Eskimo Joe's, located right across from campus, still serves up burgers, cheese fries, and other fun fare, while Mexico Joe's offers south-of-the-border food, and Joseppi's is a family-style Italian place. And the rise of online shopping and the continued cult-like status of the logo have driven Stan's Eskimo Joe's clothing business to unanticipated heights.

Refer back to **page 384** for Stan's story

MyMarketingLab™

Go to **mymktlab.com** to complete the problems marked with this icon ⭐ as well as additional Marketing Metrics questions only available in MyMarketingLab.

Objective Summary ➡ Key Terms ➡ Apply

CHAPTER 12
Study Map

---

1. Objective Summary (pp. 386–392)

Define retailing; understand how retailing evolves and consider some ethical issues in retailing.

Retailing is the process by which goods and services are sold to consumers for their personal use. The wheel-of-retailing hypothesis suggests that new retailers compete on price and over time become more upscale, leaving room for other new, low-price entrants. Four factors that motivate retailers to evolve are changing economic conditions, demographics, technology, and globalization. One of the ethical issues retailers face is shrinkage due to shoplifting, employee theft, and retail borrowing. Retailers and their employees must also be cognizant of the ethical treatment of customers.

Key Terms

retailing, p. 386

wheel-of-retailing hypothesis, p. 387

point-of-sale (POS) systems, p. 389

perpetual inventory unit control system, p. 389

automatic reordering system, p. 389

experiential shoppers, p. 390

retailtainment, p. 390

shrinkage, p. 390

retail borrowing, p. 391

customer profiling, p. 391

2. Objective Summary (pp. 392–398)

Understand how we classify traditional retailers.

Retailers are classified by NAICS codes based on product lines sold; however, new retail models, such as combination stores, offer consumers more than one product line. Merchandise assortment is described in terms of breadth and depth, which refer to the number of product lines sold and the amount of variety available for each. Retailers may also be classified by the level of service offered (self-service, full-service, and limited-service retailers) and by the merchandise assortment offered. Thus, stores are classified as convenience stores, supermarkets, box stores, specialty stores, category killers, leased departments, variety stores, general merchandise discount stores, off-price retailers, warehouse clubs, factory outlet stores, department stores, hypermarkets, and pop-up stores.

Key Terms

merchandise mix, p. 392

combination stores, p. 393

supercenters, p. 393

merchandise assortment, p. 393

merchandise breadth, p. 393

merchandise depth, p. 393

convenience stores, p. 394

supermarkets, p. 394

box stores, p. 394

specialty stores, p. 396

category killer, p. 396

leased departments, p. 396

variety stores, p. 396

general merchandise discount stores, p. 396

off-price retailers, p. 397

warehouse clubs, p. 397

factory outlet store, p. 397

department stores, p. 397

hypermarkets, p. 397

pop-up stores, p. 398

3. Objective Summary (pp. 398–403)

Describe the more common forms of nonstore retailing, including B2C e-commerce.

The three more common types of nonstore retailing are direct selling, automatic vending machines, and B2C e-commerce. In direct selling, a salesperson presents a product to one individual or a small group, takes orders, and delivers the merchandise. Direct selling includes door-to-door sales, party or network sales, and multilevel marketing (network marketing). State-of-the-art self-service vending machines can dispense products from live crabs to draft beers.

B2C e-commerce, online exchanges between companies and consumers, is growing rapidly. For consumers, B2C benefits include greater convenience, greater product variety, and increased price information. For marketers, B2C offers a world market, decreased costs of doing business, opportunities for specialized businesses, and real-time pricing. The downside of B2C e-commerce for consumers includes having to wait to receive products, security issues, and the inability to touch and feel products. For Internet-only marketers, success on the Internet may be difficult to achieve, whereas cannibalization may be a problem with traditional retailers' online operations.

Key Terms

nonstore retailing, p. 398

direct selling, p. 399

Green River Ordinances, p. 399

party plan system, p. 399

multilevel or network marketing, p. 399

pyramid schemes, p. 399

B2C e-commerce, p. 400

virtual experiential marketing, p. 401

4. Objective Summary (pp. 404–413)

Understand the marketing of services and other intangibles.

Services are products that are intangible and that are exchanged directly from producer to customer without ownership rights. Generally, services are acts that accomplish some goal and may be directed either toward people or toward an object. Important service characteristics include the following: (1) intangibility, (2) perishability, (3) variability, and (4) inseparability from the producer.

Marketers know that both the social elements of the service encounter (i.e., the employee and the customer) and the physical evidence, including the servicescape, are important to a positive service experience. To measure service quality, marketers use the SERVQUAL scale, which measures five dimensions of service quality: tangibles, reliability, responsiveness, assurance, and empathy. Gap analysis, a related measurement, gauges the difference between a customer's expectation of service quality and what actually occurs.

Managers follow the steps for marketing planning when marketing other intangibles as well. People, especially politicians and celebrities, are often packaged and promoted. Place marketing aims to create or change the market position of a particular locale, whether a city, state, country, resort, or institution. Idea marketing (gaining market share for a concept, philosophy, belief, or issue) seeks to create or change a target market's attitude or behavior. The future of services will be determined by changing demographics, globalization, technological advances, and the proliferation of information.

Key Terms

intangibles, p. 404

services, p. 404

intangibility, p. 405

perishability, p. 405

capacity management, p. 405

variability, p. 406

inseparability, p. 406

service encounter, p. 406

disintermediation, p. 382

servicescape, p. 407

SERVQUAL, p. 408

gap analysis, p. 408

place marketing, p. 410

idea marketing, p. 411

Chapter **Questions** and **Activities**

Concepts: Test Your Knowledge

12-1. What is e-tailing, and how is it different from retailing?

12-2. What are point-of-sale, perpetual inventory unit control, and automatic reordering systems? How do they fit together to create an overall system for the retailer?

12-3. In order to compete with online companies, many retailers have resorted to activities that their online competitors cannot match. What is meant by experiential shopping and retailtainment?

12-4. Distinguish between merchandise assortment, merchandise breadth, and merchandise depth.

12-5. Describe the differences in focus and in shopping experience for consumers among self-service retailers, full-service retailers, and limited-service retailers. In each case, how does the consumer interact with the retailer and what are the expectations of the consumer?

12-6. What do you understand by the term "nonstore retailing"? How does it differ from traditional retailing as a shopping experience?

12-7. Distinguish between multilevel or network marketing and pyramid schemes. What makes one of them legal and the other illegal?

12-8. What are some possible effects of B2C e-commerce on traditional retailing?

12-9. What are intangibles? How do basic marketing concepts apply to the marketing of intangibles?

12-10. What is a service? What are the important characteristics of services that make them different from goods?

12-11. What dimensions do consumers and business customers use to evaluate service quality? How should marketers respond to failures in service quality?

12-12. What do we mean by marketing people? Marketing places? Marketing ideas?

Activities: Apply What You've Learned

12-13. *Creative Homework/Short Project* Assume you are an entrepreneur who is seeking funding to start up your new retail business specializing in handcrafted artisan goods from developing and least developed countries. Customers would be able to acquire a unique product and at the same time receive a good feeling knowing that a portion of the price paid for the product would go back to the individuals who produced the product. Using the wheel of retailing as a guide, map out how you expect your business to grow and change over time while remaining profitable.

12-14. *Creative Homework/Short Project* Assume that you are the director of marketing for a national chain of convenience stores. Your firm has about 200 stores located in

43 states. The stores are fairly traditional both in design and in the merchandise they carry. Because you want to be proactive in your marketing planning, you are concerned that your firm may need to consider making significant changes because of the current economic, demographic, technological, and global trends in the marketplace. You think it is important to discuss these things with the other executives at your firm. Develop a presentation that includes the following:

a. A discussion of the economic changes that might impact your stores

b. A discussion of the demographic changes that will impact your stores

c. A discussion of the technological changes that will impact your stores

d. A discussion of how global changes may provide problems and opportunities for your organization

e. Your recommendations for how your firm might meet the challenges faced in each of these areas

12-15. *In Class, 10–25 Minutes for Teams* Retailers are faced with the problem of shrinkage and what to do about it. Shrinkage comes, of course, from shoplifting and employee theft. More subtle, however, is shrinkage that involves customers, such as "sweethearting" and "retail borrowing." Many consumers feel that such practices are okay. Conduct a short survey of students in your group to study these two sources of shrinkage. You might want to include questions about the following:

a. If and how frequently students engage in such practices

b. The attitudes of students as to whether such practices are unethical and why or why not

c. What harm comes from such practices

d. What respondents think retailers should do to prevent such shrinkage

Develop a short report on your findings and present it to your class.

⭐ **12-16.** *Creative Homework/Short Project* You just started working for a firm that sells baseball caps. Currently, the firm sells its products only in specialty stores, like Lids. You think you can improve sales by branching out to other types of retailers. Prepare a presentation that identifies the additional types of retailers your firm could sell to and what the advantages of selling to those types of retailers would be. Include at least two examples (preferably examples not used in this chapter) of each type of retailer.

12-17. *For Further Research (Individual):* One problem that traditional retailers face when they open online stores is cannibalization. Select a traditional retailer where you and your fellow students might normally shop that also sells products online. You might, for example, select Best Buy, Banana Republic, Gap, or Target. Visit the retailer's online store and make notes on the site's product offering, pricing, customer service policies, and so on. (If the store you have chosen offers many different product lines, you might wish to limit your research to one or two different product lines.) Then visit the store and compare what is offered there with the online offerings. Develop a report that summarizes your findings and discusses the potential for cannibalization and its implications for the retailer.

12-18. *Creative Homework/Short Project* Because of increased competition in its community, you have been hired as a marketing consultant by a local restaurant. You know that the characteristics of services (intangibility, perishability, variability, and inseparability) create unique marketing challenges. You also know that these challenges can be met with creative marketing strategies. Outline the challenges for marketing the restaurant created by each of the four characteristics of services. List your ideas for what might be done to meet each of these challenges.

12-19. *In Class, 10–25 Minutes for Teams* You are currently a customer for a college education, a very expensive service product. You know that a service organization can create a competitive advantage by focusing on how the service is delivered after it has been purchased—making sure the service is efficiently and comfortably delivered to the customer. Develop a list of recommendations for your school for improving the delivery of its service. Consider both classroom and nonclassroom aspects of the educational product.

12-20. *For Further Research (Individual):* Party plan systems are still a popular form of direct selling and a great way to earn some extra cash. Choose a party plan system, such as Scentsy, and then research how consultants get started, how they market themselves, and how they earn money. Prepare a report that describes these issues and that projects what your first six months' earnings potential would be if you decided to become a consultant.

12-21. *Creative Homework/Short Project* As a soon-to-be college graduate, you be will be looking for a full-time job in your field. As part of this process, you will need to learn to successfully market yourself. Prepare an outline for your marketing plan. First, list the special problems and challenges associated with marketing people rather than a physical product. Then outline your ideas for promotion strategies.

12-22. *In Class, 10–25 Minutes for Teams* Address the same issues in item 12-21 for a marketing plan for the town or city where your college is located. How would you market this town or city and the surrounding area as part of the overall college experience to potential students?

Choices: What Do You Think?

12-23. *Critical Thinking* Most retail store shrinkage can be attributed to shoplifting, employee theft, and retail borrowing. What are some ways that retail store managers can limit or stop shrinkage? What are some problems inherent in security practices? Should retailers create stricter merchandise return policies?

⭐ **12-24.** *Ethics* Studies have shown—and court rulings have confirmed—that "customer profiling" does take place in U.S. retail stores, whether intentional or not. Have you ever been the victim of profiling? What were the circumstances? Did you make a complaint? Why or why not? As the store manager of an employee who is accused of profiling, what actions would you take for both the customer and the employee?

⭐ **12-25.** *Critical Thinking* Experts predict the future of B2C e-commerce to be very rosy indeed, with exponential increases in Internet sales of some product categories within the next few years. What effect do you think the growth of e-retailing will have on traditional retailing? In what ways will this be good for consumers, and in what ways will it not be so good?

12-26. *Critical Thinking* Many consumers can be easily influenced by marketers if they use celebrities to sell products and services on their behalf. Marketers can also "sell" celebrities to consumers rather like a product. The approach differs and the degree of exposure and interest will also be different according to circumstances. What are the options, and do they really work? Try to identify some examples of celebrities being used by marketers in this way.

12-27. *Critical Thinking* Does the growth of B2C e-commerce mean the death of bricks-and-mortar stores as we know them? Are we the last generations to see street stores and shopping malls? Are traditional retailers doomed? Why or why not?

12-28. *Critical Thinking* Disintermediation is becoming more commonplace in the service industry, often eliminating a customer's interaction with, for example, bank tellers or supermarket clerks. How does this lack of interaction affect the customer's experience? How does this lack of interaction affect a firm's ability to provide superior customer service?

12-29. *Critical Thinking* Sometimes service quality may not meet customers' expectations. What problems have you experienced with quality in the delivery of the following services?
   a. A haircut
   b. A dental visit
   c. Computer repairs
   d. Your college education
   What do you think is the reason for the poor quality? How would you improve the quality of service?

12-30. *Critical Thinking* There has been a lot of criticism about the way politicians have been marketed in recent years. What are some of the ways marketing has helped our political process? What are some ways the marketing of politicians might have an adverse effect on our government?

12-31. *Ethics* Many not-for-profit and religious organizations have found that they can be more successful by marketing their ideas. What are some ways that these organizations market themselves that are similar to and different from the marketing by for-profit businesses? Is it *ethical* for churches and religious organizations to spend money on marketing? Why or why not?

12-32. *Critical Thinking* Many developed countries, including the U.S., have in recent decades become primarily service economies; that is, there is relatively little manufacturing of goods, and most people in the economy are employed by service industries. Why do you think this has occurred? In what ways is this trend a good and/or a bad thing for a country? Do you think this trend will continue?

Apply Marketing Metrics

Inventory management is an important aspect of retail strategy. For example, it is important to know *when* it is time to reorder and *how much* to order at a time, a metric called *reorder point*.

As consumers buy a product day after day, the inventory level declines. The question for retailers is how low they should allow the inventory level to decline before they place an order; that is, when is the optimal time to reorder? If you order too late, you take a chance of losing sales because you are out of stock. If you order too soon, consumer tastes may change, and you will be stuck with excess and unsellable merchandise. And generally, retailers do not want more inventory on hand than is necessary to avoid stock-outs because inventory ties up cash.

Hence, the decision of when to order and how much to order is critical to a retailer's bottom line. The simplest formula to determine the reorder point is the following:

$$\text{Reorder point} = \text{Usage rate} \times \text{Lead time}$$

Usage rate is basically how quickly the inventory sells, and lead time is the length of time from reorder to delivery. Retailers tend to keep a little extra stock on hand—"safety stock"—just in case their historical data on usage rate and lead time might vary from any one particular reorder experience. Adding in safety stock, the formula becomes the following:

$$\text{Reorder point} = (\text{Usage rate} \times \text{Lead time}) + \text{Safety stock}$$

Sam's 24-Hour Gas 'n' Sip sells 97 large sodas a day. It takes five days to place an order and receive a new shipment of large cups. But to be prepared for the possibility of extra sales or a late shipment, they need to have a safety stock equal to three days of sales.

⭐ **12-33.** What is the reorder point for large cups for Sam's gas station?

Miniproject: Learn by Doing

Miniproject 1

Select a good that you, as a consumer, would like to purchase in the next week or so. Shop for this product both online and at a physical retailer.

12-34. As you shop, record the details of both shopping experiences, including the following:
  a. Type of retailer
  b. Clerks available to assist you
  c. Website or physical facilities
  d. Product variety
  e. Product availability
  f. Product price
  g. Store hours
  h. Ease of transaction
  i. Ease of return

12-35. Explain why you would be more likely to purchase this product online or at a physical retailer in the future.

Miniproject 2

Theme and entertainment parks like Universal Studios fall in the middle of the goods/services continuum—half goods and half services. To be successful in this highly competitive market, a park must position its product? Visit the websites of three of the top theme park organizations: Walt Disney World (https://disneyworld.disney.go.com), Six Flags parks (www.sixflags.com) and Universal's Orlando Theme Park (www.universalorlando.com/Theme-Parks/World-Class-Theme-Parks.aspx).

12-36. How is this positioning communicated through the website?

12-37. What changes or improvements would you recommend for each website?

Marketing in **Action** Case Real Choices at IKEA

How would you go about becoming one of the wealthiest people in the world? Ingvar Kamprad did it by flying coach, taking public transportation, driving 10-year-old automobiles, moving from Sweden to Switzerland (to pay lower taxes), and, incidentally, founding IKEA—now the world's largest furniture store.

Kamprad founded IKEA in Sweden in 1943 when he was just 17 years old and while the world was caught up in World War II. He began by dealing pens, picture frames, wallets, and other bargain items out of a catalog. In 1951, he started to sell furniture made by local carpenters, and in 1957, he opened his first IKEA furniture store in Sweden. Today, IKEA, with $23 billion in sales and 280 retail outlets in 26 countries, is the world's largest home furnishing company, known for its contemporary designs, affordable prices, and loyal customers.

IKEA's retail locations are gigantic—roughly three times the size of a typical Home Depot—and they focus exclusively on the furniture and home decorating market. IKEA's size and focus limit the breadth of items it offers, but they do provide a great deal of merchandise depth, including furniture, decorative accessories, and lighting fixtures for all rooms of the house. While the company has historically made only low-priced, flat-packed furniture, it recently introduced a new 82-piece collection it calls "Stockholm" to offer its shoppers more expensive furniture made from higher-quality materials.

IKEA's store layout responds to consumer interest in one-stop shopping—people want to find what they need in one place rather than having to visit numerous stores. In addition, IKEA makes it easier for customers to shop once they enter the store. It sets up furniture displays in "lifestyle" themes that show the type of furniture that singles, couples, or young families might need. The company also uses vignette displays to suggest how a customer can put together various items to create a certain look. These types of displays are perfect for the generation that is no longer interested in buying furniture to last a lifetime but rather furniture that fits their lifestyles now.

IKEA has enjoyed great success throughout its history, and that success has not come by accident—IKEA got to where it is today through great marketing planning. Presently, one of the most important decisions facing IKEA is how and where it should look to expand its business and its revenues. The company has announced its desire to add new store locations in Russia, Germany, France, China, Italy, Japan, the U.K., Finland, Spain, and Switzerland.

But IKEA is more than just a bricks-and-mortar retailer. In recent years, the firm has also become a popular online store. On its website, there are self-service tools that allow the customer to plan for things like kitchens, storage, and bookcases. Additionally, there is Anna, the avatar that addresses customer questions. IKEA has developed a mobile app that gives customers the ability to download the most recent catalog. It also allows the customer to check stock and build lists. However, IKEA faces some challenges as it implements its digital experience. A major issue is that it is more difficult to implement online the strategy of using room setups to convey a particular lifestyle attractive to buyers. Despite IKEA's successful history, there are no guarantees for the future in the hypercompetitive world of retailing.

Some industry analysts believe that IKEA, in spite of maintaining an expansive website, still feels like a store-with-a-website retailer. How would IKEA be better advised to continue to structure its multichannel retail strategy?

You Make the Call

12-38. What is the decision facing IKEA?

12-39. What factors are important in understanding this decision situation?

12-40. What are the alternatives?

12-41. What decision(s) do you recommend?

12-42. What are some ways to implement your recommendation?

Sources: Based on Cora Daniels and Adam Edström, "Create IKEA, Make Billions, Take Bus," *Fortune*, May 3, 2004, 44; Emma Hall and Normandy Madden, "IKEA Courts Buyers with Offbeat Ideas," *Advertising Age*, April 12, 2004, 10; "IKEA Report," *Datamonitor*, February 10, 2008, **www .datamonitor.com**; Jon Ortiz, "Customers Drawn to IKEA 'Experience,'" *Sacramento Bee*, February 26, 2006, D1; Luisa Kroll and Allison Fass, "The World's Billionaires," **www.forbes.com/billionaires** (accessed June 19, 2006); Marianne Rohrlich, "Currents: Furniture; IKEA for the Post-Collegiate Crowd: Fancier Finishes and Less Work," *New York Times*, April 26, 2007, **http://query.nytimes.com/gst/fullpage.html?res59D00E4DF153EF935 A15757C0A9619C8B63&scp53&sq5ikea&st5nyt** (accessed May 1, 2008); Mei Fong, "IKEA Hits Home in China," *Wall Street Journal Online*, March 3, 2006, B1; Mike Duff, "IKEA Eyes Aggressive Growth," *DSN Retailing Today*, January 27, 2003, 3, 22; "News," *Chain Store Age*, February 2008, 50; "Welcome Inside, Yearly Summary FY09," **www.ikea.com/ms/en_US/about_ikea/pdf/Welcome_inside_2010.pdf**; and Aaron O'Dowling-Keane, "IKEA: Retail Strategy," *Internet Retailing*, March 18, 2013, **http://internetretailing.net/2013/03/ikea-retail-strategy** (accessed April 27, 2014).

MyMarketingLab™

Go to **mymktlab.com** for Auto-graded writing questions as well as the following Assisted-graded writing questions:

12-42. Today, traditional bricks-and-mortar retailers are faced with competition from B2C E-commerce. What are some of the benefits and limitations of B2C E-commerce?

12-43. In this chapter, we learned that the characteristics of services are intangibility, perishability, variability, and inseparability. Explain each of these characteristics and how they create challenges for marketing services.

Promotion I: Advertising and Sales Promotion

Check out the Chapter 13 **Study Map** on page 458.

Marc Brownstein

▼ A Decision Maker at Brownstein Group Brand Communication

Marc Brownstein is president and CEO of Brownstein Group Brand Communication. He went to his first client meeting at the age of three when his father, founder of what was then Brownstein Advertising, had unexpected babysitting duties and brought his son along. After graduating from Penn State, Marc spent most of his early years at Ogilvy & Mather, becoming one of the youngest members of the agency's new business development team. He has created award-winning campaigns for AT&T, American Express, *Sports Illustrated*, Hershey Foods, Hallmark, and Campbell Soup Company. In 1989, Brownstein joined the firm his father founded and assumed the responsibilities of creative director and, later, president and CEO of Brownstein Group (BG). The agency has grown fivefold since Marc took over the agency's leadership, and BG is considered an innovator in digital advertising and social media. The agency's clients include Microsoft, IKEA, Gore-Tex, and Comcast.

Marc serves on the board of directors of the National Multiple Sclerosis Society, the American Association of Advertising Agencies (AAAA), Philly Ad Club, and the Young Presidents' Organization (YPO Philadelphia and YPO International). He speaks regularly before industry groups and is a blogger for *Advertising Age* magazine. The Boy Scouts of America honored Marc in 2007 with its annual Good Scout Award for his community and business leadership. Penn State also named him an "Alumni Fellow" in 2009, the highest honor awarded by the Alumni Association.

Marc's Info

First job out of school?
Copywriter.

Career high?
Winning the Microsoft business when all odds were against us.

Business book I'm reading now?
The Outliers by Malcolm Gladwell.

My motto to live by?
1. Never discount an underdog. 2. Don't listen when others say the odds are against you. 3. Always remember that dreams *do* come true.

My management style?
I give people the opportunity to be entrepreneurial, unless they prove otherwise.

Don't do this when interviewing with me?
Make the mistake of not visiting our company's website first.

Here's my problem...

Decision Time at Brownstein Group Brand Communication

In the first quarter of 2010, one of Marc's clients (a large consumer communications company) was under siege. Its primary competitor was relentlessly attacking the company with clever advertising in major markets across the U.S. that took direct aim at a new product the client had launched.

Marc's agency took exception to these unfair attacks and his account team proactively approached the client with three possible responses. Each of these solutions was based on a strategic direction the agency formulated. The group proposed a multipronged counterattack on multiple platforms, including TV spots, outdoor billboards, print ads, online banner ads, and a landing page for the client's website.

The decision to develop these options was a risky one since the client had not requested the work and there was no budget provided to lay out these solutions. If the client didn't approve the work, Marc's agency would have invested over $200,000 worth of services for which it would not be compensated.

Still, Marc felt the competitor's campaign demanded an aggressive response. He created three integrated teams within the agency; each included creatives, public relations specialists, strategists, and account managers. He gave each team 24 hours to propose an idea. Each team then presented its idea.

Things to remember

A competitor's clever advertising campaign had attached a large consumer communications company that was a client of Brownstein Group Brand Communications. Marc created three integrated teams within the agency; each included creatives, PR specialists, strategists, and account managers, and gave each team 24 hours to propose an idea based on a strategic direction the agency formulated. The client had not requested the work and there was no budget provided to lay out these solutions. If the client didn't approve the work, Marc's agency would not be compensated for over $200,000 it had invested in the idea development.

getting. However, the client might not agree with this assessment because they had already approved the current campaign. The team's judgment was subjective; there was no formal research that actually demonstrated whether people were confused by the campaign. There's always a risk when an agency has to tell a client that its current advertising doesn't work very well.

2 Option

Fire back. This concept took direct aim at the competition's brand name and product claims. The messages mocked the rival's brand name, and they aimed to create doubt in consumers' minds about whether their product really possessed the supposedly superior product benefits it claimed. This was a very hard-hitting campaign that was also highly memorable—but it also posed a bigger risk. A direct attack response was not typical of the client's company culture; they didn't believe in starting ad wars that duked it out between two brands (like Coke vs. Pepsi). This aggressive approach would draw a lot of attention to the client and probably launch a bitter battle with the rival. However, the team argued that the competitor was already firing at them so they had no choice but to respond forcefully.

3 Option

Launch a guerrilla marketing strategy that attacked the rival more subtly than a major ad campaign. The idea was to stage a mock product comparison on the streets of various U.S. cities. Consumers would compare both products, while hidden cameras videotaped their reactions. The team intended to use this footage to launch a viral campaign that encouraged people to share the clips with their friends via *YouTube* and also post them on the client's website. Ads would follow to promote the mock comparisons; these would provide a link to the videos, and a strong public relations campaign would work in tandem to drum up awareness of the clips among the public. The team believed this approach would send the message that the client's product is superior—but that people should draw their own conclusions rather than let advertising draw it for them. This was clearly an unconventional campaign that might make the client a bit nervous, but then again, the team knew that the client wanted to ramp up its brand's "cool factor." However, the idea's success depended on the quality of the videotaped reactions people would provide. If they weren't as provocative as the team hoped, they wouldn't generate much buzz, and the campaign wouldn't go viral after all.

Now put yourself in Marc's shoes. Which option would you choose, and why?

Marc considered his **Options** 1·2·3

1 Option

Clearly define the new product. This campaign focused solely on defining exactly what the client's new product is and why it's better than the competing product. The team believed that the current advertising—which another ad agency had created—didn't do a very good job of explaining the product. The messages consumers were seeing left them confused about just what the product does and why it's superior to the competition. To respond to the rival's attack, new messages needed to inject clarity into the information people were

You Choose

Which **Option** would you choose, and **why**?
1. ☐YES ☐NO   2. ☐YES ☐NO   3. ☐YES ☐NO

See what **option** Marc chose on **page 458** ➡

MyMarketingLab™

⭐ **Improve Your Grade!**

Over 10 million students improved their results using the Pearson MyLabs.
Visit **mymktlab.com** for simulations, tutorials, and end-of-chapter problems.

Chapter 13

1

OBJECTIVE

Understand the communication process and the traditional promotion mix.
(pp. 422–428)

Communication Models in a Web 2.0 World

Test your advertising memory:*

1. Which fast-food chain encourages you to "Live Más"?

2. What product advertises that "We all go. Why not enjoy the go?"

3. What drug is known as "The Little Blue Pill"?

4. At what company could 15 minutes save you 15 percent or more on car insurance?

5. Which insurance company features a talking duck as its brand character?

Did you get them all right? You owe your knowledge about these and a thousand other trivia questions to the efforts of people who specialize in marketing communication. Of course today, these slogans are "old school" as marketers have followed consumers onto Facebook and Twitter and into virtual worlds to talk with their customers.

As we said in Chapter 1, *promotion* is the coordination of marketing communication efforts to influence attitudes or behavior. This function is the last of the famous *four Ps* of the marketing mix, and it plays a vital role—whether the goal is to sell hamburgers, insurance, ringtones, or healthy diets. Of course, virtually *everything* an organization says and does is a form of marketing communication. The ads it creates, the packages it designs, the uniforms its employees wear, and what other consumers say about their experiences with the brand contribute to the thoughts and feelings people have of the company and its products. In fact, savvy marketers should consider that *every element of the marketing mix is actually a form of communication*. After all, the price of a product, where it is sold, and, of course, the quality of the product itself contributes to our impression of it.

So far, we've talked about creating, managing, and pricing products. But it's not enough just to produce great products—successful marketing plans must also provide effective marketing communication strategies. Just what do we mean by communication? Today, messages assume many forms: quirky TV commercials, innovative websites, viral videos, sophisticated magazine ads, funky T-shirts, blimps blinking messages over football stadiums—even do-it-yourself, customer-made advertising. Some marketing communications push specific products (like the Apple iPad) or actions (like donating blood), whereas others try to create or reinforce an image that represents the entire organization (like General Electric or the Catholic Church).

Marketing communication in general performs one or more of four roles:

1. It *informs* consumers about new goods and services.

2. It *reminds* consumers to continue using certain brands.

3. It *persuades* consumers to choose one brand over others.

4. It *builds* relationships with customers.

Today, marketing experts believe a successful promotional strategy should coordinate diverse forms of marketing communication to deliver a consistent message. **Integrated marketing communication (IMC)** is the process that marketers use "to plan, develop, execute, and evaluate coordinated, measurable, persuasive brand communication programs over time to targeted audiences."[1] The IMC approach argues that consumers come in contact with a company or a brand in many different ways before, after, and during a purchase. Consumers see these points of contact, or *touch points* as we described in Chapter 5—a TV

integrated marketing communication (IMC)

A strategic business process that marketers use to plan, develop, execute, and evaluate coordinated, measurable, persuasive brand communication programs over time to targeted audiences.

---

* Answers: (1) Taco Bell, (2) Charmin toilet paper, (3) Viagra, (4) GEICO Insurance, (5) Aflac Insurance.

commercial, a company website, a coupon, an opportunity to win a sweepstakes, or a display in a store—as a whole, as a single company that speaks to them in different places and different ways.

To achieve their marketing communication goals, marketers must selectively use some or all of these touch points to deliver a consistent message to their customers in a **multichannel promotional strategy** where they combine traditional marketing communications (advertising, sales promotion, public relations, and direct marketing) activities with social media and other online buzz-building activities. That's a lot different from most traditional marketing communication programs of the past that made little effort to coordinate the varying messages consumers received. When a TV advertising campaign runs independently of a sweepstakes, which in turn has no relation to a NASCAR racing sponsorship, consumers often get conflicting messages that leave them confused and unsure of the brand's identity. We'll talk more about multichannel strategies later in this chapter.

To better understand marketing communications today, let's look at the three different models of marketing communication, shown in 📷 Figure 13.1. The first, the traditional communication model, is a "one-to-many" view in which a single marketer develops and sends messages to many, perhaps even millions of, consumers at once. The one-to-many approach involves traditional forms of marketing communication, such as *advertising*, including traditional mass media (TV, radio, magazines, and newspapers); *out-of-home*, such as

multichannel promotional strategy
A marketing communication strategy where they combine traditional advertising, sales promotion, and public relations activities with online buzz-building activities.

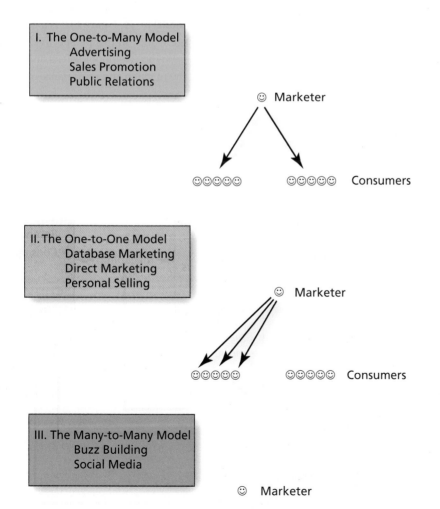

Figure 13.1 📷 *Snapshot* | Three Models of Marketing Communication

Marketers today make use of the traditional one-to-many communication model and the updated many-to-many communication model as well as talking one to one with consumers and business customers.

billboards; and Internet advertising, such as banners and pop-ups. This model also benefits from *consumer sales promotions*, such as coupons, samples, rebates, or contests, and press releases and special events that *public relations* professionals organize.

We also need to expand our traditional communication model to include the *one-to-one model*, where marketers speak to consumers and business customers individually. The one-to-one forms of marketing communication include *personal selling*, *trade sales promotion activities* used to support personal selling, and a variety of *database marketing* activities that include direct marketing.

In today's 2.0 world, the importance of the *updated* "many-to-many" model of marketing communication has increased exponentially. This newer perspective recognizes the huge impact of social media and its use in **word-of-mouth communication**, where consumers look to each other for information and recommendations. Many of us are more likely to choose a new restaurant based on users' reviews we read on Yelp than because we saw a cool commercial for the place on TV. In the updated model, marketers add new tools to their communications toolbox, including *buzz-building* activities that use *viral* and *evangelical marketing techniques* as well as new social media platforms, such as *brand communities*, *product review sites*, and *social networking sites* where consumers talk to lots of other consumers. The odds are you're using many of these platforms already. In this chapter and the following two, we'll examine each of these three different ways to communicate with our customers.

The Communication Model

Of course, promotional strategies can succeed only if we are able to get customers to understand what we're trying to say. The **communication model** in ⚡ Figure 13.2 is a good way to understand the basics of how any kind of message works. In this perspective, a *source* transmits a *message* through some *medium* to a *receiver* who (we hope) listens and understands the message. Marketers need to understand the function and importance of each of the elements of the model.

---

word-of-mouth communication
When consumers provide information about products to other consumers.

communication model
The process whereby meaning is transferred from a source to a receiver.

source
An organization or individual that sends a message.

encoding
The process of translating an idea into a form of communication that will convey meaning.

message
The communication in physical form that goes from a sender to a receiver.

medium
A communication vehicle through which a message is transmitted to a target audience.

receiver
The organization or individual that intercepts and interprets the message.

Figure 13.2 ⚡ *Process* | Communication Model

The communication model explains how organizations create and transmit messages from the marketer (the source) to the consumer (the receiver) who (we hope) understands what the marketer intends to say.

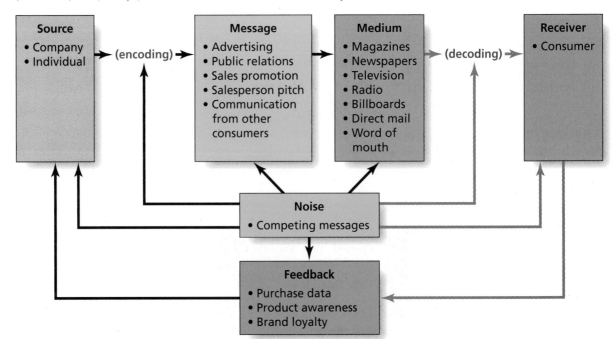

The Source Encodes

Let's start to explore this basic model from a good place: the beginning. First, there is a person or organization, the **source** that has an idea they want to communication to a receiver, such as potential customers. To do this, they must translate the idea into a physically perceivable form that conveys the desired meaning. By physically perceivable, we mean that while you can't hear or see an idea, you can hear or see a TV commercial, a billboard, or a pesky salesperson. This process called **encoding** means we can translate our idea into different forms to convey the desired meaning. We may just use words to speak to consumers. We may use music that intends to communicate excitement or peace and calm or some other product characteristic. Sometimes marketers decide to use a celebrity (Ashton Kutcher for Nikon cameras or Sofia Vergara for Cover Girl Cosmetics), an unknown actor dressed like a race-car driver, an actual customer, or an animated gecko with a Cockney accent to represent the source.[2]

The Message

The **message** is the actual content of that physically perceivable form of communication that goes from the source to a receiver. The message may be in the form of advertising, public relations, sales promotion, a salesperson's pitch, a direct marketing infomercial, or what one consumer says to another. It includes (hopefully) the information necessary to persuade, inform, remind, or build a relationship. Advertising messages may include both verbal and nonverbal elements, such as beautiful background scenery or funky music. The marketer must select the ad elements carefully so that the message connects with end consumers or business customers in its target market. Otherwise, effective communication simply does not occur, and the organization just wastes its money.

The Medium

No matter how the source encodes the message, it must then transmit that message via a **medium**, a communication vehicle that reaches members of a target audience. For marketers, this vehicle can be TV, radio, social media sites such as Facebook or Twitter, a magazine, a company website, an Internet blog, a billboard, or even a coffee mug that displays a product logo. Marketers face two major challenges when they select a medium: first, that the target market will be exposed to the medium, and, second, that the characteristics of the product are not in conflict with the medium. For example, magazines with high prestige, such as *Town and Country*, are more effective to communicate messages about expensive designer goods.[3]

The Receiver Decodes

If a tree falls in the forest and no one hears it, did it make a sound? Zen mysteries aside, communication cannot occur unless a **receiver** is there to get the message. The receiver is any individual or organization that intercepts and interprets the message. It's important to understand that the receiver interprets the message in light of his or her unique experiences. **Decoding** is the process whereby a receiver assigns meaning to a message; that is, he or she translates the message he or she sees or hears back into an idea that makes sense to him or her.

Campbell's uses the familiar symbolism of a gold star to encode a desired meaning.

decoding
The process by which a receiver assigns meaning to the message.

A simple and straightforward message.

For effective decoding to occur, the source and the receiver must share a mutual frame of reference. In this ad the receiver needs to understand the meaning of a "white flag" in order for the message to make sense.

Marketers hope that the target consumer will decode the message the way they intended, but effective communication occurs only when the source and the receiver have had similar experiences and thus share a mutual frame of reference. Too often, sources and receivers aren't on the same page, a mismatch that is especially likely to happen when the source and the receiver don't share the same cultural background or language.

Noise

The communication model also acknowledges that **noise**—anything that interferes with effective communication—can block messages. As the many arrows between noise and the other elements of the communication model in Figure 13.2 indicate, this interference can occur at any stage of communication. Marketers try to minimize noise when they place their messages where there is less likely to be distractions or competition for consumers' attention. Dior and Armani, for example, often buy multipage spreads in upscale magazines such as Condé Nast's *W* so that readers see only pictures of their clothing as they leaf through that section.

Feedback

To complete the communication loop, the source gets **feedback** from receivers. Of course, the best feedback for marketing communication is for consumers to purchase the product. Other types of feedback occur with a phone call or an e-mail to the manufacturer. More often, though, marketers must actively seek their customers' feedback through marketing research.

noise
Anything that interferes with effective communication.

feedback
Receivers' reactions to the message.

promotion mix
The total set of all products a firm offers for sale.

The Traditional Promotion Mix

As we said earlier, promotion, or marketing communication, is one of the famous four Ps. Marketers use the term **promotion mix** to refer to the communication elements that the marketer controls. The elements of the traditional promotion mix include the following:

- Advertising
- Sales promotion
- Public relations
- Personal selling
- Direct marketing

Promotion works best when the marketer skillfully combines all of the elements of the promotion mix to deliver a single consistent message about a brand. Table 13.1 presents some of the pros and cons of each element of the promotion mix.

In addition, the promotion mix must work in harmony with the overall *marketing mix* to combine elements of promotion with place, price, and product to position the firm's offering in people's minds. For example, marketers must design ads for luxury products such as Rolex watches or Jaguar automobiles to communicate that same luxury character of the product, and the ads should appear in places that reinforce that upscale image. A chic commercial that appears during the commercial breaks of an episode of *Swamp People* or *Duck Dynasty* just won't cut it.

Gillette employs a creative medium to get its message to customers.

Table 13.1 | A Comparison of Elements of the Traditional Promotion Mix

Promotional Element	Pros	Cons
Advertising	• The marketer has control over what the message will say, when it will appear, and who is likely to see it.	• Because of the high cost to produce and distribute, it may not be an efficient means of communicating with some target audiences. • Some ads may have low credibility and/or be ignored by the audience.
Sales promotion	• Provides incentives to retailers to support one's products. • Builds excitement for retailers and consumers. • Encourages immediate purchase and trial of new products. • Price-oriented promotions cater to price-sensitive consumers.	• Short-term emphasis on immediate sales rather than a focus on building brand loyalty. • The number of competing promotions may make it hard to break through the promotional clutter. • If marketers use too many price-related sales promotion activities, consumers' perception of a fair price for the brand may be lowered.
Public relations	• Relatively low cost. • High credibility.	• Lack of control over the message that is eventually transmitted and no guarantee that the message will ever reach the target. • It is difficult to measure the effectiveness of public relations efforts.
Personal selling	• Direct contact with the customer gives the salesperson the opportunity to be flexible and modify the sales message to coincide with the customer's needs. • The salesperson can get immediate feedback from the customer.	• High cost per contact with customer. • Difficult to ensure consistency of message when it is delivered by many different company representatives. • The credibility of salespeople often depends on the quality of their company's image, which has been created by other promotional strategies.
Direct marketing	• Targets specific groups of potential customers with different offers. • Marketers can easily measure the results. • Provides extensive product information and multiple offers within a single appeal. • Provides a way for a company to collect feedback about the effectiveness of its messages in an internal database.	• Consumers may have a negative opinion of some types of direct marketing. • Costs more per contact than mass appeals.

Figure 13.3 📷 *Snapshot* | Control Continuum

The messages that consumers receive about companies and products differ in terms of how much the marketer can control the content.

High	Extent of marketer's control over communication	Low

Advertising	Sales promotion	Personal selling	Direct marketing	Public relations	Word of mouth

Marketers have a lot more control over some kinds of marketing communication messages than they do others. As 📷 Figure 13.3 shows, *mass-media advertising* and *sales promotion* are at one end of the continuum, where the marketer has total control over the message he or she delivers. At the other end is *word-of-mouth (WOM) communication*, where everyday people rather than the company run the show. WOM is a vitally important component of the brand attitudes that consumers form—and of their decisions about what and what not to buy. Sandwiched between the ends we find *personal selling* and *direct marketing*, where marketers have some but not total control over the message they deliver, and *public relations*, where marketers have even less control.

McDonald's, a sponsor of the FIFA World Cup since 1994, built on its sponsorship to create promotions in its restaurants around the world. McDonald's global Player Escort Program sent 1,408 children ages 6 to 10 to the World Cup where they escorted players onto the field for all 64 FIFA matches. In Brazil, McDonald's restaurants offered customers sandwiches with flavors from countries competing in the World Cup. World Cup beverage cups were available for customers in some countries, including China and the United States, and some locations in Europe offered consumers a World Cup burger, which was 40 percent larger than McDonald's Big Mac.

mass communication
Relates to TV, radio, magazines, and newspapers.

Mass Communication: The One-to-Many Model

Some elements of the promotion mix include messages intended to reach many prospective customers at the same time. Whether a company offers customers a coupon for 50 cents off or airs a TV commercial to millions, it promotes itself to a mass audience. These are the elements of the promotion mix that use traditional **mass communication**, that is, TV radio, magazines, and newspapers:

- *Advertising:* Advertising is, for many, the most familiar and visible element of the promotion mix. Advertising reaches large numbers of consumers at one time and can convey rich and dynamic images that establish and reinforce a distinctive brand identity. Advertising also is useful to communicate factual information about the product or to remind consumers to buy their favorite brand. In recent years, Internet advertising has grown exponentially, becoming an important part of the one-to-many model. We'll talk more about Internet advertising and social media in Chapter 14.

- *Sales promotion: Consumer sales promotion* includes programs such as contests, coupons, or other incentives that marketers design to build interest in or encourage purchase of a product during a specified period. Unlike other forms of promotion, sales promotion intends to stimulate immediate action (often in the form of a purchase) rather than to build long-term loyalty.

- *Public relations: Public relations* describes a variety of communication activities that seek to create and maintain a positive image of an organization and its products among various *publics*, including customers, government officials, and shareholders. Public relations programs also include efforts to present negative company news in the most positive way so that this information will have less damaging consequences.

Personal Communication: The One-to-One Model

Sometimes, marketers want to communicate with consumers on a personal, one-to-one level. The most immediate way for a marketer to make contact with customers is simply to tell them how wonderful the product is. This is part of the *personal selling* element of the promotion mix we mentioned previously. It is the direct interaction between a company representative and a customer that can occur in person, by phone, or even over an interactive computer link.

Marketers also use direct mail, telemarketing, and other *direct marketing* activities to create personal appeals. Like personal selling, direct marketing provides direct communication with a consumer or business customer.

2 Overview of Promotional Planning

OBJECTIVE

Describe the steps in traditional and multi-channel promotional planning.

(pp. 428–434)

Now that we've talked about communication and some of the tools marketers can use to deliver messages to their customers, we need to see how to make it all happen. How do we go about the complex task of developing a promotional plan—one that delivers just the right message to a number of different target audiences when and where they want it in the most effective and cost-efficient way?

Figure 13.4 *Process* | Steps to Develop the Promotional Plan

Development of successful promotional plans involves organizing the complex process into a series of several orderly steps.

Just as with any other strategic decision-making process, the development of this plan includes several steps, as Figure 13.4 shows. First, we'll go over the steps in promotional planning, and then we'll take a look at how marketers today develop multichannel promotional strategies.

Step 1: Identify the Target Audience(s)

An important part of overall promotional planning is to identify the target audience(s). IMC marketers recognize that we must communicate with a variety of stakeholders who influence the target market. After all, we learn about a new product not just from the company that produces it but also from the news media, from our friends and family, and even from the producers of competitive products. Of course, the intended customer is the most important target audience and the one that marketers focus on the most.

Step 2: Establish the Communication Objectives

The whole point of communicating with customers and prospective customers is to let them know in a timely and affordable way that the organization has a product to meet their needs. It's bad enough when a product comes along that people don't want or need. An even bigger marketing sin is to have a product that they *do* want—but you fail to let them know about it. Of course, seldom can we deliver a single message to a consumer that magically transforms him or her into a loyal customer. In most cases, it takes a series of messages that moves the consumer through several stages.

We view this process as an uphill climb, such as the one Figure 13.5 depicts. The marketer "pushes" the consumer through a series of steps, or a **hierarchy of effects**, from initial awareness of a product to brand loyalty. At almost any point in time, different members of the target market may have reached each of the stages in the hierarchy. Marketers develop different communication objectives to "push" people to the next level.

To understand how this process works, imagine how a firm would have to adjust its communication objectives as it tries to establish a presence in the market for Hunk, a new men's cologne. Let's say that the primary target market for the cologne is single men ages 18 to 24 who care about their appearance and who are into health, fitness, working out, and looking ripped. The company would want to focus more on some promotion methods (such as advertising) and less on others (such as personal selling). Next, we'll discuss some communication objectives the company might develop for its Hunk promotion.

hierarchy of effects
A series of steps prospective customers move through, from initial awareness of a product to brand loyalty.

Figure 13.5 📷 *Snapshot* | The Hierarchy of Effects

Communication objectives move consumers through the hierarchy of effects.

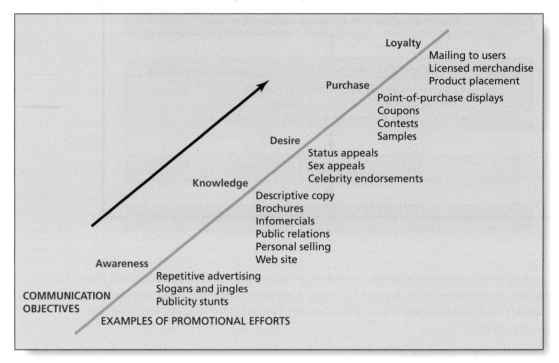

Create Awareness

The first step in the hierarchy of effects is to make members of the target market aware that there's a new brand of cologne on the market. The promotion objective might be to create an 80 percent awareness of Hunk cologne among 18- to 24-year-old men in the first two months. Note how this objective is worded. Objectives are best when they are quantitative (80 percent), when they specify the target consumer or business group (18- to 24-year-old men), and when they specify the time frame during which the plan is expected to reach the objective (in the first two months). To accomplish this, the fragrance's marketers might place simple, repetitive advertising in magazines, on TV, and on the radio that push the brand name.

Inform the Market

For those consumers who have heard the name "Hunk" but don't really know anything about it, the challenge is to provide knowledge about the benefits the new product has to offer—to *position* it relative to other colognes (see Chapter 7). The objective at this point might be to communicate the connection between Hunk and muscle building so that 60 percent of the target market develops some interest in the product in the first six months of the communication program. To accomplish this, promotion would focus on advertising and other communications that emphasize the muscle-building connection.

Create Desire

The next step in the hierarchy is desire. The task of marketing communications is to create favorable feelings toward the product and to convince at least some members of this group that they would rather splash on some Hunk instead of other colognes. The specific objective might be to create positive attitudes toward Hunk cologne among 50 percent of the target market and brand preference among 30 percent of the target market. Communication at this stage might consist of splashy advertising spreads in magazines, perhaps with an endorsement by a well-known celebrity.

Encourage Purchase and Trial

As the expression goes, "How do ya know 'til ya try it?" The company needs to get some of the men who have become interested in the cologne to try it. The specific objective now might be to encourage trial of Hunk among 25 percent of 18- to 24-year-old men. A promotion plan might encourage trial by mailing samples of Hunk to members of the target market, inserting "scratch-and-sniff" samples in bodybuilding magazines, placing elaborate displays in stores that dispense money-saving coupons, or even sponsoring a contest in which the winner gets to have WWE wrestler Triple H as his personal trainer for a day.

Build Loyalty

Loyalty, the final step in the hierarchy of effects, means customers decide to stay with Hunk after they've gone through the first bottle. The objective might be to develop and maintain regular usage of Hunk cologne among 10 percent of men from 18 to 24 years old. Promotion efforts must maintain ongoing communication with current users to reinforce the bond they feel with the product.

As a final note about objectives, at any point in time, many consumers may be stuck in each step in the hierarchy of effects. Thus, objectives must be included for the consumers at each step.

Step 3: Determine and Allocate the Marketing Communication Budget

While setting a budget for marketing communication might seem easy—you just calculate how much you need to accomplish your objectives—in reality it's not that simple. We need to make three distinct decisions to set a budget:

1. Determine the total marketing communication budget.

2. Decide whether to use a push strategy or a pull strategy.

3. Allocate spending to specific promotion activities.

Budget Decision 1: Determine the Total Marketing Communication Budget

Most firms rely on one of two budgeting techniques: top down and bottom up. With **top-down budgeting techniques**, managers establish the overall amount that the organization will allocate to promotion activities.

The most common top-down technique is the **percentage-of-sales method**, in which the marketing communication budget is based on last year's sales or on estimates for the present year's sales. The percentage may be an industry average provided by trade associations that collect objective information on behalf of member companies. The advantage of this method is that it ties spending on promotion to sales and profits. Unfortunately, this method can imply that sales cause promotional spending rather than viewing sales as the *outcome* of marketing communication efforts.

The **competitive-parity method** is a fancy way of saying "keep up with the Joneses." In other words, match whatever competitors spend. Some marketers think this approach simply mirrors the best thinking of others in the business. The competitive-parity method assumes that the same dollars spent on marketing communication by two different firms will yield the same results, but spending a lot of money doesn't guarantee a successful promotion.

Another approach is to begin at the beginning: identify promotion objectives and allocate enough money to accomplish them. That is what **bottom-up budgeting techniques** attempt. This bottom-up logic is at the heart of the **objective-task method**, which is gaining in popularity. Using this approach, the firm first defines the specific communication goals it

top-down budgeting techniques
Allocation of the promotion budget based on management's determination of the total amount to be devoted to marketing communication.

percentage-of-sales method
A method for promotion budgeting that is based on a certain percentage of either last year's sales or estimates of the present year's sales.

competitive-parity method
A promotion budgeting method in which an organization matches whatever competitors are spending.

bottom-up budgeting techniques
Allocation of the promotion budget based on identifying promotion goals and allocating enough money to accomplish them.

objective-task method
A promotion budgeting method in which an organization first defines the specific communication goals it hopes to achieve and then tries to calculate what kind of promotion efforts it will take to meet these goals.

hopes to achieve, such as increasing by 20 percent the number of consumers who are aware of the brand. It then tries to figure out what kind of promotional efforts—how much advertising, sales promotion, buzz marketing, and so on—it will take to meet that goal. Although this is the most rational approach, it is hard to implement because it obliges managers to specify their objectives and attach dollar amounts to them. This method requires careful analysis—and a bit of lucky "guesstimating."

Budget Decision 2: Decide on a Push or a Pull Strategy

The second important decision in marketing communication budgeting is whether the company will use a push or a pull strategy. A **push strategy** means that the company wants to move its products by convincing channel members to offer them and entice their customers to select these items—it pushes them through the channel. This approach assumes that if consumers see the product on store shelves, they will be motivated to make a trial purchase. In this case, marketers spend the promotion budget on personal selling, trade advertising, and trade sales promotion activities that will "push" the product from producer through the channel of distribution to consumers.

In contrast, a company that relies on a **pull strategy** is counting on consumers to demand its products. This popularity will then convince retailers to respond by stocking these items. In this case, communication budgets are used primarily for media advertising and consumer sales promotion to stimulate interest among end consumers who will "pull" the product onto store shelves and then into their shopping carts.

Budget Decision 3: Allocate the Budget to a Specific Promotion Mix

Once the organization decides how much to spend on promotion and whether to use a push or a pull strategy, it must divide its budget among the elements in the promotion mix. Although traditional advertising used to get the lion's share of the promotion budget, today sales promotion and digital marketing, such as buzz building and the use of social media, play a bigger role in marketing strategies. Overall U.S. advertising spending in 2013, for example, was $171.01 billion, up from 2012 by 3.6 percent. For the first time, however, Internet advertising at $42.8 billion overtook broadcast TV at $40.1 billion. Cable TV, however, added to total TV by $34.4 billion.[4]

In today's dynamic media environment, there are few clear guidelines for how to divide up the promotional pie. In some cases, managers may simply have a preference for advertising versus sales promotion or other elements of the promotion mix. Also, consumers vary widely in the likelihood that they will respond to various communication elements. Some thrifty consumers like to clip coupons or stock up with two-for-one offers, while others throw away those Sunday newspaper coupons without a glance. College students are especially likely to spend most of their time on the Internet (but you knew that). In larger markets, the cost of buying media, such as local TV, can be quite high. If only a small percentage of the total market includes potential customers, then mass-media advertising can be a very inefficient use of a promotion budget.

Step 4: Design the Promotion Mix

Designing the promotion mix is the most complicated step in marketing communication planning. It includes determining the specific communication tools to use, what message to communicate, and the communication channel(s) that will be used to send the message.

Planners must ask how they can use advertising, sales promotion, personal selling, public relations, direct marketing, and word-of-mouth marketing most effectively to communicate with different target audiences. Each element of the promotion mix has benefits and shortcomings, so, as we've seen, often a combination of techniques works the best.

push strategy
The company tries to move its products through the channel by convincing channel members to offer them.

pull strategy
The company tries to move its products through the channel by building desire for the products among consumers, thus convincing retailers to respond to this demand by stocking these items.

There are many ways to say the same thing, and marketers must take care when they choose how they will encode their message. To illustrate, consider two strategies that rival car companies used to promote similar automobiles. Toyota's advertising for its popular Camry sedan takes a solid, no-frills approach where consumers choose between two of their favorite cars: a Camry and another Camry. This approach works well for those who are loyal to the brand and want a trusted driving experience. The commercial for the Hyundai Sonata, however, takes it up a notch. Also a family sedan, the Hyundai ad shows a child in the backseat "racing" to the song "Real Wild Child." Rather than choosing your solid, everyday sedan, Hyundai encourages consumers to "Make every day less every day."

Step 5: Evaluate the Effectiveness of the Communication Program

The final step to manage marketing communication is to decide whether the plan is working. It would be nice if a marketing manager could simply report, "The $3 million campaign for our revolutionary glow-in-the-dark surfboards brought in $15 million in new sales!" It's not so easy. There are many random factors in the marketing environment that are out of the control of the marketer and that can impact sales: a rival's manufacturing problem, a coincidental photograph of a movie star toting one of the boards, or perhaps a surge of renewed interest in surfing sparked by a cult movie hit like *Blue Crush*. In addition, the ability of the creative design of the advertising and other promotion elements to "hit the sweet spot" with the target market makes one campaign very successful while another simply doesn't increase sales at all.

Land Rover uses attention-getting imagery to promote the adventurous side of the car.

Marketers use a variety of ways to monitor and evaluate the company's communication efforts. The catch is that it's easier to determine the effectiveness of some forms of communication than others. As a rule, various types of sales promotion are the easiest to evaluate because they occur over a fixed, usually short period, making it easier to link to sales volume. Advertising, on the other hand, has lagged or delayed advertising effects so that an ad this month might influence a car purchase next month or a year from now. Typically, researchers measure brand awareness, recall of product benefits communicated through advertising, and even the image of the brand before and after an advertising campaign. They use similar measures to assess the effectiveness of salespeople and of public relations activities.

Multichannel Promotional Strategies

As we said earlier in this chapter, marketers today recognize that the traditional one-to-many communication model in which they spent millions of dollars broadcasting ads to a mass audience is less and less effective. At the same time, it isn't yet clear how effective the new many-to-many model is—or what marketing metrics we should use to measure how well these new media work. Thus, many marketers opt for multichannel promotional strategies where they combine traditional advertising, sales promotion, public relations, and direct marketing activities with social media activities. The choice to employ multichannel marketing yields important benefits. First, these strategies boost the effectiveness of either online or offline strategies used alone. And multichannel strategies allow marketers to repeat their messages across various channels, strengthening brand awareness and providing more opportunities to convert customers.

Perhaps the best way to really understand how marketers develop multichannel strategies is to look at how some actually do it. Jaguar, for the launch of its all-new F-type sports car, left nothing to chance when it came to its multichannel strategy—the global

"Your Turn" campaign spanned TV, cinema (a short film), print, digital, mobile, experiential, and social activations. For example, in addition to TV, print, and digital ads, Jaguar partnered with USA Network's series *Covert Affairs* to feature the car, teamed up with *Playboy* to announce the Playmate of the Year, and sponsored an episode of ESPN SportsCenter. Jaguar also created a #MyTurnToJag social media contest where consumers could enter for a chance to win a drive in a Jaguar in New York, Los Angeles, Miami, or Chicago that was then shown across various social media venues.[5]

3 Advertising

OBJECTIVE

Tell what advertising is, describe the major types of advertising, discuss some of the major criticisms of advertising, and describe the process of developing an advertising campaign and how marketers evaluate advertising.

(pp. 434–452)

Advertising

Nonpersonal communication from an identified sponsor using the mass media.

A long-running Virginia Slims cigarettes advertising campaign proclaimed, "You've come a long way, baby!" We can say the same about advertising itself. Advertising has been with us a long time. In ancient Greece and Rome, ad messages appeared on walls, were etched on stone tablets, or were shouted by criers, interspersed among announcements of successful military battles, lost slaves, or government proclamations.

Advertising is nonpersonal communication from an identified sponsor using the mass media. Advertising is so much a part of marketing that many people think that advertising *"IS"* marketing. Remember, product, price, and distribution strategies are crucial as well. And, as we saw earlier, there are many ways to get a message out to a target audience in addition to advertising. But make no mistake—traditional advertising is still important. Automotive advertising tops the list with spending on measured advertising (magazines, newspapers, radio, TV, and Internet), Down from first in 2012, retail advertising was second with only a 0.2 percent increase to $16.064 billion.[6]

One thing is sure—as the media landscape continues to change, so will advertising. Sales of Internet-ready and 3DTVs are booming, as is the number of households with digital video recorders (DVRs) that let viewers skip through the commercials. Watching TV through your mobile devices is also on the rise, as many cable and satellite providers now let you use apps, like Comcast's Infinity TV Go app, to stream your favorite TV episodes. It's so popular that there's even a name for it: TV Everywhere. TV Everywhere, which is also known as **authenticated streaming**, is a term that describes using your Internet-enabled device, like a tablet or smart phone, to stream content from your cable or satellite provider.[7] Nielsen reported that in the fourth quarter of 2013, 101 million consumers viewed mobile video.[8]

Authenticated streaming

The use of an Internet enabled device, like a tablet or smart phone, to stream content from a cable or satellite provider

With all of this bleak news, is traditional advertising dead? Don't write any obituaries yet. Mass media communications are still the best way to reach a large audience. For that reason, producers of FMCGs (fast-moving consumer goods) such as P&G and Unilever will continue to rely on these traditional channels of communication to reach their customers. Indeed, wherever we turn, advertising bombards us. TV commercials, radio spots, banner ads, and huge billboards scream, "Buy me!" Advertising can be fun, glamorous, annoying, informative, and hopefully an effective way to let consumers know what a company is selling and why people should run out and buy it *today*.

Types of Advertising

Because they spend so much on advertising, marketers must decide which type of ad will work best to get their money's worth given their organizational and marketing goals. As Figure 13.6 shows, the advertisements an organization runs can take many forms, so let's review the most common kinds.

Product Advertising

When people give examples of advertising, they are likely to recall the heartwarming stories from Hallmark's ads or the cheeky reminders from the AFLAC duck. These are examples of **product advertising**, where the message focuses on a specific good or service. While not all advertising features a product or a brand, most of the advertising we see and hear is product advertising.

Institutional Advertising

Rather than a focus on a specific brand, **institutional advertising** promotes the activities, personality, or point of view of an organization or company. There are three different forms of institutional advertising:

Figure 13.6 📷 *Snapshot* | Types of Advertising

Advertisements that an organization runs can take many different forms.

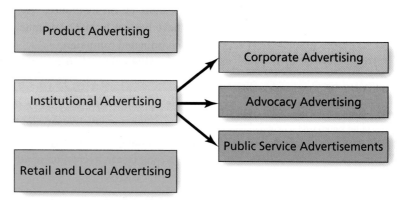

- **Corporate advertising** promotes the company as a whole instead of the firm's individual products. P&G, for example, used a corporate branding campaign called "Thank You, Mom" during the 2012 London Olympics. The ad, which focused on pictures of moms from across the globe helping their children achieve their Olympic dreams, featured a quick flash of familiar P&G brands like Tide and Duracell at the end. This particular ad was viewed more than 74 million times and garnered P&G more than $500 million in added sales.[9] According to one estimate, when consumers made such a connection between P&Gs brands, their purchasing intent increased by 20 percent.[10]

- **Advocacy advertising** states an organization's position on an issue in order to sway public opinion. For example, Focus on the Family, a conservative Christian group, aired its first-ever advocacy ad during a Super Bowl when it sponsored a 30-second pro-life commercial that featured the football player Tim Tebow. The ad tells the story of his mother's decision 23 years earlier to continue with her pregnancy, even though it was against her doctor's recommendation.[11]

- **Public service advertisements (PSAs)** are messages that promote not-for-profit organizations that serve society in some way or that champion an issue such as increasing literacy or discouraging texting while driving. Advertising agencies often take on one or more public service campaigns on a *pro bono* (for free, not the U2 singer) basis, and media run the ads free of charge.

Retail and Local Advertising

Both major retailers and small, local businesses advertise to encourage customers to shop at a specific store or use a local service. Local advertising informs us about store hours, location, and products that are available or on sale. These ads may take the form of popup ads online, text messages on your mobile device, or perhaps circulars that clog your Sunday newspaper.

Who Creates Advertising?

An **advertising campaign** is a coordinated, comprehensive plan that carries out promotion objectives and results in a series of advertisements placed in various media over a period of time. GEICO, for example, has had multiple advertising campaigns over the past few years, often with several running simultaneously. Five of its more recognized campaigns are (1) the GEICO gecko campaign; (2) the caveman campaign that even spawned a short-lived TV sitcom ("so easy a caveman can do it"); (3) the "money you could be saving" campaigns with the googly-eyed dollar bills; (4) the "Rhetorical Questions" campaign

product advertising
Advertising messages that focus on a specific good or service.

institutional advertising
Advertising messages that promote the activities, personality, or point of view of an organization or company.

corporate advertising
Advertising that promotes the company as a whole instead of a firm's individual products.

advocacy advertising
A type of public service advertising where an organization seeks to influence public opinion on an issue because it has some stake in the outcome.

public service advertisements (PSAs)
Advertising run by the media for not-for-profit organizations or to champion a particular cause without charge.

advertising campaign
A coordinated, comprehensive plan that carries out promotion objectives and results in a series of advertisements placed in media over a period of time.

that includes ads featuring Charlie Daniels, Elmer Fudd, and the Waltons; and (5) the Maxwell the pig campaign. While all of these campaigns promote the same company and its products and all use the same tagline, "Fifteen minutes could save you 15 percent or more on car insurance," each is creatively distinct. Each includes multiple ads (there have been at least 22 caveman TV commercials), but each obviously is part of a unique coordinated campaign.

Although some firms create their own advertising in-house, in most cases firms hire *outside advertising agencies* to develop an advertising campaign:

- A **limited-service agency** provides one or more specialized services, such as media buying or creative development.
- A **full-service agency** supplies most or all of the services a campaign requires, including research, creation of ad copy and art, media selection, and production of the final messages.

An advertising campaign has many elements; agencies provide the services of many different people to pull it all together:

- *Account management:* The **account executive**, or account manager, is the "soul" of the operation. This person supervises the day-to-day activities on the account and is the primary liaison between the agency and the client. The account executive has to ensure that the client is happy while verifying that people within the agency execute the desired strategy. The **account planner** combines research and account strategy to act as the voice of the consumer in creating effective advertising. It is the job of the account planner to use market data, qualitative research, and product knowledge to become intimately familiar with the consumer and to translate what customers are looking for to the creative teams who create the ads.

- *Creative services: Creatives* are the "heart" of the communication effort. The **creative services** department includes the people who actually dream up and produce the ads. They include the agency's creative director, copywriters, photographer, and art director. Creatives are the artists who breathe life into marketing objectives and craft messages that, it is hoped, will interest consumers.

- *Research and marketing services:* In **research and marketing services**, *researchers* are the "brains" of the campaign. They collect and analyze information that will help account executives develop a sensible strategy. They assist creatives in getting consumer reactions to different versions of ads or by providing copywriters with details on the target group.

- *Media planning:* The **media planner** is the "legs" of the campaign. He or she helps to determine which communication vehicles are the most effective and recommends the most efficient means to deliver the ad by deciding where, when, and how often it will appear.

Today, more and more agencies practice IMC, in which advertising is only one element of a total communication plan. Because IMC includes more than just advertising, client teams composed of people from account services, creative services, media planning, research, public relations, sales promotion, and direct marketing may work together to develop a plan that best meets the communication needs of each client.

User-Generated Advertising Content

The latest promotional innovation is to let your customers create your advertising for you. **User-generated content (UGC)**, also known as **consumer-generated media (CGM)**, includes the millions of online consumer comments, opinions, advice, consumer-to-consumer discussions, reviews, photos, images, videos, podcasts and webcasts, and product-related stories available to other consumers through digital technology. To take advantage of this

---

APPLYING ▼ Advertising Campaign

Marc's agency is responsible for creating a series of messages over a period of time for its telecommunications client.

limited-service agency
An agency that provides one or more specialized services, such as media buying or creative development.

full-service agency
An agency that provides most or all of the services needed to mount a campaign, including research, creation of ad copy and art, media selection, and production of the final messages.

account executive
A member of the account management department who supervises the day-to-day activities of the account and is the primary liaison between the agency and the client.

account planner
A member of the account management department who combines research and account strategy to act as the voice of the consumer in creating effective advertising.

creative services
The agency people (creative director, copywriters, and art director) who dream up and produce the ads.

research and marketing services
The advertising agency department that collects and analyzes information that will help account executives develop a sensible strategy and assist creatives in getting consumer reactions to different versions of ads.

media planners
Agency personnel who determine which communication vehicles are the most effective and efficient to deliver the ad.

user-generated content (UGC) or consumer-generated media (CGM)
Online consumer comments, opinions, advice and discussions, reviews, photos, images, videos, podcasts, webcasts, and product, related stories available to other consumers.

phenomenon, some marketers encourage consumers to contribute their own **do-it-yourself (DIY) ads**. For advertisers, DIY advertising offers several benefits. First, consumer-generated spots cost only one-quarter to one-third as much as professional TV and Internet ads—about $60,000 compared to the $350,000 or more to produce a traditional 30-second spot. This can be especially important for smaller businesses and emerging brands. Equally important, even to large companies with deep pockets, is the feedback on how consumers see the brand and the chance to gather more creative ideas to tell the brand's story.[12]

do-it-yourself (DIY) ads
Product ads that are created by consumers.

Perhaps the most well known promoter of UGC is PepsiCo's subsidiary Frito-Lay, which for years has featured UGC in its DIY Super Bowl ads. Rather than creating its own ads, Frito-Lay invites its customers to create their best homemade Doritos commercials. In 2014, 5,400 entrants vied for the top spot—a cool $1 million prize and airing of their ad during the big game—during Frito-Lay's "Crash the Super Bowl" contest. The winning father-and-son team spent $300 to create the "Time Machine" commercial, which showcased a time machine that "conveniently" runs only on Doritos—a clever con for getting their hands on the tasty tortilla chips.[13]

APPLYING ▼ User-Generated Content

Marc's team needs to decide if it wants to rely on consumers to help it define and spread the word about the client.

Marketers need to monitor (and sometimes encourage) UGC for two reasons. First, consumers are more likely to trust messages from fellow consumers than from companies. Second, social media is proliferating everywhere; a person who searches online for a company or product name is certain to access any number of blogs, forums, homegrown commercials, or online complaint sites that the product manufacturer had nothing to do with.

Crowdsourcing, the practice of outsourcing marketing activities to users that we discussed in Chapter 6, also can help either select a winning ad or even create one. For its 2014 Fiesta, Ford launched its Fiesta Movement remix campaign, an industry-first paid-media campaign that is completely crowdsourced by consumers. Ford gave Fiesta cars—plus gas and insurance—to 100 "social influencers" to drive and, in return, share their experiences with potential buyers. Ford's campaign includes airing some of these endorsements in commercial spots during *American Idol* and the *X Games*.[14]

crowdsourcing
A practice in which firms outsource marketing activities (such as selecting an ad) to a community of users.

Ethical Issues in Advertising

Advertising, more than any other part of marketing, has been sharply criticized as unethical for decades. Much of this criticism may be based less on actual unethical advertising and more on the high visibility of advertising and the negative attitudes of consumers who find ads an intrusion into their lives. The objections to advertising are similar to those some people have to marketing in general, as we discussed in Chapter 2. Here are the main ones:

- *Advertising is manipulative:* Advertising causes people to behave like robots and do things against their will—to make purchases they would not otherwise make were it not for the ads. However, consumers are not robots. Since they are consciously aware of appeals made in advertising, they are free to choose whether to respond to an ad or not. Of course, consumers can and often do make bad decisions that advertising may influence, but that is not the same as manipulation.

- *Advertising is deceptive and untruthful:* Deceptive advertising means that an ad falsely represents the product and that consumers believe the false information and act on it. Indeed, there is a small amount of false or deceptive advertising, but as a whole advertisers try to present their brands in the best possible light while being truthful.

  To protect consumers from being misled, the Federal Trade Commission (FTC) has specific rules regarding unfair or deceptive advertising. If the FTC finds that an ad is deceptive, they can fine the offending company and the ad agency. In addition, the FTC has the power to require firms to run **corrective advertising**—messages that clarify or qualify previous claims.[15] Yaz, a best-selling birth control pill by Bayer, was accused of overstating its ability to improve women's moods and clear up acne and not adequately communicating the drug's health risks. As a result, the Food and Drug

corrective advertising
Advertising that clarifies or qualifies previous deceptive advertising claims.

puffery
Claims made in advertising of product superiority that cannot be proven true or untrue.

greenwashing
A practice in which companies promote their products as environmentally friendly when in truth the brand provides little ecological benefit.

Administration and the attorneys generals of 27 states required Bayer to spend $20 million over six years in corrective advertising to tell consumers that they should not take the pill to cure pimples or premenstrual syndrome.

Other ads, although not illegal, may create a biased impression of products when they use **puffery**—claims of superiority that neither sponsors nor critics of the ads can prove are true or untrue. For example, Tropicana claims it has the "world's best fruit and vegetable juice," Pizza Hut claims that it has "America's best pizza," and Simply Lemonade says it's okay for other people to say it's "the best lemonade ever."

Many consumers today are concerned about **greenwashing**, a practice in which companies promote their products as environmentally friendly when in truth the brand provides little ecological benefit. This practice may refer to a company that boasts in its corporate image advertising of the cutting-edge research it does to save the planet when in fact this work accounts for only a small fraction of its activities. Carmaker Mazda received a significant amount of backlash after it released its commercial for the Mazda CX-5 compact SUV with fuel-efficient SkyActiv technology. The problem? The SUV is only slightly more environmentally friendly than similar vehicles, but because the commercial starred the popular tree-hugging Dr. Seuss character The Lorax, the ad made it seem as though the SUV was much more environmentally friendly than it really was.[16]

- *Advertising is offensive and in bad taste:* To respond to this criticism, we need to recognize that what is offensive or in bad taste to one person may not be to another. Yes, some TV commercials are offensive to some people, but then news and program content in the media can be and often are even more explicit or in poor taste. While advertisers seek to go the distance using humor, sex appeals, or fear appeals to get audiences' attention, most shy away from presenting messages that offend the very audience they want to buy their products.

- *Advertising causes people to buy things they don't really need:* The truth of this criticism depends on how you define a "need." If we believe that all consumers need is the basic functional benefits of products—the transportation a car provides, the nutrition we get from food, and the clean hair we get from shampoo—then advertising may be guilty as charged. If, on the other hand, you think you need a car that projects a cool image, food that tastes fantastic, and a shampoo that makes your hair shine and smell ever so nice, then advertising is just a vehicle that communicates those more intangible benefits.

Develop the Advertising Campaign

The advertising campaign is about much more than creating a cool ad and hoping people notice it. The campaign should be intimately related to the organization's overall communication goals. That means that the firm (and its outside agency if it uses one) must have a good idea of whom it wants to reach, what it will take to appeal to this market, and where and when it should place its messages. Let's examine the steps required to do this, as Figure 13.7 shows.

Step 1: Understand the Target Audience

The best way to communicate with an audience is to understand as much as possible about them and what turns them on and off. An ad that uses the latest teen text slang (e.g., OMG, BFF, and GR8) may relate to teenagers but not to their parents—and this strategy may backfire if the ad copy reads like an "ancient" 40-year-old trying to sound like a 20-year-old.

Figure 13.7 *Process* | Steps to Develop an Advertising Campaign

Developing an advertising campaign includes a series of steps that will ensure that the advertising meets communication objectives.

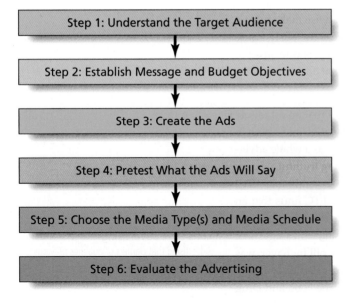

Step 1: Understand the Target Audience

Step 2: Establish Message and Budget Objectives

Step 3: Create the Ads

Step 4: Pretest What the Ads Will Say

Step 5: Choose the Media Type(s) and Media Schedule

Step 6: Evaluate the Advertising

The **Cutting Edge**

Pay-Per-Gaze

How many ads have you looked at lately? Google may soon be able to find out, using its new patent for a gaze-tracking system. It's been called **pay-per-gaze**, and it means that Google could not only track when you look at an ad but also charge advertisers every time you do.[17] And Google could charge more the longer you look at the ad.

How does it work? Using a head-mounted gaze-tracking device, Google could determine which ads a user looks at by tracking pupil direction and for how long the viewer looks at the ad. But that's not all. Google,

according to its patent, is also eventually counting on pay-per-emotion. That means Google could charge advertisers whenever an individual responds emotionally to an ad. To do that, all Google has to do is track the dilation of an individual's pupils—changes in pupil size correspond with specific emotions, such as fear or sadness.

Ultimately, then, Google could serve up content based on what an individual shows interest in. For example, if you looked at a movie ad long enough, Google could serve up the movie's trailer in an instant. How cool is that?

As we discussed in Chapter 7, marketers often identify the target audience for an advertising campaign from research. Researchers try to get inside the customer's head to understand just how to create a message that he or she will understand and to which he or she will respond. For example, USAA representatives spent a number of days with military families to get a better understanding of their customers. During this one-on-one time, USAA found out that military families place a premium on authenticity, so marketers take extreme care in making their advertising sincere. That's one reason the company uses real military families in its commercials.[18]

pay-per-gaze
A new method of charging advertisers that assesses a fee every time a viewer looks at an image in an online message.

Step 2: Establish Message and Budget Objectives

Advertising objectives should be consistent with the overall communication plan. That means that both the underlying message and the expenditures for delivering that message need to be consistent with what the marketer is trying to say about the product and the overall marketing communication budget. Thus, advertising objectives generally will include objectives for both the message and the budget.

Set Message Objectives

As we noted earlier, because advertising is the most visible part of marketing, many people assume that marketing *is* advertising. In truth, advertising alone is quite limited in what it can achieve. What advertising *can* do is inform, persuade, and remind. Accordingly, some advertisements are informational—they aim to make the customer knowledgeable about features of the product or how to use it. At other times, advertising seeks to persuade consumers to like a brand or to prefer one brand over the competition. But many ads simply aim to keep the name of the brand in front of the consumer—reminding consumers that this brand is the one to choose when they look for a soft drink or a laundry detergent.

Set Budget Objectives

Advertising is expensive. P&G, which leads all U.S. companies in advertising expenditures, spent almost $5 billion in 2013, while second- and third-place ad spenders AT&T and General Motors spent well over $3 billion each.[19]

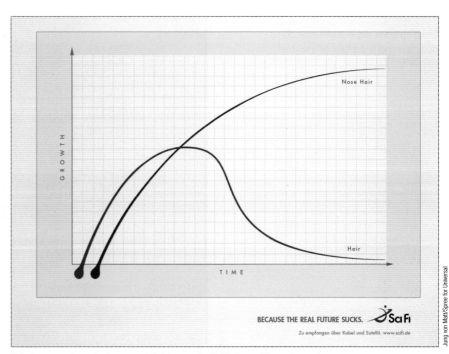

This German ad speaks to many of the viewers the SciFi channel hopes to reach.

After near bankruptcy in 1983, Harley-Davidson established a strategic objective to build a brand community: a group of people who share a common passion for a specific product. The Harley Owners Group, fondly referred to as H.O.G., is credited with helping to turn the company around. Harley supports riders' passions for their bikes by sponsoring huge rallies around the country where members can meet up.

creative strategy
The process that turns a concept into an advertisement.

creative brief
A guideline or blueprint for the marketing communication program that guides the creative process.

An objective of many firms is to allocate a percentage of the overall communication budget to advertising, depending on how much and what type of advertising the company can afford. The major approaches and techniques to setting overall promotional budgets discussed earlier in this chapter, such as the percentage-of-sales and objective-task methods, also set advertising budgets.

Step 3: Create the Ads

The creation of the advertising begins when an agency formulates a **creative strategy**, which gives the advertising creatives the direction and inspiration they need to begin the creative process. The strategy is summarized in a written document known as a **creative brief**, a rough blueprint that guides the creative process. A creative brief provides relevant information and insights about the marketing situation, the advertising objective, the competition, the advertising target and, most important, the message that the advertising must deliver.

It's one thing to know *what* a company wants to say about itself or its products and another to figure out *how* to say it. The role of the creative brief is to provide the spark that helps the ad agency come up with "the big idea," the visual and/or verbal concept that delivers the message in an attention-getting, memorable, and relevant manner. From this, the creatives develop the ads by combining already-known facts, words, pictures, and ideas in new and unexpected ways. Specifically, to come up with finished ads, they must consider four elements of the ads shown in 📷 Figure 13.8: the appeal, the format, the tonality, and the creative tactics and techniques.[20]

Figure 13.8 📷 *Snapshot* | Creative Elements of Advertising

Creating good ads includes making decisions about the four different ad elements.

Creative Element	Element Options
Appeals	Rational (Unique Selling Proposition) Emotional Reminder Advertising Teaser Ads
Execution Formats	Comparison Demonstration Testimonial Slice of Life Lifestyle
Tonality	Straightforward Humor Dramatic Romantic Apprehension/Fear
Creative Tactics and Techniques	Animation and Art Celebrities Music, Jingles, and Slogans

Advertising Appeals

An **advertising appeal** is the central idea of the ad and the basis of the advertising messages. It is the approach used to influence the consumer. Generally, we think of appeals as informational versus emotional.

Informational or rational appeals relate to consumers' practical need for the product. They emphasize the features of the product and/or the benefits we receive from using it. Often, informational appeals are based on a **unique selling proposition (USP)** that gives consumers a clear, single-minded reason why the advertiser's product is better than other products at solving a problem. For example, "15 Minutes Could Save You 15 Percent or More on Car Insurance" and "Pick Enterprise. We'll Pick You Up" are USPs. In general, a USP strategy is effective if there is some clear product advantage that consumers can readily identify and that is important to them.

Because consumers often buy products based on social or psychological needs, advertisers frequently use emotional appeals where they try to pull our heartstrings rather than make us think differently about a brand. Emotional appeals focus on an emotional or social benefit the consumer may receive from the product, such as safety, love, excitement, pleasure, respect, or approval.

Of course, not all ads fit into these two appeal categories. Well-established brands often use **reminder advertising** just to keep their name in people's minds or to be sure that consumers repurchase the product as necessary. This is the case for brands such as Coke or Pepsi.

Sometimes advertisers use **teaser ads** or **mystery ads** to generate curiosity and interest in a to-be-introduced product. Teaser ads draw attention to an upcoming ad campaign without telling the audience much about the product. Gillette introduced its new five-blade Gillette Fusion ProGlide with ads that showed the razor package but didn't say anything else about the razor.

Before the creative team can craft and polish the words and visuals to bring the big idea to life, they still must choose the most appropriate format and tonality of the advertising. We'll turn to those ideas next.

Execution format describes the basic structure of the message. Some of the more common formats, sometimes used in combination, include the following:

- *Comparison:* A comparative advertisement explicitly names one or more competitors. A commercial for the Volkswagen Passat challenged consumers to choose between the Passat and similar brands. The salesperson, with tongue in cheek, says, "The Volkswagen Passat is heads above the competition, but we're not in the business of naming names." Then, as the salesperson continues, "The fact is, it comes standard with an engine that's been the called the benchmark of its class," a bubble that reads "Sorry, Camry" pops up over the car. When the salesperson says, "It also has more rear legroom than other mid-sized sedans," another bubble pops up: "More than Altima." Finally, "The Volkswagen Passat has a lower starting price than . . ."—"Beat that, Accord." So much for not naming names!

    Comparative ads can be very effective, but there is a risk of turning off consumers who don't like the negative tone. This format is best for brands that have a smaller share of the market and for firms that can focus on a specific feature that makes them superior to a major brand.

- *Demonstration:* The ad shows a product "in action" to prove that it performs as claimed: "It slices, it dices!" Demonstration advertising is most useful when consumers are unable to identify important benefits except when they see the product in use.

Non-profit organizations often use vivid imagery to communicate the seriousness of their causes.

Humorous, witty or outrageous ads can be an effective way to break through advertising clutter.

advertising appeal
The central idea or theme of an advertising message.

unique selling proposition (USP)
An advertising appeal that focuses on one clear reason why a particular product is superior.

reminder advertising
Advertising aimed at keeping the name of a brand in people's minds to be sure consumers purchase the product as necessary.

teaser or mystery advertising
Ads that generate curiosity and interest in a to-be-introduced product by drawing attention to an upcoming ad campaign without mentioning the product.

execution format
The basic structure of the message, such as comparison, demonstration, testimonial, slice of life, and lifestyle.

tonality
The mood or attitude the message conveys (straightforward, humor, dramatic, romantic, sexy, and apprehension/fear).

- *Storytelling:* Modern storytelling commercials are like 30-second movies with a plots that involve the product in a more peripheral way. An example is the Subaru commercial that depicts a loving dad handing his six-year-old daughter the car keys and telling her to be careful. We eventually learn that she is a teenager but he still sees her as a little girl. The Subaru brand is not even revealed until we see the logo and slogan at the end.

- *Testimonial:* A celebrity, an expert, or a "man in the street" states the product's effectiveness. The use of a *celebrity endorser* is a common but expensive strategy.

- *Slice of life:* A *slice-of-life* format presents a (dramatized) scene from everyday life. Slice-of-life advertising can be effective for everyday products such as peanut butter and headache remedies that consumers may feel good about if they see that "real" people buy and use them.

- *Lifestyle:* A *lifestyle* format shows a person or persons attractive to the target market in an appealing setting. The advertised product is "part of the scene," implying that the person who buys it will attain the lifestyle. For example, a commercial on MTV might depict a group of "cool" California skateboarders who take a break for a gulp of milk and say, "It does a body good."

Tonality refers to the mood or attitude the message conveys. Some common tonalities include the following:

- *Straightforward:* Straightforward ads simply present the information to the audience in a clear manner.

- *Humor:* Consumers, in general, like humorous, witty, or outrageous ads, so these often provide an effective way to break through advertising clutter. But humor can be tricky because what is funny to one person may be offensive or stupid to another. In addition, humor can overpower the message. It's not unusual for a person to remember a hilarious ad but have no idea what product it advertised.

- *Dramatic:* A dramatization, like a play, presents a problem and a solution in a manner that is often exciting and suspenseful—a fairly difficult challenge in 30 or 60 seconds.

- *Romantic:* Ads that present a romantic situation can be especially effective at getting consumers' attention and at selling products that people associate with dating and mating. That's why fragrance ads often use a romantic format.

- *Sexy:* Some ads appear to sell sex rather than products. In an ad for the Fiat 500 Abarth, an Italian-speaking woman first angrily slaps a man for looking at her but then turns the tables and begins to seduce him. As the man leans in to kiss her, the camera pans in on the Fiat and "reality" sets in. While sex appeal ads are known to get an audience's attention, they may or may not be effective in other ways. *Sex appeal* ads are more likely to be effective when there is a connection between the product and sex (or at least romance). For example, sex appeals will work well with a perfume but are less likely to be effective when you're trying to sell a lawn mower.

- *Apprehension/fear:* Some ads highlight the negative consequences of *not* using a product. Some *fear appeal* ads focus on physical harm, while others try to create concern for social harm or disapproval. Mouthwash, deodorant, and dandruff shampoo makers and life insurance companies successfully use fear appeals. So do ads aimed at changing behaviors, such as messages discouraging drug use or smoking. In general, fear appeals can be successful if the audience perceives that the level of intensity in the fear appeal is appropriate for the product being advertised. For example, graphic photos of teens lying on the highway following an auto accident can be quite effective in public service advertisements designed to persuade teens not to text and drive, but they are likely to backfire if an insurance company tries to "scare" people into buying life insurance.

APPLYING ▼ Message Tonality

Marc's team must make a crucial decision regarding the "tone" of the messages it launches to combat a competitor's critical advertising. This tonality might be positive or negative, so they have to decide what kind of emotional response (if any) they want to arouse in the current and potential subscribers.

Creative Tactics and Techniques

In addition to ad formats and tonality, the creative process may also include a number of different creative tactics and techniques. Some of these are the following:

- *Animation and art:* Not all ads are executed with film or photography. Sometimes, a creative decision is made to use art, illustration, or animation to attract attention or to achieve the desired look for a print ad or TV commercial.

- *Celebrities:* Sometimes, celebrities appear in testimonials or for endorsements, such as Jessica Simpson's pitches for Weight Watchers.

- *Jingles:* **Jingles** are original words and music written specifically for advertising executions. Many of us remember classic ad jingles such as "I wish I were an Oscar Mayer Wiener" (Oscar Mayer) and ad slogans such as "Finger lickin' good" (KFC), "Got milk?" (the California Milk Processor Board), and "Just do it" (Nike). Today, jingles are used less frequently than in the past.

- *Slogans:* **Slogans** link the brand to a simple linguistic device that is memorable but without music. We usually have no trouble reciting successful slogans (sometimes years after the campaign has ended); think of such die-hards as "Live in your world, play in ours," "Taste the Rainbow," and "Even a caveman can do it."

Step 4: Pretest What the Ads Will Say

Now that the creatives have performed their magic, how does the agency know if the campaign ideas will work? Advertisers try to minimize mistakes by getting reactions to ad messages before they actually place them. Much of this **pretesting**, the research that goes on in the early stages of a campaign, centers on gathering basic information that will help planners be sure they've accurately defined the product's market, consumers, and competitors. As we saw in Chapter 4, this information often comes from quantitative sources, such as surveys, and qualitative sources, such as focus groups.

Step 5: Choose the Media Type(s) and Media Schedule

Media planning is a problem-solving process that gets a message to a target audience in the most effective way. Planning decisions include audience selection and where, when, and how frequent the exposure should be. Thus, the first task for a media planner is to find out when and where people in the target market are most likely to be exposed to the communication. Many college students read the campus newspaper in the morning (believe it or not, sometimes even during class!), so advertisers may choose to place ad messages aimed at college students there.

For the advertising campaign to be effective, the media planner must match the profile of the target market with specific media vehicles. For example, many Hispanic American consumers, even those who speak English, are avid users of Spanish-language media. To reach this segment, marketers might allocate a relatively large share of their advertising budget to buying Spanish-language newspapers, magazines, TV, and Spanish webcasts available on the Internet.

The choice of the right media mix is no simple matter, especially as new options, including videos and DVDs, video games, personal computers, the Internet, MP3 players, hundreds of new TV channels, and even satellite radio, now vie for our attention. In 1965, TV signals came into most consumers' living rooms through wires from the TV to a tall antenna on top of the house or via "rabbit ears" on top of the TV. Consider, however, that advertisers could reach 80 percent of 18- to 49-year-olds in the U.S. with only three 60-second TV spots placed on the three networks available: ABC, CBS, and NBC. That kind of efficiency is just a pipe dream in today's highly fragmented media marketplace.

My good man, you have a face only a mother could love.

Thank you Sir, your mother seems to agree.

For gentlemen of distinction.
www.kings1965.com

CREATIVE ORCHESTRA

Humorous ads involve the viewer, although sometimes they may push boundaries of taste for some people.

jingles
Original words and music written specifically for advertising executions.

slogans
Simple, memorable linguistic devices linked to a brand.

pretesting
A research method that seeks to minimize mistakes by getting consumer reactions to ad messages before they appear in the media.

media planning
The process of developing media objectives, strategies, and tactics for use in an advertising campaign.

Where to Say It: Traditional Mass Media

What does a 50-inch plasma TV with Dolby Surround Sound have in common with an ink pen? Each is a media vehicle that permits an advertiser to communicate with a potential customer. In this section, we'll take a look at the major categories of traditional mass media, Internet advertising, and some less traditional indirect forms of advertising. Table 13.2 summarizes some of the pros and cons of each type:

- *TV:* Because of TV's ability to reach so many people at once, it's often the medium of choice for regional and national companies. However, advertising on a TV network can be very expensive. The cost to air a 30-second ad on a popular prime-time network TV show one time normally ranges between $200,000 and $750,000 or more, depending on the size of the show's audience. Today, a single 30-second ad for the Super Bowl averages $4 million.[21] Advertisers may prefer to buy cable, satellite, or local TV time rather than network time because it's cheaper or because they want to reach a more targeted market, such as "foodies," who are into cooking. Nevertheless, 78 percent of advertisers say that TV advertising has become less effective as DVRs and video-on-demand grow in popularity,[22] and more consumers, especially younger ones, don't watch TV at all.

- *Radio:* Radio as an advertising medium dates back to 1922, when a New York City apartment manager went on the air to advertise properties for rent. One advantage of radio advertising is flexibility. Marketers can change commercials quickly, often on the spot by an announcer and a recording engineer.[23] Like TV, traditional radio advertising has declined in recent years as satellite radio, mostly by subscription only and without ads, has gained in popularity.

- *Newspapers:* The newspaper is one of the oldest communication platforms. Retailers in particular relied on newspaper ads since before the turn of the 20th century to inform readers about sales and deliveries of new merchandise. While most newspapers are local, *USA Today*, the *Wall Street Journal*, and the *New York Times* have national circulations and provide readerships in the millions. Newspapers are an excellent medium for local advertising and for events (such as store sales) that require a quick response. Today, most newspapers also offer online versions of their papers to expand their exposure, but most of these do not include the ads we see in the paper versions. Some, such as the *New York Times*, offer online subscribers downloads of the actual newspaper, including all the ads, at a much lower cost than the paper version. The future of the newspaper industry is not clear as more people choose to get their news online—or even to ignore "hard news" altogether as they get their information from sources such as TV's *The Daily Show* or online news aggregators like the *Huffington Post*.

- *Magazines:* Today, in addition to general audience magazines such as *Reader's Digest*, there are literally thousands of special-interest magazines from *Decanter* to *Garden Railways*. New technology, such as *selective binding*, allows publishers to localize their editions so that they can include advertisements for local businesses in issues they mail to specific locations. For advertisers, magazines also offer the opportunity for multipage spreads as well as the ability to include special inserts so they can deliver samples of products such as perfumes and other "scratch-and-sniff" treats.

Where to Say It: Digital Media

The term **digital media** refers to any media that are digital rather than analog. The more popular types of digital media advertisers use today include websites, social media sites such as Facebook, search engines such as Google, and digital video such as YouTube, available via a variety of devices. Marketers also send advertising text messages to consumers via mobile phones.

Owned, Paid, and Earned Media

Internet media can be classified as owned, paid, and earned.[24] Companies can control their **owned media**, including websites, blogs, Facebook, and Twitter accounts. The advantage

digital media
Media that are digital rather than analog, including websites, mobile or cellular phones, and digital video, such as YouTube.

owned media
Internet sites, such as websites, blogs, Facebook, and Twitter accounts, that are owned by an advertiser.

Table 13.2 | Pros and Cons of Media Vehicles

Vehicle	Pros	Cons
TV	• TV is extremely creative and flexible. • Network TV is the most cost-effective way to reach a mass audience. • Cable and satellite TV allow the advertiser to reach a selected group at relatively low cost. • A prestigious way to advertise. • Can demonstrate the product in use. • Can provide entertainment and generate excitement. • Messages have high impact because of the use of sight and sound.	• The message is quickly forgotten unless it is repeated often. • The audience is increasingly fragmented. • Although the relative cost of reaching the audience is low, prices are still high on an absolute basis—often too high for smaller companies. A 30-second spot on a prime-time TV sitcom costs well over $250,000. • Fewer people view network TV. • People switch from station to station and zap commercials. • Rising costs have led to more and shorter ads, causing more clutter.
Radio	• Good for selectively targeting an audience. • Is heard outside the home. • Can reach customers on a personal and intimate level. • Can use local personalities. • Relatively low cost, both for producing a spot and for running it repeatedly. • Because of short lead time, radio ads can be modified quickly to reflect changes in the marketplace. • Use of sound effects and music allows listeners to use their imagination to create a vivid scene.	• Listeners often don't pay full attention to what they hear. • Difficulty in buying radio time, especially for national advertisers. • Not appropriate for products that must be seen or demonstrated to be appreciated. • The small audiences of individual stations means ads must be placed with many different stations and must be repeated frequently.
Newspapers	• Wide exposure provides extensive market coverage. • Flexible format permits the use of color, different sizes, and targeted editions. • Provides the ability to use detailed copy. • Allows local retailers to tie in with national advertisers. • Readers are in the right mental frame to process advertisements about new products, sales, etc. • Timeliness, that is, short lead time between placing ad and running it.	• Most people don't spend much time reading the newspaper. • Readership is especially low among teens and young adults. • Short life span—people rarely look at a newspaper more than once. • Offers a very cluttered ad environment. • The reproduction quality of images is relatively poor. • Not effective to reach specific audiences.
Magazines	• Audiences can be narrowly targeted by specialized magazines. • High credibility and interest level provide a good environment for ads. • Advertising has a long life and is often passed along to other readers. • Visual quality is excellent. • Can provide detailed product information with a sense of authority.	• With the exception of direct mail, it is the most expensive form of advertising. The cost of a full-page, four-color ad in a general-audience magazine typically exceeds $100,000. • Long deadlines reduce flexibility. • The advertiser must generally use several magazines to reach the majority of a target market. • Clutter.
Directories	• Customers actively seek exposure to advertisements. • Advertisers determine the quality of the ad placement because larger ads get preferential placement.	• Limited creative options. • May be a lack of color. • Ads are generally purchased for a full year and cannot be changed.

(continues)

Table 13.2 | Pros and Cons of Media Vehicles (*continued*)

Vehicle	Pros	Cons
Out-of-home media	• Most of the population can be reached at low cost. • Good for supplementing other media. • High frequency when signs are located in heavy traffic areas. • Effective for reaching virtually all segments of the population. • Geographic flexibility.	• Hard to communicate complex messages because of short exposure time. • Difficult to measure advertisement's audience. • Controversial and disliked in many communities. • Cannot pinpoint specific market segments.
Internet websites	• Can target specific audiences and individualize messages. • Web user registration and cookies allow marketers to track user preferences and website activity. • Is interactive—consumers can participate in the ad campaign; can create do-it-yourself ads. • An entertainment medium allowing consumers to play games, download music, etc. • Consumers are active participants in the communication process, controlling what information and the amount and rate of information they receive. • Websites can facilitate both marketing communication and transactions. • Consumers visit websites with the mind-set to obtain information. • Banners can achieve top-of-mind awareness, even without click-throughs.	• Limited to Internet users only. • Banners, pop-ups, unsolicited e-mail, etc., can be unwanted and annoying. • Declining click-through rates for banners—currently less than 0.03 percent. • If Web pages take too long to load, consumers will abandon the site. • *Phishing* is e-mail sent by criminals to get consumers to go to phony websites that will seek to gain personal information, such as credit card numbers. • Because advertisers' costs are normally based on the number of click-throughs, competitors may engage in click fraud by clicking on a sponsored link. • Difficult to measure effectiveness.
Place-based media	• Effective for certain markets such a pharmaceutical companies to reach their target audience. • In retail locations, it can reach customers immediately before purchase; this provides a last opportunity to influence the purchase decision. • In locations such as airports, it receives a high level of attention because of lack of viewer options.	• Limited audience. • Difficult to measure effectiveness.
Branded entertainment	• Brand presented in a positive context. • Brand message presented in a covert fashion. • Less intrusive and thus less likely to be avoided. • Connection with a popular movie plot or TV program and with entertaining characters can help a brand's image. • Can build emotional connection with the audience. • Can create a memorable association that serves to enhance brand recall.	• Little control of how the brand is positioned—is in the hands of the director. • Difficult to measure effectiveness. • Costs of placement can be very high.
Advergaming	• Companies can customize their own games or incorporate brands into existing popular games. • Some game producers now actively pursue tie-ins with brands. • Millions of gamers play an average of 40 hours per game before they tire of it. • Millions of consumers have mobile phones "in their hands."	• Audience limited to gamers.
Mobile phones	• A large variety of different formats using different mobile phone apps.	• Consumers may be unwilling to receive messages through their phones.

Sources: Adapted from J. Thomas Russell and Ron Lane, *Kleppner's Advertising Procedure*, 15th ed. (Upper Saddle River, NJ: Prentice Hall, 2002); Terence A. Shimp, *Advertising, Promotion and Supplemental Aspects of Integrated Marketing Communications*, 8th ed. (Sydney: Thomson Southwestern, 2010); and William Wells, John Burnett, and Sandra Moriarty, *Advertising: Principles and Practice*, 6th ed. (Upper Saddle River, NJ: Prentice Hall, 2003).

of these owned media is that they are effective means for companies to build relationships with their customers while they maintain control of content. **Paid media**, the most similar model to traditional media, includes display ads, sponsorships, and paid key word searches. Consumers generally dislike paid ads, reducing their effectiveness. **Earned media** refers to word of mouth or buzz on social media. The positive of earned media is that it is the most credible to consumers. The challenge is that marketers have little control over earned media; they can only listen and respond.

Website Advertising

Online advertising no longer is a novelty; companies now spend over $121 billion a year to communicate via digital media.[25] That's because today Americans over the age of 18 spend more time on their mobile devices (just over five hours daily) than they do watching TV (about four and a half hours daily).[26]

Online advertising offers several advantages over other media platforms. First, the Internet provides new ways to finely target customers. Web user registrations and *cookies* allow sites to track user preferences and deliver ads based on previous Internet behavior. In addition, because the website can track how many times an ad is "clicked," advertisers can measure in real time how people respond to specific online messages.

Specific forms of Internet advertising include banners, buttons, pop-up ads, search engines and directories, and e-mail:

- **Banners**, rectangular graphics at the top or bottom of Web pages, were the first form of Web advertising.

- **Buttons** are small banner-type advertisements that a company can place anywhere on a page.

- A **pop-up ad** is an advertisement that appears on the screen while a Web page loads or after it has loaded. Many surfers find pop-ups a nuisance, so most Internet access software provides an option that blocks all pop-ups.

- *Search engines* provide a way for people to find Web pages of interest to them. Web **search engines**, such as Google, Bing, and Yahoo!, are programs that search for content with specified key words. Because there are millions of Web pages that include a particular word or phrase, most search engines use some method to rank their search results and provide users with the most relevant results first. As we discussed in Chapter 5, firms are increasingly paying search engines for more visibility or higher placement on results lists. Google, which has 67 percent of all U.S. Web searches,[27] has total global revenues of more than $50 billion.[28] Who have you Googled today?

- *E-mail advertising* that transmits messages to very large numbers of in-boxes simultaneously is one of the easiest ways to communicate with consumers—it's basically the same price whether you send 10 messages or 10,000. One downside to this platform is the explosion of **spam**, defined as the practice as sending unsolicited e-mail to five or more people not personally known to the sender. Many websites that offer e-mail give surfers the opportunity to allow or refuse e-mail. This **permission marketing** strategy gives the consumer the power to *opt in* or out. Marketers in the U.S. send about 258 billion e-mails to consumers every year, so they hope that a good portion of these will be opened and read rather than being sent straight to the recycle bin.[29]

paid media
Internet media, such as display ads, sponsorships, and paid key word searches, that are paid for by an advertiser.

earned media
Word-of-mouth or buzz using social media where the advertiser has no control.

banners
Internet advertising in the form of rectangular graphics at the top or bottom of Web pages.

buttons
Small banner-type advertisements that can be placed anywhere on a Web page.

pop-up ad
An advertisement that appears on the screen while a Web page loads or after it has loaded.

search engines
Internet programs that search for documents with specified key words.

spam
The use of electronic media to send unsolicited messages in bulk.

permission marketing
E-mail advertising in which online consumers have the opportunity to accept or refuse the unsolicited e-mail.

Alaska Airlines developed a system to create unique ads for individual Web surfers based on their geographic location, the number of times that person has seen an Alaska Airlines ad, the consumer's purchase history with the airline, and his experience with lost bags, delays, and flight cancellations. The program can offer different prices to different customers, even prices below the lowest published fares.

Ripped from the Headlines

Ethical/Sustainable Decisions in the Real World

Ever wonder why the sites that pop up at the top of your Google search results appear where they do? You can thank a complex algorithm that measures the popularity of the site as the number of links on other sites to that one. Links, as you probably know, are text such as a name or images on a Web page, usually underlined and often in a different color, often blue. Links connect two websites so that if you click on the link, you will automatically go to another Web page. If there are, for example, a hundred sites each having 10 or 20 links to a single site, say, a car dealer, the position for that car dealer in a Google search will be higher than if there were only 10 sites with five links each. Google's logic is that if a site that provides information on a topic, say, Chinese cuisine, has a link to another site, say, Wang's Chinese restaurant website, it is a recommendation for the restaurant. If lots of sites about Chinese cuisine have links to Wang's restaurant, Wang's must be good and should be near the top of the search results for Chinese restaurants. The problem is that some sites violate Google's guidelines—Google wants sites to earn their place in the search results based on relevance, but marketers increasingly buy their way to the top through paid links on other sites—some of which may have nothing in common with the link site.

Take, for example, some of the top flower marketers: Teleflora, FTD, ProFlowers, and 1800flowers.com. Around Mother's Day, they all paid for links that include phrases like "mothers day flowers" and "mothers day arrangements"—sometimes on sites that have nothing to do with mothers or the holiday itself.[30] 1800flowers.com posted links on sites like MyIndianRecipes.net and Johnathanduffy.net (who?). In another case, the publisher of one mom-related website, which hasn't been updated in a few years, said FTD paid her $30 a month to post a "mothers day flowers" link on her home page.

Although the outcome of these examples was inconclusive—that is, the companies were never charged with wrongdoing—companies that do pay for links certainly need to be careful. Google, in the case of J.C. Penney, for example, found that the retailer had been buying links during the Christmas holiday season and demoted the company in its search results, meaning would-be consumers were less likely to click on the J.C. Penney link because it appeared lower in the search rankings.[31]

Still, companies are willing to gamble. If the flower sellers bought links and were demoted by Google, they'd lose potential sales—but certainly not nearly as much as if they missed the chance to rank at the top of the search results for a holiday where consumers are expected to spend $1.9 billion on flowers alone.

Is it ethical for marketers to pay for links on websites in order to obtain higher rankings on search engines?

☐ YES ☐ NO

mobile advertising
A form of advertising that is communicated to the consumer via a handset.

video sharing
Uploading video recordings on to Internet sites such as YouTube so that thousands or even millions of other Internet users can see them.

vlogs
Video recordings shared on the Internet.

Mobile Advertising

The Mobile Marketing Association defines **mobile advertising** as "a form of advertising that is communicated to the consumer via a handset."[32] Mobile marketing offers advertisers a variety of ways to speak to customers, including mobile websites, mobile applications, mobile messaging, and mobile video and TV.

Newer phones with GPS features that pinpoint your location allow additional mobile advertising opportunities. In fact, the iPhone's new operating system, iOS7, comes with a new feature called iBeacon. This technology enables Apple to track consumers within a few feet of by bouncing signals off of strategically placed sensors in your favorite stores. That means advertisers can send ads to your smart phone as soon as you stand in front of the product.[33]

Video Sharing: Check It Out on YouTube

Video sharing describes the strategy of uploading video recordings or **vlogs** (pronounced "vee-logs") to Internet sites. While YouTube is certainly the most popular video sharing site, it is not the only one. After YouTube, the top seven video sharing sites include Vimeo, Vevo, Dailymotion, Veoh, Metacafe, Flickr, and Break.[34]

For marketers, YouTube provides vast opportunities to build relationships with consumers. Cuisinart and other appliance makers post videos to show consumers how to use their new products. Nike, in preparation for the World Cup kickoff, released a five-minute World Cup–themed short film featuring animated versions of some of the world's best football (or soccer, for you U.S. fans) players. Titled "Risk Everything," the video was watched by more than 18.6 million viewers in the first three months.[35] Universities and their students have gotten into video sharing. Have students in your university created a "Happy" video and placed it on YouTube or Facebook?

Where to Say It: Branded Entertainment

Today more and more marketers rely on **product placements**, also known as **branded entertainment** and **embedded marketing**, to grab the attention of consumers who tune out traditional ad messages as fast as they see them. All of these terms refer to paid placement of brands within entertainment venues including movies, TV shows, videogames, novels, and even retail settings.

Is branded entertainment a solid strategy? The idea is that when consumers see a popular celebrity who uses a specific brand in their favorite movie or TV program, they might develop a more positive attitude toward that brand. Successful brand placements include the Harley-Davidson motorcycles characters rode in FX's popular *Sons of Anarchy* show and the opening of a Subway restaurant in NBC's *Community*. And from 2001 to 2013, AT&T's name came up every time viewers were asked to vote on their favorite *American Idol* contestants.[36]

Beyond movies and TV shows, what better way to promote to the video generation than through brand placements in video games? The industry calls this technique **advergaming**. If you are a video game hound, watch for placements of real-life brands such as the Audi R7S Sportback in *Forza Motorsport 5* or the Nissan Leaf electric car in Gran Turismo. Auto marketers aren't the only ones that place their products in video games, however. All told, the in-game advertising industry is worth about $2.8 billion annually. Nissan alone spent $500,000 on advergaming in 2013, about 25 percent of its overall advertising budget.[37]

Branded entertainment on the Internet takes the form of **native advertising** in which marketing material mimics or resembles the normal content of the website that it is posted on. Even though the label "sponsored content" is placed (inconspicuously) on the ad, consumers may notice. Nationwide, for example, a regular sponsor of AMC's *Mad Men* series, aired a special commercial designed to resemble programming in which the chief marketing officer (CMO) of Nationwide discusses the company's advertising history. In the commercial, the CMO refers to a 1964 memo that resulted in the Nationwide slogan changing from "In service with the People" to "The man from Nationwide is on your side," later shortened to "Nationwide is on your side."[38]

Where to Say It: Support Media

While marketers (and consumers) normally think of advertising as mass-media messages, in reality many of the ads we see today show up in our homes, our workplaces, and public venues like restroom walls, on signs that trail behind airplanes, or in movies and TV programs. **Support media** reach people who may not have been exposed to mass-media advertising, and these platforms also support the messages traditional media delivers. Here we'll look at some of the more important support media advertisers use.

- *Directory advertising* is the most "down-to-earth," information-focused advertising medium. In 1883, a printer in Wyoming ran out of white paper while printing part of a telephone book, so he substituted yellow paper instead. Today, the Yellow Pages, including the online Yellow Pages, posts revenues of more than $16 billion in the U.S. and over $45 billion globally.[39] Often consumers look through directories just before they are ready to buy.

- **Out-of-home media** includes outdoor advertising (billboards and signs), transit advertising (signs placed inside and/or outside buses, taxis, trains, train stations, and airports), and other types of messages that reach people in public places. In recent years, outdoor advertising has pushed the technology envelope with **digital signage** that enables the source to change the message at will. Swedish carmaker Volvo placed interactive digital signs for its new V40 model at train and bus stops throughout the U.K. The signed teased, "Do you want to know more about yourself?" and let passersby use the touch screen to customize their own V40.[40] Of course, many consumers dislike out-of-home media, especially outdoor advertising, because they feel it is unattractive.

branded entertainment (also known as embedded marketing or product placements)
A form of advertising in which marketers integrate products into entertainment venues.

advergaming
Brand placements in video games.

native advertising
An execution strategy that mimics the content of the website where the message appears

support media
Media such as directories or out-of-home media that may be used to reach people who are not reached by mass-media advertising.

out-of-home media
Communication media that reach people in public places.

digital signage
Out-of-home media that use digital technology to change the message at will.

place-based media
Advertising media that transmit messages in public places, such as doctors' offices and airports, where certain types of people congregate.

media schedule
The plan that specifies the exact media to use and when to use it.

reach
The percentage of the target market that will be exposed to the media vehicle.

- **Place-based media**, like CNN's Airport Channel, transmit messages to "captive audiences" in public places, such airport waiting areas. The Airport Channel, which appears at more than 2,000 gates and other viewing areas in 50 major U.S. airports, offers on-the-go news and entertainment.[41] Similar place-based video screens are now in thousands of shops, offices, and health clubs across the country, including stores like Best Buy, Foot Locker, and Target. The Walmart Smart Network reaches more than 7.9 million consumers each week, with monitors in high-traffic marketing zones, such as checkout aisles or electronics.[42]

- And now, some retailers can even follow you around the store to deliver more up-close-and-personal messages: *RFID* technology (radio frequency identification) uses tiny sensors embedded in packages or store aisles to track customers as they pass. An unsuspecting shopper might hear a beep to remind him that he just passed his family's favorite peanut butter.[43] You're not paranoid; they really *are* watching you!

When and How Often to Say It: Media Scheduling

After choosing the advertising media, the planner then creates a **media schedule** that specifies the exact media the campaign will use as well as when and how often the message should appear. Figure 13.9 shows a hypothetical media schedule for the promotion of a new video game. Note that much of the advertising reaches its target audience in the months just before Christmas and that much of the expensive TV budget focuses on advertising during specials just prior to the holiday season.

The media schedule outlines the planner's best estimate of which media (TV or magazines for example) will be most effective to attain the advertising objective(s) and which specific media vehicles (TV shows such as Breaking Bad or the Big Bank Theory) will do the most effective job. The media planner considers qualitative factors, such as the match between the demographic and psychographic profile of a target audience and the people a media vehicle reaches, the advertising patterns of competitors, and the capability of a medium to adequately convey the desired information. The planner must also consider factors such as the compatibility of the product with editorial content. For example, viewers might not respond well to a serious commercial about preventing animal cruelty that tugs at one's heartstrings while they watch a "fun" show like *Keeping Up with the Kardashians*.

After deciding where and when to advertise, the planner must decide how often he or she wants to send the message. What time of day? And what overall pattern will the advertising follow?

A *continuous schedule* maintains a steady stream of advertising throughout the year. This is most appropriate for products that we buy on a regular basis, such as shampoo or bread. A *pulsing schedule* varies the amount of advertising throughout the year based on when the product is likely to be in demand. A suntan lotion might advertise year-round but

Figure 13.9 *Snapshot* | Media Schedule for a Video Game

Media planning includes decisions on where, when, and how much advertising to do. A media schedule, such as this one for a video game, shows the plan visually.

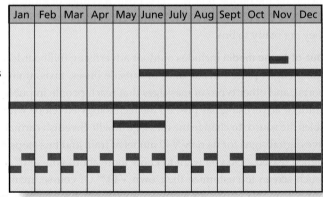

Metrics Moment

Media planners use a number of quantitative factors to develop the media schedule. **Reach** is the percentage of the target market that will be exposed to the media vehicle at least once during a given period of time, usually four weeks. For example, if the target market includes 100 million adults age 18 and over and a specific TV program has an audience that includes 5 million adults in this age-group, the program has a reach of 5. Developing a media plan with high reach is particularly important for widely used products when the message needs to get to as many consumers as possible. **Frequency** is simply the average number of times that an individual or a household will be exposed to the message. High levels of frequency are important for products that are complex or those that are targeted to relatively small markets for which multiple exposures to the message are necessary to make an impact.

Gross rating points (GRPs) are a measure of the quantity of media included in the media plan. Just as we talk about buying 15 gallons of gas or a pound of coffee, media planners talk about a media schedule that includes the purchase of 250 GRPs of radio and 700 GRPs of TV.

GRPs are calculated by multiplying a media vehicle's rating by the number of planned ad insertions. If 30 percent of a target audience watches *American Idol* and you place 12 ads on the show during a four-week period, you buy 360 GRPs of that show (30 × 12).

Although some media vehicles deliver more of your target audience, they may not be cost efficient. More people will see a commercial aired during the Super Bowl than during a 3:00 A.M. rerun of a Tarzan movie. But the advertiser could probably run late-night commercials every night for a year for less than the cost of one 30-second Super Bowl spot. To compare the *relative* cost-effectiveness of different media and of spots run on different vehicles in the same medium, media planners use a measure they call **cost per thousand (CPM)**. This figure reflects the cost to deliver a message to 1,000 people.

Assume that the cost of each 30-second commercial on *The Big Bang Theory* is $400,000, but the number of target audience members the show reaches is 20 million, or 20,000 units of 1,000 (in CPM, everything is broken down into units of 1,000). Hence, the CPM of *The Big Bang Theory* is $400,000/20,000 = $20 CPM. Compare this to the cost of advertising in *Fortune* magazine: A full-page four-color ad costs approximately $115,000, and the readership includes approximately 2 million members of our target audience, or 2,000 units of 1,000. Thus, the cost per thousand for *Fortune* is $115,000/2,000 = $57.50 CPM. As a result of this standardization to units of 1,000, you end up comparing "apples to apples," and the comparison reveals that *The Big Bang Theory*, while having a much higher total cost, actually is a much better buy!

Apply the Metrics

You have a choice of commercials during *NCIS* or ads in the *Wall Street Journal*. *NCIS* reaches 30 million members of the target audience, while *WSJ* reaches 15 million members. CBS is quoting you $500,000 per 30-second spot; *WSJ* charges $200,000 for a full-page four-color ad.

1. Calculate the CPM for each option.
2. Which one is the better financial deal?

---

more heavily during the summer months. *Flighting* is an extreme form of pulsing, in which advertising appears in short, intense bursts alternating with periods of little to no activity.

Step 6: Evaluate the Advertising

John Wanamaker, a famous Philadelphia retailer, once complained, "I am certain that half the money I spend on advertising is completely wasted. The trouble is, I don't know which half."[44] Now that we've seen how advertising is created and executed, let's step back and see how we decide if it's working.

There's no doubt that a lot of advertising is ineffective. With so many messages competing for the attention of frazzled customers, it's especially important for firms to evaluate their efforts to increase the impact of their messages. How can they do that?

frequency
The average number of times a person in the target group will be exposed to the message.

gross rating points (GRPs)
A measure used for comparing the effectiveness of different media vehicles: average reach × frequency.

cost per thousand (CPM)
A measure used to compare the relative cost-effectiveness of different media vehicles that have different exposure rates; the cost to deliver a message to 1,000 people or homes.

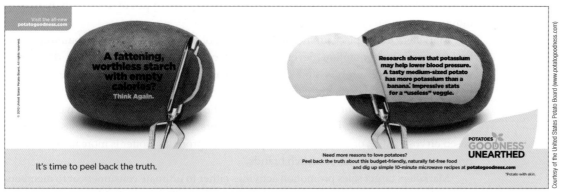

A communication objective may focus on educating consumers about a product like potatoes. The sponsor can measure the effectiveness of a campaign by assessing people's knowledge before and after the messages have run to determine if they had any impact.

posttesting
Research conducted on consumers' responses to actual advertising messages they have seen or heard.

Posttesting means conducting research on consumers' responses to advertising messages they have seen or heard (as opposed to *pretesting*, which, as we've seen, collects reactions to messages *before* they're actually placed in "the real world"). Ironically, many creative ads that are quirky or even bizarre make an advertising agency look good within the industry (and on the résumé of the creative director) but are ultimately unsuccessful because they don't communicate what the company needs to say about the product itself. Three ways to measure the impact of an advertisement are *unaided recall*, *aided recall*, and *attitudinal measures*:

unaided recall
A research technique conducted by telephone survey or personal interview that asks whether a person remembers seeing an ad during a specified period without giving the person the name of the brand.

1. **Unaided recall** tests by telephone survey or personal interview whether a person remembers seeing an ad during a specified period without giving the person the name of the brand.

2. An **aided recall** test uses the name of the brand and sometimes other clues to prompt answers. For example, a researcher might show a group of consumers a list of brands and ask them to choose which items they have seen advertised within the past week.

aided recall
A research technique that uses clues to prompt answers from people about advertisements they might have seen.

attitudinal measures
A research technique that probes a consumer's beliefs or feelings about a product before and after being exposed to messages about it.

3. **Attitudinal measures** probe a bit more deeply by testing consumers' beliefs or feelings about a product before and after they are exposed to messages about it. If, for example, Pepsi's messages about "freshness-dating" make enough consumers believe that the freshness of soft drinks is important, marketers can consider the advertising campaign successful.

4 Sales Promotion

OBJECTIVE
Explain what sales promotion is and describe the different types of consumer and B2B sales promotion activities.
(pp. 452–457)

Sometimes when you walk through your student union on campus, you might get assaulted by a parade of people eager for you to enter a contest, taste a new candy bar, or take home a free T-shirt with a local bank's name on it. These are examples of **sales promotion**, programs that marketers design to build interest in or encourage purchase of a good or service during a specified period.[45]

sales promotion
Programs designed to build interest in or encourage purchase of a product during a specified period.

How does sales promotion differ from advertising? Both are paid promotion activities from identifiable sponsors to change consumer behavior or attitudes. Often, a traditional advertising medium actually publicizes the sales promotion, as when Applebee's restaurant used TV advertising to tell military personnel and veterans about its free entree offer for Veterans Day.[46] But while marketers carefully craft advertising campaigns to create long-term positive feelings about a brand, company, or store, sales promotions are more useful if the firm has an *immediate* objective, such as bolstering sales for a brand quickly or encouraging consumers to try a new product. Indeed, the purpose of many types of sales promotion is to induce action by the consumer or business buyer.

Marketers today place an increasing amount of their total marketing communication budget into sales promotion. Several reasons account for this increase. First, due to the growth of very large grocery store chains and mass merchandisers such as Walmart, there has been a shift in power in the channels. These large chains can pressure manufacturers to provide deals and discounts. A second reason for the growth in sales promotion is declining consumer brand loyalty. This means that consumers are more likely to purchase products based on cost, value, or convenience. A special sales promotion offer is more likely to cause price-conscious customers to switch brands.

Marketers target sales promotion activities either to ultimate consumers or to members of the channel, such as retailers that sell their products. Thus, we divide sales promotion into two major categories: *consumer-oriented sales promotion* and *trade-oriented sales promotion*.

Table 13.3 | Consumer Sales Promotion Techniques: A Sampler

Technique	Description	Example
Coupons (newspaper, magazine, in the mail, on product packages, in-store, and on the Internet)	Certificates for money off on selected products, often with an expiration date, are used to encourage product trial.	Crest offers $5 off its WhiteStrips.
Price-off packs	Specially marked packages offer a product at a discounted price.	Tide laundry detergent is offered in a specially marked box for 50 cents off.
Rebates/refunds	Purchasers receive a cash reimbursement when they submit proofs of purchase.	Uniroyal offers a $40 mail-in rebate for purchasers of four new Tiger Paw tires.
Continuity/loyalty programs	Consumers are rewarded for repeat purchases through points that lead to reduced price or free merchandise.	Airlines offer frequent fliers free flights for accumulated points; a carwash offers consumers a half-price wash after purchasing 10 washes.
Special/bonus packs	Additional amount of the product is given away with purchase; it rewards users.	Maxell provides 10 free blank CDs with the purchase of a pack of 50.
Contests/sweepstakes	Offers consumers the chance to win cash or merchandise. Sweepstakes winners are determined strictly by chance. Contests require some competitive activity, such as a game of skill.	Publisher's Clearing House announces its zillionth sweepstakes.
Premiums: Free premiums include in-pack, on-pack, near pack, or in-the-mail premiums; consumers pay for self-liquidating premiums	A consumer gets a free gift or low-cost item when a product is bought; reinforces product image and rewards users.	A free makeup kit comes with the purchase of $20 worth of Clinique products.
Samples (delivered by direct mail, in newspapers and magazines door-to-door, on or in product packages, and in-store)	Delivering an actual or trial-size product to consumers in order to generate trial usage of a new product.	A free small bottle of Clairol Herbal Essences shampoo arrives in the mail.

We'll talk about the consumer type first, after which we'll discuss trade promotion. You'll see some examples of common consumer-oriented sales promotions in Table 13.3.

Sales Promotion Directed toward Consumers

One of the reasons for an increase in sales promotion is because it works. For consumer sales promotion, the major reason for this is that most promotions temporarily change the price/value relationships. A coupon for 50 cents off the price of a bottle of ketchup reduces the price, while a special "25 percent more" jar of peanuts increases the value. And if you get a free hairbrush when you buy a bottle of shampoo, this also increases the value. As shown in 📷 Figure 13.10, we generally classify consumer sales promotions as either price-based or attention-getting promotions.

Price-Based Consumer Sales Promotion

Many sales promotions target consumers where they live—their wallets. They emphasize *short-term price reductions* or *rebates* that encourage people to choose a brand—at least during the deal period. Price-based consumer promotions, however, have a downside similar to trade promotions that involve a price break. If a company uses them too frequently, this "trains" its customers to purchase the product at only the lower promotional price. Price-based consumer sales promotion includes the following:

- *Coupons:* Try to pick up any Sunday newspaper without spilling some coupons. These certificates, redeemable for money off a purchase, are the most common price promotion. Indeed, they are the most popular form of sales promotion overall. Companies

Figure 13.10 📷 *Snapshot* | Types of Consumer Sales Promotions

Consumer sales promotions are generally classified as price-based or attention-getting promotions.

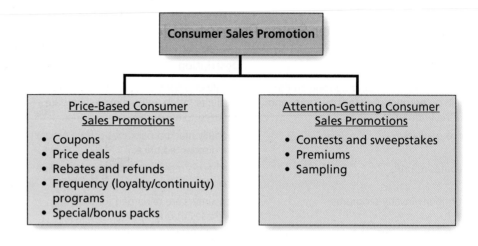

rebates
Sales promotions that allow the customer to recover part of the product's cost from the manufacturer.

frequency programs
Consumer sales promotion programs that offer a discount or free product for multiple purchases over time; also referred to as loyalty or continuity programs.

distribute billions of them annually in newspapers and magazines, in the mail, in stores, by e-mail, and through the Internet. Even industries such as pharmaceuticals that never tried this approach before now use it in a big way. This industry offers coupons that customers can redeem for free initial supplies of drugs in hopes that patients will ask their physician for the specific brand instead of a competing brand or a more economical generic version.[47]

- *Price deals, refunds, and rebates:* In addition to coupons, manufacturers often offer a temporary price reduction to stimulate sales. This price deal may be printed on the package itself, or it may be a price-off flag or banner on the store shelf. Alternatively, companies may offer refunds or **rebates** that allow the consumer to recover part of the purchase price via mail-ins to the manufacturer.

- *Frequency (loyalty/continuity) programs:* **Frequency programs**, also called *loyalty* or *continuity programs*, offer a consumer a discount or a free product for multiple purchases over time. Mike Gunn, former vice president of marketing at American Airlines, is widely credited with developing this concept in the early 1980s when he coined the phrase "frequent flyer" miles. Of course, all the other airlines were quick to follow suit, as were a host of other firms, including retailers, auto rental companies, hotels, restaurants—you name it, and they have a customer loyalty program.

- *Special/bonus packs:* Another form of price promotion involves giving the shopper more product instead of lowering the price.[48] How nice to go to Walgreens and find the normal 16-ounce jar of Planters peanuts made larger to contain four ounces or 25 percent more free! A special pack also can be in the form of a unique package, such as a reusable decorator dispenser for hand soap.

Attention-Getting Consumer Sales Promotions

Attention-getting consumer promotions stimulate interest in a company's products. Some typical types of attention-getting promotions include the following:

- *Contests and sweepstakes:* According to their legal definitions, a contest is a test of skill, while a sweepstakes is based on chance.
  - To tap into a "younger, hotter" audience, Perrier, the number one sparkling water in the world, hosted an immersive Secret Place sweepstakes, where contestants had to find clues to locate a secret bottle of Perrier that unlocked their ticket into the sweepstakes. The prize? An invite to one of five global megaparty destinations.[49]

- In an effort to launch the new AXE Apollo brand of men's grooming products and do something that's epic, the AXE Apollo Big Game Sweepstakes was designed to send 22 everyday people up to 64 miles into space where they would be weightless for up to six minutes. All contestants had to do was plead their case about why they wanted to become astronauts. Popular vote would determine the top 100 finalists, and both the brand and the transport company would determine the winners.[50]

- *Premiums:* **Premiums** are items you get free when you buy a product. General Mills Cheerios brand cereal has given away over 8 million bilingual children's books inside Cheerios boxes in the past 11 years.[51]

Oscar Mayer created an eye-catching promotion with its Weinermobile—guaranteed to draw attention from hot dog lovers.

- *Sampling:* How many starving college students at one time or another have managed to scrape together an entire meal by scooping up free food samples at their local grocery store? Some stores, like Publix and Sam's Club, actually promote Saturdays as sampling day in their advertising. **Product sampling** encourages people to try a product by distributing trial-size and sometimes regular-size versions in stores in public places such as student unions or through the mail. Companies like Procter & Gamble, Unilever, S.C. Johnson, and GlaxoSmithKline are readily taking advantage of websites such as Freesamples .com and Startsampling.com that distribute the firms' samples and then follow up with consumer-satisfaction surveys.

premiums
Items offered free to people who have purchased a product.

product sampling
Distributing free trial-size versions of a product to consumers.

Trade Sales Promotion: Targeting the B2B Customer

As we said, sales promotions also target the B2B customer—located somewhere within the supply chain. Such entities are traditionally referred to as "the trade." Hence, **trade sales promotions** focus on members of the supply chain, which include distribution channel members that we discussed in Chapter 11.

Trade promotions take one of two forms: (1) those designed as discounts and deals and (2) those designed to increase company visibility. Let's take a look at both types of trade promotions in more detail. To help you follow along, 📷 Figure 13.11 portrays several of the most important types of trade sales promotion approaches, and Table 13.4 provides more details about each approach. You will note that some of the techniques, although targeted primarily to the trade, also appeal to consumers.

Discount Promotions

Discount promotions (deals) reduce the cost of the product to the distributor or retailer or help defray its advertising expenses. Firms design these promotions to encourage stores to stock the item and be sure it gets a lot of attention. Marketers offer these discounts for a limited period of time and should not be confused with discounts that are part of the pricing strategy and are offered long term.

Figure 13.11 📷 *Snapshot* | Trade Sales Promotions

Trade sales promotions come in a variety of forms. Some are designed as discounts and deals for channel members, and some are designed to increase industry visibility.

Table 13.4 | Characteristics of Trade Sales Promotion Approaches

Technique	Primary Target	Description	Example
Allowances, discounts, and deals	Trade	Retailers or other organizational customers receive discounts for quantity purchases or for providing special merchandising assistance.	Retailers get a discount for using a special Thanksgiving display unit for Pepperidge Farm Stuffing Mix.
Co-op advertising	Trade and consumers	Manufacturers pay part of the cost of advertising by retailers who feature the manufacturer's product in their ads.	Toro pays half of the cost of Brad's Hardware Store newspaper advertising that features Toro lawn mowers.
Trade shows	Trade	Many manufacturers showcase their products to attendees.	The National Kitchen and Bath Association trade shows allow manufacturers to display their latest wares to owners of kitchen and bath remodeling stores.
Promotional products	Trade and consumers	A company builds awareness and reinforces its image by giving out "premiums" with its name on them.	Coors distributors provide bar owners with highly sought-after "Coors Light" neon signs. Caterpillar gives customers caps with the Caterpillar logo.
Point-of-purchase displays	Trade and consumers	In-store exhibits attract consumers' attention. Many point-of-purchase displays also serve a merchandising function.	The Behr's paint display in Home Depot stores allow consumers to select from over 1,600 colors, including 160 Disney colors.
Incentive programs	Trade	A prize is offered to employees who meet a prespecified sales goal or who are top performers during a given period.	Mary Kay cosmetics awards distinctive pink cars to its top-selling representatives.
Push money	Trade	A particular type of incentive program in which salespeople are given a bonus for selling a specific manufacturer's product.	A retail salesperson at a cosmetics counter gets $5 every time she sells a bottle of Glow perfume by JLo.

trade sales promotions
Promotions that focus on members of the "trade," which include distribution channel members, such as retail salespeople or wholesale distributors, that a firm must work with in order to sell its products.

merchandising allowance
Reimburses the retailer for in-store support of the product.

case allowance
A discount to the retailer or wholesaler based on the volume of product ordered.

One form of trade promotion is a short-term *price break*. A manufacturer can reduce a channel partner's costs with a sales promotion that discounts its products. For example, a manufacturer can offer a **merchandising allowance** to reimburse the retailer for in-store support of a product, such as when a store features an off-shelf display for a brand. Another way in which a manufacturer can reduce a channel partner's cost is with a **case allowance** that provides a discount to the retailer or wholesaler during a set period based on the sales volume of a product the retailer or wholesaler orders from the manufacturer.

However, allowances and deals have a downside. As with all sales promotion activities, the manufacturer expects these to be of limited duration, after which the distribution channel partner will again pay full price for the items. Unfortunately, some channel members engage in a practice the industry calls *forward buying*: They purchase large quantities of the product during a discount period, warehouse them, and don't buy them again until the manufacturer offers another discount. Some large retailers and wholesalers take this to an extreme when they engage in *diverting*. This describes an ethically questionable practice where the retailer buys the product at the discounted promotional price and warehouses it. Then, after the promotion has expired, the retailer sells the hoarded inventory to other retailers at a price that is lower than the manufacturer's nondiscounted price but high enough to turn a profit. Obviously, both forward buying and diverting go against the manufacturer's intent in offering the sales promotion.

Co-Op Advertising

Another type of trade allowance is **co-op advertising**. These programs offer to pay a portion, usually 50 percent, of the cost of any retailer advertising that features the manufacturer's product. Co-op advertising is a win-win situation for manufacturers because most local media vehicles offer lower rates to local businesses than to national advertisers. Both the retailer and the manufacturer pay for only part of the advertising, plus the manufacturer gets the lower rate. Normally, the amount available to a retailer for co-op advertising is limited to a percentage of the purchases the retailer makes during a year from the manufacturer.

co-op advertising
A sales promotion where the manufacturer and the retailer share the cost.

Sales Promotion Designed to Increase Industry Visibility

Other types of trade sales promotions increase the visibility of a manufacturer's products to channel partners within the industry. Whether it is an elaborate exhibit at a trade show or a coffee mug with the firm's logo it gives away to channel partners, these aim to keep the company's name topmost when distributors and retailers decide which products to stock and push. These forms of sales promotion include the following:

- *Trade shows:* The thousands of industry **trade shows** in the U.S. and around the world each year are major vehicles for manufacturers and service providers to show off their product lines to wholesalers and retailers. Usually, large trade shows are held in big convention centers where many companies set up elaborate exhibits to show their products, give away samples, distribute product literature, and troll for new business contacts. Today, we also see more and more online trade shows that allow potential customers to preview a manufacturer's products remotely.

trade shows
Events at which many companies set up elaborate exhibits to show their products, give away samples, distribute product literature, and troll for new business contacts.

- *Promotional products:* We have all seen them: coffee mugs, visors, T-shirts, ball caps, key chains, and even more expensive items, such as golf bags, beach chairs, and luggage emblazoned with a company's logo. They are examples of **promotional products**. Unlike licensed merchandise we buy in stores, sponsors give away these goodies to build awareness for their organization or specific brands.

promotional products
Goodies such as coffee mugs, T-shirts, and magnets given away to build awareness for a sponsor. Some freebies are distributed directly to consumers and business customers; others are intended for channel partners, such as retailers and vendors.

- *Point-of-purchase displays:* **Point-of-purchase (POP) materials** include signs, mobiles, banners, shelf ads, floor ads, lights, plastic reproductions of products, permanent and temporary merchandising displays, in-store TV, and shopping card advertisements. Marketers use POP displays because it keeps the name of the brand in front of the consumer, reinforces mass-media advertising, calls attention to other sales promotion offers, and stimulates impulse purchasing. Generally, manufacturers must give retailers a promotion allowance for use of POP materials. For retailers, the POP displays are useful if they encourage sales and increase revenues for the brand. Many are invaluable aids for shoppers. How would you like to buy paint for your bedroom without those wonderful paint displays with hundreds of color cards to take home and compare with the color of your favorite purple hippopotamus?

point-of-purchase (POP) displays
In-store displays and signs.

- *Incentive programs:* In addition to motivating distributors and customers, some promotions light a fire under the firm's own sales force. These incentives, or **push money**, may come in the form of cash bonuses, trips, or other prizes. Mary Kay Corporation—the in-home party plan cosmetics seller—is famous for giving its more productive distributors pink cars to reward their efforts. Another cosmetics marketer that uses a retail store selling model, Clinique, provides push money to department store cosmeticians to demonstrate and sell the full line of Clinique products. This type of incentive has the nickname *SPIF* for "sales promotion incentive funds."

push money
A bonus paid by a manufacturer to a salesperson, customer, or distributor for selling its product.

Here's my choice...

Real People, Real Choices

Why do you think Marc choose option 1?

1 Option **2** Option **3** Option

How It Worked Out at Brownstein Group

The client agreed with Marc, as its account executives felt their first priority was to clearly define the brand in the wake of the attacks by the rival. Marc's agency rolled out an advertising campaign that used an educational approach to better explain what the new brand was and why it should be important to consumer. Ads appeared in print, outdoor, online, and on radio. As a result of this campaign, which "punched the bully in the nose," the attack ads from the competition soon subsided.

Refer back to **page 420** for Marc's story

MyMarketingLab™

Go to **mymktlab.com** to complete the problems marked with this icon ⭐ as well as additional Marketing Metrics questions only available in MyMarketingLab.

Objective Summary ➡ Key Terms ➡ Apply

CHAPTER 13
Study Map

---

1. Objective Summary (pp. 422–428)

Understand the communication process and the traditional promotion mix.

Firms use promotion and other forms of marketing communication to inform consumers about new products, remind them of familiar products, persuade them to choose one alternative over another, and build strong customer relationships. Recognizing that consumers come in contact with a brand at many different touch points, firms today often practice IMC to reach consumers through a multichannel promotional strategy. Because marketers understand the impact of word-of-mouth communication, they are likely to supplement the traditional one-to-many communication model with a newer many-to-many model and also talk one to one with consumers.

The traditional communication model includes a message source that creates an idea, encodes the idea into a message, and transmits the message through some medium. The message is delivered to the receiver, who decodes the message and may provide feedback to the source. Anything that interferes with the communication is called "noise."

The promotion mix refers to the marketing communication elements that the marketer controls. Advertising, sales promotion, and public relations use the mass media to reach many consumers at a single time while personal selling and direct marketing allow marketers to communicate with consumers one-on-one.

Key Terms

integrated marketing communication (IMC), p. 422

multichannel promotional strategy, p. 423

word-of-mouth communication, p. 424

2. Objective Summary (pp. 428–434)

Describe the steps in traditional and multichannel promotional planning.

Recognizing the importance of communicating with a variety of stakeholders who influence the target market, marketers begin the promotional planning process by identifying the target audience(s). Next, they establish communication objectives. Objectives often are to create awareness, inform the market, create desire, encourage purchase and trial, and/or build loyalty.

Marketers develop promotion budgets from rules of thumb such as the percentage-of-sales method, the competitive-parity method, and the objective-task method. They then decide on a push or a pull strategy and allocate monies from the total budget to various elements of the promotion mix.

Next, marketers design the promotion mix by deciding how they can use advertising, sales promotion, personal selling, and public relations most effectively to communicate with different target audiences. The final step is to evaluate the effectiveness of the communication program in order to determine whether the plan is working.

Marketers today often opt for multichannel promotional strategies where they combine traditional advertising, sales promotion, and public relations activities with social media and online buzz-building activities. Multichannel strategies boost the effectiveness of either online or offline strategies used alone and allow marketers to repeat their messages across various channels, thus strengthening brand awareness and providing more opportunities to convert customers.

Key Terms

3. Objective Summary (pp. 434–452)

Tell what advertising is, describe the major types of advertising, discuss some of the major criticisms of advertising, and describe the process of developing an advertising campaign and how marketers evaluate advertising.

Advertising is nonpersonal communication from an identified sponsor using mass media to persuade or influence an audience. Advertising informs and reminds consumers and creates consumer desire. Product advertising seeks to persuade consumers to choose a specific product or brand. Institutional advertising is used to develop an image for an organization or company (corporate advertising), to express opinions (advocacy advertising), or to support a cause (public service advertising). Retail and local advertising informs customers about where to shop. Most firms rely on the services of advertising agencies to create successful advertising campaigns. Full-service agencies include account management, creative services, research and marketing services, and media planning, while limited-service agencies provide only one or a few services.

User-generated content (UGC), also known as consumer-generated media (CGM), includes online consumer comments, opinions, advice, consumer-to-consumer discussions, reviews, photos, images, videos, podcasts and webcasts, and product-related stories available to other consumers through digital technology. To take advantage of this phenomenon, some marketers encourage consumers to contribute their own do-it-yourself (DIY) ads. Crowdsourcing is a practice in which firms outsource marketing activities (such as selecting an ad) to a community of users, that is, a crowd.

Advertising has been criticized for being manipulative, for being deceitful and untruthful, for being offensive and in bad taste, for creating and perpetuating stereotypes, and for causing people to buy things they don't really need. While some advertising may justify some of these criticisms, most advertisers seek to provide honest ads that don't offend the markets they seek to attract.

Development of an advertising campaign begins with understanding the target audiences and developing objectives for the message and the ad budget. To create the ads, the agency develops a creative strategy that is summarized in a creative brief. To come up with finished ads, they must decide on the appeal, the format, the tonality and the creative tactics and techniques. Pretesting advertising before placing it in the media prevents costly mistakes.

Media planning gets a message to a target audience in the most effective way. The media planner must decide whether to place ads in traditional mass media or in digital media, including website advertising, mobile advertising, and video sharing, variously referred to as owned media, paid or bought media, and earned media. Product placements, a type of branded entertainment, integrate products into movies, TV shows, video games, novels, and even retail settings. Support media include directories, out-of-home media, and place-based media. A media schedule specifies the exact media the campaign will use and when and how often the message should appear.

The final step in any advertising campaign is to evaluate its effectiveness. Marketers evaluate advertising through posttesting. Posttesting research may include aided or unaided recall tests that examine whether the message had an influence on the target market.

Key Terms

advertising, p. 434

authenticated streaming, p. 434

product advertising, p. 411

institutional advertising, p. 435

corporate advertising, p. 435

advocacy advertising, p. 435

public service advertisements (PSAs), p. 435

advertising campaign, p. 435

limited-service agency, p. 436

full-service agency, p. 436

account executive, p. 436

account planner, p. 436

creative services, p. 436

research and marketing services, p. 436

media planner, p. 436

user-generated content (UGC) or consumer-generated media (CGM), p. 436

do-it-yourself (DIY) ads, p. 437

crowdsourcing, p. 437

corrective advertising, p. 437

puffery, p. 438

greenwashing, p. 438

pay-per-gaze, p. 439

creative strategy, p. 440

creative brief, p. 440

advertising appeal, p. 441

unique selling proposition (USP), p. 441

reminder advertising, p. 441

teaser or mystery advertising, p. 441

execution format, p. 441

tonality, p. 442

jingles, p. 443

slogans, p. 443

pretesting, p. 443

media planning, p. 443

digital media, p. 444

owned media, p. 444

paid media, p. 447

earned media, p. 447

banners, p. 447

buttons, p. 447

pop-up ad, p. 447

search engines, p. 447

spam, p. 447

permission marketing, p. 447

mobile advertising, p. 448

video sharing, p. 448

vlogs, p. 448

branded entertainment (also known as embedded marketing or product placements), p. 449

advergaming, p. 449

native advertising, p. 449

support media, p. 449

out-of-home media, p. 449

digital signage, p. 449

place-based media, p. 450

media schedule, p. 450

reach, p. 451

frequency, p. 451

gross rating points (GRPs), p. 451

cost per thousand (CPM), p. 451

posttesting, p. 452

sales promotion, p. 452

unaided recall, p. 452

aided recall, p. 452

attitudinal measures, p. 452

4. Objective Summary (pp. 452–457)

Explain what sales promotion is and describe the different types of consumer and B2B sales promotion activities.

Sales promotions are programs that marketers design to build interest in or encourage purchase of a good or service during a specified period. Marketers target sales promotion activities either to ultimate consumers or to members of the channel such as retailers that sell their products. Price-based consumer sales promotion include coupons, price deals, refunds, and rebates, frequency (loyalty/continuity) programs, and special/bonus packs. Attention-getting consumer sales promotions include contests and sweepstakes, premiums, and sampling.

Trade sales promotions come in a variety of forms. Some are designed as discounts and deals, including co-op advertising, for channel members, and some are designed to increase industry visibility. Approaches aimed at increasing industry visibility include trade shows, promotional products, point-of-purchase (POP) displays, incentive programs, and push money.

Key Terms

sales promotion, p. 452

rebates, p. 454

frequency programs, p. 454

premiums, p. 455

product sampling, p. 455

trade sales promotions, p. 455

merchandising allowance, p. 456

case allowance, p. 456

co-op advertising, p. 457

trade shows, p. 457

promotional products, p. 457

point-of-purchase (POP) displays, p. 457

push money, p. 457

Chapter **Questions** and **Activities**

Concepts: Test Your Knowledge

13-1. Describe the four key roles performed as part of the marketing communication process.

13-2. What are the three models of marketing communication?

13-3. What is noise in the communication process, and how can it be a problem for marketers?

13-4. Why is it necessary for a marketer to "push" consumers toward brand loyalty?

13-5. What are the three decisions necessary in setting a budget for marketing communications?

13-6. Distinguish between the competitive-parity and the bottom-up budgeting techniques.

13-7. What are the key purposes of institutional advertising, and what are the three different forms of it?

13-8. Firms may seek the help of full-service or limited-service advertising agencies for their advertising. Describe each.

13-9. What is consumer-generated advertising, and why is it growing in importance? What is crowdsourcing, and how is it used in advertising?

13-10. What are some of the major criticisms of advertising? What is corrective advertising? What is puffery?

13-11. Describe the steps in developing an advertising campaign. What is a creative brief? What is meant by the appeal, execution format, tonality, and creative tactics used in an ad campaign?

13-12. What is media planning? What are the strengths and weaknesses of traditional media, that is, TV, radio, newspapers, and magazines?

13-13. What is digital media? What are owned, paid, and earned media? How do marketers use website advertising, mobile advertising, and video sharing in their digital media activities?

13-14. How do marketers use branded entertainment and support media, such as directories, out-of-home media, and place-based media, to communicate with consumers?

13-15. How do marketers pretest their ads? How do they posttest ads?

13-16. What is media planning? How do media planners use reach, frequency, gross rating points, and cost per thousand in developing effective media schedules?

13-17. What is sales promotion? Explain some of the different types of consumer sales promotions marketers frequently use.

13-18. Explain some of the different types of trade sales promotions marketers frequently use.

Activities: Apply What You've Learned

⭐ **13-19.** *Creative Homework/Short Project* You work in the marketing department at your local blood center. Because donations are down, it's important that you reach out to the community for blood donor volunteers. Using the communication model, explain how you will create and transmit this message to the consumer. Then describe how you will determine whether consumers successfully received this message.

⭐ **13-20.** *Creative Homework/Short Project* Assume you are the director of marketing for a firm that markets snack foods. You are developing a promotional plan. Develop suggestions for each of the following items.

   a. Marketing communication objectives
   b. A method for determining the communication budget
   c. The use of a push strategy or a pull strategy
   d. Elements of the traditional promotion mix you will use

13-21. *Creative Homework/Short Project* Your company has developed a new high-end hand cream, designed to noticeably soften hands and reduce the appearance of age spots and scars when used daily. Using the hierarchy of effects, develop communications objectives for your product for consumers who may be at each stage in the hierarchy. Make sure your objectives are specific.

13-22. *For Further Research (Individual)* More and more firms are engaged in multichannel promotional programs. You can learn about many of these by searching library or Internet sources. Some Internet sources that may be useful are the following:

Brandchannel.com
Adweek.com (*Adweek* magazine)
NYTimes.com (*New York Times*)
Adage.com (*Advertising Age* magazine)

Gather information on one or more multichannel promotional programs. Develop a report that describes the program(s) and makes suggestions for how it or they might be improved.

13-23. *Creative Homework/Short Project* As we discussed in this chapter, many consumers are highly critical of advertising. In order to better understand this, conduct a short survey of (1) your college classmates and (2) a different group of consumers, such as your parents and their friends. In the survey, ask the respondents about the criticisms of advertising discussed in this chapter, that is, that advertising (1) is manipulative, (2) is deceptive and untruthful, (3) is offensive and in bad taste, (4) creates and perpetuates stereotypes, and (5) causes people to buy things they don't really need. Be sure to ask respondents to give you examples of ads that they feel fall in these categories. Develop a report that summarizes your results and compares the attitudes of the two consumer groups.

13-24. *In Class, 10–25 Minutes for Teams* Assume that you are a member of the marketing department for a firm that produces several brands of snack foods. Your assignment is to develop recommendations for consumer and trade sales promotion activities for a new low-fat, low-calorie, high-protein snack food. Develop an outline of your recommendations for these sales promotions. In a role-playing situation, present and defend your recommendations to your boss.

13-25. *In Class, 10–25 Minutes for Teams* Timing is an important part of a sales promotion plan. Trade sales promotions must be properly timed to ensure channel members fully maximize the opportunity to sell your product. Assume that the introduction of the new snack food in question 13.24 is planned for April 1. Place the activities you recommended in question 13.25 onto a 12-month calendar of events. (Hint: The calendar needs to start *before* the product introduction.) In a role-playing situation, present your plan to your boss. Be sure to explain the reasons for your timing of each trade sales promotion element.

Apply Marketing Metrics

13-26. You learned that media planners use a variety of metrics to help in making decisions on what TV show or which magazines to include in their media plans. Two of these are gross rating points (GRPs) and cost per thousand (CPM).

Assume you are developing a media plan for a new brand of gourmet frozen meals. Your target market includes females ages 25 to 64. The table below lists six possible media buys you are considering for the media plan, along with some relevant information about each (Note that the numbers are fictitious, created for example purposes only). The plan is based on a four-week period:

a. Calculate the GRPs for each media buy based on the information given.
b. Calculate the CPM for each media buy.
c. Based on the cost of each buy, the reach or rating of each buy, and any qualitative factors (e.g., decision criteria beyond the numbers) that you believe are important, select the top three media buys that you would recommend.
d. Explain why you would select these three.

Media Vehicle	Rating	Cost per Ad or Insertion	Number of Insertions	CPM	GRPs for This Number of Insertions
Dancing with the Stars	30	$500,000	4 (one per weekly episode)		
Big Bang Theory	20	$400,000	4 (one per weekly episode)		
CBS Evening News	12	$150,000	20 (one per weeknight news program)		
Time magazine	5	$40,000	4 (one per weekly publication)		
Better Homes and Gardens magazine	12	$30,000	1 (one per monthly publication)		
USA Today	4	$10,000	12 (three ads per week)		

Choices: What Do You Think?

13-27. *Critical Thinking* Marketers need to carefully consider and identify their target audiences before framing any kind of marketing messages. Each stakeholder group is important, but some are more important than others. At the same time, each of the stakeholder groups needs specific types of messages delivered in specific ways in order for the message to be relevant to that group and to reach it. How do marketers tackle this critical process, and which of the many stakeholders are often considered to be the most important?

13-28. *Critical Thinking* With market opportunities and threats appearing and changing so quickly, is it desirable for a business to set its marketing budgets based on information that is bound to be out of date? Should budgets be flexible? What happens when something unexpected needs to be handled?

⭐ **13-29.** *Ethics Because* of concerns about the effectiveness of mass-media advertising, more and more firms are using product placements to put their product in front of consumers. But is this practice really ethical? Are consumers deceived when they see a can of Dr. Pepper on the table of Tony Stark's house in *Iron Man 2*? Does the average consumer believe the Dr. Pepper is there because it's the favorite soft drink of a TV or movie celebrity, or are most consumers savvy enough to recognize it as a paid product placement? Should the government regulate product placements, perhaps requiring TV programs and movies to inform consumers about the paid placements? Are consumers really harmed by such practices?

⭐ **13-30.** *Critical Thinking* Greenwashing is a practice in which companies promote their products as environmentally friendly when in truth the brand provides little ecological benefit. What are your thoughts on greenwashing? How much of a product should be environmentally friendly for it to be considered a truly green brand? Fifty percent? Eighty percent? Should the practice of greenwashing be regulated?

13-31. *Ethics* Firms are increasing their use of search engine marketing in which they pay search engines such as Google and Bing for priority position listings. Social media sites such as Twitter are generating revenue by offering to sell "search words" to firms so that their posting appears on top. Are such practices ethical? Are consumers being deceived when a firm pays for priority positioning?

13-32. *Critical Thinking* Companies sometimes teach consumers a "bad lesson" with the overuse of sales promotions. As a result, consumers expect the product always to be "on deal" or have a rebate available.

What are some examples of products for which this has occurred? How do you think companies can prevent this?

Miniproject: Learn by Doing

Miniproject 1

This miniproject is designed to help you understand how important word-of-mouth marketing is to consumers like yourself. Ask several of your classmates to participate in a focus group discussion about how they communicate with others about products. Some questions you might ask are the following:

a. What products that you buy do you discuss with others at least from time to time?

b. What experiences have you had discussing products face-to-face with others?

c. What experiences have you had discussing products or reading comments of others about products on blogs, social networks, or other Internet sites?

d. What are your experiences with product-related websites? Do you participate in games and entertainment opportunities on product-related websites?

e. How do you think firms could improve their websites to provide more information for you?

13-33. Make a presentation of your findings and to your class.

Miniproject 2

The purpose of this miniproject is to give you an opportunity to experience the advertising creative process:

a. First, you should create (imagine) a new brand of an existing product (such as a laundry detergent, toothpaste, perfume, or soft drink). If you are doing a marketing plan project in your course, you might use the same product for this miniproject.

b. Next, you should decide on your creative strategy. What appeal, execution format, tonality, and creative tactics do you think are best?

c. Create a series of at least three magazine ads for your product, using the appeal you selected. Your ads should have a headline, a visual, and copy to explain your product and to persuade customers to purchase your brand.

13-34. Present your ads to your class. Explain your ad execution and the reasons for the various decisions you made in developing the ads.

Marketing in **Action** Case Real Choices at Stouffer's

When was the last time you ate a frozen meal? For many consumers, it has been a long time. That's not good news for Stouffer's, a Nestlé brand of frozen prepared foods. Sales in the U.S. have dropped 5 percent between sales of $8.48 billion in 2008 and sales of $8.04 billion in 2013. The new national focus on health and nutrition that emphasizes fresh foods is a key factor for this decline in sales. To fight this trend, Stouffer's is starting a new promotional campaign to change consumer's perceptions of the taste and nutritional value of its processed frozen meals.

The Stouffer brand began in 1922 when Abraham and Mahala Stouffer opened a small coffee shop in Cleveland, Ohio. Building on its early success, the family developed what would eventually become a national chain of restaurants. Ultimately, the company expanded into three areas: Stouffer Foods Corporation, Stouffer Hotels Corporation, and Stouffer Restaurants Corporation. Nestlé acquired the brand in 1993 with the intention to focus on the food products. Some of Stouffer's popular choices include lasagna, macaroni and cheese, meatloaf, ravioli, and Salisbury steak. They offer items in both individual and family-size portions. Additionally, the company offers the Lean Cuisine line of reduced-fat products.

According to Kantar Media, Stouffer's has an advertising budget of nearly $40 million. It is using a portion of these resources for a new advertising campaign centered on families gathered around the dinner table. One execution focuses on a young girl's reaction as she absent-mindedly puts a forkful of lasagna into her mouth. The commercial voice-over says, "She realizes that Stouffer's lasagna is topped with fresh cheese that browns beautifully." Eventually, the scene reveals that her parents are also at the table, and the voice-over says, "Made for you to love." Eric Weisberg, executive creative director of J. Walter Thompson New York, the fourth-largest advertising agency network in the world, says, "Stouffer's has been sort of this classic, warm brand, but what this campaign does is it connects it with modern families and the modern condition in a way that makes those ingredients and that food more relevant than ever before."

Stouffer's uses other tools in its promotional campaign. It sponsors a fleet of branded food trucks that travel the country serving its iconic macaroni and cheese entrée with fresh toppings. Each truck gives customers a chance to experience the dish dressed up with additions like Tabasco sauce and bacon. The company donates the proceeds from these purchases to various local charities. Tom Moe, Stouffer's director of marketing, says they're going to bring that experience and excitement to Americans across the country by delivering their good food, made with care and the best ingredients. He believes that the food trucks give the company credibility as it demonstrates that its food is made just the way that you'd make it in your own kitchen.

The company acknowledges that the Stouffer's brand is facing challenges when it comes to revenue. Moe believes those challenges "are primarily being driven by consumer misperceptions."

You Make the Call

13-35. What is the decision facing Stouffer's?

13-36. What factors are important in understanding this decision situation?

13-37. What are the alternatives?

13-38. What decision(s) do you recommend?

13-39. What are some ways to implement your recommendation?

Sources: Based on Andrew Adam Newman, "Trying to Bolster the Image of Frozen Meals as Sales Lag," *New York Times*, April 23, 2014, B5; Nestlé S.A., "About Us," **www.stouffers.com/about.aspx** (accessed May 10, 2014); and Nestlé S.A., "Stouffer's Food Trucks to Hit the Road," **www.nestleusa.com/media/pressreleases/StouffersHitsTheRoad** (accessed May 10, 2014).

MyMarketingLab™

Go to **mymktlab.com** for Auto-graded writing questions as well as the following Assisted-graded writing questions:

13-40. As an account executive for an advertising agency, you have been assigned to a new client, a company that has developed a new energy drink. As you begin development of the creative strategy, you are considering different types of ad execution formats and tonality:

   a. Comparative advertising

   b. A fear appeal

   c. A celebrity endorsement

   d. A slice-of-life ad

   e. Sex appeal

   f. Humor

Outline the strengths and weaknesses of each of these appeals for advertising the new energy drink.

13-41. *Creative Homework/Short Project.* As a marketing consultant, you are frequently asked by clients to develop recommendations for marketing communication strategies. The traditional elements used include advertising, sales promotion, public relations, and personal selling. Which of these do you feel would be most effective for each of the following clients?
   a. A bookstore
   b. An all-inclusive resort hotel
   c. A university
   d. A company that produces organic snacks
   e. A sports equipment company

Promotion II: Social Media, Direct/ Database Marketing, Personal Selling, and Public Relations

Rohan Deuskar
▼ **A Decision Maker at Stylitics, Inc.**

Rohan Deuskar was born and raised in India and came to the U.S. at the age of 18 to attend Northwestern University. After college, Rohan joined Vibes Media, a mobile marketing start-up that was pioneering the use of text messaging in interactive marketing campaigns.

At Vibes, Rohan worked in a variety of sales and account roles before starting the company's Innovation Team and helping to grow the company from six people to 80 and 15-fold revenues. He helped create some of the first marketing campaigns in the U.S. to use mobile. His work has won the Chicago Innovation Award, the Mobile Marketing Award, and many other awards as well as a U.S. patent.

Rohan left Vibes after five years to get an MBA in entrepreneurship from the Wharton School, where he became president of the entrepreneurship and rowing clubs. While at Wharton, he started Stylitics, a company designed to unlock the data in people's closets to power personalization and analytics through a "digital closet" platform. Since 2011, under Rohan's leadership, Stylitics has grown to a team of 16 people, raised over $4 million in funding, and counts a number of the world's leading fashion brands and retailers as clients. The company has been featured extensively in the *New York Times*, the *Wall Street Journal*, *Vogue*, *Women's Wear Daily*, and others. Rohan is a frequent speaker on the intersection of fashion, tech, and data at events like New York Fashion Week and DataBeat.

Rohan's Info

What I do when I'm not working?
Play guitar, read a lot, explore New York City.

First job out of school?
A tiny mobile marketing start-up called Vibes Media. I got the job after I overheard the founder discussing the idea at a coffee shop and went up to him as he was leaving!

Career high?
Picking up the *Wall Street Journal* in a New York deli and seeing a three-page profile of my year-old company, just 10 months after moving to New York City. A bit surreal.

A job-related mistake I wish I hadn't made?
Most of my mistakes have been about being too optimistic and hiring the wrong people despite warning signs.

Business book I'm reading now?
Ben Franklin's autobiography. Not a business book but the profile of an inspiring and unique man in his own words. Lots to learn.

My hero?
One of them is Ben Franklin. He not only was a creative genius but also was able to bring people together to achieve great things toward the common good.

My motto to live by?
Put in more than you take out. That applies to a job, a relationship, or the world in general.

What drives me?
The opportunity to create something that is good and useful in the world.

My management style?
(1) Listen. (2) Be kind.

My pet peeve?
Apathy. I can't stand the phrase "Whatever."

Here's my problem...

Stylitics was born from the confluence of my personal need as a consumer and a major need in the fashion industry. The spark was my frustration that, although like most people I was spending a decent amount of money and time on buying clothes and deciding what to wear, my closet was still one of the most inefficient parts of my life. I'd wear only 20 percent of my stuff, I'd forget what I owned, and I'd buy duplicates of clothes I already owned. It struck me that the closet was one of those central experiences in people's lives that is still completely analog and tied to one or two physical locations. I realized that if you had a digital version of your closet—essentially all your clothing data in one place online—then you could unlock an amazing set of new capabilities. Imagine putting together packing lists on the go, tracking stats like cost per wear of each item, or getting online outfit advice from your friend or a digital stylist. And not only would consumers be better off, but, with the user's permission, brands and retailers could see what people are wearing and buying in real time for the first time. That means better and more personal recommendations, more targeted offers, and better insights.

That's exactly what we've built. Today, we're the largest digital closet platform in the world and, for a while, the number one free fashion app in the App Store. Our apps are on iOS, Android, and the Web and used by a large number of people around the world. Our trend reports are used by some of the world's top brands and retailers to help them serve their customers better. And we're just getting started! Anyone interested in finding out more (and being more organized!) should visit Stylitics.com. Exhibit 12.1 provides a screen shot of what the app looks like on a cell phone.

In the fall of 2012, the team at Stylitics was discussing how to grow our social media presence. We'd had a year of strong user growth on our digital closet platform, driven by word of mouth and some good press. But my cofounder Zach Davis and I felt that it was time to do more to grow our brand using social media, primarily Twitter, Facebook, Instagram, and Pinterest. We had accounts on all these platforms, but they weren't really contributing very much to our goals of new user sign-ups and brand engagement. We'd seen the success that larger companies had via these channels through sophisticated campaigns. If we wanted to continue to drive user growth, we needed to step up our social media game.

As we began to discuss our options, we observed a few things. First, while we all used social media as individuals, we didn't have any experience in using social media to grow a brand. Second, while we were active on the @Stylitics Twitter and Facebook accounts, we were posting without a clear purpose or strategy. And third, and most important, we were missing a unique voice. A lot of our posts were reposts or retweets of fashion-related articles—something any company could do. Zach and I felt strongly that unless we had something to offer that was unique to our products or our vision, we should not simply add to the social media noise.

Another issue was reach. As a small company, we didn't have the budget for expensive paid social media campaigns. Even if we created an engaging and unique campaign, we still had to figure out how to make sure it would spread far enough to make an impact. Large companies hire social media agencies and invest in SEO (search engine optimization) and ads to spread the word. Our total budget was $5,000 at most—less than most large companies spend in a week. It was all very well to talk about content "going viral," but that is extremely rare, and even when it happens, it typically requires hitting a critical mass of people through paid promotion before achieving virality.

As leaders, my cofounder Zach Davis and I had to decide what our social media strategy would be. Our marketing team needed direction. Also, we knew that potential users, customers, reporters, and investors often judge young companies based on their follower counts and social media sophistication. It was not something we could ignore for much longer.

Things to remember

Rohan Deuskar created Stylitics, a "digital closet" platform that could unlock the data in people's closets to power personalization and analytics. The closet, a central experience in people's lives, was still analog and tied to one or two physical locations. Dueskar believed that if you had a digital version of your closet—essentially all your clothing data in one place online—then you could unlock an amazing set of new capabilities—putting together packing lists on the go, tracking stats like cost per wear of each item, or getting online outfit advice from your friend or a digital stylist. Stylitics was originally offered to consumers as a free fashion app in the App Store. Potential users, customers, reporters, and investors often judge young companies based on their follower counts and social media sophistication. Without much money, Stylitics considered social media as the means for growth but the marketing team needed direction.

Rohan considered his **Options** 1·2·3

1 **Spend more money.** We could increase our budget to pay a social media agency to create a campaign or pay for advertising on social platforms. We could also hire writers to create original content. This would be a safe choice, and it would require much less time and effort on our part. We could focus on other things and leave it to the experts. Of course, the funds to achieve this goal would have to come at the cost of something else. There was also no guarantee of good results, and we didn't know if consumer engagement would disappear after we exhausted our budget.

Option

2 **Create our own campaign.** We could try to come up internally with a concept for a social media campaign that would be unique and compelling. This would involve identifying external partners who would promote our content to their own followers in exchange for some kind of benefit to them. A "homegrown" strategy would be cheaper, and Stylitics would retain more control over the initiative. Engaging partners would mean extending our reach without spending money. However, an internal approach would take a lot of creativity

Option

You Choose

Which **Option** would you choose, and **why?**
1. ☐YES ☐NO 2. ☐YES ☐NO 3. ☐YES ☐NO

See what **option** Rohan chose on **page 470** ➡

MyMarketingLab™

⭐ **Improve Your Grade!**

Over 10 million students improved their results using the Pearson MyLabs.
Visit **mymktlab.com** for simulations, tutorials, and end-of-chapter problems.

Chapter 14

as well as substantial effort to convince others to participate. It could easily take up a lot of time, use up our whole budget, and still flop badly.

3

Option

Continue as before. We could also choose to continue as we had been. We could accept that until we had the resources to upgrade our social media efforts, we weren't going to be able to do much. Hopefully, as we continued to build a community of avid Stylitics users, they would spread the word organically to their social networks. We could repurpose our social media budget elsewhere and focus on other priorities. A "stay-the-course" approach would allow us to focus on the areas where we have more control. Start-ups are always strapped for time and cash—this would save us both. On the other hand, Stylitics would continue to have a generic social media presence like so many other companies.

Now, put yourself in Rohan's shoes. What option would you choose, and why?

1

OBJECTIVE

Understand how marketers communicate using an updated communication model that incorporates buzz marketing activities and new social media.

(pp. 468–475)

Social Media

In Chapter 13, we saw how advertising and sales promotion follow the one-to-many marketing communication model. In this chapter, we first look at social media that provides many-to-many marketing communication and then at two types of one-to-one communication: direct marketing and personal selling. Finally, we will learn about public relations. Public relations is the final element of the promotion mix and includes a variety of communication activities. Some of these such as lobbying are one-to-one. Others, such as press releases distributed to the news media for publication, follow the one-to-many model. Increasingly, PR professionals are not only engaged in guerilla marketing but also are moving quickly online to join in the many-to-many model.

It seems as if most of us are "on" 24/7 these days, whether we're checking our e-mail while on vacation, playing *Angry Birds* on our smart phone, tweeting about the fabulous new restaurant we discovered, or just checking Facebook on our iPad while in class. Authors Charlene Li and Josh Bernoff refer to the changing communication landscape as the **groundswell**: "a social trend in which people use technology to get the things they need from each other, rather than from traditional institutions like corporations."[1] In other words, today's consumers increasingly get their information on running shoes, nightclubs, cars, new bands, or even today's economics class lecture from one another rather than from the original source.

The Web Revolution is here! What has led to this new communication model, and how is it altering the face of marketing? Much of the answer lies in changing technology. Everyone is online now. Millions of people around the globe surf the Web, talk with their friends, watch TV, and purchase products from traditional marketers, from Internet-only marketers, and from each other on their computers, smart phones, or tablets. For example, at last report, Facebook had over 1.28 billion active users, more than the population of any country except China.[2] All these users have the potential to connect with each other and to share feedback—whether it's about how hard that statistics test was this morning or where they bought a great new swimsuit for summer and how much they paid for it. Marketers no longer are the only ones who talk about their products—millions of consumers also have the ability and the desire to spread the good (or bad) news about the goods and services they buy. That's why we're moving from a one-to-many communication model to the new world of many to many.

groundswell
A social trend in which people use technology to get the things they need from each other rather than from traditional institutions like corporations.

Game sites like Candystand are "sticky" (this one is built around candy, after all) so many advertisers find these media outlets an attractive place to advertise.

© Funtank

At the same time, traditional advertising has diminished as a way to talk to customers as consumers, especially younger ones, spend more and more time online and less time watching TV (and forget about reading newspapers!).[3] While magazine readership in general is up slightly, online readership has increased over 80 percent.[4] For those who do watch TV, the average home now has 189 channels to choose from.[5] This abundance of choice fragments the TV audience and makes the job of reaching a mass market both complex and costly.

As one telling example of this realignment, major advertisers like MasterCard and Verizon Wireless are reallocating big portions of their TV advertising budgets to focus on online videos. Verizon Wireless shifted 10 percent of its TV ad spend to online ads in 2013, and Mondelēz International, the maker of Oreos, plans to shift 10 percent of its global TV advertising dollars into online video by the end of 2014.[6]

Creative ads continue to draw our attention, but today the competition for "eyeballs" is even fiercer as traditional advertising competes with online messages and video content.

Like these big companies, many other marketers are moving money away from traditional communication vehicles such as TV advertising and investing heavily in new media. In 2013, global advertisers spent over $130 billion for online advertising! Retailers also find that their online business is growing but that the Internet customer is harder to please and less loyal. This is not surprising, as people have easy access to competing prices and to the reviews of products and sellers from other online shoppers. The growth of Internet consumer-to-consumer (C2C) shopping sites such as eBay, Etsy, and Craigslist means more and more consumers buy from each other rather than (gulp) pay retail prices. In order to better understand this new communication model and its consequences, we need to first look at how marketers encourage and enable consumers to talk about their products in "buzz-building" activities. Then we'll look at some of the specific new media trending now in the marketing communication landscape.

Buzz Marketing

Why do the heavy lifting when you can put your customers to work for you? The many-to-many communication model relies on consumers like you to talk to one another about goods, services, and organizations. Marketers think of **buzz** as everyday people helping their marketing efforts when they share their opinions with their friends and neighbors.[7] The idea is nothing new. It's basically the so-called office water-cooler effect where coworkers dish about the latest TV sitcom on Monday morning.

buzz
Word-of-mouth communication that customers view as authentic.

The trick is to create buzz that works for you, not against you. Specifically, buzz marketing refers to specific marketing activities designed to create conversation, excitement, and enthusiasm, that is, buzz, about a brand. How does this happen, or, more specifically, how do marketers make sure it happens? Let's take a look at Samsung. As part of a PR stunt to promote its new Galaxy Note III smart phone, Samsung (which sponsored the Oscars) got Oscars host Ellen DeGeneres to get a bunch of celebrities together during the show to pose for a selfie—captured, of course, with none other than the Galaxy Note III. DeGeneres then tweeted the selfie, which went on to become the most retweeted photo ever.[8]

Companies today spend millions to create consumer positive buzz. Firms like Apple specifically hire word-of-mouth (WOM) marketing managers, and the Word of Mouth Marketing Association (WOMMA) membership roster includes most of the top consumer brand companies.[9] Techniques to encourage consumers to spread information about companies and their products come under a variety of names, such as *word-of-mouth marketing, viral marketing, buzz marketing,* and *evangelist marketing*.

As we've noted, buzz isn't *really* new. In fact, we can point to the fame of none other than the *Mona Lisa* portrait as one of the first examples of buzz marketing. In 1911, the painting was stolen from the Louvre museum in Paris. The theft created buzz around the globe while it catapulted da Vinci's masterpiece into the limelight (note that we're not advocating that you arrange to get your product stolen to build buzz).

What *is* new is the magnifying effect that technology exerts on the spread of buzz: When you think of the effect of consumers talking one-on-one about the *Mona Lisa* theft a century ago, imagine the exponential increase in influence of the individual consumer "connectors" or "e-fluentials" who use Facebook, blogs, and other social media to increase their reach.[10] How many online "friends" do you have? Compared to traditional advertising and public relations activities, these endorsements are far more credible and thus more valuable to the brand.

People like to share their experiences, good or bad, with others. Truly happy customers will share their excitement about a brand. Unfortunately, the unhappy ones will be even more eager to tell their friends about their unpleasant experiences. For some brands, the difference between "good" buzz and "bad" buzz is very large; for others, it is almost the same. For example, when asked about their feelings toward the Amazon brand, 56 percent of consumers were "brand lovers," whereas only 3 percent were "brand haters." In contrast, 33 percent of consumers were "brand lovers" of McDonald's, while 29 percent were "brand haters." **Brand polarization**, the gap between good buzz and bad buzz, isn't always a bad thing, however. Bad buzz spreads faster than good buzz; in addition, it stimulates controversy, causing product lovers to vehemently defend the brand they love so much.[11]

Of course, marketers don't necessarily create the buzz around their product anyway—sometimes they just catch a wave that's building and simply ride it home.

brand polarization
The gap between good buzz and bad buzz.

Ethical Problems in Buzz Marketing

Just as firms are discovering there are a myriad of opportunities for buzz marketing, there are equally large opportunities for unethical or at least questionable marketing behavior. Some of these include the following:

tryvertising
Advertising by sampling that is designed to create buzz about a product.

f-commerce
E-commerce that takes place on Facebook.

- *Activities designed to deceive consumers:* Buzz works best when companies put unpaid consumers in charge of creating their own messages. The WOMMA Standards of Conduct include the need of its members to require their representatives to disclose their relationships or identities to consumers and to disclose aspects of their commercial relationship with a marketer, including the specific type of any remuneration or consideration received.

The **Cutting Edge**

Heinz Ketchup's Tryvertising Creates Buzz

To catch a break on Facebook, you really have to be creative. And the maker of one brand of ketchup is doing just that. Heinz opened a pop-up tryvertising page using f-commerce to launch its newest ketchup. Say what? Let's break that down: Heinz opened a pop-up (temporary) **tryvertising** (advertising by sampling that is designed to create buzz about a product) page using **f-commerce** (Facebook e-commerce) to launch its newest ketchup.[12]

The new limited-edition ketchup, one flavored with balsamic vinegar, was made available online to 3,000 of Heinz's biggest fans before the company placed just over a million bottles of the product in traditional stores. The result? Major word-of-mouth buzz among fans of the brand

due, in part, to the exclusivity of the product. Fans were definitely buzzing, and each positive product comment gets syndicated to approximately 130 other Facebook walls, generating even more buzz.

To make tryvertising work successfully, marketers do need to keep a few things in mind. Even Heinz learned some of these lessons in the process:

- Security: Keep it safe. It is e-commerce, after all.
- Privacy: Let customers know you won't share their personal details.
- Personal details: When you do collect personal details, keep it to a minimum.
- Localization: If it's available to a limited market, make sure this is clear.
- Browser compatibility: Make sure your campaign works in all major browsers.

- *Directing buzz marketing at children or teens:* Some critics say buzz marketing should never do this, as these younger consumers are more impressionable and easier to deceive than adults.[13]

- *Buzz marketing activities that damage property.* Puma encouraged consumers to stencil its cat logo all over Paris. Such activities lead to damage or vandalism, which the company will ultimately have to pay for. In addition, individual consumers could find themselves in trouble with the law, a problem that could ultimately backfire and damage the company image.

Viral Marketing

One form of buzz building is **viral marketing**. This term refers to marketing activities that aim to increase brand awareness or sales by consumers passing a message along to other consumers, it is hoped in an exponential fashion—much like your roommate passes a cold on to you and you pass it along to all your other friends.

Some of the earliest examples of viral marketing were messages at the bottom of e-mails by Yahoo! and Hotmail that advertised the free e-mail services. Apple implements viral marketing when it simply inserts the message "Sent from my iPad/iPhone" in a text message. Today, most viral marketing tactics are more subtle; they consist of marketers' use of video clips, interactive games, or other activities that consumers will find so interesting or unique that they want to share them with their friends using digital technology. To see a classic viral spot in action, visit YouTube.com and type "Hunter and bear's 2012 birthday party." This interactive viral video by Tipp-Ex, a European manufacturer of whiteout, has been viewed more than 10 million times.

viral marketing
Marketing activities that aim to increase brand awareness or sales by consumers passing a message along to other consumers.

Brand Ambassadors and Evangelists

Many marketers realize that they can't create buzz by themselves; they recruit loyal customers as **brand ambassadors or brand evangelists** to help them. These zealous consumers can be the best salespeople a company can ever find—and they often work for free. They are heavy users, take a product seriously, care a great deal about it, and want it to succeed.[14] In addition, they know the target audience better than anyone because they are a part of it.

So how do marketers identify and motivate these loyal customers to be brand ambassadors? Sometimes, they seek out customers who already blog about the product and share what they love about the brand. One way to motivate brand ambassadors is to give them special access or privileges to the company and its marketing strategies. Some might be recruited and featured through a brand contest.

brand ambassadors or brand evangelists
Loyal customers of a brand recruited to communicate and be salespeople with other consumers for a brand they care a great deal about.

New Social Media

In addition to buzz building, **social media** is an important part of the *updated communication model*. This term refers to Internet-based platforms that allow users to create their own content and share it with others who access these sites. It's hard to grasp just how much these new formats will transform the way we interact with marketers; they "democratize" messages because they give individual consumers a seat at the table where organizations shape brand meanings and promote themselves in the marketplace. This makes it much easier for companies to tap into their brand evangelists to help them spread the word. The flip side is that the bad stuff also gets out much quicker and reaches people a lot faster: In one survey, 20 percent of respondents said they had used social media to share a negative experience with a brand or service.[15]

There's no doubt that social media is the place to be in marketing communications now, even if many organizations haven't quite figured out just what to do with these platforms. Traditional brands such as McDonald's, Pizza Hut, and Church's Chicken are scrambling

social media
Internet-based platforms that allow users to create their own content and share it with others who access these sites.

to move hefty portions of their promotion budgets out of advertising and into social media. In 2012, companies spent $5.1 billion on social media advertising. That amount is expected to nearly triple to $15 billion by 2018.[16] American Express leverages social media to connect with its card members. For example, American Express used Twitter hashtags that let members load special merchant offers onto their cards, and they tweeted special hashtags so that members could make purchases from companies like Sony and Amazon.[17] American Express also boosted their social media engagement by posting historical brand images to Facebook, Twitter, and Google+. The result on Facebook alone was an astounding 127 percent increase in Facebook likes and a 100 percent increase in shares of Facebook posts.[18]

Social media include social networking sites such as Facebook, blogs and microblogs such as Twitter, picture- and video-sharing sites such as Pinterest and YouTube, product review sites such as Yelp, wikis and other collaborative projects such as Wikipedia, and virtual worlds such as Second Life. While marketers can and do use all these types of sites, we are going to focus on just a few platforms: social networking sites, virtual worlds, product review sites, mobile apps, and location-based social networks.

Social Networks

social networks

Online platforms that allow a user to represent him- or herself via a profile on a website and provide and receive links to other members of the network to share input about common interests.

Social networks are sites that connect people with other people. Successful networking sites ask users to develop profiles of themselves so that those with similar backgrounds, interests, hobbies, religious beliefs, racial identities, or political views can "meet" online. Social networks such as Facebook and LinkedIn are some of the most popular sites on the Internet with millions of users from around the globe. Once a user has created a profile, it's easy to connect with old and new friends.

So what's in all this social networking for marketers? First, by monitoring social networks, marketers learn what consumers are thinking and what they are saying to each other about their brand and about the competition. Such information can be invaluable to improve advertising messages or even to correct defects in products.

By participating in the conversations, marketers can reach influential people such as journalists and consumers who are opinion leaders. But even more important is the opportunity social networks provide to create a brand community, a group of social network users who share an attachment to a product or brand. Members of the brand community interact with each other, sharing information about the brand or just expressing their affection for it. As a result, the relationships between the consumers and the brand grow even stronger.

Sometimes, brand communities develop spontaneously among consumers, while at other times, the brand's marketers purposely create them—or at least nurture them along. Harley-Davidson, for example, set about to create a "brotherhood" of riders and met them on their own terms. To do this, the company's marketers set up outreach events and staffed them with employees. This tactic allowed the employees to get up close and personal with Harley riders so they could better understand how their customers actually relate to the bikes. In the process, some employees got interested in the bikes and became riders, and some riders wound up working for Harley.[19] Today, this extremely active community of enthusiasts, known as HOGs (Harley Owners Group), displays fierce loyalty to the brand—they wouldn't imagine riding anything but a Harley.

Now that we've discussed brand communities, let's examine a couple of the most popular social media sites.

Facebook

Facebook is the most popular of all social networking sites with, as we said earlier, over 1.28 billion active users as we write this book—and no doubt tons of new ones even as you're reading it. Users of Facebook first develop a profile that remains private unless they choose to connect with a "friend." While this social media site was originally created to

---

APPLYING ▼ Social networks

Rohan believed that growing the Stylitics brand through the use of social media was important to the continuing success of the company. He and his partner hoped to develop a unique and compelling social media campaign using sites, such as Twitter, Facebook, Instagram, and Pinerest.

allow college students to keep in touch with their friends (in those days, you had to have ".edu" in your e-mail address to join), it is no longer just for students. Today, there are many significant user segments, including baby-boomer women and even grandparents who use the platform to locate long-lost friends (and keep tabs on their grandchildren).[20]

While Facebook remains the most popular social media site for college students today, many 18- to 24-year-olds are moving away from it (maybe due to the "creep factor" as their parents increasingly sign on). Instead, they spend more time on other sites, including Instagram, Twitter, Tumblr, Snapchat, and Vine.[21] Another change is how college students access social media sites. Many prefer to use their mobile phones to access social media sites, receive and send e-mail, and otherwise interact on social media.

Twitter

Twitter is a free microblogging service that lets users post short text messages with a maximum of 140 characters. People who subscribe to an individual's Twitter feed are called "followers." Users can follow anyone they like, unlike Facebook, where you have to be recognized and accepted as a "friend." Attesting to its popularity, Twitter now has 255 million registered users who "tweet" 500 million posts a day.[22]

Thus, it is especially important that marketers monitor Twitter to understand what consumers say about their products. Unlike some other social media that work only on closed networks, Twitter is a *broadcast medium.* This means that marketers can send messages to hundreds of thousands of people at a time, and they can encourage users to rally around a cause (or brand) when they include the now familiar #. Today, it seems that everyone from political figures to music and movie celebrities uses Twitter. In fact, Twitter seems to be creating news, as newscasters request feedback from TV viewers or ask them to vote on what they like and dislike. As part of its show *Morning Express with Robin Meade*, HLN (part of CNN) hosted a 100 Days of Happiness sweepstakes. Viewers were encouraged to tweet a photo of what makes them happy in exchange for the chance to win a Caribbean vacation for two to "one happy island."[23] The sweepstakes is in response to the #100 HappyDays challenge, started by 27-year-old Dmitry Golubnichy, who lives in Switzerland and who asks people, "Can you be happy for 100 days in a row?"[24] Thousands of people signed up for the challenge.

Virtual Worlds

Virtual worlds are online, highly engaging digital environments where **avatars**—graphic representations of users—live and interact with other avatars in real time. The blockbuster movie *Avatar* exposed many people to this basic idea as it told the story of a wounded soldier who takes on a new (10 feet tall and blue) identity in the world of Pandora.

In virtual worlds, residents can hang out at virtual clubs, shop for clothing and bling for their avatars, buy furniture to deck out virtual homes, and, yes, even go to college in virtual universities. Some people find it hard to believe, but it's common for people to spend real money to buy digital products that don't exist in the real world. Indeed, the **virtual goods** market is booming: By 2016, consumers across the globe are expected to spend over $11 billion to buy items they use only in virtual worlds![25]

Second Life is one of the largest and best-known virtual worlds, although in reality there are several hundred of these environments up and running. This platform is one of many virtual worlds that have become a booming marketplace for budding fashion designers, musicians, and businesspeople who sell their products and services. A few have even become real-world millionaires by selling virtual goods to users who want to buy bling for their avatars. A sampling of other virtual worlds includes the following:

- Disney's *Club Penguin*, geared toward a younger audience, offers more than 20 games for visitors to play and earn coins, which they can then use to deck out their penguins. Players can also adopt and care for Pet Puffles in this virtual world.

Twitter
A free microblogging service that lets users post short text messages with a maximum of 140 characters.

virtual worlds
Online, highly engaging digital environments where avatars live and interact with other avatars in real time.

avatars
Graphic representations of users of virtual worlds.

virtual goods
Digital products consumers buy for use in online contexts.

- *Smeet,* a virtual world for adults, lets visitors play, flirt, and chat in 3D. Users start by building their own 3D home, but they can meet new people in public hangouts or attend live events.

- *Habbo Hotel* is a virtual world where kids inhabit a room (a "habbo") and decorate it with furniture they purchase with Habbo credits.

- *FooPets,* especially popular with 12- to 14-year-old girls, allows users to "adopt" digitally animated pets, then care for them and feed them. If the pets are not properly cared for, they will be taken to a virtual shelter.[26]

Most virtual goods, whether sold in virtual worlds or through other social media sites, have microprices—from less than $1 to $3. So what's in it for real-world marketers? Some firms enter the market for virtual goods to keep in touch with consumers, improve the brand's image, and develop loyal customers. And even micropriced items, such as digital clothing for avatars, start to add up when you sell many thousands of them.

Product Review Sites

product review sites

Social media sites that enable people to post stories about their experiences with products and services.

Product review sites are social media sites that enable people to post stories about their experiences with products and services. Marketers hope that product review sites create a connection between the consumer and the brand. Product review sites give users both positive and negative information about companies:

- *TripAdvisor* provides unbiased hotel reviews complete with photos and advice. The site gives consumers an opportunity to rate and comment on a hotel that they recently stayed in or to use other consumers' comments to select a hotel for an upcoming trip. Consumers can also rate local attractions.

- *Yelp* is a product review site that provides reviews of local businesses, such as places to eat, shop, drink, or play. Consumers can access *Yelp* through either the Internet or a mobile phone. Businesses can create pages to post photos and send messages to their customers.

- *Angie's List* is a site for consumers "tired of lousy service." Members, who cannot remain anonymous, rate service companies in more than 700 categories, and a certified data collection process ensures that companies don't report on themselves or their competitors.[27]

Mobile Apps

It's obvious to almost anyone who has a pulse today that the future of marketing communication lies in that magic little device you practically sleep with—your smart phone. Combine Web-browsing capability with built-in cameras, and the race is on to bring to the world to your belt or purse. Apple lit up this market when it introduced the iPhone, and now everyone is scrambling to "monetize" the mobile market through sales of ringtones, on-demand video, online coupons, and "apps" that entertain or educate. A few to watch include the following:[28]

- *ShopSavvy* finds the lowest prices online and at nearby bricks-and-mortar retailers. Users can like products to get price alerts or follow their favorites stores to get alerts about when items go on sale.

- *Hot5 Fitness* is a fitness app that offers hundreds of five-minute video workouts that you can add on to the end of your current fitness routine or mix together to create a longer workout. The high-quality videos feature custom music synced to the workout for maximum intensity.

- *Fastmall* provides interactive maps of malls, highlights the quickest route to stores, and even helps shoppers remember where they parked their cars. Even better: Shake your phone, and it shows you the nearest restroom location.

- *Flipboard* lets you pull content from social networks like *Facebook and Twitter*, as well as news content from the *New York Times* or *People* magazine, and organize it into a visual, magazine-like format.

Location-Based Social Networks

Location-based social networks integrate sophisticated GPS technology (like the navigation system you may have in your car) that enables users to alert friends of their exact whereabouts via their mobile phones. *Foursquare* was one of the most popular of these sites with over 50 million users, but in May 2014, the *Foursquare* folks announced they were splitting the app in two: *Foursquare* for discovering new places and *Swarm* for checking in at places you visit. Like *Foursquare*, the new *Swarm* app has the popular "Mayor" feature, but instead of competing against everyone who uses *Swarm* for the most check-ins, you compete only against your friends. The new app also offers stickers so you can let others know how you're feeling; to unlock more stickers, just check in at more places. Businesses can ride this wave by offering discounts or free services to people who check in to their locations. For example, Boloco, a burrito chain in Boston, used a feature from the *LevelUp* app, which offered customers $5 off of a food and drink purchase of $10. To "level up," customers returned to the restaurant for $10 off a $25 purchase and then $14 off a $45 purchase. Boloco saw 26 percent of its customers return for the Level 3 reward.[29]

location-based social networks
Networks that integrate sophisticated GPS technology that enables users to alert friends of their exact whereabouts via their mobile phones.

2

OBJECTIVE

Understand the elements of direct marketing.
(pp. 475–478)

Direct Marketing

Are you one of those people who loves to get lots of catalogs in the mail or pore over online catalogs for hours and then order just exactly what you want without leaving home? Maybe you're the one who ordered the Donatella Arpaia Multifunctional Pizza Oven from the Home Shopping Network for two easy payments of only $29.98 or responded to an infomercial on TV for "Flower Power," the 10-CD boxed set of music from the 1960s and 1970s. All these are examples of direct marketing, the fastest-growing type of marketing communication.

Direct marketing, a form of one-to-one marketing communication, refers to "any direct communication to a consumer or business recipient that is designed to generate a response in the form of an order, a request for further information, or a visit to a store or other place of business for purchase of a product."[30] Spending on direct marketing is increasing, while at the same time spending on traditional advertising has declined—especially fueled by ad cutbacks during the recent economic downturn. The Direct Marketing Association reported that in 2013, direct and digital spending in this category was $133.4 billion.[31]

direct marketing
Any direct communication to a consumer or business recipient designed to generate a response in the form of an order, a request for further information, and/or a visit to a store or other place of business for purchase of a product.

Clearly, direct marketing has the potential for high impact. Let's look at the four most popular types of direct marketing as portrayed in 📷 Figure 14.1: mail order (including catalogs and direct mail), telemarketing, direct-response advertising, and m-commerce. We'll start with the oldest—buying through the mail—which is still incredibly popular!

Mail Order

In 1872, Aaron Montgomery Ward and two partners put up $1,600 to mail a one-page flyer that listed their merchandise with prices, hoping to sell to farmers through the mail.[32] The mail-order industry was born, and today consumers can buy just about anything through the mail. Mail order comes in two forms: catalogs and direct mail.

Figure 14.1 📷 *Snapshot* | Key Forms of Direct Marketing

Key forms of direct marketing are mail order (including catalogs and direct mail), telemarketing, direct-response advertising, and m-commerce.

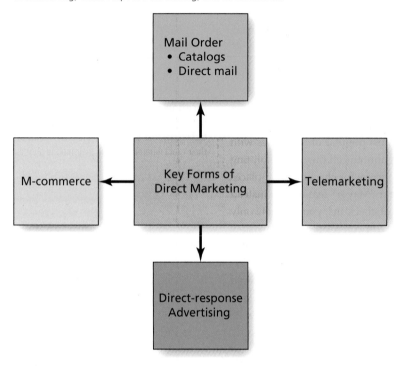

A **catalog** is a collection of products offered for sale in book form, usually consisting of product descriptions accompanied by photos of the items. The early catalogs Montgomery Ward and other innovators such as Sears and JC Penney pioneered targeted people in remote areas who lacked access to stores. Today, millions of baby boomers fondly remember spending hours poring through the *Sears Christmas Wish Book* the month before Christmas, making out their list for Santa—and changing it every day straight through Christmas Eve. (Today, Sears offers customers products through its website, *Wishbook.com*.)

The catalog customer today is less likely to live in a remote area and more likely to be an affluent career woman with access to more than enough stores but without the time or desire to go to them. According to Forbes magazine, there were more than "12,738 billion catalogs mailed in 2010 (about 35 for every man, woman, and child in the country)."[33] Catalog mania extends well beyond clothing and cosmetics purchases. Many stores use catalogs to complement their in-store efforts. Retailer Neiman Marcus is famous for its *Christmas Book*, which always includes a number of one-of-a-kind "Fantasy Gifts." The 2013 gifts included a Limited-Edition 2014 Aston Martin Vanquish Volante and the ultimate outdoor entertainment system that included a 201-inch TV screen that telescopes up from an underground hideaway.[34]

A catalog strategy allows the store to reach people in the U.S. who live in areas too small to support a store. But also, more and more U.S. firms use catalogs to reach overseas markets as well. Companies like Lands' End and Eddie Bauer do brisk sales in Europe and Asia, where consumers tend to buy more goods and services through the mail in the first place than do Americans. Lands' End opened a central warehouse in Berlin and attacked the German market with catalogs.

catalog
A collection of products offered for sale in book form, usually consisting of product descriptions accompanied by photos of the items.

Direct Mail

Unlike a catalog retailer that offers a variety of merchandise through the mail, **direct mail** is a brochure or pamphlet that offers a specific good or service at one point in time. A direct mail offer has an advantage over a catalog because the sender can personalize it. Charities, political groups, and other not-for-profit organizations also use a lot of direct mail.

Just as with e-mail spamming, Americans are overwhelmed with direct-mail offers—"junk mail"—that may end up in the trash. Of course, many consumers not only open but also respond with cold cash to their direct mail. Research from the Direct Marketing Association found that four-fifths (79 percent) of consumers will act on direct mail immediately compared to only 45 percent who say they deal with e-mail right away.[35] The direct-mail industry constantly works on ways to monitor what companies send through the mail and it allows consumers to "opt out" of at least some mailing lists.

direct mail
A collection of products offered for sale in book form, usually consisting of product descriptions accompanied by photos of the items.

Telemarketing

Telemarketing is direct marketing an organization conducts over the telephone (but why do they always have to call during dinner?). It might surprise you to learn that telemarketing actually is more profitable for business markets than for consumer markets.

telemarketing
The use of the telephone to sell directly to consumers and business customers.

When B2B marketers use the telephone to keep in contact with smaller customers, it costs far less than a face-to-face sales call yet still lets these clients know they are important to the company.

The Federal Trade Commission (FTC) established the National Do Not Call Registry to allow consumers to limit the number of telemarketing calls they receive. The idea is that telemarketing firms check the registry at least every 31 days and clean their phone lists accordingly. Consumers responded very positively to the regulation, and over 220 million have posted their home numbers and mobile numbers on the registry to date.[36] Some direct marketers initially challenged this action; they argued that it would put legitimate companies out of business while unethical companies would not abide by the regulation and continue to harass consumers. However, the National Do Not Call Registry, along with similar operations at the state level, now is an accepted part of doing business through direct marketing. The FTC maintains a list of violators on its website.[37]

Direct-Response Advertising

Direct-response advertising allows the consumer to respond to a message by immediately contacting the provider to ask questions or order the product. This form of direct marketing can be very successful. Although for many companies the Internet has become the medium of choice for direct marketing, this technique is still alive and well in magazines, in newspapers, and on TV.

As early as 1950, the Television Department Stores channel brought the retailing environment into the TV viewer's living room when it offered a limited number of products the viewer could buy when he or she called the advertised company. TV sales picked up in the 1970s when two companies, Ronco Incorporated and K-Tel International, began to peddle products such as the Kitchen Magician, Pocket Fisherman, Mince-O-Matic, and Miracle Broom on TV sets around the world.[38] And who can forget the late Billy Mays's enthusiastic hawking of Oxy Clean, Jupiter Jack, and nearly 20 other products on TV? Make a simple phone call, and one of these wonders could be yours ("but wait, there's more . . .").

Direct-response TV (DRTV) includes short commercials of less than two minutes, 30-minute or longer infomercials, and the shows that home shopping networks such as QVC and HSN broadcast. Top-selling DRTV product categories include exercise equipment, self-improvement products, diet and health products, kitchen appliances, and music. Of course, even home shopping networks have gone online, so you if you miss the show, you can still order the product.

The primitive sales pitches of the old days have largely given way to the slick **infomercials** we all know and love (?) today. These half-hour or hour-long commercials resemble a talk show, often with heavy product demonstration and spirited audience participation, but of course they really are sales pitches. Although some infomercials still carry a low-class, sleazy stereotype, in fact over the years numerous heavyweights from Apple Computer to Volkswagen have used this format.

M-Commerce

One final type of direct marketing is m-commerce. The "m" stands for "mobile," but it could also stand for "massive"—because that's how big the market will be for this platform. **M-commerce** refers to the promotional and other e-commerce activities transmitted over mobile phones and other mobile devices, such as smart phones and tablets with phone capabilities. With over 6 billion mobile phones in use worldwide—more and more of them Internet enabled—it makes sense that marketers would want to reach out and touch this large audience, which is just over 85 percent of the world's population. That means there are more mobile phones throughout the world than working toilets![39]

---

direct-response advertising
A direct marketing approach that allows the consumer to respond to a message by immediately contacting the provider to ask questions or order the product.

direct-response TV (DRTV)
Advertising on TV that seeks a direct response, including short commercials of less than two minutes, 30-minute or longer infomercials, and home shopping networks.

infomercials
Half-hour or hour-long commercials that resemble a talk show but actually are sales pitches.

m-commerce
Promotional and other e-commerce activities transmitted over mobile phones and other mobile devices, such as smart phones and personal digital assistants.

The top five countries in total mobile phones in use today are the following:[40]

China	1,100,000,000
India	893,862,000
U.S.	310,000,000
Indonesia	281,960,000
Russia	261,900,000

M-commerce through text messages (such as an ad for a concert or a new restaurant) is known as *short-messaging system* (SMS) marketing. In terms of unwanted "junk mail," m-commerce has the same potential dark side as other forms of direct marketing, such as snail mail and e-mail. And the rise of the all-in-one smart phone on which the user engages in 24/7 social networking has created an up-and-coming industry of social networking activity tracking and analytics, such as Google Analytics and similar programs.

3 OBJECTIVE
Appreciate the important role of personal selling and how it fits into the promotion mix.
(pp. 478–482)

Personal Selling: Adding the Personal Touch to the Promotion Mix

Now we turn our attention to one of the most visible—and most expensive—forms of marketing communication: personal selling. Like direct marketing, personal selling is an example of one-to-one marketing communications.

Personal selling occurs when a company representative interacts directly with a customer or prospective customer to communicate about a good or service. This form of promotion is a far more intimate way to talk to customers. Another advantage of personal selling is that salespeople are the firm's eyes and ears in the marketplace. They learn which competitors talk to customers, what they offer, and what new rival goods and services are on the way—all valuable competitive intelligence.

personal selling
Marketing communication by which a company representative interacts directly with a customer or prospective customer to communicate about a good or service.

Many organizations rely heavily on personal selling because at times the "personal touch" carries more weight than mass-media material. For a B2B market situation, the personal touch translates into developing crucial relationships with clients. Also, many industrial goods and services are too complex or expensive to market effectively in impersonal ways (such as through mass advertising). An axiom in marketing is *the more complex, technical, and intangible the product, the more heavily firms tend to rely on personal selling to promote it.*

Personal selling has special importance for students (that's *you*) because many graduates with a marketing background will enter professional sales jobs. The U.S. Bureau of Labor Statistics estimates job growth of almost 9 percent for sales representatives in manufacturing and wholesaling between 2012 and 2022. For technical and scientific products, the growth projection rises to almost 10 percent. Overall, sales job growth ranks high among all occupations surveyed.[41] Jobs in selling and sales management often provide high upward mobility if you are successful because firms value employees who understand customers and who can communicate well with them. The old business adage "nothing happens until something is sold" translates into many firms placing quite a bit of emphasis on personal selling in their promotion mixes. And the sales role is even more crucial during tricky economic times, when companies look to their salespeople to drum up new business and to maintain the business they already have.

Sold on selling? All right, then let's take a close look at how personal selling works and how professional salespeople develop long-term relationships with customers.

The Role of Personal Selling in the Marketing Mix

When a woman calls the 800 number for the MGM Grand Hotel in Las Vegas to book a room for a little vacation trip and comes away with not only a room but also show tickets, a massage booking at the hotel spa, and a reservation for dinner at Emeril's, she deals with a salesperson. When she sits in on a presentation at work by a website renewal consultant who proposes a new content management system for her firm's website, she deals with a salesperson. And when that same woman agrees over lunch at a swanky restaurant to invest some of her savings with a financial manager's recommended mutual fund, she also deals with a salesperson.

For many firms, some element of personal selling is essential to land a commitment to purchase or a contract, so this type of marketing communication is a key to the success of their overall marketing plan. To put the use of personal selling into perspective, Figure 14.2 illustrates some of the factors that make it a more or less important element in an organization's promotion.

In general, a personal selling emphasis is more important when a firm engages in a *push strategy*, in which the goal is to "push" the product through the channel of distribution so that it is available to consumers. As a vice president at Hallmark Cards once observed, "We're not selling *to* the retailer, we're selling *through* the retailer. We look at the retailer as a pipeline to the hands of consumers."[42]

Personal selling also is likely to be crucial in B2B contexts where the firm must interact directly with a client's management to clinch a big deal—and often when intense negotiations about price and other factors will occur before the customer signs on the dotted line. In consumer contexts, inexperienced customers may need the hands-on assistance that a professional salesperson provides. Firms that sell goods and services that consumers buy infrequently—houses, cars, computers, lawn mowers, and even college educations—often rely heavily on personal selling. (*Hint:* Your school didn't pick just any student at random

Figure 14.2 Snapshot | Factors That Influence a Firm's Emphasis on Personal Selling

A variety of factors influence whether personal selling is a more or less important element in an organization's overall promotion mix.

to conduct campus tours and help those clueless freshmen.) Likewise, firms whose goods or services are complex or very expensive often need a salesperson to explain, justify, and sell them—in both business and consumer markets.

If personal selling is so useful, why don't firms just scrap their advertising and sales promotion budgets and hire more salespeople? There are some drawbacks that limit the role personal selling plays in the marketing communication mix. First, when the dollar amount of individual purchases is low, it doesn't make sense to use personal selling—the cost per contact with each customer is very high compared to other forms of promotion, often hundreds of dollars. The per-contact cost of a national TV commercial is minuscule by comparison. A 30-second prime-time commercial may run $300,000 to $500,000 (or even $4 million for a 30-second commercial aired during the Super Bowl), but with millions of viewers, the cost per contact may be only $25 or $35 per 1,000 viewers. For low-priced consumer packaged goods such as Doritos or beer, personal selling to end users simply doesn't make good financial sense.

Ironically, consumer resistance to telemarketing gives a powerful boost to a form of selling that has been around for a long time: direct selling. *Direct selling is not the same thing as direct marketing*. Direct sellers bypass channel intermediaries and sell directly from manufacturer to consumer through personal, one-to-one contact. Typically, independent sales representatives sell in person in a customer's home or place of business. Tupperware, Thirty-One, Scentsy, Avon, Mary Kay, and the Pampered Chef are some well-known examples. Many direct selling firms use a *party plan* approach where salespeople demonstrate products in front of groups of friends and neighbors. Direct selling is on a big upswing. Direct retail sales in 2012 were estimated at $31.63 billion, up 5.9 percent from the previous year.[43]

Technology and Personal Selling

Personal selling is supposed to be, well, "personal." By definition, a company uses personal selling for marketing communications in situations when one person (the salesperson) interacts directly with another person (the customer or prospective customer) to communicate about a good or service. All sorts of technologies can enhance the personal selling process, and clearly today the smart phone is the communication hub of the relationship between salesperson and client. However, as anyone making sales calls knows, technology itself cannot and should not *replace* personal selling. Today, a key role of personal selling is to manage customer *relationships*—and remember that relationships occur between people, not between computers (as much as you love your *Facebook* friends or checking in on *Swarm*).

However, there's no doubt that a bevy of technological advancements makes it easier for salespeople to do their jobs more effectively. One such technological advance is *customer relationship management (CRM) software*. For years now, *account management software* such as ACT and GoldMine has helped salespeople manage their client and prospect base. These programs are inexpensive, easy to navigate, and allow salespeople to track all aspects of customer interaction. As we saw with our discussion of Oracle in Chapter 3, currently many firms turn to *cloud computing* CRM applications, which are more customizable and integrative than ACT or OnContact yet are less expensive than major companywide CRM installations. A market leader in such products is *SalesForce.com*, which is particularly user-friendly for salespeople. A key benefit of cloud computing versions of CRM systems is that firms

Telemarketing, sometimes called teleselling, involves person-to-person communication that takes place on the phone.

Dmitriy Shironosov/Shutterstock

"rent" them for a flat fee per month (at SalesForce.com, monthly prices are as low as $20 per user), so they avoid major capital outlays.[44]

Recently, some sales organizations have turned to a new-generation system called *partner relationship management (PRM)*, which links information between selling and buying firms. PRM differs from CRM in that both supplier and buyer firms share at least some of their databases and systems to maximize the usefulness of the data for decision-making purposes. Firms that share information are more likely to work together toward win-win solutions.

Beyond CRM and PRM, numerous other technology applications enhance personal selling, including teleconferencing, videoconferencing, and improved corporate websites that offer FAQ (frequently asked questions) pages to answer customers' queries. Many firms also use intranets and blogs to facilitate access to internal and external communication.

Voice-over Internet protocol (VoIP)—systems that rely on a data network to carry voice calls—get a lot of use in day-to-day correspondence between salespeople and customers. With VoIP, the salesperson on the road can just plug into a fast Internet connection and then start to make and receive calls just as if in the office. Unlike mobile phones, there are no bad reception areas, and unlike hotel phones, there are no hidden charges. One popular VoIP product is Skype, whose tagline is "The whole world can talk for free." According to its website, Skype "is a little piece of software that allows you to make free calls to other Skype users and really cheap calls to ordinary phones." Skype even offers bargain rates to fixed lines and cell phones outside the U.S.[45]

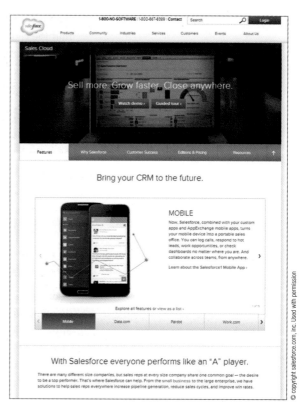

SalesForce.com is one widely used CRM system.

Thanks to Skype, built-in laptop and tablet webcams, instant messaging, and the like, customers of all types are becoming more comfortable with the concept of doing business with a salesperson who is not actually in the same room. As such, a good portion of the future of face-to-face sales calls may occur on your own computer screen. Consider the following hypothetical transaction related to buying a set of solar panels for your roof—a complex and expensive purchase.

The sales consultant calls at an appointed time. You open her e-mail message, click a link to start the presentation, and a picture of your roof appears, courtesy of satellite imaging. Colorful charts show past electricity bills and the savings from a solar-panel system. A series of spreadsheets examine the financing options available—and these are dynamic documents, not static images, so the salesperson can tinker with the figures right before your eyes. Would more panels be justified? A few keystrokes later, new charts displayed the costs and savings. Could they be shifted to another part of the roof? With a mouse, she moves some black panels from the east side to the west side. How about more cash up front? She scrolls to the spreadsheets, highlights three payment options, and computes the numbers over the next 15 years. In less than an hour, the exchange is over.

Perhaps for a few days or a week, you mull over the choices and study the fine print in the contract, but the sale was essentially closed by the time you hung up the phone. You decided to make a major, complex purchase, worth thousands of dollars, without ever meeting anyone in the flesh and without holding any product in your hands. And unlike many purchases, you had no *buyer's remorse* despite the fact it was done online—or maybe *because* it was online.[46]

For years now, all of us have been shopping online, taking in the bargains and wide selection, usually for relatively straightforward products and services and without any human contact unless a problem arises with the ordering technology itself. The brave new world of virtual selling adds another dimension and is yet another example of how the Internet transforms business and remakes job descriptions. These more sophisticated virtual selling capabilities won't replace all face-to-face salesperson/client encounters any more than e-commerce replaced bricks-and-mortar retailers. But smart sales organizations can find the right blend of technology and personal touch, tailored to their particular clientele and product offerings, that make the most of building strong customer relationships.

4 The Landscape of Modern Personal Selling

OBJECTIVE

Identify the different types of sales jobs.

(pp. 482–483)

Given what you've read about personal selling so far, you can begin to see why professional salespeople have very dynamic career opportunities. In this section, you'll get a feel for what today's jobs are like and two distinct ways salespeople approach their role.

Types of Sales Jobs

There are several different types of sales jobs from which you can choose, each with its own unique characteristics. Maybe you aspire to work in sales someday, or perhaps you've already held a sales job at some point. Let's look more closely at some of the different types of sales positions. 📷 Figure 14.3 summarizes the most important types.

As you might imagine, sales jobs vary considerably. The person who answers the phone at Zappos to take your order for a new pair of UGGs boots (if anybody orders them by phone anymore instead of online) is primarily an **order taker**—a salesperson who processes transactions the customer initiates. Many retail salespeople are order takers, but often wholesalers, dealers, and distributors also employ salespeople to assist their business customers. Because little creative selling is involved in order taking, this type of sales job typically is the lowest-paid sales position.

In contrast, a **technical specialist** contributes considerable expertise in the form of product demonstrations, recommendations for complex equipment, and setup of machinery. The technical specialist provides *sales support* rather than actually closing the sale. He or she promotes the firm and tries to stimulate demand for a product to make it easier for colleagues to actually seal the deal.

Then there is the **missionary salesperson**, whose job is to stimulate clients to buy. Like technical specialists, missionary salespeople promote the firm and encourage demand for its goods and services but don't actually take orders.[47] Pfizer salespeople do missionary sales work when they call on physicians to influence them to prescribe the latest-and-greatest Pfizer medications instead of competing drugs. However, no sale actually gets made until doctors call prescriptions into pharmacies, which then place orders for the drug through their wholesalers.

The **new-business salesperson** is responsible for finding new customers and calls on them to present the company's products. As you might imagine, gaining the business of a new customer usually means that the customer stops doing business with one of the firm's competitors (and they won't give up without a fight). New-business selling requires a high degree of creativity and professionalism, so this type of salesperson is usually very well paid. Once a new-business salesperson establishes a relationship with a client, he or she often continues to service that client as the primary contact as long as the client continues to buy from the company. In that long-term-relationship-building role, this type of salesperson is an

order taker
A salesperson whose primary function is to facilitate transactions that the customer initiates.

technical specialist
A sales support person with a high level of technical expertise who assists in product demonstrations.

missionary salesperson
A salesperson who promotes the firm and tries to stimulate demand for a product but does not actually complete a sale.

new-business salesperson
The person responsible for finding new customers and calling on them to present the company's products.

Figure 14.3 📷 *Snapshot* | Types of Sales Jobs

A wide range of different types of sales jobs are available, each of which has different job requirements and responsibilities.

order getter. Order getters are usually the people most directly responsible for a particular client's business; they may also hold the title of "account manager."[48]

More and more, firms find that the selling function works best via **team selling**. A selling team may consist of a salesperson, a technical specialist, someone from engineering and design, and other players who work together to develop products and programs that satisfy the customer's needs. When the company includes people from a range of areas, it often calls this group a *cross-functional team*.

Two Approaches to Personal Selling

Personal selling is one of the oldest forms of marketing communication. Unfortunately, over the years, smooth-talking pitchmen who will say anything to make a sale have tarnished its image. Pulitzer Prize–winning playwright Arthur Miller's famous character Willie Loman in *Death of a Salesman*—a must-read for generations of middle and high school students—didn't help. Willie Loman (as in "low man" on the totem pole—get it?) is a pathetic, burned-out peddler who leaves home for the road on Monday morning and returns late Friday evening selling "on a smile and a shoeshine." His personal life is in shambles with two dysfunctional sons and a disaffected wife who hardly knows him. Great public relations for selling as a career, right?

Fortunately, personal selling today is nothing like Miller's harsh portrayal. Selling has moved from a transactional, hard-sell approach to an approach based on relationships with customers. Let's see how.

Transactional Selling: Putting on the Hard Sell

Willy Loman practiced a high-pressure, hard-sell approach. We've all been exposed to the pushy electronics salesperson who puts down the competition when telling shoppers that if they buy elsewhere, they will be stuck with an inferior home theater system that will fall apart in six months. Or how about the crafty used car salesman who plays the good-cop/bad-cop game, gives you an awesome price, but then sadly informs you that the boss, the sales manager, won't go for such a sweet deal. These hard-sell tactics reflect **transactional selling**, an approach that focuses on making an immediate sale with little concern for developing a long-term relationship with the customer.

As customers, the hard sell makes us feel manipulated and resentful, and it diminishes our satisfaction and loyalty. It's a very shortsighted approach to selling. As we said earlier in the book, constantly finding new customers is much more expensive than getting repeat business from the customers you already have. And the behaviors transactional selling promotes (i.e., doing anything to get the order) contribute to the negative image many of us have of salespeople as obnoxious and untrustworthy. Such salespeople engage in these behaviors because they don't care if they ever have the chance to sell to you again. This is really bad business!

Relationship Selling: Building Long-Term Customers

Relationship selling is the process by which a salesperson secures, develops, and maintains long-term relationships with profitable customers.[49] Today's professional salesperson is more likely to practice relationship selling than transactional selling. This means that the salesperson tries to develop a mutually satisfying, win-win relationship with the customer. Securing a customer relationship means converting an interested prospect into someone who is convinced that the good or service holds value for him or her. Developing a customer relationship means ensuring that you and the customer work together to find more ways to add value to the transaction. Maintaining a customer relationship means building customer satisfaction and loyalty—thus, you can count on the customer to provide future business and stick with you for the long haul. And if doing business with the customer isn't profitable to you, unless you're a charitable organization, you would probably like to see that customer go somewhere else.

order getter
A salesperson who works to develop long-term relationships with particular customers or to generate new sales.

team selling
The sales function when handled by a team that may consist of a salesperson, a technical specialist, and others.

transactional selling
A form of personal selling that focuses on making an immediate sale with little or no attempt to develop a relationship with the customer.

relationship selling
A form of personal selling that involves securing, developing, and maintaining long-term relationships with profitable customers.

Figure 14.4 🎿 *Process* | Steps in the Creative Selling Process

In the creative selling process, salespeople follow a series of steps to build relationships with customers.

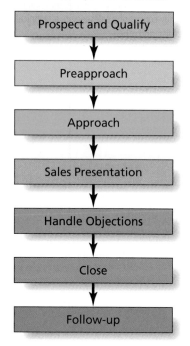

creative selling process
The process of seeking out potential customers, analyzing needs, determining how product attributes might provide benefits for the customer, and then communicating that information.

prospecting
A part of the selling process that includes identifying and developing a list of potential or prospective customers.

preapproach
A part of the selling process that includes developing information about prospective customers and planning the sales interview.

5
OBJECTIVE

List the steps in the creative selling process.
(pp. 484–487)

The Creative Selling Process

Many people find selling to be a great profession, partly because something different is always going on. Every customer, every sales call, and every salesperson is unique. Some salespeople are successful primarily because they know so much about what they sell. Others are successful because they've built strong relationships with customers so that they're able to add value to both the customer and their own firm—a win-win approach to selling. Successful salespeople understand and engage in a series of activities to make the sales encounter mutually beneficial.

A salesperson's chances of success increase when following a systematic series of steps we call the **creative selling process**. These steps require the salesperson to seek out potential customers, analyze their needs, determine how product attributes provide benefits, and then decide how best to communicate this to prospects. As 🎿 Figure 14.4 shows, there are seven steps in the process. Let's take a look at each.

Step 1: Prospect and Qualify

Prospecting is the process by which a salesperson identifies and develops a list of *prospects* or *sales leads* (potential customers). Leads come from existing customer lists, telephone directories, commercially available databases, and, of course, the diligent use of Web search engines like Google. The local library usually owns directories of businesses (including those state and federal agencies publish) and directories of association memberships. Sometimes companies generate sales leads through their advertising or sales promotion when they encourage customers to request more information.

As we discussed in Chapter 13, trade shows also are an important source of sales leads, as are visits to your company's website by potential customers. Accela Communications is one company that tracks these responses for its clients in order to generate leads. Sales organizations turn to Accela to monitor, analyze, and summarize visitors to a company's website—in essence, to develop prospect lists. Accela then turns these lists over to salespeople for follow-up by phone or in person.[50]

Another way to generate leads is through *cold calling*, in which the salesperson simply contacts prospects "cold," without prior introduction or arrangement. It always helps to know the prospect, so salespeople might rely instead on *referrals*. Current clients who are satisfied with their purchase often recommend a salesperson to others—yet another reason to maintain good customer relationships.

However, the mere fact that someone is willing to talk to a salesperson doesn't guarantee a sale. After they identify potential customers, salespeople need to *qualify* these prospects to determine how likely they are to become customers. To do this, they ask questions such as the following:

- Are the prospects likely to be interested in what I'm selling?

- Are they likely to switch their allegiance from another supplier or product?

- Is the potential sales volume large enough to make a relationship profitable?

- Can they afford the purchase?

- If they must borrow money to buy the product, what is their credit history?

Step 2: Preapproach

In the **preapproach** stage, you compile background information about prospective customers and plan the sales interview. Firms don't make important purchases lightly, and it's often difficult even to get an appointment to see a prospect. It's foolish for a salesperson to blindly call on a qualified prospect and risk losing the sale because of a lack of preparation. Salespeople try to learn as much as possible about qualified prospects early on. They may probe a prospect's prior purchase history or current needs or, in some cases, may even try to learn about their personal interests. Does the customer like for a salesperson to spend time informally talking about golf or football, or does he or she prefer a salesperson who gets to the point quickly and leaves? And, of course, it's always good to know which football team the customer roots for.

Salespeople can draw information about a prospect from a variety of sources. In the case of larger companies, they can find financial data, names of top executives, and other information about a business from outlets such as *Standard & Poor's 500 Directory* or Dun & Bradstreet's *Million Dollar Directory*. They can also find a great deal of information for the preapproach on customers' websites. And the inside scoop on a prospect often comes from informal sources, such as noncompeting salespeople who have dealt with the prospect before.

Of course, if the salesperson's firm has a CRM system, he or she can use it to see whether the database includes information about the prospect. Say, for example, a salesperson at Mike's Bikes plans to call on a buyer at Greg's Vacation Rentals to see about selling some new bikes for guests to use at Greg's various resort properties. If Mike's has had a CRM system in place for some time, any contacts with customers and potential customers (prospects) are recorded in the database. The salesperson can simply run an inquiry about Greg's Vacation Rentals, and, with luck, the CRM database will deliver information on the company, prior purchases from Mike's, when and why customers stopped buying from the company, and perhaps even the preferences of the particular buyer.

Step 3: Approach

After the salesperson lays the groundwork with the preapproach, it's time to **approach**, or contact, the prospect. During these important first minutes, several key events occur. The salesperson tries to learn even more about the prospect's needs, create a good impression, and build rapport. If the salesperson found prospect Betty Groves through a referral, he or she will probably say so to Anne up front: "Mark Gaffney with Prentice Industries suggested I call on you."

During the approach, the customer decides whether the salesperson has something to offer that is of potential value. The old saying "You never get a second chance to make a good first impression" rings true here. A professional appearance tells the prospect that the salesperson means business and is competent to handle the sale.

approach
The first step of the actual sales presentation in which the salesperson tries to learn more about the customer's needs, create a good impression, and build rapport.

sales presentation
The part of the selling process in which the salesperson directly communicates the value proposition to the customer and invites two-way communication.

Step 4: Sales Presentation

Many sales calls involve a formal **sales presentation**, which lays out the benefits of the product and its advantages over the competition. When possible and appropriate, salespeople should incorporate a great multimedia presentation shown on their tablet or laptop integrated into their sales presentations to jazz things up. A picture is worth a thousand words and a video showing how each weld in the grocery carts is triple welded—well, you know.

The focus of the sales presentation should always be on ways the salesperson, the goods and services, and the company can add value to the customer (and in a B2B setting, to the customer's company). It is important for the salesperson to present this value proposition clearly

A good salesperson is well groomed and wears appropriate business dress. She doesn't chew gum, use poor grammar or inappropriate language, mispronounce the customer's name, or seem uninterested in the call. Visible tattoos, body piercings, and the like are controversial in professional selling.

and to invite the customer's involvement in the conversation. Let the customer ask questions, give feedback, and discuss his or her needs. Canned approaches to sales presentations are a poor choice for salespeople who want to build long-term relationships. In fact, sales managers rate *listening* skills, not talking skills, as the single most important attribute they look for when they hire relationship salespeople.[51] In a sales call, it's a good idea to put the *80/20 rule* to work—that is, spend 80 percent of your time listening to the client and assessing his or her needs and only 20 percent talking (Note: This rule of thumb is a spin-off of the 80/20 rule for market segmentation we discussed in Chapter 7).

Step 5: Handle Objections

It's rare when a prospect accepts everything the salesperson offers without question. The effective salesperson anticipates *objections*—reasons why the prospect is reluctant to make a commitment—and prepared to respond with additional information or persuasive arguments. Actually, the salesperson should welcome objections because they show that the prospect is at least interested enough to consider the offer and seriously weigh its pros and cons. Handling the objection successfully can move a prospect to the decision stage. For example, the salesperson might say, "Ms. Wall, you've said before that you don't have room to carry our new line of trail bikes, although you mentioned that you may be losing some sales by carrying only one brand with very few different models. If we could come up with an estimate of how much business you're losing, I'll bet you'd consider making room for our line, wouldn't you?"

Step 6: Close the Sale

close
The stage of the selling process in which the salesperson actually asks the customer to buy the product.

The win-win nature of relationship selling should take some of the pressure off salespeople to make "the dreaded close." But there still comes a point in the sales call at which one or the other party has to move toward gaining commitment to the objectives of the call—presumably a purchase. This is the decision stage, or **close**. Directly asking the customer for his or her business doesn't need to be painful or awkward: If the salesperson has done a great job in the previous five steps of the creative selling process, closing the sale should be a natural progression of the dialogue between the buyer and seller.

There are a variety of approaches salespeople use to close the sale:

- A *last objection close* asks customers if they are ready to purchase, providing the salesperson can address any concerns they have about the product: "Are you ready to order if we can prove our delivery time frames meet your expectations?"

- An *assumptive* or *minor points close* mean the salesperson acts as if the purchase is inevitable with only a small detail or two to be settled: "What quantity would you like to order?"

- A *standing-room-only* or *buy-now close* injects some urgency when the salesperson suggests the customer might miss an opportunity if he or she hesitates: "This price is good through Saturday only, so to save 20 percent we should book the order now." When making such closes, salespeople must be sure the basis they state for buying now is truthful, or they'll lose a valuable relationship for the price of a one-time sale!

Step 7: Follow-Up

follow-up
Activities after the sale that provide important services to customers.

Understanding that the process doesn't end after the salesperson earns the client's business is basic to a relationship selling perspective that emphasizes the importance of long-term satisfaction. The **follow-up** after the sale includes arranging for delivery, payment, and purchase terms. It also means the salesperson makes sure the customer received delivery and is satisfied. Follow-up also allows the salesperson to *bridge* to the next purchase. Once a relationship develops, the selling process is only beginning. Even as one cycle of purchasing draws to a close, a good salesperson already lays the foundation for the next one.

Metrics Moment

Now you know quite a bit about selling, but how does a firm know whether a salesperson is effective? Obviously, the short answer is that he or she produces high sales volume and meets or exceeds sales goals. But just increasing total dollar or unit sales volume is not always an adequate indicator of salesperson success. The problem is that, everything else being equal, salespeople who are compensated strictly on sales volume may simply sell whatever products are easiest to sell in order to pile up total sales. And what's wrong with this, you might ask? It is that the easiest products to sell may not be the products with the highest *profit* margins, and they also may not be the products the firm believes are important to build to ensure future success in the market.

Because of these problems with using raw sales volume as the sole indicator of salesperson success, some firms turn to a variety of other metrics, including input and output measures. **Input measures** are "effort" measures—things that go into selling, such as the number and type of sales calls, expense account management, and a variety of nonselling activities, such as customer follow-up work and client service. **Output measures**, or the results of the salesperson's efforts, include sales volume but also include things like the number of orders, size of orders, number of

new accounts, level of repeat business, customer satisfaction, and quantity of particular key products sold. Profitability of the sale to the company is also an output measure, although many salespeople resist being judged on their profit contribution because they claim (not entirely incorrectly) that they cannot control many of the costs that impact product profits.

Ultimately, the best approach to measure salesperson success is to use a variety of metrics that are consistent with the goals of the particular firm, to ensure the salesperson thoroughly understands the goals and related metrics being used, and then to link salesperson rewards to the achievement of those goals.

Apply the Metrics

1. Assume that you are a professional salesperson and consider the various input and output metrics of salesperson effectiveness described above.
2. Which of the metrics would you prefer to be evaluated against? Why do you prefer these?
3. Which of the metrics would you least like being evaluated against? Why?

6

OBJECTIVE

Explain the role of public relations and the steps in developing a public relations campaign.
(pp. 487–493)

Public Relations

Public relations (PR) is the communication function that seeks to build good relationships with an organization's *publics*; these include consumers, stockholders, legislators, and other stakeholders in the organization. Today marketers use PR activities to influence the attitudes and perceptions of various groups not only toward companies and brands but also toward politicians, celebrities, and not-for-profit organizations.

The basic rule of good PR is, *Do something good, and then talk about it*. A company's efforts to get in the limelight—and stay there—can range from humanitarian acts to sponsoring band tours. For example, after Baylor University's star center Isaiah Austin, expected to be a first-round National Basketball Association (NBA) draft pick, announced that he has been diagnosed with Marfan syndrome and would never play professional basketball, Commissioner Silver invited Austin to the draft and surprised everyone by announcing that the NBA was picking Isaiah Austin for "Team NBA."[52] The next day, Austin and his family were interviewed on CNN, and the story was covered on sports Internet sites and in newspapers around the world.

The big advantage of this kind of communication is that when PR messages are placed successfully, they are more credible than if the same information appeared in a paid advertisement. As one marketing executive observed, "There's a big difference between hearing about a product from a pitchman and from your trusted local anchorman."[53]

PR strategies are crucial to an organization's ability to establish and maintain a favorable image. *Proactive PR* activities stem from the company's marketing objectives. For example, marketers create and manage **publicity**, unpaid communication about an organization that gets media exposure. It's interesting to note that this aspect of PR is blending into other promotional strategies as social media continue to mushroom. Essentially, buzz marketing is also one form of PR because it tries to motivate consumers to talk up a brand or service to one another (ideally for free).

input measures
Efforts that go into selling, such as the number and type of sales calls, expense account management, and a variety of nonselling activities, such as customer follow-up work and client service.

output measures
The results of the salesperson's efforts.

public relations (PR)
Communication function that seeks to build good relationships with an organization's publics, including consumers, stockholders, and legislators.

publicity
Unpaid communication about an organization that appears in the mass media.

crisis management
The process of managing a company's reputation when some negative event threatens the organization's image.

As many of the other functions of PR blend into buzz marketing activities, perhaps the most important function it still "owns" is **crisis management**. This refers to the process of managing a company's reputation when some negative and often unplanned event threatens the organization's image. Think about the newly hired CEO at GM, for example, who had to apologize to the public about GM's faulty ignition switches that resulted in 31 crashes and the deaths of 13 people while still trying to instill confidence in the GM brand.[54] Or what about the team at Malaysia Airlines who had to respond to the mysterious disappearance of Flight MH370, which had more than 200 passengers and crew on board?

The goal in such situations is to manage the flow of information to address concerns so that consumers don't panic and distributors don't abandon the product. Although some organizations don't seem to learn this lesson, typically the best strategy is to be honest about the problem and to quickly take responsibility for correcting it. Carnival Cruise Lines learned this lesson all too well when a fire in the engine room on its ship *Triumph* caused 3,100 passengers and crew to be stranded at sea for five days without air conditioning or working toilets. Thanks to social media, word of the conditions on the "Poop Cruise" quickly spread. Then Carnival's crisis team jumped into action, launching a Facebook page and using Twitter to send out updates and mobilizing more than 200 Carnival employees to assist disembarking passengers when the ship finally docked. Carnival also gave a full refund to passengers, reimbursement for most of their onboard expenses, a flight home, $500 cash, and a credit toward a future cruise in an effort to make up for the unplanned disaster.[55]

PR professionals know that when a firm handles a crisis well, it can minimize damage and help the company make things right. Thus, a vitally important role of PR is to prepare a *crisis management plan*. This is a document that details what an organization will do *if* a crisis occurs—who will be the spokesperson for the organization, how the organization will deal with the press, and what sort of messages it will deliver to the press and the public.

Plan a PR Campaign

public relations campaign
A coordinated effort to communicate with one or more of the firm's publics.

A **public relations campaign** is a coordinated effort to communicate with one or more of the firm's publics. This is a three-step process that develops, executes, and evaluates PR objectives. Let's review each step, and then we'll examine some of the more frequently used objectives and tactics shown in 📷 Figure 14.5.

Figure 14.5 📷 *Snapshot* | Objectives and Tactics of Public Relations

Successful PR campaigns include clearly defined objectives and the use of the right PR activities.

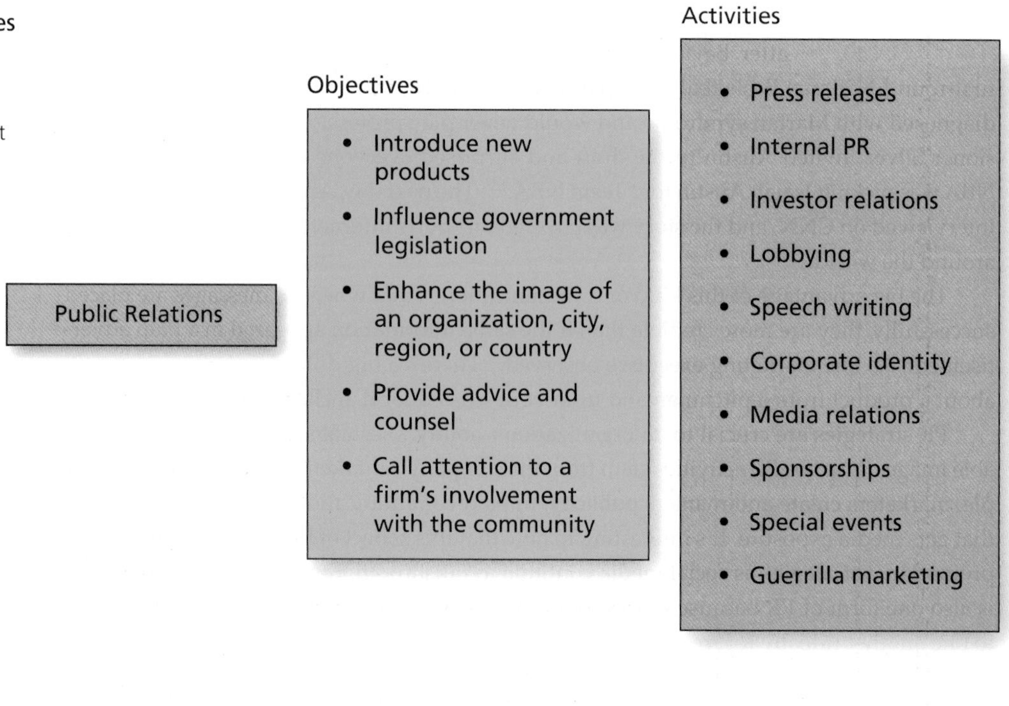

Public Relations

Objectives
- Introduce new products
- Influence government legislation
- Enhance the image of an organization, city, region, or country
- Provide advice and counsel
- Call attention to a firm's involvement with the community

Activities
- Press releases
- Internal PR
- Investor relations
- Lobbying
- Speech writing
- Corporate identity
- Media relations
- Sponsorships
- Special events
- Guerrilla marketing

Like an advertising campaign, the organization must first *develop* clear objectives for the PR program that define the message it wants people to hear. For example, the International Apple Institute, a trade group devoted to increasing the consumption of apples, had to decide if a campaign should focus on getting consumers to cook more with apples, drink more apple juice, or simply buy more fresh fruit. Because fresh apples brought a substantially higher price per pound to growers than apples used for applesauce or apple juice, the group decided to push the fresh fruit angle. It used the theme "An apple a day . . ." (sound familiar?) as it mounted a focused campaign to encourage people to eat more apples by placing articles in consumer media extolling the fruit's health benefits.

Execution of the campaign means deciding precisely how to communicate the message to the targeted public(s). An organization can get out its positive messages in many ways: news conferences, sponsorship of charity events, and other attention-getting promotions.

One of the barriers to greater reliance on PR campaigns is *evaluation*; compared to many other forms of marketing communications, it's difficult to devise metrics to gauge their effectiveness. Who can say precisely what impact an appearance by Josh Rogen on *The Tonight Show* to plug his new movie exerts on ticket sales or whether Virgin's sponsorship of the London Marathon boosted purchases of airline tickets? It is possible to tell if a PR campaign gets media exposure, though compared to advertising it's much more difficult to assess bottom-line impact. Table 14.1 describes some of the most common PR measurement techniques.

PR Objectives

Marketing communication experts know that PR strategies are best used in concert with advertising, sales promotion, and personal selling to send a consistent message to customers and other stakeholders. As part of the total marketing communication plan, they often rely on PR to accomplish the following objectives:

- *Introduce new products to retailers and consumers:* Amazon CEO Jeff Bezos created great excitement when he announced the company's work on Prime Air, a new delivery system that would deliver packages to customers in 30 minutes or less using drones. Of course, the excitement calmed down when a few months later the Federal Aviation Administration ruled that Amazon and other firms cannot use drones to deliver packages.[56]

- *Influence government legislation:* Airplane maker Boeing spent over a decade in public relations activities to persuade regulators that jetliners with two engines are as safe as those with three or four engines even for nonstop international flights, some as long as 16 hours.[57]

- *Enhance the image of an organization:* The Ladies Professional Golf Association used a variety of public relations and other promotion activities—from product endorsements to player blogs to sexy calendars—in its "These Girls Rock" campaign. The program to change the image of ladies' golf to a hip sport seems to be working, as both tournament attendance and TV audiences have increased.[58]

- *Provide advice and counsel:* Because of their expertise and understanding of the effects of communication on public opinion, PR professionals also provide *advice and counsel* for top management. When a firm needs to shut down a plant or to build a new one, to discontinue a product or add to the product line, to fire a vice president, or to give an award to an employee who spends hundreds of hours a year doing volunteer work in his community, it needs the advice of its PR staff. What is the best way to handle the situation? How should the announcement be made? Who should be told first? What is to be said, and how?

Table 14.1 | Measuring the Effectiveness of Public Relations (PR) Tactics

Method	Description	Example	Pros	Cons
Personal (subjective) evaluation of PR activities	Evaluation of PR activities by superiors may occur at all levels of the organization.	Items in employee annual reviews relate to the successful fulfillment of PR role.	Simple and inexpensive to complete; ensures that an annual assessment will be completed.	Subjective nature of the evaluation may result in biased appraisal. Employees may focus on the annual review to the exclusion of some important PR goals.
Matching of PR activity accomplishments with activity objectives	Simple counts of actual PR activities accomplished compares with activity goals set for the period.	Goal: to obtain publication of three feature articles in major newspapers in the first quarter of the year. Result: four articles published.	Focuses attention on the need for quantitative goals for PR activities and achievements. Easy and inexpensive to measure.	Focuses on activity goals rather than image or communication goals. Ignores image perception or attitudes of the firm's publics.
Evaluation of communication objectives through opinion surveys among the firm's publics	Surveys are used to determine if image/communication goals are met within key groups.	Goal: to achieve an improved image of the organization among at least 30 percent of financial community stakeholders.	Causes PR professionals to focus on actual communication results of activities.	May be difficult to measure changes in perceptions among the firm's publics. Factors not under the control of PR practitioners may influence public perceptions. It is relatively expensive. Results may take many months, thus preventing corrective actions in PR activities.
Measurement of coverage in print and broadcast media, especially those generated by PR activities	Systematic measurement of coverage achieved in print media (column inches/pages) and broadcast media (minutes of airtime).	Total number of column inches of newspaper articles resulting from PR releases. Total number of articles including those not from PR releases. Total amount of positive print and broadcast coverage. Total amount of negative print and broadcast coverage. Ratio of negative to positive print and broadcast coverage.	Very objective measurements with little opportunity for bias. Relatively inexpensive.	Does not address perceptions, attitudes, or image issues of the organization.
Impression measurement	Measure the size of the audience for all print and broadcast coverage. Often, assessment includes comparisons in terms of advertising costs for same number of impressions.	Network news coverage during the time period equaled over 15 million gross impressions. This number of impressions through advertising would have cost $4,500,000.	Objective, without any potential bias in measurement; provides a monetary measure to justify the expenditures of the PR office or consultant. Relatively inexpensive.	Does not differentiate between negative and positive news coverage. Does not consider responses of publics to the coverage. Assumes that advertising and PR communication activities are equal.

- *Enhance the image of a city, region, or country:* The city of Brooklyn Park, a suburb of Minneapolis, Minnesota, hired a PR firm to revamp its image. Once known as high-crime area, the city also suffered from "suburban blah." Brooklyn Park hopes its new PR investment can turnaround the city's image, making it a place people want to call home.[59]

- *Manage a crisis:* PR specialists handle the crucial but often difficult task of communicating with stakeholders when something goes wrong, such as when BP is involved in a massive oil spill, Honda recalls 900,000 of its minivans to due to fire risk, or GM issues a massive recall of cars with faulty ignition switches.

    Organizations respond in many ways, ranging from (unfortunately) complete denial or silence to full disclosure. For example, when Toyota started to receive reports of unsafe cars in the U.K., the director of the carmaker's operations there posted a five-minute video apologizing to consumers.[60]

- *Call attention to a firm's involvement with the community:* Marketers in the U.S. spend about $20 billion a year to sponsor sporting events, rock concerts, museum exhibits, and the ballet.[61] PR specialists work behind the scenes to ensure that sponsored events receive ample press coverage and exposure. We'll talk more about sponsorships later in this section.

Ripped from the Headlines

Ethical/Sustainable Decisions in the Real World

PR by marketers often appears out in the open, where everyone can see it—Procter & Gamble sent the Tide Loads of Hope Truck (a mobile laundromat) to Henryville, Indiana, to assist residents affected by tornadoes, for example.[62] But did you know that some PR activities are more covert and not always in the best interests of consumers?

Such is the case with two "bitter" rivals (pun intended)—the corn refinery and sugar industries—that spent tens of millions of dollars to influence public opinion about the risks and benefits of high-fructose corn syrup, sometimes without fully disclosing their efforts to the public. The rivalry began more than a decade ago when research suggested that high-fructose syrup might be a less healthy sweetener than sugar, and market share for the food additive declined as products like Gatorade and Wheat Thins changed the sweeteners they used.

So what is the Corn Refiners Association to do? Go on the defensive, of course—just not publicly. Instead, industry execs hired an advertising and PR firm to secretly fund a PR campaign to defend its products. They also paid a hefty monthly retainer to a doctor who led a research study that disputed the health consequences associated with high-fructose corn syrup to dispute claims that the product was any more dangerous than sugar.[63]

The Corn Refiners Association wasn't alone in its secretive PR efforts, however. The Sugar Association supported the nonprofit group Citizens for Health—but the group did not publicly disclose this financial support, which during one year amounted to half of its annual budget.

Both industries certainly have a right to defend their products, but the means by which they chose to do so might not have been their best efforts. Said John Bode, president of the Corn Refiners Association, "In retrospect, we could have been more clear and timely in the disclosure." Do you agree?

ETHICS CHECK: Find out what other students taking this course *would do* and *why* at **mymktlab .com**.

Is it ethical for marketers to secretly fund PR campaigns to defend their products?

☐YES ☐NO

PR Tactics

In order to accomplish their objectives, PR professionals choose from a variety of tactics, as shown in Figure 14.5. These activities include press releases, activities aimed at specific internal and external stakeholder groups, speech writing and corporate communications, sponsorships and special events, and guerilla marketing activities.

Press Release

The most common way for PR specialists to communicate is with a **press release**. This is a report of some event or activity that an organization writes and sends to the media in the hope that it will be published for free. A newer version of this idea is a video news release (VNR)

press release
Information that an organization distributes to the media intended to win publicity.

that tells the story in a film format instead. Some of the most common types of press releases include the following:

- *Timely topics* deal with topics in the news, such as Levi Strauss's efforts to promote "Casual Fridays" to boost sales of its Dockers and Slates casual dress pants by highlighting how different corporations around the country are adopting a relaxed dress code.

- *Research project stories* are published by universities to highlight breakthroughs by faculty researchers.

- *Consumer information releases* provide information to help consumers make product decisions, such as helpful tips from Butterball about how to prepare dishes for Thanksgiving dinner.

Internal PR and External Stakeholders

Internal PR activities target employees; they often include company newsletters and closed-circuit TV to keep people informed about company objectives, successes, or even plans to "downsize" the workforce. Often, company newsletters also are distributed outside the firm to suppliers or other important publics.

Investor relations activities focus on communications to those whose financial support is critical; this is especially vital for publicly held companies. It is the responsibility of the PR department to develop and distribute annual and quarterly reports and to provide other essential communications with individual and corporate stockholders, with investment firms, and with capital market organizations.

Lobbying means talking with and providing information to government officials to persuade them to vote a certain way on pending legislation or even to initiate legislation or regulations that would benefit the organization.

Speech Writing and Corporate Communications

An important job of a firm's PR department is **speech writing**; specialists provide speeches for company executives to deliver. While some executives do actually write their own speeches, it is more common for a speechwriter on the PR staff to develop an initial draft of a speech to which the executive might add her own input. PR specialists also provide input on **corporate identity** materials, such as logos, brochures, building design, and even stationery that communicates a positive image for the firm.

One of the tasks of the PR professional is to develop close **media relations** to ensure that the organization will receive the best media exposure possible for positive news, such as publicizing the achievements of an employee who has done some notable charity work or for a product the company developed that saved someone's life. And, as we've seen, good media relations can be even more important when things go wrong. News editors are less inclined to present a story of a crisis in its most negative way if they have a good relationship with PR people in the organization.

Sponsorships and Special Events

Sponsorships are PR activities through which companies provide financial support to help fund an event in return for publicized recognition of the company's contribution. Many companies today find that their promotion dollars are well spent to sponsor a golf tournament, a NASCAR driver, a symphony concert, or global events such as the Olympics or World Cup soccer competition. These sponsorships are particularly effective because they allow marketers to reach customers during their leisure time; people often appreciate these efforts because the financial support makes the events possible in the first place.

AT&T, for example, served as an exclusive "super sponsor" for South by Southwest (SXSW), the insanely popular music, film, and interactive festival held annually in

---

APPLYING ▼ Public Relations

Rohan knew the importance of press coverage that public relations could generate. It was press coverage that enabled Stylitics to achieve its early growth.

internal PR
PR activities aimed at employees of an organization.

investor relations
PR activities such as annual and quarterly reports aimed at a firm's investors.

lobbying
Talking with and providing information to government officials in order to influence their activities relating to an organization.

speech writing
Writing a speech on a topic for a company executive to deliver.

corporate identity
Materials such as logos, brochures, building design, and stationery that communicate an image of the organization.

media relations
A PR activity aimed at developing close relationships with the media.

sponsorships
PR activities through which companies provide financial support to help fund an event in return for publicized recognition of the company's contribution.

Austin, Texas. For the event, AT&T installed network resources so that fans could stay connected no matter where they went. That meant 215 WiFi spots throughout the Austin area, including a WiFi Hot Zone and charging stations. But that was just the beginning. AT&T also held a competition for the MOFILM community, hosted an AT&T Hackathon for mobile apps developers, and showed attendees the coolest places around Austin via the AT&T Teleporter.[64]

A related task is to plan and implement **special events**. Companies find special events useful for a variety of purposes. For example, a firm might hold a press conference to increase interest and excitement in a new product or other company activity. A city or state may hold an annual event such as the strawberry festivals in Florida and California or the National Cherry Blossom Festival in Washington, D.C., to promote tourism. As we noted earlier in the chapter, a company outing, such as the huge road rallies that Harley-Davidson's Harley Owners' Group (H.O.G) HOG sponsors, reinforces loyalty toward an existing product. Other special events aim simply to create buzz and generate publicity. For New York City shoppers, Unilever created its "All Small & Mighty Clothes Bus," a 40-foot bus it covered in all the shirts, shorts, and socks that one bottle of super-concentrated All laundry detergent can wash. Consumers who spotted the bus during its 12-day campaign could "clean up" if they entered a sweepstakes to win a $5,000 shopping spree or $200 gift cards.[65]

special events
Activities—from a visit by foreign investors to a company picnic—that are planned and implemented by a PR department.

Guerrilla Marketing

Organizations with tiny advertising budgets need to develop innovative—and cheap—ways to capture consumers' attention. **Guerrilla marketing** activities are an increasingly popular way to accomplish this objective. No, this term doesn't refer to marketers making monkeys out of themselves (that's "gorilla marketing"). A guerrilla marketing strategy involves "ambushing" consumers with promotional content in places where they don't expect to encounter these messages.

guerrilla marketing
Marketing activity in which a firm "ambushes" consumers with promotional content in places they are not expecting to encounter this kind of activity.

Ambient advertising is a popular type of guerilla marketing. This term describes the placement of messages in nontraditional media. Some examples include the backs of garage and theater receipts, screens attached to the back of supermarket carts, signs on elevator doors, or the ever popular signs on urinals in bars and restaurants—the possibilities are endless.

ambient advertising
Advertising placed where advertising isn't normally or hasn't ever been seen.

Another type of guerilla marketing is to stage an elaborate *flash mob*, where tens if not hundreds of people suddenly launch into a well-rehearsed dance routine in an unexpected place such as a train station or an airport. T-Mobile pulled this off at the Liverpool station in the U.K. as 350 pedestrians suddenly congregated in the center and launched into an elaborate group routine as the song *Shout!* played on huge speakers (check out the video at **www.youtube.com/watch?v=uVFNM8f9WnI**).

Today, big companies buy into guerrilla marketing strategies big time. Consider the "Wallet Drop" campaign in Singapore to help launch BK affordables—food so affordable it was like BK was putting money back in your wallet. To attract customers, BK dropped wallets loaded with BK coupons on park benches, under clothes racks, and in other locations through Singapore.[66] Now there's something you don't see every day.

Companies use guerrilla marketing to promote new drinks, cars, clothing styles, or even computer systems. Much to the annoyance of city officials in San Francisco and Chicago, IBM painted hundreds of "Peace Love Linux" logos on sidewalks to publicize the company's adoption of the Linux operating system. Even though the company got hit with a hefty bill to pay for cleaning up the "corporate graffiti," one marketing journalist noted that they "got the publicity they were looking for."[67] Given the success of many of these campaigns that operate on a shoestring budget, expect to see even more of these tactics as other companies climb on the guerrilla bandwagon.

Here's my choice...

Real **People**, Real **Choices**

1 Option   2 Option   3 Option

Why do you think Rohan choose option 2?

How It Worked Out at Stylitics

We chose option 2 and built our own campaign. We developed a concept that would leverage the strengths and appeal of the Stylitics digital closet platform while creating an incentive for people to share.

The campaign was called the Dream Closet Giveaway. We approached the Council of Fashion Designers of America (CFDA) and offered to donate a $25,000 designer closet as a prize in a drawing. Anyone who bought a T-shirt they had designed to support their breast cancer charity (see Exhibit 12.2) would be entered in the drawing. The CFDA is one of the best-known organizations in the fashion world. Once they agreed, we then approached brands and designers to see if they'd donate items to put into the Dream Closet. The incentive for the designers was that items would be shoppable on our digital closet platform, and the program would be promoted to CFDA's more than 250,000 followers. They also liked the idea of supporting the CFDA and a worthy charity. Over 25 of the world's best designers contributed products worth thousands of dollars and agreed to support the program through social media.

We handled all the design, setup, legal, and logistics, and we contributed our $5,000 budget toward adding items to the Dream Closet. We also provided all our partners with a social media kit with screen shots and copy to make it easier for them to share. It was a significant effort, but the outcome blew us away.

The campaign ran for two weeks in December 2014. Once the CFDA began promoting it, so did the brands and designers. By the end of the campaign, we had received social media promotion from brands like Calvin Klein, BCBGMAXAZRIA, Vince Camuto, and DKNY to millions of their followers. With that traction, we then contacted celebrities who had publicly supported breast cancer research in the past, leading to people like Kim Kardashian and Nicole Richie tweeting about the program. Then the media picked it up, and we received coverage, such as inclusion in Mashable's "8 Heartwarming Holiday Campaigns" alongside companies like Disney and Charity: Water.

How Stylitics Measures Success

By the final accounting, our $5,000 in social media budget had generated a campaign that reached over 25 million people and generated hundreds of tweets and retweets from celebrities, brands, and regular people. We got coverage from half a dozen publications. We also achieved our goals of new sign-ups and brand awareness, with over 50,000 page views and thousands of sign-ups. And best of all, we'd helped raise tens of thousands of dollars toward breast cancer research!

After the success of this campaign, we've changed how we look at social media. We use it to create campaigns that only we can do, including other charitable closet giveaways and hosting a weekly #stylechat on

A promotional T-Shirt for the Dream Closet Campaign.

Twitter. We also use it to share insights from our unique vantage point at the intersection of fashion and data through our blog *The Stylitics Report*. We've never hired an agency or spent much money. We've found that creativity and elbow grease can go a long way.

Refer back to **page 466** for Rohan's story ➡

MyMarketingLab™

Go to **mymktlab.com** to complete the problems marked with this icon ⭐ as well as additional Marketing Metrics questions only available in MyMarketingLab.

Objective Summary ➡ Key Terms ➡ Apply

CHAPTER 14
Study Map

---

1. Objective Summary (pp. 468–475)

Understand how marketers communicate using an updated communication model that incorporates buzz marketing activities and new social media.

Because consumers spend more time online and less time watching TV or reaching magazines, traditional advertising has diminished as a way to talk to consumers. Consumers today are increasingly getting their information on products from one another rather than from firms as technology magnifies the spread of consumer buzz. Marketers use buzz-building activities to encourage consumers to share their opinions about products with friends and neighbors. Buzz marketing can be unethical when marketers use activities designed to deceive consumers, when they direct buzz marketing to children or teens, and when buzz marketing activities encourage people to damage property.

Viral marketing refers to activities that aim to increase brand awareness or sales by consumers passing a message along to other consumers. Marketers may recruit loyal customers who care a great deal about a product and want it to succeed as brand ambassadors or brand evangelists to help create buzz.

Social media are Internet-based platforms that allow users to create their own content and share it with others. Social networking sites or social networks such as Facebook, Twitter, virtual worlds, product review sites, mobile apps, and location-based social networks connect people with other, similar people. Social networks provide opportunities for the development of brand communities formed by social network users on the basis of attachment to a product or brand.

Key Terms

groundswell, p. 468

buzz, p. 469

brand polarization, p. 470

tryvertising, p. 470

f-commerce, p. 470

viral marketing, p. 471

brand ambassadors or brand evangelists, p. 471

social media, p. 471

social networks, p. 472

Twitter, p. 473

virtual worlds, p. 473

avatars, p. 473

virtual goods, p. 473

product review sites, p. 474

location-based social networks, p. 475

2. Objective Summary (pp. 475–478)

Understand the elements of direct marketing.

Direct marketing refers to any direct communication designed to generate a response from a consumer or business customer. Some of the types of direct marketing activities are mail order (catalogs and direct mail), telemarketing, and direct-response advertising, including infomercials and m-commerce.

Key Terms

direct marketing, p. 475

catalog, p. 476

direct mail, p. 476

telemarketing, p. 476

direct-response advertising, p. 477

direct-response TV (DRTV), p. 477

infomercials, p. 477

m-commerce, p. 477

3. Objective Summary (pp. 478–482)

Appreciate the important role of personal selling and how it fits into the promotion mix.

Personal selling occurs when a company representative interacts directly with a prospect or customer to communicate about a good or service. Many organizations rely heavily on this approach because at times the "personal touch" can carry more weight than mass-media material. Generally, a personal selling effort is more important when a firm uses a push strategy in B2B contexts and for firms whose goods or services are complex or very expensive. Personal selling has been enhanced by the use of new technology, including customer relationship management (CRM) and partner relationship management (PRM), software systems and voice-over Internet protocol (VoIP) systems, such as Skype, that allow customers and salespeople to interact over the Internet.

Key Term

personal selling, p. 478

4. Objective Summary (pp. 482–483)

Identify the different types of sales jobs.

Order takers process transactions that the customer initiates. *Technical specialists* are very involved in giving product demonstrations, giving advice and recommendations, and product setup. *Missionary salespeople* work to stimulate purchase but don't take actual orders. *New-business salespeople*, or *order getters*, are responsible for finding new customers and calling on them to present the company's products. And, finally, *team selling* has become very prevalent in many industries as a way to bring together the expertise needed to better satisfy customer needs. *Transactional selling* focuses on making an immediate sale with little concern for developing a long-term relationship with the customer. It is sometimes called the "hard-sell" approach. In contrast, *relationship selling* involves securing, developing, and maintaining long-term relationships with profitable customers. Developing a customer relationship means ensuring that you and the customer find more ways to add value over time.

Key Terms

order taker, p. 482

technical specialist, p. 482

missionary salesperson, p. 482

new-business salesperson, p. 482

order getter, p. 483

team selling, p. 483

transactional selling, p. 483

relationship selling, p. 483

5. Objective Summary (pp. 484–487)

List the steps in the creative selling process.

The steps in the personal selling process include prospecting and qualifying, preapproach, approach, sales presentation, handling objections, closing the sale, and follow-up. These steps combine to form the basis for communicating the company's message to the customer. Learning the intricacies of each step can aid the salesperson in developing successful relationships with clients and in bringing in the business for their companies.

Key Terms

creative selling process, p. 484

prospecting, p. 484

preapproach, p. 484

approach, p. 485

sales presentation, p. 485

close, p. 486

follow-up, p. 486

input measures, p. 487

output measures, p. 487

6. Objective Summary (pp. 487–493)

Explain the role of public relations and the steps in developing a public relations campaign.

The purpose of PR is to build good relationships between an organization and its various publics and to establish and maintain a favorable image. Crisis management is the process of managing a company's reputation when some negative and often unplanned event threatens the organization's image.

The steps in a PR campaign begin with setting objectives, creating and executing a campaign strategy, and planning how the PR program will be evaluated. PR is useful to introduce new products; influence legislation; enhance the image of a city, region, or country; polish the image of an organization; provide advice and counsel; and call attention to a firm's community involvement.

PR specialists often use print or video news releases to communicate timely topics, research stories, and consumer information. Internal communications with employees include company newsletters and internal TV programs. Other PR activities include investor relations, lobbying, speech writing, developing corporate identity materials, media relations, arranging sponsorships and special events, and guerrilla marketing activities including ambient advertising.

Key Terms

public relations (PR), p. 487

publicity, p. 487

crisis management, p. 488

public relations campaign, p. 488

press release, p. 491

Chapter **Questions** and **Activities**

Concepts: Test Your Knowledge

14-1. What is groundswell? What did Li and Bernoff mean by this term?

14-2. What is brand polarization, and why is it often a good thing?

14-3. Define social media and explain its importance in the way marketers communicate with consumers.

14-4. What are social networks? How can marketers use them to help to build brand communities? What is the value of these brand communities?

14-5. What is direct mail? What is it also called, and what are its key advantages?

14-6. What is DRTV?

14-7. Why is personal selling particularly important in B2B contexts?

14-8. Describe the various types of sales jobs.

14-9. What is relationship selling? How does it differ from transactional selling?

14-10. What is prospecting? What does it mean to qualify the prospect? What is the preapproach? Why are these steps in the creative selling process that occur before you ever contact the buyer so important to the sale?

14-11. What are some ways you might approach a customer? Explain how some ways work better in one situation than another.

14-12. What is the objective of the sales presentation? How might you overcome buyer objections?

14-13. Why is follow-up after the sale so important in relationship selling?

14-14. What is the purpose of public relations? What is a crisis management plan? Describe some of the activities that are part of PR.

14-15. What is guerrilla marketing? What is ambient advertising?

Activities: Apply What You've Learned

14-16. *Creative Homework/Short Project* Many firms today are using a variety of buzz-building activities to encourage word-of-mouth communication about their products. Think about a business or place that you and your classmates might visit. You might, for example, think about (1) a specialty coffee shop, (2) a night spot where you and your friends might hang out on the weekends, or (3) a local theme or amusement park. For your selected product, develop ideas for at least three different buzz-building activities. Outline the details as to exactly how these activities would be implemented. Next, rank order the activities as to which you feel would be the best and tell why you feel that way. Develop a report for your class on your ideas.

14-17. *Creative Homework/Short Project* Assume that you are a marketing consultant for a client that has no presence in social media. How would you convince the client that it is advisable to establish a presence? Where would you start?

14-18. *In Class, 10–25 Minutes for Teams* In this chapter, we learned that brand polarization can be used in a positive way and that it encourages brand enthusiasts to engage with those who are negative about the brand. Find an example of bad buzz and how brand polarization affected a brand.

⭐ **14-19.** *Creative Homework/Short Project* You work for a direct marketing firm, and your client, who owns a lawn mowing and landscaping service, has enlisted your help in using various direct marketing approaches to reach out to potential customers. Consider carefully which forms of direct marketing would be most effective for your client and why. Devise a short presentation for your customer so that he can weigh the various options you recommend.

14-20. *Creative Homework/Short Project* Think of the last time you interacted with a salesperson, whether it was for a new tablet computer or a trendy pair of jeans. Identify the type of salesperson you were interacting with and explain what this person did to fulfill that particular role. Also identify whether this salesperson used a transactional selling approach or a relationship selling approach. Was this approach appropriate for the purchase you were considering? Why or why not?

⭐ **14-21.** *Creative Homework/Short Project* Assume a firm that publishes university textbooks has just hired you as a field salesperson. Your job requires that you call on university faculty members to persuade them to adopt your textbooks for their classes. As part of your training, your sales manager has asked you to develop an outline of what you will say in a typical sales presentation. Write that outline, including how you might handle a specific objective like "But this is the textbook we've always used, and it's always worked well for us."

14-22. *Creative Homework/Short Project* First, schedule an appointment with your university's marketing communication or university relations department to discuss their communication program. You will probably want to ask them about the following:

a. The target audiences for their communication program

b. The objectives of their communication program

c. The different types of traditional and nontraditional communication methods they use

d. How they evaluate the effectiveness of their communication program(s)

Based on your discussions, develop a report that (1) provides a critique of the university's communication program and (2) makes recommendations for improvement.

14-23. *In Class, 10–25 Minutes for Teams* Assume that you are the head of PR for a regional fast-food chain that specializes in fried chicken and fish. A customer has claimed that he became sick when he ate a fried roach that was in his chicken dinner at one of your restaurants. As the director of PR, what recommendations do you have for how the firm might handle this crisis?

Apply Marketing Metrics

One of the important benefits of social media such as Facebook and Twitter is that they allow marketers to easily learn what consumers are saying about their brand—and about the competition. To better understand that process, you can go out to Twitter and conduct a little detective work to see what consumers are saying about a brand:

14-24. Select a product type and particular brand of that product to study—it can be in any product category you choose. If you are doing a marketing plan project for your marketing course, you may use that product for this exercise. If not, choose a product type and brand that you use and like, one that you might use and are curious about, or one that you dislike.

14-25. Go to Twitter.com. Search for you selected brand and see what is revealed. After you have reviewed the results, provide a summary of the following information:

a. The number of tweets that are positive

b. The major aspects of your brand that people think are positive

c. The number of tweets that are negative

d. The major aspects of your brand that people think are negative

e. The number of tweets that ask questions

Choices: What Do You Think?

14-26. *Critical Thinking* A woman sued Taco Bell for deceptive advertising, claiming its tacos had far less beef than advertised. Taco Bell, understanding the potential damage to its brand, immediately went on the defense and filed a countersuit. In addition, Taco Bell's CEO posted a video statement and essentially released its recipe for seasoned beef, which contains 88 percent beef that is 100 percent USDA inspected.[68]

Was this enough for Taco Bell to do to avert a PR crisis? What else could they have done?

⭐ 14-27. *Critical Thinking* There is increasing concern about consumer privacy on social networking sites such as Facebook. How do you feel about privacy on social networks?

Is allowing personal information to be available to others without a user's specific permission unethical? Should the network owners do more to protect users' privacy? Should there be greater government regulation or should the sites be free to develop as they want to meet the needs of users? How much responsibility should users accept in protecting their own private information?

14-28. *Critical Thinking* Have you ever "liked" a company or product page on Facebook? Why did you do so? How often do you follow this company or product? Have you ever posted comments? If so, what was the purpose of your comments? Do you feel the brand owner communicates effectively with the brand community through this medium? Why or why not? What could the brand owner do better?

14-29. *Ethics* Many salespeople, especially those that sell financial products such as life insurance or annuities, earn their salary or a portion of their salary based on the product(s) they convince you to purchase. In addition, buyers are often uneducated about how the sellers make their money and about the product(s) themselves. What are the ethical obligations the seller has toward the buyer? Should the salesperson disclose how he or she earns his or her money? Is it ethical for a salesperson to try to sell the buyer a product that the salesperson receives a higher commission on? What responsibility does the buyer have in such situations?

14-30. *Critical Thinking* Recently, Twitter has joined other Internet sites in selling preferred positions on the site to generate revenue. Do you feel that such revenue-generating activities make sites such as Twitter less attractive? If you know that the top comments on a site have their positions because firms paid for them, are you likely to change your use of the sites? Are there other ways that an Internet site such as Twitter can generate revenue?

14-31. *Critical Thinking* M-commerce allows marketers to engage in *location commerce* when they can identify where consumers are and send them messages about a local store. Do you think consumers will respond positively to this? What do you think are the benefits for consumers of location commerce? Do you see any drawbacks (such as invasion of privacy)?

⭐ 14-32. *Critical Thinking* In general, professional selling has evolved from hard selling to relationship selling. Do some organizations still use the hard-sell style? If so, what types? What do you think the future holds for these organizations? Will the hard sell continue to succeed—that is, are there instances in which transactional selling is still appropriate? If so, when?

14-33. *Critical Thinking* Some critics denounce PR specialists, calling them "flacks" or "spin doctors" whose job is to hide the truth about a company's problems. What is the proper role of PR within an organization? Should PR specialists try to put a good face on bad news?

Miniproject: Learn by Doing

The purpose of this miniproject is to help you understand the advantages of following the creative selling process:

14-34. With several of your classmates, create a new product in a category that most college students buy regularly (e.g., toothpaste, shampoo, pens, pencils, soft drinks—anything that interests you that might be sold through a drugstore like Walgreens). Make up a new brand name and some creative features and benefits of the new product you come up with.

14-35. Assume you are a salesperson trying to sell your product to an organizational buyer like Walgreens for adding to their product lines. Develop a plan for executing each of the steps in the creative selling process. Make sure that you cover all the bases of how you would go about selling your product.

14-36. Report on your plan to your class and ask the other students for feedback on whether your approach will convince the Walgreens buyer to make a purchase.

Marketing in **Action** Case   Real Choices at Oreo

How do you like to eat your Oreo cookies? Oreo knows that they are many more ways to eat its iconic product than most customers would think. In addition to the classic *twist, lick, and dunk* way to enjoy an Oreo, "finding new ways to experiment with the cookie can be deliciously unexpected and fun," said Kristin Hajinlian, brand manager of Oreo at Mondelēz International, Inc.

A viral video of a fan dunking an Oreo in a glass of milk using a fork in order to keep her hands clean was the impetus for a new Oreo online Snack Hacks social media campaign. This viral video reminded Oreo marketers that eating and food were popular trends online. In reference to previous infamous tech Hackathons on the Internet, the company decided to name the campaign Snack Hacks.

The Snack Hack movement is in line with today's preference for cooking shows that highlight quirky implementation, indulgent ingredients, and exciting personalities. Oreo targeted the social media campaign toward die-hard fans who then turn around and amplify the brand on behalf of the company. "We look at our social content really as a way to connect with our fans," said Hanjinlian.

The Oreo SnackHacks campaign encouraged fans to post their own innovative ideas on eating Oreos on Twitter at #OreoSnackHack. Snack Hacks are a remixing of simple traditional recipes into new ways to be creative with food. Fans can use unusual ingredients, different kitchen utensils, or anything else to be a part of this innovative movement. Oreo fans responded with ideas such as grinding cookies in a pepper mill to create sprinkles and mixing Oreo bits with popcorn. The Twitter campaign spawned a Vine content area where fans shared a series of six-second videos.

With the success of the online fan SnackHack campaign, Oreo developed a new Web promotion with a video series showing the ideas of three top food innovators: "Top Chef" winner Michael Voltaggio making alcoholic Oreo Shandys, food truck revolutionary Roy Choi creating chicken tenders "breaded" with golden Oreos, and underground cooking sensation Nguyen Tran whipping up some Oreo bread pudding. The SnackHacks video series launched the brand's YouTube channel. Oreo fans were also encouraged to post their ideas including "how to" directions and pictures to the Oreo's Tumblr microblogging page.

While customer engagement is vital to brand success, it can be fleeting. Competition for consumers' attention is fierce. How should Oreo continue to engage customers? How does Oreo convert the social media excitement around Snack Hacks into revenue growth?

You Make the Call

14-37. What is the decision facing Oreo?

14-38. What factors are important in understanding this decision situation?

14-39. What are the alternatives?

14-40. What decision(s) do you recommend?

14-41. What are some ways to implement your recommendation?

Sources: Based on "Oreo and Celebrated Food Innovators Michael Voltaggio, Roy Choi and Nguyen Tran Team Up for New Snack Hacks Video Series," April 8, 2014, **www.reuters.com/article/2014/04/08/oreo-new-snack-hacks-idUSnPnbQFK32+9c+PRN20140408** (accessed June 27, 2014); Mondelēz International, "About Us," **www.mondelezinternational.com/about-us** (accessed May 14, 2014); and Igor Beuker, "How Oreo Refreshes Its Brand with Snack Hackaton Webisode?," April 4, 2014, **www.viralblog.com/community-marketing/how-oreo-refreshes-its-brand-with-snack-hackaton-webisode/#sthash.x1nKrFQg.dpuf** (accessed May 17, 2014).

MyMarketingLab™

Go to **mymktlab.com** for Auto-graded writing questions as well as the following Assisted-graded writing questions:

14-42. The manager of the training department at your marketing firm has asked you to help with writing a training manual that describes the selling process. To begin, include some information that describes why the creative selling process is so important. Then identify the steps and include a summary of each. Finally, include a paragraph that describes the importance of follow-up to the selling process.

14-43. What are the major differences between transactional selling and relationship selling?

Marketing Plan: The S&S Smoothie Company

This sample marketing plan includes the typical content for a marketing plan. The Executive Summary is first (highlighted in gray), followed by the various sections of the plan, beginning with the Situation Analysis. Note that in the margins, there are a number of notes to provide guidance in developing your marketing plan. Also, the relevant book part for each section is referenced.

Executive Summary

Situation Analysis

S&S Smoothie Company is a relatively young business that produces fruit-and-yogurt–based beverages with superior flavor and nutritional content and unique packaging. Within the United States, S&S has targeted a consumer market of younger, health-conscious, upscale consumers who frequent gyms and health clubs and two broad reseller markets: (1) gyms and health clubs and (2) smaller upscale food markets. S&S distributes its products through manufacturers' agents in the United States, Canada, and the United Kingdom and through Internet sales. An analysis of the internal and external environments indicates the firm enjoys important strengths in its product, its employees, and its reputation, while weaknesses are apparent in its limited size, financial resources, and product capabilities. S&S faces a supportive external environment, highlighted by a growing interest in healthy living and limited threats, primarily from potential competitive growth.

Marketing Objectives

The S&S marketing objectives are to increase awareness, gross sales (50 percent), and distribution and to introduce two new product lines over the next three years:

- A line of gourmet-flavored smoothies

- A line of low-carb smoothies

Marketing Strategies

To accomplish its growth goals, S&S will direct its marketing activities toward the following strategies:

1. *Target Market Strategy:* S&S will continue to target its existing consumer markets while expanding its organizational markets to include hotels and resorts, golf and tennis clubs, and university campuses.

500

2. *Positioning Strategy:* S&S will continue to position its products as the first-choice smoothie beverage for the serious health-conscious consumer, including those who are seeking to lower their carbohydrate intake.

3. *Product Strategy:* S&S will introduce two new product lines, each identifiable through unique packaging/labeling:
   a. *S&S Smoothie Gold:* A product similar to the original S&S Smoothie beverages but in six unique flavors
   b. *Low-Carb S&S Smoothie:* A product with 50 percent fewer grams of carbohydrates

4. *Pricing Strategy:* S&S will maintain the current pricing strategy for existing and new products.

5. *Promotion Strategy:* S&S will augment current personal selling efforts with television and magazine advertising, with sponsorships of marathons in major cities, and with a sampling program.

6. *Supply Chain Strategy:* S&S will expand its distribution network to include the organizational markets targeted. In addition, to encourage a high level of inventory in larger health clubs, S&S Smoothie will offer free refrigerated display units.

Implementation and Control

The Action Plan details how the marketing strategies will be implemented, including the individual(s) responsible, the timing of each activity, and the budget necessary. The measurement and control strategies provide a means of measurement of the success of the plan.

Situation Analysis

The S&S Smoothie Company[1] was founded in September 2008 in New York with the goal of creating and marketing healthy "smoothie" beverages for sale to health-conscious consumers. S&S Smoothie expects to take advantage of an increasing desire for healthy foods both in the United States and internationally—and to ride the wave of consumer interest in low-carb alternatives. While there are other companies both large and small competing in this market, S&S Smoothie feels it has the expertise to create and market superior products that will appeal to its target market.

Internal Environment

Mission Statement

The strategic direction and actions of the S&S Smoothie Company are driven by its mission:

> S&S Smoothie seeks to meet the needs of discriminating, health-conscious consumers for high-quality, superior-tasting smoothie beverages and other similar products.

Organizational Structure

As an entrepreneurial company, S&S Smoothie does not have a very sophisticated organizational structure. Key personnel include the following:

- Patrick Haynes, founder and co-president. Haynes is responsible for the creation, design, packaging, and production management of all S&S Smoothie products.

- William "Bill" Sartens, founder and co-president. Sartens is responsible for international and domestic distribution and marketing.

If you are developing a marketing plan for your class project, you may have the options of using a real company, an imaginary company that has been in business for a while such as S&S Smoothie or an imaginary new business that has never been in the market. Depending on which you choose, your marketing plan will have some differences. For example, if you use an existing firm you will have to find accurate information about the company for the situation analysis. If you have a fictitious company, you will have to create that information based on logical thinking. In this case, we have chosen to create an imaginary business.

PART ONE

- Allyson Humphries, chief financial officer. Humphries develops financial strategy and keeps the company's books.

- Alex Johnson, national sales manager. Johnson is responsible for maintaining the sales force of independent sales reps. He also advises on product development.

- Bob LeMay, Pam Sartens, and Paul Sartens, shareholders. Next to Patrick Haynes and William Sartens, Bob, Pam, and Paul own the largest number of shares. They consult and sit on the company's board of directors. Bob is a lawyer and also provides legal services.

Corporate Culture

S&S Smoothie is an entrepreneurial organization. Thus, a key element of the internal environment is a culture that encourages innovation, risk taking, and individual creativity. The company's beginning was based on a desire to provide a unique, superior product, and company decisions have consistently emphasized this mission.

Past and Current Marketing

The original S&S Smoothie product, introduced in mid-2008, is a fruit-and-yogurt–based beverage that contains only natural ingredients (no additives) and is high in essential nutrients. Because of the company's patented production process, S&S Smoothie beverages do not have to be refrigerated and have a shelf life of over a year. Therefore, the product can be shipped and delivered via nonrefrigerated carriers. S&S Smoothie currently sells its beverages exclusively through gyms, health clubs, and smaller upscale food markets. As a producer of dairy-based beverages, S&S Smoothie's NAICS (North American Industry Classification System) classification is 311511, Fluid Milk Manufacturers.

Current Products

For our imaginary young firm, we have decided that the company is already producing a single product. If you have a new firm, there would be no new products so this section including the discussion of current products, pricing, sales, and distribution would not exist. You will probably want to include a statement to this effect. If you are using a "real" firm, you will need to find accurate information about that firm. (Be sure to cite your sources for that information.)

At present, the single product line is the S&S Smoothie fruit and yogurt beverage. This healthy beverage product has a flavor and nutritional content that makes it superior to competing products. The present product comes in five flavors: strawberry, blueberry, banana, peach, and cherry. S&S offers each in a 12-ounce and a 20-ounce size. S&S packages the product in a unique hourglass-shaped, frosted glass bottle with a screw-off cap. The bottle design makes the product easy to hold, even with sweaty hands after workouts. The frosted glass allows the color of the beverage to be seen, but at the same time it communicates an upscale image. The labeling and lid visually denote the flavor with an appropriate color. Labeling includes complete nutritional information. In the future, S&S Smoothie plans to expand its line of products to grow its market share in the health drink market.

Current Markets

The consumer market for S&S Smoothie products is made up of anyone who is interested in healthy food and a healthy lifestyle. Although according to published research nearly 70 percent of American consumers say they are interested in living a healthy lifestyle, the number of those who actually work to achieve that goal is much smaller. It is estimated that approximately 80 million Americans actually engage in exercise and/or follow nutritional plans that would be described as healthy. As experts expect the trend toward healthier living to grow globally, the domestic market and the international market for S&S Smoothie products are expected to expand for some time.

Pricing

The suggested retail prices for S&S Smoothie beverages are $4.00 for the 12-ounce size and $6.00 for the 20-ounce container. S&S's prices to distributors are $1.20 and $1.80, respectively. At present, S&S Smoothie outsources actual production of the product. Still, the company takes care to oversee the entire production process to ensure consistent quality of its unique product. With this method of production, variable costs for the 12-ounce S&S Smoothie beverages are $0.63, and variable costs for the 20-ounce size are $0.71.

Customers/Sales

Sales of S&S Smoothie products showed slow but steady growth through 2010 due to poor economic conditions. But Actual sales figures for 2008 through 2014 are shown in Table A.1.

These sales figures plus S&S customer research show a strong and growing loyal customer base. This customer asset is important to the future of S&S. Nevertheless, research indicates that only about half of all consumers in the target market are aware of the S&S brand.

Within the U.S. consumer market, S&S Smoothie targets upscale consumers who frequent gyms and health clubs. Based on research conducted by S&S Smoothie, these consumers are primarily younger; however, there is also an older segment that seeks to be physically fit and that also patronizes health clubs.

Distribution

In order to reach its target market, S&S Smoothie places primary distribution emphasis on health clubs and other physical fitness facilities and small, upscale specialty food markets. The company began developing channel relationships with these outlets through individual contacts by company personnel. As sales developed, the company solicited the services of manufacturers' agents and specialty food distributors. Manufacturers' agents are individuals who sell products for a number of different noncompeting manufacturers. By contracting with these agents in various geographic regions, the company can expand its product distribution to a significant portion of the United States and Canada. Similar arrangements with agents in the United Kingdom have allowed it to begin distribution in that country.

The company handles large accounts such as Gold's Gym and World Gyms directly. While total sales to these chains are fairly substantial, when considering the large number of facilities within each chain the sales are very small with much room for growth.

The Internet is a secondary channel for S&S Smoothie. Online retail outlets currently account for only 5 percent of S&S Smoothie sales. Although this channel is useful for individuals who wish to purchase S&S Smoothie products in larger quantities, S&S does not expect that online sales will become a significant part of the business in the near future.

External Environment

Competitive Environment

S&S Smoothie faces several different levels of competition. Direct competitors are companies that also market smoothie-type beverages and include the following:

1. Franchise smoothie retail operations

2. Online-only smoothie outlets

Even if you are using an existing firm in your project, sales figures may not be available. Check with your instructor and ask if she would like for you to create sales records based on some logical assumptions.

Table A.1 | Company Sales Performance

Year	Gross Sales
2008	$287,850
2009	$438,770
2010	$672,146
2011	$1,211,445
2012	$1,686,228
2013	$1,918,376
2014	$1,995,120

For most of the discussion of the external environment, you should use accurate data that you normally can find on the Web. (Be sure to cite your sources for that information.) For other parts of this discussion, you may not be able to find real data and will need to create the section based on some logical assumptions.

3. Other smaller manufacturers

4. Larger companies such as Nestlé that produce similar products

Indirect competition comes from the following:

1. Homemade smoothie drinks made from powders sold in retail outlets and over the Internet

2. Homemade smoothie drinks made using a multitude of available recipes

3. Other healthy beverages, such as juices

4. A growing number of energy drinks that are especially popular with younger consumers

Economic Environment

S&S Smoothie first introduced its products during a period that proved to be the beginning of a worldwide recession. Despite this, the product gained momentum and sales steadily increased. Analysts estimate that the economic recovery will continue to be slow and take a number of years, during which time GDP and consumer sales will increase at a similarly low pace. With the continuing improvement of the economy, however, many analysts are suggesting growth opportunities for a variety of sectors of the economy.

Technological Environment

Because S&S Smoothie produces a simple food product, technological advances have minimal impact on the firm's operations. Nevertheless, the use of current technology enables and enhances many of the company's activities. For example, S&S Smoothie uses the Internet to enhance its operations in two ways. As noted previously, the Internet provides an additional venue for sales. In addition, manufacturers' agents and channel members can keep in contact with the company, allowing for fewer problems with deliveries, orders, and so on. Finally, in recent years, the company has established a presence on social media sites Facebook and Twitter through which it can communicate with consumers in a more personal way while monitoring consumers' feedback communication.

Political and Legal Environment

Because they are advertised as nutritional products, all S&S Smoothie products must be approved by the Food and Drug Administration (FDA). Labeling must include ingredients and nutritional information, also regulated by the FDA. In addition, S&S Smoothie products are regulated by the U.S. Department of Agriculture.

While there are no specific regulations about labeling or advertising products as low-carb, there is potential for such regulations to come into play in the future. In addition, there are numerous regulations that are country-specific in current and prospective global markets of which the company must constantly remain aware. Any future advertising campaigns developed by S&S Smoothie will have to conform to regulatory guidelines both in the United States and internationally.

Sociocultural Environment

S&S Smoothies uses marketing research to monitor the consumer environment. This research shows that changing cultural values and norms continue to provide an important opportunity for S&S Smoothie. The trend toward healthy foods and a healthier lifestyle has grown dramatically for the past decade or longer. In response to this, the number of health clubs across the country and the number of independent resorts and spas that offer patrons a healthy holiday have also grown. In addition, many travelers demand that hotels offer health club facilities.

During the past decade, consumers around the globe have become aware of the advantages of a low-carbohydrate diet. Low-carb menu items abound in restaurants, including fast-food chains such as McDonald's. A vast number of low-carb foods, including low-carb candy, fill supermarket shelves.

There are approximately 125 million American adults aged 15 to 44. Demographers project that this age-group will remain stable for the foreseeable future, with an increase of less than 8 percent projected to 2025. Similarly, incomes should neither decrease nor increase significantly in the near future in this segment of the population.

SWOT Analysis

The SWOT analysis provides a summary of the strengths, weaknesses, opportunities, and threats identified by S&S Smoothie through the analysis of its internal and external environments.

Strengths

The following are the strengths identified by S&S Smoothie:

- A creative and skilled employee team

- A high-quality product recipe that provides exceptional flavor with high levels of nutrition

- Because of its entrepreneurial spirit, the ability to remain flexible and to adapt quickly to environmental changes

- A strong network of manufacturers' agents and distributors

- The growth of a reputation of a high-quality product among health clubs, other retail outlets, and targeted consumer groups

Weaknesses

The following are the weaknesses identified by S&S Smoothie:

- Limited financial resources for growth and for advertising and other marketing communications

- Little flexibility in terms of personnel due to size of the firm

- Reliance on external production to maintain quality standards and to meet any unanticipated surges in demand for the product

Opportunities

The following are the opportunities identified by S&S Smoothie:

- A strong and growing interest in healthy living among both young, upscale consumers and older consumers

- Continuing consumer interest in low-carb alternatives that offers opportunities for additional product lines

Threats

The following are the threats identified by S&S Smoothie:

- The potential for competitors, especially those with large financial resources who can invest more in promotion, to develop products that consumers may find superior

- The continuation of a slowed economy that might affect sales

- Fizzling of the low-carb craze if other forms of dieting gain in popularity

- Increase in popularity of energy drinks like Rockstar, etc.

Many but not all experts recommend that the SWOT analysis should be a summary of the material covered in the discussions of the various internal and external environments. Strengths and weaknesses come from the facts presented in the internal environment, while opportunities and threats are based on discussions about the external environment. Be sure you check with your instructor on his or her perspective on the SWOT analysis.

Marketing Objectives

Remember that you will need to measure the success of your marketing strategies against your objectives. Therefore, your objectives should be quantitative, realistic, and measurable.

The following are the marketing objectives set by S&S Smoothie:

- To increase the awareness of S&S Smoothie products by at least 10 percent among the target market during the next year.

- To increase gross sales by 50 percent over the next two years

- To introduce two new product lines: a line of low-carb smoothies and a line of gourmet-flavored smoothies

- To increase distribution of S&S Smoothie products to include hotels and resorts, golf and tennis clubs, and university campuses both in the United States and globally during the next two years.

Marketing Strategies

PART TWO

Target Markets

S&S Smoothie has identified a number of consumer and organizational markets for its products.

Consumer Markets

Because the S&S Smoothie company has an existing product that was discussed in the Internal Environment Section, we were able to say we were continuing some of those same strategies in our Marketing Strategies sections. If you have determined that your marketing plan is for a new business without any marketing history, you will have to provide complete details on the target market, product, price, promotion and distribution.

S&S Smoothies will continue to target its existing consumer markets. Company research shows that the primary consumer target market for S&S Smoothie beverages can be described as follows:

Demographics

- Male and female teens and young adults

- Ages: 15–39

- Household income: $50,000 and above

- Education of head of household: College degree or above

- Primarily located in midsize to large urban areas or college towns

Psychographics

- Health-conscious, interested in living a healthy lifestyle

- Spend much time and money taking care of their bodies

- Enjoy holidays that include physical activities

- Live very busy lives and need to use time wisely to enjoy all they want to do

- Enjoy spending time with friends

- According to the VALS2™ typology, many are in the Achievers and Experiencers categories

Media Habits

- Individuals in the target market are more likely to get their news from television or the Internet than from newspapers. They are likely to view not only the news channels but also the financial news networks.

- The consumers prefer watching edgier shows such as *The Walking Dead*, *Breaking Bad*, *The Big Bang Theory*, and *Game of Thrones*.

- They are likely to have satellite radio installed in their automobiles.

- They are heavy users of social media, spending between two and three hours a day on sites including Facebook, Twitter, LinkedIn, and Foursquare.

- They frequently read magazines such as *Men's Health*, *BusinessWeek*, *Sports Illustrated*, and *The New Yorker*.

Organizational Markets

In the past, S&S Smoothie has targeted two categories of reseller markets: (1) health clubs and gyms, and (2) small, upscale specialty food markets. To increase distribution and sales of its products, S&S Smoothie will target the following in the future:

1. Hotels and resorts in the United States and in selected international markets

2. Golf and tennis clubs

3. College and university campuses

Upscale young professionals frequently visit hotels and resorts, and they demand that even business travel should include quality accommodations and first-rate health club facilities. The membership of golf and tennis clubs, while including many older consumers, also is an excellent means of providing products conveniently for the targeted groups. College and university students, probably more than any other consumer group, are interested in health and in their bodies. In fact, many universities have built large, fairly elaborate health and recreational facilities as a means of attracting students. Thus, providing S&S Smoothie beverages on college campuses is an excellent means of meeting the health beverage needs of this group.

Positioning the Product

S&S Smoothie seeks to position its products as the first-choice smoothie beverage for the serious health-conscious consumer, including those who are seeking to lower their carbohydrate intake. The justification for this positioning is as follows: Many smoothie beverages are available. The S&S Smoothie formula provides superior flavor and nutrition in a shelf-stable form. S&S Smoothie has developed its product, packaging, pricing, and promotion to communicate a superior, prestige image. This positioning is thus supported by all its marketing strategies.

Product Strategies

PART THREE

To increase its leverage in the market and to meet its sales objectives, S&S Smoothie needs additional products. Two new product lines are planned:

1. *S&S Smoothie Gold:* This product will be similar to the original S&S Smoothie beverage but will come in six unique flavors:

   a. Piña colada

   b. Chocolate banana

   c. Apricot nectarine madness

   d. Pineapple berry crush

   e. Tropical tofu cherry

   f. Peaches and dreams

The nutritional content, critical to the success of the new products, will be similar to that of the original S&S Smoothie beverages. Nutritional information is shown in Table A.2.

The packaging for the new S&S Smoothie product will also be similar to that used for the original product, utilizing the unique, easy-to-hold, hourglass-shaped, frosted glass bottle and providing the new beverage with the same upscale image. To set the product apart from the original-flavor Smoothie beverages in store refrigerator cases, labels will include the name of the beverage and the logo in gold lettering. The bottle cap will be black.

Table A.2 | Nutritional Information: S&S Smoothie Beverage

	S&S Smoothie Gold		Low-Carb S&S Smoothie	
	Amount per Serving	% Daily Value	Amount per Serving	% Daily Value
Calories	140		130	
Calories from fat	6		7	
Total fat	<0.5 g	1%	<0.5 g	1%
Saturated fat	<0.5 g	2%	<0.5 g	2%
Cholesterol	6 mg	2%	6 mg	2%
Sodium	70 mg	3%	70 mg	3%
Potassium	100 mg	3%	100 mg	3%
Total carbs	20 g	8%	10 g	4%
Dietary fiber	5 g	20%	5 g	20%
Protein	25 g	50%	25 g	50%
Vitamin A		50%		50%
Vitamin C		50%		50%
Calcium		20%		20%
Iron		30%		30%
Vitamin D		40%		40%
Vitamin E		50%		50%
Thiamin		50%		50%
Riboflavin		50%		50%
Niacin		50%		50%
Vitamin B^6		50%		50%
Vitamin B^{12}		50%		50%
Biotin		50%		50%
Pantothenic acid		50%		50%
Phosphorus		10%		10%
Iodine		50%		50%
Chromium		50%		50%
Zinc		50%		50%
Folic acid		50%		50%

Serving Size: 12 ounces

For 20-ounce sizes, multiply the amounts by 1.67.

2. *Low-Carb S&S Smoothie:* As shown in Table A.2, the Low-Carb S&S Smoothie beverage will have approximately 50 percent fewer grams of carbohydrates than the original Smoothie beverage or the S&S Smoothie Gold. Low-Carb S&S Smoothie will come in the following four flavors:

   a. Strawberry

   b. Blueberry

   c. Banana

   d. Peach

   Packaging for the Low-Carb S&S Smoothie will be similar to other S&S Smoothie beverages but will include the term "Low-Carb" in large type. The label will state that the beverage has 50 percent fewer carbs than regular smoothies.

Pricing Strategies

The current pricing strategy will be maintained for existing and new products. This pricing is appropriate for communicating a high-quality product image for all S&S Smoothie products. The company feels that creating different pricing for the new beverages would be confusing and create negative attitudes among consumers. Thus, there is no justification for increasing the price of the new products.

Pricing through the channel including margins is shown in Table A.3.

S&S Smoothie will continue to outsource actual production of the new offerings as it does with its existing product. As noted earlier, with this method of production, variable costs for the 12-ounce S&S Smoothie beverages are $0.63 and variable costs for the 20-ounce size are $0.71. Anticipated annual fixed costs for S&S Smoothie office space, management salaries, and expenses related to sales, advertising and other marketing communications are as follows:

Salaries and employee benefits	$525,000
Office rental, equipment, and supplies	$124,600
Expenses related to sales (travel, etc.)	$132,000
Advertising and other marketing communications	$450,000
Total fixed costs	$1,231,600

Sales of the two sizes of all S&S products are expected to be approximately equal; that is, half of sales will be for the 12-ounce size and half will be for the 20-ounce size. Thus, there will be an average contribution margin of $0.83 per bottle. Based on this, to achieve breakeven in units, S&S Smoothie must sell the following:

$$\frac{\$1,231,600}{.83} = 1,483,856 \text{ bottles}$$

Again, assuming equal sales of the two sizes of products, the break-even point in dollars is $2,225,784.

Promotion Strategies

In the past, S&S Smoothie has used mainly personal selling to promote its products to the trade channel. To support this effort, signage has been provided for the resellers to promote the product at the point of purchase. Posters and stand-alone table cards show appealing photographs of the product in the different flavors and communicate the brand name and the healthy benefits of the product. Similar signage will be developed for use by resellers who choose to stock the S&S Smoothie Gold and the Low-Carb Smoothies.

Selling has previously been handled by a team of over 75 manufacturers' agents who sell to resellers. In addition, in some geographic areas, an independent distributor does the selling. To support this personal selling approach, S&S Smoothie plans for additional

Even if you are using an existing firm in your project, fixed and variable costs may not be available. Check with your instructor and ask if she would like for you to create these figures based on some logical assumptions.

PART THREE

PART FOUR

Table A.3 | Pricing of S&S Smoothie Beverages

	12 Ounces	20 Ounces
Suggested retail price	$4.00	$6.00
Retailer margin	50%/$2.00	50%/$3.00
Price to retail outlets (health clubs, etc.)	$2.00	$3.00
Distributor/sales agent margin	40%/$0.80	40%/$1.20
Price to distributor/discount to sales agent	$1.20	$1.80
Variable costs	$0.63	$0.71
S&S contribution margin	$0.57	$1.09

promotional activities to introduce its new products and meet its other marketing objectives. These include the following:

1. *Television advertising:* S&S Smoothie will purchase a limited amount of relatively inexpensive and targeted cable channel advertising. A small number of commercials will be shown during prime-time programs with high viewer ratings by the target market. Television advertising can be an important means of not only creating awareness of the product, but also enhancing the image of the product.

2. *Magazine advertising:* Because consumers in the target market are not avid magazine readers, magazine advertising will be limited and will supplement other promotion activities. During the next year, S&S Smoothie will experiment with limited magazine advertising in such titles as *Men's Health*. The company will also investigate the potential of advertising in university newspapers.

3. *Sponsorships:* S&S Smoothie will attempt to sponsor several marathons in major cities. The advantage of sponsorships is that they provide visibility for the product while at the same time showing that the company supports activities of interest to the target market.

4. *Digital marketing:* S&S Smoothie will continue its use of social media to communicate with consumers and to monitor customers' postings about S&S products. In addition, S&S TV commercials will be available on the company website and on YouTube. In the latter part of the year, the company will sponsor a do-it-yourself ad competition through its website. The winning ads will be aired on cable TV.

5. *Sampling:* Sampling of S&S Smoothie beverages at select venues will provide an opportunity for prospective customers to become aware of the product and to taste the great flavors. Sampling will include only the two new products being introduced. Venues for sampling will include the following:

   a. Marathons

   b. Weightlifting competitions

   c. Gymnastics meets

   d. Student unions located on select college campuses

Supply Chain Strategies

PART FOUR

As noted earlier, S&S Smoothie distributes its beverages primarily through health clubs and gyms, and small, upscale specialty food stores. S&S Smoothie plans to expand its target reseller market to include the following:

1. Hotels and resorts in the United States and in targeted international markets

2. Golf and tennis clubs

3. College campuses

To increase leverage in larger health clubs, S&S Smoothie will offer free refrigerated display units. This will encourage the facility to maintain a high level of inventory of S&S Smoothie beverages.

Implementation

PART ONE

The action plan details the activities necessary to implement all marketing strategies. In addition, the action plan includes the timing for each item, the individual(s) responsible, and the budgetary requirements. Table A.4 shows an example of one objective (to increase distribution venues) and the action items S&S Smoothie will use to accomplish it.[2]

Table A.4 | Action Items to Accomplish Marketing Objective Regarding Supply Chain

Objective: Increase Distribution Venues

Action Items	Beginning Date	Ending Date	Responsible Party	Cost	Remarks
1. Identify key hotels and resorts, golf clubs, and tennis clubs where S&S Smoothies might be sold	July 1	September 1	Bill Sartens (consulting firm will be engaged to assist in this effort)	$25,000	Key to this strategy is to selectively choose resellers so that maximum results are obtained from sales activities. Because health club use is greater during the months of January to May, efforts will be timed to have product in stock no later than January 15.
2. Identify 25 key universities where S&S Smoothies might be sold	July 1	August 1	Bill Sartens	0	Information about colleges and universities and their health club facilities should be available on the university Web pages.
3. Make initial contact with larger hotel and resort chains	September 1	November 1	Bill Sartens	Travel: $10,000	
4. Make initial contact with larger individual (nonchain) facilities	September 1	November 1	Bill Sartens	Travel: $5,000	
5. Make initial contact with universities	August 15	September 15	Manufacturers' agents	0	Agents will be assigned to the 25 universities and required to make an initial contact and report back to Bill Sartens on promising prospects.
6. Follow up initial contacts with all potential resellers and obtain contracts for coming six months	September 15	Ongoing	Bill Sartens, manufacturers' agents	$10,000	$10,000 is budgeted for this item, although actual expenditures will be on an as-needed basis, as follow-up travel cannot be preplanned.

Measurement and Control Strategies

A variety of activities will ensure effective measurement of the success of the marketing plan and allow the firm to make adjustments as necessary. These include targeted market research and trend analysis.

Research

Firms need continuous market research to understand brand awareness and brand attitudes among their target markets. S&S Smoothie will therefore continue its program of focus group research and descriptive studies of its target consumer and reseller markets.

Trend Analysis

S&S Smoothie will do a monthly trend analysis to examine sales by reseller type, geographic area, chain, agent, and distributor. These analyses will allow S&S Smoothie to take corrective action when necessary.

PART ONE

You, Marketing, and Your Career

Although it may seem strange to think about the marketing of people, in reality we often talk about ourselves and others in marketing terms. It is common for us to speak of "positioning" ourselves for job interviews or to tell our friends not to "sell themselves short." Some people who are cruising for potential mates even refer to themselves as "being on the market." In addition, many consumers hire personal image consultants to devise a "marketing strategy" for them, while others undergo plastic surgery or makeovers to improve their "product images." The desire to package and promote ourselves is the reason for personal goods and services markets ranging from cosmetics and exercise equipment to résumé specialists and dating agencies.[1]

So the principles of marketing apply to people, just as they apply to coffee, convertibles, and computer processors. Sure, there are differences in how we go about marketing each of these, but the general idea remains the same: Marketing is a fundamental part of our lives both as consumers and as players in the business world. Perhaps a good place to start a discussion of careers is to look at the *who* and *where* of Marketing.

The *Who* and *Where* of Marketing

Marketers come from many different backgrounds. Although many have earned marketing degrees, others have backgrounds in areas such as engineering or agriculture. Retailers and fashion marketers may have training in merchandising or design. Advertising copywriters often have degrees in English or in psychology. E-marketers who do business over the Internet may have studied computer science.

Marketers work in a variety of locations. They work in consumer goods companies such as General Mills or at service companies like the Miami Heat basketball team. You'll see them in retail organizations like Sam's Club and at companies that manufacture products for other companies to use like NCR. You'll see them at philanthropic organizations such as the Red Cross or Product (RED) and at cutting-edge advertising and social media agencies like Google and Pandora.

And, although you may assume that the typical marketing job is in a large, consumer-oriented company like Disney, marketers work in other types of organizations too. There are many exciting marketing careers in companies that sell to other businesses. In small organizations, one person (perhaps the owner) may handle all the marketing responsibilities. In large organizations, marketers work on different aspects of the marketing strategy. No matter where they work, all marketers are real people who make choices that affect themselves, their companies, and very often thousands or even millions of consumers.

Marketing's Role in the Firm: Cross-Functional Relationships

What role do marketers play in a firm? The importance organizations assign to marketing activities varies a lot. Top management in some firms is very marketing oriented (especially when the chief executive officer comes from the marketing ranks), whereas in other companies marketing is an afterthought. However, analysts estimate that at least one-third of CEOs come from a marketing background—so stick with us!

Sometimes a company uses the term *marketing* when what it really means is sales or advertising. In some organizations, particularly small, not-for-profit ones, there may be no one in the company specifically designated as "the marketing person." In contrast, some firms realize that marketing applies to all aspects of the firm's activities. As a result, there has been a trend toward integrating marketing with other business functions (such as management and accounting) instead of making it a separate function.

No matter what size the firm, a marketer's decisions affect—and are affected by—the firm's other operations. Marketing managers must work with financial and accounting officers to figure out whether products are profitable, to set marketing budgets, and to determine prices. They must work with people in manufacturing to be sure that products are produced on time and in the right quantities. Marketers also must work with research-and-development specialists to create products that meet consumers' needs.

Where Do You Fit In? Careers in Marketing

Marketing is an incredibly exciting, diverse discipline that brims with opportunities. There are many paths to a marketing career; we've tried to summarize the most typical ones here. Check out Table B.1 to start thinking about which path might be best for you. Then we'll talk about how you can use your knowledge of marketing in finding a successful career whether in marketing or some other field.

Table B.1 | Careers in Marketing

Marketing Field	Where Can I Work?	What Entry-Level Position Can I Get?	What Course Work Do I Need?
Advertising	Advertising agency: Media, research, and creative departments; account work Large corporation: Advertising department: brand/product management Media: Magazine, newspaper, radio, and television selling; management consulting; marketing research	Account coordinator (traffic department); assistant account executive; assistant media buyer; research assistant; assistant brand manager	Undergraduate business degree
Brand management	Any size corporation: Coordinate the activities of specialists in production, sales, advertising, promotion, research and development, marketing research, purchasing, distribution, package development, and finance	Associate brand manager	MBA preferred, but a few companies recruit undergraduates. Expect a sales training program in the field from one to four months and in-house classes and seminars.

(continues)

Table B.1 | Careers in Marketing *(continued)*

Marketing Field	Where Can I Work?	What Entry-Level Position Can I Get?	What Course Work Do I Need?
B2B marketing	Any size corporation: Only a few companies recruit on campus, so be prepared to search out job opportunities on your own, as well as interview on campus.	Sales representative; market research administrator; product manager; pricing administrator; product administrator; assistant marketing manager; sales administrator; assistant sales manager; sales service administrator	Undergraduate business degree. A broad background of subjects is generally better than concentrating on just one area. A technical degree may be important or even required in high-technology areas. Courses in industrial marketing and marketing strategy are very helpful.
Data scientist	All types of service, manufacturing, financial, government and other organizations are hiring data scientists as the importance of collecting and analyzing big data grows.	Associate data scientist to work with a data science team. Other titles include research associate and data analyst to name a few.	A strong foundation typically in computer science and applications, modeling, statistics, analytics and math, data mining and predictive analytics. BS or higher in applied math, statistics, computer science, or related field. Some jobs require a master's or PhD in math, statistics, data mining or related field. Ability to communicate findings to both business and information technology leaders in a way that can influence how an organization approaches a business challenge is desirable. Good data scientists will not just address business problems, they will pick the right problems that have the most value to the organization.
Direct-response marketing	Any size corporation: Marketing-oriented firms, including those offering consumer goods, industrial products, financial institutions, and other types of service establishments. Entrepreneurs seeking to enter business for themselves.	Direct-response marketing is expanding rapidly and includes direct mail; print and broadcast media, telephone marketing, catalogues, in-home presentations, and door-to-door marketing. Seek counsel from officers and directors of the Direct Marketing Association and the Direct Selling Association.	Undergraduate business degree. Supplemental work in communications, psychology, and/or computer systems recommended.
Supply channel management	Any size corporation, including transportation corporations: The analysis, planning, and control of activities concerned with the procurement and distribution of goods. The activities include transportation, warehousing, forecasting, order processing, inventory control, production planning, site selection, and customer service.	Physical distribution manager; supply chain manager; inventory-control manager; traffic manager; distribution-center manager; distribution-planning analyst; customer service manager; transportation marketing and operations manager	Undergraduate business degree and MBA. Broad background in the core functional areas of business, with particular emphasis in distribution related topics such as logistics, transportation, purchasing, and negotiation.

Marketing Field	Where Can I Work?	What Entry-Level Position Can I Get?	What Course Work Do I Need?
International marketing	Large corporations: Marketing department at corporate headquarters	Domestic sales position with an international firm may be the best first step toward international opportunities.	MBA. A broad background in marketing is recommended, with some emphasis on sales management and market research.
Marketing models and systems analysis	Large corporations: Consult with managers who are having difficulty with marketing problems.	Undergraduate: Few positions available unless you have prior work experience. Graduate: market analyst, market research specialist, and management scientist.	MBA. Preparation in statistics, mathematics, and the behavioral sciences.
Marketing research	Any size corporation: Provide management with information about consumers, the marketing environment, and the competition	Assistant market analyst or assistant product analyst level.	MBA or an MS in marketing research, although prior experience and training may improve an undergraduate's chances.
New product planning	Any size corporation: Marketing of consumer products, consumer industries, advertising agencies, consulting firms, public agencies, medical agencies, retailing management	Assistant manager or director of product planning or new product development.	MBA
Retail management	Retail corporations	Assistant buyer positions; department manager positions	Undergraduate business degree
Sales and sales management	Profit and nonprofit organizations: Financial, insurance, consulting, and government	Trade sales representative who sells to a wholesaler or retailer; missionary sales representative in manufacturing who sells to retailers or decision makers (e.g., pharmaceutical representative); technical sales representative who sells to specified accounts within a designated geographic area.	Undergraduate business degree; MBA; *Helpful courses*: consumer behavior, psychology, sociology, economics, anthropology, cost accounting, computer science, statistical analysis, communications, drama, creative writing. Language courses, if you're interested in international marketing; engineering or physical science courses if you're interested in technical selling.
Services marketing	Any size corporation: Banking and financial service institutions, health care organizations, leisure-oriented businesses, and in various other service settings.	Assistant brand manager; assistant sales manager	Undergraduate business degree; MBA; additional course work in management policy, research, advertising and promotion, quantitative analysis, consumer behavior, and the behavioral sciences should prove useful.

Source: This information was based on an excellent compilation prepared by the marketing faculty of the Marshall School of Business, University of Southern California, at www.marshall.usc.edu/marketing/resources/resources-overview.htm (accessed June 11, 2010). For average salaries broken down by job type and state, consult the *Aquent/AMA Survey of Marketing Professionals* at www.marketingsalaries.com/aquent/Home.form or commercial websites, such as Payscale.com and Rileyguide.com.

Marketing and Your Career

Do you just hate it when someone asks, "What are you going to do when you graduate?" Perhaps you avoid the question by saying "Get a job—I hope."

Many college students like you have an idea of the type of career they might like but don't have a clue as to how to get there. Still others just don't even have any idea about what job they would enjoy—they just want to get one. In this appendix, we will be talking about how you can use marketing strategies to not only choose a job but also assist you in actually landing the job you want.

It's all about thinking of yourself as a product—a unique brand—and how to best market that brand. In fact, *you* are a product. That may sound weird, but companies like Linked-In couldn't exist if you were not a product with value. As we have said, *value* refers to the benefits a customer receives from buying a good or service.

You have "market value" as a person—you have qualities that set you apart from others and abilities other people want and need. After you finish this course, you'll have even more value because you'll know about the field of marketing and how this field relates to you both as a future businessperson *and* as a consumer. In addition to learning about how marketing influences each of us, you'll have a better understanding of what it means to be "Brand You"—and, it is hoped, some ideas about what you can do to increase your value to employers and maybe even to society.

Create Your Personal Marketing Plan

Because we think the best way to start a career includes much of what we know from marketing, we'll talk about developing your career as the process as creating and marketing your own personal brand. It's not about what kind of job you want after graduation—it's about what career you want and what you want to be doing 5, 10, or 15 years from now.

In Chapter 3 of this text, we talked about the steps in developing a marketing plan. We'll use those same steps in your plan to develop a great career.

Step 1: Define Your Mission

As we discussed in Chapter 3, a first step for an organization—or for you—is to define your mission—a statement of your overall purpose and what you hope to achieve. Just like a firm's mission statement guides the plans of all the functional areas of the firm, from human resources to marketing, your mission statement will guide you in your career search. It will provide the foundation of goal-directed behavior now and in the future.

As a beginning to developing a personal mission statement, you will probably want to think about what you enjoy doing the most in your life. This is important because you'll be most successful if you enjoy your career—if you like going to work every day. Some examples of what you might include in this list are the following:

- Helping people
- Developing and executing creative ideas
- Working with other people—or alone
- Working with quantitative concepts—or with words

Based on this, you can develop a concise statement of what you want in your career.

Example: "To work in a creative, value-focused environment with the goal of providing products that help make lives better."

Step 2: Perform a Situation Analysis

The next important step in any planning process is to have a clear, honest, and accurate understanding of where you are—your situation analysis. The situation analysis includes an understanding of the internal environment, an examination of the external environment in which you will look for a job and work, and a SWOT analysis.

The Internal Environment

What are your skills, talents, values, strengths, weaknesses? Are you good at writing or at persuading others to accept your ideas? Do you motivate other people? Are you good at developing strategies to achieve goals, generating innovative ideas, and/or initiating change? Are you a detail person? Do you persevere until you find the solution to a problem? Are you dependable? Can you accept criticism? Do you like or dislike being in charge? Do you hate wearing a suit and dream of a career where you can wear jeans, a T-shirt and flip-flops? Are there some things that you really hate doing such learning new things? Have you created a large debt in loans to pay for your college so that salary is critically important to you in a job? Are you tied to a specific location by family or unwillingness to relocate? Do you have any physical limitations? What are your plans and dreams for a family? It's important that you carefully and critically examine yourself before you begin a career exploration.

The External Environment

There are many factors in the external environment, factors that you have no control over and that you need to recognize and understand. These include factors that exist now, that you can expect to change in the future, and that will affect you and others who are entering the workforce. Some of these might be the following:

- Changing technology
- A changing competitive environment
- The state of the national and global economy
- Changing cultural values, tastes, and trends
- The movement of work to other locations both in and outside your home country
- Computers replacing people in jobs
- Changing population demographics
- Changing environmental and other government regulations
- The increasing importance of social media for consumers and for businesses

Your Personal SWOT Analysis

A SWOT analysis is kind of a summary of the examination of your internal and external environments. It focuses on what you have learned about yourself and identified as strengths that you can offer an employer and weaknesses that you need to address and/or make sure they will not create a road to disaster in your career.

Strengths:
- You probably have strengths that set you apart from others. You may be detail oriented, tech savvy, persistent, creative, good with quantitative analysis, and/or getting along with others.

Weaknesses:
- We all have weaknesses, but what are yours? You may be easily defeated if things don't go well. Some people find it very difficult to accept the ideas of others if they are different from their own. Your weakness may be difficulty in expressing your ideas to others.

Opportunities: What is happening in the external environment that provides good opportunities where your strengths are needed and your weaknesses are not a "deal breaker"?

- As the population ages, more job opportunities will open up.
- New opportunities in growing industries such as Internet communications, services for the aging population, and the demand for improved education including new delivery methods.

Threats: What factors that you can't control may have a negative impact on your career success?

- Predictions for the economic environment in the short term and in the long term may provide threats to career success. Of course, they may also provide opportunities.

- As marketing communication changes, new skills will be needed that you may not have.

- The increasing number of college graduates means a highly competitive hiring environment in which only the best will succeed.

Step 3: Develop Your Marketing/Career Objectives

Objectives, whether for an organization or for you as an individual seeking a career need to be specific, quantitative, measurable, attainable, and realistic. You can find out more about this in Chapter 3.

Depending on where you are in your education and career search, some examples may be the following:

- To obtain two internships in marketing areas of firms before graduation

- To obtain an entry-level marketing position with a firm that has at least $50 million in sales within the first three years after graduation

- To earn a salary of at least $30,000 within the first year after graduation

Step 4: Develop Marketing Strategies

Just as marketers know that their success in selling a new brand of toothpaste depends on developing target marketing, product, pricing, promotion, and distribution strategies, you need to develop great strategies for career success.

Target Marketing Strategy: Select Target Markets and Positioning

Firms large and small must conduct research to determine the best target market for their new brand of toothpaste or laundry detergent or jeans. You need to conduct research in order to identify your ideal job. Your research will seek to discover (1) if a potential employer is somewhere you would like to work and (2) if the employer has a job in which you can be successful.

Organizational Culture

One important aspect of a job and a career that you should consider is the organizational culture. Many young people today feel that their personal happiness is just as if not more important than the money they make. Companies like Zappos are creating a paradigm shift in terms of the work environment. At Zappos, the company's goal is to "wow" the customer, not just satisfy them. Every employee, including the top people, have the same size desk and space, which they are encouraged to decorate any way they choose. There are no private offices but lots of small conference rooms available to everyone for meetings. Healthy snacks are available for everyone for free, and less healthy snacks are in vending machines for a price. And if you ever see a coat and tie in the building, it will be a guest. Jeans and flip-flops are more the norm. Does this kind of work atmosphere appeal to you?

Of course, there are other, often more important aspects of an organization's culture. Your research should include such things as the following:

- The management philosophy

- The history of the company

- The size of the organization

- The ethical values of the firm

- The opportunities for upward mobility within the firm

- Does the firm believe in risk taking or are they conservative?

One of the best ways to find out about a company is the Web. Company websites, social media, blogs, and other sites will provide you with useful information about organizations.

Finding Potential Jobs

As we said earlier, your research should also look at identifying employers who are looking for someone with your knowledge and skills. Again, the three most important activities for finding the right job are research, research, and research. Go beyond just searching what is available today. Investigate what trends are changing the job scene. What careers are expected to be important in the future? What industries are growing? How is technology expected to influence the job market?

You will, of course, need to identify specific jobs A few sources that might be useful for you are listed in Table B.2.

Positioning Yourself

As you recall, the third step in target marketing is positioning yourself. Positioning is placing yourself in the customer's (the hiring firm's) mind in relation to the competition (other candidates for the job). If you will be applying for several different types of jobs, you may need to develop slightly different positioning for different jobs by focusing on specific

Table B.2 | Sources of Career and Job Information

What Information Is Available?	Sources
News, trends, and general information on industries.	www.hoovers.com www.bls.gov/oco www.online.onetcenter.org
Advice on career planning.	Your campus career center http://career-advice.monster.com www.salary.com
Professional trade organizations in the area which you are interested. These often include internship and full-time job listings.	www.associationjobboards.com
Individual industry publications that often include job listings.	Advertising: www.adage.com www.aaf.org Accounting and finance: www.afponline.org Marketing: www.marketingjobs.com Marketing research: www.mra-net.org Sales and marketing: www.smei.org
Local business journals provide news on local businesses and local job listings.	For business journal websites in your community, www.bizjournals.com
Lists of top businesses can provide lists of businesses that might be target companies.	Publications such as www.businessweek.com www.wsj.com For marketing related firms, www.marketingpower.com
Professional social networks allow you to create a network of people to make contacts.	www.linkedin.com

skills or experiences. There are some characteristics that are universally important that you should use in positioning yourself for a job. These include the following:

- Communication skills
- Honesty and integrity
- Teamwork
- A strong work ethic
- Initiative
- Flexibility
- Problem solving
- Computer skills

Product Strategies

Just as we discussed in Chapter 8, developing a product concept means thinking in terms of the product layers, that is, the core, the actual, and the augmented product:

- *The core product:* The benefits the firm will receive if they hire you. In your job search, you should be prepared to offer arguments and evidence that you can provide the benefits that will meet the needs of the job exceptionally well. Remember, the firm wants someone who will be an asset in helping them achieve their goals. These may be related to higher sales, increased customer satisfaction, lower costs, or something else. If they don't see you as providing that benefit, they will look for someone else.

- *The actual product:* The actual product is all about your perceivable "features." These include not only your skills related to the specific positions, such as knowledge of research methods or experience in developing branding strategies, but also those personal characteristics listed earlier.

- *The augmented product:* The augmented product for a job includes those benefits you will provide for the employer that are not requirements of the job. Are you willing to travel? Will you work overtime? Do you have some additional skills not required of the job but which you feel will be useful to the firm?

Pricing Strategies: What salary should you ask for?

When you think about price you will expect for your work, you need to consider not only the salary but also the benefits and perks the employer is offering. In many jobs, there is a base salary plus other monetary compensation in terms of a commission, bonus, or stock options. Employee benefits normally include a variety of insurance plans (medical, dental, etc.), sick leave, vacation time, day care, tuition reimbursement, and retirement plans. Perks offered by employers might be on-site cafeterias offering meals at low prices, health/workout facilities, free coffee and healthy snacks, flexible working hours, on-site day care facilities, and/or on-site basic medical care.

Sooner or later, you will have to answer the question of what salary you will need. To answer this question, some advance preparation is necessary. You may want to begin thinking about the minimum you will need to pay your basic expenses. How much more than this would you like to earn in order to have some discretionary income? Based on that, you can ask for a salary range a little above that to give yourself some negotiating room. For example, if your minimum to pay your expenses is $30,000 but you would like at least $33,000, then you might ask for $35,000 to 40,000 in order to get what you want after salary negotiations. And don't forget in your calculations to consider what you need for transportation, taxes, Social Security, deductions for retirement plans and other costs of being employed.

Most experts say that you should not bring up the subject of compensation (salary and benefits) but rather wait until the employer brings it up. If asked what you need, you may be wise not to give a specific amount unless it is demanded. A good answer might be "I'm sure you have a competitive compensation plan."

Promotional Strategies: Your Personal Marketing Communication Plan

Of course, you want to develop a great integrated marketing communication plan in order to let potential employers know about you. The opportunities for communication include the following:

- Networking: Word of mouth is probably the most influential source of information for employers. Many employers would prefer not to even post a job. You might think of networking as a sort of personal selling. Just like a salesperson practices customer relationship management by regularly contacting prospective customers, you need to keep in touch with contacts and try to be helpful to them. Your networking should begin with your family and friends. You should also be sure to obtain contact information to maintain relationships with your college peers and professors. If there is a business professional as a guest speaker in your class or for a school club, make a point to meet him or her and get his or her card before he or she leaves. Follow up with a thank-you note to ensure that the speaker remembers you.

- Career fairs can be great places to meet a number of different potential employers. Be sure to "dress for success" and bring copies of your cover letter and your résumé. Always ask for a business card so that you can follow up with the career fair contact with a note.

- Company websites based on a list of companies you have developed as discussed earlier.

- Social networking sites, such as www.Linkedin.com, www.jobster.com, and www .ryze.com.

- Online job boards and recruiting websites. Some general job boards and recruiting sites include www.collegegrad.com, www.careerbuilder.com, www.black-collegian .com, www.hotjobs.yahoo.com, www.monster.com, and your own campus career website. Some industry-specific boards include www.marketingjobs.com, www .marketingsherpa.com, and www.thebossgroup.com.

- Direct mail: To let prospective employers know about you, send them a letter—a real paper and envelope letter (not e-mail)—and your résumé. Be sure you send your letter to the right person or people at a company. A well-written letter can make you stand out from the crowd. Be sure that you don't have any spelling, grammatical, or punctuation errors in your letter or your résumé.

Advertising: Your Résumé and Cover Letter

The résumé and the cover letter are the most important elements of marketing communication for any job applicant. They're your advertising. It's important that both communicate that you have the knowledge and skills the employer is looking for. And it isn't enough just to say you know how to write a press release or create a marketing plan; you need to indicate that you have actually written the release or plan, perhaps in a class or for an internship. In this way, you can set yourself apart from your competitors, that is, the other job applicants. Most important, both your résumé and your cover letter must be well written if you want to "sell" yourself to the employer.

Résumé:

Writing a résumé for the first time can overwhelming. Fortunately, most universities have career services personnel who will help you in the task. Of course, they will probably ask that you put together a first draft, and then they will help you fine-tune it. Below are some suggestions for that first draft:

1. Get organized before you begin writing. Make notes on your jobs, internships, honors, extracurricular activities, leadership experiences, community service, class projects, and course work. But don't just create a list—you also need to describe exactly what you did, what you learned, what skills you gained, etc., with each experience. And be sure to keep a record of any names and addresses of people whom you came in contact with in these activities. Accuracy is important in these notes. One thing you must never do is to *lie or exaggerate* on your résumé.

2. Tailor to the job. Your individual experiences, skills, etc., may be more or less important for different jobs. Because you should tailor your résumé for different jobs, you should think about which are more important for the job at hand.

3. Section headings. Heading are important for any document and especially so for a résumé. The normal headings for a résumé for a college student seeking a first career position are "Education," "Honors and Scholarships," and "Work Experience." Other headings may be "Leadership Experience," "Athletic Achievements," "Professional Associations," "Extracurricular Experience," "International Language Skills," "Software Skills," and "Community Service." If you have had important internship or employment experience, you will probably want to list three to five accomplishments for each.

4. The "look" of the résumé. Looks are very important in a resume. In general, your résumé should not exceed one page, should be in a single font, and should have lots of white space so that it is easy to read.

5. Be sure there are no typos, misspellings, or grammatical errors and print on white or neutral-colored paper.

Cover Letter:

A good cover letter is as important or even more important than a good résumé. If the cover letter has typos or other errors, the employer will likely never even read the résumé. The logic is that if you can't write a good letter, they simply don't want you.

You may choose to format your cover letter with a series of paragraphs, or you may choose to use an introductory sentence or two followed by bullets. That decision is based on what and how much you want to say. The letter should do the following:

• Include your name, address, and the date

• Include an inside address

• Be addressed to an individual person by name

• Include a personal salutation: "Dear Mr. . . . ."

• Have an introductory paragraph that talks about the position you are seeking, how you learned about it, and why you are interested in the position.

• Discuss your experience and skills that make you a good candidate for the job in the body of the letter

• Make sure that each paragraph or bullet covers a single subject—when you start a new subject, you should start a new paragraph or bullet.

• Include a final paragraph that provides a strategy for an interview; that is, you will call or ask the employer to call you to set up an interview.

Supply Chain Strategies: Delivering Value with a Successful Interview

No matter how great your cover letter and résumé are, your delivery in the interview process is critical to landing the job. Planning is critical for ensuring great success in both telephone and personal interviews.

To make your interview successful, do the following:

- Be sure you know as much as possible about the job and the company. Don't be concerned that the employer will disapprove of this—employers recognize that the best candidates do their research.

- Prepare for interview questions. By this, we mean developing a list of questions you expect the interviewer to ask you and your answers. For example, in many interviews, you will be asked, "Tell us about yourself." You also need to develop a list of questions that you can ask the interviewer when requested.

- Prepare your key selling points. These are the things you would like to make sure you say to one or more of the questions. You want to focus on the benefits you can provide for the employer, but you have to do this in response to questions.

- Follow up the interview with a thank-you note within 24 hours. A handwritten note is often best, but today many businesspeople prefer the convenience of an e-mail thank-you. Also, e-mail will arrive immediately, while snail mail will take a few days. Time may be critical if the hiring decision is to be made quickly.

- Dress for success. Dressing professionally is probably the best advice for any interview, even if you have found in your research that employees of the organization dress casually. In general, this means a professional dress or suit in a conservative color for women and a suit in a conservative color for men. For both, it's best to wear conservative shoes and not to have any tattoos visible. You can probably find more information on how to dress for an interview from your school's career services advisers or online.

What to Bring to the Interview.

One of the best things you can bring to an interview is a portfolio of your work. This may include class projects and items that showcase your work in an internship or a job or a volunteer project. You will probably want to include these in a portfolio enclosed in plastic sleeves.

You should also bring extra copies of your cover letter and résumé. While you have already sent the interviewer a copy of these, they may be lost at the bottom of a pile on the desk. Having an extra copy available can save the interviewer from embarrassment and greatly enhance the interview process.

Accepting the Offer.

Experts suggest that you never accept an offer immediately. It is expected that you will take a day or so to think about the offer before you accept it. This gives you time to consider the salary and benefits offered, ask any questions that you may have, and determine if you want to negotiate anything.

After you have verbally accepted the offer, you should ask for an offer letter that includes the terms of the offer. If it includes all the elements of your verbal offer and negotiations, you can sign the offer letter, make a copy for yourself, and return the original. Then enjoy your career.

▶ Notes

CHAPTER 1

1. American Medical Association, "About AMA," www.ama.org/AboutAMA/Pages/Definition-of-Marketing.aspx (accessed April 4, 2014).

2. Alex Brownsell, "Virgin Atlantic's Top Marketer Simon Lloyd on Making the Airlines 'Irresistible,'" March 7, 2013, www.marketingmagazine.co.uk/article/1173283/virgin-atlantics-top-marketer-simon-lloyd-making-airline-irresistible (accessed April 1, 2014).

3. Brooks Barnes, "At Theme Parks, a V.I.P. Ticket to Ride," June 9, 2013, www.nytimes.com/2013/06/10/business/at-universal-park-a-vip-pass-to-help-lift-revenue.html?pagewanted=all&_r=0 (accessed April 1, 2014).

4. Lee D. Dahringer, "Marketing Services Internationally: Barriers and Management Strategies," *Journal of Service Marketing* 5 (1991): 5–17.

5. Stuart Elliott, "Introducing Kentucky, the Brand," June 9, 2004, www.nyt.com.

6. Sheila Shayon, "Break Me Off a Piece of That WASABI Kit-Kat Bar!," March 8, 2010, www.brandchannel.com/home/post/2010/03/08/Break-Me-Off-A-Piece-Of-That-WASABI-Kit-Kat-Bar!.aspx (accessed June 8, 2010).

7. Peter F. Drucker, *Management: Tasks, Responsibilities, Practices* (New York: Harper & Row, 1972), 64–65.

8. Maureen Morrison, "McDonald's to Launch 'Subway Buster': The McWrap," March 20, 2013, http://adage.com/article/news/mcdonald-s-mcwrap-subway-sandwich-share/240463 (accessed April 2, 2014).

9. Xavier de Lecaros Aquise, "The Rise of Collaborative Consumption and the Experience Economy," January 3, 2014, http://www.theguardian.com/technology/2014/jan/03/collaborative-consumption-experience-economy-startups (accessed April 14, 2014); Tammy Chung, "The New World of Ownership," November 5, 2012, www.mediapost.com/publications/article/185633/the-new-world-of-ownership.html?edition=53137 (accessed April 14, 2014); Rob Baedekker, "How to Make Money When Economy Is Failing," November 21, 2011, www.newsweek.com/how-make-money-when-economy-failing-66245 (accessed April 14, 2014).

10. Target Corporation, "2012 Corporate Responsibility Report," https://corporate.target.com/_media/TargetCorp/csr/pdf/2012-corporate-responsibility-report.pdf (accessed April 5, 2014).

11. "Henry Ford and the Model T," in *Forbes Greatest Business Stories* (New York: Wiley, 1996), www.wiley.com/legacy/products/subject/business/forbes/ford.html.

12. Serena Ng, "Pet-Food Brand's Image Bits Back Colgate," February 5, 2013, http://online.wsj.com/news/articles/SB10001424127887324761004578281832634101580 (accessed April 4, 2013).

13. Mark Strassman, "A Dying Breed: The American Shopping Mall," March 23, 2014, www.cbsnews.com/news/a-dying-breed-the-american-shopping-mall (accessed April 6, 2014).

14. Susan Berfield, "Hip Eyewear: Warby Park's New Spectacles," June 30, 2011, www.businessweek.com/magazine/hip-eyewear-warby-parkers-new-spectacles-07012011.html (accessed April 6, 2014).

15. Paula D. Englis, Basil G. Englis, Michael R. Solomon, and Aard Groen, "Strategic Sustainability and Triple Bottom Line Performance in Textiles: Implications of the Eco-Label for the EU and Beyond," Business as an Agent of World Benefit Conference, United Nations and the Academy of Management, Cleveland, OH, 2006.

16. Compare M. K. Khoo, S. G. Lee, and S. W. Lye, "A Design Methodology for the Strategic Assessment of a Product's Eco-Efficiency," *International Journal of Production Research* 39 (2001): 245–74; C. Chen, "Design for the Environment: A Quality-Based Model for Green Product Development," *Management Science* 47, no. 2 (2001): 250–64; McDonough Braungart Design, *Chemistry's Design Paradigm*, www.mbdc.com/c2c_home.htm (accessed April 15, 2006); Elizabeth Corcoran, "Thinking Green," *Scientific American* 267, no. 6 (1992): 44–46; Amitai Etzioni, "The Good Society: Goals beyond Money," *The Futurist* (2001): 68–69; and M. H. Olson, "Charting a Course for Sustainability," *Environment* 38, no. 4 (1996): 10–23. See also U.S. Environmental Protection Agency, "What Is Sustainability," www.epa.gov (accessed April 7, 2014).

17. International Ice Hockey Federation, "New Gear for Olympic Champs," August 10, 2013, www.iihf.com/home-of-hockey/news/news-singleview/?tx_ttnews[tt_news]=8171&cHash=e51cb45796cf45bf097e1226ac833cda (accessed April 6, 2014).

18. Sindya N. Bhanoo, "Those Earth-Friendly Products? Turns Out They're Profit-Friendly as Well," *New York Times*, June 12, 2010, B3.

19. Gail Nickel-Kailing, "Green Marketing: What Works, What Doesn't," January 22, 2010, http://blogs.whattheythink.com/going-green/2010/01/green-marketing-what-works-what-doesn%E2%80%99t (accessed May 4, 2010).

20. Jeff Lowe, *The Marketing Dashboard: Measuring Marketing Effectiveness*, February 2003, www.brandchannel.com/images/papers/dashboard.pdf; G. A. Wyner, "Scorecards and More: The Value Is in How You Use Them," *Marketing Research*, Summer, 6–7; C. F. Lunbdy and C. Rasinowich, "The Missing Link: Cause and Effect Linkages Make Marketing Scorecards More Valuable," *Marketing Research*, Winter 2003, 14–19.

21. Julia King, "How Analytics Helped Ford Turn Its Fortunes," December 2, 2013, www.computerworld.com/s/article/9244363/How_analytics_helped_Ford_turn_its_fortunes?taxonomyId=18&pageNumber=2 (accessed April 6, 2014).

22. Centers for Disease Control and Prevention, "Notes from the Field: Electronic Cigarette Use among Middle and High School Students—United States, 2011–2012," September 6, 2013, www.cdc.gov/mmwr/preview/mmwrhtml/mm6235a6.htm (accessed April 6, 2014).

23. Matt Richtel, "E-Cigarettes, by Other Names, Lure Young and Worry Experts," March 4, 2014, www.nytimes.com/2014/03/05/business/e-cigarettes-under-aliases-elude-the-authorities.html?action=click&module=Search&region=searchResults%230&version=&url=http%3A%2F%2Fquery.nytimes.com%2Fsearch%2Fsitesearch%2F%3Faction%3Dclick%26region%3DMasthead%26pgtype%3DHomepage%26module%3DSearchSubmit%26contentCollection%3DHomepage%26t%3Dqry940%23%2Fe-cigarettes%2F24hours%2F&_r=0 (accessed April 6, 2014).

24. Jeep, "Frequently Asked Questions," http://jeepjamboreeusa.com/faq (accessed April 6, 2014).

25. Michael E. Porter, *Competitive Advantage: Creating and Sustaining Superior Performance* (New York: Free Press, 1985).

26. Karlene Lukovitz, "Ghirardelli Streams User Content in Times Square," March 9, 2010, www.mediapost.com/publications/index.cfm?fa=Articles.showArticle&art_aid=123852 (accessed June 8, 2010).

27. CNN, "About CNN iReport," http://ireport.cnn.com/about.jspa (accessed April 6, 2014).

28. James Yang, "Here's an Idea: Let Everyone Have Ideas," *New York Times*, March 30, 2006.

29. Frito-Lay North America, "PepsiCo's Doritos Brand Reveals the Five Consumer-Created Commercials Competing for $1 Million Grand Prize," January 2, 2014, www.fritolay.com/about-us/press-release-20140102.html (accessed April 6, 2014).

30. Some material adapted from a presentation by Matt Leavey, Prentice Hall Business Publishing, July 18, 2007.

31. This section adapted from Michael R. Solomon, *Consumer Behavior: Buying, Having and Being*, 8th ed. (Upper Saddle River, NJ: Pearson Education, 2008).

32. Jeff Surowiecki, *The Wisdom of Crowds* (New York: Anchor, 2005); Jeff Howe, "The Rise of Crowdsourcing," June 2006, www.wired.com/wired/archive/14.06/crowds.html (accessed October 3, 2007).

33. Jolie Lee, "Lego to Release 'Ghostbusters' Set Tied to Anniversary," February 27, 2014, www.usatoday.com/story/news/nation-now/2014/02/17/lego-ghostbusters-ecto-1/5551069 (accessed April 6, 2014).

34. Ipsos Media CT, "Social Influence: Marketing's New Frontier," March 2014, http://go.crowdtap.com/socialinfluence (accessed April 6, 2014).

35. Susanna Kim, "Home Depot Apologizes for Racist Tweet Sent from Its Twitter Account," November 8, 2013, http://abcnews.go.com/Business/home-depot-apologizes-racist-tweet/story?id=20831402 (accessed April 6, 2014).

36. Associated Press, "GM Races to Counter Bad Publicity over Ignition Switch Recall," March 26, 2014, www.cbc.ca/news/business/gm-races-to-counter-bad-publicity-over-ignition-switch-recall-1.2587490 (accessed April 6, 2014); Chris Isidore, "GM Bankruptcy: End of an Era," June 2, 2009, http://money.cnn.com/2009/06/01/news/companies/gm_bankruptcy (accessed April 6, 2014).

37. Larry Edwards, "The Decision Was Easy," *Advertising Age*, August 26, 1987, 106. For research and discussion related to public policy issues, see Paul N. Bloom and Stephen A. Greyser, "The Maturing of Consumerism," *Harvard Business Review*, November/December 1981, 130–39; George S. Day, "Assessing the Effect of Information Disclosure Requirements," *Journal of Marketing*, April 1976, 42–52; Dennis E. Garrett, "The Effectiveness of Marketing Policy Boycotts: Environmental Opposition to Marketing," *Journal of Marketing* 51 (January 1987): 44–53; Michael Houston and Michael Rothschild, "Policy-Related Experiments on Information Provision: A Normative Model and Explication," *Journal of Marketing Research* 17 (November 1980): 432–49; Jacob Jacoby, Wayne D. Hoyer, and David A. Sheluga, *Misperception of Televised Communications* (New York: American Association of Advertising Agencies, 1980); Gene R. Laczniak and Patrick E. Murphy, *Marketing Ethics: Guidelines for Managers* (Lexington, MA: Lexington Books, 1985): 117–23; Lynn Phillips and Bobby Calder, "Evaluating Consumer Protection Laws: Promising Methods," *Journal of Consumer Affairs* 14 (Summer 1980): 9–36; Donald P. Robin and Eric Reidenbach, "Social Responsibility, Ethics, and Marketing Strategy: Closing the Gap between Concept and Application," *Journal of Marketing* 51 (January 1987): 44–58; Howard Schutz and Marianne Casey, "Consumer Perceptions of Advertising as Misleading," *Journal of Consumer Affairs* 15 (Winter 1981): 340–57; and Darlene Brannigan Smith and Paul N. Bloom, "Is Consumerism Dead or Alive? Some New Evidence," in *Advances in Consumer Research*, ed. Thomas C. Kinnear (Provo, UT: Association for Consumer Research, 1984): 569–73.

38. Parts of this section are adapted from Michael R. Solomon, *Consumer Behavior: Buying, Having, and Being*, 7th ed. (Upper Saddle River, NJ: Prentice Hall, 2007).

39. Thomas C. O'Guinn and Ronald J. Faber, "Compulsive Buying: A Phenomenological Explanation," *Journal of Consumer Research* 16 (September 1989): 154.

40. Associated Press, "Center Tries to Treat Web Addicts," September 5, 2009, www.nytimes.com/2009/09/06/us/06internet.html (accessed June 8, 2010); Samantha Manas, "Addicted to Chapstick: The World of Chapstick Addicts Revealed," July 5, 2006, www.associatedcontent.com/article/41148/addicted_to_chapstick.html (accessed May 13, 2008).

41. "Advertisers Face Up to the New Morality: Making the Pitch," July 8, 1997.

42. http://green.yahoo.com/pledge (accessed August 30, 2010).

43. www.carbonfootprint.com/carbonfootprint.html (accessed August 30, 2010).

CHAPTER 2

1. Marcella Kelly and Jim McGowen, *BUSN 5* (Mason, OH: South-Western Cengage Learning, 2013).

2. European Commission, "Clothing and Toys Top List of Dangerous Consumer Items in EU," March 26, 2014, http://ec.europa.eu/news/environment/140326_en.htm (accessed April 15, 2014).

3. Anita Chang Beattie, "Can Starbucks Make China Love Joe?," November 5, 2012, http://adage.com/china/article/china-news/can-starbucks-make-china-love-coffee/238101 (accessed April 15, 2014).

4. World Trade Organization, "Understanding the WTO: Who We Are, 2014," 2014 http://www.wto.org/english/thewto_e/whatis_e/who_we_are_e.htm (accessed April 6, 2014).

5. Katie Thomas, "Facing Black Market, Pfizer Is Looking Online to Sell Viagra," May 6, 2013, http://nytimes.com/2013/05/07/business/pfizer-begins-selling-viagra-online.htm (accessed April 14, 2014).

6. Wendy Koch, "U.S. Finalizes Steep Tariffs on China's Solar Panels," www.usatoday.com/story/news/nation/2012/11/07/us-tariffs-china-solar-panels-1689177 (accessed April 15, 2014).

7. United Nations, "World Economic Situation and Prospects 2014: Global Economic Outlook (Chapter 1)," December 18, 2013, http://www.un.org/en/development/desa/publications/wesp2014-firstchapter.html (accessed April 21, 2014).

8. "The Big Mac Index: Global Exchange Rates, to Go," January 23, 2014, www.economist.com/content/big-mac-index (accessed April 9, 2014).

9. C. K. Prahalad, *The Fortune at the Bottom of the Pyramid* (Upper Saddle River, NJ: Wharton School Publishing, 2010), xiv.

10. Alison Smale and Michael D. Shear, "Russia Is Ousted from Group of 8 by U.S. and Allies," March 24, 2014, www.nytimes.com/2014/03/25/world/europe/obama-russia-crimea.html (accessed April 15, 2014).

11. G8 Information Center, "What Is the G8?," http://www.g7.utoronto.ca/what_is_g8.html (accessed February 12, 2010).

12. EB Eggs, "About Eggland's Best," www.egglandsbest.com/egglands-eggs/why-egglands/about-us.aspx (accessed January 24, 2010).

13. www.hhs.gov/healthcare/rights/index.html (accessed April 22, 2014).

14. Katy Bachman, "Sprinkle, Eat and Pay Up Big Time: Sensa Sheds $26.5 Million to Settle FTC Charges," January 7, 2014, www.adweek.com/news/advertising-branding/sprinkle-eat-and-pay-big-time-sensa-sheds-265-million-settle-ftc-charges-154781 (accessed April 15, 2014).

15. Stephan Nielsen, "Brazil Local Content Rules Hurting Major Wind Suppliers," www.renewableenergy.com, October 7, 2013, www.renewableenergy.com/rea/news/article/2013/10/brazil-local-content-rules-hurting-major-wind-manufacturers (accessed April 16, 2014).

16. Max Nielsen, "How Nike Solved Its Sweatshop Problem," May 9, 2013, www.businessinsider.com/hwo-nike-solved-its-sweatshop-problem (accessed April 16, 2014).

17. Richard W. Pollay, "Measuring the Cultural Values Manifest in Advertising," *Current Issues and Research in Advertising* 6 (1983): 71–92.

18. Deborah Ball, "Women in Italy Like to Clean but Shun the Quick and Easy," *Wall Street Journal*, April 25, 2006, A1.

19. Daniel Goleman, "The Group and the Self: New Focus on a Cultural Rift," December 25, 1990, http://www.nytimes.com/1990/12/25/science/the-group-and-the-self-new-focus-on-a-cultural-rift.html, (accessed December 4, 2014). 37; Harry C. Triandis, "The Self and Social Behavior in Differing Cultural Contexts," *Psychological Review* 96 (July 1989): 506; Harry C. Triandis et al., "Individualism and Collectivism: Cross-Cultural Perspectives on Self-Ingroup Relationships," *Journal of Personality and Social Psychology* 54 (February 1988): 323.

20. Shaun Rein, "Shanghai Disney Must Deliver 'Big' Experience," April 11, 2011, www.cnbc.com/id/42528017 (accessed April 21, 2014).

21. McDonald's Corporation, "Getting to Know Us," www.aboutmcdonalds.com/mcd/our_company.html (accessed April 16, 2014).

22. "21 McDonald's Meals You Won't Find in America," January 19, 2013, www.huffingtonpost.com/2013/01/19/mcdonalds-international-menu_n_2507006.html (access April 16, 2014).

23. Ryan Mac, "MGM Resorts Joins Venture with Hakkasan Group to Build Non-Gaming Hotels Worldwide," April 15, 2014, www.forbes.com/sites/ryanmac/2014/04/15/mgm-resorts-joins-venture-with-abu-dhabais-hakkasan-group-to-build-non-gaming-hotels (accessed April 16, 2014).

24. Jim Thompson, "Twenty Years Later: What McDonald's in Russia Says about the Brand's Future," February 1, 2010, www.brandchannel.com/home/post/2010/02/01/Twenty-Years-Later-What-McDonalds-In-Russia-Says-About-The-Brands-Future.aspx (accessed February 1, 2010).

25. Quoted in Teri Agins, "Costume Change: For U.S. Fashion Firms, a Global Makeover," February 2, 2007, http//blogs.wsj.com/runway/2007/02/02/for-us-fashion-firms-a-global-makeover/?mod=WSJBlog (accessed February 10, 2008), A1.

26. "China's Jiangsu TV Program Goes Global in Italy," November 12, 2013, www.english.peopledaily.com/cn/90782/8453281.html (accessed April 21, 2014).

27. Matt Viser, "Dunkin' Donuts Jumps on Asia's Coffee Craze," March 30, 2014, www.bostonglobe.com/news/world/2014/03/29/from-massachusetts-seoul-dunkin-donuts-finds-new-markets-coffee-craze-sweeps-asia/aykwWhGnFNjG85ahVxJIFL/story.html (accessed April 14, 2014).

28. International Energy Agency, "Access to Electricity," World Energy Outlook, 2009, www.iea.org/weo/electricity.asp (accessed February 16, 2010).

29. Deciwatt, "The Challenge," http://deciwatt.org/the-challenge (accessed April 10, 2014).

30. Ben Schiller, "A $5 Light for the Developing World with an Ingenious Fuel: Gravity," December 14, 2012, www.fastcoexist.com/1681067/a-5-light-for-the-developing-world-with-an-ingenious-fuel-gravity#1 (accessed April 10, 2014).

31. Jack Neff, "Lipton Uses Oscars (and Muppets) to Launch Global Campaign for Unified Brand," February 26, 2014, http://adage.com/article/media/lipton-launcing-global-campaign-oscars/291873 (accessed April 17, 2014).

32. Rosa Trieu, "Chinese Company Threatens U.S. Garlic Industry," April 15, 2014, www.forbes.com/sites/rosatrieu/2014/04/15/chinese-company-threatens-u-s-garlic-industry (accessed April 17, 2014).

33. Shelly Banjo and R. Jai Krishna, "Wal-Mart Pulls Back in India," October 9, 2013, http://online.wsj.com/news/articles/SB10001424052702303382004579124703326968442 (accessed April 21, 2014).

34. Claudia Parsons, "From Madoff to Merrill Lynch: Where Was the Ethics Officer," December 9, 2009 http://www.nytimes.com/2009/01/29/business/worldbusiness/29iht-ethics.4.19786426.html?_r=1&(accessed January 25, 2010).

35. AT&T, "AT&T's Code of Business Conduct," www.att.com/Common/about_us/downloads/att_code_of_business_conduct.pdf (accessed April 16, 2014).

36. Duff Wilson, "Cigarette Giants in Global Fight on Tighter Rules," November 13, 2010, www.nytimes.com/2010/11/14/business/global/14smoke.html?_r=1 (accessed April 16, 2014).

37. Paul Lienert and Marilyn Thompson, "GM Didn't Fix Deadly Ignition Switch because It Would Have Cost $1 per Car," April 2, 2014, www.huffingtonpost.com/2014/04/02/gm-ignition-switch-dollar-per-car_n_5075680.html (accessed April 16, 2014).

38. "Foreign Corrupt Practices Act of 1977 (as Amended)," www.usdoj.gov/usao/eousa/foia_reading_room/usam/title9/47mcrm.htm (accessed May 15, 2008).

39. "Greenwashing? Marketers Actually Undersell Their Sustainable Work, Limiting the Conversation Keeps It from Advancing," March 13, 2014, http://adage.com/article/guest-columnists/marketers-underselling-sustainability-efforts/292101 (accessed December 4, 2014).

40. Sarah Vizard, "Ikea Readies First Sustainability Campaign in Marketing Switch," February 6, 2014, www.marketingweek.co.uk/sectors/retail/ikea-readies-first-sustainability-campaign-in-marketing-switch/4009417.article (accessed April 10, 2014).

41. Joan Voight, "Green Is the New Black: Nike among Marketers Pushing Sustainability," October 23, 2013, www.adweek.com/news/advertising-branding/green-new-black-levi-s-nike-among-marketers-pushing-sustainability-153318 (accessed March 10, 2014).

42. Alicia Ciccone, "H&M Launches Garment Recycling Program across All Markets," February 21, 2013, www.brandchannel.com/home/post/2013/02/21/HM-Garment-Recycling-Program-022113.aspx (accessed April 11, 2014).

43. Ross Brooks, "H&M Converts Donated Clothes into a New Denim Collection," January 23, 2014, www.sustainablebrands.com/news_and_views/Waste_Not/Ross_Brooks/HM_Converts_Donated_Clothes_New_Denim_Collection (accessed April 11, 2014).

44. www.commondreams.org/headline/2012/05/08 (accessed April 23, 2014).

45. Center for Sustainability at Aquinas College, www.centerforsustainability.org/resources.php?root=176&category=89 (accessed April 10, 2014); Jeanelle Schwartz, Beth Beloff, and Susan Beaver, "Use Sustainability Metrics to Guide Decision-Making," July 2002, http://people.clarkson.edu/~wwilcox/Design/sustain.pdf (accessed April 10, 2014).

CHAPTER 3

1. "MADD Mission Statement," www.madd.org/About-Us/About-Us/Mission-Statement.aspx (accessed January 14, 2010).

2. Western Union, "Our Rich History," http://corporate.westernunion.com/History.html (accessed April 21, 2014).

3. Serena Ng and Paul Ziobro, "At P&G, Lafley's Return Engagement," July 28, 2013, http://online.wsj.com/news/articles/SB10001424127887324170004578634133149701500 (accessed April 22, 2014).

4. CTG (Consumer Goods Technology), "P&G CEO Reveals Performance Boost Plans," October 8, 2013, http://consumergoods.edgl.com/trends/P-G-CEO-Reveals-Performance-Boost-Plans88859 (accessed April 22, 2014).

5. Michael Santoli, "'Iron Man 3' Vanquishes Doubts over Disney's Marvel Buy," May 6, 2013, http://finance.yahoo.com/blogs/michael-santoli/iron-man-3-vanquishes-doubts-over-disney-marvel-173014796.html (accessed April 22, 2014).

6. Walt Disney World, "New Fantasyland—Now Open," https://disneyworld.disney.go.com/events-tours/magic-kingdom/new-fantasyland/ (accessed April 22, 2014).

7. Michael Cieply and Brooks Barnes, "Disney Sells Miramax for $660 Million," July 30, 2010, www.nytimes.com/2010/07/31/business/media/31miramax.html?_r=0 (accessed April 22, 2014).

8. Thomas Heath, "Disney Backs Out of National Harbor, in Blow to Prince George's," November 25, 2011, www.washingtonpost.com/business/economy/in-a-blow-to-prince-georges-disney-backs-out-of-national-harbor/2011/11/25/gIQAM2OKxN_story.html (accessed April 22, 2014).

9. Dannon, "Digestive Health and Probiotic Yogurt," http://activia.us.com/probiotics-benefits/digestive-health (accessed April 24, 2014).

10. Christopher Harress, "Boeing (BA) Makes Inroads with Sale of Eight 737 MAX8s to South Africa's Comair Limited for $840 Million,"

March 19, 2014, www.ibtimes.com/boeing-ba-makes-inroads-af-rica-sale-eight-737-max-8s-south-africas-comair-limited-830-mil-lion (accessed April 22, 2014).

11. McDonald's, "Latest News from McDonald's of San Diego County," February 14, 2014, www.sdmcdonalds.com/news/archive/petite-pastries_2014.aspx#.U1kH0MdH-Hk (accessed April 24, 2014).

12. Michael Arndt, "McDonald's 24/7," *BusinessWeek*, February 5, 2007, 64–72.

13. Michael Moss, "The Extraordinary Science of Addictive Junk Food," February 20, 2013, www.nytimes.com/2013/02/24/magazine/the-extraordinary-science-of-junk-food.html?pagewanted=1&_r=0 (accessed May 2, 2014).

14. Micheline Maynard, "Delta Air Lines Rolls the Dice on a $199 Bundle of Fees," September 13, 2013, www.forbes.com/sites/michelinemaynard/2013/09/13/delta-air-lines-rolls-the-dice-on-a-199-bundle-of-fees (accessed April 22, 2014).

15. "American Airlines Wine Selection," www.aa.com/intl/cn/aboutUs_en/pr20090803.jsp (accessed January 20, 2010); American Airlines, "Fly Better. Feel Better," www.aa.com/i18n/urls/flybetter.jsp#!travelInComfort (accessed April 24, 2014).

16. Travelocity, "Today's Top Deals," www.travelocity.com (accessed April 24, 2014).

17. Michael A. Stelzner, "2013 Social Media Marketing Industry Report," May 2013, www.socialmediaexaminer.com/report, (accessed April 11, 2014).

18. Gordon A. Wyner, "Beyond ROI: Make Sure the Analytics Address Strategic Issues," *Marketing Management* 15 (May/June 2006): 8–9.

19. Guy R. Powell, *Return on Marketing Investment* (Albuquerque, NM: RPI Press, 2002), 4–6.

20. Tim Ambler, "Don't Cave In to Cave Dwellers," *Marketing Management*, September/October 2006, 25–29.

21. Ibid.

22. Quoted at http://blogs.barrons.com/techtraderdaily/2014/05/05/oracle-bernstein-ups-to-buy-cloud-clearing-up-credit-suisse-lauds-in-memory-initiative (accessed May 8, 2014).

23. "Gartner Says Worldwide PC Shipments Declined 6.9 Percent in Fourth Quarter of 2013,"," January 9, 2014, www.gartner.com/newsroom/id/2647517 (accessed April 11, 2014).

CHAPTER 4

1. Alan J. Greco and Jack T. Hogue, "Developing Marketing Decision Support Systems in Consumer Goods Firms," *Journal of Consumer Marketing* 7 (1990): 55–64.

2. "Don't Play by the Rules. Break Them," www.t-mobile.com/landing/whyt-mobile.html (accessed April 30, 2014); "Simple Choice Plan," www.t-mobile.com/cell-phone-plans/individual.html?icid=WMM_TM_WHYTMBL_CDF5EA158U200 (accessed April 30, 2014).

3. Marketing Evaluations Inc., "The Q Scores Company," www.qscores.com (accessed April 30, 2014).

4. www.citelighter.com/business/marketing/knowledgecards/q-scores (accessed May 7, 2014).

5. http://techblog.netflix.com/2012/04/netflix-recommendations-beyond-5-stars.html (accessed May 7, 2014).

6. Quoted in Dale Buss, "Unapologetically, Volvo Aims Its New Campaign at True Believers," April 15, 2013, www.forbes.com/sites/dalebuss/2013/04/15/unapologetically-volvo-aims-its-new-ads-at-true-believers (accessed May 5, 2014).

7. Experian, "Simmons National Consumer Study," www.experian.com/simmons-research/consumer-study.html (accessed May 1, 2014).

8. Michael R. Solomon, *Conquering Consumerspace: Marketing Strategies for a Branded World* (New York: AMACOM Books, 2003).

9. Charles Duhigg, "How Companies Learn Your Secrets," February 16, 2012, www.nytimes.com/2012/02/19/magazine/shopping-habits.html?pagewanted=all&_r=0 (accessed May 3, 2014).

10. Tom De Ruyck, "Inspirational Online Dialogues," October 14, 2013, rwconnect.esomar.org/inspirational-online-dialogues (accessed May 5, 2014).

11. Karl Greenberg, "Volvo Uses Twitter Chat for Digital Focus Group," May 29, 2013, www.mediapost.com/publications/article/201309/volvo-uses-twitter-chat-for-digital-focus-group.html?edition=60600 (accessed May 5, 2014).

12. Stuart Elliott and Tanzina Vega, "Trying to Be Hip and Edgy, Ads Become Offensive," May 10, 2013, www.nytimes.com/2013/05/11/business/media/trying-to-be-hip-and-edgy-ads-become-offensive.html?ref=business&_r=0 (accessed May 5, 2014).

13. Paul Marsden, "Consumer Advisory Panels," http://digitalintelligencetoday.com/downloads/Marsden_CAB.pdf (accessed May 6, 2014).

14. Matt Richtel, "The Parable of the Beer and Diapers," August 15, 2006, www.theregister.co.uk/2006/08/15/beer_diapers (accessed February 10, 2010).

15. John Carney, "Hemlines Are Plunging, Is Economy Next?" February 16, 2012, www.cnbc.com/id/46414411 (accessed May 1, 2014).

16. Uma R. Karmarkar, "Note on Neuromarketing," Harvard Business School Publication 9-512-031, 2011; Natasha Singer, "Making Ads That Whisper to the Brain," November 3, 2010, www.nytimes.com/2010/11/14/business/14stream.html?_r=0 (accessed April 22, 2014).

17. Direct Marketing Association, "Where Marketers Can Obtain State Do-Not-Call Lists," www.the-dma.org/government/donotcalllists.shtml (accessed February 7, 2010).

18. The Praxi Group, Inc., "Research Overview: Telephone versus Online Research—Advantages and Pitfalls," Fall 2007, www.praxigroup.net/TPG%20Phone%20Versus%20Online%20WP.pdf (accessed February 7, 2010).

19. Basil G. Englis and Michael R. Solomon, "Life/Style OnLine ©: A Web-Based Methodology for Visually-Oriented Consumer Research," *Journal of Interactive Marketing* 14, no. 1 (2000): 2–14; Basil G. Englis, Michael R. Solomon, and Paula D. Harveston, "Web-Based, Visually Oriented Consumer Research Tools," in *Online Consumer Psychology: Understanding and Influencing Consumer Behavior in the Virtual World*, ed. Curt Haugtvedt, Karen Machleit, and Richard Yalch (Hillsdale, NJ: Lawrence Erlbaum Associates, 2005).

20. "Nielsen Begins Largest Ever Expansion of Its National U.S. Television Ratings Panel," http://en-us.nielsen.com/main/news/news_releases/2007/september/Nielsen_Begins_Largest_Ever_Expansion_of_Its_National_U_S__Television_Ratings_Panel, September 26, 2007 (accessed March 2, 2010).

21. Nielsen, "Online Measurement," www.nielsen.com/us/en/nielsen-solutions/nielsen-measurement/nielsen-online-measurement.html (accessed May 1, 2014).

22. www.nielsen.com/us/en/press-room/2013/nielsen-launches-nielsen-twitter-tv-ratings.html (accessed May 7, 2014).

23. Tim Callahan, "Building on Success to Deliver Better Insights," http://us.acnielsen.com/pubs/2004_q4_ci_building.shtml (accessed June 10, 2008).

24. Ray Nelson, "How to Use Social Media for Marketing Research," March 19, 2013, http://socialmediatoday.com/raywilliamnelson/1313496/marketing-research-how-use-social-media-market-research (accessed April 23, 2014).

25. Peter Robison, "Tracking Every Move You Make—for a $5 Gift Card," February 14, 2014, www.businessweek.com/articles/2014-02-14/tracking-every-move-you-make-by-gps-for-a-5-gift-card-without-that-nsa-taint (accessed May 6, 2014).

26. Alexis Madrigal, "How Netflix Reverse Engineered Hollywood," January 2, 2014, www.theatlantic.com/technology/archive/2014/01/how-netflix-reverse-engineered-hollywood/282679 (accessed May 5, 2014).

27. Jack Neff, "Chasing the Cheaters That Undermine Online Research," *Advertising Age*, March 31, 2008, 12.

28. Matt Quinn, "How to Reduce Your Website's Bounce Rate," January 31, 2011, www.inc.com/guides/2011/01/how-to-reduce-your-website-bounce-rate.html (accessed April 20, 2014); Paul W. Farris, Neil T. Bendle, Phillip E. Pfeifer, and David J. Reibstein, *Marketing Metrics: The Definitive Guide to Measuring Marketing Performance* (Upper Saddle River, NJ: Pearson Education, 2010).

29. Bruce L. Stern and Ray Ashmun, "Methodological Disclosure: The Foundation for Effective Use of Survey Research," *Journal of Applied Business Research* 7 (1991): 77–82.

30. Michael E. Ross, "It Seemed Like a Good Idea at the Time," April 22, 2005, www.msnbc.msn.com/id/7209828 (accessed February 8, 2010).

31. Gary Levin, "New Adventures in Children's Research," *Advertising Age*, August 9, 1993, 17.

32. Jack Honomichl, "The 2013 Honomichl Top 50 Report," hwww.ama.org/Documents/Honomichl50Report_June2013.pdf (accessed May 6, 2014).

33. Paul W. Farris, Neil T. Bendle, Phillip E. Pheifer, and David J. Reibstein, *Marketing Metrics: 50+ Metrics Every Executive Should Master* (Upper Saddle River, NJ: Wharton School Publishing, 2006), 292.

CHAPTER 5

1. "A Crash Course in Customer Relationship Management," *Harvard Management Update*, March 2000 (Harvard Business School reprint U003B); Nahshon Wingard, "CRM Definition—Customer-Centered Philosophy," October 26, 2009, www.crmdefinition.com/2009/10/crm-definition-customer-centered-philosophy (accessed March 12, 2010).

2. Don Peppers and Martha Rogers, *The One-to-One* Future (New York: Doubleday, 1996).

3. Don Peppers, Martha Rogers, and Bob Dorf, "Is Your Company Ready for One-to-One Marketing?," *Harvard Business Review*, January–February 1999, 151–60.

4. Quoted in Cara B. DiPasquale, "Navigate the Maze," Special Report on 1:1 Marketing, *Advertising Age*, October 29, 2001, S1(2).

5. Leonard L. Berry, *On Great Service: A Framework for Action* (New York: Free Press, 1995); Paul T. Ringenbach, *USAA: A Tradition of Service* (San Antonio, TX: Donning, 1997).

6. Louis Columbus, "2013 CRM Market Share Update: 40% of CRM Systems Sold are SaaS-Based," April 26, 2013, www.forbes.com/sites/louiscolumbus/2013/04/26/2013-crm-market-share-update-40-of-crm-systems-sold-are-saas-based (accessed June 15, 2014).

7. Louis Columbus, "Gartner Predicts CRM Will Be a $36B Market by 2017," 18 June 18, 2013, www.forbes.com/sites/louiscolumbus/2013/06/18/gartner-predicts-crm-will-be-a-36b-market-by-2017 (accessed June 15, 2014).

8. Jeff Kang, "Amazon.com and Customer Relationship Management," www.iconocast.com/ZZZZResearch/eMarketing_amazon.pdf (accessed April 8, 2008).

9. MyCokeRewards, www.mycokerewards.com/beta/how-it-works (accessed June 15, 2014).

10. "My Magic Plus," http://mousehints.com/my-magic-plus (accessed June 15, 2014).

11. Robert C. Blattberg, Gary Getz, and Mark Pelofsky, "Want to Build Your Business? Grow Your Customer Equity," *Harvard Management Update*, August 2001 (Harvard Business School reprint U0108B), 3; "What Are Your Customers Really Worth?," March 6, 2007, http://www.forbes.com/2007/03/06/gm-schwab-bmw-ent-manage-cx_kw_0306whartoncustomers.html (accessed January 8, 2010).

12. SAS, "Big Data, Bigger Marketing," www.sas.com/en_us/insights/big-data/big-data-marketing.html (accessed May 31, 2014).

13. Rich Miller, "The Lessons of Moneyball for Big Data Analysis," September 23, 2011, www.datacenterknowledge.com/archives/2011/09/23/the-lessons-of-moneyball-for-big-data-analysis (accessed June 6, 2014).

14. Friedemann Mattern and Christian Floerkemeier, "From the Internet of Computers to the Internet of Things," *Informatik-Spektrum* 33 (2010): 107–21.

15. Steven Salzberg, "Why Google Flu Is a Failure," March 23, 2014, www.forbes.com/sites/stevensalzberg/2014/03/23/why-google-flu-is-a-failure (accessed July 1, 2014).

16. Amy O'Leary, "In New Tools to Combat Epidemics, the Key Is Context," June 19, 2013, http://bits.blogs.nytimes.com/2013/06/19/in-new-tools-to-combat-epidemics-the-key-is-context (accessed June 28, 2014).

17. Luke Fretwell, "'Open Data Now' Author Joel Gurin on How Businesses and Government Are Building the Data Economy," April 17, 2014, http://govfresh.com/2014/04/open-government-data-open-business-interview (accessed May 31, 2014).

18. Jim Edwards, "Yes, Your Credit Card Company Is Selling your Purchase Data to Online Advertisers," April 16, 2013, www.businessinsider.com/credit-cards-sell-purchase-data-to-advertisers-2013-4 (accessed May 31, 2014).

19. Tood Traub, "Wal-Mart used Technology to Become Supply Chain Leader," July 2, 2012, www.arkansasbusiness.com/article/85508/wal-mart-used-technology-to-become-supply-chain-leader?page=all (accessed May 30, 2014).

20. IBM, "What Is Watson?," www.ibm.com/smarterplanet/us/en/ibmwatson (accessed May 30, 2014).

21. Kate Kaye, "IBM's Watson Explores the Great E-Commerce Unknown with The North Face: Active-Gear Seller Is Mulling a New Site Featuring Watson Technology," December 13, 2013, http://adage.com/article/datadriven-marketing/ibm-watson-explores-e-commerce-unknown-north-face/245665/chan5search (accessed May 31, 2014).

22. Pan-Ning Tan, Michael Steinbach, and Vipin Kumar, *Introduction to Data Mining* (New York: Addison-Wesley, 2005).

23. Catherine Holahan, "Battling Data Monsters at Yahoo!," December 14, 2007, www.businessweek.com/technology/content/dec2007/tc20071213_341756.htm?chan5search (accessed February 8, 2010); Catherine Holahan, "Facebook: Marketers Are Your 'Friends,'" November 7, 2007, www.businessweek.com/technology/content/nov2007/tc2007116_289111.htm?chan5search (accessed February 8, 2010).

24. Kate Green, "TR10: Reality Mining," *MIT Technology Review—10 Breakthrough Technologies*, March/April 2008, www2.technologyreview.com/article/409598/tr10-reality-mining (accessed June 29, 2014); Arik Hesseldahl, "There's Gold In 'Reality Mining,'" March 24, 2008, www.businessweek.com/stories/2008-03-24/theres-gold-in-reality-miningbusinessweek-business-news-stock-market-and-financial-advice (accessed June 29, 2014).

25. Arik Hesseldahl, "A Rich Vein for 'Reality Mining,'" April 24, 2008, http://www.businessweek.com/stories/2008-04-23/a-rich-vein-for-reality-mining (accessed February 25, 2010).

26. Steve Kroft, "The Data Brokers: Selling Your Personal Information," March 9, 2014, www.cbsnews.com/news/the-data-brokers-selling-your-personal-information (accessed June 28, 2014).

27. Kashmir Hill, "How Target Figured Out Girl Was Pregnant before Her Father Did," February 16, 2012, www.forbes.com/sites/kashmirhill/2012/02/16/how-target-figured-out-a-teen-girl-was-pregnant-before-her-father-did (accessed June 28, 2014).

28. Joseph Walker, "Data Mining to Recruit Sick People," December 17, 2013, http://online.wsj.com/news/articles/SB10001424052702303722104579240140554518458 (accessed June 28, 2014).

29. Joe F. Hair Jr., "Knowledge Creation in Marketing: The Role of Predictive Analytics," *European Business Review* 19 (2007): 303–15.

30. Goutam Chakraborty and Murali Krishna Pagolu, "Analysis of Unstructured Data: Applications of Text Analytics and Sentiment Mining," *SAS Paper* 1288 (2014): 1–14.

31. IBM, "What Is a Data Scientist?," www-01.ibm.com/software/data/infosphere/data-scientist (accessed July 1, 2014).

32. Glassdoor, www.glassdoor.com/Salaries/us-data-scientist-salary-SRCH_IL.0,2_IN1_KO3,17.htm (accessed May 31, 2014); IBM, "What Is a Data Scientist?"

33. Thomas H. Davenport and D. J. Patil, "Data Scientist: The Sexiest Job of the 21st Century," October 2012, http://hbr.org/2012/10/data-scientist-the-sexiest-job-of-the-21st-century/ar/1 (accessed May 31, 2014).

34. Josh Leibowitz, Kelly Ungermena, and Maher Masri, "Know Your Customers Wherever They Are," October 16, 2012, http://blogs.hbr.org/2012/10/know-your-customers-wherever-t (accessed June 1, 2014).

35. Tan et al., *Introduction to Data Mining*.

36. Nate Nead, "Customer Acquisition vs. Retention," November 9, 2009, www.digitalsignage.com/blog/2009/11/09/signage-customer-acquisition-vs-retention (accessed February 7, 2010).

37. Robert Nelson, "Sprint May Cancel Your Service If You Call Customer Service Too Often," July 6, 2007, www.gadgetell.com/tech/comment/sprint-may-cancel-your-service-if-you-call-customer-service-to-often (accessed February 7, 2010); Samar Srivasta, "Sprint Drops Clients over Excessive Inquiries," July 7, 2007, http://online.wsj.com/public/article_print/SB118376389957059668-IpRTFYVQbLGbXKvlbPELi83M_8A_20080710.html (accessed February 7, 2010).

38. SAS, "Marketing Analytics: What It Is and Why It Matters," www.sas.com/en_us/insights/marketing/marketing-analytics.html (accessed June 1, 2014).

39. Pew Internet Research Project, "Internet Use over Time," www.pewinternet.org/data-trend/internet-use/internet-use-over-time (accessed June 1, 2014); Pew Internet Research Project, "Social Media Use over Time," www.pewinternet.org/data-trend/social-media/social-media-use-all-users (accessed June 1, 2014).

40. Gartner, "Gartner Survey Reveals Digital Marketing Budgets Will Increase by 10 Percent in 2014," April 29, 2014, www.gartner.com/newsroom/id/2723817 (accessed June 1, 2014).

41. Greg Bensinger, "Amazon Wants to Ship Your Package before You Buy It," January 14, 2014, http://blogs.wsj.com/digits/2014/01/17/amazon-wants-to-ship-your-package-before-you-buy-it (accessed August 26, 2014).

42. Hair, "Knowledge Creation in Marketing."

43. Samuel Greengard, "Predictive Analytics Helps Vodafone Ring Up Sales," June 3, 2014, www.baselinemag.com/analytics-big-data/predictive-analytics-helps-vodafone-ring-up-sales.html (accessed June 5, 2014).

44. Paul W. Farris, Neil T. Bendle, Phillip E. Pfeifer, and David J. Reibstein, *Marketing Metrics: 50+ Metrics Every Executive Should Master* (Philadelphia: Wharton School Publishing, 2006), 291.

45. Google, "Conversion Overview," https://support.google.com/analytics/answer/1006230?hl=en (accessed June 7, 2014).

46. Farris et al., *Marketing Metrics*, 294–95.

47. Wes Nichols, "Secrets of Successful Analytics Adoption," *Forbes*, July 22, 2013, www.forbes.com/sites/forbesinsights/2013/07/22/secrets-of-successful-marketing-analytics-adoption (accessed June 15, 2014).

CHAPTER 6

1. James R. Bettman, "The Decision Maker Who Came In from the Cold," Presidential Address, in *Advances in Consumer Research*, vol. 20, ed. Leigh McAllister and Michael Rothschild (Provo, UT: Association for Consumer Research, 1990); John W. Payne, James R. Bettman, and Eric J. Johnson, "Behavioral Decision Research: A Constructive Processing Perspective," *Annual Review of Psychology* 4 (1992): 87–131; for an overview of recent developments in individual choice models, see Robert J. Meyer and Barbara E. Kahn, "Probabilistic Models of Consumer Choice Behavior," in *Handbook of Consumer Behavior*, ed. Thomas S. Robertson and Harold H. Kassarjian (Englewood Cliffs, NJ: Prentice Hall, 1991), 85–123.

2. Catherine Valenti, "No Oscar? How About a Gift Bag?," March 24, http://abcnews.go.com/Business/story?id=86683&page=1 (accessed April 26, 2014).

3. Michael Lev, "No Hidden Meaning Here: Survey Sees Subliminal Ads," *New York Times*, May 3, 1991, D7.

4. "ABC Rejects KFC Commercial, Citing Subliminal Advertising," *Wall Street Journal Interactive Edition*, March 2, 2006.

5. Emily Fredrix, "TV Commercials Shrink to Match Attention Spans," October 30, 2010, http://usatoday30.usatoday.com/money/advertising/2010-10-30-shorter-v-commercials_N.htm (accessed April 25, 2014).

6. Joanna Stern, "The Biggest Tech Flops of 2013," December 29, 2013, http://abcnews.go.com/Technology/biggest-tech-flops-2013-facebook-home-galaxy-gear/story?id=21178737 (accessed April 26, 2014).

7. Abraham H. Maslow, *Motivation and Personality*, 2nd ed. (New York: Harper & Row, 1970).

8. Natasha Singer, "You've Won a Badge (and Now We Know All about You)," February 4, 2012, www.nytimes.com/2012/02/05/business/employers-and-brands-use-gaming-to-gauge-engagement.html?_r=0 (accessed April 28, 2014).

9. Robert A. Baron and Donn Byrne, *Social Psychology: Understanding Human Interaction*, 5th ed. (Boston: Allyn & Bacon, 1987).

10. Ryan Nakashima, "Disney to Create Lab to Test Ads for ABC, ESPN," May 12, 2008, www.usatoday.com/tech/products/2008-05-12-1465558386_x.htm (accessed February 24, 2010).

11. *U.S. News & World Report*, "Volkswagen Jetta Safety," http://usnews.rankingsandreviews.com/cars-trucks/Volkswagen_Jetta/Safety (accessed April 26, 2014); *U.S. News & World Report*, "Volkswagen Jetta Specs," http://usnews.rankingsandreviews.com/cars-trucks/Volkswagen_Jetta/2014/specs (accessed April 26, 2014).

12. www.jfmvipclub.com/jfm_styleguide.pdf (accessed February 24, 2010).

13. Alfred S. Boote, "Psychographics: Mind over Matter," *American Demographics*, April 1980, 26–29; William D. Wells, "Psychographics: A Critical Review," *Journal of Marketing Research* 12 (May 1975): 196–213.

14. Shiv, "Sensory Marketing: Using the Senses for Brand Building," March 3, 2014, http://marketingfaq.net/branding/sensory-marketing-and-branding (accessed April 29, 2014).

15. Aroma Marketing, "Research/Case Studies," www.sensorymax.com/aroma-marketing/research-case-studies-aroma.html (accessed April 29, 2014).

16. Ibid.

17. Jack Grant, "Shoppers Make More Purchase Decisions In-Store," June 2012, http://www.cpgmatters.com/In-StoreMarketing0612.html (accessed April 27, 2014).

18. Sally Delta, "Farmville Funeral Home Offering Drive-Thru Viewing," June 24, 2013, www.wset.com/story/22673593/farmville-funeral-home-offering-drive-thru-viewings (accessed July 14, 2014).

19. Betsy Morris, "More Consumers Prefer Online Shopping," June 3, 2013 http://online.wsj.com/news/articles/SB10001424127887324063304578523112193480212 (accessed April 27, 2014).

20. Greg Bensinger, "Amazon Wants to Ship Your Package before You Buy It," January 17, 2014, http://blogs.wsj.com/digits/2014/01/17/amazon-wants-to-ship-your-package-before-you-buy-it (accessed April 29, 2014).

21. www.amazon.com/b?node=8037720011 (accessed April 29, 2014).

22. Glenn Llopis, "Don't Sell to Me! Hispanics Buy Brands That Empower Their Cultural Relevancy," May 14, 2012, www.forbes.com/sites/glennllopis/2012/05/14/dont-sell-to-me-hispanics-buy-brands-that-empower-their-cultural-relevancy (accessed April 29, 2014).

23. Richard W. Pollay, "Measuring the Cultural Values Manifest in Advertising," *Current Issues and Research in Advertising* 6, no. 1 (1983): 71–92.

24. Michelle Saettler, "General Mills, Clorox Target Hispanic Mobile Shoppers via Bilingual Promotions App," 14, 201, www.mobile-marketer.com/cms/news/strategy/17575.html (accessed April 29, 2014).

25. Stuart U. Rich and Subhash C. Jain, "Social Class and Life Cycle as Predictors of Behavior," *Journal of Marketing Research* 5 (February 1968): 41–49.

26. Nathan Kogan and Michael A. Wallach, "Risky Shift Phenomenon in Small Decision-Making Groups: A Test of the Information Exchange Hypothesis," *Journal of Experimental Social Psychology* 3 (January 1967): 75–84; Arch G. Woodside and M. Wayne DeLozier, "Effects of Word-of-Mouth Advertising on Consumer Risk Taking," *Journal of Advertising* (Fall 1976): 12–19.

27. Everett M. Rogers, *Diffusion of Innovations*, 3rd ed. (New York: Free Press, 1983).

28. Kathleen Debevec and Easwar Iyer, "Sex Roles and Consumer Perceptions of Promotions, Products, and Self: What Do We Know and Where Should We Be Headed," in *Advances in Consumer Research*, vol. 13, ed. Richard J. Lutz (Provo, UT: Association for Consumer Research, 1986), 210–14; Lynn J. Jaffe and Paul D. Berger, "Impact on Purchase Intent of Sex-Role Identity and Product Positioning," *Psychology and Marketing*, Fall 1988, 259–71.

29. Jean Osterheldt, "Barbie Isn't 'Normal,' but Neither Is Lammily, the New 'It' Doll," March 18, 2014, www.kansas.com/2014/03/20/3353056/barbie-isnt-normal-but-neither.html (accessed April 27, 2014).

30. Melissa Dahl, "Six-Pack Stress: Men Worry More about Their Appearance Than Their Jobs," February 28, 2014, www.today.com/health/six-pack-stress-men-worry-more-about-their-appearance-their-2D12117283 (accessed April 27, 2014).

31. Matthew Boyle, "Yes, Real Men Drink Beer and Use Skin Moisturizer," October 23, 2013, www.businessweek.com/articles/2013-10-03/men-now-spend-more-on-toiletries-than-on-shaving-products (accessed April 27, 2014).

32. Catharine Skipp and Arian Campo-Flores, "Looks: A Manly Comeback," August 20, 2007, http://services.newsweek.com/search.aspx?offset50&pageSize510&sortField5pubdatetime&sortDirection5descending&mode5summary&q5Looks%2C1a1manly1comeback (accessed August 17, 2007).

33. www.boeing.com/commercial/prices (accessed March 10, 2010).

34. F. Robert Dwyer and John F. Tanner, *Business Marketing: Connecting Strategy, Relationships, and Learning* (Boston: McGraw-Hill, 2008); Edward F. Fern and James R. Brown, "The Industrial/Consumer Marketing Dichotomy: A Case of Insufficient Justification," *Journal of Marketing*, Spring 1984, 68–77.

35. Porsche, "All Boxter Models," www.porsche.com/usa/models/boxster (accessed February 22, 2010).

36. Walmart, "Where in the World Is Walmart?," http://corporate.walmart.com/our-story/our-business/locations (accessed April 26, 2014).

37. U.S. Census Bureau, *The 2012 Statistical Abstract of the United States* (Washington, DC: U.S. Census Bureau, 2012); U.S. Census Bureau, "The 2012 Statistical Abstract," www.census.gov/compendia/statab (accessed April 29, 2014).

38. U.S. Census Bureau, "North America Industry Classification System (NAICS)," www.census.gov/eos/www/naics (accessed February 23, 2010).

39. Aflac, "Aflac for Business," www.aflac.com/business/default.aspx (accessed February 23, 2010).

40. Chris Lake, "10 Kickass Crowdsourcing Sites for Your Business," August 4, 2009, http://econsultancy.com/blog/4355-10-kickass-crowdsourcing-sites-for-your-business (accessed March 16, 2010).

41. Michael Riley, Ben Elgin, Dune Lawrence, and Carol Matlack, "Missed Alarms and 40 Million Stolen Credit Card Numbers: How Target Blew It," March 13, 2014, www.businessweek.com/articles/2014-03-13/target-missed-alarms-in-epic-hack-of-credit-card-data (accessed April 26, 2014).

42. Tom Pick, "83 Exceptional Social Media and Marketing Statistics for 2014," April 20, 2014, www.business2community.com/social-media/83-exceptional-social-media-marketing-statistics-2014-0846364#!FfTg2 (accessed March 19, 2014).

43. Ryan Nakashima, "Disney to Create Lab to Test Ads for ABC, ESPN," May 12, 2008, www.usatoday.com/tech/products/2008-05-12-1465558386_x.htm (accessed February 24, 2010); Sylvia Jensen, "How Do B2B Companies Use Social Media?," www.scu.edu/ethics/practicing/decision (accessed March 21, 2014); J. J. McCorvey, "How to Use Social Media for B2B Marketing," July 29, 2010, www.inc.com/guides/2010/07/how-to-use-social-media-for-b2b-marketing.html (accessed March 15, 2014); Allen Narcisse, "Planning Your B2B Marketing Approach to Social Media: 3 Key Angles," http://contentmarketinginstitute.com/2014/01/planning-b2b-marketing-approach-social-media (accessed March 21, 2014).

CHAPTER 7

1. www.foxnews.com/leisure/2014/05/20/burger-king-ditches-have-it-your-way-slogan.

2. Ellen Neuborne and Kathleen Kerwin, "Generation Y," February 15, 1999, www.businessweek.com/1999/99_07/b3616001.htm (accessed May 31, 2014).

3. "Nike: Trying to Be the Chosen One in Action Sports," June 14, 2011, http://inthecrowds.wordpress.com/2011/06/14/nike-trying-to-be-the-chosen-one-in-action-sports (accessed May 31, 2014).

4. www.sneakerwatch.com/article/020496/the-65-most-expensive-sneakers-at-flight-club-right-now/131955 (June 2, 2014).

5. Bill Goodwin, "The Undeniable Influence of Kids," October 16, 2013, www.packagingdigest.com/packaging-design/undeniable-influence-kids (accessed May 28, 2014).

6. Karen Collier, "Teenagers Are Spending an Average of $5000 a Year of Their Parents' Hard-Earned Money, Survey Reveals," October 28, 2012, www.heraldsun.com.au/news/teenagers-are-spending-an-average-of-5000-a-year-of-their-parents-hard-earned-money-survey-reveals/story-e6frf7jo-1226504525546 (accessed May 27, 2014).

7. Amy Barrett, "To Reach the Unreachable Teen," *BusinessWeek*, September 18, 2000, 78–80.

8. Mark J. Miller, "Macy's Woos Millennials with New Brands, Digital Moxie," March 26, 2010, www.brandchannel.com/home/post/2012/03/26/Macys-Woos-Millennials-032612.aspx (accessed May 28, 2014).

9. Jacqueline Doherty, "On the Rise," April 29, 2013, http://online.barrons.com/news/articles/SB50001424052748703889404578440972842742076 (accessed May 27, 2014).

10. Bruce Drake, "6 New Findings about Millenials," March 7, 2014, www.pewresearch.org/fact-tank/2014/03/07/6-new-findings-about-millennials (accessed May 30, 2014).

11. Chipotle Mexican Grill, "Chipotle Launches 'The Scarecrow' for iPhone, iPad & iPod Touch and Animated Short Film," http://ir.chipotle.com/phoenix.zhtml?c=194775&p=irol-newsArticle&ID=1854278&highlight= (accessed May 31, 2014).

12. Bruce Horovitz, "Chipotle Targets Big Food, Skips Big Branding," www.usatoday.com/story/money/business/2013/09/12/chipotle-big-food-millennial-marketing/2798023 (accessed May 31, 2014).

13. Douglas Coupland, *Generation X: Tales for an Accelerated Culture* (New York: St. Martin's Press, 1991).

14. Robert Scally, "The Customer Connection: Gen X Grows Up, They're in Their 30s Now," *Discount Store News*, archived in Bnet.com, October 25, 1999, 38, http://findarticles.com/p/articles/mi_m3092/is_20_38/ai_57443548?tag5content;col1 (accessed June 25, 2008).

15. Scally, "The Customer Connection: Gen X Grows Up, They're in Their 30s Now"; Marshall Lager, "The Slackers' X-cellent Adventure," November 2008, www.destinationcrm.com/Articles/Editorial/Magazine-Features/The-Slackerse28099-X-cellent-Adventure-51406.aspx (accessed February 12, 2010).

16. David Crary, "Boomers Will Be Spending Billions to Counter Aging," August 22, 2011, http://usatoday30.usatoday.com/news/health/story/health/story/2011/08/Anti-aging-industry-grows-with-boomer-demand/50087672/1 (accessed May 31, 2014).

17. U.S. Census Bureau, "The Older Population: 2010," www.census.gov/prod/cen2010/briefs/c2010br-09.pdf (accessed May 27, 2014).

18. Ibid.
19. Jeffrey Zaslow, "Get Back to Where You Once Belonged," January 20, 2010, http://online.wsj.com/article/SB1000142405274870456 1004575012964067490650.html (accessed April 26, 2010).
20. Jennifer Lawrence, "Gender-Specific Works for Diapers—Almost Too Well," *Advertising Age*, February 8, 1993, S-10; Rachel Perls, "Why Is Blue for Boys and Pink for Girls?," March 16, 2007, http://hueconsulting.blogspot.com/2007/03/why-is-blue-for-boys-and-pink-for-girls.html (accessed March 1, 2010).
21. Michael Flocker, *The Metrosexual Guide to Style: A Handbook for the Modern Man* (Cambridge, MA: Da Capo Press, 2003); Lizzie Elzingre, "The Metrosexual Man," May 22, 2009, http://mens-cosmetic-health.suite101.com/article.cfm/the_metrosexual_man (accessed March 1, 2010).
22. "Spa," www.ilovethejw.com/spa.html (accessed May 27, 2014).
23. Wendy Wang, "Record Share of Wives Are More Educated Than Their Husbands," February 12, 2014, www.pewresearch.org/fact-tank/2014/02/12/record-share-of-wives-are-more-educated-than-their-husbands (accessed May 27, 2014).
24. Sonya Rhodes, "The Upside of 'Marrying Down,'" April 18, 2014, http://online.wsj.com/news/articles/SB10001424052702303663604579503800504978432 (accessed May 27, 2014).
25. John Stanton, "A Closer Look at the Single Household," July 18, 2013, www.foodprocessing.com/articles/2013/market-view-single-household (accessed May 28, 2014).
26. "Glass Baby Bottles in Demand," June 1, 2008, www.brandpackaging.com/CDA/Articles/Trends_Next_Now/BNP_GUID_9-5-2006_A_10000000000000352222 (accessed March 1, 2010).
27. Anne Fleming, "2013—The Year of the Woman Car Buyer: Capture This Powerful & Ever-Growing Segment," January 22, 2013, www.autoremarketing.com/trends/2013-%E2%80%93-year-woman-car-buyer-capture-powerful-ever-growing-segment (accessed May 31, 2014).
28. Alex Williams, "What Women Want: More Horses," June, www.nytimes.com/2005/06/12/fashion/sundaystyles/12cars.html?ex=1276228800&en=7ea4473d0aa65bb0&ei=5090&partner=rssuserland&emc=rss (accessed February 12, 2010).
29. Jack Neff, "Survey Finds the Rich Returning to Familiar Spending Habits," September 15, 2009, http://adage.com/article?article_id5139009 (accessed April 14, 2010).
30. Michael E. Ross, "At Newsstands, Black Is Plentiful," *New York Times*, December 26, 1993, F6; "Listings of Weekly, Monthly and Quarterly African American Magazines," www.blacknews.com/directory/black_african_american_magazines.shtml (accessed February 25, 2010).
31. Viacom, "BET Networks."
32. Brad Edmondson, "Asian Americans in 2001," *American Demographics*, February 1997, 16–17.
33. Greg Johnson and Edgar Sandoval, "Advertisers Court Growing Asian Population: Marketing, Wide Range of Promotions Tied to New Year Typify Corporate Interest in Ethnic Community," *Los Angeles Times*, February 4, 2000, C1.
34. Thomas Ott, "Horseshoe Casino Cleveland Makes Special Effort to Cater to Asian-American Gamblers," October 18, 2012, www.cleveland.com/metro/index.ssf/2012/10/horseshoe_casino_cleveland_wel.html (accessed June 2, 2014).
35. U.S. Census Bureau, "United States Census 2000," www.census.gov/main/www/cen2000.html (accessed March 22, 2006); "Latinas Are a Driving Force behind Hispanic Purchasing Power in the U.S.," August 1, 2013, www.nielsen.com/us/en/newswire/2013/latinas-are-a-driving-force-behind-hispanic-purchasing-power-in-.html (accessed May 28, 2014); Elinor Kinnier, "Five Trends Emerging among U.S. Hispanics: The New General Market," April, 2008, www.amg-inc.com/AMG/news/4-08-5trends-hispanicmkt.html (accessed February 25, 2010).
36. Lucette B. Comer and J. A. F. Nicholls, "Communication between Hispanic Salespeople and Their Customers: A First Look," *Journal of Personal Selling and Sales Management* 20 (Summer 2000): 121–27; Elena del Valle, "Relationship Building and Brand Loyalty," January 21, 2009, www.hispanicmpr.com/2009/01/21/relationship-building-and-brand-loyalty (accessed March 12, 2010).
37. Michael Freedman, Mythili Vutukuru, Nick Feamster, and Hari Balakrishnan, "Geographic Locality of IP Prefixes," Internet Measurement Conference, 2005.
38. Karlene Lukovitz, "McDonald's Digital Promos Geotarget College Kids," December 15, 2011, www.mediapost.com/publications/article/164279/mcdonalds-digital-promos-geo-target-college-kids.html (accessed May 29, 2014).
39. See Lewis Alpert and Ronald Gatty, "Product Positioning by Behavioral Life Styles," *Journal of Marketing* 33 (April 1969): 65–69; Emanuel H. Demby, "Psychographics Revisited: The Birth of a Technique," *Marketing News*, January 2, 1989, 21; and William D. Wells, "Backward Segmentation," in *Insights into Consumer Behavior*, ed. Johan Arndt (Boston: Allyn & Bacon, 1968), 85–100.
40. "Sample Demographics and Behaviors," www.strategicbusinessinsights.com/vals/demobehav.shtml (accessed June 1, 2014).
41. "Application of VALS™," www.strategicbusinessinsights.com/vals/applications/apps-pos.shtml (accessed June 1, 2014).
42. Alex Pham, "iTunes Crosses 25 Billion Songs Sold, Now Sells 21 Million Songs a Day," February 6, 2013, www.billboard.com/biz/articles/news/1538108/itunes-crosses-25-billion-songs-sold-now-sells-21-million-songs-a-day (accessed June 2, 2014).
43. "Lesson 3c: Language & Location Targeting," http://adwords.google.com/support/aw/bin/static.py?page5guide.cs&guide522793&topic522804 (accessed March 12, 2010).
44. "Harley Davidson and Its Aging Riders," April 20, 2012, http://knowledge.allianz.com/demography/population/?1851/harley-davidson-and-its-aging-riders (accessed May 31, 2014).
45. www.blacksocks.com (accessed March 12, 2010); Jack Ewing, "A Web Outfit with Socks Appeal," July 24, 2002, www.businessweek.com/technology/content/jul2002/tc20020724_9718.htm?chan5search (accessed March 22, 2008).
46. Chip Bayers, "The Promise of One to One (a Love Story)," *Wired*, May 1998, 130.
47. Yale Rudd Center, "Measuring Progress in Nutrition and Marketing to Children and Teens," http://fastfoodmarketing.org/media/FastFoodFACTS_Report_Summary.pdf (accessed May 31, 2014).
48. Oliver Balch, "India: Food, Marketing, and Children's Health," www.theguardian.com/sustainable-business/fast-food-marketing-childrens-health (accessed May 31, 2014).
49. Andrea K. Walker, "Under Armour in Public Eye," July 24, 2008, www.commercialalert.org/issues/culture/product-placement/under-armour-in-public-eye (accessed March 1, 2010).
50. Arundhati Parmar, "Where Are They Now? Revived, Repositioned Products Gain New Life," *Marketing News*, April 14, 2003, 1(3).
51. For an example of how consumers associate food brands with a range of female body shapes, see Martin R. Lautman, "End-Benefit Segmentation and Prototypical Bonding," *Journal of Advertising Research*, June/July 1991, 9–18.

CHAPTER 8

1. Woodstream Corp., www.victorpest.com (accessed March 27, 2010).
2. www.nytimes.com/2014/05/29/technology/apple-confirms-its-3-billion-deal-for-beats-electronics.html?_r=0 (accessed June 7, 2014).
3. Carnival Cruise Lines, "Welcome to Funville," www.carnival.com/Funville/forums (accessed June 2, 2014).
4. Associated Press, "Twinkies Make Early Return at Wal-Mart Stores, July 12, 2013, www.usatoday.com/story/money/business/2013/07/12/twinkies-make-early-return-wal-mart/2511927 (accessed June 3, 2014).
5. Olga Kharif, "Shoppers' 'Mobile Blinders' Force Checkout-Aisle Changes," March 21, 2013, www.bloomberg.com/news/2013-03-21/shoppers-mobile-blinders-force-checkout-aisle-changes.html (accessed June 4, 2014).

6. iRobotCorp., http://store.irobot.com/family/index.jsp?categoryId=2174932&s=A-ProductAge&gclid=COe3oOOA1r4CFTBk7Aod5A8AzA (accessed May 31, 2014).

7. www.wikipedia.com.

8. Michael D. Mumford, "Where Have We Been, Where Are We Going? Taking Stock in Creativity Research." *Creativity Research Journal* 15 (2003): 107–20.

9. Bruce Horovitz, "Gillette Unveils Its Costliest Cutting-Edge Razor, April 29, 2014, www.usatoday.com/story/money/business/2014/04/29/gillette-razor-shaving-personal-grooming-proglide-flexball/8420697 (accessed June 5, 2014).

10. Ibid.

11. "Gillette Declares 'Shaving Rebuilt' with Launch of New Fusion ProGlide with FlexBall™ Technology," April 29, 2014, www.marketwatch.com/story/gillette-declares-shaving-rebuilt-with-launch-of-new-fusion-proglide-with-flexball-technology-2014-04-29 (accessed June 5, 2014).

12. Darren Dahl, "Meet the Travel App That Helps You Talk Like aLocal,"February5,2014,www.forbes.com/sites/united/2014/02/05/meet-the-travel-app-that-helps-you-talk-like-a-local (accessed June 4, 2014).

13. Apple Inc., www.apple.com/ipodclassic/features.html (accessed March 28, 2010).

14. Tim Ambler, *Marketing and the Bottom Line,* 2nd ed. (Edinburgh Gate: FT Press, 2004), 172.

15. Tanya Irwin, "Lincoln Uses 'Co-Creation' to Get Design Feedback," August 21, 2011, www.mediapost.com/publications/article/156251/lincoln-uses-co-creation-to-get-design-feedback.html (accessed June 3, 2014).

16. Andrea Witt, "Adidas Releases 2010 Sustainability Report," April 1, 2011, http://news.thomasnet.com/IMT/2011/04/01/adidas-releases-2010-sustainability-report (accessed June 6, 2014).

17. Adidas Group, "Sustainability Progress Report 2013—Performance Counts," www.adidas-group.com/media/filer_public/2014/04/14/2013_sustainability_progress_report_fair_play_final_en.pdf (accessed June 6, 2014).

18. Ibid.

19. LG, "Discover OLED," www.lg.com/us/oled-tv (accessed June 6, 2014).

20. Simon Pitman, "Pfizer Sues P&G over Mouthwash Ad Claims," March 6, 2006, www.cosmeticsdesign.com/news/ng.asp?n566236-pfizer-proctor-gamble-lawsuit-mouthwash (accessed March 19, 2010).

21. www.forbes.com/sites/chancebarnett/2013/05/08/top-10-crowdfunding-sites-for-fundraising (accessed June 7, 2014).

22. Brad Stone, "Analysts Ask If the iPad Can Live Up to Its Hype," March 28, 2010, www.nytimes.com/2010/03/29/technology/29apple.html (accessed May 12, 2010).

23. Malcolm Gladwell, *The Tipping Point* (Newport Beach, CA: Back Bay Books, 2002).

24. www.chick-fil-a.com/Pressroom/Press-Releases/Grilled_Release_2014 (accessed May 31, 2014).

25. Michael McCarthy, "Tesla Generates Small Sales, Big Buzz without Paid Ads," June 10, 2013, http://adage.com/article/news/tesla-generates-small-sales-big-buzz-paid-ads/241994 (accessed June 7, 2014).

26. Simon Reynolds, "Why You Should Copy Tesla's Way of Marketing," September 1, 2013, www.forbes.com/sites/simonreynolds/2013/09/01/why-you-should-copy-teslas-way-of-marketing (accessed June 7, 2014).

27. "Tamagotchi L.i.f.e. Story," http://tamagotchilife.com/our-story (accessed June 3, 2014).

28. John M. Change, "Tamagotchis Expected to Rehatch in Stores for Fall 2014," November 26, 2013, http://abcnews.go.com/Technology/Toys/tamagotchi-friends-rebooted-fall-2014/story?id=21020541 (accessed June 3, 2014).

29. Ellen Carey, "Driving Electric Vehicle Adoption in Northern Colorado," March 31, 2014, http://blog.aee.net/driving-electric-vehicle-adoption-in-northern-colorado (accessed June 7, 2014).

30. Everett Rogers, *Diffusion of Innovations* (New York: Free Press, 1983), 247–51.

31. Sources used in this section: "Wi-Fi's Big Brother," *Economist*, March 13, 2004, 65; William J. Gurley, "Why Wi-Fi Is the Next Big Thing," *Fortune*, March 5, 2001, 184; Joshua Quittner, "Cordless Capers," *Time*, May 1, 2000, 85; Scott Van Camp, "Intel Switches Centrino's Gears," *Brandweek*, April 26, 2004, 16; Benny Evangelista, "SBC Park a Hot Spot for Fans Lugging Laptops," *San Francisco Chronicle*, April 26, 2004, A1; Todd Wallack, "Santa Clara Ready for Wireless," *San Francisco Chronicle*, April 19, 2004, D1; Glenn Fleishman, "Three Essays on Muni-Fi You Should Read," http://wifinetnews.com.

32. Christine Chen and Tim Carvell, "Hall of Shame," *Fortune*, November 22, 1999, 140.

33. "Top 10 Failed Products," www.smashinglists.com/top-10-failed-products/2 (accessed June 2, 2014).

34. Rogers, *Diffusion of Innovations*, chap. 6.

35. Patrick Sarkissian, "Why Metrics Are Killing Creativity in Advertising," March 10, 2010, http://adage.com/article/guest-columnists/viewpoint-metrics-killing-creativity-advertising/142600 (accessed May 31, 2014).

CHAPTER 9

1. David Kiley, "The MINI Bulks Up," January 17, 2006, www.businessweek.com/autos/content/jan2006/bw20060117_818487.htm?chan5search (accessed April 8, 2010).

2. Trader Joe's, "Trader Joe's Timeline," www.traderjoes.com/about/timeline.asp (accessed June 16, 2014).

3. Pepperidge Farm, "In Celebrating 75 Years, 'Pepperidge Farms Remembers' Its Beginning and Drives Innovation Ahead," August 9, 2012, http://news.pepperidgefarm.com/news/in-celebrating-75-years-pepperidge-240914 (accessed June 16, 2014).

4. www.pg.com/annualreport2011/innovating/gain.shtml (accessed June 8, 2014).

5. Rolls-Royce Motor Cars, www.rolls-roycemotorcars.com (accessed April 8, 2010).

6. Kia, "Kia Motors Brand Value Increases by 15% to USD 4.7 Billion," http://www.kia.bg/en/news/read/146/kia_motors_brand_value_increases_by_15_to_usd_4_7_billion (accessed June 18, 2014).

7. Bernie Woodall, "Kia Tries to Burnish Image with $66,000 Luxury K900 Car," May 16, 2014, http://articles.chicagotribune.com/2014-05-16/marketplace/sns-rt-us-kia-motors-k900-20140515_1_luxury-brand-bernie-woodall-k900 (accessed June 18, 2014).

8. Nivedita Bhattacharjee, "Diamond Foods Snacks on Pringles with $1.5 Billion Buy," April 5, 2011, www.reuters.com/article/2011/04/05/us-procterandgamble-diamond-idUSTRE7342D120110405 (accessed June 16, 2014).

9. www.groceryheadquarters.com/2014/04/studying-supermarket-stats (accessed June 21, 2014).

10. Sheila Shayon, "Amidst Genimgate, Levi's Breaks in New Green Jean Initiatives," May 23, 2014, www.brandchannel.com/home/post/2014/05/23/140523-Levis-Sustainability.aspx (accessed June 17, 2014).

11. Geoffrey Colvin, "The Ultimate Manager," *Fortune*, November 22, 1999, 185–87.

12. www.iso.org/iso/home/standards.htm (accessed June 7, 2014).

13. Al Ries and Laura Ries, *The Origin of Brands* (New York: Collins, 2005).

14. Laurie Burkitt and Ken Bruno, "New, Improved . . . and Failed," March 24, 2010, www.msnbc.msn.com/id/36005036/ns/business-forbescom (accessed April 4, 2010).

15. Tatiana Boncompagni, "Social Media Breathes Life into Shelved Products," May 1, 2012, www.nytimes.com/2012/05/03/fashion/social-media-breathes-new-life-into-discontinued-beauty-products.html?ref=technology&_r=0 (accessed June 17, 2014).

16. Ibid.

17. "'Apple' Wins Logo Lawsuit against Beatles," May 8, 2006, www .macnn.com/articles/06/05/08/apple.wins.logo.lawsuit (accessed April 8, 2010).

18. "The Most Famous Name in Music," *Music Trades* 118, no. 12 (September 2003).

19. Suzanne Vranica, "McDonald's Vintage T-Shirts Sizzle," April 27, 2006, www.post-gazette.com/pg/06117/685629-28.stm (accessed April 8, 2010).

20. Susan Fournier, "Consumers and Their Brands: Developing Relationship Theory in Consumer Research," *Journal of Consumer Research* 24 (March 1998): 343–73.

21. Stuart Elliott, "For One Production Company, It's All about the Power of Storytelling," November 16, 2008, www.nytimes .com/2008/11/17/business/media/17adcol.html (accessed May 31, 2010).

22. Kevin Lane Keller, "The Brand Report Card," *Harvard Business Review*, January–February 2000 (Harvard Business School reprint R00104).

23. www.brandingstrategyinsider.com/2010/08/exploring-the-value-of-sub-brands.html#.U5Ul5H7D9Mw (accessed June 6, 2014).

24. Nicholas Casey, "Can New Quiksilver Line Reach beyond the Beach," March 6, 2008, http://online.wsj.com/article_email/SB120476311128015043-lMyQjAxMDI4MDA0NjcwNjYzWj.html (accessed April 2, 2010).

25. John D. Stoll, "Eight-Brand Pileup Dents GM's Turnaround Efforts," March 4, 2008, http://online.wsj.com/article_email/SB120456874600508063-lMyQjAxMDI4MDA0NTUwNjU4Wj .html (accessed April 1, 2010).

26. www.costco.com/insider-guide-ks-products.html (accessed June 7, 2014).

27. "Psst! Wanna See Loblaws' New Products?," *Private Label Buyer* 10, no. 1 (January 2003); Len Lewis, "Turf War!," *Grocery Headquarters* 13, no. 6 (November 2002).

28. www.walmart.com/cp/1078664?povid=cat5431-env198764-moduleB120712-lLinkFC44DollarPrescriptions (accessed June 5, 2014).

29. www.tgifridays.com/eat#jack-daniels-grill (accessed June 6, 2014).

30. Lego, "Harry Potter," http://parents.lego.com/awards/awards. aspx?id5legoharrypotter (accessed April 2, 2010).

31. Zeiss, "Carl Zeiss and Sony," www.zeiss.com/camera-lenses/en_us/camera_lenses/partner/sony.html (accessed June 16, 2014).

32. D. C. Denison, "The Boston Globe Business Intelligence Column," *Boston Globe*, May 26, 2002.

33. "Putting Zoom into Your Life," *Time International*, March 8, 2004, 54.

34. Stephanie Thompson, "Brand Buddies," *Brandweek*, February 23, 1998, 26–30; Jean Halliday, "L.L. Bean, Subaru Pair for Co-Branding," *Advertising Age*, February 21, 2000, 21.

35. www.harrisinteractive.com/Insights/EquiTrendRankings/2014 EquiTrendRankings.aspx (accessed July 7, 2014).

36. Kusum L. Ailawadi, Donald R. Lehmann, and Scott A. Neslin, "Revenue Premium as an Outcome Measure of Brand Equity," *Journal of Marketing* 67 (October 2003): 1–17.

37. www.pringles.com/en_US/home.html (accessed June 4, 2014).

38. Andrew Adam Newman, "Launching a Fragrance Line (in a Manner of Speaking)," January 10, 2013, www.nytimes.com/2013/01/11/business/media/for-axes-apollo-line-a-campaign-found-in-space. html?ref=global&_r=1& (accessed June 18, 2014).

39. Aaron Baar, "Accidental Purchases: Blame Package Design, *Marketing Daily/MediaPost News*, October 29, 2010 http://www.mediapost .com/publications/article/116283/accidental-purchases-blame-package-design.html (accessed December 4, 2014)

40. "Labels to Include Trans Fat," *San Fernando Valley Business Journal*, January 19, 2004, 15.

41. Professor Jakki Mohr, University of Montana, personal communication (April 2004).

42. Russell Parsons, "Consumers Rate a Brand's Ethics before Buying, Study Finds," July 29, 2011, www.marketingweek.co.uk/consumers-rate-a-brands-ethics-before-buying-study-finds/3028851.article (accessed June 17, 2014).

CHAPTER 10

1. http://money.cnn.com/infographic/technology/what-is-bitcoin (accessed May 12, 2014); "Bitcoin FAQ," http://bitcoinfaq.com (accessed May 9, 2014).

2. http://www.bitcoinvalues.net/who-accepts-bitcoins-payment-companies-stores-take-bitcoins.html (accessed July 17, 2014).

3. Mark Andreessen, "Why Bitcoin Matters," January 21, 2014, http://dealbook.nytimes.com/2014/01/21/why-bitcoin-matters (accessed March 30, 2014); Quentin Hardy, "Bitcoin and the Fictions of Money," January 27, 2014, http://bits.blogs .nytimes.com/2014/01/27/bitcoin-and-the-fictions-of-money/?_ php=true&_type=blogs&_php=true&_type=blogs&_r=1 (accessed March 30, 2014).

4. Drew Guarini, "11 Surprising Product Fads," August 22, 2012, www.huffingtonpost.com/2012/08/22/product-fads_n_ 1819710.html (accessed May 6, 2014).

5. Paul W. Farris, Neil T. Bendle, Phillip E. Pfeifer, and David J. Reibstein, *Marketing Metrics: The Definitive Guide to Measuring Marketing Performance* (Upper Saddle River, NJ: Pearson Education, 2010).

6. Max Mason, "Virgin Battle Testing Qantas' Domestic Strategy," May 21, 2014, www.smh.com.au/business/aviation/virgin-battle-testing-qantas-domestic-strategy-20140521-38nh9 .html#ixzz32Urapa3N (accessed May 22, 2014).

7. Associated Press, "Walmart's New Tool Gives You Competitors' Prices," March 21, 2014, www.dailyfinance.com/2014/03/21/walmart-new-tool-provides-competitors-prices (accessed May 22, 2014).

8. "This Day in History," www.history.com/this-day-in-history/seventeen-states-put-gasoline-rationing-into-effect (accessed May 23, 2014).

9. Stephanie Rosenblum, "In Recession, Strategy Shifts for Big Chains," June 19, 2009, www.nytimes.com/2009/06/20/business/20retail.html?pagewanted=all (accessed May 7, 2014).

10. Jennifer Waters, "It's a New Day for Credit Cards," February 21, 2010, http://online.wsj.com/article/SB126670472534749217.htm l?KEYWORDS5credit1card1rate1regulations (accessed March 3, 2010).

11. "Key Features of the Affordable Care Act by Year," www.hhs .gov/healthcare/facts/timeline/timeline-text.html (accessed May 10, 2014); Rick Ungar, "The Real Numbers on 'The Obamacare Effect' Are In—Now Let the Crow Eating Begin," March 10, 2014, www.forbes.com/sites/rickungar/2014/03/10/the-real-numbers-on-the-obamacare-effect-are-in-now-let-the-crow-eating-begin (accessed May 20, 2014).

12. "Luxury Shoppers Seek Bargains," April 17, 2014, www.warc .com/LatestNews/News/Luxury_shoppers_seek_bargains .news?ID=32852 (accessed May 10, 2014).

13. Michael Sheehan, "Are the Rich Thrifty?," September 16, 2008, www.hcplive.com/publications/pmd/2004/28/1923 (accessed May 10, 2014).

14. Timothy Aeppel, "Chinese Willing to Pay More for Made-in-USA Goods," November 14, 2012, http://blogs.wsj.com/economics/2012/11/14/chinese-willing-to-pay-more-for-made-in-usa-goods (accessed May 8, 2014).

15. Steward Washburn, "Pricing Basics: Establishing Strategy and Determining Costs in the Pricing Decision," *Business Marketing*, July 1985, reprinted in Valerie Kijewski, Bob Donath, and David T. Wilson, eds., *The Best Readings from Business Marketing Magazine* (Boston: PWS-Kent, 1993), 257–69.

16. Robin Cooper and W. Bruce Chew, "Control Tomorrow's Costs through Today's Design," *Harvard Business Review*, January–February 1996, 88–97.

17. Emek Basker and Michael Noel, "The Evolving Food Chain: Competitive Effects of Wal-Mart's Entry into the Supermarket Industry," October 21, 2009, http://onlinelibrary.wiley.com/doi/10.1111/j.1530-9134.2009.00235.x/abstract (accessed May 8, 2014).

18. http://www.tutor2u.net/blog/index.php/business-studies/comments/qa-explain-price-skimming (accessed May 12, 2014).

19. Campbell's, "About Us," www.campbellsoupcompany.com/about-campbell (accessed May 8, 2014).

20. Laura Northrup, "QVC Bundles Some Accessories with iPad 2, Doubles the Price," March 22, 2012, http://consumerist.com/2012/03/22/qvc-bundles-some-accessories-with-ipad-2-doubles-the-price (accessed May 8, 2014).

21. Export 911, "International Commercial Terms," www.export911.com/e911/export/comTerm.htm (accessed May 27, 2008).

22. Megan Gibson, "Happy 10th Birthday, iTunes!," April 28, 2013, http://entertainment.time.com/2013/04/28/happy-10th-birthday-itunes (accessed May 8, 2014).

23. "Music Goes Mobile as More Smartphone Users Stream Songs," August 13, 2013, www.emarketer.com/Article/Music-Goes-Mobile-More-Smartphone-Users-Stream-Songs/1010126 (accessed May 10, 2014).

24. Adam Tanner, "Different Customers, Different Prices, Thanks to Big Data," March 26, 2014, www.forbes.com/sites/adamtanner/2014/03/26/different-customers-different-prices-thanks-to-big-data (accessed May 23, 2014).

25. "Definition of 'Price Discrimination,'" www.investopedia.com/terms/p/price_discrimination.asp (accessed May 23, 2014).

26. Jennifer Valentino-DeVries, Jeremy Singer-Vine, and Ashkan Soltani, "Websites Vary Prices, Deals Based on Users' Information," December 24, 2012, http://online.wsj.com/news/articles/SB10001424127887323777204578189391813881534 (accessed May 1, 2014).

27. "What Is Freemium?," www.freemium.org/what-is-freemium-2 (accessed May 22, 2014).

28. David Ackerman and Gerald Tellis, "Can Culture Affect Prices? A Cross-Cultural Study of Shopping and Retail Prices," *Journal of Retailing* 77 (2001): 57–82.

29. Shankar Vedantam, "Eliot Spitzer and the Price-Placebo Effect," March 17, 2008, www.washingtonpost.com/wp-dyn/content/article/2008/03/16/AR2008031602168.html (accessed May 27, 2008).

30. William J. Boyes, Allen K. Lynch, and William Stewart, "Why Odd Pricing?," *Journal of Applied Social Psychology* 37, no. 5 (May 2007): 1130–40; Robert M. Schindler and Thomas M. Kibarian, "Increased Consumer Sales Response through Use of 99-Ending Prices," *Journal of Retailing* 72 (1996): 187–99.

31. Sarah Kershaw, "Using Menu Psychology to Entice Diners," December 22, 2009, www.nytimes.com/2009/12/23/dining/23menus.html?scp1&sq5Using%20Menu%20Psychology%20to%20Entice%20Diners&st5cse (accessed March 3, 2010).

32. Stephanie Rosenbloom, "Back-to-School Discounts Are Deeper, More Creative," August 14, 2008, www.nytimes.com/2008/08/15/business/15retail.html?scp51&sq5Back-to-School%20Discounts%20Are%20Deeper,%20More%20Creative&st5cse (accessed March 4, 2010).

33. Sam Gustin, "Apple Found Guilty in E-Book Price Fixing Conspiracy Trial," July 10, 2013, http://business.time.com/2013/07/10/apple-found-guilty-in-e-book-price-fixing-conspiracy-trial (accessed May 8, 2014).

34. Annie Lowrey, "Is Uber's Surge-Pricing an Example of High-Tech Gouging?," January 10, 2014, www.nytimes.com/2014/01/12/magazine/is-ubers-surge-pricing-an-example-of-high-tech-gouging.html (accessed May 8, 2014).

35. Ibid.

36. Adam Bryant, "Aisle Seat Bully?," *Newsweek*, May 24, 1999, 56.

CHAPTER 11

1. Amazon, "Amazon Prime Air," www.amazon.com/b?node=8037720011 (accessed June 25, 2014).

2. Doug Goss, "Amazon's Drone Delivery: How Would It Work?," December 2, 2013, www.cnn.com/2013/12/02/tech/innovation/amazon-drones-questions (accessed June 25, 2014).

3. Rowland T. Moriarty and Ursula Moran, "Managing Hybrid Marketing Systems," *Harvard Business Review*, November–December 1990, 2–11.

4. Joan Voight, "BWM Moves into Zipcar's Territory," May 16, 2014, www.adweek.com/news/advertising-branding/bmw-moves-zipcar-s-territory-157708 (accessed June 30, 2014).

5. www.washingtonpost.com/blogs/capital-business/post/wal-mart-invites-local-business-to-join-it-on-georgia-avenue/2013/04/30/bc9a60fe-b1ae-11e2-9a98-4be1688d7d84_blog.html (accessed June 26, 2014).

6. Oneworld, "Member Airlines," www.oneworld.com/member-airlines/overview (accessed June 24, 2014).

7. John Neff, "Scion May Break Promise to Itself, Add Fourth Model," May 25, 2007, www.autoblog.com/2007/05/25/scion-may-break-promise-to-itself-add-fourth-model (accessed May 1, 2010).

8. Scion, "Pure Process," http://www.scion.com/buy/pure_process/ (accessed June 26, 2014).

9. Starbucks, "About Us," www.starbucks.com/about-us (accessed May 1, 2010).

10. Toby B. Gooley, "The Who, What, and Where of Reverse Logistics," *Logistics Management* 42 (February 2003): 38–44; James R. Stock, *Development and Implementation of Reverse Logistics Programs* (Oak Brook, IL: Council of Logistics Management, 1998), 20.

11. "Spychipped Levi's Brand Jeans Hit the U.S.," April 27, 2006, www.spychips.com/press-releases/levis-secret-testing.html (accessed May 1, 2010); Katherine Albrecht and Liz McIntyre, *Spychips: How Major Corporations and Government Plan to Track Your Every Purchase and Watch Your Every Move* (New York: Plume, 2006).

12. "Boycott Gillette," www.boycottgillette.com/index.html (accessed June 26, 2014).

13. Faye W. Gilbert, Joyce A. Young, and Charles R. O'Neal, "Buyer-Seller Relationships in Just-in-Time Purchasing Environments," *Journal of Organizational Research* 29 (February 1994): 111–20.

14. www.supplychainmetric.com/inventoryturns.htm (accessed June 14, 2014).

15. Jonathan Birchall, "Walmart Aims to Cut Supply Chain Cost," January 3, 2010, www.ft.com/cms/s/0/891c7878-f895-11de-beb8-00144feab49a.html (accessed June 28, 2010).

16. Thomas L. Friedman, *The World Is Flat 3.0: A Brief History of the Twenty-First Century* (New York: Picador, 2007).

17. Frederick Kaufman, "Former McDonald's Honchos Take on Sustainable Cuisine," July 31, 2012, www.wired.com/2012/07/ff_lyfekitchens/all (accessed June 25, 2014).

18. "Perfect Order Measure," www.supplychainmetric.com/perfect.htm (accessed May 5, 2010).

CHAPTER 12

1. "Total US Retail Sales Top $4.5 Trillion in 2013, Outpace GDP Growth," www.emarketer.com/Article/Total-US-Retail-Sales-Top-3645-Trillion-2013-Outpace-GDP-Growth/1010756 (accessed May 10, 2014).

2. Bureau of Labor Statistics, U.S. Department of Labor, "The Employment Situation—April 2014," www.bls.gov/news.release/pdf/empsit.pdf (accessed May 10, 2014).

3. Stanley C. Hollander, "The Wheel of Retailing," *Journal of Retailing*, July 1960, 41.

4. Pier 1 Imports, "About Us," www.pier1.com/company/history.aspx (accessed June 25, 2006).

5. Kim Girard, "Is JC Penney's Makeover the Future of Retailing?," March 5, 2012, http://hbswk.hbs.edu/item/6944.html (accessed May 17, 2014).

6. Matt Brownell, "Women Are Fleeing Coupon-Free J.C. Penny, New Poll Reveals," October 18, 2012, www.dailyfinance.com/2012/10/18/women-are-fleeing-coupon-free-j-c-penney-new-poll-reveals (accessed May 17, 2014).

7. Stephanie Rosenbloom and Jack Healy, "Retailers Post Weak Earnings and July Sales," August 13, 2009, www.nytimes.com/2009/08/14/business/14shop.html?scp52&sq5christmas%20sales%20percentage%20of%20annual&st5cse (accessed March 15, 2010).

8. Bruce Lambert, "Once Robust, Retail Scene on the Island Is Smarting," May 7, 2009, www.nytimes.com/2009/05/10/nyregion/long-island/10rooseveltli.html?scp55&sq5retail%20bankruptcies&st5cse (accessed March 15, 2010).

9. Christopher Durham, "Private Brand Sales Outpace National Brands—PLMA's 2013 Private Label Yearbook," June 28, 2013, http://mypbrand.com/2013/06/28/private-brands-sales-outpace-national-brands-plmas-2013-private-label-yearbook (accessed May 10, 2014).

10. Jack Neff, "Walmart Reversal Marks Victory for Brands," March 22, 2010, http://adage.com/article?article_id5142904 (accessed September 30, 2010).

11. John Ewoldt, "Total Wine & More Superstore May Steer You to Its Private Labels," November 4, 2013, www.startribune.com/blogs/230540151.html (accessed May 15, 2014).

12. www.trendhunter.com/trends/augmented-pixels-showinroom (accessed May 18, 2014); Thomas M. Anderson, "Checkups on the Run," Kiplinger Personal Finance, May 2006, 96.

13. Bill Briggs, "J.C. Penney Rings Up 25% of Store Sales via Mobile Devices," March 7, 2013, www.internetretailer.com/2013/03/07/jc-penney-rings-25-store-sales-mobile-devices (accessed May 15, 2014).

14. Barry Berman and Joel R. Evans, Retail Management: A Strategic Approach, 11th ed. (Upper Saddle River, NJ: Pearson Education 2010).

15. Rebecca Harrison, "Restaurants Try E-Menus," February 25, 2008, http://uk.reuters.com/article/internetNews/idUKL2045993 20080226.

16. Nancy D. Albers-Miller, "Utilitarian and Experiential Buyers," http://facultyweb.berry.edu/nmiller/classinfo/601/Module%203/util_and_exp.htmn (accessed May 22, 2014).

17. Retailtainment: The Future of Shopping?," May 25, 2014, www.independent.co.uk/news/business/analysis-and-features/retailtainment-the-future-of-shopping-2303942.html (accessed May 25, 2014).

18. "Thirsty for Innovation," March 28, 2014, http://saatchixlondon.wordpress.com/2014/04/10/on-the-move-with-ikea (accessed May 25, 2014); "Karl Lagerfeld Puts Social Shopping at the Heart of Its New Store," March 20, 2014, http://saatchixlondon.wordpress.com/2014/04/10/on-the-move-with-ikea (accessed May 25, 2014); "H&M's Innovative Store," January 15, 2014, http://saatchixlondon.wordpress.com/2014/04/10/on-the-move-with-ikea (accessed May 25, 2014).

19. Sean Deale, "Retailtainment: 10 Great Ideas to Increase Store-Based Retail Traffic," December 21, 2011, www.instoretrends.com/index.php/2011/12/21/retailtainment-10-great-ideas-to-increase-store-based-retail-traffic/#sthash.8u7fjeF9.dpuf (accessed May 25, 2014).

20. Toys "R" Us, Inc., "About Toys 'R' Us, Inc.," www.toysrusinc.com/about-us (accessed August 23, 2014).

21. "New Research Shows Shoplifting, Retail Crime on the Rise Globally," November 12, 2013, http://mypbrand.com/2013/06/28/private-brands-sales-outpace-national-brands-plmas-2013-private-label-yearbook (accessed May 10, 2014).

22. Center for Retail Research, "Key Findings from the Global Retail Theft Barometer 2009," www.retailresearch.org/global_theft_baromter/2009keyfindings.php (accessed March 12, 2010).

23. National Association for Shoplifting Prevention, "Shoplifting Statistics," www.shopliftingprevention.org/whatnaspoffers/NRC/PublicEducStats.htm (accessed May 11, 2014).

24. David Ovalle, "$15 Million Retail Theft Ring in South Florida Is Busted, Miami-Dade State Attorney Says," March 27, 2014, www.miamiherald.com/2014/03/27/4022792/cops-15-million-south-florida.html (accessed May 17, 2014).

25. "Dumb Mistake Leads Police to Shoplifting Suspect," August 26, 2011, http://sacramento.cbslocal.com/2011/08/26/dumb-mistake-leads-police-to-shoplifting-suspect (accessed May 15, 2014).

26. National Association for Shoplifting Prevention, "Shoplifting Statistics," www.shopliftingprevention.org/whatnaspoffers/NRC/PublicEducStats.htm (accessed May 11, 2014).

27. Jack L. Hayes International, Inc., "Shoplifter and Dishonest Employee Theft on Rise," www.hayesinternational.com/thft_srvys.html (accessed May 1, 2008).

28. Steven Greenhouse, "Shoplifters? Studies Say Keep an Eye on Workers December 29, 2009, www.nytimes.com/2009/12/30/business/30theft.html?scp56&sq5shoplifting&st5cse (accessed March 12, 2010).

29. Kelly Gates and Dan Alaimo, "Solving Shrink," Supermarket News, October 22, 2007, 43.

30. Francis Piron and Murray Young, "Retail Borrowing: Insights and Implications on Returning Used Merchandise," International Journal of Retail & Distribution Management 28, no. 1 (2000): 27–36.

31. Barbara Farfan, "Customer Service Research Reveals Profiling and Discrimination as Common Employee Practices—How Nordstrom, Costco, Trader Joe's Replace Customer Profiling with Service," March 31, 2013, http://retailindustry.about.com/b/2013/03/31/customer-service-research-reveals-profiling-and-discrimination-as-common-employee-practices-how-nordstrom-costco-trader-joes-replace-customer-profiling-with-service.htm (accessed May 17, 2014).

32. Brandon A. Perry, "Civil Rights Commission Probes Complaints about Retail Discrimination," May 16, 2013, www.indianapolisrecorder.com/news/article_87bcda4e-be36-11e2-909e-0019bb2963f4.html (accessed May 17, 2014).

33. "Abercrombie & Fitch Employment Discrimination," June 17, 2003, www.naacpldf.org/case-issue/abercrombie-fitch-employment-discrimination (accessed May 27, 2014).

34. Rebecca Leung, "The Look of Abercrombie & Fitch," November 24, 2004, http://www.cbsnews.com/news/the-look-of-abercrombie-fitch-24-11-2004/ (accessed May 27, 2014).

35. "Abercrombie & Fitch Employment Discrimination," June 17, 2003, www.naacpldf.org/case-issue/abercrombie-fitch-employment-discrimination (accessed May 27, 2014).

36. Associated Press, "Abercrombie & Fitch Settles Discrimination Lawsuit over Head Scarves," September 23, 2013, www.nydailynews.com/life-style/fashion/abercrombie-settles-discrimination-suit-article-1.1464996 (accessed May 27, 2014).

37. Linda Lisanti, "Adventure's Next Stop," Convenience Store News, March 3, 2008, 28–34; Michael Browne, "Maverik's Big Adventure," Convenience Store News, November 15, 2005, 50–54.

38. "About ALDI," www.aldifoods.com/us/html/company/about_aldi_ENU_HTML.htm?WT.z_src5main (accessed March 28, 2010).

39. Mark Albright, "Kohl's Debut with Fresh New Look," St. Petersburg Times, September 28, 2006, 1D.

40. "Proof of Club Popularity in the 64-Ounce Pudding," DSN Retailing Today, December 19, 2005, 64.

41. Quoted in Stratford Sherman, "Will the Information Superhighway Be the Death of Retailing?," Fortune, April 18, 1994, 110.

42. Direct Selling Association, Research Services Center, "2012 Direct Selling Statistics," www.dsa.org/research/industry-statistics (accessed May 15, 2014).

43. Direct Selling Association, "Ready, Set, Shop!," www.dsa.org/about/dsaoprahinsert.pdf (accessed May 16, 2014).

44. Amway, "Business Opportunity," www.amway.com/about-amway/business-opportunity (accessed May 15, 2014).

45. "Amway Corporation Company Profile," http://biz.yahoo.com/ic/103/103441.html (accessed May 15, 2014).

46. Direct Selling Association, "The Difference between Legitimate Direct Selling Companies and Illegal Pyramid Schemes,", www.dsa.org/ethics/legitimatecompanies.pdf (accessed May 19, 2014).

47. Kathleen Davis, "9 Things You Never Thought You Would Buy from a Vending Machine," July 30, 2013, www.entrepreneur.com/slideshow/227452 (accessed May 15, 2014); Ariel Knutson, "24 Vending Machines You Won't Believe Exist," www.buzzfeed.com/arielknutson/vending-machines-you-wont-believe-exist (accessed May 15, 2014).

48. Jill Becker, "Vending Machines for All Your Needs," August 16, 2012, www.cnn.com/2012/08/16/travel/odd-vending-machines (accessed May 15, 2014).

49. Kenji Hall, "High-Tech Vending Machine Is a Full-on Robo Sales-person," January 25, 2012, www.fastcodesign.com/1662222/high-tech-vending-machine-is-a-full-on-robo-salesperson-video (accessed May 18, 2014).

50. Lauren Indvik, "Forrester: U.S. Online Retail Sales to Hit $370 Bil-lion by 2017," March 12, 2013, http://mashable.com/2013/03/12/forrester-u-s-ecommerce-forecast-2017 (accessed May 15, 2014).

51. Amy Dusto, "60% of U.S. Retail Sales Will Involve the Web by 2017," October 30, 2013, www.internetretailer.com/2013/10/30/60-us-retail-sales-will-involve-web-2017 (accessed May 15, 2014).

52. Ibid.

53. Jashen Chen and Russell K. H. Ching, "Virtual Experiential Mar-keting on Online Customer Intentions and Loyalty," *Proceedings of the 41st Hawaii International Conference on System Sciences*, 2008, http://citeseerx.ist.psu.edu/viewdoc/download?doi=10.1.1.1 33.4967&rep=rep1&type=pdf (accessed May 23, 2014); Randall Stone, "Retailtainment to the Rescue, January 14, 2008, www .lippincott.com/en/insights/retailtainment-to-the-rescue (ac-cessed May 22, 2014).

54. The Network Experiential, "Creating a Storm: Two Retail Trends That Demonstrate the Real Value of Experiential Marketing," February 2, 2014, www.thenetwork-experiential.com/blogview .asp?ID={27BA6D5C-85F0-428C-833C-37D7067AB651} (accessed May 22, 2014).

55. Bob Tedeschi, "A Quicker Resort This Year to Deep Discount-ing," December 17, 2007, www.nytimes.com/2007/12/17/technology/17ecom.html?scp541&sq5forrester1research&st5nyt (accessed May 1, 2008).

56. Lauren Indvik, "Luxury Brands Still Tread Lightly with So-cial Media," October 19, 2010, www.forbes.com/2010/10/19/burberry-christian-louboutin-technology-social-media.html (ac-cessed May 20, 2014).

57. http://www.net-a-porter.com (accessed May 19, 2014).

58. "About PayPal," www.paypal-media.com/about (accessed May 15, 2014).

59. Amy Sample Ward, "Social Philanthropy: Raising Money on YouTube and Twitter," March 12, 2012, www.thenonprofittimes .com/news-articles/social-philanthropy-raising-money-on-youtube-and-twitter (accessed May 15, 2014).

60. Owen Thomas, "Amazon Has an Estimated 10 Million Members for Its Surprisingly Profitable Prime Club," *Business Insider*, March 11, 2013, www.businessinsider.com/amazon-prime-10-million-members-morningstar-2013-3 (accessed May 19, 2014).

61. Douglas A. McIntyre, "Amazon Marches toward $100 Billion in Revenue," January 30, 2013, http://247wallst.com/investing/2013/01/30/amazon-marches-toward-100-billion-in-revenue (ac-cessed May 19, 2014).

62. Bass Pro Shops, "Bass Pro Shops Announces New Features of Mega Outdoor Store in Tampa/Hillsborough County, Fla." April 4, 2014, www.basspro.com/webapp/wcs/stores/servlet/CFPage?storeId =10151&catalogId=10051&langId=-1&appID=34&template=news_ display.cfm&newsID=559 (accessed May 17, 2014).

63. Office of the United States Trade Representative, "Services," www.ustr.gov/trade-topics/services-investment/services (ac-cessed May 17, 2014).

64. Central Intelligence Agency, "The World Factbook," www.cia .gov/library/publications/the-world-factbook/fields/2012.html (accessed May 17, 2014).

65. Brad Tuttle, "Travelers Still Avoiding Carnival after 'Poop Cruise,'" May 28, 2013, http://business.time.com/2013/05/28/travelers-still-avoiding-carnival-after-poop-cruise (accessed May 26, 2014).

66. John A. Czepiel, Michael R. Solomon, and Carol F. Surprenant, eds., *The Service Encounter: Managing Employee/Customer Interac-tion in Service Businesses* (Lexington, MA: D. C. Heath, 1985).

67. Cengiz Haksever, Barry Render, Roberta S. Russell, and Robert G. Murdick, *Service Management and Operations* (Englewood Cliffs, NJ: Prentice Hall, 2000), 25–26.

68. http://businesscenter.jdpower.com/news/pressrelease .aspx?ID52010092 (accessed June 20, 2010).

69. A. Parasuraman, Leonard L. Barry, and Valarie A. Zeithaml, "SERVQUAL: A Multiple-Item Scale for Measuring Consumer Perceptions of Service Quality," *Journal of Retailing* 64, no. 1 (1988): 12–40; A. Parasuraman, Leonard L. Barry, and Valarie A. Zeithaml, "Refinement and Reassessment of the SERVQUAL Scale," *Journal of Retailing* 67, no.4 (1991): 420–50.

70. Cynthia Webster, "Influences upon Consumer Expectations of Services," *Journal of Services Marketing* 5 (Winter 1991): 5–17.

71. Michael R. Solomon, "The Wardrobe Consultant: Exploring the Role of a New Retailing Partner," *Journal of Retailing* 63 (Summer 1987): 110–28.

72. Irving J. Rein, Philip Kotler, and Martin R. Stoller, *High Visibility* (New York: Dodd, Mead, 1987).

73. Michael R. Solomon, "Celebritization and Commodification in the Interpersonal Marketplace," unpublished manuscript, Rutgers University, 1991.

74. Matt Rousch, "State Says Pure Michigan Campaign Drove $1.2 Billion Visitor Spending," March 11, 2014, http://detroit .cbslocal.com/2014/03/11/state-says-pure-michigan-campaign-drove-1-2-billion-visitor-spending (accessed May 16, 2014).

75. Gustav Niebuhr, "Where Religion Gets a Big Dose of Shopping-Mall Culture," *New York Times*, April 16, 1995, 1(2).

76. George Chen, "Hilton to Open More Waldorf, Conrad Hotels in China, Add 40,000 Jobs," June 12, 2013, www.scmp.com/business/companies/article/1258695/hilton-open-more-waldorf-conrad-hotels-china-add-40000-jobs (accessed May 16, 2014).

CHAPTER 13

1. Don E. Schultz and Heidi Schultz, *IMC. The Next Generation. Five Steps for Delivering Value and Measuring Returns Using Marketing Communication* (New York: McGraw-Hill, 2003), 20–21.

2. Barbara Lippert, "Windows Debut: Almost 7th Heaven," October 26, 2009, www.adweek.com/aw/content_display/creative/critique/e3i7a4f853fe57e4c0b5bf8e3a501635ead (ac-cessed May 12, 2009).

3. Gert Assmus, "An Empirical Investigation into the Perception of Vehicle Source Effects," *Journal of Advertising* 7 (Winter 1978): 4–10; for a more thorough discussion of the pros and cons of dif-ferent media, see Stephen Baker, *Systematic Approach to Advertis-ing Creativity* (New York: McGraw-Hill, 1979).

4. "US Total Media Ad Spend Inches Up, Pushed by Digital," August 22, 2013, www.emarketer.com/Article/US-Total-Media-Ad-Spend-Inches-Up-Pushed-by-Digital/1010154 (accessed June 28, 2014).

5. Tricia Carr, "Jaguar Sharpens F-Type Push to Reach Men Ages 25–54," May 15, 2013, www.luxurydaily.com/jaguar-sharpens-f-type-push-to-25-54-year-old-males (accessed June 12, 2014).

6. Bradley Johnson, "100 Leading National Advertisers," *Advertising Age*, June 23, 2014, 15–32.1.

7. Molly Wood, "TV Apps Are Soaring in Popularity, Report Says," June 4, 2014, http://bits.blogs.nytimes.com/2014/06/04/report-tv-apps-are-soaring-in-popularity/?_php=true&_type=blogs&_r=0 (accessed June 10, 2014).

8. Mike Temkin, "Video, Mobile, and Apps Generating Increased Usage Per Nielsen," March 5, 2014, www.shaker.com/articles/video-mobile-and-apps-generating-increased-usage-per-nielsen (accessed June 10, 2014).

9. Alexander Coolidge, "P&G Aims for Moms' Heart with Latest 'Thank You' Ad," www.usatoday.com/story/money/business/2014/01/08/pg-olympics-thank-you-ad/4380229 (ac-cessed June 9, 2014).

10. Olivia Sterns, "Procter & Gamble's Corporate Advertising Cam-paign," April 4, 2014, www.bloomberg.com/video/68293342-procter-gamble-s-corporate-advertising-campaign.html (accessed June 9, 2014).

11. Brinda Adhikari, "Tim Tebow Super Bowl Ad: Anti-Abor-tion Commercial to Air," January 26, 2010, http://abcnews .go.com/WN/tim-tebow-super-bowl-ad-cbs-air-controversial/story?id=9667638 (accessed June 11, 2014).

12. Karen E. Klein, "Should Your Customers Make Your Ads?," January 3, 2008, www.businessweek.com/stories/2008-01-02/should-your-customers-make-your-ads-businessweek-business-news-stock-market-and-financial-advice (accessed August 24, 2014).

13. Frito-Lay, "Doritos Announces Winner of $1 Million Grand Prize in Global Advertising Contest," February 3, 2014, www.fritolay.com/about-us/press-release-20140203.html (accessed June 9, 2014).

14. Dale Buss, "For Restarts Fiesta Movement on Social Media with More Focus on Sales," February 19, 2013, www.brandchannel.com/home/post/Ford-Fiesta-Movement-Remix-021913.aspx (accessed June 16, 2014).

15. Natasha Singer, "A Birth Control Pill That Promised Too Much," *New York Times*, February 11, 2009, B1.

16. Ed Gillespie, "Greenwash and Hamming It Up—Mazda Makes a Mess of CX-5 Advert," February 27, 2012, www.theguardian.com/environment/blog/2012/feb/27/mazda-advert-dr-seuss-lorax (accessed June 16, 2014).

17. Chris Taylor, "The Future of Advertising: 'Pay-Per-Gaze' Is Just the Beginning," August 15, 2013, http://mashable.com/2013/08/15/the-future-of-advertising-pay-per-gaze-is-just-the-beginning (accessed June 13, 2014).

18. E. J. Schultz, "Rookie Advertiser USAA: We Won Big with Marketing," October 5, 2013, http://adage.com/article/special-report-ana-annual-meeting-2013/rookie-advertiser-usaa-won-big-marketing/244607 (accessed June 27, 2014).

19. Johnson, "100 Leading National Advertisers."

20. Peter Cornish, personal communication, March 2010.

21. Ad Age, "Who Bought What in Super Bowl XLVIII," February 3, 2014, http://adage.com/article/special-report-super-bowl/super-bowl-ad-chart-buying-super-bowl-2014/244024 (accessed June 9, 2014).

22. "TV Advertising Is Less Effective: Survey," www.promomagazine.com/news/tvadvertising_survey_032406/index/html (accessed July 29, 2006).

23. Phil Hall, "Make Listeners Your Customers," *Nation's Business*, June 1994, 53R.

24. Sean Corcoran, "Defining Earned, Owned and Paid Media," December 16, 2009, http://blogs.forrrester.com/interactive_marketing/2009/12/defining-earned-owned-and-paid-media.html (accessed April 27, 2010).

25. Ingrid Lunden, "Internet Ad Spent to Reach $121 in 2014, 23% of $547B Total Ad Spend, Ad Tech Boosts Display," April 7, 2014, http://techcrunch.com/2014/04/07/internet-ad-spend-to-reach-121b-in-2014-23-of-537b-total-ad-spend-ad-tech-gives-display-a-boost-over-search (accessed June 9, 2014).

26. eMarketer, "Digital Set to Surpass TV in Time Spent with US Media," August 1, 2013, www.emarketer.com/Article/Digital-Set-Surpass-TV-Time-Spent-with-US-Media/1010096 (accessed June 11, 2014).

27. Ashley Zeckman, "Google Search Engine Market Share Nears 68%," May 20, 2014, http://searchenginewatch.com/article/2345837/Google-Search-Engine-Market-Share-Nears-68 (accessed June 9, 2014).

28. Tim Peterson, "Google Finally Crosses $50 Billion Annual Revenue Mark," January 22, 2013, www.adweek.com/news/technology/google-finally-crosses-50-billion-annual-revenue-mark-146710 (accessed June 9, 2014).

29. Kyle Christensen, "Still Running Marketing Campaigns? Chances Are, You're Running Out of Time," www.responsys.com/blogs/nsm/cross-channel-marketing/marketing-orchestration-still-running-marketing-campaigns-chances-youre-running-time (accessed June 10, 2014).

30. David Segal, "Trying to Game Google on 'Mother's Day Flowers,'" May 6, 2011, www.nytimes.com/2011/05/07/business/07flowers.html?_r=0 (accessed June 27, 2014).

31. David Segal, "The Dirty Little Secrets of Search," February 12, 2011, www.nytimes.com/2011/02/13/business/13search.html?pagewanted=all&module=Search&mabReward=relbias%3Ar%2C[%22RI%3A5%22%2C%22RI%3A12%22] (accessed June 30, 2014).

32. Mobile Marketing Association, "Mobile Marketing Industry Glossary," http://mmaglobal.com/uploads/glossary.pdf (accessed April 27, 2010).

33. Joshua Brustein, "If Your Phone Knows What Aisle You're in, Will It Have Deals on Groceries?," January 26, 2014, www.businessweek.com/articles/2014-01-06/apples-ibeacon-helps-marketer-beam-ads-to-grocery-shoppers-phones (accessed June 16, 2014).

34. Selin, "Top 7 Free Video Sharing Sites," March 7, 2013, www.freemake.com/blog/top-7-free-video-sharing-sites (accessed June 27, 2014).

35. Mark J. Miller, "Nike Risks Everything on Soccer Promotions as World Cup Kickoff Nears," June 9, 2014, www.brandchannel.com/home/post/2014/06/09/140609-Nike-World-Cup-Risk-Everything.aspx?utm_campaign=140609nikeriskeverything&utm_source=newsletter&utm_medium=email (accessed June 30, 2014).

36. Michael Sebastian and Nat Ives, "Top 10 Product Placements of the Last 10 Years," May 13, 2014, http://adage.com/article/media/top-10-product-placements-10-years/293140 (accessed June 27, 2014).

37. Christiaan Hetzner and Harro Ten Wolde, "Putting Cars in Video Games Is Now a $2.8 Billion Industry," August 22, 2013, www.huffingtonpost.com/2013/08/22/car-in-video-games_n_3793607.html (accessed June 10, 2014).

38. Stuart Elliott, "Nationwide Insurance Teams with 'Mad Men,'" April 4, 2013, www.nytimes.com/2013/04/05/business/media/nationwide-insurance-teams-up-with-mad-men.html?_r=0 (accessed June 27, 2014).

39. "Interactive Advertising Revenues to Reach $147B Globally, $62.4B in US," www.marketingchartscom/direct/interactive-advertising-revenues-to-reach-147b-globally-624b-in-us-3567 (accessed April 21, 2008).

40. Digital AV Magazine, "Volvo Uses a Campaign of Interactive Digital Signage for the Launch of Its New Model V40," www.digitalavmagazine.com/en/2012/09/07/volvo-recurre-a-una-campana-de-digital-signage-interactivo-para-el-lanzamiento-de-su-nuevo-modelo-v40 (accessed June 30, 2014).

41. CNN, "CNN Airport Network Adds New Entertainment and Sports Programming to Lineup," June 18, 2013, http://cnnpressroom.blogs.cnn.com/2013/06/18/cnn-airport-network-adds-new-entertainment-and-sports-programming-to-lineup (accessed June 16, 2014).

42. Walmart, "Building a Relationship with Shoppers," www.walmartsmartnetwork.info/howWePartner.htm (accessed June 16, 2014).

43. Jeremy Wagstaff, "Loose Wire—Bootleg Backlash: Software Industry Groups Are Snooping for People Using Pirated Software; But Their Assumptions about Who's a Pirate Seem Awfully Mixed Up," *Far Eastern Economic Review*, July 31, 2003, 31.

44. This remark has also been credited to a British businessman named Lord Leverhulme; see Charles Goodrum and Helen Dalrymple, *Advertising in America: The First 200 Years* (New York: Harry N. Abrams, 1990).

45. "Virgin Atlantic Rolls Out Space Miles," http://promomagazine.com/incentives/virgin_atlantic_miles_011106/index.html (accessed June 12, 2006).

46. Alex Palmer, "Applebee's, Chilie's, Outback Conduct Veterans Day Promotions," November 11, 2010, www.dmnews.com/applebees-chilis-outback-conduct-veterans-day-promotions/article/190659 (accessed June 12, 2014).

47. Michael Fielding, "C'est Délicieux," *Marketing News*, September 15, 2010, 10.

48. "Lengthy Research Leads Disney to Global 'Dreams' Theme," http://promomagazine.com/research/disney_research_061206/index.html (accessed June 12, 2006).

49. Sheila Shayon, "Perrier, at 150, Lures Younger, Hotter Audience to Its 'Secret Place,'" April 5, 2013, www.brandchannel.com/home/post/2013/04/05/Perrier-Secret-Place-040513.aspx (accessed June 27, 2014).

50. Dale Buss, "Super Bowl Ad Watch: With Space Trips, Axe Strives for 'Something That's Epic,'" January 23, 2013, www.brandchannel .com/home/post/2013/01/23/SuperBowl-ApolloUpdate.aspx (accessed June 27, 2014).

51. General Mills, "Cheerios Serves Spoonfuls of Stores for the 11th Year to Get Books into Children's Hands," April 25, 2013, www .generalmills.com/ChannelG/NewsReleases/Library/2013/ April/spoonfuls.aspx (accessed June 9, 2014).

CHAPTER 14

1. Charlene Li and Josh Bernoff, *Groundswell: Winning in a World Transformed by Social Technologies* (Boston: Harvard Business School Publishing, 2008), 9.

2. Facebook, "Company Info," http://newsroom.fb.com/company-info (accessed June 18, 2014).

3. Brian Stelter, "Nielsen Reports a Decline in Television Viewing," http://mediadecoder.blogs.nytimes.com/2012/05/03/ nielsen-reports-a-decline-in-television-viewing/?_php=true&_ type=blogs&_r=0 (accessed June 18, 2014).

4. AdWeek, "Magazine Readership Growing, Survey Shows," May 29, 2013, www.adweek.com/news/press/magazine-readership-growing-survey-shows-149863 (accessed June 18, 2014).

5. Andrew Burger, "Nielsen: Despite Hundreds of Choices, Average Number of TV Channels Watched Is 17," May 9, 2014, www. telecompetitor.com/nielsen-average-number-of-tv-channels-watched-is-17 (accessed June 18, 2014).

6. Suzanne Vranica, "TV Ad Dollars Slowly Shifting to Web Video," May 12, 2014, http://online.wsj.com/news/articles/SB10001424 052702303851804579558091795473048 (accessed June 20, 2014).

7. Lois Geller, "Wow—What a Buzz," *Target Marketing*, June 2005, 21.

8. Jay Yarow, "Apple Is +Hiring a 'Buzz Marketing Manager' to Get iPhones in the Hands of More Famous People," May 2, 2014, www.businessinsider.com/apple-is-hiring-a-buzz-marketing-manager-2014-5 (accessed June 18, 2014).

9. Matthew Creamer, "In Era of Consumer Control, Marketers Crave the Potency of Word-of-mouth," *Advertising Age*, November 28, 2005, 32.

10. Todd Wasserman, "Blogs Cause Word-of-Mouth Business to Spread Quickly," *Brandweek*, October 3, 2005, 9.

11. Pano Mourdoukoutas, "Good Buzz, Bad Buzz Brand Management: A Social Media Strategy That Pays Off," November 7, 2013, www .forbes.com/sites/panosmourdoukoutas/2013/11/07/good-buzz-bad-buzz-brand-management-a-social-media-strategy-that-pays-off (accessed June 18, 2014).

12. Paul Marsden, "F-Commerce: Heinz Innovates with New 'Tryvertising' F-Store," March 8, 2011, http://digitalintelligencetoday .com/f-commerce-heinz-innovate-with-new-tryvertising-f-store-screenshots (accessed June 23, 2014).

13. Todd Wasserman, "Word Games," *Brandweek*, April 24, 2006, 24.

14. Tamar Weinbert, *The New Community Rules: Marketing on the Social Web* (Sebastopol, CA: O'Reilly Media, 2009).

15. Erik Sass, "20% of Social Network Users Have Shared Negative Brand Experiences," April 29, 2010, www.mediapost.com/ publications/?fa5Articles.showArticle&art_aid5127224 (accessed April 30, 2010).

16. Zak Stambor, "U.S. Social Media Ad Spending Will Hit $15 Billion by 2018,"May 16, 2014, www.internetretailer.com/2014/05/16/ social-media-ad-spending-will-hit-15-billion-2018 (accessed June 18, 2014).

17. Chanelle Bessette, "Social Media Superstars 2014," January 16, 2014, http://fortune.com/2014/01/16/social-media-superstars-2014-fortunes-best-companies-to-work-for (accessed June 18, 2014).

18. Christopher Heine, "AmEx's Social Data Shows That Nostalgia Is Just Swell," October 11, 2013, www.adweek.com/news/ technology/amexs-social-data-shows-nostalgia-just-swell-153053 (accessed June 18, 2014).

19. Susan Fournier and Lara Lee, "Getting Brand Communities Right," April 2009, http://hbr.org/2009/04/getting-brand-communities-right/ar/1 (accessed June 18, 2014).

20. Myra Frazier, "The Networked Boomer Woman: Hear Us Roar," December 18, 2009, www.brandchannel.com/features_effect .asp?pf_id5496 (accessed April 4, 2010).

21. John McDermott, "Facebook Losing Its Edge among College-Aged Adults," January 21, 2014, http://digiday.com/platforms/ social-platforms-college-kids-now-prefer (accessed June 18, 2014).

22. Twitter, "About," https://about.twitter.com/company (accessed June 18, 2014).

23. HLN, "100 Days of Happiness Sweepstakes," June 5, 2014, www .hlntv.com/article/2014/05/28/100-days-happiness-sweep-stakes (accessed June 19, 2014).

24. Makenzie Bowker, "#100HappyDays: Who Is behind the Challenge?," March 18, 2014, www.hlntv.com/ article/2014/03/05/100-happy-days-photo-challenge (accessed June 19, 2014).

25. Lim Yung-Hui, " 1.6% of Facebook Users Spent Over $1 Billon on Virtual Goods," August 2, 2012, www.forbes.com/sites/ limyunghui/2012/08/02/1-6-of-facebook-users-spent-over-1-billion-on-virtual-goods (accessed June 18, 2014).

26. Sheila Shayon, "Kwedit Promise: You Can Keep That Virtual Puppy, for a Price," February 8, 2010, www.brandchannel.com/ home/post/2010/02/08/Kwedit-Promise-You-Can-Keep-That-Virtual-Puppy-For-A-Price.aspx (accessed March 5, 2010).

27. Angie's List, "How It Works," www.angieslist.com/how-it-works.htm (accessed June 19, 2014).

28. Natalie Zmuda, "An App for That, Too: How Mobile Is Changing Shopping," March 1, 2010, http://adage.com/print?article_ id5142318 (accessed March 14, 2010); Jenna Wortham, "Telling Friends Where You Are (or Not)," March 14, 2010, www.nytimes. com/2010/03/15/technology/15locate.html (accessed April 30, 2010).

29. Todd Wasserman, "5 Creative Location-Based Campaigns for Small Businesses to Learn From," http://mashable .com/2011/06/21/small-business-foursquare-scvngr (accessed June 19, 2014).

30. Direct Marketing Association, www.the-dma.org/index.php (accessed May 2, 2010).

31. Susan Taplinger, "DMA Releases 2014 'Statistical Fact Book,'" April 11, 2014, http://thedma.org/news/dma-releases-2014-statistical-fact-book-3 (accessed June 19, 2014).

32. Leslie Kaufman with Claudia H. Deutsch, "Montgomery Ward to Close Its Doors," December 29, 2000, www.nytimes .com/2000/12/29/business/montgomery-ward-to-close-its-doors.html (accessed August 29, 2014).

33. Lois Geller, "Why Are Printed Catalogs Still Around?," October 16, 2012, www.forbes.com/sites/loisgeller/2012/10/16/why-are-printed-catalogs-still-around (accessed June 30, 2014).

34. Neiman Marcus, "Neiman Marcus Presents the 2013 Christmas Book and Fantasy Gifts," October 10, 2013, http://blog .neimanmarcus.com/press-room/neiman-marcus-presents-the-2013-christmas-book-and-fantasy-gifts (accessed June 18, 2014).

35. Ishbel Macleod, "Infographic: Consumers More Likely to Deal with Direct Mail Immediately Compared to Email," October 23, 2013, www.thedrum.com/news/2013/10/23/infographic-consumers-more-likely-deal-direct-mail-immediately-compared-email (accessed June 18, 2014).

36. Alan Farnham, "Fighting Telemarketers: When Do-Not-Call List Fails, These Strategies Work," January 21, 2014, http:// abcnews.go.com/Business/best-ways-turn-tables-telemarketers/ story?id=21534413 (accessed June 19, 2014).

37. Federal Trade Commission, "National Do Not Call Registry," www.ftc.gov/donotcall (accessed May 8, 2010).

38. Alison J. Clarke, "'As Seen on TV': Socialization of the Tele-Visual Consumer," paper presented at the Fifth Interdisciplinary Conference on Research in Consumption, University of Lund, Sweden, August 1995.

39. Yue Wang, "More People Have Cell Phones Than Toilets, U.N. Study Shows," March 25, 2013, http://newsfeed.time.com/2013/03/25/more-people-have-cell-phones-than-toilets-un-study-shows (accessed June 19, 2014).

40. Central Intelligence Agency, "The World Factbook," www.cia.gov/library/publications/the-world-factbook/rankorder/2151rank.html (accessed June 18, 2014).

41. Bureau of Labor Statistics, *Occupational Outlook Handbook*, December 19, 2013, http://www.bls.gov/emp/ep_table_104.htm (accessed June 19, 2014).

42. Quoted in Jaclyn Fierman, "The Death and Rebirth of the Salesman," *Fortune*, July 25, 1994, 88.

43. Direct Selling Association, "Industry Statistics," www.dsa.org/research/industry-statistics (accessed June 18, 2014).

44. Salesforce.com, www.salesforce.com (accessed May 1, 2010).

45. Skype, www.skype.com (accessed May 1, 2010).

46. Adapted from Mitchell Schnurman, "The Game-Changing Reality of Virtual Sales Pitches," April 9, 2010, www.star-telegram.com/2010/04/09/2103717_p2/the-game-changing-reality-of-virtual.html (accessed May 1, 2010).

47. Dan C. Weilbaker, "The Identification of Selling Abilities Needed for Missionary Type Sales," *Journal of Personal Selling & Sales Management* 10 (Summer 1990): 45–58.

48. Derek A. Newton, *Sales Force Performance and Turnover* (Cambridge, MA: Marketing Science Institute, 1973), 3.

49. Mark W. Johnston and Greg W. Marshall, *Relationship Selling*, 3rd ed. (Boston: McGraw-Hill, 2010).

50. Accela Communications, www.accelacommunications.com (accessed May 6, 2010).

51. Greg W. Marshall, Daniel J. Goebel, and William C. Moncrief, "Hiring for Success at the Buyer-Seller Interface," *Journal of Business Research* 56 (April 2003): 247–55.

52. Darren Heitner, "How Isiah Austin Became NBA's Most Valuable Draft Pick," June 27, 2014, www.forbes.com/sites/darrenheitner/2014/06/27/how-isaiah-austin-became-nbas-most-valuable-draft-pick (accessed June 30, 2014).

53. Kate Fitzgerald, "Homemade Bikini Contest Hits Bars, Beach for 10th Year," *Advertising Age*, April 13, 1998, 18.

54. Jim Jelter, "General Motors CEO Mary Barra's BP Moment," March 12, 2014, http://blogs.marketwatch.com/thetell/2014/03/12/general-motors-ceo-mary-barras-bp-moment (accessed June 19, 2014).

55. Rich Thomaselli, "PR Response Has Been Swift and Active, but Test Will Come When Ship Finally Docks," February 14, 2013, http://adage.com/article/news/carnival-cruises-pr-response-triumph-crisis/239819 (accessed June 20, 2014).

56. Mark Prigg, "Amazon's Drone Dreams Come Crashing Down, U.S. Regulators Ban Package Delivery Services Using 'Model Aircraft,'" June 24, 2014, www.dailymail.co.uk/sciencetech/article-2668411/Amazons-drone-dreams-come-crashing-US-regulators-ban-package-delivery-services-using-model-aircraft.html#ixzz35rMKW4VF (accessed June 30, 2014).

57. Andy Pasztor, "FAA Ruling on Long-Haul Routes Would Boost Boeing's Designs," *Wall Street Journal*, June 5, 2006, A3.

58. Amy Chozick, "Star Power: The LPGA Is Counting on a New Marketing Push to Take Women's Golf to the Next Level," *Wall Street Journal*, June 12, 2006, R6.

59. Shannon Prather, "Identity Crisis: Brooklyn Park Hires PR Firm to Improve Its Reputation," April 8, 2014, www.startribune.com/local/north/254292091.html#FLeReIJRQyImAWVq.97 (accessed June 24, 2014).

60. Carol Driver, "Five-Minute YouTube apology from Toyota boss as first lawsuit filed over faulty pedal recall," Daily Mail, February 5, 2010, http://www.dailymail.co.uk/news/article-1248588/Five-minute-YouTube-apology-Toyota-boss-lawsuit-filed-faulty-pedal-recall.html (accessed March 15, 2010).

61. IEG Sponsorship Report, "Sponsorship Spending Growth Slows in North America as Marketers Eye New Media and Marketing Options," January 7, 2014, www.sponsorship.com/iegsr/2014/01/07/Sponsorship-Spending-Growth-Slows-In-North-America.aspx (accessed June 24, 2014).

62. Procter & Gamble, "P&G Touching, Improving Lives in Aftermath of Violent Storms," March 5, 2012, http://news.pg.com/blog/emergence-response/pg-touching-improving-lives-aftermath-violent-storms (accessed June 23, 2014).

63. Eric Lipton, "Rival Industries Sweet-Talk the Public," February 11, 2014, www.nytimes.com/2014/02/12/business/rival-industries-sweet-talk-the-public.html (accessed June 23, 2014).

64. AT&T, "AT&T Is An Exclusive 'Super Sponsor' of SXSW, March 2013, www.att.com/gen/press-room?pid=22489 (accessed June 24, 2014).

65. Quoted in Michelle Kessler, "IBM Graffiti Ads Gain Notoriety," *USA Today*, April 26, 2001, 3B.

66. Campaign Asisa, "Case Study: Burger King's Wallet Drop Stunt Creates Online Buzz in Singapore, July 22, 210, www.campaignasia.com/agencyportfolio/CaseStudyCampaign/220642,case-study-burger-kings-wallet-drop-guerilla-stunt-creates-online-buzz-in-singapore.aspx#.U6jGlKhKvDk (accessed June 23, 2014).

67. Michelle Kessler, "IBM Graffiti Ads Gain Notoriety," February 6, 2002, http://usatoday30.usatoday.com/tech/news/2001-04-25-ibm-linux-graffiti.htm (accessed August 29, 2014).

68. Maureen Morrison, "Taco Bell Counters 'Meat Filling' Charges in Lawsuit with Print, Web Effort," January 28, 2011, http://adage.com/article/news/taco-bell-launches-ad-campaign-response-lawsuit/148552 (accessed June 20, 2014).

APPENDIX A

1. S&S Smoothie Company is a fictitious company created to illustrate a sample marketing plan.

2. Note that the action plan for the final marketing plan should include objectives, action items, timing information, and budget information necessary to accomplish all marketing objectives. We have included only one objective in this sample marketing plan.

APPENDIX B

1. John W. Schouten, "Selves in Transition: Symbolic Consumption in Personal Rites of Passage and Identity Reconstruction," *Journal of Consumer Research*, March 17, 1991, 412–25; Michael R. Solomon, "The Wardrobe Consultant: Exploring the Role of a New Retailing Partner," *Journal of Retailing* 63 (1987): 110–28; Michael R. Solomon and Susan P. Douglas, "Diversity in Product Symbolism: The Case of Female Executive Clothing," *Psychology & Marketing* 4 (1987): 189–212; Joseph Z. Wisenblit, "Person Positioning: Empirical Evidence and a New Paradigm," *Journal of Professional Services Marketing* 4, no. 2 (1989): 51–82.

▶ Glossary

80/20 rule   A marketing rule of thumb that 20 percent of purchasers account for 80 percent of a product's sales.

A

account executive (account manager)   A member of the account management department who supervises the day-to-day activities of the account and is the primary liaison between the agency and the client.

account planner   A member of the account management department who combines research and account strategy to act as the voice of the consumer in creating effective advertising.

action plans   Individual support plans included in a marketing plan that provide the guidance for implementation and control of the various marketing strategies within the plan. Action plans are sometimes referred to as "marketing programs."

actual product   The physical good or the delivered service that supplies the desired benefit.

administered VMS   A vertical marketing system in which channel members remain independent but voluntarily work together because of the power of a single channel member.

adoption pyramid   Reflects how a person goes from being unaware of an innovation through stages from the bottom up of awareness, interest, evaluation, trial, adoption, and confirmation.

advergaming   Brand placements in video games.

advertising   Nonpersonal communication from an identified sponsor using the mass media.

advertising appeal   The central idea or theme of an advertising message.

advertising campaign   A coordinated, comprehensive plan that carries out promotion objectives and results in a series of advertisements placed in media over a period of time.

advocacy advertising   A type of public service advertising where an organization seeks to influence public opinion on an issue because it has some stake in the outcome.

affect   The feeling component of attitudes; refers to the overall emotional response a person has to a product.

aided recall   A research technique that uses clues to prompt answers from people about advertisements they might have seen.

AIOs   Measures of consumer activities, interests and opinions used to place consumers into dimensions.

amafessionals   Consumers who contribute ideas to online forums for the fun and challenge rather than to receive a paycheck, so their motivation is to gain *psychic income* rather than financial income.

ambient advertising   Advertising placed where advertising isn't normally or hasn't ever been seen.

anticonsumption   The deliberate defacement of products.

approach   The first step of the actual sales presentation in which the salesperson tries to learn more about the customer's needs, create a good impression, and build rapport.

attention   The extent to which a person devotes mental processing to a particular stimulus.

attention economy   A company's success is measured by its share of mind rather than share of market, where companies make money when they attract eyeballs rather than just dollars.

attitude   A learned predisposition to respond favorably or unfavorably to stimuli on the basis of relatively enduring evaluations of people, objects, and issues.

attitudinal measures   A research technique that probes a consumer's beliefs or feelings about a product before and after being exposed to messages about it.

attributes   Include features, functions, benefits, and uses of a product. Marketers view products as a bundle of attributes that includes the packaging, brand name, benefits, and supporting features in addition to a physical good.

augmented product   The actual product plus other supporting features such as a warranty, credit, delivery, installation, and repair service after the sale.

authenticated streaming   The use of an Internet enabled device, like a tablet or smart phone, to stream content from a cable or satellite provider.

automatic reordering system   Retail reordering system that is automatically activated when inventories reach a certain level.

avatars   Graphic representations of users of virtual worlds.

average fixed cost   The fixed cost per unit produced.

B

B2C e-commerce   Online exchanges between companies and individual consumers.

baby boomers   The segment of people born between 1946 and 1964.

back-translation   The process of translating material to a foreign language and then back to the original language.

backward invention   Product strategy in which a firm develops a less advanced product to serve the needs of people living in countries without electricity or other elements of a developed infrastructure.

badge   A milestone or reward earned for progressing through a video game.

bait-and-switch   An illegal marketing practice in which an advertised price special is used as bait to get customers into the store with the intention of switching them to a higher-priced item.

banners   Internet advertising in the form of rectangular graphics at the top or bottom of Web pages.

BCG growth-market share matrix   A portfolio analysis model developed by the Boston Consulting Group that assesses the potential of successful products to generate cash that a firm can then use to invest in new products.

behavior   The doing component of attitudes; involves a consumer's intention to do something, such as the intention to purchase or use a certain product.

behavioral learning theories   Theories of learning that focus on how consumer behavior is changed by external events or stimuli.

behavioral segmentation   A technique that divides consumers into segments on the basis of how they act toward, feel about, or use a good or service.

benefit   The outcome sought by a customer that motivates buying behavior that satisfies a need or want.

Big Data   A popular term to describe the exponential growth of data—both structured and unstructured in massive amounts that are hard or impossible to process using traditional database techniques.

Bitcoin   The most popular and fastest-growing digital currency.

bottom of the pyramid (BOP)   The collective name for the group of consumers throughout the world who live on less than $2 a day.

bottom-up budgeting techniques Allocation of the promotion budget based on identifying promotion goals and allocating enough money to accomplish them.

bounce rate A marketing metric for analyzing website traffic. It represents the percentage of visitors who enter the site (typically at the home page) and "bounce" (leave the site) rather than continue viewing other pages within the same overall site.

box stores Food stores that have a limited selection of items, few brands per item, and few refrigerated items.

brand A name, a term, a symbol, or any other unique element of a product that identifies one firm's product(s) and sets it apart from the competition.

brand ambassadors or brand evangelists Loyal customers of a brand recruited to communicate and be salespeople with other consumers for a brand they care a great deal about.

brand competition When firms offering similar goods or services compete on the basis of their brand's reputation or perceived benefits.

brand equity The value of a brand to an organization.

brand extensions A new product sold with the same brand name as a strong existing brand.

brand loyalty A pattern of repeat product purchases, accompanied by an underlying positive attitude toward the brand, based on the belief that the brand makes products superior to those of its competition.

brand manager An individual who is responsible for developing and implementing the marketing plan for a single brand.

brand meaning The beliefs and associations that a consumer has about the brand.

brand personality A distinctive image that captures a good's or service's character and benefits.

brand polarization The gap between good buzz and bad buzz.

brand storytelling Marketers seek to engage consumers with compelling stories about brands.

branded entertainment A form of advertising in which marketers integrate products into entertainment venues.

brandfests Events that companies host to thank customers for their loyalty.

break-even analysis A method for determining the number of units that a firm must produce and sell at a given price to cover all its costs.

break-even point The point at which the total revenue and total costs are equal and beyond which the company makes a profit; below that point, the firm will suffer a loss.

breaking bulk Dividing larger quantities of goods into smaller lots in order to meet the needs of buyers.

bribery When someone voluntarily offers payment to get an illegal advantage.

BRIC countries Refers to Brazil, Russia, India, and China, the largest and fastest growing of the developing countries with over 40 percent of the world's population.

business analysis The step in the product development process in which marketers assess a product's commercial viability.

business cycle The overall patterns of change in the economy—including periods of prosperity, recession, depression, and recovery—that affect consumer and business purchasing power.

business ethics Rules of conduct for an organization.

business plan A plan that includes the decisions that guide the entire organization.

business planning An ongoing process of making decisions that guides the firm both in the short term and for the long term.

business portfolio The group of different products or brands owned by an organization and characterized by different income-generating and growth capabilities.

business-to-business (B2B) e-commerce Internet exchanges between two or more businesses or organizations.

business-to-business marketing The marketing of goods and services from one organization to another.

buttons Small banner-type advertisements that can be placed anywhere on a Web page.

buyclass One of three classifications of business buying situations that characterizes the degree of time and effort required to make a decision.

buying center The group of people in an organization who participate in a purchasing decision.

buzz Word-of-mouth communication that customers view as authentic.

C

cannibalization The loss of sales of an existing brand when a new item in a product line or product family is introduced.

capacity management The process by which organizations adjust their offerings in an attempt to match demand.

captive pricing A pricing tactic for two items that must be used together; one item is priced very low, and the firm makes its profit on another, high-margin item essential to the operation of the first item.

case allowance A discount to the retailer or wholesaler based on the volume of product ordered.

case study A comprehensive examination of a particular firm or organization.

cash cows SBUs with a dominant market share in a low-growth-potential market.

cash discounts A discount offered to a customer to entice them to pay their bill quickly.

catalog A collection of products offered for sale in book form, usually consisting of product descriptions accompanied by photos of the items.

category killer A very large specialty store that carries a vast selection of products in its category.

causal research A technique that attempts to understand cause-and-effect relationships.

channel conflict Incompatible goals, poor communication, and disagreement over roles, responsibilities, and functions among firms at different levels of the same distribution channel that may threaten a manufacturer's distribution strategy.

channel cooperation Occurs when producers, wholesalers, and retailers depend on one another for success.

channel intermediaries Firms or individuals such as wholesalers, agents, brokers, or retailers who help move a product from the producer to the consumer or business user. An older term for intermediaries is middlemen.

channel leader A firm at one level of distribution that takes a leadership role, establishing operating norms and processes based on its power relative to other channel members.

channel levels The number of distinct categories of intermediaries that populate a channel of distribution.

channel of distribution The series of firms or individuals that facilitates the movement of a product from the producer to the final customer.

channel power The ability of one channel member to influence, control, and lead the entire channel based on one or more sources of power.

classical conditioning   The learning that occurs when a stimulus eliciting a response is paired with another stimulus that initially does not elicit a response on its own but will cause a similar response over time because of its association with the first stimulus.

click-through   A metric that indicates the percentage of website users who have decided to click on an advertisement in order to visit the website or Web page associated with it.

close   The stage of the selling process in which the salesperson actually asks the customer to buy the product.

co-op advertising   A sales promotion where the manufacturer and the retailer share the cost.

cobranding   An agreement between two brands to work together to market a new product.

code of ethics   Written standards of behavior to which everyone in the organization must subscribe.

cognition   The knowing component of attitudes; refers to the beliefs or knowledge a person has about a product and its important characteristics.

cognitive dissonance   The anxiety or regret a consumer may feel after choosing from among several similar attractive choices.

cognitive learning theory   Theory of learning that stresses the importance of internal mental processes and that views people as problem solvers who actively use information from the world around them to master their environment.

collaborative consumption   A term used to refer to the activities practiced by rentrepreneurs.

collectivist cultures   Cultures in which people subordinate their personal goals to those of a stable community.

combination stores   Retailers that offer consumers food and general merchandise in the same store.

commercialization   The final step in the product development process in which a new product is launched into the market.

common good approach   Ethical philosophy that advocates the decision that contributes to the good of all in the community.

communication and transaction functions   Happens when channel members develop and execute both promotional and other types of communication among members of the channel.

communication model   The process whereby meaning is transferred from a source to a receiver.

comparison shopping agents or shopbots   Web applications that help online shoppers find what they are looking for at the lowest price and provide customer reviews and ratings of products and sellers.

compatibility   The extent to which a new product is consistent with existing cultural values, customs, and practices.

competitive intelligence (CI)   The process of gathering and analyzing publicly available information about rivals.

competitive-parity budgeting method   A promotion budgeting method in which an organization matches whatever competitors are spending.

complexity   The degree to which consumers find a new product or its use difficult to understand.

component parts   Manufactured goods or subassemblies of finished items that organizations need to complete their own products.

concentrated targeting strategy   Focusing a firm's efforts on offering one or more products to a single segment.

consumer   The ultimate user of a good or service.

consumer addiction   A physiological or psychological dependency on goods or services including alcoholism, drug addiction, cigarettes, shopping, and use of the Internet.

consumer behavior   The process involved when individuals or groups select, purchase, use, and dispose of goods, services, ideas, or experiences to satisfy their needs and desires.

consumer ethnocentrism   Consumers' feeling that products from their own country are superior or that it is wrong to buy products produced in another country.

consumer goods   The goods individual consumers purchase for personal or family use.

consumer orientation   A business approach that prioritizes the satisfaction of customers' needs and wants.

consumer packaged good (CPG) or fast-moving consumer good (FMCG)   A low-cost good that is consumed quickly and replaced frequently.

consumer satisfaction/dissatisfaction   The overall feelings or attitude a person has about a product after purchasing it.

consumer-generated content   Everyday people functioning in marketing roles, such as participating in creating advertisements, providing input to new product development, or serving as wholesalers or retailers.

consumerism   A social movement that attempts to protect consumers from harmful business practices.

content marketing   The strategy of establishing thought leadership in the form of bylines, blogs, commenting opportunities, videos, sharable social images, and infographics.

continuous innovation   A modification of an existing product that sets one brand apart from its competitors.

contractual VMS   A vertical marketing system in which cooperation is enforced by contracts (legal agreements) that spell out each member's rights and responsibilities and how they will cooperate.

contribution per unit   The difference between the price the firm charges for a product and the variable costs.

control   A process that entails measuring actual performance, comparing this performance to the established marketing objectives, and then making adjustments to the strategies or objectives on the basis of this analysis.

convenience product   A consumer good or service that is usually low-priced, widely available, and purchased frequently with a minimum of comparison and effort.

convenience sample   A nonprobability sample composed of individuals who just happen to be available when and where the data are being collected.

convenience stores   Neighborhood retailers that carry a limited number of frequently purchased items and cater to consumers willing to pay a premium for the ease of buying close to home.

conventional marketing system   A multiple-level distribution channel in which channel members work independently of one another.

convergence   The coming together of two or more technologies to create a new system with greater benefits than its separate parts.

conversion   Signifies an event that occurs on a Web page that indicates the meeting of a predefined goal associated with the consumer's interaction with that page.

cookies   Text files inserted by a Web site sponsor into a Web surfer's hard drive that allows the site to track the surfer's moves.

core product   All the benefits the product will provide for consumers or business customers.

corporate advertising   Advertising that promotes the company as a whole instead of a firm's individual products.

corporate identity   Materials such as logos, brochures, building design, and stationery that communicate an image of the organization.

corporate VMS   A vertical marketing system in which a single firm owns manufacturing, wholesaling, and retailing operations.

corrective advertising   Advertising that clarifies or qualifies previous deceptive advertising claims.

cost per thousand (CPM) A measure used to compare the relative cost-effectiveness of different media vehicles that have different exposure rates; the cost to deliver a message to 1,000 people or homes.

cost-per-click An online ad purchase in which the cost of the advertisement is charged only each time an individual clicks on the advertisement and is directed to the Web page that the marketer placed within the advertisement.

cost-per-impression An online ad purchase in which the cost of the advertisement is charged each time the advertisement shows up on a page that the user views.

cost-per-order The cost of gaining an order in terms of the marketing investment made to turn a website visitor into a customer who has chosen to make a transaction.

cost-plus pricing A method of setting prices in which the seller totals all the costs for the product and then adds an amount to arrive at the selling price.

countertrade A type of trade in which goods are paid for with other items instead of with cash.

creating assortments Providing a variety of products in one location to meet the needs of buyers.

creative brief A guideline or blueprint for the marketing communication program that guides the creative process.

creative selling process The process of seeking out potential customers, analyzing needs, determining how product attributes might provide benefits for the customer, and then communicating that information.

creative services The agency people (creative director, copywriters, and art director) who dream up and produce the ads.

creative strategy The process that turns a concept into an advertisement.

creativity A phenomenon whereby something new and valuable is created.

crisis management The process of managing a company's reputation when some negative event threatens the organization's image.

cross-elasticity of demand When changes in the price of one product affect the demand for another item.

cross-sectional design A type of descriptive technique that involves the systematic collection of quantitative information.

crowdsourcing A practice in which firms outsource marketing activities (such as selecting an ad) to a community of users.

cultural diversity A management practice that actively seeks to include people of different sexes, races, ethnic groups, and religions in an organization's employees, customers, suppliers, and distribution channel partners.

cultural values A society's deeply held beliefs about right and wrong ways to live.

culture The values, beliefs, customs, and tastes a group of people values.

custom research Research conducted for a single firm to provide specific information its managers need.

customer equity The financial value of a customer relationship throughout the lifetime of the relationship.

customer insights The collection, deployment, and interpretation of information that allows a business to acquire, develop, and retain their customers.

customer profiling The act of tailoring the level of customer service based on a customer's perceived ability to pay.

customer reference program A formalized process by which customers formally share success stories and actively recommend products to other potential clients, usually facilitated through an on-line community.

customer relationship management (CRM) A systematic tracking of consumers' preferences and behaviors over time in order to tailor the value proposition as closely as possible to each individual's unique wants and needs. CRM allows firms to talk to individual customers and to adjust elements of their marketing programs in light of how each customer reacts.

customized marketing strategy An approach that tailors specific products and the messages about them to individual customers.

D

data Raw, unorganized facts that need to be processed.

data brokers Companies that collect and sell personal information about consumers.

data mining Sophisticated analysis techniques to take advantage of the massive amount of transaction information now available.

data scientist An individual who searches through multiple, disparate data sources in order to discover hidden insights that will provide a competitive advantage.

data warehouse A system to store and process the data that result from data mining.

database An organized collection (often electronic) of data that can be searched and queried to provide information about contacts, products, customers, inventory, and more.

decline stage The final stage in the product life cycle, during which sales decrease as customer needs change.

decoding The process by which a receiver assigns meaning to the message.

demand Customers' desires for products coupled with the resources needed to obtain them.

demand-based pricing A price-setting method based on estimates of demand at different prices.

demographics Statistics that measure observable aspects of a population, including size, age, gender, ethnic group, income, education, occupation, and family structure.

department stores Retailers that sell a broad range of items and offer a good selection within each product line.

derived demand Demand for business or organizational products caused by demand for consumer goods or services.

descriptive research A tool that probes more systematically into the problem and bases its conclusions on large numbers of observations.

developed country A country that boasts sophisticated marketing systems, strong private enterprise, and bountiful market potential for many goods and services.

developing countries Countries in which the economy is shifting its emphasis from agriculture to industry.

differential benefit Properties of products that set them apart from competitors' products by providing unique customer benefits.

differentiated targeting strategy Developing one or more products for each of several distinct customer groups and making sure these offerings are kept separate in the marketplace.

diffusion The process by which the use of a product spreads throughout a population.

digital media Media that are digital rather than analog including Web sites, mobile or cellular phones, and digital video such as YouTube.

digital signage Out-of-home media that use digital technology to change the message at will.

direct mail A brochure or pamphlet that offers a specific good or service at one point in time.

direct marketing Any direct communication to a consumer or business recipient designed to generate a response in the form of an order, a request for further information, and/or a visit to a store or other place of business for purchase of a product.

direct selling   An interactive sales process in which a salesperson presents a product to one individual or a small group, takes orders, and delivers the merchandise.

direct-response advertising   A direct marketing approach that allows the consumer to respond to a message by immediately contacting the provider to ask questions or order the product.

direct-response TV (DRTV)   Advertising on TV that seeks a direct response, including short commercials of less than two minutes, 30-minute or longer infomercials, and home shopping networks.

discontinuous innovation   A totally new product that creates major changes in the way we live.

discretionary income   The portion of income people have left over after paying for necessities such as housing, utilities, food, and clothing.

disintermediation   A service that requires the customer to obtain an outcome without the intervention of a human provider.

disintermediation (of the channel of distribution)   The elimination of some layers of the channel of distribution in order to cut costs and improve the efficiency of the channel.

distinctive competency   A superior capability of a firm in comparison to its direct competitors.

distribution center   A warehouse that stores goods for short periods of time and that provides other functions, such as breaking bulk.

distribution intensity   The number of intermediaries at each level of the channel.

distribution planning   The process of developing distribution objectives, evaluating internal and external environmental influences on distribution, and choosing a distribution strategy.

diversification strategies   Growth strategies that emphasize both new products and new markets.

do-it-yourself (DIY) ads   Product ads that are created by consumers.

dogs   SBUs with a small share of a slow-growth market. They are businesses that offer specialized products in limited markets that are not likely to grow quickly.

dual or multiple distribution systems   A system where producers, dealers, wholesalers, retailers, and customers participate in more than one type of channel.

dumping   A company tries to get a toehold in a foreign market by pricing its products lower than it offers them at home.

durable goods   Consumer products that provide benefits over a long period of time, such as cars, furniture, and appliances.

dynamic pricing   A pricing strategy in which the price can easily be adjusted to meet changes in the marketplace.

dynamically continuous innovation   A change in an existing product that requires a moderate amount of learning or behavior change.

E

e-commerce   The buying or selling of goods and services electronically, usually over the Internet.

early adopters   Those who adopt an innovation early in the diffusion process, but after the innovators.

early majority   Those whose adoption of a new product signals a general acceptance of the innovation.

earned media   Word-of-mouth or buzz using social media where the advertiser has no control.

economic communities   Groups of countries that band together to promote trade among themselves and to make it easier for member nations to compete elsewhere.

economic infrastructure   The quality of a country's distribution, financial, and communications systems.

elastic demand   Demand in which changes in price have large effects on the amount demanded.

embargo   A quota completely prohibiting specified goods from entering or leaving a country.

embedded marketing   A form of advertising in which marketers integrate products into entertainment venues. (Also know as branded entertainment or product placement.)

emergency products   Products we purchase when we're in dire need.

encoding   The process of translating an idea into a form of communication that will convey meaning.

encryption   The process of scrambling a message so that only another individual (or computer) with the right "key" can unscramble it.

enterprise resource planning (ERP) systems   A software system that integrates information from across the entire company, including finance, order fulfillment, manufacturing, and transportation and then facilitates sharing of the data throughout the firm.

equipment   Expensive goods that an organization uses in its daily operations that last for a long time.

ethical relativism   Suggests that what is ethical in one culture is not necessarily the same as in another culture.

ethnography   An approach to research based on observations of people in their own homes or communities.

evaluative criteria   The dimensions consumers use to compare competing product alternatives.

exchange   The process by which some transfer of value occurs between a buyer and a seller.

exclusive distribution   Selling a product only through a single outlet in a particular region.

execution format   The basic structure of the message such as comparison, demonstration, testimonial, slice-of-life and lifestyle.

experiential shoppers   Consumers who engage in on-line shopping because of the experiential benefits they receive.

experiments   A technique that tests predicted relationships among variables in a controlled environment.

exploratory research   A technique that marketers use to generate insights for future, more rigorous studies.

export merchants   Intermediaries a firm uses to represent it in other countries.

exposure   The extent to which a stimulus is capable of being registered by a person's sensory receptors.

expropriation   When a domestic government seizes a foreign company's assets without any reimbursement.

external environment   The uncontrollable elements outside an organization that may affect its performance either positively or negatively.

extortion   When someone in authority extracts payment under duress.

extranet   A private, corporate computer network that links company departments, employees, and databases to suppliers, customers, and others outside the organization.

F

F.O.B. delivered pricing   A pricing tactic in which the cost of loading and transporting the product to the customer is included in the selling price and is paid by the manufacturer.

F.O.B. origin pricing   A pricing tactic in which the cost of transporting the product from the factory to the customer's location is the responsibility of the customer.

f-commerce   E-commerce that takes place on Facebook.

facilitating functions   Functions of channel intermediaries that make the purchase process easier for customers and manufacturers.

factory outlet store   A discount retailer, owned by a manufacturer, that sells off defective merchandise and excess inventory.

fair trade   Companies that pledge to pay a fair price to producers in developing countries, to ensure that the workers who produce the goods receive a fair wage, and to ensure that these manufacturers rely where possible on environmentally sustainable production practices.

fairness or justice approach   Ethical philosophy that advocates the decision that treats all human beings equally.

family brand   A brand that a group of individual products or individual brands share.

family life cycle   A means of characterizing consumers within a family structure on the basis of different stages through which people pass as they grow older.

feedback   Receivers' reactions to the message.

firewall   A combination of hardware and software that ensures that only authorized individuals gain entry into a computer system.

fixed costs   Costs of production that do not change with the number of units produced.

focus group   A product-oriented discussion among a small group of consumers led by a trained moderator.

folksonomy   A classification system that relies on users rather than pre-established systems to sort contents.

follow-up   Activities after the sale that provide important services to customers.

foreign exchange rate (forex rate)   The price of a nation's currency in terms of another currency.

four Ps   Product, price, promotion, and place.

franchise organizations   A contractual vertical marketing system that includes a franchiser (a manufacturer or a service provider) who allows an entrepreneur (the franchisee) to use the franchise name and marketing plan for a fee.

franchising   A form of licensing involving the right to adapt an entire system of doing business.

free trade zones   Designated areas where foreign companies can warehouse goods without paying taxes or customs duties until they move the goods into the marketplace.

freemium strategy   A business strategy in which a product in its most basic version is provided free of charge but the company charges money (the premium) for upgraded versions of the product with more features, greater functionality, or greater capacity.

frequency   The average number of times a person in the target group will be exposed to the message.

frequency programs   Consumer sales promotion programs that offer a discount or free product for multiple purchases over time; also referred to as loyalty or continuity programs.

full-service agency   An agency that provides most or all of the services needed to mount a campaign, including research, creation of ad copy and art, media selection, and production of the final messages.

full-service merchant wholesalers   Wholesalers that provide a wide range of services for their customers, including delivery, credit, product-use assistance, repairs, advertising, and other promotional support.

functional planning   A decision process that concentrates on developing detailed plans for strategies and tactics for the short term, supporting an organization's long-term strategic plan.

G

gamer segment   A consumer segment that combines a psychographic/lifestyle component with a heavy dose of generational marketing.

gamification   A strategy in which marketers apply game design techniques, often by awarding of points, badges, or levels, to non-game experiences in order to drive consumer behavior.

gap analysis   A marketing research method that measures the difference between a customer's expectation of a service quality and what actually occurred.

gender roles   Society's expectations regarding the appropriate attitudes, behaviors, and appearance for men and women.

General Agreement on Tariffs and Trade (GATT)   International treaty to reduce import tax levels and trade restrictions.

general merchandise discount stores   Retailers that offer a broad assortment of items at low prices with minimal service.

Generation X   The group of consumers born between 1965 and 1978.

Generation Y   The group of consumers born between 1979 and 1994.

generational marketing   Marketing to members of a generation, who tend to share the same outlook and priorities.

generic branding   A strategy in which products are not branded and are sold at the lowest price possible.

geodemography   A segmentation technique that combines geography with demographics.

geographic information system (GIS)   A system that combines a geographic map with digitally stored data about the consumers in a particular geographic area.

geographic segmentation   An approach in which marketers tailor their offerings to specific geographic areas because people's preferences often vary depending on where they live.

geotargeting   Determining the geographic location of a website visitor and delivering different content to that visitor based on his or her location.

good   A tangible product that we can see, touch, smell, hear, or taste.

government markets   The federal, state, county, and local governments that buy goods and services to carry out public objectives and to support their operations.

gray market goods   Items manufactured outside a country and then imported without the consent of the trademark holder.

green customers   Those consumers who are most likely to actively look for and buy products that are eco-friendly.

green marketing   A marketing strategy that supports environmental stewardship, thus creating a differential benefit in the minds of consumers.

Green River Ordinances   Community regulations that prohibit door-to-door selling unless prior permission is given by the household.

greenwashing   A practice in which companies promote their products as environmentally friendly when in truth the brand provides little ecological benefit.

gross domestic product (GDP)   The total dollar value of goods and services produced by a nation within its borders in a year.

gross margin   The markup amount added to the cost of a product to cover the fixed costs of the retailer or wholesaler and leave an amount for a profit.

gross rating points (GRPs)   A measure used for comparing the effectiveness of different media vehicles: average reach [times] frequency.

groundswell   A social trend in which people use technology to get the things they need from each other, rather than from traditional institutions like corporations.

Group of 8 (G8)   An informal forum of the eight most economically developed countries that meets annually to discuss major economic and political issues facing the international community.

growth stage   The second stage in the product life cycle, during which consumers accept the product and sales rapidly increase.

guerrilla marketing   Marketing activity in which a firm "ambushes" consumers with promotional content in places they are not expecting to encounter this kind of activity.

H

heuristics   A mental rule of thumb that leads to a speedy decision by simplifying the process.

hierarchy of effects   A series of steps prospective customers move through, from initial awareness of a product to brand loyalty.

hierarchy of needs   An approach that categorizes motives according to five levels of importance, the more basic needs being on the bottom of the hierarchy and the higher needs at the top.

horizontal marketing system   An arrangement within a channel of distribution in which two or more firms at the same channel level work together for a common purpose.

hybrid marketing system   A marketing system that uses a number of different channels and communication methods to serve a target market.

hypermarkets   Retailers with the characteristics of both warehouse stores and supermarkets; hypermarkets are several times larger than other stores and offer virtually everything from grocery items to electronics.

I

idea generation   The first step of product development in which marketers brainstorm for products that provide customer benefits and are compatible with the company mission.

idea marketing   Marketing activities that seek to gain market share for a concept, philosophy, belief, or issue by using elements of the marketing mix to create or change a target market's attitude or behavior.

import quotas   Limitations set by a government on the amount of a product allowed to enter or leave a country.

impulse products   A product people often buy on the spur of the moment.

impulse purchase   A purchase made without any planning or search effort.

independent intermediaries   Channel intermediaries that are not controlled by any manufacturer but instead do business with many different manufacturers and many different customers.

individualist cultures   Cultures in which people tend to attach more importance to personal goals than to those of the larger community.

industrial goods   Goods individuals or organizations buy for further processing or for their own use when they do business.

inelastic demand   Demand in which changes in price have little or no effect on the amount demanded.

infomercials   Half-hour or hour-long commercials that resemble a talk show but actually are sales pitches.

information   Interpreted data.

information overload   A state in which the marketer is buried in so much data that it becomes nearly paralyzing to decide which of the data provide useful information and which do not.

information search   The process whereby a consumer searches for appropriate information to make a reasonable decision.

ingredient branding   A type of branding in which branded materials become "component parts" of other branded products.

innovation   A product that consumers perceive to be new and different from existing products.

innovators   The first segment (roughly 2.5 percent) of a population to adopt a new product.

input measures   Efforts that go into selling, such as the number and type of sales calls, expense account management, and a variety of nonselling activities, such as customer follow-up work and client service.

inseparability   The characteristic of a service that means that it is impossible to separate the production of a service from the consumption of that service.

insourcing   A practice in which a company contracts with a specialist firm to handle all or part of its supply chain operations.

instapreneur   A businessperson who produces a product only when it is ordered.

institutional advertising   Advertising messages that promote the activities, personality, or point of view of an organization or company.

intangibility   The characteristic of a service that means customers can't see, touch, or smell good service.

intangibles   Experience-based products.

integrated marketing communication (IMC)   A strategic business process that marketers use to plan, develop, execute, and evaluate coordinated, measurable, persuasive brand communication programs over time to targeted audiences.

intensive distribution   Selling a product through all suitable wholesalers or retailers that are willing to stock and sell the product.

internal environment   The controllable elements inside an organization, including its people, its facilities, and how it does things that influence the operations of the organization.

internal customers   Other employees with whom employees interact with the attitude that all activities ultimately impact external customers.

internal customer mind-set   An organizational culture in which all organization members treat each other as valued customers.

internal PR   PR activities aimed at employees of an organization.

internal reference price   A set price or a price range in consumers' minds that they refer to in evaluating a product's price.

Internet of Things   Describes a system in which everyday objects are connected to the Internet and in turn are able to communicate information throughout an interconnected system.

Internet price discrimination   An Internet pricing strategy that charges different prices to different customers for the same product.

interpretation   The process of assigning meaning to a stimulus based on prior associations a person has with it and assumptions he or she makes about it.

intranet   An internal corporate communication network that uses Internet technology to link company departments, employees, and databases.

introduction stage   The first stage of the product life cycle in which slow growth follows the introduction of a new product in the marketplace.

inventory control   Activities to ensure that goods are always available to meet customers' demands.

inventory turnover or inventory turns   The number of times a firm's inventory completely cycles through during a defined time frame.

investor relations   PR activities such as annual and quarterly reports aimed at a firm's investors.

involvement   The relative importance of perceived consequences of the purchase to a consumer.

ISO 9000   Criteria developed by the International Organization for Standardization to regulate product quality in Europe.

J

jingles   Original words and music written specifically for advertising executions.

joint demand   Demand for two or more goods that are used together to create a product.

joint venture   A strategic alliance in which a new entity owned by two or more firms allows the partners to pool their resources for common goals.

just in time (JIT)   Inventory management and purchasing processes that manufacturers and resellers use to reduce inventory to very low levels and ensure that deliveries from suppliers arrive only when needed.

K

knockoff A new product that copies, with slight modification, the design of an original product.

knowledge management A comprehensive approach to collecting, organizing, storing, and retrieving a firm's information assets.

L

laggards The last consumers to adopt an innovation.

late majority The adopters who are willing to try new products when there is little or no risk associated with the purchase, when the purchase becomes an economic necessity, or when there is social pressure to purchase.

learning A relatively permanent change in behavior caused by acquired information or experience.

leased departments Departments within a larger retail store that an outside firm rents.

least developed country (LDC) A country at the lowest stage of economic development.

level of economic development The broader economic picture of a country.

licensing An agreement in which one firm sells another firm the right to use a brand name for a specific purpose and for a specific period of time.

licensing agreement An agreement in which one firm gives another firm the right to produce and market its product in a specific country or region in return for royalties.

lifestyle The pattern of living that determines how people choose to spend their time, money, and energy and that reflects their values, tastes, and preferences.

lifetime value of a customer The potential profit that a single customer's purchase of a firm's products generates over the customer's lifetime.

limited-service agency An agency that provides one or more specialized services, such as media buying or creative development.

limited-service merchant wholesalers Wholesalers that provide fewer services for their customers.

list price or manufacturer's suggested retail price (MSRP) The price the end customer is expected to pay as determined by the manufacturer; also referred to as the suggested retail price. The appropriate price for the end customer to pay as determined by the manufacturer.

lobbying Talking with and providing information to government officials in order to influence their activities relating to an organization.

local content rules A form of protectionism stipulating that a certain proportion of a product must consist of components supplied by industries in the host country or economic community.

location-based social networks Networks that integrate sophisticated GPS technology that enables users to alert friends of their exact whereabouts via their mobile phones.

locavorism The situation when many shoppers actively look for products that come from farms within 50 to 100 miles of where they live.

logistics The process of designing, managing, and improving the movement of products through the supply chain. Logistics includes purchasing, manufacturing, storage, and transport.

long tail A new approach to segmentation based on the idea that companies can make money by selling small amounts of items that only a few people want, provided they sell enough different items.

longitudinal design A technique that tracks the responses of the same sample of respondents over time.

loss-leader pricing The pricing policy of setting prices very low or even below cost to attract customers into a store.

M

m-commerce Promotional and other e-commerce activities transmitted over mobile phones and other mobile devices, such as smartphones and personal digital assistants (PDAs).

maintenance, repair, and operating (MRO) products Goods that a business customer consumes in a relatively short time.

mall-intercept A study in which researchers recruit shoppers in malls or other public areas.

malware Software designed specifically to damage or disrupt computer systems.

market All the customers and potential customers who share a common need that can be satisfied by a specific product, who have the resources to exchange for it, who are willing to make the exchange, and who have the authority to make the exchange.

marketing An organizational function and a set of processes for creating, communicating, and delivering value to customers and for managing customer relationships in ways that benefit the organization and its stakeholders.

marketing analytics A group of technologies and processes that enable marketers to collect, measure, analyze, and assess the effectiveness of marketing efforts.

market development strategies Growth strategies that introduce existing products to new markets.

market fragmentation The creation of many consumer groups due to a diversity of distinct needs and wants in modern society.

market intelligence system A method by which marketers get information about everyday happenings in the marketing environment.

market manager An individual who is responsible for developing and implementing the marketing plans for products sold to a particular customer group.

market penetration strategies Growth strategies designed to increase sales of existing products to current customers, nonusers, and users of competitive brands in served markets.

market position The way in which the target market perceives the product in comparison to competitors' brands.

market research The process of collecting, analyzing, and interpreting data about customers, competitors, and the business environment in order to improve marketing effectiveness.

market research ethics Taking an ethical and aboveboard approach to conducting market research that does no harm to the participant in the process of conducting the research.

market segment A distinct group of customers within a larger market who are similar to one another in some way and whose needs differ from other customers in the larger market.

market share The percentage of a market (defined in terms of either sales units or revenue) accounted for by a specific firm, product lines, or brands.

marketing concept A management orientation that focuses on identifying and satisfying consumer needs to ensure the organization's long-term profitability.

marketing control The ability to identify deviations in expected performance, both positive and negative, as soon as they occur.

marketing decision support system (MDSS) The data, analysis software, and interactive software that allow managers to conduct analyses and find the information they need.

marketing information system (MIS) A process that first determines what information marketing managers need and then gathers, sorts, analyzes, stores, and distributes relevant and timely marketing information to system users.

marketing metrics Specific measures that help marketers watch the performance of their marketing campaigns, initiatives, and channels and, when appropriate, serve as a control mechanism.

marketing mix A combination of the product itself, the price of the product, the place where it is made available, and the activities that introduce it to consumers that creates a desired response among a set of predefined consumers.

marketing plan A document that describes the marketing environment, outlines the marketing objectives and strategy, and identifies who will be responsible for carrying out each part of the marketing strategy.

marketing scorecards Feedback vehicles that report (often in quantified terms) how the company or brand is actually doing in achieving various goals.

marketplace Any location or medium used to conduct an exchange.

markup An amount added to the cost of a product to create the price at which a channel member will sell the product.

mass communication Relates to television, radio, magazines, and newspapers.

mass customization An approach that modifies a basic good or service to meet the needs of an individual.

mass market All possible customers in a market, regardless of the differences in their specific needs and wants.

mass-class The hundreds of millions of global consumers who now enjoy a level of purchasing power that's sufficient to let them afford high-quality products—except for big-ticket items like college educations, housing, or luxury cars.

materials handling The moving of products into, within, and out of warehouses.

maturity stage The third and longest stage in the product life cycle, during which sales peak and profit margins narrow.

media blitz A massive advertising campaign that occurs over a relatively short time frame.

media planners Agency personnel who determine which communication vehicles are the most effective and efficient to deliver the ad.

media planning The process of developing media objectives, strategies, and tactics for use in an advertising campaign.

media relations A PR activity aimed at developing close relationships with the media.

media schedule The plan that specifies the exact media to use and when to use it.

medium A communication vehicle through which a message is transmitted to a target audience.

merchandise agents or brokers Channel intermediaries that provide services in exchange for commissions but never take title to the product.

merchandise assortment The range of products a store sells.

merchandise breadth The number of different product lines available.

merchandise depth The variety of choices available for each specific product line.

merchandise mix The total set of all products offered for sale by a retailer, including all product lines sold to all consumer groups.

merchandising allowance Reimburses the retailer for in-store support of the product.

merchant wholesalers Intermediaries that buy goods from manufacturers (take title to them) and sell to retailers and other business-to-business customers.

message The communication in physical form that goes from a sender to a receiver.

metrics Measurements or "scorecards" that marketers use to identify the effectiveness of different strategies or tactics.

metrosexual A straight, urban male who is keenly interested in fashion, home design, gourmet cooking, and personal care.

microcultures Groups of consumers who identify with a specific activity or art form.

micromarketing The ability to identify and target very small geographic segments that sometimes amount to individuals.

Millennials or Generation Z The group of consumers born after 1994.

mission statement A formal statement in an organization's strategic plan that describes the overall purpose of the organization and what it intends to achieve in terms of its customers, products, and resources.

missionary salesperson A salesperson who promotes the firm and tries to stimulate demand for a product but does not actually complete a sale.

mobile advertising A form of advertising that is communicated to the consumer via a handset.

modified rebuy A buying situation classification used by business buyers to categorize a previously made purchase that involves some change and that requires limited decision making.

monopolistic competition A market structure in which many firms, each having slightly different products, offer unique consumer benefits.

monopoly A market situation in which one firm, the only supplier of a particular product, is able to control the price, quality, and supply of that product.

motivation An internal state that drives us to satisfy needs by activating goal-oriented behavior.

multichannel promotional strategy A marketing communication strategy where they combine traditional advertising, sales promotion, and public relations activities with online buzz-building activities.

multilevel or network marketing A system in which a master distributor recruits other people to become distributors, sells the company's product to the recruits, and receives a commission on all the merchandise sold by the people recruited.

multiple sourcing The business practice of buying a particular product from several different suppliers.

N

national or manufacturer brands Brands that the product manufacturer owns.

nationalization When a domestic government reimburses a foreign company (often not for the full value) for its assets after taking it over.

native advertising An execution strategy that mimics the content of the website where the message appears.

need The recognition of any difference between a consumer's actual state and some ideal or desired state.

neuromarketing A type of brain research that uses technologies such as functional magnetic resonance imaging (fMRI) to measure brain activity to better understand why consumers make the decisions they do.

new product development (NPD) The phases by which firms develop new products including idea generation, product concept development and screening, marketing strategy development, business analysis, technical development, test marketing, and commercialization.

new-business salesperson The person responsible for finding new customers and calling on them to present the company's products.

new-task buy A new business-to-business purchase that is complex or risky and that requires extensive decision making.

noise Anything that interferes with effective communication.

nondurable goods Consumer products that provide benefits for a short time because they are consumed (such as food) or are no longer useful (such as newspapers).

nonprobability sample   A sample in which personal judgment is used to select respondents.

nongovernmental organizations (NGOs)   Another name for not-for-profit organizations.

nonstore retailing   Any method used to complete an exchange with a product end user that does not require a customer visit to a store.

North American Industry Classification System (NAICS)   The numerical coding system that the United States, Canada, and Mexico use to classify firms into detailed categories according to their business activities.

not-for-profit organizations   The organizations with charitable, educational, community, and other public service goals that buy goods and services to support their functions and to attract and serve their members.

O

objective-task method   A promotion budgeting method in which an organization first defines the specific communication goals it hopes to achieve and then tries to calculate what kind of promotion efforts it will take to meet these goals.

observability   How visible a new product and its benefits are to others who might adopt it.

observational learning   Learning that occurs when people watch the actions of others and note what happens to them as a result.

off-price retailers   Retailers that buy excess merchandise from well-known manufacturers and pass the savings on to customers.

offshoring   A process by which companies contract with companies or individuals in remote places like China or India to perform work they used to do at home.

oligopoly   A market structure in which a relatively small number of sellers, each holding a substantial share of the market, compete in a market with many buyers.

on-line auctions   E-commerce that allows shoppers to purchase products through online bidding.

one-to-one marketing   Facilitated by CRM, one-to-one marketing allows for customization of some aspect of the goods or services that are offered to each customer.

online distribution piracy   The theft and unauthorized repurposing of intellectual property via the Internet.

open-source model   A practice used in the software industry in which companies share their software codes with one another to assist in the development of a better product.

operant conditioning   Learning that occurs as the result of rewards or punishments.

operational planning   A decision process that focuses on developing detailed plans for day-to-day activities that carry out an organization's functional plans.

operational plans   Plans that focus on the day-to-day execution of the marketing plan. Operational plans include detailed directions for the specific activities to be carried out, who will be responsible for them, and time lines for accomplishing the tasks.

opinion leader   A person who is frequently able to influence others' attitudes or behaviors by virtue of his or her active interest and expertise in one or more product categories.

order getter   A salesperson who works to develop long-term relationships with particular customers or to generate new sales.

order processing   The series of activities that occurs between the time an order comes into the organization and the time a product goes out the door.

order taker   A salesperson whose primary function is to facilitate transactions that the customer initiates.

organizational markets   Another name for business-to-business markets.

out-of-home media   Communication media that reach people in public places.

output measures   The results of the salesperson's efforts.

outsourcing   The business buying process of obtaining outside vendors to provide goods or services that otherwise might be supplied in-house.

owned media   Internet sites such as Web sites, blogs, Facebook, and Twitter accounts that are owned by an advertiser.

P

package   The covering or container for a product that provides product protection, facilitates product use and storage, and supplies important marketing communication.

paid media   Internet media such as display ads, sponsorships, and paid key word searches that are paid for by an advertiser.

party plan system   A sales technique that relies heavily on people getting caught up in the "group spirit," buying things they would not normally buy if they were alone.

patent   A legal mechanism to prevent competitors from producing or selling an invention, aimed at reducing or eliminating competition in a market for a period of time.

pay-per-gaze   A new method of charging advertisers that assesses a fee every time a viewer looks at an image in an online message.

penetration pricing   A pricing strategy in which a firm introduces a new product at a very low price to encourage more customers to purchase it.

perceived risk   The belief that choice of a product has potentially negative consequences, whether financial, physical, and/or social.

percentage-of-sales budgeting method   A method for promotion budgeting that is based on a certain percentage of either last year's sales or on estimates of the present year's sales.

perception   The process by which people select, organize, and interpret information from the outside world.

perceptual map   A technique to visually describe where brands are "located" in consumers' minds relative to competing brands.

perfect competition   A market structure in which many small sellers, all of whom offer similar products, are unable to have an impact on the quality, price, or supply of a product.

perishability   The characteristic of a service that makes it impossible to store for later sale or consumption.

permission marketing   E-mail advertising in which on-line consumers have the opportunity to accept or refuse the unsolicited e-mail.

perpetual inventory unit control system   Retail computer system that keeps a running total on sales, returns, transfers to other stores and so on.

personal selling   Marketing communication by which a company representative interacts directly with a customer or prospective customer to communicate about a good or service.

personality   The set of unique psychological characteristics that consistently influences the way a person responds to situations in the environment.

physical distribution   The activities that move finished goods from manufacturers to final customers, including order processing, warehousing, materials handling, transportation, and inventory control.

place   The availability of the product to the customer at the desired time and location.

place marketing   Marketing activities that seek to attract new businesses, residents, or visitors to a town, state, country, or some other site.

place-based media   Advertising media that transmit messages in public places, such as doctors' offices and airports, where certain types of people congregate.

point-of-purchase (POP) displays   In-store displays and signs.

point-of-sale (POS) systems   Retail computer systems that collect sales data and are hooked directly into the store's inventory-control system.

pop-up ad   An advertisement that appears on the screen while a Web page loads or after it has loaded.

pop-up stores   A temporary retail space a company erects to build buzz for its products.

portfolio analysis   A management tool for evaluating a firm's business mix and assessing the potential of an organization's strategic business units.

positioning   Develop a marketing strategy to influence how a particular market segment perceives a good or service in comparison to the competition.

posttesting   Research conducted on consumers' responses to actual advertising messages they have seen or heard.

preapproach   A part of the selling process that includes developing information about prospective customers and planning the sales interview.

predatory pricing   Illegal pricing strategy in which a company sets a very low price for the purpose of driving competitors out of business.

predictive analytics   Uses large quantities of data within variables that have identified relationships to more accurately predict specific future outcomes.

predictive technology   Analysis techniques that use shopping patterns of large numbers of people to determine which products are likely to be purchased if others are.

premiums   Items offered free to people who have purchased a product.

press release   Information that an organization distributes to the media intended to win publicity.

prestige products   Products that have a high price and that appeal to status-conscious consumers.

pretesting   A research method that seeks to minimize mistakes by getting consumer reactions to ad messages before they appear in the media.

price   The assignment of value, or the amount the consumer must exchange to receive the offering.

price bundling   Selling two or more goods or services as a single package for one price.

price elasticity of demand   The percentage change in unit sales that results from a percentage change in price.

price leadership   A pricing strategy in which one firm first sets its price and other firms in the industry follow with the same or very similar prices.

price lining   The practice of setting a limited number of different specific prices, called price points, for items in a product line.

price-fixing   The collaboration of two or more firms in setting prices, usually to keep prices high.

primary data   Data from research conducted to help make a specific decision.

private-label brands   Brands that a certain retailer or distributor owns and sells.

probability sample   A sample in which each member of the population has some known chance of being included.

problem recognition   The process that occurs whenever the consumer sees a significant difference between his current state of affairs and some desired or ideal state; this recognition initiates the decision-making process.

processed materials   Products created when firms transform raw materials from their original state.

producers   The individuals or organizations that purchase products for use in the production of other goods and services.

product   A tangible good, service, idea, or some combination of these that satisfies consumer or business customer needs through the exchange process; a bundle of attributes including features, functions, benefits, and uses.

product adaptation strategy   Product strategy in which a firm offers a similar but modified product in foreign markets.

product adoption   The process by which a consumer or business customer begins to buy and use a new good, service, or idea.

product advertising   Advertising messages that focus on a specific good or service.

product category managers   Individuals who are responsible for developing and implementing the marketing plan for all the brands and products within a product category.

product competition   When firms offering different products compete to satisfy the same consumer needs and wants.

product concept development and screening   The second step of product development in which marketers test product ideas for technical and commercial success.

product development strategies   Growth strategies that focus on selling new products in existing markets.

product invention strategy   Product strategy in which a firm develops a new product for foreign markets.

product life cycle (PLC)   A concept that explains how products go through four distinct stages from birth to death: introduction, growth, maturity, and decline.

product line length   Determined by the number of separate items within the same category.

product line   A firm's total product offering designed to satisfy a single need or desire of target customers.

product management   The systematic and usually team-based approach to coordinating all aspects of a product's marketing initiative including all elements of the marketing mix.

product mix   The total set of all products a firm offers for sale.

product mix width   The number of different product lines the firm produces.

product placement   A form of advertising in which marketers integrate products into entertainment venues. (Also know as embedded marketing or branded entertainment.)

product quality   The overall ability of the product to satisfy customers' expectations.

product review sites   Social media sites that enable people to post stories about their experiences with products and services.

product sampling   Distributing free trial-size versions of a product to consumers.

product specifications   A written description of the quality, size, weight, and other details required of a product purchase.

production orientation   A management philosophy that emphasizes the most efficient ways to produce and distribute products.

promotion   The coordination of a marketer's communication efforts to influence attitudes or behavior.

promotion mix   The major elements of marketer-controlled communication, including advertising, sales promotion, public relations, personal selling, and direct marketing.

promotional products   Goodies such as coffee mugs, T-shirts, and magnets given away to build awareness for a sponsor. Some freebies are distributed directly to consumers and business customers; others are intended for channel partners such as retailers and vendors.

prospecting A part of the selling process that includes identifying and developing a list of potential or prospective customers.

protectionism A policy adopted by a government to give domestic companies an advantage.

prototypes Test versions of a proposed product.

psychographics The use of psychological, sociological, and anthropological factors to construct market segments.

public relations (PR) Communication function that seeks to build good relationships with an organization's publics, including consumers, stockholders, and legislators.

public relations campaign A coordinated effort to communicate with one or more of the firm's publics.

public service advertisements (PSAs) Advertising run by the media for not-for-profit organizations or to champion a particular cause without charge.

publicity Unpaid communication about an organization that appears in the mass media.

puffery Claims made in advertising of product superiority that cannot be proven true or untrue.

pull strategy The company tries to move its products through the channel by building desire for the products among consumers, thus convincing retailers to respond to this demand by stocking these items.

push money A bonus paid by a manufacturer to a salesperson, customer, or distributor for selling its product.

push strategy The company tries to move its products through the channel by convincing channel members to offer them.

pyramid schemes An illegal sales technique that promises consumers or investors large profits from recruiting others to join the program rather than from any real investment or sale of goods to the public.

Q

quantity discounts A pricing tactic of charging reduced prices for purchases of larger quantities of a product.

question marks SBUs with low market shares in fast-growth markets.

R

radio frequency identification (RFID) Product tags with tiny chips containing information about the item's content, origin, and destination.

raw materials Products of the fishing, lumber, agricultural, and mining industries that organizational customers purchase to use in their finished products.

reach The percentage of the target market that will be exposed to the media vehicle.

reality mining The collection and analysis of machine-sensed environmental data pertaining to human social behavior with the goal of identifying predictable patterns of behavior.

rebates Sales promotions that allow the customer to recover part of the product's cost from the manufacturer.

receiver The organization or individual that intercepts and interprets the message.

reciprocity A trading partnership in which two firms agree to buy from one another.

reference group An actual or imaginary individual or group that has a significant effect on an individual's evaluations, aspirations, or behavior.

relationship selling A form of personal selling that involves securing, developing, and maintaining long-term relationships with profitable customers.

relative advantage The degree to which a consumer perceives that a new product provides superior benefits.

reliability The extent to which research measurement techniques are free of errors.

reminder advertising Advertising aimed at keeping the name of a brand in people's minds to be sure consumers purchase the product as necessary.

rentrepreneurs Enterprising consumers who make money by rending out their possessions when they aren't using them.

repositioning Redoing a product's position to respond to marketplace changes.

representativeness The extent to which consumers in a study are similar to a larger group in which the organization has an interest.

research and development (R&D) A well-defined and systematic approach to how innovation is done within the firm.

research and marketing services Advertising agency department that collects and analyzes information that will help account executives develop a sensible strategy and assist creatives in getting consumer reactions to different versions of ads.

research design A plan that specifies what information marketers will collect and what type of study they will do.

resellers The individuals or organizations that buy finished goods for the purpose of reselling, renting, or leasing to others to make a profit and to maintain their business operations.

retailer cooperative A group of retailers that establishes a wholesaling operation to help them compete more effectively with the large chains.

retail borrowing Consumer practice of purchasing a product with the intent to return the nondefective merchandise for a refund after it has fulfilled the purpose for which it was purchased.

retailer margin The margin added to the cost of a product by a retailer.

retailing The final stop in the distribution channel in which organizations sell goods and services to consumers for their personal use.

retailtainment The use of retail strategies that enhance the shopping experience and create excitement, impulse purchases, and an emotional connection with the brand.

retro brand A once-popular brand that has been revived to experience a popularity comeback, often by riding a wave of nostalgia.

return on investment (ROI) The direct financial impact of a firm's expenditure of a resource such as time or money.

return on marketing investment (ROMI) Quantifying just how an investment in marketing has an impact on the firm's success, financially and otherwise.

reverse engineering The process of physically deconstructing a competitor's product to determine how it's put together.

reverse logistics Includes product returns, recycling and material reuse, and waste disposal.

reverse marketing A business practice in which a buyer firm attempts to identify suppliers who will produce products according to the buyer firm's specifications.

rights approach Ethical philosophy that advocates the decision that does the best job of protecting the moral rights of all.

risk-taking functions The chance retailers take on the loss of a product when they buy a product from a manufacturer because the product sits on the shelf because no customers want it.

S

sachets Single use packages of products such as shampoo often sold in developing countries.

sales presentation The part of the selling process in which the salesperson directly communicates the value proposition to the customer and invites two-way communication.

sales promotion Programs designed to build interest in or encourage purchase of a product during a specified period.

sampling The process of selecting respondents for a study.

scanner data Data derived from items that are scanned at the cash register when you check out with your loyalty card.

search engine marketing (SEM) Search marketing strategy in which marketers pay for ads or better positioning.

search engine optimization (SEO) A systematic process of ensuring that your firm comes up at or near the top of lists of typical search phrases related to your business.

search engines Internet programs that search for documents with specified keywords.

search marketing Marketing strategies that involve the use of Internet search engines.

seasonal discounts Price reductions offered only during certain times of the year.

secondary data Data that have been collected for some purpose other than the problem at hand.

segment profile A description of the "typical" customer in a segment.

segmentation The process of dividing a larger market into smaller pieces based on one or more meaningfully shared characteristics.

segmentation variables Dimensions that divide the total market into fairly homogeneous groups, each with different needs and preferences.

selective distribution Distribution using fewer outlets than intensive distribution but more than exclusive distribution.

self-concept An individual's self-image that is composed of a mixture of beliefs, observations, and feelings about personal attributes.

selling orientation A managerial view of marketing as a sales function, or a way to move products out of warehouses to reduce inventory.

sensory branding The use of distinct sensory experiences not only to appeal to customers but also to enhance their brand.

sensory marketing Marketing techniques that link distinct sensory experiences such as a unique fragrance with a product or service.

sentiment analysis The process of identifying a follower's attitude toward a brand by assessing the context or emotion of her comments.

service encounter The actual interaction between the customer and the service provider.

services Intangible products that are exchanged directly between the producer and the customer.

servicescape The actual physical facility where the service is performed, delivered, and consumed.

SERVQUAL A multiple-item scale used to measure service quality across dimensions of tangibles, reliability, responsiveness, assurance, and empathy.

share of customer The percentage of an individual customer's purchase of a product that is a single brand.

shopping products Goods or services for which consumers spend considerable time and effort gathering information and comparing alternatives before making a purchase.

shrinkage Losses experienced by retailers due to shoplifting, employee theft, and damage to merchandise.

simulated test marketing Application of special computer software to imitate the introduction of a product into the marketplace allowing the company to see the likely impact of price cuts and new packaging—or even to determine where in the store it should try to place the product.

single sourcing The business practice of buying a particular product from only one supplier.

situation analysis An assessment of a firm's internal and external environments.

Six Sigma A process whereby firms work to limit product defects to 3.4 per million or fewer.

skimming price A very high, premium price that a firm charges for its new, highly desirable product.

slogans Simple, memorable linguistic devices linked to a brand.

slotting allowance A fee paid in exchange for agreeing to place a manufacturer's products on a retailer's valuable shelf space.

social class The overall rank or social standing of groups of people within a society according to the value assigned to factors such as family background, education, occupation, and income.

societal marketing concept A management philosophy that marketers must satisfy customers' needs in ways that also benefit society and also deliver profit to the firm.

societal media Internet-based platforms that allow users to create their own content and share it with others who access these sites.

social networking platforms Online platforms that allow a user to represent him- or herself via a profile on a website and provide and receive links to other members of the network to share input about common interests.

social networks Sites used to connect people with other similar people.

social norms Specific rules dictating what is right or wrong, acceptable or unacceptable.

source An organization or individual that sends a message.

spam The use of electronic media to send unsolicited messages in bulk.

special events Activities—from a visit by foreign investors to a company picnic—that are planned and implemented by a PR department.

specialty products Goods or services that has unique characteristics and is important to the buyer and for which she will devote significant effort to acquire.

specialized services Services that are essential to the operation of an organization but are not part of the production of a product.

specialty stores Retailers that carry only a few product lines but offer good selection within the lines that they sell.

speech writing Writing a speech on a topic for a company executive to deliver.

sponsored search ads Paid ads that appear at the top or beside the Internet search engine results.

sponsorships PR activities through which companies provide financial support to help fund an event in return for publicized recognition of the company's contribution.

stakeholders Buyers, sellers, or investors in a company, community residents, and even citizens of the nations where goods and services are made or sold—in other words, any person or organization that has a "stake" in the outcome.

standard of living An indicator of the average quality and quantity of goods and services consumed in a country.

staple products Basic or necessary items that are available almost everywhere.

stars SBUs with products that have a dominant market share in high-growth markets.

status symbols Visible markers that provide a way for people to flaunt their membership in higher social classes (or at least to make others believe they are members).

stock-keeping unit (SKU) A unique identifier for each distinct product.

stock-outs Zero-inventory situations resulting in lost sales and customer dissatisfaction.

storefront The physical exterior of a store.

straight extension strategy Product strategy in which a firm offers the same product in both domestic and foreign markets.

straight rebuy A buying situation in which business buyers make routine purchases that require minimal decision making.

strategic alliance   Relationship developed between a firm seeking a deeper commitment to a foreign market and a domestic firm in the target country.

strategic business units (SBUs)   Individual units within the firm that operate like separate businesses, with each having its own mission, business objectives, resources, managers, and competitors.

strategic planning   A managerial decision process that matches an organization's resources and capabilities to its market opportunities for long-term growth and survival.

structured data   Data that (1) are typically numeric or categorical; (2) can be organized and formatted in a way that is easy for computers to read, organize, and understand; and (3) can be inserted into a database in a seamless fashion.

sub-branding   Creating a secondary brand within a main brand that can help differentiate a product line to a desired target group.

subculture   A group within a society whose members share a distinctive set of beliefs, characteristics, or common experiences.

subliminal advertising   Supposedly hidden messages in marketers' communications.

supercenters   Large combination stores that combine economy supermarkets with other lower-priced merchandise.

supermarkets   Food stores that carry a wide selection of edibles and related products.

supply chain   All the activities necessary to turn raw materials into a good or service and put it in the hands of the consumer or business customer.

supply chain management   The management of flows among firms in the supply chain to maximize total profitability.

support media   Media such as directories or out-of-home media that may be used to reach people who are not reached by mass media advertising.

surge pricing   A pricing strategy in which the price of a product is raised as demand for that product goes up and lowered as demand goes down.

sustainability   A product design focus that seeks to create products that meet present consumer needs without compromising the ability of future generations to meet their needs.

sustainability metrics   Tools that measure the benefits an organization achieves through the implementation of sustainability.

SWOT analysis   An analysis of an organization's strengths and weaknesses and the opportunities and threats in its external environment.

syndicated research   Research by firms that collect data on a regular basis and sell the reports to multiple firms.

T

take title   To accept legal ownership of a product and assume the accompanying rights and responsibilities of ownership.

target costing   A process in which firms identify the quality and functionality needed to satisfy customers and what price they are willing to pay before the product is designed; the product is manufactured only if the firm can control costs to meet the required price.

target market   The market segments on which an organization focuses its marketing plan and toward which it directs its marketing efforts.

target marketing strategy   Dividing the total market into different segments on the basis of customer characteristics, selecting one or more segments, and developing products to meet the needs of those specific segments.

targeting   A strategy in which marketers evaluate the attractiveness of each potential segment and decide in which of these groups they will invest resources to try to turn them into customers.

tariffs   Taxes on imported goods.

team selling   The sales function when handled by a team that may consist of a salesperson, a technical specialist, and others.

teaser or mystery advertising   Ads that generate curiosity and interest in a to-be-introduced product by drawing attention to an upcoming ad campaign without mentioning the product.

technical development   The step in the product development process in which company engineers refine and perfect a new product.

technical specialist   A sales support person with a high level of technical expertise who assists in product demonstrations.

telemarketing   The use of the telephone to sell directly to consumers and business customers.

test marketing   Testing the complete marketing plan in a small geographic area that is similar to the larger market the firm hopes to enter.

time poverty   Consumers' belief that they are more pressed for time than ever before.

tipping point   In the context of product diffusion, the point when a product's sales spike from a slow climb to an unprecedented new level.

tonality   The mood or attitude the message conveys (straightforward, humor, dramatic, romantic, sexy, and apprehension/fear).

top-down budgeting techniques   Allocation of the promotion budget based on management's determination of the total amount to be devoted to marketing communication.

total costs   The total of the fixed costs and the variable costs for a set number of units produced.

total quality management (TQM)   A management philosophy that focuses on satisfying customers through empowering employees to be an active part of continuous quality improvement.

touchpoint   Any point of direct interface between customers and a company (online, by phone, or in person).

trade discounts   Discounts off list price of products to members of the channel of distribution who perform various marketing functions.

trade sales promotions   Promotions that focus on members of the "trade," which include distribution channel members, such as retail salespeople or wholesale distributors, that a firm must work with in order to sell its products.

trade shows   Events at which many companies set up elaborate exhibits to show their products, give away samples, distribute product literature, and troll for new business contacts.

trademark   The legal term for a brand name, brand mark, or trade character; trademarks legally registered by a government obtain protection for exclusive use in that country.

transactional selling   A form of personal selling that focuses on making an immediate sale with little or no attempt to develop a relationship with the customer.

transportation   The mode by which products move among channel members.

transportation and storage   Occurs when retailers and other channel members move the goods from the production point to other locations where they can hold them until consumers want them.

trial pricing   Pricing a new product low for a limited period of time in order to lower the risk for a customer.

trialability   The ease of sampling a new product and its benefits.

triple-bottom-line orientation   A business orientation that looks at financial profits, the community in which the organization operates, and creating sustainable business practices.

tryvertising   Advertising by sampling that is designed to create buzz about a product.

twitter   A free microblogging service that lets users post short text messages with a maximum of 140 characters.

U

U.S. Generalized System of Preferences (GSP) A program to promote economic growth in developing countries by allowing duty-free entry of goods into the U.S.

unaided recall A research technique conducted by telephone survey or personal interview that asks whether a person remembers seeing an ad during a specified period without giving the person the name of the brand.

undifferentiated targeting strategy Appealing to a broad spectrum of people.

unfair sales acts State laws that prohibit suppliers from selling products below cost to protect small businesses from larger competitors.

uniform delivered pricing A pricing tactic in which a firm adds a standard shipping charge to the price for all customers regardless of location.

unique selling proposition (USP) An advertising appeal that focuses on one clear reason why a particular product is superior.

Universal Product Code (UPC) The set of black bars or lines printed on the side or bottom of most items sold in grocery stores and other mass-merchandising outlets. The UPC, readable by scanners, creates a national system of product identification.

unobtrusive measures Measuring traces of physical evidence that remain after some action has been taken.

unsought products Goods or services for which a consumer has little awareness or interest until the product or a need for the product is brought to her attention.

unstructured data Nonnumeric information that is typically formatted in a way that is meant for human eyes and not easily understood by computers.

usage occasions An indicator used in behavioral market segmentation based on when consumers use a product most.

usage rate A measurement that reflects the quantity purchased or frequency of use among consumers of a particular product or service.

user-generated content (UGC) or consumer-generated media (CGM) Online consumer comments, opinions, advice and discussions, reviews, photos, images, videos, podcasts, webcasts, and product, related stories available to other consumers.

utilitarian approach Ethical philosophy that advocates a decision that provides the most good or the least harm.

utility The usefulness or benefit consumers receive from a product.

V

validity The extent to which research actually measures what it was intended to measure.

VALS™ (Values and Lifestyles) A psychographic system that divides the entire U.S. population into eight segments.

value chain A series of activities involved in designing, producing, marketing, delivering, and supporting any product. Each link in the chain has the potential to either add or remove value from the product the customer eventually buys.

value co-creation The process by which benefits-based value is created through collaborative participation by customers and other stakeholders in the new product development process.

value pricing or everyday low pricing (EDLP) A pricing strategy in which a firm sets prices that provide ultimate value to customers.

value proposition A marketplace offering that fairly and accurately sums up the value that will be realized if the good or service is purchased.

variability The characteristic of a service that means that even the same service performed by the same individual for the same customer can vary.

variable costs The costs of production (raw and processed materials, parts, and labor) that are tied to and vary depending on the number of units produced.

variety stores Stores that carry a variety of inexpensive items.

venture teams Groups of people within an organization who work together to focus exclusively on the development of a new product.

vertical marketing system (VMS) A channel of distribution in which there is formal cooperation among members at the manufacturing, wholesaling, and retailing levels.

video sharing Uploading video recordings on to Internet sites such as YouTube so that thousands or even millions of other Internet users can see them.

viral marketing Marketing activities that aim to increase brand awareness or sales by consumers passing a message along to other consumers.

virtual experiential marketing An online marketing strategy that uses enhancements, including colors, graphics, layout and design, interactive videos, contests, games, and giveaways, to engage experiential shoppers online.

virtual goods Digital products consumers buy for use in online contexts.

virtual worlds Online, highly engaging digital environments where avatars live and interact with other avatars in real time.

virtue approach Ethical philosophy that advocates the decision that is in agreement with certain ideal values.

vlogs Video recordings shared on the Internet.

W

want The desire to satisfy needs in specific ways that are culturally and socially influenced.

warehouse clubs Discount retailers that charge a modest membership fee to consumers who buy a broad assortment of food and nonfood items in bulk and in a warehouse environment.

warehousing Storing goods in anticipation of sale or transfer to another member of the channel of distribution.

Web 2.0 The new generation of the World Wide Web that incorporates social networking and user interactivity.

Web scraping The process of using computer software to extract large amounts of data from websites.

wheel-of-retailing hypothesis A theory that explains how retail firms change, becoming more upscale as they go through their life cycle.

wholesaler margin The amount added to the cost of a product by a wholesaler.

wholesaling intermediaries Firms that handle the flow of products from the manufacturer to the retailer or business user.

wisdom of crowds Under the right circumstances, groups are smarter than the smartest people in them, meaning that large numbers of consumers can predict successful products.

word-of-mouth communication When consumers provide information about products to other consumers.

World Trade Organization (WTO) An organization that replaced GATT; the WTO sets trade rules for its member nations and mediates disputes between nations.

world trade The flow of goods and services among different countries—the value of all the exports and imports of the world's nations.

Y

yield management pricing A practice of charging different prices to different customers in order to manage capacity while maximizing revenues.

▶Name Index

▶Subject Index

Note: Page numbers followed by *t* indicate tables, page numbers followed by *f* indicate figures.